Second Edition

PRINCIPLES OF INSURANCE

Second Edition

PRINCIPLES OF INSURANCE

GEORGE E. REJDA

University of Nebraska

SCOTT, FORESMAN AND COMPANY

Glenview, Illinois
London, England

Acknowledgments

Acknowledgments for additional literary selections and illustrations appear within the text.

Insight 3.3, p. 60: "How Much Do Risk Managers Earn" from *National Underwriter, The Property and Casualty Insurance Edition, 1983.* Reprinted by permission.

Library of Congress Cataloging-in-Publication Data

Rejda, George E.
Principles of insurance.

Includes bibliographies and index.
1. Insurance. I. Title.
HG8051.R44 1986 368 85-25193
ISBN 0-673-18209-6

Printed in the United States of America.

12345678-RRC-908988878685

PREFACE

The academic response from students and adopters of the first edition of this textbook has been gratifying. The text has been widely used in principles of insurance courses in major universities and colleges throughout the United States. The second edition builds on the first, and it is an improved product. The fundamental objective underlying the second edition is similar to the first—I have attempted to write a clear and readable textbook that represents a blend of basic insurance principles and consumer considerations. My goal is to present basic principles in a clear, interesting, and relevant manner so that beginning students can apply these concepts immediately to their own lives by developing sound and viable insurance programs.

The second edition is completely updated and provides a thorough up-to-date treatment of the major topics in risk and insurance. Like the first edition, all major areas in risk and insurance are treated in some depth, including basic concepts, fundamental legal principles, property and liability insurance, life and health insurance, social insurance, and the functional and financial operations of insurance companies.

CHANGES IN THE SECOND EDITION

Several substantive changes have been made in the second edition to reflect current developments and trends in the insurance industry. They include the following:

1. *Boxed Readings.* Almost all chapters contain one or more mini-readings that are designed to provide additional insights with respect to the concept or principle being discussed. This is an important pedagogical aid for the benefit of students who can then see the practical significance of the concept or idea from a different perspective.
2. *1984 Homeowner Policies.* The new edition contains a detailed and complete discussion of the new 1984 homeowner policies developed by the Insurance Services Office (ISO). Chapters 7 and 10 have been completely updated to reflect the new homeowner contracts.
3. *Universal Life Insurance.* The new universal life contracts are discussed in some detail in Chapter 17, including the advantages and disadvantages of the new contracts that are now being sold by major companies. A sample universal life policy is also included in an appendix for the benefit of students and instructors.
4. *New Types of Life Insurance.* Chapter 17 provides a discussion of some new types of life insurance products, including reentry term insurance, indeterminate premium policies, and vanishing premium contracts.
5. *Replacement of Life Insurance.* Replacement of an existing life insurance policy is a highly controversial issue at the present time. In the appendix to Chapter 19, Professor Joseph Belth provides a relatively simple methodology that consumers can use to determine if replacement of an older life insurance policy is financially justified.
6. *Disability Income.* The material on individual disability income contracts in Chapter 21 has been updated to reflect current trends and developments. This includes a discussion of the loss-of-income definition of disability that some insurers are now using to determine if the insured is disabled. Optional disability income benefits are also discussed, including cost-of-living benefits, the Social Security rider, and the additional purchase option.

7. *Health Maintenance Organizations (HMOs).* Most members of HMOs are part of an employer-sponsored group. Thus, discussion of HMOs has been moved from Chapter 21 to Chapter 22 where group health insurance and employee benefits are discussed in some depth.
8. *Preferred Provider Organizations (PPOs).* Chapter 22 contains an extensive discussion of preferred provider organizations (PPOs). A PPO is a relatively new health care delivery system that has enormous potential for holding down increases in health care costs. In addition, Chapter 22 includes a discussion of new health care cost containment methods and innovations that employers and insurers are now using.
9. *Retirement Plans.* Chapter 23 has been extensively rewritten to reflect recent federal legislation that will have a profound impact on private pension and retirement plans. In particular, the text reflects the Tax Equity and Fiscal Responsibility Act of 1982 (TEFRA), the Deficit Reduction Act of 1984 (DEFRA), and the Retirement Equity Act of 1984 (REA).
10. *Social Insurance.* Chapter 24 has been updated to reflect recent amendments to the Social Security Act and legislative changes in unemployment insurance and workers' compensation laws. The objective is to present complex social insurance provisions and laws to students in a clear and relevant manner. The chapter also contains an interesting and controversial reading by A. Haeworth Robertson, former chief actuary of the Social Security Administration, concerning the future financial feasibility of the Social Security program.
11. *Banks Entering the Insurance Industry.* Chapter 28 discusses in considerable detail the highly controversial issue of entry of commercial banks into the insurance industry.
12. *Law of Large Numbers.* The empirical discussion of the law of large numbers by Professor Robert Witt has been moved from the appendix at the end of the text to a separate appendix at the end of Chapter 2. The result is an early exposure of students to some elementary statistical concepts in risk and insurance.
13. *New Objective Questions.* More than 700 new multiple-choice objective questions are now available in a supplementary instructor's manual. The objective questions are written by Professor Burton Beam, Jr., of The American College who has considerable experience in the preparation of objective examination questions for the professional Chartered Life Underwriter (CLU) examinations. The result is a test bank of high-quality objective questions for the busy instructor.

ACKNOWLEDGMENTS

A successful textbook is never written alone. I owe a heavy intellectual debt to several eminent insurance scholars and academicians for their kind and gracious assistance. Numerous educators have taken time out of their busy professional schedules to review either part or all chapters in the first or second edition or have contributed supplementary materials or offered valuable suggestions. They include the following:

Burton Beam, Jr., *The American College*

Joseph Belth, *Indiana University*

Leonard Berekson, *University of Nebraska-Lincoln*

Jerry Caswell, *Employee Benefits Consultant*

Donald Doudna, President, *Younkers Investore*

Michael Delaney, *University of Nebraska-Omaha*

Edward Graves, *The American College*

Gary Griepentrog, *University of South Carolina*

Charles Hall, Jr., *Temple University*

Robert Marshall, *Florida State University*

John McFadden, *The American College*

Robert Myers, former chief actuary, *Social Security Administration*

David Nye, *University of Florida*

Richard Phillips, *Central Michigan University*

S. Travis Pritchett, *University of South Carolina*

Barry Schweig, *Creighton University*

Donald Strand, *Illinois Wesleyan University*

Lester Strickler, *Oregon State University*

Robert Witt, *University of Texas*

Jack VanDerhei, *University of Pennsylvania*

Their comments and observations are deeply appreciated. The result, I hope, is a visually attractive text from which students can learn and professors can teach.

George E. Rejda, Ph.D., CLU
V. J. Skutt Professor of Insurance
University of Nebraska-Lincoln

CONTENTS

Second Edition

PRINCIPLES OF INSURANCE

PART

I

BASIC CONCEPTS IN RISK AND INSURANCE

CHAPTER

RISK AND ITS TREATMENT

"Risk is the spice of life, but its burdens are heavy."

Anonymous

STUDENT LEARNING OBJECTIVES

After studying this chapter, you should be able to:

- Explain the meaning of risk.
- Define the terms "chance of loss," "peril," and "hazard."
- Classify the various types of risks in our society.
- Describe the major pure risks that are associated with great financial and economic insecurity.
- Understand how risk is a burden to society.
- Explain the major methods of handling risk.

Most persons and organizations seek financial and economic security, but the presence of risk is a major impediment. We live in a risky world. We are constantly surrounded by forces, largely outside our control, that threaten our financial well-being. Thus, some of us will experience the premature and tragic death of a beloved family member; others will experience the loss or destruction of their property from earthquakes, hurricanes, floods, and other natural disasters. Still others will experience poor health from cancer, heart attacks, and other diseases. In addition, some of us will be totally and permanently disabled from a crippling automobile accident or a catastrophic illness. Finally, others will experience the traumatic effects of a liability lawsuit.

In this chapter, we will consider the nature and treatment of major risks in our society. Three major ideas will be emphasized. First, we will examine the meaning of risk. Second, we will classify the basic types of risk and examine those risks that are associated with great financial and economic insecurity. Finally, we will conclude the chapter by analyzing the major methods of handling risk in our society.

WHAT IS RISK?

There is no single definition of risk. Economists, behavioral scientists, risk theorists, statisticians, and actuaries each have their own concept of risk. But the majority of insurance authors traditionally have defined risk in terms of uncertainty. Based on this theory, ***risk** is defined as uncertainty concerning the occurrence of a loss.*[1] For example, the risk of lung cancer for smokers is present since uncertainty is present. The risk of flunking a college course is present because there is uncertainty concerning the outcome of the grade. The risk of being killed in an automobile accident is present because uncertainty is present. In short, risk is the same thing as uncertainty.

Based on this concept, if the probability of loss is either 0 or 1, there is no risk since there is no uncertainty. For example, assume that your room is on fire when you arrive home this evening. Although the loss has already occurred ($P = 1$), there is no risk since there is no uncertainty. Likewise, if you are absolutely certain that a loss cannot occur ($P = 0$), there is no risk because there is no uncertainty. For example, assume that someone attempts to burn a steel safe immersed in a tank of water. A loss from fire cannot possibly occur. Since the probability of loss is zero, there is no risk because there is no uncertainty.

Some authors who define risk as uncertainty go one step further and classify risk as objective and subjective.[2] Let us examine each of these categories of risk in greater detail.

Objective Risk

***Objective risk** is defined as the relative variation of actual loss from expected loss.* For example, assume that a fire insurer has 10,000 houses insured over a long period and, on the average, 1 percent or 100 houses burn each year. However, it would be rare for exactly 100 houses to burn each year. In some years, as few as 90 houses may burn, while in other years, as many as 110 houses may burn. Thus, there is a variation of 10 houses from the expected number of 100, or a variation of 10 percent. This relative variation of actual loss from expected loss is known as objective risk.

Objective risk declines as the number of exposures increases. More specifically, *objective risk varies inversely with the square root of the number of cases under observation.* In our previous example, 10,000 houses were insured, and objective risk was 10/100 or 10 percent. Now assume that 1 million houses are insured. The expected number of houses that will burn is now 10,000, but the variation of actual loss from expected loss is only 100. Objective risk is now 100/10,000 or 1 percent. Thus, as the square root of the number of cases increased from 100 in the first example to 1,000 in the second example (ten times), objective risk declined to one-tenth of its former level.

Objective risk can be statistically measured by some measure of dispersion, such as the standard deviation or coefficient of variation. Since objective risk can be measured, it is an extremely useful concept for an insurance company or a corporate risk manager. As the number of exposures increases, the insurance company can predict its future loss experience more accurately because it can rely on the law of large numbers. We will discuss the law of large numbers in Chapter 2.

Subjective Risk

***Subjective risk** is defined as uncertainty based on a person's mental condition or state of mind.* For example, assume that an individual is drinking heavily in a bar and foolishly attempts to drive home after the bar closes. The driver may be uncertain whether he or she will arrive home safely without being arrested by the police for drunken driving. This mental uncertainty is called subjective risk.

The impact of subjective risk varies depending on the individual. Two persons in the same situation may have a different perception of risk, and their conduct may be altered accordingly. If an individual experiences great mental uncertainty concerning the occurrence of a loss, his or her conduct may be affected. High subjective risk often results in conservative and prudent conduct, while low subjective risk may result in less conservative conduct. Thus, in the preceding example, the driver may have been previously arrested for drunken driving and is aware that he or she has consumed too much alcohol. The driver may then compensate for the mental uncertainty by getting someone else to drive him or her home or taking a cab. In contrast, another driver in the same situation may perceive the risk of being arrested for drunken driving as slight. This second driver may drive in a careless and reckless manner; a low subjective risk results in less conservative driving behavior.

CHANCE OF LOSS

Chance of loss is closely related to the concept of risk. ***Chance of loss** is defined as the probability that an event will occur.* Like risk, the term "probability" has both objective and subjective aspects.

Objective Probability

Objective probability refers to the long-run relative frequency of an event based on the assumptions of an infinite number of observations and of no change in the underlying conditions. Objective probabilities can be determined two ways. First, they can be determined by deductive reasoning. These probabilities are called *a priori probabilities.* For example, the probability of getting a head from the toss of a perfectly balanced coin is one-half, since there are two sides and only one is a head. Likewise, the probability of rolling a six with a single die is one-sixth, since there are six sides and only one side has six dots on it.

Second, objective probabilities can be determined by inductive reasoning, rather than by deduction. For example, the probability that a person age sixteen will die before age twenty-one cannot be logically deduced. However, by careful analysis of past mortality experience, life insurers can estimate the probability of death and sell a five-year term insurance policy.

Subjective Probability

Subjective probability is the individual's personal estimate of the chance of loss. Subjective probability need not coincide with objective probability. For example, some persons may buy a lottery ticket on their birthday since they believe it is their lucky day. Accordingly, they may overestimate the small objective probability of winning. A wide variety of factors have been found to influence subjective probability, including the individual's age, sex, intelligence, education, and use of alcohol. With respect to the latter, studies have shown that alcohol causes persons to overestimate their physical skills and abilities.

In addition, a person's estimate of a loss may differ from objective probability because there may be an ambiguity in the way in which the probability is presented. For example, assume that a "one-armed bandit" slot machine requires three lemons to win. The person playing the machine may perceive the probability of winning to be quite high. However, if there are ten symbols on each reel and only one is a lemon, the objective probability of hitting the jackpot with three lemons is 1/1,000. Assuming that each reel spins independently of the others, the probability that all three will simultaneously show a lemon is the product of their individual probabilities (1/10 × 1/10 × 1/10 = 1/1,000). Since most persons who gamble are not trained statisticians, they are likely to overestimate the objective probabilities of winning.

Chance of Loss Distinguished from Risk

You should not confuse chance of loss with objective risk. They are not the same thing. As we stated earlier, chance of loss is the probability that an event will occur. Objective risk is the relative variation of actual loss from expected loss. *The chance of loss may be identical for two different groups, but objective risk may be quite different.* For example, assume that a fire insurer has 10,000 homes insured in Los Angeles and 10,000 homes insured in Philadelphia. Also assume that the chance of loss in each city is 1 percent. Thus, on the average, 100 homes should burn annually in each city. However, if the annual variation in losses ranges from 75 to 125 in Philadelphia, but only from 90 to 100 in Los Angeles, objective risk is greater in Philadelphia even though the chance of loss in both cities is the same.

PERIL AND HAZARD

The terms "peril" and "hazard" should not be confused with the concept of risk discussed earlier. Let us first consider the meaning of peril.

Peril

***Peril** is defined as the cause of loss.* Thus, if your house burns because of a fire, the peril or cause of loss is the fire. If your car is totally destroyed in a collision with another motorist, collision is the peril or cause of loss. Some common perils that result in the loss or destruction of property include fire, lightning, windstorm, hail, tornadoes, earthquakes, theft, and burglary.

Hazard

*A **hazard** is a condition that creates or increases the chance of loss.* There are three major types of hazards:

- Physical hazard
- Moral hazard
- Morale hazard

Physical hazard *A **physical hazard** is a physical condition that increases the chance of loss.* Thus, if you own an older apartment building with defective wiring, the defective wiring is a physical hazard that increases the chance of a fire. Another example of physical hazard is an icy road. If you lose control of your car on an icy road and collide with another motorist, the icy road is a physical hazard while the collision is the peril or cause of loss.

Moral hazard ***Moral hazard** is dishonesty or character defects in an individual that increase the chance of loss.* For example, a dishonest merchant may be overstocked with inventories because of a severe business recession. If the inventory is insured, the merchant may deliberately burn the building to collect from the insurer. In effect, the merchant has sold the unwanted inventory to the insurer by deliberately causing the loss. A large number of fires are due to arson, which is a vivid example of moral hazard.

Moral hazard is present in all forms of insurance, and it is difficult to control. Dishonest insureds often rationalize their actions on the grounds that "the insurer has plenty of money." This is incorrect since the company can pay claims only by collecting premiums from other policyowners. Because of moral hazard, premiums are higher to all insureds, including the honest insureds. Although an individual may believe that it is morally wrong to steal from a neighbor, he or she often has no qualms about stealing from the insurer and other policyowners by either causing the loss or by inflating the size of the claim after the loss occurs.

Insurers attempt to control moral hazard by careful underwriting and by various policy provisions, such as deductibles, waiting periods, exclusions, and riders. We will examine moral hazard in greater detail in Chapter 26.

Morale hazard ***Morale hazard*** *is defined as carelessness or indifference to a loss because of the existence of insurance.* The very presence of insurance causes some insureds to be careless about protecting their property, and the chance of loss is thereby increased. For example, many motorists know their cars are insured and, consequently, they are not too concerned about the possibility of loss through theft. Their lack of concern will often lead them to leave their cars unlocked. The chance of a loss by theft is thereby increased because of the existence of insurance.

Morale hazard should not be confused with moral hazard. Morale hazard refers to insureds who are simply careless about protecting their property because the property is insured against loss. Moral hazard is more serious since it involves unethical or immoral behavior by insureds who seek their own financial gain at the expense of insurers and other policyowners.

BASIC CATEGORIES OF RISK

Risk can be classified into several distinct categories. The major categories of risk are as follows:[3]

- Pure and speculative risks
- Static and dynamic risks
- Fundamental and particular risks

Pure and Speculative Risks

A ***pure risk*** *is defined as a situation where there is only the possibility of loss.* Examples of pure risks include premature death, occupational and nonoccupational disability, catastrophic medical expenses, liability lawsuits, and damage to property from fire, lightning, flood, or earthquake. You normally do not profit if a loss occurs.

In contrast, *a* ***speculative risk*** *is defined as a situation where either profit or loss is possible.* Thus, if you should purchase 100 shares of common stock, you would profit if the stock rises in price but would lose if the price declines. Other examples of speculative risks are betting on a horse race, participating in a football pool, investing in real estate, going into business for yourself, and producing a new product in a business firm. In these situations, both profit and loss are possible.

It is important to distinguish between pure and speculative risks for several reasons. First, only pure risks are insurable by private insurers. With few exceptions, speculative risks are not insurable and other techniques for coping with risk must be used. One exception is that some insurers will insure institutional portfolio investments and municipal bonds against loss.

Second, most pure risks are more easily predictable than speculative risks. The law of large numbers can be more easily applied to pure risks whereby loss can be predicted in advance. One exception is the speculative risk of gambling where a casino can apply the law of large numbers in a most efficient manner. However, it is generally more difficult to apply the law of large numbers to speculative risks in order to predict future loss.

Finally, society may benefit from a speculative risk if a loss occurs, but it is harmed if a pure risk is present and a loss occurs. For example, a firm may develop a new technological process for producing a commodity more cheaply. As a result, a competitor may be forced into bankruptcy. Despite the bankruptcy, society benefits since the needed good is produced more efficiently at a lower cost to consumers. However, society loses when most pure risks actually occur. For example, if a flood occurs or if an earthquake devastates an area, society does not benefit.

Static and Dynamic Risks

Static risks *are risks connected with losses caused*

by the irregular action of nature or by the mistakes and misdeeds of human beings. Static risks are the same as pure risks and would, by definition be present in an unchanging economy. In contrast, ***dynamic risks*** *are risks associated with a changing economy.* Important examples of dynamic risks include the changing tastes of consumers, technological change, new methods of production, and investments in capital goods that are used to produce new and untried products.

Static and dynamic risks have several important differences. First, most static risks are pure risks, but dynamic risks are always speculative risks where both profit and loss are possible. Second, static risks would still be present in an unchanging economy, but dynamic risks are always associated with a changing economy. Also, dynamic risks usually affect more individuals and have a wider impact on society than do static risks. Finally, as we stated earlier, dynamic risks may be beneficial to society, but static risks are always harmful.

Fundamental and Particular Risks

A ***fundamental risk*** *is defined as a risk that affects the entire economy or large numbers of persons or groups within the economy.* Thus, the risk of double digit inflation is a fundamental risk since, with few exceptions, the entire economy is harmed by spiraling price increases. Other examples of fundamental risks are severe business recessions with high unemployment, wars, earthquakes that devastate large geographical areas, and floods that destroy thousands of homes.

In contrast, *a* ***particular risk*** *is a risk that affects only the individual and not the entire community or country.* Thus, the risk associated with the theft of your stereo set is an example of a particular risk. Only you are affected, not the entire community.

The distinction between a fundamental and a particular risk is important since government assistance may be necessary in order to insure fundamental risks. Social insurance, government insurance programs, and government guarantees and subsidies are used to meet certain fundamental risks in the United States. For example, the risk of unemployment cannot be insured privately by commercial insurers but can be insured publicly by state unemployment compensation programs. In addition, subsidized flood insurance can be obtained from the federal government by business firms and individuals who reside in flood areas.

TYPES OF PURE RISK

Certain types of pure risk pose a substantial threat to the financial security of both individuals and business firms. The major types of pure risk that are associated with great financial and economic insecurity include personal risks, property risks, and liability risks.

Personal Risks

Personal risks are those risks that directly affect an individual; they involve the possibility of the complete loss or reduction of earned income, extra expenses, and the depletion of financial assets. There are four major personal risks:[4]

- Risk of premature death
- Risk of old age
- Risk of poor health
- Risk of unemployment

Risk of premature death The risk of premature death means that it is possible for a person to die before attaining a certain age. At the present time, the life expectancy at birth for males in the United States is about seventy-one years, while for females, it is slightly more than seventy-eight years. Many persons die, however, before attaining these ages.

Premature death often results in great financial and economic insecurity if a family head dies prematurely. In many cases, a family head who dies prematurely has outstanding financial obligations, such as dependents to support, children to educate, and a mortgage to be paid off. But financial and economic insecurity can result from several other factors. First, the human life value of the family head is lost forever. *The* ***human life*** *value is defined as the present value of the family's share of the deceased breadwinner's future earnings.* This loss can be substantial; the human life value of most college graduates can easily exceed $250,000. Second, additional expenses may be incurred because of burial and probate costs, estate and inheritance taxes, and the expenses of last illness. Finally, the family's income from all sources may be inadequate in terms of its basic needs, quite apart from outstanding financial obligations.

It was formerly assumed that some families are made destitute only *after* the family head dies. This is clearly incorrect since in cases of a long terminal illness, the family can experience a substantial decline in its standard of living long before the death of the family head. One study of widows and orphans by the Life Underwriter Training Council and Life Insurance Agency Management Association revealed that one-fourth of all widows were living in poverty before their husband's death. As the length of the terminal illness increased, the proportion of families living in poverty also tended to increase. Forty percent of the widows whose husbands were terminally ill or disabled for two years or more before death were poor.[5] Thus, some families will experience great financial insecurity long before the family head actually dies.

Risk of old age The major risk associated with old age is the possibility of insufficient income during retirement. When older workers retire, they lose their normal work earnings. Unless they have accumulated sufficient financial assets on which to draw, or have access to other sources of income, such as a private pension or Social Security benefits, they will be confronted with a serious problem of financial and economic insecurity.

The income received by many aged persons is insufficient for maintaining a reasonable standard of living; moreover, the overall income position of the aged is far from satisfactory. The money incomes of aged families and individuals in the United States often fall substantially below the income level of the general population. The following data compare the median money incomes of families and unrelated individuals age sixty-five and over with the median family incomes of all families and unrelated individuals in the United States. The data are based on the March 1984 Current Population Survey conducted by the Bureau of the Census.[6]

Median family income for all families	$24,580
Median family income for family heads, age sixty-five and over	16,862
Median income all unrelated individuals	10,563
Median income unrelated individuals, age sixty-five and over	6,938

As the data show, the median family income for persons age sixty-five and over was only about 69 percent of the income level for all families; and for unrelated aged persons, the median income was about 66 percent of the income level for all unrelated individuals. Thus, it is clear that the aged as a group have substantially lower incomes than does the general population, which can result in serious economic insecurity for some aged.

The problem of insufficient income during retirement is also aggravated by the increased trend toward *early retirement.* More than half of the persons who retire apply for Social Security benefits before age sixty-five. Workers retire early because of poor health, technological change that eliminates jobs, plant closings, and labor union pressures to expand employment opportunities for younger workers. The result is that the duration of the retirement period has increased, while the period of productive work has decreased. Thus, some workers may be unable to save a sufficient amount of income during their working years to provide for a reasonable standard of living during the relatively longer retirement period.

Inflation can also aggravate the problem of insufficient income during retirement. Although most aged persons receive Social Security retire-

INSIGHT 1.1

Abrupt Termination of an Engineering Career

Although long-term disability often results from a progressive disease over a long period, a person can be totally disabled quickly and without warning. Consider the actual case of a thirty-two-year-old electrical engineer whose career was abruptly ended when he was seriously injured in an automobile accident where the other driver was at fault. The electrical engineer suffered horrendous burns, a complete personality change, and grotesque and deforming scars as a result of burns in the accident. He was married and had a one-year-old daughter.

The injured engineer had completed all requirements for the Ph.D. degree except for the doctoral dissertation. Because of his skills, arrangements had been made for him to continue his research and to join the staff at the University of Arizona. He had the potential of becoming a national leader in his field.

Because of the automobile accident, he endures continuous pain and suffering and must have additional surgery. He cannot continue in his field of specialization.

SOURCE: Adaptation of "Engineering Career Ended" from *FC & S Bulletins*, 1984. Reprinted by permission.

ment benefits that are periodically adjusted for inflation, the benefits are designed to provide only a minimum standard of living. Social Security benefits alone will not meet all of the income needs of most retired persons. Thus, rapid inflation can cause great financial and economic insecurity to the aged since their real incomes may be substantially reduced.

Risk of poor health Another important personal risk is the risk of poor health. Both the risk of catastrophic medical expenses and the loss of earned income must be considered. An unexpected illness or accident can often result in catastrophic medical expenses. For example, the cost of a heart or kidney transplant can easily exceed $50,000; the annual cost of kidney dialysis treatment in most hospitals exceeds $25,000. Thus, ten years of treatment would cost $250,000. Also, the costs of a crippling automobile accident that requires several major operations, plastic surgery, and rehabilitation can easily exceed $100,000. Unless the person has adequate health insurance or other sources of income to meet these expenditures, he or she will be financially insecure.

The risk of long-term disability and the consequent loss of earned income are also significant. The probability of a disability of ninety days or more is significantly higher than the probability of death at every attained age during the normal working life. For example, the probability of being disabled ninety days or more at age twenty-two is seven and one-half times greater than the probability of death at that age. This disparity decreases with age, but at sixty-two, the probability of a ninety-day disability is still twice as great as the probability of death.[7] In cases of long-term disability, there is a substantial loss of earned income, medical expenses are incurred, and someone must take care of the disabled person.

Risk of unemployment The risk of unemployment is another major threat to a person's financial security. Unemployment may result from a deficiency in aggregate demand, technological and structural economic changes, seasonal factors, and frictions in the labor market. Regardless of the cause, financial insecurity may result in at least three ways. First, of course, the worker loses his or her earned income. Unless there is adequate replacement income or past savings on which to draw, the unemployed worker will be financially insecure. Second, because of economic conditions, the worker may be able to work only part-time. Since work earnings are reduced, the income earned may be insufficient in terms of the worker's needs. Finally, if the duration of unemployment is extended over a long period, the unemployed worker may exhaust his or her accumulated financial assets.

Property Risks

Persons owning property are exposed to the risk of having their property damaged or lost from numerous perils. There are two major types of losses associated with the destruction or theft of property: direct loss and indirect or consequential loss.

Direct loss A *direct loss is defined as a financial loss that results from the physical damage, destruction, or theft of the property.* For example, assume that you own Tony and Luigi's Restaurant, and the building is insured by a fire insurance policy. If the building is damaged or destroyed from a fire, the physical damage to the property is known as a direct loss.

Indirect or consequential loss An ***indirect loss*** *is a financial loss that results from the indirect consequences of the physical damage, destruction, or theft of the property.* Thus, in addition to the physical damage loss, the restaurant would lose profits for several months while it is being rebuilt. The loss of profits would be a consequential loss. Other examples of a consequential loss would be the loss of the use of the building, the loss of rents, and the loss of a market.

Finally, extra expenses are another type of indirect or consequential loss. For example, suppose you own a newspaper, bank, or dairy. If a loss occurs, you must continue to operate regardless of cost; otherwise, you will lose customers to your competitors. It may be necessary to set up a temporary operation at some alternative location, and substantial extra expenses would then be incurred.

Natural disasters The risk of loss or damage to property from natural disasters is an important property risk that merits special treatment. Floods, hurricanes, tornadoes, earthquakes, forest and grass fires, and other violent natural disasters can result in a loss of billions of dollars in property damage as well as thousands of deaths. In 1981, 772 tornadoes killed twenty-four people and caused property damage in excess of $500 million. In 1979, hurricane Frederick caused a record $752.5 million in insured property losses, and hurricane David caused insured damages in excess of $122 million. The San Fernando Valley earthquake in 1971 caused $553 million in property damage losses. And, as newspaper headlines attest, severe floods in the United States annually cause millions of dollars of property damage.[8]

Natural disasters cause financial insecurity because of the considerable loss of human lives and the resultant loss of income to the stricken families. In addition, many property damage losses are either uninsured or underinsured, causing substantial additional expenses. Although insurance by the federal government is available for certain natural disaster perils—such as federal flood insurance under the National Flood Insurance Act of 1968—some property owners do not take advantage of this protection.

Many homeowners do not purchase insurance because they perceive the event of a natural disaster as improbable and, thus, perceive an extremely low probability of loss. Unless they have been made vividly aware of a natural disaster and have obtained useful information on insurance from other sources, such as friends and neighbors, they may not purchase the appropriate insurance, even at subsidized rates.[9]

Liability Risks

Liability risks are another important type of pure risk that most persons face. Under our system of law, you can be held legally liable if you do something that results in bodily injury or property damage to someone else. A court of law may order you to pay substantial damages to the person you have injured.

We live in a lawsuit-happy society at the present time. We have the widely held notion that the way to resolve any dispute is to sue. As a result, lawsuits of all types have increased substantially in recent years. Individuals are being held legally liable for the negligent operation of their automobiles; business firms are being sued because of defective products that result in harm or injury to someone else; physicians, attorneys, accountants, engineers, and other professionals are being sued because of alleged professional malpractice. And new types of lawsuits are constantly emerging. For example, ministers are now being sued by church members who accuse them of giving improper advice.

Liability risks are of great importance for two reasons. First, there is no maximum upper limit with respect to the amount of the loss. You can be sued for any amount. In contrast, if you own property, there is a maximum limit on the loss. For example, if your automobile has an actual cash value of $5000, the maximum physical damage loss is $5000. But if you are negligent and cause an accident that results in serious bodily injury to the other driver, you can be sued for any amount—$50,000, $500,000, or $1 million or more—by the person you have injured.

Second, although the experience is painful, you can afford to lose your present financial assets, but you can never afford to lose your future income and assets. Assume that you are sued and are required by the court to pay a substantial judgment to the person you have injured. If you do not carry liability insurance or are underinsured, your future income and assets can be attached to satisfy the judgment. In any event, your financial and economic security will be in jeopardy. We will examine the law of negligence and liability risks in greater detail in Chapter 9.

SOCIETAL BURDEN OF RISK

The presence of risk results in certain undesirable social and economic effects. Risk entails three major burdens on society:

1. The size of an emergency fund must be increased.
2. Society may be deprived of needed goods and services.
3. Mental worry and fear are present.

Larger Emergency Fund

It is prudent for both individuals and business firms to set aside funds for emergency purposes. In the absence of insurance, however, individuals and business firms must increase the size of their emergency fund in order to pay for unexpected losses. For example, assume that you have purchased a $100,000 home and wish to have the necessary funds in case the home is damaged from fire, hail, windstorm, or other perils. Without insurance, you would probably have to save at least $20,000 annually to build up an adequate fund within a relatively short period of time. Even then, an early loss could occur, and your emergency fund would be insufficient to pay the loss. If you are a middle-income wage earner, you would find such saving difficult. In any case, the higher the amount that must be saved, the more consumption spending must be reduced, which results in a lower standard of living. Moreover, as we stated earlier, a sizeable loss may occur before the fund is built up to the required level.

Loss of Certain Goods and Services

A second burden of risk is that society may be deprived of certain goods and services. Swine flu vaccine is a vivid example of how the presence of risk almost resulted in the cancellation of the vaccine. In 1976, swine flu broke out at a military base in Fort Dix, New Jersey. Because of the major flu epidemic in 1918–19 during which 548,000 Americans died, President Gerald Ford recommended a $135 million national vaccination program to meet the risk of a flu epidemic. However, because there were risks associated with the vaccine, major drug manufacturers were initially unwilling to produce it. Also, because of the potential liability to insurers if the vaccine proved defective, product liability insurers were unwilling to offer complete liability coverage without a government guarantee and ultimate acceptance of the risk. It was estimated that as many as ten million persons could have experienced adverse reactions to the vaccine, which could then result in sizeable claims against the drug manufacturers. Potential legal defense costs, in addition to the actual damage awards that would have to be paid, were estimated to be as high as $25 billion.[10] The flu vaccine eventually was manufactured. But it is safe to conclude that unless the government had stepped in, the risk was so great that society would have been deprived of the flu vaccine.

In addition, because of the presence of risk, society must pay more for needed goods and services. For example, because of the risk of a catastrophic lawsuit, professional liability insurance premiums for physicians and surgeons have soared. It is not uncommon for surgeons and anesthesiologists to pay more than $30,000 annually for medical malpractice insurance. These costs, of course, are passed on to the patients who must ultimately pay for the high risk associated with the practice of medicine.

Mental Worry and Fear

A final burden of risk is that mental worry and fear are present. This mental unrest must be recognized as a true cost of risk to society. Numerous examples can illustrate the mental unrest and fear because of risk. A college student who needs a grade of C in a required course in order to graduate may enter the final examination room with a feeling of apprehension and fear. Parents may be fearful if a son or daughter departs on a skiing trip during a blinding snowstorm since the risk of freezing to death or being killed on an icy road is present. Finally, some passengers in a Boeing 727 jet may become extremely nervous and fearful if the jet flies into rough turbulence and bounces all over the sky.

METHODS OF HANDLING RISK

As we stressed earlier, risk is a burden not only to the individual but to society as well. Thus, it is important to examine some techniques for meeting the problem of risk. There are five major methods of handling risk. They are as follows:

- Risk avoidance
- Risk retention
- Risk transfer
- Loss control
- Insurance

Risk Avoidance

Risk avoidance is one method of handling risk. For example, you can avoid the risk of being mugged in North Philadelphia by staying out of the area; you can avoid the risk of divorce by not marrying; a career employee who is frequently transferred can avoid the risk of selling a home in a depressed real estate market by renting instead of owning; and a business firm can avoid the risk of being sued for a defective product by not producing the product.

But as a practical matter, not all risks can or even should be avoided. For example, you can avoid the risk of death or disability in a plane crash by refusing to fly. But is this practical and desirable? The alternatives are not appealing. You can drive or take a bus or train, all of which take considerable time and often involve great fatigue. Although the risk of a plane crash is present, the safety record of commercial airlines is outstanding, and flying is a reasonable risk to assume. Or, you may wish to avoid the risk of business failure by refusing to go into business for yourself. But you may have the necessary skills and capital to be successful in business, and risk avoidance may not be the best approach for you to follow in this case.

Risk Retention

Risk retention is a second method of handling

risk. An individual or a business firm may retain all or part of a given risk. Risk retention can be either active or passive.

Active risk retention Active risk retention means that an individual is consciously aware of the risk and deliberately plans to retain all or part of it. For example, a motorist may wish to retain the risk of a small collision loss by purchasing an automobile collision insurance policy with a $200 deductible. A homeowner may retain a small part of the risk of damage to the home by purchasing a homeowners policy with a substantial deductible. A business firm may deliberately retain the risk of petty thefts by employees, shoplifting, or the spoilage of perishable goods. Or a business firm may use risk retention in a self-insurance program, which is a special application of risk retention.[11] In these cases, the individual or business firm makes a conscious decision to retain part or all of a given risk.

Active risk retention is used for two major reasons. First, risk retention can save money. Insurance may not be purchased at all, or it may be purchased with a deductible; either way, there is often a substantial saving in the cost of insurance. Second, the risk may be deliberately retained because commercial insurance is either unavailable or can be obtained only by the payment of prohibitive premiums. Some physicians, for example, practice medicine without professional liability insurance because they perceive the premiums to be inordinately high.

Passive risk retention Risk can also be retained passively. Certain risks may be unknowingly retained because of ignorance, indifference, or laziness. This is often very dangerous if a risk that is retained has the potential for destroying a person financially. A simple example can illustrate the danger of passive risk retention. Most students who work are retaining the risk of long-term disability without being aware of the catastrophic nature of such a risk. As we pointed out earlier, the probability of being disabled ninety days or more at age twenty-two is seven and one-half times greater than the probability of death. If you are not presently insured for this risk by either an individual or group long-term disability income policy, then you are using the technique of risk retention in an inappropriate and dangerous manner.[12]

In summary, risk retention can be an extremely useful technique for handling risk, especially in a modern corporate risk management program, which we will examine in Chapter 3. Risk retention, however, is appropriate mainly for handling high-frequency, low-severity type risks where potential losses are relatively small. Except under unusual circumstances, an individual should not use the technique of risk retention to retain low-frequency, high-severity risks, such as the risk of catastrophic medical expenses, long-term disability, or a liability lawsuit.

Risk Transfer

Risk transfer is another technique for handling risk. Risks can be transferred by several methods, among which are the following:

- Transfer of risk by contracts
- Hedging price risks
- Incorporation of a business firm

Transfer of risk by contracts Unwanted risks can be transferred by contracts. For example, the risk of a defective television or stereo set can be transferred to the retailer by purchasing a service contract, which makes the retailer responsible for all repairs after the warranty expires. The risk of a substantial increase in rent can be transferred to the landlord by a long-term lease. The risk of a substantial price increase in construction costs can be transferred to the builder by having a firm price in the contract rather than a cost-plus contract. Finally, a risk can be transferred by a **hold-harmless agreement.** For example, if a manufacturer of scaffolds inserts a hold-harmless clause in a contract with a retailer, the retailer agrees to hold the manufacturer harmless in case a scaffold collapses and someone is injured.

Hedging price risks Hedging price risks is another example of risk transfer. Hedging is a technique for transferring the risk of unfavorable price fluctuations to a speculator by purchasing and selling future contracts on an organized commodity exchange, such as the Chicago Board of Trade.

Both selling and buying hedges are possible, but only a buying hedge is illustrated here.[13] The buying hedge is the purchase of a future contract to protect against a possible price increase of the actual commodity prior to its purchase. For example, assume that a soybean oil exporter receives an order to export 180,000 pounds of crude soybean oil that must be shipped in three months at a certain price. The soybean exporter sets the price for this order on the basis of the cash price of the soybean oil on the day he or she makes the deal. However, the soybean oil will not be purchased until shortly before the delivery is made to the exporter. Meanwhile, the exporter must have protection against the risk of an upward price fluctuation. The price of soybean oil could decline, of course, in which case he or she would make more money. The exporter would probably prefer not to speculate, but would rather have a modest but certain profit.

That profit can be protected by hedging. The exporter has sold 180,000 pounds of soybean oil for future delivery, so 180,000 pounds of soybean oil should be purchased on the futures market. The bookkeeping entries appear as follows after the transactions:

Cash	Future
April 1 Sell 180,000 pounds of soybean oil at $28.00 per 100 lbs.	*April 1* Buy 180,000 pounds of August soybean oil at $23.00 per 100 lbs.

Now assume that three months later (or when the exporter buys the oil to complete his or her part of the contract), both cash and future prices for soybean oil have risen $10 per hundred-weight. The bookkeeping entries now appear as follows:

Cash	Future
April 1 Sell 180,000 pounds of soybean oil at $28.00 per 100 lbs.	*April 1* Buy 180,000 pounds of August soybean oil at $23.00 per 100 lbs.
July 1 Buy 180,000 pounds of soybean oil at $38.00 per 100 lbs.	*July 1* Sell 180,000 pounds of August soybean oil at $33.00 per 100 lbs.
loss $10.00	gain $10.00

net result $0.00

Ignoring commissions, the net difference in the transactions is zero. The exporter's gain in the futures market has offset the loss in the cash market. However, the basic profit in selling the soybean oil is preserved, since the risk of an adverse price fluctuation has been transferred.

Incorporation of a business firm A final example of risk transfer is by incorporation. If a firm is a sole proprietorship, the owner's personal assets, as well as the assets of the firm, can be attached by creditors for satisfaction of debts. If a firm incorporates, on the other hand, the personal assets of the stockholders cannot be attached by creditors for payment of the firm's debts. In essence, by incorporation, the liability of the stockholders is limited, and the risk of the firm having insufficient assets to pay business debts is shifted to the creditors.

Loss Control

Loss control is another important method for handling risk. Loss control consists of certain activities undertaken to reduce both the frequency and severity of losses. Thus, loss control has two major objectives: loss prevention and loss reduction.

"Tables on Hedging Futures" from *Introduction to Hedging*. Source: Chicago Board of Trade.

Loss prevention Loss prevention aims at reducing the probability of loss so that the frequency of losses is reduced. Several examples of personal loss prevention can be given. Automobile accidents can be reduced if motorists pass a safe driving course and drive defensively. Flunking out of college can be prevented by intensive study on a regular basis. The number of heart attacks can be reduced if individuals watch their weight, give up smoking, and follow good health habits.

Loss prevention is also important for business firms. For example, a boiler explosion can be prevented by periodic inspections by a safety engineer; occupational accidents can be reduced by the elimination of unsafe working conditions and by strong enforcement of safety rules; and fires can be prevented by forbidding workers to smoke in an area where highly flammable materials are being used. In short, the goal of loss prevention is to prevent the loss from occurring.

Loss reduction Although stringent loss prevention efforts can reduce the frequency of losses, some losses will inevitably occur. Thus, the second objective of loss control is to reduce the severity of a loss after it occurs. For example, a department store can install a sprinkler system so that a fire is promptly extinguished, thereby reducing the loss; highly flammable materials can be stored in a separate area to confine a possible fire to that area; a plant can be constructed with fire resistant materials to minimize a loss; and fire doors and fire walls can be used to prevent a fire from spreading.

Ideal method for handling risk From the viewpoint of society, loss control is the ideal method for handling risk. This is true for two reasons. *First, the indirect costs of losses may be large, and, in some instances, they can easily exceed the direct costs.* For example, a worker may be injured on the job. In addition to being responsible for the worker's medical expenses and a certain percentage of earnings (direct costs), the firm may also incur sizeable indirect costs. For example, a machine may be damaged and must be repaired; the assembly line may have to be shut down; costs are incurred in training a new worker to replace the injured worker; and a contract may be cancelled because goods are not shipped on time. By preventing the loss from occurring, both indirect costs and direct costs are reduced.

Second, the social costs of losses must also be considered. For example, assume that the worker in the preceding example dies from the accident. Substantial social costs are incurred because of the death. Society is deprived forever of the goods and services that the deceased worker could have produced. The worker's family loses its share of the worker's earnings and may experience great financial insecurity. And the worker may personally experience great pain and suffering before he or she finally dies. In short, these social costs can be reduced through an effective loss control program.

Insurance

A final technique for handling risk is by insurance. For most individuals, this is the most practical method for handling a major risk. Although commercial insurance has several characteristics, three of its major characteristics should be emphasized. First, *risk transfer* is used since a pure risk is transferred to the insurer. Second, the *pooling technique* is used to spread the losses of the few over the entire group so that average loss is substituted for actual loss. Finally, the risk may be reduced by application of the *law of large numbers*, whereby an insurer can predict future loss experience with some accuracy. Each of these characteristics will be treated in greater detail in Chapter 2.

SUMMARY

- There is no single definition of risk. Risk traditionally has been defined as uncertainty concerning the occurrence of a loss.
- Objective risk is the relative variation of actual loss from expected loss. Subjective risk is uncertainty based on an individual's mental condition or state of mind. Chance of loss is defined as the probability that an event will occur; it is not the same thing as risk.
- Peril is defined as the cause of loss. Hazard is any condition that creates or increases the chance of loss. There are three types of hazards. Physical hazard is a physical condition present that increases the chance of loss. Moral hazard is dishonesty or character defects in an individual that increase the chance of loss. Morale hazard is carelessness or indifference to a loss because of the existence of insurance.
- The basic categories of risk include:
  a. Pure and speculative risks.
  b. Static and dynamic risks.
  c. Fundamental and particular risks.

  A pure risk is a risk where there is only the possibility of loss. A speculative risk is a risk where both profit and loss are possible.

  Static risks are risks connected with losses caused by the irregular action of nature or by the mistakes and misdeeds of human beings; they are normally present even if the economy is unchanging. Dynamic risks are risks associated with a changing economy, such as technological change and innovation. Dynamic risks normally affect more persons than static risks and may be beneficial to the economy. Static risks are usually harmful to the economy.

  A fundamental risk is a risk that affects the entire economy or large numbers of persons or groups within the economy, such as inflation, war, or recession. A particular risk is a risk that affects only the individual and not the entire community or country.
- There are certain types of pure risk that can threaten an individual's financial security. They include:
  a. Personal risks.
  b. Property risks.
  c. Liability risks.
- Personal risks are those risks that directly affect an individual. Major personal risks include:
  a. Risk of premature death.
  b. Risk of old age.
  c. Risk of poor health.
  d. Risk of unemployment.
- Property risks affect persons who own property. If property is damaged or lost, two principal types of losses may result:
  a. Direct loss to property.
  b. Indirect or consequential loss.

  A direct loss is a financial loss that results from the physical damage, destruction, or theft of the property. An indirect or consequential loss is a financial loss that results from the indirect consequences of the physical damage, destruction, or theft of the property. Examples of indirect losses are the loss of use of the property, loss of profits, loss of rents, and extra expenses.
- Liability risks are extremely important because there is no maximum upper limit on the

amount of the loss and if a person must pay damages, future income and assets can be attached to pay the judgment.

- Risk entails three major burdens on society:
  a. The size of the emergency fund must be increased.
  b. Society may be deprived of needed goods and services.
  c. Mental worry and fear are present.
- There are five major methods of handling risk:
  a. Risk can be avoided.
  b. Risk can be retained.
  c. Risk can be transferred.
  d. Loss control can be used.
  e. Risk can be insured.

QUESTIONS FOR REVIEW

1. Explain briefly the meaning of risk.
2. How does objective risk differ from subjective risk?
3. Define chance of loss.
4. Distinguish between an objective probability and a subjective probability.
5. Define peril, hazard, physical hazard, moral hazard, and morale hazard.
6. Explain the difference between pure and speculative risk, static and dynamic risk, and fundamental and particular risk.
7. List the major types of pure risk that are associated with great financial and economic insecurity.
8. Why is pure risk harmful to society?
9. What is the difference between a direct loss and an indirect or consequential loss?
10. Describe briefly the five major methods of handling risk. Give an example of each method.

QUESTIONS FOR DISCUSSION

1. The Apex Fire Insurance Company receives an application to provide fire insurance on a frame building located near an oil refinery in an industrial section of the city. In considering this property for insurance, the fire insurer is concerned with the concepts of risk, peril, and hazard.
   a. Explain what is meant by *risk*, *peril*, and *hazard*.
   b. Based on the above situation, give an example of a risk, a peril, and a hazard.
   c. Risk managers are normally concerned with pure risks rather than speculative risks. Explain the difference between a pure risk and a speculative risk, and give an example of each with respect to the operation of a business firm.
2. Identify the types of financial losses likely to be incurred by each of the following parties:
   a. A person who negligently injures another motorist in an automobile accident.
   b. A restaurant that is shut down for six months because of a tornado.
   c. A family whose family head dies prematurely.

3. Chance of loss can be defined as the probability that an event will occur.
   a. Give an example of this definition of chance of loss.
   b. Are chance of loss and risk the same thing? Explain.
4. Mary operates a pawn shop in a large city. Her shop is in a high crime area, and she is complaining that the high cost of burglary insurance is threatening the existence of her business. A trade association points out that noninsurance methods can be used to handle the burglary exposure. Identify and illustrate how three different noninsurance methods might be used to deal with this exposure.
5. Various methods can be used to handle risk. For each of the following, what method for handling risk is illustrated? Explain.
   a. The decision not to carry earthquake insurance on a firm's main manufacturing plant.
   b. The installation of an automatic sprinkler system in a hotel.
   c. The decision not to produce a product that might result in a product liability lawsuit.
   d. The requirement that retailers who sell a firm's product sign an agreement releasing the firm from liability if the product should injure someone.

KEY CONCEPTS AND TERMS TO KNOW

Risk
Objective risk
Subjective risk
Chance of loss
Objective probability
Subjective probability
Peril
Hazard
Physical hazard
Moral hazard
Morale hazard
Pure risk
Speculative risk
Static risk
Dynamic risk
Fundamental risk
Particular risk
Personal risks
Property risks
Liability risks
Human life value
Direct loss
Indirect or consequential loss
Risk avoidance
Risk retention
Risk transfer
Loss control
Hold-harmless clause

SUGGESTIONS FOR ADDITIONAL READING

Athearn, James L. and S. Travis Pritchett. *Risk and Insurance*, 5th ed. St. Paul, Minnesota: West Publishing Company, 1984, chapter 1.

Bickelhaupt, David L. *General Insurance*, 11th ed. Homewood, Illinois: Richard D. Irwin, Inc., 1983, chapters 1 and 2.

Crane, Frederick G. *Insurance Principles and Practices*, 2nd ed. New York: John Wiley and Sons, 1984, chapter 1.

Crowe, Robert M. and Ronald C. Horn. "The Meaning of Risk." *The Journal of Risk and Insurance* 34 (September 1967): 459–74.

Dorfman, Mark S. *Introduction to Insurance*, 2nd ed. Englewood Cliffs, New Jersey: Prentice-Hall, Inc., 1982, chapter 1.

Greene, Mark R. and James S. Trieschmann. *Risk and Insurance*, 6th ed. Cincinnati, Ohio: Southwestern Publishing Company, 1984, chapter 1.

Hammond, J. D., ed. *Essays in the Theory of Risk*. Glenview, Illinois: Scott, Foresman and Co., 1968.

Head, George L. "An Alternative to Defining Risk as Uncertainty." *The Journal of Risk and Insurance* 34 (June 1967): 205–14.

Kunreuther, Howard. "The Changing Societal Consequences of Risks from Natural Disasters." *The Annals of the American Academy of Political and Social Science* 443 (May 1979): 104–16.

Mehr, Robert I. and Emerson Cammack. *Principles of Insurance*, 7th ed. Homewood, Illinois: Richard D. Irwin, Inc., 1980, chapters 1 and 2.

Pfeffer, Irving and David R. Klock. *Perspectives on Insurance*. Englewood Cliffs, New Jersey: Prentice-Hall, Inc., 1974, chapter 14.

Rejda, George E., special ed. "Risk and Its Treatment: Changing Societal Consequences," *The Annals of the American Academy of Political and Social Science* 443 (May 1979).

Schoemaker, Paul J. H. *Experiments on Decisions under Risk: The Expected Utility Hypothesis*. Hingham, Massachusetts: Kluwer-Nijhoff Publishing, 1980.

Vaughan, Emmett J. *Fundamentals of Risk and Insurance*, 3rd ed. New York: John Wiley & Sons, 1982, chapter 1.

Williams, Jr., C. Arthur and Richard M. Heins. *Risk Management and Insurance*, 5th ed. New York: McGraw-Hill Book Company, 1985, chapter 1.

NOTES

1. Risk has also been defined as (1) chance of loss, (2) possibility of an adverse deviation from a desired outcome that is expected or hoped for, (3) the variation in the possible outcomes that exist in a given situation, and (4) possibility that a sentient entity can incur a loss. For a critical discussion of the uncertainty theory of risk, the interested student should read George L. Head, "An Alternative to Defining Risk as Uncertainty," *The Journal of Risk and Insurance*, 34 (June 1967), pp. 205–14; and Robert M. Crowe and Ronald C. Horn, "The Meaning of Risk," *The Journal of Risk and Insurance*, 34 (September 1967), pp. 459–74.
2. For example, see Mark R. Greene and Oscar N. Serbein, *Risk Management: Text and Cases* (Reston, Virginia: Reston Publishing, Inc., 1978), pp. 30–32.
3. A. H. Mowbray made the distinction between pure and speculative risk; Alan H. Willett classified risk into static and dynamic risks; and C. A. Kulp treated risk as either fundamental or particular. See A. H. Mowbray, R. H. Blanchard, and C. A. Williams, Jr., *Insurance*, 6th ed. (New York: McGraw-Hill Book Company, 1969), pp. 6–8; Alan H. Willett, *The Economic Theory of Risk and Insurance* (Homewood, Illinois: Richard D. Irwin, Inc., 1951), pp. 14–23; and C. A. Kulp, *Casualty Insurance*, 3rd ed. (New York: The Ronald Press Company, 1956), pp. 3–14.
4. George E. Rejda, *Social Insurance and Economic Security* (Englewood Cliffs, New Jersey: Prentice-Hall, Inc., 1976), pp. 5–6.
5. Rejda, p. 51.
6. U.S. Bureau of the Census, Current Population Reports, Series P-60, No. 145, *Money Income and Poverty Status of Families and Persons in the United States: 1983 (Advance Data from March 1984 Current Population Survey)*, U.S. Government Printing Office, Washington, D.C., 1984, Table 6, p. 11.
7. Herbert Denenberg et al., *Risk and Insurance*, 2nd ed. (Englewood Cliffs, New Jersey: Prentice-Hall, Inc., 1974), p. 302.
8. Insurance Information Institute, *Insurance Facts*, 1982–83 Edition, pp. 55–57.
9. Howard Kunreuther, "The Changing Societal Consequences of Risks from Natural Disasters," *The Annals of the American Academy of Political and Social Science*, 443 (May 1979), p. 105.
10. Mark R. Greene, "A Review and Evaluation of Selected Government Programs to Handle Risk," *The Annals of the American Academy of Political and Social Science*, 443 (May 1979), p. 140.
11. Self-insurance is discussed in Chapter 3.
12. This is based on the assumption that you are working either part-time or full-time and have work earnings that will terminate if you should become disabled.
13. For a complete discussion of hedging, see Chicago Board of Trade, *Introduction to Hedging* (Chicago, Illinois: Board of Trade of the City of Chicago, 1972).

CHAPTER 2

THE INSURANCE MECHANISM

"If, in meeting hazard, average is substituted for actual loss, the result is insurance."

C.A. Kulp, Casualty Insurance

STUDENT LEARNING OBJECTIVES

After studying this chapter, you should be able to:

- Define insurance and explain the basic characteristics of insurance.
- Explain the law of large numbers.
- Describe the requirements of an insurable risk from the viewpoint of the insurer.
- List the major insurable and uninsurable risks in our society.
- Show how insurance differs from gambling and speculation.
- Describe the major fields of insurance.
- Explain the social benefits and social costs of insurance.

For most persons and families, insurance is the major technique for handling risk. In this chapter, we will discuss the meaning of insurance and examine its basic characteristics. We will then examine the requirements that must be fulfilled before a risk can be insured privately. We will also point out how insurance differs from both gambling and speculation. We will conclude the chapter by describing the major fields of insurance and the social benefits and social costs of insurance in our society.

DEFINITION OF INSURANCE

In Chapter 1, we noted that risk can be defined several ways. Likewise, there is no single definition of insurance. Insurance can be defined from the viewpoint of any of several disciplines, including law, economics, history, actuarial science, risk theory, and sociology. But we will not examine the pros and cons of each possible definition.[1] Instead, we will focus our attention on those common elements that are typically present in any insurance plan. However, before we proceed, a working definition of insurance—one that captures the essential characteristics of a true insurance plan—must be established.

After careful study, the Commission on Insurance Terminology of The American Risk and Insurance Association has defined insurance as follows:[2]

> ***Insurance*** *is the pooling of fortuitous losses by transfer of such risks to insurers who agree to indemnify insureds for such losses, to provide other pecuniary benefits on their occurrence, or to render services connected with the risk.*

Although this definition may not be acceptable to all insurance scholars, it is useful for analyzing the common elements of a true insurance plan.

BASIC CHARACTERISTICS OF INSURANCE

Based on the preceding definition, insurance typically has several distinct characteristics. They include the following:

- Pooling of losses
- Payment of fortuitous losses
- Risk transfer
- Indemnification

Pooling of Losses

Pooling or the sharing of losses is the heart of insurance. ***Pooling*** *or combination is the spreading of losses incurred by the few over the entire group, so that in the process, average loss is substituted for actual loss.* In addition, pooling involves the grouping of a large number of homogeneous exposure units so that the law of large numbers can operate to provide a substantially accurate prediction of future losses. Thus, pooling implies: (1) the sharing of losses by the entire group, and (2) the prediction of future losses with some accuracy based on the law of large numbers. Let us examine each of these concepts in greater detail.

With respect to the first concept—loss sharing—consider this simple example. Assume that 1,000 farmers in Southeastern Nebraska agree that if any farmer's home is damaged or destroyed by a fire, the other members of the group will indemnify or cover the actual costs of the unlucky farmer who has a loss. Assume also that each home is valued at $75,000, and, on the average, one burns each year. In the absence of insurance, the maximum loss to each farmer is $75,000 if the home should burn. However, by pooling the loss, it can be spread over the entire group, and if one farmer has a total loss, the maximum amount that each farmer would have to pay is only $75 ($75,000/1,000). In effect, the pooling technique results in the substitution of an average loss of $75 for the actual loss of $75,000.

In addition, by pooling or combining the loss experience of a large number of homogeneous exposure units, an insurer may be able to predict future losses with some accuracy. From the viewpoint of the insurer, if future losses can be predicted, objective risk is reduced. Thus, another characteristic often found in many insurance schemes is risk reduction based on the law of large numbers.

The law of large numbers *means that the greater the number of exposures, the more closely will the actual results approach the probable results that are expected from an infinite number of exposures.*[3] For example, if you flip a balanced coin into the air, the *a priori probability* of getting a head is 0.5. If you flip the coin only ten times, you may get a head eight times. Although the observed probability of getting a head is 0.8, the true probability is still 0.5. If the coin were flipped one million times, however, the actual number of heads would be approximately one-half. Thus, as the number of random tosses increases, the actual results approach the expected results.

A practical illustration of the law of large numbers is the National Safety Council's prediction of the number of automobile deaths during a typical holiday weekend. Because millions of automobiles are on the road, the National Safety Council has been able to predict with great accuracy the number of motorists who will die during a typical July 4 holiday weekend. For example, 500 to 700 motorists may be expected to die during a typical July 4 weekend. Although individual motorists cannot be identified, the actual number of deaths for the group of motorists as a whole can be predicted with some accuracy.

However, for most insurance lines, the actuary seldom knows the true probability of loss. Estimates of both the average frequency and the average severity of loss must be based, therefore, on previous loss experience. If there is a sufficiently large number of homogeneous exposure units, the actual loss experience of the past may be a good approximation of future losses. This is so because, as we noted in Chapter 1, objective risk varies inversely with the square root of the number of cases under observation: As the number of exposures increases, the relative variation of actual loss from expected loss will decline. Thus, the insurer can predict future losses with a greater degree of accuracy as the number of exposures increases. This is important since the actuary must charge a premium that will be adequate for paying all losses and expenses during the policy period. The lower the degree of objective risk, the more confidence an insurer has that the actual premium charged will be sufficient to pay all claims and expenses and provide a margin for profit.

Payment of Fortuitous Losses

A second characteristic of private insurance is the payment of fortuitous losses. *A **fortuitous loss** is one that is unforeseen and unexpected and occurs as a result of chance.* In other words, the loss must be accidental. Insurance contracts will not pay for intentionally caused losses. The law of large numbers is based on the assumption that losses are accidental and occur randomly.

Risk Transfer

Risk transfer is another essential element of insurance. With the exception of self-insurance,[4] a true insurance plan always involves risk transfer. ***Risk transfer*** *means that a pure risk is transferred from the insured to the insurer, which typically is in a stronger financial position to pay the loss than the insured.* From the viewpoint of the individual, pure risks that are typically transferred to insurers include the risks of premature death, poor health, disability, destruction and theft of property, and liability lawsuits.

Indemnification

A final characteristic of insurance is indemnification for losses. The insured is indemnified if a covered loss occurs. ***Indemnification*** *means compensation to the victim of a loss, in whole or in part, by payment, repair, or replacement.* Thus, if your home burns in a fire, the homeowners policy will indemnify you for the loss. If you are sued because of the negligent operation of an automobile, your automobile liability insurance policy will pay on your behalf those sums that you are legally obligated to pay. Similarly, if you are seriously disabled, a disability income policy will indemnify you for part of the wage loss.

This concludes our discussion of the essential characteristics of insurance. A more rigorous statement of the law of large numbers can be found in the Appendix at the end of the chapter. Let us next examine the requirements of an insurable risk.

REQUIREMENTS OF AN INSURABLE RISK

Insurers normally insure only pure risks. However, not all pure risks are insurable. Certain requirements usually must be fulfilled before a pure risk can be privately insured. From the viewpoint of the insurer, there are ideally six requirements of an insurable risk:

1. There must be a large number of homogeneous exposure units.
2. The loss must be accidental and unintentional.
3. The loss must be determinable and measurable.
4. The loss should not be catastrophic.
5. The chance of loss must be calculable.
6. The premium must be economically feasible.

Large Number of Homogeneous Exposure Units

The first requirement of an insurable risk is the existence of a large number of homogeneous exposure units. The purpose of this requirement is to enable the insurer to predict loss based on the law of large numbers. Exposure units with similar loss-producing characteristics are grouped by classes. If a sufficiently large number of exposure units are present within a class, the insurer can accurately predict both the average frequency and the average severity of loss.

You should keep in mind that a large number of heterogeneous exposure units would not fulfill this requirement of an insurable risk. The exposure units must be roughly similar to each other in terms of loss-producing characteristics. If heterogeneous exposure units were grouped together, it would be difficult for the insurer to accurately predict the average frequency and severity of claims. For this reason, frame dwellings, manufacturing plants, churches, schools, office buildings, and other structures are not grouped together in one class. Because of their dissimilar nature, the chance of loss would be difficult to calculate accurately.

Accidental and Unintentional Loss

A second requirement is that the loss should be accidental and unintentional; ideally, it should be fortuitous and outside the insured's control. This means that if an individual deliberately causes a loss, it should not be paid.

The requirement of an accidental and unintentional loss is necessary for two reasons. First, if intentional losses were paid, moral hazard would be substantially increased, and premiums would rise as a result. The substantial increase in premiums could result in relatively fewer persons purchasing the insurance. The insurer may not then have a sufficient number of homogeneous exposure units to predict future losses.

Second, the loss should be accidental because the law of large numbers is based on the random occurrence of events. A deliberately caused loss is not a random event, since the insured knows when the loss will occur. Thus, since prediction of future losses is based on past loss experience, the prediction of future experience may be highly inaccurate if a large number of intentional or nonrandom losses occur.

Determinable and Measurable Loss

A third requirement is that the loss should be both determinable and measurable. This means the loss must be definite as to cause, time, place, and amount. Death comes closest to meeting this requirement, since death can be easily determined in most cases, and if the person is insured, the face amount of the life insurance policy is the amount paid.

Some losses, however, are difficult to determine and measure. For example, under a disability-income policy, the insurer promises to pay a monthly or weekly benefit to the disabled person if the definition of disability stated in the policy is satisfied. Some dishonest claimants may deliberately fake an illness or injury in order to collect from the company. Even if the claim is legitimate, the company must still determine whether the insured satisfies the definition of disability as stated in the policy. Sickness and disability are highly subjective, and the same event can affect two persons quite differently. For example, two accountants who are insured under separate disability-income contracts may be injured in an automobile accident, and both may be classified as totally disabled. One accountant, however, may be stronger willed and be more determined to return to work. If he or she undergoes rehabilitation and returns to work, the disability-income benefits are terminated. Meanwhile, the other accountant would still continue to receive disability-income benefits according to the terms of the policy. In short, it is difficult to determine when a person is actually disabled. However, all losses ideally should be both determinable and measurable.

The basic purpose of this requirement is that the insurer must be able to determine if the loss is covered under the policy, and if it is covered, how much the company will pay. For example, Mary may have a fur coat insured under the homeowners policy. It makes a great deal of difference to the insurer whether a thief breaks into her home and steals the coat, or the coat is missing merely because her husband stored the coat in a dry cleaning establishment but forgot to tell her. The loss is covered in the first example but not in the second.

No Catastrophic Loss

The fourth requirement of an ideal insurable risk is that the loss should not be catastrophic. This means that a large proportion of exposure units should not incur losses at the same time. As we stated earlier, pooling is the essence of insurance. If most or all of the exposure units in a certain class simultaneously incur a loss, then the pooling technique breaks down and becomes unworkable. Premiums must be increased to prohibitive levels, and the insurance technique is no longer a viable arrangement by which losses of the few are spread over the entire group.

Insurers ideally wish to avoid all catastrophic losses, but in the real world, this is impossible, since catastrophic losses periodically result from floods, hurricanes, tornadoes, earthquakes, forest fires, and other natural disasters.

Fortunately, two approaches are available for meeting the problem of a catastrophic loss. First, *reinsurance can be used*, whereby insurance companies are indemnified by reinsurers for catastrophic losses. We will study reinsurance later in Chapter 26.

Second, insurers can avoid the concentration of risk by *dispersing their coverage over a large geographical area.* The concentration of loss exposures in some areas due to frequent floods, tornadoes, hurricanes, or other natural disasters can cause periodic catastrophic losses. If loss exposures are geographically dispersed, the possibility of a catastrophic loss is reduced.

Calculable Chance of Loss

Another important requirement of an insurable risk is that the chance of loss must be calculable. The insurer must be able to calculate both the average frequency and the average severity of future losses with some accuracy. This is necessary so that a proper premium can be charged that is sufficient to pay all claims and expenses and yield a profit during the policy period.

Certain losses, however, are difficult to insure because the chance of loss cannot be accurately estimated. For example, floods, war, and cyclical unemployment occur on an irregular basis, and prediction of the average frequency and the severity of losses is therefore difficult. Thus, without government assistance, these losses are difficult for private carriers to insure.

Economically Feasible Premium

A final requirement is that the premium must be economically feasible. The insured must be able to afford to pay the premium. In addition, for the insurance to be an attractive purchase, the premiums paid must be substantially less than the face value or amount of the policy.

In order to have an economically feasible premium, the chance of loss must be relatively low. One view is that if the chance of loss exceeds 40 percent, the cost of the policy will exceed the amount that the insurer must pay under the contract. For example, an insurer could issue a $1,000 life insurance policy on a man age ninety-nine, but the pure premium would be about $980, and an additional amount for expenses would have to be added. The total premium would exceed the face amount of the insurance.[5]

Based on these requirements, personal risks, property risks, and liability risks can be privately insured, since the requirements of an insurable risk generally can be met. By contrast, *most market risks, financial risks, production risks, and political risks* are normally uninsurable by private insurers.[6] These risks are uninsurable for several reasons. First, these risks are speculative and so are difficult to insure privately. Second, the potential of each to produce a catastrophic loss is great; this is particularly true for political risks, such as the risk of war. Finally, calculation of the proper premium for such risks may be difficult because the chance of loss cannot be accurately estimated. For example, insurance that protects a retailer against loss because of a change in consumer tastes, such as a style change, cannot be purchased today. Accurate loss data are not available, and there is no accurate way to calculate a premium. The premium charged may or may not be adequate to pay all losses and expenses. Since private insurers are in business to make a profit, certain risks are uninsurable because of the possibility of substantial losses.

TWO APPLICATIONS: THE RISKS OF FIRE AND UNEMPLOYMENT

You will understand more clearly the requirements of an insurable risk if you can apply these requirements to a specific risk. For example, let us first consider the risk of fire to a private dwelling. This risk can be privately insured, since the requirements of an insurable risk are generally fulfilled. Figure 2.1 illustrates that the risk of fire in a private dwelling fulfills the requirements of an insurable risk.

As you can see, the risk of fire to a private dwelling generally meets the requirements of an insurable risk. Let us next examine the risk of unemployment, which generally is not privately insurable at the present time. How well does the risk of unemployment meet the requirements of an insurable risk? As is evident in Figure 2.2, the risk of unemployment does not completely meet the requirements.

First, labor is heterogeneous in nature. There are professional, highly skilled, semi-skilled, unskilled, blue collar, and white collar workers. Moreover, unemployment rates vary significantly by occupation, age, sex, education, marital status, city, state, and a host of other factors, including government programs and policies that frequently change. Also, the duration of unemployment varies widely among the different groups. In addition, since a large number of workers can become unemployed at the same time, a potential catastrophic loss is present. Finally, since the different types of unemployment occur irregularly, it is difficult to calculate accurately the chance of loss. For these reasons, the risk of unemployment generally cannot be privately insured at the present time, but can be insured by social insurance programs. We will examine social insurance programs later in the chapter.

ADVERSE SELECTION

An effective insurance plan must also consider the problem of adverse selection. *Adverse selection means that the exercise of choice by insureds results in higher than average loss levels.* Unless insurance companies protect themselves against this exercise of choice, the people who obtain insurance tend to be those who need it most—

Figure 2.1
The Risk of Fire as an Insurable Risk

Requirements	Does risk of fire qualify as insurable?
1. Large number of homogeneous exposure units	Yes. A large number of homogeneous exposure units are present.
2. Accidental and unintentional loss	Yes. With the exception of arson, most fire losses are accidental and unintended.
3. Determinable and measurable loss	Yes. If there is disagreement over the amount paid, the standard fire policy has provisions for resolving disputes.
4. No catastrophic loss	Yes. Although catastrophic fires have occurred, all exposure units normally do not burn at the same time.
5. Calculable chance of loss	Yes. Chance of fire can be calculated, and the average severity of a fire loss can be estimated in advance.
6. Economically feasible premium	Yes. Premium rate per $100 of fire insurance is relatively low.

those with a greater probability of loss than the average. For example, we can expect that a person with no insurance who needs a costly surgical operation will seek health insurance, that a business person who operates in a high crime-rate area will seek crime insurance, and that a person who resides in a flood zone will desire flood insurance. If this tendency goes unchecked, a disproportionate number of insureds who may experience an early loss will enter each insured class, so that actual losses will be higher than expected. The higher level of losses will result in a premium increase, which only worsens the problem, since the superior insureds within each class will probably seek insurance elsewhere at a lower cost. The substandard insureds, however, will still retain their coverage. This process will continue until the only insureds covered are the worst ones. At that point, the insurance plan would fail, since the pooling technique cannot work if all or a large part of the group incur losses at the same time.

Insurers attempt to control adverse selection by underwriting and policy provisions. ***Underwriting*** *refers to the selection and classification of profitable insureds.* Applicants for insurance who do not meet underwriting standards will be denied insurance or charged an extra premium.

Policy provisions are also used to control adverse selection. Examples of such provisions are the suicide clause in life insurance, and the preexisting condition clause and probationary period in health insurance. We will examine these policy provisions in greater detail later in the text when we analyze specific contracts.

INSURANCE AND GAMBLING COMPARED

Insurance is often erroneously confused with gambling. But they are not the same thing. There are two important differences between them. First, gambling creates a new speculative risk that did not exist before, while insurance is a technique for handling an already existing pure risk. Thus, if you bet $200 on a horse race, a new speculative risk is created, but if you pay $200 to the insurer for fire insurance, the risk of fire is already present and is transferred to the insurer by a contract.

The second difference between insurance and gambling is that gambling is socially unproductive, since the winner's gain comes at the expense of the loser. In contrast, insurance is always socially productive, since neither the insurer nor the insured is placed in a position where the gain of the winner comes at the expense of the loser.[7] The insurer and the insured have a common interest in the prevention or nonoccurrence of loss. Both parties win if the loss does not occur. Moreover, the gambling transaction never restores the loser to his or her former financial position, but insurance financially restores the insured in whole or in part if a loss occurs.

INSURANCE AND SPECULATION COMPARED

In Chapter 1, we examined the concept of hedging, by which a risk can be transferred to a speculator by purchase of a futures contract. An insurance contract, however, is not the same thing as speculation. Although both techniques are similar in that risk is transferred by a contract, and no new risk is created by the transaction, there are some important differences between them. First, an insurance transaction normally involves the transfer of risks that are insurable, since the requirements of an insurable risk generally can be met. However, speculation is a technique for handling risks that are typically uninsurable, such as protection against a substantial decline in the price of agricultural products and raw materials.

A second difference between insurance and speculation is that insurance can reduce the ob-

Figure 2.2
The Risk of Unemployment as an Insurable Risk

Requirements	Does risk of unemployment qualify as insurable?
1. Large number of homogeneous exposure units	Not completely. Exposure units are heterogeneous in nature (professional, skilled, semi-skilled, and unskilled workers).
2. Accidental and unintentional loss	No. A certain proportion of unemployment is due to individuals who voluntarily quit their jobs.
3. Determinable and measurable loss	Not completely. The level of unemployment can be determined, but the measurement of loss is difficult. Some unemployment is involuntary, some is voluntary.
4. No catastrophic loss	No. A severe national recession or depressed local business conditions could result in a catastrophic loss.
5. Calculable chance of loss	No. The different types of unemployment are too irregular to estimate accurately the chance of loss.
6. Economically feasible premium	No. Adverse selection, moral hazard, and the potential for a catastrophic loss could make the premium unattractive.

jective risk of an insurer by application of the law of large numbers. As the number of exposure units increases, the insurer's prediction of future losses improves, since the relative variation of actual loss from expected loss will decline. Thus, many insurance transactions reduce objective risk. In contrast, speculation typically involves only risk transfer, not risk reduction. The risk of an adverse price fluctuation is transferred to a speculator who feels he or she can make a profit because of superior knowledge of forces that affect market price. The risk is transferred, not reduced, since the speculator's prediction of loss may be based only on a relatively small number of transactions.

FIELDS OF INSURANCE

The various fields of insurance can be divided into private and government insurance. Private insurance, in turn, can be classified into life and health insurance on the one hand, and property and liability insurance on the other. Government insurance can usefully be classified into social insurance programs and all other government insurance plans. Thus, the major fields of insurance, both private and public, can be classified as follows:

- Private Insurance
  - Life and health insurance
  - Property and liability insurance
- Government insurance
  - Social insurance
  - Other government insurance

Private Insurance

Life and health insurance More than 2,000 life and health insurers are now operating in the United States. The names of many of these companies are household words, and include such financial giants as Prudential Insurance Company of America, Metropolitan Life, New York Life, Mutual of Omaha, and Northwestern Mutual.

Life insurers pay death benefits to beneficiaries upon the death of the insureds. Death benefits typically cover burial expenses and provide periodic income payments to the deceased's dependents. In addition, life insurers sell private pensions and individual annuities to meet the need for income after retirement. Life and health insurers also sell health insurance that provides for the payment of medical expenses in the event of sickness or injury. Finally, both types of insurers sell disability-income coverages to meet the problem of the loss of earnings during a period of disability.

Property and liability insurance At the present time, about 3,000 property and liability insurers are operating in the United States. Many of these are large, well-known companies such as State Farm, Allstate, Travelers, and Aetna Life and Casualty.

The property and liability industry can be classified by several major lines of insurance (see Figure 2.3).

Fire insurance and allied lines. Fire insurance covers the loss or damage to real estate and personal property because of fire, lightning, or removal from the premises. Other perils can be added, such as windstorm, hail, tornadoes, and vandalism. Indirect losses can also be covered,

Figure 2.3
Fire insurance and allied lines

Marine insurance
a. Ocean marine
b. Inland marine

Casualty insurance
a. Automobile insurance
b. General liability insurance
c. Burglary and theft insurance
d. Workers' compensation
e. Glass insurance
f. Boiler and machinery insurance
g. Nuclear insurance
h. Crop-hail insurance
i. Health insurance
j. Other miscellaneous lines

Multiple-line insurance

Fidelity and surety bonds

including the loss of profits and rents and the extra expenses incurred as a result of a business interruption loss.

Marine insurance. Marine insurance is often called transportation insurance because it covers goods in transit against most pure risks connected with transportation.

Marine insurance is divided into ocean marine and inland marine insurance. *Ocean marine insurance* provides protection for all types of ocean-going vessels and their cargoes; contracts can be written to cover the legal liability of the owners and shippers. *Inland marine insurance* provides coverage for goods being shipped on land. This includes imports, exports, domestic shipments, and the instrumentalities of transportation (for example, bridges, tunnels, and pipelines). In addition, inland marine insurance also covers personal property such as fine art, jewelry, and furs.

Casualty insurance. Casualty insurance is a broad field of insurance and covers whatever is not covered by fire, marine, and life insurers.

Automobile insurance provides for legal liability arising out of the operation of an automobile, physical damage coverage for the automobile itself, medical payments insurance, and protection against uninsured motorists.

General liability insurance provides protection against claims arising out of property damage or bodily injury to others. Legal liability for claims of this kind may arise out of the ownership of property, sales or distribution of products, manufacturing or contracting operations, operation of elevators and the like, and professional services.

Burglary and theft insurance covers the loss of property, money, and securities because of burglary, robbery, or larceny. In addition, the loss of money and securities because of destruction or disappearance can also be insured.

Workers' compensation insurance provides protection to covered workers against an occupational accident or job-related disease. The insurance normally pays for the costs of medical care, rehabilitation and lost wages for injured employees and death benefits to the dependents of employees who die from work-related accidents or occupational disease.

Glass insurance provides broad coverage for glass breakage. Because of architectural demands, merchandising trends, and decorative uses, there has been an increasing need for glass insurance.

Boiler and machinery insurance is a highly specialized line covering a wide variety of power-producing equipment, including boilers, turbines, and generators. Here loss prevention is emphasized to the extent that major insurers provide for safety inspections and other engineering services to prevent losses. The rapid growth of automation and sophisticated production techniques have intensified the need for loss prevention in the area.

Nuclear insurance provides protection against losses resulting from nuclear accidents. Three insurance company groups—American Nuclear Insurers, Mutual Atomic Energy Liability Underwriters, and the Mutual Atomic Energy Reinsurance Pool—together can provide up to $160 million of liability coverge and $30 million of contingent liability insurance to nuclear facilities. Also, the industry groups can provide up to $527 million of insurance to cover damage to the property of nuclear facility operators on an all-risk basis.

Crop-hail insurance provides protection against loss of growing crops as a result of hail storms and other perils.

Health insurance coverages are also sold by casualty insurers. These are similar to the coverages discussed earlier and include medical expense insurance, disability income, and accident policies.

Other miscellaneous casualty lines include *title insurance,* which provides protection against financial loss because of a legal defect in a title to real estate, and *credit insurance,* which provides protection to manufacturers and wholesalers against financial loss because an account receivable from a customer is not collectible.

Multiple-line insurance. Multiple-line insurance is a type of insurance that combines both property and liability coverages into one contract.

Prior to passage of multiple-line laws in the 1940s, the insurance business was strictly compartmentalized. This meant that a company writing fire insurance could not write casualty insurance, and a casualty insurer could not write fire insurance. Since then, all states have passed some type of multiple-line legislation that permits insurers to write fire and casualty insurance in one contract. For example, the typical homeowners policy now combines fire insurance and other perils with liability insurance in one contract. Other multiple-line policies are the Businessowners Policy and Special Multi-peril Policy (SMP) for motels, apartments, and other business firms. We will examine multiple-line contracts in greater detail in Chapter 13.

Fidelity and surety bonding. Fidelity bonds provide protection against loss caused by the dishonest or fraudulent acts of employees, such as embezzlement and the theft of money. *Surety bonds* provide for monetary compensation in case of failure by bonded persons to perform certain acts, such as the failure of a contractor to construct a building on time. Surety bonds include contract, license and permit, court, and fiduciary bonds. We will examine the major characteristics of bonding later in Chapter 15.

Government Insurance

Social insurance Government social insurance programs have basic characteristics that distinguish them from other government insurance plans. They are financed entirely or in large part by special contributions from employers, employees, or both, not primarily by government's general revenues. These contributions are usually earmarked for special funds that are kept separate from ordinary government accounts; the benefits, in turn, are paid from these funds. In addition, the right to receive benefits is ordinarily either derived from or linked to the recipient's past contributions or coverage under the program; the benefits and contributions generally vary among the beneficiaries, according to their prior earnings, but the benefits are heavily weighted or skewed in favor of low-income groups. Moreover, most social insurance programs are compulsory; certain covered workers and employers are required by law to pay contributions and participate in the programs. Finally, qualifying conditions and benefit rights are usually prescribed exactly in the statutes, leaving little room for administrative discretion in the award of benefits.[8]

The major social insurance programs in the United States include the following:

- Old-Age, Survivors, Disability, and Health Insurance (Social Security)
- Unemployment insurance
- Workers' compensation
- Compulsory temporary disability insurance
- Railroad Retirement Act
- Railroad Unemployment Insurance Act

The *Old-Age, Survivors, Disability, and Health Insurance (OASDHI)* program is the most important social insurance program in the United States. It protects individuals against financial insecurity from premature death and old age. It also provides valuable protection against the loss of earnings from disability and high medical expenses of the aged. The OASDHI program is a massive income-maintenance program that provides an important layer of income protection to most individuals and families. More than nine out of ten workers are currently covered for OASDHI benefits, about one out of six people currently receives monthly cash benefits, and more than 29 million of the aged and the disabled have coverage for their medical expenses under the Medicare program.

Unemployment insurance programs provide weekly cash benefits to workers who experience short-term involuntary unemployment. *Workers' compensation* provides benefits to workers who are injured or disabled because of a job-related accident or disease. *Compulsory temporary disability insurance,* which exists in five states, Puerto Rico, and the railroad industry, provides for the partial replacement of wages that may be lost because of a temporary disability. The *Railroad Retirement Act* provides retirement benefits, survivorship benefits, and disability income benefits to railroad workers who meet certain eligibility requirements. Finally, the *Railroad Unemployment Insurance Act* provides unemployment and sickness benefits to railroad employees. Most social insurance programs provide a high degree of protection to covered workers. We will return to social insurance in Chapter 24, where the programs will be analyzed in greater detail.

Other government insurance programs Other government insurance programs that do not exhibit the distinguishing characteristics of social insurance exist at both the federal and state level. Important federal insurance programs include the Civil Service Retirement System, various life insurance programs for veterans, pension termination insurance, insurance on savings accounts and checking accounts (Federal Deposit Insurance Corporation), insurance on funds deposited with savings and loan institutions (Federal Savings and Loan Insurance Corporation), federal flood insurance, federal crop insurance, federal crime insurance, student loan insurance fund, war risk insurance, and numerous other programs.

Government insurance programs also exist at the state level. These programs include the Wisconsin State Life Insurance Fund, crop-hail programs in six states, title insurance programs in four states, and the Maryland State Automobile Insurance Fund.

This concludes our discussion of the major lines of private and government insurance. Let us next consider the benefits of insurance to society.

BENEFITS OF INSURANCE TO SOCIETY

The existence of insurance results in great benefits to society. The major social and economic benefits of insurance include the following:

- Indemnification for loss
- Less worry and fear
- Source of investment funds
- Loss prevention
- Enhancement of credit

Indemnification for Loss

Indemnification for losses is an important benefit to society. Indemnification permits individuals and families to be restored to their former financial position after a loss occurs. As a result, they can maintain their economic security. Since they are restored either in part or in whole after a loss occurs, they are less likely to apply for public assistance or welfare, or to seek financial assistance from relatives and friends.

Indemnification to business firms also results in great benefits to society. After a loss occurs, indemnification permits the firm to remain in business and employees to keep their jobs. Suppliers continue to receive orders, and customers can still receive the goods and services they desire. The community also benefits because its tax base is not eroded. In short, the indemnification function contributes greatly to family and business stability and therefore is one of the most important social and economic benefits of insurance.

Less Worry and Fear

A second benefit of insurance is that worry and fear are reduced. This is true both before and after a loss. For example, if family heads have adequate amounts of life insurance, they are less likely to worry about the financial security of their dependents in the event of premature death; persons insured for long-term disability do not have to worry about the replacement of their earnings if a serious illness or accident occurs; and property owners who are insured enjoy greater peace of mind since they know they are covered if a loss occurs. Worry and fear are also reduced after a loss occurs, since the insureds know that they have insurance that will pay for the loss.

Source of Investment Funds

Another important social and economic benefit is that the insurance industry is an important source of funds for capital investment and accumulation.

INSIGHT 2.1

Social Investments of Life and Health Insurers

Life and health insurers invest in a wide variety of social investments. A social investment is one that benefits society as a whole or is designed to meet a specific social problem. During 1967–1972, the life and health insurance industry made a formal commitment to invest $2 billion in social investments, such as housing for low income persons, revitalization of declining neighborhoods, better educational and health facilities, and investments that lead to job creation. Since that time, social investments have become an important part of the investment portfolios of many insurers.

In 1983, life and health insurers invested more than $2.2 billion in social investments as indicated by the following table:

Selected types of social investments (in millions): Trend companies

	1979	1980	1981	1982	1983
Housing, 1-4 family	$466	$257	$273	$471	$922
Housing, multifamily	147	69	27	44	140
Hospitals	94	124	21	24	52
Nursing homes	42	8	8	7	19
Clinics	12	15	3	*	14
Other health facilities	28	7	21	5	24
Commercial	301	446	325	228	670
Industrial	52	105	107	56	95
Land	2	6	6	1	*
Social service	4	7	4	*	2
Environment	478	63	182	131	61
Minority deposits	56	22	56	354	27
Education	15	43	70	50	115
Other	43	91	30	41	67
Total	$1,740	$1,263	$1,133	$1,412	$2,208

Number of Trend Companies (79)
*Less than 500,000.
Source: Table, "Selected Types of Social Investments" from *Twelfth Annual Social Report of the Life and Health Insurance Business, 1984.* Reprinted by permission.

The largest investments are loans for family and multi-family housing units. Funds are also deposited in minority held financial institutions. In addition, an increasing number of companies are participating in the College Endowment Funding Plan, which raises capital for financially troubled black colleges by obtaining below-market loans from insurers. In view of the serious economic and social problems now facing American cities, social investments may become even more important in the future.

Premiums are collected in advance of the loss, and funds not needed to pay immediate losses and expenses can be loaned to business firms. These funds typically are invested in shopping centers, hospitals, new plants, housing developments, and new machinery and equipment. Such investments increase society's stock of capital goods, and so tend to promote economic growth and full employment. Moreover, since the total supply of loanable funds is increased by the advance payment of insurance premiums, the cost of capital to business firms that borrow is lower than it would be in the absence of the insurance industry.

Loss Prevention

Loss prevention is another important social and economic benefit of insurance. Insurance companies are actively involved in numerous loss prevention programs and also employ a wide variety of loss prevention personnel, including safety engineers and specialists in fire prevention, occupational safety and health, and products liability. Some important loss-prevention activities that property and liability insurers strongly support include:

- Highway safety and reduction of automobile deaths
- Fire prevention
- Reduction of work-related disabilities
- Prevention of automobile thefts
- Prevention and detection of arson losses
- Prevention of defective products that could injure the user
- Prevention of boiler explosions

The loss-prevention activities reduce both the direct and indirect or consequential losses. Society benefits since both types of losses are reduced.

Enhancement of Credit

A final benefit is that insurance enhances a person's credit. Insurance makes a borrower a better credit risk because it guarantees the value of the borrower's collateral, or gives greater assurance that the loan will be repaid. For example, when a house is purchased, the lending institution normally requires property insurance on it before the mortgage loan is granted. Mortgage life insurance can pay off the loan if the mortgagee dies prematurely; and so makes the homeowner a better credit risk. Similarly, a business firm seeking a temporary loan for Christmas, Easter, or other seasonal business may be required to insure its inventories before the loan is made. And if a new automobile is purchased and financed by a bank or other lending institution, physical damage insurance on the automobile may be required before the loan is made. Thus, insurance can enhance a person's credit.

COSTS OF INSURANCE TO SOCIETY

Although the insurance industry provides enormous social and economic benefits to society, the social costs of insurance must also be recognized. The major social costs of insurance include the following:

- Cost of doing business
- Fraudulent claims
- Inflated claims

Cost of Doing Business

One important cost is the cost of doing business. Insurers consume scarce economic resources—land, labor, capital, and business enterprise—in providing insurance to society. In financial terms, an *expense loading* must be added to the pure premium to cover the expenses incurred by companies in their daily operations. An expense loading is the amount needed to pay all expenses, including commissions, general administrative expenses, state premium taxes, acquisition expenses, and an allowance for contingencies and profit. Sales and administrative expenses by property and liability insurers account for about 25 percent of each premium dollar; operating expenses of life insurers account for about 16 percent of each premium dollar.[9] As a result, the

INSIGHT 2.2

Arson: A Growing Problem

The arson problem is widespread and growing steadily every day. The National Fire Protection Association reports a 377 percent increase in arson since 1964; 32 percent in the last two years alone. Basically, arson is committed for three reasons: profit, revenge, and "fun". Based on statistics reported to Aetna's Arson/Fraud Unit in 1980 for major losses the categories break out this way:

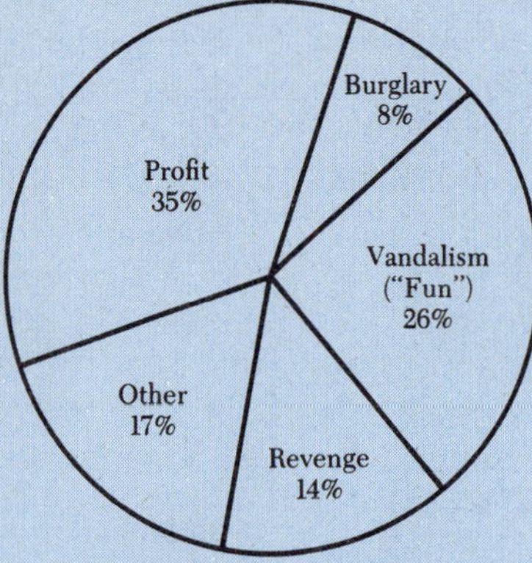

Arson for Profit
The profit-minded arsonist might be a building owner who finds the hope of profit gained through insurance more desirable than the property itself. The owner may be in debt, or just want to make a quick profit from an insurance company. Or, the arsonist may be starting a blaze to hide another crime, to profit by burning the evidence which might put him or her behind bars. Tenants wishing to break leases, persons wishing to acquire newer material possessions, or homeowners wishing to get the best price for their holdings may also engage in arson for profit.

Arson for Revenge
Here, the arsonist is a citizen with a grudge. It might be someone who was fired from a job, jilted by a lover, or who had a political or social statement to make. In this case, the arson is an outgrowth of the person's more violent feelings.

Arson for "Fun"
It is difficult to pinpoint the motivation in arson for "fun". The arsonist may be a juvenile seeking thrills from the burning and destruction of property, or the arsonist may be a pyromaniac, finding deeper meaning in setting fires.

SOURCE: Excerpt from "Our Town is Burning Down" from *Arson: A Growing Problem.* Reprinted by permission of Aetna Life & Casualty Co.

total costs to society are increased. For example, assume that a small country with no insurance has an average of $100 million of fire losses each year. If fire insurers now provide fire insurance, assume that the expense loading is 35 percent of the losses. Thus, the total costs to this country are increased to $135 million.

But these additional costs are justified for several reasons. First, objective risk is reduced because of insurance. Second, the costs of doing business are not necessarily wasteful, since insurers engage in a wide variety of loss-prevention activities. Finally, the insurance industry provides meaningful employment to millions of workers. About two million workers are employed by life insurers and property and liability insurers.[10] However, since economic resources are used up in providing insurance to society, a real economic cost is incurred.

Fraudulent Claims

A second cost of insurance is the submission of fraudulent claims. We noted in Chapter 1 that moral hazard is present in all forms of insurance. A dishonest person may deliberately incur a loss or fake a loss and then submit the claim to the insurer for payment. Numerous examples of fraudulent claims can be given. Arson losses have increased substantially over time. In 1983 alone, incendiary fires in buildings and other structural fires of suspicious origin caused property damage of about $1.4 billion and took 970 lives.[11] Some persons fraudulently report the theft of valuable property, such as a diamond ring or fur coat, and then submit the claim to the insurer for reimbursement. Dishonest pawnbrokers report fictitious burglaries and then attempt to collect from the insurer. And organized gangs of car thieves steal automobiles with the specific purpose of collecting the insurance.

The payment of fraudulent claims results in higher premiums to all insureds. Financial costs are also incurred by insurers in their efforts to detect and prosecute dishonest claimants; if a conviction is obtained, society must then support the wrongdoer if he or she is incarcerated. In short, the presence of insurance encourages intentional losses and invites the submission of fraudulent claims. These social costs fall directly on society.

Inflated claims

Many claims are inflated because of insurance. The loss may not be intentionally caused by the insured, but the claim may be inflated; in other words, it may exceed the actual economic loss experienced by the insured. Examples of inflated claims include the following:

- Attorneys for plaintiffs may seek high liability judgments that often exceed the true economic loss of the victim.
- Physicians may charge above-average fees for surgical procedures covered by major medical health insurance.
- Disabled persons may malinger to collect disability-income benefits for a longer duration.
- Insureds may inflate the amount of an automobile collision loss to cover the deductible in an automobile insurance policy.

These inflated claims must be recognized as an important social cost of insurance. Premiums must be increased to cover the losses, and disposable income that could be used for the consumption of other goods or services is thereby reduced.

In summary, the social and economic benefits of insurance appear to outweigh the social costs. Insurance reduces worry and fear; the indemnification function contributes greatly to social and economic stability; the economic security position of individuals and firms is preserved; and from the viewpoint of insurers, objective risk in the economy is reduced. The social costs of insurance can be viewed as the sacrifice that society must make to obtain these benefits.

SUMMARY

- There is no single definition of insurance. However, a typical insurance plan contains four elements:
  a. Pooling of losses
  b. Fortuitous losses
  c. Risk transfer
  d. Indemnification

  Pooling means that the losses of the few are spread over the group and average loss is substituted for actual loss. Fortuitous losses are unforeseen and unexpected and occur as a result of chance. Risk transfer involves the transfer of a pure risk to an insurer. Indemnification means that the victim of a loss is restored in whole or in part by payment, repair, or replacement by the insurer.
- The law of large numbers means that as the number of exposures increases, the more likely it is that the actual results will approach the expected results. The law of large numbers permits an insurer to estimate future losses with some accuracy.
- There are several ideal requirements of an insurable risk:
  a. There must be a large number of homogeneous exposure units.
  b. The loss must be accidental and unintentional.
  c. The loss must be determinable and measurable.
  d. The loss should not be catastrophic.
  e. The chance of loss must be calculable.
  f. The premium must be economically feasible.

  Personal risks, property risks, and liability risks can be privately insured, since the requirements of an insurable risk generally can be met. However, market risks, financial risks, production risks, and political risks generally are uninsurable, since these requirements are difficult to meet.
- Adverse selection means that persons who may have an early loss apply for insurance. Without adequate controls, the insured group would contain a disproportionate number of substandard insureds who may experience an early loss. If losses occur simultaneously to a large proportion of insureds, then the pooling technique becomes unworkable.
- Insurance is not the same as gambling. Gambling creates a new speculative risk, while insurance is designed to handle an existing pure risk. Also, gambling is socially unproductive, since the winner's gain comes at the expense of the loser. Insurance is always socially productive, since both the insured and insurer win if the loss does not occur.
- Insurance is not the same as speculation. Insurance involves the transfer of a pure risk, while speculation involves the transfer of a speculative risk. Also, insurance may often reduce the objective risk of an insurer because of the law of large numbers. Speculation typically involves only risk transfer and not risk reduction.
- The principal fields of insurance can be divided into private and government insurance. Private insurance consists of life and health insurance and property and liability insurance. Government insurance consists of social insurance and other government insurance programs.
- The major benefits of insurance to society are as follows:
  a. Indemnification for loss

b. Less worry and fear
c. Source of investment funds
d. Loss prevention activities
e. Enhancement of credit

- Insurance entails certain social costs to society. They include the following:
  a. Cost of doing business
  b. Fraudulent claims
  c. Inflated claims

QUESTIONS FOR REVIEW

1. Explain the major characteristics of a typical insurance plan.
2. Why is the pooling technique essential to insurance?
3. Explain the law of large numbers and show how the law of large numbers can be used by an insurer to estimate future losses.
4. Explain the major requirements of an insurable risk.
5. Why are most market risks, financial risks, production risks, and political risks considered to be uninsurable by private insurers?
6. Why are insurance companies concerned about adverse selection?
7. How does insurance differ from gambling? How does insurance differ from speculation?
8. List the major fields of private and government insurance.
9. How is insurance beneficial to society?
10. Explain the social costs of insurance to society.

QUESTIONS FOR DISCUSSION

1. One author states that "the law of large numbers forms the basis of insurance." Do you agree or disagree with this statement?
2. Although no risk completely meets all of the ideal requirements of an insurable risk, some risks come much closer to meeting them than others.
   a. List the ideal requirements of an insurable risk.
   b. Compare the risks of (i) automobile collision, and (ii) war in terms of how well they meet the requirements of an insurable risk.
3. The federal government agreed to reimburse financial institutions against loss if they made loans to the Chrysler Corporation.
   a. Do the loan guarantees to financial institutions by the federal government constitute insurance? Your answer must include a discussion of the basic characteristics of a true insurance plan.
   b. Is it financially feasible for a private insurer to sell commercial insurance that would insure the risk of a loan default by the Chrysler Corporation? Your answer must include an application of each of the requirements of an insurable risk.

4. One critic of private insurance stated that "insurance is wasteful and socially unproductive because it encourages the submission of false and fraudulent claims. As a result, honest persons must pay more for their insurance than is necessary."
   a. Do you agree or disagree with the above statement?
   b. In view of the social costs of insurance, would society be better off if the institution of insurance were not in existence?
5. Explain how insurance is socially productive while gambling is socially unproductive.

KEY CONCEPTS AND TERMS TO KNOW

Insurance
Pooling
Fortuitous loss
Risk transfer
Indemnification
Law of large numbers
Requirements of an insurable risk
Adverse selection
Underwriting
Multiple-line insurance
Life and health insurance
Property and liability insurance
Casualty insurance
Ocean marine insurance
Inland marine insurance
Social insurance

SUGGESTIONS FOR ADDITIONAL READING

Athearn, James L. and S. Travis Pritchett. *Risk and Insurance,* 5th ed. St. Paul, Minnesota: West Publishing Company, 1984, chapter 3.

Bickelhaupt, David L. *General Insurance,* 11th ed. Homewood, Illinois: Richard D. Irwin, Inc., 1983.

Greene, Mark R. and James S. Trieschmann. *Risk and Insurance,* 6th ed. Cincinnati, Ohio: Southwestern Publishing Company, 1984, chapter 2.

Mehr, Robert I., Emerson Cammack and Terry Rose, *Principles of Insurance,* 8th ed. Homewood, Illinois: Richard D. Irwin, 1985.

Pfeffer, Irving. *Insurance and Economic Theory.* Homewood, Illinois: Richard D. Irwin, Inc., 1956.

Vaughan, Emmett J. *Fundamentals of Risk and Insurance,* 3rd ed. New York: John Wiley & Sons, 1982, chapter 2.

Williams, Jr., C. Arthur, George L. Head, Ronald C. Horn, and G. William Glendenning. *Principles of Risk Management and Insurance,* 2nd ed. Volume I. Malvern, Pennsylvania: American Institute for Property and Liability Underwriters, 1981, chapters 6 and 7.

NOTES

1. For a discussion of insurance from several disciplines, see Irving Pfeffer, *Insurance and Economic Theory* (Homewood, Illinois: Richard D. Irwin, Inc., 1956). This book is a classic in analyzing the various definitions of insurance. A more recent discussion of the various definitions of insurance can be found in C. Arthur Williams, Jr., George L. Head and G. William Glendenning, *Principles of Risk Management and Insurance,* Volume I (Malvern, Pennsylvania: American Institute for Property and Liability Underwriters, Inc., 1978), pp. 274–304.
2. *Bulletin of the Commission on Insurance Terminology of the American Risk and Insurance Association,* 1, No. 4 (October 1965), p. 1.
3. Robert I. Mehr, *Life Insurance: Theory and Practice* (Dallas, Texas: Business Publications, 1977) p. 40.
4. Self-insurance is discussed in Chapter 3.

5. Robert I. Mehr and Emerson Cammack, *Principles of Insurance*, 7th ed. (Homewood, Illinois: Richard D. Irwin, 1980), p. 33.
6. Market risks include the risks of adverse price changes in raw materials, general price level changes (inflation), changes in consumer tastes, new technology, and increased competition from competitors. Financial risks include the risks of adverse price changes in the price of securities, adverse changes in interest rates, and the inability to borrow on favorable terms. Production risks include the risks associated with strikes and labor problems, shortages of raw materials, depletion of natural resources, and technical problems in production. Finally, political risks include the risks of war, overthrow of government, adverse government regulations, and the withholding of oil by Arab countries.
7. Charles O. Hardy, *Risk and Risk-Bearing* (Chicago, Illinois: University of Chicago Press, 1923), p. 373.
8. George E. Rejda, *Social Insurance and Economic Security*, 2nd ed. Englewood Cliffs, NJ: Prentice-Hall, Inc., 1984.
9. Insurance Information Institute, *Insurance Facts, 1984–85 Property/Casualty Fact Book*, p. 16; and American Council of Life Insurance, *1983 Life Insurance Fact Book*, p. 61.
10. *Insurance Facts, 1984–85 Property/Casualty Fact Book*, p. 5.
11. *Insurance Facts, 1984–85 Property/Casualty Fact Book*, p. 58.

APPENDIX*

THE LAW OF LARGE NUMBERS AND SOME ELEMENTARY STATISTICAL CONCEPTS IN RISK AND INSURANCE

An elementary knowledge of probability distributions is essential in order to understand the basic foundations of insurance. A probability distribution shows the probability of occurrence for each possible outcome of some contingent event, such as the amount of loss resulting from a fire or an automobile accident. Because the outcomes are mutually exclusive, the sums of these probabilities must equal one.

In order to understand risk and insurance theory, you should be familiar with three probability distributions: (1) the probability distribution of total dollar losses for some time period; (2) the distribution of the number of losses or accidents for each year (the claim frequency distribution); and (3) the distribution of dollar losses per accident (the claim severity distribution).[1] The total dollars of loss (or the pure premium) for the entity during a given time period can be obtained by summing the dollar losses associated with each accident during the period.

As indicated above, the probability distribution of total losses for an entity during some time period is usually referred to as the pure premium distribution. This distribution can be for an individual, for an insurance company with a group of risks, or for a business firm with more than one exposure unit subject to loss from some peril. The total loss or pure premium distribution for an individual for some type of peril shows the total losses for an individual risk during a given time period, such as a year. An aggregate loss or pure premium distribution for a given line of insurance or for a class of risks within a given line of insurance shows the potential total losses for such a group of insured individuals or exposure units. An aggregate pure premium distribution for some type of exposure retained or self-insured by a business firm or corporation shows the total losses that might be incurred during a given time period. Thus, this total loss distribution can be used to represent somewhat different pure loss situations, depending on the exposure to loss and the entity being considered. However, the basic concepts associated with these distributions are exactly the same, as will be clearer shortly.

TOTAL LOSS DISTRIBUTION DERIVED FROM THE CLAIM FREQUENCY AND CLAIM SEVERITY DISTRIBUTIONS

It can be shown statistically that the total loss distribution or pure premium distribution for an entity can be obtained by combining the claim frequency distribution with the claim severity distribution. The *claim frequency distribution*, or the distribution of the numbers of losses, shows the probability of having various numbers of claims or losses during a given time period. The *claim severity distribution* shows the probability associated with each possible amount of loss given that a loss has occurred. This distribution of loss amounts is a conditional probability distribution since it shows the potential size of losses given that an accident or loss has occurred.

By combining the claim frequency and claim severity distributions, a total loss distribution (or pure premium distribution) for an entity during a given time period can be obtained. In statistics,

* Prepared by Robert C. Witt, University of Texas at Austin.

this combinatorial process is referred to as convoluting these distributions. For beginning insurance students, however, knowledge of the exact statistical techniques used in combining these distributions is not essential. It is only important to understand that a total loss distribution is derived from the associated claim frequency and claim severity distributions.

For illustrative purposes, assume that the *number* of accidents or losses, Z, for an entity during some time period and the potential *size* of these losses, Y, are random variables with known probability distributions, P(z) and P(y), respectively. Similarly, let X represent the total possible losses that a risk could develop during the time period with a probability distribution denoted by P(x). The arithmetic means or expected values for these random variables will be denoted as E(Z), E(Y), and E(X), respectively, where E(·) is the expected value operator which merely denotes the average or mean value for a random variable. The variances associated with these variables will be denoted as Var(Z), Var(Y), and Var(X), respectively. Recall that the variance of a random variable merely shows the dispersion of the values of the variable around its mean.

Now it can be shown that the mean of the total loss distribution is merely the product of the expected *number* of losses (or mean claim frequency) and the expected *size* of loss (or mean claim severity) for the individual risk; that is:

$$(1)\ E(X) = E(Z) \cdot E(Y).$$

If all individual risks were perfectly homogeneous, then their mean or expected losses would be identical.[2]

It can also be shown that the variance for the total loss distribution is given by the following relationship.

$$(2)\ Var(X) = Var(Z) \cdot E(Y)^2 + Var(Y) \cdot E(Z)$$

Thus, it can be seen that the variance of total losses, Var(X), can be derived from the means and variances associated with the claim frequency and claim severity distributions.[3]

An Illustration

The above formulas for the mean and variance of a total loss distribution can be illustrated by using the data from the fire insurance example in this chapter. For example, in Chapter 2, we saw that 1,000 farmers in Nebraska formed a mutual fire insurance association where the fire losses of the unfortunate few were shared by all members of the association (the loss pooling concept). In this example, it was assumed that the number of losses incurred by the group of farmers followed a binomial distribution.

$$P_n(z) = \frac{n!}{z!(n - z)} p^z (1 - p)^{n-z}$$

where Z = the number of fire losses for 1,000 exposures during the year (it can range from 0 to 1,000),

n = 1,000, the number of insured farm houses or exposure units,

p = 1/1,000 = the probability that an individual farmer's house will burn to the ground,

$p_n(z)$ = the probability that z of the n farmers' houses exposed to the fire peril burn down during the year.

Note that the number of losses for a *single* farmer follows a Bernoulli probability distribution with a probability of p for a total fire loss and a probability of $(1 - p)$ for no loss; that is:

$$P(z) = p^z \cdot (1 - p)^{1-z}$$
$$\text{where } z = 0 \text{ or } 1$$

Thus, $P(z = 1) = p$, and $P(z = 0) = 1 - p$ for a single farmer. The *expected number* of fire losses during a year for a *single* farmer also turns out to equal p.

$$E(Z) = \sum_{z=0}^{1} z \cdot P(z)$$
$$= 0 \cdot p(z = 0) + 1 \cdot p(z = 1)$$
$$= 0 \cdot (1 - p) + 1 \cdot p$$
$$= p$$
$$= 1/1{,}000.$$

Thus, the probability of one loss and the expected number of losses, p, is the same for one farmer.

The variance in the *number of losses* for a single farmer is calculated in the usual manner, as follows:

$$V(Z) = \sum_{z=0}^{1} [z - E(z)]^2 \cdot P(z)$$
$$= [0 - p]^2 \cdot P(z = 0) + [1 - p]^2 \cdot P(z = 1)$$
$$= (0 - p)^2 \cdot (1 - p) + (1 - p)^2 \cdot P$$
$$= p^2 \cdot (1 - p) + (1 - p)^2 \cdot p$$
$$= p(1 - p) \cdot [p + (1 - p)]$$
$$= p(1 - p)$$
$$= (1/1{,}000) \cdot (1 - 1/1{,}000)$$
$$= (1/1{,}000) \cdot (999/1{,}000)$$
$$= 999/(1{,}000)^2.$$

An elementary statistics book will show that the mean and variance for n Bernoulli trials is the mean and variance of a binomial probability distribution with n trials. In this case, there are $n =$ 1,000 farmers who are exposed to a total fire loss of their homes (each exposure unit is a trial). Thus, the *expected number of losses* and the associated variance in the number of losses for 1,000 farm homes exposed to the fire peril can be shown to equal the following:

$$E_n(Z) = \sum_{z=0}^{1000} z \cdot P_n(Z)$$
$$= n \cdot p$$
$$= 1{,}000 \cdot (1/1{,}000) = 1$$
$$= \text{the expected number of losses for } n = 1{,}000 \text{ exposure units.}$$

$$Var_n(Z) = \sum_{t=0}^{1000} [z - E_n(Z)]^2 \cdot P_n(Z)$$
$$= n \cdot p \cdot (1 - p)$$
$$= 1{,}000 \cdot (1/1{,}000)(1 - 1/1{,}000)$$
$$= 999/1{,}000.$$

Thus, it can be seen that expected total number of fire losses for n farmers is merely n times the expected number of losses for a *single* farmer or exposure unit; that is:

$$E_n(Z) = n \cdot E(Z) = n \quad p$$

Similarly, the variance for the total number of losses is merely n times the variance of the number of losses for a single exposure:

$$Var_n(Z) = n \cdot Var(Z)$$
$$= n \cdot p(1 - p).$$

In summary, the mean *number* of fire losses expected by the mutual insurance association of 1,000 farmers is one per year over a long-term period. Alternatively, a single farmer would expect a total fire loss only once in 1,000 years.

Given that a fire occurred, it was assumed in this chapter that the fire destroyed the entire home. Therefore, the size of loss could only assume one value, \$75,000. This is a somewhat simplified severity distribution because no partial losses are recognized. This means the expected value of a loss, Y, given a fire has occurred, is \$75,000; that is:

$$E(Y) = \$75{,}000$$

As suggested in formula (1), the expected total fire losses for one farmer or exposure unit, $E(X)$, is merely the product of the expected *number* of losses, $E(Z)$, times the expected size of a loss, $E(Y)$:

$$E(X) = E(Z) \cdot E(Y)$$
$$= p \cdot E(Y)$$
$$= (1/1{,}000) \cdot \$75{,}000 = \$75.$$

This is the long-run expected fire loss for one farmer. For n farmers, it can be shown that expected total fire losses, $E_n(X)$, is equal to n times $E(X)$:

$$\begin{aligned} E_n(X) &= n \cdot E(X) \\ &= 1{,}000 \cdot \$75 \\ &= \$75{,}000. \end{aligned}$$

Thus, the farmers' mutual insurance association would expect $75,000 in fire losses per year. Since losses are pooled, however, each member would only expect to pay $75 for the fire insurance.

It should be emphasized that $E(X)$ and $E_n(X)$ are only expected values because actual total losses could turn out to be smaller or larger than $75 and $75,000, respectively, for the individual farmer and the group of farmers, depending on the actual number of homes that burned during a year. Thus, the variability of potential total losses must be considered for insurance purposes.

As shown in Equation (2), the variance of total losses for a single exposure unit is determined by the means and variances associated with the claim frequency and claim severity distributions for a single exposure.

$$\begin{aligned} Var(X) &= Var(Z) \cdot E(Y)^2 + Var(Y) \cdot E(Z) \\ &= p(1-p) \cdot E(Y)^2 + Var(Y) \cdot p \\ &= [999/(1{,}000)^2] \cdot (\$75{,}000)^2 + 0 \cdot (1/1{,}000) \\ &= (999)(\$75)^2 = (\$2{,}370.52)^2 \end{aligned}$$

Since the variance is expressed in "squared dollars," the standard deviation of total losses, σ_x, is a more relevant measure of dispersion because it is the square root of the variance.

$$\sigma_x = \sqrt{Var(x)} = \sqrt{(\$2{,}370.52)^2} = \$2{,}370.52.$$

All of the values in the above equation were previously calculated except the variance of the claim severity distribution, Var(Y). The variance for loss severity is equal to zero here because only a single loss size (a total loss) was assumed possible for illustrative purposes.[4] Obviously, this is a somewhat unrealistic assumption for fire insurance, but it allows presentation of basic concepts in a simplified framework.

In summary, the mean of the total loss distribution for a single exposure unit, $E(x)$, is $75, and the standard deviation, σ_x, is $2,370.52. Although the average expected loss cost per farmer, $E(x)$, is $75, the actual average could deviate substantially from this expected value due to the random nature of fire losses. The nature of the distribution of *average losses* is analyzed below in order to illustrate the law of large numbers, which is a fundamental component of the insurance mechanism.

The Law of Large Numbers

As stated earlier, after the claim frequency and claim severity distributions for an entity have been combined, the total loss (or pure premium) distribution for some type of peril is obtained. If it is assumed we are dealing with fire insurance or automobile insurance and that all exposure units or risks are homogeneous, the total loss distribution for an individual exposure unit can be used as the basic probability distribution. That is, if it is assumed that all risks who purchase fire or automobile insurance are homogeneous, then they will have the same total loss distributions with identical means and variances.

Now, if underwriting considerations are ignored and it is assumed that the insurer basically takes a random sample from this basic total loss distribution, it can be shown that the average losses for a random sample of n exposure units will follow a normal distribution because of the *central limit theorem. This theorem indicates that the distribution of any average value for a random variable will approach a normal distribution as the sample size increases.*[5] Assuming that a sufficiently large sample size is taken, the value of average losses, $\bar{X}$, for this random sample should be normally distributed in repeated sampling experiments. That is, average losses for a sample of n exposure units is a random variable with normal distribution under some reasonable conditions.

If a random sample of size n were repeatedly taken, the distribution of the sample average losses, $\bar{X}$ would follow a normal distribution, as indicated above. The mean of this average loss distribution, $E(\bar{X})$, would be the same as the mean of the parent population, $E(X)$, which is the expected total loss for one exposure unit.[6] The variance associated with the potential average losses, $\text{Var}(\bar{X})$, however, is the variance of the parent population, $\text{Var}(X)$, divided by the number of exposure units, n. The *standard deviation* for the average loss distribution is the square root of the variance and is generally referred to as the *standard error* of the average loss distribution. Thus, the standard error of the average loss distribution, $\sigma_{\bar{x}}$, is merely the standard deviation of the parent pure premium distribution, σ_x, divided by the square root of the number of exposure units or insureds; that is:

$$\sigma_{\bar{x}} = \sigma_x/\sqrt{n}$$

In our fire insurance example, we found that the standard deviation of losses, σ_x, for one exposure unit was $2,370.52. Thus, the standard error for 1,000 exposure units would equal $74.96.

$$\begin{aligned} \sigma_{\bar{x}} &= \sigma_x / \sqrt{n} \\ &= \$2{,}370.52 / \sqrt{1{,}000} \\ &= \$2{,}370.52 / 31.62 \\ &= \$74.96. \end{aligned}$$

If the number of exposure units or insured farm homes were increased to 10,000, $\sigma_{\bar{x}}$ would decrease to $23.71. As explained below, this decrease in the standard error of average losses as the number of exposure units increases basically illustrates the law of large numbers.

The law of large numbers can be explained by reference to the standard error of the average loss (or sample mean pure premium) distribution. Since the standard deviation of the total loss distribution, σ_x, is fixed, the standard error of average losses, $\sigma_{\bar{x}}$, decreases if one increases the number of exposure units. This merely indicates that the variance of the average loss distribution decreases as a sample size or number of exposure units increases. This is a simple intuitive statement of the law of large numbers. This statistical theorem has extremely important implications in insurance. It is important because it shows that the variation in the average loss distribution decreases as the number of exposure units or insureds increases. Thus, an insurer or business firm is better able to estimate its true expected losses for some type of peril as the number of exposure units increases because the variance in the distribution decreases. This basic concept is illustrated in Figure 2A.1 by showing the distribu-

Figure 2A.1 Distribution of Average Losses

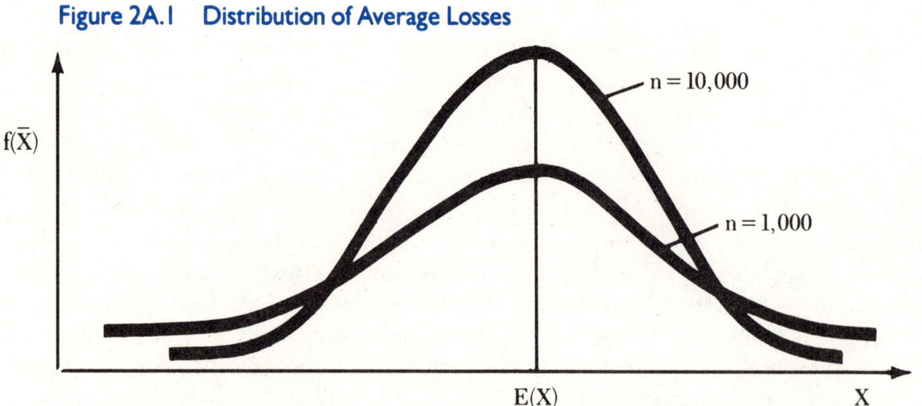

tion of average losses, $\bar{X}$, for $n = 1{,}000$ and $n = 10{,}000$.

Once one understands how the distribution of average losses behaves as the number of exposures increases, one can understand how insurance rates are developed. In essence, insurers attempt to estimate the true expected losses or mean pure premium, $\mu = E(X)$, by using the sample mean pure premium, $\bar{X}$, as an estimate of it. This is based on the assumption that there will be no changes in the underlying distribution.[7] However, the insurers also have to allow for underwriting risk. That is, there is variability in their estimate, and they have to allow for this risk.[8] Thus, a risk charge has to be added into their insurance rate along with an expense loading to cover commissions for agents, salaries for insurance employees, and various other expenses associated with administering the insurance mechanism. Some of these concepts will be illustrated in a simplified fashion below.

Since average losses, $\bar{X}$, are normally distributed for a sufficiently large sample size, it is an unbiased estimator of the true expected losses, $U = E(X)$. Thus, one can make statements about the accuracy of the estimate by using confidence intervals. Moreover, the accuracy of the estimate increases as the number of risks increases because the variation in the distribution of average losses decreases as the sample size, n, increases, as is shown below:

$$\sigma_{\bar{x}} = \sigma/\sqrt{n} \rightarrow o \text{ } as \text{ } n \rightarrow \infty$$

That is, $\sigma_{\bar{x}}$ approaches zero as n approaches infinity or gets very large.

If it is assumed that underwriting risk is basically a variance concept, the standard error of average losses can be used as a measure of the underwriting risk faced by the insurer. This measure allows for the inherent variation in the pure premium distribution and also for the variation due to random sampling. By utilizing this measure, some insights about the ratemaking process can be gained.

Since the standard error of average losses decreases as the number of exposure units, n, increases, it can be shown that the underwriting risk per individual insured or exposure unit decreases as the size of the insurer increases. This is shown in Figure 2A.2, where an underwriting risk function is shown. However, it should be noted that, even though the underwriting risk per individual insured decreases, the total underwriting risk faced by the insurer increases.[9]

Figure 2A.2 Illustration of Individual (Average) Underwriting Risk Faced by the Insurer

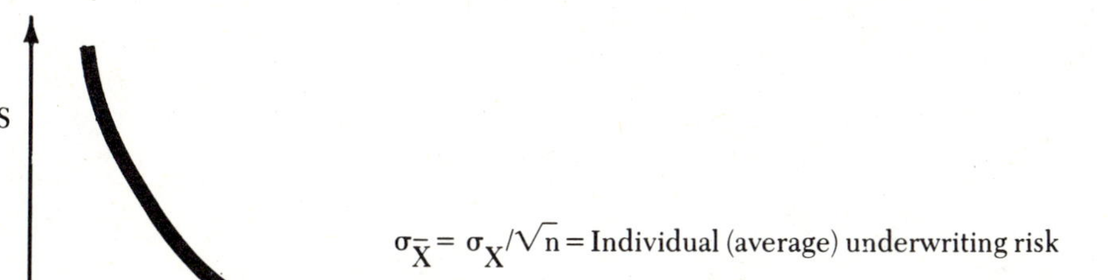

1. For convenience and ease of exposition, it is assumed that only one claim can result from an accident. This simplifying assumption allows one to focus on basic aspects of the loss generating process without being distracted with some practical complexities.
2. In the real world, risks are usually not completely homogeneous with respect to their loss potentials, but this fact will be ignored here in order to simplify the exposition.
3. For a more detailed explanation of how Equations (1) and (2) were obtained, see: Robert C. Witt, "Pricing and Underwriting Risk in Automobile Insurance: A Probabilistic View," *The Journal of Risk and Insurance*, Vol. XL, No. 4 (December 1973), pp. 509–31.
4. For n exposure units, the variance of total losses, $\text{Var}_n(x)$, is merely n times the variance of losses for a single exposure, that is:

$$\text{Var}_n(x) = n \cdot \text{Var}(x)$$

The standard deviation of total losses for n exposures, ${}_n\sigma_x$, is merely the square root of n times the standard deviation of total losses for a single exposure:

$$\begin{aligned} {}_n\sigma_x &= \sqrt{n \cdot \text{Var}(x)} \\ &= \sqrt{n} \cdot \sigma_x \end{aligned}$$

5. This theorem holds for any random variable with a finite mean and variance. However, the sample size must be larger for some random variables than others before the central limit theorem comes into play.
6. In our fire insurance example, $E(\bar{x})$ would equal \$75. The expected loss for a single exposure unit would also equal \$75. Recall $E_n(x) = \$75{,}000$ in our example was for $n = 1{,}000$ exposure units.
7. In practice, one would have to trend losses and make other adjustments in the loss data in order to allow for the impact of inflation on loss costs and the effect of other economic and social changes.
8. A distinction between systematic and unsystematic components of underwriting risk could be made, but it would unduly complicate the analysis here.
9. The total underwriting risk faced by the insurer is reflected by the product of the number of exposure units times the standard error of the average loss distribution; that is, $n \cdot \sigma_{\bar{x}}$. Based on some elementary algebra, it can also be shown that the total underwriting risk is the product of the square root of the number of exposure units times the standard deviation of the parent loss distribution; that is:

$$n \cdot \sigma_{\bar{x}} = n \cdot \sigma_x/\sqrt{n} = \sqrt{n} \cdot \sigma_x$$

Thus, the total underwriting risk faced by the insurer increases at a decreasing rate. That is, the insurer's total underwriting risk increases as the number of insured exposure units increases, but it increases at a decreasing rate due to the impact of the law of large numbers.

RISK MANAGEMENT

"Risk management deals with the systematic identification of a company's exposure to the risk of loss . . . ."

Insurance Company of North America, Risk Management

STUDENT LEARNING OBJECTIVES

After studying this chapter, you should be able to:

- Define risk management.
- Explain the basic objectives of risk management.
- List and explain the four functions of a risk manager.
- Explain the various methods for handling losses, including avoidance, retention, noninsurance transfers, loss control, and insurance.
- Explain the various situations under which each of the above techniques can be used in a risk management program.

In recent years, an increasing number of business firms, governmental units, and other organizations have turned to risk management as a device for handling pure risks. In Chapter 2, we saw how insurance can be used to meet pure risk. But insurance is only one of several methods for dealing with risk. Risk management attempts to identify the pure risks faced by the firm or organization and uses a wide variety of methods, including insurance, for handling these risks.

In this chapter, the principles of risk management will be discussed. We will first examine more precisely the meaning of risk management and the basic objectives of a risk management program. We will then consider the risk management process, which is a systematic procedure for identifying and evaluating potential losses, selecting the most appropriate methods for paying losses, and administering the overall program.

MEANING OF RISK MANAGEMENT

***Risk management** can be defined as executive decisions concerning the management of pure risks.* It is a discipline that provides for the systematic identification and analysis of loss exposures faced by the firm or organization, and for the best methods of handling these loss exposures in relation to the firm's profitability. As a general rule, the risk manager is concerned only with the management of pure risks, not speculative risks. All pure risks are treated, including those that are uninsurable.

Risk Management and Insurance Management

Risk management should not be confused with insurance management. Risk management is a much broader concept and differs from insurance management in several respects. First, risk management places greater emphasis on the identification and analysis of pure loss exposures. Second, insurance is only one of several methods that can be used to meet a particular loss exposure; as you will see, the techniques of avoidance, loss control, transfer, and retention are also widely used in a modern risk management program. Third, risk management provides for the periodic evaluation of all techniques for meeting losses, not just insurance. Finally, a successful risk management program requires the cooperation of a large number of individuals and departments throughout the firm, and risk management decisions have a greater impact on the firm than insurance management decisions. Insurance management affects a smaller number of persons.

Risk and Insurance Management Society

Most large corporations, governmental units, and education institutions have some type of formal or informal risk management program in existence today. Most risk managers belong to a national professional organization known as the Risk and Insurance Management Society, or RIMS. The objectives of RIMS are to promote risk management principles and assist risk managers in their daily risk management activities. A wide variety of risk management reports and studies are made available to risk managers. In addition, RIMS publishes a monthly journal, *Risk Management*, and national and regional conferences are periodically held to disseminate information about risk management. Finally, monthly meetings are also held where risk managers discuss common problems.

OBJECTIVES OF RISK MANAGEMENT

Risk management has several important objectives. These objectives can be classified into two categories: (1) objectives prior to a loss, and (2) objectives after a loss occurs.[1]

Objectives Prior to a Loss

A firm or organization has several risk management objectives prior to the occurrence of a loss. The most important of these include the following:

- Economy
- Reduction of anxiety
- Meeting externally imposed obligations

The *economy goal* means that the firm should prepare for potential losses in the most economical way. This involves a financial analysis of safety program expenses, insurance premiums, and the costs associated with the different techniques for handling losses.

The second objective, the *reduction of anxiety,* is more complicated. Certain loss exposures may create greater worry and fear for the risk manager than other exposures. But the risk manager wants to minimize the anxiety and fear associated with all loss exposures.

The third preloss objective is to *meet any externally imposed obligations.* This means the firm must meet certain obligations imposed on it by outsiders. For example, government regulations may require a firm to install safety devices to protect workers from harm. Similarly, a firm's creditors may require that property pledged as collateral for a loan must be insured. The risk manager must see that these externally imposed obligations are met.

Objectives After a Loss

After a loss occurs, the risk manager has the following objectives:

- Survival of the firm
- Continued operation
- Stability of earnings
- Continued growth
- Social responsibility

Let us briefly examine each of these important postloss objectives.

The first and most important risk management objective after a loss occurs is *survival of the firm.* Survival means that after a loss occurs, the firm can at least resume partial operation within some reasonable time period if it chooses to do so.

The second postloss objective is to *continue operating.* For some firms, the ability to continue operating after a severe loss is an extremely important objective. This is particularly true of certain firms, such as a public utility firm, which is obligated to provide continuous service. But it is also extremely important for those firms that may lose some or all of their customers to competitors if they cannot operate after a loss occurs. This would include banks, bakeries, dairy farms, and similar firms.

Stability of earnings is the third postloss objective. This objective is closely related to the objective of continued operations. The goal of stability of earnings may be achieved if the firm continues to operate. However, there may be substantial costs involved in achieving this goal (such as operating at another location), and perfect stability of earnings may not be attained.

The fourth postloss objective is *continued growth* of the firm. A firm may grow by developing new products and markets or by acquisitions and mergers. The risk manager must consider the impact that a loss will have on the firm's ability to grow.

Finally, the goal of *social responsibility* is to minimize the impact that a loss has on other persons and society in general. A severe loss by a firm can adversely affect employees, customers, suppliers, creditors, taxpayers, and the community in general. For example, a severe loss that requires the shutting down of a plant in a small community for an extended period can lead to depressed business conditions and substantial unemployment in the community. The risk manager must therefore be concerned about the social responsibility of the firm to the community after a loss occurs.

THE RISK MANAGEMENT PROCESS

In order to attain the preceding goals and objectives, the risk manager must perform certain functions. There are four basic functions of a risk manager. They are:

- Identifying potential losses
- Evaluating the potential losses
- Selecting the appropriate technique or combination of techniques for handling losses
- Administering the program

In the following sections, we will examine each of these important functions of a risk manager in some detail.

IDENTIFYING POTENTIAL LOSSES

The first function of a risk manager is to identify all pure loss exposures. This involves a painstaking identification of all potential losses to the firm. The risk manager normally tries to identify six types of potential losses. They are:

1. Property losses
2. Business interruption losses
3. Liability losses
4. Death or disability of key persons
5. Losses resulting from workplace injuries
6. Losses from fraud, criminal acts, and employee dishonesty

The risk manager has several sources of information that can be used to identify major and minor loss exposures. *Physical inspection* of company plants and operations can identify major loss exposures. Extensive **risk analysis questionnaires** can be used to discover hidden loss exposures that are common to many firms. **Flow charts** that depict the production and delivery processes can reveal production bottlenecks where a loss can have severe financial consequences to the firm. *Financial statements* can be used to identify the major assets that must be protected. And, of course, *reports on past losses* experienced by the firm can be invaluable in identifying major loss exposures.

EVALUATING POTENTIAL LOSSES

After the loss exposures are identified, the next step is to evaluate and measure the impact of losses on the firm. This involves an estimation of the potential frequency and severity of loss. ***Loss frequency*** *refers to the probable number of losses that may occur during some given time period.* ***Loss severity*** *refers to the probable size of the losses that may occur.*

The risk manager must estimate the frequency and severity of loss for each type of loss exposure. The various loss exposures can then be ranked according to their relative importance. For example, a loss exposure with the potential for bankrupting the firm—such as a liability judgment in excess of the firm's assets—is much more important in a risk management program than one with a small loss potential.

In addition, the relative frequency and severity of each loss exposure must be estimated so that the risk manager can select the most appropriate techniques, or combination of techniques, for handling the loss exposure. For example, if certain losses regularly appear and are fairly predictable, they can be budgeted for out of the firm's income and treated as a normal operating expense. However, if the annual loss experience of a certain type of exposure fluctuates widely, an entirely different approach may be required.

Although the risk manager must consider both loss frequency and loss severity, severity is more important, since a single catastrophic loss could wipe out the firm. Therefore, the risk manager must also consider all losses that can result from a single event. Both the maximum possible loss and maximum probable loss must be estimated. *The* ***maximum possible loss*** *is the worst loss that could possibly happen to the firm during its lifetime. The* ***maximum probable loss*** *is the worst loss that is likely to happen.*[2] For example, a firm may own a building valued at $500,000; thus the maximum possible loss is $500,000. The risk manager may estimate that once every fifty years, the building will incur property damage from a flood in excess of $400,000; so the maximum probable loss is only $400,000.

Catastrophic losses are difficult to predict in advance because they occur so infrequently. However, their potential impact on the firm must be considered. In contrast, certain losses, such as physical damage losses to automobiles and trucks, occur with greater frequency, are usually relatively small, and can be predicted with greater accuracy.

SELECTING THE APPROPRIATE TECHNIQUE FOR HANDLING LOSS

After the frequency and severity of losses are estimated, the risk manager must then select the most appropriate technique, or combination of techniques, for handling each loss exposure. In Chapter 1, we examined the various methods of handling risk. These same techniques are widely used in risk management programs. To refresh your memory, they are as follows:[3]

- Avoidance
- Retention
- Noninsurance transfers
- Loss control
- Insurance

In the following sections, we will examine each of these techniques in greater detail to see how they can be applied to specific loss exposures in a risk management program.

Avoidance

*Loss **avoidance** means that a certain loss exposure is never acquired, or an existing loss exposure is abandoned.* For example, the firm can avoid a flood loss by not building a plant in a flood plain. An existing loss exposure may also be abandoned. For example, a firm that produces a highly toxic product may stop manufacturing that product.

The major advantage of avoidance is that the chance of loss is reduced to zero, or the chance of loss that previously existed is eliminated because the activity that produced the chance of loss has been abandoned. Thus, it is not necessary to use other risk management techniques for the loss exposures that have been avoided because there is no remaining exposure to be treated.

Avoidance, however, has two disadvantages. First, it may not be possible to avoid all losses. For example, the premature death of a key executive cannot be avoided. Second, it may not be practical or feasible to avoid the exposure. For example, a paint factory can avoid losses arising out of the production of paint. However, without any paint production, the firm will not be in business.

Retention

Retention is another risk management technique for handling losses. ***Retention** means that the firm retains part or all of the losses that result from a given loss exposure.*

Conditions for Using Retention Retention can be used in a risk management program if certain conditions are met. They include the following:[4]

- No other method of treatment is available
- The worst possible loss is not serious
- Losses are highly predictable

Retention may be used when no other method of treating the exposure is available. Insurers may not be willing to write a certain coverage or noninsurance transfers may not be available. Or loss control measures may reduce the frequency of some losses, but not all losses can be eliminated. In these cases, the retention technique is a residual method. If the exposure cannot be transferred or insured, then it must be retained. Property damage from war would be included in this category.

Retention can also be used when the worst possible loss is not serious. For example, physical damage loss to automobiles in a large firm's fleet will not bankrupt the firm if the automobiles are separated by wide distances and, thus, are not likely to be simultaneously damaged.

Finally, retention is appropriate when losses are highly predictable. Workers' compensation claims, physical damage loss to automobiles, and shoplifting losses fall in this category. From past experience, the risk manager should be able to determine a probable range of frequency and severity of actual losses. If most losses fall within that range each year, they can be budgeted for out of the firm's income.

Determining retention levels The risk manager must also determine the dollar amount of losses the firm will retain. An important consideration here is the firm's overall financial position. A financially strong firm can have a higher **retention level** than one whose financial position is weaker. Retention levels should therefore be reviewed annually in light of the firm's present financial position, recent loss experience, and the cost of insurance in the marketplace.

Retention levels should be established for both single occurrences and aggregate annual amounts. Determining the maximum dollar amount of losses to retain annually may be done in several ways.[5] A publicly held corporation can determine its maximum annual retention in terms of the maximum uninsured loss the company can absorb without adversely affecting the stockholders. The company's dividend policy and the extent to which the company's earnings will be adversely affected by losses must be reviewed in this light. A common rule of thumb is that the maximum retention can be set at 5 percent of the company's annual earnings before taxes from its current operation.

Another approach is to determine the maximum annual retention as a percentage of the firm's net working capital; typically, this figure is between 1 and 5 percent. Although this method does not reflect the firm's overall financial position for absorbing a loss, it is a measure of the firm's ability to fund a loss.

A third approach is based on the recognition that retained losses typically are paid out of retained earnings, or pretax dollars. Under this formula, the maximum annual retention is equal to some percentage of current earned surplus (typically 1 to 3 percent), plus an equal or lower percentage of average pretax earnings over the past few years. This latter percentage has the effect of smoothing out the highs and lows.

Paying losses If retention is used, the risk manager must have some established method for paying losses. The following methods of financing losses can be used.[6]

1. *Current Net Income.* The firm can pay losses out of its current net income, and the losses would be treated as expenses for that year. However, payments to cover large numbers of losses could exceed current net income. Other assets of the firm may then have to be liquidated to pay losses. Moreover, a profitable year could easily turn into an unprofitable one because of an unexpected loss, such as an explosion, liability lawsuit, or work-related accident.

2. *Earmarked Assets.* Another method is to earmark liquid assets, such as short-term securities, to pay losses. However, there is no assurance that the assets will be sufficient to pay an unusually large loss. Moreover, keeping assets in liquid form may substantially reduce their rate of return; they may yield a much higher rate of return by being used in the business.

3. *Borrowing.* A third method is to borrow the necessary funds from a bank. However, this approach requires a line of credit from a commercial bank, and arrangements for the loan must be made before the loss occurs. Furthermore, interest must be paid on the loan, and the periodic repayment of the loan can aggravate any cash flow problems the firm may have. Finally, a compensating cash balance may also be required.

4. *Captive Insurer.* Finally, a firm can establish a **captive insurer**—an insurance company established and owned by the parent firm for the purpose of insuring the firm's loss exposures—to pay losses. More than 1,000 captive insurers exist at the present time. Most of them are located in Bermuda because of the favorable regulatory climate, low capitalization requirements, and low taxes. About one-third of the 500 largest corporations in the United States have established captive insurers.[7]

There are several reasons why corporations have formed captive insurers. They are summarized as follows.

a. *Reduction in premium costs.* The captive insurer may be able to provide coverage more economically than commercial insurers. Also, the parent firm may have diffi-

INSIGHT 3.1

Self-Insurance and Workers' Compensation

Although the term "self-insurance" has become an industry and media buzz-word in recent years, it's still relatively misunderstood. Self-insurance means that a business or industry takes upon itself the burden of risk retention—of making itself liable for a particular type of risk—rather than insuring the risk through an insurance company.

Workers compensation statutes require employers to insure their full liability in a manner satisfactory to the state overseeing the employer's workers compensation. At present, 47 states and the District of Columbia have compulsory statutes on the books requiring employers to have workers compensation coverage. However, nearly all states allow an employer to be exempted from this requirement if the employer can meet certain qualifications for self-insurer status.

In addition to *total risk retention,* two other types of workers compensation self-insurance are permitted by state exemption:

Limited self-insurance, in which the employer retains part of the risk but buys excess insurance above the retained risk. Frequently, states require a security deposit from the employer for limited status.

Group self-insurance, now allowed by about 20 states. In most cases, group members insure each other's obligations by agreeing to be "jointly and severally liable"—in other words, each group member is liable, not only for his own risks, but also for those of all the other group members as well in the event of a loss. Group self-insurance operates on the theory that a number of employers who join together can achieve the aggregate size, strength and capabilities of a single large employer and thus qualify for group status. This differs from individual self-insurance where the self-insurer retains only his *own* risk. Primary support for group self-insurance has come mainly from small and medium-sized employers not otherwise eligible for self-insurance status, and from employer trade associations.

SOURCE: "Understanding Self-Insurance" from *Journal of American Insurance,* Fall, 1982.

culty in obtaining certain types of insurance from commercial insurers.

b. *Greater stability of earnings.* A captive insurer can provide for greater stability of earnings over time, since the adverse impact of chance fluctuations on the firm's income is reduced.

c. *Easier access to a reinsurer.* A captive insurer has easier access to a reinsurer, since many reinsurers will deal only with insurance companies and not with insureds.

d. *Profit center.* The captive insurer can be a profit center by insuring other parties as well as providing insurance to the parent firm and its subsidiaries.

e. *International advantages.* Captive insurers also have some advantages in the international insurance markets. For example, some foreign countries require business firms to insure their local operations by purchasing insurance from local insurers. A captive insurer may be able to reinsure the local insurer, which may then be in a position to write broader lines of insurance than would otherwise be possible.

Self-insurance **Self-insurance** is a special form of retention. A retention program can be considered self-insurance if it possesses certain characteristics that are typically found in commercial insurance.

In order for a retention program to be considered self-insurance, the following two requirements must be met.[8] (1) A large number of homogeneous exposure units must exist, so that losses can be predicted based on the law of large numbers. (2) Losses are paid by earmarked liquid assets or by a captive insurer.

One requirement is that the firm must have a large number of homogeneous exposure units so that losses are fairly predictable based on the law of large numbers. Since the firm has numerous exposure units, its actual loss experience may vary within a narrow range around its expected losses, thereby making it possible to predict losses in the short-run. However, some risk management experts believe that if a vigorous standard is set for predictability, few retention programs would qualify as self-insurance.

The second requirement is that the program must be funded by earmarked assets or by a captive insurer. The firm must have a liquid fund of assets to pay losses, or, alternatively, a captive insurer can be used to pay claims. However, since relatively few retention programs have specifically earmarked assets for the payment of losses or have access to a captive insurer, few programs would be considered self-insurance under this second requirement.

Some authorities believe only the first requirement must be satisfied to have self-insurance, while another group believes that only the second requirement has to be met. A third group believes that both requirements must be satisfied.

Advantages and disadvantages of retention The retention technique has both advantages and disadvantages in a risk management program. The major advantages are summarized as follows.[9]

1. *Save money.* The firm can save considerable money in the long run if its actual losses are less than the loss allowance in the insurer's premium.
2. *Lower expenses.* There may also be sizeable expense savings. The services provided by the insurer may be provided by the firm at a lower cost. Some expenses may be reduced, including loss-adjustment expenses, general administrative expenses, commissions and brokerage fees, loss control expenses, taxes and fees, and the insurer's profit.
3. *Encourage loss prevention.* Since the exposure is retained, there may be a greater incentive for loss prevention within the firm.
4. *Cash flow advantages.* Cash flow may be increased by retention, since the firm can use the funds that normally would be held by the insurer.

The retention technique, however, has several disadvantages. They are summarized as follows.

1. *Possible higher losses.* The losses retained by the firm may be greater than the loss allowance in the insurance premium that is saved by not purchasing the insurance. Also, in the short-run, there may be great volatility in the firm's loss experience.
2. *Possible higher expenses.* Expenses may actually be higher. Outside experts such as safety engineers and loss-prevention specialists may have to be hired. Insurers may be able to provide loss control services more cheaply.
3. *Higher taxes.* Income taxes may also be higher. The premiums paid to an insurer are income-tax deductible. However, if retention is used, only the amounts actually paid out are deductible.

This concludes our discussion of retention. Let us next consider noninsurance transfers as a technique for handling potential losses.

Noninsurance Transfers

***Noninsurance transfers** refer to the various methods other than insurance by which a pure risk and its potential financial consequences can be transferred to another party.* Some noninsurance techniques that are commonly used in risk management programs include *contracts, leases,* and *hold-harmless agreements.* For example, a company's contract with a construction firm to build a new plant can specify that the construction firm is responsible for any damage to the plant while it is being built. A firm's computer lease can specify that maintenance, repairs, and any physical damage loss to the computer are the responsibility of the computer firm. Or a firm may insert a hold-harmless clause in a contract, by which one party assumes legal liability on behalf of another party. Thus, a publishing firm may insert a hold-harmless clause in a contract, by which the author, and not the publisher, is held legally liable if the publisher is sued for plagiarism.

In a risk management program, noninsurance transfers have several advantages. They are summarized as follows.[10]

1. The risk manager can transfer some potential losses that are not commercially insurable.
2. Noninsurance transfers often cost less than insurance.
3. The potential loss may be shifted to someone who is in a better position to exercise loss control.

However, noninsurance transfers have several disadvantages. They are summarized as follows.

1. The transfer of potential loss may fail because the contract language is ambiguous. Also, there may be no court precedents for the interpretation of a contract that is tailor-made to fit the situation.
2. If the party to whom the potential loss is transferred is unable to pay the loss, the firm is still responsible for the claim.
3. Noninsurance transfers may not always reduce insurance costs, since an insurer may not give credit for the transfers.

Loss Control

Loss control is another method for handling loss in a risk management program. *Loss control activities are designed to reduce both the frequency and severity of losses.* Unlike the technique of avoidance of loss, loss control deals with an exposure that the firm does not wish to abandon. The purpose of loss control activities is to change the characteristics of the exposure so that it is more acceptable to the firm; the firm wishes to keep the exposure but wants to reduce the frequency and severity of losses.

Several examples can illustrate how loss control measures can reduce the frequency and severity of losses. Examples of measures that reduce loss frequency are quality control checks, driver examinations, strict enforcement of safety rules, and improvements in product design. Examples of measures that reduce loss severity are installation of automatic sprinkler or burglar alarm systems, early treatment of injuries, limiting the amount of cash on the premises that can be stolen, and rehabilitation of injured workers.

Insurance

Commercial insurance can also be used in a risk management program. Insurance can be advantageously used for the treatment of loss exposures that have a low probability of loss but the severity of a potential loss is high.

Risk management and insurance If the risk manager decides to use insurance to treat certain loss exposures, five key areas must be emphasized. They are as follows.[11]

- Selection of insurance coverages
- Selection of an insurer
- Negotiation of terms
- Dissemination of information concerning insurance coverages
- Periodic review of the insurance program

First, the risk manager must select the insurance coverages that are needed. Since there may not be enough money in the insurance budget to insure all possible losses, the need for insurance can be divided into several categories depending on importance. One useful approach is to classify the need for insurance into three categories: (1) essential, (2) desirable, and (3) available. **Essential insurance** includes those coverages required by law or by contract, such as workers' compensation insurance. Essential insurance also includes those coverages that will protect the firm against a catastrophic loss or a loss that threatens the firm's survival; liability insurance would fall into this category. **Desirable insurance** is protection against losses that may cause the firm financial difficulty, but not bankruptcy. **Available insurance** is coverage for slight losses that merely inconvenience the firm.

The risk manager must also determine if a ***deductible*** *is needed and what size of deductible is warranted.* A deductible is used to eliminate small claims and the administrative expense of adjusting these claims. Substantial premium savings are possible if a deductible is used. In essence, then, a deductible is a form of risk retention.

Most risk management programs combine the retention technique discussed earlier with commercial insurance. In determining the size of the deductible, the firm may decide to retain only a relatively small part of the maximum exposure to loss. The insurer normally adjusts any claims, and only losses in excess of the deductible are paid.

Another approach is to purchase ***excess insurance.*** A firm may be financially strong and may wish to retain a relatively large proportion of the maximum exposure to loss. Under an excess insurance plan, the insurer does not participate in the loss until the actual loss exceeds the amount a firm has decided to retain. The retention limit may be set at the maximum probable loss (not maximum possible loss), which is the worst possible loss likely to occur. For example, a retention limit of $1 million may be established for a single fire loss to a plant valued at $25 million. The $1 million would be viewed as the maximum probable loss. In the unlikely event of a total loss, the firm would absorb the first $1 million of loss, and the commercial insurer would pay the remaining $24 million.

Second, the risk manager must select an insurer or several insurers. Several important factors come into play here. These include the financial strength of the insurer, risk management services provided by the insurer, and the cost of protection. The insurer's financial strength is determined by the size of policyholders' surplus, underwriting and investment results, adequacy of reserves for outstanding liabilities, types of insurance written, and the quality of management.[12] Several trade publications are available to the risk manager for determining the financial strength of a particular insurer. One of the most important of these is *Best's Insurance Reports,* which rates the companies on the basis of their relative financial strength.

The risk manager must also consider the availability of risk management services in selecting a particular insurer. Such services include assistance in identification of loss exposures, in loss control, and in claim adjustment. The risk manager must also determine whether a particular insurer is willing to provide the desired insurance coverages. Other factors are the willingness of an insurer to accept all loss exposures the risk manager wants to insure, regardless of their quality, and the insurer's policy on cancellation. Some insurers may cancel the insured if a major loss occurs.

The cost of insurance protection must also be studied. All other factors being equal, the risk manager would prefer to purchase the insurance at the lowest possible price. Many risk managers will therefore solicit competitive premium bids from several insurers to get the necessary protection and services at the lowest price.

Third, after the insurer or insurers are selected, the terms of the insurance contract must be negotiated. The risk manager and insurer must agree on the contract language. If printed policies, endorsements, and forms are used, the risk manager and insurer must agree on the documents that will form the basis of the contract. If a specially tailored ***manuscript policy*** is written for the firm,[13] the language and meaning of the

INSIGHT 3.2

Cash Flow Insurance Plans

Cash flow insurance plans are alternative arrangements for paying insurance premiums by business firms. The major advantage of these plans in a risk management program is that they permit the policyholder to delay payment of insurance premiums so that the firm's cash flow can be improved. The premiums that ordinarily would be paid to the insurer can be invested by the firm or retained in the business until the funds are actually needed to pay losses.

Two important cash flow plans include the *compensating balance plan* and the *paid loss retro plan.* Both plans enable the company to use its cash flow more efficiently.

1. *Compensating balance plan.* Under this plan, the full premium is paid at the beginning of the period. The insurer deducts its initial expenses from the premium, and the remainder is deposited in the policyholder's checking account to support a line of credit. This procedure releases the funds that the firm must keep in its checking account as a "compensating balance." The released funds can then be invested by the policyholder at a higher rate of return. Funds are returned to the compensating balance checking account only as losses and expenses are paid by the insurer.

2. *Paid loss retro plan.* Under this plan, the firm initially pays a relatively small part of the total premium to cover early administrative expenses and loss costs. The firm gives a promissory note or letter of credit to the insurer for the balance of the premium. The policyholder is then billed for the insurance costs as they are actually paid by the insurer. Thus, most premiums are paid retroactively based on the actual dollar cost of insured losses. This plan, in effect, permits the policyholder to maintain control over the remaining funds that ordinarily would be paid to the insurer as an advance premium.

SOURCE: Adaptation of "Cash Flow Insurance Plans" from *Principles of Risk Management and Insurance* by Williams, Head, Horn and Glendenning. Copyright © 1981. Reprinted by permission of American Institute for Property and Liability Underwriters.

contractual provisions must be clear to both parties. In any case, the various risk management services the insurer will provide must be clearly stated in the contract. Finally, if the firm is large, the premiums may be negotiable between the firm and insurance company. Even if the premiums are not negotiable, the risk manager may be able to persuade the insurer that the firm belongs in an underwriting classification with a lower rate.

Fourth, information concerning insurance coverage must be disseminated to others in the firm. The firm's employees and managers must be informed about the insurance coverages, the various records that must be kept, the risk management services that the insurer will provide, and the changes in hazards that could result in a suspension of insurance. And, of course, those persons responsible for reporting a loss must be informed. The firm must comply with policy provisions concerning how notice of a claim is to be given and how the necessary proofs of loss are to be assembled and presented.

Finally, the insurance program must be periodically reviewed. The risk manager has to decide whether claims are paid promptly or not and to assess the quality of the insurer's loss control services. Even the basic decision—whether to purchase insurance—must be periodically reviewed.

Advantages and disadvantages of insurance The use of commercial insurance in a risk management program has both advantages and disadvantages.[14] The major advantages are summarized as follows.

1. The firm will be indemnified after a loss occurs. The firm can continue to operate, and there may be little or no fluctuation in earnings.
2. Uncertainty is reduced, which permits the firm to lengthen its planning horizon. Worry and fear are reduced for managers and employees, which should improve their performance and productivity.
3. Insurers can provide valuable risk management services, such as loss control services, exposure analysis to identify loss exposures, and claims adjusting.
4. Insurance premiums are income-tax deductible as a business expense.

However, the use of insurance entails certain disadvantages and costs. They are summarized as follows.

1. The payment of the insurance premium is a major cost, since the premium consists of a component to pay loss costs, an amount for expenses, and an allowance for profit and contingencies. There is also an opportunity cost. Under the retention technique discussed earlier, the premium could be invested or used in the business until needed to pay claims. If insurance is used, premiums must be paid in advance.
2. Considerable time and effort must be spent in negotiating for insurance. An insurer or insurers must be selected, policy terms and premiums must be negotiated, the firm must cooperate with the loss control activities of the insurer, and proof of loss must be filed with the insurer following a loss.
3. The risk manager may have less incentive to follow a program of loss control, since the insurer will pay the claim if a loss occurs. Such a lax attitude toward loss control could increase the number of noninsured losses as well.

In summary, the risk manager can use avoidance, retention, noninsurance transfers, loss control, and commercial insurance in a risk management program. Let us next consider the appropriate situations for using each of these methods.

Which Method Should Be Used?

In determining the appropriate method or methods, a matrix can be used that classifies the various loss exposures according to frequency and severity. The following matrix can be a useful guide to the risk manager.

Type of Loss Exposure	*Loss Frequency*	*Loss Severity*
1	Low	Low
2	High	Low
3	Low	High
4	High	High

The first loss exposure is one that is characterized by both low frequency and low severity of loss. This type of exposure can be best handled by retention, since the loss occurs infrequently and, when it does occur, it seldom causes financial harm. One example of this type of exposure would be the potential theft of a secretary's dictionary.

The second type of exposure is more serious. A loss occurs frequently, but its severity is relatively low. Examples of this type of exposure include physical damage losses to automobiles, workers' compensation claims, shoplifting, and food spoilage. Loss control should be used here to reduce the frequency of losses. In addition, since losses regularly occur and are predictable, the retention technique can also be used. However, since these relatively small losses in the aggregate can reach sizeable levels over a one-year period, commercial insurance could also be purchased on an excess basis.

The third type of exposure should be met by insurance. Insurance is best suited for low-frequency, high-severity losses. The high severity means that a catastrophic potential is present, while a low probability of loss indicates that purchase of insurance is economically feasible. Examples of this type of exposure include fires, explosions, tornadoes, and liability lawsuits. The risk manager could also use a combination of retention and commercial insurance with the retention limit determined by the principles that we have discussed earlier.

The fourth and most serious type of exposure is one characterized by both high frequency and high severity. This type of exposure is best handled by avoidance. Retention is not advisable because of the catastrophic loss potential, and commercial insurance may not be available or available only at prohibitively high premiums. One example of this type of exposure is someone who applies for a truck driving job with a trucking firm. Assume that the applicant has been previously arrested and convicted three times for driving while intoxicated and has also served a prison term for drunken driving. If the driver is hired and then kills several passengers in another vehicle because he or she is drunk, the liability exposure to the firm would be enormous. This type of exposure can be avoided by not hiring the applicant.

ADMINISTERING THE RISK MANAGEMENT PROGRAM

We have examined three of the four risk management functions at this point. Let us examine the fourth and final function of the risk manager—administration of the program.

The Risk Manager's Position

In most large corporations, the risk manager is fairly high in the organizational structure, and, in most cases, he or she is at least at the middle management level. One survey of risk managers who are members of RIMS indicated that about half of the United States' respondents held the title of manager, director was the next most popular title, 4 percent vice-presidents, and 4 percent treasurers. About 46 percent of the risk managers reported directly to a vice-president.[15]

Common activities of the risk managers included loss exposure identification and measurement, arrangement of insurance handling claims, design and installation of employee benefit plans, participation in loss control measures, safety, group insurance, and self-insurance administration. It is apparent from these activities that the risk manager is considered an important part of the management team.

Policy Statement

A **risk management policy statement** is necessary in order to have effective administration of the risk management program. This statement outlines the risk management objectives of the firm as well as company policy with respect to treatment of loss exposures. It also educates top level executives in regard to the risk management process, gives the risk manager greater authority in the firm, and provides standards for judging the risk manager's performance.

The following is a selection on retention from a typical risk management policy statement.[16]

> *Risk Retention.* Generally, the Special Chemical Company will retain a risk under the following circumstances:
>
> 1. When the amount of annual potential loss is relatively so small that it may conveniently be treated as a normal operating expense;
> 2. When
>   a. the probability of loss (frequency) is so great that loss is almost certain to occur; and
>   b. the rates for insurance or other transfer mechanisms are disproportionately high; and
>   c. potential loss amounts are within the financial ability of the Company to retain; and
>   d. no accessory insurance services are required;
> 3. When the probability of occurrence is so remote that the ordinarily prudent businessman will not incur any amount of premium expense; and

INSIGHT 3.3

How Much Do Risk Managers Earn?

Risk managers earn a median annual salary that falls between $50,000 and $59,000. They also receive bonuses, stock options and/or profit sharing in 70 percent of companies they work for.

Those were the findings of a survey conducted by The Bureau of National Affairs, a Washington, D.C., publisher of specialized information services.

Of the 194 risk managers surveyed, 74 percent have had prior work experience in the insurance field, and 62 percent have college degrees in business.

SOURCE: *National Underwriter*, Property and Casualty Insurance Edition, November 25, 1983, p. 28.

4. When insurance is not available, or only available at prohibitive cost.

In addition, a **risk management manual** may be developed and used in the program. The manual describes in some detail the risk management program of the firm and can be a very useful tool for training new employees who will be participating in the program. Writing such a manual also forces the risk manager to state precisely his or her responsibilities, objectives, and available techniques.

Cooperation with Other Departments

The risk manager does not work in isolation. Other functional departments within the firm are extremely important in identifying pure loss exposures and methods for treating these exposures. These departments can cooperate in the risk management process in the following ways:

1. *Accounting*. Internal accounting controls can reduce employee fraud and theft of cash.
2. *Finance*. Information can be provided showing how losses can disrupt profits and cash flow and the impact that losses will have on a firm's balance sheet and income statement.
3. *Marketing*. Accurate packaging can prevent liability lawsuits. Safe distribution procedures can prevent accidents.
4. *Production*. Quality control can prevent production of defective goods and so prevent liability lawsuits. Adequate safety in the plant can reduce accidents.
5. *Personnel*. This department may be responsible for employee benefit programs, pension programs, and safety programs.

This list indicates how the risk management process involves the entire firm. Indeed, without the active cooperation of the other departments, the risk management program will be a failure.

Periodic Review

To be effective, the risk management program must be periodically reviewed. In particular, those activities relating to risk management costs, safety programs, and loss prevention must be carefully monitored. Loss records must also be examined to detect any changes in frequency and severity. Any new developments that affect the original decision on handling a loss exposure must also be examined. Finally, the risk manager must determine if the firm's overall risk management policies are being carried out and if he or she is receiving the total cooperation of the other departments in carrying out the risk management functions.[17]

SUMMARY

- Risk management is defined as executive decisions concerning the management of pure risks. All pure risks are considered, including those that are uninsurable.
- There are several important differences between risk management and insurance management. First, risk management places greater emphasis on the identification and analysis of pure loss exposures. Second, insurance is only one of several methods for handling losses; the risk manager uses a wide variety of methods to handle losses. Third, risk management provides for the periodic evaluation of all methods for meeting losses, not just insurance. Finally, risk management requires the cooperation of other individuals and departments throughout the firm.
- Risk management has several important objectives. Objectives prior to a loss include the goal of economy, reduction of anxiety, and meeting externally imposed obligations. Objectives after a loss include survival of the firm, continued operation, stability of earnings, continued growth, and social responsibility.
- The risk manager performs several basic functions: (a) potential losses must be identified; (b) the potential losses must then be evaluated in terms of loss frequency and loss severity; (c) an appropriate method or combination of methods for handling losses must be selected; and (d) the risk management function must be properly administered.
- The major methods for handling losses in a risk management program are avoidance, retention, noninsurance transfers, loss control, and insurance.
- The major advantage of avoidance is that the chance of loss is reduced to zero. The major disadvantages are that it may not be possible to avoid all losses, and that it is neither practical nor feasible to avoid all loss exposures.
- Retention can be used if no other method of treatment is available, the worst possible loss is not serious, and losses are highly predictable. If retention is used, some method for paying losses must be selected. Losses can be paid out of the firm's current net income; liquid assets can be earmarked to pay losses; the necessary funds can be borrowed; or a captive insurer can be formed.
- A captive insurer may be formed because the firm wants to reduce its premium costs; a captive insurer provides for greater stability of earnings; access to a reinsurer is easier; the captive insurer can be a profit center by selling insurance to other parties; and a captive insurer may provide certain international advantages in the world markets.
- Self-insurance is a special case of retention. In order for a retention program to be considered self-insurance, two requirements must generally be satisfied. First, there must be a large number of homogenous exposure units so that losses can be predicted based on the law of large numbers. Second, losses must be paid either by earmarked assets or by a captive insurer.
- The advantages of retention are that the firm may be able to save money on insurance premiums; there may be a reduction in expenses; loss prevention is encouraged; and cash flow may be increased. The major disadvantages are the possibility of greater volatility in losses in the short run, of higher expenses if loss control personnel must be hired, and of possible higher taxes.
- There are several advantages of noninsurance transfers. The risk manager may be able to transfer some uninsurable exposures; noninsurance transfers may cost less than insurance; and

the potential loss may be shifted to someone who is in a better position to exercise loss control. However, there are several disadvantages. The transfer of a potential loss may fail because the contract language is ambiguous; the firm is still responsible for the loss if the party to whom the potential loss is transferred is unable to pay the loss; and an insurer may not give credit for the transfers.

- Loss control is extremely important in a risk management program. Loss control activities are designed to reduce both loss frequency and loss severity.
- Commercial insurance can also be used in a risk management program. Use of insurance involves a selection of insurance coverages, selection of the insurer, negotiation of contract terms with the insurer, dissemination of information concerning the insurance coverages, and periodic review of the insurance program.
- The major advantages of insurance include indemnification after a loss occurs, reduction in uncertainty, availability of valuable risk management services, and the income-tax deductibility of the premiums. The major disadvantages of insurance include the cost of insurance, time and effort that must be spent in negotiating for insurance, and a possible lax attitude toward loss control.
- A risk management program must be properly administered. This involves preparation of a risk management policy statement, close cooperation with other individuals and departments, and periodic review of the entire risk management program.

QUESTIONS FOR REVIEW

1. Define risk management. How does risk management differ from insurance management?
2. Explain the objectives of a risk management program both before and after a loss.
3. Explain the four basic functions of a risk manager.
4. How can the risk manager identify potential losses? How does the risk manager evaluate and analyze each potential loss?
5. Explain the various methods for handling potential losses in a risk management program.
6. What conditions must be fulfilled before retention is used in a risk management program?
7. Define the term *captive insurer* and explain why captive insurers are formed.
8. Is self-insurance the same as insurance? Explain.
9. List some examples of noninsurance transfers and loss control.
10. Explain the basic factors that a risk manager must consider if commercial insurance is used in a risk management program.

QUESTIONS FOR DISCUSSION

1. The Smith Corporation manufactures and sells ladders and scaffolds that are used by construction firms. These products are sold to more than 1,000 independent retailers in the United States. The management of Smith Corporation is concerned that the company may be sued if one of its products is defective and someone is injured. Since the cost of products liability in-

surance has increased sharply in recent years, the Smith Corporation is looking for ways to control its loss exposures.

For each of the following risk management techniques, describe a specific action utilizing that technique that may be helpful in dealing with the products liability exposure of the Smith Corporation:

a. Avoidance
b. Loss prevention
c. Loss reduction
d. Noninsurance transfer

2. A risk manager recently stated that "avoidance is a meaningless technique to risk managers since loss exposures must be dealt with and not avoided."
   a. Do you agree or disagree with the above statement? Explain your answer.
   b. Compare the risk management techniques of *avoidance* and *loss control* with respect to the following:
      1. The effect on the loss exposure itself.
      2. The financing of losses if they should occur.
3. The Goat Corporation has 10,000 salespersons and employees in the United States who drive company cars. Mary, risk manager of the Goat Corporation, has recommended to the firm's management that they should implement a *partial retention program* for collision losses to the company's cars.
   a. Describe the factors that the Goat Corporation should consider in deciding whether or not it should partially retain the collision loss exposure to company cars.
   b. If the partial retention program is implemented, explain the various methods that the Goat Corporation can use to pay for any collision losses to the company's cars.
   c. Explain the advantages and disadvantages of a partial retention program to the Goat Corporation.
4. Bill argues that the term self-insurance is a misnomer and is not insurance since a pure risk is not transferred to a commercial insurer. He argues that self-insurance is only another name for retention. Do you agree or disagree with Bill? Explain your answer.
5. Gerald has just been appointed head of the risk management department of Gates Manufacturing. His first action as a risk manager is to prepare a formal risk management policy statement.
   a. What benefits can the firm expect to receive from a well-prepared risk policy statement?
   b. Describe the different techniques that Gerald might use to identify the firm's pure loss exposures.

KEY CONCEPTS AND TERMS TO KNOW

Risk management
Risk analysis questionnaire
Flow chart
Loss frequency
Loss severity
Maximum possible loss
Maximum probable loss
Avoidance
Retention
Retention level
Noninsurance transfer
Loss control
Deductible
Captive insurer
Self-insurance
Essential insurance
Desirable insurance
Available insurance
Excess insurance
Manuscript policy
Risk management policy statement
Risk management manual

SUGGESTIONS FOR ADDITIONAL READING

Athearn, James L. and S. Travis Pritchett. *Risk and Insurance,* 5th ed. St. Paul, Minnesota: West Publishing Co., 1984, chapter 2.

Bickelhaupt, David L. *General Insurance*, 11th ed. Homewood, Illinois: Richard D. Irwin, Inc., 1983, chapters 1 and 2.

Doherty, Neil A. *Corporate Risk Management: A Financial Exposition,* New York: McGraw-Hill, 1985.

Greene, Mark R. and Oscar N. Serbein. *Risk Management: Text and Cases,* 2nd ed. Reston, VA: Reston Publishing Company, 1983.

Greene, Mark R. and James S. Trieschmann. *Risk and Insurance,* 6th ed. Cincinnati, Ohio: Southwestern Publishing Company, 1984, chapter 3.

Insurance Company of North America. *Insurance Decisions: Determining Risk Retention Levels.* Philadelphia, Pennsylvania: INA Corporation, n.d.

Insurance Company of North America. *Insurance Decisions: Self-Insurance.* Philadeiphia, Pennsylvania: INA Corporation, n.d.

Insurance Company of North America. *Risk Management: Some Professional Considerations.* Philadelphia, Pennsylvania: INA Corporation, n.d.

Insurance Institute of America. *Readings on Risk Control.* Malvern, Pennsylvania: Insurance Institute of America, 1983.

Insurance Institute of America. *Readings on Risk Financing.* Malvern, Pennsylvania: Insurance Institute of America, 1983.

Insurance Institute of America. *Readings on the Risk Management Function.* Malvern, Pennsylvania: Insurance Institute of America, 1983.

Mehr, Robert I. and Bob A. Hedges. *Risk Management: Concepts and Applications.* Homewood, Illinois: Richard D. Irwin, Inc., 1974.

Williams, Jr., C. Arthur and Richard M. Heins. *Risk Management and Insurance,* 5th ed. New York: McGraw-Hill Book Company, 1985.

Williams, Jr., C. Arthur, George L. Head, Ronald C. Horn, and G. William Glendenning. *Principles of Risk Management and Insurance,* 2nd ed., Volume I. Malvern, Pennsylvania: American Institute for Property and Liability Underwriters, 1981, chapters 1–5.

Williams, Numan A., ed. *Risk Retention: Alternate Funding Methods.* Malvern, Pennsylvania: The Society of Chartered Property and Casualty Underwriters, 1983.

NOTES

1. Robert I. Mehr and Bob A. Hedges, *Risk Management: Concepts and Applications* (Homewood, Illinois: Richard D. Irwin, Inc., 1974), chapters 1 and 2. See also C. Arthur Williams, Jr., George L. Head, Ronald C. Horn, and G. William Glendenning, *Principles of Risk Management and Insurance,* 2nd ed, Volume I (Malvern, Pennsylvania: American Institute for Property and Liability Underwriters, 1981), pp. 15–18.
2. Williams, Jr., 2nd ed., pp. 158–159.
3. These techniques are analyzed in some detail in Williams, Jr., 2nd ed., Vol. I, chapters 2, 3, 4, and 5. The author drew heavily on this source in preparing this section.
4. Williams, Jr., 2nd ed., pp. 125–126.
5. *Insurance Decisions Determining Risk Retention Levels* (Philadelphia, Pennsylvania: Insurance Company of North America, n.d.), pp. 3–12.
6. Williams, Jr., 2nd ed., pp. 135–142.
7. Mark R. Greene, "Analyzing Captives—How, and What, Are They Doing?" *Risk Management,* 26 (December 1979), p. 13.
8. C. Arthur Williams, Jr., George L. Head, and G. William Glendenning, *Principles of Risk Management and Insurance,* Volume I (Malvern, Pennsylvania: American Institute for Property and Liability Underwriters, 1978), pp. 160–161.

9. The advantages and disadvantages of retention are discussed in some detail in Williams, Jr., 2nd ed., pp. 126–133.
10. Williams, Jr., 2nd ed., pp. 103–104.
11. For an extensive discussion of insurance in a risk management program, see Williams, Jr., 2nd ed., pp. 107–23, 146–51.
12. The financial aspects of insurers are discussed in Chapters 26 and 27.
13. A manuscript policy is one that is specifically designed for a business firm to meet its specific needs and requirements.
14. Williams, Jr., 2nd ed., pp. 108–16.
15. Williams, Jr., pp. 35–36.
16. Williams, Jr., 2nd ed., pp. 41–42.
17. Insurance Company of North America, *Risk Management, Some Professional Considerations* (Philadelphia, Pennsylvania: Insurance Company of North America, n.d.), p. 12.

PART

2

LAW AND THE INSURANCE CONTRACT

CHAPTER

4

FUNDAMENTAL LEGAL PRINCIPLES

"The education of those engaged in the important functions of the insurance business calls for an understanding of the essentials of insurance law."

Edwin W. Patterson, Essentials of Insurance Law

STUDENT LEARNING OBJECTIVES

After studying this chapter, you should be able to:

- Explain the fundamental legal principles that are reflected in insurance contracts, including:
    - Principle of indemnity
    - Principle of insurable interest
    - Principle of subrogation
    - Principle of utmost good faith
- Explain how the legal concepts of representations, concealment, and warranty support the principle of utmost good faith.
- Describe the basic requirements for the formation of a valid insurance contract.
- Show how insurance contracts differ from other contracts.
- Explain the law of agency and how it affects the actions of insurance agents.

Insurance contracts are complex legal documents that reflect the general rules of law. In this chapter, we will examine some fundamental legal principles that are reflected in insurance contracts. We will also examine the basic requirements that must be met to have a valid insurance contract. We will then discuss the distinct legal characteristics of insurance contracts and show how insurance contracts differ from other contracts. We will conclude the chapter by examining the law of agency and analyzing how it affects the actions of insurance agents.

PRINCIPLE OF INDEMNITY

The principle of **indemnity** is one of the most important legal principles in the field of insurance. Most property insurance contracts are contracts of indemnity. *A contract of indemnity specifies that the insured should not collect more than the actual cash value of the loss.* The principle of indemnity has two fundamental purposes. *The first purpose is to prevent the insured from profiting from insurance.* The insured should not profit if a loss occurs, but should be restored to approximately the same financial position as existed before the loss. For example, if Mary's home is insured for $80,000, and a $20,000 loss occurs, the principle of indemnity would be violated if $80,000 were paid to her. She would be profiting from insurance.

The second purpose of the principle of indemnity is to reduce moral hazard. If dishonest insureds can profit from a loss, they may deliberately cause a loss with the intention of collecting the insurance. Thus, if the loss payment does not exceed the actual cash loss, moral hazard is reduced.

Actual Cash Value Rule

The concept of **actual cash value** underlies the principle of indemnity. In property insurance, the standard method for indemnifying the insured is based on the actual cash value of the damaged property at the time of loss. Actual cash value is determined as follows:

Replacement Cost − Depreciation
= Actual Cash Value

This rule takes into consideration both inflation in and depreciation of property values over time. Replacement cost is the current cost of restoring the damaged property with new materials of like kind and quality. Depreciation accounts for wear and tear and economic obsolescence.

The actual cash value rule is designed to restore the insured to approximately the same financial position after the loss as existed before the loss. For example, assume that Gerald has a favorite couch that burns in a fire. Assume also that he bought the couch five years ago, that the couch is 50 percent depreciated, and that a similar couch would today cost $1,000. Under the actual cash value rule, Gerald will collect $500 for the loss of his couch because replacement cost is $1,000, but depreciation is $500, or 50 percent. If Gerald were paid the full replacement value of $1,000, the principle of indemnity would be violated, since he would receive the value of a brand new couch instead of one that is five years old. In short, the $500 payment represents indemnification for the loss of a five-year-old couch. This can be summarized as follows:

Replacement cost	=	$1,000
Depreciation	=	$500 (couch is 50 percent depreciated)
Replacement cost − depreciation	=	Actual cash value
$1,000 − $500	=	$500

Replacement cost less depreciation is not the only method for determining the amount of a loss. In some cases, *fair market value* can be used as the basis for determining the amount of loss. The fair market value of a building may be below its actual cash value based on replacement cost less depreciation. This may be due to several reasons, including poor location, a deteriorating neighborhood, or economic obsolescence of the building. For example, in major cities, large homes in older residential areas often have a market value well below replacement cost less depreciation. If a loss occurs, the fair market value may be used to determine the value of the loss. In one case, a building valued at $170,000 based on replacement cost less depreciation had a market value of only $65,000 when a loss occurred. The court ruled that the actual cash value of the property should be based on the fair market value of $65,000 rather than on $170,000.[1]

Although the actual cash value rule is the normal rule for paying losses in property insurance, different procedures are followed for other types of insurance. In liability insurance, the amounts paid are the actual damages that the insured is legally obligated to pay because of bodily injury or property damage to someone else. In business interruption insurance, the amount paid is usually based on the loss of profits plus continuing expenses incurred when the firm is shut down because of a loss from a covered peril. In life insurance, the amount paid upon the insured's death is the face amount of the policy.

Exceptions to the Principle of Indemnity

There are several important exceptions to the principle of indemnity. They include the following:

- Valued policy
- Valued policy laws
- Replacement cost insurance
- Life insurance

Valued policy A valued policy is a departure from the principle of indemnity. *A **valued policy** is one that pays the face amount of insurance regardless of actual cash value if a total loss occurs.* Valued policies typically are used to insure antiques, fine arts, rare paintings, and family heirlooms. Because of the difficulty in determining the actual value of the property at the time of loss, the insured and insurer both agree on the value of the property when the policy is first issued. For example, you may have an antique clock that was owned by your great-grandmother. You may feel that the clock is worth $10,000 and have it insured for that amount. If the clock is totally destroyed in a fire, you would be paid $10,000 regardless of the actual cash value of the clock at the time of loss.

Valued policy laws **Valued policy laws** are another exception to the principle of indemnity.[2] *These laws generally require payment of the face amount of insurance if a total loss occurs from a peril specified in the law, even though the policy states that only the actual cash value will be paid.* The specified perils typically are fire, lightning, and tornado.[3] The laws generally apply only to real property, and the loss must be total. For example, a building insured for $200,000 may have an actual cash value of $175,000. If a total loss from a fire occurs, the face amount of $200,000 would be paid. Since the insured would be paid more than the actual cash value, the principle of indemnity would be violated.

The original purpose of a valued policy law was to protect the insured from an argument with the company if an agent had deliberately overinsured property in order to receive a higher commission. After a total loss, the company might offer less than the face amount for which the insured had paid premiums, on the grounds that the building was overinsured. However, the importance of a valued policy law has declined over time because inflation of property values has made overinsurance relatively uncommon. Underinsurance is now the greater problem, since it results in both inadequate premiums for the insurer and inadequate protection for the insured.

Despite their reduced importance, valued policy laws can lead to overinsurance and an increase in moral hazard. Most buildings are not physically inspected before they are insured. If a company fails to inspect a building for valuation purposes, overinsurance and possible moral hazard may result. The insured may not be concerned about loss prevention, or may even deliberately cause a loss to collect the proceeds. Although valued policy laws may provide a defense for the insurer when fraud is suspected, the burden of proof is on the insurer to prove fraudulent intent. This is often difficult. For example, a house advertised for sale at $1,800 was insured for $10,000 under a fire insurance policy. About six months later, the house was totally destroyed by a fire. The insurer denied liability on the grounds of misrepresentation and fraud. However, an appeals court ordered the face amount of insurance to be paid. The court held that nothing prevented the company from inspecting the property to determine its value, and the insured's statement concerning the value of the house was an expression of *opinion*, not a representation of *fact.*[4]

Replacement cost insurance **Replacement cost insurance** is a second exception to the principle of indemnity. *Replacement cost insurance means there is no deduction taken for depreciation in determining the amount paid after a loss.* For example, assume that the roof on your home is five years old and has a useful life of twenty years. The roof is damaged by a tornado, and the current cost of replacement is $10,000. Under the actual cash value rule, you would receive only $7,500 ($10,000 − $2,500 = $7,500). Under a replacement cost policy, you would receive the full $10,000. Since you receive the value of a brand new roof instead of one that is five yers old, the principle of indemnity is technically violated.

However, replacement cost insurance is based on the recognition that payment of the actual cash value can still result in a substantial loss to the insured, since few persons budget for depreciation. The deduction for depreciation means that you must come up with the necessary cash to restore the property to its original condition after a loss occurs. In our earlier example, you would have had to pay $2,500 to restore the damaged roof, since it was one-fourth depreciated. To deal with this problem, property insurers are now making replacement cost insurance available on homes, buildings, and personal and business property.

Life insurance Life insurance is another exception to the principle of indemnity. A life insurance contract is a valued policy that pays a stated sum to the beneficiary upon the insured's death. The indemnity principle is difficult to apply to life insurance for the obvious reason that the actual cash value rule (replacement cost less depreciation) is meaningless in determining the value of a human life. Moreover, in order to plan for personal and business purposes, such as the need to provide a specific amount of monthly income to the deceased's dependents, a certain amount of life insurance must be purchased before death occurs. For these reasons, a life insurance policy can also be considered an exception to the principle of indemnity.

PRINCIPLE OF INSURABLE INTEREST

The principle of **insurable interest** is another important legal principle that you should understand. *The principle of insurable interest specifies that the insured must lose financially if a loss occurs, or must incur some other kind of harm if the loss takes place.* For example, you have an insurable interest in your automobile since you may lose financially if the car is damaged or stolen. You have a similar insurable interest in your stereo set since you may lose financially if the set is damaged. You also have an insurable interest in a house that you own, since you may lose financially if the home is damaged or destroyed.

To be enforceable, all insurance contracts must be supported by an insurable interest; otherwise, insureds could collect even though a loss had not occurred. This would be contrary to the public interest. Let us examine this important point in greater detail by describing the basic purposes of the insurable interest requirement.

Purposes of an Insurable Interest

Insurance contracts must be supported by an insurable interest for the following reasons.[5]

- To prevent gambling
- To reduce moral hazard
- To measure the loss

First, an insurable interest is necessary *to prevent gambling.* If an insurable interest were not required, the contract would be a gambling contract and would be against the public interest. For example, you could insure the property of another and hope for an early loss. You could similarly insure the life of another person and hope for an early death. These contracts clearly would be gambling contracts and would be against the public interest.

Second, an insurable interest *reduces moral hazard.* If an insurable interst is not required, a dishonest person can purchase a property insurance contract on someone else's property and then deliberately cause a loss to receive the proceeds. But if the insured stands to lose financially, nothing is gained by causing the loss. Thus, moral hazard is reduced. In life insurance, an insurable interest requirement reduces the incentive to murder the insured for the purpose of collecting the proceeds.

Finally, an insurable interest *measures the amount of the insured's loss.* In property insurance, most contracts are contracts of indemnity, and one measure of recovery is the insurable interest of the insured. You can never collect more than your insurable interest, since this would be a violation of the principle of indemnity.

Examples of an Insurable Interest

Let us briefly examine some situations that satisfy the insurable interest requirement. It is helpful at this point to distinguish between an insurable interest in property and liability insurance and in life insurance.

Property and liability insurance *Ownership of property* can support an insurable interest, since owners of property will lose financially if their property is damaged or destroyed.

Potential legal liability can also support an insurable interest. For example, a dry-cleaning firm has an insurable interest in the property of the customers, since the firm may be legally liable for damage to the customer's goods because of the firm's negligence.

Those who are **secured creditors** have an insurable interest as well. A commercial bank or savings and loan institution that grants mortgages has an insurable interest in the property pledged. The property serves as collateral for the mortgage, so that if the building is damaged, the collateral behind the loan is impaired. A bank that makes an inventory loan to a business firm has the same insurable interest in the stock of goods, since it serves as collateral for the loan. However, the courts have ruled that unsecured or general creditors normally do not have an insurable interest in the debtor's property.[6]

Finally, a *contract right* can support an insurable interest. For example, a business firm that contracts to purchase goods from abroad on the condition that they arrive safely in the United States has an insurable interest in the goods because of the loss of profits if the merchandise does not arrive.

Life insurance The question of an insurable interest does not arise when you purchase life insurance on your own life. The law considers the insurable interest requirement to be met whenever a person voluntarily purchases life insurance on his or her life. This means that you can purchase as much life insurance as you desire, and you can name anyone as beneficiary. The beneficiary is not required to have an insurable interest in your life. However, as a practical matter, life insurers will limit the amount of life insurance they will write on any single life.

INSIGHT 4.1

Insurable Interest in Life Insurance

Facts

Jack was employed by Pioneer Foundry for nine years. During Jack's employment, the company had an insurable interest in Jacks's life, and it purchased a $50,000 policy on his life, the company being named as beneficiary on the policy. When Jack later left the company, the company continued to pay the premiums on the policy until Jack's death. Is the company, which had no insurable interest at the time of Jack's death entitled to recover $50,000 on the policy?

Decision

The company is entitled to recover the proceeds.

Reasoning

If the insurable interest requirement is met when the policy is issued, the policy proceeds must be paid even if there is no insurable interest at death. The company is not limited in its recovery to the amount of its financial loss, which in this case was nothing.

Secor v. Pioneer Foundry Co., Inc., 173 N.W. 2d 780 (Mich. 1970).

SOURCE: Joseph L.Frascona, *Business Law, Texts and Cases* (Dubuque, Iowa: Wm. C. Brown, 1980), p. 904.

If you wish to purchase a life insurance policy on the life of another person, you must have an insurable interest in that person's life. Close ties of love, affection, blood, and marriage will satisfy the insurable interest requirement in life insurance. For example, a husband or wife can purchase a life insurance policy on the other's life based on love and affection. A grandparent can purchase a life insurance policy on the life of a grandchild. However, remote family relationships will not support an insurable interest. Thus, a son-in-law does not have an insurable interest in the life of a mother-in-law unless he can show that a pecuniary interest is involved. Likewise, a mother-in-law does not have an insurable interest in the life of the son-in-law.

If a **pecuniary interest** is involved, the insurable interest requirement in life insurance can be met. Even when there is no relationship by blood or marriage, one person may be financially harmed by the death of another. For example, a corporation can insure the life of an outstanding salesperson, since the firm's profits may decline if the salesperson should die. One business partner can insure the life of the other partner in order to purchase the deceased partner's interest if he or she should die. And an unsecured creditor has an insurable interest in the life of a debtor, since the loan may not be repaid if the debtor should die.

When Must an Insurable Interest Exist?

In property insurance, the insurable interest must exist at the time of loss. There are two reasons for this requirement. First, most property insurance contracts are contracts of indemnity. If an insurable interest did not exist at the time of loss, financial loss would not occur. Hence the principle of indemnity would be violated if payment were made. For example, if Charles sells his home to Susan, and a fire occurs before the insurance on the home is canceled, Charles cannot collect since he no longer has an insurable interest in the property. Susan cannot collect either since she is not named as an insured under the policy.

Second, you may not have an insurable interest in the property when the contract is first written, but may expect to have an insurable interest in the future, at the time of possible loss. For example, in ocean marine insurance, it is common to insure a return cargo by a contract entered into prior to the ship's departure. However, the policy may not cover the goods until they are on board the ship as the insured's property. Although an insurable interest does not exist when the contract is first written, you can still collect if you have an insurable interest in the goods at the time of loss.

In contrast, in life insurance, the insurable interest requirement must be met only at the inception of the policy, not at the time of death. Life insurance is not a contract of indemnity but is a valued policy that pays a stated sum upon the insured's death. Since the beneficiary has only a legal claim to receive the policy proceeds, the beneficiary does not have to show that a loss has been incurred by the insured's death. For example, if Susan takes out a policy on her husband's life and later gets a divorce, she is entitled to the policy proceeds upon the death of her former husband if she has kept the insurance in force. The insurable interest requirement must be met only at the inception of the contract.

PRINCIPLE OF SUBROGATION

The principle of **subrogation** strongly supports the principle of indemnity. *Subrogation means substitution of the insurer in place of the insured for the purpose of claiming indemnity from a third person for the loss covered by insurance.*[7] *Stated simply, this means that the insurer is entitled to recover from a negligent third party any loss payments made to the insured.* For example, assume that a negligent motorist fails to stop at a red light and smashes into Mary's car, causing damages in the amount of $5,000. If she has collision insurance on her car, her company will pay the physical damage loss to the car (less any deductible) and then attempt to collect from the negligent motorist who caused the accident. Alternatively, Mary could attempt to collect directly from the negligent motorist for the damage to her automobile. Subrogation does not apply if a loss payment is not made. However, to the extent that a loss payment is made, the insured gives to the insurer legal rights to collect damages from the negligent third party.

Purposes of Subrogation

Subrogation has three basic purposes. They are:

1. To prevent the insured from collecting twice for the same loss.
2. To hold the negligent person responsible for the loss.
3. To hold down insurances rates.

First, subrogation prevents the insured from collecting twice for the same loss. In the absence of subrogation, it is possible for the insured to collect from the insurer and from the person who caused the loss. The principle of indemnity would therefore be violated, since the insured would be profiting from a loss.

Second, subrogation is used to hold the guilty person responsible for the loss. By exercising its subrogation rights, the insurer can collect from the negligent person who caused the loss.

Finally, subrogation tends to hold down insurance rates. Subrogation recoveries can be reflected in the rate-making process, which tends to hold rates below the level at which they would otherwise be. If subrogation were not allowed, insurance rates would be substantially higher for many lines of insurance.

Importance of Subrogation

You should keep in mind five important corollaries of the principle of subrogation.

1. *In the absence of any policy provision stating how subrogation recoveries are shared, the insurer can retain any amounts recovered through subrogation only after the insured is fully indemnified.* Some persons may not be fully indemnified after a loss because of (1) insufficient insurance, (2) satisfaction of a deductible, or (3) legal expenses in trying to recover from a negligent third party. For example, Charles may have his $100,000 home insured for only $80,000 under a homeowners policy. Assume that the

house is totally destroyed in a fire because of faulty wiring by an electrician. The insurer would pay $80,000 to Charles and then attempt to collect from the negligent electrician. Assume that the insurer has a net recovery of $50,000 (after deduction of legal expenses) after exercising its subrogation rights against the negligent electrician. Charles would receive $20,000, and the insurer can retain the balance of $30,000.

There are some exceptions to the general rule of full recovery by the insured when the insurer exercises its subrogation rights. In automobile collision insurance, many companies will indemnify the insured for any deductible if full recovery is received from the negligent third party. However, if the insurer incurs legal expenses in exercising its subrogation rights, the deductible may be prorated with the insured. For example, if the company incurs legal expenses of $250 in recovering $1,000 from the negligent third party, only three-fourths of the deductible will be remitted to the insured. Finally, some insurance contracts may specify that a subrogation recovery will be shared by the insured and insurer based on the proportion that the loss incurred by each party bears to the total loss.

2. *The insured cannot impair the insurer's subrogation rights.* The insured cannot do anything after a loss that prejudices the insurer's right to proceed against a negligent third party. For example, if the insured waives the right to sue the negligent party, the right to collect from the insurer for the loss is also waived. This could happen if the insured settles an automobile collision loss with the negligent driver without the company's consent. If the company's right to subrogate against the negligent motorist is adversely affected, the insured's right to collect from the insurer is forfeited.[8]

3. *The insurer can waive its subrogation rights in the contract.* To meet the special needs of some insureds, the insurance company may waive its subrogation rights by a contractual provision for losses that have not yet occurred. For example, in order to rent an apartment house, a landlord may agree to release the tenants from potential liability if the building is damaged. If the landlord's insurer waives its subrogation rights, and if a tenant negligently starts a fire, the insurer would have to reimburse the landlord for the loss, but could not recover from the tenant since the subrogation rights were waived.

The company can also decide not to exercise its subrogation rights after a loss occurs. The legal expenses may exceed the possible recovery; a counterclaim against the insured or insurer may be filed by the alleged wrongdoer; the insurer may wish to avoid embarrassment of the insured; or the company may wish to maintain good public relations. For these reasons, subrogation rights after a loss may not be exercised.[9]

4. *Subrogation does not apply to life insurance and to most individual health insurance contracts.* Life insurance is not a contract of indemnity, and subrogation has relevance only for contracts of indemnity. Individual health insurance contracts usually do not contain subrogation clauses.[10] Thus, if Mary is injured in an automobile accident by a negligent driver, she can collect for her medical expenses under an individual health insurance contract and can also sue the negligent motorist for her bodily injuries.

5. *The insurer cannot subrogate against its own insureds.* If the company could recover a loss payment for a *covered loss,* the basic purpose of owning the insurance would be defeated.

PRINCIPLE OF UTMOST GOOD FAITH

An insurance contract is based on the principle of **utmost good faith.** *This means that a higher degree of honesty is imposed on both parties to an insurance contract than is imposed on parties to other contracts.* This principle has its historical roots in ocean marine insurance—the marine underwriter had to place great faith in statements made by the applicant for insurance concerning the cargo to be shipped. The property to be insured may not have been visually inspected, and the contract may have been formed in a location far removed from the covered cargo and ship. Thus, the principle of utmost good faith imposed a high degree of honesty on the applicant for insurance.

The principle of utmost good faith is supported by three important legal doctrines. They are:

- Representations
- Concealment
- Warranty

Representations

***Representations** are statements made by the applicant for insurance.* For example, if you apply for life insurance, you may be asked questions concerning your age, weight, height, occupation, state of health, family history, and other relevant questions. These statements are called representations.

The legal significance of a representation is that the insurance contract is voidable at the insurer's option if the representation is (1) material and (2) false. *Material means that if the insurer knew the true facts, the policy would not have been issued, or would have been issued on different terms.* For example, Gerald may apply for life insurance and state in the application that he has not visited a doctor within the last five years. However, he may have undergone surgery for lung cancer six months earlier. In this case, he has made a statement that is both false and material, and the policy is voidable at the insurer's option. If Gerald dies shortly after the policy is issued, the company could contest the death claim on the basis of a material misrepresentation.

But if an applicant for insurance states an *opinion or belief* that later turns out to be wrong, the insurer must prove that the applicant spoke fraudulently and intended to deceive the company before it can avoid the policy. For example, assume that Charles is asked when he applies for health insurance if he has high blood pressure and that he answers no to the question. If the insurer later discovers that Charles has high blood pressure, in order to avoid the policy, it must prove that Charles intended to deceive the company. Thus, a statement of opinion or belief must be *material, false,* and *fraudulent* before the company can deny payment of a claim.

An **innocent** (unintentional) **misrepresentation** of a **material fact** also makes the contract voidable. A majority of court opinions has held that an innocent misrepresentation of a material fact makes the contract voidable. The important case of *McDowell v. Fraser* in 1779 illustrates the historical basis of an innocent misrepresentation. A broker applied for insurance on a ship that was sailing from New York to Philadelphia and stated that the ship was safely observed in the Delaware River on 11 December by another ship that landed in New York. Based on this representation, the underwriter insured the ship. However, the ship had in fact sunk two days earlier. It was conceded that the broker honestly believed the ship was safe when the statement was made. However, the court considered only the question of materiality and ruled in favor of the insurer on the grounds that the exact day was important in estimating the risk of a short voyage.

Thus, the test of materiality is the effect that the statement has on the insurer, not whether the insured makes a careless or fraudulent statement.[11] If the applicant for insurance misrepresents a material fact, the contract is voidable by the insurer.

Concealment

The doctrine of **concealment** also supports the principle of utmost good faith. *A concealment is failure of the applicant for insurance to reveal a material fact to the insurer.* Concealment is the same thing as nondisclosure; that is, the applicant for insurance is silent and deliberately withholds material information from the insurer. The legal effect of a material concealment is the same as a misrepresentation—the contract is voidable at the insurer's option.

We stated earlier that an insurance policy is a

INSIGHT 4.2

Misrepresentaiton of a Material Fact

Facts

In applying for automobile insurance, Johnny stated in his application that he had no arrests for offenses other than traffic violations, that he had not been fined or convicted for a moving violation, and that he did not use alcoholic beverages. In fact, Johnny had a number of convictions for traffic violations, forgery, and drunkenness. The company issued the policy, and Johnny's car was later involved in an accident. Johnny was not driving the car at the time of the accident. May the company cancel the policy and avoid liability because of Johnny's false statement?

Decision

The company is not liable.

Reasoning

Johnny's misrepresentations were material to the risk. Consequently the policy was void.

Countryside Casualty Co. v. Orr, 523 F.2d 870 (1975).

SOURCE: Joseph L. Frascona, *Business Law, Text and Cases* (Dubuque, Iowa: Wm. C. Brown, 1980), p. 906.

contract of utmost good faith. The applicant for insurance is required to disclose material information to the insurer even though the disclosure may result in a denial of the insurance or require the payment of higher premiums. For example, James may intentionally conceal the fact that he has high blood pressure when he applies for life insurance on a nonmedical basis. High blood pressure is a serious health problem and is an important cause of heart disease. If the company had known the true facts, he either would have been refused the insurance or would have been required to pay higher premiums. Although he may not have been asked whether he ever had high blood pressure, he is required to volunteer this information to the insurer. If the policy were issued and James dies shortly thereafter, the company could contest the claim.

Warranty

The doctrine of **warranty** also reflects the principle of utmost good faith. *A warranty is a statement of fact or a promise made by the insured, which is part of the insurance contract and which must be true if the insurer is to be liable under the contract.*[12] For example, in exchange for a reduced premium, the owner of a liquor store may warrant that an approved burglary and robbery alarm system will be operational at all times. Likewise, a bank may warrant that a guard will be on the premises twenty-four hours a day. The clause describing the warranty becomes part of the contract.

In its strictest form based on the common law, a warranty is a harsh legal doctrine. Any breach of the warranty, even if minor or not material, allows the insurer to avoid the policy. Thus, if the liquor store in the earlier example is burglarized while the central alarm system is being repaired, the company could deny liability for the loss. But the courts have softened and modified the harsh doctrine of warranty. With the exception of ocean marine insurance, most American courts do not follow the strict common law. Some modifications of the doctrine of warranty are summarized as follows:

1. Statements made by the applicant for insurance are considered to be representa-

tions and not warranties. Thus, the insurer cannot deny liability for a loss if a misrepresentation is not material.

2. Most courts will interpret a breach of warranty liberally in those cases where a minor breach affects the risk only temporarily or insignificantly.
3. "Increase in hazard" statutes have been passed which state that the company cannot deny a claim unless the breach of warranty increases the hazard.

This concludes our discussion of the fundamental legal principles that are embodied in insurance contracts. Let us next examine the basic requirements for a valid insurance contract.

REQUIREMENTS OF AN INSURANCE CONTRACT

An insurance policy is based on the law of contracts. To be legally enforceable, an insurance contract must meet four basic requirements. They are:

- Offer and acceptance
- Consideration
- Competent parties
- Legal purpose

Offer and Acceptance

The first requirement of a binding insurance contract is that there must be an offer and an acceptance of its terms. *The general rule is that the applicant for insurance makes the offer, and the company accepts or rejects the offer.* An agent merely solicits or invites the prospective insured to make an offer. Let us examine the concept of **offer and acceptance** in greater detail by making a careful distinction between property and liability insurance and life insurance.

In property insurance, the offer and acceptance can be oral or in writing. In the absence of specific legislation to the contrary, oral insurance contracts are valid. However, as a practical matter, most property and liability insurance contracts are in written form. The applicant for insurance fills out the application and pays the first premium (or promises to pay the first premium). This constitutes the offer. The agent then accepts the offer on behalf of the insurance company. In property and liability insurance, agents typically have the power to bind their companies.[13] Thus, the insurance contract can be effective immediatley, since the agent accepts the offer on behalf of the company he or she represents. This is the normal procedure followed in personal lines of property and liability insurance, including homeowners policies and automobile insurance. However, in some cases, the agent is not authorized to bind the company, and the application must be sent to the company for approval. The company may accept the offer and issue the policy. Assuming that the other basic requirements of an insurance contract have been met, the insurance is then in force.

In life insurance, the procedures followed are different. A life insurance agent normally does not have the power to bind the company. Therefore, the application for life insurance is always in writing, and the applicant must be approved by the company before the life insurance is in force. The normal procedure is for the applicant to fill out the application and pay the first premium, which constitutes the offer. *A conditional binding receipt* is then given to the applicant. If the applicant is found insurable according to the company's normal underwriting standards, the life insurance is effective as of the date of the application or the date of the medical examination, whichever is later. For example, assume that Michael applies for a $50,000 life insurance policy on Monday. He fills out the application, pays the first premium, and receives a conditional binding receipt. On Tuesday morning, he takes a physical examination, and on Tuesday afternoon, he is accidentally killed in a boating accident. The application and premium will still be forwarded to the company, as if he were still alive. If he is found insurable according to the normal underwriting rules of the company, the life insurance is in force, and $50,000 would be paid to his beneficiary.

However, if the applicant for life insurance does not pay the first premium when the application is filled out, a different set of rules applies. The insurer must approve the application and then issue the policy, which constitutes an offer to the applicant. The prospective insured accepts the offer by paying the first premium and accepting delivery of the policy. In addition, most life insurers require the applicant to be in good health when the policy is delivered. Before the life insurance is in force, therefore, the policy must be issued and delivered to the applicant, the first premium must be paid, and the applicant must be in good health when the contract is delivered. These requirements are considered to be "conditions precedent"—in other words, they must be fulfilled before the life insurance is in force.[14]

Consideration

The second requirement of a valid insurance contract is **consideration.** Consideration refers to the value that each party gives to the other. The insured's consideration is payment of the first premium (or a promise to pay the first premium) plus an agreement to abide by the conditions specified in the policy. The insurer's consideration is the promise to do certain things as specified in the contract. This can include paying for a loss from an insured peril, providing certain services, such as loss prevention and safety services, or defending the insured in a liability lawsuit.

Competent Parties

The third requirement of a valid insurance contract is that each party must be legally **competent.** This means the parties must have legal capacity to enter into a binding contract. Most adults are legally competent to enter into insurance contracts, but there are some exceptions. Insane persons, intoxicated persons, and corporations that act outside the scope of their authorized authority cannot enter into enforceable insurance contracts. Minors normally are not legally competent to enter into binding insurance contracts; but some states have enacted laws that permit minors as young as age fourteen and a half to enter into a valid life or health insurance contract.

Legal Purpose

A final requirement is that the contract must be for a **legal purpose.** An insurance contract that encourages or promotes something illegal or immoral is contrary to the public interest and cannot be enforced. For example, a street pusher of heroin and other hard drugs cannot purchase a property insurance policy that would cover seizure of the drugs by the police. A numbers runner cannot purchase a holdup policy to cover the loss of daily receipts. A professional check writer cannot purchase a business interruption policy that will cover the loss of profits if he or she is sent to prison. These contracts obviously are not enforceable, since they would promote illegal ventures that are contrary to the public interest.

DISTINCT LEGAL CHARACTERISTICS OF INSURANCE CONTRACTS

Insurance contracts have distinct legal characteristics that make them different from other contracts. These are:

- Aleatory contract
- Unilateral contract
- Conditional contract
- Personal contract
- Contract of adhesion

Aleatory Contract

An insurance contract is aleatory rather than commutative. *An **aleatory contract** is one in which the values exchanged are not equal.* Depending on chance, one party may receive a value out of all proportion to the value that is given. For example, assume that Susan pays a premium of $300 for $80,000 of homeowners insurance on her home. If the home were totally destroyed by fire shortly thereafter, she would collect an amount that greatly exceeds the premium paid.

In contrast, other commercial contracts are commutative. *A commutative contract is one in which the values exchanged by both parties are theoretically even.* For example, the purchaser of real estate normally pays a price that is viewed to be equal to the value of the property.

Although the essence of an aleatory contract is chance, or the occurrence of some fortuitous event, an insurance contract is not a gambling contract. Gambling creates a new speculative risk that did not exist before the transaction. Insurance, however, is a technique for handling an already existing pure risk. Thus, although both gambling and insurance are aleatory in nature, an insurance contract is not a wagering contract, since no new risk is created.

Unilateral Contract

An insurance contract is a unilateral contract. *A **unilateral contract** means that only one party makes a legally enforceable promise.* In this case, only the insurer makes a legally enforceable promise to pay a claim or provide other services to the insured. After the first premium is paid, and the insurance is in force, the insured cannot be legally forced to pay the premiums or to comply with the policy provisions. Although the insured must continue to pay the premiums in order to receive payment for a loss, he or she cannot be legally forced to do so. However, if the premiums are paid, the insurer must accept them and must continue to provide the protection promised under the contract.

In contrast, most commercial contracts are *bilateral* in nature. Each party makes a legally enforceable promise to the other party. If one party fails to perform, the other party can insist on performance or can sue for damages because of the breach of contract.

Conditional Contract

An insurance contract is a **conditional contract.** This means the insurer's obligation to pay a claim depends on whether or not the insured or the beneficiary has complied with all policy conditions. *Conditions are provisions inserted in the policy that qualify or place limitations on the insurer's promise to perform.* The conditions section imposes certain duties on the insured if he or she wishes to collect for a loss. Although the insured is not compelled to abide by the policy conditions, he or she must do so in order to collect for a loss. The insurer is not obligated to pay a claim if the policy conditions are not met. For example, under the standard fire policy, the insured must give immediate written notice of a loss. If the insured delays for an unreasonable period in reporting the loss, the company can refuse to pay the claim on the grounds that a policy condition has been violated.

Personal Contract

In property insurance, insurance is a **personal contract.** *This means the contract is between the insured and the insurer.* Strictly speaking, a property insurance contract does not insure property, but insures the owner of property against loss. The owner of the insured property is indemnified if the property is damaged or destroyed. Since the contract is personal, the applicant for insurance must be acceptable to the company and must meet certain underwriting standards regarding character, morals, and credit. Since a property insurance contract is a personal contract, it normally cannot be assigned to another party without the insurer's consent. If property is sold to another person, the new owner may not be acceptable to the insurer. Thus, the insurer's consent is normally required before the policy can be validly assigned to another party. In contrast, a life insurance policy is not a personal contract. Therefore, it can be freely assigned to anyone without the insurer's consent.

A property insurer's loss payment can, however, be freely assigned to another party without the insurer's consent. Although the insurer's consent is not required, the contract may require that the insurer be notified of the assignment of the proceeds to another party.

Contract of Adhesion

A ***contract of adhesion*** *means the insured must accept the entire contract, with all of its terms and conditions.* The insurer drafts and prints the policy, and the insured generally must accept the entire document and cannot insist that certain provisions be added or deleted or the contract rewritten to suit the insured. Although the contract can be altered by the addition of endorsements or forms, the endorsements and forms are drafted by the insurer. However, to redress the imbalance that exists in such a situation, the *courts have ruled that any ambiguities or uncertainties in the contract are construed against the insurer.* If the policy is ambiguous, the insured gets the benefit of the doubt.

Manuscript policies are an exception to this statement. In contrast to a printed policy prepared by the insurer, a manuscript policy is a contract prepared to meet specific needs of any individual client or corporation. These policies are normally prepared by a large brokerage firm or a risk management department, and then agreed to by an insurer. In these cases, the courts have modified the common law doctrine pertaining to contracts of adhesion when policy provisions are disputed. This is only fair because it is reasonable to assume that both parties have access to professional advice.

LAW AND THE INSURANCE AGENT

An insurance contract normally is sold by an agent who represents the principal. An agent is simply someone who has the authority to act on behalf of someone else. The principal is the party for whom action is to be taken. Thus, if Gerald has the authority to solicit, create, or terminate an insurance contract on behalf of Apex Fire Insurance, Gerald would be the agent, and Apex Fire Insurance would be the principal.

General Rules of Agency

There are three important rules of law that govern the actions of agents and their relationship to insureds. They are:[15]

1. There is no presumption of an agency relationship.
2. An agent must have the authority to bind the principal.
3 A principal is responsible for the acts of agents.

No presumption of an agency relationship

There is no presumption that one person legally can act as an agent for another. Some visible evidence of an agency relationship must exist. For example, a person who claims to be an agent for an automobile insurer may collect premiums and then abscond with the funds. The automobile insurer is not legally responsible for the person's actions if it has done nothing to create the impression that an agency relationship is in existence. However, if the person has a calling card, rate book, and application blanks, then it can be presumed that a legitimate agent is acting on behalf of that company.

Authority to bind the principal An agent must be authorized to act on behalf of the principal. An agent's authority to bind the principal is derived from three sources: (1) expressed powers, (2) implied powers, and (3) apparent authority.

Expressed powers are powers specifically conferred on the agent. These powers are normally stated in the *agency agreement* between the agent and the company. The agency agreement may also withhold certain powers. For example, a life insurance agent may be given the power to solicit applicants and arrange for physical examinations. Certain powers, such as the right to extend the time for payment of premiums, or the right to alter contractual provisions in the policy, may be denied.

Agents also have **implied powers.** Implied powers refer to the authority of the agent to perform all incidental acts necessary to fulfill the purposes of the agency agreement. For example, an agent may have the expressed authority to deliver a life insurance policy to the client. It follows that the agent also has the implied power to collect the first premium. The legal significance of implied powers is that the agent's power to bind the principal may be extended far beyond the scope of the principal's expressed authorization as stated in the agency agreement.

Finally, an agent may bind the principal by **apparent authority.** If an agent acts with apparent authority to do certain things, and a third party is led to believe that the agent is acting within the scope of reasonable and appropriate authority, the principal can be bound by the agent's actions. Third parties only have to show that they have exercised due diligence in determining the agent's real authority. Authority created or exercised in this manner is known as apparent authority. For example, an agent for an automobile insurer may frequently grant his or her clients an extension of time to pay overdue premiums. If the company has not expressly granted this right to the agent and has not taken any action to deal with the violation of company policy, it could not later deny liability for a loss on the grounds that the agent lacked authority to grant the time extension. The insurer first would have to notify all policyowners of the limitations on the agent's powers.

Principal responsible for acts of agents A final rule of agency law is that the principal is responsible for all acts of agents when they are acting within the scope of their authority. This responsibility also includes fraudulent acts, omissions, and misrepresentations.

In addition, knowledge of the agent is presumed to be knowledge of the principal with respect to matters within the scope of the agency relationship. For example, if a life insurance agent knows that an applicant for life insurance is addicted to alcohol, this knowledge is imputed to the insurer even though the agent deliberately omits this information from the application. Thus, if the insurer issues the policy, it cannot later attack the validity of the policy on the grounds of alcohol addiction and the concealment of a material fact.

Waiver and Estoppel

The doctrines of waiver and estoppel have direct relevance to the law of agency and to the powers of insurance agents. The practical significance of these concepts is that an insurer legally may be required to pay a claim which it ordinarily would not have to pay.

***Waiver** is defined as the voluntary relinquishment of a known legal right.* If the insurer voluntarily waives a legal right under the contract, it cannot later deny payment of a claim by the insured on the grounds that such a legal right was violated. For example, under the standard fire policy, the insured is required to give immediate written notice of a loss to the insurer. But most persons incurring a loss normally will telephone their agent to notify the company that a loss has occurred. Even so, knowledge of the agent is presumed to be knowledge of the company. Thus, the company cannot deny payment of the claim on the grounds that written notice of the loss was not given. In effect, it has waived the policy provision of written notice by the practice of accepting a telephone call from the insured who experiences a loss.

The legal term *estoppel* was derived centuries ago from the English common law. It literally means that an individual has his or her mouth stopped when he or she tries to take back something already said. The law of estoppel is designed to prevent persons from changing their minds to the detriment of another party.

Technically, ***estoppel** is a representation of fact made by one person to another which is reasonably relied upon by that person to such an extent that it would be inequitable to allow the first person to deny the truth of the representation.*[16] Stated simply, if one person makes a statement to another person who then relies on the statement to his or her detriment, the first person cannot later deny the statement was made. For example, assume that George has an automobile insurance premium due. He calls his agent and asks for an extension of time. The agent states, "Don't worry. The company has a ten-day grace period for overdue premiums." If George has an accident during the so-called grace period, the company cannot deny liability for the loss on the grounds that the premium was not paid on time. In effect, the company would be estopped or prevented from denying payment of the claim. George has relied on the statement by his agent, and the insurer cannot later change its mind to George's detriment.

SUMMARY

- The principle of indemnity means that the insured should not profit from a loss but should be restored to approximately the same position after the loss as existed before the loss. In property insurance, the standard method of indemnifying the insured is based on actual cash value. Actual cash value is defined as replacement cost less depreciation. There are several exceptions to the principle of indemnity. These exceptions include a valued policy, valued policy laws, replacement cost insurance, and life insurance.
- The principle of insurable interest means that the insured must stand to lose financially if a loss occurs, or must incur some other kind of harm if the loss takes place. All insurance contracts must be supported by an insurable interest to be legally enforceable.
  There are three purposes of the insurable interest requirement:
  a. to prevent gambling
  b. to reduce moral hazard
  c. to measure the amount of loss
- In property insurance, the ownership of property, potential legal liability, secured creditors, and contractual rights can support the insurable interest requirement. In life insurance, the question of an insurable interest does not arise when a person purchases life insurance on his or her life. However, if life insurance is purchased on the life of another person, there must be an insurable interest in the person's life. Close ties of love, affection, blood, and marriage, or a pecuniary interest will satisfy the insurable interest requirement in life insurance.
- In property insurance, the insurable interest requirement must be met at the time of loss. In life insurance, the insurable interest requirement must be met only at the inception of the policy.
- The principle of subrogation means that the insurer is entitled to recover from a negligent third party any loss payments made to the insured. The purposes of subrogation are to prevent the insured from collecting twice for the same loss, to hold the negligent person responsible for the loss, and to hold down insurance rates. If the insurer exercises its subrogation rights, the insured must be fully restored before the company can retain any sums collected from the negligent third party. Also, the insured cannot do anything that might impair the insurer's subrogation rights. However, the insurer can waive its subrogation rights in the contract either before or after the loss. Finally, subrogation does not apply to life insurance contracts and to most individual health insurance contracts.
- The principle of utmost good faith means that a higher degree of honesty is imposed on both parties to an insurance contract than is imposed on parties to other contracts.

- The legal doctrines of representations, concealment, and warranty support the principle of utmost good faith. Representations are statements made by the applicant for insurance. The company can deny payment for a claim if the representation is both material and false. In the case of statements of belief or opinion, the misrepresentation must be material, false, and fraudulent before the company can deny a claim. An innocent misrepresentation of a material fact makes the contract voidable at the insurer's option. Concealment of a material fact has the same legal effect as a misrepresentation: The contract is voidable at the insurer's option.
- A warranty is a clause in the insurance contract that prescribes, as a condition of the insurer's liability, the existence of a fact affecting the risk. Based on common law, any breach of the warranty, even if not material, allows the insurer to avoid the policy. The harsh, common law doctrine of a warranty has been modified and softened by court decisions and statutes.
- In order to have a valid insurance contract, four requirements must be met:
  a. There must be an offer and acceptance.
  b. Consideration must be exchanged.
  c. The parties to the contract must be legally competent.
  d. The contract must be for a legal purpose.
- Insurance contracts have distinct legal characteristics. An insurance contract is an *aleatory contract* where the values exchanged are not equal. An insurance contract is *unilateral* where only the insurer makes a legally enforceable promise. An insurance contract is *conditional* when the insurer's obligation to pay a claim depends on whether or not the insured or beneficiary has complied with all policy provisions. A property insurance contract is considered to be a *personal contract* between the insured and insurer and cannot be validly assigned to another party without the insurer's consent. A life insurance policy is not considered to be a personal contract and is freely assignable. Finally, insurance is a *contract of adhesion,* which means the insured must accept the entire contract, with all of its terms and conditions.
- There are three general rules of agency that govern the actions of agents and their relationship to insureds. They are:
  a. There is no presumption of an agency relationship.
  b. An agent must have the authority to bind the principal.
  c. A principal is responsible for the actions of the agents.

  An agent can bind the principal based on expressed powers, implied powers, and apparent authority.
- Based on the legal doctrines of waiver and estoppel, an insurer legally may be required to pay a claim which it ordinarily would not have to pay.

QUESTIONS FOR REVIEW

1. Explain the principle of indemnity. How does the concept of actual cash value support the principle of indemnity?
2. Explain how a valued policy, valued policy laws, replacement cost insurance, and life insurance are exceptions to the principle of indemnity.
3. What is an insurable interest? Why is an insurable interest required in every insurance contract?

4. Explain the principle of subrogation. Why is subrogation used?
5. Explain the principle of utmost good faith. How do the legal doctrines of representations, concealment, and warranty support the principle of utmost good faith?
6. Explain the four requirements that must be met in order to have a valid insurance contract.
7. Insurance contracts have distinct legal characteristics that distinguish them from other contracts. Explain these characteristics.
8. Explain the three general rules of agency that govern the actions of agents and their relationship to insureds.
9. What are the various sources of authority that enable an agent to bind the principal?
10. Explain the meaning of *waiver* and *estoppel.*

QUESTIONS FOR DISCUSSION

1. Although some insurance authorities believe that replacement cost insurance violates the principle of indemnity, numerous property insurance contracts are now written on this basis.
   a. Explain the arguments advanced by those who believe replacement cost insurance violates the principle of indemnity.
   b. What arguments can you present to show that replacement cost insurance does not violate the principle of indemnity?
2. Explain how the principle of indemnity tends to reduce moral hazard and gambling.
3. Charles borrowed $200,000 from the Gateway Bank to purchase a fishing boat. He keeps the boat at a dock owned by the Marina Company. He uses the boat to earn an income by fishing. Charles also has a contract with the Blue Fin Fishing Company to transport shrimp from one port to another.
   a. Do any of the following parties have an insurable interest in Charles or his property? If an insurable interest exists, explain the extent of the interest.
      Gateway Bank.
      Marina Company.
      Blue Fin Fishing Company.
   b. If Charles did not own the boat but operated it on behalf of the Blue Fin Fishing Company, would he have an insurable interest in the boat? Explain.
4. Representations and warranties exist in many contracts, but they are particularly important with respect to insurance contracts. Explain the difference(s) between representations and warranties that are found in insurance contracts, and give an example of each.
5. *a.* Insurance is a *conditional contract.* Explain the meaning of the term.
   b. Explain some additional characteristics of insurance contracts that distinguish them from other contracts.
6. One requirement for the formation of a valid insurance contract is that the contract must be for a legal purpose.
   a. Identify three factors, other than the legal purpose requirement, that are essential to the formation of a binding insurance contract.
   b. Show how each of the three requirements in (a) above is fulfilled when the applicant applies for an automobile liability insurance policy.

7. In each of the following cases, indicate whether a person is legally competent to enter into a valid insurance contract.
   a. A young man, age fifteen, who applies for a life insurance contract on his life.
   b. A married woman, age twenty-one, who applies for an automobile liability policy and is the named insured.
   c. A young woman, age twenty-one, who signs an application for life insurance when she is intoxicated.
   d. A young man, age twenty-one, who has been convicted of drunken driving and has been cancelled by an insurer.
8. Mary is applying for a health insurance policy. She has a chronic liver ailment and other health problems. She honestly discloses the true facts concerning her medical history to the insurance agent. However, the agent did not include all the facts in the application. Instead, the agent stated that he was going to cover the material facts in a separate letter to the insurance company's underwriting department. However, the agent did not furnish the material facts to the insurer, and the contract was issued as standard. A claim occurred shortly thereafter. After investigating the claim, the insurer denied payment. Mary contends that the company should pay the claim since she honestly answered all questions that the agent asked.
   a. On what basis can the insurance company deny payment of the claim?
   b. What legal doctrines can Mary use to support her argument that the claim should be paid?

KEY CONCEPTS AND TERMS TO KNOW

Indemnity
Actual cash value
Valued policy
Valued policy law
Replacement cost insurance
Insurable interest
Secured creditor
Pecuniary interest
Subrogation
Utmost good faith
Representations
Concealment
Warranty
Material fact
Innocent misrepresentation
Offer and acceptance
Consideration
Competent parties
Legal purpose
Aleatory contract
Unilateral contract
Conditional contract
Personal contract
Contract of adhesion
Rules of agency
Expressed powers
Implied powers
Apparent authority
Waiver
Estoppel

SUGGESTIONS FOR ADDITIONAL READING

Greene, Mark R., and James S. Trieschmann. *Risk and Insurance,* 6th ed. Cincinnati, Ohio: Southwestern Publishing Company, 1984, chapter 8.

Grieder, Janice E., Muriel L. Crawford, and William T. Beadles. *Law and the Life Insurance Contract,* 5th ed. Homewood, Illinois: Richard D. Irwin, Inc., 1984.

Horn, Ronald C. *Subrogation in Insurance Theory and Practice.* Homewood, Illinois: Richard D. Irwin, 1964.

Keeton, Robert E. *Insurance Law: Basic Text.* St. Paul, Minnesota: West Publishing Company, 1971.

Mehr, Robert I., Emerson Cammack, and Terry Rose. *Principles of Insurance,* 8th ed. Homewood, Illinois: Richard D. Irwin, Inc., 1985.

National Underwriter Company. *Fire Casualty & Surety Bulletins,* Fire and Marine Volume. These bulletins contain interesting cases concerning the meaning of actual cash value, insurable interest, and other legal concepts.

Patterson, Edwin W. *Essentials of Insurance Law,* 2nd ed. New York: McGraw-Hill Book Company, 1957.

Vaughan, Emmett J. *Fundamentals of Risk and Insurance,* 3rd ed. New York: John Wiley & Sons, 1982, chapter 11.

Williams, Jr., C. Arthur, George L. Head, Ronald C. Horn, and G. William Glendenning. *Principles of Risk Management and Insurance,* 2nd ed. Volume II. Malvern, Pennsylvania: American Institute for Property and Liability Underwriters, 1981.

NOTES

1. *Jefferson Insurance Company of New York* v. *Superior Court of Alameda County,* C.C.H. Fire & Casualty (1970), p. 658.
2. Valued policy laws are in force in Arkansas, California (optional), Florida, Georgia, Kansas, Louisiana, Mississippi, Missouri, Montana, Nebraska, New Hampshire, North Dakota, Ohio, South Carolina, South Dakota, Tennessee, Texas, West Virginia, and Wisconsin.
3. In a few states, the valued policy law applies to all perils covered by the policy.
4. *Gamel* v. *Continental Ins. Co.,* 463 S.W. (2nd.) 590 (1971). For additional information concerning valued policy laws, the interested student should consult the *Fire, Casualty, & Surety Bulletins,* Fire and Marine Volume (Cincinnati: The National Underwriter Company). The bulletin service is regularly updated and can be found in many libraries.
5. Edwin W. Patterson, *Essentials of Insurance Law,* 2nd ed. (New York: McGraw-Hill Book Company, 1957), pp. 109–11 and 154–59.
6. Patterson, p. 114.
7. Patterson, pp. 147–48.
8. Patterson, p. 149.
9. C. Arthur Williams, Jr., George L. Head, Ronald C. Horn, and G. William Glendenning, *Principles of Risk Management and Insurance,* 2nd ed., Volume II (Malvern, Pennsylvania: American Institute for Property and Liability Underwriters, 1981), p. 228.
10. Group health insurance contracts may contain subrogation clauses. Most group health insurance plans include coordination-of-benefit provisions, and these provisions include subrogation rights against other *group health insurers.* Group health insurance and coordination-of-benefit provisions are discussed in Chapter 22.
11. Patterson, pp. 383–84.
12. Joseph L. Frascona,*Business Law, Text and Cases* (Dubuque, Iowa: W. C. Brown, 1980), p. 905.
13. This can be done by a *binder*. A binder is a temporary contract of insurance and can be either written or oral. It is used to bind the company immediately prior to the receipt of the application and issuance of the policy.
14. Dan M. McGill, *Life Insurance,* rev. ed. (Homewood, Illinois: Richard D. Irwin, 1967), p. 485.
15. McGill, pp. 544–51.
16. Patterson, pp. 495–96.

CHAPTER 5

ANALYSIS OF INSURANCE CONTRACTS

"The insurance contract is one of the most important inventions of the human mind in modern times."

Edwin W. Patterson, Essentials of Insurance Law

STUDENT LEARNING OBJECTIVES

After studying this chapter, you should be able to:

- Explain the basic parts of any insurance contract, including the declarations, insuring agreement, exclusions, conditions, and miscellaneous provisions.
- Define the insured and show how more than one person can be insured under the same policy.
- Understand the meaning of endorsements or riders and show how they modify the basic policy.
- Explain the nature and purposes of deductibles in insurance contracts.
- Explain the meaning of coinsurance and how coinsurance achieves the fundamental purpose of equity in rating.
- Explain how losses are paid when more than one insurance contract covers the same loss.

In this chapter, we will continue our discussion of insurance contracts. Although insurance contracts differ, they contain some common elements. In this chapter, we will examine those basic contractual provisions that are common to all contracts. Your understanding of specific insurance contracts will be greatly enhanced by an understanding of these common provisions.

BASIC PARTS OF AN INSURANCE CONTRACT

Insurance contracts are complex legal documents. Despite their complexities, insurance contracts generally can be divided into five parts.[1] They are as follows:

- Declarations
- Insuring agreement
- Exclusions
- Conditions
- Miscellaneous provisions

Although all insurance contracts do not necessarily contain all five parts in the order given, such a classification provides a simple and convenient framework for analyzing most insurance contracts.

Declarations

The declaration section is the first part of an insurance contract. ***Declarations** are statements that provide information about the property or life to be insured.* Information contained in the declarations section is used for underwriting and rating purposes and for identification of the property or life to be insured. The declarations section can be found on the first page of the policy or on a policy insert. In some contracts, however, the declarations are part of the written application that is attached to the policy. In property insurance, the declarations section contains information concerning the identification of the insurer, the name of the insured, the location of the property, the period of protection, the coinsurance percentage, the deductible (if any), and other relevant information. In life insurance, the first page of the policy typically contains the name and age of the insured, the types and amounts of life insurance, the premium, the issue date of the contract, and the policy number.

Insuring Agreement

The insuring agreement is the heart of an insurance contract. *The **insuring agreement** summarizes the major promises of the insurer.* The company, in other words, agrees to do certain things, such as paying losses from insured perils, providing certain services (for example, loss prevention services), or agreeing to defend the insured in a liability lawsuit. The promises of the insurer and the conditions under which losses are to be paid are described in the insuring agreement.

There are two basic forms of an insuring agreement: (1) named-perils coverage and (2) all-risk coverage. *Under a **named-perils policy,** only those losses specifically listed in the policy are covered.* If the peril is not listed, it is not covered. For example, in the homeowners policy (broad form), certain perils are specifically listed. Only losses caused by these perils are covered. Thus, property damage from fire or lightning is covered, since these perils are listed in the contract. However, flood damage is not covered, since flood is not a listed peril.

*Under an **all-risk policy,** all losses are covered except those losses specifically excluded.* If the loss is not excluded, then it is covered. For example, under the physical damage section of a personal auto policy, physical damage losses to the automobile are covered. Thus, if a horse licks the paint off a freshly painted car, or goats tear up the convertible roof of an automobile, the losses would be covered since they are not excluded.

Exclusions

Exclusions are the third basic part of any insurance contract. There are three major types of exclusions:

- Excluded perils
- Excluded losses
- Excluded property

INSIGHT 5.1

All-risk vs. Named-perils Coverage

All-risk coverage generally is preferable to a named-perils contract, since the protection is broader, and there are fewer gaps in coverage. All-risk coverage has two major advantages. *First, if the loss is not excluded, then it is covered.* The following are actual examples of unusual losses that have been paid under all-risk contracts but would not have been covered under a typical named-perils contract:[1]

1. A Civil War cannonball was accidentally dropped into a toilet, completely destroying the toilet.
2. The insured was in the attic, lost his balance, and put his foot through the ceiling.
3. A child tore the arm of a leather chair with a toy, and the entire chair had to be reupholstered.

Second, a greater burden of proof is placed on the insurer. To deny payment, the insurer must prove that the loss is excluded. In contrast, the burden of proof is on the insured under the named-perils contract; to be covered, the insured must show that the loss is caused by a named peril.

All-risk coverage, however, has certain disadvantages. *First, it is more expensive than a named-perils contract.* Some insureds cannot afford the higher premiums that all-risk contracts require.

Second, in some cases, a loss that would be paid by a less expensive named-perils contract may not be covered under an all-risk contract. This could happen if the all-risk contract contained a lengthy list of exclusions; in contrast, the named-perils contract may have numerous listed perils but fewer exclusions.

Adaptation of "All Risks Loss Examples" from *Methods Fire & Allied of FC & S Bulletins,* 1983. Reprinted by permission.

Excluded perils The contract may exclude certain perils or causes of loss. Several examples can illustrate this type of exclusion. Under the typical homeowners policy, the perils of flood, earth movement, and nuclear radiation or radioactive contamination are specifically excluded. In the physical damage section of a personal auto policy, collision is specifically excluded if the automobile is used as a public taxicab. Finally, in life insurance and disability income policies, the peril of war is often excluded.

Excluded losses Certain types of losses may also be excluded. For example, in the standard fire policy, indirect or consequential losses are not covered, such as the loss of profits or rents, or the loss of use of the building. Similarly, in an accident policy that covers only accidents, losses due to sickness and disease are not covered. In the personal liability section of the homeowners policy, a liability lawsuit arising out of the negligent operation of an automobile is excluded. Nor are professional liability losses covered; a specific professional liability policy is needed to cover this exposure.

Excluded property The contract may also exclude or place limitations on the coverage of certain property. For example, the standard fire policy excludes money, deeds, evidence of debt, and similar types of property. In a homeowners policy, certain types of personal property are excluded, such as automobiles, airplanes, animals, birds, and fish. In a liability insurance policy, property of others in the care, control, and custody of the insured is usually excluded.

Reasons for exclusions Exclusions are necessary for the following reasons:[2]

- Uninsurable perils
- Presence of extraordinary hazards
- Coverage provided by other contracts
- Moral hazard
- Coverage not needed by typical insureds

Exclusions are necessary because the peril may be considered uninsurable by commercial insurers. A given peril may depart substantially from the requirements of an insurable risk, which we studied earlier in Chapter 2. There may be an incalculable catastrophic loss, a loss may be within the direct control of the insured, or a loss may be due to a predictable decline in value, and hence, not insurable. For example, most property and liability insurance contracts exclude losses for potential catastrophic events such as war or exposure to nuclear radiation. A health insurance contract may exclude losses within the direct control of the insured, such as an intentional self-inflicted injury. Finally, predictable declines in the value of property, such as depreciation, wear and tear, and inherent vice, are not insurable. Inherent vice refers to the destruction or damage of property without any tangible external force, such as the tendency of fruit to decompose and rot and the tendency of diamonds to crack.

Exclusions are also used because extraordinary hazards are present. In Chapter 1, we defined a hazard as a condition that increases the chance of loss. Because of an extraordinary increase in hazard, a loss may be excluded. Insurance is based on the pooling of losses. Exposure units with roughly the same loss-producing characteristics are grouped, and losses are pooled or spread over the entire group. In the process, aggregate losses are more easily predictable. The pooling technique is based on the assumption that each exposure unit is charged a premium that accurately reflects the long run chance of loss. Thus, if an exposure unit faces an extraordinary hazard that is peculiar to it and is not shared by the other exposure units, the premium charged to the exposure unit is too low. This results in an inadequate premium for the insurer and an inequity for the other exposure units, since they are subsidizing the exposure unit faced with the extraordinary increase in hazard.

For example, the premium for liability insurance under a personal auto policy is based on the assumption that the automobile is normally used for personal and recreational use and not as a public taxicab. The chance of an accident, and a resulting liability lawsuit, is much higher if the automobile is used as a public taxi. Therefore, to provide coverage for a public taxicab at the same premium rate for a family automobile could result in inadequate premiums for the insurer and unfair rate discrimination against other insureds who are not using their vehicles as taxicabs. To avoid this problem, public taxicabs are in a separate rating category, and losses due to the operation of the vehicle as a public taxicab are specifically excluded under the personal auto policy. The exclusion is necessary because of the extraordinary increase in hazard.

Exclusions are also necessary because coverage is provided by other contracts. Exclusions are used to avoid the duplication of coverage and to confine the coverage to the policy best designed to provide it. For example, an automobile is excluded under a homeowners policy because it is covered under the personal auto policy and other automobile insurance contracts. If both policies covered the loss, there would be unnecessary duplication. Likewise, plate glass insurance excludes a fire loss, because the policy that provides fire insurance on a building typically includes coverage for glass. Coverage under a glass insurance policy would be redundant.

In addition, certain property is excluded because of moral hazard, or difficulty in determining and measuring the amount of loss. For example, the standard fire policy excludes money, and the new 1984 homeowner contracts limit the coverage of money to $200. If unlimited amounts of money were covered, fraudulent claims could increase. Also, loss adjustment problems in determining the exact amount of the loss could also increase. Thus, because of moral hazard, exclusions are used.

Finally, exclusions are used because the protection is not needed by the typical insured. Since a particular peril may not be common to a large group of persons, the insureds should not be required to pay for coverage that they will not need or use. For example, most homeowners do not own private airplanes. To cover aircraft as personal property under the homeowners policy would be grossly unfair to the majority of insureds who do not own airplanes but who would be required to pay substantially higher premiums. Therefore, aircraft is specifically excluded under a homeowners policy, since the coverage is not needed by the typical insured.

Conditions

The conditions section is another important part of an insurance contract. As we noted in Chapter 4, ***conditions** are provisions inserted in the policy that qualify or place limitations on the insurer's promise to perform.* In effect, the conditions section imposes certain duties on the insured if he or she wishes to collect for a loss. If the policy conditions are not met, the insurer can refuse to pay the claim. Common conditions in a contract include the requirement to protect property after a loss, to file a proof of loss with the company, and to cooperate with the company in the event of a liability lawsuit. For example, if your house is on fire, you cannot simply call your agent and tell him or her to fix the house and then call you in Bermuda when the house is restored. You must actively cooperate with the company in determining the amount of the loss.

Miscellaneous Provisions

Insurance contracts contain some miscellaneous provisions that are common to all insurance contracts. These provisions treat the relationship between the insured and insurer, or the relationship and responsibility of the insurer toward third parties. These common provisions also establish working procedures for carrying out the terms of the contract. For example, in property and liability insurance, some common provisions refer to cancellation, subrogation, requirements if a loss occurs, assignment of the policy, and other-insurance provisions. In life and health insurance, some common provisions refer to the grace period, the reinstatement of a lapsed policy, and the misstatement of age. We will not examine the details of these common provisions at this point. They will be discussed later in the text when specific insurance contracts are analyzed.

DEFINITION OF THE INSURED

Insurance contracts typically contain a definition of the insured under the policy. The contract must indicate the person or persons for whom the protection is provided. Several possibilities exist concerning the persons who are insured under the policy. First, the policy may insure only *one person.* For example, in many life and health insurance contracts, only one person is specifically named as insured under the policy.

Second, the policy may contain a formal definition of the **named insured.** The named insured is the person or persons named in the declarations section of the policy as opposed to someone who may have an interest in the policy but is not named as an insured. For example, the named insured under the personal auto policy includes the person(s) named in the declarations and his or her spouse if a resident of the same household. Thus, Charles may be the named insured under the personal auto policy. His wife is also included in the definition of the named insured as long as she resides in the same household.

The policy may also cover *additional in-*

sureds even though they are not specifically named in the policy. For example, in addition to the named insured, a homeowners policy also covers resident relatives of the named insured or spouse, such as a son or daughter, or any person under age twenty-one who is in the care of the insured, such as a child in a foster home. The personal auto policy covers the named insured and spouse, resident relatives, and any other person using the automobile with the permission of the named insured. In short, a contract may provide broad coverage with respect to the number of persons who are insured under the policy.

ENDORSEMENTS AND RIDERS

Insurance contracts frequently contain **endorsements and riders.** The terms "endorsements and riders" are often used interchangeably and mean the same thing. *An endorsement is a written provision that adds to, deletes, or modifies the provisions in the original contract.* In life and health insurance, the term "rider" is used to describe a document that amends or changes the original policy.

There are numerous endorsements in property and liability insurance that modify, extend, or delete provisions found in the original policy. For example, when added to the standard fire policy, the extended coverage endorsement extends the fire insurance policy to cover additional specified perils.

In life and health insurance, numerous riders can be added that increase or decrease benefits, waive a condition of coverage present in the original policy, or amend the basic policy. For example, a waiver-of-premium provision can be added to a life insurance policy. After a six-month waiting period, all future premiums are waived as long as the insured remains disabled according to the terms of the rider.

An endorsement attached to a contract normally has precedence over any conflicting terms in the contract, unless a law or regulation requires that a standard policy be used or that a policy contain certain provisions. An endorsement cannot be used to subvert the purpose of legislation by modifying the terms of the standard policy or by changing the wording of a required provision. If an endorsement is contrary to a law or regulation, the policy is read and applied as if that endorsement did not exist.[3]

DEDUCTIBLES

A deductible is another common policy provision. *A* ***deductible*** *is a provision that requires the insured to pay part of the loss before the insurer makes any payment under the terms of the policy.* Deductibles typically are found in property, health, and automobile insurance contracts. A deductible is not used in life insurance because the insured's death is always a total loss, and a deductible would only reduce the face amount of insurance. Also, a deductible is not widely used in personal liability insurance because the insurer must provide a legal defense, even for a small claim. The insurer wants to be involved from the first dollar of loss in order to minimize its ultimate liability for a claim. Also, the premium reduction that would result from a small deductible in personal types of third-party liability coverages would be relatively small.[4]

Purposes of Deductibles

Deductibles have several important purposes. They include the following:

- To eliminate small claims
- To reduce premiums
- To reduce morale hazard

A deductible eliminates small claims that are expensive to handle and process. For example, an insurer can easily incur expenses of $50 or more in processing a $25 claim. Since a deductible eliminates small claims, the insurer's loss adjustment expenses are reduced.

Deductibles are also used to reduce pre-

miums. Since small losses are eliminated, more of the premium dollar can be used for the larger claims that can cause serious financial insecurity if a loss should occur. Insurance is not an appropriate technique for paying small losses that can be better budgeted for out of personal or business income. Insurance should be used to cover large catastrophic events, such as medical expenses of $250,000 from a terminal illness. Insurance that protects against a catastrophic loss can be purchased more economically if deductibles are used. This concept of using insurance premiums to pay for large losses rather than for small losses is often called the **large-loss principle.**

Other factors being equal, a large deductible is preferable to a small one. For example, many motorists with automobile collision insurance have policies that contain a $100 deductible instead of a $200 or $250 deductible. They may not be aware of how expensive the extra insurance really is. For example, let us assume that you can purchase collision insurance on your car with a $100 deductible at an annual premium of $300, while a policy with a $200 deductible can be purchased for an annual premium of $270. If you select the $100 deductible over the $200 deductible, you will obtain an additional $100 of collision insurance, but you must also pay an additional $30 in annual premiums. Using a simple benefit-cost analysis, you are paying an additional $30 for an additional $100 of insurance, a relatively expensive increment of insurance. When analyzed in this manner, larger deductibles are preferable to smaller ones.

Finally, deductibles can reduce morale hazard. Morale hazard is carelessness because insurance is in force, which increases the chance of loss. Deductibles encourage persons to be more careful with respect to the protection of their property and prevention of a loss. Loss prevention is thereby encouraged, since the insured must pay part of any loss.

Types of Deductibles

More than twenty distinct types of deductibles can be found in property insurance, health insurance, and automobile physical damage insurance. Examples of deductibles include the following:

- Straight deductible
- Aggregate deductible
- Franchise deductible
- Disappearing deductible
- Waiting (elimination) period

Straight deductible The ***straight deductible*** means that *the insured must pay a certain number of dollars of loss before the insurer is required to make a payment.* Such a deductible typically applies to each loss. An example can be found in automobile collision insurance. For example, assume that Mary has her 1985 Chevrolet automobile insured for a collision loss, subject to a $250 deductible. If a collision loss is $5,000, she would receive only $4,750.

Aggregate deductible *In some property insurance contracts, an* ***aggregate deductible*** *may be used, by which all covered losses during the year are added together until they reach a certain level.* If total covered losses are below the aggregate deductible, the insurer pays nothing. Once the deductible is satisfied, all losses thereafter are paid in full. For example, assume that a property insurance contract contains a $1,000 aggregate deductible for the calendar year. If a loss of $500 occurs in January, the insurer pays nothing. If a $2,000 loss occurs in February, the insurer would pay $1,500. At this point, the aggregate deductible of $1,000 has now been satisfied for the year. If a $5,000 loss occurs in March, it is paid in full. Any other covered losses occurring during the year would also be paid in full.

A *calendar-year deductible* is another type of aggregate deductible that is frequently found in health insurance contracts. Eligible medical expenses are accumulated during the calendar year, and once they reach a certain amount, the insurer must then pay the benefits promised under the contract. Once the deductible is satisfied during the calendar year, no additional deductibles are imposed on the insured.

Franchise deductible A franchise deductible is commonly found in ocean marine insurance and can be expressed either as a percentage or dollar amount. *A **franchise deductible** means that the insurer has no liability if the loss is under a certain amount, but once this amount is reached, the entire loss is paid in full.* For example, assume that an exporter is shipping goods to England that are valued at $100,000, and a 5 percent franchise deductible is present in the contract. If a $4,000 loss occurs, the shipper must pay the entire amount, since it is below the deductible amount of $5,000. However, if the actual loss is $5,000 or greater, the entire amount is paid in full by the insurer. In effect, this type of deductible acts as a disappearing deductible, since small losses are not paid, but a large loss exceeding the deductible amount is paid in full. A franchise deductible is used in ocean marine insurance because shippers expect minor losses from bad weather, rolling ships, and the frequent handling of cargo. This kind of deductible is workable in ocean marine insurance because the property is in the carrier's possession, and there is less incentive to inflate the loss to collect in full.

Disappearing deductible *Under a **disappearing deductible**, the amount of the deductible decreases as the size of the loss increases.* In effect, small claims are not paid, but large losses are paid in full. For example, assume that a $500 disappearing deductible is present in the contract. Claims in excess of $500 are indemnified at the rate of 111 percent. This has the effect of causing the deductible to disappear when the loss reaches $5,000.

Disappearing deductibles are not widely used at the present time. If used at all, they are limited to contracts covering direct property damage by fire and allied perils. Disappearing deductibles cannot be written with business interruption insurance or time element coverages.

Waiting (elimination) period A deductible can also be expressed as a waiting period. *A **waiting period** is a stated period of time at the beginning of a loss during which no insurance benefits are paid.* A waiting period is appropriate for a single loss that occurs over some time period, such as continuing hospital expenses or the loss of work earnings. Waiting periods are commonly used in health insurance and disability income contracts. For example, a hospital policy may have a three-day waiting period for sickness before any benefits are paid. In addition, disability income contracts that replace part of a disabled worker's earnings typically have waiting periods of seven to ninety days, or even longer. Some contracts pay disability income benefits from the first day of an accident, but they may require a waiting period in the event of sickness.

COINSURANCE

A coinsurance clause is another common provision that frequently appears in property insurance contracts covering commercial property. Coinsurance is also used in health insurance and is called a percentage participation clause. Let us first consider the coinsurance provisions that frequently appear in property insurance contracts.

Nature of Coinsurance

*A **coinsurance** clause inserted in a property insurance contract requires the insured to insure the property for a stated percentage of its actual cash value at the time of loss. If the insured fails to meet the coinsurance requirement at the time of loss, he or she must share in the loss as a coinsurer.* If the insured wants to collect in full for a *partial loss*, the coinsurance requirement must be satisfied. Otherwise, the insured will be penalized if a partial loss occurs.

A coinsurance formula is used to determine the amount paid for a covered loss. The coinsurance formula is as follows:

$$\frac{\textit{Amount of Insurance Carried}}{\textit{Amount of Insurance Required}} \times \textit{Loss} = \textit{Amount Paid}$$

For example, assume that a commercial building

Figure 5.1
Insurance to Full Value

Assume that 10,000 buildings are valued at $75,000 each and are insured to full value for a total of $750 million of fire insurance. The following fire losses occur:

2 total losses	$150,000
30 partial losses at $10,000 each	300,000
Total fire losses	$450,000

$$\text{Pure premium rate} = \frac{\$\ 450{,}000}{\$750{,}000{,}000}$$
$$= 6 \text{ cents per } \$100 \text{ of insurance}$$

Figure 5.2
Insurance to Half Value

Assume that 10,000 buildings are valued at $75,000 each and insured only to half value, for a total of $375 million of fire insurance. The following fire losses occur:

2 total losses	$ 75,000
30 partial losses at $10,000 each	300,000
Total fire losses	$375,000

$$\text{Pure premium rate} = \frac{\$\ 375{,}000}{\$375{,}000{,}000}$$
$$= 10 \text{ cents per } \$100 \text{ of insurance}$$

has an actual cash value of $500,000 but that its owner has insured it for only $300,000. If an 80 percent coinsurance clause is present in the policy, the required amount of insurance based on actual cash value is $400,000.[5] If a $10,000 loss occurs, only $7,500 will be paid. This can be illustrated as follows:

$$\frac{\$300{,}000}{\$400{,}000} \times \$10{,}000 = \$7{,}500$$

Since the insured has only three-fourths of the required amount of insurance at the time of loss, only three-fourths of the loss, or $7,500 will be paid. Since the coinsurance requirement is not met, the insured must absorb the remaining $2,500 of the loss.

Purpose of Coinsurance

The fundamental purpose of coinsurance is to achieve ***equity in rating.*** Most property insurance losses are partial and not total losses. But if everyone insures only for the partial loss rather than for the total loss, the premium rate for each $100 of insurance must be higher. This would be inequitable to the insured who wishes to insure his or her property to its full value. (See Figure 5.1.)

If everyone insures to full value, the pure premium rate for fire insurance is 6 cents for each $100 of insurance. (We will ignore the expense and profit allowance of the insurer.) Now let us see what happens when everyone insures their property for only half value. (See Figure 5.2.)

If each person insures only for a partial loss, the pure premium rate will increase from 6 cents per $100 of fire insurance to 10 cents per $100. (We again ignore expenses and a profit allowance.) This would be inequitable to the individual who wants to insure his or her building to its proper value. If full insurance to value is desired, the individual would have to pay a higher rate of 10 cents, which we calculated earlier to be worth only 6 cents. This would be inequitable. *So, if the insured meets the coinsurance requirement, he or she will receive a rate discount, and the person who is underinsured will be penalized through application of the coinsurance formula.*

As an alternative to coinsurance, *graded rates* could be used, by which rate discounts would be given as the amount of insurance to value is increased. But this would require an accurate appraisal of each property to determine the required amount of insurance, an expensive proposition for the insurer. In addition, the appraisal method is unsatisfactory if property values fluctuate widely during the policy period. For these reasons, the coinsurance formula, rather than a table of graded rates, is used to achieve equity in rating.

Coinsurance Problems

Some practical problems are present when a coinsurance clause is present in a contract. First, *inflation* can result in a serious coinsurance penalty if the amount of insurance is not periodically increased for inflation. The insured may be in compliance with the coinsurance clause when the policy first goes into effect. However, rapid price inflation can cause the replacement cost of the property to increase sharply. The result is that the insured may not be carrying the required amount of insurance at the time of loss, and he or she will then be penalized if a loss occurs. Thus, if a coinsurance clause is present, the amount of insurance carried should be periodically evaluated to determine if the coinsurance requirement is being met.

Second, the insured may incur a coinsurance penalty if property values fluctuate widely during the policy period. For example, there may be a substantial increase in inventory values because of the unexpected arrival of a shipment of goods. If a loss occurs, the insured may not be carrying sufficient insurance to avoid a coinsurance penalty. One solution to this problem is an *agreed amount endorsement*, by which the insurer agrees in advance that the amount of insurance carried meets the coinsurance requirement. Another solution is a *reporting form*, by which property values are periodically reported to the insurer.[6]

Third, if a small loss occurs, the insured may incur a financial hardship if he or she is required to take a physical inventory of the undamaged and damaged goods for purposes of determining if the coinsurance requirement has been met. Under a *waiver of inventory clause*, the insured is relieved of the obligation of taking a physical inventory of the undamaged goods if the loss is less than 2 percent of the amount of insurance.

Percentage Participation Clause

A **percentage participation clause** is another form of coinsurance that is found in health insurance contracts. Most major medical policies contain a percentage participation clause that requires the insured to pay a certain percentage of eligible medical expenses in excess of the deductible. A typical plan requires the insured to pay 20 or 25 percent of covered expenses in excess of the deductible. For example, assume that Susan incurs eligible hospital and medical expenses in the amount of $20,500, and that she has a $50,000 major medical policy with a $500 deductible and an 80-20 participation clause. The insurer will pay $16,000 of the total bill, and Susan will pay $4,500.

The purposes of the percentage participation clause are (1) to reduce premiums and (2) to prevent overutilization of policy benefits. Since the insured pays part of the cost, premiums are reduced. It is also argued that physicians and other suppliers of medical care will be more restrained in setting their fees if the patient pays part of the cost, and that the patient will not demand the most expensive medical facilities if he or she pays part of the cost.

OTHER-INSURANCE PROVISIONS

Other-insurance provisions typically are present in property and liability insurance and health insurance contracts. These provisions apply when more than one contract covers the same loss. The purpose of these provisions is to reduce profiting from insurance and violation of the principle of indemnity. If the insured could collect the full amount of the loss from each insurer, there would be profiting from insurance and a substantial increase in moral hazard. Some dishonest insureds would deliberately cause a loss in order to collect multiple benefits.

Some important other-insurance provisions in property and liability insurance include (1) the pro rata liability clause, (2) contribution by equal shares, and (3) primary and excess insurance.

Figure 5.3
Pro Rata Liability Clause

Company A	$\frac{\$100,000}{\$200,000}$ or ½ × $10,000 =	$ 5,000
Company B	$\frac{\$50,000}{\$200,000}$ or ¼ × $10,000 =	$ 2,500
Company C	$\frac{\$50,000}{\$200,000}$ or ¼ × $10,000 =	$ 2,500
	Total loss payment	$10,000

Pro Rata Liability Clause

The **pro rata liability clause** applies when more than one policy covers the same insurable interest in the property. *Each company's share of the loss is based on the proportion that its insurance bears to the total amount of insurance on the property, whether collectible or not.* For example, assume that Charles owns an apartment house and wishes to insure it for $200,000. For underwriting reasons, insurers may limit the amount of insurance they will write on a given property. Assume that an agent places $100,000 of insurance with Company A, $50,000 with Company B, and $50,000 with Company C, for a total of $200,000. If a $10,000 loss occurs, each company will pay only its pro rata share of the loss. (See Figure 5.3.)

Thus, Charles would collect $10,000 for the loss and not $30,000. However, you should also be aware of the significance of the words "whether collectible or not." For example, if Company A should deny liability for the loss for some reason (such as material increase in hazard), the other companies will still pay only their pro rata share of the loss. They will not pay Company A's share of the loss.

The basic purpose of the pro rata liability clause is to preserve the principle of indemnity and to prevent profiting from insurance. In the preceding example, if the pro rata liability clause were not present, the insured would collect $10,000 from each insurer, or a total of $30,000 for a $10,000 loss. The increase in moral hazard is obvious.

Contribution by Equal Shares

Contribution by equal shares is another type of other-insurance provision that is frequently found in liability insurance contracts. *Each company shares equally in the loss until the share of each*

Figure 5.4
Contribution by Equal Shares

Amount of Loss = $15,000

Amount of insurance		Contribution by equal shares	Total paid
Company A	$10,000	$5,000	$5,000
Company B	$20,000	$5,000	$5,000
Company C	$30,000	$5,000	$5,000

Figure 5.5
Contribution by Equal Shares

Amount of loss = $50,000

Amount of insurance		Contribution by equal shares	Total paid
Company A	$10,000	$10,000	$10,000
Company B	$20,000	$10,000 + $10,000	$20,000
Company C	$30,000	$10,000 + $10,000	$20,000

insurer equals the lowest limit of liability under any policy, or until the full amount of the loss is paid. (See Figure 5.4.)

However, if the loss were $50,000, how much would each company pay? In this case, each company would pay equal amounts until its policy limits are exhausted. The remaining insurers then continue to share equally in the remaining amount of the loss until each insurer has paid its policy limit in full, or until the full amount of the loss is paid. Thus, Company A would pay $10,000, Company B would pay $20,000, and Company C would pay $20,000. (See Figure 5.5.) If the loss were $60,000, Company C would pay the remaining $10,000.

Primary and Excess Insurance

Primary and excess insurance is another type of other-insurance provision. *The primary insurer pays first, and the excess insurer pays only after the policy limits under the primary policy are exhausted.*

An automobile liability insurance policy is an excellent example of primary and excess coverage. For example, assume that Bob goes on vacation ands rents a car. He has liability insurance in the amount of $100,000 per person for bodily injury liability under his automobile policy. Also assume that the rental firm carries liability insurance on the rented car, and that the bodily injury liability limits are $200,000 per person. If Bob negligently injures another person while driving the rental car, both policies will cover the loss. The normal rule is that liability insurance on the borrowed (rental) car is primary, and any other insurance is excess. Thus, if a court of law awards a $250,000 judgment against Bob, the rental firm's insurer will pay the first $200,000 of loss. Bob's policy is excess, so his insurer will pay the remaining $50,000 of loss.

The **coordination-of-benefits provision** in group health insurance is another example of primary and excess coverage. This provision is designed to prevent overinsurance and the duplication of benefits if one person is covered under more than one group health insurance plan. For example, assume that Jack and Jane McVay work, that each is covered under a different group health insurance plan, and that each is insured as a dependent under the other's plan. *In a typical coordination-of-benefits provision, the employee's coverage is primary, and coverage as a dependent is excess.* Thus, if Jack incurs covered medical expenses, his policy will pay first as primary coverage. Jane's coverage will apply as excess insurance. No more than 100 percent of the eligible medical expenses are paid under both plans.

SUMMARY

- There are five basic parts in an insurance contract. They are:
  a. Declarations
  b. Insuring agreement
  c. Exclusions
  d. Conditions
  e. Miscellaneous provisions
- Declarations are statements concerning the life or property to be insured. The insuring agreement summarizes the promises of the insurer. There are two basic types of insuring agreements:
  a. Named-perils coverage
  b. All-risk coverage
- All policies contain one or more exclusions. There are three major types of exclusions:
  a. Excluded perils
  b. Excluded losses
  c. Excluded property
  Exclusions are necessary for several reasons. The peril may be uninsurable by private insurers; extraordinary hazards may be present; coverage is provided by other contracts; moral hazard is present to a high degree; and coverage is not needed by the typical insureds.
- Conditions are provisions that qualify or place limitations on the insurer's promise to perform. The conditions section imposes certain duties on the insured if he or she wishes to collect for a loss.
- The contract also contains a definition of the insured. The contract may cover only one person, or it may cover other persons as well even though they are not specifically named in the policy.
- An endorsement or rider is a written provision that adds to, deletes, or modifies the provisions in the original contract. An endorsement normally has precedence over any conflicting terms in the contract to which the endorsement is attached.
- A deductible requires the insured to pay part of the loss before the insurer makes any payment under the terms of the policy. Deductibles are used to eliminate small claims, to reduce premiums, and to reduce moral hazard. Examples of deductibles include the straight deductible, aggregate deductible, franchise deductible, disappearing deductible, and waiting periods.
- A coinsurance clause requires the insured to insure the property to a stated percentage of its actual cash value at the time of loss. If the coinsurance requirement is not met at the time of loss, the insured must share in the loss as a coinsurer. The fundamental purpose of coinsurance is to achieve equity in rating.
- A percentage participation clause is a form of coinsurance that is used in major medical health insurance contracts. A typical provision requires the insured to pay 20 percent of covered expenses in excess of the deductible, and the insurer pays 80 percent.
- Other-insurance provisions are present in many insurance contracts. These provisions apply when more than one policy covers the same loss. The purpose of these provisions is to prevent profiting from insurance and violation of the principle of indemnity. Some important other-in-

surance provisions include the pro rata liability clause, contributions by equal shares, and primary and excess insurance.

QUESTIONS FOR REVIEW

1. Describe the five basic parts of an insurance contract.
2. List the major types of exclusions that are typically found in insurance contracts. Why are exclusions used by insurers?
3. Define the term *conditions*. What is the significance of the conditions section to the insured?
4. How can an insurance contract cover other persons even though they are not specifically named in the policy?
5. What is an endorsement or rider? If an endorsement conflicts with a policy provision, how is the problem resolved?
6. Why are deductibles found in insurance contracts? Describe some deductibles that may appear in insurance contracts.
7. Explain how a coinsurance clause works. Why is coinsurance used?
8. Explain how coinsurance achieves equity in rating.
9. What is the purpose of other-insurance provisions? Give an example of the pro rata liability clause and contributions by equal shares.
10. Show how a statement in a policy concerning primary and excess insurance can prevent the duplication of policy benefits.

QUESTIONS FOR DISCUSSION

1. Jason owns a light plane that he flies on weekends. He is upset when you inform him that aircraft are excluded as personal property under the homeowners policy. As an insured, he feels that his plane should be covered just like any other personal property he owns.
   a. Explain to Jason the rationale for excluding certain types of property such as aircraft under the homeowners policy.
   b. Explain some additional reasons why exclusions are present in insurance contracts.
2. Property insurance contracts contain different types of deductibles that can affect the amount the insured will receive after a covered loss occurs. Assume that the insured incurs a covered loss of $1,000. For each of the following deductibles, indicate the amount that the insured would collect if the policy contained:
   a. a $100 straight deductible.
   b. an aggregate deductible of $750.
   c. a $500 franchise deductible.
   d. a deductible that pays nothing for losses under $500 and 111 percent of the excess over $500 for losses between $500 and $5,000, but in no case more than the loss.
   e. a one-week waiting period (assuming that the $1,000 loss is the loss of earned income that the insured would have earned uniformly over a four-week period).

3. Charles owns a warehouse that is insured for $200,000 under the standard fire policy. The policy contains an 80 percent coinsurance clause. The warehouse is damaged by fire to the extent of $50,000. The actual cash value of the warehouse at the time of loss is $500,000.
   a. What is the insurer's liability, if any, for the above loss? Show your calculations.
   b. Assume that Charles carried $500,000 of fire insurance on the warehouse at the time of loss. If the amount of loss is $10,000, how much will he collect?
   c. Explain the theory or rationale of coinsurance.
4. Mary owns a commercial office building that is insured under three fire insurance contracts. She has $100,000 of insurance in Company A, $200,000 in Company B, and $200,000 in Company C.
   a. If a $100,000 loss occurs, how much will Mary collect from each insurer? Explain your answer.
   b. If Company B is insolvent and cannot pay the claim, how much will Mary collect from each insurer?
   c. What is the purpose of the other-insurance provisions that are frequently found in insurance contracts?
5. Assume that a $60,000 liability claim is covered under two liability insurance contracts. Policy A has a $100,000 limit of liability for the claim, while Policy B has a $25,000 limit of liability. Both contracts provide for *contributions by equal shares.*
   a. How much will each insurer contribute toward the above claim? Explain your answer.
   b. If the claim were only $10,000, how much would each insurer pay?
6. Assume that Bob drives Mary's car with her permission, and negligently injures another person while driving Mary's car. Bob has an automobile liability insurance contract with basic liability limits of $100,000 per person for bodily injury liability. Mary has a similar policy with liability limits of $50,000 per person.
   a. If a court of law awards a liability judgment of $75,000 against Bob, how much will each insurer pay?
   b. If the liability judgment is $200,000, how much will each insurer pay?

KEY CONCEPTS AND TERMS TO KNOW

Declarations
Insuring agreement
Exclusions
Conditions
Named-perils coverage
All-risk coverage
Endorsements and riders
Named insured
Deductible
Large-loss principle
Straight deductible
Aggregate deductible
Franchise deductible
Disappearing deductible
Waiting (elimination) period
Coinsurance
Percentage participation clause
Equity in rating
Other-insurance provisions
Pro rata liability clause
Contribution by equal shares
Primary and excess insurance
Coordination-of-benefits provision

SUGGESTIONS FOR ADDITIONAL READING

Athearn, James L. and S. Travis Pritchett. *Risk and Insurance,* 5th ed. St. Paul, Minnesota: West Publishing Company, 1984, chapter 6.

Bickelhaupt, David L. *General Insurance,* 11th ed. Homewood, Illinois: Richard D. Irwin, Inc., 1983, chapter 4.

Greene, Mark R. and James S. Trieschmann. *Risk and Insurance,* 6th ed. Cincinnati, Ohio: Southwestern Publishing Company, 1984, chapter 9.

Greider, Janice E., Muriel L. Crawford, and William T. Beadles. *Law and the Life Insurance Contract,* 5th ed. Homewood, Illinois: Richard D. Irwin, Inc., 1984.

Mehr, Robert L., Emerson Cammack, and Terry Rose. *Principles of Insurance,* 8th ed. Homewood, Illinois: Richard D. Irwin, Inc., 1985.

Pritchett, S. Travis. "Primacy in Insurance," in *Issues in Insurance,* Volume I, John D. Long, ed. Malvern, Pennsylvania: American Institute for Property and Liability Underwriters, 1978.

Williams, Jr., C. Arthur, George L. Head, Ronald C. Horn, and G. William Glendenning. *Principles of Risk Management and Insurance,* 2nd ed., Volume II. Malvern Pennsylvania: American Institute for Property and Liability Underwriters, 1981, chapters 9–14.

Williams, Jr., C. Arthur and Richard M. Heins. *Risk Management and Insurance,* 5th ed. New York: McGraw-Hill Book Company, 1985, chapters 16–17.

NOTES

1. C. Arthur Williams, Jr., George L. Head, Ronald C. Horn, and G. William Glendenning, *Principles of Risk Management and Insurance*, 2nd ed., Vol. II (Malvern, Pennsylvania: American Institute for Property and Liability Underwriters, 1981), pp. 49–50.
2. Williams, Jr., pp. 50–56.
3. Williams, Jr., pp. 60–61.
4. Williams, Jr., p. 201.
5. If a replacement cost contract is used, the coinsurance percentage would be applied to the cost of replacing the property to determine the required amount of insurance.
6. Reporting forms are discussed in Chapter 13.

PART
3 PROPERTY AND LIABILITY INSURANCE

CHAPTER

6

FIRE INSURANCE

"There is no fire without some smoke."

John Heyword, Proverbs

STUDENT LEARNING OBJECTIVES

After studying this chapter, you should be able to:

- Describe the historical development of fire insurance in the United States, and explain why a standard fire policy was necessary.
- Describe the basic provisions of the standard fire policy, including
  - covered perils
  - covered property
  - persons insured
  - exclusions
- Explain the limitations on the amounts recoverable under the standard fire policy.
- Describe the situations that may result in a suspension of insurance.
- Describe the various methods for protecting the mortgagee's interest.
- Explain the requirements that must be met if a loss occurs.
- Show how the appraisal clause can be used to resolve a dispute between the insurer and insured.

Fires are an alarming cause of financial insecurity. The destruction of property values and the loss of human lives can be a traumatic experience to families and business firms alike. In 1983 alone, more than 800,000 fires occurred in the United States, which resulted in property damage of about $5.9 billion and the loss of an estimated 4,600 lives. About 74 percent of these fires were residential fires.[1]

In this chapter and the following chapters, we begin our study of specific property insurance contracts that provide protection against the destruction or theft of property. We will first study the basic provisions in the standard fire policy (SFP), which is a basic insurance contract for insuring most forms of property against the risk of fire.

HISTORICAL DEVELOPMENT OF THE STANDARD FIRE POLICY

Let us begin by briefly examining the historical development of the SFP in the United States.

Lack of Uniformity

During the early years of fire insurance, insurers drafted their own policies, and the contracts lacked uniformity. The contracts were lengthy and restrictive; numerous moral hazard clauses and other restrictive provisions were inserted in the contracts, which permitted insurers to deny claims; and the contracts were cumbersome and difficult to understand. In addition, adverse court decisions against fire insurers resulted in even more restrictive contracts. The need for a uniform policy was obvious. In 1873, Massachusetts became the first state to adopt a standard policy for the writing of fire insurance. New York passed a similar law in 1886. The standard fire policy was later revised in 1918 and 1943. The 1943 New York Standard Fire Policy is now used in most states, and minor variations of it are used in the other states.

Two major advantages result from a standard policy, such as the SFP. First, loss adjustment problems are reduced, since the possibility of two contracts with different policy provisions is reduced. Second, there are fewer legal difficulties, since the words, phrases, and provisions of the standard contract have been interpreted repeatedly by the courts and their meaning is known more precisely.

Incomplete Contract

The SFP is an incomplete contract, and an appropriate *form* must be added to it. A form must be added because property has different characteristics, and the insurance needs of individuals and business firms vary widely. For example, private dwellings, churches, manufacturing plants, schools, motels, and other properties have different physical characteristics that require different forms. More than 200 forms can be added to the SFP to meet the specific needs of individuals and business firms. Thus, a complete contract consists of the standard fire policy and an appropriate form or forms.

In recent years, the SFP has declined in importance. Many states have passed laws that require insurance contracts to be more readable. In view of the trend towards readable contracts, the SFP has been eliminated as a separate contract for certain types of insurance, and its basic provisions are now incorporated into the newer readable contracts.

However, despite its reduced importance, the SFP remains an important document. The basic provisions of the SFP have been incorporated into the newer readable contracts, and students of insurance should understand these basic provisions. Moreover, many basic property insurance concepts were first legally defined in the SFP—for example, the principles of indemnity, insurable interest, actual cash value, and pro rata sharing of losses. So the SFP is an excellent example of fundamental legal principles and concepts. Finally, the SFP is still widely used to insure commercial buildings and business property that do not qualify for coverage under the newer contracts. For these reasons, the SFP is worth our attention.

BASIC PROVISIONS OF THE STANDARD FIRE POLICY

In this section we will examine the basic provisions of the standard fire policy. The complete contract is reproduced in Appendix B.

Insuring Agreement

The first page of the SFP contains the declarations, which provide relevant information concerning the property to be insured. The *insuring agreement* appears at the bottom of the declarations page and includes the following provisions:

- Consideration
- Policy term
- Persons insured
- Limitations on recovery
- Covered perils
- Assignment of the policy

Consideration Consideration by both parties is necessary to have a valid insurance contract. *The insurer's consideration is the promise to pay a loss from a covered peril. The insured's consideration is payment of the first premium plus acceptance of the policy provisions and stipulations.* The insured must comply with the policy provisions and stipulations to receive any benefits under the contract. The insurer's promise to pay presupposes the fulfillment of the agreements by the insured.

Policy term Although the SFP can be written for one, two, or three years, most fire insurance contracts are written for a policy term of one year. The insuring agreement states that the period of protection begins at noon standard time and ends at noon standard time exactly one year later at the location of the covered property. However, in 1977, the Insurance Services Office, a rate-making organization, changed the inception of coverage to 12:01 A.M. In some states, the period of protection now begins and ends at 12:01 A.M. standard time at the location of the covered property.

Standard time (not daylight savings time) refers to the time zone where the property is located. Thus, if you live in New York City and own property in Los Angeles, California, the period of protection is based on standard time in California, not New York.

Persons insured *The SFP covers the named insured and his or her legal representatives.* The named insured can be an individual, business association, or corporation. A party not specified as a named insured has no legal right to receive a loss payment directly even though that party has an insurable interest in the property at the time of loss. Thus, to ensure complete protection, all parties with an insurable interest should be named as insureds in the declarations section.[2]

Legal representatives of the named insured are also covered under the SFP. This prevents an insurer from denying payment of a claim if the insured dies, is declared insane, or is bankrupted. Thus, if Sam owns a building insured under the SFP and dies shortly after a fire occurs, the loss payment would be made to his legal representative, such as the executor of his estate.

Limitations on recovery There are six limitations on recovery in the insuring agreement. They are as follows:

- Face amount of the policy
- Actual cash value
- Amount to repair or replace the property with similar materials
- No allowance for increased cost of repair due to some ordinance or law
- No coverage for business interruption or other indirect losses
- Insurable interest of the insured

The maximum loss payment is the face amount of the policy. The insured can never receive more than the amount of insurance specified in the declarations page. Payment of the maximum amount of insurance is normally relevant only if a total loss occurs. However, most losses are partial, and payment for a total loss under the SFP is not common.

Most forms attached to the SFP specify that the face amount of the policy is not reduced by any loss payments. However, in the absence of such a provision, the maximum amount paid during the policy term would be limited to the face amount of insurance stated in the policy.

A second limitation is the ***actual cash value*** *of the destroyed or damaged property.* As we stated in Chapter 4, actual cash value is usually defined as replacement cost less depreciation. For example, assume that Tom owns a building insured for $500,000, that replacement cost is $500,000, that depreciation is $100,000, and that a total loss from a fire occurs. Under the actual cash value rule, Tom would receive only $400,000. In those states where a valued policy law is in effect, the face amount of the policy must be paid in the event of a total loss, regardless of the actual cash value of the property at the time of loss. Thus, in a valued policy state, the entire $500,000 would be paid.

A third limitation is the amount required to repair or replace the property with materials of like kind and quality. For example, if Sam owns a frame dwelling insured under the SFP, and a total loss occurs, he cannot expect the insurer to restore the property with brick masonry. He would be in a better financial position after the loss than he was before the loss occurred. The principle of indemnity would be violated if higher-quality materials were used to restore the property.

Still another limitation is that the insurer is not liable for the increased cost of repair or reconstruction due to some ordinance or law. For example, a new building code may require all buildings to be constructed with fire resistive materials and steel supporting framework. If an older building is damaged by a fire and must be rebuilt according to the building code, the increased construction costs are not covered by the SFP.

In addition, business interruption losses are not covered. The SFP covers only a direct loss. A business interruption loss such as the loss of profits or additional expenses is an indirect or consequential loss that is not covered by the SFP. However, a separate business interruption policy or a package policy can be purchased to cover the loss of profits and other continuing expenses when a business incurs a loss covered by the SFP or by its endorsements.[3]

A final limitation is that the insured can never recover more than his or her insurable interest. As we stated earlier, all parties with an insurable interest must be named in the policy in order to have complete protection. If a loss occurs, the amount paid cannot exceed the insurable interest of each party. For example, assume that Bob and Bill each have an equal interest in an apartment house with an actual cash value of $200,000. Also assume that each party purchases a $100,000 fire insurance policy to cover his interest. If a $10,000 loss occurs, which is well within the policy limits of both insurers, Bob would collect $5,000 from his company and Bill would collect $5,000 from his company. Since each party has a 50 percent interest in the property, each receives 50 percent of the total loss payment.

Covered perils The SFP is an extremely narrow contract. Only three perils are covered in the insuring agreement. The SFP covers only a *direct loss* to property because of fire, lightning, and removal from the premises. Indirect losses such as business interruption loss and loss of profits are not covered.

To have coverage under the SFP, an insured peril must be the proximate cause of the loss. **Proximate cause** means there is an unbroken chain of events between the occurrence of an insured peril and damage or destruction of the property. For example, assume that your neighbor's house is razed by a fire and that one wall is left standing. Assume further that the wall collapses onto your property several days later, causing considerable property damage to your garage. The loss is covered under the SFP, since fire is the proximate cause of loss.

As we noted earlier, only a direct loss from a **fire** is covered. However, what is a fire, and how is it defined? You can search the SFP in vain, but you will find no definition of a fire in the policy. Instead, we must examine the various court decisions that have clarified the meaning of a fire. Two requirements must be fulfilled in order to have a fire covered by the SFP:

- **There must be combustion accompanied by a flame or glow.**
- **The fire must be hostile or unfriendly.**

First, there must be combustion or rapid oxidation that causes a flame or at least a glow. Thus, scorching, heating, and charring that occur without a flame or glow are not covered. *Second, the fire must be hostile or unfriendly.* A **hostile fire** is outside its normal confines. A **friendly fire** is intentionally kindled and is where it is supposed to be. If it escapes its normal confines, it then becomes an unfriendly fire.

Several examples can illustrate the meaning of a fire:

1. A child playing with matches causes a fire. The fire is covered because it is hostile.
2. A fire occurs in a home, and firefighters spray the contents of the other rooms and chop a hole in the roof. The entire loss is covered, since fire is the proximate cause of loss.
3. You are smoking a cigarette. The flame or glow at the end of the cigarette is where it should be. The cigarette is not covered under the SFP.
4. A box of cigars is accidentally thrown into a burning fireplace. The loss is not covered since the fire is friendly. However, if the cigars were on a table, and sparks escaped from the fireplace causing a fire, the entire loss would be covered since the fire is hostile.
5. You are using a hot iron to press a garment. The iron accidentally falls over and scorches the garment. The loss is not covered since there is no flame or glow.

The SFP policy also covers the peril of *lightning.* Thus, if lightning strikes a house, the property damage is covered. It is not necessary for a fire to occur. Lightning frequently causes considerable property damage even though no fire ensues. The loss is covered, however.

Finally, the SFP covers the **removal of property** from the premises because of a loss caused by an insured peril. The property is covered on a pro rata basis for up to five days if it is moved to another location for safekeeping after a loss. The removal-from-premises coverage is very broad and generally covers the physical loss of property on an all-risk basis. For example, if property is being removed from Gerald's home because it is threatened by a fire, and the removal occurs during the middle of a cloudburst, the rain damage would be covered. For the same reason, if workers carelessly break a mirror that is being moved to another location for safekeeping after a fire occurs, the loss would be covered.

Assignment of the policy The assignment provision is also part of the insuring agreement. *The SFP cannot be validly assigned to someone else without the insurer's written consent.* The SFP is considered to be a personal contract between the named insured and insurer, by which the insured is indemnified if a loss occurs. This assignment provision enables the insurer to select its own insureds and provides some protection against moral hazard. Thus, the insurer's written consent is necessary to have a valid assignment; without it, the assignment is invalid.

Conditions, Exclusions and Other Provisions

The second page of the SFP consists of 165 lines. Important conditions, exclusions, and other miscellaneous provisions are contained in this section. As you study this section, you may find it helpful to refer to the SFP in Appendix B.

Concealment and fraud In Chapter 4, we noted that an insurance contract is a contract of utmost good faith, and that a high standard of honesty is imposed on both parties to an insurance contract. This principle is clearly reflected in the SFP's provision concerning concealment and fraud.

If the insured willfully conceals a material fact or makes a material misrepresentation, either before or after a loss, the insurer can void the policy. For example, an applicant with twenty unsatisfied judgments against him applied for a fire insurance policy on some personal property, but the application was in his son's name. A fire occurred, and the insurer refused to pay the claim on the grounds that the policy would not have been issued if the true identity of the owner had been known.[4] The concealment of a material fact resulted in the denial of the claim.

Excluded property The SFP excludes certain types of property. These include accounts, bills, currency, deeds, evidence of debt, money, and securities. Manuscripts and bullion are also excluded unless carefully described in writing in the policy.

Certain types of property are excluded for two reasons. *First, moral hazard and fraudulent claims would increase without such exclusions.* If money were insured, for example, some persons would undoubtedly submit fraudulent claims. *Second, loss-adjustment problems would increase,* since it would be difficult to determine the exact amount of money burned and to place an exact monetary value on accounts, deeds, evidence of debt, and similar property.

Excluded perils The SFP also excludes certain perils. They are:

- **Enemy attack**
- **Invasion**
- **Insurrection**
- **Rebellion**
- **Civil war**
- **Usurped power**
- **Order of any civil authority**
- **Neglect of the insured to protect the property**
- **Loss by theft**

War, enemy attack, and similar perils are not insurable under the SFP because of the catastrophic exposure the insurer is unwilling to assume. In addition, loss by order of any civil authority, such as by a duly authorized law officer who burns a building to flush out snipers, would not be covered. An exception to this rule is the destruction of property to prevent spreading of a fire that did not originate from an excluded peril. For example, if a row home is on fire, and the home next to it is destroyed by dynamite in an effort to contain the fire, the loss would be covered by the SFP.

The insurer is not liable for any loss due to neglect of the insured to protect the property at or after a loss. The purpose of this exclusion is to reduce the size of those losses that can be substantially increased because of neglect or carelessness.

Finally, the SFP excludes the theft of property. For example, if you are on vacation and a stereo set is stolen from your home, the loss would be excluded under the SFP.[5] However, the theft of property that occurs during its removal from the premises because of danger from an insured peril is generally covered. For example, assume that a fire occurs in your home, and you move the stereo set to a public warehouse for safekeeping. If the set is stolen during a burglary of the warehouse, the loss would be covered.

Other insurance Other insurance on the property is normally permitted under the SFP. However, the insurer can either prohibit other fire insurance on the property or limit the amount of insurance by an endorsement. The purpose of this provision is to reduce the problem of overinsurance on certain types of property. The intent is not to prevent *different* interests in the prop-

INSIGHT 6.1

What Does Vacant or Unoccupied Mean?

The courts have held that occupancy of a dwelling means the actual use of the premises by human beings as their customary residence. A recent court decision highlights this point.[1] In this case, the vacancy or unoccupancy exclusion was held to apply to the loss of an insured home from which the owners had moved four months earlier before the home was destroyed by fire. Although the insureds had left some furniture in the house, had made periodic visits to care for their dogs kept on the premises and to tend their garden, and had also stayed overnight in the house several times, the court ruled that these activities did not constitute occupancy within the meaning of the fire policy. *The court ruled that occupancy entails use of the building for the purpose for which it is insured—as a residence.* Thus, coverage was suspended under the fire policy.

[1] *Carroll v. Tennessee Farmers Mutual Insurance Company*, 1979 C.C.H. (Fire & Casualty) 1264.

SOURCE: Adaptation of material from *FC & S Bulletins*, November 1981. Reprinted by permission.

erty from being insured (such as the owner and mortgagee), but to prevent the *same insured* from obtaining several different contracts without the knowledge of the insurer.[6]

Suspension of insurance Under certain conditions, the SFP is suspended, and the insurance is not in force. There are three conditions that can suspend or restrict the insurance:

- Material increase in hazard
- Vacancy or unoccupancy beyond sixty days
- No coverage for riot or explosion, unless a fire ensues

The insurer is not liable if there is a material increase in hazard by any means within the control or knowledge of the insured. For example, assume that Homer has a fire insurance policy on his home and establishes a paint factory in the basement. In this case, he has changed the basic character of the risk assumed by the insurer. If a fire occurs, the loss is not covered because the hazard has been materially increased, and the insured had knowledge of the increased hazard.

In addition, loss occurring after the building is vacant or unoccupied beyond sixty consecutive days is not covered. A vacant building is one in which no one is living and from which the furnishings and contents have been removed. An unoccupied building is one in which no persons are living, but in which the furnishings and contents remain. The insurance is suspended after sixty consecutive days because a vacant or unoccupied building is subject to a greater probability of loss than a building that is occupied. A vacant or unoccupied building may attract vandals or transients who could start a fire. Moreover, a partial loss can easily turn into a total loss in a vacant or unoccupied building because a fire is less likely to be discovered before it gains considerable headway. Also, moral hazard may be greater since a vacant or unoccupied building may not be producing an income. Unless the insurer grants special permission, the insurance is suspended after sixty days if the building is vacant or unoccupied.

Finally, losses due to riot or explosion are not covered unless a fire ensues, and in that case, only the fire loss is covered. However, when the appropriate form is added to the SFP to make it a complete contract, both riot and explosion losses are covered.

Other perils and added provisions This section permits other perils and policy provisions to be added to the SFP. Additional perils and other types of insurance, such as business interruption coverages, can be added by an endorsement. One common use of this section is the addition of the Extended Coverage Endorsement, which broadens the SFP to cover additional perils. Extended coverage perils are discussed in Chapter 8.

Prohibition of waiver This section states that no policy provision can be waived unless it is in writing and attached to the policy. For example, an agent cannot orally waive any of the provisions in the SFP.

However, this issue is far from settled because court decisions concerning the waiver provision are not in agreement. Some courts have ruled that an agent cannot orally waive any policy provision. Other courts have ruled that an agent has the authority to conduct oral negotiations for the insurer, and that he or she can orally waive the very clause that states that no provision can be waived. In view of the conflicting decisions, you are well advised to abide by the terms of the policy, regardless of any oral statements made by an agent.

Cancellation The SFP can be cancelled by either the insured or the insurer. The insured may decide to cancel because the property has been sold, because the insurance can be obtained more cheaply elsewhere, or because the protection is no longer needed. If the insured cancels, the cancellation is effective when it is received by the company or when specified by the insured. In either case, a premium refund based on the **short-rate table** will be made to the insured rather than a pro rata refund based on the unearned premium. Thus, if you pay an annual premium of $100 and then cancel after six months, a premium refund of 40 percent or $40 rather than $50 will be paid to you based on the short-rate table.

The short-rate table is used for two reasons. *First, expenses are incurred by the insurer when the policy is first issued and then later cancelled.* To compensate for these expenses, the short-rate table is used. Most administrative expenses are incurred when the policy is first issued rather than spread evenly over the policy term. The costs of issuing and printing the policy are obvious examples. Also, additional expenses are incurred if the policy is later cancelled.

Second, a short-rate table is used to offset adverse selection. Although the premium received by the insurer is earned uniformly over the policy period, the probability of a fire is not constant, but is considerably higher during the winter months. Since the insured may cancel at the most advantageous time (for example, just after the winter season), the company would obviously be selected against and would experience higher than expected losses. To compensate for this, the short-rate table is used.

The insurer also has the right of cancellation. A company may wish to cancel for various reasons, including the desire to avoid an increase in physical or moral hazard, to withdraw from an unprofitable line of insurance, or to withdraw from a certain geographical area. *The insurer can cancel by giving the insured five days' written notice of cancellation.* For example, if the cancellation notice is received on Monday, the cancellation becomes effective at midnight on Saturday evening. As a practical matter, many states now require a longer cancellation notice, such as ten, twenty, or thirty days. In addition, the cancellation notice must be accompanied by a full **pro rata refund of the premium,** or a statement that the unearned premium will be tendered on demand.

Protection of the mortgagee's interest The mortgagee also has an insurable interest in the property being insured. The mortgagee usually is a savings and loan institution, commercial bank, or other lending institution that makes a loan to the mortgagor so that the property can be purchased. The property serves as collateral for the mortgage, and if the property is damaged or destroyed, the collateral behind the loan is impaired, and the mortgagee may not be repaid.

There are several ways of protecting the mortgagee's interest. They are:[7]

- Purchase of separate insurance
- Assignment of the policy by the insured
- Loss payable clause
- Standard Mortgage Clause

The mortgagee can purchase separate insurance equal to its insurable interest. But this is seldom done because there would then be more insurance on the property than is necessary. Furthermore, if the mortgagee must pay the premiums on the separate policy and keep track of policy renewals, the interest rate charged to the borrower would have to be increased to reflect the higher cost of doing business. For these reasons, a separate policy is seldom purchased.

The mortgagee can also protect its interest in the property by an ***assignment.*** For example, the insured may insure the property and then assign the policy to the mortgagee. However, the mortgagee's insurable interest is not completely protected by an assignment, because the assignee (lending institution) legally has no greater rights than the assignor (insured). If the insured should violate a policy provision, or if the insurance protection should terminate because of nonpayment of premiums, nothing would be paid to the mortgageee in case of a loss. Thus, the mortgagee's interest would not be protected by an assignment of an insurance policy.

A ***loss payable clause*** *is another way to protect the mortgagee's interest.* This clause directs the insurer to make a loss payment to the mortgagee in the event of a loss. However, this method is also defective in protecting the mortgagee's interest. If the insured violates a policy provision or fails to pay the premium, the insurer would not pay the loss, and the mortgagee would receive nothing.

The best method for protecting the mortgagee's interest is the **Standard Mortgage Clause.** This clause may appear in the form which is added to the SFP, or it may be attached to the policy as a separate endorsement. Under this clause, the mortgagee has the following rights:

- To receive loss payments as its interest may appear, regardless of any violation of policy provisions by the owner, and regardless of any change in occupancy or increase in hazard.
- To receive ten days' written notice of cancellation.
- To sue under the policy in its own name.

The most important characteristic of the Standard Mortgage Clause is that the mortgagee is entitled to receive a loss payment from the insurer regardless of any policy violation by the insured. For example, the hazard may be materially increased, which as we stated earlier, would suspend the insurance. Thus, if Sam stores several large drums of gasoline in his garage to beat a price increase in gasoline, and a fire occurs, the insurer must still make a loss payment to the mortgagee. The mortgagee's interest is protected despite the policy violation by the insured. In addition, the mortgagee is entitled to ten days' cancellation notice, rather than five days' notice, which is provided to the owner under the SFP. Finally, the mortgagee has the right to sue under the policy in its own name, even though the mortgagee has not paid any premiums for the protection provided.

The Standard Mortgage Clause imposes certain duties upon the mortgagee in exchange for these rights. The duties are as follows:

- To notify the insurer of any change in ownership, occupancy, or increase in hazard.
- To pay the premium if the owner or mortgagor fails to do so.
- To provide proof of loss if the owner or mortgagor fails to do so.
- To surrender subrogation rights to the insurer in those cases where the insurer denies liability to the owner or mortgagor,

but must still make a loss payment to the mortgagee under the Standard Mortgage Clause.

The practical implications of the Standard Mortgage Clause can be illustrated by two simple examples. In the first example, the claim is valid, but in the second example, the insurer denies liability to the owner but must still make a loss payment to the mortgagee. Assume that Sam owns an $80,000 home with a $50,000 mortgage on it from Lincoln Federal, and that a $10,000 loss occurs. In most cases, the insurer will make the check for the loss payment payable to both parties. Both Sam and Lincoln Federal would endorse the check, and the proceeds would be used to restore the property. Note, however, that the mortgagee is technically entitled to the loss payment under the Standard Mortgage Clause. Thus, if Lincoln Federal retains the proceeds, Sam's mortgage would be reduced by $10,000.

Now, let's see what happens when the owner violates a policy provision, but a loss payment must still be made to the mortgagee. Assume that Sam comes home drunk, throws gasoline on the carpet, and burns the living room. Assume also that the loss is $10,000. In this case, the insurer will deny liability for the loss to Sam, since he deliberately caused the loss. But under the terms of the Standard Mortgage Clause, a $10,000 loss payment must be made to Lincoln Federal. Lincoln Federal then gives subrogation rights to the insurer in the amount of $10,000. Sam now owes the insurer $10,000. Alternatively, the insurer could pay off the entire mortgage and then obtain an assignment of the mortgage from Lincoln Federal. Sam would then owe the insurer the balance of the mortgage. In either case, Sam receives no benefits from his insurance, since he deliberately caused the loss.

Pro rata liability clause The SFP also contains a **pro rata liability clause** that applies when more than one policy covers the same insurable interest in the property. Each company is liable according to the proportion that its insurance bears to the total amount of insurance on the property, whether collectible or not. We discussed the pro rata liability clause in Chapter 5.

Requirements in case loss occurs If a loss occurs, several requirements must be fulfilled in order to receive a loss payment. *First, the insured must give immediate written* ***notice of the loss*** *to the company.* If you call your agent immediately after a loss, you would be in compliance with this requirement. Note, however, that you are required to notify the company as soon as practical after a loss occurs. If there is unreasonable delay, the insurer can deny payment of the claim. Thus, if Charles notifies his company two months after his home burns, the insurer could deny payment of the claim. The purpose of this requirement is to enable the insurer to investigate promptly all details of the loss, including the cause of the loss. Unreasonable delay defeats this purpose because evidence of the cause of loss may disappear with the lapse of time.

Second, the insured is required to protect the property from further damage. Thus, if a home burns, and the owner does not protect the property from further loss, such as boarding up or locking the home to keep vandals from entering, the insurer is not liable for any additional loss. The purpose of this requirement is to reduce the amount of loss due to the insured's carelessness or negligence. Stated differently, the insured cannot walk away from the loss and abandon the property to the insurer.

Finally, unless extended in writing by the company, the insured must file a satisfactory proof of loss within sixty days. Proof of loss consists in the completion of a claim form furnished by the insurer. The claim form must provide detailed information concerning the time and origin of the loss, all interests in the property, actual cash value of the property, the amount of loss claimed, and numerous other details. The purposes of this requirement are to provide satisfactory proof to the company that the property has been damaged or destroyed and to determine the amount of the loss for purposes of payment.

Appraisal clause An **appraisal clause** is used when the insured and insurer cannot agree on the actual cash value or amount of the loss. Either party can demand that the dispute be resolved by an appraisal. Each party selects a competent and disinterested appraiser. The appraisers then select an umpire. If they cannot agree on an umpire after fifteen days, a judge in a court of record will appoint one. If the appraisers fail to agree on the amount of the loss, only their differences are submitted to the umpire. An agreement in writing by any two of the three is then binding on both parties. Each party pays for his or her own appraiser, and the appraisal expenses and umpire's fees are shared equally by both parties.

The purpose of the appraisal clause is to reduce litigation and provide an equitable and fair procedure for resolving any disagreement concerning the amount of the loss.

Company's option The company has the option of paying the claim in dollars, or it can repair, rebuild, or replace the property with materials of like kind and quality. The purpose of this provision is to provide some protection to the insurer against the payment of an inflated claim. The company can restore the property rather than pay the claim in cash. However, this option is seldom exercised, since most insurers prefer not to be in the construction or repair business. A cash payment is simpler, and disputes about the quality of the repair job are avoided.

No abandonment of property There can be no abandonment of any property to the company. The company has the option to take salvage at its agreed or appraised value, but the company cannot be forced to take salvage, and the insured cannot abandon the property. For example, assume that the inventory of Susan's small dress shop is insured for $100,000. A fire occurs, and the salvage value of the property after the loss is $25,000. The company can pay Susan $75,000, or it can take all the damaged property and pay her $100,000. However, she cannot abandon the property to the insurer and demand payment of $100,000.

Other provisions Analysis of several miscellaneous provisions will complete our analysis of the SFP. First, the insurer must pay the loss within sixty days after proof of loss is received; as we have seen, determination of the loss is made either by agreement or by appraisal.

Second, a lawsuit against the company concerning the loss must be made within twelve months after the loss and only upon compliance with all policy provisions pertaining to the insured's obligations at the time of and after the loss.

Finally, the insurer is subrogated to the insured's right of recovery from other parties to the extent of payment of the loss. Thus, if faulty wiring results in a $20,000 fire to Val's home, the insurer will pay Val $20,000, and may then attempt to recover from the negligent electrician.

SUMMARY

- The standard fire policy covers only a direct loss from fire, lightning, and removal from the premises. In order for a fire to be covered, there must be a flame or glow, and the fire must be hostile or unfriendly.
- There are several limitations on recovery under the standard fire policy. The amount paid is subject to the following limits:
  a. Face amount of the policy.
  b. Actual cash value.
  c. Amount to repair or replace the property with similar materials.
  d. No allowance for increased cost due to some ordinance or law.
  e. No coverage for business interruption or other indirect losses.
  f. Insurable interest of the insured.
- In order to have a valid assignment of the standard fire policy, the insurer must consent to the assignment. The assignment provision protects the insurer from moral hazard and gives the company the right to select its own insureds.
- The standard fire policy can be suspended under certain conditions. They are as follows:
  a. Material increase in hazard.
  b. Vacancy or unoccupancy beyond sixty days.
  c. No coverage for riot or explosion, unless a fire ensues and then only the fire loss is covered.
- The insurer can cancel the standard fire policy by giving five days' written notice to the insured. If the insurer cancels, the insured receives a full pro rata refund of the unearned premium. If the insured cancels, the premium refund is based on the short-rate table.
- The mortgagee can protect its interest by several methods. They are:
  a. Purchase of separate insurance.
  b. Assignment of the policy by the insured.
  c. Loss payable clause.
  d. Standard Mortgage Clause.
- The Standard Mortgage Clause provides the greatest protection to the mortgagee. The mortgagee is still entitled to receive a loss payment from the insurer regardless of any policy violation by the insured.
- Certain requirements must be fulfilled if a loss occurs. The insured is required to do the following:
  a. Give immediate written notice to the company of a loss.
  b. Protect the property from further damage.
  c. File proof of loss within sixty days.
- The appraisal provision is designed to resolve disputes. Each party selects its own appraiser. The appraisers then select an umpire. An agreement by any two is binding on all parties.

QUESTIONS FOR REVIEW

1. Describe the three perils that are covered under the SFP. What is the meaning of a fire?
2. Explain the various limitations on recovery under the SFP.

3. Why must the insurer consent to an assignment of the SFP to another party?
4. Describe the various exclusions in the SFP.
5. Explain the three situations that may lead to a suspension of fire insurance.
6. Describe the cancellation provision of the SFP.
7. Explain the various methods for protecting the mortgagee's interest in property.
8. Describe briefly the mortgagee's rights and duties under the Standard Mortgage Clause.
9. Under the SFP, certain requirements must be fulfilled in the event of a loss. Explain these requirements.
10. Explain the *nature* and *purpose* of the appraisal clause in the SFP.

QUESTIONS FOR DISCUSSION

1. With reference to each of the following situations, explain whether or not the loss would be covered by the 1943 New York Standard Fire Policy. (Assume no special endorsements.)
   a. Damage by firefighters in attempting to extinguish a fire in an adjoining building.
   b. Destruction by fire of a $5,000 government bond and $100 in money.
   c. Damage to woodworking equipment by fire started by a worker who negligently drops a lighted cigarette into a pile of shavings.
   d. Damage to a plastic basket that melts upon contact with the heating element of an electric stove.
   e. Loss of a roast that burns from a grease fire in the oven.
   f. Damage to the insured's house by a fire truck that skids on an icy street while going to a fire.
   g. Charring of a table from a lighted cigarette that is carelessly left on the edge of the table.
2. Jerome owns the Lake Marina Company. He has purchased a standard fire policy that provides $100,000 of insurance on the building and $40,000 on its contents. The policy does not contain any coinsurance requirement or deductible. A fire damaged the building to the extent of 60 percent of its value and destroyed $20,000 of contents. During the fire, Jerome moved his remaining personal property to a nearby dock for protection. During the removal, property worth $2,000 was accidentally knocked into the water and lost. Jerome's building had an actual cash value of $100,000 prior to the loss.
   a. How much would Jerome recover under the standard fire policy for the damage to his *building* and the loss of *contents?* Show your calculations and explain the reasons for your answer.
   b. Assume that in the above loss, the building must be rebuilt according to the specifications contained in a new building code. The additional cost of construction is $20,000. How much, if anything, will Jerome recover, in addition to the amount indicated in *a*. above?
3. You are a risk management consultant to the Gateway Bank, and you are asked to prepare an insurance program to cover the bank's loss exposures.
   a. Describe the various insurance methods available to the Gateway Bank to protect its interest in property on which it has made loans.
   b. Explain briefly the advantages and disadvantages of each method described in *a*. above.

   c. Assume that the bank's trust department is named as executor of an estate. What rights will the trust department have under a fire insurance policy that covers property in that estate? Explain your answer.

4. Bill owns a building with an actual cash value of $200,000 that is subject to a $100,000 mortgage held by First Federal as the mortgagee. Bill has the building insured for $150,000 under the standard fire policy, and First Federal is named as mortgagee under the Standard Mortgage Clause.
   a. Assume there is a covered fire loss to the building in the amount of $50,000. To whom would the loss be paid? Explain your answer.
   b. Assume instead that the insurer denies liability for the same claim on the basis of a material increase in hazard that was within Bill's knowledge and control. First Federal was not aware of the material increase in hazard. How would the loss be settled under these conditions? Explain your answer.
5. Jane owns a building that is covered by the 1943 New York Standard Fire Policy. The policy has three months to run before it expires. Jane sells the building to Bob and assigns the fire insurance policy to Bob without notifying the insurance company. One month after the sale is completed, the building is damaged by fire to the extent of $10,000.
   a. To what extent, if any, is the insurer liable for the loss? Explain your answer.
   b. What recommendations might have been given to Jane and Bob to avoid problems with respect to fire insurance coverage on the building that was sold?
6. The standard fire policy imposes certain definite obligations upon the insured immediately upon the occurrence of a loss.
   a. Explain the requirements imposed on the insured immediately following a fire loss.
   b. Assume that the insured is vacationing in Europe and is not notified of the fire until two weeks after its occurrence. Can the fire insurer deny payment of the claim on the basis that immediate written notice of the loss was not given? Explain your answer.
7. A fire destroyed the building and contents of the Lastovica Construction Company. Mike, the owner of the company, contends that the insured loss is $100,000. Mike's insurer maintains that the recovery should be $80,000. Assume that the Lastovica Construction Company is insured under the standard fire policy. Describe the provision in the policy that provides the means of resolving the disagreement over the amount of loss.

KEY TERMS AND CONCEPTS TO KNOW

Fire
Friendly fire
Hostile fire
Proximate cause
Actual cash value
Removal from premises
Suspension of insurance
Short-rate table
Pro rata premium refund
Standard Mortgage Clause
Assignment
Loss payable clause
Pro rata liability clause
Appraisal clause
Notice of loss

SUGGESTIONS FOR ADDITIONAL READING

Bickelhaupt, David L. *General Insurance,* 11th ed. Homewood, Illinois: Richard D. Irwin, Inc., 1983, chapter 13.

Fire, Casualty, & Surety Bulletins, Fire and Marine Volume. Cincinnati, Ohio: The National Underwriter Company. The bulletins are published monthly. Up-to-date information on fire insurance can be found in this volume.

Greene, Mark R. and James S. Trieschmann. *Risk and Insurance,* 6th ed. Cincinnati, Ohio: Southwestern Publishing Company, 1984, chapter 10.

Huebner, S. S., Kenneth Black, Jr., and Robert S. Cline, *Property and Liability Insurance,* 3rd ed. Englewood Cliffs, New Jersey: Prentice-Hall, Inc., 1982, chapters 2 and 3.

Riegel, Robert, Jerome S. Miller, and C. Arthur Williams, Jr. *Insurance Principles and Practices: Property and Liability,* 6th ed. Englewood Cliffs, New Jersey: Prentice-Hall, Inc., 1976, chapter 7.

Vaughan, Emmet J. *Fundamentals of Risk and Insurance,* 3rd ed. New York: John Wiley & Sons, 1982, chapter 24.

Williams, Jr., C. Arthur, George L. Head, Ronald C. Horn, and G. William Glendenning. *Principles of Risk Management and Insurance,* 2nd ed., Volume II. Malvern, Pennsylvania: American Institute for Property and Liability Underwriters, 1981, chapter 15.

NOTES

1. Insurance Information Institute, *Insurance Facts, 1984–85 Property/Casualty Fact Book,* pp. 57–59.
2. C. Arthur Williams, Jr., George L. Head, Ronald C. Horn, and G. William Glendenning, *Principles of Risk Management and Insurance,* 2nd ed., Volume II (Malvern, Pennsylvania: American Institute for Property and Liability Underwriters, 1981), p. 285.
3. See Chapter 13 for a discussion of business interruption insurance.
4. *United States Fidelity & Guaranty Co. v. Haywood,* 177 S.E. (2nd.) 530.
5. However, the theft loss would be covered under a homeowners policy. See Chapter 7 for a discussion of the various homeowners policies.
6. Robert Riegel, Jerome S. Miller, and C. Arthur Williams, Jr., *Insurance Principles and Practices: Property and Liability,* 6th ed. (Englewood Cliffs, New Jersey: Prentice-Hall, Inc., 1976), p. 162.
7. Riegel, pp. 50–54.

CHAPTER

7

HOMEOWNERS INSURANCE

"For a man's house is his castle."

Sir Edward Coke, Third Institute (1644)

STUDENT LEARNING OBJECTIVES

After studying this chapter, you should be able to:

- Describe the different types of homeowner policies that are used in the United States.
- Explain the basic provisions of the new 1984 Homeowners 3 policy including: basic coverages, insured perils, exclusions, and duties after a loss occurs.
- Explain and give an illustration of the replacement cost provision in the homeowners policy.
- Describe the important rules that a consumer should follow when shopping for a homeowners policy.

In this chapter, we will examine the popular homeowner policies that are widely used to insure private dwellings and the personal property of individuals and families. Homeowners insurance is a **package policy** that combines two or more separate contracts into one policy. Prior to the introduction of homeowners insurance in the 1950s, property insurance on a private dwelling and personal property, theft coverage, and personal-liability insurance could not be obtained in one policy. However, as a result of multiple-line laws, these coverages can now be combined into a single contract. As a result, the insured has gained several advantages. First, the total premium is lower than if the insured had purchased several separate contracts from different insurers. The premium reduction is due to reduced administrative expenses, stricter underwriting, reduction in adverse selection since the entire package must be accepted, and higher minimum insurance amounts. Second, there are fewer gaps in coverage, and the major insurance needs of a typical policyowner are more easily met in one contract. Finally, there is the advantage of convenience, since the insured deals with only one agent and insurer.[1] It is estimated that at least 75 percent of all eligible private dwellings are insured under some type of homeowner policy.[2]

1984 HOMEOWNERS PROGRAM

Homeowner contracts were first written in the early 1950s. Since that time, they have been revised several times. The 1976 version by the Insurance Services Office (ISO), which resulted in the Homeowners 76 Policy Program, was particularly significant. The standard fire policy was eliminated as a separate document, and its basic provisions were incorporated into the homeowner policy itself. The policy language was also simplified. The Homeowners 76 Policy referred to the policyholder as "you" and the insurer as "we."

However, the Homeowners 76 Program was not adopted in several states, and the older forms were used instead. Elimination of the standard fire policy as a separate document caused problems in some states, since it was mandated by law. Also, some agents and brokers objected to certain provisions in the Homeowners 76 Policy. In response to these criticisms, the Insurance Services Office revised the homeowners policy in 1982, and it was initially introduced on a trial basis in six states in 1982 and early 1983. Shortly after the 1982 policy was introduced, several adverse court decisions concerning the interpretation of policy provisions made it apparent that additional revision was necessary. The 1982 homeowners policy was revised in 1983 and again in 1984 to clarify further the scope of coverage under the program.

The Insurance Services Office planned to introduce the new 1984 Homeowners Program in about 25 percent of the states in 1984, and in most of the remaining states in 1985.

Eligible Dwellings

The homeowner contracts are carefully underwritten, and the eligibility requirements are fairly strict. A homeowner contract on a private dwelling can be written only on an *owner-occupied* dwelling that does not contain more than two families (four families in some states). Each family is limited to a maximum of two boarders or roomers. Separate homeowner forms are written for renters and condominium owners. Minimum amounts of insurance must be purchased under all forms.

Types of Homeowner Policies

Six homeowner forms are now used in the new 1984 ISO program.[3] They are:

- HO-1 (basic form)
- HO-2 (broad form)
- HO-3 (special form)
- HO-4 (contents broad form)
- HO-6 (unit-owners form)
- HO-8 (modified coverage form)

Under the older Homeowners 76 program,

HO-5 (Comprehensive Form) was another form that was also used; it provided all-risk coverage on both the building and contents. However, under the new 1984 program, HO-5 has been eliminated as a separate contract. An endorsement is now added to HO-3 to provide the same protection that the older HO-5 provided.

Each homeowner form is divided into two major sections. Section I covers the dwelling, other structures, and personal property,[4] as well as additional living expenses or fair rental value from a covered loss. Section II provides personal liability insurance and coverage for the medical payments of others. The Section II coverages are identical in all homeowner policies.

Homeowners 1 (basic form) **Homeowners 1** is a *basic form* that insures the dwelling and other structures and also covers the insured's personal property. Additional living expenses and fair rental value are also covered in the event that a loss makes the dwelling uninhabitable.

Homeowners 1 is a *named perils* policy. The insured perils are (1) fire, (2) lightning, (3) windstorm, (4) hail, (5) explosion, (6) riot or civil commotion, (7) aircraft, (8) vehicles, (9) smoke, (10) vandalism or malicious mischief, (11) theft, (12) breakage of glass or safety glazing material that is part of a building, storm door, or storm window, and (13) volcanic eruption.

Homeowners 2 (broad form) **Homeowners 2** is a *broad form* that expands the coverage under the basic form and adds several new perils. They include loss from falling objects; weight of ice, snow, or sleet; accidental discharge from a plumbing, heating, air conditioning, or automatic fire protective sprinkler system, or from a household appliance; tearing, cracking, burning, or bulging of a steam or hot water heating system, air conditioning or automatic fire protective sprinkler system, or an appliance for heating water; freezing of a plumbing, heating, air conditioning, or automatic fire protective sprinkler system, or household appliance; and damage from an artificially-generated electrical current.

Homeowners 3 (special form) **Homeowners 3** is a *special form* that insures the dwelling and other structures *against risks of direct loss to property except those losses specifically excluded.* All direct physical damage losses to the dwelling and other structures are covered, except certain losses specifically excluded. Personal property is covered by the same *broad named perils* listed in HO-2, plus the peril of damage by glass or safety glazing material. Homeowners 3 is a popular and widely used form that will be discussed in greater detail later in the chapter.

Homeowners 4 (contents broad form) **Homeowners 4** is specifically designed for tenants of rented premises. There is no insurance on the dwelling or building, since the landlord normally is responsible for insurance on the building. Homeowners 4 covers the tenant's personal property against loss or damage, and it also provides personal-liability insurance as well. Personal property is covered by the same named-perils listed in Homeowners 2. In addition, up to 10 percent of the insurance on personal property can be applied to cover any building additions or alterations to the building. A minimum amount of $6,000 of insurance on personal property is required under this form.

Homeowners 6 (unit-owners form) **Homeowners 6** is designed exclusively for condominium owners. The policy covers the personal property of the insured on a broad form, named-perils basis. Generally, a minimum amount of $6,000 of insurance on personal property is required; but many companies require higher minimum amounts. There is no insurance on the building, since the condominium association carries insurance on the building and other property that is owned in common by the owners of the different units.

In addition, there is also $1,000 of insurance for building improvements and alterations, such as carpeting, wallpaper, wall paneling, and additional kitchen cabinets. The $1,000 limit can be increased to a higher amount. Finally, the policy also provides loss assessment coverage of up to $1,000 that covers the insured if he or she is assessed for a loss not covered by the condominium association.

Homeowners 8 (modified coverage form) **Homeowners 8** is a modified HO-1 form by which losses to the dwelling and other structures are paid based on the amount required to repair or replace the property using common construction materials and methods. Thus, payment is not based on replacement cost. In addition, theft coverage is limited to losses that occur on the residence premises up to a maximum of $1,000 per occurrence.

The HO-8 form is designed for older homes in urban neighborhoods where the replacement cost of a house may substantially exceed its market value. For exmple, a house may have a market value of $50,000, but its replacement cost may be $100,000. Under the other homeowner forms, to be indemnified on the basis of replacement cost, the homeowner must carry insurance at least equal to 80 percent of the replacement cost of the property. But a homeowner may be reluctant to insure a house for $80,000 (80% × $100,000) when its current market value is only $50,000, and the insurer may be unwilling to insure a house for $80,000 under a standard homeowners policy when its current market value is considerably lower. Thus, to make homeowners coverage available on older homes in residential neighborhoods, and to reduce the problem of moral hazard, the HO-8 form has been developed.

Figure 7.1 compares the various homeowner forms, minimum limits, and insured perils.

ANALYSIS OF HOMEOWNERS 3 POLICY (SPECIAL FORM)

In this section, we will examine the basic coverages that appear in the Homeowners 3 policy (special form). As you study this section, you may find it helpful to refer to the Homeowners 3 policy in Appendix C of this text.

There are five basic coverages in Section I of the Homeowners 3 policy. They are as follows:

1. Coverage A—Dwelling
2. Coverage B—Other structures
3. Coverage C—Personal property
4. Coverage D—Loss of use
5. Additional coverages

Let us briefly examine each of these coverages.

Coverage A—Dwelling

Coverage A covers the dwelling on the residence premises as well as any structure attached to the dwelling. Thus, the home and attached garage or carport would be insured under this section.

Materials and supplies intended for construction, alteration, or repair of the dwelling or other structures are also covered. For example, lumber in a garage that will be used to add on to the house would be covered if a loss occurs.

Coverage A specifically excludes land. Thus, if the land on which the dwelling is located is damaged from an insured peril—such as from a volcanic eruption—the land is not covered.

Coverage B—Other Structures

Coverage B insures other structures on the residence premises that are separated from the dwelling by clear space. This includes a detached garage, tool shed, or horse stable. Structures connected to the dwelling by a fence, utility line, or other connection are also considered to be other structures.

The amount of insurance under Coverage B is based on the amount of insurance on the dwelling (Coverage A). Under the Homeowners 3 policy, 10 percent of the insurance on the dwelling applies as *additional insurance* to the other structures. For example, if the home is insured for $80,000, the other structures are covered for $8,000.

Coverage B has three major exclusions. First, the coverage does not apply to land, which includes land on which the other structures are located. Second, there is no coverage if the structure is used for business purposes. For example, if Charles repairs automobiles in a detached garage, there is no coverage if the garage burns in a fire.

Finally, with the exception of a private garage, there is no coverage if the other structure is rented to someone who is not a tenant of the dwelling. For example, assume that Sam owns and occupies a house which has a horse stable. If Sam rents the horse stable to another person, there would be no coverage on the stable if a loss occurs.

Coverage C—Personal Property

Personal property owned or used by an insured is covered anywhere in the world. This also includes borrowed property. In addition, at the insured's request, the insurance can be extended to cover the personal property of a guest or resident employee while the property is in any residence occupied by an insured. For example, Susan may invite a guest to dinner. If the guest's coat burns in a fire, the loss is covered under Susan's policy.

The amount of insurance on personal property is equal to 50 percent of the insurance on the dwelling.[5] This limit can be increased. Thus, if Sam's home is insured for $80,000, an *additional* $40,000 of insurance applies to personal property. *The full amount of insurance on personal property applies both on and off the premises anywhere in the world.* An exception to this rule is that if personal property is usually located in another residence of the insured, other than the residence premises, the off-premises coverage is limited to 10 percent of Coverage C, or $1,000, whichever is greater. For example, assume that Sam has $40,000 of insurance on his personal property. He could take that property on an extended trip to Europe and have coverage up to a maximum of $40,000 on it while it is off the premises. Assume by contrast that Sam owns a cabin or summer home on a river, and that fishing gear is normally kept there. In this case, a maximum of $4,000 would apply to the loss of the fishing gear and other personal property because it is personal property normally located at this location (10 percent of $40,000 or $1,000, whichever is greater).

Personal property moved by the insured to a newly acquired principal residence is not subject to the preceding limitation for 30 days after the move begins. This means that the insured's personal property is covered for the perils insured against while the property is being moved to the new location, as well as at the new principal residence itself. After 30 days, the insurer must be notified for full protection to continue.

Special limits of liability Because of moral hazard and loss-adjustment problems, and a desire by the insurer to limit its liability, certain types of property have maximum dollar limits on the amount paid for any loss. Some limits can be increased by an endorsement. The special limits of liability are as follows:

1. $200 on money, bank notes, bullion, gold, silver, platinum, coins, and medals.
2. $1,000 on securities, valuable papers, manuscripts, passports, tickets, and stamp collections.
3. $1,000 on watercraft, including trailers and equipment.
4. $1,000 on other trailers not used with boats.
5. $1,000 on grave markers.
6. $1,000 for the theft of jewelry, watches, furs, precious and semiprecious stones.
7. $2,000 for the theft of firearms.
8. $2,500 for the theft of silverware, goldware, and pewterware.
9. $2,500 on property, on the residence premises, that is used at any time or in any manner for any business purpose.
10. $250 on property, away from the residence premises, that is used at any time or in any manner for any business purpose.

The $200 limit on money includes coin collections. If you have a valuable coin collection worth several thousand dollars, it should be scheduled and insured for a specific amount of

Figure 7.1
Comparison of 1984 Homeowner Coverages

Coverage	HO-1 (basic form)	HO-2 (broad form)	HO-3 (special form)
		Section I Coverages	
A. Dwelling	$15,000 minimum	$15,000 minimum	$20,000 minimum
B. Other structures	10% of A	10% of A	10% of A
C. Personal property	50% of A	50% of A	50% of A
D. Loss of use	10% of A	20% of A	20% of A
Covered perils	Fire or lightning Windstorm or hail Explosion Riot or civil commotion Aircraft Vehicles Smoke Vandalism or malicious mischief Theft Breakage of glass or safety glazing material (limit of $100) Volcanic eruption	Fire or lightning Windstorm or hail Explosion Riot or civil commotion Aircraft Vehicles Smoke Vandalism or malicious mischief Theft Breakage of glass or safety glazing material Falling objects Weight of ice, snow, or sleet Accidental discharge or overflow of water or stream Sudden and accidental tearing, cracking, burning, or bulging of a steam, hot water, air conditioning, or automatic fire protective sprinkler system, or appliance for heating water Freezing Sudden and accidental damage from artificially generated electrical current Volcanic eruption	Dwelling and other structures covered against risks of direct physical loss to property except losses specifically excluded Personal property covered by same perils as HO-2 plus damage by glass or safety glazing material, which is part of a building, storm door, or storm window
		Section II Coverages	
E. Personal liability	$100,000	$100,000	$100,000
F. Medical payments to others	$ 1,000 per person	$ 1,000 per person	$ 1,000 per person

HO-4 (contents broad form)	HO-6 (unit owners form)	HO-8 (modified coverage form)
	Section I Coverages	
Not applicable Not applicable $ 6,000 min. 20% of C	Not applicable Not applicable $ 6,000 min. 40% of C	Same as HO-1 except losses are paid based on the amount required to repair or replace the property using common construction materials and methods.
Same perils as HO-2 for personal property	Same perils as HO-2 for personal property	Same perils as HO-1 except theft coverage applies only to losses on the residence premises up to a maximum of $1,000; certain other coverage restrictions also apply.
	Section II Coverages	
$100,000	$100,000	$100,000
$ 1,000 per person	$ 1,000 per person	$ 1,000 per person

insurance. A **schedule** is a list of covered property or specific amounts of insurance. The coin collection should be listed and specifically insured for its true value. A valuable stamp collection should also be specifically insured, since there is a $1,000 limit on stamps.

Boats have limited coverage under the homeowners policy. Coverage on boats is limited to $1,000, including the equipment, furnishings, and outboard motors. A boat with a value in excess of this limit should be specifically insured. This can be done by purchasing an all-risk policy on the boat.

Grave markers have a limit of $1,000. Vandalism, destructive tornadoes, and windstorms can cause serious property damage to grave markers in cemeteries. Under the new contracts, this property is now covered up to $1,000.

The theft of jewelry and furs is limited to a maximum of $1,000 for any loss. Expensive jewelry and furs should be scheduled and specifically insured. There is also a $2,000 limit on the theft of firearms and a $2,500 limit on the theft of silverware, goldware, and pewterware. In recent years, the theft of guns and silverware has become a prime objective of burglars. So valuable gun or silverware collections should be specifically insured based on the current value of the collection. Note also that the limits on jewelry and furs, guns, silverware and goldware apply only to the *theft peril*. The full amount of insurance applies to losses from other covered perils.

Finally, property used for any business purpose ls limited to $2,500 on the premises and $250 off the premises. Thus, a personal computer that you use at home for business purposes is limited to a maximum of $2,500.

Property not covered Certain types of property are excluded under Coverage C. The following property is not covered:

1. *Articles separately described and specifically insured.* Articles separately described and specifically insured under either the homeowners policy or some other policy are not covered under Coverage C. The intent here is to avoid duplicate coverage. Valuable property such as a diamond ring, furs, boats, and coin collections may have to be specifically insured because of the dollar limits on losses discussed earlier. In such cases, the homeowners policy will not contribute toward any loss, not even on an excess basis.
2. *Animals, birds, and fish.* Pets are excluded because they are difficult to value.[6] Specialized coverages can be used to insure valuable animals, such as thoroughbred horses and racing dogs.
3. *Motor vehicles and motorized land conveyances.* Motor vehicles and motorized land vehicles are specifically excluded. Thus, automobiles, motorcycles, and motorscooters are not covered. The intent of this exclusion is to cover automobiles and similar vehicles under an automobile insurance policy.

   The exclusion also applies to (a) equipment and accessories and (b) any device or instrument for the transmitting, recording, receiving, or reproduction of sound or pictures, which is operated by power from the electrical system of the motor vehicle or conveyance, including accessories, antennas, tapes, wires, records, or discs, *while in or upon the vehicle or conveyance*. Thus, stereo tape players, stereo tapes, citizen band radios, police scanners, television sets, and videocassette recorders are excluded from coverage. You should remember that the sound equipment exclusion applies only while the property is in or upon the vehicle or conveyance. A stereo tape or CB radio that is removed from an automobile and taken into the house would be covered under the homeowners policy.

   Finally, vehicles or conveyances that are not subject to motor vehicle registration and are (a) used to service an insured's residence or (b) designed to assist the handicapped are exempt from the exclusion. Thus, a garden tractor, riding lawn mower, or electric wheel chair would be covered under the policy.

4. *Aircraft and parts.* Aircraft and parts are specifically excluded. However, hobby or model aircraft not used or designed to carry people or cargo in flight are not subject to the exclusion.
5. *Property of roomers, boarders, and other tenants.* The property of roomers and boarders who are not related to an insured is also excluded. Thus, if the insured rents a room to a student, the student's property is not covered under the insured's homeowners policy. However, the property of roomers, boarders, and tenants related to the insured can be covered at the insured's option. The purpose of the exclusion is to require other persons to obtain their own insurance.
6. *Property in a regularly rented apartment.* Property in an apartment regularly rented or being held for rental to others is specifically excluded. For example, Susan may have a furnished apartment on the second floor of her home, which is rented to students. Furniture inside the apartment is not covered under Susan's policy.
7. *Property rented or held for rental to others off the residence premises.* Property away from the residence premises that is rented to others is specifically excluded. For example, if Mary owns a bike rental business and rents a bicycle to a customer, the bicycle is not covered under her homeowners policy.
8. *Business records.* The 1984 homeowners policy excludes books of account, drawings or other paper records, and electronic data processing tapes, wires, records, discs, or other software media that contain business data. However, the cost of blank or unexposed records and media is covered. The overall effect of this exclusion is to eliminate coverage for the expense of reproducing business records.

Coverage D—Loss of Use

Coverage D provides protection when the residence premises cannot be used because of an insured loss. The amount of additional insurance under this coverage is 20 percent of the amount of insurance on the dwelling (Coverage A). Three benefits are provided: (1) **additional living expense,** (2) **fair rental value,** and (3) **prohibited use.**

Additional living expense If a covered loss makes the residence premises not fit to live in, the company pays, at the insured's option, either (1) the increase in additional living expense or (2) the fair rental value of the residence premises. *Additional living expense* is the increase in living expenses actually incurred by the insured to maintain the family's normal standard of living. *Fair rental value* refers to the rental value of that part of the residence premises where the insured resides (less any expenses that do not continue while the premises are not fit to live in). For example, assume that Fred's home is damaged by a fire, and he rents a furnished apartment for three months at $500 per month. The $1,500 would be covered as an additional living expense. However, Fred may decide instead to move in with his parents for three months while his house is being rebuilt. He would be paid the cost of renting comparable housing (less any expenses that are discontinued, such as utilities).

Payment under either option will be for the shortest time to repair or replace the damage or, if the insured permanently relocates, for the shortest time for the household to settle elsewhere.

Fair rental value The loss of rents is also covered if part of the premises is rented or held for rental to others. For example, Gerald may rent a room to a student for a monthly rent of $100. If the home is uninhabitable from a fire, and it takes three months to rebuild, Gerald would receive $300 for the loss of rents (less any expenses that do not continue).

Prohibited use If a civil authority prohibits the insured from using the premises because of a loss to a neighboring premises from an insured peril, additional living expenses and fair rental value can be paid for a maximum period of two weeks. For example, Mary may be ordered out of her home by a fire marshal because the house next door had an explosion from a leaking gas main. Her additional living expense or fair rental value loss would be covered for up to two weeks.

Finally, any loss or expense due to cancellation of a lease or agreement is not covered. Thus, if you have a favorable lease that is cancelled because of a severe fire, the additional increase in housing costs would not be covered.

Additional Coverages

In addition to Coverages A, B, C, and D, eight additional coverages are provided. They are as follows:

1. Debris removal.
2. Reasonable repairs.
3. Trees, shrubs, and other plants.
4. Fire department service charge.
5. Property removed.
6. Credit card, fund transfer card, forgery, and counterfeit money.
7. Loss assessment.
8. Collapse.

Debris removal The homeowners policy pays the reasonable expense of removing debris of covered property from an insured peril. The cost of removing debris is included in the limit of liability that applies to the damaged property. However, when the policy limits are exhausted, an *additional* 5 percent of the amount of insurance is available to cover the expenses of removing the debris. For example, assume that a detached garage is covered for $5,000 under Coverage B (other structures), and a total loss occurs. An additional 5 percent or $250 would be paid to remove the debris.

Debris removal also pays the cost of removing volcanic ash, dust, or particles from a volcanic eruption that cause a direct loss to a building or property in a building.

Finally, if an uninsured tree falls and damages covered property, the cost of removing the tree from the residence premises is now covered. The coverage applies only when a Coverage C peril insured against causes the tree to fall. The maximum limit for any one loss is $500. For example, if a tree falls on the dwelling and damages it during a heavy windstorm, the cost of removing the tree is covered.

Reasonable repairs The policy also pays the reasonable cost incurred by the insured to protect the property from further damage after a covered loss occurs. For example, a broken picture window may have to be repaired immediately after a severe windstorm to protect personal property from further damage. The reasonable cost would be paid. This provision does not increase the total amount of insurance on the property being repaired.

Trees, shrubs, and other plants The homeowners policy also covers trees, shrubs, plants, or lawns on the residence premises against loss from a limited number of perils. *Coverage is provided only for fire, lightning, explosion, riot, civil commotion, aircraft, vehicles not owned or operated by a resident of the premises, vandalism, malicious mischief, and theft.* Note that *windstorm* is not listed. Therefore, it is not covered. If an expensive tree is blown over in a severe windstorm, the cost of replacing the tree is not covered. However, as we noted earlier, if the fallen tree damages covered property, such as the dwelling, the cost of removing the tree is covered under debris removal.

The maximum limit for a loss under this coverage is 5 percent of the insurance that covers the dwelling. Loss to any one tree, plant, or shrub (but not lawns) is limited to a maximum of $500. However, property grown for business purposes, such as nursery trees, is not covered. The amount of insurance provided under this provision is considered additional insurance.

Fire department service charge The policy pays up to $500 for a fire department service charge if the named insured is liable by a contract or agreement for fire department charges incurred when firefighters are called to protect covered property from an insured peril. However, coverage does not apply if the property is located within the governmental unit or protection district that provides the fire department protection.

This coverage is considered additional insurance and is not subject to any deductible.

Property removal If property is removed from the premises because it is endangered by an insured peril, direct loss from *any cause* is covered for a maximum of thirty days while the property is removed. Thus, furniture being moved and stored in a public warehouse because of a fire in the home is covered for a direct loss from any cause for a maximum of thirty days. This coverage does not increase the amount of insurance on the property being removed.

Credit card, fund transfer card, forgery, and counterfeit money Under federal law, there is a maximum liability of $50 if a credit card is stolen or lost and is used by someone else. There is no liability if the loss is promptly reported to the credit card company. However, a wallet or purse containing several credit cards may be stolen or lost. Under the homeowners policy, if credit cards are stolen or lost and used in an unauthorized manner, any loss to the insured is covered up to a maximum of $500. Likewise, loss that results from the theft or unauthorized use of an insured's fund transfer card is also covered. If a forged or altered check results in a loss to the insured, it is also covered. If the insured accepts counterfeit money in good faith, that loss is covered, too.

Several exclusions apply to this coverage. First, unauthorized use of a credit card or fund transfer card by a resident of the named insured's household is not covered. Thus, if a son, age sixteen, steals his father's credit card and makes an unauthorized purchase, the loss is not covered. Second, losses by any person who has been entrusted with either type of card are also excluded. Third, if an insured does not comply with all terms and conditions under which the cards are issued, the loss is not covered. Finally, losses arising out of business use or dishonesty of an insured are not covered.

This coverage is also considered to be additional insurance and is not subject to any deductible.

Loss assessment The policy pays up to $1,000 for any loss assessment charged against the named insured as owner or tenant of the residence premises by a corporation or association of property owners because of the direct loss to property collectively owned by all members. However, the loss to the property owned collectively must be caused by a peril insured against in Coverage A (other than by an earthquake or volcanic eruption).

Collapse Under the new 1984 homeowners policy, collapse has been eliminated as a separate peril, and a more restrictive definition of collapse has been added instead as an additional coverage. Collapse of a building (or any part of a building) is covered only if the loss is caused by any of the following:

1. *Perils insured against in Coverage C (Personal Property); however, these perils apply to both the covered building and personal property.*
2. *Hidden decay.*
3. *Hidden insects or vermin damage.*
4. *Weight of contents, equipment, animals, or people.*
5. *Weight of rain that collects on a roof.*
6. *Use of defective materials or methods in construction, remodeling, or renovation if the collapse occurs during the course of construction, remodeling, or renovation.*

Two exclusions apply to the collapse coverage. First, loss to an awning, fence, patio, pavement, swimming pool, underground pipes, and certain other property is not covered under perils 2–6 above unless the loss is the direct result of the collapse of a building. Second, collapse does not include settling, cracking, shrinking, building, or expansion.

Deductible A base deductible of $250 applies to each covered loss. However, the insured has the option of purchasing the $100 deductible that was used earlier in the 1976 homeowners contracts. The $250 deductible does not apply to a fire department service charge or to losses involving a credit card, fund transfer card, forgery, or counterfeit money.

SECTION I—PERILS INSURED AGAINST

Dwelling and Other Structures

The older Homeowners 76 policy covered the dwelling and other structures for *all risks* of direct physical loss except certain losses that were excluded. In the new 1984 homeowners policy, the word "all" has been deleted from the all-risks description of perils insured against under Coverages A and B. *The 1984 homeowners policy now insures the dwelling and other structures against risk of direct physical losses, except certain losses specifically excluded.* The deletion of any reference to an all-risk policy is intended to avoid creating reasonable expectations among policyholders that the policy covers all losses, even losses that are specifically excluded in the policy.

In addition, the new wording is designed to meet the problem of *concurrent causation* (discussed later) by which the courts ruled that, in certain cases, coverage existed under the homeowners policy even though the loss was specifically excluded in the policy.

The following losses, however, are not covered:

1. *Collapse.* Losses involving collapse are specifically excluded, except those collapse losses covered under "additional coverages."
2. *Freezing.* Freezing of a plumbing, heating, air conditioning or automatic fire protection sprinkler system, or household appliance, or discharge, leakage, or overflow from within the system or appliance is not covered while the building is vacant or unoccupied, unless heat is maintained in the building, or the water supply is shut off and drained.
3. *Fences, pavement, patio, and similar structures.* Damage to fences, pavements, patios, swimming pools, foundations, retaining walls, and similar structures is not covered if the damage is caused by freezing and thawing, or from the pressure of weight of water or ice.
4. *Dwelling under construction.* Theft in or to a dwelling under construction, or of materials and supplies used in construction, is not covered until the dwelling is both completed and occupied.
5. *Vandalism and malicious mischief.* Damage from vandalism, malicious mischief, or breakage of glass and safety glazing materials is not covered if the dwelling is vacant for more than thirty consecutive days prior to the loss.
6. *Constant seepage or leakage.* Constant or repeated seepage or leakage of water or steam over a period of weeks, months, or years from within a plumbing, heating, air conditioning, or automatic fire protective sprinkler system, or from a household appliance is not covered.
7. *Other exclusions.* The following losses are also excluded:
   a. Wear and tear, marring, deterioration.
   b. Inherent vice, latent defect, mechanical breakdown.
   c. Smog, rust, mold, wet or dry rot.
   d. Smoke from agricultural smudging or industrial operations.

e. Release, discharge or dispersal of contaminants or pollutants.
f. Settling, cracking, shrinking, bulging, or expansion of pavements, patios, foundations, walls, floors, roofs, or ceilings.
g. Birds, vermin, rodents, insects, or domestic animals.

If any of the preceding perils cause water damage not otherwise excluded from a plumbing, heating, air conditioning, or automatic fire protector sprinkler system, or household appliance, the damage caused by the water is covered. This includes the cost of tearing out and replacing any part of a building which is necessary to repair the system or appliance. However, the policy specifically excludes loss to the system or appliance from which the water escapes.

8. *Losses excluded under Section I—Exclusions.* Certain additional losses to the dwelling and other structures are also excluded under Section I—Exclusions (discussed later). *Thus, with the exception of losses caused by the preceding perils, all other losses to the dwelling and other structures are covered.*

Personal Property

Personal property (Coverage C) is covered on a *named-perils* basis. The following perils are covered:

1. Fire or lightning.
2. Windstorm or hail.
3. Explosion.
4. Riot or civil commotion.
5. Aircraft.
6. Vehicles.
7. Smoke.
8. Vandalism or malicious mischief.
9. Theft.
10. Falling objects.
11. Weight of ice, snow, or sleet.
12. Accidental discharge or overflow of water or steam.
13. Sudden and accidental tearing apart, cracking, burning, or bulging of a steam, hot water, air conditioning, or automatic fire protective sprinkler system, or appliance for heating water.
14. Freezing of a plumbing, heating, air conditioning or automatic fire protective sprinkler system, or household appliance.
15. Sudden and accidental damage from an artificially generated electrical current.
16. Damage by glass or safety glazing material.
17. Volcanic eruption.

Fire or lightning Both fire and lightning are covered under the homeowners policy. We explained the meaning of these perils in Chapter 6 as part of our analysis of the standard fire policy.

Windstorm or hail Windstorm or hail damage is also covered. However, damage to the interior of the building and its contents because of rain, snow, sand, or dust is not covered unless there is an opening in the roof or wall from the wind or hail which then allows the elements to enter. For example, if Patti carelessly leaves a window open in the living room, rain damage to a sofa is not covered. But if the wind or hail should break the window, allowing rain to enter through the opening, the water damage to property inside the room would be covered.

An important exclusion applies to boats. Boats and related equipment are covered only while inside a fully enclosed building. For example, if a boat is stored in the driveway of the home and is damaged by a severe windstorm, the loss is not covered.

Explosion Broad coverage is provided from an explosion. Any type of explosion loss is covered. For example, if a furnace explodes or a sonic boom breaks a window, the damage is covered.

Riot or civil commotion Property damage during a riot or civil commotion is also covered.

Each state defines the meaning of a riot. It is usually defined as an assembly of three or more persons who commit a lawful or unlawful act in a violent or tumultuous manner, to the terror or disturbance of others. Civil commotion is a large or sustained riot that involves an uprising of the citizens.

Aircraft Aircraft damage, including damage from self-propelled missiles and spacecraft, is also covered. For example, if a commercial jet crashes into a residential area, damage to the home and personal property is covered. Likewise, if a missile from a nearby military base goes astray, the insured property is covered against loss.

Vehicles Property damage from vehicles is also covered. For example, if a motorist loses control of an automobile and smashes into the foundation of your home, the loss is covered. Or if you carelessly back out of the garage and damage the garage door, the loss is covered.

Smoke Sudden and accidental damage from smoke is also covered. This includes smoke damage from a fireplace. For example, if the fireplace malfunctions and smoke pours into the living room, any smoke damage to the drapes is covered. However, smoke damage from agricultural smudging or industrial operations is specifically excluded.

Vandalism or malicious mischief Vandalism and malicious mischief are increasing in importance, so this is an important coverage. For example, if someone breaks into your home and destroys some wall paintings, the loss is covered.

Theft Theft losses are covered, including the attempted theft and the loss of property when it is likely that the property has been stolen. For example, if you hang your raincoat and umbrella on a rack in the student union on a rainy day, and the items are gone when you return, the loss is covered.

Although coverage of theft is fairly broad, there are several exclusions. They include the following:

1. Theft by an insured is excluded. For example, if Mary, age sixteen, steals $50 from her mother's purse before running away from home, the theft is not covered.
2. Theft in or to a dwelling under construction, or of materials and supplies used in the construction of a dwelling, is not covered until the dwelling is completed and occupied.
3. Theft from any part of the premises rented to someone other than an insured is not covered. For example, if the insured rents a room to a student, the theft of a radio in the room would not be covered.

In addition, several important exclusions also apply when the theft occurs away from the residence premises. They include the following:

1. *Secondary residence.* If property is located at any other residence owned, rented to, or occupied by an insured, the loss is not covered unless an insured is temporarily residing there. For example, Sam may own a cabin on the river. Theft of property inside the cabin is not covered unless Sam is temporarily residing there. He may be fishing at the river when the theft occurs. As long as he can show he was temporarily residing at the cabin when the theft occurred, the loss would be covered.

   In addition, theft of personal property of a student while at a residence away from home is covered if the student has been there any time during the forty-five days immediately preceding the loss. For example, assume you are attending college and are temporarily living away from home. If a thief steals some personal property from your college residence, the loss is covered if you have been there anytime during the forty-five day period preceding the loss.

2. *Watercraft.* Theft of a boat, its furnishings, equipment, and outboard motor is excluded if the theft occurs away from the premises.
3. *Trailers and campers.* The theft of trailers or campers away from the premises is not covered. Trailers and campers can be insured under the personal auto policy, which we will study later in Chapter 11.

Falling objects Damage to personal property from falling objects is covered. However, loss to property contained inside the building is not covered unless the roof or outside wall of the building is first damaged by the falling object. For example, if a mirror falls from a wall and breaks, the loss is not covered. But if the mirror falls and breaks because the exterior of the dwelling is first damaged from a falling object (such as from a falling tree), the loss would be covered.

Weight of ice, snow, or sleet Damage to property contained in a building from the weight of ice, snow, or sleet is also covered. For example, the heavy weight of snow may cause the roof to collapse, and snow falls on personal property inside the dwelling. The damage to the personal property would be covered.

Accidental discharge or overflow of water or steam If loss results from an accidental discharge or overflow of water or steam from a plumbing, heating, air conditioning, or automatic fire protective sprinkler system, or from a household appliance, the property damage is covered. For example, if an automatic dishwasher malfunctions and floods the kitchen, the water damage to the kitchen carpet would be covered.

Sudden and accidental tearing apart, cracking, burning, or bulging of a steam, hot water, air conditioning, or automatic fire protective sprinkler system, or appliance for heating water If a steam, hot water, air conditioning, or automatic fire protective sprinkler system, or an appliance for heating water, suddenly tears apart, cracks, burns, or bulges, the property damage is covered. For example, damage to personal property from a hot water heater that suddenly explodes is covered.

Freezing of a plumbing, heating, air conditioning, or automatic fire protective sprinkler system, or household appliance The policy also covers damage from the freezing of a plumbing, heating, air conditioning, or automatic fire protective sprinkler system, or household appliance. Freezing is not covered if the dwelling is unoccupied unless heat is maintained in the building, or the water supply is shut off, and the system is drained.

Sudden and accidental damage from an artificially generated electrical current Sudden and accidental property damage from an artificially generated electric current is also covered. For example, if a short circuit causes an electric dryer to burn out, the loss is covered. However, loss to tubes, transistors, or similar electronic components is specifically excluded. Thus, a television picture tube that burns out is not covered.

Damage by glass or safety glazing material Damage by glass or safety glazing material that is part of a building, storm door, or storm window is also covered. For example, if furniture is damaged by the shattering of glass from a broken window or door, the property damage is covered.

Volcanic eruption Loss covered by a volcanic eruption is also covered, except losses caused by an earthquake, land shock waves, or tremors. For example, property damage because of volcanic explosion, volcanic ash, lava flow, or airborne shock waves would be covered under this peril.

This ends our discussion of the covered perils. Let us next examine some specific exclusions in Section I.

SECTION I—EXCLUSIONS

In addition to the specific exclusions discussed earlier, several *general exclusions* are also included in the policy.

Ordinance or Law

Loss due to an ordinance or law that regulates the construction, repair, or demolition of a building or structure is not covered, unless specifically provided for under the policy. For example, a city ordinance may require certain changes in a home's wiring, plumbing, or foundation, or may require a partly damaged building to be completely razed. These losses are not covered.

Earth Movement

Property damage from earth movement is also excluded. This includes damage from earthquake, volcanic eruption, or landslide. However, direct loss by fire, explosion, theft, or breakage of glass or safety glazing material which is part of a building, storm door, or storm window, resulting from the earth movement is covered.

Water Damage

Property damage from certain water losses is specifically excluded. The following types of water damage losses are not covered:

1. Floods, surface water, waves, tidal water, and overflow or spray from a body of water.
2. Water backing up through sewers or drains.
3. Water below the surface of the ground that exerts pressure on or seeps through a building, sidewalk, driveway, foundation, swimming pool, or other structure.

Power Failure

There is no coverage for loss caused by the failure of power or other utility service if the failure takes place off the residence premises. For example, if the contents of a freezer thaw and spoil because a public utility plant malfunctions, the loss is not covered. However, if the power failure is caused by an insured peril on the residence premises, any resulting loss is covered. Thus, if lightning strikes the home and power is interrupted, the spoilage of food in a freezer is covered.

Neglect

If the insured neglects to use all reasonable means to save and preserve the property at or after the loss, or when the property is endangered by an insured peril, the loss is not covered.

War

Property damage from war is also specifically excluded. This exclusion is similar to the war exclusion clause contained in the standard fire policy.

Nuclear Hazard

Nuclear hazard losses are also excluded, including nuclear reaction, radiation, or radioactive contamination. For example, if a radiation leak from a nuclear power plant contaminates your property, the loss is not covered.

Intentional Loss

An intentional loss committed by or at the direction of an insured is specifically excluded. The new 1984 homeowners policy takes away coverage for *all insureds* when there is an intentional loss committed by or at the direction of *any insured.* Thus, no payment would be made to the innocent spouse of an arsonist who torched the family home.

Additional General Exclusions

The preceding eight general exclusions are now combined in one paragraph in the new 1984 policy. In addition, three new additional general exclusions have been added. They are:

1. *Weather conditions* that contribute to the loss in any way with a cause or event excluded by the general exclusions. (The general exclusions discussed earlier are found in paragraph one of the Section I—Exclusions section.)

2. *Acts or decisions*, including failure to act or decide by any person, group, organization, or government body.
3. *Faulty, inadequate, or defective* planning, zoning, design, workmanship, materials, or maintenance.

However, any ensuing loss to property described in Coverages A and B (dwelling and other structures) not excluded or excepted in the policy would be covered.

The purpose of the three new general exclusions is to eliminate coverage for losses that would be payable under the doctrine of **concurrent causation** which the courts in several jurisdictions, particularly California, have invoked with respect to flood and earth movement losses. *The doctrine of concurrent causation states that when a property loss is attributable to two causes, one that is excluded and one that is covered, the policy provides coverage.* For example, in one case, the court ruled that the exclusion of earth movement in an all-risk homeowners policy did not exclude damage to the insured's house from a landslide, because the faulty installation of a water drain by a third party was considered to be a covered, concurrent cause of loss.[7] In effect, the court said that the concurrence of an excluded peril (earth movement) along with a peril that was not excluded (third-party negligence in constructing the water drainage system) was sufficient for coverage to exist under the all-risks homeowners policy.

The new wording now eliminates coverage, even of an otherwise insured peril, when the loss is caused concurrently, or in any sequence, by any excluded peril. *However, it should be noted that the three new exclusions do not apply to any ensuing loss that is not excluded by the policy.* For example, if the insured claims that flooding or earth movement (excluded perils in paragraph one) has been caused by excessive rain, the loss would not be covered. But there would be coverage for losses caused by weather conditions if none of the paragraph one exclusions contributes to the loss. Thus, loss by windstorm alone would be covered.

This concludes our discussion of the general exclusions contained in Section I of the Homeowners 3 policy. Let us next examine some important policy conditions.

SECTION I—CONDITIONS

The conditions section of the homeowners policy contains numerous conditions. Only two of the most important will be discussed here.

Duties After a Loss

Certain duties are clearly imposed on the insured after a loss occurs. The following duties must be performed:

1. *Give immediate notice.* The insured must give immediate notice to the company or agent. In case of a theft, the police must also be notified. The credit card company must also be notified in case of loss or theft of a credit or fund transfer card.
2. *Protect the property.* The insured must protect the property from further damage, make reasonable and necessary repairs to protect the property, and keep an accurate record of the expenditures. For example, the windows may be broken and boarded up to protect against vandalism. The cost of boarding up is covered by the homeowners policy.
3. *Prepare an inventory of damaged personal property.* The inventory must show in detail the quantity, description, actual cash value, and the amount of loss.
4. *Exhibit the damaged property.* The insured may be required to show the damaged property to the insurer as often as is reasonably required. The insured may also be required to submit to an examination under oath.
5. *File a proof of loss within 60 days.* The proof of loss must include the time and cause of loss, interest of the insured and all others in the property, all liens on the property, other insurance covering the loss, and other relevant information.

Loss Settlement

Covered losses to *personal property* are paid on the basis of *actual cash value* at the time of loss but are not to exceed the amount necessary to repair or replace the property. However, it is possible to add an endorsement to the policy that covers personal property on the basis of replacement cost. This endorsement will be discussed later in the chapter.

Carpets, domestic appliances, awnings, outdoor antennas, and outdoor equipment, whether attached to the dwelling or not, are also indemnified on the basis of actual cash value.

Covered losses to the *dwelling and other structures* are paid on the basis of *replacement cost* with no deduction for depreciation. Replacement cost insurance is one of the most valuable and generous features of the homeowner policies. *If the amount of insurance carried is equal to at least 80 percent of the replacement cost of the damaged building at the time of loss, full replacement cost is paid with no deduction for depreciation up to the limits of the policy.* Replacement cost is the amount necessary to repair or replace the dwelling with material of like kind and quality at current prices. For example, assume that a home has a current replacement value of $100,000 and is insured for $80,000. If the home is damaged from a tornado, and damages are $20,000, the full $20,000 is paid with no deduction for depreciation. If the home is totally destroyed, however, the maximum amount paid is the face amount of the policy—in this case, $80,000.

A new set of rules applies if the amount of insurance is less than 80 percent of the replacement cost at the time of loss. Stated simply, *if the insurance carried is less than 80 percent of the replacement cost, the insured receives the larger of the following two amounts:*

1. *Actual cash value of that part of the building damaged*

or

2. $$\frac{\text{Amount of insurance carried}}{80\% \times \text{replacement cost}} \times \text{Loss} = \text{Amount paid}$$

For example, assume that a dwelling has a replacement cost of $100,000, but is insured for only $60,000. The roof of the house is ten years old and has a useful life of twenty years, or is 50 percent depreciated. Assume that the roof is severely damaged by a tornado, and that the replacement cost of a new roof is $20,000. Based on the preceding rules, the insured receives the larger of:

1. *Actual cash value* = *$10,000*

2. $$\frac{\$60{,}000}{\$80\% \times \$100{,}000} \times \$20{,}000 = \$15{,}000$$

The insured receives $15,000 for the loss. The entire loss would have been paid if the insured had carried a minimum of $80,000 of insurance.

Whenever the cost to repair or replace the damage is more than $1,000, or more than 5 percent of the amount of insurance on the building, whichever is less, the insured must actually repair or replace the damaged property to receive full replacement cost. Otherwise, the loss is paid on the basis of actual cash value until the actual repairs or replacement are completed. The insured can submit a claim for the actual cash value and then collect any additional amount he or she may have coming under the replacement cost provision as long as the additional claim is made within 180 days after the loss.

SECTION II—LIABILITY COVERAGES

The homeowners policy also covers the insured for personal liability and medical payments to other persons. *Personal liability coverage (Coverage E)* protects the insured and resident relatives against bodily injury or property damage liability claims made by third parties. The minimum amount of personal liability insurance that can be carried is $100,000 for each occurrence. This amount can, of course, be increased.

Medical payments insurance (Coverage F) is not based on legal liability and covers the medical expenses of persons, other than an insured, who are injured while on the insured premises, or are injured by some act of the insured, or by an animal of the insured. The minimum amount of coverage is $1,000 for each person. This amount can also be increased. The Section II liability coverages will be analyzed in greater detail in Chapter 10, after we have examined the law of negligence and legal liability.

SHOPPING FOR HOMEOWNERS INSURANCE

Careful insurance consumers should consider several important factors when a homeowners policy is purchased. You should remember the following suggestions when you shop for a homeowners policy:

1. Have adequate insurance amounts.
2. Don't ignore inflation.
3. Add necessary endorsements.
4. Consider cost.

Have Adequate Insurance

The first suggestion is to have adequate amounts of insurance on both your home and personal property. This is particularly important if a room is added to the house or substantial home improvements are made, since the value of the house may be substantially increased by the improvements. In any case, however, if you own your home, insurance at least equal to 80 percent of the replacement costs at the time of loss should be carried; otherwise, you will not collect the full replacement cost in the event of a partial loss. You might also consider carrying insurance equal to 100 percent of the replacement cost of the dwelling, because even if you meet the 80 percent requirement, you would still be seriously underinsured in the event of a total loss.

Don't Ignore Inflation

Many homeowners are underinsured because of inflation. This means that if you have a loss, the replacement cost provision with respect to the 80 percent rule may not be met. You will then be penalized, since the full replacement cost will not be paid.

To deal with inflation, you should add an **inflation-guard endorsement** to your homeowners policy. There are various inflation-guard endorsements. These endorsements provide for an annual pro rata increase, such as 6 or 8 percent in the limits of liability under Coverages A, B, C, and D. For example, if the policyholder selects an 8 percent inflation-guard endorsement, the various limits are increased by 8 percent annually. The specified annual percentage increase is prorated throughout the policy year. Thus, a house originally insured for $100,000 would be covered for $104,000 at the end of six months.

In some territories, the inflation-guard increases are not prorated over the entire year. Instead, the various limits are increased by some specified percentage, such as 1½ or 2 percent, every three months. Also, some inflation-guard endorsements are based on a *construction cost index*, which is a more accurate measure of determining the correct amount of insurance to own.

But a word of caution is in order. Although an inflation-guard endorsement is helpful in keeping your homeowners insurance up to date, it may not provide complete protection against inflation. The various limits may not increase precisely along with the inflation in property values. So you should periodically examine your insurance coverage to determine if it is adequate. The inflation-guard endorsement is no substitute for regular and careful review of insurance amounts on both the dwelling and the personal property contained within it.

Add Necessary Endorsements

In addition to the inflation-guard endorsement, certain other endorsements may be necessary in view of either local conditions or high values for certain types of property. Numerous endorsements can be added to the homeowners policy, but only a few will be mentioned here.

1. *Earthquakes.* If the homeowner lives in an area where earthquakes frequently occur, such as southern California, an **earthquake endorsement** can be added that covers earthquakes, landslides, volcanic eruption, and earth movement. A 2 percent deductible, expressed as a percentage of the amount of insurance, is applied to each loss. In some western states where the incidence of earthquakes is above average, a 5 percent deductible is frequently used. In either case, there is a minimum deductible of $250 for any loss. The deductible applies separately to the dwelling, other structures, and personal property.

2. *Scheduled personal property endorsement.* If the insured has valuable jewelry, furs, silverware, cameras, musical instruments, fine arts, antiques, stamp collections, or coin collections, this property should be scheduled and specifically insured to provide full coverage. This can be done by adding a **scheduled personal property endorsement** that provides all-risk (special) coverage on the scheduled items.

3. *Replacement cost endorsement.* As we noted earlier, a personal property **replacement cost endorsement** can be added to a homeowners policy that provides replacement cost coverage on personal property, which includes awnings, carpets, domestic appliances, and outdoor equipment. For example, assume that Mary's television set is stolen. The set originally cost $500. The replacement cost of a new comparable model is $1,000. If Mary has a $250 deductible, and the set is 50 percent depreciated, she would collect $250 under a conventional homeowner contract ($1000 – 500 – 250 = $250). However, with the replacement cost endorsement, she would collect $750 ($1000 – $250 = $750).

The replacement cost endorsement for personal property has several important limitations. The amount paid is limited to the *smallest* of five amounts. They are:

1. Replacement cost at the time of loss.
2. Full repair cost at the time of loss.
3. 400 percent of actual cash value.
4. Any special dollar limits in the policy (such as limits on jewelry, furs, and silverware).
5. Limit of liability on personal property.

In addition, if the replacement cost of the loss exceeds $500, the property must actually be repaired or replaced for the replacement cost provision to apply. Otherwise, only the actual cash value is paid.

The replacement cost endorsement also excludes certain types of property. They are:

- Antiques, fine arts, and similar property
- Collector's items and souvenirs
- Property that is not in good or workable condition
- Obsolete property that is stored or not used

These items are excluded because of loss adjustment problems and possible moral hazard. In particular, the last two items are excluded because payment of replacement cost would violate the principle of indemnity and cause an increase in moral hazard.

The cost of the replacement cost endorsement varies by company. In one company, the replacement cost endorsement will increase the premium by an additional 15 percent.

Consider Cost

The cost of homeowners insurance should also be considered. Homeowner premiums are based on a number of factors. They include the following:

- Construction
- Location
- Type of policy
- Deductible
- Company selected

First, the *construction* of the home is extremely important in determining the premium rate. The more fire-resistant the home is, the lower is the premium rate. Thus, a brick or stone home will have a lower rate than a frame home.

Second, the *location* of the home is an important factor in determining the premium rate. For rating purposes, the loss experience of each territory is determined. If the loss experience in a particular territory is poor, the rate will, of course, be higher than in territories with more favorable loss experience.

With respect to location, the *quality of the local fire department and available water supply* are extremely important factors in determining property insurance rates. The Insurance Services Office rates public fire departments in towns and cities on a scale of 1 to 10. The lower the score, the better the fire department is, and the lower is the normal rate. *Accessibility of the home* to the fire department is another factor in determining the rate. This is why homes in rural areas usually have higher rates than homes in large cities.

The *type of policy* is also important in determining the total premium. The Homeowners 3 policy (special form) is more expensive than the Homeowners 2 (broad form) because it gives broader coverage. Likewise, Homeowners 2 is more expensive than Homeowners 1 (basic form) since it covers additional perils.

The *size of the deductible and the company from which the policy is purchased* are also important. The higher the deductible, the lower is the premium. And the price of homeowners insurance depends on the company selected. Let us examine each of these two factors in greater detail.

The premiums for a homeowners policy can be substantially reduced by following two rules:

- **Select a higher deductible**
- **Shop around**

Select a higher deductible A flat $250 deductible now applies to all covered perils. However, as we noted earlier, the deductible does not apply to a fire department service charge; coverage for credit or fund transfer cards, forgery, or counterfeit money; scheduled property that is specifically insured; and the personal liability coverages under Section II.

Higher optional deductibles are now available with a substantial savings in premiums. For example, a $500 deductible could save you at least 10 percent of the standard premium in many companies.

Shop around The second rule for reducing homeowner premiums is to shop around. There is considerable price variation among property insurers, depending on loss experience, underwriting standards, and locality. Some states have prepared shoppers' guides to assist consumers when homeowner policies are purchased. For example, see Figure 7.2 for a comparison of homeowner premiums in Phoenix and Tucson,

Figure 7.2
1984 Annual Homeowners Premium Comparison

Company	Phoenix Premium	Tuscon Premium
Liberty Mutual Fire Insurance Co. (Liberty Mutual Insurance Group)	$158.00	$165.00
American Casualty Co. of Reading Pennsylvania (CNA Insurance Group)	174.00	171.00
Western Home Insurance Co. (Farmers Home Group)	178.00	166.00
Safeco Insurance Co. (Safeco Group)	179.00	182.00
United Services Automobile Association (USAA Group)	181.00	173.00
Westfield Insurance Co. (Westfield Companies Group)	185.00	185.00

Figure 7.2

Company	Phoenix Premium	Tuscon Premium
Unigard Mutual Insurance Co. (Unigard Insurance Group)	186.00	186.00
Fidelity and Guaranty Insurance Co. (United States Fidelity and Guaranty Insurance Group)	188.00	187.00
Civil Service Employees Insurance Co. (Civil Service Employees Group)	192.00	186.00
Transamerica Insurance Co. (Transamerica Group)	193.00	193.00
Farmers Insurance Co. of Arizona (Farmers Insurance Group)	195.00	180.00
American National Fire Insurance Co. (American Financial Insurance Group)	196.00	196.00
Sentry Insurance, a Mutual Co. (Sentry Insurance Group)	197.00	225.00
INA Underwriters Insurance Co. (CIGNA Group)	197.60	197.60
Travelers Indemnity Co. of Illinois (Travelers Group)	200.00	181.00
Twin City Fire Insurance Co. (Hartford Group)	200.00	191.00
Union Mutual Insurance Co. of Providence (Employers Mutual Group)	201.00	201.00
Continental Insurance Co. (Continental Corporation Group)	202.00	195.00
Standard Fire Insurance Co. (Aetna Life & Casualty Group)	203.00	192.00
All American Insurance Co. (Central Mutual Insurance Group)	204.00	215.00
United Pacific Insurance Co. (Reliance Group)	205.00	177.00
Allstate Insurance Co. (Allstate Group)	208.00	193.00
Royal Indemnity Insurance Co. (Royal Insurance Group)	208.00	208.00
Associated Indemnity Corporation (Fireman's Fund Insurance Group)	210.00	193.00
Federal Insurance Co. (CHUBB Group)	210.00	210.00
Home Insurance Co. (Home Insurance Group)	219.00	209.00
Northern Assurance Co. of America (Commercial Union Assurance Group)	221.00	223.00
State Farm Fire and Casualty Co. (State Farm Group)	223.00	189.00
Prudential Property and Casualty Insurance Co. (Prudential of America Group)	228.00	213.00
St. Paul Guardian Insurance Co. (St. Paul Group)	244.00	218.00
American Fire and Casualty Co. (Ohio Casualty Group)	245.00	245.00

Note: The premium comparison is based on a hypothetical residence built in 1980, having 2,200 square feet of living area and a current value of $80,000. Coverage for the following, after a $250 deductible, is included in the premiums listed: dwelling, $80,000; contents, $40,000; additional living expense, $8,000; personal liability, $100,000; and medical payments, $2,000. Many companies give discounts for newer homes and credits for smoke detectors, fire alarms, and other safety features.

SOURCE: "1984 Annual Homeowners Premium Comparison". Reprinted by permission of the Insurance Department of Arizona.

INSIGHT 7.1

Homeowner Discounts

Insurers offer a surprisingly wide variety of rate discounts and premium credits to policyholders who qualify. They include the following:

1. *Security devices.* A premium credit of 2 to 10 percent is frequently given for the installation of certain security devices, such as deadbolt locks on main doors, fire extinguishers, or electronic burglary and fire alarm systems.

2. *Smoke detector.* A 2 percent premium credit may be given for an approved smoke detector, which can prevent fire deaths and reduce property damage.

3. *Marking of valuables.* Rate discounts may be given if the policyholder marks easily stolen valuables, such as cameras, television sets, and stereo equipment. The insurer or agent usually provides a free marking device to mark the items.

4. *Nonsmokers.* Smoking is a leading cause of fires. Some insurers give a special discount for nonsmokers. To be eligible, all residents in the household must be nonsmokers who have not smoked for at least one year.

5. *New Home.* Many insurers give a rate discount for a newly built home. The discount typically ranges from 15 percent for a home less than two years old to 5 percent for a home four to five years old.

6. *Renovation of older home.* Some insurers give a sizeable rate discount if an older home is renovated, which usually includes revamping of the electrical, heating and cooling, and plumbing systems, and repair of the roof.

7. *Loss free experience.* Some insurers give a discount to homeowners who have not submitted a claim for a certain period, such as one to two years. The discount is lost when a loss is incurred.

8. *Inspection of the home.* In at least one state (Alaska), a premium credit can be given for a dwelling that is inspected.

SOURCE: Adaptation of "Homeowners Insurance" from *Journal of American Insurance*, Spring, 1981. Copyright © 1981 by the Alliance of American Insurers. Reprinted with permission.

Arizona. These guides have indicated a wide variation in premiums. Consequently, it will pay you to get a price quotation from several insurers before you buy a homeowners policy.

Also, when you shop for a homeowners policy, you should inquire whether you are eligible for any rate discounts or premium credits. Premiums can be further reduced by these discounts and credits (see Insight 7.1).

However, in shopping for a homeowners policy, price is not the only factor you should consider. Other important considerations include the financial strength and reputation of the insurer, quality of the agent and services provided, claim practices of the insurer, and policy provisions or limitations. However, all other factors being equal, a low-cost policy is preferable to a high-cost policy.

SUMMARY

- The homeowners policy is a package policy that covers the dwelling and other structures, personal property, additional living expenses, and personal-liability lawsuits.
- There are six homeowner forms under the 1984 Homeowners Program. HO-1 is a basic form that covers the dwelling and personal property on a named-perils basis. HO-2 is a broad form that expands the coverage under the basic form and adds additional perils. HO-3 is a special form that provides special coverage on the dwelling and named-perils coverage on personal property. HO-4 is designed for renters. HO-6 is designed for condominium owners. HO-8 is similar to the HO-1 form except that losses are indemnified on the basis of the amount required to repair or replace the property using common construction materials and methods.
- The homeowner forms contain two sections. Section I provides coverage on the dwelling, other structures, personal property, loss of use benefits, and additional coverages. Section II provides personal-liability insurance to the insured and also covers the medical expenses of others who may be injured while on the insured premises or by some act of the insured or by an animal of the insured.
- The conditions section imposes certain duties on the insured after a loss occurs. The insured must give immediate notice of the loss; the property must be protected from further damage; the insured must prepare an inventory of the damaged personal property and may be required to show the damaged property to the insurer as often as is reasonably required; and proof of loss must be filed within 60 days.
- The replacement cost provision is one of the most valuable features of the homeowners policy. Losses to the dwelling and other structures are paid on the basis of replacement cost if the insured carries insurance equal to at least 80 percent of the replacement cost at the time of loss. Losses to personal property are paid on the basis of actual cash value. However, an endorsement can now be added that covers personal property on a replacement cost basis.
- Certain rules should be followed when shopping for a homeowners policy. They are:
  a. Have adequate insurance amounts.
  b. Don't ignore inflation.
  c. Add necessary endorsements.
  d. Consider cost.

QUESTIONS FOR REVIEW

1. Explain the advantages of a package policy to the insured.
2. Describe the basic types of homeowner policies and indicate the groups for which each form is designed.
3. List the major coverages that are provided in Section I of the homeowners policy.
4. What additional coverages are provided in Section II of the homeowners policy?
5. Explain the special limits of liability that apply to certain types of property. Why are these limits used?
6. Describe the various exclusions that are found in the Homeowners 3 policy.
7. Explain the duties that are imposed on the insured after a loss occurs.

8. Explain the replacement cost provisions of the homeowners policy and give an example.
9. Explain briefly the rules that should be followed when shopping for a homeowners policy.
10. Explain briefly several endorsements that can be added to the homeowners policy.

QUESTIONS FOR DISCUSSION

1. Mary has her home and personal property insured under a Homeowners 3 (special form) policy. Indicate whether or not each of the following losses is covered. If the loss is not covered, explain why it is not covered.
   a. Mary carelessly spills a can of black enamel paint while painting a bedroom. A white wall-to-wall carpet is badly damaged and must be replaced.
   b. Water backs up from a clogged drainpipe, floods the basement, and damages some books stored in a box.
   c. Mary's house is totally destroyed in a tornado. Her valuable Doberman Pincher attack dog was killed in the tornado.
   d. Smoke from a nearby industrial plant damages Mary's freshly painted house.
   e. Mary is on vacation, and a thief breaks into her hotel and steals a suitcase containing jewelry, money, clothes, and an airline ticket.
   f. Mary's son is playing baseball in the yard. A line drive breaks the living room window.
   g. A garbage truck accidentally backs into the garage door and shatters it.
   h. Defective wiring causes a fire in the attic. Damage to the house is extensive. Mary is forced to move to a furnished apartment for three months while the house is being rebuilt.
   i. Mary's son is attending college but is home for Christmas vacation. A stereo set is stolen from his dormitory room during his absence.
   j. During the winter, heavy snow damages part of the front lawn, and the sod must be replaced.
   k. During a severe windstorm, a picket fence and an elm tree are blown over.
2. James has his home and personal property insured under a Homeowners 3 (special form) policy. The dwelling is insured for $48,000. The replacement cost of the home is $80,000, and its actual cash value is $60,000. Indicate the extent to which each of the following losses would be covered under James' Homeowners 3 policy. (Assume there is no deductible.)
   a. Lightning strikes the roof of the house and severely damages it. The actual cash value of the damaged roof is $10,000, and it will cost $16,000 to replace the damaged portion.
   b. A window in the living room is carelessly left open during a heavy rainstorm. The drapes are water stained and must be replaced. The actual cash value of the damaged drapes is $200, and their replacement cost is $300.
   c. The hot water heater explodes and damages some household contents. The actual cash value of the damaged property is $1,000, and the cost of replacing the property is $1,600.
3. Sarah owns a valuable diamond ring that has been in her family for generations. She is told by an appraiser that the ring has a current market value of $20,000. She feels that the ring is adequately insured since she owns a Homeowners 3 (special form) policy. Is Sarah correct in her thinking? If not, how would you advise her concerning proper protection of the ring?
4. Paul has his home and its contents insured under a Homeowners 3 (special form) policy. He carries $80,000 of insurance on the home which has a replacement cost of $100,000. Explain

the extent to which each of the following losses is covered. (Assume there is no deductible). If Paul's policy does not cover the loss, or inadequately covers any of these losses, show how full coverage can be obtained.

a. Paul's coin collection, which is valued at $5,000, is stolen from his home.

b. Teenage vandals break into Paul's home and rip up a painting owned by Paul's wife. The painting is valued at $1,000.

c. A motorboat stored in the driveway of Paul's home is badly damaged during a hailstorm. The actual cash value of the damaged portion is $1,000, and its replacement cost is $1,500.

5. Margaret is an elderly widow who is disabled and must live on a relatively fixed income. She has an inflation-guard endorsement attached to her homeowners policy. She gets upset when she receives her annual premium notice, since every year the premiums appear to be substantially higher than the year before. She feels that she should drop the inflation-guard endorsement so that her premiums will not continually increase.

   a. Explain the *nature* and *purpose* of the inflation-guard endorsement.

   b. Do you agree with Margaret? Explain why or why not.

   c. Explain to Margaret how she can reduce the premiums under her homeowners policy without dropping the inflation-guard endorsement.

6. The new 1984 Homeowners Program by the Insurance Services Office is designed to meet the legal doctrine of *concurrent causation.*

   a. Explain the legal doctrine of concurrent causation. In your answer, give an example of concurrent causation.

   b. Give one illustration of how the legal doctrine of concurrent causation is effectively met by a policy provision in the new 1984 Homeowners Program.

KEY CONCEPTS AND TERMS TO KNOW

Package policy
HO-1 (basic form)
HO-2 (broad form)
HO-3 (special form)
HO-4 (contents broad form)
HO-6 (unit-owners form)
HO-8 (modified coverage form)
Additional living expenses
Fair rental value
Prohibited use
Replacement cost provisions
Schedule
Concurrent causation
Inflation-guard endorsement
Earthquake endorsement
Scheduled personal property endorsement
Replacement cost endorsement

SUGGESTIONS FOR ADDITIONAL READING

Fire, Casualty & Surety Bulletins. Personal Lines Volume, Dwelling Section. Cincinnati, Ohio: The National Underwriter Company.

Greene, Mark R. and James S. Trieschmann. *Risk and Insurance,* 6th ed. Cincinnati, Ohio: Southwestern Publishing Company, 1984, chapter 11.

"ISO's New Homeowners '84," *Independent Agent* 81, No. 8 (April 1984), pp. 63–65.

Wood, Glenn L., Claude C. Lilly, III, Donald S. Malecki, and Jerry S. Rosenbloom. *Personal Risk Management and Insurance*, 3rd ed., Volume I. Malvern, Pennsylvania: American Institute for Chartered Property and Liability Underwriters, 1984, chapter 4.

NOTES

1. David L. Bickelhaupt, *General Insurance*, 10th ed. (Homewood, Illinois: Richard D. Irwin, Inc., 1979), pp. 776–77.
2. Robert S. Cline and George B. Flanigan, "The Homeowner's Program Revisited," *The Journal of Insurance Issues and Practices*, 2 (Winter 1978–79), p. 81.
3. The discussion of homeowners insurance in this chapter is based on material drawn from Glenn L. Wood, Claude C. Lilly, III, Donald S. Malecki, and Jerry S. Rosenbloom, *Personal Risk Management and Insurance*, 3rd ed., Volume I (Malvern, Pennsylvania: American Institute for Chartered Property and Liability Underwriters, 1984), chapter 4; *Fire, Casualty & Surety Bulletins*, Personal Lines Volume, Dwelling Section; and George E. Guinane, *Homeowners Guide* (Indianapolis, Indiana: The Rough Notes Company, 1977).
4. The Section I coverages are not applicable to HO-4 and HO-6.
5. The amount of insurance on personal property (Coverage C) can be reduced to a minimum of 40 percent of the insurance on the dwelling.
6. Wood, p. 197.
7. *Premier Insurance Company v. Welch*, 1983 C.C.H. Fire & Casualty 1274.

CHAPTER 8

OTHER PROPERTY INSURANCE COVERAGES

"Variety is the very spice of life."
William Cowper, Olney Hymns (1779)

STUDENT LEARNING OBJECTIVES

After studying this chapter, you should be able to:

- Describe the four forms that are used in the Dwelling 77 Program.
- Explain how a mobile home can be adequately insured.
- Show how recreational boats can be insured.
- Describe the types of property that can be insured under the Personal Articles Floater.
- Explain the major provisions of the following federal property insurance programs:
  - flood insurance
  - FAIR plans
  - crime insurance

In this chapter, we will continue our discussion of property insurance by examining some additional coverages that can be used by individuals and families. We will first consider the Dwelling 77 Policy Program, which is another example of the trend toward simplified and readable contracts. We will then discuss some property insurance contracts that can be used to insure mobile homes, recreational boats, and valuable personal property such as jewelry and furs. We will conclude the chapter by examining some federal property insurance programs, including federal flood insurance, FAIR plans, and federal crime insurance.

DWELLING 77 POLICY PROGRAM

The Dwelling 77 Program is designed for dwellings that are ineligible for coverage under the standard homeowner contracts and for persons who do not want or need a homeowners contract. Most of these homes can be insured under a Dwelling 77 policy.

Eligible Dwellings

Several types of residential properties are eligible for coverage. The dwelling forms can be used to insure a one to four family building that is occupied as a residence. Certain incidental business operations are permitted in the dwelling. They include a private school, a studio, an office, and a small service operation, such as a beauty parlor or telephone answering service. A completed home or a home under construction can also be insured under the dwelling forms; the home may be occupied by its owner or by a renter. A townhouse or rowhome can be similarly covered if the structural unit does not exceed four families in size. Even a mobile or trailer home can be insured if the policy period does not exceed one year, and if the mobile home or trailer remains at a permanent location described in the property.

Certain types of dwellings are ineligible for coverage. Farm dwellings and dwellings that house more than five boarders or roomers cannot be insured under the dwelling forms.

Types of Dwelling Forms

There are four dwelling property forms that can be used to insure the dwelling and personal property.[1] They are:

- Dwelling Property 1 (basic form)
- Dwelling Property 2 (broad form)
- Dwelling Property 3 (special form)
- Dwelling Property 8 (modified coverage form)

Let us briefly examine each of these forms.

Dwelling Property 1 (basic form) The *basic form* can be used to insure any of the eligible dwellings described earlier. Several coverages are provided, which are similar to the homeowner coverages discussed in Chapter 7. Coverage A insures the *dwelling* and structures attached to the dwelling. *However, losses are indemnified on the basis of actual cash value, not replacement cost.*

Coverage B provides insurance on *other structures,* such as a detached garage, tennis court, or tool shed. Under the basic form, 10 percent of the amount of the insurance on the dwelling can be applied to cover other structures. However, this is not additional insurance.

Coverage C insures *personal property* that is owned or used by the insured and residing family members. Personal property away from the premises is also covered. The insured can apply up to 10 percent of the insurance under Coverage C to cover personal property anywhere in the world. Again, the extension of coverage is not additional insurance.

Coverage D covers the *fair rental value* if a loss makes part of the dwelling rented to others or held for rental unfit for normal use. A maximum of 10 percent of the insurance on the dwelling can be applied to cover the loss of rents, subject to a maximum monthly limit of 1/12 of that 10 percent. For example, if the dwelling is insured for \$48,000, a total of \$4,800 can be applied to cover the loss of rents, with a maximum monthly limit of \$400 (1/12 × \$4800). This insurance is not additional insurance.

Finally, *other coverages* are also provided. These coverages include the cost of removing debris, the cost of reasonable repairs to protect the property from further damage, and coverage on property being removed from the premises because it is endangered by an insured peril.

The basic form covers only a limited number of perils. The perils of fire, lightning, and internal explosion can be purchased alone. The insured also has the option of adding the extended coverage perils plus vandalism and malicious mischief by payment of an additional premium. The **extended coverage perils** are windstorm or hail, explosion, riot or civil commotion, aircraft, vehicles, and smoke. Thus, the following perils can be covered:

1. Fire, lightning, internal explosion.
2. Windstorm or hail.
3. Explosion.
4. Riot or civil commotion.
5. Aircraft.
6. Vehicles.
7. Smoke.
8. Vandalism or malicious mischief.

Dwelling Property 2 (broad form) The *broad form* extends the coverages contained in the basic form. Covered losses to the dwelling and other structures are indemnified on the basis of *replacement cost* rather than actual cash value. The replacement cost provisions are similar to those found in the homeowner contracts. In addition to Coverages A, B, C, and D, the broad form adds a new benefit for additional living expenses (Coverage E). If a covered loss makes the property unfit for normal use, the additional increase in living expenses is paid.

The broad form covers all of the perils that can be insured under the basic form, plus other perils. The covered perils are as follows:

Perils 1–7. Fire, lightning, and extended-coverage perils.

8. Vandalism or malicious mischief.
9. Breakage of glass or safety glazing material.
10. Burglars.
11. Falling objects.
12. Weight of ice, snow, or sleet.
13. Collapse of buildings or any part of a building.
14. Accidental discharge or overflow of water or steam.
15. Explosion of steam or hot water system, air conditioning system, or appliances for heating water.
16. Freezing of a plumbing, heating, air conditioning system, or household appliance.
17. Sudden and accidental damage from an artificially generated electrical current.

Dwelling Property 3 (special form) The *special form* covers the dwelling, other structures, and any other property covered under Coverage A or Coverage B *against direct physical loss from any peril except for those perils otherwise excluded.* Personal property is covered for the same *named perils* that are found in the Dwelling Property 2 (broad form) policy discussed earlier.

Dwelling Property 8 (modified coverage form) The Insurance Services Office has introduced the *modified coverage form* in some states; it is designed for a homeowner who has an older home with a market value substantially below its replacement cost. The modified coverage form is identical to the basic form described earlier with one major exception—buildings are indemnified on the basis of *repair cost* rather than actual cash value.

Under the repair cost provisions, the amount paid is based on the actual cost of repairing the damaged building using common construction materials and methods that are functionally equivalent to and less costly than obsolete, antique, or custom materials. For example, a plaster wall would be repaired with less costly drywall and slate shingles with asphalt shingles. Of course, if the total repair cost exceeds the policy limit, the smaller amount is paid.

The repair cost provisions require the insured to restore the damaged building on the same site and for the same occupancy and use within 180 days after the loss. If the insured does not restore the building according to the repair cost provisions, the repair cost option is forfeited, and settlement is based on the smallest of (1) policy limit, (2) market value of the building (excluding the value of the land), or (3) the cost to repair or replace the damaged building with materials of like kind and quality less depreciation. Thus, if a building is highly depreciated, the insured has a greater incentive to restore the building rather than receive the actual cash value.

MOBILE HOME INSURANCE

Mobile homes are becoming increasingly popular. Because of the rapid increase in the prices of both older and newer homes, many middle-income and low-income families are being priced out of the market for conventional housing. Thus, there is greater interest in the less expensive forms of housing, such as mobile homes.

Mobile home insurance is presently written by an endorsement to either Homeowners 2 or Homeowners 3, which tailor the homeowners policy to meet the characteristics of mobile homes.[2]

Eligibility

To be eligible for coverage, the mobile home must cost at least $4,000 when new and must be at least ten feet wide and forty feet long. In addition, it must be capable of being towed on its own chassis, and it must be designed for year-round living. The policy can be issued only to the owner-occupant of the mobile home, and the occupancy must be only for private residential purposes. These requirements are imposed to eliminate coverage for camper trailers that are pulled by automobiles and are insured under an automobile policy.

Coverages

The coverages on a mobile home are similar to those found in homeowner contracts (see Figure 8.1). Coverage A insure the mobile home on a replacement cost basis. In addition, floor coverings, household appliances, dressers, cabinets, and other built-in furniture are also covered when installed on a permanent basis. Coverage A also applies to utility tanks and other structures attached to the mobile home such as a carport or small storage shed.

Some mobile homes have depreciated to the point where replacement cost coverage is inappropriate. In such cases, an optional cash value endorsement can be added, which limits the insurer's obligation to the lowest of: (1) repair cost, (2) replacement with similar property but not necessarily from the same manufacturer, or (3) actual cash value of the damaged property.

Company B insures other structures subject to a minimum limit of $2,000. Coverage C insures unscheduled personal property and is limited to 40 percent of Coverage A. Coverage D provides

Figure 8.1
Mobile Home Policy Coverage Provisions

Coverage A—Dwelling	$10,000 minimum
Coverage B—Other structures	10% of Coverage A ($2,000 minimum)
Coverage C—Personal property	40% of Coverage A
Coverage D—Loss of use	20% of Coverage A
Coverage E—Personal liability	$100,000
Coverage F—Medical payments to others	$1,000 for each person

for loss of use coverage and is 20 percent of the Coverage A limit.

In addition, the mobile home endorsement provides for an additional coverage that pays up to $500 for the cost incurred in transporting the mobile home to a safe place when it is endangered from a covered peril. The $500 limit can be increased to a maximum of $2,500 by an additional premium.

Finally, Coverages E and F provide for comprehensive personal liability insurance and medical payments to others. This coverage is identical to the coverage provided in the homeowner contracts. Comprehensive personal liability insurance will be discussed in Chapter 10.

INSURANCE ON PLEASURE BOATS

Millions of boats are used in the United States each year for pleasure purposes. But the homeowner contracts provide only limited coverage of boats, up to a maximum of $1,000 and theft of the boat away from the premises is excluded. Consequently, specific insurance on a valuable boat is often needed.

Insurance on pleasure boats generally can be divided into two major categories:

- Personal yacht insurance
- Boat owners package policy

Let us briefly examine each of these categories.

Personal Yacht Insurance

Personal yacht insurance is a form of ocean marine insurance that is designed for larger boats, such as cabin cruisers, inboard motorboats, and sailing vessels. Personal yacht insurance provides several coverages. They include the following:

1. **Hull insurance.** Hull insurance is the term used to describe physical damage coverage on the boat. In addition to the boat, the sails, tackle, machinery, furniture, and other equipment are also covered. The insurance is typically written on an all-risk basis, which means all physical damage losses from external causes are covered, except those losses specifically excluded. Thus, if the boat is damaged by heavy seas, high winds, flood, collision with another vessel, or sinks because of an insured peril, the loss is covered. A deductible of varying amounts normally applies to all physical damage losses.
2. **Protection and indemnity insurance.** This coverage is a form of marine liability insurance. The owner of the vessel is covered for property damage and bodily injury liability on an indemnity basis. For example, if the owner of the boat carelessly damages the dock of a marina and is sued, the property damage to the marina is covered under this section.
3. **Medical payments insurance.** This is similar to the medical payments coverage in an automobile insurance policy. If an insured person is injured while in or upon the boat, reasonable medical expenses incurred are paid up to some maximum limit.
4. **Federal compensation.** Longshoremen and harbor workers who are injured on vessels and drydocks are typically excluded from coverage under a state workers' compensation law. A federal law called the United States Longshoremen and Harbor Workers Compensation Act covers these workers for a job-related accident or disease. The personal yacht policy covers the possible liability of the insured under that act for the accidents and injuries to maritime workers during the course of their employment.

Boat Owners Package Policy

Many companies have developed special package policies for boat owners, such as owners of large outboard motorboats. Although the package policies are not uniform, they contain certain common features. The major coverages are summarized as follows.

1. *Physical damage coverage.* Most boat owner policies are currently written on an *all-risk basis*. Under the physical damage

section of a boat owners package policy, the boat, equipment, accessories, motors, and trailer are covered on an all-risk basis. All losses are covered except those losses specifically excluded. For example, if the boat is damaged from heavy winds, collides with another boat, or is stolen, the loss is covered.

2. *Liability coverage.* Liability insurance is also included that covers the insured for property damage and bodily injury liability from the negligent operation of the boat. For example, if an operator carelessly runs into another boat and damages it, swamps another boat, or accidentally injures some swimmers, these losses are covered under liability insurance.
3. *Medical payments coverage.* This coverage is similar to those found in automobile insurance contracts. Medical payments coverage pays the reasonable expenses of any person who is injured in an accident while in, on, boarding, or leaving the insured boat, or while being towed as a water skier. The medical expenses must be incurred within a certain time period, which usually ranges from one to three years.

PERSONAL ARTICLES FLOATER

The **Personal Articles Floater** (PAF) is the principal contract that is now used to insure certain types of valuable personal property that are moved frequently among different locations. As we have seen, the homeowner contracts contain limitations on certain types of valuable property. Coin collections are limited to a maximum of $200; stamp collections are limited to $1,000; the theft of jewelry and furs is limited to $1,000; and the theft of silverware and goldware is limited to $2,500. Higher amounts of insurance can be obtained on a scheduled basis under the PAF.

All-Risk Coverage

The PAF covers listed personal property on an *all-risk basis.* With the exception of fine arts, coverage for most classes of property is worldwide in scope.

In addition, certain types of newly acquired property are automatically covered. *This extension applies only to jewelry, watches, furs, cameras, and musical instruments.* Protection is automatically provided for thirty days if insurance is already written on that class of property. For example, a professional photographer may have insured a $10,000 camera under the PAF. If a new camera is acquired, the coverage automatically applies for thirty days. Any new acquisitions must be reported to the company, and an additional premium must be paid. The amount of insurance that can be acquired under this extension is limited to a maximum of 25 percent of the amount of insurance that applies to each class, or $10,000, whichever is less.

Although the PAF is an all-risk contract, certain general exclusions apply to all classes of scheduled property. Losses from the following perils are not covered:

- Wear and tear
- Gradual deterioration
- Damage from insects and vermin
- Inherent vice
- Nuclear energy
- War

Types of Covered Property

A wide variety of personal property can be insured under the PAF. The form is especially valuable if expensive personal property is moved frequently to different locations.

Cameras Most photographic equipment, including cameras, projection machines, portable sound and recording equipment, films, binoculars, and telescopes, can be insured under the PAF. Each item must be individually described and valued. Miscellaneous small items, such as carrying cases, filters, and holders can be written on a *blanket basis* without scheduling each item, provided the amount is not more than 10 percent of the total amount insured in the schedule. Television cameras and equipment, coin operated devices, and cameras of dealers or manufacturers are not covered under this form.

Fine arts Fine arts can also be insured under the PAF. This includes paintings, antique furniture, rare books, statuary, rare glass and bric-a-brac, and manuscripts. *Coverage of fine arts is on a valued basis.* Thus, if a rare painting burns in a fire, the amount of insurance listed in the schedule for that item is the amount paid.

In addition, newly acquired property is automatically covered for ninety days. The insured must notify the company within ninety days and pay an additional premium.

Several important exclusions apply to fine arts. The following losses are specifically excluded:

1. Damage from any repairing, restoration, or retouching process is specifically excluded.
2. There is no coverage for the breakage of art glass windows, statuary (except metal statuary), marbles, glassware, and similar fragile articles. Breakage can be covered with an additional premium. However, loss from fire, lightning, aircraft, theft, windstorm, earthquake, flood, explosion, malicious damage, collision, derailment, or overturn of a conveyance would be covered.
3. There is no coverage for property on exhibition at fair grounds or on the premises of national or international expositions unless the premises are specifically described in the contract.

Golfer's equipment Golf clubs, golf carts, and other golf equipment are covered on an all-risk basis anywhere in the world. The golfer's clothes in a clubhouse locker or other building used in connection with the game of golf are also covered. Golf balls are covered only for loss by fire and by burglary (when there are visible marks of forcible entry).

Furs Personal furs and garments trimmed with fur, imitation fur, items consisting principally of fur, and fur rugs can be insured under the PAF. Each item must be listed separately with a specific amount of insurance for each item.

Because of moral hazard, insurance on furs is carefully underwritten. Coverage is restricted to persons of high integrity and satisfactory financial resources. The company requires information concerning the insured's background, occupation, and sources of income. The insured may also be required to complete a form showing where the furs were purchased and the price paid or provide an appraisal from a reputable furrier. Many companies will not insure furs for more than the original purchase price regardless of their appraisal value. In addition, many underwriters require a bill of sale, even when an appraisal is furnished.

Personal jewelry Coverage for personal jewelry applies on an all-risk basis anywhere in the world. Each item must be described and a specific amount of insurance shown for it. This includes watches, precious stones, and necklaces.

Because of moral hazard, insurance on jewelry is carefully underwritten. The insured must be of high moral character, have satisfactory financial resources, and not be in the habit of misplacing or losing articles. Original bills of sale or a signed appraisal from a reputable jeweler are normally required. Some companies require an appraisal only if the insurance exceeds $1,000, but the purchase price and the date of purchase are still required. If the jewelry is in need of repair, or the stones must be reset, they must be restored to a first-class condition before the insurance can be issued.

Musical instruments Musical instruments can also be insured under the PAF. Instrument cases, sound and amplifying equipment, and similar equipment can also be insured. Coverage is on an all-risk basis anywhere in the world.

An important exclusion applies to this coverage. Instruments played for *remuneration* during the policy period are not covered unless an endorsement is added to the policy and a higher premium paid. For example, a professional musician who plays in a night club or bar would have to pay a higher premium to have his or her musical instruments covered. This exclusion also applies to amateur musicians who are sometimes paid for their performances.

Silverware Silverware and goldware collections are often extremely valuable. As we noted earlier, the homeowners policy provides only maximum coverage of $2,500. Higher amounts can be obtained by the PAF.

Stamp and coin collections Stamp and coin collections are covered against all risks of physical loss on a worldwide basis. The items can be insured on a *blanket basis* by which each item is not specifically described, and the insurance applies to the entire collection. But if the items are valuable, they should be *scheduled*, so that each item is specifically listed and insured. There is no automatic coverage for newly acquired stamps or coins. When new additions to the collection are made, the coverage can be increased by an immediate endorsement to the policy.

Certain losses to coins and stamps are specifically excluded. They include the following:

1. There is no coverage for fading, creasing, denting, scratching, tearing, thinning, transfer of colors, inherent defect, dampness, extremes of temperature, gradual depreciation, or damage from handling or working on the property.
2. Theft from an unattended automobile is excluded unless the property is being shipped by registered mail.
3. Mysterious disappearance of unscheduled items is not covered unless they are mounted in a volume and the page to which they are attached is also lost.
4. Stamps or coins in the custody of transportation companies are excluded. Shipments by mail are also excluded except shipments by registered mail.
5. Property that is not actually part of a stamp or coin collection is not covered.

In the case of loss to *unscheduled property*, the cash market value is the basis of recovery. However, there is a $1,000 maximum limit on numismatic property, and a $250 maximum limit on any stamp, coin, or individual article, or any one pair, block, or series. Thus, items worth over $250 should be scheduled and specifically insured.

FEDERAL PROPERTY INSURANCE PROGRAMS

Federal insurance programs are necessary because certain perils are difficult to insure privately, and because insurance may not be available at affordable premiums from private insurers. Although there are numerous federal insurance programs, we will limit our discussion to the following:

- Federal flood insurance
- FAIR plans
- Federal crime insurance

Federal Flood Insurance

Buildings exposed to damage from a flood are difficult to insure privately without some government assistance. The requirements of an insurable risk that we explained in Chapter 2 are not easily met. The exposure units in flood-prone areas are not independent of each other, so that if a flood occurs, a catastrophic loss may result. Hence the premiums for property insurance in flood areas would be too high for most insureds to pay. The problem of adverse selection also makes the flood peril difficult to insure privately, since only property owners in flood-prone areas are likely to seek protection. So financial assistance from the federal government is necessary.

The **federal flood insurance** program was created by the National Flood Insurance Act of 1968. The purpose of the Act was to provide flood insurance at subsidized rates to persons who reside in flood areas. Flood insurance is provided by the Federal Insurance Administration (FIA), which is a department of the Federal Emergency Management Agency (FEMA). Flood insurance is now available to property owners in flood zones in every state, as well as the District of Columbia, Puerto Rico, and the Virgin Islands.

The program originally was a joint undertaking of the federal government and private insurers. The partnership between the federal government and private insurers ended in 1978 when the federal government took over the program. However, in late 1983, the federal government enacted a *write-your-own-program* to encourage private insurers to write flood insurance with financial assistance provided by the federal government.

Under the write-your-own-program, private insurers will sell flood insurance under their own names, collect the premiums, retain a specified percentage for commissions and expenses, and invest the remaining premiums. The companies service the flood insurance contracts, adjust losses, and pay their own claims. If the insurers' losses are not covered by premiums and investment income, they will be reimbursed for the difference. However, any flood insurance profits will be turned over to the United States Treasury.[3]

The FIA will continue to determine eligibility, rates, and coverage limitations. Flood insurance can be obtained from any licensed insurance agent or broker. Agents and brokers who are not affiliated with the private insurers can continue to write federal flood insurance directly with the National Flood Insurance Program (NFIP). Let us briefly examine some major features of the current flood insurance program.[4]

Eligibility requirements Most buildings and their contents can be insured for flood insurance if the community agrees to adopt and enforce sound flood control and land use measures. More than 17,000 communities are now participating in the program.

When a community first joins the program, it is provided with a flood hazard boundary map that shows the general area of flood losses, and residents are allowed to purchase limited amounts of insurance at subsidized rates under the emergency portion of the program.

FEMA then studies the community and prepares a flood insurance rate map, which divides the community into specific zones to determine the degree of flooding to which the insurable buildings are exposed. When this map is prepared, and the community agrees to adopt more stringent flood control and land use measures, the community enters the regular phase of the program, and substantially higher amounts of flood insurance can then be purchased at actuarial rates.

To encourage community participation in the flood insurance program, lending institutions that make federally insured loans cannot approve mortgages on property in flood zones unless federal flood insurance is purchased. In addition, property owners in flood zones are ineligible for federal disaster relief benefits if they have not purchased flood insurance. As a result of these requirements, the sales of federal flood insurance policies have increased dramatically.

Finally, certain dwellings are ineligible for coverage. They include (1) homes built over water or below a high tide line, (2) unanchored mobile homes in special hazard areas, and (3) mobile homes placed in parks that were opened in coastal high hazard areas after April 1, 1982.

Amounts of insurance Under the *emergency* program, the amount of federal insurance that can be purchased at subsidized rates is limited to $35,000 on a single-family dwelling and $10,000 on the contents. The owner of a single-family dwelling pays 45¢ for each $100 of coverage on the dwelling. For other residential structures, the maximum amount of insurance is limited to $100,000.

Under the *regular* program, the maximum amount of coverage for a single-family home is $185,000 and $60,000 on the contents. Other residential structures can be insured up to $250,000. Rates under the regular program vary according to the type of construction and location of the property.

A $500 deductible applies separately to both the building and contents. In addition, there is a $250 aggregate limit on jewelry, precious metals, and furs. A similar $250 limit applies to paintings and other art objects.

Definition of flood **Flood** is defined as a general and temporary condition of partial or complete inundation of normally dry areas from (1) the overflow of inland or tidal waters, (2) the unusual and rapid accumulation of runoff or surface waters from any source, and (3) mudslide. Thus, flood damage caused by an overflow of rivers, streams, or other bodies of water, by abnormally high waves, or by severe storms is covered. Mudslide damage is also covered if the mudslide is caused by the accumulation of water on the earth's surface or under the ground.

Mudslide damage that is caused by conditions on the property or by conditions within the insured's control is not covered. A general condition of flooding must first exist. For example, water damage from a broken water pipe or clogged sewer is not covered. Property damage from water seepage or from the backup of sewers is covered only if the loss results from a general flooding condition.

FAIR Plans

During the 1960s, major riots occurred in many cities in the United States, resulting in millions of dollars of property damage. Consequently, many property owners in riot-prone areas were unable to obtain property insurance at affordable premiums. This problem resulted in the creation of **FAIR plans** (Fair Access to Insurance Requirements), which were enacted into law as a result of the Urban Property and Reinsurance Act of 1968. The basic purpose of a FAIR plan is to make property insurance available to urban property owners who are unable to obtain coverage in the normal markets. FAIR plans typically provide coverage for fire and extended-coverage insurance, vandalism, malicious mischief, and, in a few states, crime insurance. FAIR plans exist in twenty-six states, the District of Columbia, and Puerto Rico. In addition, beach and windstorm plans exist in seven states along the Atlantic and Gulf Coast seaboard where property is highly vulnerable to damage from severe windstorms and hurricanes.[5]

If a property owner is unable to obtain insurance in the normal markets, he or she can apply for coverage through a FAIR plan. The property is inspected before the policy is issued. The inspection reveals the true physical condition of the property and eliminates the possibility that the owner of insurable property will be denied insurance solely because of location. If the property meets certain reasonable underwriting standards, it can be insured at standard rates that the state periodically determines. If the building is substandard, it may still be insurable at substantially higher premiums. In some cases, the insurance may be refused unless the property owner makes certain improvements in the property to bring it up to acceptable underwriting standards. Once the improvements are made, the property is reinspected, and the insurance is granted if the recommendations have been followed. Finally, the insurance may be denied because the property is considered uninsurable. The applicant must be told why the property cannot be insured. However, the insurance cannot be denied because the property is located in a riot-prone area or is exposed to other environmental hazards.

Each state with a FAIR plan has a central placement facility and a reinsurance association or pool. The placement facility assigns the approved applications to individual insurers who are members of the reinsurance association or pool. The applications are assigned according to a formula that considers the proportion of premiums written in the state by each participating insurer. The participating insurers pay their share of losses and expenses based on the proportion of property insurance premiums that they write in the state.

In addition, under the original act, insurers participating in the state's FAIR plan were eligible to purchase federal riot reinsurance that provided protection against catastrophic losses from riots or civil disorders. However, in 1983, Congress enacted legislation that would terminate the offering of riot reinsurance to reinsurers. Contracts that were still in force at the time the legislation was enacted were permitted to expire (on September 30, 1984), but no new reinsurance contracts were to be written. The primary purpose for the legislation was the relatively small number of insurers that purchased the reinsurance.

FAIR plans are highly controversial at the present time. It was argued that FAIR plans are no longer needed and should be phased out, since the social threat of widespread riot losses has subsided. Also, some critics charge that property insurers have used the FAIR plans to rid themselves of undesirable business, such as bowling alleys, bars, and restaurants. In rebuttal, property insurers maintain that FAIR plan premiums are inadequate, and that they have incurred sizable underwriting losses since the plans began operating.

Federal Crime Insurance

Persons residing in high crime rate areas often find it difficult to obtain crime insurance at *affordable rates.* For that reason, **federal crime insurance** became operational in 1971. Since then, the federal government has provided crime insurance at subsidized rates in those areas where the Federal Insurance Administration has determined that insurance is not available at affordable rates. Federal crime insurance can be purchased in twenty-seven states, the District of Columbia, Puerto Rico, and the Virgin Islands.[6] The insurance is sold by licensed agents and brokers in the eligible states, and the policies are issued and maintained by servicing insurers. A servicing insurer has a contract with the Federal Insurance Administration to perform various insurance functions in selling crime insurance in a specific area. However, the Federal Insurance Administration is the actual insurer.

There are two federal crime insurance contracts: (1) a residential policy and (2) a commercial crime policy. Only the residential policy is discussed here.[7]

Eligibility To qualify for federal crime insurance, homeowners or renters must maintain certain protective devices, such as door and window locks that meet certain specifications. In addition, all covered losses must be reported to the police even if a claim is not filed.

Federal crime insurance can be written on property located in a dwelling (one to four family unit) or in the insured's living quarters in an apartment building or dormitory. However, the insurance cannot be written for residents in a hotel unless the hotel is a residence hotel where the average stay of a tenant exceeds six months.

Coverages The residential crime policy covers the loss of personal property from a burglary or robbery while the property is on the insured premises or is in the presence of the insured. **Burglary** is the unlawful taking of property from within the premises by someone who uses force or violence to gain entry, and there are visible marks of entry on the exterior of the premises. **Robbery** is the unlawful taking of another person's property by violence or threat of violence. For example, if a thief breaks into your apartment when you are gone and steals a television or stereo set, the loss is covered. If a robber mugs you in a subway and steals your wallet or purse, the loss is covered.

The residential crime policy also covers damage to the insured premises from a burglary or robbery and damage to the insured's living quarters or personal property caused by vandalism or malicious mischief.

Insurance amounts The minimum amount of federal crime insurance that can be carried is $1,000, and the maximum is $10,000. All covered losses are subject to a deductible of 5 percent of the amount of the gross loss, or $100, whichever is higher.

Regardless of the number of claims submitted, the Federal Insurance Administration has only a limited right of cancellation. The insurance can be cancelled or not renewed only under certain conditions stated in the policy.

Despite the high incidence of crime, federal crime insurance is not widely sold. At the end of 1982, only 44,710 residential crime policies were in force. New York alone accounted for about 59 percent of the residential policies and about 62 percent of the total insurance in force.[8] The slow growth is due partly to the lack of enthusiasm by agents and brokers, relatively low commission rates, and stringent federal standards for protective devices. Vocal critics of government insurance programs are pushing hard for the elimination of federal crime insurance, and, unless extended by Congress, the program is scheduled to expire in September 1985.

SUMMARY

- The Dwelling 77 Program further illustrates the trend towards more readable and simplified contracts. This program is designed for dwellings that are ineligible for coverage under the homeowner contracts and for persons who do not want or need a homeowner policy.
- The Dwelling Property 1 policy is a *basic form* that provides fire and extended-coverage insurance and coverage for vandalism or malicious mischief. Losses to the dwelling and other structures are paid on the basis of actual cash value rather than replacement cost. The Dwelling Property 2 policy is a *broad form* that includes all perils covered under the basic form and additional perils. Under this form, losses to the dwelling and other structures are paid on the basis of replacement cost. The Dwelling Property 3 policy is a *special form* that covers the dwelling and other structures against direct physical loss from any peril except for those perils otherwise excluded; personal property is covered on a named-perils basis. Finally, the Dwelling Property 8 policy is a *modified coverage form* that is similar to the basic form except that buildings are indemnified on the basis of repair cost rather than actual cash value.
- A mobile home can be insured by an endorsement to Homeowners 2 or Homeowners 3. Thus, the coverages on a mobile home are similar to those found in homeowner contracts.
- Insurance on recreational or pleasure boats can be classified into two categories. *Personal yacht insurance* is designed for larger boats, such as cabin cruisers and inboard motorboats. The personal yacht policy provides hull insurance, protection and indemnity insurance, medical payments insurance, and also covers the possible liability of the insured to maritime workers injured in the course of employment. Boats can also be insured by a special boat owners package policy. A *boat owners policy* provides physical damage insurance on an all-risk basis for the boat, equipment, accessories, motors, and trailer. Liability insurance and medical payments coverage are also included.

- The Personal Articles Floater is an all-risk contract that can be used to insure valuable personal property that may be moved to different locations. The floater can be used to cover valuable cameras, fine arts, golfer's equipment, furs, personal jewelry, musical instruments, silverware, and stamp and coin collections. Under this form, individual items are listed or scheduled and are insured for specified amounts.
- The flood peril is difficult to insure privately because of the problems of a catastrophic loss, prohibitively high premiums, and adverse selection. Federal flood insurance is now available that covers buildings and personal property in flood zones.
- The maximum amount of flood insurance that can be written on a single-family dwelling is $35,000 under the emergency program and $185,000 under the regular program. A $500 deductible applies separately to the buildings and contents.
- FAIR plans provide basic property insurance to individuals who are unable to obtain coverage in the normal markets. The property is inspected before the policy is issued. If the property meets reasonable underwriting standards, it can be insured at standard or surcharged rates. In some cases, the owner may be required to make certain improvements in the property before the policy is issued. If the insurance is denied, the applicant must be informed of the reasons why the property cannot be insured. The insurance cannot be denied solely on the basis of the location or exposure to environmental hazards.
- Federal crime insurance is available to persons who reside in high crime-rate areas and cannot purchase crime insurance at affordable rates. The residential crime policy covers the loss of personal property from burglary or robbery while the property is on the insured premises or is in the presence of the insured. The maximum amount of insurance that can be purchased is $10,000. All covered losses are subject to a deductible of 5 percent of the amount of the gross loss, or $100, whichever is higher. The right of cancellation under the policy is limited.

QUESTIONS FOR REVIEW

1. Why is the Dwelling 77 Program used?
2. Describe briefly the four forms that are now used in the dwelling program.
3. List the basic coverages in a policy covering mobile homes.
4. Describe the major features of a personal yacht policy.
5. List the coverages found in a typical boat owners package policy.
6. Explain how a valuable silverware, coin, or stamp collection can be insured under the Personal Articles Floater.
7. Why is the flood peril difficult to insure privately?
8. Describe briefly the major provisions of the federal flood insurance program.
9. What is the basic purpose of a FAIR plan? Describe how a FAIR plan works.
10. Describe the basic provisions of the federal residential crime insurance policy.

QUESTIONS FOR DISCUSSION

1. Gerald owns a four-plex and lives in one unit. The four-plex is insured under the Dwelling Property 1 (basic form) policy for $160,000. The replacement cost of the building is $200,000. To what extent, if any, will Gerald recover for the following losses?
   a. A fire occurs in one of the apartments because of defective wiring. The actual cash value of the damage is $10,000, and the replacement cost is $12,000.
   b. Gerald's tenants move out because the apartment is unfit for normal living. It will take three months to restore the apartment to its former condition. The apartment is rented for $400 monthly.
   c. The tenant's personal property is damaged in the fire. The actual cash value of the damaged property is $5,000, and its replacement cost is $7,000.
2. Susan owns a mobile home that is insured by an endorsement to a Homeowners 3 policy. To what extent, if at all, would this policy pay for each of the following losses?
   a. A severe windstorm damages the roof of the mobile home.
   b. A built-in range and oven are also damaged in the storm.
   c. A canoe stored outside the mobile home is completely destroyed.
   d. A window air conditioner is badly damaged in the storm.
   e. Susan must move to a furnished apartment for three months while the mobile home is being repaired.
3. "A typical personal yacht policy can be viewed as a package policy." Do you agree or disagree with this statement?
4. Mary is a professional entertainer who performs in night clubs and bars in different cities. She is concerned that her musical instruments may be damaged or stolen while she is on the road. She asks your advice concerning the type of insurance she should purchase to protect her musical instruments. How would you advise Mary?
5. The federal flood insurance program is designed to provide flood insurance to property owners who reside in flood-prone areas.
   a. Explain the extent to which flood damage to fixed property meets the requirements of an insurable risk.
   b. Describe the major features of the current flood insurance program.
   c. The federal flood insurance program has grown substantially in recent years. What factors account for the recent growth in the federal flood insurance program?

KEY TERMS AND CONCEPTS TO KNOW

Dwelling Property 1
Dwelling Property 2
Dwelling Property 3
Dwelling Property 8
Extended-coverage perils
Mobile home insurance
Hull insurance
Protection and indemnity insurance
Personal Articles Floater
Scheduled coverage
Blanket coverage
Federal Flood insurance
Flood
FAIR plan
Federal crime insurance
Burglary
Robbery

SUGGESTIONS FOR ADDITIONAL READING

Fire, Casualty, & Surety Bulletins. Fire and Marine Volume and Casualty and Surety Volume. Cincinnati, Ohio: The National Underwriter Company. See also the Personal Lines Volume. The bulletins are published monthly.

Golonka, Nancy. *How to Protect What's Yours.* New York: Acropolis Books Ltd. and the Insurance Information Institute, 1983, chapter 6.

Greene, Mark R. "A Review and Evaluation of Selected Government Programs to Handle Risk," *The Annals of the American Academy of Policy and Social Science* 443 (May 1979), pp. 129–44.

Williams, Jr., C. Arthur and Richard M. Heins. *Risk Management and Insurance,* 5th ed. New York: McGraw-Hill, 1985, chapter 34, pp. 702–708.

Wood, Glenn L., Claude C. Lilly, III, Donald S. Malecki, and Jerry S. Rosenbloom. *Personal Risk Management and Insurance,* 3rd ed., Volume I. Malvern, PA: American Institute for Property and Liability Underwriters, 1984, chapter 5.

NOTES

1. The Dwelling 77 Program is described in some detail in *FC & S Bulletins,* Personal Lines Volume, Dwelling section. The author drew on this source in preparing this section.
2. For a detailed explanation of insurance on mobile homes, the interested student should consult Glenn L. Wood, Claude C. Lilly, III, Donald S. Malecki, and Jerry S. Rosenbloom, *Personal Risk Management and Insurance,* 3rd ed., Volume I (Malvern, PA: American Institute for Property and Liability Underwriters, 1984), pp. 258–62.
3. *National Underwriter,* Property & Casualty Insurance edition, November 11, 1983, p. 2.
4. See *National Underwriter,* November 11, 1983 for additional details.
5. FAIR plans are in operation in California, Connecticut, Delaware, District of Columbia, Georgia, Illinois, Indiana, Iowa, Kansas, Kentucky, Louisiana, Maryland, Massachusetts, Michigan, Minnesota, Missouri, New Jersey, New Mexico, New York, North Carolina, Ohio, Oregon, Pennsylvania, Puerto Rico, Rhode Island, Virginia, Washington, and Wisconsin. Beach and windstorm plans exist in Alabama, Florida, Louisiana, Mississippi, North Carolina, South Carolina, and Texas.
6. Federal crime insurance is available in Alabama, Arkansas, California, Colorado, Connecticut, Delaware, District of Columbia, Florida, Georgia, Illinois, Iowa, Kansas, Louisiana, Maryland, Massachusetts, Minnesota, Missouri, New Jersey, New Mexico, New York, North Carolina, Ohio, Pennsylvania, Rhode Island, Tennessee, Virginia, Washington, Wisconsin, Puerto Rico, and the Virgin Islands.
7. The federal commercial crime policy is discussed in Chapter 15.
8. *Insurance Facts,* 1983–84 ed., p. 48.

CHAPTER 9

THE LIABILITY RISK

"The law of damages in tort cases—that is, when and how much payment has to be made—is a nightmare of inefficiency and inequity."

Jeffrey O'Connell, Ending Insult to Injury

STUDENT LEARNING OBJECTIVES

After studying this chapter, you should be able to:

- Define a tort and explain the major classes of torts.
- Explain the law of negligence and the elements of a negligent act.
- Explain some legal defenses that can be used in a lawsuit.
- Explain the meaning of imputed negligence and *res ipsa loquitor*.
- Apply the law of negligence to specific liability situations.
- Discuss the special problems of products liability and professional liability.
- Show how elective no-fault insurance can be an acceptable alternative to the law of negligence.

The number of liability lawsuits has increased substantially in recent decades. Operators and owners of automobiles are being sued for negligent operation of their vehicles; business firms are being sued because of defective products that injure others; physicians, attorneys, and other professionals are being sued for malpractice, negligence, and incompetence; even governments and charitable institutions are being sued more often because they no longer enjoy complete immunity from lawsuits. Thus, exposure to liability is becoming more important to those who wish to avoid or minimize potential losses.

In this chapter, we will examine the law of negligence and the elements of a negligent act. We will also discuss the various legal defenses that can be used to defeat a claim for damages. In addition, we will examine some situations that can result in a negligent act and the awarding of damages. We will conclude the chapter by examining the concept of elective no-fault insurance as an alternative to the present system.

BASIS OF LEGAL LIABILITY

Each person has certain legal rights. A **legal wrong** is a violation of a person's legal rights, or a failure to perform a legal duty owed to a certain person or to society as a whole.

There are three broad classes of legal wrongs. A *crime* is a legal wrong against society that is punishable by fines, imprisonment, or death. A *breach of contract* is another class of legal wrongs. Finally, a **tort** is a legal wrong. *A tort can be defined as a legal wrong, other than a breach of contract, for which the law allows a remedy in the form of money damages.* The person who is injured or harmed (called the **plaintiff** or claimant) by the actions of another person (called the defendant or **tortfeasor**) can sue for damages.

Torts generally can be classified into three categories. They are as follows:

- Intentional torts
- Absolute liability
- Negligence

Intentional Torts

Legal liability can arise from an intentional act or omission that results in harm or injury to another person or damage to the person's property. Examples of intentional torts include assault, battery, trespass, false imprisonment, fraud, libel, slander, and patent or copyright infringement.

Absolute Liability

Because the potential harm to an individual or society is so great, some persons may be held liable for the harm or injury done to others even though negligence cannot be proven. **Absolute or strict liability** means that persons are liable for damages even though fault or negligence cannot be proven. Some common situations of absolute liability include the following:

- Occupational injury and disease of employees in cases where employers are held absolutely liable under a workers' compensation law
- Blasting operations that injure another person
- Manufacturing of explosives
- Owning wild or dangerous animals
- Crop spraying by airplanes

Negligence

Negligence is another type of tort that can result in substantial liability. Since this concept is so important in liability insurance, we will examine the law of negligence in some detail.

LAW OF NEGLIGENCE

Negligence is a legal wrong or tort that results in harm or injury to another person. *Negligence typically is defined as the failure to exercise the standard of care required by law to protect others from harm.* The meaning of the term "standard of care" is based on the care required of a reasonably prudent person. Your actions are compared, in other words, with the actions of a reasonably prudent person under the same circumstances. If your conduct and behavior are below the standard of care required of a reasonably prudent person, you may be considered negligent.

The standard of care required by law is not the same for each wrongful act. Its meaning is complex and depends on the age and knowledge of the parties involved, court interpretations over time, skill, knowledge, and judgment of the claimant and tortfeasor, seriousness of the harm, and a host of additional factors.

Elements of a Negligent Act

In order to collect damages, the injured person must show that the tortfeasor is guilty of negligence. There are four essential **elements of a negligent act.** They are:

1. Existence of a legal duty to use reasonable care.
2. Failure to perform that duty.
3. Damages or injury to the claimant.
4. Proximate cause relationship between the negligent act and the infliction of damages.

All four requirements must be satisfied before the tortfeasor can be found guilty of negligence.

Existence of a legal duty The first requirement is the existence of a legal duty to protect others from harm. For example, a motorist has a legal duty to stop at a red light and to drive an automobile safely within the speed limits. A manufacturer has a legal duty to produce a safe product. A physician has a legal duty to provide a high degree of care to the patients.

If there is no legal duty imposed by law, you cannot be held liable. For example, you may be a champion swimmer, but you have no legal obligation to dive into a swimming pool to save a two-year-old child from drowning. Nor do you have a legal obligation to stop and pick up a hitchhiker at night when the temperature is 30 degrees below zero. To be guilty of negligence, there must first be a legal duty or obligation to protect others from harm.

Failure to perform that duty The second requirement of a negligent act is the failure to perform the legal duty required by law. You fail to comply with the standard of care required by law to protect others from harm. As we noted earlier, your actions would be compared with the actions of a reasonably prudent person under similar circumstances. If your conduct falls short of this standard, the second requirement would be satisfied.

The tortfeasor's conduct can be either a *positive or negative act*. For example, a driver who speeds in a residential area or runs a red light is an example of a positive act that a reasonably prudent person would not do. A negative act is simply the failure to act. You fail to do something that a reasonably prudent person would have done. For example, if you injure another person because you failed to repair the faulty brakes on your automobile, you could be found guilty of negligence. In this case, the failure to act has caused the injury.

Damages or injury The third requirement of a negligent act is damages or injury to the claimant. The injured person must show that he or she has suffered damages or injury as a result of the actions of the alleged tortfeasor. For example, a speeding motorist may run a red light, smash into your car, and seriously injure you. Since you are injured, the third requirement of a negligent act has been satisfied.

The dollar amount of money damages awarded by a jury depends on several factors. **Special damages** may be awarded that compensate the claimant for determinable, itemized losses, such as medical expenses, loss of earnings, or damage to property. **General damages** may be awarded for losses that cannot be specifically itemized, such as pain and suffering, disfigurement, the loss of companionship of a spouse, and the loss of future earnings because of partial or permanent disability. Finally, **punitive damages** may be awarded where the objective is to punish the tortfeasor so that others are deterred from committing the same wrongful act.

INSIGHT 9.1

Structured Settlement

In the past, a lump sum payment was the only way to settle a large bodily injury claim. That is changing. One of the most successful new settlement options is called a *structured settlement.* Unlike a lump sum settlement which provides a one-time cash payment, a structured settlement consists of payments spread out over a period of time. Since these installments can be scheduled monthly, quarterly, annually, or on whatever basis the recipient prefers, a structured settlement is actually a financial package tailored to meet the claimant's immediate and future needs.

In practice, structured settlements offer claimants long-term financial security and protection from mismanagement of their awards. However, recipients of large amounts of cash are often not physically or psychologically able to manage the money. Too often they squander it or fall victim to a swindle or bad investments. In the case of minors or severely disabled persons, this is particularly tragic as they may become a long-term burden on their families or wards of the state. In fact, these are the type of claimants for whom structured settlements are especially useful.

Another advantage of a structured settlement is that time-phased payments are usually totally exempt from the federal income tax. Even though a lump sum settlement is also tax-free, the income from the investment of that lump sum is usually fully taxable at the same rate as ordinary income. With a structured settlement, the claimant receives a larger amount of money in the long run because the money is invested by the insurance company and the investment earnings are passed on to the claimant tax-free.

Insurers often finance structured settlements by purchasing annuities from life insurance companies. An annuity allows for the tax-free status of both the principal and the interest income of the award. It also enables insurers to set up payment plans to suit individual needs. Payments may vary from two payments—one at the time of settlement followed by another at a later date—to hundreds of payments spanning a claimant's lifetime. If the claimant dies before full payment, the

---

Damage awards are increasingly being paid to injured persons in the form of a structured settlement rather than a lump sum cash payment. As a result, the financial security of severely disabled accident victims should be substantially improved. (See Insight 9.1.)

Proximate cause relationship The final requirement of a negligent act is that a **proximate cause** relationship must exist. *This means there must be an unbroken chain of events between the negligent act and the infliction of damages.* For example, a beautician who carelessly burns the scalp of a customer with a hair dryer could be held liable for the injury. A drunk driver who kills another motorist would also meet the proximate cause requirement. So would the owner of a building if a sign falls from the building and injures a passing pedestrian.

However, a *new and independent intervening cause* could absolve the original tortfeasor from legal liability. If the injury normally would not have occurred except for the new intervening cause, then the new cause is the proximate cause of the injury. For example, assume that a speeding motorist's brakes fail because of a faulty repair job and that consequently an accident with another motorist occurs. A new intervening cause—a faulty brake job—is the proximate cause of the accident. Thus, the automobile repair shop and not the speeding motorist could be held liable for the accident. Note, however, that the intervening cause is effective only if the new cause is not reasonably foreseeable by the person who com-

remaining payments are made to the survivors or estate as they fall due.

For example, one claimant was a 20-year-old student who was injured in an automobile accident caused by an insured policyholder. Because of the claimant's permanent disability, the insurer's financial liability was estimated to be about $375,000.

Instead of a lump sum payment, this insurer set up a structured settlement, which provided initial payments of $50,000 to the claimant and $100,000 for his attorney's fees. Then, an annuity was established to provide long-term income. After two years, the claimant will receive monthly payments of $2,000. Every five years, the monthly payments will increase by $250 for a period of 40 years.

Altogether, the claimant will receive a guaranteed settlement of $1,530,000; the insurer's costs totalled about $330,000—$150,000 in initial payments and approximately $180,000 for the annuity premium.

Structured settlements have quickly become a popular alternative to the lump sum method of claim settlement, largely because everyone wins in such an arrangement. The claimant receives a guaranteed future income with a payment schedule customized to meet his or her needs. A structured settlement eliminates the worry and risk involved in managing a large lump sum payment, and the claimant enjoys the tax-exempt status of the settlement income. Insurers benefit because claim costs are reduced and cash reserves are protected. By being able to offer a flexible and attractive settlement alternative, insurers are often able to reach agreement with a claimant sooner and avoid possible court expenses and costly delays. The general public also benefits because structured settlements reduce demands on the court system, lead to lower insurance costs, and provide guaranteed long-term financial security to severely disabled persons.

SOURCE: Adaptation of "Nothing Left" from pp. 26–27 of *Aide*, Fall 1983. Reprinted with permission.

mits the original act. Thus, in our previous example, if the speeding motorist is not aware that the brakes are faulty, and an accident subsequently occurs, the proximate cause of the accident is a faulty repair job. As we stated earlier, the automobile repair shop would be primarily responsible for the accident, not the speeding driver.

Defenses Against Negligence

Although you may be sued, there are certain legal defenses that can be used to defeat a claim for damages. Some important legal defenses include the following:

- Contributory negligence
- Comparative negligence
- Last clear chance rule
- Assumption of risk

Contributory negligence Under a **contributory negligence** law, if you contribute in any way to your own injury, you cannot recover damages. Thus, under the strict common law doctrine of contributory negligence, even if you are only 1 percent responsible for an accident, and the other party is 99 percent responsible, you cannot collect any damages for the accident. For example, if a motorist on an expressway suddenly slows down without signaling and is rear-ended by another driver, the failure to signal could constitute contributory negligence. The first motorist cannot collect damages for injuries if contributory negligence is established.

INSIGHT 9.2

Types of Comparative Negligence Laws

There are four types of comparative negligence laws. They are:

1. Pure
2. Georgia plan
3. 50-50
4. Slight and gross

Under a *pure* comparative negligence law, the person bringing suit is entitled to damages regardless of the amount of his or her fault. For example, Bob who is 80 percent at fault is entitled to proceed against Mary who is 20 percent at fault. Bob's recovery would be limited to a maximum of 20 percent of his actual damages. Mary's recovery is limited to 80 percent of her damages.

Under the *Georgia* or *49 percent plan,* the initiator of the suit is entitled to recover only if his or her negligence is *less than* the negligence of the defendant. This means you can recover from the other party only if you are 49 percent or less at fault.

Under the 50-50 plan, the plaintiff can recover if his or her negligence does not exceed the negligence of the defendant. *This means the plaintiff can recover if he or she is not more than 50 percent at fault.* The 50-50 plans should not be confused with the Georgia plan. Unlike the Georgia plan, the 50-50 plan allows each party to recover damages when both parties are equally at fault. Each party's recovery would be limited to 50 percent of the actual damages.

Finally, two states have a peculiar comparative law based on *slight and gross negligence.* Under this law, the plaintiff is entitled to recover only if his or her negligence is slight and the defendant's negligence is gross.[1]

1. *Pure* comparative negligence laws are in existence in Alaska, California, Florida, Illinois, Iowa, Kentucky, Louisiana, Michigan, Mississippi, Missouri, New Mexico, New York, Rhode Island, and Washington. The *Georgia plan* is followed in Arkansas, Colorado, Georgia, Idaho, Kansas, Maine, North Dakota, Utah, West Virginia, and Wyoming. The *50-50* system is followed in Connecticut, Delaware, Hawaii, Indiana, Massachusetts, Minnesota, Montana, Nevada, New Hampshire, New Jersey, Ohio, Oklahoma, Oregon, Pennsylvania, Texas, Vermont, and Wisconsin. Finally, the *slight and gross* system is followed in Nebraska and South Dakota.

SOURCE: Adaptation of "Comparative Negligence" from *FC & S Bulletins,* 1985. Reprinted by permission.

Comparative negligence Because of the harshness of the contributory negligence rule, forty-three states have enacted **comparative negligence** *laws* that permit the injured person to recover damages even though he or she may have contributed to the accident. Under a comparative negligence law, if both the plaintiff (injured person) and the defendant contributed to the plaintiff's injuries, the financial burden of the injury is shared by both parties according to their respective degrees of fault. For example, if you are 20 percent responsible for an automobile accident, and the other driver is 80 percent responsible, you can collect for your injury, but your damage award will be proportionately reduced. Thus, if actual damages are $10,000, the damage award would be reduced to $8,000.

Comparative negligence laws vary among the states, but they all have a common element in that negligence by the plaintiff does not necessarily bar a recovery for damages (see Insight 9.2).

Last clear chance rule The doctrine of last clear chance is another statutory modification of the contributory negligence doctrine. Under the

last clear chance rule, a plaintiff who is endangered by his or her own negligence can still recover damages from the defendant if the defendant has a last clear chance to avoid the accident but fails to do so. For example, a jaywalker who walks against a red light is breaking the law. But if a motorist has a last clear chance to avoid hitting the jaywalker and fails to do so, the injured jaywalker can recover damages for the injury.

Assumption of risk The **assumption of risk doctrine** is another defense that can be used to defeat a claim for damages. Under this doctrine, a person who understands and recognizes the danger inherent in a particular activity cannot recover damages in the event of injury. In effect, the assumption of risk bars recovery for damages even though another person's negligence causes the injury. For example, assume that while you are voluntarily teaching a friend to drive an automobile, your friend negligently crashes into a telephone post and injures you. You could not collect for damages since you willingly assumed the risk inherent in teaching a novice how to drive.

IMPUTED NEGLIGENCE

Under certain conditions, the negligence of one person can be imputed to another. Several examples can illustrate this principle. First, an *employer-employee relationship* may exist where the employee is acting on behalf of the employer. The negligent acts of the employee can be imputed to the employer. For example, assume that you are driving a car to deliver a package for your employer. If you should negligently injure another motorist, your employer could be held liable for your actions.

Second, many states have passed some type of **vicarious liability** law, by which the negligence of the driver of an automobile can be imputed to its owner. Under these laws, if the owner of an automobile gives permission to a friend to drive the automobile, and the friend negligently causes an accident, the owner can be held liable. In addition, many states have passed laws with respect to the operation of an automobile by a family member. Under the **family purpose doctrine,** the owner of an automobile can be held liable for the negligent acts committed by immediate family members while they are operating the family car. For example, if Mary, age sixteen, negligently injures another motorist while driving her father's car and is sued for $100,000, her father could be held liable.

Third, imputed negligence may arise out of a *joint business venture.* For example, two brothers may be partners in a business. One brother may negligently injure a customer with a company car, and the partnership is then sued by the injured person. Both partners could be held liable for the injury.

A **dram-shop law** is a final example of imputed negligence. Under such a law, a business that sells liquor can be held liable for damages that may result from the sale of liquor. For example, assume that a bar owner continues to serve a customer who is drunk, and that after the bar closes, the customer injures three people while trying to drive home. The bar owner could be held legally liable for the injuries.

RES IPSA LOQUITOR

An important modification of the law of negligence is the doctrine of ***res ipsa loquitor***—the thing speaks for itself. Under this doctrine, the injured person can collect damages without first having to prove negligence. The very fact that the event occurs is sufficient proof that the defendant is negligent. The accident or injury normally would not have occurred if someone had not been careless. Examples of the doctrine of *res ipsa loquitor* include the following:

1. A dentist extracts the wrong tooth.
2. A surgeon leaves a surgical sponge in the patient's abdomen.
3. X-ray burns are on a patient's body.
4. A surgical operation is performed on the wrong patient.

To apply the doctrine of *res ipsa loquitor,* four major requirements must be met. They are:

1. The event is one that normally does not occur in the absence of negligence.
2. The defendant has superior knowledge of the cause of the accident, and the injured party cannot prove negligence.
3. The defendant has exclusive control over the instrumentality causing the accident.
4. The injured party has not contributed to the accident in any way.

SPECIFIC APPLICATIONS OF THE LAW OF NEGLIGENCE

Property Owners

Property owners have a legal obligation to protect others from harm. However, the standard of care owed to others depends upon the situation. Traditionally, three groups have been recognized: (1) trespasser, (2) licensee, and (3) invitee:[1]

Trespasser A **trespasser** is a person who enters or remains on the owner's property without the owner's consent. With the exception of children (discussed later), the property owner owes the least degree of care to the trespasser. If the trespasser is injured, the property owner normally has no liability. The property owner has no legal obligation to eliminate a dangerous condition, and the trespasser is viewed as assuming the risk of any such condition on the premises. For example, a pond may be obscured by weeds on the owner's farm. The farmer normally has no liability if a trespassing hunter falls into the pond and drowns.

However, the property owner cannot deliberately set a trap to injure the trespasser. If the trespasser is injured by the trap, the owner can be held liable. For example, a farmer in Iowa owned an unoccupied house. To discourage vandalism, a shotgun was triggered to go off mechanically in the case of a break-in. An admitted prowler was severely injured by a blast from the shotgun. He sued the owner and was awarded $30,000 in damages. The law is clear on this point—trespassers cannot be deliberately harmed by a trap.

Licensee A **licensee** is a person who enters or remains on the premises with the occupant's permission. Examples of licensees include door-to-door salespersons, solicitors for charitable or religious organizations, police officers, fire fighters, and social guests. The occupant is required to warn the licensee of any dangerous condition or activity on the premises, which may not be readily apparent to the licensee. The licensee must accept the premises as he or she finds them. Thus, the occupant must only give warning of unsafe hidden conditions, but there is no obligation to inspect the premises for the benefit of the licensee.

Invitee An **invitee** is someone who is invited on to the premises for the benefit of the occupant. Examples of invitees include customers in a store, milk truck drivers, letter carriers, and garbage collectors.

A higher degree of care is owed to an invitee. In addition to warning the invitee of any dangerous condition, the occupant has the obligation to inspect the premises and to eliminate any dangerous condition revealed by the inspection. For example, a store owner may be aware that an escalator is faulty. The customers must be warned of the unsafe escalator (perhaps by a sign) and prevented from using the escalator. The faulty escalator must be repaired; otherwise customers in the store could be injured, and the owner would be liable.

At the present time, the traditional distinction between and among trespasser, licensee, and invitee is being challenged by some courts. Although the courts still maintain this distinction, the number of exceptions to the different categories has increased. In those cases where the trespasser has been elevated to the status of a licensee, the courts have generally been willing to accept mitigating circumstances to the general rules. Also, some courts have disregarded the traditional classifications in certain situations, and others have expressed dissatisfaction with the arbitrary and inflexible nature of these categories.[2]

Attractive Nuisance Doctrine

An **attractive nuisance** is a condition that can attract and injure children. Under the attractive nuisance doctrine, the occupants of land are liable for the injuries of children who may be attracted by some dangerous condition, feature, or article. This doctrine is based on the principles that children may not be able to recognize the danger involved and may be injured, and that it is in the best interest of society to protect them rather than protect the owner's right to the land. Many courts consider children to be invitees, and a high degree of care is imposed on the occupants of land to protect them from harm.

Several examples can illustrate the attractive nuisance doctrine, by which the occupant or owner can be held liable:

1. The gate to a swimming pool is left unlocked, and a three-year-old child drowns.
2. A homeowner has a miniature house for the children. A neighbor's child enters through an unlocked window, which falls on her neck and strangles her.
3. A building contractor carelessly leaves the keys in a tractor. While driving the tractor, two small boys are seriously injured when the tractor overturns.

Owners and Operators of Automobiles

The owner of an automobile who drives in a careless and irresponsible manner can be held liable for property damage or bodily injury sustained by another person. There is no single rule of law that can be applied here. The legal liability of the owner who is also the operator has been modified over time by court decisions, comparative negligence laws, the last clear chance rule, no-fault automobile insurance laws (see Chapter 12), and a host of additional factors. However, the laws in all states clearly require the owner of an automobile to exercise a high degree of care while operating the automobile.

With respect to the liability of the owner who is not the operator, the general rule is that the owner is not liable for the negligent acts of operators. But there are exceptions to this general principle. In all states the owner is liable for an operator's negligence if an *agency relationship* exists. For example, if you injure someone while on a personal or business errand for a friend, your friend can be held liable. Also, some states have passed **permissive use statutes** that impose liability on the owner for the negligence of anyone who is operating the automobile with the owner's expressed or implied consent. For example, if James borrows his father's car for a date, his father could be held liable if he lets his girlfriend drive and she negligently injures someone.

Governmental Liability

Until recently, federal, state, and local governments were granted immunity from lawsuits because the doctrine of sovereign immunity held that "the king can do no wrong." This doctrine has been modified over time by both statutory law and court decisions. At present, a government can be held liable if it is negligent in the performance of a **proprietary function.** Proprietary functions of government typically include the operation of water plants, electrical transportation, and telephone systems, municipal auditoriums, and similar moneymaking activities that could be carried on by private enterprise. Thus, if some seats collapse at a rock concert in a city auditorium, the city can be held liable for injuries to spectators. With respect to **government functions**—for example, street and sewer maintenance—municipalities normally are immune from liability lawsuits. Yet this immunity has also been eroded. Since the distinction between a government and a proprietary function is often a fine line, many courts have tried to find exceptions to the doctrine of governmental immunity or eliminate it entirely.[3]

Governments can also be held liable under the provisions of tort claim acts that permit an individual to sue for damages. At the federal level, the Federal Tort Claims Act provides that the United States is liable for money damages to the same extent as private individuals. Many states have also passed comprehensive tort claim acts that expose municipalities to the same legal actions now taken against corporations.

Charitable Institutions

Like governments, charitable institutions were generally immune from lawsuits until recently. This immunity has been gradually eliminated by state law and court decisions.[4] The trend today in many states is to hold a charitable institution liable with respect to its fund-raising or money-making activities. For example, a hospital operated by a religious order can now be successfully sued for medical malpractice; a church sponsoring a dance or carnival can now be held liable for an injury to a customer. Where charitable immunity still exists, the immunity is largely restricted to nonsecular activities of religious institutions that lack substantial financial resources.[5]

Employer and Employee Relationships

Under the doctrine of **respondeat superior,** an employer can be held liable for the negligent acts of employees who are acting on the employer's behalf. Thus, if a sales clerk in a sporting goods store carelessly drops a barbell set on a customer's toe, the owner of the store can be held liable.

In order for an employer to be held liable for the negligent acts of the employees, two requirements must be fulfilled. First, the worker's legal status must be that of an employee. A person typically is considered an employee if he or she is given detailed instructions on how to do a job, is furnished tools or supplies by the employer, and is paid a wage or salary at regular intervals. Second, the employee must be engaged in furthering the employer's business. At present, a broad standard is applied here. The employer can be held liable for the negligent acts of an employee who is acting on the employer's behalf even where there is a reasonably foreseeable deviation from the employer's instructions. For example, if a truck driver is instructed to make a delivery 100 miles from the place of employment, and travels an additional 20 miles to visit some relatives, the employer is vicariously liable for any accidents during the entire trip due to the driver's negligence.[6]

Parents and Children

The general rule is that parents normally are not responsible for their children's torts. Children who reach the age of reason (typically age seven and older) are responsible for their own wrongful acts. However, there are several exceptions to this general principle. First, a parent can be held liable if a child uses a dangerous weapon, such as a gun or knife, to injure someone. For example, if a ten-year-old child is permitted to play with a loaded revolver, and someone is thereby injured or killed, the parents can be held responsible. Second, the parent may be legally liable if the child is acting as an agent for the parent. For example, if a son or daughter is employed in the family business, the parents can be held liable for any injury to a customer caused by the child's actions. Third, if a family car is operated by a minor child, the parents can be held liable under the family purpose doctrine discussed earlier. Finally, several states have passed laws that hold the parents liable for the willful and intentional acts of children that result in property damage to others.

Animals

Owners of wild animals are held absolutely liable for the injuries of others even if the animals are domesticated. Thus, owners of a zoo containing lions and tigers are absolutely liable for damage if one of the animals should escape and injure someone. This is true even if the owner is meticulously careful in protecting the public from harm, or if the animal escaped accidentally. For example, if some wild animals in a zoo escape because the cages are broken open by an earthquake, the owners are still absolutely liable for any injuries.

The owners of animals with vicious propensities are also held absolutely liable if someone is injured. For example, a bull breeder can be held liable if an escaped bull gores a person.

With respect to domestic pets without known dangerous tendencies, such as an ordinary house dog or cat, the doctrine of absolute liability does not apply if the owner uses due care in controlling the animals. However, there is one important exception. Some states have passed laws holding the owner liable for injury to another even if the pet does not have a known vicious propensity. Under such a law, you could be held liable if your gentle beagle bites someone.

SPECIAL NEGLIGENCE PROBLEMS

In recent years, special negligence problems have emerged that have caused serious problems to consumers, purchasers of insurance, products liability insurers, providers of medical care, and legislators. Two major negligence problems are (1) products liability and (2) professional liability.

Products Liability

Products liability refers to the legal liability of a manufacturer, wholesaler, or retailer of products to persons who incur bodily injuries or property damage from a defective product. Prior to the 1960s, products liability lawsuits were rare. In 1961, 50,000 lawsuits were filed. By the end of 1966, the annual number of products liability lawsuits had increased to 100,000. Since that time, the number of products liability lawsuits has continued to increase at an alarming rate.[7]

The size of the damage awards has also increased. For example, in 1978, a California jury awarded $128 million to a youth who was seriously burned when a Ford Pinto in which he was riding was struck from behind, and the gas tank exploded. The award was later reduced to $6 million upon appeal. In another case, a jury awarded $2.4 million to an unemployed Michigan man who was blinded as a result of taking a drug manufactured by a pharmaceutical firm.

More recently, thousands of lawsuits have been filed against firms that use asbestos in the production of products. Asbestos can cause a latent form of cancer where the cancer appears years after exposure to asbestos. In particular, the Manville Corporation, the world's largest producer of asbestos, filed for court protection under Chapter 11 of the Federal Bankruptcy Code in order to suspend thousands of asbestos lawsuits that threatened the company's solvency.

Several reasons account for the substantial increase in products liability lawsuits.[8] First, the courts have gradually rejected the older **privity of contract** doctrine. Under this doctrine, the original seller of the goods was not liable to anyone for a defective product except the immediate buyer or one in privity with him. This meant that only the person who was a party to the contract could bring action against the manufacturer of a defective product. Since a manufacturer sells to wholesalers and retailers, the injured person had recourse only against the retailer. However, as a result of adverse court decisions, injured persons in most states can now directly sue the manufacturer of a defective product. Second, emphasis on *consumerism* and enactment of consumer legislation have encouraged individuals to sue because of defective products. In particular, the Consumer Product and Safety Act of 1972 has been credited with stimulating an increase in products liability lawsuits. Finally, the substantial number of *new products* has resulted in an increase in products liability.

Basis for lawsuits A person who is injured or incurs property damage from a defective product can sue for damages based on several legal principles. They include the following:

- Breach of warranty
- Strict liability
- Negligence

A **breach of warranty** is based on contract law rather than tort law. Since it is a contract action, it does not require proof of negligence. A warranty means that the manufacturer or seller of products warrants that the good is reasonably fit for the purpose for which it is intended. If the product is defective, the injured person can sue for breach of warranty.

The warranty can be either *expressed* or *implied.* For example, in a lawsuit against the Ford Motor Company, the court ruled that statements made in advertising material concerning a shatterproof windshield made the company liable for damages due to windshield breakage, since an expressed warranty was violated. Similarly, with respect to an implied warranty, an injured plaintiff argued that her husband's new automobile had a defective steering mechanism which caused her to be injured. She won the case based on a breach of implied warranty.

A person injured by a defective product can also collect damages based on *strict liability.* Under strict liability, the injured person does not have to prove negligence on behalf of the manufacturer or seller. The injured person only has to show that there is a defect in the product, and that the product caused injury or damage.

Finally, the injured person can sue because the manufacturer or seller failed to exercise the standard of care required in producing its product and so was negligent. A manufacturer or seller can be held liable for negligence as a result of:

- Improper product design
- Improper assembly of the product
- Failure to test and inspect the product
- Failure to warn of inherently dangerous characteristics
- Deceptive advertising
- Failure to foresee possible abuse or misuse of the product

Solutions to the problem Several solutions have been proposed to reduce the magnitude of the products liability problem. They include the following:

1. *Statute of limitations.* The manufacturer or seller's liability for a defective product would be subject to a nine-year statute of limitations.
2. *State of the art defense.* If the product conformed to the prevailing state of the art at the time it was manufactured, it would not be considered a defective product today.
3. *Alteration of the product defense.* The manufacturer would have a defense if the injury were produced by alteration, modification, or misuse of the product by the defendant.
4. *Limitation on attorney's fees.* This would discourage some attorneys from attempting to persuade injured persons to bring suit.
5. *Elimination of punitive damages.* This would reduce the magnitude of the damage award.
6. *Recovery from collateral sources.* The damage award would be reduced if the injured person collected from other sources, such as private health and disability income insurance.

Product Liability Risk Retention Act of 1981 As a result of increased lawsuits, many business firms have found it difficult to obtain products liability insurance at affordable premiums, and some smaller firms have altogether dropped their products liability insurance. Other firms have decided to go out of business because the increase in premiums was greater than the previous year's net profit, or they have decided not to develop new programs. In response to the preceding problems, the Product Liability Risk Retention Act of 1981 was enacted. The Act permits firms to form *risk retention groups* in which group members can self-insure the product liability loss exposures rather than purchase commercial insurance. In addition, the new law allows *purchasing groups* to be formed in which the firms can band together and purchase products liability insurance on a group basis from commercial insurers.

Professional Liability

In recent years, the number of liability lawsuits and jury awards against professionals has also increased. Let us briefly examine some important professional liability problems.

Medical malpractice Medical malpractice is defined as *negligence in doing some act which a reasonable physician would not have done under the same circumstances or as a failure to do something which a physician would have done.*[9] Stated simply, malpractice is improper or negligent medical treatment in the eyes of the law. For example, a surgeon who performs an incorrect surgical procedure can be held legally liable if the patient is paralyzed after the operation.

The number of medical malpractice lawsuits has increased sharply in recent years, and premiums for malpractice insurance have soared. It is not uncommon for a neurosurgeon in New York to pay more than $60,000 annually for malpractice insurance. Moreover, in some hospitals in New York, malpractice costs have increased the daily room-and-board charge by at least $15 per day.[10]

Medical malpractice lawsuits have increased for several reasons.[11] First, according to experts who have studied the problem, there is a disturbing level of *improper or negligent medical care* provided by some physicians. All physicians do not offer high quality medical care. In many cases, physicians attempt some medical procedure beyond their normal skills or make errors in judgment. As a result, the patient is harmed, and the physician is sued.

Second, medical malpractice lawsuits have escalated because of *unrealistic patient expectations.* Advances in medical science and medical technology often result in high medical expectations. When patient expectations are high, failure to fulfill them often leads to a lawsuit.

Third, medical malpractice claims have increased because of the **philosophy of entitlement.** This means that Americans increasingly believe that somebody owes them something when things are not quite right. Jurors occasionally leave the impression that the key question is not whether negligence is present, but who is better able to bear the burden of loss. The real attitude is "someone is injured, and therefore someone should collect."

Finally, there has been a *deterioration in the physician-patient* relationship. The medical profession as a group no longer commands the prestige it once enjoyed. This is due partly to the sharp increase in the cost of medical care, partly to publicized fraud by some physicians under the Medicare and Medicaid programs, and partly to studies that suggest large numbers of unneeded medical procedures, especially surgery, are performed each year. The result is that patients are more willing to sue than formerly.

Several suggestions and approaches have been taken to solve the medical malpractice problem. They include the following:

1. *Joint underwriting associations.* Joint underwriting associations (JUA) have been formed that require liability insurers in the state to write their share of professional liability insurance.
2. *Arbitration panels.* Many states have formed arbitration panels to resolve disputes between physicians and patients.
3. *Limit on damage awards.* Many states have enacted laws that limit damage awards.
4. *Attorney's fees.* Limitations would be placed on contingent fees charged by attorneys.
5. *Statute of limitations.* The statute of limitations for filing lawsuits against physicians would be shortened.
6. *Res ipsa loquitor.* The use of the *res ipsa loquitor* doctrine (thing speaks for itself) would be prohibited.

Legal malpractice Lawsuits against attorneys for legal malpractice have also increased. Between 1974 and 1976, legal malpractice lawsuits increased by more than 40 percent. In 1977 alone, more than 72,500 malpractice suits came to trial or were settled out of court.[12] The problem continues today.

Several reasons explain the rapid increase in legal malpractice lawsuits. First, the standards for judging legal negligence have been broadened. Earlier, only a blatant legal error or omission could produce a malpractice suit. Today, because of adverse court decisions, attorneys are held to a higher standard of care than formerly. Second, the old rule of privity, which made an attorney responsible only to his or her clients, has lost its former force. An attorney today may be held liable by a party who may benefit from the attorney's performance but is not a client. Third, there has been an increased willingness on the part of attorneys to testify against each other and even sue each other. Testimony by one attorney against another was uncommon until recently.

Finally, because of an increase in the scope of government, there are more complex laws, rules, and regulations. New laws with respect to pollution, ecology, consumerism, and privacy have produced an entirely new bundle of individual rights. Thus, the margin for legal errors or omissions continually increases, resulting in additional lawsuits for legal malpractice.

Several solutions to the legal malpractice problem have been offered. They include the following:

1. *Defensive practice of law.* Attorneys are now specializing in limited areas of law. Questionable matters of law in other areas are referred to other legal specialists.
2. *Educational seminars.* Local bar associations are conducting seminars on complex government regulations. Classes are also held on how an attorney can avoid a legal malpractice lawsuit.
3. *Waiver of rights.* In some cases, clients are asked to waive certain rights if the attorney's legal work or advice is in error.

Liability of architects and engineers The number of malpractice lawsuits against architects and engineers has also increased sharply in recent years. In 1976 alone, about 30 percent of all insured architects and engineers faced malpractice lawsuits.[13]

The increased number of lawsuits in this professional area can be explained by several factors. Similar to the trend in medicine and law, the increase in malpractice suits against architects is partly due to a broader interpretation of liability by the courts. Architects and engineers are being held legally liable for injuries to the general public as well as to the building owners, and to workers injured by a hazardous condition on the construction site. New building materials and techniques have also increased the risk of a lawsuit. And in some jurisdictions, the courts have interpreted the statute of limitations as starting when a construction defect is discovered, rather than when the building was first designed. The result is a substantial increase in the architect's or engineer's potential liability exposure.

The substantial increase in building costs has greatly increased the size of claims. Multimillion dollar judgments in the construction industry are not uncommon. This means an architect or engineer who is involved in a large operation needs at least $5 million of professional liability insurance, which may cost $100,000 annually.[14]

Two approaches are now used to control this enormous liability exposure. First, professional architectural and engineering societies have sponsored loss-control seminars through which loss frequency and loss severity can be reduced. Second, many architects and engineers are analyzing the financial feasibility of proposed projects more carefully, in order to avoid those projects where lawsuits may be brought for the purpose of eliminating or reducing their professional fees.

Professional liability in other fields Other professional groups are experiencing similar liability problems. Public accounting firms have experienced a gradual increase in both the number and size of claims. Pharmacists are being sued in large numbers. Even education has come under the malpractice attack. In one case, a young woman sued a university for a tuition refund on the grounds that she learned nothing in a particular course because of poor teaching. Also, in many states, parents have sued the school districts because their children can barely read, even though they have received diplomas. With the cost of education increasing, especially college costs, educational malpractice suits from dissatisfied students or parents are likely to increase in the future.

ELECTIVE NO-FAULT INSURANCE

Critics argue that the present tort system has numerous defects, and that new approaches for compensating accident victims are necessary. They argue that under the present system, too few persons are adequately compensated for their injuries; claim settlements are slow and expensive; small claims are overpaid, while larger ones are underpaid; only a small fraction of the liability insurance premiums is received by accident victims in the form of benefits; and numerous inequities in the system now exist. In view of these defects, Professor Jeffrey O'Connell has proposed an **elective no-fault insurance** plan as an alternative to the present tort system.[15]

Under Professor O'Connell's proposal, an insured would voluntarily purchase no-fault insurance from an insurer in increments of $10,000 up to $1 million or more. If the accident occurs, the insured would receive benefits without first having to prove negligence against the third party who caused the accident. Payment of no-fault benefits would be made only for economic losses, including the loss of wages, medical expenses, and rehabilitation expenses. No payment would be made for pain and suffering, nor would any payment be made if the injured person received benefits from some collateral source, such as sick leave or private health insurance.

In addition, the insurer would also pay the insured the equivalent of any amount in excess of the no-fault benefits that the insured could receive in a fault-finding claim against the third party who caused the accident. Legal expenses incurred in gaining such a payment would not be deducted, since the insurer's attorneys would have to be paid anyway in pressing its claim against the third party who caused the accident. Thus, the insured would be guaranteed a certain level of no-fault benefits, plus whatever amount of economic loss in excess of that limit which he or she is eligible for under a fault-finding claim.

In exchange for these benefits, the insured would transfer to the insurer the entire fault-based claim against the third party who actually caused the accident. The transfer of the fault-finding claim would be made prior to the injury when the no-fault benefits are first purchased.

Under Professor O'Connell's proposal, the complex legal issues of the determination of fault and the value of pain and suffering would still have to be settled. However, those legal issues could be settled more quickly and efficiently by the no-fault insurer and by the insurer of the third party who caused the accident. Both insurers would be more willing to settle the claim informally without expensive litigation. But even if litigation is necessary, it would take place between large, impersonal organizations without forcing the agonies of expense, trickery, delay, and uncertainty on lonely and frightened accident victims.

SUMMARY

- A tort is a legal wrong, other than breach of contract, for which the law allows a remedy in the form of money damages. There are three categories of torts: intentional torts, absolute liability, and negligence.
- Negligence is defined as the failure to exercise the standard of care required by law to protect others from harm. There are four elements of a negligent act:
  a. Existence of a legal duty to use reasonable care.
  b. Failure to perform that duty.
  c. Damages or injury to the claimant.
  d. Proximate cause relationship.
- Under a *contributory negligence law,* if the injured person contributed in any way to the accident, he or she cannot collect damages. Under the *comparative negligence law,* the injured person could collect, but the damage award would be reduced. Under the *last clear chance rule,* the plaintiff who is endangered by his or her own negligence can still recover damages from the defendant if the defendant has a last clear chance to avoid the accident but fails to do so. Under the *assumption of risk* doctrine, a person who understands and recognizes the danger inherent in a particular activity cannot recover damages in the event of injury.
- Under certain conditions, the negligence of one person can be imputed to another. Imputed negligence may arise from an employer-employee relationship, vicarious liability law, family-purpose doctrine, joint business venture, or a dram-shop law.
- Under the doctrine of *res ipsa loquitor* (thing speaks for itself), the injured person can collect damages without first having to prove negligence.
- The standard of care required by law varies with the situation. Specific liability situations can involve property owners, an attractive nuisance, owners and operators of automobiles, governmental units and charitable institutions, employers and employees, parents and children, and the owners of animals.
- Products liability lawsuits have increased over time because of rejection of the privity of contract doctrine by the courts, increased emphasis on consumerism, new consumer protection laws, and the substantial number of new products that are produced each year. A person injured by a defective product can sue the manufacturer, wholesaler, or retailer. The suit can be based on a breach of warranty, strict liability, or negligence.
- Large numbers of physicians have been sued for medical malpractice. Medical malpractice lawsuits have increased because of improper or negligent care by physicians, unrealistic patient expectations, the philosophy of entitlement, and a deterioration in the physician-patient relationship.
- Other professionals are being sued in large numbers, including attorneys, accountants, architects, and engineers.
- Because of defects in the present tort liability system, elective no-fault insurance has been proposed. Under this concept, a person would voluntarily purchase no-fault insurance from the insurer. If an accident occurs, the insured would receive benefits from the insurer without first having to prove negligence against the party who caused the accident. In exchange for these benefits, the insured would transfer to the insurer the entire fault-based claim against the third party who actually caused the accident.

QUESTIONS FOR REVIEW

1. Define the meaning of a tort and list the three broad classes of torts.
2. Define negligence. What are the essential elements of a negligent act?
3. Describe some legal defenses that can be used if a person is sued.
4. How does comparative negligence differ from contributory negligence?
5. Explain the meaning of imputed negligence.
6. What is a vicarious liability law?
7. Explain the meaning of *res ipsa loquitor*.
8. Briefly describe the standard of care to protect others from harm for each of the following liability situations:
   a. property owners
   b. an attractive nuisance
   c. owners and operators of automobiles
   d. governmental units and charitable institutions
   e. employers and employees
   f. parents and children
   g. owners of animals
9. Why have *products liability* and *professional liability lawsuits* increased substantially over time?
10. Describe some defects in the present tort-liability system.
11. Explain how elective no-fault insurance can be an acceptable alternative to the law of negligence.

QUESTIONS FOR DISCUSSION

1. Bill went deer hunting with Ed, a professional guide. After seeing the bushes move, Bill quickly fired his rifle at what he thought to be a deer. However, Ed caused the movement in the bushes and was seriously wounded by the bullet. Ed survived and later sued Bill on the ground that "Bill's negligence was the proximate cause of the injury."
   a. Based on the above facts, is Bill guilty of negligence? Your answer must include a definition of *negligence* and the *essential elements* of a negligent act.
   b. Bill's attorney believes that if *contributory negligence* could be established, it would greatly influence the outcome of the case. Do you agree with Bill's attorney? Your answer must include a definition of contributory negligence.
   c. If Bill can establish *comparative negligence* on the part of Ed, would the outcome of the case be changed? Explain your answer.
2. Smith Construction is building a warehouse for Gerald. The construction firm routinely leaves certain construction machinery at the building site overnight and on weekends. Late one night, Fred, age ten, began playing on some of Smith's construction equipment. Fred accidentally released the brakes of a tractor on which he was playing, and the tractor rolled down a hill and smashed into the building under construction. Fred was severely injured in the accident. Fred's parents sue both Smith Construction and Gerald for the injury.

a. Based on the elements of a negligent act, describe the requirements that must be met for Smith Construction to be held liable for negligence.

b. Describe the various classes of persons that are recognized by the law with respect to entering upon the property of another. In which class of persons would Fred belong?

c. What other legal doctrine is applicable in this case because of Fred's age? Explain your answer.

3. Parkway Distributors is a wholesale firm that employs several outside salespersons. Mary, a salesperson employed by Parkway Distributors, was involved in an automobile accident with another motorist while she was using her automobile in making regular sales calls for Parkway Distributors. Mary and the motorist are seriously injured in the accident. The motorist sues both Mary and Parkway Distributors for the injury based on negligence.
   a. Describe the requirements that the motorist must establish to show that Mary is guilty of negligence.
   b. On what legal basis might Parkway Distributors be held legally liable for the injury to the motorist? Explain your answer.
   c. Is Parkway Distributors responsible for Mary's injury? Explain your answer.
4. Tom asks his girlfriend, Susy, to go to a supermarket and purchase some steaks for dinner. While driving Tom's car to the supermarket, Susy ran a stop sign and seriously injured a pedestrian. Does Tom have any legal liability for the injury? Explain your answer.
5. The number of products liability lawsuits has increased substantially over time, and the dollar amount of the damage awards has also increased.
   a. Explain the factors that have caused products liability lawsuits to increase over time.
   b. Discuss some possible solutions for reducing the magnitude of this problem.
6. Whirlwind Mowers manufactures and sells power lawn mowers to the public and distributes the products through its own dealers. Tom is a homeowner who has purchased a power mower from an authorized dealer on the basis of the dealer's recommendation that "the mower is the best one available to do the job." Tom was cutting his lawn when the mower blade flew off and seriously injured his leg.
   a. Tom sues Whirlwind Mowers and asks damages based on negligence in producing the power mower. Is Whirlwind Mowers guilty of negligence? Explain your answer.
   b. The doctrine of *res ipsa loquitor* can often be applied to cases of this type. Show how this doctrine can be applied to this case. Your answer must include a discussion of *res ipsa loquitor.*
   c. Explain the various types of damage awards that Tom might receive if Whirlwind Mowers is found guilty of negligence.
7. Medical malpractice lawsuits have sharply increased over time. How do you explain the substantial increase in the number of malpractice lawsuits against physicians?

KEY CONCEPTS AND TERMS TO KNOW

Legal wrong
Tort
Absolute liability (strict liability)
Negligence
Elements of negligent act
Tortfeasor
Plaintiff
Special damages
General damages
Punitive damages
Proximate cause
Contributory negligence
Comparative negligence
Last clear chance rule
Assumption of risk
Imputed negligence
Vicarious liability
Family purpose doctrine
Res ipsa loquitor
Dram-shop law
Trespasser
Licensee
Invitee
Attractive nuisance
Permissive use statute
Respondeat superior
Governmental function
Proprietary function
Privity of contract
Breach of warranty
Philosophy of entitlement
Elective no-fault insurance

SUGGESTIONS FOR ADDITIONAL READING

Donaldson, James H. *Casualty Claim Practice*, 4th ed. Homewood, Illinois: Richard D. Irwin, Inc., 1984. Chapters 3 and 4.

Hall, Jr., Charles P. "Medical Malpractice Problem," *The Annals of the American Academy of Political and Social Science* 443 (May 1979).

Malecki, Donald S., ed. *Professional Liability: Impact in the Eighties*. Malvern, Pennsylvania: The Society of Chartered Property and Casualty Underwriters, 1983.

Malecki, Donald S., James H. Donaldson, and Ronald C. Horn. *Commercial Liability Risk Management and Insurance*, Volume 1. Malvern, Pennsylvania: American Institute for Property and Liability Underwriters, 1978, chapter 1.

Nardi, Joseph B. "Medical Malpractice Insurance: Crisis or Opportunity?" *Insurance Review* XLV, No. 2 (March/April 1984).

O'Connell, Jeffrey. "No-Fault Insurance: What, Why, and Where?" *The Annals of the American Academy of Political and Social Science* 443 (May 1979).

Prosser, William L. *Handbook of the Law of Torts*. St. Paul, Minnesota: West Publishing Company, 1971.

Schweig, Barry B. "Products Liability Problem," *The Annals of the American Academy of Political and Social Science* 443 (May 1979).

Williams, Jr., C. Arthur, George L. Head, and G. William Glendenning. *Principles of Risk Management and Insurance*, Vol. II. Malvern, Pennsylvania: American Institute for Property and Liability Underwriters, 1978, chapter 10.

Williams, Jr., C. Arthur and Richard M. Heins. *Risk Management and Insurance*, 5th ed. New York: McGraw-Hill Book Company, 1985, chapters 7–9.

NOTES

1. Defense Research Institute, "Liability to Trespasser, Licensee and Invitee," *For the Defense* (November, 1972), pp. 103–106.
2. Defense Research Institute, p. 106.
3. *Municipal Liability* (Philadelphia, Pennsylvania: Insurance Company of North America, n.d.), p. 3.
4. C. Arthur Williams, Jr., George L. Head, and G. William Glendenning, *Principles of Risk Management and Insurance,* Volume II (Malvern, Pennsylvania: American Institute for Property and Liability Underwriters, 1978), p. 195.
5. Williams, Jr., p. 196.
6. Williams, Jr., p. 178.
7. Barry B. Schweig, "Products Liability Problem," *The Annals of the American Academy of Political and Social Science,* 443 (May 1979), p. 99.
8. Schweig, pp. 94–103.
9. Charles P. Hall, Jr., "Medical Malpractice Problem," *The Annals of the American Academy of Political and Social Science,* 443 (May 1979), p. 84.
10. Hall, Jr., p. 92.
11. Hall, Jr., pp. 82–93.
12. *Insurance Decisions: The Liability Threat to Professionals* (Philadelphia, Pennsylvania: Insurance Company of North America, n.d.), p. 3.
13. *Insurance Decisions*, p. 8.
14. *Insurance Decisions*, pp. 9–10.
15. Jeffrey O'Connell, "No-Fault Insurance: What, Why and Where?" *The Annals of the American Academy of Political and Social Science*, 443 (May 1979), pp. 72–81.

PERSONAL LIABILITY INSURANCE

"He who defends himself in a court of law is a fool."

Anonymous

STUDENT LEARNING OBJECTIVES

After studying this chapter, you should be able to:

- Describe the persons who are insured for personal liability under Section II of the homeowners policy.
- Describe the different locations that are insured under Section II in the homeowners policy.
- Explain the insuring agreements found in Section II of the homeowners policy.
- List the major exclusions that apply to the Section II coverages in the homeowners policy.
- Describe some important liability endorsements that can be added to the homeowners policy.
- Explain the major features of the personal umbrella policy.

In this chapter, we will study personal liability insurance that can protect you against a lawsuit or claim arising out of your personal actions. Our attention will be focused primarily on Section II in the homeowners policy. The Section II coverages provide *comprehensive personal liability insurance* that protects the named insured and other household members against a claim or suit arising out of bodily injury or property damage to someone else. Finally, we will study the major features of the *personal umbrella policy,* which provides valuable protection against a catastrophic lawsuit.

COMPREHENSIVE PERSONAL LIABILITY INSURANCE

Comprehensive personal liability insurance protects the named insured and household members for legal liability arising out of their personal acts. In the event of a lawsuit involving bodily injury or property damage to someone else, the company will defend you and pay out those sums that you are legally obligated to pay up to the limits of the policy.

Comprehensive personal liability insurance can be purchased as a separate policy, or it can be provided by the homeowners policy. Both coverages generally are the same, so we will limit our discussion to the Section II liability coverages in the new 1984 homeowners contracts. Section II provides comprehensive personal liability insurance to homeowners, family members, and renters. With the major exception of business and professional liability, and liability arising out of the operation of an automobile, most personal acts are covered. Fortunately for the student, the Section II liability coverages are identical for all homeowner forms.[1]

Persons Insured

There is broad coverage of persons who are insured for personal liability under the homeowners policy. The following persons and organizations are insured under the Section II coverages in the homeowners policy.

Named insured and spouse The named insured and spouse, if the spouse is a resident of the same household, are insured for personal liability. However, if the couple gets a divorce or separates, or if one spouse establishes a separate household, the liability insurance would not cover that spouse.

Family members Relatives who reside in the named insured's household are also covered. If children are attending college and temporarily living away from home, they are insured under their parents' policy. But relatives must reside in the same household to be covered. Relatives who are visiting are not covered under the named insured's policy.

Other persons under age twenty-one Other persons under age twenty-one in the care of an insured are covered if they reside in the same household. This would include a foster child, a foreign exchange student, or a ward of the court. However, guests in the home are not covered. For example, if you have overnight guests, they are not covered since they are not residents of the household.

Person or organization responsible for animals or watercraft Any person or organization legally responsible for covered animals or watercraft is also insured. For example, if you go on vacation and leave your dog with a neighbor, your neighbor is covered if the dog should bite someone. However, an important exclusion applies to this section. A person or organization using or having custody of the animal or watercraft for business purposes, or without the owner's permission, is not covered. For example, if you board your dog in a kennel or dog hospital, the operator of the kennel or hospital is not covered. Likewise, the operators of boat marinas or persons who repair boats are not covered. Of course, if the animal or boat is stolen, the thief has no coverage under your policy.

Employees of an insured With respect to any vehicle to which the insurance applies, employees of an insured are covered while they are working for the insured. For example, if a gardener injures someone while operating a tractor or power mower, he or she is covered under the insured's policy.

Other persons With respect to any vehicle to which the insurance applies, other persons who are using the vehicle on an insured location with the named insured's consent are also insured under the policy.

Insured Locations

Several locations are insured under the Section II coverages in the homeowners policy. The following locations are insured:

Residence premises The **residence premises** where the insured resides are insured under the Section II coverages in the homeowners policy. The residence premises are defined as a one or two family dwelling, other structures, and grounds, or that part of the building where the insured resides, which is listed in the declarations section of the policy. The insured premises can be a private dwelling, apartment, or room.

Other locations Any other residence acquired during the policy period is covered automatically until the policy expiration date, at which time it must be reported for the protection to continue. This could include a house or a summer or winter home that is purchased or inherited during the policy period. Any premises used by the insured in connection with the residence premises, such as a garage or horse stall, are also insured.

Temporary residence If the insured is *temporarily* residing in any part of premises which he or she does not own, this location is also insured. For example, if you go on vacation and rent a motel or hotel room, a lake cottage, or a cabin in a resort area, you are covered at these locations.

Vacant land Vacant land owned or rented by an insured is also covered. For example, if children are playing on a vacant lot owned by the insured and part of the ground collapses, a claim or suit would be covered. Vacant farmland is an exception. However, farmland can be insured by an endorsement to the policy. Coverage also applies to land on which a one or two family dwelling is being constructed for use as a residence.

Land on which a residence is being built Land owned or rented by an insured on which a one or two family dwelling is being built as a residence for an insured is also an insured location.

Cemetery or burial plots Individual or family cemetery plots or burial vaults are also covered. For example, a family grave in an old cemetery may be slowly sinking into the ground. If someone steps on the grave site and is injured, any claim or suit would be covered.

Occasional rental of premises Any part of the premises occasionally rented to an insured for other than business purposes is also covered. For example, if Betty and Ed rent a hall to celebrate their twenty-fifth wedding anniversary, personal liability coverage applies to that location.

Insuring Agreements

Section II of the homeowners policy provides the following two coverages:

1. Coverage E—Personal Liability
   $100,000 per occurrence
2. Coverage F—Medical payments to others
   $1,000 per person

The minimum limits for Coverages E and F can both be increased to higher amounts by the payment of a small additional premium.

Coverage E—Personal Liability **Personal liability** insurance protects the insured against a claim or suit for damages because of bodily injury or property damage caused by the insured's negligence. This means that if you are liable for damages, the company will pay up to the policy limits those sums that you are legally obligated to pay. As we stated earlier, the minimum amount of liability insurance is $100,000 for each occurrence. The insurance amount is a *single limit* that applies to both bodily injury and property damage on a per occurrence basis. In the new 1984 homeowner contracts, **occurrence** is defined as an accident, including exposure to conditions, which results in bodily injury or property damage during the policy period. An occurrence can be a sudden accident, or it can be a gradual series of incidents that occur over time. For example, if your charcoal grill causes smoke damage over a period of time to the white stone on the side of your neighbor's house, the property damage would be covered as an occurrence.

In addition, the company provides a legal defense and agrees to defend you even if the suit is groundless, false, or fraudulent. The company has the right to investigate and settle the claim or suit by either defending you in a court of law or by settling out of court. As a practical matter, most personal liability suits are settled out of court. However, the company's obligation to defend you ends when the amount paid for damages from the occurrence equals the policy limits.

Personal liability coverage is broad. The following examples can illustrate the types of lawsuits covered:

1. Your dog bites a neighbor's child and you are sued.
2. While burning leaves in the yard, you accidentally set fire to your neighbor's house.
3. You install a wood-burning stove to save fuel, and billows of impure smoke and soot cause damage to your neighbor's property.
4. You are playing golf and accidentally hit a golfer playing ahead of you in the head with a golf ball.
5. You are playing basketball or football and accidentally injure another player.
6. You carelessly run over another student with your ten-speed bicycle.
7. A guest in your home trips over a turned-up carpet and sues you for bodily injury.
8. You are shopping in an antique shop and carelessly break an expensive Chinese vase.

Finally, you should remember that personal liability insurance in Coverage E is based on legal liability and the law of negligence. Before the company will pay out any sums for damages, you must be legally liable. In contrast, the next coverage we will examine is not based on negligence and legal liability.

Coverage F—Medical Payments to Others This coverage is a mini-accident policy that is part of the homeowners policy. The policy pays up to $1,000 per person for the reasonable medical expenses of another person who may be accidentally injured on the premises, or by the activities of an insured, resident employee, or animal owned by or in the care of an insured. The $1,000 limit may be increased by an additional premium. This coverage can be illustrated by the following examples:

1. A guest slips in your home and breaks an arm. The reasonable medical expenses are paid up to the policy limits.
2. A neighbor's child falls off a swing in your backyard and is injured. The child's medical expenses are covered.
3. You accidentally bump into another student who is getting a drink of water and chip his or her tooth. The dental expenses are covered.
4. Your dog bites a neighbor. The neighbor's medical expenses are paid up to the policy limits.

The company will pay all necessary medical expenses incurred or medically ascertained within three years from the date of the accident. The medical expenses covered are the reasonable charges for medical and surgical procedures, x-rays, dental care, ambulances, hospital stays, professional nursing, prosthetic devices, and funeral services.

Several important points are worth noting with respect to this coverage. *First, medical payments coverage is not based on the law of negligence and the establishment of legal liability.* If a person is accidentally injured, he or she does not have to prove that the insured was at fault. The policy will pay the medical expenses of the covered injury up to the policy limits. Also, you are still protected under Coverage E if a lawsuit results from the injury. For example, your dog may bite a child who is taken to a hospital for emergency treatment. Assume that medical expenses of $1,000 are paid by your company. If you are later sued because of the injury, your insurer will defend you and pay out those sums that you are legally obligated to pay.

Second, medical payments coverage does not apply to you or to regular residents of your household, other than a residence employee. For example, assume that you have a swimming pool in your backyard. Your daughter and a neighbor's child are roughhousing near the pool. Both children fall on the wet concrete and are injured. Only the medical expenses of the neighbor's child are covered. An exception is a **residence employee** who is injured on the premises. For example, your cook may burn his or her hand while cooking dinner. The medical expenses would be covered under your policy.

Finally, with respect to the medical expenses of others, the policy states the situations under which the benefits are paid. Coverage F applies only to the following persons and situations:

- To a person on the insured location with the permission of an insured; or
- To a person off the insured location, if the bodily injury:

  arises out of a condition on the insured location or the ways immediately adjoining.

  is caused by the activities of an insured.

  is caused by a residence employee in the course of the residence employee's employment by an insured.

  is caused by an animal owned by or in the care of an insured.

If the injury occurs on the insured location, the injured person must be on the premises with the permission of an insured. For example, a trespasser who is injured on the premises has no coverage. If injury to the person occurs off the insured location, there is coverage if the injury arises out of a condition on the insured location or the ways immediately adjoining. For example, if a pedestrian slips on an icy sidewalk in front of your house, the medical expenses are covered under your policy.

Finally, if someone is injured away from the insured location, the injury must be caused by the activities of an insured, by a residence employee in the course of employment by an insured, or by an animal owned by or in the care of an insured. For example, if you are playing basketball and accidentally injure another player, the injured player's medical expenses would be paid by your policy.

This concludes our discussion of the Section II coverages in the homeowners policy. Let us next consider the various Section II exclusions that are present in the policy.

SECTION II EXCLUSIONS

Three major groups of exclusions appear in Section II of the homeowners policy. The first group of exclusions applies to both personal liability and medical payments to others. The second group applies only to personal liability, while the third group applies only to medical payments to others.

Personal Liability and Medical Payments Exclusions

Several exclusions apply to both personal liability and medical payments to others. Let us briefly examine these exclusions.

Intentional injury If the insured deliberately injures another person or intentionally causes property damage, the loss is not covered. For example, if you get into an argument with someone and break his or her nose, a claim or suit for damages would not be covered. Likewise, if you give your Doberman Pinscher dog a command to attack someone, coverage does not apply. Intentional acts that cause bodily injury or property damage are against the public interest, and hence, they are properly excluded.

Business pursuits **Business pursuits** are also excluded, but coverage can be added by an endorsement. For example, if you operate a beauty shop in your home and carelessly burn a customer with a hair dryer, a lawsuit by the customer is not covered. However, homeowners often have garage sales or patio sales to sell unwanted personal property. Coverage ordinarily applies if the garage sale is not conducted as a regular business.

Legal liability associated with the renting of property is also excluded. For example, if you own a twelve-plex apartment house that is rented to students, personal liability coverage under the homeowners policy does not apply. The intent here is to exclude a professional landlord who owns a large apartment complex from paying the same premium that the individual homeowner would pay.[2]

There are several exceptions to the business pursuits exclusion. First, activities that are usual to nonbusiness pursuits are covered. For example, self-employed carpenters or painters are not covered in the course of doing business. However, if they should work on or paint their own homes, coverage applies since these activities are something that a typical homeowner would do.

Second, if the residence is occasionally rented for exclusive use as a residence, coverage applies. For example, if a professor rents his or her home while on sabbatical leave, there would be coverage. Also, if part of the premises is rented to no more than two roomers or boarders, or if part of the premises is rented as an office, school, studio, or private garage, coverage also applies. For example, if a homeowner rents the garage to a motorist to park his or her automobile, the coverage would apply.

Professional services Legal liability arising out of professional services is also excluded. Physicians and dentists are not covered for acts of malpractice under the homeowners policy. Also, attorneys, accountants, nurses, architects, engineers, and other professionals are not covered for legal liability for rendering or failing to render professional services. The loss exposures involving professional activities are substantially different from those faced by the typical homeowner. Negligent acts of professionals often result in the payment of substantial damage awards far in excess of those paid on behalf of negligent homeowners. For this reason, a professional liability policy is necessary to cover professional activities. Professional liability insurance will be examined in greater detail in Chapter 14.

Uninsured locations In addition, uninsured locations are not covered for personal liability and medical payments to others. We have already examined the meaning of an insured location. If the event occurs at an uninsured location, a suit or claim for damages is not covered.

Motor vehicles Motor vehicles, motorized land conveyances, and trailers, owned, operated, or rented by an insured, are also excluded. *Thus, automobiles, trucks, motorcycles, mopeds, and motorbikes clearly are not covered.* These vehicles can be insured by an appropriate automobile insurance policy. In addition, if you are towing a boat trailer, horse trailer, or rental trailer, the coverage does not apply.

The 1984 homeowners policy also adds two new exclusions with respect to motor vehicles. First, there is no coverage for liability arising out of the entrustment of an excluded vehicle or motorized land conveyance to any person. Second, there is no coverage for statutorily imposed vicarious parental liability for the actions of a

INSIGHT 10.1

What is a Business Pursuit?

The business pursuits exclusion has resulted in considerable litigation and confusion with respect to the exclusion of business liability under the homeowners policy. Despite the large number of court decisions, there is no clear consensus with respect to the meaning of a business pursuit. However, most courts that have examined the business pursuits exclusion generally agree that two criteria must be satisfied for the exclusion to apply: (1) expectation of gain and (2) at least some degree of continuity. If either element is absent, the business pursuits exclusion does not apply.

1. *Business in the home.* Many insureds operate a full-time business out of their homes, such as babysitting for pay, telephone solicitation, dressmaking, tailoring, haircutting, or cosmetology. Liability exposures arising out of these business operations generally are not covered since the two tests referred to earlier are usually met. Also, professional liability is excluded. Thus, physicians, dentists, attorneys, and other professionals who operate out of their homes are not covered for professional liability.

2. *Hobbies.* Many insureds have hobbies that gradually evolve into a business liability exposure. These hobbies include photography, music, painting, ceramics, woodworking, or other activities. The insured may sell hobby items on a regular basis with the expectation of earning a profit or may receive income or fees from paid instruction on a regular basis. Once again, the two tests of profit and continuity can be applied. If both tests are met, the business pursuits exclusion applies.

3. *Youth employment.* Many youths work part time and earn income by delivering newspapers, babysitting children, mowing lawns, shoveling snow, or other activities. Does the business pursuits exclusion apply to these activities? Once again, the various court decisions are inconsistent with respect to the business pursuits exclusion. As a general principle, part-time or casual employment by youths would not be considered a business pursuit and, therefore, coverage would apply.[1] Thus, if a teenager accidentally breaks a window while delivering newspapers, the loss would be covered. However, the part-time activity could become so extensive that it is considered a business pursuit. In one case, the court ruled that the business pursuits exclusion applied to a fifteen-year-old boy who operated a lawn care business, devoted twenty to twenty-five hours a week to the business, adopted a trade name that was advertised in the local newspaper, and purchased several pieces of lawn-care equipment.[2] Thus, because of conflicting court decisions, you should check with your agent to determine if a particular business activity is excluded by the company's homeowner policy.

[1] Emmett J. Vaughan, *Fundamentals of Risk and Insurance,* 3rd ed. (New York: John Wiley & Sons, 1982), p. 450.
[2] *Hanover Insurance Co. vs. Ransom,* 448 Atl. (2nd) 399 (1982).

SOURCE: Adaptation of "Watch Out for 'Business' Exposures" from *Methods Multi-Peril Section* of *FC & S Bulletins,* 1985. Reprinted by permission.

child or minor using an excluded motor vehicle or motorized land conveyance.

The exclusion of motor vehicles and motorized land conveyances, however, does not apply to the following:

1. *A trailer not towed by or carried on a motorized land conveyance is covered.* Thus, a home trailer that is parked and used as living quarters on a July 4th weekend would be covered.

2. *A motorized land conveyance designed for recreational use off public roads and not subject to motor vehicle registration is covered if (a) it is not owned by an insured or (b) it is owned by the insured and on an insured location.* Thus, a rented snowmobile would be covered. Also, a snowmobile owned by the insured and used on an insured location would also be covered. However, an endorsement can be added to cover an owned snowmobile that is used away from an insured location.
3. *A motorized golf cart when used to play golf on a golf course is also covered.* Thus, you are covered if you accidentally run over a golfer on the golf course. But if you use the golf cart for transportation home, you are not covered if you injure someone.
4. *A vehicle or conveyance not subject to motor vehicle registration is also covered if it is (a) used to service an insured residence, (b) designed for assisting the handicapped, or (c) in dead storage.* Thus, if you injure someone with a power lawn mower, the coverage applies. Also, if a handicapped insured injures someone with a motorized wheelchair, the coverage applies. Likewise, a vehicle not subject to motor vehicle registration that is in dead storage on an insured location is also covered.

Watercraft The 1984 homeowners policy excludes several categories of watercraft from coverage. They are as follows:

1. *Owned watercraft of any size with inboard or inboard-outdrive motor power is excluded from coverage.* However, coverage for this loss exposure can be purchased if desired.
2. *Rented watercraft with an inboard or inboard-outdrive motor power of more than 50 horsepower is also excluded.*
3. *An owned or rented sailing vessel, with or without auxiliary power, that is 26 feet or more in length is also excluded.*
4. *Watercraft powered by one or more outboard motors with more than 25 total horsepower is not covered if the outboard motor is owned by an insured.* However, outboard motors of more than 25 total horsepower are covered for the policy period if (a) you acquire them prior to the policy period and declare them at the policy inception, or (b) your intention to insure is reported in writing to the company within 45 days after you acquire the outboard motors.

Finally, negligent entrustment of and vicarious parental liability for the excluded watercraft described above are also excluded from coverage.

Aircraft Liability arising out of the ownership, maintenance, or use of an aircraft is not covered. An aircraft is any device used or designed to carry people or cargo in flight, such as an airplane, helicopter, glider, or balloon. However, model or hobby aircraft not used or designed to carry people or cargo are not subject to this exclusion.

War The Section II coverages also exclude war, undeclared war, civil war, insurrection, rebellion, and other hostile military acts. The homeowner contracts also exclude discharge of a nuclear weapon even if accidental. For example, if a National Guard pilot accidentally fires a nuclear weapon into a residential area, a claim or suit would not be covered.

Personal Liability Exclusions

The second group of exclusions applies only to personal liability (Coverage E). Let us briefly examine this set of exclusions.

Contractual liability **Contractual liability** means that you agree to assume the legal liability of another party by a written or oral contract. The 1984 homeowners policy excludes certain contractual liability exposures. They include the following:

1. *Liability of an insured for his or her share of any loss assessment charged against the owners of a condominium, cooperative unit, or community property is excluded.* However, an additional coverage (discussed later) provides $1,000 of coverage for a loss assessment if certain conditions are met.
2. *Liability under any contract or agreement is excluded.* However, the exclusion does not apply to written contracts (a) that directly relate to the ownership, maintenance, or use of an insured location, or (b) where the liability of others is assumed by the insured prior to an occurrence. Thus, there would be coverage for liability assumed under a written lease, equipment rental agreement if the equipment is used to maintain the residence premises, easement, and other written contracts where legal liability of a nonbusiness nature is assumed by an insured.

Property owned by the insured Property damage to property owned by the insured is also excluded. The insured cannot legally be liable to himself or herself. Thus, if the insured carelessly damages a lawn mower by running over a rock, the property damage is excluded.

In addition, keep in mind that the definition of an insured excludes not only the named insured and spouse, but also relatives residing in the household, and anyone under age twenty-one in the care of any insured. Thus, if a teenage son becomes angry at his parents and breaks some furniture, a lawsuit by the parents against their son would not be covered.

Property in the care of the insured Property damage to property rented to, occupied or used by, or in the care of the insured is not covered. For example, if you rent some power tools from a rental firm and carelessly damage one of the tools, the property damage is not covered if you are sued.

An important exception applies to this exclusion. The exclusion does not apply to property damage caused by fire, smoke, or explosion. For example, if you rent an apartment and carelessly start a fire with a cigarette, you can be held liable for the loss. In such a case, the homeowners policy would cover the loss.

Workers' compensation Bodily injury to any person who is eligible to receive benefits provided by the named insured under a workers' compensation, nonoccupational disability, or occupational disease law is not covered. This is true if the workers' compensation benefits are either mandatory or voluntary. In some states, domestic workers must be covered for workers' compensation benefits by their employers, while in other states, the coverage is voluntary. In either case, if an insured employee is eligible for workers' compensation benefits, there is no coverage for **bodily injury liability.**

Nuclear energy The homeowners policy excludes liability arising out of nuclear energy. If an insured under the homeowners policy is also insured under a nuclear energy liability policy, coverage does not apply. A nuclear energy policy is one issued by American Nuclear Insurers, Mutual Atomic Energy Liability Underwriters, Nuclear Insurance Association of Canada, or any of their successors. Under a nuclear energy policy, the definition of an insured is broad. If any person is involved in a nuclear incident, the nuclear energy liability policy covers the loss. For example, if an engineer carelessly causes a nuclear meltdown in a utility plant powered by atomic energy, the nuclear energy liability policy covers the loss. It is not covered by the homeowners policy.

Bodily injury to an insured There is no coverage for bodily injury to the named insured or to any resident of the household who is a relative or under age twenty-one and in the care of an insured. Thus, if one spouse is negligently injured by the other spouse, the injured spouse cannot collect damages.

Medical Payments Exclusions

The third group of exclusions under Section II applies only to medical payments to others (Coverage F). Let us briefly examine these exclusions.

Injury to a resident employee off an insured location If an injury to a resident employee occurs off an insured location and does not arise out of or in the course of employment by an insured, medical payments coverage does not apply. For example, if Mary is employed by the insured as a babysitter and is injured on her way home, her medical expenses are not covered.

Workers' compensation This is similar to the workers' compensation exclusion that we discussed earlier under personal liability insurance. Medical payments coverage does not apply to any person who is eligible to receive benefits provided by the named insured under a workers' compensation, nonoccupational disability, or occupational disease law. The injured employee's medical expenses are covered by workers' compensation insurance.

Nuclear energy Medical payments do not cover any person for bodily injury that results from nuclear reaction, radiation, or radioactive contamination. For example, bodily injury or disease resulting from a radiation leak in a nuclear power plant is not covered.

Persons regularly residing on the insured location There is no medical payments coverage for any person (other than a residence employee of an insured) who regularly resides on any part of the insured location. Thus, a tenant injured in a household accident cannot receive payment for medical expenses. The intent here is to minimize collusion among household members.

Additional Coverages

Section II also provides four additional coverages. They are: (1) claim expenses, (2) first aid expenses, (3) damage to the property of others, and (4) loss assessment.

Claim expenses In addition to payment of the liability limits, **claim expenses** are also paid. The company pays the court costs, attorney fees, and other legal expenses incurred in providing a legal defense.

The company also pays the premiums on bonds required in a suit defended by the insurer. For example, a decision may be appealed to a higher court, and if an appeal bond is required, the company pays the premiums.

In addition, the reasonable expenses incurred by the insured at the company's request to assist in the investigation and defense of a claim or suit are also paid. For example, if you are asked to attend a hearing, and you incur meal and transportation expenses, the company pays these expenses. This obligation includes payment for the actual loss of your earnings up to $50 per day. Finally, interest on the judgment that accrues after the judgment is awarded, but before payment is made, is also paid by the insurer.

First aid expenses The company also pays any **first aid expenses** incurred by the insured for bodily injury covered under the policy. For example, a guest may slip in your home and break a leg. If you call an ambulance to take the injured person to the hospital and are later billed for $150 by the ambulance company, this amount would be paid as a first aid expense.

Damage to property of others The company will pay up to $500 per occurrence for property **damage to the property of others** caused by an insured. The damaged property is valued on the basis of replacement cost. This coverage can be illustrated by the following examples:

1. A son, age ten, accidentally breaks a neighbor's window while playing softball.

2. At a party, you carelessly burn a hole in the owner's carpet with your cigarette.
3. You borrow your neighbor's lawn mower and accidentally damage the blade by running over a rock.
4. You are visiting a friend and accidentally break an expensive lamp.

The law of negligence does not apply to this coverage. Payment is made even though there is no legal liability to do so. The purpose of this coverage is to preserve personal friendships and keep peace in the neighborhood. Also, in some states, the parents are held responsible for the property damage caused by a young child. If this coverage were not provided, the person whose property is damaged would have to file a claim for damages against the insured who caused the damage. In addition, only a maximum of $500 is paid under this coverage. Amounts in excess of this limit are paid only by proving negligence and legal liability by the person who caused the damage.

Damage to the property of others also contains a unique set of exclusions. The major exclusions are summarized as follows:

1. *Property covered under Section I.* Property damage is excluded to the extent of any amount recoverable under Section I of the policy. The new 1984 homeowners policy now coordinates the Section II coverages with Section I coverages so that they complement each other. For example, assume that you borrow an expensive camera, which has a replacement cost of $1,500 and an actual cash value of $1,250. If the camera is destroyed in a tornado, the insurer would pay under Section I the actual cash value of $1,250 less the $250 deductible, or $1,000. Damage to the property of others under Section II would pay $500. Thus, both coverages would pay the full replacement cost of the destroyed camera, with no deductible.
2. *Intentional property damage by insureds, age thirteen or older.* If the property damage is intentionally caused by an insured, age thirteen or older, the coverage does not apply. This exclusion is extremely relevant to teenage vandalism, which is a serious national problem. For example, if a teenager damages a plate glass window with a sling shot, runs over a homeowner's lawn with an automobile, or maliciously breaks a tree, the parents' policy will not cover the property damage. In such cases, the $500 maximum benefit will not be paid.
3. *Property owned by an insured.* Property damage to property owned by an insured is also excluded. For example, if a son damages some power tools owned by his parents, the damage would not be covered.

   However, under the new 1984 homeowners policy, damage to the property of others now includes rented property, as well as rented, nonregistered recreational vehicles. Thus, if you rent a portable television set and accidentally drop it, the damage is covered. Likewise, if you rent a golf cart and damage it, the loss is covered. Under the 1976 homeowners policy, damage to the property of others did not apply to rented property.
4. *Business pursuits.* Property damage arising out of business pursuits is excluded. For example, if you operate a lawn maintenance business and accidentally cut down a shrub while mowing a customer's lawn, the damage is not covered.
5. *Property damage because of an act or omission.* Property damage caused by an act or omission in connection with a premise owned, rented, or controlled by the insured at any *insured location* is not covered. For example, without an endorsement, farmland is not covered under the homeowners policy. If the insured should accidentally damage the tractor of the ten-

ant who is farming the land, the coverage does not apply.

6. *Motor vehicles, aircraft, or watercraft.* Property damage that is caused by a motor vehicle, aircraft, or watercraft is not covered. For example, if you run over a neighbor's ten-speed bicycle with your automobile, the loss is not covered.

Loss assessment The 1984 homeowners policy also provides coverage of $1,000 for certain liability loss assessments. Higher limits are available by endorsement.

ENDORSEMENTS TO SECTION II COVERAGES

Numerous endorsements can be added to the Section II coverages under the homeowners policy. Only three of them will be discussed here. They are as follows:

- Business pursuits
- Personal injury
- Watercraft and recreational vehicles

Business Pursuits

A **business pursuits endorsement** can be added to the homeowners policy to cover any legal liability as a result of business activities. The exclusion of business pursuits under the policy usually is not a problem for the person who operates his or her own business, since a general liability insurance policy covering the business usually is in force. However, it can be a serious problem for an employee who is not insured under the owner's general liability policy or for someone who engages in business activities and has no liability insurance coverage. For example, if you are an employee in a lumber yard and accidentally drop a fifty-pound bag of cement on a customer's head, the owner is covered for a lawsuit because of your actions. But if you are not included as an insured under the employer's liability policy, and you are also sued by the injured customer, you have no coverage. Even if you are not legally liable, the costs of having an attorney defend you can be staggering. Another example is a housewife who regularly babysits for a working neighbor. If she should accidentally injure one of the children, the homeowners policy would not cover the loss.

The business pursuits endorsement contains several exclusions. The major exclusions are summarized as follows:

1. *If the insured owns or financially controls a business, or is a partner or member in a partnership, the insurance does not apply.* Specific liability insurance covering the business is needed.
2. *Professional services other than teaching are excluded.* The endorsement specifically excludes legal liability from architectural, engineering, or industrial design services; medical, surgical, and dental services; treatment conducive to the health of persons or animals; and beauty or barber services. A professional liability policy is needed to cover the legal liability of professionals in these occupations.
3. *If the insured causes bodily injury to a fellow employee in the course of employment, the insurance does not apply.* The intent here is to exclude a loss covered under a workers' compensation law.
4. *Certain activities of faculty members and teachers are also excluded.* Liability arising out of draft or saddle animals such as horses is not covered. Liability arising out of aircraft, motor vehicle, recreational motor vehicle, or watercraft is not covered. For example, if a high school instructor is teaching a driving course, and a student driver injures someone because of faulty directions from the instructor, the injury is not covered. Finally, bodily injury claims against a teacher arising out of corporal punishment can be added as an optional coverage.

Personal Injury

The homeowners policy only covers legal liability arising out of *bodily injury or prope[illegible] damage to someone else.* **Personal injury,** which should not be confused with bodily injury, can be added to the homeowners policy as an endorsement. Personal injury means legal liability arising out of the following:

- False arrest, detention or imprisonment, or malicious prosecution
- Libel, slander, or defamation of character
- Invasion of privacy, wrongful eviction, or wrongful entry

For example, if you have a person arrested who is later found innocent, or if you make false or slanderous statements about a person's reputation, you may be liable for damages. These losses are not covered under the homeowners policy but can be covered by the personal injury endorsement.

Watercraft and Recreational Vehicles

As we noted earlier, boats and recreational vehicles such as snowmobiles have specific limitations and exclusions under Section II of the homeowners policy. Separate endorsements can be added to provide additional liability coverages on boats and recreational vehicles. For example, legal liability involving an owned snowmobile away from an insured location is not covered unless specified by an endorsement.

PERSONAL UMBRELLA POLICY

Personal liability claims occasionally reach catastrophic levels. They may exceed the liability limits of the basic contracts. After these basic limits are exhausted, the insured may be required to pay thousands of dollars out of his or her personal assets. This is a particularly important consideration for wealthy professionals and successful businesspersons whose personal assets can be attached if a judgment substantially exceeds the amount of insurance in force. Thus, protection is needed for a catastrophic lawsuit. In particular, physicians, surgeons, dentists, businesspersons, attorneys, accountants, farmers, and persons with large amounts of financial assets need protection against catastrophic lawsuits.

The **personal umbrella policy** is designed to provide protection against a catastrophic lawsuit or judgment. Most comapnies will write this coverage in amounts ranging from $1 million to $10 million. The policy covers the entire family anwhere in the world. Coverage is broad and typically includes coverage for catastrophic liability exposures associated with the home, boats, automobiles, and sports, and recreational vehicles.

Major Features

Although personal umbrella policies are not standard contracts, they contain common features. They are summarized as follows:

1. The umbrella policy provides excess liability insurance over basic underlying contracts.
2. Certain losses not covered by the underlying contracts are also covered, subject to a retained limit or deductible.
3. Basic underlying policies must be at least equal to certain minimum amounts.
4. The umbrella policy is reasonable in cost.

Excess liability insurance The personal umbrella policy is excess over any basic underlying contracts that may apply. The policy pays only after the basic limits of the underlying coverages are exhausted. The company agrees to pay losses for which the insured is legally liable, which exceed the retained limit. The **retained limit** is either (1) the amount recoverable under the underlying contract, or (2) a stated sum (deductible) if the loss is not covered by the underlying insurance.

Losses not covered by underlying contracts The personal umbrella policy also covers many losses that are not covered by the underlying contracts, including personal injury. If the loss is covered by the personal umbrella policy but not by any underlying contract, a *retained limit or deductible* must be satisfied. Most personal umbrella policies require a retention of at

Figure 10.1
Minimum Underlying Coverage Amounts Required to Qualify for a Personal Umbrella Policy

Automobile liability insurance	$250,000/$500,000/$50,000 or $300,000 single limit
Comprehensive personal liability insurance (separate contract or homeowners policy)	$100,000
Watercraft	$100,000 ($300,000 for large watercraft)
Employers' liability insurance (where required or permitted by law)	$100,000

least $250 per occurrence, but it could be considerably higher. Examples of claims not covered by the underlying contracts, but insured under the umbrella policy, include libel, slander, defamation of character, and contractual liability.

Several examples can illustrate how the personal umbrella policy works. Assume that Sam has a $1 million personal umbrella policy. He also has an automobile liability policy with limits of $250,000/$500,000/$50,000, and he has $100,000 of personal liabilty coverage under the homeowners policy.[3] Assume that Sam injures another motorist in an accident and incurs a $650,000 judgment. The underlying automobile insurance policy pays the first $250,000, and the personal umbrella policy pays the remaining $400,000, since the underlying limits of $250,000 per person have been exhausted.

If Sam's German shepherd bites and mauls a neighbor's child, and Sam incurs a judgment of $150,000, the homeowners policy would pay $100,000 and the umbrella policy would pay $50,000.

Finally, assume that Sam is sued by his divorced wife for defamation of character and must pay damages of $10,000. If there is no underlying coverage and a retention of $250, the umbrella policy would pay $9,750.

Minimum underlying coverages A third feature of the personal umbrella policy is that the insured must carry certain minimum insurance amounts before the company assumes the personal catastrophic exposure. Although the required amounts of underlying insurance vary among insurers, the amounts shown in Figure 10.1 are typically required.

Reasonable cost The personal comprehensive umbrella policy is extremely reasonable in cost in view of the catastrophic protection provided. The actual cost depends on several variables, including the number of automobiles, boats, and motorcycles to be covered. However, for most families, the protection can be obtained by an annual premium of less than $125. Payment of a relatively modest premium will provide you with a greater peace of mind, since you are covered for a catastrophic lawsuit involving personal liability.

Umbrella Liability Exclusions

You may mistakenly believe that the personal umbrella policy provides catastrophic protection against all claims. This is incorrect. Although the policy provides broad coverage, certain exclusions typically are present. Some common exclusions are as follows:[4]

1. Any obligation under a workers' compensation, disability benefits or similar law.

INSIGHT 10.2

Umbrellas, point by point

In comparing umbrella liability policies, note the following especially carefully:

The total cost. A company may charge low rates for umbrellas but require high limits of auto and residential insurance—or vice versa. If you'd have to increase your underlying insurance, factor the costs into your outlay.

Discounts. The company that insures your car or home may give you a price break on an umbrella. Check with it first.

Legal defense costs. Note whether these would be included in the policy limit.

Who is covered. Umbrellas typically protect you and family members living with you. Find out who are considered family members and whether they would be covered while temporarily away from home, such as children attending a distant school.

Where you'd be protected. Most umbrellas pay claims brought only in the U.S. or Canada; other protect you anywhere in the world.

Exclusions. These generally include intentional personal injury or property damage unless inflicted in protecting people or property, liabilities under worker's compensation and similar programs, and damage to your own property or losses through your handling or use of aircraft. As mentioned, work-related activities usually aren't covered. For those you may need a business insurance policy. Personal protection could be added with an endorsement. If you moonlight, inquire about a rider on your residential insurance.

An umbrella may also stop short of covering volunteer service on the board of a church, charity, civic group or condominium association. Accordingly, be sure to find out whether the organization has a liability policy that would protect you

SOURCE: Reprinted with permission from *Changing Times* Magazine, © Kiplinger Washington Editors, Inc., "Umbrellas, point by point," from "What If You're Sued for a Million," Dec. 1984. This reprint is not to be altered in any way, except with permission from *Changing Times.*

2. Damage to property a covered person owns.
3. An auto or watercraft owned by a family member or furnished for his or her regular use. This exclusion does not apply to the named insured or to an auto or watercraft owned by the named insured.
4. Nuclear energy exclusion.
5. An act committed or directed by a covered person with intent to cause personal injury or property damage.
6. Aircraft.
7. Watercraft. This exclusion does not apply to watercraft with inboard motor(s) of fifty horsepower or less, outboard motor(s) of twenty-five horsepower or less, or to sailing vessels less than twenty-six feet long.
8. Business activity or business property. This exclusion does not apply to the named insured's or family member's use of a private passenger auto. Business property does not include farms.
9. Professional liability.
10. An act or failure to act as an officer, trustee, or director of a corporation or association. This exclusion does not apply to a not-for-profit corporation or association.

SUMMARY

- Section II of the homeowners policy protects the named insured, household members, and other persons for legal liability arising out of their personal acts.
- Several groups of persons are insured under Section II of the homeowners policy. This includes the named insured and spouse if a resident of the same household, resident relatives, other persons under age twenty-one in the care of an insured, persons or organizations responsible for the insured's animals or watercraft, and employees of an insured while operating a vehicle to which the insurance applies.
- Insured locations include the resident premises described in the declarations, other residences acquired during the policy period, a residence where the insured is temporarily residing, vacant land other than farmland, cemetery or burial plots, land on which a residence is being built, and occasional rental of a premise for other than business purposes.
- Personal liability insurance (Coverage E) protects the insured against a claim or suit for damages because of bodily injury or property damage caused by the insured's negligence. The company will defend the insured and pay out those sums that the insured is legally obligated to pay up to the policy limits.
- Medical payments to others (Coverage F) pays the reasonable medical expenses of another person who may be accidentally injured on the premises, or by the activities of an insured, resident employee, or animal owned by or in the care of an insured. It is not necessary to prove negligence and establish legal liability before the medical expenses are paid. The coverage does not apply to the named insured and regular residents of the household, other than residence employees.
- Section II also provides four additional coverages. They are: (1) claim expenses, (2) first aid expenses, (3) damage to the property of others, and (4) coverage for a loss assessment charge.
- Several liability endorsements can be added to the homeowners policy. They include coverage for business pursuits, personal injury, and coverage for watercraft and recreational vehicles.
- The new 1984 homeowner policies increase the basic underlying limits in Section II, expand certain provisions, and also add new exclusions.
- The personal umbrella policy is designed to provide protection against a catastrophic lawsuit or judgment. The major features of the personal umbrella policy are as follows:
  a. The policy provides excess liability insurance over basic underlying insurance contracts.
  b. Certain losses not covered by the underlying contracts are also covered, subject to a retained limit or deductible.
  c. The basic underlying contracts must be at least equal to certain minimum amounts.
  d. The umbrella policy is reasonable in cost.

QUESTIONS FOR REVIEW

1. Who are the persons insured under Section II of the homeowners policy?
2. Does the homeowners policy provide personal liability coverage only at the residence described in the declarations? Explain.
3. Describe the coverage for personal liability (Coverage E) in Section II of the homeowners policy.
4. What is an occurrence?
5. Describe the coverage for medical payments to others (Coverage F) in Section II of the homeowners policy.
6. Who are the persons covered for medical payments to others (Coverage F) in the homeowners policy?
7. List the exclusions that apply to the Section II coverages in the homeowners policy.
8. In addition to coverage for personal liability (Coverage E) and medical payments to others (Coverage F), several additional coverages are provided in Section II of the homeowners policy. Describe the additional coverages that are found in Section II.
9. Describe some endorsements that can be added to the Section II coverages in the homeowners policy.
10. Explain the meaning of personal injury. Is personal injury covered under the homeowners policy?
11. Describe the major features of the personal umbrella policy.

QUESTIONS FOR DISCUSSION

1. Indicate whether the following losses are covered under Section II in the homeowners policy. Assume there are no special endorsements. Give reasons for your answer.
   a. The insured's dog bites a neighbor's child and also chews up the neighbor's coat.
   b. The insured accidentally injures another player while playing softball.
   c. A guest slips on a waxed kitchen floor and breaks an arm.
   d. A neighbor's child falls off a swing in the yard and breaks an arm.
   e. The insured accidentally falls on an icy sidewalk and breaks a leg.
   f. The insured rents a power rake and damages the rake because of negligence.
   g. While driving to the supermarket, the insured hits another motorist with the automobile.
   h. A ward of the court, age ten, in the care of the insured, deliberately breaks a neighbor's window.
   i. The insured paints houses for a living. A can of paint accidentally falls on the roof of a customer and discolors it.
   j. The insured falls asleep while smoking a lighted cigarette, and a rented apartment is badly damaged by the fire.
   k. The insured borrows a camera and it is stolen from a motel room while the insured is on vacation.

2. Joseph is the named insured under a Homeowners 3 policy (special form) with a liability limit of $100,000 per occurrence and $1,000 medical payments. For each of the following situations, indicate whether or not the loss is covered under Section II of Joseph's homeowners policy.
   a. Joseph is a self-employed accountant who works in his home. One of Joseph's clients sues him for negligence in preparing an incorrect financial statement and recovers a $3,000 judgment against him.
   b. A maid who works for Joseph's wife falls from a ladder in the home and is injured. The maid incurs medical expenses of $1,000. The maid sues Joseph for $10,000 alleging that his wife was negligent. The maid is not covered by workers' compensation insurance.
   c. Joseph's nineteen-year-old son, who recently was married and now lives in his own apartment, negligently killed another hunter in a hunting accident. The son is sued for $100,000 in a wrongful death accident.
3. Mary rents an apartment and is the named insured under a Homeowners 4 policy (contents broad form) with a liability limit of $100,000 per occurrence and $1,000 medical payments. For each of the following situations, indicate whether or not the loss is covered under Section II of Mary's homeowners policy. Assume there are no special endorsements, and each situation is an independent event.
   a. Mary is at a party at a friend's house. She accidentally burns a hole in the living room couch with her lighted cigarette. It will cost $500 to repair the damaged couch.
   b. Mary rents a snowmobile at a ski resort and accidentally collides with a skier. Mary is sued for $200,000 by the injured skier.
4. Liability insurance can be written either on an *occurrence basis* or an *accident basis.*
   a. Explain the difference between an occurrence and an accident. Give an illustration of each in your answer.
   b. On what basis is the personal liability coverage in the homeowners policy written?
5. The personal umbrella policy provides broad protection against catastrophic lawsuits or judgments.
   a. Explain several liability loss exposures that typically are covered by the personal umbrella policy but generally are not covered by the Section II coverages in the homeowners policy.
   b. Explain how the *retained limit or deductible* in the personal umbrella policy applies to a loss that is not covered by an underlying contract. Give an illustration in your answer.

KEY CONCEPTS AND TERMS TO KNOW

Residence premises
Personal liability
Medical payments to others
Occurrence
Business pursuits
Intentional injury
Bodily injury liability
Contractual liability
Residence employee
Claim expenses
First aid expenses
Damage to property of others
Business pursuits endorsement
Personal injury
Personal umbrella policy
Retained limit
Underlying coverages

SUGGESTIONS FOR ADDITIONAL READING

Crane, Frederick G. *Insurance Principles and Practices,* 2nd ed. New York: John Wiley & Sons, 1984, chapter 10.

Fire, Casualty, & Surety Bulletins, Personal Lines Volume, Dwelling Section. Cincinnati, Ohio: The National Underwriter. The bulletins are published monthly.

Greene, Mark R. and James S. Trieschmann. *Risk and Insurance,* 6th ed. Cincinnati, Ohio: Southwestern Publishing Company, 1984, chapter 15.

Vaughan, Emmett J. *Fundamentals of Risk and Insurance,* 3rd ed. New York: John Wiley & Sons, 1982, chapter 29.

Wood, Glenn L., Claude C. Lilly III, Donald S. Malecki, and Jerry S. Rosenbloom. *Personal Risk Management and Insurance,* 3rd ed., Volume I. Malvern, Pennsylvania: American Institute for Property and Liability Underwriters, 1984, chapter 5.

NOTES

1. The discussion of Section II liability coverages in this chapter is based on Glenn L. Wood, Claude C. Lilly III, Donald S. Malecki, and Jerry S. Rosenbloom, *Personal Risk Management and Insurance,* 3rd ed., Volume I (Malvern, Pennsylvania: American Institute for Property and Liability Underwriters, 1984), chapter 5; George E. Guinane, *Homeowners Guide* (Indianapolis, Indiana: The Rough Notes Company, 1977); "ISO's New Homeowners '84," *Independent Agent,* 81, No. 8 (April 1984), pp. 63–68; "The '82 Homeowners," *Independent Agent,* 80, No. 10 (June 1983), pp. 30–31; Insurance Services Office, *Homeowners Policy Program, 1984 Edition,* Supplementary Information to Circular HO-84-234 (August 23, 1984); *Fire, Casualty, & Surety Bulletins,* Personal Lines Volume, Dwelling Section, (Cincinnati, Ohio: The National Underwriter); and Philip Gordis, *Property and Casualty Insurance,* 26th ed. (Indianapolis, Indiana: The Rough Notes Company, 1980), pp. 447–56.
2. George E. Guinane, *Homeowners Guide* (Indianapolis, Indiana: The Rough Notes Company, 1977), p. 76.
3. The figures $250,000/$500,000 refer to a limit of $250,000 per person and $500,000 per accident for bodily injury liability. The $50,000 figure is the limit for property damage liability.
4. Alliance of American Insurers, *Policy Kit for Students of Insurance,* 1983, p. 295.

AUTOMOBILE INSURANCE

". . . If you can't pay, you can lose your driving privileges."

Consumer Shopping Guide for Automobile Insurance, State of Missouri

STUDENT LEARNING OBJECTIVES

After studying this chapter, you should be able to:

- Identify the persons who are covered for liability insurance under the PAP.
- Describe the liability coverage in the PAP.
- Explain the medical payments coverage in the PAP.
- Describe the uninsured motorists coverage in the PAP.
- Explain the coverage that insures your automobile against physical damage or theft.
- Explain the duties imposed on the insured after an accident or loss occurs.

In 1983, about 29 million automobile accidents occurred, and about 45,000 persons were killed in these accidents. The economic cost of these accidents was staggering. Automobile accidents in 1983 resulted in an economic loss of about $63 billion, which was the equivalent of about $260 for each person in the United States. These costs included the cost of paying for the property damage; medical, hospital, and legal expenses; lost productivity; costs of emergency services; public assistance costs; and the administrative costs of insurance.

In this chapter, we begin our study of automobile insurance. Automobile insurance is extremely important in maintaining an individual's or a family's financial security. Legal liability arising out of the negligent operation of an automobile can reach catastrophic levels. Medical expenses, pain and suffering, the unexpected death of a family member, and the damage or loss of an expensive automobile can have a traumatic financial impact on the individual or family.

In this chapter, we will study the **Personal Auto Policy** (PAP). The PAP was first introduced in several states by the Insurance Services Office in 1977. The PAP is easier to read and understand than the older Family Auto Policy (FAP). The language has been simplified and is more personal. The named insured is referred to as "you" and "your," and the insurer is referred to as "we" and "our."

The PAP is divided into six parts. They are as follows:

1. Part A—Liability Coverage.
2. Part B—Medical Payments Coverage.
3. Part C—Uninsured Motorists Coverage.
4. Part D—Coverage for Damage to Your Auto.
5. Part E—Duties after an Accident or Loss.
6. Part F—General Provisions.

In the following sections, we will examine each of these major parts in some detail.[1] Let us begin by examining the liability section of the PAP.

PART A—LIABILITY COVERAGE

Liability coverage (Part A) is the most important part of the PAP. It protects a covered person against a suit or claim arising out of the negligent operation of an automobile.

Insuring Agreement

In the insuring agreement, the company agrees to pay any damages for bodily injury or property damage for which you are legally responsible because of an automobile accident. The company also agrees to defend you and pay all legal defense costs. This is a valuable provision, since, in effect, you are being provided with a team of defense attorneys prior to an accident.

The liability coverage is written as a **single limit** for both bodily injury and property damage liability. The liability limit is applied on a *per accident basis* without a separate limit for each person. However, if desired, the policy can be written with split limits. A **split limit** means the amount of insurance for bodily injury liability and property damage liability is stated separately, such as $50,000 per person and $100,000 per accident for bodily injury liability and $50,000 for property damage liability.

The liability coverage is written on an accident rather than on an occurrence basis to reduce confusion and misunderstanding and not to restrict the coverage. Because of numerous court decisions, the term "accident" also includes an occurrence.

In addition, all states have financial responsibility or compulsory insurance laws that require motorists to carry a minimum amount of liability insurance or to post a bond at the time of an accident. The minimum liability limits in most states are $30,000 to $50,000 (see Figure 12.1 in Chapter 12) per each accident and are woefully inadequate in view of the high damage awards in recent years. If you are a standard driver, the minimum liability limits can be substantially increased without a proportionate increase in premiums. For example, if the minimum liability limits were increased from $30,000 to $100,000, the premiums in many jurisdictions would increase by less than 40 percent.

Covered Auto

A wide variety of vehicles can be insured under the PAP. They include the following:

- Any vehicle shown in the Declarations
- Pickup, panel truck, or van if not used in any business or occupation
- Newly acquired vehicles
- Trailers
- Temporary substitute automobile

First, a **covered auto** is *any vehicle shown in the declarations*. This can include a private passenger automobile, station wagon, or jeep owned by the named insured. In addition, a private passenger automobile that is leased for at least six months is also considered an owned automobile.

Second, a *pickup, panel truck, or van* is also covered if it is not used in any business or occupation. Farming is an exception. These vehicles would be covered while being used on a farm or ranch.

Third, *newly acquired* vehicles are also covered. If the vehicle is an *additional* vehicle, you are automatically covered as long as you notify the company within thirty days. An additional premium for the extra vehicle must be paid. For example, if you own one car and purchase another, you are automatically covered when you drive away from the lot. The automatic protection applies to a private passenger automobile and also to a pickup, panel truck, or van that is not used in any business or occupation.

If the new vehicle *replaces* an automobile shown in the declarations, it is automatically insured for all coverages provided on the previous auto. However, if you want physical damage insurance on the replacement car, you must request coverage from the company within thirty days. This is known as Coverage for Damage to Your Auto (Part D). For example, Joseph has a 1977 Buick Skylark which is traded in for a 1986 Pontiac. The Skylark is insured under the PAP with full coverage, including physical damage insurance. Assume that Joseph forgets to notify his insurer of the trade-in. Two months later, he skids on an icy road and hits a telephone pole. The property damage to the telephone pole would be covered under the liability section of the PAP. However, the physical damage to Joseph's car is not covered, since the PAP requires that the company must be notified within thirty days after the insured car is replaced in order for the physical damage insurance to be in force. If he had notified the company within thirty days after the trade-in, and had requested physical damage coverage, the damage to the 1986 Pontiac would have been covered.

In addition, if you own a *trailer*, it is also covered for liability insurance under the policy. A trailer is defined as a vehicle designed to be pulled by a private passenger automobile or by a pickup, panel truck, or van. It also includes a farm wagon or farm implement while being towed by a private passenger automobile, or by a pickup, panel truck, or van. For example, you may be pulling a boat trailer which upsets and injures another motorist. The liability section of the PAP would cover the loss.

Finally, a **temporary substitute automobile** is also covered. A temporary substitute automobile is a **nonowned automobile** or trailer that the insured is temporarily using because of mechanical breakdown, repair, servicing, loss, or destruction of a covered vehicle. For example, if you drive a loaner car while your car is in the garage for repairs, it is insured for liability coverage under the PAP.

Covered Persons

Numerous persons are insured under the liability section of the PAP. They are as follows:

- Named insured and any family member.
- Any person using the named insured's covered auto.
- Any person or organization, but only for li-

ability arising out of a covered person's use of a covered auto on behalf of that person or organization.

- Any person or organization legally responsible for the named insured's or family members' use of any automobile or trailer (other than a covered auto or one owned by that person or organization).

First, *the named insured and family members* are covered for the ownership, maintenance, or use of any automobile or trailer. The liability coverage extends to nonowned automobiles as well. The named insured also includes a spouse if a resident of the same household. A family member is a person related to the named insured by blood, marriage, or adoption who resides in the same household, including a ward or foster child. Thus, the husband, wife, and children are covered while using any automobile, owned or nonowned.

Keep in mind that family members residing in the same household are automatically insured. *They do not have to obtain permission of the named insured or spouse before the coverage applies*. For example, Robert, age fourteen, is covered if he takes his father's car without his permission and injures someone in an accident. Father is also covered if he is sued because of his son's negligence.

In addition, as we noted earlier, the family member must be a resident in the named insured's household. If children are attending college, and are temporarily away from home, they are still insured under their parents' policy.

Second, *any other person using the named insured's covered auto* is also covered, if there is a reasonable belief that permission to use the automobile exists. The PAP excludes coverage only if the nonowner cannot establish a reasonable belief that he or she was granted permission to use the covered automobile. The older FAP required the borrower to obtain permission from the owner or owner's spouse. This is no longer the case. For example, Sam may have permitted his girlfriend, Mary, to drive his car several times over the past six months. If Mary takes Sam's car without his expressed permission, she is covered under his policy as long as she can show a reasonable belief that Sam would have given her permission.

Third, *any person or organization* legally responsible for the acts of a covered person while using a covered auto is also insured. For example, if James permits a fellow worker to drive his car on an errand for their mutual employer, and the fellow worker injures someone, the employer is covered for any suit or claim.

Finally, there is coverage for *any person or organization legally responsible* for the named insured's or family members' use of any automobile or trailer (other than a covered auto and one owned by the person or organization). For example, James may borrow the car of a fellow worker to mail a package for his employer. If James injures someone while driving that car, the employer is also covered for any suit or claim. However, the PAP does not extend coverage to the employer when the named insured is using an automobile owned by the employer.

Supplementary Payments

In addition to the policy limits and a legal defense, certain **supplementary payments** are also made. Premiums on a bail bond can be paid up to $250 because of an accident that results in property damage or bodily injury. However, payment is not made for a traffic violation except if an accident occurs. For example, assume that Henry is drunk and injures another motorist in an accident. If he is arrested, and bond is set at $2,500, the company will pay the premium up to a maximum of $250.

Premiums on an appeal bond and a bond to release an attachment of property in a lawsuit defended by the insurer are also paid as supplementary payments. If interest accrues after a judgment is handed down, the interest is also paid.

In addition, the company will pay up to $50 daily for the loss of earnings (but not other income) due to attendance at a hearing or trial at the insurer's request.

Finally, other reasonable expenses incurred at the insurer's request are paid. For example, you may be a defendant in a trial and be requested to testify. If you have meal or transportation expenses, they would be paid as a supplemental payment.

Exclusions

The liability section of the PAP has a lengthy list of exclusions. They are summarized as follows:

1. Intentional bodily injury or property damage is excluded. Thus, if you intentionally run over a bicycle, the damage is not covered.
2. Liability coverage is not provided to any person for damage to property owned or being transported by that person. For example, a friend may ask you to take a television set to a repair shop. You have an accident, and the set is damaged. The damage is not covered.
3. Property damage to property that is rented to, used by, or in the care of a covered person is not covered. For example, you may rent some power tools that are damaged in an accident. The damage is not covered. There are two exceptions to this exclusion. First, property damage to a nonowned private garage or residence is covered. For example, if you rent a house and carelessly back into a partly opened garage door, the damage would be covered.

   Second, an extremely important exception applies when you borrow someone else's vehicle. Property damage to a *nonowned* private passenger automobile, trailer, pickup, panel truck, or van is covered under the liability section of the PAP if the vehicle is not furnished for your regular use. For example, if you borrow a friend's car and damage it, *the property damage is covered under the liability section of your policy if you are legally liable.* Your company will pay the damage to the borrowed vehicle if you are liable.[2]
4. Bodily injury to an employee of any person seeking protection under the policy is not covered. The intent here is to cover the employee's injury under a workers' compensation law. However, domestic employees would be covered if workers' compensation benefits are not available.
5. There is no liability coverage on a vehicle while it is being used to carry persons or property for a fee. For example, if taxicab drivers are on strike, and you transport passengers for a fee, the liability coverage does not apply. This exclusion does not apply to a share-the-expense car pool.
6. If a person is employed or engaged in the automobile business, liability arising out of the operation of vehicles in the automobile business is excluded. For example, if you are a mechanic in a garage and have an accident while roadtesting a customer's car, your policy will not cover you. Liability arising out of the accident would be covered instead under the employer's liability policy, such as a Garage Liability policy. However, the exclusion does not apply to the operation of any covered auto by the named insured, family member, or partner. For example, referring back to our earlier illustration, you would be covered while driving your own car to and from work or on an errand for your employer, such as driving to a parts shop to pick up a part.
7. This exclusion is similar to the preceding, except that it applies to all businesses other than the automobile business. The intent here is to exclude liability coverage for commercial vehicles and trucks that are used in the business. For example, if you drive a large cement truck, your liability coverage does not apply. However, this exclusion does not apply

to a private passenger automobile (owned or nonowned) or to a pickup, panel truck, or van that you own.

8. If a person uses a vehicle without having a reasonable belief that he or she is entitled to do so, there is no coverage.
9. Liability of insureds who are covered under special nuclear energy contracts is also excluded.
10. Liability arising out of motorized vehicles having less than four wheels is excluded. Thus, motorcycles, mopeds, motorscooters and motorized bicycles are not covered under the PAP. We will discuss later how these vehicles can be insured.

In addition, a vehicle other than a covered auto which is owned by, furnished, or made available for the regular use of the named insured is also excluded. You can drive someone else's automobile occasionally and still have coverage. But if the automobile is driven regularly, or made available for your use on a regular basis, there is no coverage. For example, if your employer furnishes you with a car, or a car is available for your use in a carpool, the liability coverage does not apply. The key point here is not how frequently you drive a borrowed automobile, but whether it is made available for your regular use.

A similar exclusion applies to automobiles furnished or made available for the regular use of another family member. For example, if a son or daughter drives a nonowned automobile on a regular basis, there is no coverage. However, the exclusion does not apply to the named insured and spouse. Thus, if father drives his son's car, father's liability coverage will cover him while driving the son's car.

For an additional premium, the *extended nonowned coverage endorsement* can be added to the PAP that covers the insured while operating a nonowned auto on a regular basis.

Out-of-State Coverage

An important feature applies if the accident occurs in a state other than where the covered automobile is normally garaged. If the accident occurs in a state that has a financial responsibility law which requires higher liability limits than the limits shown in the Declarations, the PAP will automatically provide higher specified limits.

In addition, if the state has a compulsory insurance or similar law that requires a nonresident to have insurance whenever he or she uses a vehicle in that state, the PAP will also provide the required minimum amounts and types of coverage. This insures compliance with an out-of-state no-fault law and the payment of required benefits. We will examine no-fault automobile insurance in Chapter 12.

Other Insurance

In some cases, more than one automobile policy covers a liability claim. The PAP has a provision for determining the amount and priority of payments.

If there is other applicable insurance covering the loss, the insurer pays only its pro rata share. The insurer's share is the proportion that its limit of liability bears to the total applicable limits of liability under all policies. However, if the insurance applies to a *nonowned automobile*, the company's insurance is excess over any other collectible insurance. (See Fig 11.1.)

PART B—MEDICAL PAYMENTS COVERAGE

Medical payments coverage is a special benefit that can be added to the PAP. Let us briefly examine the major features of this coverage.

Insuring Agreement

Under this provision, the company pays all reasonable medical and funeral expenses incurred by a covered person within three years from the date of the accident. This includes medical, surgical, x-ray, dental, and funeral services. The benefit limits typically range from $1,000 to $10,000 per person and apply to each covered person injured in an accident.

Figure 11.1

1. Mary carelessly injures another motorist while driving her own car and must pay damages of $30,000. If two automobile liability policies cover the loss, each company pays its pro rata share of the loss. Assume that Mary is insured for $50,000 in Company A and $100,000 in Company B. Company A pays $10,000 and Company B pays $20,000. This can be illustrated by the following:

Company A

$$\frac{\$\ 50{,}000}{150{,}000} \times \$30{,}000 = \$10{,}000$$

Company B

$$\frac{\$100{,}000}{150{,}000} \times \$30{,}000 = \underline{\$20{,}000}$$

Total $30,000

2. Bob is the named insured and borrows Mary's car with her permission. Both policies will cover any loss. Bob has $50,000 of liability insurance and Mary has $100,000. Bob negligently injures another motorist and must pay damages of $125,000. *The rule is that insurance on the borrowed car is primary, and other insurance is excess.* Each company pays as follows:

Mary's insurer (primary)	$100,000
Bob's insurer (excess)	25,000
Total	$125,000

Mary's insurer pays $100,000, while Bob's insurer pays the remaining $25,000.

Covered Persons

Two groups of persons are covered for medical payments. They are: (1) named insured and family members, and (2) other persons.

The named insured and family members are covered while occupying a motor vehicle,[3] or while pedestrian(s) when struck by a motor vehicle designed for use mainly on public roads. Thus, if the parents and children are hurt in an automobile accident while on vacation, their medical expenses are covered up to the policy limits. Likewise, if the named insured or any family member is struck by a motor vehicle or trailer while walking, their medical expenses are also paid. However, as we stated earlier, the vehicle must be designed for use on a public road for the coverage to apply. Thus, if the pedestrian is injured by a farm tractor, bulldozer, or snowmobile, the injury is not covered, since these vehicles are not designed for use mainly on public roads.

Other persons are covered for their medical expenses as well, but only while they are occupying a *covered auto.* For example, if Joseph owns his car and is the named insured, all passengers in his car are covered for their medical expenses under his policy. However, if he is driving a *nonowned automobile,* any nonrelated passengers in the car are not covered for their medical expenses under his policy. Thus, if Joseph *borrows* a car and picks up a hitchhiker, the hitchhiker's medical expenses would not be covered under his policy.

Exclusions

Medical payments coverage has numerous exclusions. They are summarized as follows:

1. Bodily injury while occupying a motorized vehicle with less than four wheels is excluded.
2. If the covered auto is used to carry persons or property for a fee, the medical payments coverage does not apply. This exclusion does not apply to a share-the-expense car pool.
3. If the injury occurs while the vehicle is being occupied as a residence or premises, the coverage does not apply.
4. If the injury occurs during the course of employment, medical payments coverage does not apply if workers' compensation benefits are available.
5. There is no coverage for an injury sustained while occupying or when struck by a vehicle (other than your covered

auto) which is owned by you or is made available for your regular use. The intent here is to exclude medical payments coverage on an owned or regularly used car that is not described in the policy and an appropriate premium paid.

6. A similar exclusion applies to any vehicle (other than a covered auto) owned by or made available for the regular use of any family member. However, the exclusion does not apply to the named insured and spouse. For example, if a son owns a car that is separately insured, and if the parents are injured while occupying the son's car, their medical expenses are covered under their policy.
7. There is no coverage if the injury occurs while occupying a vehicle without a reasonable belief of being entitled to do so. Thus, if a covered auto is stolen, the thief has no coverage for medical payments.
8. There is no coverage while occupying a vehicle used in a covered person's business or occupation. The intent here is to exclude medical payments coverage for *nonowned trucks and commercial vehicles* used in the business of an insured person. However, the exclusion does not apply to a private passenger automobile (owned or nonowned), or to a pickup, panel truck, or van that you own.
9. Injury because of war or discharge of a nuclear weapon, even if accidental, is not covered.
10. There is no coverage for nuclear reaction, radiation, or radioactive contamination.

Other Insurance

If other automobile medical payments insurance covers the loss, the company pays its pro rata share of the loss based on the proportion that its limits bear to the total applicable limits. However, with respect to a *nonowned vehicle*, the insurance is excess. For example, assume that Patti has medical payments coverage and is also covered for auto medical payments insurance by her employer while operating her car on company business. Both policies have medical payments coverage in the amount of $5,000. If she is injured in an automobile accident and her medical expenses are $2,000, each company pays $1,000.

However, as we stated earlier, medical payments coverage is excess with respect to a *nonowned vehicle*. For example, assume that Kim picks up Patti for lunch. Kim loses control of the car, hits a tree, and Patti is hurled out of the car. Her medical bills are $6,000. Kim has $2,000 of medical expenses coverage, and Patti has $5,000. Kim's insurer pays the first $2,000 as primary insurer, and Patti's company pays the remaining $4,000 as excess insurance.

This ends our discussion of Medical Payments Coverage. Let us next consider the Uninsured Motorists Coverage.

PART C—UNINSURED MOTORISTS COVERAGE

Some persons foolishly drive without liability insurance. The **uninsured motorists coverage** is designed to pay for the bodily injury caused by an uninsured motorist, hit-and-run driver, or by a driver whose company is insolvent. Let us examine the major features of this important coverage.

Insuring Agreement

The company pays the damages that a covered person is legally entitled to receive from the owner or operator of an uninsured motor vehicle because of bodily injury caused by an accident. For example, if you are injured by a negligent driver, and your bodily injuries are $10,000, your insurer will pay the loss. Several important points must be emphasized with respect to this coverage:

1. The coverage applies only if the uninsured motorist is legally liable. If the uninsured motorist is not liable, the company will not pay for the bodily injury.
2. In most states, the uninsured motorists coverage applies only to a bodily injury

and not to property damage. Thus, if an uninsured driver runs a red light and smashes into your car, the property damage is not covered.

3. The maximum amount paid for a bodily injury usually is limited to the state's financial responsibility requirement, typically $15,000 to $25,000 per person. Higher limits can be purchased.
4. The amounts paid under the uninsured motorists coverage can be reduced under certain conditions. The amount paid is reduced by any sums paid by the negligent driver or organization legally responsible for the accident and by any benefits received under a workers' compensation, disability benefits, or similar law.
5. The claim is subject to *arbitration* if the covered person and insurer disagree over the amount of damages or whether the injured person is entitled to receive any damages.

Covered Persons

Three groups of persons are covered under the uninsured motorist provision. First, the *named insured and family members* are covered if they are injured by an uninsured motorist. Second, *other persons* are covered while they are occupying a covered auto. A third group of covered persons are *persons who may not be physically involved in the accident, but are entitled to recover damages from the person or organization legally responsible for the bodily injury to the covered person.* For example, if the named insured is killed by an uninsured motorist, the named insured's legal representative could still collect damages under the uninsured motorists coverage.

Uninsured Vehicles

An extremely important provision defines an uninsured motor vehicle. Four groups of vehicles are considered to be an uninsured vehicle:

1. An uninsured vehicle is a motor vehicle or trailer for which no bodily injury liability insurance policy or bond applies at the time of the accident.
2. There may be a bodily injury liability policy or bond in force, but the amount is less than the amount required by the state's financial responsibility law. This vehicle is also considered to be an uninsured motor vehicle.
3. A hit-and-run vehicle is considered to be an uninsured vehicle. Thus, if the named insured or any family member is struck by a hit-and-run driver while occupying a covered auto or while walking, the uninsured motorists provision will pay for the injury.
4. A vehicle whose bonding or insurance company denies that coverage exists or becomes insolvent is also considered to be an uninsured vehicle. For example, if you have a valid claim against a negligent driver, but the insurer becomes insolvent before the claim is paid, the uninsured motorist coverage would pay the claim.

However, certain vehicles are specifically considered not to be an uninsured motor vehicle. If you are injured by one of these vehicles, your uninsured motorists coverage will not apply. These include the following:

1. Any vehicle owned by or furnished for the regular use of the named insured or any family member.
2. Any vehicle owned or operated by a qualified self-insurer.
3. Any vehicle owned by a governmental unit or agency.
4. Any vehicle operated on rails or crawler treads.
5. Farm type tractor or equipment designed mainly for use off public roads, while not on a public road.
6. Any vehicle used as a residence or premises.

Exclusions

There are several general exclusions under the

INSIGHT 11.1

Why are Drivers Uninsured?

Who drives without insurance? In California, most likely he is a young male of lower socioeconomic status with a record of accidents and major traffic convictions. Or so says a recent study conducted by the California Department of Motor Vehicles, which examined more than 125,000 drivers whose licenses were suspended in 1978 for not supplying evidence of insurance following a reportable accident.

The study noted three main reasons for the results. First, many poor young people simply cannot afford the cost of liability insurance. Second, young people are more likely to be uninsured because as a group they have fewer assets to protect and tend to take more risks. In addition, young males are more likely to be involved in traffic accidents, which might explain their overrepresentation.

The study also reported that the uninsured motorists had 72 percent more accidents than the average of their counterparts in the general population. Further, the uninsured group had approximately three times as many traffic convictions and eight times as many major convictions. Major convictions include drunk, impaired, or reckless driving and hit and run.

SOURCE: "Why Are Drivers Uninsured?" from *Journal of American Insurance,* Summer, 1981.

uninsured motorists provisions. They are summarized as follows:

1. There is no coverage for any person who occupies or is struck by a motor vehicle or trailer owned by the named insured or family member that is not insured under the policy. The intent is to prevent "free" coverage of automobiles owned by the named insured or family members.
2. The coverage does not apply if a person settles a bodily injury claim without the insurer's consent. The purpose of this exclusion is to protect the insurer's interest in the claim.
3. If a person occupies a covered automobile when it is used to carry persons or property for a fee, the uninsured motorists coverage does not apply.
4. Any person who uses a vehicle without a reasonable belief that he or she is entitled to do so is not covered. For example, if a thief steals your car and is later injured by an uninsured motorist, the thief is not covered under your policy.
5. Uninsured motorist benefits cannot directly or indirectly benefit a workers' compensation insurer or self-insurer. In some states, a workers' compensation insurer has a legal right of action against a third party who has injured an employee. This exclusion prevents the uninsured motorists coverage from providing benefits to the workers' compensation insurer.

Other Insurance

If other uninsured motorists insurance applies to the loss, the PAP pays only its pro rata share, which is the proportion that its limit of liability bears to the total of all applicable limits. However, with respect to a *nonowned* vehicle, the uninsured motorists coverage is excess. If the primary insurer's limits are exhausted, the PAP will pay any remaining expenses up to its policy limits. For example, assume that Sam has $25,000 of uninsured motorists coverage with his insurer. He is seriously injured by an uninsured motorist while riding in his friend's car. The friend also has $25,000 of coverage. If Sam has

$35,000 of bodily injuries, the friend's insurer pays the first $25,000, and Sam's insurer pays the remaining $10,000.

Underinsured Motorists Coverage

The **Underinsured Motorists Coverage** can be added to the PAP to provide more complete protection. This coverage promises to pay damages for a bodily injury caused by the operation of an *underinsured* motor vehicle. Under this provision, you can recover the difference between your actual damages for a bodily injury and the amount of liability insurance paid by the other driver's insurance, subject to the maximum limit of liability for the underinsured motorists coverage. For example, assume that your PAP is endorsed with the underinsured motorists coverage in the amount of $50,000. You are injured by a negligent driver who has liability limits of $15,000/$30,000, which satisfy the state's financial responsibility law. If your bodily injuries are $50,000, you would receive only $15,000 from the negligent driver's insurance, since that is the applicable limit of liability. However, under the underinsured motorists coverage, you would recover another $35,000 from your insurer, which is the difference between your actual damages and the other driver's limit of liability.

This concludes our discussion of the uninsured motorists coverage. Let us next consider how you can insure your automobile against a physical damage loss.

PART D—COVERAGE FOR DAMAGE TO YOUR AUTO

Part D (**coverage for damage to your auto**) provides coverage for the damage or theft of your automobile. Let us briefly examine the major features of this coverage.

Insuring Agreement

In the insuring agreement, the company agrees to pay any direct and accidental loss to your covered auto, including its equipment, less any applicable deductible. Two optional coverages are available. A covered auto can be insured for (1) a *collision loss* and (2) *other than a collision loss* (formerly called comprehensive). A collision loss, however, is covered only if the declarations page indicates that collision coverage is in effect. Thus, you have the option of purchasing the coverage with or without collision insurance.

Collision loss Collision means the covered auto is in contact with another object or is upset. The following are examples of a collision loss:

1. You strike another motorist with your automobile, or some other driver hits your car.
2. Your car strikes a tree, telephone pole, or building.
3. Your car is parked, and the fender is dented when you return.
4. You suddenly open the car door, and hit the car parked next to you.

Collision losses are paid regardless of fault. If you cause the accident, your insurer will pay for the damage to your automobile, less any deductible. If some other driver damages your car, you can either collect from the negligent driver (or from his or her insurer), or look to your insurer to pay the claim. If you collect from your own company, you must give up subrogation rights to the company. Your insurer will then attempt to collect from the negligent driver who actually caused the accident.

As we stated earlier, collision insurance is normally sold with a deductible. Although a wide variety of deductibles can be used, two types are commonly used. First, the deductible may be a straight deductible, whereby the first $100, $250, or some higher amount of loss is paid by the insured. Second, the deductible can be an 80-20 deductible, where the insurer pays 80 percent of the loss, and the insured pays the remaining 20 percent, up to a maximum of $50. Thus, if the collision loss is $250, the insured pays $50. If the loss is $1,000, the maximum payment of the insured is limited to $50. The 80-20 deductible has little to recommend it. It is more expensive than a straight deductible, and, more importantly, it encourages the submission of small claims.

Other than collision loss This coverage formerly was called *comprehensive insurance* under the older FAP. Under the PAP, certain losses are considered not to be a collision loss. This distinction is important, since a collision loss is paid only if collision coverage is elected and an additional premium is paid.

Loss from any of the following perils is considered not to be a collision loss:

- Missiles and falling objects
- Fire, theft, or larceny
- Explosion and earthquake
- Windstorm, hail, water, and flood
- Malicious mischief or vandalism
- Riot or civil commotion
- Contact with a bird or animal
- Glass breakage

These losses are self-explanatory, but a few comments are in order. Remember that colliding with a bird or animal is not a collision loss. Thus, if you hit a bird or a deer with your car, the loss would be covered even if you did not elect collision coverage. In addition, if glass breakage is caused by a collision, you can elect to have it covered as a collision loss. This distinction is important since both coverages (collision loss and other than a collision loss) may be written with deductibles. Without this qualification, the named insured would have to pay two deductibles if the car has both body damage and glass breakage in a single collision (assuming both coverages are elected).

Covered Vehicles

The Part D coverage applies only to a covered auto that is owned by the named insured or spouse. Thus, any vehicle described in the declarations is covered. A newly acquired private passenger automobile, trailer, camper body, pickup, panel truck, or van is also covered, provided the named insured asks the company to insure it within thirty days of acquisition.

In addition, the insuring agreement refers only to "your covered auto." Thus, *a physical damage loss to a nonowned automobile is not covered.* As we stated earlier, if you are driving a borrowed automobile and damage it, the liability section of the PAP will pay for the damage if you are legally liable.[4] This approach has at least two advantages to many insureds. First, there is no deductible under liability insurance. Second, under the new PAP, there would be coverage (under liability) for the damage to the borrowed car, even though the owner has no physical damage insurance on it.

Transportation Expenses

Part D also provides a supplementary payment. If a covered automobile is stolen, after forty-eight hours the company will pay for any transportation expenses. Both the police and insurer must be notified. The amount paid is limited to $10 daily up to a maximum of $300. Payments can be for a train, bus, taxi, rental car, or any other transportation expense. Thus, if your covered automobile is stolen, and you rent a car for seven days at $20 daily, the insurer will pay $50 for the rental car. (Note that the first two days are not paid.)

An optional endorsement can be added for rental reimbursements if a covered auto sustains any covered damage and is withdrawn from normal service for more than twenty-four hours. The amount paid is limited to $15 daily up to a maximum of $450 for the expenses incurred in renting a *substitute auto.*

Coverage for *towing and labor costs* can also be added by an endorsement. This coverage pays for towing and labor costs if a covered automobile breaks down, provided the labor is performed at the place of the breakdown. The maximum amount paid is $25, $50, or $75 for each disablement depending on the named insureds' preference. For example, if you call a repair truck because your car fails to start in cold weather, the labor costs and any tow-in costs will be paid. This coverage also has little to recommend it, since it encourages the submission of small claims.

Exclusions

There are numerous exclusions under coverage for damage to your auto (Coverage D). They are summarized as follows:

1. Loss to a covered automobile is excluded while it is used to carry persons or property for a fee. The exclusion does not apply to a share-the-expense car pool.
2. There is no coverage for damage due to wear and tear, freezing, mechanical or electrical breakdown, or road damages to tires. The exclusion does not apply if the damage results from the theft of the covered automobile. The intent is to cover tire defects under the tire manufacturer's warranty and to exclude normal maintenance costs of operating an automobile.
3. Loss due to radioactive contamination or war is not covered.
4. Loss to equipment designed for the reproduction of sound is excluded, unless the equipment is permanently installed in the covered automobile. For example, the theft of a stereo tape recorder not permanently attached to an automobile would be excluded.
5. Another important exclusion applies to the loss of tapes, records, or other devices for use with equipment designed for the reproduction of sound. For example, the theft of stereo tapes from your automobile would not be covered.
6. Loss to a camper or trailer not shown in the declarations is excluded. The exclusion does not apply to a newly acquired camper body or trailer if you ask the company to insure it within thirty days after you become the owner.
7. A temporary substitute automobile is not covered. Remember that damage to a temporary substitute automobile is covered under the liability section of the PAP for nonowned vehicles, which we described earlier.
8. Loss to television antennas, awnings, cabanas, or equipment designed to create additional living facilities is also excluded.
9. There is no coverage for loss to any sound receiving and transmitting equipment designed for use as a citizen's band radio, two-way mobile radio, telephone, or scanning monitor receiver, or their accessories. The exclusion does not apply if the equipment is permanently installed in the opening of the dash or console of the auto.
10. Loss to any custom furnishings or equipment in a pickup, panel truck, or van is not covered. For example, customized equipment in a van, such as carpeting, furniture, bars, television sets, and cooking and sleeping facilities would be excluded.

However, an appropriate endorsement can be added to the policy that permits you to buy back the coverage on excluded property. Thus, a citizen's band radio, stereo tapes and decks, and customized van equipment can be covered by an appropriate endorsement and payment of an additional premium.

Payment of Loss and Limit of Liability

The company has several options for payment of a loss to a covered automobile. First, the loss can be paid in money. In most cases, the insurer's liability is the lower of the actual cash value of the stolen or damaged property, or the amount necessary to repair or replace the property. For example, if an automobile is totaled in an accident, and the repair costs exceed its actual cash value, the company's liability is limited to the actual cash value of the automobile.

Second, the company has the right to repair or replace the stolen or damaged automobile. If

INSIGHT 11.2

Replacement Cost Insurance for a New Car

When the cost of repairing a damaged automobile exceeds its current market value, the automobile is normally declared a total loss. The owner is paid the actual cash value of the car, and the insurer takes title to the damaged car and can sell it as salvage. An increasing problem in such claims is that, even though the insured receives the current value of the car, the amount paid is often less than the amount still owed on the car loan. This frequently happens when the car is damaged beyond repair early in the loan period. The owner must continue to make the loan payments on a wrecked car that cannot be driven, and worse yet, he or she must then take out a new loan for a replacement car.

Because of sharply rising repair costs, the proportion of wrecked cars that are declared a total loss has increased over time. For example, one large insurer reports that the proportion of wrecked cars declared a total loss has increased from 3.5 percent in 1971 to 11.1 percent in 1982. This is due largely to rising repair costs for automobile parts and labor where the cost of repairing a damaged car often exceeds its current market value.

To reduce the financial hardship upon insureds when a new car is totaled, several insurers are now selling automobile physical damage insurance on a replacement cost basis. An endorsement can be added to an automobile insurance contract that pays the cost of repairing or replacing a damaged vehicle even though the cost exceeds the car's current market value. *Under the endorsement, if the wrecked car is declared a total loss because it cannot be repaired, or because the repair costs exceed the cost of a comparable new car, it is replaced with a new car of the same model, size class, body type, and equipment.* The insurer generally has the right to pay in money or to repair or replace the damaged car.

Most insurers allow the endorsement to be added up to 90 days after a new car is purchased. The cost varies by company. One insurer charges an additional premium equal to 10 percent of the combined comprehensive and collision premium.

SOURCE: Adaptation of "Automobile Repair or Replacement Coverage" from *FC & S Bulletins*, November 1982. Reprinted by permission.

the car is stolen, the company will pay the cost of returning the stolen car to the named insured and will also pay for any damages resulting from the theft. The company also has the right to keep all or part of the property at an agreed or appraised value.

Finally, in the case of an expensive antique or customized car, a **stated amount endorsement** can be inserted in the policy. However, this endorsement does not create a valued policy. If the stated amount is *less* than the actual cash value, or the amount necessary to repair or replace the property, then the stated amount will be paid. However, if the stated amount *exceeds* the actual cash value, or the amount necessary to repair or replace the property, the lower of these latter two figures will be the amount paid.

Other Insurance

If other insurance covers the physical damage loss, the company will pay only its pro rata share, which is the proportion that its limits of liability bear to the total of all applicable limits.

Trailers

At this point, it is worthwhile to distinguish between liability coverage and physical damage coverage on trailers. *Liability insurance* automatically applies to most trailers designed to use with a private passenger automobile. This includes both owned and nonowned trailers. Thus, a boat trailer, horse trailer, camper trailer, rental trailer, and house trailer are insured for liability coverage.[5]

With respect to *physical damage insurance*, Coverage for Damage to Your Auto (Part D) also applies to trailers if they are described in the Declarations. If Part D is in effect, a newly acquired trailer or camper body is insured from the date of acquisition if the insured asks the company to insure it within thirty days after he or she becomes the owner.

With respect to a *nonowned trailer*, there is no coverage for a collision loss or other loss under Part D. Remember that Coverage for Damage to Your Auto (Part D) applies only to your covered auto, not to any nonowned vehicle, such as a rental trailer. Instead, any property damage to the nonowned trailer caused by the named insured would be covered under the liability section of the PAP if you are legally liable.

Finally, if collision coverage is in force, the deductible applies to both vehicles in an accident. For example, assume Mary has a $100 deductible on her collision coverage. If she is pulling a boat trailer with her automobile, and both vehicles are damaged in a collision loss, the $100 deductible applies separately to each vehicle. Thus, if damages to the car and trailer are $2,000 and $500, respectively, she will collect only $2,300.

PART E—DUTIES AFTER AN ACCIDENT OR LOSS

You should know what to do if you have an accident or loss. You should first determine if anyone in the other vehicle is hurt. If someone is injured, an ambulance should be called. If there are bodily injuries, or the property damage exceeds a certain amount (such as $200), you are also required to notify the police in most jurisdictions. You should give the other driver your name, address, and the name of your agent and insurer and request the same information from him or her. Under no circumstances should you admit that you caused the accident. The question of negligence and legal liability will be resolved by the insurers involved (or court of law if necessary) and not by you. You do not have the right to admit that you are responsible for the accident.

Your agent should be promptly notified of the accident, even if there are no injuries or property damage. Failure to report the accident promptly to your insurer could jeopardize your coverage if you are later sued by the other driver.

After the accident occurs, a number of duties are imposed upon you. You must cooperate with the insurer in the investigation and settlement of a claim. You must send to the insurer copies of any legal papers or notices received in connection with the accident. If you are claiming benefits under the uninsured motorists, underinsured motorists, or medical payments coverages, you may be required to take a physical examination at the company's expense. You must also authorize your insurer to obtain medical reports and other pertinent records. Finally, you must submit a proof of loss at the company's request.

Some additional duties are imposed upon you if you are seeking benefits under the uninsured motorists coverage. The police must be notified if a hit-and-run driver is involved. Also, if you bring a lawsuit against the uninsured driver, you must send copies of the legal papers to your insurer.

If your automobile is damaged, and you are seeking indemnification under Coverage D other duties are imposed upon you. You must take reasonable steps to protect the covered automobile from further damage; your insurer will pay for any expense involved. You must also permit the company to inspect and appraise the automobile before it is repaired. If you and the company cannot agree on the amount of the physical damage loss, the claim will be submitted to arbitration.

This concludes our discussion of physical damage insurance. Let us next examine some general policy provisions.

INSIGHT 11.3

Pack Your Policy

Crossing international borders is probably easier in North America than anywhere else in the world. Drivers may need to take precautions to be adequately insured, however, especially in Mexico.

Under Mexican law, all cars involved in an accident are impounded until fault is determined. You can be liable for criminal as well as civil penalties and be required to have your car repaired in Mexico. Having an agent who knows the system with you can be invaluable.

Some U.S. companies sell additional coverage good within 25 miles of the U.S. border. Anywhere else you'll need a policy from a Mexican insurance company. Buy your Mexican insurance before leaving the U.S. Look in almost any U.S. city near the border for an agent who also represents U.S. insurance companies. Carry your policy and a list of Mexican agents at all times while in that country. If you have a problem with a claim, then contact the U.S. agent you bought the policy from. If necessary, take your complaint next to the state insurance department that licensed the agent.

U.S. drivers will need to obtain proof of current insurance coverage before driving in Canada. Your agent will give you a "Canada Non-Resident Inter-Province Motor Vehicle Liability Insurance Card" on request. This relieves you of the need to carry a photocopy of your insurance policy.

Canadian auto insurance policies automatically cover Canadian drivers in the continental U.S.

SOURCE: "Pack Your Policy." Reprinted with permission from the Winter 1984 issue of *Everybody's Money*, published by Credit Union National Association, Inc., Madison, Wisconsin.

PART F—GENERAL PROVISIONS

This section contains eight general provisions. Only two of them are discussed here.

Policy Period and Territory

The PAP provides coverage only in the United States, its territories or possessions, and in Canada. The policy also insures the covered automobile while it is being transported between the ports of any of these places. For example, if you rent a car while vacationing in England or Germany, you are not covered. Likewise, you are not covered if you drive your car on an extended vacation into Mexico. Additional automobile insurance must be purchased to be covered while driving in foreign countries. With respect to driving in Mexico, the safest approach is not to do it without first obtaining liability insurance from a Mexican insurer. A motorist from the United States who has not purchased insurance from a Mexican insurer could be detained in jail after an accident, have his or her automobile impounded, and be subject to other penalties as well.

Termination

A very important provision applies to termination of the insurance by either the insured or insurer. There are four parts to this provision:

- Cancellation
- Nonrenewal
- Automatic termination
- Other termination provisions

Cancellation The named insured can cancel at any time by returning the policy to the company or by giving advance written notice of the effective date of **cancellation.**

The insurer also has the right of cancellation. If the policy has been in force for *less than sixty days*, the insurer can cancel after giving at least ten days notice. Thus, the company has sixty days to investigate a new insured to determine if he or she is acceptable to the company.

If the policy is in force for sixty days, and if it is not a renewal or continuation policy, the company can cancel for only two reasons: (1) the premium has not been paid, or (2) the driver's license of an insured has been suspended or revoked during the policy period. If the policy is cancelled for nonpayment of the premium, at least ten days notice must be given. If the policy is cancelled because of a revoked or suspended driver's license, at least twenty days notice must be given.

Nonrenewal The company may decide *not to renew* the policy when it comes up for renewal. If the insurer decides not to renew the policy, the named insured must be given at least twenty days notice before the end of the policy period. However, if the policy period is other than one year, the company has the right of **nonrenewal** only at the anniversary date of the policy's original effective date. Thus, a PAP written for only six months will not be subject to nonrenewal more than once a year.

Automatic termination If the company decides to renew the policy, an automatic termination provision becomes effective. This means that if the named insured does not accept the company's offer to renew, the policy automatically terminates at the end of the current policy period. Thus, once the company bills the named insured for another period, the insured must pay the premium, or the policy automatically terminates upon its expiration date. However, some companies may provide a short grace period, such as ten days, to pay the renewal premium.

Other termination provisions Some states have placed additional restrictions on the insurer's right to cancel or not renew. If the state law requires a longer period of advance notice to the named insured, or modifies any termination provision, the PAP is modified to comply with those requirements. In addition, the company can deliver any notice instead of mailing it. Also, if the policy is cancelled, the named insured will receive any premium refund; however, making or offering to make a premium refund is not a condition for cancellation. Finally, the effective date of cancellation stated in the cancellation notice becomes the end of the policy period.

INSURING MOTORCYCLES AND MOPEDS

Because of excellent gasoline mileage and relatively low cost, motorcycles and mopeds are becoming more popular as modes of transportation. However, the PAP excludes coverage for motorcycles, mopeds, and similar vehicles.

A **Miscellaneous Type Vehicle Endorsement** can be added to the PAP to insure motorcycles, mopeds, motorscooters, golf carts, motor homes, dune buggies, and similar vehicles. One exception is a snowmobile, which requires a separate endorsement to the PAP. The Miscellaneous Type Vehicle Endorsement can be used to provide the same coverages found in the PAP, including liability, medical payments, uninsured motorist, collision, and comprehensive physical damage insurance. The endorsement has a schedule that describes the vehicles to be insured and the premium and limits of liability for each coverage.

You should be aware of several points if the Miscellaneous Type Vehicle Endorsement is added to the PAP. First, the liability coverage does not apply to a nonowned vehicle. Although other persons are covered while operating your motorcycle with your permission, the liability coverage does not apply if you operate a nonowned motorcycle (other than as a temporary substitute vehicle).

Second, property damage to a nonowned vehicle is excluded. Thus, if you borrow or rent a motorcycle and damage it, the physical damage loss is not covered even if you are legally liable for the damage.

Third, a *passenger hazard exclusion* can be activated, which excludes liability for bodily injury to any passenger on the motorcycle. When the exclusion is activated, the insured pays a lower premium.

Finally, when Part D (Coverage for Damage to Your Auto) is added to cover physical damage losses to the motorcycle, the amount paid is the lowest of (1) the stated amount shown in the endorsement, (2) actual cash value, or (3) amount necessary to repair or replace the property (less any applicable deductible).

SUMMARY

- The Personal Auto Policy (PAP) consists of six major parts. They are:
  a. Part A—Liability Coverage.
  b. Part B—Medical Payments Coverage.
  c. Part C—Uninsured Motorists Coverage.
  d. Part D—Coverage for Damage to Your Auto.
  e. Part E—Duties after an Accident or Loss.
  f. Part F—General Provisions.
- Liability coverage protects the insured from bodily injury or property damage liability arising out of the negligent operation of an automobile or trailer. A single limit of liability applies to both bodily injury and property damage.
- Covered vehicles include any vehicle shown in the Declarations; a pickup, panel truck, or van not used in any business or occupation; newly acquired vehicles; trailers; and a temporary substitute automobile.
- Covered persons include the named insured and spouse, family members, other persons using a covered automobile if there is a reasonable belief that permission to use the automobile exists, and any person or organization legally responsible for the acts of a covered person.
- Medical payments coverage pays all reasonable medical, dental, and funeral expenses incurred by a covered person within three years from the date of the accident.
- Uninsured motorists coverage pays for the bodily injury of a covered person caused by an uninsured motorist, hit-and-run driver, or by a driver whose insurer is insolvent.
- Underinsured motorists coverage can be added as an endorsement to the PAP. A covered person can recover the difference between the actual damages for a bodily injury and the negligent driver's applicable limit of liability, subject to the maximum limit of liability for the underinsured motorists coverage.
- Coverage for Damage to Your Auto pays for any direct or accidental physical loss to a covered automobile less any deductible. A collision loss is covered only if the Declarations page indicates that collision coverage is in effect. The insured can purchase Coverage D either with or without collision insurance.
- Certain duties are imposed on the insured after an accident occurs. A person seeking coverage must cooperate with the insurer in the investigation and settlement of a claim and send to the insurer copies of any legal papers or notices received in connection with the accident.

- After the policy has been in force for sixty days, and it is not a renewal or continuation policy, the company can *cancel* the insured only if the premium has not been paid, or the driver's license of an insured has been suspended or revoked during the policy period. However, if the company decides *not to renew* the policy when it comes up for renewal, the named insured must be given at least twenty days notice before the end of the policy period.
- Motorcycles and mopeds can be insured by adding the miscellaneous type vehicle endorsement to the Personal Auto Policy.

QUESTIONS FOR REVIEW

1. Describe the major coverages that are found in the Personal Auto Policy.
2. Indicate the types of vehicles that can be insured under the Personal Auto Policy.
3. Who are the persons insured for liability coverage under the Personal Auto Policy?
4. Describe the supplementary payments that can be paid under the liability section of the Personal Auto Policy.
5. If you drive a borrowed automobile and damage it, will the Personal Auto Policy pay for the damage? Explain.
6. Who are the persons insured for medical payments coverage under the Personal Auto Policy?
7. Explain the major features of the uninsured motorists coverage in the Personal Auto Policy.
8. Describe the insuring agreement under Coverage for Damage to Your Auto in the Personal Auto Policy.
9. Explain the duties imposed on the insured after an accident or loss occurs.
10. How can motorcycles and mopeds be insured?

QUESTIONS FOR DISCUSSION

1. Fred has a Personal Auto Policy that provides the following coverages: $30,000 liability coverage, $5,000 medical payments coverage, $15,000 uninsured motorists coverage, $200 deductible for collision loss, and a $50 deductible for other than a collision loss. With respect to each of the following situations, indicate whether or not the losses are covered. Assume that each situation is a separate event.
   a. Fred's son, age sixteen, takes the family car without permission and kills a pedestrian in a drag-racing contest. The heirs of the deceased pedestrian sue for $100,000.
   b. Fred borrows a friend's car to go to the supermarket. He fails to stop at a red light and negligently smashes into another motorist. The other driver's car, valued at $5,000, is totally destroyed. In addition, damages to the friend's car are $1,000.
   c. Fred's daughter, Mary, attends college in another state and drives a family automobile. Fred tells her that no other person is to drive the family car. Mary lets her boyfriend drive the car, and he negligently injures another motorist. The boyfriend is sued for $10,000.
   d. Fred's wife is driving a family car in a snowstorm. She loses control of the car on an icy street and smashes into the foundation of a house. The property damage to the house is $20,000. Damages to the family car are $5,000. Fred's wife has medical expenses of $3,000.
   e. Fred is walking across a street and is struck by a motorist who fails to stop. He has bodily injuries in the amount of $15,000. His suit, valued at $250, is ripped in the accident.

f. Fred's car is being repaired for faulty brakes. While road testing the car, a mechanic injures another motorist and is sued for $50,000.

g. Fred hits a steer crossing a highway. Damages to Fred's car are $700.

h. A thief breaks a car window and steals a camera and golf clubs locked in the car. It will cost $200 to replace the damaged window. The stolen property is valued at $500.

i. Fred's wife goes shopping at a supermarket. When she returns, she finds that the left rear fender has been damaged by another driver who did not leave a name. Damages to the car are $500.

j. Fred works for a construction company. While driving a large cement truck, he negligently injures another motorist. The injured motorist sues Fred for $20,000.

k. Fred's son drives a family car on a date. He gets drunk, and his girlfriend drives him home. The girlfriend negligently injures another motorist who has bodily injuries in the amount of $10,000.

2. Mary is the named insured under a Personal Auto Policy which provides coverage for bodily injury and property damage liability, medical payments, and the uninsured motorists coverage. For each of the following situations, briefly explain whether the claim is covered by Mary's Personal Auto Policy.

   a. Mary ran into a telephone pole and submitted a medical expense claim for Jason, a passenger in Mary's car at the time of the accident.

   b. Mary loaned her car to Susan. While operating Mary's car, Susan damaged Smith's car in an accident caused by Susan's negligence. Susan is sued by Smith for damages.

   c. Mary's husband ran over a bicycle while driving the car of a friend. Her husband is sued for damages by the owner of the bicycle.

   d. In a fit of anger, Mary deliberately ran over the wagon of a neighbor's child that had been left in Mary's driveway after repeated requests that the wagon be left elsewhere. The child's parents seek reimbursement.

3. Victor rented a twenty-foot camping trailer while on a vacation in the Rocky Mountains. He turned his car too sharply on a hairpin curve, and the trailer overturned. The trailer was damaged beyond repair. Its value at the time of the accident was $12,000. Indicate whether or not Victor's Personal Auto Policy will cover the loss.

4. Ben was driving a neighbor's pickup truck to get a load of firewood. A child darted out between two parked cars and ran into the street in front of the truck. In an unsuccessful attempt to avoid hitting the child, Ben lost control of the vehicle and hit a telephone pole. The child was critically injured, the pickup truck was badly damaged, and the telephone pole collapsed. Ben has liability coverage and collision coverage under his personal auto policy. The neighbor also has a Personal Auto Policy with liability coverage and collision coverage on the pickup.

   a. If Ben is found guilty of negligence, which insurer will pay for the bodily injuries to the child and the property damage to the telephone pole? Explain.

   b. Which insurer will pay for the physical damage to the neighbor's pickup? Explain.

5. Jack traded in his 1978 Ford for a new 1986 Ford. Two weeks later, he hit an oily spot in the road on his way to work and skidded into a parked car. The 1978 Ford was insured under the Personal Auto Policy with full coverage, including a $200 deductible for a collision loss. At the time of the accident, Jack had not notified his insurer of the trade-in. The physical damage to the parked car was $5,000. Damage to Jack's car was $3,000. Will Jack's Personal Auto Policy cover either or both of these losses? Explain.

KEY TERMS AND CONCEPTS TO KNOW

Personal auto policy
Liability coverage
Single limit
Split limit
Covered auto
Nonowned auto
Temporary substitute automobile
Supplementary payments
Medical payments coverage
Uninsured motorists coverage
Underinsured motorists coverage
Coverage for damage to your auto
Collision loss
Other than a collision loss
Stated amount endorsement
Cancellation
Nonrenewal
Miscellaneous Type Vehicle Endorsement

SUGGESTIONS FOR ADDITIONAL READING

Athearn, James L. and S. Travis Pritchett. *Risk and Insurance*, 5th ed. St. Paul, Minnesota: West Publishing Company, 1984, chapter 16.

Bickelhaupt, David L. *General Insurance*, 11th ed. Homewood, Illinois: Richard D. Irwin, Inc., 1983, chapter 20.

Crane, Frederick G. *Insurance Principles and Practices*, 2nd ed. New York: John Wiley & Sons, 1984, chapters 5 and 6.

Fire, Casualty, & Surety Bulletins. Personal Lines Volume. Cincinnati, Ohio: The National Underwriter Company. The bulletins are published monthly. Up-to-date information on the Personal Auto Policy can be found in the Personal Lines Volume, Personal Auto section.

Greene, Mark R. and James S. Trieschmann. *Risk and Insurance*, 6th ed. Cincinnati, Ohio: Southwestern Publishing Company, 1984, chapter 16.

Vaughan, Emmett J. *Fundamentals of Risk and Insurance*, 3rd ed. New York: John Wiley & Sons, 1982, chapter 31.

Wood, Glenn L., Claude C. Lilly, III, Donald S. Malecki, and Jerry S. Rosenbloom. *Personal Risk Management and Insurance*, 3rd ed., Volume I. Malvern, Pennsylvania: American Institute for Property and Liability Underwriters, 1984.

NOTES

1. For a detailed explanation of the PAP, the interested student should consult the *Fire, Casualty, & Surety Bulletins*, Personal Lines Volume, Personal Auto section. The author drew heavily on this material in preparing this chapter.
2. Under the older FAP, if the insured carried physical damage insurance on his or her car, the insurance also applied to a nonowned car driven with the permission of the owner or the owner's spouse. Thus, collision and comprehensive insurance on the insured's car also applied to the nonowned car. Under the PAP, this is not true. Physical damage insurance to the owned automobile does not extend to borrowed vehicles. Instead, property damage to the borrowed vehicle would be covered under the liability section of the PAP, but this requires the insured to be legally liable for the damage to the borrowed vehicle.
3. Occupying means in, upon, getting in, on, out, or off the automobile.
4. There is an exception to this statement. In Illinois, the PAP is subject to an amendatory endorsement, which broadens Coverage D so that it provides *comprehensive coverage* on a *nonowned auto* (as defined) if the insured has purchased that coverage on a covered auto. Thus, if the insured borrows a car that is damaged by a comprehensive peril, the loss is covered under Coverage D of the borrower's policy, regardless of whether the borrower is legally liable. However, if the insured borrows a car and is legally liable for a *collision loss*, the loss is covered under the borrower's liability coverage.
5. However, mobile homes or land yachts are not considered trailers and require specific coverage.

CHAPTER 12

ADDITIONAL TOPICS IN AUTOMOBILE INSURANCE

"The basic difficulty with the automobile insurance system is that the insured event is too complicated. . . ."

Jeffrey O'Connell, The Injury Industry and the Remedy of No-Fault Insurance

STUDENT LEARNING OBJECTIVES

After studying this chapter, you should be able to:

- Describe the following approaches for compensating automobile accident victims:
  - financial responsibility laws
  - compulsory insurance laws
  - unsatisfied judgment fund
  - uninsured motorists coverage
- Explain no-fault automobile insurance with respect to the following:
  - meaning of no-fault insurance
  - arguments for and against no-fault insurance
  - effectiveness of no-fault plans
- Describe the various methods for providing automobile insurance to high-risk drivers.
- Explain the various factors that determine the cost of automobile insurance.
- Describe the rules that should be followed in shopping for automobile insurance.

In this chapter, we will continue our discussion of automobile insurance. We will first discuss some legal approaches to the problem of compensating innocent accident victims because of the negligence of irresponsible motorists. This will include an analysis of financial responsibility laws, compulsory insurance laws, unsatisfied judgment funds, and the uninsured motorists coverage. We will also consider no-fault automobile insurance as an alternative technique for compensating automobile accident victims. In addition, the problem of providing automobile insurance to high-risk drivers will also be discussed. We will conclude the chapter by examining the cost of automobile insurance and the factors that should be considered in shopping for automobile insurance.

PROTECTION AGAINST IRRESPONSIBLE MOTORISTS

In many cases, innocent persons who are involved in automobile accidents are unable to recover financial damages from the negligent motorists. Although the accident victim may have incurred property damage or a bodily injury, he or she often recovers nothing or receives less than full indemnification from the negligent motorist who caused the accident. To deal with this problem, the states have passed laws that provide some protection to accident victims from irresponsible drivers. The following types of laws have been enacted:[1]

1. Financial responsibility laws.
2. Compulsory automobile liability insurance.
3. Unsatisfied judgment funds.
4. Uninsured motorists coverage.
5. No-fault automobile insurance.

In the following section, we will discuss the major features of each of these approaches.

Financial Responsibility Laws

Most states have enacted some type of **financial responsibility law** that requires persons involved in automobile accidents to furnish proof of financial responsibility up to certain minimum dollar limits. Proof of financial responsibility is generally required under the following circumstances:

1. After an automobile accident involving bodily injury or property damage over a certain amount.
2. Conviction for certain offenses, such as driving while intoxicated or reckless driving.
3. Failure to pay a final judgment resulting from an automobile accident.

Under these conditions, if a motorist does not meet the state's financial responsibility law requirements, the state can revoke or suspend the motorist's driving privileges.

Financial responsibility laws can be divided into three broad categories: (1) accidents, (2) judgments, and (3) convictions for certain offenses. To deal with accidents, most states have a **security-type law.** Under this type of law, a person involved in an automobile accident is required to furnish proof of financial responsibility up to certain minimum dollar limits. Both the driver's license and vehicle registration can be suspended unless the person can provide security to pay a judgment arising out of a current accident up to the statutory requirements.

Evidence of financial responsibility can be provided by producing an automobile liability policy with certain minimum limits. Most states have minimum limits of $15,000/$30,000/$10,000 or $25,000/$50,000/$10,000.[2] Other ways in which the financial responsibility law can be satisfied are by posting a bond, depositing securities or money in the amount required by law, or by showing that the person is a qualified self-insurer. If evidence of financial responsibility is not provided by one of these methods, the right to drive is suspended until the security is posted or the claim is settled. Figure 12.1 shows the financial responsibility law requirements in the various states and Canadian provinces.

A more stringent law for dealing with accidents is the **security and proof method.** Under this type of law, the driver's license and vehicle registration can be suspended unless the involved person submits security to pay for a judgment arising out of a *current accident* and also shows proof of financial responsibility for *future accidents*. Thus, this type of law requires proof of financial responsibility not only for present accidents, but for future accidents as well.

Judgments that arise out of automobile accidents are treated differently. The person against whom a judgment is obtained must both pay the judgment and provide proof of financial responsibility for future accidents. Both conditions must be fulfilled before the driver's license and registration are restored. A judgment is considered paid when the amount equal to the minimum liability limits has been paid, even though the original judgment may exceed these limits.

Finally, with respect to a *conviction for certain offenses*, most states require proof of financial responsibility before driving privileges are restored. The majority of states require proof of financial responsibility for three years. These convictions include the failure to stop after an accident, loss of a license because of too many violations of traffic laws, reckless driving, driving while intoxicated or under the influence of drugs, and conviction of a felony in which an automobile was used.

Although financial responsibility laws provide considerable protection against irresponsible motorists, they have several defects. The major defects are summarized as follows:

1. There is no guarantee that all accident victims will be paid. Financial responsibility laws normally have no penalties other than the loss of driving privileges. Thus, the accident victim may not be paid if he or she is injured by an uninsured driver, hit-and-run driver, or driver of a stolen car. An irresponsible motorist often drives without a license, so the law fails to achieve the objective of getting the irresponsible driver off the road.
2. Accident victims may not be fully indemnified for their injuries. Most financial responsibility laws require only minimum liability insurance limits in the amount of $15,000, $20,000, or $25,000 per person. If the bodily injury exceeds the minimum limit, the accident victim may not be fully compensated.
3. There may be considerable delay in compensating the accident victim if the case goes to trial. The delay in payment may result in financial hardship for some accident victims.

Compulsory Insurance Laws

Compulsory insurance laws are the second method for protecting innocent accident victims against irresponsible motorists. These laws require the owners and operators of automobiles to carry certain types of liability insurance as a condition for driving legally within the state. Prior to 1971, three states—Massachusetts, New York, and North Carolina—required each automobile owner to carry automobile liability insurance at least equal to a certain amount before the automobile could be registered and licensed.[3] At the present time, more than half of the states have enacted some type of compulsory automobile liability insurance law as a condition for driving within the state.

Compulsory insurance laws have both desirable and undesirable features. These laws are considered superior to financial responsibility laws because they provide a stronger guarantee of protection to the public against loss. Supporters of compulsory insurance laws also argue that about one out of eight registered vehicles is uninsured in those states with financial responsibility laws.[4] Thus, compulsory laws are necessary.

Critics of compulsory insurance laws, however, point out the following defects:[5]

1. Insurers have less freedom to select profitable insureds. In addition, claims have substantially increased, and the courts are therefore congested.
2. Automobile rates are politically controlled, resulting in underwriting losses.

Figure 12.1
Table of Limits

Financial Responsibility and Compulsory Insurance Laws

The table that follows displays the minimum financial responsibility or compulsory liability insurance limits for all states, the District of Columbia, and the Canadian provinces.

The laws of all states express the requirement in terms of *split limits*. For example, if the chart shows "25/50/10," the law requires that the policy provide at least $25,000 for bodily injury to each person, $50,000 for all bodily injury, and $10,000 for property damage, each accident.

The insurance laws of some states also state the requirement in terms of a *combined single limit*. For example, if the chart shows "15/30/10 or 40," the law provides that a policy with a combined single limit of at least $40,000 will also satisfy the requirement. A combined single limit of $40,000 means that the insurance will pay up to $40,000 for all bodily injury and property damage arising out of each accident. The required limits for the Canadian provinces are expressed as combined single limits only.

State	*Liability limits*
Alabama	20/40/10 or 50
Alaska	50/100/25 or 125
Alberta	100
Arizona	15/30/10
Arkansas	25/50/15
British Columbia	100
California	15/30/5
Colorado	25/50/15
Connecticut	20/40/10
Delaware	15/30/10 or 40
District of Columbia	10/20/5
Florida	10/20/5
Georgia	15/30/10
Hawaii	25/Unlimited/10
Idaho	25/50/15
Illinois	15/30/10
Indiana	25/50/10
Iowa	20/40/15
Kansas	25/50/10
Kentucky	25/50/10 or 60
Louisiana	10/20/10
Maine	20/40/10
Manitoba	200
Maryland	20/40/10

Moreover, lower rates can be secured only by limiting policy coverage.

3. Property damage claims may be fraudulently converted into bodily injury claims, since most laws require coverage only for bodily injury.
4. Compulsory insurance laws do not result in complete coverage of all drivers; nor do they assure payment to accident victims in all cases. For example, injuries may occur from (1) hit-and-run drivers, (2) out-of-state drivers, (3) drivers who have let their insurance lapse, (4) drivers of stolen cars, and (5) fraudulently registered automobiles.
5. Compulsory laws provide less than complete protection since the required minimums do not meet the full needs of accident victims.
6. Compulsory laws (as well as financial responsibility laws) do nothing to prevent automobile accidents, which is the heart of the problem.
7. Compulsory laws fail to reduce the number of uninsured motorists. Some persons let their policies lapse. Forged insurance certificates have been used to circumvent the law.

Unsatisfied Judgment Funds

Five states have established **unsatisfied judgment funds** for compensating innocent accident vic-

State	Liability limits	State	Liability limits
Massachusetts	10/20/5	Ontario	200
Michigan	20/40/10	Oregon	25/50/10
Minnesota	25/50/10	Pennsylvania	15/30/5
Mississippi	10/20/5	Prince Edward Island	100
Missouri	25/50/10	Quebec	50 †
Montana	25/50/5	Rhode Island	25/50/10
Nebraska	25/50/25	Saskatchewan	100
Nevada	15/30/10	South Carolina	15/30/5
New Brunswick	100	South Dakota	15/30/10
Newfoundland	200	Tennessee	15/30/10 or 40
New Hampshire	25/50/25	Texas	15/30/15
New Jersey	15/30/5	Utah	20/40/10 or 30
New Mexico	25/50/10	Vermont	20/40/10
New York	10/20/5 *	Virginia	25/50/10
Northwest Territories	50	Washington	25/50/10
North Carolina	25/50/10	West Virginia	20/40/10
North Dakota	25/50/10	Wisconsin	25/50/10
Nova Scotia	200	Wyoming	10/20/5
Ohio	12.5/25/7.5	Yukon	200
Oklahoma	10/20/10		

*50/100 for wrongful death.

†Because Quebec has a complete no-fault system for bodily injury, the minimum limit applies only to property damage within Quebec and combined bodily injury and property damage outside Quebec.

SOURCE: "Table of Limits" from *FC & S Bulletins*, January 1985. Reprinted by permission.

tims.[6] An **unsatisfied judgment fund** is a fund established by the state to compensate accident victims who have exhausted all other means of recovery. Let us briefly examine the basic characteristics of these funds.[7]

First, the accident victim must obtain a judgment against the negligent motorist who caused the accident and must show that the judgment cannot be collected. Thus, there must be an unsatisfied judgment.

Second, the negligent motorist is not relieved of legal liability when payments are made out of the fund. The negligent motorist must repay the fund or lose his or her driver's license until the fund is reimbursed.

Finally, the method of financing benefits varies among the states. Funds can be obtained by assessing the uninsured motorists in the state, by charging each motorist a fee, or by assessing insurers according to the amount of automobile liability premiums written in the state.

There are both advantages and disadvantages of unsatisfied judgment funds. The major advantages are:

1. An innocent accident victim has some protection against irresponsible motorists.
2. Some uninsured drivers are kept off the road until the fund is repaid.

The major disadvantages include the following:

1. The financing is inequitable, since insured motorists are charged a fee. Some states,

however, charge a higher fee to the uninsured driver.
2. The administration of the funds is cumbersome and slow.
3. The amounts repaid into the funds by uninsured motorists are relatively small.
4. The unsatisfied judgment funds have experienced financial problems in recent years.

Uninsured Motorist's Coverage

Uninsured motorist's coverage is another approach for compensating innocent automobile victims. As we noted in Chapter 11, the insurer agrees to pay the accident victim who has bodily injuries caused by an uninsured motorist, by a hit-and-run driver, or by a driver whose company is insolvent.

The uninsured motorists coverage has several advantages. First, motorists have some protection against an uininsured driver. Many states require that the coverage be mandatorily included in all automobile liability insurance policies sold within the state. In other states, coverage is included unless the insured voluntarily declines the protection. Second, the coverage is relatively inexpensive, costing less than $20 annually in most states. Finally, claim settlement is faster and more efficient than a tort liability lawsuit. Although the accident victim must establish negligence by the uninsured driver, it is not necessary to sue the negligent driver and win a judgment.

The uninsured motorist's coverage typically is used in connection with one of the other methods for compensating automobile accident victims. For example, it may be used in a state with a compulsory insurance law or in one with an unsatisfied judgment fund. In addition, the *underinsured motorist's coverage*, which we discussed earlier in Chapter 11, is also available in most states for drivers who are particularly concerned about collecting when they are injured by an uninsured or underinsured motorist.

No-Fault Automobile Insurance

There is considerable controversy concerning the methods of compensating accident victims for their injuries. The accident victim must overcome many obstacles before he or she can collect under the tort liability system, in which negligence must be established.[8] First, the injured driver must make a claim against the other driver's insurer, which owes him or her no loyalty. Second, under the present liability system, the accident victim must show that the other driver is negligent, and this may be difficult to prove if the cause of the accident cannot be accurately determined. Third, the amount the injured person can collect is not specified; it depends on such things as lost wages, pain and suffering, medical expenses, property damage, and numerous other factors. In addition, the present system is marred by delays, inequities in claim payments, and considerable legal cost in determining fault. Finally, critics argue that automobile accident claims are dominated by attitudes of distrust, confusion, and outright hostility.

In view of these criticisms and widespread dissatisfaction with the tort liability system, about half the states have enacted some type of no-fault law. Massachusetts enacted the first no-fault law in 1971. Nevada has since repealed its no-fault law, effective January 1, 1980. The Illinois no-fault law was declared unconstitutional shortly after it took effect. Pennsylvania repealed its no-fault law in 1984 and replaced it with a selective system of tort law and no-fault elements.

Meaning of no-fault insurance ***No-fault insurance** means that after an automobile accident, each party collects from his or her own insurer, regardless of fault.* It is not necessary to determine who is at fault and prove negligence before a loss payment is made. Regardless of who caused the accident, each party collects from his or her insurer. In addition, a true no-fault law typically places some restriction on the right to sue the negligent driver who actually caused the accident.

Types of no-fault laws No-fault laws can be classified into three categories.[9] They are:

- Modified no-fault laws
- Add-on plans
- Pure no-fault law

Under a **modified no-fault law,** the right to sue is restricted but not completely eliminated. If the claim is under a certain dollar threshold, the accident victim collects from his or her own insurer. However, if the injury is serious or the claim exceeds a certain dollar threshold, the accident victim has the right to sue the person who allegedly caused the accident. Payments for pain and suffering are not made. Thus, modified no-fault laws only partially restrict the right to sue.

Add-on plans pay modest benefits to accident victims without regard to fault, but the injured person still has the right to sue the negligent driver who caused the accident. This also includes the right to sue for pain and suffering (general damages). Hence the name add-on: the laws add on benefits but take nothing away. Since an injured person still retains the right to sue, add-on laws are not true no-fault laws. A pure no-fault plan places restrictions on the right to sue.

Finally, under a **pure no-fault law,** the injured person cannot sue at all, regardless of the seriousness of the claim, and no payments are made for pain and suffering. In effect, the tort liability system for bodily injury is abolished, since the injured accident victim cannot sue for damages. Instead, the injured person receives unlimited benefits from his or her own insurer for medical expenses and the loss of wages. No state has enacted a pure no-fault law at this time, but Michigan's law comes closest to this concept.

Arguments for no-fault laws Critics argue that no-fault laws are necessary because of serious defects in the present tort liability system. Since auto liability insurance is based on fault, critics point out the following defects:

1. *Difficulty of determining fault.* Automobile liability insurance does not automatically pay when a motorist or pedestrian is injured in an accident. The insured person must prove negligence by the person responsible for the accident in order to collect damages.

However, most accidents occur suddenly and unexpectedly, and details surrounding them can seldom be accurately determined. It is estimated that a driver averages 200 observations and twenty decisions per mile; a normally cautious driver could be held negligent because an incorrect split-second decision results in an accident. In addition, whether an injured motorist can collect anything often depends on court testimony several months or years later, by which time memory of the exact details of the accident may have faded. Also, since fault must be determined in order for damages to be paid, either party to the accident may be tempted to suppress or fabricate evidence to show that the other party is at fault. Finally, the legal doctrine of contributory negligence and the last clear chance rule are often difficult to apply in determining negligence.

2. *Limited scope of reparations system.* Another major shortcoming is that the coverage under the present liability system is deficient in its scope of reparations. The Department of Transportation found that only 45 percent of the seriously injured or the beneficiaries of those killed benefited in any way from the tort liability system.[10] One out of every ten victims received no compensation from any source whatsoever.

3. *Inequities in claim payments.* In the present system, smaller claims may be overpaid, while serious claims may be underpaid. The Department of Transportation study showed that, for small claims with an economic loss of $500 or less, the average settlement was four and one-half times the actual economic loss. For seriously or fatally injured victims with an economic loss of $25,000 or more, only about one-third was recovered.

Small claims may be overcompensated because inflated settlements cost insurers less than taking claims into court. In contrast, a large claim is likely to be vigorously resisted. Thus, despite the popular viewpoint that automobile personal injury awards are large, the evidence indicates that large awards are relatively rare when measured against the entire population and total losses.

A large percentage of each premium dollar is used to pay lawyers, claims investigators, and other costs of fixing blame. The Department of Transportation study showed that for each dollar of liability-insurance premiums collected, twenty-three cents were used for the salaries and fees of defense attorneys, plaintiffs' attorneys, claims investigators, and other claim costs. Only forty-four cents went to automobile accident victims to compensate them for their losses.

4. *Delay in payments.* Large numbers of claims may not be promptly paid because of investigations, negotiations, and waiting for court dates. The Department of Transportation study revealed that only about half of the claims were settled in six months or less. Moreover, the system is unduly slow in those cases where the need for prompt payment is the greatest. Seriously injured persons or their survivors had to wait an average of sixteen months for final payment from automobile liability insurance.

Arguments against no-fault laws On the other hand, supporters of the present system argue that no-fault laws are also defective. Major arguments against no-fault laws include the following:[11]

1. *Moral accountability would be eroded.* It is argued that the negligence system is based on individual moral accountability. In effect, the guilty motorist would escape the consequences of his or her negligent act.

2. *The defects of the negligence system are exaggerated.* Problems and difficulties in applying the law of negligence to automobile accidents are exaggerated. Generations of judges, lawyers, and juries have successfully applied negligence concepts to automobile accidents. Moreover, most automobile claims are settled out of court, which suggests the present system is working fairly well.

3. *Claims of efficiency and premium savings are exaggerated.* Predictions and assertions of greater efficiency and resulting premium savings from no-fault laws are exaggerated and unreliable. Under some federal no-fault proposals, automobile premiums would actually increase, not decrease.

4. *Court delays are not universal.* The problem of court delay is greatly exaggerated by supporters of no-fault laws. Court delay resulting from congestion is a problem only in large metropolitan areas, and this delay can be avoided by providing more adequate courts and improved procedures. Moreover, court delay is a separate problem and should be attacked as such rather than used as an argument for a no-fault system. The courts are burdened because of a rising tide of divorce cases, criminal actions, and other types of civil suits.

5. *Safe drivers may be penalized.* Rating systems under a no-fault plan may penalize safe drivers and provide a bonus for the irresponsible motorists who actually cause accidents. The rating system may inequitably allocate the accident costs to the persons who are not responsible for the accident and their premiums may go up as a result. However, the persons who actually caused the accident may not have their premiums increased at all.

6. *There is no payment for pain and suffering.* Attorneys representing injured accident victims argue that true loss to the victim cannot be measured only by the actual dollar amount of medical expenses and loss of wages. Pain and suffering must also be considered. For example, a married woman who is pregnant may be injured by a negligent motorist. She may have a traumatic abortion and lose the child. Although her medical expenses would be paid, she would receive nothing for the loss of her child.

7. *The present system only needs to be reformed.* The defects of the negligence system only need to be eliminated. This could be done by increasing the number of judges and courts, enacting a comparative negligence law in lieu of contributory negligence, limiting the contingency fees of attorneys, and using arbitration rather than the courts in small cases to settle disputes. Rather than replacing the old system with a new system of no-fault, the old system only needs to be reformed, not abandoned.

Basic characteristics of no-fault laws No-fault laws vary widely among the states with respect to type of law, benefits, right to sue, benefit amounts, property damage, and payment for pain and suffering. The major features of no-fault laws are summarized as follows:

1. *Types of plans.* About half the states had no-fault plans in existence at the beginning of 1985. The majority of states have modified no-fault plans where restrictions are placed on the right to sue. A minority of states have add-on plans through which the insured person receives additional benefits from his or her insurer but still has the right to sue a negligent driver. As we noted earlier, no state has enacted a pure no-fault law.[12]

2. *Benefits.* Most states have a minimum overall limit that insurers must provide as no-fault benefits to any single person, and some states have aggregate limits on the maximum recovery by all covered persons in one accident.

The no-fault benefits are provided by adding an endorsement to the automobile insurance policy. The endorsement typically is called *Personal Injury Protection (PIP)* coverage, which describes the no-fault benefits to be provided. Benefits are restricted to the disabled person's *economic loss.* First, *medical expenses* are paid up to some maximum limit. Most states have relatively low limits on medical expenses, ranging from $2,000 up to $50,000 for any covered person. A few states provide for unlimited medical expenses (as defined by the policy). *Rehabilitation expenses* incurred by an injured accident victim are also paid.

Second, payments are made for the *loss of earnings.* The no-fault benefits are limited to a stated percentage of the disabled person's weekly or monthly earnings, with a maximum limit in terms of time and duration. For example, New York pays benefits equal to 80 percent of the disabled person's earnings up to a maximum limit of $1,000 monthly for three years.

Third, benefits are also paid for **replacement services,** such as payments for housekeeping services which the injured person would have performed for himself or herself. For example, New York pays a maximum benefit of $25 per day up to one year for essential services that cannot be performed by the injured person.

In addition, *funeral expenses* are paid that typically range from $1,000 to $2,000. Finally, **survivors' loss benefits** are paid to the survivors to compensate them if a covered person is killed. The reduction in expenses by the deceased person's death is usually subtracted from the amount paid.

Several states also require that **optional no-fault benefits** above the prescribed minimums be made available. And many states require insurers to offer **optional deductibles** that may be used to restrict or eliminate certain no-fault coverages.

3. *Right to sue.* In those states with add-on plans, there are no restrictions on the right to sue. The accident victim can receive first party no-fault benefits from his or her insurer and still sue the negligent driver for damages. However, in many of these states, the insurer paying no-fault benefits has subrogation rights against any negligent party to the extent of benefits paid.

In the remaining states that have modified no-fault laws, the right to sue is restricted. In general, the accident victim can sue the negligent driver for general damages, including pain and suffering, only if the dollar threshold for medical expenses exceeds a certain amount, or the injury is serious and results in death, disfigurement, dismemberment, bone fracture, permanent disability, or permanent loss of a bodily function. In states with a threshold for medical expenses, the thresholds are unrealistically low, such as $500 in Massachusetts, $400 in Connecticut, and $200 in New Jersey.

All states permit a lawsuit in the event of a serious injury. A serious injury typically is a personal injury that results in death, dismemberment, disfigurement, bone fracture, permanent loss of a bodily function or organ, or permanent disability. Under these circumstances, the injured person can sue for damages, including payment for pain and suffering.

4. *Exclusion of property damage.* Most no-fault laws cover only bodily injury and exclude property damage. Thus, if a negligent driver smashed into your automobile, you would still be permitted to sue for the property damage to your

car. It is argued that the defects inherent in the tort liability system with respect to bodily injuries are not normally present to the same degree in property damage claims; thus, a lawsuit for property damage does not normally result in long court delays, expensive legal fees, and similar defects now found in bodily injury lawsuits.[13]

How effective are no-fault laws? Although a few states have repealed or modified their original laws, various research studies suggest that, on balance, no-fault laws are working fairly well.[14] Although no-fault laws contain some defects, the original objectives of these laws generally are being attained. An extensive research study by the All Industry Research Advisory Committee (AIRAC), which represents about 85 percent of the property-liability insurance business in the United States, provides a wealth of useful information concerning the compensation of automobile victims in both no-fault and tort liability states. More than 53,000 automobile accident claims were analyzed. Some major conclusions from this study include the following:[15]

1. *Less delay in claim payments.* In the no-fault states, 81 percent of the accident victims received payments within three months. In contrast, only 46 percent of the automobile accident victims in other states received payments within the same time period.
2. *More claims paid on a no-fault basis.* In no-fault states, about 77 percent of all automobile injury claims were paid on a no-fault basis, compared with 34 percent of the states that still operated under the traditional tort liability system.
3. *Substantial reduction in potential liability lawsuits.* The various tort thresholds and restrictions on the right to sue in the no-fault states have eliminated about 42 percent of the potential liability claims for injured persons who are now being paid on a no-fault basis. Prior to the enactment of no-fault laws, these persons would have been eligible to sue based on the tort liability system.
4. *More groups being paid.* No-fault laws are now covering groups who formerly would have been ineligible for payments based on the fault system. For example, almost 50 percent more persons who were injured in single-vehicle accidents received payments in the no-fault states than in the tort liability states.
5. *Increased efficiency in reimbursing automobile victims.* In the no-fault states, a large portion of the automobile insurance claims dollar is paid to accident victims for their economic losses and a small portion for general damages or intangible losses. In the no-fault states, accident victims received fifty-two cents out of each dollar of claim payments in the form of reimbursement for economic losses (such as medical expenses and lost wages) and only forty-eight cents for general damages. In contrast, in the tort liability states, only forty-three cents out of each dollar paid went for the economic losses, and fifty-seven cents were paid out for general damages.
6. *Fewer attorneys needed.* No-fault laws also appear to be reducing the need for attorneys. Only 17 percent of the persons who were collecting benefits under their no-fault personal injury protection coverages (PIP) had hired attorneys. However, about half of the persons who were collecting payments under the liability coverages hired attorneys to represent them.

Let us next examine the important issue of the cost of automobile insurance. Proponents of no-fault laws have argued that these laws will substantially reduce automobile insurance premiums. When the first no-fault law was passed by Massachusetts in 1971, and later by Florida in 1972, automobile insurance liability premiums in these states declined by about 50 percent[16] and 25 percent, respectively. Since that time, automobile insurance premiums have increased substantially in most states. Proponents of no-fault laws argue that the increase in premiums has been due largely to inflation rather than to the no-fault laws, and that premiums would have increased even more rapidly without these laws. One research study revealed that between 1972 and 1977, total personal injury premiums for fault-based liability insurance and other supplemental coverages increased 22 percent in the tort liability states, but only 18 percent in states with modified no-fault laws that provided low no-fault benefits. In the modified no-fault states with high benefits, premiums increased only 13 percent. In contrast, in those states with add-on laws, such premiums (including premiums for no-fault coverages) increased about 50 percent.[17]

In Michigan, whose law is close to a pure no-fault law, the same study found an 11 percent decrease in total personal injury premiums for both no-fault and fault-finding claims. The study also showed a 53 percent reduction in personal injury premiums covering fault-finding claims, and an 87 percent reduction in the *number* of such claims.[18] In short, Michigan's powerful no-fault law has reduced both premiums and the number of fault-based claims.

However, there is some evidence that suggests that defects in no-fault laws have contributed to premium increases in some states. *Critics of no-fault laws point out that the dollar thresholds on medical expenses in some states are too low to discourage lawsuits, and the result is that a large number of minor cases end up in litigation.* For example, in New Jersey, automobile rates have risen 70 to 80 percent since the no-fault law went into effect in 1973.[19] Although much of this increase was due to inflation, part of the increase in rates was also due to the relatively low **dollar threshold** of $200 for medical expenses. Because of the low threshold, liability lawsuits increased, which was ultimately reflected in higher automobile liability insurance premiums. Nevada similarly experienced an increase in claims because of the low dollar threshold of $750, and automobile insurance rates rapidly increased as a result; Nevada has since repealed its no-fault law.

Since a low dollar threshold may encourage lawsuits, some states are now defining the threshold in terms of a verbal threshold rather than an absolute dollar amount. A **verbal threshold** means that a lawsuit is permitted only in serious injury cases, such as death, disfigurement, dismemberment, or permanent loss of a bodily function or member. Thus, an injured person with only a minor injury cannot sue at all.

In summary, the available evidence pertaining to no-fault laws suggests that more persons are being paid, that claims are being paid more promptly, that there is less need for an attorney, and that a larger portion of the premium dollar is being paid out in benefits to automobile accident victims. However, the evidence concerning the impact of no-fault laws on the cost of automobile insurance is mixed and inconclusive. Two guarded conclusions that can be drawn from the research completed *to date* are that strong no-fault laws may hold down the rate of increase in automobile liability insurance premiums, but that claims of a substantial reduction in liability insurance premiums in all no-fault states are largely unproven.

Let us next consider the problem of providing automobile insurance to high-risk drivers.

AUTOMOBILE INSURANCE FOR HIGH-RISK DRIVERS

Some drivers have difficulty in obtaining automobile insurance through normal market channels. This is especially true of younger drivers, who account for a disproportionate number of automobile accidents, and drivers who have poor driving records. Several plans have been designed for high-risk drivers who have difficulty in obtaining insurance in the standard markets.[20] They include the following:

- Automobile insurance plans
- Joint underwriting associations
- Reinsurance facility
- State fund
- High-risk automobile insurers

Automobile Insurance Plan

Each state has an **automobile insurance plan** (formerly called an assigned risk plan) or some alternate method for providing automobile insurance to persons who are unable to get protection in the voluntary market. Automobile insurers are assigned their proportionate share of high-risk drivers based on the amount of automobile liability insurance premiums written in the state. Let us briefly examine the basic characteristics of these plans.[21]

First, persons applying for insurance in an automobile insurance plan must show that they have tried but were unsuccessful in obtaining automobile insurance within sixty days of the date of application.

Second, the liability insurance limits are at least equal to the state's financial responsibility law requirement, typically \$25/\$50/\$10. Most states offer higher limits on an optional basis. In addition, medical payments coverage and physical damage insurance are also available in most states.

Third, the premiums paid for the insurance are substantially higher than insurance obtained in the voluntary markets. Each driver is rated on his or her record and is surcharged based on the number of accidents or moving traffic offenses. It is not uncommon for a high-risk driver to pay two to three times the normal premium.

In addition, certain persons are ineligible for insurance through an automobile insurance plan. They include individuals who are engaged in an illegal enterprise, such as drugs and gambling, who have been convicted of a felony during the preceding thirty-six months, or who are habitual violaters of state and local laws.

Finally, a company is not required to insure a high-risk driver for more than three years. The insurance can also be canceled under certain conditions, such as nonpayment of premiums, obtaining the policy through fraud or misrepresentation, or no longer being eligible for or entitled to insurance in good faith.

Considerable controversy surrounds automobile insurance plans at present. The major advantage of these plans is that a high-risk driver generally has at least one source for obtaining liability insurance. Thus, the social objective of protecting innocent accident victims is at least partially met.

The major disadvantages of automobile insurance plans include the following:

1. Despite higher premiums paid by high-risk drivers, the automobile insurance plans have incurred substantial underwriting losses. Thus, the good drivers in the voluntary markets must subsidize the substandard drivers. Moreover, the greater the percentage of drivers in a state who are placed in an automobile insurance plan, the greater is the subsidy on insureds in the voluntary market.
2. High premiums may cause many substandard drivers to go uninsured. This produces the exact opposite of what the plans are intended to accomplish.
3. Many drivers who are "clean risks" with no driving convictions are often arbitrarily placed in the plans.
4. The consumer does not have a choice of companies.

Joint Underwriting Associations

Four states (Florida, Hawaii, Michigan, and Missouri) have established joint underwriting associations to make automobile insurance available to high-risk drivers. A **joint underwriting association (JUA)** is an organization of all automobile insurers operating in the state. The JUA designs the high-risk automobile policy and sets the rates that are charged. All underwriting losses are proportionately shared by the companies on the basis of premiums written in the state.

In addition, each agent or broker is assigned a company that provides claim services and other services to the policyowners. This arrangement provides all agents and brokers within the state with a market for placing high-risk drivers. Although only a limited number of large insurers provide for policyholder services, all companies share in the underwriting losses as noted earlier.

Reinsurance Facility

Four states (Massachusetts, New Hampshire, North Carolina, and South Carolina) have established a **reinsurance facility** or pool for placing high-risk automobile drivers. Under this arrangement, the company must accept all applicants for insurance, both good and bad drivers. If the applicant is considered a high-risk driver, the company has the option of placing the driver in the reinsurance pool. The applicant is not aware of this transfer, and thus, the stigma of being in an assigned risk plan is avoided. Although the high-risk driver is in the reinsurance pool, the original company services the policy. Underwriting losses in the reinsurance facility are shared by all automobile insurers in the state. In recent years, the reinsurance facilities have experienced substantial underwriting losses. The result is that good drivers are heavily subsidizing the poor drivers in the plans.

The *Maryland Automobile Insurance State Fund* was created in 1973 for the purpose of providing insurance to state motorists who could not obtain insurance in the voluntary markets. The state fund came into existence because of high rates charged by private insurers, large numbers of motorists who had been placed in the assigned risk plan, and difficulties in obtaining insurance by the high-risk drivers. The fund limits the insurance to drivers who have been canceled or refused insurance by private insurers.

The financial results have been dismal. During the first six years of operation alone, the fund experienced underwriting losses of about $50 million.[22] State law requires private automobile insurers in the state to subsidize any losses by the state fund. The result, again, is that good drivers in the voluntary standard markets are heavily subsidizing the poorer drivers in the fund.

High-Risk Automobile Insurers

Some private insurers specialize in insuring motorists with poor driving records. These companies typically insure drivers who have been canceled or refused insurance, teenage drivers, and drivers convicted of drunk driving. The premiums are substantially higher than premiums paid in the normal or standard markets. The actual premium paid is based on the individual's driving record, typically over the past three years. The higher the number of chargeable accidents or moving vehicle traffic violations, the higher the premium charged. The liability insurance limits are at least equal to the financial responsibility law requirement in the state, and many companies offer higher limits on an optional basis. In addition, because the drivers have a high probability of being involved in an accident, medical payments coverage is often limited to $1,000 per person, and collision insurance may require a $250 deductible.

Some companies have driver incentive plans to encourage safe driving: premiums are periodically reduced, say 5 percent each quarter, if the insured has had no chargeable offenses against him or her. However, if another accident or traffic violation occurs during the policy period, the driver typically is surcharged and must pay higher premiums.

This concludes our discussion of high-risk automobile insurance. Let us next consider the important issue of the cost of automobile insurance.

COST OF AUTOMOBILE INSURANCE

In this section, we will briefly examine how automobile insurance premiums for private automobiles are determined. We will limit our discussion to liability and physical damage insurance, since these two coverages account for a large proportion of the total premiums paid. Medical payments and uninsured motorist coverages are relatively low-cost items in the total premium.

The major **rating factors** for determining private passenger automobile premiums are as follows:[23]

- Territory
- Age, sex, and marital status
- Use of the automobile
- Driver education

- Good student discount
- Number and type of automobiles
- Driving record

Territory

A base rate for liability insurance is first determined. This basic rate is determined largely by the territory where the automobile is principally used and garaged. Each state is divided into rating territories—for example, a large city, a part of a city, a suburb, or a rural area. Claims data are compiled for each territory in determining the basic rate. Thus, a city driver normally pays a higher rate than a rural driver because of the higher number of automobile accidents in congested cities.

After the basic rate is determined, it is modified by other rating factors. Let us briefly examine these factors.

Age, Sex, and Marital Status

Age, sex, and marital status are important in determining the total premium. Most states permit these factors to be used in determining premiums.

Age is an extremely important rating factor, since young drivers account for a disproportionate number of accidents. In 1983, drivers under age thirty comprised 33.6 percent of the motoring population but accounted for 50.8 percent of the drivers involved in all accidents and 50.2 percent of the drivers in fatal accidents.[24]

The sex of the driver is also important since younger unmarried female drivers as a group have relatively fewer accidents than unmarried male drivers in the same age category. Also, marriage appears to make drivers more responsible, especially married male drivers: young married men also have relatively fewer accidents than unmarried male drivers in the same age category.

Young, male drivers who own or are the principal operators of automobiles normally pay the highest rates, since this group has the highest accident rate and the most costly accidents. Some insurers use four rating classes for young drivers under age thirty. They are:[25]

Under age twenty
Age twenty and twenty-one
Age twenty-two through twenty-four
Age twenty-five through twenty-nine

Certain credits and rate discounts are allowed with respect to the rating factor of age. A premium credit may be given if the youthful driver of a family car is attending a school or college more than 100 miles from home. Also, female drivers ages thirty through sixty-four may be eligible for a rate discount if they are the only drivers in their households. Older drivers age sixty-five or over are also eligible for rate discounts in many companies.

Use of the Automobile

Use of the automobile is another important rating factor. Insurers classify automobiles on the basis of how the car is driven, such as the following:

1. Pleasure use—not used in business or customarily driven to work, unless the one-way mileage to work is under 3 miles.
2. Drive to work—not used in business but is driven 3–15 miles to work each way.
3. Drive to work—not used in business, but is driven 15 or more miles each way.
4. Business use—customarily used in business or professional pursuits.
5. Farm use—principally garaged on a farm or ranch, and not used in any other business or driven to school or other work.

A car classified for farm use has the lowest rating factor, followed next by pleasure use of the car. Driving the car to work or using it for business purposes requires a higher rating factor.

With respect to youthful operators, only two categories are used. Although the same use categories are used, they are combined: (1) pleasure or farm use, or (2) drive to work or business use.

Driver Education

If a youthful operator successfully completes an approved driver education course, he or she can receive a driver training credit. The rate credit is based on the premise that driver education courses for teenage drivers can reduce accidents and hold down insurance rates.

Good Student Discount

A **good student discount** is available in many companies. This is based on the premise that good students are better drivers. The psychological makeup and intellectual capacity of the superior student also contribute to the safer operation of an automobile. Also, a superior student will probably spend more time studying and less time driving the family car. To qualify for the discount, the individual must be a full-time student in high school or college, be at least age 16, and meet one of the following:

1. Rank in the upper 20 percent of the class.
2. Have a B average, or the equivalent.
3. Have at least a 3.0 average.
4. Be on the Dean's List or honor roll.

A school official must sign a form indicating that the student has met one of the scholastic requirements.

Number and Type of Automobiles

A **multi-car discount** is also available if the insured owns two or more automobiles. This discount is based on the assumption that two cars owned by the same person will not be driven as frequently as only one car owned by the same person.

The year, make, and model of the automobile also affect the cost of physical damage insurance on the car. Premiums on a new car will be considerably higher than premiums on a car several years old. As the car gets older, the comprehensive and collision premiums decline.

Also, the damageability and repairability of the car are important rating factors for physical damage insurance. New cars are now rated based on susceptibility to damage and cost of repairs.

Individual Driving Record

Many companies have **safe driver plans** where the premiums paid are based on the individual driving record of the insured and operators who live with the insured. The insured who has a clean driving record qualifies for a lower rate than drivers who have poor records. A *clean driving record* means the insured or household resident has not been involved in any accident where he or she is at fault and has not been convicted of a serious traffic violation in the last three years. A driver without a clean record must pay higher premiums.

Accident points are assessed for accidents and traffic violations, and rate surcharges are applied accordingly. Points are charged for a conviction of drunken driving, failure to stop and report an accident, homicide or assault involving an automobile, driving on a suspended or revoked driver's license, and other offenses. The actual premium paid is based on the total number of accumulated points.

This concludes our discussion of the cost of automobile insurance. Let us next consider some rules to follow when automobile insurance is purchased.

SHOPPING FOR AUTOMOBILE INSURANCE

The thrifty insurance consumer should observe several rules in shopping for automobile insurance. Consumer experts typically make the following suggestions:

- Have adequate liability insurance.
- Purchase higher deductibles on collision and comprehensive insurance.
- Take advantage of discounts.
- Shop around for insurance.
- Improve your driving record.

Have Adequate Liability Insurance

Adequate liability insurance is the most important consideration in automobile insurance. Damage awards in recent years have soared because of inflation, higher hospital and medical costs, higher wage losses, changing concepts of damages, and more liberal juries. A negligent driver who is underinsured could have a deficiency judgment filed against him or her, whereby both present and future income and assets can be attached to satisfy the judgment. This can be avoided by adequate liability limits.

Purchase Higher Deductibles

Another important recommendation is to purchase higher deductibles on collision and comprehensive insurance. Most insureds carry collision insurance with a deductible of $100, but it is much too low in view of the rapid inflation in automobile prices over time. A deductible of $100 made sense years ago, when car prices were considerably lower—but not today. As the following figures indicate, the deductible of $100 as a percentage of the value of the car has declined over time:

$$\underset{1952}{\frac{\$100 \text{ deductible}}{\underset{\text{cost of the car}}{\$2{,}000}}} = 5\% \qquad \underset{1986}{\frac{\$100 \text{ deductible}}{\underset{\text{cost of the car}}{12{,}000}}} = .83\%$$

Collision insurance premiums can be reduced by increasing the deductible amount from $100 to some higher amount. Increasing the deductible to $200 or $250 will reduce the collision insurance premium by at least 10 percent in most companies.

Finally, you should consider dropping the physical damage insurance on your car if it is an older model with a low market value. The cost of repairs after an accident will often exceed the value of an older car, but the company will pay not more than its current market value. One rough rule of thumb is that when a standard size automobile (such as a Chevrolet, Ford, or Plymouth) is six years old, the physical damage insurance should be dropped.

Take Advantage of Discounts

When you purchase automobile insurance, you should determine if you are eligible for a discount. Companies currently make available a wide variety of discounts that can reduce your premium by a substantial amount. Figure 12.2 shows the various discounts offered by ten leading automobile insurers. You should review your eligibility for all the discounts shown, since you may be eligible for more than one.

Shop Around for Automobile Insurance

Another important principle is to shop carefully for automobile insurance. Several insurers should be contacted so that premiums can be compared. There is intense price competition among automobile insurers, and considerable variation in underwriting standards, loss experience, and claim practices. All insurers do not charge the same premium for comparable coverages. Several states have prepared shoppers' guides to help insurance consumers make a better decision when automobile insurance is purchased. (For example, see a comparison of auto insurance rates in Pennsylvania in the Appendix to this chapter.)

It should be stressed that price should not be the only consideration in selecting an automobile insurer. Other important factors include company claim practices, services provided by agents and companies, financial strength of the company, and particular coverages offered by a company that meet an individual's special needs.

Improve Your Driving Record

If you are a high-risk driver and are paying exorbitant premiums in an automobile insurance plan or with a high-risk automobile insurance plan or with a high-risk automobile insurer, a clean accident record over the last three years will substantially reduce your premiums. Meanwhile, other alternatives should be considered. An older model car can be driven with no collision or comprehensive insurance; physical damage insurance on a later model car can easily double your premiums if you are a high-risk driver. You might also consider riding a motorcycle, bicycle, or using a bus. In the last analysis, however, there is no substitute for a good driving record. Finally, you should not drive when you are drinking. A conviction for drunk driving can be extremely costly when purchasing automobile insurance.

Figure 12.2
Discounts Offered by 10 Leading Auto Insurers

Type of Discount	Companies (of the 10)	Savings Offered	Coverages Applicable to
Driver training	9	Range 5–40%; most commonly 10%. Offered by one company only in Nebraska and Pennsylvania	Generally, all coverages (may not apply to UM)
Good student	9	Range 5–30%; commonly 25%	Generally, all coverages (may not apply to UM)
Student away at school	10	Some companies put policyholders in a lower price bracket; others offer percentage discounts, usually 10–15%	Most coverages
Car pool	10	Some companies put policyholders in a lower price bracket; others offer percentage discounts of 15–20%	Usually, all coverages
Multi-car	10	Range 10–25%; usually about 15%	Generally, all coverages (may not apply to UM)
Passive restraints	7	Range 10–30%	Commonly applies to no-fault and medical payments only
Anti-theft devices	9	Range 5–15%. Most companies offer only in a few states including Illinois, Massachusetts, and New York	Usually, comprehensive only
Female age 30–64, sole driver in household	4	Usually 10%	All coverages
Senior citizen	9	Range 5–15%. Usually offered at age 65; by one company at age 55	Most coverages
Farmer	10	Range 10–30%; most commonly 10%	Generally, all coverages (may not apply to UM)
Defensive driving	7	Range 10–15%. Usually offered in only a few states, including Arkansas, Delaware, Illinois, Louisiana, New York, and Texas	Most coverages (with some companies, liability only)
Non-smoker	1	12–25%	Liability, collision, no-fault, medical payments

SOURCE: Reprinted with permission from *How to Protect What's Yours*, by Nancy Golonka, copyright © 1983 by Acropolis Books and The Insurance Information Institute; Washington, DC 20009.

INSIGHT 12.1

What "One Too Many" Can Cost

In addition to fines and legal fees, a DWI conviction can have a serious impact on auto insurance premiums. The chart below is based on sample rates by one insurer for a conventional package of insurance coverages and limits on a 1982 car in the $6,500 to $8,000 price range. Here's how a DWI conviction would influence the annual premiums. Remember, the DWI charge continues for three years.

Location	Clean Record	DWI	Additional DWI Cost
Baltimore, MD	$577	$1,186	$609
Chevy Chase, MD	$439	$ 892	$453
Denver, CO	$423	$ 990	$567
Fairfax, VA	$332	$ 767	$435
Montgomery, AL	$275	$ 644	$369
San Diego, CA	$370	$ 841	$471
Seattle, WA	$384	$ 886	$502
Tampa, FL	$400	$ 889	$489

The middle column shows premium samples for policyholders after a DWI. A history of convictions and claim frequency above the norm often results in nonrenewal of policy. This may force the former policyholder into the state's Auto Insurance Plan if other companies are unwilling to voluntarily provide insurance. AIP's usually charge considerably higher premiums than those available in the voluntary market.

SOURCE: Adaptation of "What 'one too many' can cost" from p. 18 of *Aide*, Spring 1983. Reprinted with permission.

SUMMARY

- Financial responsibility laws require motorists to show proof of financial responsibility at the time of an accident involving a bodily injury or property damage over a certain amount, for conviction of certain offenses, and for failure to pay a final judgment resulting from an automobile accident. Most motorists meet the financial responsibility law requirements by carrying automobile liability insurance limits of a certain minimum amount.
- Compulsory insurance laws require the owners and operators of automobiles to carry automobile liability insurance as a condition for driving legally within the state.
- Five states have unsatisfied judgment funds to compensate accident victims who have exhausted all other means of recovery. The accident victim must obtain a judgment against the negligent driver who caused the accident and show that the judgment cannot be collected.
- The uninsured motorists coverage is another approach for compensating automobile accident victims. The uninsured motorists coverage compensates the accident victim who has bodily injuries caused by an uninsured motorist, by a hit-and-run driver, or by a driver whose company is insolvent.

- No-fault automobile insurance means that after an accident has occurred, each party collects from his or her own insurer, regardless of fault. There are three types of no-fault laws:
  a. Modified no-fault laws.
  b. Add-on plans.
  c. Pure no-fault law.
- The arguments for no-fault automobile insurance laws are summarized as follows:
  a. Difficulty of determining fault.
  b. Limited scope of the reparations system.
  c. Inequities in claim payments.
  d. High cost and inefficiency.
  e. Delay in payments.
- The arguments against no-fault automobile insurance laws are summarized as follows:
  a. Moral responsibility may be eroded.
  b. The defects of the negligence system are exaggerated.
  c. Dubious claims of efficiency and premium savings are exaggerated.
  d. Court delays are not universal.
  e. Safe drivers may be penalized.
  f. There is no payment for pain and suffering.
  g. The present system only needs to be reformed.
- Several approaches are used to provide automobile insurance to high-risk drivers. They are:
  a. Automobile insurance plans.
  b. Joint underwriting association (JUA).
  c. Reinsurance facility.
  d. Maryland Automobile Insurance State Fund.
  e. High-risk automobile insurers.
- The premium charged for automobile insurance is a function of numerous variables, including territory, age, sex, marital status, use of automobile, driver education, good student discount, number and types of automobiles, and the insured's driving record.
- Consumer experts suggest several rules to follow when shopping for automobile insurance. They are:
  a. Have adequate liability insurance.
  b. Purchase higher deductibles on collision and comprehensive insurance.
  c. Take advantage of discounts.
  d. Shop around for insurance.
  e. Improve your driving record.

QUESTIONS FOR REVIEW

1. What is a financial responsibility law?
2. Explain the meaning of a compulsory insurance law.
3. What is an unsatisfied judgment fund? How do these funds work?

4. Explain the meaning of no-fault automobile insurance. Describe the three major types of no-fault laws.
5. List the arguments for and against no-fault automobile insurance.
6. Explain the *nature* and *purpose* of an automobile insurance plan.
7. What is a joint underwriting association (JUA)?
8. How does a reinsurance facility work?
9. What factors determine the premium charged for automobile liability and physical damage insurance?
10. Explain the suggestions that a person should follow when shopping for automobile insurance.

QUESTIONS FOR DISCUSSION

1. All states have passed some type of financial responsibility or compulsory insurance law to compensate accident victims.
   a. Describe how a financial responsibility law functions. In your answer, indicate the various ways in which proof of financial responsibility can be satisfied.
   b. Does a compulsory automobile liability insurance law adequately protect innocent accident victims? In your answer, state the arguments for and against compulsory insurance laws.
2. Unsatisfied judgment funds are used in some states to compensate innocent accident victims.
   a. Describe the major features of an unsatisfied judgment fund.
   b. How effective are unsatisfied judgment funds in meeting the problem of compensating innocent accident victims?
3. About half of the states have passed some type of no-fault automobile insurance law to compensate accident victims.
   a. Describe the benefits that are typically paid under a no-fault law.
   b. Explain the rationale for enactment of a no-fault automobile insurance law.
   c. What is a "threshold" in a no-fault automobile insurance law?
   d. How well have no-fault automobile insurance laws worked? Explain your answer.
4. Automobile insurance plans (assigned risk plans) are used in most states to meet the problem of providing automobile insurance to high-risk drivers.
   a. Describe the eligibility requirements for obtaining insurance from an automobile insurance plan.
   b. Explain the process for assigning high-risk drivers to individual insurers.
   c. Are the automobile insurance plans financially self-supporting? Explain your answer.
5. Several states have established *reinsurance facilities* or a *joint underwriting association* for providing automobile insurance to high-risk drivers.
   a. Describe how a reinsurance facility works.
   b. Describe how a joint underwriting association (JUA) functions.
   c. Is the problem of providing automobile insurance to certain high-risk drivers adequately met by these approaches? Explain your answer.
6. Automobile insurance premiums can be substantially reduced by a safe driver plan.
   a. Describe how a safe driver plan functions.
   b. Are all accidents chargeable to the individual driver involved in the accident? Explain your answer.

7. Mary is terribly upset when she receives a current premium notice for her automobile insurance. She is looking for ways to reduce the premiums she is currently paying for automobile insurance and comes to you for advice. Explain to Mary how she may be able to reduce her annual premium outlay for automobile insurance.

KEY CONCEPTS AND TERMS TO KNOW

Financial responsibility law
Security-type law
Security and proof law
Compulsory insurance law
Unsatisfied judgment fund
No-fault automobile insurance
Modified no-fault law
Add-on plan
Pure no-fault law
Replacement services
Survivors' loss benefits
Optional no-fault benefits
Optional deductibles
Dollar threshold
Verbal threshold
Automobile insurance plan
Joint underwriting association
Reinsurance facility
High-risk automobile insurer
Rating factors
Multi-car discount
Good student discount
Safe driver plan

SUGGESTIONS FOR ADDITIONAL READING

"Auto Insurance: How It Works." *Consumer Reports,* Vol. 49, No. 9 (September 1984), pp. 501–10.

"Benefits of No-Fault Auto Insurance." *Journal of American Insurance,* 59, #3 (1983).

Bickelhaupt, David L. *General Insurance,* 11th ed. Homewood, Illinois: Richard D. Irwin, Inc., 1983, chapter 19.

"Do Defensive Driving Courses Make Better Drivers?" *Journal of American Insurance,* Vol. 60, No. 3 (1984), pp. 25–27.

Fire, Casualty & Surety Bulletins. Cincinnati, Ohio: The National Underwriter Company. The bulletins are published monthly. Detailed information on the material discussed in this chapter can be found in the Personal Lines Volume and Casualty-Surety Volume.

Golonka, Nancy. *How to Protect What's Yours.* Washington, D.C.: Acropolis Books Ltd., 1983, chapters 11–13.

Greene, Mark R. and James S. Trieschmann. *Risk and Insurance,* 6th ed. Cincinnati, Ohio: Southwestern Publishing Company, 1984, chapter 16.

Lee, J. Finley. *Servicing the Shared Automobile Insurance Market.* New York: National Industry Committee on Automobile Insurance Plans, Mutual Insurance Rating Bureau, 1977.

O'Connell, Jeffrey. "No-Fault Insurance: What, Why, and Where?" *The Annals of the American Academy of Political and Social Science* 443 (May 1979).

Vaughan, Emmett J. *Fundamentals of Risk and Insurance,* 3rd ed. New York: John Wiley & Sons, 1982, chapters 30 and 32.

"What Ever Happened to No-Fault?" *Consumer Reports,* Vol. 49, No. 9 (September 1984), pp. 511–13 and p. 546.

Williams, Jr., C. Arthur and Richard M. Heins. *Risk Management and Insurance,* 5th ed. New York: McGraw-Hill Book Company, 1985, chapter 8, pp. 142–53.

Witt, Robert C. and Jorge Urrutia. "A Comparative Economic Analysis of Tort Liability and No-Fault Compensation Systems for Automobile Insurance." *The Journal of Risk and Insurance* 50, #4 (December 1983).

Wood, Glenn L., Claude C. Lilly III, Donald S. Malecki, and Jerry S. Rosenbloom. *Personal Risk Management and Insurance,* 3rd ed., Volume I. Malvern, Pennsylvania: American Institute for Property and Liability Underwriters, 1984, chapter 4.

NOTES

1. A complete discussion of these laws can be found in *Fire, Casualty & Surety Bulletins*, Personal Lines Volume, Personal Auto section.
2. The first two figures refer to *bodily injury* liability limits, and the third figure refers to *property damage* liability.
3. An alternative would be to post a bond.
4. David L. Bickelhaupt, *General Insurance*, 11th ed. (Homewood, Illinois: Richard D. Irwin, Inc., 1983), p. 587.
5. Bickelhaupt, pp. 587–89.
6. Unsatisfied judgment funds exist in New Jersey, Maryland, Michigan, North Dakota, and New York.
7. Bickelhaupt, pp. 591–92.
8. Jeffrey O'Connell and Wallace H. Wilson, *Car Insurance and Consumer Desires* (Champaign-Urbana: University of Illinois Press, 1969), pp. 1–2.
9. For an excellent discussion of no-fault insurance, see Jeffrey O'Connell, "No-Fault Insurance: What, Why, and Where?" in *Risk and Its Treatment: Changing Societal Consequences, The Annals of the American Academy of Political and Social Science*, 443 (May 1979), pp. 72–81.
10. A summary of the major defects of the tort liability system in automobile liability lawsuits can be found in U.S. Department of Transportation, *Major Vehicle Crash Losses and Their Compensation in the United States, A Report to the Congress and the President* (Washington, D.C.: U.S. Government Printing Office, 1971), pp. 15–100. The statistics cited in this section are based on this study.
11. Robert E. Keeton, "The Impact on Insurance of Trends in Tort Law," in John D. Long, ed. *Issues in Insurance*, Volume I (Malvern, Pennsylvania: American Institute for Property and Liability Underwriters, 1978), pp. 196–97.
12. Michigan's no-fault law comes closest to the concept of a pure no-fault law.
13. Robert I. Mehr and Gary W. Eldred, "Should the No-Fault Concept be Applied to Property Damage?" *The Journal of Risk and Insurance*, 42 (March 1975), p. 17.
14. See Jeffrey O'Connell, "No-Fault Insurance: What, Why, and Where?" pp. 75–77 and Robert E. Keeton, pp. 197–98.
15. All Industry Research Advisory Committee, *Automobile Injuries and Their Compensation in the United States*, Volumes I and II (Chicago, Illinois: Alliance of American Insurers, 1979). A summary of this study can be found in, "Automobile Injuries and Compensation: The AIRAC Study," *Journal of American Insurance* (Winter, 1978–79), pp. 6–10. See also "Benefits of No-Fault Auto Insurance: Why Does It Work?" *Journal of American Insurance*, 59, #3 (1983), pp. 6–9.
16. Part of the decline in premiums in Massachusetts was due to mandated reductions by the Commissioner of Insurance.
17. O'Connell, "No-Fault Insurance: What, Why, and Where?" p. 75.
18. O'Connell, p. 75.
19. *The Wall Street Journal*, June 14, 1979, p. 14.
20. The market for high-risk drivers is often called the "residual market."
21. Glenn L. Wood, Claude C. Lilly, III, Donald S. Malecki, and Jerry S. Rosenbloom, *Personal Risk Management and Insurance*, 3rd ed., Volume I (Malvern, Pennsylvania: American Institute for Property and Liability Underwriters, 1984), pp. 146–48.
22. *Insurance Facts*, 1980–81, p. 30.
23. *A Family Guide to Auto and Home Insurance*, 10th ed. (New York: Insurance Information Institute, 1978), pp. 8–12. See also Nancy Golonka, *How to Protect What's Yours* (Washington, D.C.: Acropolis Books, Ltd., 1983), chapter 12. A detailed explanation of these ratings factors can be found in the *Fire, Casualty, & Surety Bulletins*, Personal Lines Volume, Personal Auto section.
24. *Insurance Facts*, 1984–85 Edition, p. 75.
25. Wood, p. 131.

APPENDIX

COMPARISON OF AUTOMOBILE INSURANCE RATES IN PENNSYLVANIA

The annual rates shown are for a married adult, age 26–65, with one car. It is assumed that the driver does not use the car for business, drives approximately 12,000 miles a year, and has had no accidents or violations in the past three years. The rates shown do not include physical damage (collision or comprehensive) coverage.

Coverages included in this rate comparison are basic first-party benefits ($10,000 medical, $5,000 wage loss, $1,500 funeral); $15,000/$30,000 bodily injury liability; $5,000 property damage liability; and $15,000/$30,000 uninsured and underinsured motorist coverage. This is the minimum automobile insurance package required by law in Pennsylvania except for self-insured vehicle owners.

First locate the company name in the left margin. Then read across to your county of residence. Some companies divide some counties into more than one rating territory. Typically, the higher rate applies to a more urban area within the county.

The rates for the 20 largest companies and the Insurance Services Office (ISO) have been included in the chart. These companies insure more than 90 percent of the insured vehicles in Pennsylvania. (ISO is an industry rating organization that files rates jointly for many of the smaller insurance companies.) However, companies may deviate considerably from the ISO rates shown; for exact figures, check with your agent.

Also shown are the rates for the Pennsylvania Automobile Insurance Plan, the "Assigned Risk Plan," which assigns you to a company if your driving record is such that you cannot obtain insurance elsewhere. All companies must charge you the same rate for assigned risk coverage.

A WORD OF CAUTION: Automobile insurance rates vary not only by company, but among classifications within each company. Although a company may have a lower rate for the example used in this guide, it may not necessarily be lower for your particular classification.

TABLE SOURCE: "Comparison of Private Passenger Auto Companies" reprinted with permission of Pennsylvania Insurance Department.

Company	Adams	Allegheny	Armstrong	Beaver	Bedford	Berks	Blair	Bradford	Bucks	Butler	Cambria	Cameron	Carbon	Center	Chester
Aetna Cas. & Sur. Co.	162	170 218	170	174 198	150	162 170	198	206	228 318	170	184	166	182	166	236 282
Allstate Ins. Co.	183	199 249	199	215 225	193	183 209	221	231	305 487	199	203 225	227	201	201	277 363
Automobile Ins. Co. of Hartford, Conn.	208	220 286	220	226 258	194	208 224	260	270	302 424	220	240	218	234	214	310 376
Erie Ins. Co.	176	199 235	199	206 209	178	172 185	210	205	238 363	199	187 203	197	167	180	238 363
Erie Ins. Exchange	121	136 160	136	143	122	118 127	143	140	162 246	136	128 139	135	115	123	162 246
Federal Kemper Ins. Co.	136	194 270	162	204 218	148	166 198	196	172	194 232	162	174 178	172	174	142	218 250
Harleysville Mutual Insurance Company[1]	195	219 251	225	231 237	199	195 203	221	263	281 361	225	211 225	253	209	195	251 357
Insurance Company of North America[1]	234	254 292	258	283 304	240	227 234	249	299	351 430	258	238 245	288	247	252	326 411
Keystone Ins. Co.	161	146 194	146	184 193	206	161 201	188	189	316 391	146	163 166	175	170	146	289 367
Liberty Mutual Fire Insurance Company[2]	148	191 220	152	220	128	157 160	219	207	152 401	152	160 202	146	194	151	279 282
Metropolitan Property & Liability Ins. Co.[3]	146	159 212	159	171 176	156	145 164	149 177	191	255 334	159	165 174	182	175	149	207 307
Motorists Mutual Insurance Company	179	196 237	218	211 240	185	179 198	209	245	285 336	218	198 206	255	198	187	226 310
Nationwide Mutual Insurance Company	150	166 210	174	175	144	156 171	155 191	177	215 313	174	170 180	174	172	155	215 285
Pa. National Mutual Casualty Ins. Co.	164	176 216	176	192 200	168	216 176	184	206	250 322	176	190 194	208	180	182	234
Prudential Prop. & Cas. Insurance Company	200	260 368	256	310	280	236 244	272 280	276	394 574	256	232 252	246	254	236	360 390
State Farm Mutual Automobile Ins. Co.[4]	142	161 220	161	174 264	142	168 171	162 231	218	319 431	161	171 212	161	205	162	294 298
Travelers Indemnity Co.	156	164 222	164	184 202	144	138 180	202	180	248 254	164	178 206	172	166	164	200 264
United States F&G Co.	228	244 286	254	276 300	234	218 228	240	288	340 416	254	232 236	278	242	246	314 394
Valley Forge Ins. Co.	125	149 178	149	154 160	127	125 141	146	148	182 220	149	145 145	149	135	125	154 214
West American Insurance Company	170	204 228	209	211 218	176	170 198	209	209	289 296	209	177 183	231	194	182	235 311
Insurance Services Office (ISO)	236	252 296	262	286 310	242	226 236	248	300	356 438	262	240 244	290	250	254	326 414
PA Automobile Ins. Plan (A.I.P.S.O.)	358	400 522	400	437 472	413	358 458	455	457	545 699	400	389 446	435	439	415	536 638

[1]$35,000 single limit liability; $35,000 single limit uninsured

[2]Property damage $10,000

[3]$35,000 single limit liability

[4]Initial membership fee $7–$10

Clarion	Clearfield	Clinton	Columbia	Crawford	Cumberland	Dauphin	Delaware	Elk	Erie	Fayette	Forest	Franklin	Fulton	Greene	Huntingdon	Indiana	Jefferson	Juniata
170	170	166	158 182	166	162 192	158 192	236 282	166	182 206	180	166	162	150	184	166	184	170	166
199	199	201	181 211	227	183 203	183 203	277 363	227	239 245	239	227	183	193	203	201	203	199	201
220	220	214	206 234	218	208 248	202 248	310 376	218	236 272	234	218	208	194	240	214	240	220	214
199	199	180	167 170	197	172 197	171 197	238 363	197	200 238	201	197	176	178	187	180	187	199	180
136	136	123	115 117	135	118 135	118 135	162 246	135	137 162	137	135	121	122	128	123	128	136	123
162	162	142	128 186	172	150 184	136 184	222 250	172	160 190	172	150	136	148	164	152	164	162	152
225	225	195	203 215	253	195 217	195 217	251 357	253	245 251	215	253	195	199	211	195	211	225	195
258	258	252	225 265	288	225 243	222 243	326 411	288	286 328	259	288	222 234	240	238	252	238	258	252
146	146	146	160 178	175	138 161	138 161	289 367	206	167 206	170	175	161	206	166	146	166	146	146
152	152	151	151 194	146	148 181	140 181	282 397	146	146 180	186	146	148	128	160	151	160	152	151
159	159	149	149 175	172	145 163	146 163	207 326	182	168 194	167	182	146	156	165	149	165	159	149
218	218	187	171 200	255	174 187	174 187	226 310	255	220 240	204	255	179	185	198	187	198	218	187
174	174	155	155	174	150 171	162 171	215 290	174	170 206	181	174	150	144	170	155	170	174	155
176	176	182	164 190	208	164 194	164 194	234 306	208	212 214	204	206	164	168	190	182	190	176	182
256	256	236	254	256	224 226	200 226	390 494	246	256 308	300	246	200	280	232	236	232	256	236
161	161	162	162	161	142 190	142 190	298 420	161	161 224	196	161	142	142	171	162	161	161	162
164	164	164	166 174	172	154 194	154 194	200 264	172	182 202	186	172	156	144	178	164	178	164	164
254	254	246	216 260	278	212 234	214 234	314 394	278	280 326	254	278	212 228	234	232	246	232	254	246
149	149	125	130 136	149	125 141	125 141	154 214	149	155 168	148	149	125	127	145	125	145	149	125
209	209	182	161 200	231	170 175	166 172	235 311	231	219	216	231	170	176	183	182	183	209	182
262	262	254	224 270	290	220 242	220 242	326 414	290	290 336	262	290	236	242	240	254	240	262	254
400	400	415	427 460	435	358 418	358 472	536 638	435	432 442	437	435	358	413	389	415	389	400	415

Company	Lackawanna	Lancaster	Lawrence	Lebanon	Lehigh	Luzerne	Lycoming	McKean	Mercer	Mifflin	Monroe	Montgomery	Montour	Northampton
Aetna Cas. & Sur. Co.	182 204	162 166	174 198	162 166	164 166	182 186	166 182	166	174	166	206	228 282	158	164 166
Allstate Ins. Co.	201 271	181 183	215 225	181 183	187 207	201 231	201 235	227	215	201	231	305 363	181	187 207
Automobile Ins. Co. of Hartford, Conn.	234 268	208 218	226 258	208 218	212	234 240	214 238	218	226	214	270	302 376	206	212
Erie Ins. Co.	167 218	176 177	206 209	176 177	177	167 191	180 202	197	206	180	205	238 363	170	177
Erie Ins. Exchange	115 149	121 122	141 143	121 122	121 122	115 131	123 138	135	141	123	140	162 246	117	121 122
Federal Kemper Ins. Co.	174 200	136 162	204 218	136 162	158 160	146 174	152 172	172	218	142	172	194 250	128	158 160
Harleysville Mutual Insurance Company[1]	209 249	195 205	231 237	195 205	207 209	209 231	195 235	253	231	195	263	281 357	203	207 209
Insurance Company of North America[1]	247 290	234 241	283 304	234 241	231 232	247 261	252 304	288	304	252	299	351 411	225	231 232
Keystone Ins. Co.	170 188	148 201	184 193	148 161	152 167	161 170	146 162	175	184	146	189	316 391	160	152 167
Liberty Mutual Fire Insurance Company[2]	194 228	148 155	163 220	148 155	157 168	182 194	151 178	146	163	151	207	245 379	151	157 168
Metropolitan Property & Liability Ins. Co.[3]	175 210	142 156	171 174	145 156	146 158	175 184	149 165	182	171	149	194	208 307	149	146 158
Motorists Mutual Insurance Company	198 229	179 207	211 240	179 207	179 181	198 208	187 228	255	240	187	245	285 310	245	179 181
Nationwide Mutual Insurance Company	167 213	146 152	175	146 152	156 165	167 182	155 173	174	175	155	191	215 285	155	156 165
Pa. National Mutual Casualty Ins. Co.	180 224	164 178	192 200	164 178	174 178	180 186	182 208	208	200	182	206	250 306	164	174 178
Prudential Prop. & Cas. Insurance Company	254 272	200 218	310	200 218	226 230	252 254	236 242	246	310	236	276	310 414	254	226 246
State Farm Mutual Automobile Ins. Co.[4]	205 239	157 165	174 264	161 168	168 179	192 205	162 188	161	161	162	238	265 400	162	168 179
Travelers Indemnity Co.	166 210	156 168	184 202	156 168	152 164	166 182	164	172	202	164	180	200 264	172	152 164
United States F&G Co.	242 282	220 232	276 300	228 232	222	256 242	246 298	278	300	246	288	340 394	216	222
Valley Forge Ins. Co.	135 161	125 134	154 160	125 134	129 133	135 142	125 148	149	154	148	148	182 214	130	129 133
West American Insurance Company	194 214	170 191	211 218	170 191	171 172	194 206	182 215	231	211	182	209	289 311	161	171 172
Insurance Services Office (ISO)	250 292	236 240	286 310	236 240	230	250 266	254 308	290	310	254	300	356 414	224	230
PA Automobile Ins. Plan (A.I.P.S.O.)	439 494	358 431	437 472	358 431	385 396	439 513	415 474	435	472	415	457	545 638	427	385 396

[1]$35,000 single limit liability; $35,000 single limit uninsured

[2]Property damage $10,000

[3]$35,000 single limit liability

[4]Initial membership fee $7–$10

Northumber-land	Perry	Philadelphia	Pike	Potter	Schuylkill	Snyder	Somerset	Sullivan	Susquehanna	Tioga	Union	Venango	Warren	Washington	Wayne	Westmoreland	Wyoming	York
158 182	166	424 466	206	166	176 182	162	184	166	206	206	162	158 170	166	186	206	192	166	162 192
181 201	201	681 763	231	227	201 211	183	203	201	231	231	183	199 219	227	239	231	215	201	181 203
206 234	214	572 628	270	218	228 234	208	240	214	270	270	208	206 220	218	242	270	252	214	208 248
167 170	180	574 646	205	197	167	158	187	180	205	205	158	199	197	205	205	205	180	176 197
115 117	123	386 434	140	135	0 115	109	128	123	140	140	109	136	135	140	140	140	123	121 135
128 174	152	362 430	172	172	186 188	138	164	158	172	172	138	162 184	172	196	172	188	158	136 184
203 209	195	521 571	263	253	209 215	195	211	195	263	263	195	221 225	253	219	263	225	195	205
225 247	252	619 726	299	288	247 265	234	238	252	299	299	234	258	288	270	299	268	252	234 243
160 170	146	598 644	188	175	170 178	161	166	146	189	189	161	139 146	175	146 194	189	146 194	146	148 161
151 194	151	582 595	207	146	194	148	160	151	207	207	148	152	146	200	207	191	151	140 155
149 175	149	577 590	194	182	163 175	146	165 174	191	191	191	146	159 171	182	185	194	174	188	142 163
171 198	187	482 562	245	255	198 200	179	198	187	245	245	179	194 218	255	204	245	196	187	207 179
155 167	155	423 482	191	177	155 167	150	159	167	177	177	150	174	174	204	191	186	167	146 171
164 180	182	468 476	206	208	180 190	164	190	182	206	206	164	176 184	208	196	206	196	182	178
254	236	610 894	276	246	254	200	232	276	276	276	200	246 256	246	272	276	272	276	200 226
162 205	162	635 641	238	161	168 205	142	171 212	218	218 238	218	142	161	161	211	238	201	238	157 190
166 172	164	444 452	180	172	166 174	156	178	164	180	180	156	162 164	172	196	180	202	164	156 194
216 288	246	606 704	288	278	242 260	228	232	246	288	288	228	254	278	262	288	266	246	228 234
130 135	125	316 363	148	149	135 136	125	145	125	148	148	125	143 149	149	166	148	162	125	125 141
161 194	182	458 517	209	231	194 200	170	183	182	209	209	170	209 240	231	214	209	204	182	191
224 250	254	640 744	300	290	250 270	236	240	254	300	300	236	262	290	272	300	274	254	236 242
427 439	415	1104 1285	457	435	439 460	358	389	415	457	457	358	400 445	435	522	457	443	415	358 431

CHAPTER 13

COMMERCIAL PROPERTY INSURANCE

"Knowledge of commercial property insurance is absolutely essential to a successful risk management program."

L. Berekson, Risk Management Consultant

STUDENT LEARNING OBJECTIVES

After studying this chapter, you should be able to:

- Describe the major characteristics of the general property form that is used to insure commercial property.
- List some coverages that fall under the category of allied lines.
- Explain the major coverages for insuring a business interruption loss, including the gross earnings form and extra-expense insurance.
- Describe the major classes of ocean marine and inland marine insurance.
- Explain the major characteristics of the Special Multi-Peril (SMP) Policy.
- Explain the major characteristics of the Businessowners Policy (BOP).

Business firms own commercial buildings, inventories, machinery, equipment, and other valuable business property that are exposed to physical damage losses from numerous perils. Firms can also incur substantial consequential or indirect losses, such as the loss of profits, extra expenses, or loss of use of the property.

In this chapter, we begin our study of commercial property insurance. We will briefly survey each of the major property insurance lines for business firms. Our survey will include commercial fire insurance and fire insurance forms, allied lines, business interruption insurance, miscellaneous casualty coverages, transportation insurance, and multiple-line coverages for business firms.

FIRE INSURANCE AND FIRE INSURANCE FORMS

Commercial buildings and business personal property are exposed to the risk of fire and numerous other perils. In this section, we will briefly examine some commercial fire insurance coverages.

Standard Fire Policy

Commercial buildings and their contents can be insured against the risk of fire by the standard fire policy. The New York Standard Fire Policy is the foundation document for most fire and allied lines policies covering commercial property. The standard fire policy, which we discussed in Chapter 6, can be issued as a separate document with an appropriate form or forms attached. However, in the newer package policies, the standard fire policy has been eliminated as a separate contract, and its major provisions have been incorporated into the policy itself. The result is a more readable and understandable contract.

Fire Insurance Forms

Commercial fire insurance forms can be classified as follows: (1) specific coverage, (2) blanket coverage, (3) reporting forms, and (4) floaters.

Specific coverage **Specific coverage** means that a definite amount of insurance applies to a specific item of property. This form is commonly used to insure property at a fixed location. For example, a commercial warehouse at a certain location may be specifically insured for $1 million.

Blanket coverage Business property can also be insured on a *blanket* basis. **Blanket coverage** has two meanings. First, it refers to a specific amount of insurance that applies to property at different locations. Second, it also refers to coverage of different types of property at the same location. The major advantage of blanket coverage is that it is not necessary to adjust the amount of insurance when the property values at each location change, but the total value of property remains roughly constant over time.[1]

Reporting forms A firm may have wide fluctuations in its inventories throughout the year. A **reporting form** requires the insured to report monthly or quarterly the value of the insured inventory. As long as the report is accurate, the amount of insurance on the inventory is automatically adjusted based on the amount of insured values. A maximum amount of insurance is selected by the insured, and a provisional premium is paid at the beginning of the year. The premium is later adjusted at the end of the year based on the actual property values reported. For example, assume that the insured correctly reports an inventory of $1 million at the last reporting date, and the inventory is increased to $5 million before the next reporting date. If a total loss occurs, the entire inventory of $5 million would be covered.[2]

A reporting form requires the insured to report honestly. If the insured is dishonest and underreports, he or she will be penalized if a loss occurs. Under the *full value reporting clause*, if the insured underreports the property values at a location, and a loss occurs at that location, recovery is limited to the proportion that the last value reported bears to the true value that should have been reported. For example, if the actual inventory on hand is $500,000, and the insured reports only $400,000, only four-fifths of any loss will be paid.

Floaters A **floater policy** is one that covers personal property that can be moved from one location to another. The property is insured for both transportation perils and perils that affect property at a fixed location. We will discuss floater policies later in the chapter.

General Property Form

The general property form is a widely used form that can be added to the standard fire policy to insure commercial buildings and their contents. The form can be used to insure retail stores, automobile garages, schools, churches, lumberyards, apartments, and other firms. The building and contents can both be insured, or each can be separately insured. Let us briefly examine the basic characteristics of this form.

Property covered Three types of property can be covered by the general property form. They are: (1) the building, (2) personal property of the insured, and (3) personal property of others.

The general property form can be used to insure the *building*, which also includes coverage on machinery and equipment used to service and maintain the building, and yard fixtures.

Personal property of the insured can also be covered. This is *business personal property* owned by the named insured and is usual to the occupancy of the named insured. For example, baked goods in a bakery shop would be covered if the contents are insured. In addition, the insured's interest in the personal property of others is also covered to the extent of labor, materials, and other charges. For example, a television shop may repair a customer's set. If the parts and labor are $125, and the set is damaged from an insured peril, the insured's interest of $125 would be covered. Likewise, unless excluded, tenants' improvements and betterments are also covered. An example would be the installation of a new air conditioning unit by the insured when a building is leased to open a new bar and restaurant.

Finally, *personal property of others* in the care, control, and custody of the insured is also covered. For example, if a television repair shop has a fire, and several television sets belonging to the customers are damaged, the loss would be covered.

Insured perils The general property form covers fire, lightning, removal from the premises, the extended coverage perils, and vandalism or malicious mischief. A $100 deductible applies to a loss in any occurrence. Thus, if a furniture store is set on fire in a riot, the loss would be covered.

Extensions of coverage If a coinsurance requirement of 80 percent or higher is met, the general property form provides for six extensions of coverage. They are:

1. *Personal property of others.* An additional 2 percent of the insurance on personal property ($2,000 maximum) can be applied to cover the property of others in the custody of the insured.
2. *Off-premises coverage.* An additional 2 percent of the insurance on both the building and personal property ($5,000 maximum) can be applied to insured property temporarily away from the premises for cleaning, repairing, reconstruction, or restoration.
3. *Newly acquired property.* Up to 10 percent of the insurance on the building ($25,000 maximum) can be applied to a newly acquired building. Also, up to 10 percent of the insurance on personal property ($10,000 maximum) can be applied to cover business property at a newly acquired location. The automatic coverage under both extensions is limited to a maximum of thirty days after the property is acquired.
4. *Personal effects.* Up to 5 percent of the insurance on personal property ($500 maximum) can be applied to cover the per-

sonal effects of the named insured, officers, partners, and employees. A $100 limit applies to any single individual. The extension does not apply if other insurance covers the loss.

5. *Valuable papers and records.* Up to 5 percent of the insurance on personal property ($500 maximum) can be applied to cover a direct loss to valuable papers and records from an insured peril.
6. *Outdoor trees, shrubs, and plants.* Up to 5 percent of the amount of insurance on both the building and personal property ($1,000 maximum) can be applied to outdoor trees, shrubs, and plants (but not lawns). A limit of $250 applies to any single tree, shrub, or plant.

Builders' Risk Forms

A new building under construction is exposed to numerous perils, especially the peril of fire. A builders' risk form can be used to cover the insurable interest of a general contractor, subcontractor, or building owner. Two forms are commonly used. Under the *completed value form,* insurance is purchased equal to the full value of the completed building. Since the building is substantially overinsured during the initial stages of construction, the rate charged is only 50 to 55 percent of the 100 percent coinsurance rate. Under a *builders' risk reporting form,* the builder periodically reports the value of the building under construction. As construction progresses, the amount of insurance on the building is increased, based on the reported values. The final premium paid is based on the actual values reported.

Replacement Cost Insurance

Several types of commercial property are now written on a replacement cost basis, through which the insured is indemnified on the basis of replacement value with no deduction for depreciation. **Replacement cost insurance** can be written on buildings; improvements and betterments; furniture and fixtures; machinery, equipment, and supplies connected with them; and on the contents of educational, govenmental, nonprofit hospital, and religious institutions.

Replacement cost insurance is carefully underwritten, and the insured must meet certain requirements to collect on the basis of replacement cost. First, a minimum coinsurance requirement of 80 percent of replacement cost must be met in most states. Second, the damaged property must be repaired or replaced. Otherwise, the insured is indemnified on the basis of actual cash value.

ALLIED LINES

Allied lines refer to coverages that are closely related to fire insurance and to lines of insurance that have been traditionally written by property insurers. Allied line coverages are often issued as separate policies rather than by attaching an appropriate form to the standard fire policy.

Sprinkler Leakage Insurance

An automatic sprinkler system is an effective risk management tool for reducing the amount of damage from a fire. However, there is always the danger that the sprinkler system may accidentally discharge water because of a broken pipe, faulty valve, improper maintenance, or from some other cause. The standard fire policy does not cover water damage from the accidental discharge of water from a sprinkler system, so sprinkler leakage insurance is needed. **Sprinkler leakage insurance** covers direct damage to insured property because of leakage or discharge of water or other substances from an automatic sprinkler system, or loss caused by the collapse or fall of a tank that is part of the system. Thus, if the automatic sprinkler system in Ben Simon's Department Store should accidentally discharge because of a broken pipe, causing $10,000 of water damage to men's suits, the loss would be covered.

Earthquake Insurance

Commercial property in certain areas is highly vulnerable to damage from earthquakes. In 1971, the earthquake in San Fernando, California, caused property damage of $553 million. More recently, in 1979, the earthquake in Imperial County, California, caused an estimated $30 million in property damage.[3]

Earthquake insurance can be provided by an endorsement to the standard fire policy or by a separate earthquake form. In the western states, earthquake insurance on commercial buildings is typically provided by an endorsement to the standard fire policy. For commercial buildings, a minimum coinsurance requirement of 80 percent must be met. In addition, in the western states, there is also a mandatory deductible of 5 to 10 percent of the value of the property; in other states, the deductible is 2 percent.

Even with an earthquake endorsement, the deductible can result in a large loss to the insured, especially if the foundation of a commercial building is badly damaged or cracked. For example, a 5 percent deductible on a commercial office building worth $40 million produces a deductible amount of $2 million. Since the deductible can be large, there is a market for "first loss" or "primary" coverage to cover the deductible amount. The policy covering the deductible is often purchased separately from another insurer. Even so, it also contains a deductible of one-half of 1 percent, or $1,000, whichever is larger. Thus, in our previous example, the $2 million deductible on the $40 million building would be substantially reduced to $200,000.[4]

Crop Insurance

Crop insurance provides protection against damage to growing crops from hail or other perils. *Crop hail insurance* is particularly important to grain farmers who have borrowed large amounts of money to finance the purchase of land and equipment.

Crop hail insurance can be written on a named perils basis, such as hail or wind damage associated with hail, or on an all-risks basis, such as drought or insect damage. The amount of insurance is stated in terms of a certain number of dollars per acre, and the amount paid for a loss is based on the reduction in yield. Crop hail insurance is usually sold with various types of deductibles, which equal at least 5 percent of the amount of the destroyed crops.

Crop insurance can be purchased from private insurers, from state funds in a few states, and from the Federal Crop Insurance Corporation (FCIC), an agency of the U.S. Department of Agriculture. Since federal crop insurance is so important, let us briefly examine the major features of this coverage.

Federal crop insurance provides *all-risk coverage* for unavoidable crop losses due to adverse weather conditions, including drought, excessive rain, hail, wind, hurricane, tornado, freezing, winterkill, snow, and lightning. The insurance also covers unavoidable losses due to insects, plant disease, flood, wildlife, fire, and earthquake.

The basic purpose of all-risk insurance is to guarantee the insured a certain amount of crop production expressed in terms of bushels, pounds, or other commodity unit. If the insured's actual production is less than the guarantee because of an insured loss, a payment will be made for the lost production at a price selected by the insured before the growing season starts. However, federal crop insurance does not guarantee full production, but only 75 percent or less of the average production over a representative period of years. Thus, the producer bears the loss until the yield drops 25 percent or more below the average or usual production. This is the part of the loss that the producer can bear with the least difficulty. This approach is followed since crop insurance that covers the full loss of production would require unusually high and impractical rates.[5]

In recent years, farmers have become increasingly dissatisfied with the federal crop insurance program and have dropped their coverage. (See Insight 13.1.)

Difference in Conditions Insurance (DIC)

Difference in Conditions insurance (DIC) is an all-risk policy that covers other perils not insured by basic property insurance contracts. DIC insur-

INSIGHT 13.1

Dissatisfied Farmers Dropping Federal Crop Insurance Coverage

Congressional investigators say complaints about high premiums and poor coverage prompted the nation's farmers to remove millions of acres from federal crop insurance coverage last year.

In reviewing operations of the Federal Crop Insurance Corp., the investigators from the General Accounting Office found:

FCIC coverage is often too high or low for individual farmers.

Indemnity payments take more than 30 days to process in over half the claims.

State and local governments have declined to join the federal government in subsidizing FCIC premiums for farmers.

Under the crop insurance program, farmers in nearly every county of the nation can obtain insurance on any of 28 crops that guarantees production at 50 percent, 65 percent or 75 percent of their average yield. In an effort to encourage participation, the government pays up to 30 percent of the premium costs.

But, according to the report, "Farmers insuring almost 22 percent of the acres for crop year 1981 canceled their insurance for crop year 1982."

Of those 9 million acres pulled out of the program last year, the GAO said, "The major reasons cited by 46 percent of the farmers . . . were the high cost of premiums and/or low yield coverage."

The report said the six states accounting for the bulk of the cropland enrolled in the FCIC program withdrew from it at much higher rates than the national average. They were South Dakota with a 49 percent withdrawal rate; Iowa, 35 percent; Nebraska, 32 percent; Texas, 31 percent; Kansas, 27 percent; and North Dakota, 26 percent.

The GAO survey also found 6.5 percent of those pulling out of the program either misunderstood it or felt service and claims payment were inadequate. Another 5.3 percent believed the insurance was unnecessary.

SOURCE: "Dissatisfied farmers dropping federal crop insurance coverage," from *The Lincoln Star*, March 14, 1983. Reprinted by permission of The Associated Press.

ance is written as a separate contract to supplement the coverage provided by the underlying contracts. As such, it excludes perils covered by the underlying contracts (such as fire and extended coverage perils, riot and civil commotion, vandalism and malicious mischief, and sprinkler leakage). However, most other insurable perils are covered. The policy can also be written to cover flood, earthquake, and building collapse. However, a substantial deductible must be satisfied for losses not covered by the underlying contracts.

DIC insurance has several advantages. First, it can be used to fill gaps in coverage. Many large multinational corporations use a DIC policy to insure their overseas property. Many foreign countries require property insurance to be purchased locally; if the local coverage is inadequate, a DIC policy can fill the gap in coverage.

Second, DIC insurance can be used to insure unusual and catastrophic exposures that are not covered by the underlying contracts. Some unusual losses that have been paid include the following:[6]

1. An accident caused molasses to spill into a complicated machine, which cost $38,000 to clean out.
2. Dust collection on a roof solidified and the weight caused the roof to collapse.
3. A city water main broke, which flooded the basement of an industrial plant, causing hundreds of thousands of dollars of damage.

Finally, DIC is less expensive than the purchase of separate contracts for flood and earthquake. It is cheaper because it is excess over the underlying coverages, and it does not require either coinsurance or insurance to full value.

BUSINESS INTERRUPTION INSURANCE

The standard fire policy does not cover a consequential or indirect loss, such as the loss of profits, rents, or extra expenses. Business interruption insurance is designed to cover the loss of earnings or extra expenses because of a direct physical damage loss to insured property. In this section, we will examine the fundamentals of business interruption insurance.

Gross Earnings Form

When a firm has a business interruption loss, profits are lost, and certain expenses may still continue, such as rent, interest, and officers' salaries. However, other expenses may be discontinued or sharply reduced during the shutdown period. For example, regular employees may be laid off, and expenses for telephone, heat, water, and light may be discontinued or reduced.

The **gross earnings form** covers the loss of gross earnings less any expenses that can be discontinued during the shutdown period.[7] Thus, we have the following:

Amount paid =
Gross earnings − Discontinued expenses

In effect, the amount paid represents the loss of profits plus expenses that still continue during the shutdown period. For example, a retail shoe store may be totally destroyed in a fire. Let us assume that all regular employees are laid off during the shutdown period. Assume also that the firm's estimated net sales and expenses for the next twelve months are as shown in Figure 13.1.

If the store is shut down for one year, it will lose net profits of $50,000 and also incur continuing expenses of $100,000. Thus the total business interruption loss is $150,000. This can be summarized as follows:

Gross earnings	*$200,000*
Less discontinued expenses	*50,000*
Amount paid	*$150,000*

The $150,000 loss payment represents the loss of net profits plus an amount for continuing expenses.

Figure 13.1

Net sales	$400,000	
Less cost of merchandise sold	200,000	
Gross earnings	$200,000	
Ordinary payroll	45,000	Discontinued expenses
Water, heat, and light (discontinued portion)	5,000	Discontinued expenses
Officers' salaries	80,000	Continuing expenses
Rent and interest	20,000	Continuing expenses
Net profit	$ 50,000	

The gross earnings form has a coinsurance requirement of 50, 60, 70, or 80 percent based on the firm's annual gross earnings. The actual coinsurance percentage selected will depend on the length of time it will take to resume operations, and also on the period of time during which most of the business is done. If the firm expects to be shut down for no more than six months, a coinsurance percentage of 50 percent could be selected.[8] However, when seasonal peak periods are considered, this percentage may be inadequate, since 50 percent of the firm's business may not occur within a consecutive six-month period. Thus, when seasonal or peak periods are present, a higher coinsurance percentage may be advisable to provide greater protection during a prolonged shutdown period which continues during the peak period.

Finally, ordinary payroll is covered unless it is excluded by an endorsement to the policy. The endorsement can exclude ordinary payroll, or it can be covered for a limited period, such as ninety days.

Earnings Form

The **earnings form** is designed for smaller firms. This form covers the loss of gross earnings when the firm is shut down. Coinsurance is not required, but there is a monthly limit on the amount payable. The insured can select a limitation on recovery of one-sixth, one-fourth, or one-third of the face amount of insurance for any shutdown period of thirty consecutive days. For example, if the insured has $30,000 of insurance and a one-third limit, maximum recovery is limited to $10,000 for any consecutive thirty-day period.

Extra Expense Insurance

Certain firms such as banks, newspapers, and dairies must continue to operate after a loss occurs; otherwise, customers will be lost to competitors. **Extra expense insurance** covers the extra expenses incurred to continue operations. Loss of profits are not covered, since the firm will still be operating. However, the additional expenses to continue operating are covered subject to certain limits on the amount of insurance that can be used. A common limitation is that up to 40 percent of the insurance can be used during the first month following the loss, up to 80 percent for two months, and up to 100 percent when the restoration period exceeds two months.

Some firms need both business interruption and extra expense insurance—for example, a firm that is partly shut down but continues part of its normal operations by incurring extra expenses. For that reason, the Insurance Services Office has designed a *business interruption and extra expense form* which incorporates the gross earnings form and extra expense insurance into one policy. The combination form is essentially the gross earnings form with extra expense insurance provided as an extension of insurance (not additional insurance). When the combination form is used, ordinary payroll cannot be excluded from the basic business interruption coverage.

Contingent Business Interruption Insurance

Contingent business interruption insurance covers the interruption of the insured's business because of property damage to another firm not owned, operated, or controlled by the insured. There are three property situations in which this coverage may be needed. These properties are frequently called contributory, recipient, and leader properties:

1. *Contributory property.* The insured may depend on one or a few manufacturers or suppliers for most of its materials. The firm that supplies most or all of the materials and supplies is called the contributory property.
2. *Recipient property.* The insured depends on one or a few business firms to purchase most of its products. The firm to which most or all of the insured's products are sold is known as a recipient property.
3. *Leader property.* The insured depends on a neighboring business to help attract customers to its place of business. The attract-

ing business firm is called the leader property.

For example, a specialized cheese manufacturer may sell the bulk of its cheese production to a resort hotel. If the hotel is closed because of a fire, the cheese factory would also have to shut down. This type of loss would be covered by a contingent business interruption policy (recipient property).

Rent and Rental Value Insurance

Rent insurance is another type of business interruption coverage. **Rent insurance** covers the insured against the loss of rents when a building is untenantable because of loss from an insured peril. For example, an apartment house may be damaged in a fire, and several apartments are totally destroyed. Rent insurance would cover the loss of rents.

Rental value insurance refers to insurance that indemnifies the occupant for the loss of use of the premises. If the owner occupies the building and a covered loss occurs, rental value insurance indemnifies the owner for the amount needed to rent similar quarters. For example, assume that Homer owns a building where he operates a furniture store, and that it will cost him $2,000 monthly to rent a comparable building if a loss should occur. If the building is damaged from a fire, rental value insurance would pay him $2,000 monthly for a reasonable length of time to restore the damaged building.

Rental value insurance can also be used by a tenant who occupies the premises under a lease that does not allow for rent abatement if a loss should occur. Because of the lease provisions, the tenant may be obligated to pay monthly rent even though the damaged building cannot be occupied. Rental value insurance can be used to cover this loss.

Leasehold Interest Insurance

Leasehold interest insurance covers the loss that may result from the cancellation of a valuable lease when the building is damaged from an insured peril. An insurable value can also result if the insured makes substantial leasehold improvements that are expected to be amortized over the life of the lease, or a nonrefundable bonus is paid to obtain the lease. The amount paid is the present value of the leasehold interest for the remaining months of the lease. For example, assume that Oscar has signed a fifteen-year lease that has five years left to run. The lease requires a monthly rent of $2,000. However, if the lease is cancelled because of a fire, and Oscar must now pay a monthly rent of $3,000 at a new location, he would receive the present value of $1,000 monthly (at 6 percent discount) for sixty months or $51,593.

This concludes our discussion of business interruption insurance. Let us next examine some miscellaneous coverages.

MISCELLANEOUS COVERAGES

Casualty insurers write certain types of insurance that cannot be neatly classified as property or liability insurance. However, these coverages are important since property values are exposed to loss.

Plate Glass Insurance

Because of architectural and decorative considerations, the use of glass in construction has increased; this has led to an increasing need for glass insurance. The *comprehensive glass policy* is an all-risk policy that covers glass breakage from any cause (except fire, war, and nuclear damage). Lettering and ornamentation are also covered if separately described. The policy also covers glass damage from the accidental or malicious application of chemicals. For example, the store front window of a retail store may be broken by windstorm or hail, or vandals may throw acid on the glass. However, if the window is only scratched or marred and not broken, the loss is not covered (except if etched by chemicals).

There is no policy face amount since the insurer *replaces* the broken glass. Certain other items are also paid. They include the following:

1. Repairing or replacing frames that encase the glass.
2. Installing temporary plates or boarding up openings.
3. Removing or replacing any obstructions when necessary to replace the damaged glass.

Each additional feature is limited to a maximum of $75 for each occurrence. Higher limits are available by the payment of an additional premium.

Boiler and Machinery Insurance

A boiler explosion can cause substantial property damage to a firm and may also result in bodily injury and property damage to others. *Boiler and machinery insurance* can be used to insure boilers for both a direct and indirect loss. Business firms often purchase boiler and machinery insurance for the extensive loss prevention services that casualty insurers provide. Safety engineers will periodically inspect the boiler and other machinery for structural defects and other weaknesses that can cause a loss. Because of this emphasis on loss prevention, boiler and machinery insurance has a relatively low loss ratio.

Insuring agreement The insured is covered against loss from an accident to any object. An **object** is the boiler or machinery that is insured. An *accident* is defined as the sudden and accidental breakdown of an object, such as an explosion, bursting flywheel, or electrical short circuit.

The insuring agreement has five mandatory coverages. A sixth coverage (bodily injury liability) is also available. Some insurers include it in the basic policy, while others offer it as an optional coverage. A boiler and machinery policy is unique since the losses are paid in sequence; that is, a single amount of insurance first applies to Coverage A, then to Coverage B, then to Coverage C, and so on. The basic coverages are summarized as follows:

1. *Loss to property of the insured.* This coverage provides property insurance on the insured object. The insurance applies first to the object and then to all other property of the insured damaged in the accident.
2. *Expediting expenses.* The insurance is next applied to cover expediting expenses. This covers the cost of temporary repairs and expediting repairs. Overtime and extra costs of express or other means of transportation are also paid. This coverage has a maximum limit of $5,000, which can be increased by an additional premium.
3. *Liability for property of others.* This section protects the insured against legal liability if the property of others in the insured's care, custody, or control is directly damaged in an accident.
4. *Bodily injury liability (optional).* If included in the policy, the insured is covered for bodily injury liability that arises out of an insured accident. Also, expenses incurred by the insured for immediate medical and surgical relief to others are also paid regardless of legal liability.
5. *Defense costs and supplementary payments.* The policy provides for a legal defense if the insured is sued because of an insured accident. Defense costs, interest on the judgment, and premiums on appeal, release, or attachment bonds are also paid as supplementary payments.
6. *Automatic coverage.* Newly acquired objects similar to those described in the schedule are automatically covered. The insured must notify the company within ninety days and pay an additional premium.

Indirect losses Indirect or consequential losses can also be covered by an appropriate endorsement to the policy. The indirect losses that can be covered include the following:

1. *Business interruption insurance* can be added to the boiler and machinery policy to cover the interruption of business from an insured loss. Two types of business interruption forms are available. Under a *valued form,* a specified daily

indemnity is paid for each day of total shutdown regardless of the firm's actual loss of earnings. If the firm is partially shut down, a proportionate part of the daily indemnity is paid. Under the *actual loss sustained form,* the insured's actual loss of earnings and continuing expenses are paid (subject to certain limitations).

2. The boiler and machinery policy can be endorsed to cover consequential damage (indirect loss). **Consequential damage insurance** covers the spoilage of a specified property from the lack of power, light, heat, steam, or refrigeration if an accident occurs to an insured object. For example, the loss of oven heat in a bakery would result in spoilage of dough or batter. In addition, the form also covers the insured's legal liability for spoilage to the property of others, such as the contents of a public meat-locker plant which would thaw and spoil. There is also coverage for expenses incurred by the insured to prevent or reduce spoilage.

3. *Extra expense insurance* can also be added to the boiler and machinery policy. Extra expense insurance covers the additional cost of maintaining operations after an accident to an insured object until the firm can resume its normal operations. For example, a firm may have its own power plant to produce electricity and have an emergency standby connection with an outside public utility firm in case power is interrupted. If an accident occurs, and the power is interrupted, the extra costs of the outside power would be covered.

Credit Insurance

Credit insurance protects a firm against abnormal credit losses because of customer insolvency and for past due accounts when they are filed for collection within a specified time stated in the policy. Credit insurance is written only for manufacturers, wholesalers, and service organizations. Retail firms are ineligible for coverage. Only abnormal credit losses are covered; normal credit losses (called the primary loss) are seldom covered. Credit insurance is designed to cover only those losses that exceed the firm's normal credit losses in the regular course of business. There usually is a limit on the amount paid on any one account, which is based on the debtor's credit rating. There is also a maximum limit on total losses paid during the policy term.

Credit losses generally are subject to two deductibles. First, credit losses are reduced by the **primary loss amount,** which reflects the firm's normal credit losses. The primary loss amount for a firm is a percentage of the firm's net annual sales based on the bad-debt experience of similar firms, or the firm's actual loss experience. If normal credit losses were covered, the premiums for credit insurance would be considerably higher.

Second, the insured is expected to bear a portion of any credit loss by a *coinsurance percentage* that acts as a deductible. The coinsurance percentage typically is 10 to 20 percent and applies to each covered loss. The purpose of this deductible is to encourage the insured to be careful in the granting of credit, especially to firms with marginal credit ratings.

Accounts Receivable Insurance

A firm may incur a sizeable loss if its accounts receivable records are destroyed by a fire, theft, or other peril, and the amount owed by customers cannot be collected. *Accounts receivable insurance* is an all-risk policy that indemnifies the firm if it is unable to collect outstanding customer balances because of damage or destruction of the records. Certain additional expenses are also paid, including interest charges on a loan to offset the impaired collections, extra collection expenses, and the cost of reconstructing the records. The basic accounts receivable policy requires the insured to report monthly. The policy may be written on a nonreporting form basis if the firm has a credit history of at least two years, and its coverage needs do not exceed $100,000.

Valuable Papers Insurance

Business firms often have valuable papers to protect. *Valuable papers insurance* can be written to cover customers' lists, maps, deeds, abstracts,

INSIGHT 13.2

Age of Automation Inspires EDP Insurance

In this age of automation, there's at least one thing that computers can't calculate: the potential losses that businesses could suffer if their electronic brains should be crippled or destroyed. Losses in one or more areas of a firm's day-to-day operations (production or shipping, for example) could run into thousands of dollars and would *not* be covered under conventional insurance policies.

An Electronic Data Processing policy is an *all-risk* form of coverage which provides protection for physical damage to hardware, damage to the media (such as cards or disks) or software, business interruption, and extra expenses. Areas often excluded in fire and physical damage policies, such as change in temperature or breakdown, *are* covered under most EDP policies.

SOURCE: "Tenants Often Liable for Fire Damage" and "Age of Automation Inspires EDP Insurance" from *Insurance and Risk Management*, June/July 1982. Reprinted by permission of Insurance Marketing Services, Inc.

drawings, or other documents. Each item can be specifically insured, or a blanket policy can be written covering all valuable papers. One example of a valuable papers exposure is a university's file of student transcripts. Several years ago, Bradley University had a fire that destroyed the transcripts in the Registrar's office. Fortunately, duplicate transcripts were available on microfilm in the library, and the university was able to reproduce them. A valuable papers policy would have covered this loss.

Title Insurance

Title insurance protects the owner of property or the lender of money against any unknown defects in the title to the property under consideration.[9] Defects to a clear title can result from an invalid will, incorrect description of the property, forgery of the title, defective probate of a will, undisclosed liens, easements, and numerous other legal defects. Thus, the owner could lose the property to someone with a superior claim, or incur other losses because of an unknown lien, unmarketability of the title, and attorney expenses. Title insurance is designed to provide protection against these losses.

Any liens, encumbrances, or easements against real estate are normally recorded in a courthouse in the area where the property is located. This information is recorded in a legal document known as an *abstract*, which is a history of ownership and title to the property. When real estate is purchased, the purchaser may hire an attorney to search the abstract to determine if there are any defects to a clear title to the property. However, the purchaser is not fully protected by this method, since there may be an unknown lien, encumbrance, or other title defect not recorded in the abstract. Thus, the owner could still incur a loss despite a diligent and careful title search by the abstractor. If the attorney has made a careful abstract search, or has not certified something as being incorrect, he or she cannot be considered negligent if the title is later found to be defective. Thus, the owner needs a stronger guarantee that he or she will be indemnified if a loss occurs. Title insurance can provide that guarantee.

Title insurance policies have certain characteristics that distinguish them from other contracts. They are:

1. *The policy provides protection against title defects that have occurred in the past prior to the effective date of the policy.* In effect, title insurance refers to past defects that are discovered in the future after the policy goes into effect.

2. *The policy is written by the insurer based on the assumption that no losses will occur.* Any known title defects or facts that have a bearing on the title are listed in the policy and excluded from coverage.
3. *The policy term runs indefinitely in the future.* As long as the title defect occurred before the issue date of the policy, any insured loss is covered no matter when it is discovered in the future.
4. *The premium is paid only once when the policy is issued.* No additional premiums are required even though the policy term runs indefinitely in the future. However, if the policy is sold or transferred, the new owner must pay a new premium if he or she wants the protection continued.
5. *If a loss occurs, the insured is indemnified in dollar amounts up to the policy limits.* The policy does not guarantee that the owner will keep possession, or remove any title defects, or provide a legal remedy against known defects.

This concludes our discussion of miscellaneous property and casualty coverages. Let us next consider transportation insurance.

TRANSPORTATION INSURANCE

Billions of dollars of goods are shipped by business firms each year. These goods are exposed to damage or loss from numerous transportation perils. The goods can be protected by ocean marine and inland marine contracts. *Ocean marine insurance* provides protection for goods transported over water. All types of ocean-going vessels and their cargo can be insured by ocean marine contracts; the legal liability of ship owners and cargo owners can also be insured.

Inland marine insurance provides protection for goods shipped on land. This includes insurance on imports and exports, domestic shipments, and instrumentalities of transportation, such as bridges and tunnels. In addition, inland marine insurance can be used to insure fine arts, jewelry, furs, and other forms of property insurance.[10]

Ocean Marine Insurance

Ocean marine insurance is one of the oldest forms of transportation insurance. It dates back almost 300 years. The ocean contracts covering ocean-going vessels and cargo are incredibly complex. The policy provisions are written in archaic English, which reflects basic marine law, trade, and customs, as well as court interpretations of the various policy terms and provisions. In this section, we will briefly examine the fundamentals of ocean marine insurance.

Major classes of ocean marine insurance Ocean marine insurance can be divided into four major classes that reflect the various insurable interests. They are:

- Hull insurance
- Cargo insurance
- Liability insurance
- Freight insurance

Hull insurance covers the physical damage to the ship or vessel. It is similar to automobile collision insurance that covers physical damage to an automobile by a collision. Hull insurance is frequently written with a deductible. The deductible can be a stated dollar amount, or it can be a **franchise deductible** where the loss is not paid if it is under a certain limit, but is paid in full if it equals or exceeds this limit. Thus, if a hull insurance policy with a 3 percent franchise deductible is written on a ship valued at $1 million, a loss under $30,000 is paid entirely by the insured. If the loss equals or exceeds $30,000, the insurer pays the loss in full.

Cargo insurance protects the shipper of the goods against financial loss if the goods are damaged or lost. The policy can be written to cover a single shipment if goods are shipped infrequently. If regular shipments are made, an **open cargo policy** can be used, by which the goods are automatically insured when the shipment is made. The shipper is required to report periodically the number of shipments that are made. The open cargo policy has no expiration date and is in force until it is canceled.

Liability insurance is also provided. A hull insurance policy contains a **running down clause** (RDC) that covers the owner's legal liability if the ship causes damage to another ship or to its cargo. The running down clause covers only a collision loss to another ship and its cargo. It does not cover legal liability arising out of injury or death to other persons, damage to piers and docks, and personal injury and death of crew members.

Because liability coverage under the running down clause is incomplete, **protection and indemnity insurance** (P&I) can be added to provide broad and comprehensive liability insurance for property damage and bodily injury to third parties. Protection and indemnity insurance is usually written as a separate contract. It covers the legal liability of the shipowner for damage to other ships and cargo; damage to fixed objects such as piers and docks; injury or death to crew members; injury or death to other persons, such as stevedores working on the ship; and fines and penalties.

Finally, *freight insurance* indemnifies the shipowner for the loss of earnings if the ship is damaged or loss, and the goods are not delivered.

Basic Concepts in Ocean Marine Insurance

Ocean marine insurance is based on certain fundamental concepts. Let us briefly examine these concepts and some related contractual provisions.

Implied warranties Ocean marine contracts contain three **implied warranties.** They are: (1) seaworthy vessel, (2) no deviation from course, and (3) legal purpose. The shipowner implicitly warrants that the vessel is *seaworthy,* which means that the ship is properly constructed, maintained, and equipped for the voyage to be undertaken. The warranty of *no deviation* means that the ship cannot deviate from its original course, no matter how slight. However, an intentional deviation is permitted in the event of an unavoidable accident, to avoid bad weather (e.g., hurricane), to save the life of an individual on board, or to rescue persons from some other vessel. The warranty of *legal purpose* means that the voyage should not be for some illegal venture, such as the smuggling of drugs into a country.

The implied warranties are based on court decisions, and they are just as binding as any expressed warranty stated in the contract. A violation of an implied warranty, such as an unexcused deviation, permits the insurer to deny liability for the loss. The implied warranties are strictly enforced, since a breach of them would cause an increase in hazard to the insurer.

Covered perils An ocean marine policy provides broad coverage for certain specified perils. They include perils of the sea, such as damage or loss from bad weather, high waves, collision, sinking, and stranding. Other covered perils include loss from fire, enemies, pirates, thieves, jettison (throwing goods overboard to save the ship), barratry (fraud by the master or crew at the expense of the ship or cargo owners), and all other similar perils.

Although the ocean marine policy provides broad coverage, certain losses are excluded. Damage to goods from dampness or discoloration is not covered unless there is actual contact with sea water due to a peril of the sea. In addition, loss caused by a delay or the loss of a market is not covered unless specifically endorsed. War damage is excluded under a clause with a peculiar name called the *free of capture and seizure* (FC&S) clause. However, war damage can be covered by a separate policy or by an endorsement and payment of an additional premium. Finally, loss from strikes, riots, and civil commotion are excluded under the *strikes, riots, and civil commotion* (SR&CC) clause.

Particular average loss In marine insurance, the word "average" refers to a partial loss. A **particular average loss** is a loss that falls entirely on a particular interest as contrasted with a general average loss that falls on all parties to the voyage. Under the **free-of-particular-average** (FPA) clause, partial losses are not covered unless the loss is caused by certain perils, such as stranding, sinking, burning, or collision of the vessel.

The free-of-particular-average clause is often written as a franchise deductible, where the franchise amount is stated as a percentage of the insured property. Thus, a free-of-particular-average clause under 5 percent means that a loss under 5 percent falls entirely on the insured; but if it equals or exceeds 5 percent, the insurer pays the claim in full.

General average loss A **general average loss** is a loss incurred for the common good that is shared by all parties to the venture. For example, if a ship damaged by heavy waves is in danger of sinking, part of the cargo may have to be jettisoned to save the ship. The loss falls on all parties to the voyage, including the shipowner, cargo owners, and freight interests. Each party must pay its share of the loss based on the proportion that its interest bears to the total value in the venture. For example, assume that the value of the ship, cargo, and freight totals $10 million, and that $1 million worth of goods are jettisoned to save the ship. If the ship is valued at $5 million, or one-half of the total value in the venture, the shipowner is responsible for one-half of the general average loss, or $500,000.

Four conditions must be satisfied to have a general average loss.[11] They are as follows:

1. *Necessary.* The sacrifice is necessary to protect all interests in the venture—ship, cargo, and freight.
2. *Voluntary.* The sacrifice must be voluntary.
3. *Successful.* The effort must be successful. At least part of the value must be saved.
4. *Free from fault.* Any party that claims a general average contribution from other interests in the voyage must be free from fault with respect to the risk that threatens the venture.

Coinsurance Although a marine policy does not contain a specific coinsurance clause, the insured is expected to carry insurance equal to 100 percent of value. An ocean marine policy is a *valued contract,* by which the face amount is paid if a total loss occurs. If the insurance carried does not equal the full value of the goods at the time of loss, the insured must share in the loss. Thus, if $50,000 of cargo insurance is carried on goods worth $100,000, only one-half of any partial loss will be paid. The policy face is paid in the event of a total loss.

Sue and labor clause This clause requires the insured to take all reasonable means to preserve and protect the property from further damage if a loss or misfortune occurs. The insured is reimbursed for any reasonable expenses incurred in protecting and saving the property.

Inland Marine Insurance

Inland marine insurance grew out of ocean marine insurance. Ocean marine insurance first covered property from the point of embarkation to the place where the goods were landed. As commerce and trade developed, the goods had to be shipped over land as well. Inland marine insurance developed in the 1920s to cover property being transported over land, instrumentalities of transportation, such as bridges and tunnels, and property of a floating or mobile nature.

Marine insurers initially wrote much of the insurance covering transportation risks, so that fire and casualty companies were limited in their ability to compete. Several reasons explain why marine insurers wrote much of the early inland marine business. First, marine insurers had broad charter powers that enabled them to write fire and casualty lines in one contract. Prior to the enactment of multiple-line laws, the insurance business was compartmentalized. Fire and casualty lines had to be written separately. However, under an inland marine policy, both lines could be written together in one contract. Second, marine insurers had considerable experience in writing all-risk policies, and inland marine policies could be designed to provide broad coverage on the same basis. Third, marine insurers had considerable flexibility in rating and were not bound by rate regulation or rating bureaus, while fire and casualty insurers were limited in their ability to engage in rate competition. Finally, marine insurers could adapt a policy to meet a particular situation, since marine insurance contracts were not standardized. In contrast, fire insurers were required to use standard fire forms and did not have the flexibility to tailor a contract to meet a specific situation. For these reasons, marine insurers initially wrote much of the business on inland transportation risks.

Nationwide Marine Definition

As inland marine insurance developed, conflicts arose between fire insurers and marine insurers. To resolve the confusion and conflict, the companies drafted a **Nationwide Marine Definition** in 1933 to define the property that marine insurers could write. The definition was approved by the National Association of Insurance Commissioners (NAIC) and was later revised and broadened in 1953. In 1976, the NAIC drafted a new definition of marine insurance which has been adopted by most states. At present, marine insurers can write insurance on the following types of property:

1. Imports.
2. Exports.
3. Domestic shipments.
4. Instrumentalities of transportation and communication.
5. Personal property floater risks.
6. Commercial property floater risks.

Major Classes of Inland Marine Insurance

Based on the Nationwide Marine Definition, inland marine contracts can be classified into four major categories. They are:

- Shipment of goods
- Instrumentalities of transportation and communication
- Floater policies
- Bailee forms

Shipment of goods Inland marine contracts can be used to insure the domestic shipment of goods from one location to another. The goods may be shipped by common carrier, such as by a trucking company, railroad, airline, or the firm's own trucks. Although a common carrier is legally liable for safe delivery of the goods, not all losses are covered. For example, damage that results from an "act of God" is not covered. In addition, shipping charges are reduced if the shipper agrees to value the goods at less than their full value (called a released bill of lading). If the common carrier assumes liability for any loss or damage of the goods based on their full value, the shipping charges are considerably higher. Consequently, the shipper may save money by agreeing to a lower valuation and then purchase insurance to cover the shipment.

Some basic forms that can be used to insure the domestic shipment of goods include the following:

- Annual transit policy
- Trip transit policy
- Motor truck cargo policy (owner's form)

An **annual transit policy** can be used by manufacturers, wholesalers, and retailers to cover the shipment of goods on public trucks, railroads, and coastal vessels. Both outgoing and incoming shipments can be insured. These forms are not standardized, but they have similar characteristics. They can be written either on an all-risk or named perils basis. The named perils typically include fire, lightning, windstorm, flood, earthquake, landslide, and the perils of transportation, such as collision, derailment, and overturn of the transporting vehicle. For example, assume that the Fine Furniture Manufacturing Company in North Carolina ships a load of furniture to a retailer in Nebraska. If the furniture is shipped on the truck of a common carrier, and the truck overturns in a collision with another motorist, damage to the furniture would be covered.

Although a transit policy provides broad coverage, certain exclusions are present. The policy can be written to cover the theft of an entire shipment, but pilferage of the goods generally is not covered. Other common exclusions are losses from strikes, riots, or civil commotion, leakage and breakage (unless caused by an insured peril), marring, scratching, dampness, molding, and rotting.

A **trip transit policy** is used by firms and individuals to cover a single shipment. For example, an electrical transformer worth several thousands of dollars that is shipped from an eastern factory to the west coast, or the household goods of executives who are transferred can be insured under a variation of the trip transit policy.[12]

If the goods are shipped in the owner's trucks, a *motor truck cargo policy* (owner's form) can be used to insure the shipment. The owner forms principally provide coverage on property belonging to the insured which is shipped on the insured's own vehicles. Although motor cargo forms are not standardized, the coverage is similar to that provided by the transit policies.

Instrumentalities of transportation and communication This refers to property at a fixed location that is used in transportation or communication. Inland marine insurance can be used to provide all-risk coverage on bridges, tunnels, piers, docks, wharves, pipelines, power transmission lines, radio and television towers, outdoor cranes, and loading bridges. For example, a bridge may be damaged by a flood, icejam, or collision from a ship; a television tower or power line may be blown over in a windstorm; or a fire may start in a tunnel when a gasoline truck overturns and explodes. These losses can be insured under inland marine contracts.

Some bridges are toll bridges. Damage to the bridge may result in a substantial loss of toll revenues. This is a business interruption loss that can be insured under a bridge use and occupancy form that covers the loss of revenues because of physical damage to the bridge.

Floater policies Business property is often mobile and moved from one location to another. Floater policies can be used to insure the property while it is either in transit or at the new location. A wide variety of floater policies are used to insure commercial business property. The following are examples of business floaters:

- Contractors' equipment floater
- Installation floater
- Salesperson's floater
- Garment contractor floater
- Physicians' and surgeons' equipment floater

A *contractors' equipment floater* is used to insure the property of contractors, such as bulldozers, tractors, cranes, earth movers, and scaffolding equipment. An *installation floater* provides all-risk coverage on equipment and machinery while the property is in transit for installation and also while the property is being installed. A *salesperson's floater* covers damage or loss to samples used by salespersons in their business. A *garment contractor floater* is a processing floater that covers the property of a firm when it is sent to another firm for processing—for example, the trousers of men's suits that are sent to another firm to have zippers installed. Finally, a *physicians' and surgeons' equipment floater* covers medical, surgical, and dental equipment, supplies of a physician or dentist, and can also be extended to cover furniture, fixtures, and improvements.

In addition, inland marine policies can be used to cover the property of dealers. Most inland marine contracts are designed to cover property away from the policyholder's premises, but policies covering the property of dealers are an exception. A dealer's policy covers property located principally on the policyowner's premises, and coverage away from the premises is provided on an incidental basis.[13] It also covers the property of others, such as the property of others being repaired and property of other dealers on consignment. A dealer's policy can be illustrated by the following forms:

- Jewelers' block policy
- Furriers' block policy
- Camera and musical instruments floater

A *jewelers' block policy* is an all-risk contract that covers jewelry, watches, and precious stones of retail and wholesale jewelers, jewelry manufacturers, pawnbrokers, watch dealers, and diamond wholesalers. A *furriers' block policy* provides all-risk protection on stocks of furs, such as furs sold by wholesalers and retail furriers. Finally, a *camera and musical instruments floater* provides all-risk coverage on the insured's stock in trade that consists principally of cameras and their accessories, or musical instruments and their accessories.

Bailee forms A **bailee** is someone who has temporary possession of property that belongs to another. Examples of bailees are dry cleaners, laundries, and television repair shops. Under common law, bailees are legally liable for damage to customers' property only if they or their employees are negligent. However, to ensure customer good will, many bailees purchase insurance to cover the damage or loss to customers' property while in the bailee's possession. A *bailees' customer policy* can be used to provide protection to customers' property, as well as to insure legal liability for damage to the property of customers. We will discuss the various bailee forms and the legal liability of bailees in Chapter 14.

MULTIPLE-LINE INSURANCE COVERAGES FOR BUSINESS FIRMS

Business firms increasingly are using multiple-line package policies to meet their basic insurance needs. A *package policy* is one that combines two or more separate contracts into a single policy. If both property and casualty insurance lines are combined into a single policy, it is known as a *multiple-line* contract. In this section, we will briefly examine some basic package policies for business firms.

Special Multi-Peril Policy (SMP)

The **special multi-peril policy** (SMP) is a popular package policy that covers most commercial property and liability loss exposures in a single contract. The SMP policy can be written to insure motels, apartment houses, condominiums, office buildings, retail stores, institutions such as churches and schools, processing firms such as dry cleaners, manufacturing firms, and similar commercial firms. The SMP policy can be tailored to cover most property and liability loss exposures in a single policy, with the exception of workers' compensation, automobile insurance, and surety bonds.

By use of a package policy, the firm has the advantage of broader coverage with fewer gaps in protection, relatively lower cost since individual policies are not purchased, and the convenience of a single contract. Let us briefly examine the basic characteristics of the SMP policy.

Eligibility The SMP policy can be used to insure almost any business, institutional, governmental, or nonprofit organization. However, farms, granaries, rooming or boarding houses, apartment houses with fewer than three units, firms whose principal business involves motor vehicles (such as automobile garages), and firms subject to special rating plans (such as petrochemical plants) are not eligible for coverage.

Policy jacket The SMP policy contains a policy jacket that describes the general policy conditions and definitions used in the contract. Appropriate forms and endorsements are then added to tailor the SMP policy to meet the specific needs of a particular firm.

Coverages The SMP policy has four broad areas of coverage. They are:

- ▶ Section I Property Coverage
- ▶ Section II Liability Coverage
- ▶ Section III Crime Coverage
- ▶ Section IV Boiler and Machinery Coverage

Section I (property coverage) and Section II (liability coverage) are mandatory. Under Section I, the building and business personal property can be insured on a named perils or all-risk basis. In addition, several optional coverages can be added to the policy depending on the specific needs of the firm. Some *optional coverages* are replacement cost insurance, sprinkler leakage insurance, earthquake insurance, business interruption or extra expense insurance, accounts receivable and valuable papers insurance, glass insurance, and insurance on fine arts and outdoor signs.

Section II (liability insurance) provides general liability insurance for bodily injury and property damage liability arising out of the business operations of the firm. Commercial liability insurance will be discussed in greater detail in Chapter 14.

Section III (crime coverage) provides several crime insurance coverages that can be written on an optional basis. The various loss exposures that can be insured include employee dishonesty, burglary, robbery, theft inside or outside the premises, money orders and counterfeit paper currency, and depositors' forgery. We will discuss these coverages in greater detail in Chapter 15.

Finally, Section IV (boiler and machinery coverage) can be used to cover boilers and machinery. This coverage is similar to the standard boiler and machinery policy discussed earlier in the chapter.

Deductible A $100 deductible applies to loss in each occurrence. A separate deductible applies to each building (or its contents) and personal property in the open. A maximum deductible of $1,000 applies to the loss of all property in a single occurrence.

Businessowners Policy (BOP)

The **businessowners policy (BOP)** is a package policy specifically designed for smaller retail stores, office buildings, and apartment buildings. It was introduced nationally by the Insurance Service Office in 1976. The businessowners policy is designed to meet the basic property and liability insurance needs of smaller business firms in one contract.[14]

Eligible firms The BOP can be written to cover buildings and business personal property of the owners of apartments, office buildings, and stores. Apartments cannot exceed six stories in height and are limited to a maximum of 60 dwelling units and 7,500 square feet of mercantile space. Office buildings are limited to a maximum of three stories and a maximum area of 100,000 square feet; mercantile space cannot exceed 7,500 square feet. Stores must be occupied principally for mercantile purposes, and the total area cannot exceed 7,500 square feet. Tenants of offices and stores can also insure their business property under the BOP as long as office space does not exceed 10,000 square feet, or the store's total area does not exceed 7,500 square feet.

Certain business firms and property cannot be insured under the BOP. They include automobile repair or service stations and dealers in automobiles, motorcycles, motor homes, or mobile homes; bars, grills, or restaurants; condominiums; contractors; buildings used in manufacturing or processing; household personal property of the businessowners; places of amusement; wholesalers; and financial institutions. These firms are ineligible for the BOP because the loss exposures are outside that contemplated for the average small-to-medium size firm.

Coverages The BOP is designed to meet the property insurance needs of most small-to-medium size firms on one contract. The following is a summary of the basic characteristics of the BOP:

1. *Buildings.* All buildings are insured on a *replacement cost basis.* There is no coin-

surance requirement. However, the insured is expected to carry insurance equal to the full cost of the property. The insurance on the building is automatically increased by a stated percentage each quarter to keep pace with inflation.

2. *Business personal property.* Business personal property is also insured on a *replacement cost basis.* A peak season provision provides for a temporary increase of 25 percent of the amount of insurance when inventory values are at their peak. Tenants' improvements and betterments are also covered. Property in transit or temporarily away from the store is also covered up to a maximum of $1,000.

   In addition, business personal property at newly acquired locations is also covered for a maximum of $10,000 for 30 days. This provides automatic protection until the BOP can be endorsed to cover the new location.

3. *Deductibles.* A deductible of $100 per occurrence applies to most property losses. The deductible applies separately to each building (including its contents), to the contents if the building is not insured, and to personal property in the open. Concurrent damage to another building on the premises is subject to another deductible, and damage to merchandise to be loaded on a truck at the premises is subject to a third deductible.

   The combined deductibles in any single occurrence are limited to a maximum of $1,000. The deductible does not apply to loss-of-income coverage.

   A separate deductible of $250 applies to crime losses, such as burglary and robbery or employee dishonesty.

4. *Loss of income.* The BOP provides automatic coverage for the loss of income. The loss of income includes business interruption losses, extra expenses, and the loss of rents. The insured who has a loss in all three areas may recover on the basis of all three. The amount paid is limited to the *actual loss sustained* by the firm for a maximum period not to exceed twelve months.

5. *Covered perils.* Two forms are used under the BOP. Under the *standard form,* the insured is protected against loss on a *named perils basis.* The covered perils are fire and extended coverage, vandalism and malicious mischief, sprinkler leakage, and transportation perils. Under the *special form,* protection is provided on an *all-risks basis.*

6. *Optional property insurance.* Both forms can be endorsed to cover employee dishonesty, outdoor signs, comprehensive plate glass, earthquakes, and boiler and machinery insurance. The standard form can also be endorsed to provide burglary and robbery insurance to covered business personal property. The special form automatically includes this coverage since it is an all-risk form.

   When burglary and robbery insurance is included in the BOP, the coverage also applies to money and securities used in the insured's business. Money and securities are covered up to $5,000 on the premises and $2,000 away from the premises. (The special form has an on-premises limit of $10,000.)

7. *Business liability insurance.* Liability insurance is provided in the amount of $300,000, $500,000, or $1 million. Medical payments insurance is also provided in the amount of $1,000 for each person and $10,000 for each accident. Comprehensive liability protection is provided, including premises and operations liability, products and completed operations liability, fire legal liability, and coverage for other specialized liability exposures. We will explain the meaning of these terms in Chapter 14.

SUMMARY

- Commercial fire insurance forms can be classified as specific coverage, blanket coverage, reporting forms, and floaters.
- The general property form can be used to insure a commercial building, business property of the insured, and personal property of others.
- Allied lines refers to coverages that are closely related to fire insurance; they include sprinkler leakage insurance, earthquake insurance, crop insurance, and difference in conditions insurance.
- The gross earnings form can be used to insure a business interruption loss where the amount paid is equal to the firm's gross earnings less discontinued expenses. The firm receives a payment that represents the loss of profits plus expenses that still continue during the shutdown period.
- Other types of business interruption insurance include extra expense insurance, contingent business interruption insurance, and rents or rental value insurance.
- Certain miscellaneous coverages are important to business firms, including plate glass insurance, boiler and machinery insurance, credit insurance, accounts receivable insurance, valuable papers insurance, and title insurance.
- Ocean marine insurance can be divided into four categories that reflect the various insurable interests. They are:
  a. Hull insurance.
  b. Cargo insurance.
  c. Liability insurance.
  d. Freight insurance.
- A particular average loss in marine insurance is a loss that falls entirely on a particular interest as contrasted with a general average loss that falls on all parties to the voyage.
- Inland marine insurance can be classified into four major categories. They are:
  a. Shipment of goods.
  b. Instrumentalities of transportation and communication.
  c. Floater policies.
  d. Bailee forms.
- The special multi-peril policy (SMP) is a package policy that can be used to cover most commercial property and liability loss exposures in a single contract. The SMP policy can be used to provide insurance on buildings and business personal property, liability insurance, crime insurance, and boiler and machinery insurance in one policy.
- The Businessowners Policy is a package policy for smaller business firms. It covers the building, business personal property, loss of income to the firm, and liability exposures. The policy can be endorsed to cover employee dishonesty, outdoor signs, plate glass, earthquakes, and boiler and machinery insurance.

QUESTIONS FOR REVIEW

1. Briefly describe the coverage under the general property form and builder's risk forms.
2. Why does a business firm normally require sprinkler leakage insurance?

3. Explain the major features of earthquake insurance.
4. Explain the gross earnings form, extra expense insurance, and contingent business interruption insurance that can be used to insure a business interruption loss.
5. List the major coverages under a boiler and machinery policy.
6. Describe each of the major categories of ocean marine insurance.
7. What is the difference between a particular average loss and general average loss in ocean marine insurance? What conditions must be fulfilled in order to have a general average loss?
8. Describe the different types of property that can be insured under an inland marine policy.
9. Briefly describe the major features of the special multi-peril (SMP) policy.
10. Briefly describe the major features of the businessowners policy.

QUESTIONS FOR DISCUSSION

1. Commercial fire insurance forms can be classified as *specific, blanket, reporting,* or *floater.* Explain the meaning of each of these terms.
2. Fred owns a department store that is protected by an automatic sprinkler system. The building and its contents are insured under the 1943 New York Standard Fire Policy with a General Property Form attached to it. Fred has been advised by his insurance agent that he should also carry sprinkler leakage insurance. Do you agree or disagree with the agent's advice? Explain your answer.
3. Jack owns a retail shoe store. He has purchased business interruption insurance on the store under the Gross Earnings Form with no exclusion of payroll and a 50 percent coinsurance provision. He estimates the following values for the next twelve months.

Net sales	$300,000
Cost of merchandise sold	180,000
Expenses that will continue in the event of a business interruption loss	60,000
Expenses that can be discontinued in the event of a business interruption loss	36,000
Net profit	24,000

   a. How much business interruption insurance should Jack carry to meet the coinsurance requirement? Explain your answer.
   b. Assuming that the 50 percent coinsurance requirement is met, how much will Jack collect for a covered business interruption loss if the business is totally interrupted for a period of six months? Explain your answer.
   c. How does extra expense insurance differ from the gross earnings form?
4. Joseph rents an office in a desirable city office building under a long-term lease. The rental is $2,000 monthly. Joseph's lease has ten more years to run and states that if the premises are damaged by a fire and are rendered untenantable, either Joseph or the landlord can cancel the lease by giving thirty days notice to the other party. Joseph has been advised by a rental agent that a comparable office would cost $3,000 per month to rent today.
   a. What type of insurance would you recommend to Joseph in this situation?
   b. Explain how the recommended coverage would cover Joseph's loss exposure.

5. *a.* The *Mary Queen,* an ocean-going oil tanker, negligently collided with a large freighter. The *Mary Queen* is insured by an ocean marine hull insurance policy with a collision or running down clause included in the policy. For each of the following losses, explain whether the ocean marine coverage would apply to the loss:
   (1) damage to the *Mary Queen.*
   (2) damage to the freighter.
   (3) death or injury to the crew members on the freighter.

   b. Briefly explain each of the following ocean marine terms or provisions:
   (1) free of particular average loss.
   (2) general average loss.
   (3) open cargo policy.
6. Edward owns and operates a small furniture store in a suburban shopping center. His agent advises him that the store can be insured under the Businessowners Policy. Edward comes to you for advice. List the various loss exposures to Edward's furniture store that can be covered by the Businessowners Policy.

KEY CONCEPTS AND TERMS TO KNOW

Specific coverage
Blanket coverage
Reporting forms
Floater policy
Replacement cost insurance
Sprinkler leakage
Difference in conditions
Gross earnings form
Earnings form
Extra expense insurance
Contingent business interruption insurance
Rent insurance
Rental value insurance
Object
Expediting expenses
Consequential damage
Primary loss amount
Hull insurance
Franchise deductible
Open cargo policy
Running down clause
Protection and indemnity insurance
Implied warranties
Particular average loss
Free-of-particular average loss
General average loss
Nationwide Marine Definition
Annual transit policy
Trip transit policy
Instrumentalities of transportation and communication
Bailee
Special multi-peril (SMP) policy
Businessowners policy

SUGGESTIONS FOR ADDITIONAL READING

Bickelhaupt, David L. *General Insurance,* 11th ed. Homewood, Illinois: Richard D. Irwin, Inc., 1983, chapters 14, 15, 23, and 27.

Fire, Casualty, & Surety Bulletins. Fire and Marine Volume and Casualty-Surety Volume. Cincinnati, Ohio: The National Underwriter Company. The bulletins are published monthly and provide detailed information on all commercial property insurance lines.

Gordis, Philip. *Property and Casualty Insurance,* 26th ed. Indianapolis, Indiana: The Rough Notes Company, Inc., 1980.

Greene, Mark R. and James S. Trieschmann. *Risk and Insurance,* 6th ed. Cincinnati, Ohio: Southwestern Publishing Company, 1984, chapters 12, 13, and 17.

Huebner, S. S., Kenneth Black, Jr., and Robert S. Cline. *Property and Liability Insurance,* 3rd ed. Englewood Cliffs, New Jersey: Prentice-Hall, Inc., 1982.

Mehr, Robert I. and Emerson Cammack. *Principles of Insurance.* Homewood, Illinois: Richard D. Irwin, Inc., 1980, chapters 11, 12, and 15.

Rodda, William H., James S. Trieschmann, Eric A. Wiening, and Bob A. Hedges. *Commercial Property Risk Management and Insurance,* 2nd ed. Volumes I and II. Malvern, Pennsylvania: American Institute for Property and Liability Underwriters, 1983.

Vaughan, Emmett J. *Fundamentals of Risk and Insurance,* 3rd ed. New York: John Wiley & Sons, 1982, chapter 33.

Williams, Jr., C. Arthur and Richard M. Heins. *Risk Management and Insurance,* 5th ed. New York: McGraw-Hill, 1985, chapters 18 and 19.

NOTES

1. A *pro rata distribution clause* is usually added to a blanket policy. The amount of insurance at each location is based on the proportion that the property values at that location bears to the total property values at all locations. However, a pro rata distribution clause is not required if the contract contains a coinsurance clause of 90 percent or higher.
2. This assumes that the maximum amount of insurance carried is at least equal to this amount.
3. *Insurance Facts,* 1983–84 edition, p. 65.
4. William H. Rodda, James S. Trieschmann, and Bob A. Hedges, *Commercial Property Risk Management and Insurance,* Volume I (Malvern, Pennsylvania: American Institute for Property and Liability Underwriters, 1978), p. 223.
5. Complete details on federal crop insurance can be found in *An Inside Look at All-Risk Crop Insurance* (Washington, D.C.: Federal Crop Insurance Corporation, U.S. Department of Agriculture, 1980).
6. Rodda, p. 231.
7. These are two gross earnings forms. One is used for manufacturing, and the other is used for mercantile and nonmanufacturing risks.
8. However, if ordinary payroll is excluded, or there is limited coverage of ordinary payroll, the lower coinsurance percentages usually are not available.
9. A complete description of title insurance can be found in S. S. Huebner, Kenneth Black, Jr., and Robert S. Cline, *Property and Liability Insurance,* 3rd ed. (Englewood Cliffs, New Jersey: Prentice-Hall, Inc., 1982), chapter 23.
10. Transportation insurance is discussed in detail in *Fire, Casualty, & Surety Bulletins,* Fire and Marine Volume, Aircraft-Boats and Inland Marine sections; William H. Rodda, James S. Trieschmann, and Bob A. Hedges, *Commercial Property Risk Management,* Volumes I and II (Malvern, PA: American Institute for Property and Liability Underwriters, 1978); and Philip Gordis, *Property and Casualty Insurance,* 26th ed. Indianapolis, IN: The Rough Notes Co., 1980. The author drew on these sources in preparing this section.
11. Rodda, p. 395.
12. William H. Rodda, James S. Trieschmann, and Bob A. Hedges, *Commercial Property Risk Management and Insurance,* Volume II (Malvern, Pennsylvania: American Institute for Property and Liability Underwriters, 1978), p. 53.
13. Emmett J. Vaughan, *Fundamentals of Risk and Insurance,* 3rd ed. (New York: John Wiley & Sons, Inc., 1982), p. 526.
14. A detailed explanation of the businessowners policy can be found in *Fire, Casualty, & Surety Bulletins,* Fire and Marine Volume, Commercial Multiple-peril section.

CHAPTER 14

COMMERCIAL LIABILITY INSURANCE

"If a firm wants to survive in this jungle, it must have protection against catastrophic legal liability lawsuits."

Jack Willhoft, President, Spartan Arch Skate Company

STUDENT LEARNING OBJECTIVES

After studying this chapter, you should be able to:

- Explain the important general liability loss exposures of business firms.
- Describe the major features of the Comprehensive General Liability Policy.
- Explain why separate coverage for employers' liability is provided in a workers' compensation policy.
- Describe the major liability coverages in the Business Auto Policy and Garage Policy.
- Explain the nature and purpose of Bailees' Customer Insurance.
- Describe the major characteristics of the Commercial Umbrella Policy.
- Explain the general liability loss exposures that are covered by the Businessowners Policy.
- Describe the major features of a professional liability policy.

Business firms operate in an intense competitive environment where liability lawsuits are routine. Firms are sued for defective products, bodily injuries to customers or employees, property damage, pollution of the environment, and a host of other reasons. In this chapter, we will continue our study of business insurance by examining some major commercial liability insurance coverages. We will begin by examining the general liability loss exposures of business firms. We will then survey some important commercial liability contracts that can be used to meet those exposures. Our survey will include a discussion of general liability insurance, workers' compensation and employers' liability insurance, commercial automobile liability insurance, aviation liability insurance, bailees' liability insurance, the commercial umbrella liability policy, and liability insurance in the new businessowners policy. We will conclude the chapter by examining professional liability insurance.

GENERAL LIABILITY LOSS EXPOSURES

General liability refers to the legal liability arising out of business operations other than liability for automobile or aviation accidents or employee injuries.[1] The most important general liability loss exposures of commercial firms are as follows:

- Premises and operations
- Elevators and escalators
- Products liability
- Completed operations
- Contractual liability
- Contingent liability

Premises and Operations

Legal liability can arise out of the *ownership and maintenance of the premises* where the firm does business. Firms are legally required to maintain the premises and elevators in a safe condition and are also responsible for the actions of their employees. Customers in a store fall into the legal category of *invitees*, and the highest degree of care is owed to them. The customers must be warned and protected against any dangerous condition on the premises. For example, a firm can be held liable if a customer trips on a torn carpet and breaks a leg, or if a ceiling collapses and a customer is injured.

Legal liability can also arise out of the firm's *operations*, either on or off the premises. For example, a sales clerk in a paint store may carelessly spill some paint on a customer's coat; employees unloading lumber in a lumber yard may accidentally damage a customer's truck; or a construction worker on a high-rise building may carelessly drop a steel beam that injures a pedestrian.

In a general liability insurance policy, the coverage that protects the firm for legal liability arising out of the ownership and maintenance of the premises and its business operations is known as **premises and operations coverage.**

Elevators and Escalators

A firm can also be sued because of *defective elevators and escalators*. For example, a passenger elevator may fall several flights, causing injuries to customers inside the elevator, or a customer's toe may be crushed because of a defective escalator. Liability arising out of elevators and escalators can also be insured by a general liability policy.

Products Liability

Products liability refers to the legal liability of manufacturers, wholesalers, and retailers to persons who are injured or incur property damage from defective products. We noted in Chapter 9 that the number of products liability lawsuits and the size of the damage awards have increased substantially over time. Firms can be successfully sued on the basis of negligence, breach of warranty, and strict liability. Products liability coverage can be added to a general liability policy to cover this exposure. We have already discussed the products liability problem in Chapter 9, so further treatment is not needed here.

Completed Operations

Completed operations refers to liability arising out of faulty work performed away from the premises after the work or operations are completed. Contractors, plumbers, electricians, repair shops, and similar firms are liable for bodily injuries and property damage to others after their work is completed. When the work is in progress, it is part of the operations exposure. But after the work is completed, it is a completed operations exposure. For example, a hot water tank may explode if it is improperly installed; ductwork in a supermarket may collapse and injure a customer because of improper installation; and a highway contractor may leave a deep rut in the shoulder of a highway that causes injury to a passing motorist.

In a general liability policy, a firm can obtain protection against legal liability arising out of completed operations by *products and completed operations insurance.*

Contractual Liability

A business firm may also have a contractual liability exposure. **Contractual liability** means that the business firm agrees to assume the legal liability of another party by a written or oral contract. For example, a manufacturing firm may rent a building, and the lease specifies that the building owner is to be held harmless for any liability arising out of use of the building. Thus, by a written lease, the manufacturing firm is assuming some potential legal liability that it ordinarily would not assume. Certain types of contractual liability are automatically covered under premises and operations insurance. However, other contracts must be specifically insured under *contractual liability insurance.*

Contingent Liability

Contingent liability refers to liability arising out of work done by independent contractors. As a general rule, business firms are not legally liable for work done by independent contractors. However, under certain conditions, a firm can be held liable for work performed by independent contractors. Firms can be held liable if (1) the activity is illegal, (2) it is a situation that does not permit delegation of authority, or (3) the work is inherently dangerous.[2] For example, a general contractor may hire a subcontractor to perform a blasting operation. If someone is injured in the blast, the general contractor can be held liable even though the subcontractor is primarily responsible. Even if the general contractor has no legal liability, the legal costs of defense against the lawsuit can be enormous. To obtain protection against contingent legal liability for work performed by independent contractors, *independent contractors* coverage can be added to a general liability policy.[3]

Other General Liability Loss Exposures

Business firms are often exposed to other important general liability loss exposures. Some important loss exposures are summarized as follows:

1. *Environmental pollution.* Chemical, manufacturing, and other firms may pollute the environment by impure smoke, fumes, acids, toxic chemicals, waste materials, and other pollutants.
2. *Fire legal liability.* A firm may rent or use property that belongs to another party, such as a building. If a fire occurs because of the negligence of the firm or its employees, the firm can be held legally liable for the loss. Many general liability insurance policies do not cover this exposure because of the care, custody, or control exclusion. **Fire legal liability insurance** can be added to a general liability policy to cover this exposure.
3. *Liquor liability laws.* Most states have **liquor liability laws** (often called dram-shop laws) that make bars, restaurants, taverns, and other firms that sell liquor legally liable for injuries caused by intoxicated customers. Most general liability policies exclude legal liability arising out of the manufacturing, selling, distributing, or serving of alcoholic beverages. This ex-

INSIGHT 14.1

Tenants Often Liable for Fire Damage

If you are a businessowner, you probably operate from rented or leased premises. Assume that three weeks from now a fire broke out in your office and caused extensive damage to the building. Although your landlord's fire insurance will probably cover the cost of repairs, *you* could wind up footing the bill.

Here's why: As a tenant you can be held liable for damage to the portion of your landlord's property that you occupy, which gives the insurance company the right to sue you for negligence in allowing the fire to start or spread. The chances are that a general liability insurance contract would not cover you in this instance, because most of these policies specifically exclude coverage for damage to rented or leased property which is under your "care, custody and control." So, if you lost the suit, you would have to reimburse the insurance company for the cost of repairs. Even if you won, the time, effort and expense of a lawsuit (on top of the trauma of the fire itself) could drain you.

You can protect yourself against this type of situation with fire legal liability insurance that will: (1) pay amounts up to the limit of the policy for which you might be held liable resulting from damage by fire to the property of a third party in your "care, custody and control"; and (2) provide a legal defense for any suit involving liability from a fire. Coverage does not include liability assumed under any agreement or contract. Fire legal liability can be written as an "add-on" either to the basic fire policy or to a general liability policy, depending on the insured's needs.

SOURCE: "Tenants Often Liable for Fire Damage" and "Age of Automation Inspires EDP Insurance" from *Insurance and Risk Management*, June/July 1982. Reprinted by permission of Insurance Marketing Services, Inc.

posure can be covered by a *liquor liability policy* that is usually written by specialty insurers, such as Lloyds of London.

4. *Directors and officers liability.* An increasing number of officers and directors of business firms have been sued in recent years. The lawsuits are often initiated by angry stockholders who claim that mismanagement by officers and directors has resulted in financial losses to the stockholders. This exposure of directors and officers to liability lawsuits can be covered by a *directors and officers liability insurance policy.*
5. *Personal injury.* In addition to bodily injury and property damage liability, a business firm may be sued for personal injury. **Personal injury** refers to false arrest, detention or imprisonment, malicious prosecution, libel, slander, defamation of character, violation of the right of privacy, and unlawful entry or eviction. For example, a department store may be successfully sued by an innocent customer who is erroneously arrested for shoplifting. The personal injury exposure can be insured by adding *personal injury liability coverage* to a general liability policy.
6. *Property in the insured's care, custody, or control.* Liability can also arise out of damage to property in the insured's care, custody, or control. Many general liability policies exclude this exposure. This can be a problem for firms that work on the property of others, such as an automobile repair garage. In some cases, this exposure can be insured by an endorsement to the policy, and certain specialized general liability policies may also provide coverage for this exposure.

COMPREHENSIVE GENERAL LIABILITY INSURANCE

The *Comprehensive General Liability* (CGL) policy is designed to meet most general liability loss exposures of business firms in a single contract. The CGL policy consists of three separate documents: (1) a *declarations page*, (2) a *policy jacket* that contains the policy definitions, conditions, and provisions common to all general liability contracts, and (3) the CGL *coverage parts* that contain the insuring agreements, exclusions, and other provisions.

Coverages

The CGL policy automatically provides coverage for (1) premises and operations, (2) independent contractors, (3) completed operations, (4) products liability, and (5) incidental contractual exposures.

The CGL also automatically covers any newly acquired insurance exposures that arise during the policy period after the contract is first written. The new exposures are automatically insured without first giving notice to the insurer. Since there is automatic coverage of unknown eligible loss exposures, the CGL is one of the broadest commercial liability policies available today.

In addition, other coverage parts and endorsements can also be added (such as contractual liabililty and premises medical payments) to meet the specialized insurance needs and liability loss.

Insuring Agreements

The company agrees to pay on behalf of the insured all sums up to the policy limits that the insured is legally obligated to pay because of *bodily injury or property damage* caused by an occurrence. An *occurrence* includes not only an accident, but also any continuous or repeated exposure to conditions that result in bodily injury or property damage that is neither expected nor intended by the insured. For example, rain and water seepage over a period of time may rot a roof, which may cause it to collapse and injure a customer. A drug manufacturer may produce a defective batch of flu vaccine, and, over a period of time, several persons may become violently ill from the vaccine and sue the drug manufacturer. These exposures would be considered occurrences and can be covered by the CGL. (Note, however, that the Insurance Services Office has made available a new CGL policy on a claims-made basis.[4] A claims-made policy is discussed later in the chapter.)

Defense Costs

The insurer also agrees to defend any lawsuit against the insured even if the allegations in the lawsuit are groundless, false, or fraudulent. The court costs and legal defense costs are paid in addition to the amounts paid as damages. However, the company's obligation to defend the insured ends when the policy limits are exhausted by payment of a judgment or settlement.

Exclusions

The CGL policy contains numerous exclusions. These exclusions are necessary for several reasons.[5] First, they eliminate loss exposures that require additional premiums such as coverage of contractual liability and liquor liability. Second, the exclusions eliminate exposures covered under other contracts, such as legal liability for automobiles, aircraft, workers' compensation, and nuclear energy. Finally, the exclusions eliminate certain exposures that are considered to be uninsurable, such as war in all its forms, and faulty workmanship.

The major exclusions in the CGL policy are summarized as follows:

1. *Contractual liability.* The policy excludes contractual liability other than liability for incidental contracts. **Incidental contracts** include written leases, easements, agreements required by municipalities, sidetrack agreements, and elevator maintenance agreements. Contractual liability can be covered more completely by adding *contractual liability coverage* to the CGL.

2. *Automobiles and aircraft.* The policy generally excludes liability coverage for automobiles and aircraft. The intent here is to exclude legal liability covered by other policies.
3. *Mobile equipment during hazardous activities.* Mobile equipment, such as bulldozers, power cranes, graders, or rollers, is not covered while it is being used in any organized racing, speed, or demolition contest, or in any stunting activity. Also, bodily injury or property damage caused by a snowmobile is not covered.
4. *Mobile equipment transported by automobiles.* Mobile equipment being transported by an automobile owned, operated, rented, or loaned to the insured is not covered. This is considered to be part of the automobile liability exposure which the CGL excludes.
5. *Watercraft.* Legal liability arising out of any watercraft owned, operated, rented, or loaned to any insured is excluded. However, the exclusion does not apply to the watercraft while ashore on the premises owned, rented, or controlled by the insured. Property damage to owned or nonowned watercraft is not covered because of the care, custody, and control exclusion.
6. *Pollution exclusion.* Most pollution and contamination claims are also excluded.
7. *War.* Liability assumed by the insured under any incidental contract or for first aid expenses under the supplementary payments provision is not covered if the bodily injury or property damage arises out of war in all of its forms.
8. *Liquor liability.* Firms engaged in the manufacturing, distributing, selling, or serving of alcoholic beverages are not covered for liquor liability. Also, the owners and lessees of premises used for those purposes are also excluded. Finally, legal liability arising out of the serving or sale of alcohol to minors or to intoxicated persons who injure someone is not covered. This exposure can be covered by adding *liquor liability coverage* to the CGL.
9. *Workers' compensation.* Any legal obligation of the insured under a workers' compensation or similar law is excluded.
10. *Care, custody, or control exclusion.* Damage to property owned, rented to, or in the care, custody, or control of the insured is also excluded. The exclusion does not apply to claims arising out of written sidetrack agreements or the negligent use of elevators owned, rented, or controlled by the insured. However, damage to the elevator itself is not covered. This exposure can be insured by adding elevator collision insurance to the policy.
11. *Property damage to premises by the insured.* There is no coverage for property damage to premises sold (alienated) by the insured. For example, a building with defective wiring may be sold to a purchaser. The insured may fail to inform the new owner of the latent defect, and a fire ensues. If the purchaser sues for property damage to the premises, the lawsuit is not covered.

In addition to the exclusions just discussed, the CGL contains several important exclusions that deal primarily with the products liability and completed operations exposure. They are summarized as follows:

1. *Failure to perform.* There is no coverage for the loss of use of undamaged tangible property of others that results from failure of the product to perform as the insured warrants or represents. However, the exclusion does not apply when the firm's product causes sudden and accidental damage to the tangible property of others, including the loss of use after the damage occurs.

   For example, a manufacturer sells a

steam turbine to another firm and guarantees that the turbine will produce a specified level of power. The turbine may produce an inadequate supply of power which results in the loss of use of certain machinery dependent on that power. As a consequence, the owner of the turbine loses production and revenues. Since this is a loss of use of undamaged tangible property, it is excluded under the CGL. However, if the steam turbine should explode, the insured would have liability coverage against the owner's loss of use of tangible property (other than the turbine). The intent is to exclude exposures that properly should be considered part of the cost of producing the product. If the product does not perform properly, the burden of any loss stemming from that product should fall on the manufacturer and not on the insurer.[6]

2. *Damage to the named insured's products*. The CGL excludes damage to the named insured's products. The intent is to avoid payment by an insurer for a product that is incorrectly designed or defectively produced.
3. *Work performed*. Property damage to work performed by or on behalf of the named insured, when damage arises out of the work, is also excluded. For example, if a roof collapses after being built, the cost to redo the work is excluded. The intent is to prevent the insurer from having to pay for faulty work performed by the named insured.
4. *Recall of products*. Manufacturers, automobile manufacturers, drug firms, toy manufacturers, and other firms frequently discover defects in a product and must recall their goods. If a product is recalled because it is defective or is suspected of being defective, the costs of recalling the product are not covered.

Broad Form CGL Endorsement

The broad form endorsement can be added to the CGL policy to provide even broader liability coverage. The endorsement automatically provides a broad range of additional coverages that firms often need, but which they ignore.

The additional coverages provided by the broad form CGL endorsement are listed as follows:

1. Contractual liability.
2. Personal injury and advertising injury liability.
3. Premises medical payments ($1000 maximum for each person).
4. Host liquor liability.
5. Fire legal liability on real property ($50,000 per occurrence).
6. Broad form property damage liability (including completed operations).
7. Incidental medical malpractice.
8. Nonowned watercraft liability (under twenty-six feet in length).
9. Limited worldwide coverage.
10. Additional persons insured (spouses of partners and any employee of the named insured).
11. Extended bodily injury coverage (coverage of an intentional act resulting solely from the use of reasonable force for the protection of property or persons).
12. Automatic coverage on newly acquired organizations (ninety days).

WORKERS' COMPENSATION AND EMPLOYER LIABILITY INSURANCE

All states have workers' compensation laws that require covered employers to provide workers' compensation benefits to employees who are disabled from work-related accidents or occupational disease. Most employers meet their legal obligations by buying a workers' compensation policy from a private insurer. In this section, we will briefly discuss the new 1984 workers' compensation policy by the Insurance Services Of-

INSIGHT 14.2

Retroactive Liability Insurance

Insurance generally cannot be written retroactively to cover losses that have already occurred. *Retroactive liability insurance* is an exception. Under this novel type of coverage, liability insurance can be obtained after a loss occurs. It is argued that this type of coverage can be written, since there is considerable uncertainty concerning the actual amounts that must be paid and the timing of the loss payments after a liability loss occurs. The tragic hotel fire in the MGM Grand Hotel in Las Vegas in 1980 where 84 persons died spurred the development of this coverage. Since MGM's liability policy fell far short of covering estimated claims, the hotel increased retroactively its liability coverage from $30 million to $200 million. According to a press report, the hotel paid $37.5 million in premiums to Frank B. Hall & Co. for the additional $170 million of coverage, which was purchased from several insurers and reinsurers.

The retroactive arrangement was allegedly designed to benefit both MGM and the insurers involved. The hotel could immediately deduct the premiums for federal income tax purposes; its balance sheet would be improved, since a qualified financial statement could be avoided; existing credit lines could be maintained; and stockholder confidence could be increased. The insurers involved believed that the large premiums could be invested at high rates of return over a long period, since claims were expected to be settled slowly over a seven-year period. However, MGM settled the liability claims quickly and generously, which resulted in high claims and relatively low investment profits for the insurers. As a result, the companies became involved in a legal dispute with MGM where the companies have denied payment of claims considered to be excessive.

fice. The historical development of workers' compensation as a form of social insurance will be treated in Chapter 24.[7]

Insuring Agreements

There are three distinct coverages in the insuring agreements. They are:

- Part one—workers' compensation insurance
- Part two—employers' liability insurance
- Part three—other states insurance

Workers' Compensation Insurance

Part one is the *workers' compensation* section of the policy. Under this section, the insurer agrees to pay *all* workers' compensation and other benefits that the employer must legally provide to covered employees who are occupationally disabled. There are no policy limits for part one. The insurer instead agrees to pay all benefits required by the workers' compensation law of any state listed in the declaration.

Part two is the *employers' liability* section of the policy. Under this section, the insurer agrees to pay damages that the employer is legally obligated to pay because of an accident or disease incurred by employees arising out of and in the course of employment. This section is similar to other liability insurance policies where the employer's negligence must be established before the insurer is legally obligated to pay.

Employers' Liability Insurance

Part two covers employers against lawsuits by

employees who are injured in the course of employment, but whose injuries (or disease) are not compensable under the state's workers' compensation law.

Employers' liability coverage is needed for several reasons. First, a few states do not require workers' compensation coverage unless the employer has three or more employees. In such cases, an employer is covered under the employers' liability section if an employee with a work-related injury or disease sues for damages. Second, an injury or disease that occurs on the job may not be considered to be work related, and, therefore, it is not covered under the state's workers' compensation law. However, the injured employee may still believe that the employer should be held accountable, and the employer would be covered if sued. Third, some state workers' compensation laws permit lawsuits by spouses and dependents for the *loss of consortium* (loss of companionship, affection, and comfort). The employer would be covered under part two in such a case. Finally, in a growing number of cases, employers are confronted with lawsuits because of *third-party actions*. An injured employee may sue a negligent third party, and the third party, in turn, sues the employer for contributory negligence. The lawsuit would be covered under part two (unless the employer assumed the liability of the third party). For example, assume that a machine is defective, and its operator is injured. In addition to payment of workers' compensation benefits, many states allow the injured employee to sue the negligent third party. If the insured employee sues the manufacturer of the defective machine, the manufacturer, in turn, could sue the employer for failure to provide proper operating instructions, or for failure to enforce safety rules. The employer would be covered in such cases.

Other States Insurance

Part three of the workers' compensation and employers' liability policy provides *other states insurance*. Workers' compensation coverage applies only to those states listed on the information page (declarations page) of the policy. However, the employer may be faced with a workers' compensation claim under the law of another state. This possibility could arise if an employee is unexpectedly sent into a state that was not considered at all when the workers' compensation policy was first written, or the law of a particular state is broadened so that employees are now covered under that state's workers' compensation law. Also, the employer's operations may be expanded in a particular state, which brings the employees under the state's workers' compensation law.

Other states insurance applies only if one or more states are shown on the information page of the policy (item 3 C). *In such cases, if the employer begins work in any of the states listed, the policy applies as if that state were listed in the policy for workers' compensation purposes.* Thus, the employer has coverage for any workers' compensation benefits that it may have to make under that state's workers' compensation law.

Voluntary Compensation Coverage

Some employers wish to provide workers' compensation benefits to employees even though they are not required by law to do so (such as domestic employees). A **voluntary compensation endorsement** can be added to the policy by which the insurer agrees to pay workers' compensation benefits to employees not covered under the law.

Exclusions

A workers' compensation policy contains several exclusions and limitations. The exclusions for part one (workers' compensation insurance) are listed in the section titled "Payments You Must Make." The employer is responsible for any payments in excess of the benefits regularly provided by the workers' compensation law including those required because of the following:

1. Serious and willful misconduct by the insured.
2. Employing a person who is hired in violation of the law with the knowledge of the insured.

3. Failure to comply with a health or safety law or regulation.
4. Discharging, coercing, or discriminating against any employee in violation of the workers' compensation law.

Part two (employers' liability insurance) also contains several exclusions. The exclusions are summarized as follows:

1. *Liability assumed under contract.* However, the exclusion does not apply to a warranty that work by the insured will be done in a workmanlike manner.
2. *Punitive damages.* Punitive or exemplary damages because of bodily injury to an employee hired in violation of law are excluded.
3. *Bodily injury to an employee employed in violation of law.* Part two also excludes bodily injury to an employee while employed in violation of law with the actual knowledge of the insured or executive officers.
4. *Workers' compensation.* Part two excludes any obligation imposed by a workers' compensation, occupational disease, unemployment compensation, disability benefits, or similar law. (Note that workers' compensation is covered under part one.)
5. *Intentional injury.* Bodily injury intentionally caused or aggravated by the insured is also excluded.
6. *Bodily injury outside the United States.* Part two also excludes bodily injury that occurs outside the United States, its territories and possessions, and Canada. However, the exclusion does not apply to a citizen or resident of the United States or Canada who is temporarily outside these countries.
7. *Discharge, coercion, or discrimination against employees.* Part two excludes damages that arise out of the discharge, coercion, or discrimination against any employee in violation of law.

BUSINESS AUTOMOBILE INSURANCE

Legal liability arising out of the ownership and use of automobiles and trucks is another important loss exposure for business firms. In this section, we will briefly examine some important automobile liability coverages that can be used to meet this exposure.

Business Auto Policy (BAP)

The *Business Auto Policy* (BAP) is widely used by business firms to insure the liability exposure from automobiles. In 1978, the BAP was nationally introduced by the Insurance Services Office to replace the Basic Auto Policy and Comprehensive Automobile Liability insurance. The BAP is a simplified and readable contract similar to the new homeowner policies and Personal Auto Policy. The language is informal and simple, and complex technical terms have been eliminated.[8]

Liability insurance coverage The BAP provides considerable flexibility to business firms with respect to the automobiles that can be covered by liability insurance. The insured can select precisely those automobiles to be covered under the policy. There are nine numerical classifications, and each has a numerical symbol. They are as follows:

1. Any auto.
2. Owned autos only.
3. Owned private passenger autos only.
4. Owned autos other than private passenger autos only.
5. Owned autos subject to no-fault.
6. Owned autos subject to a compulsory uninsured motorists law.
7. Specifically described autos.
8. Hired autos only.
9. Nonowned autos only.

If any one or more of the symbols 1 through 6 are selected, there is *automatic coverage* on any new owned automobiles that the firm acquires during the policy period. If symbol 7 is used, new cars are covered only if two conditions are met: (1) the company must already insure all autos that the insured owns for the coverage provided, or the new auto replaces one that the insured previously owned that had that coverage, and (2) the firm informs the company within thirty days after acquisition that it wants the auto insured for that coverage.

In addition, when liability insurance is provided, there is automatic free coverage on all trailers that have a load capacity of 2,000 pounds or less, and the trailer is designed primarily for travel on public roads. Also, mobile equipment, such as bulldozers, graders, or scrapers, is also covered while being carried or towed by a covered automobile. Both coverages are broader than the coverage provided by the older Comprehensive Automobile Liability policy.

Finally, by use of the appropriate symbol, covered autos can also be insured for auto medical payments insurance, uninsured motorists insurance, and any no-fault provisions required by law.

Physical damage insurance The insured has a choice of physical damage coverages that can be used to insure covered autos against damage or loss. Four physical damage coverages are available. They are summarized as follows:

1. *Comprehensive coverage.* The company will pay for loss to a covered auto or its equipment from any cause except the covered auto's collision with another object or its overturn.
2. *Specified perils coverage.* Only losses from specified perils are covered. They are:
   a. fire or explosion.
   b. theft.
   c. windstorm, hail, or earthquake.
   d. flood.
   e. mischief or vandalism.
   f. the sinking, burning, collision, or derailment of any conveyance transporting the covered auto.
3. *Collision coverage.* Loss caused by the coverd auto's collision with another object or its overturn is covered under this provision.
4. *Towing.* The company will pay up to $25 for towing and labor costs incurred each time a covered auto of the private passenger type is disabled. However, the labor must be performed at the place of disablement.

In addition, the company will pay up to $10 per day (after forty-eight hours) up to a maximum of $300 for transportation expenses incurred by the insured because of the total theft of a covered auto of the private passenger type. The coverage applies only to covered autos that are insured for either comprehensive or specified perils coverage.

Nonownership Liability Coverage

Salespersons, repair and maintenance employees, route persons, inspection personnel, and other employees frequently drive their automobiles on company business. A business firm can be held legally liable for damages caused by employees while they are using their own automobiles on company business. If the employee carries liability insurance on his or her car, the firm is also protected as an additional insured. But the liability limits may be inadequate, or the policy may have lapsed. The firm may also be exposed to liability claims arising from the operation of other nonowned automobiles—for example, a restaurant or hotel that parks cars for the guests. These nonownership exposures can also be insured under the BAP.

Garage Policy

The *Garage Policy* is a highly specialized contract that is designed to meet the insurance needs of service stations, parking garages, automobile dealerships, repair shops, and similar firms. The latest Garage Policy offered by the Insurance Services Office is a simplified and readable contract and is similar in format to the business auto policy. The major coverages include (1) liability insurance, (2) garagekeepers insurance, and (3) automobile physical damage insurance.

Liability insurance The liability section of the Garage Policy is very broad and is the equivalent of the Business Auto Policy and Comprehensive General Liability Policy combined. The company agrees to pay all sums that the insured must legally pay as damages because of bodily injury or property damage caused by an accident in the course of garage operations. *Garage operations* are defined to include automobiles, business premises, and business activities. As such, the liability section automatically includes premises and operations liability coverage, products and completed operations coverage, elevator and escalator liability insurance, and incidental contractual liability, as well as automobile liability insurance.

The insured has a choice of autos that can be covered under the Garage Policy. Numerous numerical symbols are used to denote the covered autos (symbols 21–31), an approach similar to the BAP. The following classes of automobiles can be covered:

21. Any auto.
22. Owned autos only.
23. Owned private passenger autos only.
24. Owned autos other than private passenger autos only.
25. Owned autos subject to no-fault.
26. Owned autos subject to a compulsory insured motorists law.
27. Specifically described autos.
28. Hired autos only.
29. Nonowned autos used in your garage business.
30. Autos left with you for service, repair, or storage.
31. Dealers' autos and autos held for sale by nondealers or trailer dealers (physical damage coverages).

The policy also includes symbol 32, which is open ended and is designed for special situations and particular coverages that the insurer agrees to cover. In addition, the liability section of the garage policy contains several exclusions. Only two of them are discussed here. First, damage to the property of others in the insured's care, custody, or control is excluded. Thus, damage to a customer's car on an automobile servicing hoist, or damage to a customer's car while it is being road tested by a mechanic would not be covered. These common exposures can be covered by adding *Garagekeepers Collision Insurance* to the policy.

Second, there is no coverage for property damage to any of the insured's products if the product is defective at the time it is sold. This exclusion is important for firms that sell automobiles, gasoline, parts, tires, batteries, or other products. For example, assume that a tire dealer sells a pair of radial tires, and that one tire has a hidden defect. The defective tire later blows out, and the car and other tire are damaged in a collision loss. This exclusion eliminates coverage for the defective tire, but the property damage caused by the defective tire would be covered. The intent of this exclusion is to cover property damage or bodily injury caused by a defective product but not any damage to the product itself.

Garagekeepers insurance This coverage can be added to the Garage Policy. The owner of a parking lot, automobile repair shop, or storage garage who keeps a customer's car for storage or repair and makes a charge is legally considered a bailee for hire. Regardless of signs to the contrary posted on the premises, the garage owner can be held legally liable for the loss or damage to a customer's car because of the failure to exercise ordinary care. We noted earlier that the Garage Policy excludes coverage for property of others in the care, custody, or control of the insured. This exclusion can be eliminated by adding Garagekeepers Insurance to the Garage Policy. Under this coverage, the company agrees to pay all sums that the insured legally must pay as damages for loss to customers' automobiles while in the garage owner's care for service, repairs, parking, or storage. Three coverages are available: (1) comprehensive, (2) specified perils, and (3) collision. These coverages are based on the legal liability of the insured. For example, if a customer's car is stolen because the garage owner carelessly left the garage door unlocked, the loss would be covered. However, it is possible to broaden the coverage on customers' automobiles without regard to legal liability by the payment of additional premiums.

Physical damage insurance Physical damage insurance on covered automobiles can also be added to the garage policy. The following three coverages are available:

1. *Comprehensive coverage.* The company will pay for a loss from any cause except for the covered auto's collision with another object or its overturn.
2. *Specified perils coverage.* Covered perils are fire, explosion, theft, hail, windstorm, earthquake, flood, mischief, vandalism, and the sinking, burning, collision, or derailment of any conveyance transporting the covered auto.
3. *Collision coverage.* Loss caused by the covered auto's collision with another object or its overturn is covered under this provision.

This concludes our discussion of the Garage Policy. Let us next consider aviation insurance.

AVIATION INSURANCE

Business firms often own aircraft that are used on company business. A company plane that crashes can result in bodily injury or death to the passengers and substantial property damage to buildings within the area where the crash occurred. It is also possible for an executive aircraft to collide in mid-air with a commercial jet, resulting in millions of dollars in claims against the firm. Commercial airlines own fleets of expensive jets, and the liability exposure is enormous. The potential legal liability of a fully loaded DC-10 aircraft that crashes can easily exceed $300 million.

Most states apply the common law rules of negligence to aviation accidents. However, some states have absolute liability laws that hold the owners or operators of aircraft absolutely liable for certain aviation accidents. In addition, as a result of international treaties and agreements among countries, absolute liability is imposed on commercial airlines for aviation accidents that occur during international flights.[9]

Use Classification

Aircraft are classified by use in several categories.[10] This classification is necessary for purposes of rating and underwriting.

Use of the aircraft is commonly classified into six categories. They are:

1. *Pleasure and business.* The aircraft is used for personal, pleasure, family, and business purposes.
2. *Industrial aid.* This classification includes item one above and transportation of executives, employees, guests, and customers. This classification is usually assigned to business firms.
3. *Limited commercial.* The aircraft is owned and used for pleasure or business; for transporting executives, salespersons, employees, or guests without charge; or is used in furthering the business enterprise. Although the plane can be used for instruction or rented to others, it cannot be used to carry passengers for a charge.
4. *Commercial ex instruction.* This classification includes items one and two above plus transportation of cargo and passengers for a fee. Aircraft rented to others or used for instruction cannot be included in this class.
5. *Commercial.* This includes all uses that are permitted under limited commercial and commercial ex instruction.
6. *Special uses.* Unusual use of the aircraft would be assigned this classification, such as crop dusting or aircraft used in testing.

Aircraft Liability Insurance

Aircraft liability insurance is used to insure the legal liability of the owners and operators of airplanes and other aircraft.

A typical aircraft liability policy has several optional insuring agreements as indicated by the following:

- Bodily injury liability insurance excluding passengers.
- Passenger bodily injury liability insurance.
- Property damage liability insurance.
- Single limit bodily injury and property damage liability insurance (excluding passenger liability).
- Single limit bodily injury and property damage liability insurance (including passenger liability).

The bodily injury liability coverage is similar to that found in automobile liability insurance. However, a distinction is made between bodily injury of persons other than passengers and passenger bodily injury. This distinction is important for two reasons. First, the seating capacity of airplanes varies considerably, and the premiums for passenger bodily injury are partly based on the number of seats in the insured aircraft. Thus, a plane with fifty passenger seats would be charged a higher premium than one with only eight seats. Second, this distinction permits the use of different liability limits for passenger liability and bodily injury to persons other than passengers. For example, passenger liability may be written for $100,000 per seat, but for bodily injury to persons other than passengers, the liability limit may be considerably lower, such as $25,000 per person.

In addition, the policy can be written with a single limit for bodily injury and property damage, since all liability coverages frequently apply to the same accident. For example, the policy may be written with a single limit of $5 million per occurrence which applies to both bodily injury and property damage.

Admitted Liability Coverage

Business firms frequently transport customers, employees, or employees of customers in company planes. For business reasons, a firm may wish to make a voluntary settlement with an injured passenger. **Admitted liability coverage** (also called voluntary settlement insurance) can be used to meet this need. If a passenger is injured in an aircraft accident, the insurer will offer a voluntary settlement, regardless of the insured's legal liability for the accident. If a voluntary settlement is used, the injured passenger or heirs of a deceased passenger must agree to release the insured from further liability as a result of the accident. If the injured party refuses to sign the release, the voluntary offer is withdrawn, and the regular bodily injury coverage applies if the insured is later sued because of the accident.

Medical Payments

Medical payments insurance for passengers can also be added to the policy. This coverage is similar to the medical payments section found in automobile insurance, and payment is made without regard to legal liability of the insured.

Under this coverage, the insurer agrees to pay all reasonable medical, surgical, and funeral expenses incurred within one year from the date of the accident for each person who sustains a bodily injury while in or while boarding or alighting from the aircraft. The pilot is not covered unless included in the declarations.

Aircraft Hull Insurance

Physical damage insurance on aircraft is called **hull insurance** and is similar to collision insurance in an automobile policy. Hull insurance on aircraft and aircraft liability insurance are commonly combined in a single policy.

Two different versions of hull insurance are commonly used. First, the insured has the option of insuring aircraft for (1) *all risks* of physical damage while not in flight and *named perils coverage* while in flight, or (2) for *all risks* in any circumstances whether in flight or not. Under the first option, the aircraft is covered on an all-risks basis only while it is not in flight. The aircraft is covered while in flight only for the perils of fire, explosion, lightning, theft, robbery, or pilferage (but excluding damage from a fire or explosion if the aircraft collides with the ground, water, or any object). Under the second option, the aircraft is covered on an all-risks basis whether in flight or on the ground.

Second, other insurers do not offer the named perils option. Instead, two separate all-risk coverages are made available—while *in motion* or while *not in motion*. Either or both may be purchased.

Aircraft hull insurance is commonly sold with a deductible. For smaller aircraft, the basic deductible is $250 while in motion and $50 while not in motion. On larger aircraft, such as a corporate jet, the deductible can range from zero to several thousand dollars, depending on the insured's option.

In some cases, the deductible is based on the amount of hull insurance on the aircraft, such as 2½, 5, or 10 percent, depending on the insured's option.

Other Aviation Liability Insurance Coverages

Other aviation liability insurance coverages are available to meet specialized needs. A *hangar keepers liability policy* can be used to cover the operators or owners of hangars who have aircraft in their care, custody, or control for storage, safekeeping, or repairs. The liability exposure is substantial, since a hangar may contain aircraft worth several millions of dollars.

In addition, an *airport liability policy* can be written to cover bodily injury and property damage that may result from the ownership, operation, or control of an airport. For example, the owner of a private airport may fail to keep a runway free from obstructions, which results in property damage to a light plane. The operator of the airport would be covered if a lawsuit results from the accident.

BAILEES' LIABILITY INSURANCE

We noted in Chapter 13 that a bailee is someone who has temporary possession of property that belongs to another party. Bailees, such as a laundry or dry cleaner, are legally liable for damage to the customers' goods only if they or their employees are guilty of negligence. However, the customers expect to be paid for the loss or damage to their goods regardless of who is at fault. If the customers are not reimbursed, the bailee may lose his or her future business. In the case of a destructive fire or tornado, the firm may be financially ruined if the customers are not reimbursed for their damaged property.

The **Bailees Customer Policy** can be used to cover the loss or damage to the property of customers regardless of the bailee's legal liability. Different forms are used for laundries and dry cleaners, tailors, television repair shops, rug cleaners, upholsterers, and similar firms.

The policy can be written either on an all-risk or named perils basis. The named perils policy provides coverage against loss or damage by fire, lightning, explosion, collision, burglary and theft, windstorm, flood, sprinkler leakage, earthquake, strikes, riots, transportation perils, and confusion of goods.[11] For example, if a suit or dress is damaged in a fire, or the garment is damaged when the delivery truck overturns in a collision, the loss would be covered.

Certain exclusions are commonly found in the bailees' customer policy. They include damage to goods in the custody of other laundries or cleaners; theft of goods left on delivery vehicles overnight unless the vehicle is locked in a garage or other building; shortages of individual pieces, unless caused by a burglary or holdup; loss to goods in the custody of other processors, unless there is an endorsement for such coverage; misdelivery; careless destruction of goods; and unaccountable shortages.

Finally, the bailees' customer policy may allow the insured to handle and adjust small claims, usually under $100 or some other modest amount. Often it is convenient and less expensive for the insured to adjust the claim. Larger losses are handled by a company adjustor.[12]

COMMERCIAL UMBRELLA LIABILITY POLICY

Because firms are sometimes sued for large amounts, they seek protection against catastrophic liability judgments not adequately insured under a standard liability policy. The *Commercial Umbrella Liability Policy* can provide protection against catastrophic liability judgments that may bankrupt a firm. The amount of insurance is frequently written for $1 million, $5 million, $10 million, or even higher limits.

Basic Features

Although Commercial Umbrella Liability Policies are not standard, they have certain features.

Excess liability insurance The liability insurance is excess over any basic underlying limits that may apply. The umbrella policy pays only after the basic limits of the underlying coverages are exhausted. The insured is indemnified for the **ultimate net loss** in excess of the underlying limit. Ultimate net loss is the total amount that the insured is legally obligated to pay. (Legal defense costs may or may not be included.) The *underlying limit* is either (1) the amount recoverable under the underlying insurance contract, or (2) the retained limit if the loss is not covered by the underlying insurance.

The umbrella policy also covers many losses that are excluded by the underlying contracts. If the loss is covered by the commercial umbrella policy but not by any underlying contract, a *deductible or* **retained limit** must be satisfied. Commercial umbrella policies typically require retained limit of at least $25,000, but it may be a lower amount for smaller firms.

Minimum underlying coverages The insured is required to carry certain minimum amounts of liability insurance before the company assumes the umbrella liability exposures. Many umbrella insurers require the underlying coverages to be at least equal to the following limits:

general liability insurance
$500,000 (bodily injury)
$100,000 (property damage)
automobile liability insurance
$250,000/$500,000 (bodily injury)
$100,000 (property damage)
employer liability and
bailee liability insurance
$100,000

The commercial umbrella liability applies when the loss exceeds the underlying limits.

Liability coverages The commercial umbrella policy generally indemnifies the insured for the following types of liability losses:

- Personal injury
- Property damage
- Advertising liability

Personal injury is defined to include bodily injury, and also includes coverage for mental injury, false arrest, wrongful eviction, malicious prosecution, libel, slander, defamation of character, humiliation, and invasion of privacy.

Property damage refers to physical damage to property not owned by the insured, or the loss of use of tangible property that has not been physically damaged or destroyed, provided the loss of use is caused by an occurrence during the policy period.

Finally, *advertising liability* covers losses that arise out of the insured's advertising activities, including libel, slander, or defamation; infringement of a copyright, title or slogan; piracy or misappropriation of an idea under the contract; and invasion of the right of privacy.

Exclusions

Some important exclusions typically are found in the commercial umbrella liability policy. They include the following:

1. Obligations of the insured under a workers' compensation or similar law.
2. Liability arising out of any aircraft, or watercraft over a certain length.
3. Pollution losses.
4. Property damage to the insured's products, or work performed by one on behalf of the insured.
5. Expenses in recalling defective products.

6. Failure of the insured's products or work to meet the standards warranted or represented by the insured.
7. Damage to property owned by the insured, or in the care, custody, or control of the insured.
8. Under advertising liability, claims against the insured for failure of performance of contract, and infringement of a registered trademark or name (other than titles or slogans), incorrect description of an item, and mistake in an advertised price.

Finally, if the commercial umbrella liability policy contains an exclusion that is also found in an underlying contract, the firm has no coverage under either contract for the loss.

LIABILITY INSURANCE—BUSINESSOWNERS POLICY

The Businessowners Policy (BOP) that we examined in Chapter 13 also provides comprehensive liability insurance (Section II) to business firms. The liability coverages in the Businessowners Policy provide broad protection against most liability exposures of smaller firms. Let us briefly examine the liability coverages in the Businessowners Policy.

Basic Coverages

The BOP provides comprehensive liability protection to a businessowner. The policy covers bodily injury, property damage, and personal injury caused by an occurrence. Note that personal injury claims are covered as well as bodily injury and property damage. The liability insurance is written in the amounts of $300,000, $500,000, or $1 million.

In addition, the BOP provides other important coverages to the businessowner. In effect, the BOP provides the equivalent of *premises and operations liability; products and completed operations; personal injury liability; blanket contractual liability; broad form property damage; host liquor liability; nonowned automobile liability; and fire and explosion legal liability.*

Legal Defense

The company also pays the legal costs of defending the insured. The legal costs are in addition to the amount that the insurer is legally obligated to pay because of the insured's negligence.

Definition of Insured

General liability policies generally do not include the employees as insureds. Thus, if a clerk should injure a customer, both the clerk and storeowner would be sued. The storeowner would be covered under the firm's general liability policy for the employee's negligence, but the employee usually is not named as an insured and would have no coverage under the firm's policy. Likewise, the clerk may not be insured for the negligent act under the homeowners policy because of the business pursuits exclusion.

Under the Businessowners Policy, the definition of an insured now includes employees while acting within the scope of their activities. This feature protects a negligent employee who might be named in the lawsuit along with the employer.

Medical Payments

Medical payments are also part of the Businessowners Policy. The payments are made regardless of legal liability. Thus, if a woman falls and breaks her arm in a shoe store, her medical expenses would be paid. The amount of medical expenses paid is limited to a maximum of $1,000 for each person and $10,000 for each accident.

Exclusions

The exclusions are similar to those found in the comprehensive general liability policy. However, several exclusions have been modified to provide coverage that normally is provided by an endorsement or by separate insurance. In general, most liability claims involving owned automobiles,[13] aircraft, watercraft, workers' compensation, and professional liability (except pharmacological services of a retail drug store) are not covered. In addition, the policy contains the usual liquor liability exclusion discussed earlier, but there is an important exception. *Host liquor liability coverage* is provided if alcohol is served at functions incidental to the insured's business. Thus, if the company has a Christmas party, and an intoxicated employee injures someone, the firm is covered if a lawsuit ensues.

This concludes our discussion of the liability coverages in the businessowners policy. Let us next consider professional liability insurance.

PROFESSIONAL LIABILITY INSURANCE

In Chapter 9, we examined the problem of professional liability and the increased number of lawsuits against physicians, surgeons, attorneys, accountants, professors, and other professionals. In this section, we will briefly discuss some professional liability insurance coverages that provide protection against a malpractice lawsuit or lawsuit involving a substantial error or omission.

Medical Malpractice Insurance

Physicians, surgeons, dentists, and hospitals require substantial amounts of liability insurance which provide protection in case of acts of malpractice that result in harm or injury to patients. A commonly used malpractice form is the Physicians, Surgeons, and Dentists Professional Liability insurance policy. The latest version of this important contract contains the following features.[14]

1. Broad coverage is provided.
2. Liability is not restricted to accidental acts.
3. The insured is protected against the negligent acts of an employee.
4. There is a maximum limit per medical incident and an aggregate limit for each coverage.
5. Professional liability insurance is not a substitute for general liability insurance.
6. Newer forms permit the company to settle a claim without the insured physician's or surgeon's consent.
7. Most new policies are written on a claims-made basis.

First, the insuring agreement provides broad coverage. The company agrees to pay all sums that the insured is legally obligated to pay as damages because of injury caused by a medical incident. A *medical incident* is any act or omission in the furnishing of professional medical or dental services by the insured, an employee of the insured, or any person acting under the personal direction or supervision of the insured. Since *injury* is not defined, it includes bodily injury, property damage, and also intangible damages such as mental suffering, humiliation, undue familiarity, invasion of privacy, libel, and slander, if such acts arise out of professional services. Thus, if Dr. Jones operates on a patient, and the patient is paralyzed after the operation, Dr. Jones would be covered for a malpractice lawsuit.

Second, liability is not restricted to accidental acts of the physician or surgeon. In many cases, the physician or surgeon deliberately intends to do a certain act; however, the professional diagnosis may be faulty, and the patient is injured. Thus, Dr. Jones may intend to operate on a patient by using a certain surgical procedure. If the patient is harmed or injured by the operation and alleges that a different surgical procedure should have been used, Dr. Jones would still be covered for his willful, intentional act to operate in a certain way.

Third, the policy covers the physician against the negligent acts of an employee, such as the nurse. However, the nurse typically is not covered under the physician's policy but must secure his or her own professional liability policy. Thus, if the office nurse gives a wrong shot to a patient, the physician is covered if the patient is harmed. If desired, coverage for employees can be provided by an endorsement to the policy.

Fourth, there is a maximum limit per medical incident and an aggregate limit for each coverage. Under the older forms, a per claim limit applied to each claim regardless of the number of claims that could result from a single malpractice act or omission. For example, a patient harmed by the physician and the patient's family could file separate lawsuits, and the full limit of liability would apply to each claim. Under the newer forms, the per medical incident limit is the maximum that would be paid for both claims.

Professional liability insurance is not a substitute for other necessary forms of liability insurance. General liability insurance is also needed that covers liability arising out of a hazardous condition on the premises or acts of the insured that are not professional in nature. For example, a patient may trip on a torn carpet in the doctor's office and break an arm. The professional liability policy would not cover this event. A general liability policy is also needed.

Another important characteristic is that the *newer forms permit the insurer to settle the claim without the physician's or surgeon's consent.* The older forms generally required the company to have the insured's written consent to settle a claim. This provision was designed to protect the professional reputation of the physician or surgeon, since payment of a claim could be viewed as an admission of guilt.

The newer forms typically give the insurer the right to settle without the physician or surgeon's consent, since an occasional claim against certain high-risk categories is not viewed as being overly detrimental to his or her character.

Finally, malpractice liability policies are currently written on a claims-made basis rather than on an occurrence basis. A **claims-made policy** means the contract in force at the time the claim is reported is responsible for the loss, regardless of when the negligent act or error occurred. In contrast, on an *occurrence basis,* the insurer providing the coverage at the time the negligent act occurred would be responsible for the claim. For example, a surgeon may be sued by a patient because of an operation that was performed five years earlier. Under an occurrence policy, the original liability insurer would be responsible for the claim; under a claims-made policy, the current insurer would defend the claim. Companies have resorted to claims-made policies because of the problem of the **long tail** on losses, and the determination of the proper premium. The *long tail* refers to a relatively small number of professional liability claims that occur years after the policy was first written. Under an occurrence policy, the original liability insurer would be responsible for the claim. Since insurers found it difficult to estimate accurately the size of these delayed claims, the correct premium to charge became difficult to determine. Since liability premiums can be computed more accurately by a claims-made policy, this approach is now used.

Finally, a physician with a claims-made policy may retire, change insurers, or drop his or her malpractice insurance. To protect the physician, companies also offer what is known as a *buy-out policy,* which covers future claims arising out of incidents that occurred during the period the claims-made policy was in force.[15]

Errors and Omissions Insurance

Errors and omissions insurance provides protection against loss incurred by a client because of some negligent act, error, or omission by the insured. Professionals who need errors and omission insurance include insurance agents and brokers, travel agents, real estate agents, stockbrokers, attorneys, consultants, engineers, architects, and other individuals who give advice to clients. The errors and omissions coverage is designed to meet the needs of each profession.

This type of coverage can be illustrated by the Insurance Agents' and Brokers' Errors and Omissions Policy.[16] Although there is no standard form, certain characteristics are common to all forms. First, the company agrees to pay all sums that the insured is legally obligated to pay because of any negligent act, error, or omission by the insured (or by any other person for whose acts the insured is legally liable) in the conduct of business as general agents, insurance agents, or insurance brokers. For example, assume that Joseph is an independent agent who fails to renew a property insurance policy for a client. The policy lapses, and a subsequent loss is not covered. If the client sues for damages, Joseph would be covered for his omission.

INSIGHT 14.3

High-Risk Baby Deliveries

An increasing number of physicians who specialize in obstetrics (the branch of medicine dealing with childbirth) and gynecology (the branch dealing with diseases of the female reproductive organs) are relinquishing the obstetrics portion of their practice.

The major reason is the high cost of malpractice insurance, which in turn is based on the large sums that juries have awarded to plaintiffs in lawsuits filed against obstetricians. And such lawsuits have been growing in number.

In Suffolk County, N.Y., for example, the yearly insurance premium for an "ob-gyn" is $52,000, which the Medical Liability Insurance Co. wants to increase. In Florida and California, the average annual malpractice insurance premium is about $20,000. As a result, 6.4 percent of obstetricians in New York stopped delivering babies last year; in Florida, 17.8 percent stopped; in California, 10.4 percent.

"The risk for obstetricians practicing in New York, Florida and California," explains Mort Lebow, director of public affairs for the American College of Obstetricians and Gynecologists, "has become very high in our litigious society. If an obstetrician is found guilty of damaging a baby at birth, the jury can award millions on the grounds that the child has been damaged for life. Neurosurgeons, orthopedists [specialists in diseases of the bones, joints, muscles and tendons] and obstetricians pay the highest insurance fees of all medical specialists. And an increasing number of obstetricians have decided that the risk outweighs the reward."

Dr. Simon Sayre of Los Angeles, who stopped deliverying babies 13 years ago to enter the field of public health, used to average 25 deliveries a month. "I can tell you," he points out, "that maternity work is very demanding. You have to be available at all hours, day after day, and it becomes very wearing. Some obstetricians I know in California are finding that the monetary remuneration is too small for the time spent."

Another California ob-gyn notes that office overhead can cost 45 percent of his gross. He must deliver 70 babies, he says, just to pay his malpractice insurance and overhead.

SOURCE: "High Risk Baby Deliveries" by Lloyd Shearer, *Parade Magazine*, November 13, 1983. Reprinted with permission.

Second, the policy normally is sold with a sizable deductible. A $1,000 deductible is common. Insurers may offer higher deductibles so that the agent has an incentive to minimize his or her mistakes and errors.

Third, the coverage applies to claims made during the policy period that arise out of events occurring during the policy period. However, insurers differ concerning the coverage of events that occur *before the inception of the policy* when a claim is made during the policy period. Generally, events that occurred prior to the policy's inception are covered if a claim is made during the policy period. However, most contracts require that the insured must not have any knowledge of or grounds for reasonable expectation that there was some circumstance that could lead to a claim.

With respect to lawsuits brought *after expiration of the policy*, most contracts provide coverage if the error or omission occurred during the policy period. However, there may be some time limitations or restrictions imposed on the insured. At least one company limits its liability to a maximum of five years after the event occurred; another company provides that if the insured gives notice of any event that could subsequently result in a claim, the claim is considered to have been made during the policy period even though the contract has expired. Still other contracts are silent and state that coverage applies if the error or omission occurs during the policy period.

Finally, the policy contains relatively few exclusions. However, claims that result from dishonest, fraudulent, criminal, or malicious acts by the insured, libel and slander, bodily injury, or destruction of tangible property are specifically excluded.

SUMMARY

- General liability refers to the legal liability of business firms arising out of business operations other than liability for automobile or aviation accidents or employee injuries. The most important general liability loss exposures are as follows:
  a. Premises and operations.
  b. Elevators and escalators.
  c. Products liability.
  d. Completed operations.
  e. Contractual liability.
  f. Contingent liability.
- Legal liability can arise out of the *ownership and maintenance of the premises* where the firm does business. A firm can also be liable for defective *elevators and escalators. Completed operations* refers to liability arising out of faulty work performed away from the premises after the work is completed. *Contractual liability* means the business firm agrees to assume the legal liability of another party by a written or oral contract. *Contingent liability* means the firm can be held liable for work by independent contractors.
- Other important general liability loss exposures include environmental pollution, property in the insured's care, custody, or control, fire legal liability, liability arising out of a liquor or dramshop law, directors and officers liability, and personal injury.
- The Comprehensive General Liability Policy covers most general liability loss exposures in a single policy. Liability coverage can be provided for the premises and operations, independent contractors, completed operations, products liability, and incidental contractual exposures. The broad form endorsement can be added to cover other liability exposures.
- All states have workers' compensation laws that require covered employers to provide workers' compensation benefits to employees who are disabled from work-related accidents or occupational disease. The workers' compensation insurer pays all benefits that the employer must legally provide to employees who are occupationally disabled.
- The Business Auto Policy can be used by business firms to insure the liability exposure from automobiles. The employer can select those automobiles to be covered under the policy.
- The Garage Policy is designed to meet the insurance needs of service stations, parking garages, repair shops, and similar firms. The major coverages include liability insurance, garagekeepers insurance, and physical damage insurance. Garagekeepers insurance covers the garage owner's liability for damage to customers' automobiles while in the garage owner's care for service or repairs.

- Aircraft insurance can be used to insure the legal liability of the owners and operators of aircraft. The policy typically combines into a single form liability insurance on the aircraft and physical damage insurance on the plane itself.
- A Bailees' Customer Policy can be used to cover the loss or damage to the property of customers regardless of the bailee's legal liability.
- The Commercial Umbrella Liability Policy provides protection to firms against a catastrophic judgment that may bankrupt the firm. The umbrella policy is excess insurance over the underlying coverages.
- Section II of the Businessowners Policy provides comprehensive liability insurance to smaller business firms. The policy covers property damage and bodily injury liability, personal injury, products and completed operations, blanket contractual liability, broad form property damage, host liquor liability, nonowned automobile liability, and fire and explosion legal liability. The insured's employees are also covered for their negligent acts while acting within the scope of their employment.
- Medical malpractice insurance is designed to cover liability arising out of a medical incident. Medical malpractice insurance has several important features:
  a. Coverage is broad.
  b. Liability is not restricted to accidental acts.
  c. The insured is protected against the negligent acts of employees.
  d. There is a maximum limit for each medical incident and an aggregate limit for each coverage.
  e. Newer forms permit the company to settle a claim without the physician's or surgeon's consent.
  f. Most new policies are written on a claims-made basis.

QUESTIONS FOR REVIEW

1. List the major general liability loss exposures of business firms.
2. What is contractual liability?
3. Explain the meaning of completed operations.
4. Define contingent liability. Under what conditions can the firm be held liable for work done by independent contractors?
5. Explain the meaning of a liquor liability or dramshop law.
6. Briefly describe the major coverages in the Comprehensive General Liability Policy.
7. Describe the three distinct coverages in the insuring agreements of a workers' compensation policy. Why is coverage for employer liability (part two) needed?
8. Describe the major features of the Business Auto Policy and Garage Policy.
9. Briefly explain the major coverages that are used to insure aircraft.
10. Why is liability insurance needed by a bailee? In your answer, give a brief description of the bailees' customer policy.
11. Briefly describe the major features of the Commercial Umbrella Liability Policy.
12. Explain the major features of a professional liability policy.

QUESTIONS FOR DISCUSSION

1. Mary leases a store building where she operates a retail dress shop. The premises are insured under a Comprehensive General Liability (CGL) policy with limits of $200,000 for bodily injury liability and $50,000 for property damage. The lease contains a hold-harmless agreement by which Mary agrees to hold the landlord harmless for any liability claims arising out of the operation of the dress shop. A light fixture falls from the ceiling and injures a customer. The customer sues the landlord and obtains a $10,000 judgment. The landlord then attempts to collect from Mary under the terms of the lease.
   a. What types of general liability loss exposure are represented by this situation?
   b. Will Mary's CGL policy cover her for any liability she may have for the judgment? Explain your answer.
2. Lastovica Construction agrees to build a new plant for the Smith Corporation. A heavy machine used by Lastovica Construction accidentally falls from the roof of the partially completed plant. Mike, an employee of Lastovica Construction, is severely injured when the falling machine crushes his foot. Mary, a member of the public, is also injured when she is passing by on the public sidewalk.
   a. Mary sues both Lastovica Construction and the Smith Corporation for her injury. What legal defense could the Smith Corporation use to counter Mary's claim based on the nature of its relationship with Lastovica Construction? Explain your answer.
   b. Does Lastovica Construction have any responsibility for Mike's medical expenses and lost wages? Explain.
3. Fred owns and operates a small retail food store in a suburban shopping center. The store is insured for liability coverage under a Businessowners Policy. Indicate with reasons whether or not the following situations are covered under Fred's Businessowners Policy. Treat each situation separately.
   a. A clerk accidentally injures a customer with a shopping cart. Both Fred and the clerk are sued.
   b. A customer slips on a wet floor and breaks a leg.
   c. Fred has a customer arrested for shoplifting. The customer is innocent and sues for damages.
   d. A housewife returns a spoiled package of gourmet cheese and demands her money back.
   e. Fred has a Christmas party for his employees after the store closes. One employee gets drunk and injures another motorist while driving home. The injured motorist sues both Fred and the employee.
4. The Sheldon Art Gallery has a Comprehensive General Liability (CGL) policy with liability limits of $500,000 for bodily injury and $100,000 for property damage. The Sheldon Art Gallery also has a Commercial Umbrella Liability Policy with a limit of $5 million and a *retained limit* (deductible) of $25,000. With respect to each of the following losses, indicate the extent of liability, if any, of the insurer writing the commercial umbrella policy. Explain your answers.
   a. A jury awards damages of $600,000 to a customer for injuries sustained when a flight of stairs in the gallery collapsed. The CGL pays up to its liability limit.
   b. A painting valued at $10,000 is left with Sheldon Art Gallery to be framed. An employee accidentally tears the painting while framing it. The CGL policy denies liability because the property is in the insured's care, custody, and control.

5. A surgeon is insured under a Physicians, Surgeons, and Dentists Professional Liability Policy. Indicate with reasons whether or not the following situations are covered by the professional liability policy. Treat each situation separately.
   a. An office nurse gives a patient a wrong drug. Both the physician and the nurse are sued.
   b. The surgeon sets a broken arm of a patient. The patient sues because the arm is deformed and crooked.
   c. A patient waiting to see the doctor is injured when the legs of an office chair collapse.
6. Explain the difference between a *claims-made* professional liability policy and one written on an *occurrence* basis.

KEY CONCEPTS AND TERMS TO KNOW

Premises and operations coverage
Products liability
Completed operations
Contractual liability
Contingent liability
Fire legal liability
Liquor liability law (dramshop law)
Personal injury
Incidental contracts
Failure to perform
Voluntary compensation endorsement
Nonownership liability coverage
Hull insurance
Admitted liability coverage
Bailees' customer policy
Ultimate net loss
Retained limit
Claims-made policy
Long tail

SUGGESTIONS FOR ADDITIONAL READING

Athearn, James L. and S. Travis Pritchett. *Risk and Insurance,* 5th ed. St. Paul, Minnesota: West Publishing Company, 1984, chapter 18.

Bickelhaupt, David L. *General Insurance,* 11th ed. Homewood, Illinois: Richard D. Irwin, Inc., 1983, chapters 17 and 18.

Crane, Frederick G. *Insurance Principles and Practices,* 2nd ed. New York: John Wiley & Sons, 1984, chapter 18.

Donaldson, James H. *Casualty Claim Practice,* 4th ed. Homewood, IL: Richard D. Irwin, Inc., 1984, chapter 16.

Fire, Casualty, & Surety Bulletins. Casualty and Surety Volume. Cincinnati, Ohio: The National Underwriter. The bulletins are published monthly. Detailed information on all forms of liability insurance can be found in this volume.

Greene, Mark R. and James S. Trieschmann. *Risk and Insurance,* 6th ed. Cincinnati, Ohio: Southwestern Publishing Company, 1984, chapter 15.

Malecki, Donald S., James H. Donaldson, and Ronald C. Horn. *Commercial Liability Risk Management and Insurance.* Volumes I and II. Malvern, Pennsylvania: American Institute for Property and Liability Underwriters, 1978.

Morrison, John W. *The Insurability of Punitive Damages.* Cincinnati, OH: The National Underwriter Co., 1985.

Smith, Michael L. and Robert C. Witt. "The Case for Retroactive Liability Insurance," *Risk Management,* Vol. 31, No. 8 (August 1984).

Vaughan, Emmett J. *Fundamentals of Risk and Insurance,* 3rd ed. New York: John Wiley & Sons, 1982, chapter 34.

NOTES

1. Frederick G. Crane, *Insurance Principles and Practices* (New York: John Wiley & Sons, 1980), p. 337.
2. S. S. Huebner, Kenneth Black, Jr., and Robert S. Cline, *Property and Liability Insurance*, 2nd ed. (Englewood Cliffs, New Jersey: Prentice-Hall, Inc., 1976), p. 435.
3. This is also known as owners and contractors protective insurance.
4. The Insurance Services Office has introduced a Commercial General Liability policy on a claims-made basis. An occurrence policy could still be purchased at a higher premium.
5. Donald S. Malecki, James H. Donaldson, and Ronald C. Horn, *Commercial Liability Risk Management and Insurance*, Volume I (Malvern, Pennsylvania: American Institute for Property and Liability Underwriters, 1978), pp. 99–107.
6. Malecki, p. 240.
7. The new 1984 workers' compensation and employers' liability policy is discussed in detail in *Fire, Casualty, & Surety Bulletins*, Casualty & Surety Volume, Workers' Compensation section.
8. The interested student should consult the *Fire,Casualty, & Surety Bulletins*, Casualty & Surety Volume, Auto section for detailed information on the Business Auto Policy.
9. Donald S. Malecki, James H. Donaldson, and Ronald C. Horn, *Commercial Liability Risk Management and Insurance*, Volume II (Malvern, Pennsylvania: American Institute for Property and Liability Underwriters, 1978), p. 290.
10. Aviation insurance is discussed in considerable detail in *Fire, Casualty, & Surety Bulletin*, Fire & Marine Volume, Aircraft-Boats section.
11. Confusion of goods is the inability to identify the owner of the goods even though they may not be destroyed.
12. William H. Rodda, James S. Trieschmann, and Bob A. Hedges, *Commercial Property Risk Management and Insurance*, Volume II (Malvern, Pennsylvania: American Institute for Property and Liability Underwriters, 1978), p. 64.
13. With the exception of the parking of automobiles, the businessowners policy does not cover any insured for liability arising out of an owned automobile. However, the exclusion does not apply to a nonowned private passenger car or station wagon used in the business of the named insured. Thus, although employees would not be covered under the BOP for their own negligence while driving their cars on company business, there would be coverage for the named insured. Likewise, the exclusion does not apply to the occasional and infrequent use of a nonowned commercial vehicle used by an employee of the named insured in the business.

CHAPTER 15

CRIME INSURANCE AND FIDELITY AND SURETY BONDS

"The cost of non-violent crimes by individuals against business is $30 billion to $40 billion a year."

—*Insurance Facts*

STUDENT LEARNING OBJECTIVES

After studying this chapter, you should be able to:

- Define burglary, robbery, and theft.
- Explain the major features of the Mercantile Open Stock Burglary Policy and Mercantile Robbery Policy.
- Describe the major coverages found in the Comprehensive Dishonesty, Disappearance, and Destruction (3D) Policy.
- Explain the three parties to a bond and show how surety bonds differ from insurance.
- List the major types of fidelity and surety bonds and give an example where each can be used.

The annual cost of crime to business firms is enormous. The dollar amount of reported crimes against property from robbery, burglary, larceny, and motor vehicle theft totalled about $9.4 billion in 1983.[1] However, the total cost of crime is much higher when other costly offenses such as employee embezzlement, arson, and vandalism are taken into consideration. Moreover, since many crimes go unreported, the true cost of crime is understated. Finally, certain groups are affected more severely by crime than other groups. In particular, the burden of crime falls heavily on small businesspersons who are frequently robbed, burglarized, beaten, threatened, or even killed by criminals in their unlawful acts.

In this chapter, we will discuss some basic crime insurance coverages for business firms. We will also examine fidelity and surety bonds, which are closely related to crime perils. Fidelity bonds protect employers against the dishonest acts of employees, while surety bonds provide indemnification if the bonded party fails to perform.

CRIME INSURANCE

Crime insurance generally refers to burglary and theft coverages that cover the loss of property (including money and securities) from robbery, burglary, or theft, and the loss of money and securities because of destruction or disappearance. Many crime insurance coverages are now included in package policies.[2]

Basic Definitions

Most property crimes against business firms are due to burglary, robbery, and theft. For purposes of insurance, **burglary** is defined as the unlawful taking of property from within the premises by someone who uses actual force or violence to gain entry, and there are visible marks of entry on the exterior of the premises. **Robbery** is defined as the unlawful taking of another person's property by violence or the threat of violence. **Theft** is a much broader term and is defined as any act of stealing. It includes both burglary and robbery.

Mercantile Open Stock Burglary Policy

The **Mercantile Open Stock Burglary Policy** is designed for firms that have merchandise of high value that can be stolen and easily converted into cash. *The policy covers the loss of merchandise, furniture, fixtures, and equipment from a burglary, attempted burglary, or robbery of a watchman. The coverage applies only when the premises are closed for business.* Damage to the premises is also covered if the insured owns the building or is liable for damages. For example, if a burglar breaks into Charlie's Pawnshop by sawing off the bars on a ground-level window, and steals several cameras, both the building damage and the loss of cameras are covered.

The policy contains several exclusions and limitations. The policy does not cover money or securities, fraudulent or dishonest acts of employees, manuscripts and records, and furs removed from a showcase or shop window by a person who has broken the glass from *outside* the premises. A special limitation also applies to items pledged as collateral for loans, such as a pawnshop loan. The loss is limited to the value shown on the insured's records, or if the records are not available, to the unpaid balance of the loan plus accrued legal interest. There is also a $50 limit on any single article of jewelry, and a $100 limit applies to the loss of the contents of any showcase or show window located outside of the insured's premises but inside the building line where the property is located. These limits can be increased.

The mercantile open stock burglary policy contains a unique coinsurance clause. The amount of required insurance is stated as a coinsurance percentage or coinsurance limit. *The **coinsurance percentage** varies from 40 to 80 percent depending on the territory.* The variation by territory reflects the fact that burglary losses are much higher in certain areas than in others. Thus, the coinsurance percentage would be higher in New York City than in Lincoln, Nebraska.

*The **coinsurance limit** is a maximum dollar amount that varies depending on how easily the*

INSIGHT 15.1

Computer Fraud: A New Loss Exposure

Computer fraud is a rapidly growing area of sophisticated criminal activity. For example, the Wells Fargo Bank lost $21 million in illegally transferred assets; a former computer consultant for a Los Angeles bank gained access to the bank's electronic transfer codes and transferred more than $10 million to a Swiss bank account. The average loss from computer crime is estimated to be about $500,000, and an estimated three to five billion dollars are annually lost to computer criminals.

The sharp increase in computer crime is due to several factors, including the rapid growth of computers in business, the increased numbers of persons who are skilled in computer use, the ease of access to many EDP programs, and the relatively lax security practices of many firms.

In response to the growing problem of computer fraud, *computer fraud insurance* can now be added as an endorsement to the Blanket Crime policy, Comprehensive 3D policy, or Money and Securities Broad Form. Previous coverage for computer fraud was either severely limited or nonexistent.

SOURCE: Adaptation of "Computer Fraud Insurance" from *F C & S Bulletins*, November 1982. Reprinted by permission.

goods can be stolen. It is based on the theory that a burglar is unlikely to steal more than the amount specified as the coinsurance limit. Thus, for a given territory, the coinsurance limit may be $30,000 for a film shop but only $10,000 for a retail dress shop, since film can be stolen more easily.

To avoid a coinsurance penalty, *the insured must carry insurance at least equal to the coinsurance percentage multiplied by the cash value of the inventory at the time of loss, or the coinsurance limit, whichever is less.* For example, assume that the coinsurance percentage is 60 percent, and the coinsurance limit for a camera shop is $30,000. The owner has $10,000 of insurance. Assume further that $8,000 of films are stolen, and the actual cash value of the inventory at the time of loss is $20,000. The amount of required insurance is the lower of (1) the coinsurance percentage multiplied by the actual cash value of the inventory (60% × $20,000 = $12,000), or (2) the coinsurance limit ($30,000). In this case, the insured is penalized, since only $10,000 of insurance is carried, but $12,000 is required (lower of the two amounts). Since only ten-twelfths of the required amount of insurance is carried, only ten-twelfths of the loss is paid, or $6,667. This can be summarized as follows:

$$\frac{\$10,000}{\$12,000} \times \$8,000 = \$6,667$$

Mercantile Safe Burglary Policy

This policy covers the loss of money, securities, and other property from within a locked vault or safe as a result of a burglary. To have a covered loss, the safe must be closed and locked, entry into the safe or vault must be made by actual force and violence, and there must be visible signs of entry caused by tools, explosives, electricity, or chemicals upon the exterior of the insured unit through which entry is made. If the burglar opens the safe by successful manipulation of the combination lock, the loss is not covered. But if the safe is removed from the premises to be opened at the safecracker's leisure, the loss would be covered.

The policy also covers damage to the safe or vault, as well as damage to furniture, fixtures, equipment, and other property outside of the safe or vault. Property damage to the building is covered if the insured is the owner or is liable for damages to the building.

Each safe or vault must be described in the policy. Rate discounts are available depending on the type of safe, nature of the operations, and special protective devices. It is important for the insured to maintain any special protective devices, such as a central alarm system. If a rate discount is given, and the protective device cannot be maintained for reasons beyond the insured's control, the amount of insurance is reduced to the amount the premium would have purchased without the discount. However, if the insured deliberately fails to maintain the protective device, the insurer has a valid reason for denying coverage.

Mercantile Robbery Policy

Business firms are frequently held up and robbed. The **Mercantile Robbery Policy** is designed to cover the loss of money, securities, and other property from a robbery or attempted robbery. There are two insuring agreements: (1) robbery inside the premises, and (2) robbery outside the premises. The coverages can be written together or separately.

The inside holdup coverage pays for the loss of money, securities, and other property as a result of robbery or attempted robbery within the premises. For example, if the Clocktower Liquor Store is held up, and the robber escapes with $500 and several bottles of whiskey, both losses would be covered. In addition, damage to the building is covered if the insured owns the building or is liable for damages.

Robbery outside the premises covers the loss of money, securities, and other property by robbery or attempted robbery outside the premises while the property is being conveyed by a messenger. For example, if the owner is robbed while taking the day's receipts to the bank, the loss is covered.

The mercantile robbery policy covers only the peril of robbery. Robbery is defined as the taking of insured property in any of the following ways:

- By violence inflicted upon a messenger or custodian.
- By putting a messenger or custodian in fear of violence.
- By any overt felonious act committed in the presence of the messenger or custodian of which he or she is actually cognizant.
- From the person or direct care and custody of a messenger or custodian who has been killed or rendered unconscious.
- Kidnapping and window smashing.

With respect to the first two parts of the definition, it is not necessary for the robber to be armed, nor is it necessary for the robber to threaten openly the custodian of money. For example, if the robber looks menacingly at the victim and places him or her in fear of violence, the coverage would apply.

The third part of the definition covers the theft of property even if violence is not inflicted or threatened, provided the custodian is aware that a criminal act is taking place. For example, if an employee in a liquor store sees someone snatch a carton of cigarettes from a counter and then dash out of the door, the loss would be covered. The fourth part of the definition covers the loss of property if the messenger or custodian is killed or knocked unconscious.

The last part of the definition—kidnapping and window smashing—applies only to coverage for robbery inside the premises. Thus, a loss from kidnapping would be covered. For example, if the owner of a liquor store is apprehended by a robber on the way home and is forced to return to the store and open the cash register and safe, the loss would be covered. Likewise, if the store is open for business and someone outside the building breaks a show window and steals property within it, the loss would also be covered. However, the coverage applies only while the firm is open for business.[3]

Money and Securities Broad Form Policy

This policy is an all-risk policy that provides broad coverage for the destruction, disap-

pearance, or wrongful abstraction of money and securities, plus limited coverage on other property. There are two separate insuring agreements that apply to loss inside the premises and loss outside the premises. The coverages can be written separately or together.

The most important coverage involves the loss of money and securities. Loss from almost any cause is covered, including fire, flood, robbery, burglary, safe burglary, and theft. A classic example of how broad this coverage is would be the loss of a stack of money blown out of an open window by a strong wind.

The policy has several exclusions, including dishonest acts of employees; giving or surrendering money or securities in an exchange or purchase; accounting or arithmetic errors, such as giving a customer too much change; and loss of money in a coin-operated amusement device or vending machine unless the amount of money deposited is recorded on a continuous recording instrument. The intent of this latter exclusion is to exclude some "confidence games" and swindling losses.

The off-premises coverage covers the actual destruction, disappearance, or wrongful abstraction of money and securities if the property is being conveyed by a messenger or armored car company, or if the property is within the living quarters in the home of the messenger. Thus, if a messenger is robbed while taking money to a bank for deposit, the loss would be covered.

Storekeepers Burglary and Robbery Policy

This contract is a package policy for small retail firms that need a variety of crime coverages in modest amounts. *There are seven insuring agreements, and a basic limit of $250 applies to each agreement.* This limit can be increased to a maximum of $1,000 for each insuring agreement.

The coverages are listed as follows:

- Robbery inside the premises.
- Robbery outside the premises.
- Kidnapping.
- Burglary: safe burglary.
- Theft—night depository or residence.
- Burglary: robbery of a watchman.
- Damage.

The first three agreements have already been explained. The fourth agreement covers the loss of money, securities, and other property from a locked safe or vault by forcible entry, including the felonious abstraction of the safe from the premises. The fifth agreement covers the theft of money and securities from a night depository or from the living quarters of a messenger. The sixth agreement covers burglary and the taking of insured property by violence or threat of violence to a security guard on duty within the premises. The seventh agreement covers damage to the building and property from any of the insured crimes.

There can be a recovery under more than one coverage. For example, if the premises are damaged when a burglar breaks into the building, and money is stolen from a safe, both the property damage and the loss of money would be covered.

Comprehensive Dishonesty, Disappearance, and Destruction (3D) Policy

This policy is commonly referred to as the *3D* policy and is designed to provide broad protection against a wide variety of crime perils. *The policy has numerous insuring agreements, each of which has a separate premium and separate amount of insurance.* None of the coverages is mandatory, and the insured can select those coverages specifically needed. The first five coverages are printed in the form, and the others can be added by separate endorsements. The five basic coverages are as follows:

1. *Employee dishonesty.* This section covers the loss of money, securities, and other property through fraudulent or dishonest acts of employees, acting alone or in collusion with others.
2. *Loss inside the premises.* This section provides the same protection as that provided

by the inside premises portion of the Money and Securities Broad Form Policy.

3. *Loss outside the premises.* This section provides the same protection as the outside premises coverage of the Money and Securities Broad Form Policy.
4. *Money orders and counterfeit paper currency.* This section covers the insured against loss in accepting in good faith any post office or express money order in exchange for merchandise, money, or services. Any loss from accepting counterfeit paper currency is also covered.
5. *Depositor's forgery coverage.* This section covers losses due to forgery or to alteration of outgoing checks and other instruments of the insured.

There are numerous additional coverages that can also be added. They include forgery insurance on incoming checks, robbery of a paymaster, burglary and theft insurance on merchandise or office equipment, safe deposit box coverage, forgery of credit cards, and extortion.

Federal Crime Insurance

Private insurers often find it difficult to insure commercial crime exposures at a profit. This is because of the high frequency and severity of crime losses in certain areas, problems of adverse selection since firms that are repeatedly burglarized or robbed (target risks) want crime insurance, and moral hazard since some employers are dishonest and may fake claims or may be careless in protecting their property.

Federal crime insurance was enacted in 1971 because crime insurance was unavailable at affordable rates in many parts of the country. Under this program, insurance is provided by the federal government at subsidized rates for the perils of burglary, robbery, and larceny in those areas where the Federal Insurance Administrator has determined that insurance is not available at affordable rates. In 1983, federal crime insurance was available in twenty-seven states, the District of Columbia, Puerto Rico, and the Virgin Islands.[4]

Federal crime insurance is sold by licensed property and casualty agents and brokers in the eligible states, and the policies are issued and serviced by private servicing insurers. A servicing company has a contract with the Federal Insurance Administrator to perform the various insurance functions in selling of crime insurance in a specific area. However, the federal government is the actual insurer.

There are two basic policy forms—a commercial crime policy and a residential policy. Only the commercial crime policy will be discussed here, since we discussed the residential crime policy in Chapter 8.

The **commercial crime policy** is designed to cover industrial, commercial, nonprofit, or public property against certain crime perils. The maximum amount of insurance that can be written is $15,000 per occurrence. The policy provides coverage for robbery inside or outside of the premises, safe burglary, theft from a night depository, burglary or robbery of a security guard when the premises are closed for business, and damage to the premises and property from a burglary or robbery.

The policy is sold with a deductible, which ranges from $250 to $500, or 5 percent of the gross amount of the loss, whichever is greater.

Finally, the insured is required to maintain certain protective devices, such as locks on doors and bars on windows. If a required protective device is not maintained, the claim can be denied.

This ends our discussion of crime insurance. Let us next look at a closely related line—fidelity and surety bonds.

FIDELITY AND SURETY BONDS

Many persons are dishonest, corrupt, or inept. A dishonest employee who needs money may embezzle or steal company funds. A marginal contractor may be financially overextended and is thus unable to complete a building project. A public official may embezzle public funds, or an executor of an estate may illegally convert part of the estate assets to his or her own use. These acts cause millions of dollars of loss each year to individuals, employers, and government. Fidelity and surety bonds can be used to meet these loss exposures.

*A **fidelity bond** is a bond that protects an employer against the dishonest or fraudulent acts of employees,* such as embezzlement, fraud, or the theft of money. *A **surety bond** is a bond that provides monetary compensation if the bonded party fails to perform certain acts,* such as a contractor who fails to complete a project according to contract specifications. Let us first consider surety bonds.

Parties to a Surety Bond

There are always three parties to a surety bond. They are:

- Principal
- Obligee
- Surety

*The **principal** is the party who agrees to perform certain acts or fulfill certain obligations.* For example, Smith Construction may agree to build an office building for the city of Omaha. If Smith Construction is required to obtain a performance bond before the contract is awarded, it would be known as the principal.

*The **obligee** is the party who is reimbursed for damages if the principal fails to perform.* Thus, the city of Omaha would be reimbursed for damages if Smith Construction failed to complete the building on time or according to contract specifications.

The surety is the final party to a bond. *The **surety** is the party who agrees to answer for the debt, default, or obligation of another.* For example, Smith Construction may purchase a performance bond from United Fidelity. If Smith Construction (principal) fails to perform, the city of Omaha (obligee) would be reimbursed for any loss by United Fidelity (surety).

Comparison of Surety Bonds and Insurance

Surety bonds are similar to insurance contracts since both provide protection against specified losses. However, there are some important differences between them. The major differences are illustrated in Figure 15.1.

Figure 15.1
Comparison of Insurance and Surety Bonds

Insurance	Bonds
1. There are two parties to an insurance contract.	1. There are three parties to a bond.
2. The insurer expects to pay the losses. The premium reflects the losses that will be paid.	2. The surety theoretically expects no losses to occur. The premium is viewed as a service fee, by which the surety's credit is substituted for that of the principal.
3. The insurer normally does not have the right to recover a loss of payment from the insured.	3. The surety has the legal right to recover a loss payment from the defaulting principal.
4. Insurance is designed to cover losses that are outside of the insured's control.	4. The surety guarantees the character, honesty, integrity, and ability to perform. These qualities are within the insured's control.

You should note, however, that most insurance authors believe that fidelity bonds are similar to insurance, since losses are expected and are reflected in the premiums charged.

Types of Fidelity Bonds

We noted earlier that a fidelity bond protects an employer against the dishonest or fraudulent acts of employees. Fidelity bonds are similar to insurance, since losses are expected and are reflected in the premiums charged.

There are several types of fidelity bonds. They include the following:

- Individual bond
- Name schedule bond
- Position schedule bond
- Blanket bonds
  - commercial blanket bond
  - blanket position bond

Individual bond Under an **individual bond,** the employee is specifically named in the bond, and coverage applies only to that person. Other employees are not covered.

Name schedule bond Under a **name schedule bond,** each person to be bonded is specifically named in the bond and is bonded for a specified amount. For example, a name schedule bond may cover the following employees:

Jim Jones, President	*$10,000*
Mary Smith, Treasurer	*50,000*
Susan James, Cashier	*25,000*
Tom Hall, Routeman	*5,000*

Thus, if Mary Smith embezzled $20,000 over a period of time, the entire loss is covered. However, if Tom Hall steals company funds, the loss would be covered only to a maximum of $5,000. The advantage of a name schedule bond is that the firm has only one bond instead of several individual bonds based on the number of employees to be bonded.

Position schedule bond Under a **position schedule bond,** there is no reference to any named employee. Instead, the various positions to be bonded and the number of employees occupying these positions are listed in the bond. For example, if the positions are treasurer, cashier, and accountant, the number of persons in each position would be listed in the position schedule bond.

The major advantage of a position schedule bond is that notification of the bonding company is not necessary if there is a change in personnel. The bonding company must be notified only if there is a change in the number of persons occupying a bonded position. This is important since the employer may have to absorb part of the loss if the number of persons occupying the bonded position exceeds the number stated in the bond at the time of loss. For example, the bond may specify that a cashier is covered for $25,000, and there are four cashiers in the position. Assume that a fifth cashier is hired, and the employer fails to notify the bonding company. If a cashier causes a loss, the surety's liability is limited to a maximum of four-fifths of $25,000, or $20,000.

Blanket bonds A blanket bond provides much broader coverage to the employer than a position bond. Under the blanket bond, all employees are covered without exception. New employees are automatically covered without notice to the company.

One major advantage of the blanket bond is that it is not necessary to identify the dishonest employee or employees in order to collect for a loss. The loss is paid even though the dishonest employee cannot be identified. In contrast, under an individual or name schedule bond, the employee who caused the loss must be specifically identified, and under a position bond, the loss must be due to a person occupying the bonded position. Another advantage is that all employees are covered. Under a name schedule or individual bond, the firm may not bond certain trusted, long-service employees who may later steal from the firm.

Two types of blanket bonds are commonly used today—a **Commercial Blanket Bond** and **Blanket Position Bond.** *The major distinction between them is that, under the Commercial Blanket Bond, the bond's limit of liability (called a* ***bond penalty****) is the maximum limit that applies to any single loss, regardless of the number of employees involved. Under a Blanket Position Bond, the bond penalty applies to each employee.* For example, assume that three employees acting together embezzle $30,000. Under a $10,000 Commercial Blanket Bond, the employer would collect only $10,000. Under a Blanket Position Bond, the bond penalty applies to each employee. If the three employees can be identified, the employer would collect $30,000. However, if the employees cannot be identified, recovery is limited to the bond penalty of $10,000.

Common Features of Fidelity Bonds

All fidelity bonds have certain common features. Some common provisions are summarized as follows:

1. *Continuous coverage.* Most fidelity bonds provide continuous coverage. The bond does not expire at the end of the period of protection as insurance policies do. The bond remains in force until it is cancelled by either party. However, a premium must be paid annually or every three years to keep the bond in force. Thus, a bond has an anniversary date, not an expiration date.

2. *Bond penalty.* The maximum amount paid for a covered loss is called the penalty of the bond. Since a bond provides continuous protection, the bond penalty does not apply to each separate year but to the entire period the bond is in force. For example, if the bond penalty is $10,000, and a dishonest treasurer embezzles $50,000 over a five-year period, the maximum amount paid for the loss is $10,000.

3. *Termination of the bond on a dishonest employee.* Once the employer becomes aware of any loss committed by a bonded employee, coverage on the dishonest employee is terminated. The employer is required to notify the surety of the loss. If the employer fails to notify the surety, there is no further coverage on the employee who may later steal again from the company. Also, under a name schedule or position schedule bond, if the employer fails to notify the surety of a dishonest employee, a policy condition is violated, and the entire fidelity coverage is in jeopardy.

4. *Discovery period (cutoff period).* A fidelity bond provides coverage only while the bond is in force. *If the bond is terminated, the employer has a certain period to discover losses that have occurred while the bond was in force (often called a cutoff period).* The **discovery period** typically ranges from six months to three years. For example, assume that the employer cancels a bond with a bond penalty of $25,000 and a two-year discovery period. If a $10,000 loss is discovered during the discovery period and is traced to an employee who was working for the firm before the bond was cancelled, the loss would be covered.

5. *Superseded suretyship clause.* Most bonds have a **superseded suretyship clause** by which a new bond provides coverage for a loss that occurred while a prior bond was in effect. *Under this provision, if a bond is cancelled, the new bond picks up any losses that occurred while the old bond was in effect, but the loss was not discovered until after the discovery period under the old bond had run out.*

The maximum recovery under this provision is limited to the bond penalty under the old bond, or the limit of liability under the new bond, whichever is less. For example, assume that the bond penalty is $20,000 under the old bond and $30,000 under the new bond. The new company is liable only for a maximum loss of $20,000 if the loss occurred while the prior bond was in force, but is discovered after the discovery period under the prior bond has run out.

The purpose of this provision is to permit an employer to change bonding companies without penalty. The provision applies only if there is no break in the continuity of coverage under both bonds. The new bond must replace the old bond on the same day the old bond is cancelled.

6. *Inventory shortage.* An inventory shortage is not covered unless the employer can prove that the loss is caused by a dishonest employee or employees.

7. *Salvage.* After a loss is paid, the surety may recover part or all of the stolen property from the dishonest employee. Under the **full salvage clause,** the employer is entitled to any recovery until the firm is restored in full for the loss. Some bonds contain a **pro rata salvage clause** which provides for a pro rata sharing of the salvage between the surety and employer based on the proportion of loss incurred by each.

Types of Surety Bonds

There are six major classes of **surety bonds.** They are listed as follows:

1. Contract bonds
   - bid bond
   - performance bond
   - payment bond
   - maintenance bond
2. License and permit bonds
3. Public official bonds
4. Judicial bonds
   - fiduciary bond
   - court bond
5. Federal surety bonds
6. Miscellaneous surety bonds

Contract bonds A **contract bond** guarantees that the principal will fulfill all contractual obligations. There are several types of contract bonds. Under a *bid bond,* the owner (obligee) is guaranteed that the party awarded a bid on a project will sign a contract and furnish a performance bond. Under a *performance bond,* the owner is guaranteed that work will be completed according to the contract specifications. For example, if a building is not completed on time, the surety is responsible for completion of the project and the extra expense in hiring another contractor.

A *payment bond* guarantees that the bills for labor and materials used in building the project will be paid when the bills are due. Finally, a *maintenance bond* guarantees that poor workmanship by the principal will be corrected, or defective materials will be replaced. This maintenance guarantee is often included in a performance bond for one year without additional charge.

License and permit bonds This type of bond is commonly required of persons who must obtain a license or permit from a city or town before they can engage in certain activities. A **license and permit bond** guarantees that the person bonded will comply with all laws and regulations that govern his or her activities. For example, a liquor store owner may post a bond guaranteeing that liquor will be sold according to law. A plumber or electrician may post a bond guaranteeing that the work performed will comply with the local building code.

Public official bonds This type of bond is usually required by law for public officials who are elected or appointed to public office. A **public official bond** guarantees that public officials will faithfully perform their duties for the protection of the public.

Judicial bonds These bonds are used for a wide variety of court proceedings and guarantee that the party bonded will fulfill certain obligations specified by law. There are two classes of **judicial bonds.** First, a *fiduciary bond* guarantees that the person responsible for the property of another will faithfully exercise his or her duties, give an accounting of all property received, and make up any deficiency for which the courts hold the fiduciary liable. For example, administrators of estates, receivers or liquidators, or guardians of minor children may be required to post a bond guaranteeing their performance.

The second type of judicial bond is a court bond. A *court bond* is designed to protect one person (obligee) against loss in the event that the person bonded does not prove that he or she is legally entitled to the remedy sought against the obligee. For example, an *attachment bond* guarantees that if the court rules against the plaintiff who has attached the property of the defendant in a lawsuit, the defendant will be reimbursed for damages as a result of having the property attached.

Finally, a *bail bond* is another type of court bond. If the bonded person fails to appear in court at the appointed time, the entire bond penalty may be forfeited.

Federal surety bonds These bonds are required by federal agencies that regulate the actions of business firms such as manufacturers, wholesalers, and large import firms. A federal surety bond guarantees that the bonded party will faithfully comply with federal standards, pay all taxes or duties that accrue, or pay the penalty if the bondholder fails to do so.

Miscellaneous surety bonds This category consists of bonds that cannot be classified in any other group. For example, an *auctioneer's bond* guarantees the faithful accounting of sales proceeds by an auctioneer; a *lost instrument bond* guarantees the obligee against loss if the original instrument (such as a lost stock certificate) turns up in the possession of another party; and an *insurance agent bond* indemnifies an insurer for any penalties that may result from the unlawful acts of agents.

SUMMARY

- The Mercantile Open Stock Burglary Policy covers the loss of merchandise, furniture, and fixtures from a burglary, attempted burglary, or robbery of a security guard. The coverage applies only when the premises are closed for business.
- The Mercantile Open Stock Burglary Policy contains a unique coinsurance clause. The amount of required insurance is stated as a coinsurance percentage or coinsurance limit, whichever is lower.
- The Mercantile Safe Burglary Policy covers the loss of money, securities, and other property from within a locked vault or safe as a result of a burglary.
- The Mercantile Robbery Policy is designed to cover the loss of money, securities, and other property from a robbery or attempted robbery. Coverage for robbery inside the premises and robbery outside the premises can be written together or separately.
- The Money and Securities Broad Form Policy provides broad coverage for the destruction, disappearance, or wrongful abstraction of money and certificates. Loss from almost any cause is covered.
- The Storekeepers Burglary and Robbery Policy is a package policy for small retail firms that need a variety of crime coverages in modest amounts. Seven coverages are available.
- The Comprehensive Dishonesty, Disappearance, and Destruction Policy is designed to provide broad protection against a wide variety of crime perils. There are eighteen separate coverages that can be included in the policy. The five basic coverages that are printed in the form are:
  a. Employee dishonesty.
  b. Loss inside the premises.
  c. Loss outside the premises.
  d. Money orders and counterfeit paper currency.
  e. Depositor's forgery coverage.

- A federal crime insurance program is available to business firms in twenty-seven states. The program is subsidized by the federal government in those areas where crime insurance is not available at affordable rates.
- There are three parties to a bond. The *principal* is the party who agrees to perform certain obligations. The *obligee* is the party who is reimbursed for damages if the principal fails to perform. The *surety* is the party who agrees to answer for the debt, default, or obligation of another.
- Fidelity bonds are similar to insurance contracts since losses are expected. However, there are several major differences between surety bonds and insurance:
  a. There are two parties to an insurance contract; there are three parties to a bond.
  b. The insurer expects to pay losses; the surety theoretically expects no losses to occur.
  c. The insurer normally does not have the right to recover a loss payment from the insured; the surety has the right to recover from a defaulting principal.
  d. Insurance is designed to cover losses outside of the insured's control; the surety guarantees the character, honesty, integrity, and ability to perform, which are within the insured's control.
- Fidelity bonds are designed to protect employers against the dishonest or fraudulent acts of employees. They include an individual bond, name schedule bond, position schedule bond, and blanket bond.
- Surety bonds guarantee the performance of the principal. Surety bonds include various contract bonds, license and permit bonds, public official bonds, judicial bonds, federal surety bonds, and miscellaneous surety bonds.

QUESTIONS FOR REVIEW

1. Briefly describe the major features of the Mercantile Open Stock Burglary Policy.
2. Explain the coinsurance provision in the Mercantile Open Stock Burglary Policy.
3. Briefly describe the major features of the Mercantile Safe Burglary Policy and Mercantile Robbery Policy.
4. Money can be insured against certain losses under the Money and Securities Broad Form Policy. Briefly describe the major features of this policy.
5. List the basic coverages that are provided under the Comprehensive Dishonesty, Disappearance, and Destruction Policy (3D).
6. Why is it necessary to have a federal crime insurance program for business firms?
7. Describe the three parties to a bond.
8. How do surety bonds differ from insurance contracts?
9. How does a commercial blanket bond differ from a blanket position bond?
10. Explain the following features of fidelity bonds:
    a. Bond penalty.
    b. Termination of a bond on a dishonest employee.
    c. Discovery period.
    d. Superseded suretyship clause.

QUESTIONS FOR DISCUSSION

1. Mary owns a retail shoe store that is insured by a Mercantile Open Stock Burglary Policy in the amount of $30,000. The Mercantile Open Stock Burglary Policy has a coinsurance percentage of 60 percent and a coinsurance limit of $40,000. The store currently has an inventory of $60,000.
   a. Briefly describe the perils that are covered by the Mercantile Open Stock Burglary Policy.
   b. Explain the meaning of a burglary in the Mercantile Open Stock Burglary Policy.
   c. If a covered burglary loss of $12,000 occurs, how much will Mary collect?
2. What type of crime insurance policy do you recommend for each of the following losses?
   a. A robber holds up the owner of an automobile service station during business hours, and $500 is taken from the cash register.
   b. A pawnshop is broken into after business hours. Several diamond rings and watches are stolen.
   c. A liquor store operator is robbed of the day's receipts while driving to the bank to make a deposit.
3. The Comprehensive Dishonesty, Disappearance, and Destruction Policy (3D) is designed to provide broad coverage for various crime perils.
   a. Describe several crime exposures that can be insured under the 3D policy.
   b. Explain how the 3D policy can provide considerable flexibility to business firms with respect to the insuring of crime exposures.
4. Lastovica Construction has been awarded a contract by a school board to build a new public school and must provide a performance bond.
   a. With respect to the performance bond, identify the principal, surety, and obligee.
   b. If Lastovica Construction fails to complete the building according to the terms of the contract, what would be the surety's obligation?
   c. Does the surety have any recourse against Lastovica Construction in the above example? Explain your answer.
5. Carmine owns several retail shoe stores. The employees are bonded under a blanket position bond with a penalty of $10,000. Carmine discovered that Susan, a long-time accountant, had embezzled $3,000 from the firm in order to pay the gambling debts of her son, who had been threatened with bodily harm. Susan agreed to repay the firm, and the embezzlement was not reported to the bonding company. Several months later, Susan stole $2,000 from the company's cash receipts and then disappeared. What is the liability of the bonding company, if any, for the loss? Explain your answer.
6. An executive with 500 employees must decide whether to purchase a blanket position bond or a commercial blanket bond.
   a. From the executive's viewpoint, what are the major differences between a blanket position bond and a commercial blanket bond?
   b. Assume that a commercial blanket bond is purchased with a bond penalty of $50,000. Assume that three employees acting together embezzle $100,000. What would be the bonding company's liability for the loss? Explain your answer.
   c. If a blanket position bond had been purchased, what would be the bonding company's liability for the above loss? Assume that the three employees can be identified.

KEY CONCEPTS AND TERMS TO KNOW

Burglary
Robbery
Theft
Mercantile Open Stock Burglary Policy
Coinsurance percentage
Coinsurance limit
Mercantile Safe Burglary Policy
Mercantile Robbery Policy
Money and Securities Broad Form
Storekeepers Burglary and Robbery Policy
Comprehensive Dishonesty, Disappearance, and Destruction Policy (3D)
Pro rata salvage clause
Surety bond
Contract bonds
License and permit bonds
Commercial crime policy
Principal
Obligee
Surety
Fidelity bond
Surety bond
Individual bond
Name schedule bond
Position schedule bond
Commercial blanket bond
Blanket position bond
Bond penalty
Discovery period
Superseded suretyship clause
Full salvage clause
Public official bonds
Judicial bond
Federal surety bonds

SUGGESTIONS FOR ADDITIONAL READING

Bickelhaupt, David L. *General Insurance*, 11th ed. Homewood, Illinois: Richard D. Irwin, Inc., 1983, chapter 21.

Fire, Casualty & Surety Bulletins. Casualty and Surety Volume. Cincinnati, Ohio: The National Underwriter Company. The bulletins are published monthly. Detailed information on crime insurance and fidelity and surety bonds can be found in this volume.

Gordis, Philip. *Property and Casualty Insurance*, 26th ed. Indianapolis, Indiana: The Rough Notes Company, 1980.

Greene, Mark S. and James S. Trieschmann. *Risk and Insurance*, 6th ed. Cincinnati, Ohio: Southwestern Publishing Company, 1984, chapter 18.

Huebner, S. S., Kenneth Black, Jr., and Robert S. Cline. *Property and Liability Insurance*, 3rd ed. Englewood Cliffs, New Jersey: Prentice-Hall, Inc., 1982.

Mehr, Robert I. and Emerson Cammack. *Principles of Insurance*, 7th ed. Homewood, Illinois: Richard D. Irwin, Inc., 1980, chapter 15.

Vaughan, Emmett J. *Fundamentals of Risk and Insurance*, 3rd ed. New York: John Wiley & Sons, 1982, chapter 35.

NOTES

1. *Insurance Facts, 1984–85 Property/Casualty Fact Book*, p. 87.
2. Crime insurance and bonding are discussed in considerable detail in *Fire, Casualty, & Surety Bulletins*, Casualty & Surety volume. The author drew on this source in preparing this chapter.
3. The Mercantile Open Stock Burglary Policy would cover the loss if the business were closed.
4. Federal crime insurance for business firms is available in Alabama, Arkansas, California, Colorado, Connecticut, Delaware, District of Columbia, Florida, Georgia, Illinois, Iowa, Kansas, Louisiana, Maryland, Massachusetts, Minnesota, Missouri, New Jersey, New Mexico, New York, North Carolina, Ohio, Pennsylvania, Rhode Island, Tennessee, Virginia, Washington, Wisconsin, Puerto Rico, and the Virgin Islands.

PART

4

LIFE AND HEALTH INSURANCE

CHAPTER 16 FUNDAMENTALS OF LIFE INSURANCE

"The human life value, expressed in dollars, should be carefully appraised for life and health insurance purposes."

S. S. Huebner, The Economics of Life Insurance

STUDENT LEARNING OBJECTIVES

After studying this chapter, you should be able to:

- Explain the economic justification for the purchase of life insurance.
- Describe the basic methods for estimating the amount of life insurance to own.
- Explain the yearly renewable term method for providing life insurance protection to an individual.
- Explain the level-premium method for providing life insurance protection to an individual.
- Explain the nature and purpose of the legal reserve.

We begin our study of life insurance in this chapter. Life insurance is important in providing financial security to individuals and families. The purchase of life insurance can be justified if you have an earning capacity and others are dependent on your earnings for at least part of their financial support. If a family head dies prematurely, the family's share of the deceased breadwinner's earnings is lost forever. Life insurance can be used to restore all or part of this loss.

In this chapter, we will examine some important fundamental concepts in life insurance. Two important areas will be heavily emphasized. First, we will consider the problem of how much life insurance to own and the various methods for estimating the amount of life insurance to own. Second, we will discuss the different ways of providing life insurance to an individual, which include the yearly renewable term method and the level-premium method.

AMOUNT OF LIFE INSURANCE TO OWN

The amount of life insurance to own is often a difficult problem to resolve. Several methods can be used to determine the proper amount of life insurance to own. They include the following:

- Human life value approach
- Income replacement approach
- Needs aproach

Human Life Value Approach

We stated earlier that the family's share of the deceased breadwinner's earnings is lost forever if the family head dies prematurely. This loss is called the **human life value.** *More specifically, the human life value can be defined as the present value of the family's share of the deceased breadwinner's future earnings.* It can be calculated by the following steps:

1. Estimate the individual's average annual earnings over his or her productive lifetime.
2. Deduct federal and state income taxes, social security taxes, life and health insurance premiums, and the costs of self-maintenance. The remaining amount is used for the family.
3. Determine the number of years from the person's present age to the contemplated age of retirement.
4. Using a reasonable discount rate, determine the present value of the family's share of earnings for the period determined in step 3.

For example, assume that Gerald, age twenty-five, is married and has two children. He earns \$25,000 annually and plans to retire at age sixty-five. (For the sake of simplicity, we will assume that his earnings will remain constant.) Of this amount, \$10,000 is used for federal and state taxes, life and health insurance, and Gerald's personal needs. The remaining \$15,000 is used to support his family. This stream of income is then discounted back to the present to determine Gerald's human life value. Using a reasonable discount rate of 6 percent, the present value of \$1 payable annually for 40 years is \$15.05. Therefore, Gerald has a human life value of \$225,750 (\$15,000 × \$15.05 = \$225,750). This sum represents the present value of the family's share of Gerald's earnings that would be lost if he should die prematurely. As you can see, the human life has an enormous economic value when earning capacity is considered. The major advantage of the human life value concept is that it crudely measures the economic value of a human life.

However, the human life value approach has several defects that limit its usefulness in trying to measure accurately the correct amount of life insurance to own. *The major defects are, first, that other sources of income are not considered, such as Social Security survivor benefits.*

Second, in its simplest form, work earnings and expenses are assumed to remain constant. This is clearly unrealistic. Moreover, it is difficult to estimate accurately the future increase in earnings.

Third, the amount of income allocated to the family is a critical factor in determining the human life value. This amount can quickly change depending on several factors, such as divorce, birth, or death in the family.

Fourth, the long-run discount rate is critical. The human life value can be substantially increased merely by assuming a lower discount rate.

Fifth, the effects of inflation on earnings and expenses are ignored. Inflation can quickly erode the real purchasing power of the policy proceeds.

Finally, insuring the human life value to its full amount is neither necessary nor affordable for most persons. The amount of income a person can afford to spend on life insurance depends on the person's spending priorities, value judgments, level of income, and family obligations.[1]

Income Replacement Approach

The **income replacement approach** is similar to the human life value approach, but it is more refined. The amount of life insurance needed is assumed to be directly related to the income lost by premature death. *The amount of life insurance needed is expressed in terms of multiples of earned income.* The amount of earned income to be replaced is based on the percentage of earnings after taxes that is used to meet the family's needs. This approach also considers the availability of Social Security survivor benefits, and can provide a modest inflation hedge in determining the amount of life insurance to own.

Some life insurance companies have constructed special tables to show the amount of life insurance needed based on the income replacement approach. Figure 16.1 indicates the amount of life insurance needed, expressed as a multiple of gross earnings, if the objective is to restore 75 percent of the earnings after taxes from the date of death to age sixty-five. It is based on the assumption that the family head has a nonworking spouse and two children who were born at the insured's age of twenty-six and twenty-nine, respectively. Social Security survivor benefits are also taken into consideration in the table. For example, a family head, age thirty, who earns $30,000 annually would need $222,000 of life insurance (7.4 × $30,000) to replace 75 percent of his or her earnings after taxes for thirty-five years.

Inflation is a troublesome problem in life insurance financial planning. Under the income replacement approach, the loss of purchasing power after death occurs can be a major problem if the replacement income after death remains constant. Thus, Figure 16.1 is based on an inflation factor of 3 percent annually, if the life insurance proceeds can be invested to earn 6 percent annually. The extra interest earnings will allow the monthly income to increase rather than remain level during a period of inflation. Social Security survivor benefits, which are also payable in addition to the insurance amounts obtained from Figure 16.1 are automatically adjusted for inflation if the Consumer Price Index increases by at least 3 percent from one year to the next.

Although the income replacement approach measures more accurately the proper amount of life insurance to own, it also has several defects. *First, the income replacement approach assumes the insured has dependents who rely on his or her earnings for their financial support.* If there are no dependents, the need for replacement income largely disappears. Thus, the life insurance needs of single persons cannot be accurately meausred by this approach.

Second, there is nothing magic or special about 75 percent or any replacement percentage. Some family heads may prefer to leave 50 percent of their net earnings to their families, while others may prefer a higher or lower percentage.

Finally, this approach ignores retirement income that may be lost if the family head dies before age sixty-five. The income replacement approach does not replace the retirement income that the insured (and spouse) might have received if he or she had lived to retirement.

Needs Approach

The final method for estimating the amount of life insurance to own is the **needs approach.** Under this method, the various family needs that must

Figure 16.1
Insurance Requirements in Addition to Social Security to Replace 75% of Earnings After Taxes to Insured's Age 65—Children Born at Insured's Age 26 and 29

	Age of Insured						
Gross Annual Pay	**25**	**30**	**35**	**40**	**45**	**50**	**55**
$ 7500	15.3	5.3	6.2	7.3	8.5	7.9	5.6
9000	15.0	5.1	6.0	7.0	8.1	7.8	5.5
12,000	14.6	5.0	5.8	6.7	7.9	7.6	5.4
15,000	14.3	4.9	5.7	6.7	7.9	7.4	5.3
20,000	14.1	4.9	6.5	7.4	8.1	7.3	5.2
30,000	13.9	7.4	8.2	8.4	8.3	7.2	5.1
40,000	13.4	8.4	8.7	8.6	8.2	6.9	4.9
60,000	12.5	9.0	8.9	8.4	7.8	6.5	4.6

SOURCE: The Bankers Life, *How Much Life Insurance Do I Need—How Much Life Insurance Can I Afford*, Table 2, n.d.

be met if the family head should die are analyzed. After considering other sources of income and financial assets, these needs are then converted into specific amounts of life insurance. The total amount of life insurance needed is then compared with the amount of life insurance on the family head to determine if the amount of life insurance is adequate. The most basic family needs are as follows:

- Estate clearance fund
- Income during readjustment period
- Income during the dependency period
- Life income to the widow
- Special needs
  Mortgage redemption fund
  Educational fund
  Emergency fund
- Retirement needs

Estate clearance fund An **estate clearance fund** or cleanup fund is immediately needed when the family head dies. Cash is needed for burial expenses, expenses of last illness, installment debts, estate administration expenses, and estate, inheritance, and income taxes. In a typical estate, a fund of $10,000 should be adequate.

Income during the readjustment period The **readjustment period** is a one- or two-year period following the breadwinner's death. During this period, the family should receive approximately the same amount of income it received while the family head was alive. The purpose of the readjustment period is to give the family time to adjust their living standards to a different level. There is normally an emotional shock and considerable grief when the family head dies, especially if the death is unexpected. By providing an equivalent amount of income to the family during this period, a financial shock that would only compound the family's grief is avoided.

Income during the dependency period The **dependency period** follows the readjustment period. It is the period until the youngest child reaches age eighteen. The family should receive income during this period so that the surviving spouse can remain home, if necessary, to care for the children during their critical formative years. For example, at present, many wives with children are in the labor force and plan to continue working even if their husbands should die. But it is still advisable to supplement the family's income during this period to compensate for the loss of financial support and also to cover any extra expenses that may be incurred by the working spouse, such as child care expenses.

Life income for widow Although many married women are in the labor force when their husbands die, some women have been out of the labor force for several years. When the children are grown, the surviving spouse may be middle-aged. The occupational skills that she possesses may be obsolete, and it may be difficult for her to find a job that will pay an adequate salary. Thus, it is often desirable to plan for a life income to the widow.

There are two income periods to consider: (1) income during the blackout period, and (2) income to supplement Social Security benefits after the blackout period. The **blackout period** refers to the period from the time Social Security survivor benefits terminate to the time they are resumed, at age sixty.[2] Thus, it is desirable to provide income during the blackout period and also to supplement Social Security benefits at retirement.

If a woman has a career of her own, the need for a life income is greatly reduced. However, this is clearly not true of an older woman who has been out of the labor force for several years. Many elderly widows are living in poverty, and the need for an adequate lifetime income becomes especially important.

Special needs Certain special needs must also be considered. These needs include a mortgage redemption fund, educational fund, and emergency fund.

1. *Mortgage redemption fund.* Often it is desirable to provide the family with a mortgage free home. The amount of monthly income needed is greatly reduced when monthly mortgage payments or rent payments are not required.

There are two circumstances that may make it inadvisable to pay off the mortgage. First, the interest rate on the existing mortgage may be well below the current interest rate in the money market. For example, treasury bills may have a 10 percent rate, while the old mortgage may have a 7 or 8 percent rate. The family would then be better off financially if it invested the funds in higher yielding investments than if it prepaid the mortgage. Second, the house may be sold more easily with a large mortgage that has a relatively low rate of interest. The new owner may be able to assume the attractive mortgage.

2. *Educational fund.* The family head may also wish to provide an educational fund for the children. Since the funds will not be needed until the children reach college age, they can be invested to provide income to the family during the readjustment and dependency periods. But how much life insurance is needed? If the child intends to go to a private college or university, the costs will be considerably higher than at a public institution. If a college education at a private college or university is desired, a college fund of at least $40,000 for four years of school will be required for each child.

3. *Emergency fund.* An emergency fund should also be provided. An unexpected event, such as the need for a new furnace or roof, a serious illness, dental work, or replacement of an older automobile, may require large amounts of cash. A fund of $10,000 should be adequate for most families.

Retirement needs The family head may survive to retirement, so the need for an adequate retirement income must also be considered. In most cases, the typical wage earner will be eligible for Social Security retirement benefits, and may be eligible for private pension benefits from an employer. If retirement income from these sources is inadequate, or if the individual is not covered under a private pension plan, it may be necessary to supplement the Social Security benefits from other sources. Additional income can be obtained from cash value life insurance, individual investments, a retirement annuity, or an Individual Retirement Account.[3] Failure to plan for retirement could result in serious financial hardship because of inadequate income during old age.[4]

INSIGHT 16.1

Life Insurance: Three Families' Needs

Life insurance needs vary depending on individual and family situations. The amount of life insurance needed can be determined by the needs approach. First, you estimate what your future financial needs would be less any Social Security benefits you expect. (Contact your local Social Security office for more information.) Second, you determine what current assets you have, including your present life insurance, to meet these needs. (Omit assets like automobiles and your personal residence that would not likely be sold by your family.) Third, subtract your assets from your needs to determine the amount of additional life insurance you should have, if any. (While certain assets will generate investment income, it has been assumed that all such income will be offset by the effects of inflation.)

The needs approach tailors your life insurance protection to your individual needs. Three hypothetical family situations are described below to illustrate how the needs approach identifies the type and amount of financial security different members require.

Paul Hayes

1. Financial needs		
(a) Family living expenses	$ 83,000	
(b) Retirement fund	137,000	
(c) College education	12,000	
(d) Other (emergency, final expenses, etc.)	22,000	
Total financial needs		$254,000
2. Current assets		
(a) Cash, savings, securities, etc.	$ 23,000	
(b) Equity in real estate, excluding home	16,000	
(c) Life insurance	110,000	
Less: Current assets		—$149,000
3. Additional life insurance needed		$105,000

Example

Paul Hayes is 39 and earns $30,000 a year. He has a wife and two children ages 12 and 6. He has four primary financial needs—(a) provide income to support his family for 12 years until the younger child is 18, (b) build a 20-year retirement fund for his wife, (c) establish a college education fund for his children, and (d) provide for other miscellaneous expenses (e.g., emergencies, funeral, etc.). He calculated his total financial needs taking into account the Social Security benefits his family would receive if he died (including benefits for children attending college). In spite of these benefits and his current assets, his present insurance provides only about ½ of what he needs. He needs an additional $105,000 of insurance.

Advantages and disadvantages of the needs approach The major advantage of the needs approach is that it is a reasonably accurate method for determining the amount of life insurance to own when specific family needs and objectives are recognized. In addition, the needs approach also considers other sources of income and financial assets in determining the amount of life insurance to own. If present life insurance and financial assets are insufficient for meeting these needs, the inadequacy is quickly recognized. Finally, the needs approach can also be used to recognize needs during a period of disability or retirement.

David Russell

1. Financial needs		
(a) Retirement fund	300,000	
(b) Other (emergency, final expenses, etc.)	22,000	
Total financial needs		$322,000
2. Current assets		
(a) Cash, savings, securities, etc.	$ 47,000	
(b) Equity in business	100,000	
(c) Life insurance	100,000	
Less: Current assets		—$247,000
3. Additional life insurance needed		$ 75,000

Example
David Russell is married, 49 years old and earns $48,000 a year. He has three children, all of whom are out of college, so he has no education or family living expense needs. (He assumes his wife could support herself until age 62 if he died.) Dave has two primary financial needs— (a) establish a 20 year retirement fund for his wife to provide income beyond what Social Security will provide, and (b) provide for other expenses that might occur. He needs an additional $75,000 of insurance.

Linda Gardner

1. Financial needs		
(a) Dependent support	$165,000	
(b) Other (emergency, final expenses, etc.)	17,000	
Total financial needs		$182,000
2. Current assets		
(a) Cash, savings, securities, etc.	$ 6,000	
(b) Equity in real estate, excluding home	36,000	
(c) Life insurance	50,000	
Less: Current assets		—$ 92,000
3. Additional life insurance needed		$ 90,000

Example
Linda Gardner is single, 29 years of age and earns $22,000 a year. She rents an apartment but has investment real estate holdings. She provides a modest amount of financial support for her 62-year-old widowed mother. However, if Linda died, she would like to provide $7,500 a year to support her mother for the rest of her life. Linda has two primary financial needs—(a) provide income to support her mother, and (b) provide for other miscellaneous expenses that might occur. Linda can insure her mother's financial support for life by $90,000 of additional life insurance with her mother as beneficiary.

SOURCE: New York Life Insurance Co.

The needs approach, however, has several disadvantages.[5] First, the family head is assumed to die immediately, which is unrealistic.

Second, life insurance programming and settlement options are required, which can be complex and difficult to understand. The use of a computer may be necessary to determine the exact amount of insurance required.

Third, family needs must be periodically evaluated to determine if they are still appropriate as circumstances change.

Fourth, in its simplest version, the needs

approach ignores inflation which can result in a substantial understatement of the amount of life insurance to own.

This concludes our discussion of the various methods for determining the amount of life insurance to own. Let us next consider the basic methods for providing life insurance protection.

METHODS FOR PROVIDING LIFE INSURANCE PROTECTION

Two basic methods can be used to provide life insurance to individuals. They are:[6]

- Yearly renewable term method
- Level-premium method

Yearly Renewable Term Method

Yearly renewable term insurance *provides life insurance protection for only one year.* The insured is permitted to renew the policy for successive one-year periods with no evidence of insurability. This means that evidence of good health or a physical examination is not required when the policy is renewed.

The pure premium for yearly renewable term insurance is determined by the death rate at each attained age. For the sake of simplicity, we will ignore interest and operating expenses of the company. The insurance protection is only for one year, and individuals within the group must pay their pro rata share of death claims. For example, based on the 1958 C.S.O. Mortality Table, the death rate at age twenty-five is 1.93 for each 1,000 lives. If 100,000 individuals at age twenty-five are insured for $1,000 for one year, the insurance company must pay 193 death claims, or $193,000. If interest and expenses are ignored, each insured must pay a premium of $1.93 ($193,000/100,000 = $1.93). You will notice that the $1.93 in premiums is the same as the death rate at age twenty-five. At age twenty-six, the death rate is 1.96 per 1,000 lives. If the 99,807 survivors want the protection for another year, the insurer must pay 196 death claims, or $196,000. Each of the 99,807 insureds must pay their pro rata share of the death claims, or $1.96 ($196,000/99,807 = $1.96). Finally, if the 99,611 survivors wish to insure their lives for another year, the insurer must pay $198,000 in death claims. Each insured's share of the total death claims would be $1.99 ($198,000/99,611 = $1.99).

You can see that the yearly renewable term insurance premium increases as the individual gets older. The premium increase is gradual during the early years, but it rises sharply during the later years. The following illustration shows the pure premiums for $1,000 of yearly renewable term insurance at various attained ages. (We again ignore interest and expenses.)

Age 25	*$ 1.93*	*Age 75*	*$ 73.37*
Age 35	*$ 2.51*	*Age 85*	*$ 161.14*
Age 45	*$ 5.35*	*Age 95*	*$ 351.24*
Age 55	*$13.00*	*Age 98*	*$ 668.15*
Age 65	*$31.75*	*Age 99*	*$1,000.00*

The premiums tend to increase at an increasing rate.[7] The yearly renewable term insurance premium eventually becomes prohibitive in cost, so some insureds may drop their insurance. The healthier members may drop their life insurance as the premiums increase, but the unhealthy persons will still continue to renew their policies despite the premium increase. This leads to adverse selection against the insurer. The insurer may then have a disproportionate number of impaired lives in the group, which drives the death rate up even more.

You can see that under the yearly renewable method, the premiums are substantial at the older ages. *Therefore, if the insured wants lifetime protection, the yearly renewable term method is impractical because the premiums are prohibitive in cost at the older ages.* Some other method must be used to provide lifetime protection. This method is called the level-premium method.

Level-premium Method

Under the **level premium method,** premiums are level and do not increase with age, and the in-

Figure 16.2 Comparison of Net Premiums Under the Level-premium Method and Yearly Renewable Term Method; 1958 C.S.O. Table, 2.5 Percent Interest

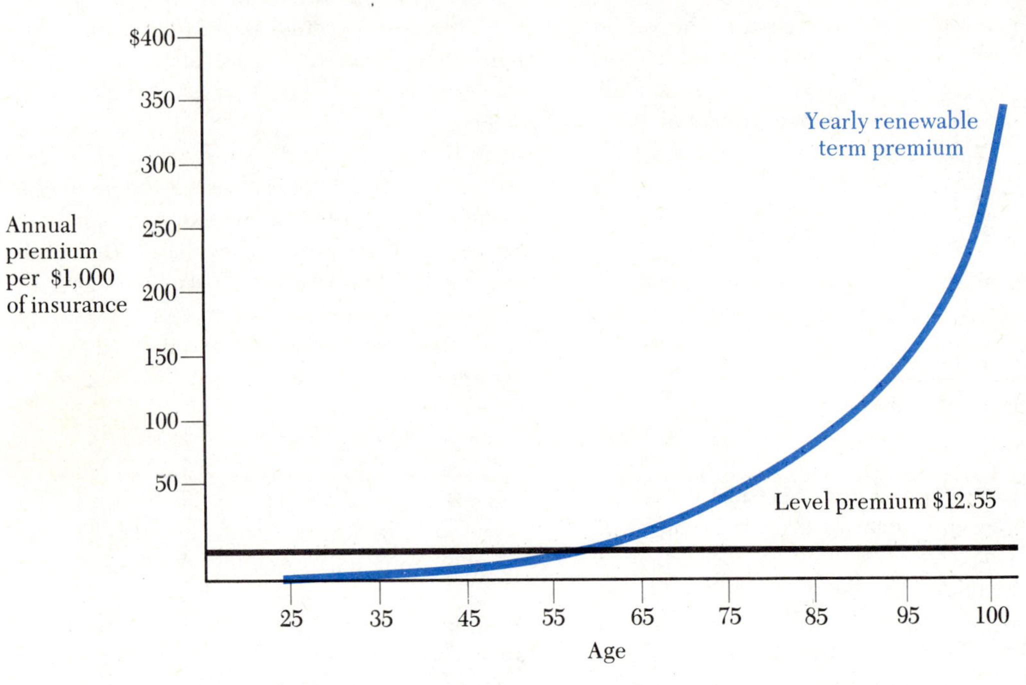

sured has lifetime protection to age 100. Under this method, premiums paid during the early years of the policy are higher than is necessary to pay current death claims, while those paid in the later years are inadequate for paying death claims. The redundant or excess premiums paid during the early years are invested at compound interest, and the accumulated funds are then used to supplement the inadequate premiums paid during the later years of the policy. Since the method of investing and accumulating the fund is regulated by state law, it is referred to as a **legal reserve.** The legal reserve technically is a composite liability account of the insurer and should not be allocated to individual contracts. However, for our purposes, we can view the legal reserve as the aggregate of the individual accounts established for the individual policyowners.[8]

The significance of the level-premium method can be illustrated by Figure 16.2, which compares the level-premium method with the yearly renewable term method for a $1,000 policy issued at age twenty-five. As you can see, the premiums are level and do not increase with age. *A level premium is possible since the excess premiums are invested at compound interest and are used to supplement the deficiency in premiums during the later years.* In contrast, under the yearly renewable term method, the premiums are very low during the early years but gradually increase to a point where they become prohibitive in cost. For this reason, lifetime protection cannot be provided to most insureds under the yearly renewable term method.

Fundamental purpose of the legal reserve We noted earlier that the redundant pre-

Figure 16.3 Proportion of Protection and Investment Elements in Ordinary Life Contract, Issued as of Age 25; 1958 C.S.O. Table, 2.5 Percent Interest

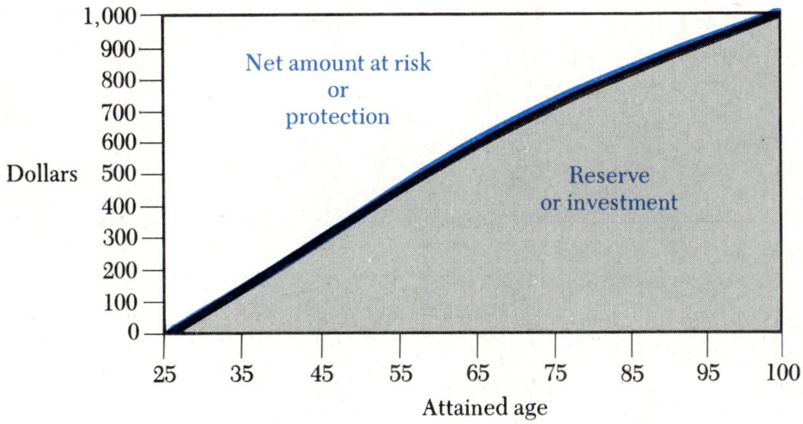

miums paid during the early years are reflected in a legal reserve. The concept of a legal reserve can be illustrated in greater detail by Figure 16.3, which represents the legal reserve under an ordinary life policy. The legal reserve steadily increases over time and is equal to the face amount of the policy at age 100. If the insured is still alive at age 100, the face amount of the policy is paid at that time. *The difference between the face amount of the policy and the legal reserve is called the* ***net amount at risk.*** The net amount at risk represents the pure insurance portion of the policy. It declines over time as the legal reserve increases. Thus, from a conceptual standpoint the death claims can be viewed as consisting of two elements—a legal reserve (savings element) and the net amount at risk (protection element).[9] As the legal reserve increases, the net amount at risk declines. *It follows that the fundamental purpose of the legal reserve is to provide lifetime protection.* As the death rate increases with age, the legal reserve also increases, and the net amount at risk declines, which produces a cost of insurance within practicable limits.[10] Therefore, by the level premium method, the company can provide the insured with lifetime protection.

Cash values **Cash values** should not be confused with the legal reserve. Under the level-premium method, a legal reserve results. Because of the legal reserve, cash values become available. The policyowner may no longer want the insurance, and the policy can be surrendered for its cash surrender value. However, cash values and the legal reserve are not the same thing and are computed separately. The cash values are below the legal reserve for several years, but after the policy has been in force over an extended period, such as fifteen years, the cash surrender value will equal the full reserve. We will examine the various cash surrender options in Chapter 18.

You should remember that cash values are the by-product of the level-premium method, not the purpose of it. The fundamental purpose of the level-premium method is to provide lifetime protection and not to build up a savings account in the form of cash values. This is not to say that an individual cannot save by purchasing cash value life insurance. Indeed, in the aggregate, large amounts are annually saved by policyowners in the form of accumulated cash values. However, the savings feature is incidental to the fundamental goal of lifetime protection.

SUMMARY

- The purpose of life insurance can be economically justified if a person has an earning capacity, and someone is dependent on those earnings for at least part of their financial support.
- The human life value is defined as the present value of the family's share of the deceased breadwinner's earnings. This approach crudely measures the economic value of a human life.
- The income replacement approach can be used to determine the amount of insurance to own. The amount of life insurance is expressed in terms of multiples of earned income.
- The needs approach can be used to determine the amount of life insurance to own. After considering other sources of income and financial assets, the various family needs are converted into specific amounts of life insurance. The most important family needs are as follows:
  a. Estate clearance fund.
  b. Income during readjustment period.
  c. Income during dependency period.
  d. Life income to the widow.
  e. Special needs: mortgage redemption fund, education fund, emergency fund.
  f. Retirement needs.
- Under the yearly renewable term method, life insurance protection is provided for only one year. The policy can be renewed for successive one-year periods with no evidence of insurability. The method is not suitable for lifetime protection because premiums increase with age until they reach prohibitively high levels.
- Under the level-premium method, premiums are level and do not increase with age. The insured has lifetime protection to age 100. Under this method, premiums paid during the early years are higher than is necessary to pay current death claims. The excess or redundant premiums paid during the early years are invested and used to supplement the inadequate premiums paid during the later years.
- The legal reserve is a liability item that reflects the redundant premiums paid during the early years of the policy. It steadily increases until it reaches the face amount of the policy by age 100. The fundamental purpose of the legal reserve is to provide lifetime protection.
- Because a legal reserve is necessary for lifetime protection, cash values become available. However, cash values are the by-product of the level-premium method, not the purpose of it. Since the insured has paid in more than is actuarially necessary during the early years of the policy, he or she should receive something back if the policy is surrendered.

QUESTIONS FOR REVIEW

1. Explain the economic justification for the purchase of life insurance.
2. Define the human life value. How is the human life value measured?
3. Explain the income approach for determining the amount of life insurance to own.
4. Describe the needs approach for determining the amount of life insurance to own.
5. Explain the advantages and limitations of the needs approach in determining the amount of life insurance to own.
6. Explain the yearly renewable term method for providing life insurance to individuals.
7. Is the yearly renewable term method suitable for lifetime protection?

8. Explain the level-premium method for providing life insurance to individuals.
9. Describe the *nature* and *purpose* of the legal reserve in cash-value life insurance.
10. Why does a level-premium whole life policy provide cash values?

QUESTIONS FOR DISCUSSION

1. The human life value concept provides a method for estimating the amount of life insurance to own.
   a. Describe the steps in the calculation of an individual's human life value.
   b. All other factors unchanged, explain the effect, if any, of a reduction in the interest rate used to calculate the individual's human life value.
   c. Explain the defects in the human life value approach as a technique for determining the amount of life insurance to own.
2. Joseph, age twenty-three, is married and has one child. He has been told that he should purchase life insurance to protect his family.
   a. Describe each of the basic family needs for which Joseph may need life insurance.
   b. Explain the limitations in the needs approach as a method for determining the amount of life insurance to own.
3. A significant aspect of a whole life policy is the fact that the net amount at risk decreases over the duration of the contract.
   a. What is the net amount at risk?
   b. Explain why the net amount at risk in a whole life policy decreases over the duration of the contract.
   c. What is the significance of a decreasing net amount at risk in a whole life insurance policy?
4. An agent remarked that "the fundamental purpose of the legal reserve is to accumulate cash values and provide a means of saving money." Do you agree or disagree with this statement? Explain your answer.

KEY CONCEPTS AND TERMS TO KNOW

Human life value
Income replacement approach
Needs approach
Estate clearance fund
Readjustment period
Dependency period
Blackout period
Yearly renewable term method
Level-premium method
Legal reserve
Net amount at risk
Cash values

SUGGESTIONS FOR ADDITIONAL READING

Athearn, James L. and S. Travis Pritchett. *Risk and Insurance,* 5th ed. St. Paul, Minnesota: West Publishing Company, 1984, chapter 8.

Belth, Joseph M. *Life Insurance: A Consumer's Handbook,* 2nd ed. Bloomington, Indiana: Indiana University Press, 1985.

Bickelhaupt, David L. *General Insurance,* 11th ed. Homewood, Illinois: Richard D. Irwin, Inc., 1983, chapter 5.

Greene, Mark R. and James S. Trieschmann. *Risk and Insurance,* 6th ed. Cincinnati, Ohio: Southwestern Publishing Company, 1984, chapters 19 and 20.

Huebner, S. S. and Kenneth Black, Jr. *Life Insurance,* 10th ed. Englewood Cliffs, New Jersey: Prentice-Hall, Inc., 1982, chapters 1 and 2.

Mehr, Robert I. and Sandra G. Gustavson. *Life Insurance Theory and Practice,* 3rd ed. Dallas, Texas: Business Publications, Inc., 1984, chapter 3.

NOTES

1. Robert I. Mehr, *Life Insurance Theory and Practice,* rev. ed. (Dallas, Texas: Business Publications, Inc., 1977), p. 5.
2. Reduced Social Security survivor benefits to a surviving spouse are payable at age sixty. Full benefits are payable at age sixty-five.
3. For an explanation of the Individual Retirement Account (IRA), see Chapter 23.
4. The problem of insufficient income during retirement was discussed in Chapter 1.
5. Glenn L. Wood, Claude C. Lilly III, Donald S. Malecki, and Jerry S. Rosenbloom, *Personal Risk Management and Insurance,* 2nd ed., Volume I (Malvern, Pennsylvania: American Institute for Property and Liability Underwriters, 1980), p. 369. However, Professors Terry Rose and Robert Mehr have designed a new programming model that would eliminate many of the defects found in the *static* needs approach model. See, Terry Rose and Robert I. Mehr, "Flexible Income Programming," *The Journal of Risk and Insurance,* 47 (March 1980), pp. 44–60.
6. Dan M. McGill, *Life Insurance,* rev. ed. (Homewood, Illinois: Richard D. Irwin, 1967), pp. 29–39.
7. However, between ages zero and ten, the death rate declines, then increases at an increasing rate. Thus, term insurance premiums must eventually increase at an increasing rate.
8. McGill, pp. 32–33. The legal reserve technically is a liability item that must be offset by sufficient assets. Otherwise, regulatory authorities may declare the insurer to be insolvent.
9. This is only a concept. In practice, the death claim paid by the insurer does not consist of two separate benefits that equal the face value of the policy.
10. McGill, p. 36. The cost of insurance is a technical term and is obtained by multiplying the net amount at risk by the death rate at the insured's attained age. Under the level-premium method, the cost of insurance can be kept within reasonable bounds at all ages.

TYPES OF LIFE INSURANCE AND ANNUITIES

"The life insurance needs of virtually any buyer can be met satisfactorily with just two policy forms—straight life and five-year renewable term."

Joseph M. Belth, Life Insurance, A Consumer's Handbook

STUDENT LEARNING OBJECTIVES

After studying this chapter, you should be able to:

- Describe the major characteristics of term insurance.
- Explain the essential features of ordinary life insurance.
- Describe the major characteristics of limited-payment life insurance.
- Explain how universal life insurance differs from conventional cash-value policies.
- Describe the major chacteristics of the family income, family maintenance, and family policies.
- Describe some special-purpose life insurance policies that are designed to meet certain needs and objectives.
- Explain the nature of an annuity and how it differs from life insurance.
- Describe the major types of individual annuities that are sold today.

We will continue our study of life insurance in this chapter. We will first examine the major characteristics of the three basic types of life insurance policies—term, whole life, and endowment insurance. We will next consider some special-purpose life insurance policies that have unique features or are designed to meet special needs. We will conclude the chapter by examining the nature of an annuity and the major types of annuities that are sold today.

TYPES OF LIFE INSURANCE

Although there are many variations of life insurance policies, there are only three basic types of life insurance. They are:

- Term insurance
- Whole life insurance
- Endowment insurance

Let us examine each of these forms.

Term Insurance

Term insurance has several basic characteristics.[1] First, the insurance protection is *temporary*. Term insurance provides protection for a temporary period such as one, five, ten, or twenty years, or until the insured reaches a stated age, such as sixty-five or seventy. If the insured dies within the term period, the face amount is paid to the beneficiary. If the insured is still alive after the period expires, and the policy is not renewed, the contract expires, and the company has no further obligations.

Most term insurance policies are **renewable.** This means that the policy can be renewed for additional periods without evidence of insurability. The premium is increased at each renewal and is based on the insured's attained age. The purpose of the renewal provision is to protect the insurability of the insured. However, this leads to adverse selection against the company. Since premiums increase with age, some individuals in good health will drop their insurance, while those in poor health will continue to renew, regardless of the premium increase. To minimize adverse selection, many companies place an age limitation beyond which renewal is not permitted, such as age 70.

Most term insurance contracts are also **convertible.** This means that the term insurance policy can be exchanged for a permanent policy without evidence of insurability. There are two methods for converting a term insurance policy. Under the **attained age method,** the premium charged is based on the insured's attained age at the time of conversion, and the policy is one currently issued by the company. Under the **retroactive method,** the premium paid is based on the insured's original age, and the policy issued is one that would have been issued originally. If the conversion is retroactive, the insured pays a lower premium based on his or her attained age. The original policy may also offer more liberal benefits or have better actuarial assumptions than policies currently issued by the company. However, these advantages are offset by a financial adjustment that is required under a retroactive conversion. The insured must pay a sum equal to (1) the difference in cash values or reserves under the policies being exchanged, or (2) the difference in premiums paid on the term policy and those that would have been paid on the permanent policy, with interest on the difference at a specified rate.[2] The purpose of the financial adjustment is to place the company in the same financial position it would have enjoyed if the policy had been issued at the original age. The insured normally should not convert a term insurance policy based on original age if he or she is unhealthy. The face amount of insurance would be the same as the face amount under an attained age conversion, but a substantial financial adjustment would also be necessary.

Finally, term insurance policies usually have *no cash values* or savings element. The insurance consists of pure protection. Although some long-term policies develop a small reserve, it is used up by the end of the period.

Types of term insurance A wide variety of term insurance products are sold today. They include the following:

- Yearly renewable term
- Five, ten, fifteen, or twenty year term
- Term to age sixty-five
- Decreasing term
- Reentry term

Let us briefly examine each of them.

As we stated in Chapter 16, *yearly renewable term insurance* is issued for a one-year period, and the policyowner can renew for successive one-year periods to some stated age without evidence of insurability. Premiums increase with age at each renewal date. Most yearly renewable term policies also allow the policyowner to convert to a cash-value policy.

Term insurance can also be issued for *five, ten, fifteen, or twenty years*, or for even longer periods. The premiums paid during the term period are level, but they increase when the policy is renewed. Some life insurance experts believe that the five-year term insurance policy provides the highest degree of flexibility to the policyowner.

A term to age sixty-five policy provides protection to age sixty-five, at which time the policy expires. The policy can be converted to a permanent plan of insurance, but the decision to convert must be exercised before age sixty-five. For example, the company may require conversion to a permanent policy before age sixty. Since premiums are level, the policy develops a small reserve that is used up by the end of the period.

Decreasing term insurance is a form of term insurance where the face amount gradually declines each month or year. The reduction in insurance may look something like this.[3]

If death occurs in year	The death benefit is
1	$30,000
5	28,470
10	25,470
15	21,150
20	14,520
40	2,520

Although the face amount gradually declines, the premium is level throughout the period. In some policies, the policyowners are not required to pay premiums for the entire period. For example, a twenty-year decreasing term policy may require premium payments for seventeen years. This is to avoid paying a relatively large premium for only a small amount of insurance near the end of the term period. Finally, decreasing term insurance can be written as a separate policy, or it can be added as a rider to an existing contract.

Reentry term is a relatively new term insurance product sold by some insurers. Because of intense price competition in recent years, some insurers have designed term insurance products based on select mortality rates, that is, lower rates based on the mortality experience of persons who are known to be in good health within the last few years.

Under a reentry term policy, the renewal premiums are based on select mortality rates (lower rates) if the insured can periodically demonstrate acceptable evidence of insurability. To remain on the low-rate schedule, the insured must periodically show that he or she is in good health and is still insurable. Evidence of insurability generally is required at intervals of one to five years, depending on the company, amount of insurance, and type of policy. The rates are substantially increased if the insured is unable to provide satisfactory evidence of insurability.

Uses of term insurance Two major situations justify the use of term insurance: (1) income is limited, or (2) a temporary need is present. If the policyowner's income is limited and substantial amounts of life insurance are needed, a term insurance policy can be effectively used. Because of mortality improvements and keen price competition, term insurance rates have declined sharply in recent years. As a result, substantial amounts of life insurance can be purchased for a relatively modest annual premium outlay. (See Figure 17.1 for premiums by one insurer.)

Term insurance can also be used if the need for protection is temporary. For example, if the insured borrows money to buy an automobile or

Figure 17.1
Annual Renewable Term Life Insurance Annual Premiums

Non-smoker

	$100,000	$250,000	$500,000	$1,000,000
Male age:				
25	96.00	196.88	352.50	652.50
35	96.00	196.88	352.50	652.50
45	138.75	288.75	525.00	997.50
55	258.75	603.75	1170.00	2002.50
65	655.50	1541.25	2913.75	5722.50
75	2015.00	4942.50	9805.00	19,530.00
Smoker				
25	104.00	257.50	505.00	950.00
35	110.00	272.50	535.00	1010.00
45	199.00	492.50	960.00	1860.00
55	453.00	1122.50	2165.00	4160.00
65	1155.00	2862.50	5515.00	10,500.00
70	1880.00	4165.00	8300.00	16,570.00

has a mortgage to pay off, term insurance can be used to pay off the loan if the debtor dies prematurely. In particular, decreasing term insurance can be effectively used to pay off the mortgage if the family head dies prematurely.

Finally, term insurance can also be used to guarantee future insurability. A person may need large amounts of permanent insurance, but may be financially unable to purchase the needed protection today. A large amount of inexpensive term insurance can be purchased, which can then be converted later into a permanent insurance policy without evidence of insurability.

Limitations of term insurance Although term insurance can be used effectively at younger ages, it is not suitable for lifetime protection. For some individuals, the need for substantial amounts of life insurance will continue beyond age sixty-five or seventy. Term insurance is not appropriate at the older ages, since term insurance premiums increase with age and eventually reach prohibitive levels. Because of the premium increase, some insureds will drop their term insurance policies. Thus, after years of premium payments, they may die uninsured.

In addition, term insurance is not suitable for lifetime protection, since term insurance contracts generally cannot be renewed beyond some stated age, such as age 70. The insured may be financially unable to convert the term insurance into a permanent policy, and the protection would be lost.

Decreasing term insurance should also be used with caution. It has several disadvantages, and so should not be used to meet all of your life insurance needs. For example, if you become uninsurable, the balance of the insurance must be converted into a permanent plan in order to freeze the insurance at its present level. But some decreasing term policies can be converted in an amount equal only to 75 or 80 percent of the remaining insurance. Thus, if the policy is converted, part of the protection is lost, and a much higher premium for the permanent insurance must be paid. If the policy is not converted, the insurance protection continues to decline even though the insured is uninsurable. In contrast, a five-year term insurance policy can avoid this problem. If the insured becomes uninsurable, it is not necessary to convert the term insurance into a permanent policy. Instead, the insurance can be renewed for successive periods. If it becomes necessary to convert the policy, the original face amount of insurance is still available. Most companies will not permit the insured to convert the remaining amount of decreasing term insurance to its original level without furnishing evidence of insurability.

Moreover, decreasing term insurance does not provide for changing needs, such as a birth or adoption of a child. Nor does it provide an effective hedge against inflation. Because of inflation, the amount of life insurance in most families should be periodically increased just to maintain the real purchasing power of the original policy. Thus, decreasing term insurance is a poor inflation hedge. Finally, term insurance cannot be used to provide income for the retirement period or to save money, since most term policies do not accumulate cash values.

Whole Life Insurance

Whole life insurance is permanent insurance that provides lifetime protection. There are several types of whole life insurance. They include:

- Ordinary life insurance (straight life)
- Limited-payment life insurance
- Universal life insurance

Let us examine the major characteristics of each of these forms of whole life insurance.

Ordinary life insurance **Ordinary life insurance** (also called straight life) provides lifetime protection to age 100 and the death claim is a certainty. If the insured is still alive at age 100, the face amount of insurance is paid to the insured.

In addition, premiums are level and do not increase with age. Under a whole life policy, the policyowner is overcharged for the insurance protection during the early years and undercharged during the later years when premiums are inadequate to pay death claims. As we noted in Chapter 16, the excess or redundant premiums are reflected in a liability item known as a legal reserve. The legal reserve makes it possible to provide lifetime protection.

Ordinary life insurance also have an investment or savings element called **cash surrender values.** The cash values are due to the overpayment of insurance premiums during the early years. As a result, the policyowner builds a cash equity in the policy. The policy may be surrendered for its cash value, or the cash may be borrowed under a loan provision. The cash values are relatively small during the early years, but increase over time until they become significant. For example, a $100,000 ordinary life policy issued at age twenty-five would have about $60,000 of cash value at age sixty-five.

Finally, ordinary life insurance provides considerable flexibility. It is the least expensive form of permanent life insurance available. It contains cash surrender or nonforfeiture options, dividend options (if participating), and settlement options that can be used to meet a wide variety of financial needs and objectives. We will examine these options in Chapter 18.

Uses of ordinary life insurance There are two general situations where ordinary life insurance can be used: (1) lifetime protection is needed, and (2) additional savings are desired.

An ordinary life policy can be used in those situations where lifetime protection is needed. This means that the need for life insurance will continue beyond age sixty-five or seventy. Some financial writers and consumer experts point out that the average person does not need large amounts of life insurance beyond age sixty-five, since the need for life insurance declines with age. This is an oversimplification of a complex issue and can be misleading. Some persons may need substantial amounts of life insurance beyond age sixty-five. For example, a cleanup fund is still needed at the older ages; there may be a federal estate tax problem, so substantial amounts of life insurance may be needed for estate liquidity; a divorce settlement may require the purchase and maintenance of a life insurance policy on a divorced spouse, regardless of his or her age; and the policyowner may wish to leave a sizable bequest to the spouse, the children, or a charitable organization, regardless of when death occurs. Since an ordinary life policy can provide lifetime protection, these objectives can be realized even though the insured dies at an advanced age.

Ordinary life insurance can also be used when additional savings are desired. Some insureds wish to meet their protection and saving needs by an ordinary life policy. As we stated earlier, ordinary life insurance builds cash values that can be obtained by surrendering the policy or by borrowing the cash value. However, the desirability of saving through life insurance is highly controversial, and there are some disadvantages of saving through a cash value policy. We will examine life insurance as a method of saving in Chapter 19.

Limitation of ordinary life insurance The major limitation of ordinary life insurance is that some persons will be underinsured even after the policy is purchased. The fundamental objective of life insurance is protection of the human life value. You should make every effort to insure your human life value to its proper level as quickly as possible. However, most persons are limited in the amounts they can spend on life insurance. Unfortunately, because of the savings feature, some persons may voluntarily purchase or else be persuaded by a life insurance agent to purchase an ordinary life policy when term insurance would be the better choice. For example, assume that James, age twenty-five, is a married graduate student with two dependents to support. He estimates that he can spend only $500 annually on life insurance. This premium would purchase about $34,000 of ordinary life insurance. The same premium would purchase about $500,000 of yearly renewable term insurance in many companies. It is difficult to justify the purchase of an ordinary life insurance policy and still be inadequately insured at the same time.

Limited-payment life insurance A **limited-payment policy** is the second form of whole life insurance. The insurance is permanent, and the insured has lifetime protection. The premiums are level, but they are paid only for a certain period. For example, Mary, age twenty-five, may purchase a twenty-year limited payment policy in the amount of $10,000. After twenty years, the policy is completely paid up, and no additional premiums are required. A paid-up policy should not be confused with one that *matures*. A policy matures when the face amount is paid as a death claim or as an endowment. A policy is *paid up* when no further premium payments are required.

The most common limited-payment policies are for ten, twenty, twenty-five, or thirty years. A policy paid up at age sixty-five or seventy is another form of limited-payment insurance. Since the premiums under a limited-payment policy are higher than under an ordinary life policy, cash values are also higher.

A limited-payment policy should be used with caution. It is extremely difficult for a person with a modest income to insure his or her life adequately with a limited-payment policy. Because of relatively high premiums, the amount of permanent life insurance that can be purchased is substantially lower than if an ordinary life policy were purchased. If permanent life insurance is desired, most persons will find that their need for permanent protection can be met more adequately by an ordinary life policy.

For example, based on the rates of one insurer, a male age twenty-five could purchase a $10,000, twenty-year limited-payment policy for about $172. The same premium would purchase about $13,000 of ordinary life insurance, or 30 percent more.

The short term limited-payment policies can be used by individuals whose peak earnings are confined to relatively short periods, such as major league baseball players. The longer term policies, such as a life paid-up at age sixty-five or seventy, may also be appropriate if the policyowner wants the insurance paid up by retirement. However, for most insureds, the need for permanent protection can be adequately met by an ordinary life policy.

Universal life insurance **Universal life** insurance is another type of whole life insurance that is rapidly growing in importance. Conventional cash-value policies have been criticized in recent years because the rates of return on the savings component are relatively low and are not disclosed to policyowners. As a result, many policyowners have replaced their older cash-value policies with newer life insurance products that may offer them higher returns. In addition, because of relatively high interest rates paid by financial institutions in recent years, life insurers have experienced keen competition from money market mutual funds, commercial banks, savings and loan institutions, stock brokerage firms, and other financial institutions. To be more competitive with other financial institutions and to overcome the criticisms against cash-value policies, life insurers now make available a variety of *interest sensitive products. Universal life insurance* is one such product. First introduced in 1979, universal life insurance is growing rapidly. About $124 billion of universal life insurance was in force in the United States at the end of 1983, up sharply from $4.9 billion at the end of 1981.[4]

Basic characteristics *Universal life insurance can be viewed conceptually as a flexible premium deposit fund combined with monthly renewable term insurance.* As such, universal life has certain characteristics that distinguish it from conventional cash-value contracts. They include the following:

- Unbundling of component parts
- Two forms of universal life available
- Relatively higher investment returns
- Considerable flexibility
- Cash withdrawals permitted
- Favorable income tax treatment

Let us briefly examine each of these characteristics.

Unbundling of component parts A distinct characteristic of universal life insurance is the separation or unbundling of three component parts: (1) protection component, (2) savings component, and (3) expense component.[5] The separation of these parts is reported annually to the policyowner in a disclosure statement covering the prior year.

The policyowner determines the amount and frequency of the premium payments, such as a one-time payment, or monthly, quarterly, semiannually, or annually. A deduction is made from each premium payment for commissions, sales, and marketing expenses. The balance of the premium goes into the policy's cash value and interest is credited monthly. A monthly deduction from the cash value is also made for the cost of the insurance protection.

For example, assume that Fred, age thirty-five, buys a universal life policy with a specified death benefit of $200,000 in excess of the cash value. The annual premium payment is $3,000.[6] For sake of simplicity, we will assume that expense charges, mortality charges, and the crediting of interest are made on an annual basis. (Current universal life policies, however, have monthly expense charges, monthly mortality charges, and monthly crediting of interest.)

Assume that each premium is subject to an 8 percent expense charge. Also assume a *first-year* expense charge of a flat $400, plus $1 for each $1,000 of the specified death benefit. In addition, the policy provides for a maximum mortality charge based on the 1958 CSO mortality table, but the current mortality charge is only 80 percent of the maximum rate. Finally, the policy provides a guaranteed interest rate of at least 4 percent on the cash value and a higher return based on current interest rates. Assume that 4 percent interest is being credited on the first $1,000 of cash value, and 11 percent on the cash value in excess of $1,000.

When Fred pays the first $3,000 premium, there is an expense charge of $240 (8 percent of $3,000) and a first-year expense charge of $600 ($400 plus $1 for each $1,000 of the specified $200,000 death benefit). The first year mortality charge is $402 ($2.01 per $1,000 of the specified $200,000 death benefit). The remaining cash value of $1,758 is credited with $123 of interest at the end of the first year (4 percent on the first $1,000 and 11 percent on the excess). Thus, the cash value at the end of the first year is $1,881.

When Fred pays the second premium, there is a deduction of $240 (8 percent of $3,000) for expenses. The balance of the premium ($2,760) is added to the first-year cash value ($1,881), and a deduction of $422 is made for the cost of insurance protection for the second year ($2.11 per $1,000 of the specified $200,000 death benefit). The remaining cash value ($4,219) is credited with $394 of interest at the end of the second year (4 percent on the first $1,000 and 11 percent on the excess). Thus, the second-year cash value is $4,613. This can be summarized as follows:

Policy Year	Premium	Expense Charges	Mortality Charges	Cash Values
1	$3,000	$840	$402	$1,881
2	3,000	240	422	4,613

Two forms of universal life insurance available Two forms of universal life insurance are typically available. *The first form pays a level death benefit;* as the cash value increases over time, the amount of pure insurance protection declines. *The second form provides for a specified amount of insurance plus the accumulated cash value.* Thus, the death benefit will be greater than the original amount of insurance for which you applied.

Relatively higher investment returns Universal life insurance generally provides relatively higher investment returns on the savings element than conventional cash value contracts. Two rates of interest are usually quoted. First, there is a *guaranteed minimum rate return* on the policy's cash value, such as 4 or 4½ percent. Second, *excess interest* is also paid, which is the difference between the current advertised rate (say 11 percent) and the guaranteed rate (say 4½ percent). Some companies pay excess interest only on cash values that exceed $1,000 or outstanding policy loans.

Several methods are currently used to determine the current rate of interest on the cash value.[7] Some companies declare a current rate of interest annually, which rate varies depending on market interest rates. Other companies use an *investment index* to determine the interest rate, such as the current rate of return on ninety-day Treasury bills with an adjustment made for company expenses and profits. Still other companies use a *dual index*, such as the higher of the ninety-day Treasury bill rate or the twenty-year U.S. Government Bond rate, adjusted for company expenses and profits.

Considerable flexibility Universal life insurance has several desirable features that provide considerable flexibility. They include the following:

- Premiums can be increased or decreased, and the frequency of premium payments can be varied.
- Premium payments can be any amount as long as there is sufficient cash value to cover mortality costs and expenses.
- The specified death benefit can be increased or decreased. (Evidence of insurability is usually required to increase the amount of insurance.)
- The policy form can be changed from a level death benefit to a death benefit equal to a specified face amount plus the policy cash value (with evidence of insurability).
- The policyowner can add to the cash value at any time. The amounts that can be added are subject to maximum guideline limits that govern the relationship of the cash value to the death benefit.

INSIGHT 17.1

It's the Rate That Counts

Insurance companies guarantee a minimum interest rate for accumulating universal life cash values, but the actual rates they pay are usually closer to those earned on their investments. The table shows how much difference higher rates can make. The figures are for a $100,000 universal life policy for a 35-year-old male nonsmoker. The premium is $2,000 a year. The 11% rate was being paid recently and guaranteed for 30 days. The 8% figures are included for illustration purposes only. In this type of policy the death benefit is the amount you specify in your application or the cash value plus $25,000, whichever is greater. With other types of policies the beneficiary receives only the face amount.

Year	Guaranteed cash value at 4½%	Death benefit	Cash value at 8%	Death benefit	Cash value at 11%	Death benefit
1	$1,717	$100,000	$1,875	$100,000	$1,930	$100,000
5	9,487	100,000	11,190	100,000	12,226	100,000
10	20,878	100,000	27,499	100,000	32,722	100,000
15	34,457	100,000	51,245	100,000	67,222	100,000
20	50,755	100,000	86,292	111,292	125,614	150,614
25	70,876	100,000	137,548	162,548	223,436	248,436
30	95,828	120,828	212,017	237,017	387,374	412,374

SOURCE: Reprinted with permission from *Changing Times* Magazine, © Kiplinger Washington Editors, Inc., "It's the rate that counts," from "Universal Life Insurance. . ," November 1983. This reprint is not to be altered in any way, except with permission from *Changing Times*.

- ▶ A partial cash withdrawal (not a loan) can be made without terminating the policy.
- ▶ Policy loans are also permitted at competitive interest rates.
- ▶ If the policy permits, additional insureds can be added to the policy.

Insight 17.2 shows how a universal life policy can be changed over time, as the policyowner's financial condition, family responsibilities, and investment objectives change.

Cash withdrawals permitted Part or all of the cash value can also be withdrawn. Interest is not charged on the amounts withdrawn, but the death benefit is reduced by the amount of the withdrawal. Most companies also charge a surrender fee for each cash withdrawal.

Policy loans are also permitted. A fixed annual rate of 8 percent or a variable interest rate is typically charged on the amounts borrowed. In addition the cash value borrowed is normally credited with only the lower guaranteed rate of interest (e.g., 4½ percent).

Favorable tax treatment Universal life insurance generally enjoys the same favorable federal income tax advantages as conventional cash value policies. The death benefit paid to a named beneficiary is normally received income tax free. Interest credited to the cash value is not

INSIGHT 17.2

A Policy that Changes When You Do

To illustrate the flexibility of the new universal life policy, *Changing Times* asked First Penn-Pacific Life Insurance Co. to project the values for a $50,000 policy with a $500 annual premium for a male age 30. The cash values for the company's model, called the Economist, were computed on the basis of two rates of interest—the 4% guaranteed rate and the 9.75% rate the company was paying at the time the table was prepared.

Put into the program were these changes: At 33 the man marries and buys a policy rider providing $20,000 of insurance on his wife's life. That amount is not included in the death benefits shown in the table. When he is 35, a child is born and he increases his insurance by $10,000. From 52 through 55, he withdraws $2,000 a year from the cash value for education expenses, thereby reducing the death benefit. At the 4% rate the cash value would be depleted and his policy would lapse, as would his wife's. At the 9.75% rate, however, enough cash value remains to keep the policy in force. At 66 the man begins withdrawing $3,000 a year to bolster his retirement income, ultimately depleting the cash value and voiding both his and his wife's insurance.

		At 4%		At 9.75%	
Age	Annual premium or withdrawal	Cash value	Death benefit	Cash value	Death benefit
30	$ 500	$ 37	$50,000	$ 37	$50,000
31	500	417	50,000	417	50,000
32	500	812	50,000	812	50,000
33	500	1,183	50,000	1,195	50,000
34	500	1,569	50,000	1,617	50,000
35	500	1,951	60,000	2,059	60,000
36	500	2,339	60,000	2,535	60,000
37	500	2,734	60,000	3,049	60,000
38	500	3,136	60,000	3,605	60,000
39	500	3,537	60,000	4,197	60,000
40	500	3,946	60,000	4,840	60,000
41	500	4,354	60,000	5,528	60,000
42	500	4,751	60,000	6,258	60,000

SOURCE: Reprinted with permission from *Changing Times* Magazine © Kiplinger Washington Editors, Inc., "A Policy that Changes When You Do," August 1981. This reprint is not to be altered in any way, except with permission from *Changing Times.*

taxable to the policyowner in the year credited. The cash value of the policy also accumulates on a tax-deferred basis.

Limitations of universal life insurance Universal life insurance has been widely promoted as an ideal whole life policy that everyone should buy. Although universal life insurance is superior to conventional cash value policies in many respects, it has several limitations. Consumer experts point out the following defects in present universal life insurance contracts.[8]

1. *Misleading rates of return.* As noted earlier, advertised rates of return on most

Age	Annual premium or withdrawal	At 4% Cash value	At 4% Death benefit	At 9.75% Cash value	At 9.75% Death benefit
43	500	5,148	60,000	7,043	60,000
44	500	5,535	60,000	7,880	60,000
45	500	5,902	60,000	8,766	60,000
46	500	6,259	60,000	9,717	60,000
47	500	6,605	60,000	10,739	60,000
48	500	6,931	60,000	11,832	60,000
49	500	7,236	60,000	13,004	60,000
50	500	7,519	60,000	14,265	60,000
51	500	7,772	60,000	15,617	60,000
52	−2,000	5,393	58,000	14,328	58,000
53	−2,000	2,870	56,000	12,879	56,000
54	−2,000	196	54,000	11,253	54,000
55	−2,000	0	0	9,416	52,000
56	500	0	0	10,059	52,000
57	500	0	0	10,695	52,000
58	500	0	0	11,324	52,000
59	500	0	0	11,941	52,000
60	500	0	0	12,544	52,000
61	500	0	0	13,121	52,000
62	500	0	0	13,668	52,000
63	500	0	0	14,163	52,000
64	500	0	0	14,586	52,000
65	500	0	0	14,924	52,000
66	−3,000	0	0	11,556	40,000
67	−3,000	0	0	7,689	37,000
68	−3,000	0	0	3,237	34,000
69	−3,000	0	0	0	0

universal life insurance contracts currently range from about 8 to 11 percent, depending on the company. *However, the rates advertised are gross rates of return and not net rates.* The advertised rates are the rates credited to the money that goes into the savings component after sizable expense charges and the cost of insurance protection are deducted. Also, as noted earlier, some companies pay less than the advertised rates if the cash value is under a certain amount, such as $1,000. After expense charges and the cost of the insurance protection are deducted, the effective yearly returns are substantially lower than the advertised rates and are often negative for the first one to three years after the policy is purchased.

2. *Incomplete disclosure.* We noted earlier that the protection, savings and expense components in a universal life policy are unbundled or separated. *However, this disclosure is incomplete and not rigorous, since the policyowner is not given information on how the expenses are allocated between the protection and savings components in the policy.* Professor Joseph Belth, a widely respected consumer insurance expert, maintains that the cost of the insurance protection and the yearly rate of return on the savings component cannot be accurately determined without making some assumptions concerning the allocation of expenses between the protection and saving components.[9] The early rates of return will vary widely depending on how the expenses are allocated between the protection and savings components. Professor Belth argues that the advertising of universal life insurance policies is often misleading and deceptive because the ads quote a high gross return on the savings component and may also quote a low cost for the protection component, but neither figure includes an allocation of the expense charges. Thus, he argues that net rates of return rather than gross rates should be disclosed to the policyowners.
3. *Decline in interest rates.* A major attraction of universal life insurance is the expectation of relatively high tax-sheltered investment returns in the future. Universal life insurance may not be as attractive to investors if interest rates should decline sharply in the future. Interest rates in recent years have reached historically high levels. Premiums for universal life insurance are generally invested at the present time in short-term investments. If short-term rates should decline sharply relative to long-term rates, universal life insurance could lose much of its competitive edge.

New developments in universal life Many life insurers have modified their initial universal life products one or more times to make them more competitive. Some newer developments include the following:

1. *Reduced loading.* Many companies have reduced the front-end load on universal life products, such as 3 percent instead of 7 to 10 percent. However, the persistency on universal life products in some companies has been poor, so a *rear-end load* is now being used. There is a relatively heavy rear-end surrender charge on the amounts withdrawn that decreases linearly over some time period, such as ten, fifteen, or twenty years.
2. *Elimination of first-year extra expense charge.* Some insurers have eliminated the first-year extra expense charge (such as a flat $400 plus $1 for each $1,000 of insurance).
3. *Payment of current interest rate on all cash value.* Some universal life products now pay current interest rates on all cash values rather than on cash values exceeding $1,000. However, the amount borrowed as a policy loan is still credited with a lower rate of interest (such as 4½ percent).

Endowment Insurance

Endowment insurance is the third basic form of life insurance. An *endowment policy* is one that pays the face amount of insurance if the insured dies within a specified period; if the insured survives to the end of the period, the face amount is paid to him or her at that time. For example, assume that Mary, age twenty-two, purchases a twenty-year endowment policy in the amount of $10,000. If she dies any time within the twenty-year period, the face amount of $10,000 is paid to her beneficiary. If she is alive at the end of the period, the face amount is paid to her.

An endowment policy is a combination of *level term insurance and a pure endowment*. The level term insurance pays the face amount if the insured dies within the stated period. A pure endowment pays the face amount only if the insured is alive at the end of the period.

Most endowment policies are sold for periods of ten, fifteen, twenty, twenty-five, or thirty years. An endowment at age sixty-five or seventy is also available from most companies. Since endowment policies require the payment of relatively high premiums, the cash values are substantially higher than for other policies. Stated differently, the investment element in an endowment policy is relatively high, and the pure insurance protection is relatively low.

Uses of endowment insurance An endowment policy has been sold in the past as a savings plan for individuals who otherwise would not save without the compulsion of regular life insurance premium payments. In addition, an endowment policy can also be used for retirement purposes, such as an endowment at age sixty-five or seventy. The policy matures at the specified retirement age, and the cash is used to provide a life income to the insured.

Finally, an endowment policy can be used to provide for a college education. An educational endowment at age eighteen is often used to provide funds for the children's education. However, an educational endowment is expensive and should not be used if the family head is inadequately insured. We will discuss an educational endowment policy in greater detail later in this chapter.

Limitations of endowment insurance Endowment insurance has three major limitations. First, an endowment policy is expensive, and the family head may be *underinsured* if it is used for basic protection.

A second disadvantage is that the rate of return on the savings element of an endowment policy is dismal. The annual rate of return on an endowment policy is less than 4 percent in many companies.[10] If the objective is to save money, other financial instruments are more desirable, since their rates of return are considerably higher. Such instruments include savings accounts in a commercial bank, savings bank, or savings and loan institution, time certificates, and money market mutual funds.

Finally, when the endowment policy matures, the need for life insurance protection may still be present. For example, a twenty-year endowment purchased at age twenty-five will mature at age forty-five, but the need for protection may still exist. The family head, however, may be uninsurable or substandard in health, and he or she may be unable to purchase a new policy at standard rates.[11]

SPECIAL LIFE INSURANCE POLICIES

Term insurance can be effectively combined with whole life insurance to meet certain needs. In addition, certain life insurance contracts have unique features and are designed for specific purposes. Let us briefly examine some special life insurance policies.

Family Income Policy

The **family income policy** is a combination of decreasing term and whole life insurance. It pays a monthly income of $10 for each $1,000 of life insurance if the insured dies within the family income period. The monthly income is paid to the end of the family income period, at which time the face amount of insurance is paid.

For example, assume that a $10,000, twenty-year family income policy is purchased. If the insured dies five years after the policy is issued, the beneficiary receives $100 monthly for the next 15 years, at which time the face amount of $10,000 is paid. This can be illustrated by Figure 17.2. If a twenty-year family income policy is issued in 1986, and the insured dies in 1990, monthly income of $100 will be paid to 2006, and the face amount of insurance will be paid at that time. If the insured dies, say in 2016, only the face amount of $10,000 will be paid.

As we noted earlier, the family income policy is a combination of decreasing term and whole life

Figure 17.2 $10,000 Family Income Policy, 20-Year Income Period

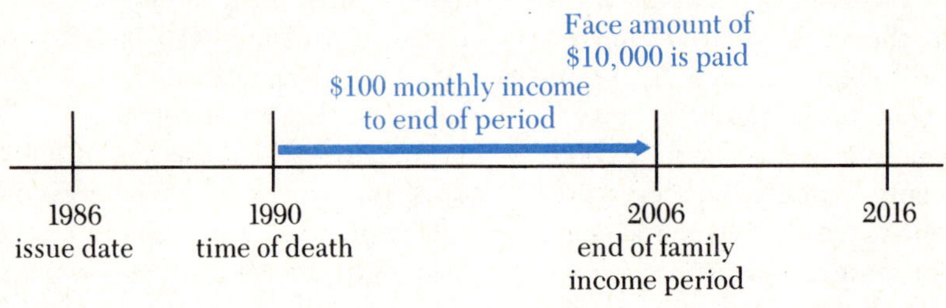

Figure 17.3 $10,000 Family Income Policy, 20-Year Income Period, Issue Age 20; 1958 C.S.O. Table, 2.5 Percent Interest

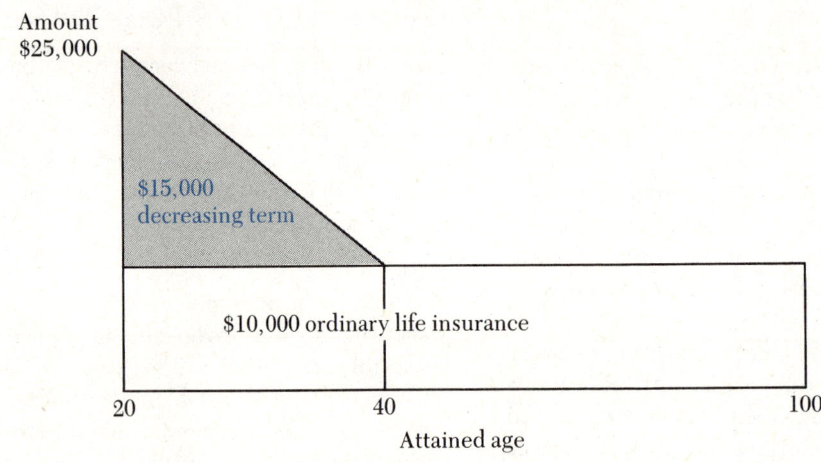

insurance. The monthly income payments are derived from decreasing term insurance and interest on the policy proceeds of the basic contract. The structure of the family income policy can be illustrated by Figure 17.3. About $15,000 of decreasing term and $10,000 of ordinary life insurance are needed to provide monthly income payments of $100 for twenty years.

Family Maintenance Policy

The **family maintenance policy** is a combination of level term and whole life insurance. It pays a monthly income of $10 for each $1,000 of life insurance for a definite time period if the insured dies anytime during the family maintenance period. After the monthly payments expire, the face amount of insurance is then paid. For example, assume that an individual, age twenty, purchases a $10,000, twenty-year family maintenance policy. If *the insured dies anytime within the twenty-year family maintenance period, the beneficiary receives $100 monthly for the full twenty years.* The face amount of insurance on the basic policy is then paid at the end of the payment period.

Figure 17.4 $10,000 Family Maintenance Policy, 20-Year Income Period

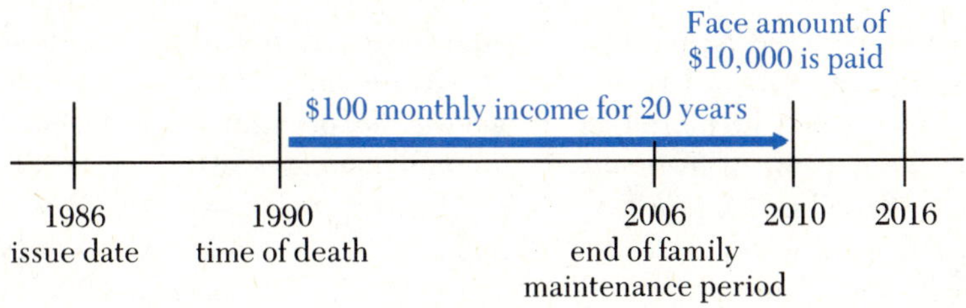

Figure 17.5 $10,000 Family Maintenance Policy, 20-Year Income Period, Issue Age 20; 1958 C.S.O. Table, 2.5 Percent Interest

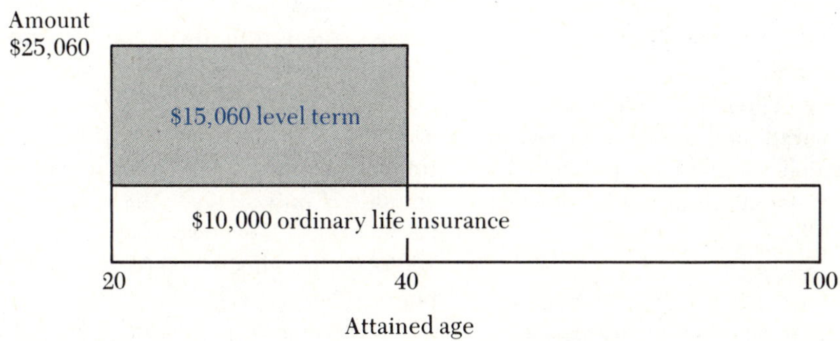

The family maintenance policy can be illustrated by Figure 17.4. If the policy is issued in 1986, and the insured dies in 1990, the beneficiary will receive $100 monthly until 2010, at which time the face amount of insurance will be paid. If the insured dies after the family maintenance period expires, say in 2016, only the face amount will be paid.

As we noted earlier, the family maintenance policy is a combination of level term and whole life insurance. The term insurance is level because the company agrees to make payments for a definite period if death occurs anytime within the family maintenance period. The structure of a family maintenance policy is illustrated in Figure 17.5. About $15,000 of level term and $10,000 of ordinary life insurance are needed to provide monthly income payments of $100 for a full twenty years if death occurs anytime during the family maintenance period.

Family Policy

The **family policy** insures all family members in one policy. The insurance usually is sold in units. One unit typically consists of $5,000 of permanent insurance on the family head, $1,000 of term to age sixty-five on the spouse, and $1,000 of term to age twenty-five on each child's life. The term insurance on the spouse is convertible with no evidence of insurability. Each child can convert up to five times the amount of insurance on his or her life with no evidence of insurability at the end of the term period. There is no increase in premiums if additional children are born. Newborn children are covered after fourteen or fifteen days.

The premium is normally based on the husband's life. If the wife is younger than her husband, the amount of insurance may be more than $1,000; if she is older, the amount of insurance will be less than $1,000. If the husband dies, no additional premium payments are required.

The family policy has several advantages. All family members are insured in one policy, and only one premium is periodically paid. Inexpensive term insurance is provided on the wife and children for burial purposes. The future insurability of the children is also guaranteed, up to some maximum amount.

One disadvantage of the family policy, however, is that the insurance on the family head is permanent insurance. The husband (or wife) may be inadequately insured, and the same premium paid for the family policy could have purchased a substantially higher amount of term insurance on the breadwinner's life.

Specials

Many companies issue policies known as *specials.* These contracts either require the purchase of a minimum amount of life insurance or feature reduced rates as the size of the policy increases. A **special policy** can also refer to a contract that is sold to a preferred group of persons. Special policies are commonly based on the following.[12]

- Minimum insurance amounts
- Quantity discounts
- Preferred risk plans

Some companies require the purchase of a *minimum amount of life insurance,* such as $50,000, $75,000, $100,000 or more. If the minimum amount is purchased, the premium rate per $1,000 of insurance is relatively lower. The purpose of the minimum insurance amount is to reduce the expense rate per $1,000 of life insurance sold. This is based on the recognition that certain fixed expenses are incurred when the policy is sold, regardless of its size. These expenses can be spread over a larger base when minimum amounts of insurance are required.

A *quantity discount* may also be offered where the premium rate declines as the policy amount increases. This can be accomplished by the *band approach* where ranges are established, and a reduced rate is applied to each range. For example, the rate may be $20 per $1,000 if the face amount of insurance is less than $10,000, $19 for policies between $10,000 and under $20,000, and $18 if the policy amounts exceeds $20,000.

A quantity discount can also be granted by the *policy fee* method. This is the most common method used today. Under the policy fee approach, the rate is the same for each policy regardless of size, and a policy fee is added. For example, the basic premium may be $20 per $1,000 for an ordinary life policy issued at age thirty-five plus a $10 policy fee. If the face amount is only $1,000, the effective rate is $30 per $1,000. However, if the face amount is $50,000, the effective rate is reduced to $20.20 per $1,000.

A lower rate may also be charged when the policy is sold to *preferred risks.* These are individuals whose mortality experience is expected to be lower than average. The policy is carefully underwritten and is sold only to individuals whose build, health history, occupation, and habits indicate more favorable mortality than the average. In addition, the company may also require the purchase of a minimum amount of insurance, such as $50,000.

The *nonsmoker's discount* is a current example of a preferred risk policy. Many companies offer substantially lower rates to nonsmokers in recognition of the more favorable mortality that can be expected of this group.

Modified Life Insurance

A **modified life policy** is a whole life policy in which premiums are reduced for the first three to five years and are higher thereafter. The initial premium is slightly higher than for term insurance, but considerably lower than an ordinary life policy issued at the same age.

There are several variations of the modified life policy. Under one version, the premium increases only once at the end of three or five years, and a dividend is paid that can be used to offset most or all of the premium increase. Under another version, the premiums gradually increase each year for five years and remain level thereafter. Finally, term insurance can be used for the first three to five years, which automatically converts into an ordinary life policy at a slightly higher premium than a regular ordinary life policy issued at the same age.

The major advantage of a modified life policy is that insureds can purchase permanent insurance immediately even though they cannot afford the higher premiums for a regular policy. Modified life insurance is particularly attractive to persons who expect that their incomes will increase in the future and that higher premiums will not be financially burdensome.

One major disadvantage of a modified life policy, however, is that premiums may increase during a period of rapid inflation. Some persons may find the premium increases to be financially burdensome, and as a result, they may drop their insurance. Wages may have increased less than expected, or the wage increase may lag behind increases in the cost of living. Thus, during a period of rapid inflation, some insureds may decide to reduce their expenses by dropping their life insurance, especially if the premium has just increased.

Multiple Protection Policy

A **multiple protection policy** is one in which the face amount doubles or triples if death occurs during some specified period. Only the face amount is paid if death occurs after expiration of the period. The period of multiple protection may be ten, fifteen, or twenty years, or it may run to some stated age such as sixty or sixty-five. For example, a $25,000 multiple protection policy with a twenty-year period pays $50,000 if the insured dies within the twenty-year period, but only $25,000 if death occurs after the period expires.

The multiple protection policy consists of permanent insurance and level term insurance for the multiple protection period. A double death benefit consists of permanent insurance and an equal amount of level term insurance. If a triple death benefit is desired, the level term insurance is double the amount of permanent insurance. The term insurance usually can be converted to a permanent policy with no evidence of insurability.

Juvenile Insurance

Juvenile insurance refers to life insurance purchased by a parent or adult on the lives of children under a certain age, such as age fifteen or sixteen. Some common forms of juvenile life insurance are as follows:

- Limited payment or endowment insurance
- Educational endowment at age eighteen
- Jumping juvenile insurance

Limited payment or endowment policies are commonly issued on the lives of children. They typically include life-paid-up-at-age-sixty-five, twenty- or thirty-year limited-payment policies, twenty-year endowment, and an endowment at age eighty-five. These policies build cash values quickly because of the relatively high premiums.

An *educational endowment at age eighteen* is another form of juvenile insurance. The policy matures as an endowment at age eighteen to provide funds for a college education. Many life insurance experts do not recommend an educational endowment policy because it is an expensive method for building a college education fund. The parent often is better off by investing the funds separately or by purchasing an ordinary life policy on his or her life, the cash values of which can provide the necessary college funds. For example, one large insurer charges about

$450 for a $10,000 educational endowment at age eighteen issued on the life of a child under six months of age. If the father, age twenty-five, used the same dollars to purchase a $40,000 ordinary life insurance policy on his life, about $8,400 in cash values would be available in eighteen years, which is only $1,600 less than would be available under the educational endowment policy.[13] If the father died before the child reaches college age, $40,000 would be paid, whereas the juvenile insurance policy may have accumulated only a few thousand dollars of cash value.

In addition, a *payor benefits clause* is frequently included in an educational endowment policy or other juvenile contracts, which increases the premium even more. A payor clause provides that all premiums are waived if the premium payor (such as the father) dies or is totally disabled before the child reaches a specified age.

A **jumping juvenile insurance** policy is another form of permanent life insurance in which the face amount is increased five times at age twenty-one without evidence of insurability or an increase in premiums. Thus, a $5,000 policy issued on a child age five jumps to $25,000 at age twenty-one without evidence of insurability or a premium increase. This contract is often sold as a savings program for college. It can also be used to guarantee the future insurability of the child.

The major danger in insuring children is that the family head may be inadequately insured. Scarce premium dollars that could be used to increase the life insurance on the family head are instead diverted to the children. Moreover, most wives are also underinsured, and a working wife has an enormous human life value. In many cases, the total life insurance on her life is less than $15,000. A child's death normally does not cause a financial hardship to the family, but if the husband or wife dies prematurely, the family may experience great economic insecurity. One study of widows and orphans revealed that the median amount of life insurance benefits received by the family was only $12,160. Thirty-seven percent of the widows in this study received no private life insurance benefits after their husbands' deaths.[14] Therefore, it is clear that children should be insured only after both parents have adequate amounts of life insurance on their lives.

Arguments advanced for life insurance on children are not convincing and often are misleading. One common argument is that insurance on children is cheaper because it is purchased at a younger age. This argument is deceptive. Although insurance premiums on children are lower, they are paid over a much longer time period. Premiums at the older ages are higher, but they are paid for shorter periods of time. Moreover, when present values are taken into account, the child's policy often is more expensive. One study indicated that the present value of a $20,000 life-paid-up-at-age-sixty-five policy issued by one insurer on a child, at age fifteen is $5,584 at a 4 percent discount rate. However, the present value of the same type policy issued by the same insurer at age 35 was only $3,905.[15] In short, a juvenile insurance policy may be no bargain when it comes to cost.

Another argument is that life insurance should be purchased to guarantee the future insurability of the children. This argument has greater validity, but only if the husband and wife are adequately insured. Unfortunately, a guaranteed insurability option cannot be purchased separately but must be added to the permanent life insurance policy. However, the children's future insurability can be guaranteed to a limited extent by the family policy that we discussed earlier; the family policy also provides a modest amount of insurance for burial purposes. Even if the future insurability of the children cannot be guaranteed, the odds are they will still be able to purchase insurance in the future. More than 90 percent of all policies are issued at standard rates.

Variable Life Insurance

Due to inflation, many life insurers are now selling variable life insurance contracts. A **variable life policy** is a policy in which the death benefit varies according to the investment experience of a separate account maintained by the insurer. The purpose of variable life insurance is to maintain the real purchasing power of the death benefit. For example, if the inflation rate is 6 percent, the purchasing power of a $50,000 ordinary life policy will be reduced to $25,000 in only twelve years. The amount of life insurance would have to be increased from $50,000 to $100,000 just to maintain the real purchasing power of the benefits during the same period.

Although there are different policy designs, variable life policies have certain common features. First, a variable life policy is a permanent contract with a level premium.[16] Second, the entire reserve is held in a separate account and is invested largely in equities or other investments. If the investment experience is favorable, the original amount of insurance will be increased. If the investment experience is poor, the amount of insurance can be reduced, but it can never be reduced below the original face amount. Thus, regardless of investment experience, the minimum death benefit will be at least equal to the original face amount, but it could be considerably higher depending on the investment performance of the account. Finally, the risk of excessive mortality and expenses is borne by the insurer, but the investment risk is borne by the insured.

Cost-of-Living Rider

The **cost-of-living rider** is another approach to inflation. Under this provision, the policyowner can purchase one-year term insurance equal to the percentage change in the Consumer Price Index with no evidence of insurability. The amount of term insurance changes each year and reflects the cumulative change in the CPI from the issue date of the policy, although the total amount of term insurance may be limited to one or two times the face amount of insurance. The policyowner pays the entire premium for the term insurance, which means the risk of inflation is borne by the policyowner.

The cost-of-living provision of one large insurer can be illustrated as follows. Assume that George, age twenty-five, purchases an ordinary life policy in the amount of $20,000, and that the cumulative increases in the CPI for the first two years are 13 percent and 20 percent, respectively. The amounts of insurance are as follows:

(Issue date)	*Original policy*	*$20,000*
(Year 1)	*Original policy*	*20,000*
	Term insurance	*2,600*
	Total insurance	*$22,600*
(Year 2)	*Original policy*	*$20,000*
	Term insurance	*4,000*
	Total insurance	*$24,000*

The policyowner can keep the term insurance until the anniversary date of the policy nearest age sixty-five, or until premiums are no longer payable, whichever occurs first, at which time the term insurance terminates. The term insurance can be converted into a permanent plan of insurance with no evidence of insurability.

Adjustable Life Insurance

Life insurance needs are not constant but change over time. For example, marriage, birth or adoption of a child, lay-off from work, responsibility to aged parents, purchase of a home or business, and retirement needs may require substantial adjustments in a personal life insurance program. **Adjustable life insurance** permits certain changes to be made in the amount of life insurance, premiums, period of protection, and duration of the premium-paying period. These adjustments are made within the confines of one contract.

Basic characteristics Adjustable life insurance has four distinct characteristics.[17] First, it combines both term insurance and permanent insurance elements into a single policy. Depending on how the adjustment provisions are exercised, the policy can be changed from term insurance to whole life insurance, and vice versa. The contract can be changed from a low-premium paying policy such as term insurance to a higher-premium policy such as an ordinary life policy or limited-payment contract. The reverse is also true.

Second, adjustable life insurance has the usual features of cash-value life insurance. This includes cash surrender options, dividend options, settlement options, policy loan provision, and other standard provisions. The guaranteed purchase option can also be added, whereby additional insurance can be purchased every three years without evidence of insurability.

Third, and this is the most distinctive feature, the policy is designed to provide considerable flexibility. As financial objectives and needs change, the policyowner can make the following adjustments within certain limits:

- Raise or lower the face amount
- Increase or decrease the premium
- Lengthen or shorten the protection period
- Lengthen or shorten the premium-paying period

Finally, a cost-of-living provision can be attached to most adjustable life policies without any extra premium. Under this provision, the face amount of insurance is automatically increased every three years based on changes in the Consumer Price Index during that period. However, the maximum increase on any option date is limited to 20 percent of the existing face amount, or $20,000, whichever is lower. The policyowner pays for the extra insurance, and evidence of insurability is not required.

Advantages and disadvantages of adjustable life insurance An adjustable life insurance policy has the following advantages:

1. The life insurance can easily be adjusted to changing insurance needs over the life cycle of the insured.
2. It is not necessary to purchase multiple life insurance policies. The life insurance needs of a typical insured can be met with a single policy.
3. The policyowner may benefit from the economies of a single policy versus multiple policies. Premiums are sent to only one company; a change in address, or changes in dividend options, settlement options, beneficiary, policy loans, or other provisions involve only one company.

The disadvantages of adjustable life insurance policies include the following:

1. The policy is more expensive than a traditional term or ordinary life policy.
2. Extra services must be provided to the policyowners, and administrative expenses will be higher under this policy than for traditional policies.

Economatic Policy

An **economatic policy** is a special form of participating whole life insurance in which the dividends are used to buy some combination of term insurance and cash-value insurance equal to the difference between the face amount of insurance and some guaranteed amount. For example, assume that Kenneth, age thirty-five, purchases a $100,000 policy from a large insurer with a guaranteed amount of $65,000. The $35,000 difference is made up by using the dividends to buy a combination of one-year term insurance and paid-up additions. As the years pass, the paid-up additions increase, and the term component declines. After twenty or more years, Kenneth has a whole life policy with a guaranteed amount of insurance equal to the full $100,000. At that time, Kenneth can receive the dividends in cash or use them to buy additional insurance.

The economatic policy has the major advantage of substantially reduced premiums for a permanent policy. In effect, the dividends are used to reduce the premiums but are not directly applied to them. In the preceding illustration, the annual premium for the economatic policy is $1,416. A conventional ordinary life policy issued by the same insurer at the same age would be $2,004, or about 42 percent more.

The disadvantage, however, is that dividends are not guaranteed, and if dividends should be reduced in the future because of adverse economic conditions, the policyowner could have a reduced amount of insurance. Moreover, there is no flexibility in the use of dividends, since they are already committed to keeping the face amount of insurance level.[18]

Deposit Term

A **deposit term policy** is a combination of term insurance for some initial time period (such as ten years) and a modest pure endowment feature.[19] The first-year premium is substantially higher than the renewal premium paid in the second and subsequent years. The difference between the higher first-year premium and subsequent premiums is often referred to as the *deposit.* At the end of the ten years, the policy endows in an amount equal to a multiple of the premium deposit (such as two or three). If the multiple is two times, this is equivalent to a tax-free return of 7.2 percent on the premium deposit.

Several options are available to the policyowner at the end of each ten-year period. The policyowner can (1) renew the policy for another ten-year period with another higher first-year premium, (2) continue the policy as decreasing term insurance to age 100, or (3) convert to some form of whole life or endowment insurance.[20]

The purpose of deposit term insurance is to encourage policyowners to keep their insurance in force. All or part of the extra first-year premium is forfeited if the policy is terminated during the initial term period.

Indeterminate Premium Policies

Stock life insurers sell both participating and nonparticipating life insurance. Because of the substantial decline in life insurance premiums in recent years, nonparticipating policies have become less attractive to insurance purchasers.

An **indeterminate premium policy** is a nonparticipating policy (either whole life, term, or endowment) that permits the company to adjust premiums based on anticipated *future experience.* The maximum premium that can be charged is stated in the policy. The actual premium paid when the policy is issued is considerably lower and may be guaranteed for some initial period, such as two to three years. The intent is to have the actual premium paid reflect current market conditions. After the initial guaranteed period expires, the company can increase premiums up to the maximum limit if future anticipated experience with respect to mortality, investments, and expenses is expected to worsen. However, the premiums may not change if future experience is expected to be similar to past experience. Conversely, if future experience is expected to improve, then the company can reduce the premiums if it desires to do so.

Vanishing Premium Policy

A **vanishing premium policy** is a form of participating whole life insurance in which the premium disappears after a short period, such as five to seven years. For example, one life insurer charges an annual premium of $1,058 for a $100,000 policy issued to a male age thirty-five. After five years, the premiums disappear, and no further premium payments are required.

The mechanics of a vanishing premium policy are simple to understand. Premium projections are based on relatively high current interest rates (such as 11 percent). The dividends are allowed to accumulate at interest or used to purchase paid-up additions to the policy. After a number of years, the accumulated dividends under the policy, plus future dividends, are used to pay future premiums. Alternatively, the paid-up additions can be periodically liquidated as needed and, along with future dividends, used to pay all future premiums. As a result, the premium "vanishes" at the end of some stated time period.

OTHER TYPES OF LIFE INSURANCE

In addition to the basic and special forms of life insurance, other types of life insurance are available, including savings bank life insurance, industrial life insurance, and group life insurance.

Savings Bank Life Insurance

Savings bank life insurance is life insurance that is sold over the counter in mutual savings banks of three states—Massachusetts, New York, and Connecticut. To be eligible, a person must either reside or regularly work in the state where the insurance is sold. Thus, summer residents or nonresident traveling salespersons would be ineligible. The insurance is sold over the counter, so soliciting agents are not used. The objective is to avoid the substantial acquisition expenses incurred by commercial insurers when life insurance is initially sold.

The amount of life insurance that can be purchased is strictly limited by law. The maximum limit on individual coverage is $62,000 in Massachusetts, $30,000 in New York, and $25,000 in Connecticut.[21] Because of political pressures from commercial life insurers and life insurance agents, the amount of insurance that can be purchased has been limited to relatively low levels.

Savings bank life insurance is low-cost life insurance. Thus, there are some substantial price advantages for thrifty insurance consumers who reside or work in the three states where the insurance is sold. Based on the interest adjusted cost method, the net cost of the life insurance is substantially lower than policies sold by many commercial life insurers.[22] This is partly due, of course, to the method of selling. The insurance is sold only on a walk-in basis, so there are no overhead expenses for a field force of agents.

Industrial Life Insurance

Industrial life insurance is a class of insurance in which the policies are sold in small amounts, usually $1,000 or less, and the premiums are paid monthly or weekly to an insurance agent (called a **debit agent**) at the policyowner's home. Nine out of ten industrial policies in force have cash values.

Industrial life insurance rates generally are substantially higher than rates charged for ordinary insurance. The higher cost is due to three reasons. First, mortality costs are relatively higher since the policies typically are written on low-income persons without a medical examination. Second, selling and administrative costs are relatively higher since agents collect the premiums at the policyowners' homes. Third, lapse rates are much higher than other forms of life insurance.

Industrial life insurance has gradually declined in relative importance. It now accounts for less than 1 percent of the total life insurance in force. It has declined in importance because of the rapid increase in group life insurance plans provided by employers, and also because of the desire and increased financial ability of American workers to purchase larger amounts of life insurance.

Group Life Insurance

Group life insurance is an important form of life insurance that provides life insurance on a number of persons in a single master contract. Physical examinations are not required, and certificates of insurance are issued to members of the group as evidence of insurance.

Group life insurance is rapidly growing and now accounts for about 46 percent of the total amount of life insurance in force in the United States. It is an important fringe benefit provided by employers. We will examine group life insurance in greater detail in Chapter 22.

This concludes our discussion of life insurance in this chapter. Let us next consider annuities.

ANNUITIES

Annuities are designed to provide retirement income to individuals. They can greatly enhance the economic security of individuals during their old age. Let us begin by examining the concept of an annuity.

Annuity Concept

An **annuity** can be defined as a periodic payment to an individual that continues for a fixed period or for the duration of a designated life or lives.

The person who receives the periodic payments or whose life governs the duration of payments is known as the **annuitant.** *The fundamental purpose of a **life annuity** is to provide a lifetime income to an individual that cannot be outlived.* An annuity is the opposite of life insurance. Life insurance creates an immediate estate and provides protection against dying too soon before financial assets can be accumulated. An annuity is designed to liquidate a principal sum and provides protection against living too long. It provides protection against the loss of income because of excessive longevity and the exhaustion of one's savings.

Annuities are possible because the risk of excessive longevity is pooled by the group. Individuals acting alone cannot be certain that their savings will be sufficient during retirement. Some persons may die early before exhausting their savings, while others will still be alive after their principal is exhausted. These persons can come together as a group, deposit their savings with an insurance company, and receive a guarantee of a lifetime income. Although the insurer cannot predict how long an individual member of the group will live, the company can determine the approximate number of annuitants who will still be alive at the end of each successive year. Thus, the company can calculate the amount that each person must contribute to the pool. Interest can be earned on the funds before they are paid out. Also, some annuitants will die early, and their unliquidated principal can be used to provide additional payments to those annuitants who survive beyond their life expectancy. Thus, the annuity payments consist of three sources: (1) premium payments, (2) interest earnings, and (3) the unliquidated principal of annuitants who die early. By pooling the risk of excessive longevity, annuitants can be provided with a periodic income that they cannot outlive.

Finally, annuitants tend to be healthy individuals who live longer than most persons. In recognition of their increased life expectancy, special annuity tables are used to compute the premium payments. The 1958 C.S.O. Mortality Table is not used. The annuity tables used to compute premiums run to age 115 rather than to age 100 for a mortality table.

Types of Annuities

A wide variety of annuities are presently sold by insurers. For sake of convenience, the different types of annuities can be classified as follows:

1. Time when payments begin
   a. Immediate annuity
   b. Deferred annuity
2. Nature of the insurer's obligation
   a. Life annuity (no refund)
   b. Life annuity with installments certain
   c. Installment or cash refund annuity
   d. Joint-and-survivor annuity
3. Fixed or variable benefits
   a. Fixed annuity
   b. Variable annuity

Let us briefly examine each of them.

Time when payments begin Annuities can be classified according to the time when the payments begin. The annuity payments can be made monthly, quarterly, semiannually, or annually. The payments can start immediately or be deferred until some later date.

1. **Immediate annuity.** *An immediate annuity is one where the first payment is due one payment interval from the date of purchase.* If the income is paid monthly, the first payment starts one month from the purchase date, or one year from the purchase date if the income is paid annually.

Immediate annuities are typically purchased in a lump sum by people near retirement. For example, assume that Joseph retires at age sixty-five, and wishes to supplement his Social Security retirement benefits. He has $60,000 of savings which he uses to buy a single-premium immediate annuity that will pay him a monthly lifetime income of $680.

2. **Deferred annuity.** A *deferred annuity provides an income at some future date.* Several

INSIGHT 17.3

Single Premium Deferred Annuity

Single premium deferred annuities (SPDA) have become attractive investments in recent years because of favorable income tax advantages and relatively high yields. A SPDA can also be used to fund an Individual Retirement Account (IRA), Keogh plan for the self-employed, or other qualified pension plan (see Chapter 23).

A SPDA has certain basic features. They include the following:

1. *Tax-deferred interest accumulation.* Although income on a SPDA does not eliminate your income tax liability, all interest income earned accumulates on a tax-deferred basis. As such, sizable amounts can be accumulated during your working career. This can be illustrated by the following example, which is based on an annual contribution of $2,000, 8 percent interest, and representative annuity rates for males in early 1983.[1]

Invested over 30 years	Total accumulated	Annual payout starting at age 65
$60,000	$244,692	$27,750
Invested over 20 years		
$40,000	$ 98,846	$11,200
Invested over 10 years		
$20,000	$ 31,291	$ 3,550

2. *Guarantee of principal.* Despite the default on annuities sold by the Baldwin-United Companies in 1983, SPDA's are generally considered safe investments for conservative investors. The principal is usually guaranteed, which means that if the annuity is surrendered, you will never re-

types of deferred annuities are sold today. A popular form of deferred annuity is the *retirement* annuity. It is essentially a plan for accumulating a sum of money for retirement purposes. The premium for the annuity is usually based on $10 of monthly retirement income that will begin at some selected age, usually age sixty-five. The premiums are accumulated at interest (less expenses) prior to retirement. At the maturity date, the annuitant can elect to have the accumulated sum applied under one of the annuity options stated in the contract. Typical options include the pure life annuity, life income with five, ten, fifteen, or twenty years certain, installment refund, and cash refund options. The *cash option* is also available, by which cash is elected rather than the annuity. But this leads to adverse selection since those in poor health will elect to take the cash rather than the annuity.

If the annuitant dies during the period prior to retirement (called the *accumulation period)*, the death benefit is paid equal to the sum of the premiums paid, or the cash value, if higher. If the annuitant dies during the liquidation period, any death benefit paid will depend on the annuity option selected. For example, if a life annuity option is selected, nothing is paid. If a life income with ten years certain is selected, payments continue to the beneficiary if fewer than ten years of payments have been received. Prior to the matu-

ceive less than the original single premium (less any cash withdrawals and state premium taxes, if any). In addition, twenty-nine states have state guaranty funds that protect the policyowners in failed companies.

3. *Guarantee of interest.* The quoted interest rate on the single premium deposit is usually guaranteed from some initial time period, such as three months to four years. After that time, the interest rate will vary, depending on current market conditions. In 1985, insurers generally were guaranteeing a return of 10 to 11½. percent on newly issued contracts depending on the company. Companies also guarantee a minimum interest rate on the cash value, such as 4½ or 5½ percent, regardless of actual interest rates.

4. *No load.* Most SPDA's are sold without any sales charges or fees. The entire premium is credited with the initial interest rate from the date the contract is issued. However, as will be pointed out later, there may be a *back-end load* if you make a withdrawal that exceeds the maximum allowed during a contract year.

5. *Withdrawal of funds.* If a need arises, most SPDA's permit the withdrawal of a specified percentage of the account during the contract year, such as 7 to 10 percent annually. However, withdrawals in excess of the allowed amounts are subject to a surrender charge which declines over time. For example, one insurer imposes a surrender charge of 7 percent of the excess amount withdrawn during the first contract year, which declines to zero after the seventh contract year.

In addition, most companies have a bail-out provision that permits the withdrawal of funds without penalty if the current interest rate declines substantially below the initial interest rate. For example, one company permits the withdrawal of funds with no surrender charge if the interest rate declared for the current contract year is more than one percentage point below the initial two-year rate.

6. *Minimum premium.* Most companies require a minimum single premium of $5,000. However, for tax-qualified contracts, such as an IRA, the minimum single premium required is $2,000.

[1]American Council of Life Insurance, *What You Should Know About Annuities* (December 1983), p. 9.

rity date, the retirement annuity has a cash surrender value and loan provision. The annuity can be surrendered for its cash value, or the cash value can be borrowed.

The *retirement income policy* (often called a retirement endowment) is a variation of the retirement annuity. The retirement income policy is similar to the retirement annuity except that it provides a substantial amount of life insurance equal to $1,000 for each $10 of monthly retirement income, or the cash value, if higher. For example, a $500 monthly retirement income policy would initially provide $50,000 of life insurance. The cash value in the policy eventually will exceed the face amount of insurance, and it then becomes the death benefit paid prior to retirement. Any death benefit after retirement will depend on the annuity option selected.

A deferred annuity can be purchased with a lump sum, or the contract may permit flexible premiums. If you purchase a deferred annuity with a lump sum, it is called a *single premium deferred annuity.* Because of relatively high investment returns and tax-free buildup during the accumulation period, single premium deferred annuities have been increasingly popular with investors in recent years (see Insight 17.3).

A deferred annuity can also be purchased with flexible premiums. A *flexible premium annuity* is a contract that permits the annuity owner to vary the premium deposits. There is no requirement that a specified amount must be deposited each year. The amount of retirement income will depend on the accumulated sum in the annuity at retirement.

Nature of the insurer's obligation Annuities can also be classified in terms of the insurer's obligation under the contract. Payments may be made only during the lifetime of the annuitant or the annuity may guarantee a certain number of payments. In addition, the annuity payments may be based on two or more lives.

1. *Life annuity (no refund).* A **life annuity** provides a lifetime income to the annuitant only while he or she is alive. No further payments are made after the annuitant dies. A pure life annuity pays the highest amount of lifetime income for each dollar spent. It is suitable for a person who needs maximum lifetime income and has no dependents or has provided for them through other means.
2. *Life annuity with installments certain.* A *life annuity with installments certain* is one that pays a life income to the annuitant with a certain number of guaranteed payments. If the annuitant dies before receiving the guaranteed number of payments, the remaining payments are paid to a designated beneficiary.

   This option can be used by someone who needs lifetime income and also wishes to provide income to the beneficiary in the event of an early death. Due to the guaranteed payments, the income paid is relatively less than the income paid by a pure life annuity.
3. *Installment or cash refund annuity.* An **installment refund annuity** pays the annuitant a lifetime income. However, if the annuitant dies before receiving total payments equal to the premiums paid, the income payments continue to the beneficiary until they equal the sum of the premiums paid.

   Another version of this option is the *cash refund annuity.* If the annuitant dies before receiving total payments equal to the sum of the premiums paid, the balance is paid in one lump sum to the beneficiary.
4. *Joint-and-survivor annuity.* A **joint-and-survivor annuity** is based on the lives of two or more annuitants, such as a husband and wife or brother and sister. The annuity income is paid until the death of the last annuitant. Some contracts pay the full amount of original income until the last survivor dies. Other plans pay only two-thirds or one-half of the original income when the first annuitant dies.

Fixed or variable benefits Annuities can also be classified in terms of fixed or variable benefits.

1. *Fixed annuity.* Under a *fixed annuity,* the periodic payment is a guaranteed fixed amount; during the accumulation period, the premiums are invested in bonds, mortgages, and other fixed income securities with a guaranteed return.
2. *Variable annuity.* In contrast, a **variable annuity** is an annuity that provides a lifetime income, but the periodic income payments will vary depending on the level of common stock prices. *The fundamental purpose of the variable annuity is to provide an inflation hedge by maintaining the real purchasing power of the periodic payments during retirement.* It is based on the assumption that a long run correlation exists between the cost of living and common stock prices. The variable annuity was first issued by the College Retirement Equities Fund (CREF) in July, 1952. Since that time, most major life insurers have offered variable annuity products to the public.

Figure 17.6
CREF Annuity Unit Values Since 1952 (Annuity Year: May through April)

1952	$10.00	1963	22.68	1974	26.21
1953	9.46	1964	26.48	1975	21.84
1954	10.74	1965	28.21	1976	26.24
1955	14.11	1966	30.43	1977	24.80
1956	18.51	1967	31.92	1978	23.28
1957	16.88	1968	29.90	1979	27.28
1958	16.71	1969	32.50	1980	26.27
1959	22.03	1970	28.91	1981	35.86
1960	22.18	1971	30.64	1982	30.56
1961	26.25	1972	35.74	1983	42.52
1962	26.13	1973	31.58		

Basic characteristics of a variable annuity The variable annuity has certain basic characteristics. The premiums are invested in a portfolio of common stocks or other investments which presumably will increase in value during a period of inflation. The premiums are used to purchase **accumulation units** during the period prior to retirement, and the value of each accumulation unit varies depending on common stock prices. For example, assume that the accumulation unit is initially valued at $1, and the annuitant makes a monthly premium payment of $100. During the first month, 100 accumulation units are purchased.[23] If common stock prices increase during the second month, and the accumulation unit rises to $1.10, about 91 accumulation units can be purchased. If the stock market declines during the third month, and the accumulation unit declines to $0.90, about 111 accumulation units can be purchased. Thus, accumulation units are purchased over a long period of time in both rising and falling markets.

At retirement, the accumulation units are then converted into **annuity units.** The number of annuity units remains constant, but the value of each unit will change each month or year depending on the level of common stock prices. For example, at retirement, let us assume that the annuitant has 10,000 accumulation units that have a current market value of $60,000. Assume that the accumulation units are converted into 100 annuity units.[24] As we stated earlier, the number of annuity units remains constant, but the value of each unit will change over time. Let us assume that the annuity unit is initially valued at $5 when the annuitant retires. A monthly income of $500 will be paid. During the second month, if the annuity unit increases in value to $5.10, the monthly income also increases to $510. During the third month, if the annuity units decline to $4.90 because of a stock market decline, the monthly income is reduced to $490. Thus, the monthly income depends on the level of common stock prices.

How well has the variable annuity worked? We stated earlier that the variable annuity is based on the assumption of a long run correlation between common stock prices and the Consumer Price Index. In the short run, however, the assumption that common stocks are a good inflation hedge is highly questionable. The variable annuity can become an extremely dangerous financial instrument, since monthly retirement benefits may decline during a period of rapid inflation. This can be illustrated by Figure 17.6,

Figure 17.7
Comparision of CREF Annuity Unit with the Consumer Price Index 1970–1983

Year	Percent increase in Consumer Price Index	Percent increase or decrease in CREF annuity unit
1970	5.9%	−11.0%
1971	4.3	6.0
1972	3.3	16.6
1973	6.2	−11.6
1974	11.0	−17.0
1975	9.1	−16.7
1976	5.8	20.1
1977	6.5	− 5.5
1978	7.7	− 6.1
1979	11.3	17.2
1980	13.5	− 3.7
1981	10.4	36.5
1982	6.1	−14.8
1983	3.2	39.1
1970–83	156.6	47.1

Source: *Economic Report of the President* (Washington, D.C.: U.S. Government Printing Office, 1984), Table B54, pp. 282–83. and Table 1.

which shows the value of the CREF annuity unit from 1952 through 1983.

The annuity unit initially increased from $10 in 1952 to $42.52 in 1983. However, during specific periods of rapid inflation, the value of the annuity unit has declined. In particular, the variable annuity performed poorly during the 1970s. This can be illustrated by Figure 17.7, which compares the annual increase of the CPI with the percentage increase or decrease in the value of the CREF annuity unit from 1970 through 1983. Although the CPI increased each year during this fourteen-year period, the value of the annuity unit increased in only seven years. For the entire period, the CPI increased about 157 percent, while the annuity unit increased about 47 percent.

How can wc explain this undesirable result? In recent years, common stock prices have been extremely sensitive to rising interest rates during periods of rapid inflation. During periods of rapidly rising prices, interest rates have increased sharply, and the stock market has reacted by moving in the opposite direction. Thus, the variable annuity benefit may be reduced at the wrong point of time. Instead of having an inflation hedge, the annuitant suffers a further decline in the purchasing power of the monthly benefit.

SUMMARY

- There are three basic types of life insurance. They are: term insurance, whole life insurance, and endowment insurance.
- *Term insurance* provides temporary protection and is renewable and convertible without evidence of insurability. Term insurance is appropriate when income is limited, or temporary needs must be fulfilled. However, since term insurance usually has no cash values, it cannot be used for retirement or savings purposes.
- There are several forms of whole life insurance. *Ordinary life insurance* is a form of whole life insurance that provides lifetime protection to age 100. The premiums are level and are payable for life. The policy develops an investment or savings element called cash surrender values, which result from the overpayment of premiums during the early years. An ordinary life policy is appropriate when lifetime protection is desired or additional savings are desired.
- A *limited-payment policy* is another form of whole life insurance. The insured also has lifetime protection. However, the premiums are paid only for a limited period, such as ten, twenty, or thirty years, or until age sixty-five.

- *Universal life insurance* is another form of whole life insurance. Conceptually, universal life can be viewed as a flexible premium deposit fund combined with monthly renewable term insurance. Universal life insurance has the following features:
  a. Unbundling of protection, savings, and expense components.
  b. Two forms of universal life available.
  c. Relatively higher investment returns.
  d. Considerable flexibility.
  e. Cash withdrawals permitted.
  f. Favorable income tax treatment.
- *Endowment insurance* is the third type of life insurance. An endowment policy pays the face amount of insurance if the insured dies within a specified period. If the insured survives to the end of the endowment period, the face amount of insurance is paid to him or her at that time.
- The *family income policy* is a combination of decreasing term and whole life insurance. It pays a monthly income of $10 for each $1,000 of life insurance if the insured dies within the family income period. The monthly income is paid to the end of the period, at which time the face amount of insurance is paid.
- The *family maintenance policy* is a combination of level term and whole life insurance. Monthly income is paid for a definite period of time if the insured dies within the family maintenance period. The face amount of insurance is paid after the monthly payments expire.
- The *family policy* insures all members in one policy. It provides permanent insurance on the family head and term insurance on the spouse and children. The term insurance is convertible with no evidence of insurability. Each child can convert up to five times the amount of insurance on his or her life.
- Companies also offer various types of *special policies* in which the rate decreases as the amount of insurance purchased increases. Special policies are based on the purchase of minimum policy amounts, quantity discounts, or the sale of insurance only to preferred risks.
- A *modified life policy* is a whole life policy in which premiums are reduced for the first three to five years and are higher thereafter. A *multiple protection policy* is one in which the face amount is doubled or tripled if death occurs within some specified period.
- *Juvenile insurance* refers to life insurance purchased by a parent or adult on the lives of children under a certain age, such as age fifteen or sixteen. An *educational endowment policy* is an example of juvenile insurance in which the policy matures at age eighteen to provide funds for a college education.
- A *variable life policy* is designed as an inflation hedge. The death benefit varies according to the investment experience of a separate account maintained by the insurer. The *cost-of-living rider* is another approach to inflation whereby the policyowner can purchase one-year term insurance equal to the percentage change in the Consumer Price Index with no evidence of insurability.
- *Adjustable life insurance* allows the policyowner to adjust the life insurance to changing insurance needs. Certain changes can be made in the amount of life insurance, premiums, period of protection, and duration of the premium-payment period.
- An *economatic policy* is a special whole life policy in which the dividends are used to buy some combination of term insurance and cash-value insurance equal to the difference between the face amount of insurance and some guaranteed amount.

- A *deposit term policy* requires a substantially higher first-year premium. The extra premium or deposit earns a relatively high tax-free rate of return if the insurance is kept in force. Part or all of the deposit is forfeited if the policy lapses during some initial term period, such as ten years.
- An *indeterminate premium policy* is a special nonparticipating policy that permits the company to increase premiums up to some minimum limit based on future anticipated experience. The actual premiums paid are substantially lower when the policy is first issued.
- A *vanishing premium policy* is a participating whole life policy in which the premiums disappear after a short time period, such as five to seven years.
- Other types of life insurance include savings bank life insurance, industrial life insurance, and group life insurance.
- An annuity is a plan that provides periodic payments to an individual, which continue for a fixed period or for the duration of a designated life or lives. The fundamental purpose of life annuity is to provide a lifetime income to an individual that cannot be outlived.
- Annuities can be classified in terms of the following:
  a. Time when payments begin
    1. Immediate annuity
    2. Deferred annuity

  b. Nature of the insurer's obligations
    1. Life annuity (no refund)
    2. Life annuity with installments certain
    3. Installment or cash refund annuity
    4. Joint-and-survivor annuity

  c. Fixed or variable benefits
    1. Fixed annuity
    2. Variable annuity

QUESTIONS FOR REVIEW

1. Describe the three basic forms of life insurance.
2. Why is term insurance not suitable for lifetime protection?
3. Under what situations can an ordinary life policy be used?
4. Explain the essential features of universal life insurance.
5. Explain the limitations of endowment insurance.
6. Describe briefly the family income, family maintenance, and family policies.
7. What is a *special* policy?
8. Should life insurance be purchased on the lives of children? Explain.
9. Describe the major features of a variable life insurance policy.
10. What is the fundamental objective of an annuity?
11. Describe the basic types of individual annuities that are sold today.

QUESTIONS FOR DISCUSSION

1. Stanley wants to purchase a five-year term insurance policy in the amount of $50,000. The policy is both renewable and convertible.
   a. Describe the situations under which term insurance can be used.
   b. What rights does Stanley have because the policy is *renewable* and *convertible?* Explain your answer.
   c. If Stanley wishes to save money for retirement purposes, do you recommend the purchase of this contract?
2. Mary is age thirty-five and is considering the purchase of the following individual life insurance policies with a face amount of $50,000:
   Five-year renewable and convertible term policy (renewable until age sixty-five)
   Ordinary life policy
   Twenty-payment life policy
   Endowment at age sixty-five
   a. Which of these contracts requires the *highest* and *lowest* current annual premium outlay?
   b. Which contract will provide the highest amount of retirement income at age sixty-five? Explain your answer.
   c. If Mary intends to keep the insurance until age sixty-five, under which of these contracts will the annual premium increase?
   d. Which of these contracts will allow Mary to continue her life insurance beyond age sixty-five? Explain your answer.
3. Five years ago, Jeffrey purchased a twenty-year family income policy in the amount of $40,000. The policy provides for a family income benefit of $10 for each $1,000 of insurance.
   a. If Jeffrey died today, what benefits would be paid to his beneficiary?
   b. If Jeffrey died twenty years from today, would your answer to *(a)* be different? Explain.
   c. Briefly describe the structure of the family income policy.
4. For each of the following situations, describe a life insurance policy that can be used to meet the situation. Treat each item separately.
   a. Retirement income to supplement Social Security benefits at age sixty-five.
   b. Protection of the face amount of life insurance against the effects of inflation.
   c. Monthly income to the family if the insured dies prematurely.
   d. Insuring the human life value of an individual, age twenty-two, at the lowest possible annual premium.
   e. Life insurance that is paid up when the insured retires at age sixty-five.
   f. Life insurance that reflects a quantity discount as the amount of life insurance increases.
   g. Funds for college when a child reaches age eighteen.
   h. A policy that adjusts the amount of life insurance to changing insurance needs.
   i. Insurance that is sold over the counter.
   j. A policy in which the face amount is doubled if the insured dies within a certain period.
5. *a.* How is universal life insurance similar to conventional cash-value policies?
   b. How does universal life insurance differ from conventional cash-value policies?
6. Although annuities and life insurance are based on the principles of pooling and compound interest, there are some important differences between them.

a. Describe the major differences between life insurance and annuities.
b. Explain briefly each of the following type of individual annuities:
retirement income policy
life annuity with twenty years certain
variable annuity

KEY CONCEPTS AND TERMS TO KNOW

Term insurance
Reentry term
Ordinary life insurance
Limited-payment insurance
Universal life
Endowment insurance
Renewable
Convertible
Attained age method
Retroactive method
Cash surrender values
Family income policy
Family maintenance policy
Family policy
Special policies
Modified life policy
Multiple protection policy
Educational endowment
Jumping juvenile policy
Variable life insurance
Cost-of-living rider
Adjustable life insurance
Economatic policy
Deposit term policy
Indeterminate premium policy
Vanishing premium policy
Savings bank life insurance
Industrial life insurance
Debit agent
Annuity
Annuitant
Life annuity
Installment refund annuity
Immediate annuity
Deferred annuity
Joint-and-survivor annuity
Variable annuity
Accumulation unit
Annuity unit

SUGGESTIONS FOR ADDITIONAL READING

American Council of Life Insurance. *A Consumer's Guide to Life Insurance*. Washington, D.C.: American Council of Life Insurance, 1982.

Belth, Joseph M. *Life Insurance: A Consumer's Handbook*, 2nd ed. Bloomington, Indiana: Indiana University Press, 1985.

Buechner, Robert W., Thomas F. Eason, and David L. Manzier. *Why Universal Life?* 2nd ed. Cincinnati, Ohio: The National Underwriter Company, 1983.

Consumers Union. *The Consumers Union Report on Life Insurance: A Guide to Planning and Buying the Protection You Need*, 4th ed. Mount Vernon, New York: Consumers Union, 1980.

Consumers Union. "Life Insurance—A Special Two-Part Report," *Consumer Reports*, Vol. 45, No. 2 (February 1980), and No. 3 (March 1980).

Huebner, S. S. and Kenneth Black, Jr. *Life Insurance*, 10th ed. Englewood Cliffs, New Jersey: Prentice-Hall, 1982.

Hunt, James H. *Universal Life: How Good Is It?* Alexandria, Virginia: National Insurance Consumer Organization, 1982.

Mehr, Robert I. and Sandra G. Gustavson. *Life Insurance: Theory and Practice*, 3rd ed. Dallas, Texas: Business Publications Inc., 1984.

Williams, Jr., C. Arthur and Richard M. Heins. *Risk Management and Insurance*, 5th ed. New York: McGraw-Hill Book Company, 1985, chapter 23.

NOTES

1. These characteristics are discussed in greater detail in Dan M. McGill, *Life Insurance*, rev. ed. (Homewood, Illinois: Richard D. Irwin, Inc., 1967), pp. 43–57.
2. McGill, p. 47.
3. Consumers Union, *The Consumers Union Report on Life Insurance* (Mount Vernon, New York: Consumers Union, 1980), p. 65.
4. *Life Insurance Fact Book*, 1984, p. 26.
5. For a complete analysis of the unbundling of universal life policies, see Joseph M. Belth, ed., "The War Over Universal Life—Part 1," *The Insurance Forum*, Vol. 8, No. 11 (November 1981), pp. 137–140.
6. The figures in this illustration are derived from Belth, "The War Over Universal Life—Part 1," p. 138.
7. Robert W. Buechner, Thomas F. Eason, and David L. Manzier, *Why Universal Life?* 2nd ed. (Cincinnati, Ohio: The National Underwriter Company, 1983), p. 57.
8. The limitations of universal life are discussed in considerable detail in Belth, ed., "The War Over Universal Life—Part 1," pp. 137–140, and "The War Over Universal Life—Part 2," *The Insurance Forum*, Vol. 8, No. 12 (December 1981), pp. 141–144. See also, "Universal Life Insurance," *Consumer Reports*, Vol. 47, No. 1 (January 1982), pp. 42–44.
9. See Belth, "The War Over Universal Life—Part 1," pp. 137–140.
10. See Joseph M. Belth, "Watch Out for Those Endowment Policies," *The Insurance Forum*, Vol. 5, No. 3 (March 1978) and Joseph M. Belth, "More on Endowment Policies," *The Insurance Forum*, Vol. 6, No. 1 (January 1979).
11. Some companies will permit the policyowner to keep the endowment policy in force beyond the normal maturity date.
12. McGill, pp. 68–70, 250–51.
13. Claude C. Lilly, Glenn L. Wood, and Jerry S. Rosenbloom, *Personal Risk Management and Insurance*, Volume I (Malvern, Pennsylvania: The American Institute for Chartered Property and Casualty Underwriters, 1978), pp. 362–63.
14. George E. Rejda, *Social Insurance and Economic Security*, 2nd ed. (Englewood Cliffs, New Jersey: Prentice-Hall, Inc., 1984), p. 56.
15. Lilly, p. 363.
16. In some variable life policies, premiums can vary depending on the investment experience.
17. Charles L. Trowbridge, "Adjustable Life—A New Solution to an Old Problem," *Journal of the American Society of Chartered Life Underwriters*, Vol. 31, No. 4 (October 1977).
18. *The Consumers Union Report on Life Insurance*, pp. 129–132.
19. S. S. Huebner and Kenneth Black, Jr., *Life Insurance*, 10th ed. (Englewood Cliffs, New Jersey: Prentice-Hall, Inc., 1982), p. 127.
20. Huebner, p. 127.
21. American Council of Life Insurance, *Life Insurance Fact Book*, 1984, p. 101.
22. The interest adjusted method for determining the cost of life insurance is discussed in Chapter 19.
23. We will ignore any deduction for administrative and sales expenses. Many individual variable annuity contracts have a front-end load.
24. The actual number of annuity units will depend on the age of the annuitant, the number of guaranteed payments, the conversion rates, the assumed investment return, and other factors.

CHAPTER 18

LIFE INSURANCE CONTRACTUAL PROVISIONS

"Nearly every family buys life insurance; yet few policyholders ever read a life contract with any effort to understand its provisions."

Robert I. Mehr, *Life Insurance: Theory and Practice*

STUDENT LEARNING OBJECTIVES

After studying this chapter, you should be able to:

- Explain the important contractual provisions that are present in life insurance policies.
- Describe the different types of dividend options.
- Explain the nonforfeiture options that are found in cash-value life insurance contracts.
- Describe the settlement options for the payment of life insurance proceeds.
- Describe some additional benefits and riders that can be added to a life insurance policy, including:
  - waiver of premium
  - guaranteed purchase option
  - double indemnity rider

Although most persons own life insurance, they seldom read their policies in order to understand the basic provisions. As a result, they fail to obtain the maximum benefits and financial flexibility from their policies.

In this chapter, we will discuss some common life insurance policy provisions. We will first examine some important contractual provisions that appear in life insurance policies. We will then consider the basic options that are frequently found in life insurance contracts, including dividend options, nonforfeiture options, and settlement options. We will conclude the chapter by describing some additional benefits and riders that can be added to a life insurance policy.

LIFE INSURANCE CONTRACTUAL PROVISIONS

Life insurance policies contain important contractual provisions. Let us briefly examine the major contractual provisions that are found in life insurance contracts.

Ownership Clause

The owner of a life insurance policy can be the insured, the beneficiary, or other party. In most cases, the applicant, insured, and owner are the same person. *Under the **ownership clause**, the policyowner possesses all contractual rights in the policy while the insured is living.* These rights include naming and changing the beneficiary, surrendering the policy for its cash value, borrowing the cash value, receiving dividends, and electing settlement options. These rights generally can be exercised without the beneficiary's consent.

The policy also provides for a change of ownership. The policyowner can designate a new owner by filing an appropriate form with the company. The insurer may require the policy to be endorsed to show the new owner.

Entire Contract Clause

*The **entire contract clause** states that the life insurance policy and attached application constitute the entire contract between the parties.* All statements in the application are considered to be representations rather than warranties. No statement can be used by the company to void the policy unless it is a material misrepresentation, and is part of the application. In addition, no officer of the company can change the policy terms unless the policyowner consents to the change.

There are two basic purposes of the entire contract clause. First, it prevents the company from modifying the policy without the knowledge or consent of the owner by changing its charter or bylaws. Second, it protects the beneficiary, since a statement made in connection with the application cannot be used by the company to deny a claim unless the statement is a material misrepresentation and is part of the application.

Incontestable Clause

*The **incontestable clause** states that the company cannot contest the policy after it has been in force two years during the insured's lifetime.*[1] This means that after the policy has been in force for two years during the insured's lifetime, the company cannot later contest a death claim on the basis of material misrepresentation, concealment, or fraud when the policy was first issued. The company has two years in which to discover any irregularities in the contract. With few exceptions, the death claim must be paid after the incontestable period expires. For example, if Charles, age twenty-two, applies for a life insurance policy, conceals the fact that he has high blood pressure, and dies within the two-year period, the company could contest the claim on the basis of a material concealment. But if he dies *after* expiration of the period, the company must pay the claim.

The purpose of the incontestable clause is to protect the beneficiary from financial hardship if the company tries to deny payment of the claim years after the policy was first issued. Since the insured is dead, he or she cannot refute the insurer's allegations. As a result, the beneficiary could be financially harmed if the claim is denied on the grounds of a material misrepresentation or concealment.

The incontestable clause is normally effective against fraud. If the insured makes a fraudulent misstatement to obtain the insurance, the company has two years to detect the fraud. Otherwise, the death claim must be paid. However, there are certain situations where the fraud is so outrageous that payment of the death claim would be against the public interest. In these cases, the company can contest the claim after the incontestable period runs out. They include the following.[2]

1. The beneficiary takes out a policy with the intent of murdering the insured.
2. The applicant for insurance has someone else take a medical examination.
3. An insurable interest does not exist at the inception of the policy.

Suicide Clause

Most life insurance policies contain a suicide clause. *The **suicide clause** typically states that if the insured commits suicide within two years after the policy is issued, the face amount of insurance will not be paid; there is only a refund of the premiums paid.* In some life insurance policies, suicide is excluded for only one year. If the insured commits suicide after the period expires, the policy proceeds are paid just like any other claim.

In legal terms, death is normally considered an unintentional act because of the strong instinct of self-preservation. *Therefore, the burden of proving suicide always rests on the insurer.* The company must prove conclusively that the insured has committed suicide to deny payment of the claim.

The purpose of the suicide clause is to reduce adverse selection against the insurer. By having a suicide clause, the company has some protection against the individual who wishes to purchase life insurance with the intention of committing suicide.

Grace Period

*A life insurance policy also contains a **grace period** during which the policyowner has a period of twenty-eight to thirty-one days to pay an overdue premium.* The insurance remains in force during the grace period. If the insured dies within the grace period, the overdue premium is usually deducted from the policy proceeds.

The purpose of the grace period is to prevent the policy from lapsing by giving the policyowner additional time to pay an overdue premium. The policyowner may be temporarily short of funds or may have forgotten to pay the premium. In such cases, the grace period provides considerable financial flexibility.

Reinstatement Clause

A policy may lapse if the premium has not been paid by the end of the grace period, or if an automatic premium loan provision is not in effect. *The **reinstatement provision** permits the owner to reinstate a lapsed policy.* Several requirements must be fulfilled to reinstate a lapsed policy. They are summarized as follows:

1. Evidence of insurability is required.
2. All overdue premiums plus interest must be paid from their respective due dates.
3. All policy loans must be repaid.
4. The policy must not have been surrendered for its cash value.
5. The policy must be reinstated within five years.

Most companies do not require evidence of insurability if the reinstatement payment is received within thirty-one days after the grace period expires, and if the insured is still alive when payment is received. Reinstatement after that time generally requires evidence of insurability.

It is often advantageous for a policyowner to reinstate a lapsed policy rather than purchase a new one. First, the premium is lower since the reinstated policy was issued at an earlier age. Second, the acquisition expenses incurred in is-

INSIGHT 18.1

Is This Death a Suicide?

Facts

A twenty-year-old Marine served in a fighter squadron as a radar technician. He was familiar with .45 calibre automatic pistols and had given instructions on their use. The Marine was a happy-go-lucky, cheerful person who sometimes tried to "shake up" his friends by placing a .45 to his head and pulling the trigger. One day when the Marine was apparently in good spirits, he suddenly put a pistol to his head, said "Here's to it" to a friend, and pulled the trigger. The gun fired, killing the Marine. The insurance company that insured him claimed this was a suicide.

Decision

The death is not a suicide.

Reasoning

The company must prove that the death was intentional. The burden of proof was not met here.

Angelus v. Government Personnel Life Ins. Co., 321 P. 2d 545 (Wash. 1958).

SOURCE: Joseph L. Frascona, *Business Law, Text and Cases*, 2nd ed. (Dubuque, Iowa: Wm. C. Brown, 1984), p. 911.

suing the policy must be paid again under a new policy. Third, cash values and dividends are usually higher under the reinstated policy; the new policy may not develop any cash values until the end of the third year. Fourth, the incontestable period and suicide period under the old policy may have expired. Reinstatement of a lapsed policy does not reopen the suicide period, and a new incontestable period generally applies only to statements contained in the application for reinstatement. Statements contained in the original application cannot be contested after the original incontestable period expires. And the reinstatement policy may contain more favorable policy provisions, such as a 5 or 6 percent loan rate.

A major disadvantage, however, of reinstating a lapsed policy is that a substantial cash outlay is required if the policy lapsed several years earlier.

Misstatement of Age

When the insured dies, there may be a discrepancy between the insured's actual age and age stated in the policy. *Under the **misstatement of age clause**, if the insured's age is misstated, the amount payable is the amount that the premium would have purchased at the correct age.* For example, assume that Gerald, age thirty-five, applies for a $20,000 ordinary life policy, but his age is incorrectly stated as age thirty-four. If the premium is $20 per $1,000 at age thirty-five and $19 per $1,000 at age thirty-four, the insurer will pay only 19/20 of the death proceeds. Thus, only $19,000 would be paid (19/20 × $20,000 = $19,000).

The provision also works in the opposite direction. If the age listed in the policy is overstated, the amount payable will be increased. However, although some insurers follow this method, most companies limit the amount paid to the original face amount and refund the excess premium to the beneficiary.

Beneficiary Designation

The beneficiary is the party named in the policy to receive the policy proceeds. The principal types of beneficiary designations are as follows:

- Primary and contingent beneficiary
- Revocable and irrevocable beneficiary
- Specific and class designation

Primary and contingent beneficiary A **primary beneficiary** is the beneficiary who is first entitled to receive the policy proceeds upon the insured's death. A **contingent beneficiary** is entitled to the proceeds if the primary beneficiary dies before the insured. If the primary benficiary dies before receiving the guaranteed number of payments under an installment settlement option, the remaining payments are paid to the contingent beneficiary.

In many families, the husband will name his wife primary beneficiary (and vice versa), and the children will be named as contingent beneficiaries. The legal problem in naming *minor children* as beneficiaries is that they lack the legal capacity to receive the policy proceeds directly. Most insurers will not pay the death proceeds directly to minor children.[3] Instead, they will require a guardian to receive the proceeds on the minors' behalf. If a court of law appoints a guardian, payment of the proceeds may be delayed, and legal expenses will be incurred. One solution is to have a guardian named in your will who can legally receive the proceeds on the children's behalf. Another approach is to pay the proceeds to a *trustee* (normally a commercial bank with a trust department) which has the discretion and authority to use the funds for the children's welfare.

The insured's estate can be named as primary or contingent beneficiary. However, many financial planners do not recommend designation of the estate as beneficiary. The death proceeds may be subject to probate expenses, state inheritance taxes, and claims of creditors. Payment of the proceeds may also be delayed until the estate is settled.

Revocable and irrevocable beneficiary Most beneficiary designations are revocable. *A **revocable beneficiary** means that the policyowner reserves the right to change the beneficiary designation and the beneficiary's consent is not required.* The revocable beneficiary has only the expectation of benefits, and the policyowner can change the beneficiary whenever desired. All policy rights under the contract can be exercised without the consent of the revocable beneficiary.

In contrast, *an **irrevocable beneficiary** designation is one that cannot be changed without the beneficiary's consent.* If the policyowner wishes to change the beneficiary designation, the irrevocable beneficiary must consent to the change. However, with respect to the exercise of other policy rights, such as obtaining a policy loan, election of dividend and settlement options, and assignment of the policy, there are conflicting legal opinions. One view is that the irrevocable beneficiary is a co-owner of the policy and must consent to the exercise of any policy rights. The other view is that the irrevocable beneficiary's consent is not needed to exercise any policy rights with the exception of changing the beneficiary.[4] In any case, under most current contracts, if the irrevocable beneficiary dies before the insured, all rights revert to the policyowner who can then name a new beneficiary.

Specific and class beneficiary A specific beneficiary means the beneficiary is specifically named and identified. In contrast under a **class beneficiary designation,** a specific person is not named but is a member of a group designated as beneficiary, such as children of the insured. A class designation is appropriate whenever the insured wishes to divide the policy proceeds equally among members of a particular group.

Most companies restrict the use of a class designation because of the problem of identifying members of the class. Although all companies permit the designation of children as a class, they will not permit this designation to be used when the class members cannot be identified, or the relationship to the insured is remote. For example, the class designation "my children" means that all children of the insured share in the policy proceeds, whether legitimate, illegitimate, or adopted. But if "children of the insured" is used as the designation, the insured's children by any marriage would be included, but the wife's children by a former marriage would be excluded. Thus, a class designation must be used with great care.

Change of Plan

Life insurance policies usually contain a **change of plan provision** that allows policyowners to exchange their present policies for different contracts. The purpose of this provision is to provide flexibility to the policyowner, since when individual and family needs, objectives, and circumstances change, the original policy may no longer be appropriate.

If the change is to a *higher premium policy,* such as changing from an ordinary life to a limited-payment policy, the policyowner must pay the difference in cash values between the two policies plus interest at a stipulated rate. Evidence of insurability is not required, since the pure insurance protection (net amount at risk) is reduced.

In addition, based on company practice, the policyowner may be allowed to change to a *lower premium policy,* such as changing from an endowment policy to an ordinary life contract. In such a case, the insurer refunds the difference in cash values under the two policies to the policyowner. Evidence of insurability is required in this type of change, since the pure insurance protection is increased (higher net amount at risk).

Exclusions and Restrictions

A life insurance policy contains remarkably few exclusions and restrictions. *Suicide* is usually excluded only for the first two years. During a period of war, some companies may insert a **war clause** in their policies, which exclude payment if the insured dies as a direct result of war. The purpose of the war clause, of course, is to reduce adverse selection against the insurer when large numbers of new insureds may be exposed to death during a war time.

In addition, **aviation exclusions** may be present in some policies. Most newly issued policies do not contain any exclusions with respect to aviation deaths, and aviation death claims are paid like any other claim. However, some companies exclude aviation deaths other than as a fare-paying passenger on a regularly scheduled airline. Military aviation may also be excluded, or covered only by payment of an extra premium. Or a private pilot who does not meet certain flight standards may have an aviation exclusion rider inserted in the policy, or be charged a higher premium.

During the initial underwriting of the policy, the company may discover certain *undesirable activities* by the insured. These activities may be excluded or covered only by payment of an extra premium. They include automobile racing, sky diving, flying a hang glider, and travel or residence in a dangerous country.

Payment of Premiums

Life insurance premiums can be paid annually, semiannually, quarterly, or monthly. If the premium is paid other than annually, the policyowner must pay a carrying charge, which can be relatively expensive when the true rate of interest is calculated. For example, the semiannual premium may be 52 percent of the annual premium and so could be viewed as a carrying charge of only 4 percent. However, the actual charge is 16.7 percent. Let us see why. Assume that your annual premium is $100. You pay the semiannual premium of $52 and defer payment of $48. Six months later, the $48 and $4 carrying charge are due. This means that you are paying $4 for the use of $48 for six months, which is the equivalent of an annual charge of 16.7 percent.[5]

Assignment Clause

A life insurance policy is freely assignable to another party. There are two types of assignments. *Under an* ***absolute assignment,*** *all ownership* *rights in the policy are transferred to a new owner.* For example, the policyowner may wish to donate a life insurance policy to a church, charity, or educational institution. This can be accomplished by an absolute assignment. The new owner can then exercise the ownership rights in the policy.

Under a **collateral assignment,** *the policyowner assigns a life insurance policy as collateral for a loan.* The assignment form used is typically the American Banking Association's assignment form. *Under this form, only certain rights are transferred to the creditor to protect its interest, and the policyowner retains the remaining rights.* The party to whom the policy is assigned can receive the policy proceeds only to the extent of the loan; the balance of the proceeds is paid to the beneficiary.

The purpose of the **assignment clause** is to protect the insurer from paying the policy proceeds twice if an unrecorded assignment is presented to the company after the death claim is paid to the beneficiary. If the company is not notified of the assignment, the proceeds are paid to the named beneficiary when the policy matures as a death claim or endowment. Under general rules of law, the company is relieved of any further obligation under the policy, even though a valid assignment is in existence at the insured's death. However, if the insurer is notified of the assignment, a new contract exists between the insurer and assignee (one who receives the assignment, such as a bank), and the company then recognizes the assignee's rights as being superior to the beneficiary's rights.

Policy Loan Provision

A **policy loan** provision appears in a cash value life insurance policy which allows the policyowner to borrow the cash value. The interest rate is stated in the policy, and the loan typically bears interest at 5, 6, or 8 percent. However, a large number of states have enacted legislation that permits insurers to charge a *flexible policy loan interest rate* patterned after the national Association of Insurance Commissioner's model bill. In these states, life insurers can now issue new contracts with policy loan rates of up to 8 percent or with flexible interest rates based on Moody's index of seasoned corporate bonds. The policy loan rates can be revised as often as every three months. Some companies have offered a higher dividend scale to policyholders who have their old policies endorsed to provide for a flexible loan rate.

Interest on a policy loan must be paid annually, and it is added to the outstanding loan if not paid. If the loan is not repaid by the time the policy matures as a death claim or endowment, the face amount of the policy is reduced by the amount of indebtedness. Except for the payment of a premium, the company can defer granting the loan for up to six months, but this is rarely done.

Persons who borrow their cash values often believe that they are paying interest on their own money. This is clearly incorrect. The cash legally belongs to the insurance company. Although you have the contractual right to surrender or borrow the cash value, the cash is an asset of the insurance company and legally belongs to them. Interest must be paid on the loan because the company assumes a certain interest rate when premiums, legal reserves, dividends, and surrender values are calculated. The insurer's assets must be invested in interest-bearing securities and other investments so that the contractual obligations can be met. A policyowner must pay interest on the loan to offset the loss of interest to the insurer. If the loan had not been granted, the company could have earned interest on the funds.

Notice, too, that policy loan provisions make it necessary for the company to keep some assets in lower yielding, liquid investments to meet the demand for policy loans. Since these funds could have been invested in higher-yielding investments, policyowners who borrow should pay interest because higher yields must be forsaken.

Advantages of policy loans The major advantage of a policy loan is the relatively low rate of interest that is paid. The low policy loan rates of 5, 6, or 8 percent are real bargains in today's economy. In addition, there is no credit check on the policyowner's ability to repay the loan; there is no fixed repayment schedule; and the policyowner has complete financial flexibility in determining the amount and frequency of loan repayments.

Disadvantages of policy loans The major disadvantage is that the policyowner is not legally required to repay the loan, and the policy could lapse if the total indebtedness exceeds the available cash value. In addition, rather than repay the loan, the policyowner may let the policy lapse or may surrender the policy for any remaining cash value. Finally, as we stated earlier, if the loan has not been repaid by the time the policy matures, the face amount of insurance is reduced by the amount of the debt.

Automatic Premium Loan

The **automatic premium loan** *provision* can be added to most cash-value policies. Under this provision, an overdue premium is automatically borrowed from the cash value after the grace period expires, provided the policy has a loan value sufficient to pay the premium. The policy continues in force just as before but a premium loan is now outstanding. The premium loan bears interest at the stated contractual rate. Premium payments can be resumed at any time without evidence of insurability.

The basic purpose of an automatic premium loan is to prevent the policy from lapsing because of nonpayment of premiums. The policyowner may be temporarily short of funds, or may carelessly forget to pay the premium. Thus, the automatic premium loan provides considerable financial flexibility to the policyowner.

The automatic premium loan provision, however, has two major disadvantages. First, it may be overused. The policyowner may get into the habit of using the automatic premium loan provision too frequently. If the cash values are relatively modest, and are habitually borrowed over an extended period, the cash values could eventually be exhausted, and the contract would terminate. A second disadvantage is that the policy proceeds will be reduced if the premium loans are not repaid by the time the policy matures.

To guard against possible overuse, some companies limit the number of times that the automatic premium provision can be used—for example, no more than six consecutive premium payments if they are paid monthly, or no more than two consecutive premiums if they are paid other than monthly.

DIVIDEND OPTIONS

Life insurance contracts frequently contain dividend options. If the policy pays dividends it is known as a **participating policy**; the policyowner has the right to share in the divisible surplus of the company, and the dividend represents largely a refund of part of the gross premium if the company has favorable experience with respect to mortality, interest, and expenses. In contrast, a contract that does not pay dividends is known as a *nonparticipating policy* (often called a guaranteed cost policy).

Policy dividends generally are derived from three sources: (1) the difference between expected and actual mortality experience; (2) excess interest earnings on the assets required to maintain legal reserves; and (3) the difference between expected and actual operating expenses. Since the dividends paid are determined by the actual operating experience of the company, they cannot be guaranteed.

There are several ways in which dividends can be taken. They are as follows:

- Cash
- Reduction of premiums
- Accumulate at interest
- Paid-up additions
- Term insurance (fifth dividend option)

Cash

A dividend usually is payable after the policy has been in force for a stated period, typically one or two years. The dividend can be paid in cash. The policyowner receives a check equal to the dividend, usually on the anniversary date of the policy.

Reduction of Premiums

The dividend can be used to reduce the next premium coming due. The dividend notice will indicate the amount of the dividend, and the policyowner must then remit the difference between the premium and actual dividend paid. This option is appropriate whenever premium payments become financially burdensome. It can also be used if the policyowner has a substantial reduction in earnings, and expenses must be reduced.

Accumulate at Interest

The dividend can be retained by the company and accumulated at interest. The contractual rate of interest is 3 percent or more, but the actual interest rate credited to the dividend accumulations is much higher. Most companies are now paying 6 percent or more on the accumulated dividends. However, the interest rate credited to the accumulated dividends is generally below that paid by savings and loan institutions, savings banks, commercial banks, and credit unions.

In most companies, the accumulated dividends can be withdrawn at any time. If not withdrawn, they are added to the amount paid when the policy matures, or the contract is surrendered for its cash value. The dividend itself is not taxable for income tax purposes. However, the interest income on the accumulated dividends is taxable income and must be reported annually for federal and state income tax purposes. Thus, the interest option may be undesirable for policyowners who wish to minimize income taxes.

Paid-up Additions

Under the paid-up additions option, the dividend is used to purchase a reduced amount of paid-up whole life insurance. For example, assume that Patti, age twenty, owns a $10,000 ordinary lfie policy. If a dividend of $50 were paid, about $200 of paid-up whole life insurance could be purchased.

The paid-up additions option has both favorable and unfavorable features. *First, the paid-up additions are purchased at net rates, not gross rates;* there is no loading for expenses. *A second advantage is that evidence of insurability is not required.* Thus, if the insured is substandard in health or is uninsurable, this option may be appealing, since additional amounts of life insurance can be purchased.

However, the paid-up additions option has some unfavorable features. *First, in some companies, the paid-up increments of insurance may be overpriced.* The frequently advanced argument that paid-up additions are relatively inexpensive since they are purchased at net rates is somewhat misleading. In a careful price analysis of paid-up additions, Professor Joseph Belth found that the paid-up additions purchased in some companies were indeed low-priced, but in other companies, they were high-priced increments of life insurance.[6]

A second disadvantage is that reduced paid-up insurance is a form of single premium whole life insurance. Consumer experts point out that rarely is a single premium policy appropriate for most insureds. For example, if $100,000 of ordinary life insurance is desired, the insured normally does not pay a single premium of $40,000 to obtain the protection. Why, then, should a $40 dividend be used to buy a $100 paid-up addition. Since most persons are underinsured, a better approach would be to use the dividends to purchase another policy, assuming, of course, that the person is insurable.[7]

Term Insurance (Fifth Dividend Option)

A few companies have a fifth dividend option, whereby the dividend is used to purchase term insurance. Two forms of this option are typically used. *First, the dividend can be used to purchase one-year term insurance equal to the cash value of the basic policy, and the remainder of the dividend is then used to buy paid-up additions or is accumulated at interest.* This option may be appropriate if the policyowner regularly borrows the cash value. The face amount of the policy

INSIGHT 18.2

Which Dividend Option is Best?

There is no one best dividend option. *The best dividend option is the one that is best for you in terms of your financial circumstances, needs, and objectives.* If your income is limited or if premium payments are financially burdensome, the dividend can be paid in cash or used to reduce the next premium. If you are substandard in health or uninsurable, then the paid-up additions option is appropriate. If income tax considerations are important, you should not use the interest option since the interest is taxable. Instead, the paid-up additions option would be more appropriate, since the dividend becomes the legal reserve under the paid-up addition, and interest accumulations on the legal reserve are not taxed as current income of the policyowner. If your objective is to have a paid-up policy at retirement, then the paid-up additions option is desirable. If you need additional life insurance, the fifth dividend option can be used if it is available. In short, no single dividend option is best for all insureds. Each insured must choose an option suited to his or her situation.

would not be reduced by the amount of any outstanding loans at the time of death.

A *second form of this option is to use the dividend to purchase yearly renewable term insurance.* The actual amount of term insurance purchased depends on the amount of the dividend, the insured's attained age, and the company's term insurance rates. However, it is not uncommon for a $40 dividend to purchase $10,000 or more yearly renewable term insurance under this option. Unfortunately, this desirable option is offered by only a small number of companies.

Other Uses of Dividends

The dividends can also be used to convert a policy into a *paid-up contract.* If the paid-up option is used, the policy becomes paid-up whenever the reserve value under the basic contract plus the reserve value of the paid-up additions or deposits equal the net single premium for a paid-up policy at the insured's attained age. For example, an ordinary life policy issued at age twenty-five could be paid up by age forty-eight by using this option.

The dividend can also be used to *mature a policy as an endowment.* When the reserve value under the basic policy plus the reserve value of the paid-up additions or deposits equal the face amount of insurance, the policy matures as an endowment. For example, a $50,000 ordinary life policy issued at age twenty-five would mature as an endowment at age fifty-eight by using this option.[8]

NONFORFEITURE OPTIONS

If a cash-value policy is purchased, the policyowner has paid more than is actuarially necessary for the protection. Thus, he or she should get something back if the policy is surrendered. The payment to a withdrawing policyowner is known as a **nonforfeiture value** or cash surrender value.

All states have standard **nonforfeiture laws** that require companies to provide at least a minimum nonforfeiture value to policyowners who surrender their policies. There are three nonforfeiture or cash surrender options. They are:

- Cash value
- Reduced paid-up insurance
- Extended term insurance

Cash Value

The policy can be surrendered for its cash value, at which time all benefits under the policy cease. A policy normally does not build any cash value until the end of the second or third year, although a few policies have a small cash value at the end of the first year. The cash values are relatively small during the early years because the relatively heavy first-year acquisition expenses incurred by the company in writing the policy have not yet been recovered. However, over a long period, the cash values are substantial.

The company can delay payment of the cash value for six months if the policy is surrendered. This provision is a carryover from the great depression of the 1930s, when cash demands on life insurers were excessive. The delay clause is rarely used today.

The cash surrender option can be used if the insured no longer needs life insurance. Although it is usually not advisable to surrender a policy for cash, since other options may be more appropriate, there are circumstances where the cash surrender option can be used. For example, if an insured is retired and no longer has any dependents to support, the need for substantial amounts of life insurance may be reduced. In such a case, the cash surrender option could be used.

Reduced Paid-up Insurance

Under this option, the cash surrender value is applied as a net single premium to purchase a reduced paid-up policy. The amount of insurance purchased depends on the insured's attained age, the cash surrender value, and the mortality and interest assumptions stated in the original contract. The reduced paid-up policy is the same as the original policy, but the face amount of insurance is reduced. An ordinary life or limited-payment policy would be converted to a reduced paid-up policy. An endowment policy would mature at the same date but for a reduced amount. If the original policy is participating, the reduced paid-up policy also pays dividends.

The reduced paid-up insurance option is appropriate if life insurance is still needed, but the policyowner does not wish to pay premiums. For example, assume that Joseph has a $10,000 ordinary life policy which he purchased at age twenty-one. He is now age sixty-five and wants to retire, but he does not want to pay premiums after retirement. The cash surrender value can be used to purchase a reduced paid-up policy of about $8,300.

Extended Term Insurance

Under this option, the net cash surrender value is used as a net single premium to extend the full face amount of the policy (less any indebtedness) into the future as term insurance for a certain number of years and days. In effect, the cash value is used to purchase a paid-up term insurance policy equal to the original face amount (less any indebtedness) for a limited period. The length of the term insurance protection is determined by the insured's attained age when the option is exercised, the net cash surrender value, and the company's premium rates for extended term insurance. For example, in our earlier illustration, if Joseph stopped paying premiums at age sixty-five, the cash value would be sufficient to keep the $10,000 policy in force for another fifteen years and 272 days. If he is still alive after that time, the policy is no longer in force.

If the policy lapses for nonpayment of premiums, and the policyowner has not elected another option, the extended term option automatically goes into effect in most companies. This means that many policies are still in force even though the policyowners mistakenly believe their policies have lapsed for nonpayment of premiums. However, if the automatic premium loan provision has been added to the policy, it has priority over the extended-term option.

A whole life or endowment policy contains a table of nonforfeiture values that indicates the benefits under the three options at various ages. Figure 18.1 illustrates the nonforfeiture values for an ordinary life policy issued at age twenty-one. The nonforfeiture values are usually stated in terms of benefits for each $1,000 of insurance.

SETTLEMENT OPTIONS

Settlement options or *optional methods of settlement* refer to the various ways that the policy

Figure 18.1
Nonforfeiture Options (Dollar Amount for Each $1,000 of Face Amount of Insurance)

End of policy year	Cash or loan value	Paid-up insurance	Extended term insurance	
			Years	Days
1	$ 0.00	$ 0	0	0
2	0.00	0	0	0
3	4.79	15	1	315
4	16.21	48	6	161
5	27.91	81	11	15
6	39.91	113	14	275
7	52.20	145	17	158
8	64.78	176	19	157
9	77.66	206	20	342
10	90.84	236	22	29
11	104.33	265	22	351
12	118.13	294	23	231
13	132.25	322	24	54
14	146.69	350	24	191
15	161.43	377	24	290
16	176.47	403	24	356
17	191.79	429	25	28
18	207.38	454	25	42
19	223.22	478	25	36
20	239.29	502	25	13
Age 60	563.42	806	17	26
Age 65	608.49	833	15	272

proceeds can be paid other than in a lump sum. The policyowner may elect the settlement options prior to the insured's death, or the beneficiary may be granted the right. In addition, most cash-value policies permit the surrender values to be paid under the settlement options if the policy is surrendered. The most common settlement options are as follows:

- Interest option
- Fixed period option
- Fixed amount option
- Life income options

Interest Option

Under the *interest option,* the policy proceeds are retained by the company, and interest is periodically paid to the beneficiary. The interest can be paid monthly, quarterly, semiannually, or annually. Most companies guarantee a minimum interest rate of at least 3 percent on the policy proceeds retained under the interest option. If the policy is participating, a higher rate of interest is paid based on excess interest earnings. For example, a company may pay 6 percent on the proceeds even though the contractual rate is only 3 percent.

The beneficiary can be given withdrawal rights, whereby part or all of the proceeds can be

Figure 18.2
Fixed Period Option (Minimum Monthly Income Payments per $1,000 Proceeds)

Period (years)	Monthly payment	Period (years)	Monthly payment	Period (years)	Monthly payment
1	$84.50	11	$8.86	21	$5.32
2	42.87	12	8.24	22	5.15
3	29.00	13	7.71	23	4.99
4	22.07	14	7.26	24	4.84
5	17.91	15	6.87	25	4.71
6	15.14	16	6.53	26	4.59
7	13.17	17	6.23	27	4.48
8	11.69	18	5.96	28	4.37
9	10.54	19	5.73	29	4.27
10	9.62	20	5.51	30	4.18

withdrawn. The beneficiary may also be given the right to change to another settlement option.

The interest option provides considerable flexibility, and it can be used in a wide variety of circumstances. In particular, it can be effectively used if the funds will not be needed until some later date. For example, educational funds could be retained at interest until the children are ready for college. Meanwhile, the interest income can be paid to supplement the family's income during the readjustment and dependency periods. Also, if the proceeds cannot be paid directly to a minor, the funds can be accumulated at interest until the child reaches legal age.

One disadvantage of the interest option however, is that many financial institutions are currently paying higher rates of interest than life insurers. Although life insurers currently pay 6 percent or more on funds retained under the interest option, savings and loan institutions, commercial banks, and money market mutual funds may pay higher rates.

Fixed Period Option

Under the *fixed period or installment time option*, the policy proceeds are paid to a beneficiary over some fixed period of time. The payments can be monthly, quarterly, semiannually, or annually. Both principal and interest are systematically liquidated under this option. If the primary beneficiary dies before receiving all of the payments, the remaining payments will be paid to a contingent beneficiary or to the primary beneficiary's estate.

Figure 18.2 illustrates the fixed period option for various years for each $1,000 of proceeds at 3 percent interest. The length of the period determines the amount of each payment. For example, if the fixed period is five years, a $50,000 policy would provide a monthly income of $895.50. However, the monthly benefit would be only $481 if a ten-year period is elected.

The fixed period option can be used in those situations where income is needed for a definite time period, such as during the readjustment, dependency, and blackout periods. The fixed period option, however, should be used with caution. It is an extremely inflexible option. Partial withdrawals by the beneficiary normally are not allowed because of the administrative expense of recomputing the amount of the payment during the fixed period. However, many companies will permit the beneficiary to withdraw the commuted value of the remaining payments in a lump sum.

Figure 18.3
Fixed Amount Option

Policy proceeds	Length of time $500 monthly can be paid
$20,000	3 years 6 months
10,000	1 year 8 months
5,000	0 years 10 months

Fixed Amount Option

Under the *fixed amount or installment amount option,* a fixed amount is periodically paid to the beneficiary. The payments are made until both the principal and interest are exhausted. If excess interest is paid, the period is lengthened, but the amount of each payment is unchanged.

Figure 18.3 illustrates the fixed amount option for a monthly payment of $500 if the policy proceeds are varying amounts.[9] If the proceeds are $20,000, a monthly income of $500 can be provided for three years and six months. If the proceeds are $10,000, the same monthly income can be paid for only one year and eight months.

The fixed amount option provides considerable flexibility. The beneficiary can be given limited or unlimited withdrawal rights, and also the right to switch the unpaid proceeds to another option. The beneficiary may also be allowed to increase or decrease the fixed amount. It is also possible to arrange a settlement agreement, by which the periodic payments can be increased at certain times, such as in August and September when grown children start college. Unless there is some compelling reason for using the fixed period option, life insurance experts generally recommend using the fixed amount option because of its flexibility.

Life Income Options

The policy proceeds can also be paid to the beneficiary under a life income option. The cash surrender value can also be disbursed under a life income option. The major life income options are as follows:

- Life income
- Life income with period certain
- Refund annuity
- Joint-and-survivor income

Under the life income options, installment payments are paid only while the beneficiary is alive. All further payments cease upon the beneficiary's death. Although this option provides the highest amount of installment income, there may be substantial forfeiture of the proceeds if the beneficiary dies shortly after the payments start. Since there is no refund feature or guarantee of payments, other life income options usually are more desirable.

Under a life income with period certain, a lifetime income is paid to the beneficiary with a certain number of guaranteed payments. If the primary beneficiary dies before receiving the guaranteed number of payments, the remaining payments are paid to a contingent beneficiary. For example, assume that Mary is receiving $500 monthly under a life income option with ten years certain. If she dies after receiving only one year of payments, the remaining nine years of payments will be paid to a contingent beneficiary or to her estate.

Under a *refund annuity,* a lifetime income is paid to the beneficiary. *If the beneficiary dies before receiving payments equal to the amount of insurance, the difference is refunded in installment payments or in a lump sum to another beneficiary.* For example, assume that Mary has $50,000 of life insurance paid to her under a refund annuity. If she dies after receiving total payments of only $10,000, the remaining $40,000 is paid to another beneficiary or to her estate.

Under a joint-and-survivor income option, income payments are paid to two persons during their lifetimes, such as a husband and wife. For example, Michael and Mary may be receiving

Figure 18.4
Life Income Options (Minimum Monthly Income Payments per $1000 Proceeds)

Adjusted age		Certain period			
male	female	none	10 years	20 years	refund
50	55	$4.62	$4.56	$4.34	$4.36
51	56	4.72	4.65	4.40	4.44
52	57	4.83	4.75	4.46	4.52
53	58	4.94	4.85	4.53	4.61
54	59	5.07	4.96	4.59	4.69
55	60	5.20	5.07	4.66	4.79
56	61	5.33	5.19	4.72	4.88
57	62	5.48	5.31	4.78	4.99
58	63	5.64	5.43	4.84	5.09
59	64	5.80	5.57	4.90	5.20
60	65	5.98	5.70	4.96	5.32
61	66	6.16	5.85	5.02	5.44
62	67	6.36	5.99	5.07	5.57
63	68	6.57	6.14	5.13	5.71
64	69	6.79	6.30	5.17	5.85
65	70	7.03	6.45	5.22	6.00
66	71	7.28	6.62	5.26	6.15
67	72	7.54	6.78	5.30	6.31
68	73	7.83	6.95	5.33	6.48
69	74	8.13	7.11	5.36	6.66
70	75	8.45	7.28	5.39	6.85
71	76	8.79	7.45	5.41	7.05
72	77	9.16	7.62	5.43	7.26
73	78	9.55	7.79	5.45	7.48
74	79	9.96	7.95	5.46	7.71
75	80	10.41	8.11	5.48	7.95

$600 monthly under a joint-and-survivor income annuity. If Michael dies Mary continues to receive $600 monthly during her lifetime. There are also special versions of this option, such as a joint-and-two-thirds annuity or joint-and-one-half annuity. In the preceding illustration, the monthly income of $600 would be reduced to $400 or $300 upon the death of the first person.

The various life income options for single lives can be illustrated by Figure 18.4, which shows the amount of monthly income for each $1,000 of insurance.

Females normally receive lower periodic payments than males because of a longer life expectancy. For example, if the proceeds are $50,000, a female beneficiary, age sixty-five, would receive $285 monthly under the life income option with ten years certain, while the male beneficiary the same age would receive $322.50.

Figure 18.5
Joint-and-survivor Life Income Option (Minimum Monthly Payments per $1000 Proceeds)

Adjusted age		Joint payee adjusted age						
male		45	50	55	60	65	70	75
	female	50	55	60	65	70	75	80
45	50	$3.68	$3.80	$3.90	$3.97	$4.02	$4.06	$4.10
50	55	3.80	3.97	4.13	4.25	4.34	4.41	4.46
55	60	3.90	4.13	4.35	4.56	4.72	4.84	4.92
60	65	3.97	4.25	4.56	4.86	5.13	5.33	5.48
65	70	4.02	4.34	4.72	5.13	5.51	5.85	6.10
70	75	4.06	4.41	4.84	5.33	5.85	6.33	6.73
75	80	4.10	4.46	4.92	5.48	6.10	6.73	7.28

Figure 18.5 illustrates the joint-and-survivor income option at various ages for each $1,000 of insurance. For example, an ordinary life policy may have a cash surrender value of $50,000. If the policy is surrendered, and the cash is paid out under the joint-and-survivor income option, a monthly income of $256.50 would be paid during the lifetime of both persons, age sixty-five.

Advantages of Settlement Options

Settlement options have several advantages. The major advantages are summarized as follows:

1. *Periodic income is paid to the family.* Settlement options can restore part or all of the family's share of the deceased breadwinner's earnings. The economic security of the family can then be maintained.
2. *Principal and interest are guaranteed.* The insurance company guarantees both principal and interest. There are no investment worries and administrative problems, since the funds are invested by the insurer.
3. *The first $1,000 of interest income is excluded from income taxes.* If the proceeds are paid to the spouse of the deceased under an installment settlement option, the first $1,000 of interest income is excluded from federal income taxation. The $1,000 interest exclusion does not apply to the interest option.
4. *Settlement options are extremely valuable in life insurance programming.* Life insurance can be programmed to meet the policyowner's needs and objectives. Settlement options can be used to meet these needs and objectives. Life insurance programming will be examined in Chapter 20.

Disadvantages of Settlement Options

Settlement options have several disadvantages that limit their usefulness. The major disadvantages are summarized as follows:

1. *Higher yields often can be obtained elsewhere.* Interest rates offered by other financial institutions may be considerably higher than the rates paid by insurers under the settlement options.
2. *The settlement agreement may be inflexible and restrictive.* The policyowner may have a settlement agreement that is too restrictive. The beneficiary may not have withdrawal rights or the right to change options. As a result, the beneficiary's financial needs may not be satisfied. For example, the funds may be paid over a

twenty-year period under the fixed period option with no right of withdrawal. An emergency may arise, but the beneficiary could not withdraw the funds.

3. *Life income options have limited usefulness at the younger ages.* Life income options should rarely be used before age sixty-five or seventy, which restrict their usefulness at the younger ages. If a life income option is elected at a younger age, the income payments are substantially reduced. Also, if a life income option is used, it is the equivalent of purchasing a single premium life annuity. Because of competition, a single premium annuity may be purchased more cheaply from another insurer.

Use of a Trust

The policy proceeds can also be paid to a trustee, such as the trust department of a commercial bank. Under certain circumstances, it may be desirable to have the policy proceeds paid to a trustee rather than disbursed under the settlement options. This would be the case if the amount of insurance is substantial; if considerable flexibility and discretion in the amount of timing of payments are needed; if there are minor children or mentally or physically handicapped adults who cannot manage their own financial affairs; or if the amounts paid must be periodically changed as the beneficiary's needs and desires change. However, these advantages are partly offset by the payment of a trustee's fee. Moreover, the investment results cannot be guaranteed.

OTHER LIFE INSURANCE BENEFITS

Other benefits can often be added to a life insurance policy by the payment of an additional premium. These additional benefits provide valuable protection to the insured.

Waiver-of-Premium

A **waiver-of-premium provision** can be added to a life insurance policy. In some policies, the waiver-of-premium is automatically included. Under this provision, if the insured becomes totally disabled from bodily injury or disease before some stated age, all premiums coming due during the period of disability are waived. During the period of disability, death benefits, cash values, and dividends continue as if the premiums had been paid.

Before any premiums are waived, the insured must meet the following requirements:

1. Become disabled before some stated age, typically age sixty.
2. Be continuously disabled for six months.
3. Satisfy the definition of total disability.
4. Furnish proof of disability satisfactory to the company.

The disability must occur before some stated age, typically before age sixty. A six-month waiting period must also be satisfied. Some companies use a shorter waiting period of four months. During the waiting period, the insured must be continuously disabled. There is a retroactive refund of premiums paid by the insured during the first six months of disability if all premiums are being waived under the contract.

The insured must also satisfy the definition of disability stated in the policy. Several definitions of total disability are used.

1. The insured cannot engage in *any occupation* for which he or she is reasonably fitted by education, training, and experience.
2. During the first two years, total disability means that the insured cannot perform all duties of *his or her occupation.* After the initial period, total disability means that the insured cannot engage in *any* occupation reasonably fitted by education, training, and experience.

3. Total disability is the entire and irrecoverable loss of sight of both eyes, or the use of both hands or both feet, or one hand and one foot.

The first definition of total disability appears in many older life insurance policies. Under this definition, the insured is considered totally disabled if he or she cannot work in *any occupation* reasonably fitted by education, training, and experience. For example, assume that Dr. Harry Crockett is a chemistry professor who has throat cancer and cannot teach. If he can find some other job for which he is reasonably fitted by training and education, such as a research scientist for a chemical firm, he would not be considered disabled. However, if he cannot work in any occupation reasonably fitted by his education, training, and experience, then he would be considered totally disabled.

The second definition of total disability is more liberal and is found in many newer life insurance policies. For the first two years of disability (in some companies five years), total disability means the insured cannot perform all the duties of *his or her own occupation*. After the initial period expires, the definition becomes stricter. The insured is considered totally disabled only if he or she cannot engage in *any occupation* reasonably fitted by education, training, and experience. For example, assume that Dr. Myron Pudwill is a dentist who has a hand blown off in a hunting accident. For the first two years, he would be considered totally disabled, since he is unable to perform all duties of his occupation. Premiums during this initial period would be waived. However, after the initial period expires, if he could work in any occupation for which he is reasonably fitted by his education and training, he would not be considered totally disabled. Thus, if he could get a job as a research scientist with a drug firm or teach in a dental school, he would not be considered disabled. He would then have to resume premium payments.

Total disability can also be defined in terms of the loss of use of bodily members. For example, if Fred loses his eyesight in an explosion, or if both legs are paralyzed from some crippling disease, he would be considered totally disabled.

Before any premiums are waived, the insured must furnish satisfactory proof of disability to the insurer. The company may also require continuing proof of disability once each year. If satisfactory proof of disability is not furnished, no further premiums will be waived.

Most life insurance experts recommend adding this provision to a life insurance policy, especially if the face amount of life insurance is large. During a period of long-term disability, premium payments can be financially burdensome. Since most persons are underinsured for disability income benefits, waiver of premiums during a period in which income is reduced is highly desirable. The rider is relatively inexpensive and generally costs about 1 to 3 percent of the premiums if it is added to the policy before age forty.

Life Insurance Disability Income Rider

Some older life insurance contracts contain a **disability income rider** that typically pays monthly disability income benefits in the amount of $10 for each $1,000 of insurance if the insured is totally disabled. The monthly payments range from $5 to $20, but $10 monthly is the most common. Thus, if James has a $30,000 ordinary life policy with a disability income rider, he will receive $300 monthly in the event of total disability.

The insured must meet certain requirements before benefits are paid. They are summarized as follows:

1. The disability must occur before some stated age, such as age fifty-five or sixty.
2. The definition of total disability must be satisfied. The typical definition of total disability is similar to the *any occupation* definition discussed earlier.

3. Most companies will not pay disability income benefits beyond age sixty-five. If the insured is still disabled at age sixty-five, the face amount of the policy is paid as an endowment.
4. A six-month waiting period is required before the monthly benefits are paid. Some riders require only four-month waiting period. Unlike the waiver-of-premium provision, the disability income rider does not pay retroactive benefits for the first six months of disability.
5. The insured must meet strict underwriting requirements. The rider is typically restricted to carefully selected full-time employed persons. The amount of monthly income is limited to a stated percentage of the insured's earnings. Also, the rider is usually restricted to cash value contracts.

Because of the growth of individual and group disability income contracts, life insurance disability income riders are not widely sold at the present time. However, many older cash-value policies contain this provision.

Guaranteed Purchase Option

A ***guaranteed purchase option*** *permits the insured to purchase additional amounts of life insurance at specified times in the future without evidence of insurability.* The purpose of the option is to guarantee the insured's future insurability. Additional amounts of life insurance may be needed in the future, or the insured may be unable to afford additional amounts of life insurance today. The guaranteed purchase option guarantees the ability to purchase additional amounts of life insurance at standard rates, even though the insured may be substandard in health or be uninsurable.

Amount of insurance The typical option permits additional amounts of life insurance to be purchased with no evidence of insurability when the insured attains age twenty-five, twenty-eight, thirty-one, thirty-four, thirty-seven, and forty. The option usually is not available after age forty.

The amount of life insurance that can be purchased at each option date is limited to the face amount of the basic policy subject to some minimum and maximum amount. The minimum amount of each additional policy is $5,000, and the maximum amount is stated in the rider. In some companies, the additional policy is limited to a maximum of $25,000. For example, assume that Robert, age twenty-two, purchases a $25,000 ordinary life policy with a guaranteed purchase option and becomes uninsurable after the policy is issued. Assuming that he elects to exercise each option, he would have the following amount of insurance:

Age 22	*$25,000 (basic policy)*
	+
Age 25	*$25,000*
Age 28	*25,000*
Age 31	*25,000*
Age 34	*25,000*
Age 37	*25,000*
Age 40	*25,000*
Total insurance	*$175,000*

Although uninsurable, Robert has increased his insurance estate from $25,000 to $175,000.

Advanced purchase privilege Most companies have some type of advance purchase privilege, whereby an option can be immediately exercised upon the occurrence of some event. If the insured marries, has a birth in the family, or legally adopts a child, an option can be immediately exercised prior to the next option due date. Some companies will provide automatic term insurance for ninety days if the insured marries or a child is born. The insurance expires after ninety days unless the guaranteed insurability option is exercised. If the insured dies within the ninety-day period, the term insurance is paid in addition to the face amount of the basic policy.

If an option is exercised under the advance purchase privilege, the number of total options is not increased. If an option is exercised early, each new policy eliminates the next regular option date. Finally, the policyowner typically has only thirty to sixty days to exercise an option. If the option expires without being used, it cannot be exercised at some later date. This is to protect the company from adverse selection.

Other considerations Four additional points should be noted concerning the guaranteed insurability rider. One important consideration is whether the waiver-of-premium rider can be added to the new policy without furnishing evidence of insurability. Company practices vary in this regard. The most liberal provision permits the waiver-of-premium rider to be added to the new policy if the basic policy contains such a provision. If the premiums are waived under the basic policy, they are also waived under the new policy. Thus, in our earlier example, if premiums are being waived under Robert's basic policy of $25,000 because he is totally disabled, the premiums for each new policy will also be waived as long as he remains disabled. A less liberal approach is to permit the disabled insured to purchase a new policy with no evidence of insurability, but not to waive the new premiums under the waiver-of-premium rider.

Second, the guaranteed insurability option usually cannot be added to a term insurance policy. It is restricted to ordinary life, limited payment, or endowment policies.

Third, when an option is exercised, the premium is based on the insured's attained age. As each option is exercised, the premium rate increases because the insured is older. However, even though the insured may be substandard in health or uninsurable, the premium rate is a standard rate based on the insured's then attained age.

Fourth, the incontestable clause in each additional policy is effective from the date of issue of the basic policy. If the incontestable period under the basic policy has expired, a new incontestable period does not apply to each additional policy. However, the treatment of suicide is different. The suicide provision in each additional policy is effective from the date of issue of the additional policy.

Most consumer experts recommend purchase of the guaranteed purchase option for individuals who will probably need additional life insurance in the future. The cost is relatively low. Depending on the insured's age, the premium ranges from about $0.50 to $2.00 for each $1,000 of life insurance.

Double Indemnity Rider

A **double indemnity rider** doubles the face amount of life insurance if death occurs as a result of an accident. In some companies, the face amount is tripled. The cost of the rider is relatively low and typically ranges from $0.75 to $1.00 for each $1,000 of accidental death benefits. Thus, the rider may cost about $25 annually if it is added to a $25,000 policy. If the insured dies as a result of an accident, $50,000 would be paid.

Requirements for collecting benefits Several requirements must be satisfied before a double indemnity benefit is paid. They are as follows:

- Death must be caused directly and independently of any other cause by accidental bodily injury.
- Death must occur within ninety days of the accident.
- Death must occur before some specified age, such as age sixty, sixty-five, or seventy.

The first requirement is that accidental injury must be the direct cause of death. If death occurs from some other cause, such as disease, the double indemnity benefit is not paid. For example, assume that Sam is painting his two-story house. If the scaffold collapses, and Sam is killed, a double indemnity benefit would be paid because the direct cause of death is an accidental bodily injury. However if Sam is killed because he had a heart attack and fell from the scaffold, the double payment would not be made. In this case, heart disease is the direct cause of death, not accidental bodily injury.

A second requirement is that death must occur within ninety days of the accident. The purpose of this requirement is to establish the fact that accidental bodily injury is the proximate cause of death. However, since modern medical technology can prolong life for extended periods, many companies are using longer time periods, such as 120 or 180 days.[10]

Finally, the accidental death must occur before some specified age. Although some policies provide lifetime accidental death benefits, coverage usually terminates on the policy anniversary date just after the insured reaches a certain age, such as age seventy. In order to limit their liability, insurers typically impose some age limitation.

Exclusions The double indemnity provisions vary widely with respect to exclusions. The most common exclusions are as follows:

- Any disease or infirmity of mind or body.
- Suicide whether sane or insane.
- Traveling in or descending from any aircraft if the insured during the flight acts in any capacity other than as a passenger.
- Declared or undeclared war.
- Inhalation of gas or fumes.
- Commission of a felony.

Insurance advisors generally do not recommend purchase of the double indemnity rider. Although the cost is relatively low, there are three major objections to the rider. *First, most persons will die as a result of a disease and not from an accident.* Since most persons are underinsured, the premiums for the double indemnity rider could be better used to purchase an additional amount of life insurance, which would cover both accidental death and death from disease. *Second, the insured may be deceived and believe that he or she has more insurance than is actually the case.* For example, a person with a $50,000 policy may believe that he or she has $100,000 of life insurance. *Finally, the economic value of a human life is not doubled or tripled if death occurs from an accident.* Therefore, it is economically unsound to insure an accidental death more heavily than death from disease.

SUMMARY

- The *incontestable clause* states that the company cannot contest the policy after it has been in force two years during the insured's lifetime.
- The *suicide clause* states that if the insured commits suicide within two years after the policy is issued, the face amount is not paid. There is only a refund of the premiums paid.
- The *grace period* allows the policyowner a period of twenty-eight to thirty-one days to pay an overdue premium. The insurance remains in force during the grace period.
- There are several types of beneficiary designations. A *primary beneficiary* is the party who is first entitled to receive the policy proceeds upon the insured's death. A *contingent beneficiary* is entitled to the proceeds if the primary beneficiary dies before the insured or dies before receiving the guaranteed number of payments under an installment settlement option. A *revocable beneficiary* designation means that the policyowner can change the beneficiary without the beneficiary's consent. An *irrevocable beneficiary* designation is one that cannot be changed without the beneficiary's consent.
- A *dividend* represents a refund of part of the gross premium if the experience of the company is favorable. Dividends can be taken in several ways. They are:

a. Cash.
b. Reduction of premiums.
c. Accumulate at interest.
d. Paid-up additions.
e. Term insurance (in some companies).

- There are three *nonforfeiture* or cash surrender options. They are:
  a. Cash value.
  b. Reduced paid-up insurance.
  c. Extended term insurance.
  The cash can also be borrowed under the policy loan provision. An automatic premium loan provision can also be added to the policy, whereby an overdue premium is automatically borrowed from the cash value.
- *Settlement options* are the various ways that the policy proceeds can be paid other than in a lump sum. The most common settlement options are:
  a. Interest option.
  b. Fixed period option.
  c. Fixed amount option.
  d. Life income options.
- A *waiver-of-premium provision* can be added to a life insurance policy, whereby all premiums coming due during a period of total disability are waived. Before any premiums are waived, the insured must meet the following requirements:
  a. Become disabled before some stated age, such as age sixty.
  b. Be continuously disabled for six months.
  c. Satisfy the definition of total disability.
  d. Furnish proof of disability satisfactory to the company.
- Some companies permit a *disability income rider* to be attached to a life insurance policy. The typical rider pays $10 monthly for each $1,000 of insurance if the insured is totally disabled.
- The *guaranteed purchase option* permits the insured to purchase additional amounts of life insurance at specified times in the future without evidence of insurability. The purpose of the option is to guarantee the insured's future insurability.
- A *double indemnity rider* doubles the face amount of life insurance if death occurs as a result of an accident. Consumer experts generally do not recommend purchase of the double indemnity rider.

QUESTIONS FOR REVIEW

1. Briefly explain the ownership clause and entire contract clause in a life insurance contract.
2. Describe the *nature* and *purpose* of the incontestable clause and suicide clause.
3. Explain the requirements for reinstating a lapsed policy.
4. If the insured's age is misstated, can the company refuse to pay the policy proceeds? Explain.
5. Describe the various beneficiary designations in life insurance.
6. Can a life insurance policy be assigned to another party? Explain.
7. Can dividends be guaranteed? Explain.

8. Explain the nonforfeiture or cash surrender options that are found in cash-value life insurance.
9. List the various settlement options for the payment of life insurance proceeds.
10. Explain the definition of total disability that is found in a typical waiver-of-premium provision.

QUESTIONS FOR DISCUSSION

1. A policy that pays dividends is known as a participating policy. The dividends can be paid several ways.
   a. Explain the nature of a life insurance dividend.
   b. Describe the dividend options that are typically found in life insurance policies.
   c. For each of the options described above in *(b)*, indicate an appropriate situation where it can be used.
2. Life insurance proceeds can be paid under the fixed period or fixed amount settlement options. Compare the *fixed period option* and the *fixed amount option* with respect to the degree of flexibility that can be obtained if they are used in a settlement plan or agreement.
3. Jim, age twenty-two, purchased a $30,000 five-year renewable and convertible term insurance policy. In answer to the health questions, Jim told the agent that he had not visited a doctor within the last five years. However, he had visited the doctor two months earlier. The doctor told Jim that he had a serious heart disease. Jim did not reveal this information to the agent when he applied for life insurance. Jim died three years after the policy was purchased. At that time, the life insurer discovered the heart ailment. Explain the extent of the insurer's obligation, if any, with respect to payment of the death claim.
4. Mary, age twenty-five, recently purchased a $20,000 ordinary life insurance policy. The waiver-of-premium rider, guaranteed purchase option, and disability income rider are attached to the policy. For each of the following situations, indicate the extent of the insurer's obligation, if any, to Mary or to Mary's beneficiary. Identify the appropriate policy provision or rider that applies in each case. Treat each event separately.
   a. Mary failed to pay the second annual premium due on January 1. She died fifteen days later.
   b. Mary committed suicide three years after the policy was purchased.
   c. At Mary's death, the life insurer discovered that Mary had deliberately lied about her age. Instead of being twenty-five years old, as she had indicated, she was actually twenty-six years old at the time the policy was purchased.
   d. Two years after the policy was purchased, Mary was told that she had leukemia. She is uninsurable but would like to obtain additional life insurance.
   e. Mary is seriously injured in an automobile accident. After six months, she is still unable to return to work. She has no income from her job, and the insurance premium payments are financially burdensome.
   f. Mary has a mentally retarded son. She wants to make certian that her son will have a continuous income after her death.
   g. Mary let her policy lapse. After four years, she wants to get the policy reinstated. Her health is fine. Point out to Mary how she can get her life insurance back.

h. Mary wants to retire and does not wish to pay the premiums on her policy. Indicate the various options that are available to her.
i. Ten years after the policy is purchased, Mary is fired from her job. She is unemployed and is in desperate need of cash.

5. Additional riders and benefits often can be added to a life isurance policy to provide greater protection to the insured. Describe the nature and purpose of each of the following riders and options:
a. waiver-of-premium rider.
b. guaranteed purchase option.
c. life insurance disability income rider.
d. double indemnity rider.

KEY CONCEPTS AND TERMS TO KNOW

Ownership clause
Entire contract clause
Incontestable clause
Suicide clause
Grace period
Reinstatement provision
Misstatement of age clause
Primary and contingent beneficiary
Revocable and irrevocable beneficiary
Class beneficiary designation
Change of plan provision
War clause
Aviation exclusions
Assignment clause
Absolute assignment
Collateral assignment
Policy loan
Automatic premium loan
Participating policy
Nonforfeiture value
Nonforfeiture law
Settlement options
Waiver-of-premium provision
Disability income rider
Guaranteed purchase option
Double indemnity rider

SUGGESTIONS FOR ADDITIONAL READING

Belth, Joseph M. *Life Insurance: A Consumer's Handbook*, 2nd ed. Bloomington, Indiana: Indiana University Press, 1985.

Consumers Union. *The Consumers Union Report on Life Insurance: A Guide to Planning and Buying the Protection You Need*, 4th ed. Mount Vernon, New York: Consumers Union, 1980.

Consumers Union. "Life Insurance—A Special Two-Part Report," *Consumer Reports*, Vol. 45, No. 2 (February 1980), and Vol. 45, No. 3 (March 1980).

Greider, Janice E., Muriel L. Crawford, and William T. Beadles. *Law and the Life Insurance Contract*, 5th ed. Homewood, Illinois: Richard D. Irwin, Inc., 1984.

Huebner, S. S. and Kenneth Black, Jr. *Life Insurance*, 10th ed. Englewood Cliffs, New Jersey: Prentice-Hall, Inc., 1982.

Mehr, Robert I. and Sandra G. Gustavson. *Life Insurance: Theory and Practice*, 3rd ed. Dallas, Texas: Business Publications, Inc., 1984.

Wood, Glenn L., Claude C. Lilly, III, Donald S. Malecki, and Jerry S. Rosenbloom. *Personal Risk Management and Insurance*, 3rd ed., Volume I. Malvern, Pennsylvania: American Institute for Property and Liability Underwriters 1984.

NOTES

1. In some policies, the incontestable period is limited to one year.
2. Dan M. McGill, *Life Insurance*, rev. ed. (Homewood, Illinois: Richard D. Irwin, Inc., 1967), pp. 562–63.
3. There are some exceptions. In some states, minors who have attained age eighteen can receive a limited amount of proceeds, such as $2,000 or $3,000 annually.
4. Claude C. Lilly, Glenn L. Wood, and Jerry S. Rosenbloom, *Personal Risk Management and Insurance*, Volume I (Malvern, Pennsylvania: American Institute for Property and Liability Underwriters, 1978), p. 413.
5. Joseph M. Belth, *Life Insurance: A Consumer's Handbook*, 2nd ed. (Bloomington, Indiana: Indiana University Press, 1985), pp. 152–53.
6. Belth, p. 109.
7. A qualification is necessary here. If the insured is substandard or uninsurable, then the paid-up additions option obviously makes sense. However, if a person is insurable, a reasonable approach would be to let the dividends accumulate either at interest or under the paid-up additions option for several years. The accumulated cash could then be used to purchase a new policy. If the new policy is participating, the dividends from both contracts could pay a large portion of the annual premium under the new policy.
8. Robert I. Mehr, *Life Insurance: Theory and Practice*, rev. ed. (Dallas, Texas: Business Publications, 1977), p. 227.
9. A 3.5 percent interest assumption is used.
10. Lilly, p. 427.

CHAPTER 19

BUYING LIFE INSURANCE

"Many people buy life insurance backward."

Consumer Reports

STUDENT LEARNING OBJECTIVES

After studying this chapter, you should be able to:

- Describe the traditional method of determining the cost of life insurance and explain its defects.
- Explain the interest-adjusted surrender cost index and net payments index for determining the cost of life insurance.
- Describe the annual rates of return that consumers can expect to earn on the saving element in traditional cash-value life insurance policies.
- Explain the rules that should be followed when life insurance is purchased.

Most people buy life insurance without much thought. They usually do not shop carefully for life insurance; they often purchase the insurance from the first agent who contacts them; and they are not usually aware of the huge cost differences among different policies. The result is that many persons pay far more than is necessary for the protection they receive.

In this chapter, we will discuss the fundamentals of life insurance buying. We will first discuss the important issue of the cost of life insurance. We will next consider the rates of return consumers can earn on the savings element in traditional cash-value policies. We will conclude the chapter by describing some important rules to follow when buying life insurance.

COST OF LIFE INSURANCE

Once you have decided on the best type of policy to own, you still have the problem of purchasing the insurance at the lowest possible cost. There are enormous cost variations among similar policies offered by different companies. *If you make a mistake and purchase a high-cost policy rather than a low-cost policy, this mistake can cost you thousands of dollars over your lifetime.* In their report on life insurance costs, Consumers Union found huge differences in the cost of life insurance, especially for cash-value policies. For example, assume that you are a male, age thirty-five, and you decide to purchase a $100,000 participating whole life policy. If you purchase the policy from Fidelity Life Association (a high-cost policy) rather than from Central Life Assurance Company (a low-cost policy), the theoretical cost difference between the two policies over a twenty-year period would be $22,949.[1] So we are talking about big bucks if you make the wrong choice.

The cost of life insurance is a complex subject. In general, cost can be viewed as the difference between what you pay for a life insurance policy and what you get back. If you pay premiums and get nothing back, the cost for the insurance equals the premiums paid. However, if you pay premiums and later get something back, such as cash values and dividends, your cost will be reduced. Thus, in determining the cost of life insurance, four major cost factors must be considered: (1) annual premiums, (2) cash values, (3) dividends, and (4) time. Several cost methods consider some or all of these factors. We will examine only two of these methods here. They are:

- Traditional net cost method
- Interest-adjusted cost method

Traditional Net Cost Method

The **traditional net cost method** is commonly used by life insurers and agents to illustrate the net cost of life insurance. Under this method, the annual premiums for some time period (usually ten or twenty years) are added together. The total dividends received during the same period and the cash value at the end of the period are then subtracted from the total premiums to determine the net cost of life insurance. For example, assume that Susan, age twenty, is approached by a life insurance agent who wants to sell her a $10,000 ordinary life policy. The policy has an annual premium of $132.10. She will receive $599 in dividends over a twenty-year period, and the cash surrender value at the end of the twentieth year will be $2,294. (See Figure 19.1.) Her net cost for the 20 years is a minus $251, or an average cost per year of minus $12.55 (− $1.26 per $1,000). Susan is delighted, since her agent points out not only that the life insurance is "free," but that she has an additional gain of $251. Susan should keep in mind, however, that in life insurance, there is no such thing as a free lunch. The traditional net cost method has several defects and is misleading. The most glaring defects are as follows:

1. *The time value of money is ignored.* Interest that the policyowner could have earned on the premiums by investing them elsewhere is ignored.

Figure 19.1
Traditional Net Cost Method

Total premiums for 20 years		$2,642
Subtract dividends for 20 years		599
Net premiums for 20 years		$2,043
Subtract the cash value at the end of 20 years		$2,294
Insurance cost for 20 years	–	$ 251
Net cost per year (– $251 ÷ 20)	–	$12.55
Net cost per $1,000 per year (– $12.55 ÷ 10)	–	$ 1.26

2. *The insurance is often shown to be free.* This is contrary to common sense, since no life insurer can provide free life insurance to the public and stay in business.
3. *The steepness of the dividend scale is ignored.* Some companies pay small dividends at first and then pay ballooning dividends in later years. The timing and amount of each dividend are ignored.
4. *The dividend scale is assumed to remain unchanged.* However, in most companies dividends will change over time.
5. *The net cost is based on the assumption that the policy will be surrendered.* The assumption that the policyowner will keep the insurance exactly twenty years (or some other period) and then surrender the policy is questionable.

Interest-Adjusted Method

The **interest-adjusted method** is a more accurate measure of life insurance costs. *Under this method, the time value of money is taken into consideration by applying an interest factor to each element of cost.* The interest-adjusted method was developed by the National Association of Insurance Commissioners, and most states have regulations or laws requiring that this information be furnished on request.

There are two principal types of interest-adjusted cost indexes. They are:

- Surrender cost index
- Net payment cost index

The surrender cost index is useful if you believe you may surrender the policy at the end of ten or twenty years, or some other time period. The net payment cost index is useful if you intend to keep your policy in force, and if cash values are of secondary importance to you. Let us examine each of these cost indexes.

Surrender cost index The surrender cost index measures the cost of life insurance if you surrender the policy at the end of some time periods, such as ten or twenty years. (See Figure 19.2.)

The annual premiums are accumulated at 5 percent interest, which recognizes the fact that the policyowner could have invested the premiums elsewhere. Dividends are also accumu-

Figure 19.2
Surrender Cost Index

Total premiums for 20 years, each accumulated at 5%	$4,586
Subtract dividends for 20 years, each accumulated at 5%	824
Net premiums for 20 years	$3,762
Subtract the cash value at the end of 20 years	2,294
Insurance cost for 20 years	$1,468
Amount to which $1 deposited annually will accumulate in 20 years at 5%	$34.719
For the interest-adjusted cost per year, divide $1,468 by $34.719	$42.28
For the cost per $1,000 per year, divide $42.28 by 10	$ 4.23

INSIGHT 19.1

Should You Replace a Life Insurance Policy?

Replacement of life insurance contracts has increased sharply in recent years. Should you replace an older life insurance policy with a new one? This is a complex question to answer, and persuasive arguments can be made both for and against replacement. The major industry arguments against replacement are summarized as follows:

1. *A new incontestable clause and suicide clause are usually present in the new policy.* Thus, the company could deny payment of the death claim if you make a material misrepresentation or concealment or commit suicide within two years of the effective date of the policy.
2. *First-year acquisition expenses must again be paid.* Replacing an older policy with a new one means that you must again pay the agent's commission and other sales and administrative expenses. The new front-end load may be reflected in a higher premium and relatively lower cash values and dividends during the early years of the policy.
3. *The replacement policy may require a higher premium.* The new policy may require a higher premium because you are older when the replacement is made.
4. *Your health may be poor.* You should not replace your present policy if you are substandard in health or uninsurable, since you may be rated up or refused a replacement policy.

On the other hand, replacement of an older policy can be justified under certain conditions. If you are healthy and insurable, it may be to your financial advantage to make the switch. Two major arguments for replacement are as follows:

1. *There are huge variations in cost among policies.* Despite the precautions mentioned earlier, if your present policy is a high-cost policy, it may pay you to replace it with a lower cost policy. Professor Joseph Belth has devised a simple method for determining if a replacement is justified. This method is discussed in the Appendix to this chapter.
2. *Higher amounts of life insurance can often be purchased for the same premium.* This is especially true if the older policy is replaced with a newer universal life contract.

lated at 5 percent interest, which considers interest earnings on the dividends as well as the amount and timing of each dividend. The net premiums for twenty years are $3,762.

The next step is to subtract the cash value at the end of twenty years from the net premiums, which results in a total insurance cost of $1,468. This is the amount the policyowner pays for the insurance protection for twenty years, after considering the time value of money.

The final step is to convert the total interest-adjusted cost for twenty years ($1,468) into an annual cost. This is done by dividing $1,468 by the factor $34.719. This factor means that a $1 deposit each year at 5 percent interest will accumulate to $34.719 at the end of twenty years. By dividing the total cost of $1,468 by $34.719, we end up with an annual interest-adjusted cost of $42.28, or $4.23 for each $1,000 of insurance. As you can see, in our illustration, the interest-adjusted cost is positive and not negative, which means that it costs something to own life insurance after foregone interest is considered. In this case, Susan has an average annual cost of $42.28 if she surrenders the policy after twenty years.

Net payment cost index The net payment cost index measures the relative cost of a policy if death occurs at the end of some specified time period, such as ten or twenty years. It is based on

Figure 19.3
Net Payment Cost Index

Total premiums for 20 years, each accumulated at 5%	$4,586
Subtract dividends for 20 years, each accumulated at 5%	824
Insurance cost for 20 years	$3,762
Amount to which $1 deposited annually will accumulate in 20 years at 5%	$34.719
For the interest-adjusted cost per year, divided $3,762 by $34.719	$108.36
For the cost per $1,000 per year, divide $108.36 by 10	$10.84

the assumption that you will continue the policy in force and not surrender it. Therefore, it is the appropriate cost index to use if you intend to keep your life insurance in force.

The net payment cost index is calculated in a manner similar to the surrender index except that the cash value is not subtracted. (See Figure 19.3.)

If the policy is kept in force for twenty years, Susan has an annual cost of $108.36 ($10.84 per $1,000) after interest is considered.

Substantial Cost Variation Among Insurers

There are enormous cost variations in cash value life insurance based on the interest-adjusted cost indexes. Figure 19.4 shows interest-adjusted cost data for a select group of *participating* whole life policies in the amount of $25,000 at ages twenty-five, thirty-five, and forty-five. Of the companies shown, Central Life Assurance had the lowest surrender cost index at the end of twenty years for a $25,000 participating whole life policy issued at age twenty-five (−$3.30 per $1,000). Republic National had the highest surrender cost index at the end of the twenty-year period ($5.14 per $1,000). *This wide variation in costs highlights the point we stressed earlier—you can save thousands of dollars over a long period by paying careful attention to the cost index when you shop for life insurance.*

Figure 19.5 provides similar information for a select group of *nonparticipating (guaranteed cost)* policies. There is also a wide variation in cost based on the surrender cost index at the end of twenty years. Of the companies shown, Monarch Life had the lowest surrender cost index at the end of twenty years for a nonparticipating policy issued at age twenty-five ($2.18 per $1,000), while National Fidelity had the highest surrender cost index at the end of the twenty-year period ($6.02 per $1,000).

Obtaining Cost Information

Interest-adjusted cost data can be found in a special report on life insurance costs by Consumers Union.[2] In addition, you can ask a life insurance agent to give you this information if you are approached to buy life insurance. Interest-adjusted cost data can also be obtained from *Life Rates & Data*, which is published annually by the National Underwriter Company and may be available in your city or college library. And certain states such as New York have issued *shoppers' guides* that provide cost data on life insurance.

However, if you use interest-adjusted cost data, you should keep in mind the following points:

1. *Shop for a policy and not the company.* Some companies have excellent low-cost policies at certain ages and amounts, but they are not as competitive when other ages and amounts are considered.
2. *Compare only similar plans of insurance.* You should compare policies of the same type with the same benefits. Otherwise, the comparison can be misleading.
3. *Ignore small variations in the cost index*

Figure 19.4
Interest Adjusted Cost Indexes $25,000 Participating Policies (per $1,000 basis)

	Age 25				Age 35				Age 45			
	Payment		Cost		Payment		Cost		Payment		Cost	
	10	20	10	20	10	20	10	20	10	20	10	20
ALEXANDER HAMILTON												
WLNCS (Heritage)	9.05	7.65	4.05	1.66	13.56	11.30	5.23	2.89	20.69	17.31	8.43	6.16
AMERICAN GENERAL COS												
WLNCS (Business Life)	9.65	7.46	4.45	1.75	14.01	10.89	5.40	2.60	21.06	16.71	8.31	5.51
BANKERS LIFE NE												
WLNCS	8.01	6.04	3.50	. . .	11.95	8.80	4.09	.09	18.45	13.74	6.47	1.97
BOSTON MUTUAL												
L95M/98F	11.17	10.32	5.57	3.72	15.73	14.67	6.83	5.62	23.77	22.03	10.99	10.30
CENTRAL LIFE ASSUR												
WL-DIVOPT (EOL)	9.63	9.18	.88	−3.30	14.10	13.26	.88	−4.55	21.73	19.99	2.23	−4.75
CONTINENTAL AMERICAN												
L98	9.27	8.39	4.80	2.16	13.84	12.27	6.20	3.43	21.66	19.51	9.92	7.64
DOMINION LIFE												
WL	10.95	8.43	3.76	1.23	15.21	11.85	4.68	2.20	22.59	18.31	8.20	6.01
EQUITABLE LIFE ASSUR												
WL (Adj WL)	9.52	6.64	1.12	−1.33	13.87	9.83	1.99	−.84	21.15	15.74	5.10	2.04
FARM BUREAU IA												
L95 (Exec Pref)	10.53	8.12	2.66	.78	15.19	11.96	3.99	2.08	22.21	18.04	6.99	5.39
FRANKLIN COMPANIES												
WL (Exec Sel 1)	13.28	9.45	5.29	1.69	17.54	12.29	6.21	2.14	24.62	17.61	9.46	4.88
GENERAL AMERICAN												
WLNCS (WL 100) (Pref)	8.34	6.48	2.36	.59	12.55	9.58	3.31	1.07	19.61	14.93	6.13	3.36
GUARANTEE MUTUAL, NE												
WL 4.5%NCS	8.95	6.60	3.50	.75	12.84	9.35	4.14	.91	19.35	14.32	6.63	2.92
GUARDIAN												
WLNCSBOF	7.72	4.25	1.08	−2.43	10.78	5.63	.82	−3.75	16.14	9.01	2.11	−3.44
INDEP ORDER OF FORESTERS												
WL (Exec Life)	10.94	9.08	4.65	2.46	15.42	12.83	5.73	3.73	22.88	19.37	9.25	7.47
LINCOLN NATIONAL												
WLNCS	10.29	8.96	4.27	2.66	14.70	12.54	5.26	3.66	21.02	17.92	7.44	6.12
MINNESOTA MUTUAL LIFE												
WL/T65NCS (Adj Life II)(PEI)	7.75	7.75	2.97	.44	10.79	10.79	3.10	−.77	16.14	16.14	4.31	−1.65
MONARCH LIFE, MA												
WL	12.91	11.27	4.74	3.06	18.01	15.92	6.35	5.12	26.95	24.14	11.35	10.49
NATIONAL LIFE VT												
VPNCS (Value Life)	8.02	6.16	2.82	−.13	11.42	8.70	2.88	−.31	17.61	12.72	4.88	.61

	Age 25				Age 35				Age 45			
	Payment		Cost		Payment		Cost		Payment		Cost	
	10	20	10	20	10	20	10	20	10	20	10	20
NEW ENGLAND LIFE												
WLNCSB	6.82	5.13	.94	−1.01	10.60	7.55	1.50	−1.25	16.32	11.65	3.17	−.19
NEW YORK LIFE COS												
WL	10.39	8.10	5.02	2.11	14.92	11.46	6.37	2.82	22.72	17.83	10.15	6.14
NEW YORK LIFE COS												
WLNCS	9.94	7.65	4.57	1.66	13.96	10.50	5.41	1.86	20.80	15.91	8.23	4.22
NORTHWESTERN MUTUAL												
L90NCS	8.50	5.42	2.01	−.71	12.27	7.59	2.51	−1.06	18.04	11.54	4.22	.01
PENN MUTUAL												
L95NCSB	8.32	6.98	3.78	.73	12.42	9.76	4.24	.80	18.38	14.74	6.34	2.70
PILOT LIFE												
WLNCSB	9.46	7.98	5.60	2.71	13.62	11.38	6.58	3.43	20.46	17.24	9.40	6.18
PROVIDENT MUTUAL												
M2 (Prot)	10.12	8.82	3.23	2.11	14.50	12.57	4.13	3.15	22.09	19.36	7.40	6.89
REPUBLIC NATIONAL												
WL	15.20	13.46	8.08	5.14	20.07	17.75	9.70	6.92	27.76	24.80	13.75	11.38
SECURITY BENEFIT LIFE												
WL (Exec)	9.76	8.23	4.76	2.24	13.56	11.54	5.23	3.13	20.66	17.92	8.40	6.78
SHENANDOAH LIFE												
WL (Pres Life LXXX)	9.15	7.84	5.52	3.03	13.72	11.58	6.83	3.98	21.62	18.04	10.56	7.18
STATE MUTUAL COMPANIES												
WLNCS	8.88	7.08	1.86	.21	12.77	10.06	2.55	.63	18.67	14.96	4.57	2.72
SUN LIFE, CN												
WL (Sun Permanent)	9.83	8.44	4.84	2.29	13.89	11.94	5.60	3.29	21.35	18.69	9.11	7.25
TRANSAMERICA OCCIDENTAL												
GP26 (Parsetter WL)	6.34	6.30	4.67	2.90	10.06	9.99	6.50	4.90	16.89	16.79	11.37	10.05
UNITED STATES LIFE												
WL	14.22	12.75	6.27	4.60	20.05	17.69	8.92	7.07	30.32	26.28	15.48	13.06

Abbreviations used:

WL	Whole life/ordinary life
NCS	Noncigarette smoker
L	Number following L is age plan becomes paid up (L95)
DIVOPT	Dividend option used
NCSB	NCS risk plus favorable build weight history
NCS BOF	NCSB risk plus other factors
T	Term plan; number following T is age plan expires
VP	Number of years to pay up or endow; varies by age at issue
M	Modified plan; number following M, if under 50, is number of years of reduced premiums (M3)
GP	Graded premium WL plan; number following GP is number of different premiums

SOURCE: From 1984 "Life Rates & Data." Reprinted by permission of National Underwriter Company.

Figure 19.5
Interest Adjusted Cost Indexes $25,000 Nonparticipating (Guaranteed Cost) Policies (per $1,000 basis)

	Age 25			Age 35			Age 45		
	Payment	Cost		Payment	Cost		Payment	Cost	
	20	10	20	20	10	20	20	10	20
AETNA COMPANIES									
WLNCS	9.33	5.01	3.77	13.64	6.30	5.66	21.32	10.27	10.58
AETNA COMPANIES									
WL	9.54	5.22	3.98	14.04	6.70	6.06	22.12	11.07	11.38
ALEXANDER HAMILTION									
WL (Heritage)	8.52	5.19	4.23	13.19	6.75	6.42	21.16	10.86	11.48
AMERICAN GENERAL COS									
L95NCS (Pref Exec WL)	11.53	2.70	3.26	15.76	3.64	4.96	22.79	6.85	9.28
COVENANT LIFE									
WL 5.5%	7.29	3.96	3.00	11.62	5.18	4.85	19.57	9.27	9.89
DOMINION LIFE									
WL	9.52	4.52	3.96	14.05	5.72	5.99	21.47	9.20	10.64
FIDELITY & GUARANTY									
WL	8.08	4.80	3.81	12.45	6.06	5.69	19.65	9.36	10.00
FRANKLIN COMPANIES									
L95 (Pref 95 1)	10.96	5.34	4.81	15.43	6.54	6.78	23.96	11.15	12.52
GREAT-WEST LIFE									
WLNCSB (Estatemaster)	9.47	6.14	5.18	13.38	6.94	6.61	20.29	9.99	10.61
HARTFORD COMPANIES									
WL	9.76	4.76	4.20	14.54	6.21	6.48	22.71	10.44	11.88

numbers. Small cost differences can be offset by other policy features or by services that you can expect to get from an agent or insurer.

4. *Cost indexes apply only to a new policy.* The cost data should not be used to determine whether to *replace* an existing policy with a new one.
5. *The type of policy you buy should not be based solely on a cost index.* You should buy the right type of policy that meets your needs, such as term, whole life, or some combination. Once you have decided on the type of policy, then compare costs.
6. *Consider other factors besides cost.* The financial strength and reputation of the insurer should also be considered in addition to cost. Also, a higher policy cost can be justified if you have a good agent who gives you good service and proper advice.

RATES OF RETURN ON CASH-VALUE POLICIES

Another important consideration is the average annual rate of return on the savings element in a traditional cash-value policy. Consumers normally do not know the annual rate of return they earn on the savings element in their policies.

	Age 25			Age 35			Age 45		
	Payment	Cost		Payment	Cost		Payment	Cost	
	20	10	20	20	10	20	20	10	20
IDS LIFE, MN									
WLNCS	8.19	4.40	3.44	12.59	5.78	5.42	20.17	9.57	10.15
LIBERTY NATIONAL									
WLNCS (Est WL)	8.93	3.94	3.39	13.73	5.44	5.69	21.84	9.60	11.02
MONARCH LIFE, MA									
WL	7.85	4.44	2.18	12.24	5.65	4.03	20.67	9.99	9.58
NATIONAL FIDELITY									
WLNCS	11.72	7.25	6.02	16.15	8.58	7.94	23.45	12.09	12.39
PAUL REVERE COMPANIES									
WL	9.20	5.87	4.91	15.01	8.57	8.24	23.30	13.00	13.62
PILOT LIFE									
L95NCSB	8.13	4.65	3.69	12.46	5.72	5.43	19.32	8.49	9.27
PYRAMID LIFE									
WL	11.23	6.23	5.07	16.37	8.04	7.70	25.27	13.00	13.81
REPUBLIC NATIONAL									
WL	10.80	7.47	5.27	15.53	9.09	7.58	23.51	13.21	12.80
UNITED STATES LIFE									
WL (Business WL)	12.28	2.13	3.78	16.85	3.75	6.05	24.69	8.64	11.30
WILLIAM PENN LIFE									
M1 (Exec)	11.18	2.45	3.26	15.10	3.17	4.79	21.12	5.41	8.27
WISCONSIN NATIONAL									
WL	10.90	5.22	4.74	15.96	7.03	7.29	24.44	11.64	12.98

Note: For abbreviations used, see Figure 19.4.

SOURCE: From 1984 "Life Rates & Data." Reprinted by permission of National Underwriter Company.

However, a consumer who buys a traditional cash-value policy with a low return can lose a considerable amount of money over the life of the policy. A difference of only 1 percent in the annual rate of return can amount to a sizable loss when compound interest is considered. For example, if $1,000 is deposited annually into a savings account for thirty years (which can be the duration of a whole life policy), the amount in the account at various rates of compound interest is as follows:

0%	$30,000	5%	$ 69,761
2%	41,379	6%	83,802
3%	49,003	7%	101,073
4%	58,328	8%	122,346

Thus, the annual rate of return that you receive on a cash-value policy is critical if you intend to save money over a long period of time.

Linton Yield

The **Linton yield** is one method that can be used to determine the rate of return on the savings portion of a cash-value policy. It was developed by M. Albert Linton, a well-known life insurance actuary. In essence, the Linton yield is the average annual rate of return on a cash-value policy if it is held for a specified number of years. It is based on the assumption that a cash-value policy can be viewed as a combination of insurance protection and a savings fund. To determine the average annual rate of return for a given period, it is first necessary to determine that part of the annual premium that is deposited in the savings fund. This can be determined by subtracting the cost of the insurance protection for that year from the annual premium (less any dividend). The balance of the premium is the amount that can be deposited into the savings fund. Thus, the average annual rate of return is the compound interest rate that is required to make the saving deposits equal the guaranteed cash value in the policy at the end of a specified period.

Federal Trade Commission Report

Based on the Linton yield method, Figure 19.6 summarizes the average annual rates of return for new whole life policies issued in 1977. The data are based on financial information provided by seventy-one large life insurers to the Federal Trade Commission. Each company was asked to submit information on the three best-selling whole life policies.

The five-year rates of return for participating policies ranged from about a minus 8 percent to about a minus 12 percent. For nonparticipating policies, the five-year rates ranged from about a minus 11 percent to about a minus 20 percent. The ten-year rates of return are under 2 percent for the participating policies and are still negative for the nonparticipating contracts. The twenty-year rates for participating policies ranged from about 3.6 percent to about 4.6 percent. The twenty-year rates for the nonparticipating policies ranged from about 1 percent to about 2.8 percent.

The negative returns during the early years are explained by the heavy first-year acquisition and administrative expenses that are incurred when the policy is first sold. An agent receives a commission equal to at least one-half of the first year's premium. And there may be a medical examiner's fee, an inspection report, and other expenses in issuing the policy. In recognition of these first-year expenses, most cash-value policies do not have any cash value at the end of the first year, and the cash values are relatively low in the first few years of the policy. Thus, if you surrender or lapse the policy during the early years of the policy, you will lose a substantial amount of money.

Consumers Union Report on Life Insurance

Consumers Union has also provided valuable information on the annual rates of return on the savings element in certain cash-value policies at the end of nine, nineteen, and twenty-nine years.[3] Based on a study of the 40 *lowest-cost* policies and the Linton yield method, the average annual rate of return for a *participating* whole life policy in the amount of $25,000 issued to a male age twenty-five ranged from −0.85 percent to 8.54 percent at the end of nine years; from 4.96 percent to 7.97 percent at the end of nineteen years; and from 4.69 percent to 7.88 percent at the end of twenty-nine years. Most of the 40 lowest-cost policies had an average annual return in excess of 5 percent at the end of twenty-nine years.

The average annual returns, however, for the highest-cost policies were substantially lower. The average annual return for the five *highest-cost* participating policies ranged from a −6.40 percent to −0.99 percent at the end of nine years; from 1.22 percent to 2.84 percent at the end of nineteen years; and from 2.32 percent to 3.61 percent at the end of twenty-nine years.

Similar information was also provided for *nonparticipating* policies. A study of the 35 *lowest-cost* nonparticipating policies showed that the average annual rate of return for a $25,000 policy issued to a male age twenty-five ranged from −8.60 percent to 6.94 percent at the end of nine years; from 1.85 percent to 5.10 percent at the end of nineteen years; and from 2.94 percent to 5.63 percent at the end of twenty-nine years.

Similar data for the five *highest-cost* nonparticipating policies showed average annual rates of return that ranged from −6.29 percent to 0.65 percent for nine years; from 1.02 percent to 2.71 percent for nineteen years; and from 1.61 percent to 2.49 percent for twenty-nine years.

The annual yields for both the lowest- and highest-cost nonparticipating policies are substantially lower than the average yields on the

Figure 19.6
Average Rates of Return on Whole-Life Policies: 1977

Age at issue	Face amount of policy	If policy is held for	Dividend paying	Nondividend paying
25	$ 10,000	5 years	−12.28%	−19.78%
		10 years	1.93	− 1.25
		20 years	4.61	2.34
	25,000	5 years	−11.99	−17.51
		10 years	1.25	− 0.61
		20 years	4.21	2.71
	100,000	5 years	−12.25	−16.81
		10 years	0.96	− 0.38
		20 years	4.09	2.83
35	10,000	5 years	− 8.43	−14.31
		10 years	1.74	− 1.25
		20 years	4.32	1.91
	25,000	5 years	− 8.36	−11.96
		10 years	1.43	− 0.26
		20 years	4.12	2.47
	100,000	5 years	− 8.53	−11.28
		10 years	1.28	− 0.05
		20 years	4.06	2.64
45	10,000	5 years	− 9.84	−14.11
		10 years	0.63	− 2.48
		20 years	3.56	0.94
	25,000	5 years	− 9.13	−11.65
		10 years	0.68	− 1.34
		20 years	3.57	1.60
	100,000	5 years	− 9.08	−10.88
		10 years	0.62	− 0.96
		20 years	3.57	1.82

SOURCE: Bureau of Consumer Protection, Bureau of Economics, *Life Insurance Cost Disclosure, Staff Report to the Federal Trade Commission* (Washington, D.C.: U.S. Government Printing Office, 1979), pp. 29–30.

participating policies described earlier. Thus, if you intend to save money through cash-value life insurance, the policy that you select is critical. Consumer experts and the Federal Trade Commission have recommended that annual rates-of-return data should be furnished to the purchasers of cash-value life insurance. But the life insurance industry has vigorously opposed this recommendation. Life insurance cost disclosure is an extremely sensitive and controversial issue which we will examine in greater detail in Chapter 28.

SHOPPING FOR LIFE INSURANCE

You should consider several important factors when you are thinking about purchasing life insurance. Consumer experts typically make the following suggestions:[4]

1. Decide on the best type of insurance for you.
2. Estimate the amount of insurance needed.
3. Decide whether you want a policy that pays dividends.

4. Shop around for the lowest-cost policy.
5. Pay annual premiums.
6. Don't sign a promissory note.
7. Consider other factors in addition to cost.

Decide on the Best Type of Insurance for You

The first step in purchasing life insurance is to decide on the best type of policy for you. *The best policy is the one that best meets your needs.* If your income is limited, or you have a temporary need, consider term insurance. If you need lifetime protection, consider ordinary life insurance. If you feel that you cannot save money without being forced, then consider ordinary life insurance as a savings vehicle. However, remember that the annual rates of return on cash-value policies vary enormously. The Consumers Union report on life insurance can be extremely valuable in selecting companies whose policies generally have relatively high rates of return.

In addition, avoid purchasing a policy that you cannot afford. If you drop the policy after a few months or years, you will lose a substantial sum of money. Make certain that you can afford the premiums.

Estimate the Amount of Insurance Needed

The needs approach is probably the most practical method for determining the amount of life insurance needed. Persons with dependents need surprisingly large amounts of life insurance. In determining the amount needed, you must consider your family's present and future financial needs, potential survivor benefits from Social Security, present financial assets, and inflation. These factors will be discussed in greater detail in Chapter 20, when life insurance programming is considered.

Decide Whether You Want a Policy That Pays Dividends

In recent decades, participating life insurance policies have generally been better buys than nonparticipating policies. Dividends have been increased substantially in most companies because of excess interest earnings. However, dividends are not guaranteed and can change over time as economic conditions change. Nonparticipating policies have a guaranteed cost and initially require a lower premium outlay. If you believe that high interest rates will continue in the future, then you should consider a participating policy, since excess interest earnings have a powerful effect on the dividends paid. If you expect interest rates to fall sharply and remain at lower levels in the future, then consider a nonparticipating policy. Note, however, that many economists do not expect long-term interest rates to decline sharply and remain permanently at lower levels in the near future.

Shop Around for the Lowest-cost Policy

We must again stress the importance of shopping around. You should not purchase a life insurance policy from the first agent who approaches you. Shop around and get the interest-adjusted cost indexes for several policies. *Compare the index costs with the **benchmark net cost indexes** contained in the Consumers Union report on life insurance.*[5] Otherwise, you may only be comparing two high-cost policies with each other. The benchmark cost indexes of Consumers Union can help you determine if the policy that you intend to buy is a low-cost, average-cost, or high-cost policy.

Pay Annual Premiums

Pay annual premiums if possible. More than 80 percent of life insurance premiums are paid other than annually, but this can be expensive. The **annual percentage rate (APR)** for paying life insurance premiums other than annually can be relatively high. In a study of fifteen major life insurance companies, Professor Joseph Belth found considerable variation in the annual percentage rates when premiums were paid other than annually.[6]

The APRs ranged from 5 percent to 14.2 percent for semiannual premiums, from 4.9 percent to 28.7 percent for quarterly premiums, and from 4.9 percent to 29.3 percent for regular monthly premiums. If special monthly premiums were paid, for example, by a preauthorized check drawn on a checking account, the APRs ranged from 4.3 percent to 12.4 percent.

Don't Sign a Promissory Note

You may be short on cash, and a life insurance agent may persuade you to buy a cash-value policy by signing a promissory note. The sales pitch is often presented in an attractive manner, and you may think you are receiving something for nothing. For example, you may be asked to buy a cash-value policy with triple indemnity, waiver of premium, and a guaranteed purchase option. The annual premium is $400. You are asked to pay only $15, and you sign a five-year promissory note for $385 at 8 percent interest. The agent then explains that the policy will pay off the note and interest at the end of five years. It sounds as if you have received something for nothing. Wrong! A pure endowment pays off the note at the end of five years, and the cost of a pure endowment is included in the premium charged. It is a relatively expensive benefit. Moreover, *if you fail to pay the second and subsequent premiums before the note is due, the entire note is due immediately.* For example, you may not be able to pay the second annual premium of $400. After the grace period expires, the policy lapses for nonpayment of premiums. Although the policy is not in force, you still owe $385 plus interest, which is due immediately. Finally, the policy sold in connection with a promissory note often is a high-cost policy with some unnecessary benefits, such as a double or triple indemnity. If your income is limited and you need life insurance, consider term insurance as an alternative.

Consider Other Factors in Addition to Cost

In addition to cost, you should consider the financial strength and stability of the company. You can determine a company's financial rating by consulting *Best's Insurance Reports,* which can be found in a public library. The companies are rated A+ (excellent), A (excellent), B+ (very good), B (good), C+ (fairly good), and C (fair). Consumer experts generally recommend a general policyholder's rating of A or higher, since companies with this grade are unlikely to have financial problems that will result in unpaid death claims.

Finally, you should deal with a professional competent agent. If you have an agent who has given you good service in the past, that may be a factor in selection of a company. Also, an agent who is a **Chartered Life Underwriter (CLU)** should be technically competent to give you proper advice. Holders of the CLU designation are also expected to abide by a code of ethics that places their clients' interests ahead of their own. However, the life insurance industry is characterized by a high turnover of agents, so that in some cases, the agents are neither experienced nor competent.

SUMMARY

- There are enormous cost variations among similar life insurance policies. Purchase of a high-cost policy can cost thousands of dollars over the insured's lifetime.
- The traditional net cost method has been used to illustrate the cost of life insurance. However, this method has several defects and is misleading. It does not consider the following:
  a. The time value of money is ignored.
  b. The insurance is often shown to be free.
  c. The steepness of the dividend scale is ignored.
  d. The dividend scale is assumed to remain unchanged.
  e. The net cost is based on the assumption that the policy will be surrendered.

- The interest-adjusted method is a more accurate measure of life insurance costs. The time value of money is taken into consideration by applying an interest factor to each element of cost. If you are interested in surrendering the policy at the end of a certain period, the *surrender cost index* is the appropriate cost index to use. If you intend to keep your policy in force, the *net payment cost index* should be used.
- The annual rates of return on the savings element in most traditional cash-value life insurance policies are negative during the early years and relatively modest over a long-run period, such as twenty years. Annual rates-of-return data are not readily available to purchasers of cash-value life insurance. The recent reports by Consumers Union on the cost of life insurance can be helpful in this regard.
- Life insurance experts generally recommend several rules to follow when shopping for life insurance. They are:
  a. Decide on the best type of insurance for you.
  b. Estimate the amount of insurance needed.
  c. Decide whether you want a policy that pays dividends.
  d. Shop around for the lowest-cost policy.
  e. Pay annual premiums.
  f. Don't sign a promissory note.
  g. Consider other factors in addition to cost.

QUESTIONS FOR REVIEW

1. Describe the traditional net cost method for determining the cost of life insurance.
2. Explain the defects of the traditional net cost method.
3. Explain the surrender cost index and net payment cost index. How are these indexes an improvement over the traditional net cost method?
4. Where can interest-adjusted cost information be obtained?
5. List the rules that should be followed if interest-adjusted data are used.
6. Describe the annual rates of return that consumers can expect to earn on the savings element in their cash-value policies.
7. Why are the rates of return on the savings element in most cash-value policies negative during the early years?
8. List the rules that should be followed when shopping for life insurance.
9. Is it desirable to replace an older life insurance policy with a new policy? Explain.
10. Should cost be the only factor to consider when a life insurance policy is purchased? Explain.

QUESTIONS FOR DISCUSSION

1. A life insurance agent remarked that "most life insurance policies cost about the same, and it really is not necessary to be concerned about cost." Do you agree or disagree with the agent's remarks? Explain.

2. A participating ordinary life policy in the amount of $10,000 is issued to an individual, age thirty-five. The following cost data are given.

Annual premium	$ 230
Total dividends for 20 years	1,613
Cash value at end of 20 years	3,620
Accumulated value of the annual premiums at 5 percent for 20 years	$7,985
Accumulated value of the dividends at 5 percent for 20 years	$2,352
Amount to which $1 deposited annually will accumulate in 20 years at 5 percent	$34.719

a. Based on the above information, compute the annual net cost for each $1,000 of life insurance at the end of twenty years using the *traditional net cost method.*

b. Compute the annual *surrender cost index* for each $1,000 of life insurance at the end of twenty years.

c. Compute the annual *net payment index* for each $1,000 of life insurance at the end of twenty years.

3. A friend remarked that "cash-value life insurance is a good place to save money, since the annual return is reasonable, and the money is safe." Do you agree or disagree with this statement? Explain your answer.
4. Assume that you are short of cash, and a life insurance agent tries to sell you an ordinary life policy by asking you to sign a promissory note for most of the first year's premium. Do you think this is a good way to buy life insurance? Explain your answer.
5. You have been asked for some advice on how to buy life insurance. What suggestions can you give for buying life insurance?

KEY CONCEPTS AND TERMS TO KNOW

Traditional net cost method
Interest-adjusted method
Surrender cost index
Net payment cost index
Linton yield
Benchmark net cost indexes
Annual percentage rate (APR)
Chartered Life Underwriter (CLU)

SUGGESTIONS FOR ADDITIONAL READING

Auxier, Albert L. and W. W. Dotterweich. "An Exante Study of Justifiable Replacements Among Nonparticipating Straight Life Policies," *Journal of Insurance Issues and Practices*, Vol. 2, No. 3, 4 (Spring-Summer 1979).

Belth, Joseph M. *Life Insurance: A Consumer's Handbook,* 2nd ed. Bloomington, Indiana: Indiana University Press, 1985.

Bureau of Consumer Protection, Bureau of Economics. *Life Insurance Cost Disclosure, Staff Report to the Federal Trade Commission,* Washington, D.C.: Government Printing Office, 1979.

Consumers Union. "Life Insurance—A Special Two-Part Report," *Consumer Reports,* Vol. 45, No. 2 (February 1980), and No. 3 (March 1980).

Consumers Union. *The Consumers Union Report on Life Insurance: A Guide to Buying and Planning the Protection You Need,* 4th ed. Mount Vernon, New York: Consumers Union, 1980.

Murray, Michael L. "Analyzing the Investment Value of Cash Value Life Insurance," *The Journal of Risk and Insurance,* Vol. 45, No. 1 (March 1976).

Scheel, William C. "How to Tell When It Is Advisable for an Insured to Replace an Existing Policy," *Estate Planning* (November 1978).

Scheel, William C. and Jack Van Derhei. "Replacement of Life Insurance: Its Regulation and Current Activity," *The Journal of Risk and Insurance,* Vol. 45, No. 2 (June 1978).

The National Underwriter Company. *1984 Life Rates & Data, Successor to Little Gem.* Cincinnati, Ohio: The National Underwriter Company, 1984.

NOTES

1. Consumers Union, "Life Insurance—A Special Two-Part Report," *Consumer Reports,* Vol. 45, No. 3 (March 1980), p. 165.
2. Consumers Union, "Life Insurance—A Special Two-Part Report," *Consumer Reports,* Vol. 45, No. 2 (February 1980), pp. 79–106; and "Life Insurance—A Special Two-Part Report," (March 1980), pp. 163–68.
3. "Life Insurance—A Special Two-Part Report," (February 1980), pp. 79–106.
4. "Life Insurance—A Special Two-Part Report," (February 1980), p. 79.
5. The benchmark cost indexes can be found in the tables of *Consumer Reports,* Vol. 45, No. 2 (February 1980), p. 88 and Vol. 45, No. 3 (March 1980), p. 165.
6. Joseph M. Belth, "A Forgotten Aspect of Life Insurance Disclosure," *The Insurance Forum,* Vol. 5 (December 1978).

APPENDIX

Is Your Life Insurance Reasonably Priced?* (How to Evaluate an Existing Life Insurance Policy)

If you own a life insurance policy on which you have paid premiums for some years, and if you are wondering whether you are receiving fair value for your money, this article is aimed at you.

The Players

Many of those in the life insurance business are legitimate and ethical sales people; however, the business is plagued by a significant number of replacement artists and conservation artists. A replacement artist is a person who uses dubious methods to convince you—the owner of an existing life insurance policy—to replace your policy with a new one. Some replacement artists attempt to discredit the agent and the company from whom you bought your existing policy. Some of what replacement artists say may be accurate, but some of it may be deceptive or even false. The problem is that most policyholders cannot determine what is accurate and what is not.

A conservation artist, on the other hand, is a person who uses dubious methods to convince you—the owner of an existing life insurance policy—that your policy should not be replaced. Some conservation artists attempt to discredit the replacement artist. Some of what conservation artists say may be accurate, but some of it may be deceptive or even false. The problem is that most policyholders cannot determine what is accurate and what is not.

In short, a war is going on between replacement artists and conservation artists. As the owner of an existing life insurance policy, you are caught in the middle. You probably do not know enough about life insurance to be able to distinguish accurate information from inaccurate information, and you probably do not know whom to believe. The purpose of this article is to arm you with the ability to find out for yourself whether the life insurance protection you own is reasonably priced.

The General Approach

This article describes three steps you must follow in order to determine whether the life insurance protection you own is reasonably priced: (1) gather certain information about each policy you wish to evaluate, (2) perform certain calculations using the information gathered in the first step, and (3) compare the results of your calculations with certain benchmarks.

Gathering Information

The most difficult step is not the arithmetic, but rather is the assembling of the necessary information. Some of what you need is in the policy itself, but you may find the information difficult to extract. And some of what you need may not be in the policy. It is suggested that you obtain the information by writing a carefully worded letter to the president of the life insurance company that issued the policy. A suggested letter is shown [on page 405].

You may find the address of the company on the policy itself, on a recent premium notice, or

* The material in this appendix was written by Joseph M. Belth, Ph.D., professor of insurance in the School of Business at Indiana University (Bloomington), and author of *Life Insurance: A Consumer's Handbook* (1985). It was first published in the June 1982 issue of *The Insurance Forum*, of which Professor Belth is the editor, and was modified slightly for the purposes of this appendix. Copyright © 1982 by Insurance Forum, Inc., P.O. Box 245, Ellettsville, IN 47429. Used by permission.

by calling your local library. You may find the policy number on the policy itself or on a recent premium notice. Your letter should request the following items of information:

(1) The amount that the insurance company would have paid to your beneficiary if you had died at the end of the most recently completed policy year. This is the face amount (*F*) of your policy.
(2) The amount that the insurance company would have paid to you if you had surrendered your policy at the end of the most recently completed policy year. This is the cash value (*CV*) of your policy. (Some policies do not have cash values, so the amount here could be zero.)
(3) The amount that the insurance company would have paid to you if you had surrendered your policy at the end of the year preceding the most recently completed policy year. This (*CVP*) corresponds to item (2), but for one year earlier.
(4) The premium (*P*) for the most recently completed policy year. (Policies that are "paid up" require no further premiums, so the amount here could be zero.)
(5) The dividend (*D*) for the most recently completed policy year. (Some policies do not pay dividends, so the amount here could be zero.)
(6) The date on which the most recently completed policy year began.
(7) Your insurance age, in accordance with the company's method of determining age, on the date referred to in item (6) above.

It is recommended that you word the letter exactly as illustrated, and that you keep a copy of the letter. If you receive no response, or if you receive an inadequate response, you should file a written complaint with your state insurance commissioner. You may obtain the address of your state insurance commissioner from your local library.

The Calculations

Once you have acquired the information listed in the preceding section, you are ready to perform certain calculations, except for the choice of an interest rate (*i*). It is suggested that you use an interest rate of 6 percent (.06) in your calculations. (For comments concerning the interest rate, see the explanatory appendix at the end of this article.)

Now you are ready to perform certain calculations in order to arrive at a yearly price per $1,000 of protection for the most recently completed policy year. The formula is as follows:

$$\frac{(P + CVP)(1 + i) - (CV + D)}{(F - CV)(.001)}$$

To illustrate, suppose the response to your letter provided the following information:

(1) Face amount (*F*): $25,000
(2) Cash value at end of most recently completed policy year (*CV*): $10,450
(3) Cash value at end of year preceding most recently completed policy year (*CVP*): $10,000
(4) Premium (*P*): $550
(5) Dividend (*D*): $400
(6) Date on which most recently completed policy year began: March 10, 1981.
(7) Your insurance age on March 10, 1981: 56

Your next step is to plug these figures into the formula. The calculations are as follows:

$$\frac{(550 + 10{,}000)(1 + .06) - (10{,}450 + 400)}{(25{,}000 - 10{,}450)(.001)}$$

$$= \frac{(10{,}550)(1.06) - 10{,}850}{(14{,}550)(.001)}$$

$$= \frac{11{,}183 - 10{,}850}{14.550} = \frac{333}{14.550} = 22.89$$

In other words, the yearly price per $1,000 of protection in the most recently completed policy year (which began on March 10, 1981) is $22.89, assuming 6 percent interest.

The Comparison

The benchmarks against which to compare yearly prices per $1,000 of protection are shown on this page. The suggested interpretations of the benchmark figures are as follows:

(1) If the yearly price per $1,000 of protection is less than the benchmark figure, the price of your protection is low, and you should not consider replacing your policy.
(2) If the yearly price per $1,000 of protection is more than the benchmark figure but less than double that figure, the price of your protection is moderate, and again you should not consider replacing your policy.
(3) If the yearly price per $1,000 of protection is more than double the benchmark figure, the price of your protection is high, and you should consider replacing your policy.

To illustrate, the benchmark figure for age 56 is $15, and the yearly price per $1,000 of protection that came out of your calculations is $22.89. Since the latter is more than the benchmark figure but less than double that figure, the price of your protection is moderate, and you should not consider replacing your policy.

Benchmarks

Age	Price
Under 30	$ 1.50
30–34	2.00
35–39	3.00
40–44	4.00
45–49	6.50
50–54	10.00
55–59	15.00
60–64	25.00
65–69	35.00
70–74	50.00
75–79	80.00
80–84	125.00

Several Warnings

Life insurance policies are complex financial instruments. In this article, we have tried to simplify the subject so that you can find out for yourself whether your life insurance protection is reasonably priced. The simplification process, however, makes it necessary to voice warnings in several areas.

(1) If your policy carries an extra premium because of a health impairment or other problem, the analysis of such a policy is beyond the scope of this article.

(2) If your policy covers more than one life, the analysis of such a policy is also beyond the scope of this article. Examples are family policies (in which husband, wife, and children are covered in one policy) and joint life policies (which cover two lives and pay the face amount on the first death).

(3) It is possible that the year for which you perform the calculations—the most recently completed policy year—is not representative of other policy years. For example, the price of the protection in the first one or two policy years is often quite high, reflecting sales commissions and the other expenses associated with the issuance of a life insurance policy. As another example, the price in a single isolated year may be quite low or quite high because of certain structural characteristics of the policy. For these reasons, you might wish to gather the information and perform the calculations for a few other years, especially if the figure for the most recently completed policy year is either very low or very high. The postscript of the suggested letter is optional; it is designed to help you obtain the information for a few other years, should you wish to perform the calculations.

(4) You may obtain a negative result. This may arise because of an unusual year, as mentioned in the preceding paragraph, or because the price of the protection in your policy is extremely low. A negative figure does not mean the company is crazy—remember that you are using a modest interest rate of 6 percent in your calculations.

(5) If the amount payable on surrender of your policy is equal to the amount payable on death, you have no life insurance protection, and

the yearly price per $1,000 of protection is without meaning. Under these circumstances, you should view your policy as a savings account. Calculate the yearly rate of return (expressed as a decimal) with the following formula:

$$\frac{CV + D}{P + CVP} - 1$$

You can then judge your policy by comparing the yearly rate of return with what you can earn in a savings bank, savings and loan association, or credit union. In making such a comparison, however, you should consider the income tax situation, as discussed in the explanatory appendix below.

(6) If the amount payable on surrender of your policy is only slightly smaller than the amount payable on the death (less than, say, 5 percent below the amount payable on death), you have very little life insurance protection, and the yearly price per $1,000 of protection has very little meaning. Under these circumstances, you should view your policy as essentially a savings account. Use the above formula to approximate the yearly rate of return.

(7) If yours is a small policy—less than, say, $3,000 in face amount, the yearly price per $1,000 of protection may be high because of the expenses associated with the maintenance of a small policy. It may not be worth the bother to replace a small policy; indeed, a small policy may not be worth keeping unless you have some emotional attachment to it.

(8) We were careful to say that, if the price of the protection in your policy is high, you should *consider* replacing your policy. We did *not* say you should necessarily replace your policy. There are several reasons for you to proceed with caution: a replacement necessarily involves the purchase of a new policy, and the purchase of a new policy requires care if you wish to acquire low-priced protection; surrendering an existing policy may involve the sacrifice of certain valuable policy provisions; surrendering an existing policy may involve certain income tax considerations; purchasing a new policy may involve significant expenses in the first one or two years, as mentioned earlier; and because of a health impairment or other problem, you may find it difficult to qualify for a new policy.

An Explanatory Appendix

Instead of following the suggestions in this article blindly, you may prefer to acquire some understanding of the formula and the benchmarks. The purpose of this appendix is to provide a brief explanation.

Let's consider the numerator of the formula. The first parenthetical expression $(P + CVP)$ is the amount that you would have had available to put into some other savings vehicle if you had decided to surrender the policy at the end of the year preceding the most recently completed policy year. You would have received the cash value (CVP) and you would have been relieved of the premium (P).

Multiplying the above expression by $(1 + i)$ tells you what you would have had in that other savings vehicle by the end of the most recently completed policy year if you had invested the $(P + CVP)$ at an annual interest rate of i. This leads us to a discussion of the interest rate.

The interest rate you choose is not important if your policy has little or no cash value. However, the interest rate you choose is quite important if your policy has a substantial cash value. If your policy has a cash value, it probably has a loan clause that permits you to borrow against the policy up to approximately the cash value at an interest rate of 5 to 8 percent. If you believe you could put the money in some other savings vehicle at a much higher interest rate and with a high degree of safety, and if the amount available is substantial, you should consider borrowing against your policy and investing the proceeds of the loan. Bear in mind, however, that the savings vehicle you are thinking about may produce interest income that is subject to current income tax. The interest earnings built into cash-value life insurance, on the other hand, are income-tax-deferred and eventually will be either partially or fully income-tax-exempt. For simplicity, we suggested you use an interest rate of 6 percent in the calculations.

The last parenthetical expression in the numerator of the formula ($CV + D$) is the amount that you had available, at the end of the most recently completed policy year, having continued the policy for that year. The difference between the product of the first two expressions ($11,183 in the example) and the last expression ($10,850) is the price you paid ($333) for the life insurance protection in that year (assuming 6 percent interest).

Now let's consider the denominator of the formula. The cash value is the savings component of the policy, and is an asset from your point of view. Therefore, the life insurance protection you had ($14,550) is the difference between the face amount $25,000) and the cash value ($10,450). The other expression in the denominator moves the decimal point three places to the left, so that the denominator represents the amount of life insurance protection in thousands of dollars (14.550).

Since the price you paid for the protection (assuming 6 percent) was $333, and since the amount of protection in thousands of dollars was 14.550, the yearly price per $1,000 of protection (assuming 6 percent) was $22.89.

Finally, the benchmarks were derived from certain United States population death rates. The benchmark figure for each five-year age bracket is slightly above the death rate per 1,000 at the highest age in that bracket. What we're saying is that, if the price of your life insurance protection per $1,000 is in the vicinity of the "raw material cost" (that is, the amount needed just to pay death claims based on population death rates), your life insurance protection is reasonably priced.

SUGGESTED LETTER

President
XYZ Life Insurance Company
Post Office Box 245
Ellettsville, IN 47429

Dear President:

Please furnish me with the following information concerning my policy number 1 234 567:

(1) The amount that you would have paid in a single sum to my beneficiary if I had died at the end of the most recently completed policy year, including any supplemental term life insurance benefits. Please disregard any accidental death benefits, any dividends, and any loan against the policy.

(2) The amount that you would have paid in a single sum to me if I had surrendered the policy at the end of the most recently completed policy year. Please disregard any dividends and any loan against the policy.

(3) The amount that you would have paid in a single sum to me if I had surrendered the policy at the end of the year preceding the most recently completed policy year. Please disregard any dividends and any loan against the policy.

(4) The premium for the most recently completed policy year, including the premiums for any supplemental term life insurance benefits. Please exclude the premiums for any accidental death benefits, disability benefits, or guaranteed insurability benefits. Please exclude the interest on any loan against the policy, and assume I paid the year's premium in full at the beginning of the year.

(5) The dividend for the most recently completed policy year, including the dividends for any supplemental term life insurance benefits. Please exclude any dividends for

any accidental death benefits or disability benefits. Please exclude any dividends credited to dividend accumulations or additions.

(6) The date on which the most recently completed policy year began.

(7) My age, according to your records, when the most recently completed policy year began.

Thank you for providing the information that I have requested.

Sincerely yours,

[*Editor's note:* The following postscript is optional. See the third point in the section entitled "Several Warnings."]

PS: Also, please furnish the above information for the two policy years preceding the most recently completed policy year, and for the two policy years following the most recently completed policy year. In the case of amounts payable in future years, please identify any nonguaranteed amounts and base the figures on your company's current scale.

LIFE INSURANCE PROGRAMMING AND ESTATE PLANNING

"The primary question to answer is: How much money would my dependents need if I died tomorrow?"

Consumer Reports

STUDENT LEARNING OBJECTIVES

After studying this chapter, you should be able to:

- Describe the four basic steps in the life insurance programming process.
- Determine the amount of life insurance needed to meet certain financial goals and objectives.
- Explain the approaches that can be used to reduce the adverse effects of inflation on a life insurance program.
- Describe the general objectives of estate planning and the basic steps in the estate planning process.
- Explain the estate planning tools that can be used to meet the insured's objectives.
- Explain the special advantages of life insurance in estate planning, and describe how life insurance is taxed.

The fundamental purpose of life insurance is to replace the family's share of the deceased breadwinner's earnings. In developing a sound life insurance program, the basic question that must be answered is the amount of income the family will receive if the breadwinner dies prematurely.

In this chapter, we will study the fundamentals of life insurance programming, which is a method of determining the family's financial requirements and the amount of life insurance needed to satisfy them. We will also examine the basic principles of estate planning, which is a systematic process for the conservation of estate assets and the orderly distribution of estate property. Estate planning is part of the overall programming process, since it involves the distribution of property to family members for their financial well-being after the insured dies.

FUNDAMENTALS OF LIFE INSURANCE PROGRAMMING

Life insurance programming is a systematic method of determining the insured's financial goals, which are then translated into specific amounts of life insurance. The insured's financial assets are taken into consideration in determining the net amount of life insurance needed. The various life insurance settlement options are also used to meet these goals.

Life insurance programming involves four basic steps:[1]

1. Determine the insured's financial goals.
2. Compare present life insurance and financial assets with the amount needed for attaining these goals.
3. Determine the amount of new life insurance needed.
4. Periodically review the program.

Let us briefly examine each of these four steps.

Determination of Financial Goals

The first step in programming is to determine the insured's financial goals. A life underwriter can determine the client's financial goals after a detailed interview. In our earlier discussion of the needs approach in Chapter 16, we noted that there are several basic needs that should be considered in determining the proper amount of life insurance to own. They are:

- Estate clearance fund
- Income during the readjustment period
- Income during the dependency period
- Life income to widow
- Special needs
  Mortgage redemption
  Educational fund
  Emergency fund
- Retirement needs

For example, assume that Joe Friend, age thirty, is an accountant who is interested in having his insurance programmed with these financial needs in mind. Joe presently earns $30,000 annually. He has a wife, age twenty-five, and a son, age one. If Joe should die prematurely, he estimates that his family will need $10,000 for burial expenses, installment debts, and other expenses; $60,000 to pay off the mortgage, which has twenty years to run; $10,000 for an emergency fund; and $20,000 for an educational fund. In addition, he wants the family to have a monthly income of $1,500 during the readjustment and dependency periods. He also wants his wife to have a lifetime income of $800 monthly after his son is grown. These financial needs are summarized as follows:

- Cash needs

Estate clearance	$10,000
Mortgage redemption	60,000
Emergency fund	10,000
Educational fund	20,000

- Income needs
  $1,500 monthly for two years
  1,500 monthly for fifteen years
  800 lifetime income to widow

Figure 20.1 Joe's Life Insurance Needs and Present Coverages and Resources

Cash needs		Present insurance and financial assets	
Estate clearance	$10,000	OASDI lump sum death benefit	$ 255
Mortgage redemption	60,000	Group life insurance	30,000
Emergency fund	10,000	Individual life insurance	25,000
Education fund	20,000	Savings accounts	10,000
	$100,000	Checking account	5,000
			$70,255

Income needs	
Readjustment period	$1,500 monthly for 2 years
Dependency period	1,500 monthly for 15 years
Blackout period	800 monthly for 20 years
Life income	800 monthly for life

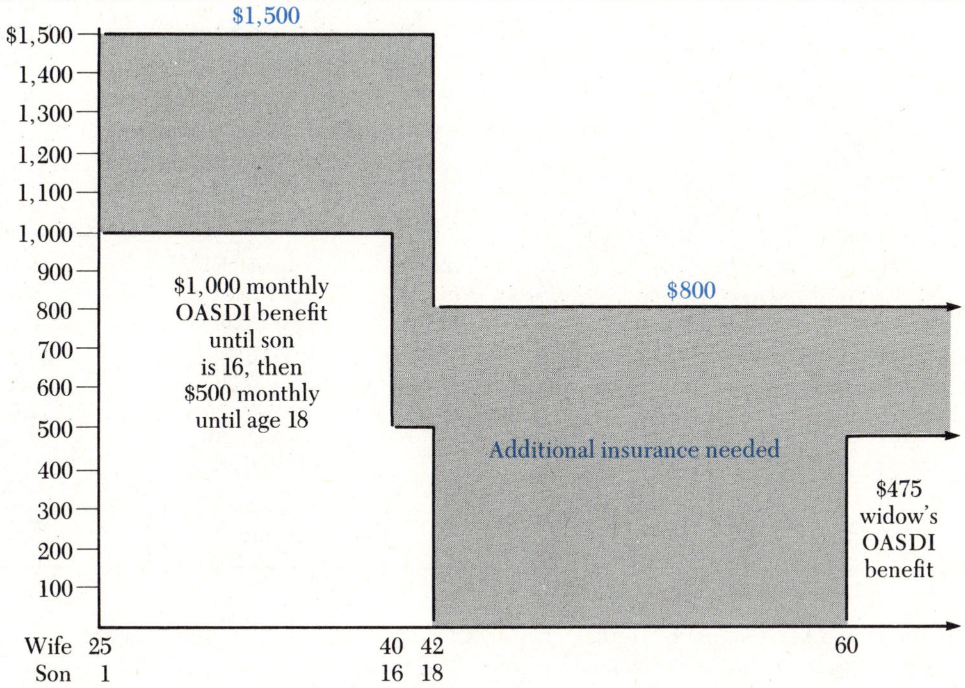

Comparison of Present Life Insurance and Assets with the Amount Needed

The second step is to compare the client's present life insurance and financial assets with the amount needed to attain the financial goals described earlier. In most cases, substantial amounts of life insurance must be purchased to achieve these goals.

Joe is now insured for $30,000 under his employer's group life insurance plan. He also

Figure 20.2
Minimum Monthly Income Payments Per $1,000 of Proceeds Life Income Settlement Options

Single Life Monthly Payments

Adjusted age		Certain period			
male	**female**	**none**	**10 years**	**20 years**	**refund**
50	55	$ 4.62	$4.56	$4.34	$4.36
51	56	4.72	4.65	4.40	4.44
52	57	4.83	4.75	4.46	4.52
53	58	4.94	4.85	4.53	4.61
54	59	5.07	4.96	4.59	4.69
55	60	5.20	5.07	4.66	4.79
56	61	5.33	5.19	4.72	4.88
57	62	5.48	5.31	4.78	4.99
58	63	5.64	5.43	4.84	5.09
59	64	5.80	5.57	4.90	5.20
60	65	5.98	5.70	4.96	5.32
61	66	6.16	5.85	5.02	5.44
62	67	6.36	5.99	5.07	5.57
63	68	6.57	6.14	5.13	5.71
64	69	6.79	6.30	5.17	5.85
65	70	7.03	6.45	5.22	6.00
66	71	7.28	6.62	5.26	6.15
67	72	7.54	6.78	5.30	6.31
68	73	7.83	6.95	5.33	6.48
69	74	8.13	7.11	5.36	6.66
70	75	8.45	7.28	5.39	6.85
71	76	8.79	7.45	5.41	7.05
72	77	9.16	7.62	5.43	7.26
73	78	9.55	7.79	5.45	7.48
74	79	9.96	7.95	5.46	7.71
75	80	10.41	8.11	5.48	7.95

owns $25,000 of individual life insurance. He has $10,000 in a savings account and $5,000 in a checking account. He is also insured for Social Security survivor benefits. If he should die, his widow and son would receive monthly Social Security survivor benefits in the amount of $1,000 until the son reaches age sixteen. At that time, the mother's benefit ($500) will terminate, but the son's benefit ($500) will continue until age eighteen. His widow will also receive a lifetime monthly income of $475 from Social Security starting at age sixty.

As a starting point, a needs analysis chart should be prepared. Figure 20.1 illustrates Joe's financial needs and present resources. It is clear that Joe cannot attain his financial goals based on his present program. The cash needs alone exceed his present insurance coverages and financial assets by almost $30,000. The income needs also cannot be met. An additional $500 of monthly income is required until the son reaches age sixteen, and $1,000 monthly is required for an additional two years until the son reaches age eighteen. The blackout period requires $800 of monthly income; and an additional $325 of monthly income is needed to provide a lifetime income to the widow. In short, additional life insurance is needed to fill these gaps.

Determining the Amount of New Life Insurance

The third step is to determine the amount of new life insurance that must be purchased to complete the program. Two basic principles must be emphasized.[2] *First, the insured is assumed to die immediately.* Since the time of death is uncertain, the only safe assumption is to assume that the various needs must be met immediately. *Second, the most distant need in time is considered first.* You then work backward to the present. Interest income on the funds needed later can provide part of the income needed during the earlier periods.

Let us first start with the *lifetime income* need. From Figure 20.1, we note that Joe's widow will receive $475 of monthly income from Social Security starting at age sixty, so an additional $325 of monthly lifetime income must be provided. By referring to the table in the policy that shows the various life income settlement options, the additional amount of life insurance can be easily determined. Figure 20.2 indicates the minimum monthly income payments for each $1,000 of policy proceeds for the various life income settlement options. Under the life income option, with ten years certain, a female, age sixty, will receive a minimum monthly income of $5.07 for each $1,000 of policy proceeds. About $64,100 of life insurance is needed to produce the additional income. ($325/5.07 × $1,000 = $64,103 or $64,100). If Joe purchases $64,100 of additional life insurance, this amount will provide a lifetime income of $325 starting at age sixty. When added to the monthly Social Security benefit of $475, a life income of $800 monthly can be provided.

The next step is to determine the amount of insurance required to provide income during the *blackout period.* We again refer to Figure 20.1 and note that $800 monthly will be needed for eighteen years. Since the $64,100 of life insurance for the life income need will not be needed until age sixty, interest income on this amount can provide part of the income needed during the blackout period. If a conservative interest rate of 3 percent is assumed, monthly income in the amount of $160 can be paid to the family. We are deliberately assuming a relatively low rate of interest, since any excess interest over this amount can be used to meet the problem of inflation (discussed later).

Since $800 of monthly income must be provided during the blackout period, an additional $640 of monthly income is required. Either the fixed period or fixed amount option can be used to meet this need. Figure 20.3 shows the minimum monthly income for each $1,000 of proceeds paid under the fixed period option. About $107,400 of additional life insurance is required to produce the needed income ($640/$5.96 × $1,000 = $107,383 or $107,400). If Joe purchases $107,400 of life insurance, this sum will provide $640 of monthly income to his widow for eighteen years. When added to the $160 of interest income on $64,100, a total monthly income of $800 can be provided during the blackout period.

The next step is to provide $1,500 of monthly income during the *readjustment and dependency periods.* Social Security survivor benefits to the widow and son will provide $1,000 of monthly income until the son reaches the age of sixteen. At that time, the monthly benefit will be reduced to $500 and will be paid until the son attains age eighteen. In addition, interest income can be earned on $171,500 of life insurance, which will be needed later for the blackout period and life income needs ($107,400 + $64,100). Assuming a 3 percent return, $429 of interest income can be provided each month. (The reason for assuming a relatively low interest assumption is to provide an inflation hedge as will be discussed later.) This income can be used to offset part of the reduction in Social Security survivor benefits when the son reaches age sixteen. An additional $571 of monthly income is needed for another two years to offset the reduction in Social Security benefits and to meet Joe's goal of $1,500 monthly to the

Figure 20.3
Minimum Monthly Income Payments Per $1,000 of Proceeds

Period (years)	Monthly payment
1	$84.50
2	42.87
3	29.00
4	22.07
5	17.91
6	15.14
7	13.17
8	11.69
9	10.54
10	9.62
11	8.86
12	8.24
13	7.71
14	7.26
15	6.87
16	6.53
17	6.23
18	5.96
19	5.73
20	5.51
21	5.32
22	5.15
23	4.99
24	4.84
25	4.71
26	4.59
27	4.48
28	4.37
29	4.27
30	4.18

family. About $13,300 of additional life insurance will provide $571 monthly to the family during the two-year period in which Social Security benefits are reduced ($571/42.87 × $1,000 = $13,319 or $13,300). Thus, the family will receive a total of $1,500 monthly ($500 + $429 + $571 = $1,500) during the two-year period in which Social Security survivor benefits are reduced.

The final step is to provide monthly income to the family during the remainder of the readjustment and dependency periods. The family will receive $1,000 monthly from Social Security until the son reaches age sixteen. Also $462 of monthly interest can be earned on $184,800 of life insurance that will not be needed until a later date ($64,100 + $107,400 + $13,300). Finally, an additional $38 monthly is needed for fifteen years to meet the required monthly income goal of $1,500. This income need can be met by an additional $5,600 of life insurance ($38/$6.87 × $1,000 = $5,531 or $5,600). Thus, these three sources will provide a total monthly income of $1,500 until the son reaches age sixteen.

With respect to *retirement income,* Joe is covered for both Social Security retirement benefits and private pension benefits under his employer's pension plan. He also has an Individual Retirement Account (IRA) that will provide additional retirement income. Since the mortgage on the home will be paid off by retirement, and the son will be self-supporting, Joe believes that no additional life insurance will be necessary to provide income during the retirement period.

In summary, Joe's cash and income needs total $290,400. Since his present financial assets and life insurance are only about $70,000, an additional $220,400 of life insurance must be purchased to accomplish his goals. This is a substantial amount of new life insurance that must be purchased. In many cases, an individual cannot afford to purchase a large amount of new insurance, and the financial goals and aspirations must be scaled downward. However, Joe wants to complete his program, but feels that he cannot spend more than $400 annually for new life insurance at the present time.

Joe decides to purchase a participating five-year renewable and convertible term insurance policy in the amount of $190,400. Since he is a nonsmoker, he is eligible for life insurance at reduced rates. This policy will cost about $260 annually (after dividends) and will enable him to meet the various income needs described earlier. In addition, he also decides to purchase a twenty-year decreasing term insurance policy in the amount of $30,000, which together with the group insurance proceeds of $30,000 will pay off the remaining mortgage of $60,000. The decreasing term policy will cost less than $100 annually.

The $30,000 policy on Joe's life can be used as an estate clearance fund and educational fund. Since the educational fund requires $20,000, the remaining $10,000 can be used for cleanup purposes and estate clearance needs. Cash in the checking account and the Social Security death benefit are allocated for cleanup purposes. Thus, a maximum of $10,255 is available for the estate clearance fund. Finally, Joe feels that the $10,000 savings account can be used as an emergency fund if necessary. Thus, for an additional annuity outlay of less than $400, Joe has accomplished his goals. The complete program for Joe is illustrated in Figure 20.4

Problem of inflation Our discussion of life insurance programming would not be complete without a brief discussion of the problem of inflation. A sharp increase in consumer prices can seriously erode the purchasing power of the life insurance proceeds. For example, if prices double, the purchasing power of the life insurance proceeds is reduced 50 percent. Since the economy has experienced inflation in recent years, it is only prudent to consider the impact of inflation on your life insurance program.

At present, there is no perfect solution to the problem of inflation when life insurance is programmed. However, several approaches can be used to reduce the adverse effects of inflation on life insurance benefits. *First, Social Security monthly income benefits are completely inflation proof.* Whenever the Consumer Price Index increases by at least 3 percent annually, Social Security benefits are correspondingly increased. Since Social Security survivor benefits provide a relatively large proportion of the income required during the readjustment, dependency, and life income periods, an especially effective inflation hedge is present during these periods. However, Social Security benefits are not paid during the blackout period, which is a critical income period for many widows.

A second approach is to assume a relatively low interest rate in determining the interest that can be earned on the life insurance proceeds. We have taken this approach in our earlier programming illustrations. Although life insurers typically guarantee 3 or 3.5 percent interest on the policy proceeds paid under the various settlement options, many companies currently are paying 6 percent or more on these funds. Excess interest earned can then be used to offset part of the loss in purchasing power due to inflation.

Another approach is to purchase additional life insurance that can be used as an inflation fund. Amounts can be periodically withdrawn to supplement the monthly income payments, depending on the rate of inflation.

Finally, a variable life insurance policy can be purchased as an inflation hedge. However, since the premiums are invested in common stocks that may decline in value during a period of rapid inflation, the desired increase in the policy face amount during a period of rapid inflation may not be forthcoming. As an alternative, *a cost of living rider* can be added to the policy that increases the face amount of insurance during the period of inflation. The dividends paid under a participating policy can help pay the cost of the rider.

Periodic Review of the Program

The final step in life insurance programming is a periodic review of the program. Cash and income needs can quickly change depending on circumstances. A birth, death, disability, divorce, legal separation, remarriage, or early retirement can affect the amount of life insurance needed. At a minimum, a life insurance program should be periodically reviewed every two years. If the insured's financial goals and circumstances have substantially changed, a new program may be necessary.

Figure 20.4 Joe's Additional Life Insurance Requirements

Cash needs		Present insurance and financial assets	
Estate clearance	$10,000	OASDI lump sum death benefit	$ 255
Mortgage redemption	60,000	Group life insurance	30,000
Emergency fund	10,000	Individual life insurance	25,000
Education fund	20,000	Savings accounts	10,000
	$100,000	Checking account	5,000
			$70,255

Income needs	
Readjustment period	$1,500 monthly for 2 years
Dependency period	1,500 monthly for 15 years
Blackout period	800 monthly for 20 years
Life income	800 monthly for life

Additional amount of life insurance required = $220,400

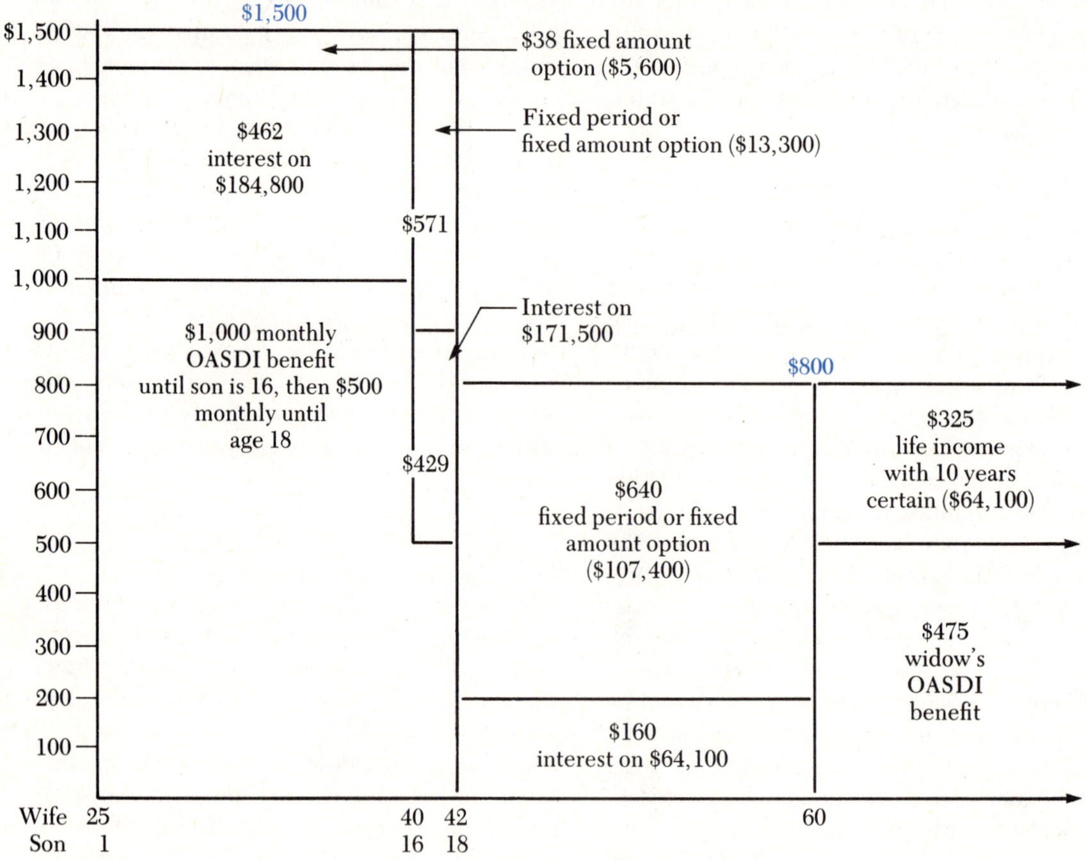

Finally, the rate of return paid by other financial institutions should also be determined when the program is reviewed. If the interest rate on invested funds is substantially higher than that paid by life insurers, the beneficiary should be given the option to withdraw the proceeds and invest them elsewhere.

PRINCIPLES OF ESTATE PLANNING

Estate planning is a process for the conservation and distribution of a person's property and wealth. The general objectives of estate planning are to (1) conserve estate assets both before and after death, (2) distribute property according to the individual's wishes, (3) minimize federal estate and state inheritance taxes, (4) provide estate liquidity to meet the costs of estate settlement, and (5) provide for the family's financial needs. As such, estate planning includes all of the elements of life insurance programming, and adds an additional dimension of estate conservation and distribution.[3]

Estate Shrinkage

Without a proper plan, the value of an estate can be substantially reduced after an individual dies. Estate planners can point to numerous examples of substantial **estate shrinkage** due to the lack of an estate plan or an improperly designed plan. For example, it is not uncommon for an $800,000 estate to shrink to less than $500,000 before the property is distributed to the heirs.

What causes estate shrinkage? It is due to several factors.[4] First, there are the costs associated with the death itself, such as funeral expenses and the expenses of the last illness. Also, there may be installment debts, mortgage debt, and business claims against the estate that must be paid. The estate can also shrink because of legal costs of settling the estate. These costs include attorney fees, court costs, administrator and executor fees, and bond costs. Attorneys generally receive fees equal to 2 to 5 percent of the estate. The fees are substantially higher if the estate is complex, or the attorney must defend the estate in a contested claim.

Forced liquidation of property can also reduce the value of the estate. The estate may lack liquidity to pay the estate clearance costs and federal and state death taxes, so property may have to be liquidated at reduced prices to obtain needed cash. Finally, payment of the federal estate tax and state inheritance tax can substantially reduce the size of the estate before the property is distributed to the heirs. Since one goal of estate planning is to minimize the federal estate tax, let us examine this important tax in greater detail.

Federal Estate Tax

Federal estate and gift taxes are now unified, and the same tax rates apply to both estate property and gifts. The federal estate tax ranges from 18 percent on the smaller estates to 55 percent on taxable estates exceeding $3 million (declining to 50 percent in 1988 and thereafter on transfers in excess of $2.5 million). However, a **unified tax credit** can reduce the amount of tax. The tax credit is $155,800 for 1986 and will gradually increase to $192,800 by 1987. Thus, beginning in 1987, a taxable estate of $600,000 or less will be exempt from the federal estate tax.

The gross estate can also be reduced by certain deductions in determining the **taxable estate.** Allowable deductions include administrative costs, debts, funeral expenses, and any losses that occur while the estate is being settled because of a fire, storm, theft, or other casualty loss. A marital deduction is also allowed, which can result in a substantial reduction of the taxable estate. We will discuss the marital deduction later in the chapter.

The federal estate tax is usually payable within nine months of the deceased's death. For this reason, liquidity is an extremely important consideration in estate planning, because the necessary cash must be available.

Steps in Estate Planning

Estate planning involves five basic steps. They are as follows:[5]

1. Obtain facts about the estate.
2. Evaluate any estate impairment items.
3. Design an appropriate plan.
4. Prepare legal documents.
5. Periodically review the plan.

The first step is to *obtain relevant facts* about the individual's estate. A questionnaire is filled out showing the property owned, family facts, state law that governs the validity of the will, current estate plan, objectives of the individual, and other relevant facts.

The second step is to *evaluate any **estate impairment items.*** This means that potential claims against the estate must be evaluated. This includes an estimate of burial and last illness expenses, attorney fees and probate costs, unpaid federal income taxes at the time of death, and other expenses that will be charged to the estate.

The third step is to *design an appropriate plan.* This involves the judicious selection of various estate planning tools, such as a will, trust, life insurance, and the marital deduction. The plan must then be hypothetically tested to determine if the estate objectives will be accomplished. The fourth step is *preparation of legal documents* by an attorney to carry out the plan. Finally, the plan must be *periodically reviewed.* Many estate planners recommend an annual review of the client's situation to see if the estate plan must be changed.

Estate Planning Instruments

Several estate planning instruments or tools can be used in estate planning. They include the following:[6]

- Will
- Marital deduction
- Gifts
- Trusts
- Life insurance

Will A **will** is a key tool in estate planning. A will is a legal instrument by which property is disposed of in accordance with the individual's wishes. A properly drawn will simplifies the distribution of estate property, minimizes legal and financial obstacles in distributing property to the heirs, and speeds up the estate settlement process. A properly drawn will can also reduce federal estate taxes and ensure the equitable distribution of property to family members.

Many persons die without a will. This is known as **dying intestate.** The property is then distributed according to the intestate provisions of state law where the individual lived. Dying without a will often results in property being distributed to persons whom the deceased would not have wanted to receive the property. For example, in a typical state, if an individual with children dies without a will, the surviving spouse receives only one-third of the estate property, and the other two-thirds goes to the children. The deceased may have intended that the surviving spouse should receive all the property. If there are no children, then part of the estate passes to the deceased's parents in many states. Thus, the surviving spouse may be deprived of needed financial assets for self-support.

Marital deduction The **marital deduction** is a powerful estate planning tool that can substantially reduce federal estate taxes. The marital deduction applies when property is left to a surviving spouse. As a result of the Economic Recovery Tax Act of 1981, the marital deduction is now *unlimited.* This means that, except for certain terminable interests, unlimited amounts of property can be transferred to a current spouse free of federal estate or gift taxes. For example, assume that Gerald dies in 1987 and has a gross estate valued at $1,300,000. He leaves $600,000 of property outright to his wife. In this case, the marital deduction is $600,000. Debts, administrative costs, and funeral expenses total $100,000. The taxable estate is $600,000 and the tentative federal estate tax is $192,800. However, as a result of the unified tax credit of $192,800 for

Figure 20.5
Figuring Federal Estate Taxes

Gross estate			$1,300,000
Less:			
	Debts	$60,000	
	Administrative costs	35,000	
	Funeral expenses	5,000	
			100,000
	Adjusted gross estate		$1,200,000
Less:	Marital deduction		600,000
	Taxable estate		$ 600,000
Tentative tax			$ 192,800
Less:	Unified tax credit		192,800
	Federal estate tax		$ 0

1987, the federal estate tax is zero. (See Figure 20.5.)

If the estate is large, estate planners generally do not recommend leaving the entire estate outright to the surviving spouse by use of an unlimited marital deduction. Although all property would pass free of federal estate taxes to the surviving spouse, it would be subject to the federal estate tax when the surviving spouse dies. The federal estate tax payable at that time on the second estate generally is higher than that paid on the first, since the second estate does not qualify for the marital deduction (unless the surviving spouse remarries). This can result in higher federal estate taxes and a shrinkage in the estate property that can be passed on to the heirs, such as children.

Gifts Living gifts can also be used to reduce the amount of the taxable estate. An individual can give a maximum of $10,000 annually to as many persons as he or she wishes without incurring a federal gift tax on the transfer. If the spouse joins in the gift, a total of $20,000 can be given annually to each person.

Gifts can be effectively used as an estate planning tool, since they can reduce the size of the taxable estate. As we stated earlier, an individual can give a maximum of $10,000 annually to as many persons as he or she wishes free of federal gift taxes ($20,000 if the spouse joins in the gift).

Also, as a result of the Economic Recovery Tax Act of 1981, the value of any gifts (other than gifts of life insurance) made by the deceased within three years of death will not be included in the gross estate for federal estate tax purposes. In general, property can be given away, and the value of the property will not be included in the deceased's gross estate. However, with the exception of gifts to the spouse, a gift tax may have to be paid if the value of the gift to any person exceeds $10,000 annually ($20,000 if the spouse joins in the gift). The unified tax credit can be used to reduce the amount of gift tax payable.

If a federal gift tax is payable, part or all of the unified tax credit can be used to defray the tax. However, any portion of the unified tax credit that is used to defray gift taxes is no longer available for reducing federal estate taxes.

Trusts **Trusts** can also be used as an estate planning tool. A trust is an arrangement whereby property is legally transferred to a trustee, who manages the property for the benefit of named beneficiaries. A trustee can be a bank, trust company, or an adult. A trust can provide security to the beneficiaries and insure competent management of estate property after the individual dies. Certain types of trusts can also reduce estate taxes and administrative costs in settling an estate.

There are two broad categories of trusts: (1) living or **inter vivos** and (2) testamentary. In a living trust, property is placed in the trust while the individual is still alive. If the creator of the trust has the right to revoke the trust and receive the property back, this is known as a **revocable trust.** A revocable trust does not reduce estate taxes, but probate costs can be reduced if the trust is still in existence at the creator's death. In addition, there are some income tax advantages, since the trust income can be taxed to the beneficiaries, such as the children, who may be in a lower tax bracket.

If the creator of the trust gives up the right to receive the property back, this is known as an **irrevocable trust.** An irrevocable trust can reduce estate taxes, since property is taken out of the estate. Probate costs are also reduced. However, there are gift tax implications when property is placed in an irrevocable trust. A gift tax may have to be paid if it exceeds the amount of the unified tax credit.

A second broad category of trusts is a testamentary trust. A **testamentary trust** is provided for in the will and does not come into existence until the creator dies. The testamentary trust can be used to protect minors, handicapped family members, or spendthrift heirs. This type of trust adds flexibility to the estate plan, since the trustee can be granted discretionary powers to deal with the beneficiary's problems and needs as they arise.

Finally, certain testamentary trusts can also be used to reduce federal estate taxes (see Insight 20.1).

Life insurance Life insurance is a widely used estate planning tool. It has several advantages in estate planning. First, life insurance can create an immediate estate, which ordinarily might take years to accumulate. For example, an average wage earner may need a long period to save $100,000. An estate of $100,000 can be created immediately by the purchase of life insurance.

Life insurance also provides estate liquidity. Cash is immediately available for funeral expenses, estate clearance costs, and death taxes. Thus, if the amount of life insurnce is adequate, forced liquidation of property to raise the needed cash is unnecessary. Also, life insurance proceeds paid to a named beneficiary are not subject to probate costs. The proceeds are paid immediately to the heirs without first having to go into a probate court.

And life insurance can provide for the equitable treatment of heirs. For example, assume that a farmer has a son and daughter, and that the son helps manage the farm. The farm is valued at $250,000 and is left to the son in the farmer's will. The farmer can then purchase a $250,000 life insurance policy and name the daughter both owner and beneficiary of the policy. Both children would then be treated equally upon the farmer's death.

Taxation of Life Insurance

Our discussion of estate planning would not be complete without a brief discussion of the taxation of life insurance.

Federal estate tax If the insured has any **incidents of ownership** in a life insurance policy at the time of death, the entire proceeds are included in the deceased's estate for federal estate tax purposes. Incidents of ownership include the right to change the beneficiary, right to borrow the cash value or surrender the policy, and the right to select a settlement option. The proceeds are also included in the insured's gross estate if they are payable to the estate. It is possible to remove the life insurance proceeds from the gross estate if the policyowner makes an *absolute assignment* of the policy to someone else and has no incidents of ownership in the policy at the time of death. However, if the assignment is made within three years of death, the policy proceeds will be included in the deceased's gross estate for federal estate tax purposes.

Federal income tax Life insurance proceeds paid in a lump sum are received income tax free by the beneficiary. If the proceeds are periodically liquidated under the settlement option, the payments consist of both principal and interest. The interest income generally is taxable to the beneficiary. However, if the proceeds are paid to a surviving spouse under either the fixed amount, fixed period, or life income settlement

INSIGHT 20.1

Estate Tax: Not a Dead Issue

While death is obviously a certainty, should you assume the same for estate tax? In light of the 1981 tax cut, the answer, it seems, is no—if you take wise steps now. True, you can leave your entire estate tax-free to your spouse. You also can bequeath $325,000 tax-free to anyone other than your spouse if you die this year [1984] an amount that rises gradually to $600,000 in 1987.

Right now your estate may be small enough to pass tax-free to any heirs. But times change. Prosperity or another period of double-digit inflation might swell the value of your assets, pushing your estate once again into the clutches of the federal tax collector. For example, assume that you come to an unexpected end in 1987, by which time your net worth has grown to $850,000. If your will leaves everything to your spouse, he or she will get the whole sum untaxed all right. But at your spouse's death, only a total of $600,000 can pass tax-free to your children or other heirs. They will lose about $70,800 of their inheritance to the federal tax collector.

You can prevent that possible loss by revising your will so that only $600,000 goes to your spouse on your death and the rest—in our example, $250,000—into something called a *bypass trust*. Depending on how you set it up, your spouse could draw income from the trust and even invade its principal in case of need. When he or she dies, the heirs named in the trust would receive the remaining principal tax-free. The $600,000 that you left to your spouse also would be sheltered from tax as part of his or her estate.

You can put property into a bypass trust during your lifetime. But to qualify for tax advantages the trust must be irrevocable—meaning that its provisions can never be altered—at your death. Although couples with [taxable] estates worth more than $1.2 million can't escape estate taxes altogether, they too can use bypass trusts to reduce them.

A variation of a bypass trust, the so-called *Q-tip trust* (short for qualified terminable interest property), lets you shelter a large estate and control its ultimate disposition from the grave. Assume again that your estate totals $850,000. Make your children a tax-free bequest of $250,000 and put $600,000 in a Q-tip trust for your spouse. It qualifies for the 100 percent marital deduction and provides lifetime income to your spouse, but the principal passes to your chosen heirs after your spouse's death. To put it bluntly, your estate is out of a fortune hunter's reach should your spouse remarry.

A simpler way to avoid taxes is to reduce the size of your estate during your lifetime. A married couple can make annual tax-free gifts of up to $20,000 to each of as many people as they like.

Do you still swear that you'll never be worth enough to worry about estate planning? Visit your lawyer anyway to find out how state taxes will affect your estate. They range from very low in Florida, for example, to highly costly in Connecticut. Also, change your will if it was written before Sept. 12, 1981 and states that you leave your spouse the maximum marital deduction allowed by law. That wording could be construed to mean that you want to leave your spouse only what was tax-free under the old law: half your estate, or $250,000, whichever is greater.

SOURCE: Adapted from the February 1984 issue of *Money* by special permission;

INSIGHT 20.2

Costly Errors and Omissions in Estate Planning

Joint Tenancy

Jerry and Tina Marigold had been married for more than 50 years. Although they were childless, both came from large families, and they were very fond of their nieces and nephews. They had a comfortable estate, consisting of their home and furnishings, several savings accounts, some stocks, an automobile and a piece of undeveloped land in the Arizona desert.

Last May the Marigolds were driving home on a black, rain-slashed night. The road was nearly invisible, and neither saw the washed-out bridge until too late. The car plunged into the swollen river and was swept downstream several hundred feet where it was ensnared on a drowned tree. There it was discovered six hours later by highway patrolmen. Tina apparently had died instantly. Jerry was still alive, but he died on the way to the hospital.

When it was time to settle the Marigolds' estate, it was found that everything they owned except the furnishings was in both of their names as joint tenants—and neither had a will. The result: Everything went to Jerry's family, nothing to Tina's.

This was not what either Jerry or Tina wanted; they wanted their property divided equally between both sets of nieces and nephews. What went wrong?

To begin with, each wanted the other to inherit everything on the first death, and they were told—correctly—that joint tenancy would achieve this very simply, without probate or federal taxes. And that's just what happened. As the survivor, Jerry inherited Tina's interest in all the property—the furnishings as surviving spouse under the laws of intestacy (that is, no will) and the rest as surviving joint tenant. On Jerry's death, everything passed to *his* heirs—his relatives, not Tina's—under the laws of intestacy.

This could have been prevented easily. All they needed were simple wills stating that on their simultaneous deaths or on the death of the survivor, everything would be divided equally between their sets of nieces and nephews. The Marigolds' half-understanding defeated half their purpose.

Some states have ancestral property laws. Under these laws, property inherited by one spouse from another passes, on the second spouse's death without a will, to the first spouse's relatives. The aim is clear, but it may not be too reliable. For example, the ancestral property law in California applies only to the first spouse's separate property, not to his/her share of community property.

Problems With Wills

Joint tenancies caused a different problem for the Andersons—Ed, Jan and their three children. Late in 1982, Ed and Jan had a lawyer draw up new wills for them. The wills conformed to the

option, the first $1,000 of interest income is received income tax free each year. The $1,000 interest exclusion does not apply to the interest option.

Premiums paid for individual life insurance policies generally are not deductible for income tax purposes. Dividends on life insurance policies are received income tax free unless the dividends are retained under the interest option, in which case the interest income is taxable to the policyowner. However, if the dividends are used to buy paid-up additions to the policy, the cash value of the paid-up additions accumulates income tax free. Thus, compared with the interest

Economic Recovery Tax Act of 1981. This act granted married couples an unlimited marital deduction—no estate tax on property passing between them—and increased the *unified credit.* The effect of the latter is to exempt certain amounts from the estate tax, increasing from $225,000 for deaths in 1982 to $325,000 for deaths in 1984 and leveling off at $600,000 for deaths in 1987 and later. These amounts are for *each* decedent, so a married couple with proper wills could pass double the exemption to their children tax free. That's what the Andersons sought to achieve when they had their new wills drawn.

The new wills provided for an *exemption equivalent trust.* This meant that, on the first death, an amount equal to the decedent's exemption would pass into a trust for the benefit of the surviving spouse for life, then to the children on the survivor's death. The property would pass tax free at both deaths: going into the trust on the first death (exempt) and coming out on the second death (not owned by the surviving spouse).

Ed died in the summer of 1984. Under his will, $325,000 should have passed to his exemption equivalent trust for Jan's benefit. It should have passed—but it didn't. It didn't because Ed and Jan held all their property in joint tenancy and everything passed outright to Jan. That was because joint tenancy titles override wills. There was no tax at Ed's death; the marital deduction prevented that. But now the $325,000 will be part of Jan's taxable estate when she dies—increasing the tax by $125,000 as the property passes to the children.

Who's to blame? Certainly the initial responsibility for explaining the effects of joint tenancy under the will pattern belonged to the lawyer, who should have supervised the dissolution of those joint tenancies. But the ultimate responsibility belonged to Ed and Jan. Perhaps they were told what needed to be done but neglected to do it; often people sign their wills, put them away and forget them. Follow-up action is just as important as the wills themselves. In the Andersons' case, their failure to follow up on title changes rendered the wills wholly useless.

The Family Farm

Bjorg Svendsen and his bride, Greta, immigrated to the United States in 1864, pulled by the 1862 Homestead Act that gave them, absolutely free, 160 acres of land if they would improve it and live on it for at least five years. Bjorg did better than that. By the time of his death in 1912, he'd expanded the original 160 acres to 2,000—more than three square miles. Bjorg and Greta had 59 children, grandchildren and great-grandchildren, and from his death until 1942, at least one of his descendants actively farmed the land. That year the last of them left for urban defense work or the armed services. The land from then on was farmed by tenants supervised by a farm management company.

By 1976 the family had become scattered, and several members convinced the others that it

option, the paid-up additions option provides a small tax advantage.

In addition, the annual increase in cash value under a permanent life insurance policy is income tax free. However, if the policy is surrendered for its cash value, any gain is taxable as ordinary income. If the cash value exceeds the premiums paid less any dividends, the excess usually is taxable as ordinary income.

In summary, estate planning is a complex process. We have only touched the basic principles of estate planning in this chapter, and actual case situations can be extremely complicated. For this reason, estate planning is not a do-it-yourself

was time to sell. A prospective buyer was found at a top price. Then the troubles began. By this time Bjorg and Greta had 135 living descendants. Of these, 93 actually owned various fractions of the land through five generations of inheritances, but recorded title listed only 27 owners, some dating as far back as Greta's death in 1920. Her own children, all long since gone, appeared as record owners of fully half the property.

What happened? When someone died, the family simply divided his share of the farm's income among his heirs. Often as not, they took the easy way, and no one bothered to probate his share or record the new ownership. This tangle of titles worked well enough as long as family members cooperated and no one wanted to sell the farm.

Sad to say, here it is 1984 and the tangle is not yet unraveled. Several probates had to be opened or reopened and dozens of affidavits taken. The light has been seen at tunnel's end, but some titles remain dangling. Meanwhile, of course, the prospective buyer has long since gone elsewhere. The lesson is clear: The easy way to handle things often turns out to be the hardest. The family should have kept the recorded titles current so that the true owners could readily be lined up to sign the deed of sale. Even better, if the farm had been held by a corporation or a trust, the sale could have been readily made by the directors or trustees without need of all the title clearances.

Medical Insurance

Don Moser and his wife, Georgia, had two children, Steve and Alice. From the time of her birth, Alice suffered from a chronic illness of indeterminate cause. The medical and hospital bills were sky-high, but Don's employer provided a first-rate group insurance plan that covered all but a small fraction of the cost.

This medical protection lasted as long as Don remained with the employer. But if his employment ceased for any reason—including death—the group protection would end. The policy, however, gave Don or his family 30 days in which to convert the coverage to an individual policy. Don was vaguely aware of this conversion right, but he never thought of telling Georgia about it. So when he died in a hunting accident, no one converted the policy and it lapsed. All Georgia's efforts to get a new policy for Alice have been in vain.

Don should have read carefully his group medical plan, particularly as it applied to his family, and checked its conversion features. He should have discussed the plan with his wife. He even should have posted a notice about those conversion features in the medicine cabinet. It would have been a lot more important to his family's health than any of the pills in there.

SOURCE: William B. Lynch, J.D., C.L.U., "Costly Errors and Omissions in Estate Planning," *Dollar$ense* (Fall 1984, pp. 12–13. © 1984 E. F. Baumer & Co.

scheme, and a team of highly competent professionals is required. A *chartered life underwriter (CLU)* can make valuable suggestions but cannot give legal advice. Therefore, a *competent attorney* is also necessary. He or she can give legal advice and draw up the necessary legal documents. A *tax accountant* may also be needed, especially if there are complex business interests that must be considered. Finally, if a trust is required, a *trust officer* of a commercial bank or trust company can provide valuable advice on the conservation and investment of estate assets. Failure to obtain proper advice can often result in costly errors in estate planning (see Insight 20.2).

SUMMARY

- Life insurance programming is a systematic plan for determining the insured's financial goals, which are then translated into specific amounts of life insurance.
- There are four steps in life insurance programming. They are:
  a. Determine the insured's financial goals.
  b. Compare present life insurance and financial assets with the amount needed for attaining these goals.
  c. Determine the amount of new life insurance needed.
  d. Periodically review the program.
- Inflation can seriously erode the purchasing power of life insurance. If life insurance is programmed, several approaches can be used to reduce the adverse effects of inflation. They are:
  a. Social Security survivor benefits are completely inflation proof.
  b. A relatively low interest rate can be assumed in determining the interest that can be earned on the life insurance proceeds. The excess interest earned can then be used to offset part of the loss in purchasing power.
  c. Additional life insurance can be purchased and used as an inflation fund.
  d. A variable life insurance policy can be purchased, or a cost-of-living rider can be used to increase the face amount of insurance during a period of inflation.
- Estate planning is a system for the conservation and distribution of a person's property and wealth. Without a proper estate plan, the value of an estate can be substantially reduced after an individual dies.
- There are five basic steps in the estate planning process. They are:
  a. Obtain facts about the estate.
  b. Evaluate any estate impairment items.
  c. Design an appropriate plan.
  d. Prepare legal documents.
  e. Periodically review the plan.
- Several estate planning tools can be used in the estate planning process. They are:
  a. Will.
  b. Marital deduction.
  c. Gifts.
  d. Trusts.
  e. Life insurance.

QUESTIONS FOR REVIEW

1. Explain the various steps in life insurance programming.
2. In determining the amount of new life insurance that may have to be purchased, explain the two basic principles that should be emphasized.
3. To what extent should the availability of Social Security benefits be considered in life insurance programming?
4. Why is it necessary to review periodically a life insurance program?
5. Explain the general objectives of estate planning.
6. Describe the factors that may contribute to shrinkage of the estate after an individual dies.

7. Briefly describe the unified tax credit that applies to both the federal estate and federal gift taxes.
8. Explain the five basic steps in the estate planning process.
9. Briefly describe how the following can be effectively used in estate planning:
   a. Will.
   b. Marital deduction.
   c. Gifts.
   d. Trusts.
   e. Life insurance.
10. With respect to the federal estate tax and the federal income tax, briefly explain how life insurance is taxed.

QUESTIONS FOR DISCUSSION

1. A life insurance agent remarked that "life insurance programming offers several advantages to the insured, but certain precautions should be observed."
   a. Explain the advantages that can result from life insurance programming.
   b. What precautions should be followed if you have your life insurance programmed?
2. In life insurance programming, describe an appropriate settlement option or options that can be used to meet the following family needs:
   a. education fund.
   b. funds for federal estate taxes.
   c. income during the dependency period.
   d. income during the blackout period.
   e. life income to the surviving spouse.
3. A life insurance author remarked that "rapid inflation can complicate the life insurance programming process."
   a. Explain how inflation can complicate the life insurance programming process.
   b. Describe the various approaches that can be taken to minimize the adverse effects of inflation on a life insurance program.
4. One important objective of estate planning is to minimize the federal estate tax. Explain how the following estate planning tools can be used to reduce federal estate taxes:
   a. gifts.
   b. marital deduction.
   c. irrevocable trust.
5. An attorney who specializes in estate planning stated that "life insurance can be an effective estate planning tool if properly used."
   a. Explain how the payment of life insurance proceeds can be arranged to reduce the federal estate tax.
   b. Are there any advantages of having the life insurance proceeds paid to a named beneficiary rather than to the insured's estate? Explain.
   c. What federal income tax disadvantage could result from the use of the interest option rather than an installment settlement option?

KEY CONCEPTS AND TERMS TO KNOW

Life insurance programming
Estate planning
Estate shrinkage
Federal estate and gift tax
Unified tax credit
Taxable estate
Estate impairment items
Will
Dying intestate
Marital deduction
Trusts
Intervivos trust
Revocable trust
Irrevocable trust
Testamentary trust
Incidents of ownership

SUGGESTIONS FOR ADDITIONAL READING

Ackerman, Lawrence K. "Estate Planning Principles." In Davis W. Gregg and Vane B. Lucas, eds., *Life and Health Insurance Handbook,* 3rd ed. Homewood, Illinois: Richard D. Irwin, Inc., 1973, chapter 55.

Greene, Mark R. and James S. Trieschmann. *Risk and Insurance,* 6th ed. Cincinnati, Ohio: Southwestern Publishing Company, 1984, chapter 23.

Huebner, S. S. and Kenneth Black, Jr. *Life Insurance,* 10th ed. Englewood Cliffs, New Jersey: Prentice-Hall, Inc., 1982, chapter 2.

Mehr, Robert I. and Sandra G. Gustavson. *Life Insurance: Theory and Practice,* 3rd ed. Dallas, Texas: Business Publications, Inc., 1984, chapters 20 and 21.

Stone, Gary K. and Jerry S. Rosenbloom, eds. *Personal and Business Estate Planning—Selected Readings.* East Lansing, Michigan: Michigan State University Graduate School of Business Administration, 1976.

Waggoner, Leland T. "Concepts of Programming." In Davis W. Gregg and Vane B. Lucas, eds., *Life and Health Insurance Handbook,* 3rd ed. Homewood, Illinois: Richard D. Irwin, Inc., 1973, chapter 52.

Wood, Glenn L., Claude C. Lilly, III, Donald S. Malecki, and Jerry S. Rosenbloom. *Personal Risk Management and Insurance,* 3rd ed., Volume II. Malvern, PA: American Institute for Property and Liability Underwriters, 1984, chapter 14.

NOTES

1. Leland Waggoner, "Concepts of Programming," in Davis W. Gregg and Vane B. Lucas, eds., *Life and Health Insurance Handbook,* 3rd ed. (Homewood, Illinois: Richard D. Irwin, Inc., 1973), pp. 797–815.
2. Dad M. McGill, *Life Insurance,* rev. ed. (Homewood, Illinois: Richard D. Irwin, Inc., 1967), pp. 674–76.
3. For additional information, the interested student should consult Lawrence J. Ackerman, "Estate Planning Principles," in Davis W. Gregg and Vane B. Lucas, eds., *Life and Health Insurance Handbook,* pp. 844–55. For a readable treatment of estate planning for the lay person, see also Philip A. Henderson, *Estate Planning* (Lincoln, Nebraska: Institute of Agricultural and Natural Resources, University of Nebraska at Lincoln, 1977).
4. Ackerman, pp. 845–46.
5. Ackerman, pp. 846–53.
6. Henderson, pp. 12–30.

HEALTH INSURANCE

"Get a company that will pay your claims, not fight them."

Herbert S. Denenberg, The Shopper's Guidebook

STUDENT LEARNING OBJECTIVES

After studying this chapter, you should be able to:

- Describe the basic medical expense coverages, including hospital expense and surgical expense insurance.
- Explain the characteristics of major medical insurance.
- Describe the major features of disability income contracts.
- Explain the meaning of certain health insurance contractual provisions.
- Discuss the major characteristics of Blue Cross and Blue Shield plans.
- Discuss the major factors that should be considered when health insurance is purchased.

Millions of Americans become sick or disabled each year. A serious illness or injury can result in great financial and economic insecurity. Two major problems are encountered if the sickness or disability is serious and prolonged. The disabled person loses his or her work earnings, and medical expenses must be paid. In a typical year, about one in six Americans will be hospitalized, and an average person will visit a physician about five times during the year. If you are hospitalized, the cost of medical care is expensive. An average hospital stay lasts about eight days. In 1981, the average cost per patient stay was about $2,161.[1] Although most persons have some type of health insurance to cover their medical bills, the quality of coverage varies widely. Some contracts are extremely limited in scope of coverage and benefits paid, while others provide broad comprehensive protection.

In this chapter, we begin our study of health insurance contracts. We will first discuss the individual basic forms of individual medical expense insurance. We will next consider major medical insurance and disability income plans. We will also examine some important health insurance contractual provisions. Next, we will discuss the major features of Blue Cross and Blue Shield plans. We will conclude the chapter by describing some important rules that you should follow when health insurance is purchased.

TYPES OF HEALTH INSURANCE

In general, individual health insurance contracts can be classified into five categories. They are:

- Hospital expense insurance
- Surgical expense insurance
- Physicians' expense insurance
- Major medical insurance
- Disability income insurance

In the following section, we will examine each of these individual coverages in some detail. Group health insurance will be discussed in Chapter 22.

Hospital Expense Insurance

Hospital expense insurance pays for medical expenses incurred while in a hospital. A typical hospital policy provides two basic benefits: (1) daily hospital benefit, and (2) a benefit for miscellaneous expenses.

A daily benefit is paid for room and board charges. The plans typically pay a stated amount for each day in the hospital up to some maximum number of days. For example, the insured may be allowed to select a daily benefit of $100 or $150 for 90, 120, or 360 days.

There are three basic approaches for paying the daily room and board benefit. They are:

1. *Indemnity approach.* The plan pays the actual costs of the daily services up to some maximum limit.
2. *Valued approach.* A fixed amount is paid for each day of hospitalization regardless of the actual cost of the services provided.
3. *Service approach.* Service benefits rather than cash benefits are provided to the insured. For example, the full cost of hospital services in a semiprivate room may be paid for each day of hospitalization up to some maximum number of days.

A hospital policy also provides a lump sum benefit for miscellaneous expenses, such as laboratory charges, x-rays, drugs, and the use of the operating room.

There are several methods for determining the amount paid for miscellaneous expenses. They are:

1. *Choice of maximum dollar amounts.* Many newer plans offer the insured a choice of maximum dollar amounts, such as $2,000 or $3,000.
2. *Multiple of daily room benefit.* Another approach is to pay a benefit for miscellaneous expenses that is a multiple of the daily room benefit, such as ten, fifteen, or twenty times the daily benefit.
3. *Percentage participation clause.* Another method is to use a percentage participation clause (coinsurance), such as payment

of 80 percent of the miscellaneous expenses up to some maximum limit.

With respect to maternity benefits, newer individual policies tend to cover only the *complications of pregnancy*, and not the normal costs of childbirth. A complication of pregnancy means a sickness for which the diagnosis is distinct from normal pregnancy, but is caused by the pregnancy.

The normal costs of pregnancy are not usually covered in individual policies because the risk insured against does not meet the requirements of an insurable risk. Since many married couples determine when a child will be born, the event is not accidental and fortuitous. Policies that provide pregnancy benefits generally do not pay the full costs, and usually require a probationary (waiting) period of at least nine months.[2]

Surgical Expense Insurance

Surgical expense insurance can be added to a hospital policy. It provides for the payment of physicians' fees for surgical operations performed in a hospital or elsewhere. The benefits paid are usually determined by a schedule of surgical operations. The schedule lists the different surgical procedures and the maximum amount paid for each operation. The insured has a choice of **surgical schedules**, such as a $900, $1,200, or $1,500 schedule. For example, the policy may pay $1,000 for removal of a lung but only $200 for a tonsillectomy.

A **relative value schedule** can also be used to determine the maximum amounts paid for surgical operations. Instead of having a stated dollar amount for each surgical procedure, a relative value schedule assigns a number of units or points for each operation. The actual dollar amount paid for each operation is determined by multiplying the number of units by the value of the unit (stated in the policy). The advantage of this approach is that it determines the amounts paid based on the complexity and degree of difficulty of each operation. For example, a complex eye operation may have a value of 100, while a simple tonsil operation may have a value of 15. Thus, if the unit value is $10, the policy pays $1,000 for the eye operation but only $150 for the tonsil operation.

Another advantage of a relative value schedule is that it can be conveniently adapted to differences in the cost of living and in surgeons' fees in different geographical areas.

Physicians' Expense Insurance

Physicians' expense insurance pays a benefit for *nonsurgical care* provided by a physician in the hospital, the patient's home, or in the doctor's office. A few plans also pay for diagnostic x-ray and laboratory expenses performed outside the hospital.

Major Medical Insurance

Major medical insurance is designed to pay a large proportion of the covered expenses of a catastrophic illness or injury. A typical major medical policy has the following characteristics:[3]

- Broad coverage
- Few exclusions
- High maximum limits
- Deductible
- Percentage participation (coinsurance)

Broad coverage Major medical insurance provides broad coverage of all reasonable and necessary medical expenses and other related expenses from a covered illness or injury. The policy covers eligible expenses incurred while in the hospital, in the doctor's office, or at home.

Eligible medical expenses include charges for hospital room and board and general nursing care, miscellaneous hospital services and supplies, treatment by licensed physicians and surgeons, and private duty nursing care by a registered nurse. Also, a major medical plan covers prescription drugs, wheelchairs, iron lungs, artificial limbs and eyes, and mechanical equipment for treatment. Some plans even cover transportation expenses to places where specialized care is given.

Few exclusions When compared with other medical expense plans, major medical insurance has relatively few exclusions. Some common exclusions include the following:

1. Expenses caused by war or military conflict.
2. Elective cosmetic surgery.
3. Dental care except as a result of an accident.
4. Eye and hearing examinations, eyeglasses, and hearing aids.
5. Pregnancy and childbirth, except complications of pregnancy.
6. Expenses covered by workers' compensation and similar laws.
7. Treatment received while in a federal or state hospital.

In addition to the above exclusions, major medical plans typically contain **internal limits** to control costs. Some common internal limits are as follows:

1. *Hospital room and board.* The plans place a dollar limit on the daily room benefit paid, such as a maximum of $200 daily. Another approach is to limit the maximum daily amount paid for a semiprivate room.
2. *Surgeons' fees.* Surgical and medical fees may be limited to a maximum dollar amount, such as $5,000.
3. *Private duty registered nurse.* Some plans limit covered nursing expenses to 80 percent if the nursing services are provided in a hospital, and 50 percent elsewhere.
4. *Mental illness, nervous disorders, alcoholism, and drug addiction.* There are often maximum dollar or percentage limits in the policy for persons receiving treatment for any of these diseases.

High maximum limits Major medical policies are commonly written with limits of $50,000, $100,000, $250,000, or even higher limits. A few plans have no limits at all. The maximum amount paid may apply to each separate disability, or it may be a lifetime maximum. High limits are necessary to meet the crushing financial burden of a major catastrophic illness or injury.

The maximum amount paid under a major medical policy depends partly on the length of the benefit period. A **benefit period**, typically one to three years, refers to the length of time major medical benefits will be paid after the deductible is satisfied. When that benefit period ends, the insured must then satisfy a *new deductible* in order to establish a new benefit period. For example, assume that Sam has a $50,000 major medical expense policy with a $250 deductible and a three-year benefit period. Assume that he is hospitalized from a heart attack and satisfies the deductible on the first day of his illness. A three-year benefit period for that illness is then established. At the end of three years, Sam must again satisfy a new deductible if the maximum amount of $50,000 has not been paid.

The purpose of the benefit period is to provide a definite time period within which eligible medical expenses for a specific disease or injury must be incurred in order to be reimbursed under the policy. The objective is to limit recovery to the seriously and acutely ill individual without including the prolonged, chronically ill person.[4]

Deductible A major medical policy usually contains a deductible that must be satisfied before benefits are paid. The purpose of the deductible is to eliminate payment of small claims and the relatively high administrative expenses of processing small claims. By eliminating small claims, the insurer can provide higher and more adequate policy limits and still keep premiums reasonable.

Several types of deductible are used in individual major medical policies. They include the following:[5]

- Each illness
- Each individual
- Family budget
- Common accident provision

A separate deductible can apply to **each covered illness** or injury. The deductible can be $50,

$100, $250, or even higher. Medical expenses relating to a specific disability must be incurred by the insured within a certain time period, such as 90 or 120 days. The important point to remember is that only the medical expenses of a specific disability can be accumulated to satisfy the deductible.

The deductible can apply to **each individual.** This means that all medical expenses incurred by a covered person during some time period can be used to satisfy the deductible regardless of the number of causes or separate disabilities involved. For example, a $100 deductible may have to be met only once during the calendar year. After the deductible is met, the major medical policy starts to pay.

The **family budget deductible** means that medical expenses for all family members are accumulated for purposes of satisfying the deductible. The accumulation period typically is one month, but a longer period could be used. For example, a $50 monthly deductible may be used. If medical expenses for the entire family exceed $50 during the month, the major medical policy starts to pay.

Finally, many individual major medical policies contain a **common accident provision**, which means that only one deductible has to be satisfied if two or more family members are injured in a common accident, such as an automobile accident.

Percentage participating clause Most major medical policies contain a **percentage participation clause** (or **coinsurance**) that requires the insured to pay a certain percentage of eligible medical expenses in excess of the deductible. A typical plan requires the insured to pay 20 percent or 25 percent of covered expenses in excess of the deductible. For example, assume that Susan incurs eligible hospital and medical expenses in the amount of $20,500, and that she has a $50,000 major medical policy with a $500 deductible and an 80-20 percentage participation clause. The insurer will pay $16,000 of the total bill, and Susan will pay $4,500.

The purposes of the percentage participation clause are to reduce premiums and prevent overutilization of policy benefits. Since the insured pays part of the cost, premiums are reduced. It is also argued that physicians and other suppliers of medical care will be more restrained in setting their fees if the patient pays part of the cost, and that the patient will not demand the most expensive medical facilities if he or she pays part of the cost.

Newer major medical policies may contain a **stop limit** by which 100 percent of the eligible medical expenses are paid after the insured incurs out-of-pocket expenses of a certain amount, such as $2,000. Under the traditional major medical plans, the percentage participation clause applies across the board to all eligible expenses in excess of the deductible. Thus, with an 80-20 percentage participation clause, and ignoring any deductible, the insured must pay $10,000 out of a covered loss of $50,000. This could result in a heavy financial burden to many insureds. With a $2,000 stop limit, the major medical policy would pay $48,000, and the insured would pay only $2,000, again ignoring any deductible.

DISABILITY INCOME INSURANCE

A serious disability can result in a substantial loss of work earnings. Unless you have replacement income from disability income insurance, or income from other sources, you may be financially insecure. Many persons seldom think about the financial consequences of a long-term disability. However, *the probability that an individual will experience a long-term disability of 90 or more days is higher than is commonly believed and is significantly higher than the probability of death at every attained age during the normal working life.* For example, the probability of being disabled 90 or more days at age 22 is about seven and one-half times greater than is the probability of death at that age. This disparity decreases with age, but at age 62, the probability of being disabled 90 or more days is still about twice the probability of death.[6]

You should also remember that the economic loss from a long-term disability is greater than the economic loss that results from premature death at the same age. In the case of premature death, the family loses its share of the deceased breadwinner's future earnings, and burial expenses are also incurred. However, in the case of a long-term disability, especially permanent total disability, there is the loss of earned income, payment of medical expenses, loss of employee benefits, depletion of savings, and other expenses, such as getting someone to care for the disabled person. Thus, the economic loss to the family is substantially higher from a long-term disability than from premature death.

It is clear that many individuals are not adequately protected against the loss of earned income during a period of disability. For example, it is estimated that American workers lost about $36 billion in earnings in 1979 for short-term nonoccupational sickness or injury. Of this amount, about $13.4 billion, or only about 37 percent, was restored from private individual and group disability income insurance, sick leave, government insurance programs, and income from other programs.[7] The proportion of earned income restored during the period of long-term disability is undoubtedly much lower.

Disability income insurance provides income payments when the insured is unable to work because of an illness or injury. The income payments are designed to restore at least part of the work earnings lost during a period of disability.

Individual disability income policies typically have the following characteristics:

- Periodic income payments
- Waiting period
- Waiver of premium
- Rehabilitation benefit
- Accidental death and dismemberment benefits

Periodic Income Payments

Weekly or monthly cash disability income payments are paid to a person who is totally disabled because of sickness or an accident. Both sickness and accidents are usually covered, but it is possible to purchase a policy that covers only accidents. An *accident only* policy is less expensive than one covering both sickness and accidents. However, an accident policy is more restrictive and provides incomplete protection, since most disabilities are caused by disease.

The amount of the disability income benefit is related to the insured's work earnings. To reduce moral hazard and malingering that can result from being overinsured, most companies generally limit the amount of disability income to no more than 60 to 70 percent of the person's earned income.

The length of time an insured will receive the disability income payments depends on the duration of the *benefit period.* The insured can select an appropriate benefit period. After a waiting period (discussed later), benefits are typically paid for thirteen to fifty-two weeks, for two, five, ten, or twenty years, up to age sixty-five, or even for life. The benefit period may be the same for both accidents and sickness, but it is often shorter for sickness. For example, a policy may pay lifetime benefits for an accident, but only to age sixty-five for sickness. The benefit period for sickness may be shorter because sickness is subjective, and it is often difficult to determine if a person is truly sick. However, a disability that results from an accident can be determined more precisely, and the insured usually does not cause an accident to collect benefits. A dishonest insured, however, may fake an illness to collect benefits. Also, sickness occurs more frequently than an accident. For these reasons, there may be greater restrictions placed on the length of the benefit period for a covered illness.

Waiting Period

Most individual disability income policies are written with waiting periods, during which time disability income benefits are not paid. Waiting periods typically range from seven to ninety days, up to six months and one year. The purposes of the waiting period are to reduce moral hazard and to reduce premiums. Some persons may fake a

INSIGHT 21.1

How Much Disability Income Insurance Do You Need?

Most persons ignore the risk of disability in their personal insurance program. The correct amount of disability income insurance should be carried so that you are not financially hurt if you are sick or injured for a long time. Consumers Union has provided a simple and convenient method for determining the proper amount of insurance to carry. It involves the following considerations:

1. Disability benefits are generally taxfree, so you need to replace only your take-home (after-tax) pay. Estimate this roughly from your last year's Fedearl income-tax return by subtracting the taxes paid, including Social Security taxes, from your gross earned income (salary only, since any dividend and interest income you now receive should continue). Divide this total by 12 to get your monthly take-home pay.

2. You may already have disability benefits from Government or employer programs. Estimate them as follows:

a. The local Social Security office may help you estimate your Social Security benefits, but don't count on it. An insurance agent can often help you make the estimate, since many insurance companies have a computer program that can easily calculate it. Recently, the average Social Security disability benefit was $851 a month for a wage earner with dependents. To be "disabled" under Social Security, however, you must be unable to do any job whatever. Benefits are payable only if your disability is expected to last at least a year (or to be fatal). Payments don't begin until you have been disabled for at least five months. The amount paid is a percentage of your previous monthly earnings, with some statistical adjustments. The percentage is higher for people with low earnings. When you've received benefits for two years, you're eligible to have medical expenses covered by Medicare.

b. Other Government programs that provide certain disability benefits, if you qualify, include Armed Services Disability Benefits, Veterans Administration Pension Disability Benefits, Civil Service Disability Benefits, the Federal Employees Compensation Act, and state workers' compensation systems. There are also special programs for railroad workers, longshoremen, and people with black-lung disease.

c. Ask your company benefits supervisor to help you calculate the company benefits. In a few states (including California, Hawaii, New Jersey, New York, and Rhode Island, plus Puerto Rico), employers must provide a certain minimum level of benefits. But the state-mandated minimums

sickness and then attempt to collect from the company. This possibility is reduced by a waiting period.

Premiums can be substantially reduced by waiting periods, since they will eliminate many smaller claims. For example, one large health insurer charges the following premiums for a guaranteed renewable disability income policy in the amount of $500 monthly issued to a male office worker, age twenty-six.[8]

Waiting period	*Annual premium*	*Percentage reduction in premium*
7 days	$300	—
15 days	246	18%
30 days	192	36
60 days	150	50
90 days	138	54
6 months	114	62
1 year	96	68

tend to be small ($95 a month in New York, for example), and benefits typically expire after 26 weeks.

Ask first about sick pay or wage-continuation plans (for all practical purposes, these are disability income insurance). Then ask about any plans formally designated as insurance. For any benefit your employer offers, check on the tax treatment. Some disability income benefits, if funded entirely by an employer, are taxable or partially taxable.

d. Your company may have sponsored a group disability insurance plan. A private insurer provides the coverage and you pay for it, often through a payroll deduction. The big advantage of a group plan is that it is usually considerably less expensive than individual coverage, sometimes half as much. A disadvantage is that if you change jobs, you may lose the coverage. The benefits from a group plan in which you pay the premiums are tax-free.

3. Add up the monthly disability benefits to which you are already entitled.

4. Subtract these from your current take-home pay. The result will show the monthly disability benefits you'll need in order to maintain your present after-tax income.

Disability-income worksheet
(Follow instructions 1 to 4 above.)

1. Estimate amount of current monthly take-home (after-tax) pay $ __________

2. Estimate existing disability benefits:
- **a.** Social Security benefits $__________
- **b.** Other Government benefits __________
- **c.** Company programs __________
- **d.** Group disability policy benefits __________

3. Total existing disability benefits $ __________

4. Subtract existing benefits from current take-home pay to determine monthly disability benefits needed $ __________

SOURCE: "Use our worksheet to calculate the disability insurance you need." Copyright 1983, by Consumers Union of United States, Inc., Mount Vernon, NY 10553. Reprinted by permission from *Consumer Reports*, March 1983.

Notice that the percentage reductions in premiums beyond a ninety-day waiting period are relatively modest, since most disabilities have a duration of less than ninety days. Consequently, most insureds can adequately meet their disability income needs by selecting a waiting period of thirty to ninety days.

Waiver of Premium

Many disability income policies contain a *waiver-of-premium* provision, by which premiums are waived during a period of total disability. A typical provision states that if the insured is totally disabled for at least ninety consecutive days, all premiums due during the period of disability are waived. If the insured recovers from the disability, the premium payments must be resumed.

Rehabilitation Benefit

A rehabilitation benefit is also provided in many plans. The company and insured may agree on a vocational rehabilitation program. In order to encourage rehabilitation, the disability income benefits are paid during the training period. At the end of training, if the insured is still totally disabled, the benefits continue as before. But if the individual is fully rehabilitated and is capable of returning to work, the benefits will terminate. The costs of rehabilitation are usually paid by the company.

Accidental Death, Dismemberment, and Loss of Sight Benefits

Some disability income policies also pay accidental death, dismemberment, and loss of sight benefits in the event of an accident. The maximum amount paid, known as the *principal sum*, is based on a schedule. Part of the principal sum is paid for less serious injuries. The following is an example of an accidental death, dismemberment, and loss of sight benefit:

Life	the principal sum
Both hands or both feet or sight of both eyes	the principal sum
One hand and one foot	the principal sum
One hand or foot and sight of one eye	the principal sum
One arm or leg	two-thirds the principal sum
One hand or foot	one-half the principal sum
Sight of one eye	one-third the principal sum

Meaning of Total Disability

Most disability income contracts require the insured to be totally disabled from an accident or sickness. The definition of total disability is stated in the policy. There are several definitions of total disability. The most common include the following:

- Inability to perform all duties of the insured's own occupation
- Inability to perform the duties of any occupation for which the insured is reasonably fitted by education, training, and experience
- Inability to perform the duties of any gainful occupation
- Loss-of-income test

Total disability can be defined in terms of the insured's *own* occupation. **Total disability** is the complete inability of the insured to perform each and every duty of his or her own occupation. An example would be a surgeon whose hand is blown off in a hunting accident. The surgeon could no longer operate and would be totally disabled under this definition.

The second definition is more restrictive. Total disability in this case is defined as the complete inability to perform the duties of *any* occupation for which the insured is reasonably fitted by education, training, and experience. Thus, if the surgeon who lost a hand in a hunting accident could get a job as a professor in a medical school or as a research scientist, he or she would *not* be considered totally disabled, since these occupations are consistent with the surgeon's education, training, and experience.

The third definition is the most restrictive. Total disability is defined as the inability to perform the duties of any gainful occupation. Strict application of the definition would make the disability income policy worthless, since the insured could sell pencils and apples even if confined to a wheel chair. The courts have wisely intervened and generally have interpreted this definition to mean that the person is totally disabled if he or she cannot work in any gainful occupation reasonably fitted by education, training, and experience.

Finally, some companies are now using a loss-of-income test to determine if the insured is disabled under the contract. You are considered disabled if your income goes down as a result of a sickness or accident. A disability income policy containing this definition typically pays a percentage of the maximum monthly benefit equal to the percentage of earned income that is lost. For example, assume that Sam earns $5,000 monthly and has a disability income contract with a maximum monthly benefit of $3,000. If Sam's work earnings are reduced to $1,500 monthly because of the disability (or 70 percent), the policy pays $2,100 monthly (70 percent of $3,000).[9]

The loss-of-income test makes sense, since the loss of earned income is the event that you are insured against. However, at the present time, most newer individual disability income policies *combine* the first two definitions. For an initial period of disability—typically one to five years—total disability is defined in terms of the insured's own occupation. After the initial period expires, the second definition is applied.

For example, assume that Dr. Myron Pudwill is a dentist who can no longer practice because he has arthritis in his hands. For the first two years, he would be considered totally disabled. However, after two years, if he could work as a dental supply salesperson or even as a professor in a dental school, he would no longer be considered disabled since he is reasonably fitted for these occupations by his education and training.

A presumptive proof of total disability exists, according to many companies, if the insured suffers the total and irrecoverable loss of the sight of both eyes, or the total loss of use of both hands, both feet, or one hand and one foot. For example, if Susan loses her eyesight in both eyes because of an eye disease, she would be considered totally disabled under this definition.

Meaning of Partial Disability

Some disability income policies also pay partial disability benefits. **Partial disability** is defined as the inability of the insured to perform one or more important duties of his or her occupation. Partial disability benefits are paid at a reduced rate for a shorter period. For example, a person may be totally disabled from an automobile accident. If the person recovers and goes back to work on a part-time basis to see if recovery is complete, partial disability benefits may be paid.

Meaning of Accident

The definition of an accident is also stated in the policy. An accident can be defined in terms of (1) accidental means, or (2) accidental bodily injury.

If the injury is defined in terms of **accidental means**, both the *cause* of the accident and the *result* (injury) must be unintended and unexpected. However, if the injury is defined as an **accidental bodily injury**, only the result has to be accidental or unexpected. A simple example can make this distinction clear. If James dives off a 100-foot tower into a swimming pool and breaks his neck, he could not collect under an accidental means policy. Although the broken neck was unintentional and unexpected, the cause of the accident was his deliberate act to dive into the pool. Thus, the cause of the accident would not be accidental. In contrast, under an accidental bodily injury policy, he could collect, since only the result (broken neck) has to be accidental or unexpected.

Fortunately, newer disability income policies typically define an injury in terms of accidental injury. However, some older disability income policies and limited accident-only policies still contain the more restrictive definition of accidental means.

COMMON HEALTH INSURANCE POLICY PROVISIONS

In this section we will examine some common health insurance contractual provisions that appear in *individual* policies. The states have enacted laws that require certain contractual provisions to appear in all individual health insurance contracts, while other provisions are optional. The required and optional provisions are based on the model bill drafted by the National Association of Insurance Commissioners. There are twenty-three uniform policy provisions. Of this number twelve are required provisions, and eleven are optional.

Continuance Provisions

A *continuance provision* refers to the length of time that an individual health insurance policy

INSIGHT 21.2

Optional Disability Income Benefits

Several highly desirable benefits can also be added to a disability income policy. Most companies make available the following optional benefits:

1. *Cost of living rider.* Under this option, the disability benefits are periodically adjusted for increases in the cost of living, usually measured by the Consumer Price Index. Two limitations generally apply to the cost of living adjustment. First, the annual increase in benefits typically is limited to a certain maximum percentage (such as 5 percent per year); second, there is usually a maximum limit on the overall increase in benefits (such as a 100 percent maximum increase in benefits.)

2. *Option to purchase additional insurance.* Your income may increase, and you may need additional disability income benefits. Under this option, the insured has the right to purchase additional disability income benefits at specified times in the future with no evidence of insurability. The premium generally is based on the insured's age at the time the additional benefits are purchased.

3. *Social Security substitute.* Social Security disability benefits are difficult to obtain because of the harsh definition of disability and stringent eligibility requirements. The Social Security substitute option pays you an additional amount if you are turned down for Social Security disability benefits.

will remain in force. There are five basic types of continuance provisions. They are:

- Cancellable
- Renewable at the insurer's option
- Conditionally renewable
- Guaranteed renewable
- Noncancellable

Cancellable From the consumer's viewpoint, the lease desirable policy is one that can be cancelled. The insurer can cancel by giving at least five days written notice to the insured. Fortunately, cancellable policies are rare today. Cancellable policies are not used at all in individual basic medical expense and major medical plans. Many states prohibit this type of policy, and if it is used, cancellation is generally restricted to the renewal date of the policy.

Renewable at the insurer's option Under a policy that is **renewable at the insurer's option**, the company cannot cancel during the policy term, but the right to renew the policy for another period is at the insurer's option. This policy is not much better than a cancellable policy, since the insured has no guarantee that the policy will be continued. Although the company cannot cancel during the policy term, it can cancel indirectly by refusing to renew the policy.

Conditionally renewable A **conditionally renewable** policy cannot be cancelled during the policy term, but the company can refuse to renew the policy under certain conditions stated in the contract. For example, the company may refuse to renew the policy if premiums are not paid, if renewals are declined on all similar policies in the state, or if the insured attains age sixty-five, when Medicare coverage begins. In addition, the company may agree to renew the policy beyond age sixty-five only if the insured is employed full-time. The insurance may terminate at the end of the month if full-time employment ceases.

Guaranteed renewable A **guaranteed renewable** policy is one by which the company guarantees to renew the policy to a stated age, typically age sixty-five. The policy can not be cancelled, and renewal of the policy is at the insured's sole discretion. However, the company has the right to increase premium rates for the underwriting class in which the insured is placed. Although an individual insured cannot be singled out for a rate increase, premium rates can be increased for the class as a whole.

This type of policy provides considerable protection. The policy cannot be cancelled regardless of the number of claims or of an individual's deterioration in health. Although premium rates can be increased for broad classes of insureds, this feature should not be viewed as undesirable, since a fixed premium guarantee requires substantially higher premiums.

Noncancellable A **noncancellable** policy provides the greatest protection to the insured. A noncancellable policy is one that cannot be cancelled: the insurer guarantees renewal of the policy to a stated age, such as age sixty-five, and the premium rates cannot be increased. The noncancellable policy is similar to the guaranteed renewable policy described earlier, except that the premiums or rate structure are guaranteed. The premium may be level from the issue date or increase according to a rate schedule inserted in the policy. However, after the policy is issued, the company can neither change the premiums (or rate schedule) nor place any restrictive riders on the policy.

Although the noncancellable policy provides the greatest protection to the insured, its cost is a major disadvantage. Because of inflation, this type of policy is substantially more expensive than the guaranteed renewable policy.

Preexisting Conditions Clause

To control adverse selection, individual health insurance contracts often contain a **preexisting conditions clause.** A preexisting condition is a physical or mental condition of the insured that existed prior to issuance of the policy. A typical clause states that preexisting conditions are not covered until the policy has been in force for a specified period, generally one or two years. For example, James may have been treated for alcoholism six months prior to issuance of the policy. If that condition is not excluded, it is covered only after the policy has been in force for a specified period, such as two years.

Probationary Period

Some individual policies contain a probationary period that applies only at the inception of the policy. The **probationary period** is a specified number of days after the policy is issued, such as fourteen days, during which sickness is not covered. Accidents are covered immediately, but sickness is excluded for a short period. The purpose of the probationary period is to reduce adverse selection by eliminating coverage for sickness that existed before the policy went into effect.

Another type of probationary period applies to maternity benefits. In those individual contracts that provide maternity benefits, a waiting period of nine or ten months must typically be satisfied. Here again the purpose is to reduce adverse selection.

Recurrent Disability

In disability income insurance, a problem may arise if the insured becomes disabled, recovers from the disability, and then shortly thereafter incurs a second disability. Is the second disability a continuation of the first disability, or is it a new disability? This question is important because if the second disability is merely a continuation of the first, the remainder of the original benefit period applies, but no new waiting period has to be met. But if the second disability is a new disability, then a new benefit period is available, and a new waiting period must be satisfied.

Most disability income policies contain a **recurrent disability clause** to resolve the problem. In general, the second disability is considered to be a continuation of the first disability, unless the insured returns to work on a full-time basis for at least six months. For example, assume that

George has a disability income policy with a one-year benefit period for both sickness and accident and a thirty-day waiting period. Assume also that George has a heart attack and is totally disabled for four months. He would receive benefits for three months. Assume that he recovers and returns to work on a full-time basis. One month later, he has a second heart attack. The second attack is a continuation of the first disability. No new waiting period has to be satisfied, but only nine months of benefits remain. However, assume the second heart attack occurs several years later. This would be considered as a new disability with a new benefit period, but a new waiting period must then be satisfied.

Time Limit on Certain Defenses

The **time limit on certain defenses** provision is required and has the same effect as the incontestable clause in life insurance. After the policy has been in force for two years (three years in some states), the company cannot void the policy or deny a claim on the basis of a preexisting condition or misstatements in the application, except for fraudulent misstatements. After two years, the company could deny a claim if it could prove that the insured made a fraudulent misstatement when the policy was first issued.

Relation of Earnings to Insurance

The **relation of earnings to insurance** provision is often called the *average earnings clause*, and is found in most guaranteed renewable or noncancellable disability income policies. It applies when more than one disability income policy covers the same loss. *The clause states that if disability income benefits payable from all policies exceed the insured's monthly earnings at the time of disability, or average monthly earnings for the two-year period preceding the disability (whichever is greater), the company's liability is limited to the proportion of policy benefits that such earnings bear to the total disability benefits from all contracts.* The clause further states that benefits under all policies cannot be reduced to less than $200 a month. If the benefits are reduced, a pro rata refund of the premium is paid to the insured.

For example, assume Joseph becomes disabled. His monthly earnings are $800, and his average monthly earnings over the last two years are $500. He has $400 per month disability income policy with Company A and $600 monthly with Company B. Both policies contain the relation of earnings to insurance clause. He would collect $320 from Company A and $480 from Company B, or a total of $800. This can be summarized as follows:

$$\frac{\text{Monthly earnings or average earnings over the last two years, whichever is higher}}{\text{Total disability income benefits payable}} \times \text{Benefit stated in the policy} = \text{Amount paid by the policy}$$

$$\text{Company A} \quad \frac{\$\ 800}{\$1{,}000} \times \$400 = \$320$$

$$\text{Company B} \quad \frac{\$\ 800}{\$1{,}000} \times \$600 = \underline{\$480}$$

$$\text{Total paid} = \$800$$

The purpose of the average earnings clause is to prevent profiting from insurance when disability income benefits from all policies exceed the insured's normal earnings. Since a noncancellable or guaranteed renewable policy cannot be cancelled, the insurer must have some protection against an increase in moral hazard and malingering that can result from overinsurance.

Change of Occupation

Disability income premiums are usually based on the insured's occupation. If the insured changes to a more hazardous occupation, the risk to the company is substantially increased without a corresponding increase in premiums.

Under the **change of occupation** clause, if the insured changes to a *more* hazardous occupation, the benefits are reduced based on the amount of benefits the premium would have purchased for the more hazardous occupation. Thus, if James changes jobs from an office worker to a construction worker, and becomes disabled, his benefits are reduced accordingly.

The provision also works in reverse. If the insured changes to a *less* hazardous occupation, the premiums are reduced, but the benefits remain the same. Also, there is a refund of the excess premiums paid by the insured based on the date of the change in occupation, or the anniversary date of the policy, whichever is more recent. Thus, if James is originally classified as a construction worker, and is now working as an office worker, his premiums will be reduced, and any excess premiums will be refunded upon request.

Grace Period

A *grace period* is a required provision. If the premiums are paid weekly, a grace period of at least seven days must be given. If the premiums are paid monthly, the grace period must be at least ten days. When the premium is paid on any other basis, the required grace period is thirty-one days. As a practical matter, most companies today provide a grace period of thirty-one days.

Reinstatement

If the premium is not paid within the grace period, the health insurance policy lapses. The **reinstatement provision** permits the insured to reinstate a lapsed policy. If the insured pays the premium to the company or agent, and an application is not required, the policy is reinstated. However, if an application for reinstatement is required, the policy is reinstated only when the company approves the application. If the company has not previously notified the insured that the application has been denied, the policy is automatically reinstated on the forty-fifth day following the date of the conditional receipt. The reinstated policy is subject to a ten-day waiting period for sickness, but accidents are covered immediately.

BLUE CROSS AND BLUE SHIELD PLANS

Blue Cross plans are nonprofit, community-oriented, prepayment plans that provide coverage primarily for hospital services. *Blue Shield plans* are also nonprofit, prepayment plans that provide payments mainly for physician services. However, within the past few years, most Blue Cross and Blue Shield plans have merged into single entities. In 1983, forty-two plans jointly wrote Blue Cross and Blue Shield benefits. Also, twenty-six separate Blue Cross plans and twenty-five separate Blue Shield plans were in operation.[10]

Blue Cross

The origin of Blue Cross can be traced to a prepayment hospital expense plan for school teachers at Baylor University Hospital in Dallas. The plan was first developed in 1929 by Justin Ford Kimball and provided twenty-one days of hospital coverage in a semiprivate room for a prepayment of 50 cents monthly. Since that time, Blue Cross plans have been developed in all parts of the United States.

Blue Cross plans generally provide **service benefits** rather than cash benefits to the subscribers. Most plans cover the full cost of a semiprivate room in the hospital. Payment is made directly by Blue Cross to the hospital or other providers of care rather than to the subscriber.

Blue Cross plan members can be individuals, families, or groups. About 85 percent of the members are in group plans. The benefits generally are broad and comprehensive. In addition to daily room and board benefits, outpatient services for accidental injury and minor surgery are also covered. The plans also cover medical emergencies, diagnostic testing, physical therapy, kidney dialysis, and chemotherapy treatments. Preadmission testing is also covered in most plans. Also, under many family plans, handicapped dependent children are also covered regardless of age as long as a physical or mental condition exists. Maternity benefits are also provided in most plans.

Most Blue Cross plans also offer *supplemental major medical coverage* for the costs of a catastrophic illness or injury. This coverage is a form of major medical insurance that has variable front-end deductibles and 80-20 percent coinsurance. The maximum benefits range from a low of $5,000 in some plans to a high of $250,000 in others. Some plans provide an unlimited amount of extended benefits beyond the basic certificate.

Blue Cross subscribers can freely transfer from one plan to another anywhere in the United States. Members can transfer from one area plan to another; they can also change their coverage from family to single, single to family, family member to an individual, and group to nongroup without losing continuity of coverage and without having to fulfill any new waiting periods.

Blue Shield

Blue Shield plans are nonprofit, prepayment plans that provide coverage for physicians' and surgeons' fees and other medical costs. The origin of Blue Shield plans can be traced to a number of county medical prepayment bureaus that were in existence shortly before the turn of the century in the northwestern part of the United States. Today, the Blue Shield plans in various communities in the United States are strongly supported and controlled by local physicians and local and state medical societies.

Blue Shield plans presently use two major methods for the payment of claims. The first and newest method is to pay physicians and other suppliers of medical care on the basis of their **usual, customary, and reasonable charges** (UCR). The usual charge refers to the physician's normal or usual charge for a specific procedure. The customary charge refers to the amount charged for the same procedure by physicians with similar training in the same geographical area. The charge is considered reasonable if the physician's usual charge does not exceed the customary charge for the same procedure by doctors with similar training within the community. However, the fee charged by a physician could exceed the usual and customary charge and still be considered reasonable because of some extenuating circumstances, such as complications of surgery.

The second method of payment is the *indemnity approach,* by which a fixed dollar amount is paid for medical care. Predetermined cash benefits are paid for a listed schedule of surgical procedures.

Comparison of Blue Cross and Blue Shield with Commercial Health Insurers

There are several important differences between Blue Cross and Blue Shield plans and commercial health insurers. The major differences are summarized as follows.[11]

1. *Service benefits.* Blue Cross and Blue Shield plans emphasize service benefits rather than cash benefits. Commercial health insurers normally pay cash benefits directly to the insureds.
2. *Nonprofit status.* Blue Cross and Blue Shield plans are classified as nonprofit organizations. As such, they receive favorable tax treatment and are exempt from most taxes. Commercial health insurers pay numerous taxes, including the federal and state income tax and state premium taxes.
3. *Contractual relationship with hospitals.* A Blue Cross plan enters into contracts with local hospitals to provide certain services to Blue Cross members. Blue Cross pays the hospitals directly for the services provided. Commercial health insurers normally have no contractual relationship with hospitals. Instead, cash benefits are paid directly to the insured.
4. *First dollar coverage.* Blue Cross and Blue Shield plans traditionally have emphasized first dollar coverage of claims with respect to base plan benefits. Historically, commercial health insurers have emphasized deductibles and waiting periods in the payment of claims.

SHOPPING FOR HEALTH INSURANCE

When you shop for health insurance, you should consider several important factors. Consumer experts typically make the following suggestions.[12]

1. Insure for the large loss.
2. Avoid limited policies.
3. Consider service benefits.
4. Watch out for restrictive policy provisions.
5. Use deductibles and elimination periods to reduce premiums.
6. Beware of mail-order health insurers.
7. Deal with a reputable insurer.
8. Shop around for health insurance.

Insure for the Large Loss

Insurance should be purchased to cover a large, catastrophic loss that can financially ruin an individual or family. Thus, a high-quality major medical policy and long-term disability income contract should be purchased to provide protection against a catastrophic loss. Try to purchase a major medical policy with a stop limit rather than one that applies the coinsurance percentage to all losses in excess of the deductible. In addition, the disability income policy should pay benefits to age sixty-five and be either noncancellable or guaranteed renewable.

Avoid Limited Policies

A **limited policy** is one that covers only certain specified diseases or accidents, or pays limited benefits or places serious restrictions on the right to receive them. A *hospital indemnity policy* is one example of a limited policy. It pays a fixed daily, weekly, or monthly benefit during a hospital stay. The amount paid is on an unallocated basis without regard to the actual expenses of hospital confinement. For example, the policy may promise to pay $1,500 monthly ($50 daily) for five years if you are hospitalized, no health questions are asked, and the first month's premium is only $1. It sounds like a good deal, but in health insurance, there is no such thing as a "free lunch." The policy is limited. Few persons will ever collect benefits for an extended period. The average hospital stay for persons under age sixty-five is about eight days. If you are confined for only eight days, the total benefit paid would be only $400. During that time, you may have incurred several thousands of dollars of medical expenses, but only a small amount would be paid by the hospital indemnity policy. Also, the policy covers you only while in the hospital. If you recover at home, no payment is made. A preexisting conditions clause is also contained in the hospital indemnity application. For example, if you receive medical treatment within twelve months preceding the effective date of the coverage, the condition is not covered until the policy has been in force for at least one year. Finally, the low $1 premium is a "come on" to induce you to buy the policy. After the first month, the premium is substantially higher, such as $18.10 monthly for an adult age forty and over. If a rough benefit-cost analysis is made, a hospital indemnity policy is expensive. For example, in one company, an adult age forty who is hospitalized only once during the year for an average period of eight days would pay an annual premium of $217.20 to collect a benefit of only $400 ($50 daily).

A **dread disease policy** is another limited contract. It provides high maximum limits for a single disease or for certain specified diseases, such as cancer, encephalitis, or spinal meningitis. A *cancer policy* is one example of a dread disease policy. Some health insurance experts recommend that a cancer policy should not be purchased. They argue that it is illogical to insure yourself more heavily against only one disease because you don't know how you will become disabled.

Finally, *accident only policies* should be avoided, since they are limited in coverage and benefits. A list of these contracts is endless, and includes a travel accident policy while on vacation, a freeway or turnpike accident policy, accident policies sold by newspapers, and travel ticket policies sold over the counter or from vending machines in airports.

Consider Service Benefits

Many consumer experts recommend the purchase of a policy that pays service benefits rather than indemnity or cash benefits. This means that Blue Cross and Blue Shield plans should be considered, because they typically provide full or partial service benefits. These plans generally provide comprehensive service benefits that automatically keep pace with inflation.

However, Blue Cross and Blue Shield plans are usually more expensive than policies sold by commercial insurers. As the costs of covered medical services rise because of inflation, premiums must also rise. Most Blue Cross and Blue Shield plans have substantially increased premiums to policyowners in recent years. However, for persons who can afford to pay higher premiums, plans that provide service benefits have much to recommend.

Watch Out for Restrictive Policy Provisions

Even the best health insurance policies contain restrictions. You should be aware of them. Some common restrictions include a preexisting conditions clause, probationary period, exclusionary riders, and a house confinement clause in some contracts.

Consumer advisors generally recommend that a policy with a *preexisting conditions clause* longer than one year should not be purchased. Also, you should determine how far back the company will go in determining whether you have a preexisting condition. The most liberal is to exclude a condition only if medical treatment has been received within one year of the issuance of the policy. Some companies go back five years, while others go back as far as birth.

A *probationary period* should be as short as possible. We noted earlier that a probationary period excludes sickness or certain types of disease for a short period after the contract is first issued. The most liberal is an exclusion period of only fourteen days; other companies will exclude sickness for the first thirty days, while others will require a waiting period of six months or more for certain diseases such as heart disease, cancer, or tuberculosis.

You should also avoid purchasing a policy in which an **exclusionary rider** appears. Many insurers require you to fill out a health questionnaire before the policy is issued. If the questionnaire reveals that you have been treated for a certain disease, such as cancer or heart disease, the company may add a rider to the policy that excludes the condition. As an alternative, some companies will cover the impairment but charge a higher premium or else pay reduced benefits. In any event, exclusionary riders that limit coverage should be avoided if possible.

Finally, you should determine whether the policy has a *house confinement* clause which limits the payment of benefits while the insured is confined to the home or hospital. A small number of policies still contain this obsolete provision.

Use Deductibles and Elimination Periods to Reduce Premiums

A good individual health insurance policy is expensive. A high quality basic medical expense contract and major medical policy that covers the entire family can easily cost more than $1,000 annually. The premiums can be reduced by purchasing the policy with a sizable deductible. Most individual health insurance policies pay *first dollar benefits*, which means they start to pay with the first dollar of loss. The result is that many persons are adequately covered for small loss, but are underinsured for the large, catastrophic loss. A deductible can reduce small claims that are better budgeted for out of an individual's income. As a general rule, a deductible of at least $100 should be purchased to hold down premiums.

Likewise, elimination or waiting periods should be used when a disability income policy is purchased. We saw earlier how premiums can be substantially reduced by buying a policy with at least a thirty-day waiting period.

Beware of Mail-Order Health Insurers

In recent years, mail-order health insurance has become increasingly popular. Many companies advertise heavily in newspapers, TV, radio, and the mails. Often a movie star or other celebrity will endorse the policy and recommend it as a "good buy for the American family."

Careful shoppers should exercise great caution in purchasing health insurance from mail-order companies. The advertising is often deceptive, despite efforts by state insurance departments to force certain mail-order insurers to clean up their advertising. In addition, the hospital indemnity policy is widely promoted by mail-order companies. We noted earlier how little this policy can pay. Finally, some mail-order insurers have relatively low loss ratios because of restrictive claims practices. A United States Senate study showed that one mail-order insurer rejected 38.5 percent of its first year's claims.[13] The restrictive claims practices are often due to a liberal interpretation of the preexisting conditions clause.

Deal with a Reputable Insurer

You should deal with a company that will pay your claims and not fight them. The payoff under a health insurance policy occurs when a claim is submitted. A reputable insurer will have a fair, efficient, and courteous claims policy. Unfortunately, not all companies fit this category.

It is difficult for the average person to know the claims practices of a certain insurer. One suggestion is to call or write the complaint division of your state insurance department and inquire about the company. If a large number of complaints are lodged against a particular insurer, you may want to deal with another company. Another suggestion is to ask a friend or acquaintance who may be a policyowner in that company how fairly he or she has been treated. In any event, a company with a legalistic, narrow, or restrictive claims policy should be avoided.

In addition, you should deal only with a financially strong company. A liberal claims policy is of no value if the company is broke when you file a claim. You should insure with companies that receive one of the two highest ratings for financial stability (A+ or A) from *Best's Insurance Reports*, a journal that can be found in most major libraries. If you are really serious, you should go back several years to see if the recommendation for a particular company has changed. A lowered rating, or no recommendation at all, is a definite warning signal that the financial condition of the company has changed.

Shop Around for Health Insurance

You should contact more than one company before a policy is purchased. Although price is important, it is not the only consideration. A low-premium policy may contain restrictive provisions or pay limited benefits, or may reflect a restrictive claims policy. Herbert S. Denenberg, a nationally known consumer advisor, recommends that you get answers to the following fifteen questions before you buy a policy.[14]

1. Is the company's loss ratio over 50%? (The higher, the better)[15]
2. Does the policy cover both illnesses and accidents? (It should.)
3. Does it cover all or most accidents and illnesses that may put you in a hospital? (The more it covers, the better.)
4. Does the policy offer service benefits (full coverage) or does it offer benefits on an indemnity basis up to specified dollar amounts only? (Service benefits are most advantageous.)
5. If it provides indemnity benefits, do the benefits cover at least a major portion of the daily hospital costs and surgeon's fees in your area? (The higher, the better.)
6. Is there a waiting period, for instance thirty days, during which new illnesses will not be covered? Is there a longer waiting period, for instance six months, during which coverage for specified illnesses or diseases is likewise excluded? (The shorter the waiting period and the less it covers, the better.)
7. Is there an exclusion against coverage for preexisting conditions? Is it longer than one year? (More than one year is too long.)

8. Are there exclusionary riders limiting your coverage in important respects? (There shouldn't be, except in unusual cases.)
9. Does the company receive one of the two highest ratings for financial stability from *Best's Insurance Reports*? (It should.)
10. Does the company offer fair, efficient, and courteous claim service? (It should.)
11. If you are applying for family coverage, does the policy provide automatic coverage for infants from date of birth? (It should.)
12. If you are applying for family coverage, is there a waiting period for maternity coverage? Is it longer than eight or nine months? Are the benefits adequate to cover the costs of pregnancy and delivery in your area? (If you need maternity coverage, make sure you have it.)
13. Can the company cancel your policy? If so, when and under what circumstances?
14. Can the company raise your premiums? If so, when and under what circumstances?
15. Are you buying a mail-order policy? (Beware of deceptive advertising.)

SUMMARY

- Health insurance policies generally can be classified into five categories. They are:
  a. Hospital expense insurance
  b. Surgical expense insurance
  c. Physicians' expense insurance
  d. Major medical insurance
  e. Disability income plans
- A hospital policy pays a daily room and board benefit for each day of hospitalization. A benefit for miscellaneous expenses or hospital extras is also paid. A surgical policy provides for the payment of physicians' fees for surgical operations. Physicians' expense insurance pays a benefit for nonsurgical care provided by a physician in the hospital, office, or home.
- Major medical insurance is designed to cover the expenses of a catastrophic illness or injury. A typical major medical plan has certain characteristics. They are:
  a. Broad coverage.
  b. Few exclusions.
  c. High maximum limits.
  d. Deductible.
  e. Percentage participation clause (coinsurance).
- Disability income plans provide for the periodic payment of income to an individual who is totally disabled. The benefits are paid after a waiting period is satisfied. The insured generally has a choice of benefit periods. After ninety days, all premiums are waived if the insured is totally disabled.
- The definition of disability is stated in a disability income policy. For the first two years, total disability is typically defined as the inability to perform all duties of the insured's own occupation. After that time, total disability is defined as the inability to perform the duties of any occupation for which the insured is reasonably fitted by education, training, and experience.

- A continuance provision refers to the length of time that an individual health insurance policy can remain in force. The basic types of continuance provisions are:
  a. Cancellable.
  b. Renewable at the insurer's option.
  c. Conditionally renewable.
  d. Guaranteed renewable.
  e. Noncancellable.
- Health insurance policies contain certain contractual provisions. Some provisions are required by state law, while others are optional.
- Blue Cross plans are nonprofit, community-oriented, prepayment plans that provide coverage primarily for hospital services. Blue Shield plans are nonprofit, prepayment plans that provide payments mainly for physician services.
- Consumer experts recommend certain rules to follow when health insurance is purchased. They are:
  a. Insure for the large loss.
  b. Avoid limited policies.
  c. Consider service benefits.
  d. Watch out for restrictive policy provisions.
  e. Use deductibles and elimination periods to reduce premiums.
  f. Beware of mail-order health insurers.
  g. Deal with a reputable insurer.
  h. Shop around for health insurance.

QUESTIONS FOR REVIEW

1. Describe the benefits typically payable under a hospital expense and surgical expense policy.
2. Explain the basic characteristics of a major medical policy. Why are deductibles and coinsurance used in a major medical policy?
3. Describe the various types of deductibles that may be found in major medical policies.
4. Explain the major features of a disability income policy.
5. Explain the various definitions of total disability that are found in individual disability income contracts.
6. Explain the distinction between *accidental means* and *accidental bodily injury*.
7. Describe the basic types of continuance provisions in individual health insurance policies.
8. Briefly describe the following clauses:
   a. Preexisting conditions.
   b. Probationary period.
   c. Recurrent disability.
   d. Time limit on certain defenses.
   e. Relation of earnings to insurance.
   f. Change in occupation.
9. Describe the basic characteristics of Blue Cross and Blue Shield plans.
10. Explain the options that can be added to a disability income policy.

QUESTIONS FOR DISCUSSION

1. Explain the major differences between a typical individual hospital-surgical expense policy and an individual major medical policy with respect to the following:
   a. Use of a surgical schedule.
   b. Use of deductibles.
   c. Benefit limits.
2. Compare a typical guaranteed renewable disability income policy with a noncancellable disability income policy with respect to each of the following:
   a. Continuance of coverage.
   b. Use of waiting periods.
   c. Premium guarantees.
3. Mary's average earnings over the last two years are $900 per month. She is totally disabled as a result of an automobile accident. At the time of the accident, she was earning $1,500 monthly. She has a $1,000 guaranteed renewable disability income policy with Company A. Benefits are payable to age sixty-five for both accidents and sickness after a thirty-day waiting period. She owns a similar disability income policy with Company B in the amount of $1,000 monthly. Both policies contain the relation of earnings to insurance clause (average earnings clause).
   a. What is the purpose of the relation of earnings to insurance clause?
   b. Based on the above information, how much will Mary collect during the period of disability?
4. The definition of disability in a disability income policy is stated in the contract.
   a. How is total disability defined in a typical disability income policy?
   b. How is an accident defined in a disability income policy?
5. Compare Blue Cross and Blue Shield plans with commercial health insurers with respect to the following:
   a. Benefits provided.
   b. Use of deductibles.
   c. Protection against inflation in medical care.
6. If you are shopping for a health insurance policy, what important factors should you consider? Explain your answer.

KEY CONCEPTS AND TERMS TO KNOW

Hospital expense insurance
Surgical expense insurance
Physicians' expense insurance
Indemnity approach
Valued approach
Service approach
Surgical schedule
Relative value schedule
Major medical insurance
Percentage participation clause (coinsurance)
Internal limits
Benefit period
Each illness deductible
Each individual deductible
Family budget deductible

Common accident provision
Stop limit
Disability income insurance
Total disability
Partial disability
Accidental means
Accidental bodily injury
Renewable at insurer's option
Conditionally renewable
Guaranteed renewable
Noncancellable
Preexisting conditions clause
Probationary period
Recurrent disability clause
Time limit on certain defenses clause
Relation of earnings to insurance clause
Change of occupation clause
Reinstatement provision
Blue Cross and Blue Shield plans
Service benefits
Usual, customary, and reasonable charges
Limited policy
Dread disease policy
Exclusionary rider

SUGGESTIONS FOR ADDITIONAL READING

"Disability Income Insurance," *Consumer Reports*, Vol. 48, No. 3 (March 1983) and "Follow-up: Disability Insurance," *Consumer Reports*, Vol. 48, No. 7 (July 1983).

Glenn L. Wood, Claude C. Lilly III, Donald S. Malecki, and Jerry S. Rosenbloom. *Personal Risk Management and Insurance*, 3rd ed., Volume II. Malvern, Pennsylvania: American Institute for Property and Liability Underwriters, 1984, chapter 9.

Hall, Jr., Charles P. "The Future of Health Insurance and Medicare: A 20 Year Forecast," *The Journal of Insurance Issues and Practices*, Vol. 6, No. 2 (June 1983).

Henderson, Robert R. *Health Care in the United States*. New York: Metropolitan Life Insurance Company, 1982.

Huebner, S. S. and Kenneth Black, Jr. *Life Insurance*, 10th ed. Englewood Cliffs, New Jersey: Prentice-Hall, Inc., 1982, chapters 17, 18, and 19.

Mehr, Robert I. and Sandra G. Gustavson. *Life Insurance: Theory and Practice*, 3rd ed. Dallas, Texas: Business Publications, Inc., 1984, chapter 12.

Soule, Charles E. *Disability Income Insurance: The Unique Risk*, Homewood, IL: Dow Jones-Irwin, 1984.

Williams, Jr., C. Arthur and Richard M. Heins. *Risk Management and Insurance*, 5th ed. New York: McGraw-Hill Book Company, 1985, chapter 24.

NOTES

1. *Source Book of Health Insurance Data: 1982–1983* (Washington, D.C.: Health Insurance Association of America, 1983), pp. 6, 69, 71.
2. Some older policies pay a flat amount for childbirth, such as $500. A waiting period of nine or ten months is required. Some companies permit maternity benefits to be added as an optional coverage, but the cost is relatively high for the limited benefits provided. Blue Cross plans pay most or all of the hospital costs of childbirth.
3. A detailed description of major medical expense can be found in Harry M. Johnson, "Major Medical Expense Insurance," *CLU Study Guide, CLU Course HS 323, Financial Statement Analysis/Individual Insurance* (Bryn Mawr, Pennsylvania: The American College, 1984).
4. Johnson, p. 4.33.
5. Johnson, pp. 4.30–4.31.
6. George E. Rejda, *Social Insurance and Economic Security*, 2nd ed. (Englewood Cliffs, N.J.: Prentice-Hall, Inc., 1984), p. 199.
7. *Source Book of Health Insurance Data: 1982–1983*, p. 24.
8. Benefits are paid to age sixty-five for both sickness and accidents.

9. "Disability Income Insurance," *Consumer Reports,* Vol. 48, No. 3 (March 1983), p. 368.
10. Burton T. Beam, Jr., and John J. McFadden, *Employee Benefits* (Homewood, IL: Richard D. Irwin, 1985), p. 133.
11. S. S. Huebner and Kenneth Black, Jr. *Life Insurance,* 10th ed. (Englewood Cliffs, N.J.: Prentice-Hall, Inc., 1982), pp. 258–260.
12. Herbert S. Denenberg, *The Shopper's Handbook* (Washington, D.C.: Consumer News, Inc., 1974), pp. 91–101.
13. Denenberg, p. 100.
14. Denenberg, pp. 97–98.
15. The loss ratio is the ratio of incurred losses and loss-adjustment expenses to earned premiums.

CHAPTER 22

EMPLOYEE BENEFIT PLANS

"There's safety and savings in numbers. Try to get group coverage."

Herbert S. Denenberg, The Shopper's Guidebook

STUDENT LEARNING OBJECTIVES

After studying this chapter, you should be able to:

- Show how group insurance differs from individual insurance.
- Explain the basic underwriting principles that are followed in group insurance to obtain favorable experience.
- Describe some common eligibility requirements in group insurance.
- Describe the basic types of group life insurance plans.
- Explain the major characteristics of group medical expense plans.
- Describe the basic characteristics of group disability income and dental insurance plans.
- Describe the basic characteristics of health maintenance organizations (HMOs) and explain the advantages and disadvantages of HMOs.
- Explain the characteristics of a preferred provider organization (PPO).

Most large firms have a wide variety of employee benefit plans that provide considerable financial security to covered employees and their dependents. Employee benefit plans generally are employer-sponsored plans that pay benefits if the workers die, become sick or disabled, or lose their work earnings as a result of retirement or unemployment.

In this chapter, we begin our study of employee benefit plans. Our discussion will be limited largely to group life and health insurance plans, since these plans are widely used by most employers. Private pensions and other retirement plans will be discussed in Chapter 23. We will first examine the nature of group insurance, basic underwriting principles and eligibility requirements. We will then discuss group life insurance, which is the most basic type of employee benefit provided today. We will also examine the major types of group health insurance plans that are used by employers today. We will conclude the chapter by examining alternative health care delivery systems, such as health maintenance organizations (HMOs) and preferred provider organizations (PPOs).

NATURE OF GROUP INSURANCE

Group insurance is a form of insurance that provides benefits to a number of persons under a single contract. Medical examinations usually are not required, and certificates of insurance are issued to the members as evidence of their insurance.

Group insurance differs from individual insurance in several respects. The most important differences are as follows:[1]

- Coverage of many persons under one contract
- Low-cost protection
- Evidence of insurability usually not required
- Subject to experience rating

A distinctive characteristic of group insurance is the coverage of many persons under one contract. A **master contract** is formed between the insurance company and group policyowner for the benefit of the individual members. In most plans, the group policyowner is the employer.

A second characteristic is that group insurance provides low-cost protection to the members. Group insurance rates generally are lower than individual rates. The relatively lower cost is due to reduced administrative and marketing expenses that result from mass distribution methods. Also, employers usually pay part or all of the cost, which reduces or eliminates premium payments by the employees.

Another characteristic is that individual evidence of insurability is usually not required. Group selection of risks is used, not individual selection. The insurance company is concerned with the insurability of the group as a whole rather than with the insurability of any single member within the group.

Finally, **experience rating** is used in group insurance plans. If the group is sufficiently large, the actual loss experience is a major factor in determining the premiums that are charged.

BASIC PRINCIPLES OF GROUP INSURANCE

Since individual evidence of insurability is usually not required, group insurers must observe certain underwriting principles so that the mortality of the group is favorable. They are:[2]

- Insurance incidental to the group
- Flow of persons through the group
- Automatic determination of benefits
- Minimum participation requirements
- Third-party sharing of cost
- Simple and efficient administration

Insurance Incidental to the Group

Insurance must be incidental to the group; that is, the group should not be formed for the sole purpose of obtaining insurance. This requirement is necessary to reduce adverse selection against the insurer. If the group is formed for the specific purpose of obtaining insurance, a disproportionate number of unhealthy persons would join the group to obtain low-cost insurance.

Flow of Persons Through the Group

Ideally, there should be a flow of younger persons into the group and a flow of older persons out of the group. Without a flow of younger persons into the group, the *average age* of the group will increase, and premium rates will likewise increase. The higher premiums may cause some younger and healthier members to drop out of the plan, while the older and unhealthy members will still remain, which would lead to still higher rates. However, turnover of employees should not be so significant that administrative costs are high.

Automatic Determination of Benefits

The benefits should be automatically determined by some formula that precludes the individual selection of insurance amounts by either the employer or the employees. The amount of insurance can be based on earnings, position, length of service, or some combination of these factors. The purpose of this requirement is to reduce adverse selection against the insurer. If individual members were permitted to select the amount of insurance, unhealthy persons would select larger amounts, while healthier persons would be likely to select smaller amounts. The result would be a disproportionate amount of insurance on the impaired lives. However, some group insurance plans allow employees to select their own benefit levels subject to certain maximum limits.

Minimum Participation Requirements

A minimum percentage of the eligible employees must participate in the plan. If the plan is **noncontributory**, 100 percent of the eligible employees must be covered. If the plan is **contributory**, a large proportion of the eligible employees must elect to participate in the plan. In a contributory plan, it may be difficult to get 100 percent participation, so a lower percentage such as 50 or 75 percent is typically required.

There are two reasons for the minimum participation requirement. First, if a large proportion of eligible employees participate, adverse selection is reduced, since the possibility of insuring a large proportion of unhealthy lives is reduced. Second, if a high proportion of eligible members participate, the expense rate per insured member or per unit of insurance can be reduced.

Third-party Sharing of Cost

Ideally, the individual members should not pay the entire cost of their protection. A third-party sharing of costs avoids the problem of increasing premiums for older members. In a plan in which the members pay the entire cost, the younger persons help pay for the insurance provided to older persons. Once they become aware of this, some younger persons may drop out of the plan and obtain their insurance more cheaply elsewhere. However, the older persons will still remain, causing premiums to increase even more.

Also, if the plan is contributory, a third-party sharing of costs makes the plan more attractive to individual members and encourages greater participation in the plan. This is especially true of group term insurance, which is the predominant type of group insurance in existence today. The employer pays part of the cost in a contributory group term insurance plan and absorbs any increase in premiums because of adverse mortality experience. The result is that the premium rates paid by the employees can be kept fairly stable.

Simple Administration

There should also be simple and efficient administration of the plan. If the plan is noncontributory, the employer remits the premiums directly to the insurer. If the plan is contributory, the premiums are collected from the employees by payroll deduction. This reduces administrative expenses for the insurer and keeps participation in the plan at a high level.

ELIGIBILITY REQUIREMENTS IN GROUP INSURANCE

Certain eligibility requirements must be satisfied in group insurance. Let us briefly examine some common eligibility requirements.

Eligible Groups

The types of groups that are eligible for group insurance are determined by company policy and state law. Most groups today are eligible for group insurance benefits. They include individual employer groups, multiple-employer groups, labor unions, creditor-debtor groups, and miscellaneous groups, such as fraternities and sororities.

Group insurers require the group to be a *certain size* before the group is insured. The most common requirement is *ten lives.* Some insurers will insure groups with as few as two or three members, but the typical requirement is at least ten lives. There are two reasons for a minimum-size requirement. First, the company has some protection against insuring a group that consists largely of substandard individuals, so that the financial impact of one impaired life on the loss experience of the group is reduced. Second, there are certain fixed expenses that must be met regardless of the size of the group. The larger the group, the broader is the base over which these expenses can be spread, and the lower is the expense rate per unit of insurance.

Eligibility Requirements

Employees must meet certain eligibility requirements before they can participate in a group insurance plan. They include the following:[3]

- Be a full-time employee
- Satisfy a probationary period
- Apply for insurance during the eligibility period
- Be actively at work

Employers usually require the workers to be employed full-time before they can participate in the plan. Also, in some group insurance plans, a new employee may have to satisfy a **probationary period**, which typically is a waiting period of one to six months, before he or she can participate in the plan. The purpose of the probationary period is to eliminate transient workers who will be with the firm for only a short period. It is administratively expensive to maintain records and insure workers who will not be working permanently for the firm.

After the probationary period (if any) expires, the employee is eligible to participate in the plan. However, if the plan is contributory, the employee must request coverage either before or during the eligibility period. The **eligibility period** is a short period of time—typically thirty-one days—during which the employee can sign up for the insurance without furnishing evidence of insurability. If the employee signs up for the insurance after the eligibility period expires, evidence of insurability is required. This is necessary to protect the company against adverse selection.

Finally, the employee must be *actively at work* on the day the insurance becomes effective. The employee who is actively at work is presumably meeting certain minimum health standards, which also gives the insurer some protection against adverse selection.

This concludes our discussion of eligibility requirements. Let us next consider group life insurance plans.

GROUP LIFE INSURANCE

Life insurance can be classified into three broad categories: (1) group, (2) ordinary, and (3) industrial. Of these categories, group life insurance is the fastest growing. At the end of 1983, group life insurance accounted for about 45 percent of the total life insurance in force in the United States.[4]

Group life insurance plans generally can be classified into five distinct categories.[5] They are:

- Group term
- Group creditor
- Group paid-up

- ▶ Group ordinary
- ▶ Group survivor income benefit insurance (SIBI)

Let us briefly examine each of these plans.

Group Term Life Insurance

Group term life insurance is the most important form of group life insurance in existence today. More than 99 percent of the group life insurance in force is group term insurance. The insurance provided is yearly renewable term insurance, which provides low-cost protection to the employees during their working careers.

Under a typical group term plan, the employee has the *right to convert* group life insurance to some form of cash-value life insurance after he or she leaves the group. You normally have thirty-one days in which to convert to an individual policy without furnishing evidence of insurability. But you are not allowed to convert to an individual term insurance policy.[6] If the master contract is terminated, you can convert up to $2,000 of life insurance (less any replacement coverage from another insurer) if you have been insured for at least five years under the plan. As a practical matter, relatively few employees convert their group insurance because of the problem of cost and because group insurance will probably be provided by another employer. Those employees who do convert are usually substandard in health or uninsurable, which results in strong adverse selection against the insurer.

Group term insurance has the major advantage of providing low-cost protection to employees, which can be used to supplement individual life insurance policies. However, it has several disadvantages. The insurance is temporary; it is expensive for an older worker to convert to an individual policy after retirement; and the problem of securing life insurance after retirement is still present.

Group Creditor Life Insurance

Commercial banks, finance companies, savings and loan institutions, and other lending institutions frequently make credit life and health insurance available to debtors. **Group creditor** life insurance provides for the cancellation of any outstanding indebtedness if the borrower dies. The lending institution is both the policyowner and beneficiary. The balance of the loan is paid to the creditor at the debtor's death.

Term insurance is normally used to insure the debtor's life. The amount of insurance is usually limited to the amount of the loan, and the insurance on the debtor's life declines as the loan is repaid. The insurance protection expires when the loan is repaid. In contrast to group term insurance, group creditor life insurance cannot be converted into an individual policy.

Group creditor life insurance generally can be obtained without individual evidence of insurability. Adverse selection against the insurer is minimized, since the protection declines as the loan is repaid. Also, the individual must usually be employed and show that the loan can be repaid. Thus, the characteristics that make a person a good credit risk also tend to reduce adverse selection against the insurer.

Although group creditor life insurance has the principal advantage of paying off an outstanding loan when the debtor dies, it has been criticized as being detrimental to consumers' best interests. Consumer advocates argue that credit life insurance rates are excessive in some states. Although maximum life credit life insurance rates are regulated by the states, some debtors are overcharged for their protection. In some plans, insurers pay out less than fifty cents in death benefits for each dollar of premiums collected. Also, some debtors can purchase an individual policy more cheaply elsewhere rather than obtaining protection through a group creditor plan. One reason for the excessive rates in some plans is that perverse price competition is often present. In other words, a lending institution has a strong financial incentive to negotiate a group credit life insurance contract with an insurer at the highest possible rate (subject to state law) rather than at the lowest possible rate. Since group insurance is experience rated, and death claims are relatively low, a sizable dividend is

INSIGHT 22.1

Firms Offering Universal Life In Benefit Plans

The name may be mind-numbing, but an employee benefit offered by a growing number of companies can be worth a closer look. Called "group universal life insurance," it could be a better deal than most people can get on their own.

Whether written on an individual or a group basis, universal life gives policyholders more flexibility and a higher return than traditional whole life insurance. Buying it through a group plan offered by an employer reduces the cost because the built-in charges for sales commissions are lower than for individual policies.

Employees can also generally take group universal policies with them if they switch companies or retire. The conventional group life insurance offered by most companies either can't be transferred or can be converted to permanent policies only at substantial cost.

But before rushing to sign up, employees should scrutinize the coverage they are offered, ask questions about commissions and compare the policy with those available through individual agents or through associations.

Whole life insurance guarantees a death benefit whenever the policyholder dies. It also provides a growing cash value that can be borrowed against. Policyholders pay a fixed annual premium, and the insurance company determines how much goes for death benefits and how much for building the policy's cash value.

With universal life, policyholders are essentially buying less-expensive term life insurance, which provides a death benefit over a certain number of years, and investing the savings in a "side fund" that accumulates tax-deferred interest. Policyholders can decide each year how much coverage they want and how much they want to put in the side fund.

Although the tax overhaul proposed by the Treasury Department last fall would eliminate the side fund's favorable tax treatment, congressional action is uncertain. If such a provision were enacted, existing policies would probably be exempted.

Companies large and small have been paying part or all of the cost of group term life insurance for their employees for years. Employees at many companies also have the option of buying additional term insurance at group rates.

often paid to a lending institution because of favorable mortality experience. Thus, the higher the rate, the greater is the profit to the lending institution, which comes at the expense of debtors who must pay higher premiums for their protection.

Group Paid-up Insurance

Group paid-up *insurance* provides a certain amount of paid-up insurance at retirement, depending on the age of entry into the plan. *Group paid-up life insurance consists of accumulating units of single premium whole life insurance and decreasing term insurance, which together equal the face amount of the policy.* The employee's contributions are used to purchase units of single premium whole life insurance. The employer's contributions are used to purchase term insurance equal to the difference between the paid-up insurance and the face amount of the policy.

Some employees may enter the plan at an older age, and there may be an insufficient amount of paid-up insurance at retirement. In such a case, the employee can convert any re-

Optional Coverage

Recently some companies have been replacing the optional term coverage with universal life. Although both types of insurance are paid for out of employees' own pockets, the death-benefit premium for universal life can be cheaper than term coverage. One reason: Optional term coverage is sometimes offered at what the Internal Revenue Service considers to be a subsidized price, and the IRS taxes the amount of the subsidy as imputed, additional income; with universal life, there is no such subsidy.

Other companies are offering universal life as a substitute for company-paid insurance that could subject employees to additional taxes. For example, the IRS considers the cost of coverage above $50,000 to be taxable income. And, if a group plan favors key employees with coverage exceeding that provided for the rank and file, the full cost of the key empoyees' coverage could be taxable under tax-law revisions enacted last year.

Still other companies are offering universal life as an additional benefit.

ITT Plan

One of the largest companies trying universal life is ITT Corp., which will offer the coverage in place of optional term insurance for its 30,000 salaried employees in the U.S. starting July 1. [1985]

ITT employees will be able to buy coverage of from one to five times their annual salary, up to $500,000. As with regular term insurance policies, the cost of the death benefit portion of universal life increases as the policyholder gets older. For example, under the ITT plan, $100,000 of coverage costs $8 a month at age 32, $14 a month at age 42, $36 a month at age 52 and $65 a month at age 62.

To illustrate how the side fund will work, John T. Brophy, a senior vice president at Johnson & Higgins, a New York insurance brokerage and consulting firm that is administering the ITT plan, offers this example: If a 32-year-old employee pays in $8.40 a month, the fund would have a cash value of $23,000, assuming a 10% annual interest rate, by the time the employee is 65. The accumulated cash value could then be used to convert the policy into paid-up permanent life insurance with a death benefit of $50,000 to $102,000, depending on subsequent interest rates.

SOURCE: "Firms Offering 'Universal Life' in Benefit Plans" by David B. Hilder from *Wall Street Journal*. Reprinted by permission of the *Wall Street Journal*,

maining term insurance at retirement to an individual policy without evidence of insurability.

Group paid-up life insurance has the principal advantage of providing some life insurance to older workers after retirement. However, it has several disadvantages. Less insurance is provided for a given premium; the plan is usually limited to groups with strong administration and low labor turnover; and the plan has little appeal to some younger workers who are not concerned about retirement.

In recent years, relatively few new group paid-up plans have been written. However, a number of older plans, usually plans of large employers, are still in existence.

Group Ordinary

Many insurers offer group ordinary plans, which is another method for providing life insurance for employees after retirement. The distinctive characteristic of a **group ordinary** plan is that a *traditional whole life policy is split into two component parts—decreasing insurance protection and increasing cash values.*[7] The practices of insurers vary in this regard. Some companies issue only one policy with the premiums and dividends allocated separately to each part, while other insurers issue two separate contracts that are independent of each other. Regardless of the approach used, there are two separate and distinct component parts, and each part has separate tax consequences.

The employee's contributions are used to fund the cash value or permanent portion of the plan. The employer's contributions are used to fund the term insurance portion of the plan. If the employer's contributions were used to fund the permanent insurance, the premiums would be considered taxable income to the employee. For this reason, the employee pays the premiums for the permanent insurance benefits.

Group ordinary plans have the principal advantage of providing employees with permanent insurance after retirement. The major disadvantage is that these plans must meet complex rules and regulations set forth in the Internal Revenue Code in order for the employees to receive favorable income tax treatment.[8]

Group Survivor Income Benefit Insurance

Group **survivor income benefit insurance (SIBI)** is a form of group life insurance that differs significantly from the group insurance plans already discussed.[9] *If the covered employee dies, an SIBI plan pays monthly income benefits to eligible dependents of the deceased; a lump-sum cash benefit is not paid.* The objective is to provide a monthly income to the family which, together with Social Security benefits, will restore part or all of the family's share of the deceased employee's earnings.

The monthly benefit can be based on the employee's salary, or it can be a flat amount. In a typical plan, the surviving spouse receives a monthly benefit equal to 25 percent of the deceased employee's earnings. Each eligible child receives 15 percent, and the overall family maximum is 40 percent. For example, if James dies suddenly from a heart attack, leaving behind a wife and son, and if his monthly earnings were $2,000, the wife and son would receive monthly SIBI benefits of $800 ($500 + $300).

The monthly benefits are paid to the widow until she reaches age sixty-two, remarries, or dies, whichever occurs first. However, some SIBI plans place a maximum limit of two to five years on the length of time that benefits can be paid to the surviving spouse. The children's benefits are paid as long as a qualified survivor is present. The benefits are paid until the youngest child reaches age nineteen (twenty-three if a student), marries, or dies, whichever occurs first.

The principal advantage of SIBI plans is that continuous income is provided to the family after the employee's death. Thus, a properly designed SIBI plan, along with Social Security survivor benefits, can reduce the economic problem of premature death discussed in Chapter 1.

This concludes our discussion of group life insurance. Let us next consider group health insurance.

GROUP HEALTH INSURANCE

Most employers have established group health insurance plans for their employees to help meet the costs of medical care from nonoccupational accidents or illness. Also, many employers have group disability income plans that replace at least part of the wages lost during a period of disability. In this section, we will examine the major types of group health insurance plans for employees. They include the following:

- Group basic medical-expense insurance
- Group major medical insurance
- Group disability income insurance
- Group dental insurance

Let us briefly examine the characteristics of these plans.

Group Basic Medical-Expense Insurance

Most of the individual basic medical-expense benefits discussed in Chapter 21 are also marketed on a group basis. A group basic medical-expense plan usually provides the following benefits:

- Hospital-expense insurance
- Surgical-expense insurance
- Physicians' visits
- X-ray and laboratory benefits

Basic hospital-expense insurance covers medical expenses incurred while in a hospital. A small number of plans pay a fixed minimum benefit for daily room and board charges, such as $100 for each day of hospitalization. However, most new plans pay the *full cost of a semiprivate room* if the employee is hospitalized. In one recent survey of new group health insurance cases, 87 percent of the employees with basic hospital-expense benefits were covered in full for a semiprivate room for seventy or more days. In addition to daily room and board benefits, most new plans also provide *unlimited coverage* for miscellaneous hospital expenses. In the same survey, 85 percent of the employees had unlimited coverage for miscellaneous hospital expenses.[10]

Basic surgical-expense insurance is usually included in a basic group medical-expense plan. Surgical-expense insurance pays the fees of physicians for surgical operations. Several methods are commonly used to compensate physicians under a basic plan. Under the **schedule approach**, the various surgical operations are listed, and a maximum dollar amount is specified for each procedure. The employer has a choice of surgical schedules, such as $1,000, $1,400, $1,800, and $2,200. A variation of the schedule approach is a **relative value schedule** where units or points are assigned to each operation based on the degree of difficulty. A conversion factor is then used to convert the relative value of the operation into a dollar amount that is paid to the physician.

Another approach for compensating physicians is on the basis of *reasonable and customary fees*. Under this approach, the physician is paid his or her usual fee as long as it is considered reasonable and customary.

Group basic medical-expense plans also provide benefits for physicians' visits other than for surgery. Most plans cover physician visits only while the employee is hospitalized; but some plans cover office or home visits as well. The amount paid can be a fixed amount, such as $20 per visit, or it can be based on the physician's reasonable and customary charges.

Finally, most basic plans provide diagnostic X-ray and laboratory benefits. This benefit helps pay for the costs of diagnostic X-rays and laboratory services performed outside of the hospital. The amounts paid are relatively small, such as $50 or $100 each year.

Coordination-of-benefits provision Most group medical-expense plans contain a **coordination-of-benefits provision**, which is designed to prevent overinsurance and the duplication of benefits when one person is covered under more than one group plan. For example, the husband and wife may both work and be covered under different group medical-expense plans. Each is insured as a dependent under the other's plan. In a typical coordination-of-benefits provision, the plan covering the employee is primary, and the dependent's plan is excess insurance. No more than 100 percent of the eligible medical expenses are paid under both plans.

Group Major Medical Insurance

Many employers also provide group major medical insurance for their employees. Group major medical insurance can be written as a supplement to a basic medical-expense plan, or it can be combined with a basic plan to form a comprehensive major medical policy.

Major medical-expense insurance A group major medical plan is frequently written to *supplement* the benefits provided under a basic plan. Group major-medical insurance has characteristics similar to the individual policies described in Chapter 21, but the benefits have much higher limits and are more comprehensive.

Most group major medical plans that supplement a basic plan have high lifetime maximum limits. Maximum limits of $100,000 to $250,000 for each individual are common. An increasing number of plans have maximum limits of $1 million, and a few plans have no limits at all. These high limits reflect the rapid increase in medical costs over time.

A coinsurance provision of 80 percent is typically found in group major medical plans. However, in most new plans, the coinsurance provision is modified by a **stop-loss limit**, which places a dollar limit on the maximum amount that an individual must pay. Under a stop-loss provision, once the individual's total outlay from deductibles and coinsurance exceeds a certain level, such as $1,000, all remaining eligible medical expenses are paid in full.

Group major medical plans also contain deductibles. Some common deductibles are as follows:

- Individual deductible
- Calendar-year deductible
- Corridor deductible

An **individual deductible** applies to each person. A deductible of $100 or $200 or some higher amount is present in most plans. Some plans require that eligible medical expenses equal to the deductible must be accumulated within a given time period, such as ninety days. Also, many plans limit the maximum number of deductibles by the family during the year to three.

A **calendar-year deductible** is used in many plans. The deductible has to be satisfied only once during the calendar year. Once the deductible is met, no additional deductibles are imposed during the calendar year. To avoid paying for two deductibles within a short period, some plans permit eligible medical expenses incurred during the last three months of the calendar year to be carried over and applied to the next year's deductible.

Finally, a **corridor deductible** is used to integrate a basic medical-expense plan with a group major medical policy. In this case, the group major medical policy excludes benefits provided by the basic plan. After the basic plan benefits are exhausted, a corridor deductible must be met before the major medical policy pays any benefits. The corridor deductible applies only to eligible medical expenses that are not covered by the basic medical-expense plan. A deductible of $100 or $200 is commonly used. This type of deductible can be illustrated by the following:

$30,000	total medical expenses
−20,000	paid by medical-expense plan
$10,000	remaining medical expenses
− 100	corridor deductible
$ 9,900	balance of medical expenses to be paid
− 7,920	80 percent paid by group major medical plan
$ 1,980	20 percent paid by the insured

Comprehensive major medical insurance A **comprehensive major medical** policy is a combination of basic plan benefits and major medical insurance in one policy. It is designed for employers who want both basic benefits and major medical protection in a single policy. This type of plan is characterized by a low deductible, such as $50 or $100 per year, by high maximum limits of up to $250,000 or even higher, and by coinsurance. In addition, the deductible and coinsurance provisions are not applied to certain medical expenses. The deductible does not usually apply to hospital expenses, and some plans do not impose a deductible for surgical expenses as well. Also, coinsurance is not applied to a certain amount of covered hospital expenses. For example, in one plan, the deductible does not apply to hospital expenses. The first $3,000 of hospital expenses are paid in full, and a coinsurance rate of 80 percent is applied to the remaining hospital expenses. No deductible is aplied to surgical expenses, and 80 percent of the reasonable and customary charges of the physician are paid.

This concludes our discussion of group medical-expense plans. Let us next consider the basic characteristics of group disability income plans.

Group Disability Income Insurance

Group disability income plans pay weekly or monthly cash payments to employees who are disabled from accidents or illness. There are two basic types of plans: (1) short-term disability income, and (2) long-term disability income.

Short-term disability income Many employers provide short-term disability income benefits to their employees.[11] The disability income benefits are paid for relatively short periods, ranging from thirteen weeks to two years. Most plans sold today pay benefits for a maximum period of twenty-six weeks. In addition, most plans have a short waiting period of three to seven days for sickness, while accidents typically are covered from the first day of disability. The waiting period eliminates nuisance claims, holds down costs, and discourages malingering and excessive absenteeism.

Most short-term plans cover only **nonoccupational disability**, which means that an accident or illness must occur off the job. Disability is usually defined in terms of the worker's *own* occupation. You are considered totally disabled if you are unable to perform all of the duties of your own occupation. Partial disability is seldom covered under a group short-term plan. You must be totally disabled and must be unable to perform all duties of your own job.

The amount of disability income benefits is related to the worker's normal earnings and typically is equal to some percentage of weekly earnings, such as 50 to 67 percent. Thus, if Gerald's weekly earnings are $300, he could collect a maximum weekly benefit of $200 if he becomes disabled.

In addition, short-term plans have relatively few exclusions. As we noted earlier, a disability that occurs on the job usually is not covered, since occupational disability is covered under a workers' compensation law.[12] Also, except for very small groups, preexisting conditions are immediatley covered. Most plans also cover alcoholism, drug addiction, and nervous and mental disorders. Finally, as a result of an amendment to the Civil Rights Act of 1964, maternity benefits can no longer be excluded in a group disability income plan; nor can disability benefits for pregnancies be limited to a shorter period than that applicable to other disabilities.[13]

Long-term disability income Many employers also provide long-term disability income benefits.[14] The long-term plans pay disability income benefits for longer periods, which typically range from two years to age sixty-five or even for life.

A dual definition of disability is typically used to determine if a worker is totally disabled. For the first two years, you are considered disabled if you are unable to perform all of the duties of your *own* occupation. After two years, you are still considered disabled if you are unable to work in *any* occupation for which you are reasonably fitted by education, training, and experience. In addition, in contrast to short-term plans, long-term plans typically cover ***both occupational and nonoccupational*** *disability*.

The disability income benefits are usually paid monthly, and the maximum monthly benefits are substantially higher than the short-term plans. The maximum monthly benefit is generally limtied to 60 to 67 percent of the employee's normal earnings. Since long-term plans are designed largely for executives and upper-income employees, maximum monthly benefits generally range from $1,000 for the smaller groups up to $3,000 for larger groups. Some plans provide for even higher maximum monthly benefits.

To reduce malingering and moral hazard, other disability income benefits paid for by the employer are taken into consideration. If the disabled worker is also receiving Social Security or workers' compensation benefits, the long-term disability benefit is reduced accordingly. However, many plans limit the reduction only to the amount of the initial Social Security disability benefit. Thus, if Social Security disability benefits are increased because of increases in the cost of living, the long-term disability income benefit is not reduced further.

Some long-term plans also have a cost-of-living adjustment and pension accrual benefit. Under the **cost-of-living adjustment**, benefits paid to the disabled employee are adjusted annually for increases in the cost of living. However, to keep the cost of this benefit reasonable, the annual benefit increase may be limited to the maximum of two or three percent.

Under the **pension accrual benefit**, the plan makes a pension contribution so that the disabled employee's pension benefit remains intact. For example, if both James and his employer contribute 6 percent of his salary into a pension plan, and he is disabled, the plan would pay an amount equal to 12 percent of his monthly salary into the company's pension plan for as long as he remains disabled. Thus, James would still receive his pension at the normal retirement age.

Group Dental Insurance

Group dental insurance helps pay the costs of normal dental care as well as damage to teeth from an accident. Group dental insurance is a rapidly growing form of health insurance. In 1967, about two million persons were insured under group dental expense plans by private health insurers. By the end of 1981, the number of persons covered under the group plans of private health insurers increased to about 61 million.[15]

Types of plans There are two basic types of group dental insurance plans.[16] Under a **comprehensive plan**, practically all types of dental services are covered. This includes oral examinations, X-rays and cleaning, fillings, extractions, inlays, bridgework and dentures, oral surgery, root canal therapy, and orthodontia. Under this approach, dentists are reimbursed on the basis of their reasonable and customary charges subject to any limitations on benefits stated in the plan.

Under a **schedule plan**, the various dental services are listed in a schedule, and a flat dollar amount is paid for each service. If the dentist charges more than the specified amount, the patient must pay the differences.

Cost controls In order to control costs and reduce adverse selection against the insurer when the plan is initially installed, several cost controls are used.[17] They include the following:

- Deductibles and coinsurance
- Maximum limit on benefits
- Waiting periods
- Exclusions
- Predetermination of benefits

Most dental insurance plans use various deductibles and coinsurance to control costs. For example, an annual deductible of $50 may apply to all covered dental services. Coinsurance is also used to control costs. After the deductible is met, the plan may pay 80 percent of the dentist's eligible charges. However, the coinsurance percentage may vary depending on the type of service. To encourage regular visits to a dentist, some plans do not impose any coinsurance requirements for one or two routine dental examinations each year. However, fillings and oral surgery may be paid only at a rate of 80 percent, while the cost of orthodontia or dentures is typically paid at a lower rate of 50 percent.

Maximum limits on benefits are also used to control costs. There may be a maximum annual limit on the amount paid, such as $1,000 during the calendar year. Another approach is to impose a lifetime maximum on certain types of dental services, such as a lifetime maximum of $800 for dentures.

Waiting periods for certain types of services are also used to control costs. For example, some plans do not cover dentures until the employee is insured for at least one year, and there may be only one replacement of dentures for each five-year period.

Certain exclusions are used to reduce costs. Common exclusions include cosmetic dental work, such as capping a tooth; replacement of lost or stolen dental devices, such as dentures or a space retainer; and benefits provided under a workers' compensation or similar law.

Finally, a **predetermination of benefits provision** is commonly used to control costs. Under this provision, if the cost of dental treatment exceeds $100, the dentist submits a plan of treatment to the insurer. The insurer then specifies the services that are covered and how much the plan will pay. The employee is then informed of the amount the plan will pay and makes a rational decision on whether or not to proceed with the proposed plan of treatment.

Dental insurance has the principal advantage of helping employees meet the costs of regular dental care. Also, it encourages persons to see their dentists on a regular basis thereby preventing or detecting dental problems before they become serious.

HEALTH MAINTENANCE ORGANIZATIONS (HMOs)

A **health maintenance organization (HMO)** is an alternative to traditional group health insurance. *An HMO can be defined as an organized system of health care that provides comprehensive health services to its members for a fixed, prepaid fee.* In 1982, 277 HMOs provided comprehensive health services to 10.8 million persons.[18] Examples of HMOs include the Kaiser-Permanente Medical Group, the Health Insurance Plan of Greater New York (HIP), and the Group Health Association Plan in Washington, D.C.

Basic Characteristics

HMOs have certain characteristics that distinguish them from private health insurance and Blue Cross-Blue Shield service plans. They include the following:[19]

- Organized plan to deliver health services to the members
- Broad comprehensive health services
- Fixed prepaid fee
- Dual choice
- Physicians generally not compensated by fee-for-service

Organized plan to deliver health services to the members The HMO has the responsibility for organizing and delivering comprehensive health services to its members. The HMO owns or leases medical facilities, enters into agreements with hospitals and physicians to provide medical services, hires ancillary personnel, and has general managerial control over the various services provided.

There are two basic types of HMOs. First, under a *group practice plan*, physicians usually are employees of the HMO or an organization that contracts with the HMO and are paid a salary. Most HMOs have a closed panel of physicians, and members are limited in their choice of physicians to those employed by the plan. The physicians typically are general practitioners or family practice specialists and other medical specialists who practice medicine as a group and share facilities. About 80 percent of HMO subscribers are covered under group practice plans.

The second type of HMO is an *individual practice association plan* (IPA). An IPA is an open panel of physicians who work out of their own offices. The individual physicians contract with HMOs to treat members on a per capita basis, modified fee-for-service basis or some combination. One modification is to pay individual physicians 80 to 90 percent of their usual fee. The balance goes into a risk pool for absorbing a portion of the loss if the costs of services exceed the IPA's income. The amounts in the risk pool can also be used to pay physicians later if the IPA's income exceeds its expenses. Most IPAs have risk-sharing agreements with participating physicians.

Broad comprehensive health services An HMO also provides broad comprehensive health services to its members. Most services are covered in full, with relatively few maximum limits on individual services. Covered services typically include the full costs of hospitalization, all necessary medical services for acute care, surgeons' and physicians' fees, maternity care, laboratory and X-ray services, outpatient services, special duty nursing, and numerous other services. All office visits to HMO physicians are also covered, either in full or at a nominal charge for each visit.

Fixed prepaid fee A member of an HMO pays a fixed prepaid fee (usually paid monthly) and is provided with a wide range of comprehensive health services. Deductibles and coinsurance are not normally used. However, some HMOs charge a nominal fee for certain services, such as $2 for each office visit or $2 for prescription drugs. The payment of an annual fixed fee is an important advantage to the member, since it eliminates any financial barriers to needed medical care and assures a wide range of health services. Aside from the fixed annual fee and nominal charges for certain services, a member pays nothing for the medical care provided, even if these expenses reach catastrophic levels.

Dual choice Some persons are dissatisfied with the medical care provided by an HMO. Therefore, the members generally have the opportunity each year to elect to remain in the HMO or participate in a group health insurance plan, including Blue Cross and Blue Shield. The objective is to offer the members an alternative to the HMO in the event they become dissatisfied, thereby conforming to the traditional concept of freedom of choice.

Physicians generally not compensated by fee-for-service With the exception of individual practice association plans, physicians generally are not usually compensated based on a fee-for-service basis. Some physicians are employees of the HMO and are paid an annual salary. Some are paid according to the *capitation method*. This means that a medical group of physicians and other health care professionals engage in the group practice of medicine. The medical group receives income for the health services provided in the form of a fixed monthly charge for each member, often referred to as a per capita income or a capitation charge. The medical group then pays its physicians any way it wishes. Since the medical group is charged for the costs of hospitalization, it may provide financial incentives for physicians to achieve lower hospital rates. These financial incentives include profit-sharing schemes, bonuses, and shares in the net earnings at the end of the year.

Many critics of health care in the United States believe the traditional fee-for-service method often works in a perverse way. Under this method, physicians are compensated based on the services provided, and the more services they provide, the higher are their incomes. As a result, some surgical operations are unnecessary, and other medical services are often provided that are not needed. In contrast, under an HMO, a physician generally is not compensated based on the services he or she provides. Thus, the traditional relationship between the amount of services rendered by a physician and the income received is altered, which removes the financial incentive to perform unnecessary services.

Advantages of HMOs

The major advantage of an HMO is that broad comprehensive health care is provided to the members. There are fewer gaps in coverage; service benefits are provided; relatively few exclusions are present; deductibles and coinsurance generally are not emphasized; and with the exception of nominal charges for certain services, the annual fixed fee is the only payment made.

Another advantage is the stress on loss prevention. Many loss prevention services are typically provided to keep the members healthy. They include multiphasic screenings, regular physical examinations, access to medical specialists, well-child care, eye exams, prenatal and postnatal maternity care, and immunizations. There is a strong incentive to treat a disease in its early stage in order to promote a prompt recovery.

In addition, the member may save time in receiving medical care. Since a full range of comprehensive services is available from one organization, often at a single location, the patient is not forced to visit numerous specialists in different locations, and time is saved. Moreover, the members have access to medical care at night or over the weekend as opposed to the situation under the solo-practice approach, where the family's physician is often unavailable during those times.

Disadvantages of HMOs

Critics of HMOs point out certain disadvantages of HMOs. First, some HMOs have failed, and many are in financial difficulty. The startup costs are enormous, and many HMOs are too small to achieve substantial economies of scale. To achieve such economies of scale, an HMO should have at least 20,000 members. Many smaller HMOs are well below this figure.

Another disadvantage is that the freedom to select an individual physician is restricted. As we noted earlier, group practice HMOs have a closed panel of physicians, and the member must choose among those available in the group. Some members also feel that the medical care provided to them is too impersonal, and a close physician-patient relationship is difficult to attain.

There is also the problem of receiving medical care outside the geographical area of the HMO. The HMO will usually pay the cost of emergency medical services when the member requires medical care outside the immediate geographical area served by the HMO. However, the member may have to pay the physician or hospital directly and then seek reimbursement from the HMO, or funds may have to be wired from the HMO to the out-of-area supplier of medical care.

Finally, some physicians argue that the quality of medical care is not as high as that provided by the physicians engaged in solo practice. They suggest that the incentives for cost savings under an HMO could result in a reduction in the quality of medical care. Some members may not receive prompt hospitalization when necessary, outpatient service may be rushed, and in some HMOs, a member may wait a long time to get an appointment.

This concludes our discussion of HMOs. Let us next consider personal provider organizations (PPOs), a relatively new alternative to traditional group health insurance plans.

PREFERRED PROVIDER ORGANIZATIONS (PPOs)

Because of the rapid use in health-care costs in recent years, employers and insurers have introduced a wide variety of new innovations and approaches to control health-care costs. (See Insight 22.2.)

Preferred provider organizations (PPOs) have also been enacted as a new approach for holding down health-care costs. *A preferred provider organization can be defined as a group of health-care providers that contracts with employers, insurers, or other third-party payers to provide health-care services to the group members at a reduced fee.*[20] The employer, insurer, or other group negotiates a contract with the providers of care to provide certain physicians, hospitals, and health-care services to the group members. The providers of care, however, provide their services at a reduced fee. A special utilization review program to control medical expenses may also be established. In return, the employer or insurer promises prompt payment and an increased patient volume. To encourage patients to use the PPO providers, deductibles or copayment charges may be reduced or waived. Also, the patient may be charged a lower fee for certain routine treatments, or offered increased benefits such as preventive health care.

PPOs should not be confused with HMOs. There are two important differences between them. First, PPOs do not provide medical care on a prepaid basis. The PPO providers are paid on a fee-for-service basis as their services are used. However, as stated earlier, the fees charged are below the providers' regular fee. Second, unlike an HMO, employees are not required to use the PPO, but have freedom of choice each time they need care. However, as stated earlier, employees have a financial incentive to use PPO providers, since deductibles may be waived and copayment charges reduced.

INSIGHT 22.2

How Can Health Care Costs Be Controlled?

An estimated $322 billion was spent on health care in the United States in 1982, or 10.5 percent of the gross national product. To meet the problem of spiraling health care costs, major employers and group health insurers have introduced a wide variety of new approaches and techniques for controlling health care costs. They include the following:

1. *Preadmission testing.* A patient may be scheduled for surgery or for admission into a hospital. Various tests are given on an outpatient basis before the patient is admitted into the hospital. In most cases, one or two days of hospital room and board charges can be eliminated. Thus, claim costs can be reduced.
2. *Second opinions.* Many group plans now pay for a second opinion where the patient consults another physician to determine if surgery is needed. The objective is to reduce unnecessary surgery.
3. *Out-of-hospital surgery.* Many plans now pay for ambulatory surgery where the patient enters a facility other than a hospital for minor surgery and recovers at home.
4. *Home health care.* An employee may be discharged early from a hospital to recover at home. A typical home health care plan covers part-time nursing in the home; physical, occupational, or speech therapy; and medical equipment used in the home. The cost of care at home is less expensive than care provided in the hospital.
5. *Nursing home coverage.* Many plans now pay for medical care in a less costly nursing home or extended-care facility.
6. *Claim audits.* Hospitals frequently make mistakes in billing patients. Under a claim audit, independent auditing firms are used to verify hospital bills and to avoid duplicate charges. Substantial savings have been realized.

PPOs have the major advantage of controlling health-care costs, since fees are negotiated at a discount with the participating providers of health-care services. PPOs also help physicians to build up their practice.

However, there are several obstacles to the growth of PPOs. First, there are legal barriers to the formation of PPOs, since not all states allow the formation of PPOs. There are also antitrust implications, since PPOs are not exempt from federal antitrust laws under the McCarran-Ferguson Act. The insurance laws in some states also prohibit insurers from influencing a patient's choice of a healthcare provider by offering financial incentives.

Second, some physicians are reluctant to join a PPO. When a physician charges a reduced fee to PPO patients, he or she may become known as a discount physician. If other patients become aware of the discounts, they may demand the same rates as those charged PPO patients.

Finally, legal problems can arise if a physician is denied privileges at a designated PPO facility, or is dropped as a provider because of a poor utilization record. The physician may bring a conspiracy suit against the PPO similar to the lawsuits brought by some physicians against hospitals who have denied them hospital privileges.

7. *Additional benefits for outpatient surgery or treatment.* The deductible and coinsurance charges are frequently waived if the patient has outpatient surgery or treatment for less serious ailments.
8. *Fee negotiation.* Some physicians or hospitals may overcharge their patients. Many insurers have their own medical-cost staff personnel who deal directly with physicians and hospitals to ensure that their charges are fair and reasonable.
9. *Hospice coverage.* Many insurers now cover hospice care where the cost of treating terminally ill patients is substantially lower than traditional forms of treatment.
10. *Prospective reimbursement formulas.* Under this arrangement, the amounts paid to hospitals or other providers for medical care are negotiated in advance. If actual costs are below the negotiated charge, the hospital or provider can retain the profit. If actual costs, however, rise above the predetermined fixed amount, the hospital or provider must absorb the extra cost. Thus, there is a strong financial incentive to keep costs down.
11. *Cash incentive programs.* Some plans provide cash incentives to employees to conserve on the use of medical services. For example, in Mendocino County in California, the Office of Education deposits $500 annually for each employee into a trust account. The worker can draw on the $500 reserve when medical expenses are incurred. When expenses exceed $500, a Blue Cross-Blue Shield plan pays the remaining costs. Any part of the $500 that is not used during the year is kept on deposit. Upon retirement or departure from the district, the workers may withdraw their accumulated savings. Interest on the fund is used to help pay Blue Cross-Blue Shield premiums. The results are encouraging. Premiums have not been increased in two years, vision benefits have been added without an additional charge, and there has been a noticeable decline in the number of visits to doctors.
12. *Wellness programs.* Many firms have wellness programs that are designed to keep employees healthy by promoting a healthy life style. Thus, medical costs can be held down.

SOURCE: George E. Rejda, *Social Insurance & Economic Security*, 2nd Ed., © 1984, pp. 220–221. Reprinted by permission of Prentice-Hall, Inc., Englewood Cliffs, N.J.

SUMMARY

- Group insurance provides benefits to a number of persons under a single master contract. Low-cost protection is provided, since the employer pays part or all of the cost. Evidence of insurability is usually not required. Large groups are subject to experience rating, by which the group's loss experience determines the premiums that are charged.
- Certain underwriting principles are followed in group insurance to obtain favorable loss experience. They are:
  a. Insurance must be incidental to the group.
  b. There should be a flow of persons through the group.
  c. The benefits should be automatically determined by some formula that precludes individual selection of insurance amounts.
  d. A minimum percentage of eligible employees must participate in the plan.
  e. There should be a third-party sharing of costs.
  f. There should be simple and efficient administration.

- Most groups today are eligible for group insurance benefits. However, group insurers generally require the group to have at least ten members before it can be insured. Individual employees must meet certain eligibility requirements. They are:
  a. Be a full-time employee.
  b. Satisfy a probationary period.
  c. Apply for insurance during the eligibility period.
  d. Be actively at work.
- There are five categories of group life insurance plans. They are:
  a. Group term.
  b. Group creditor.
  c. Group paid-up.
  d. Group ordinary.
  e. Group survivor income benefit insurance (SIBI).
- Numerous group health insurance plans have been established for employees. The most common plans are:
  a. Group basic medical-expense insurance.
  b. Group major medical insurance.
  c. Group disability income insurance.
  d. Group dental insurance.
- A health maintenance organization (HMO) is an organized system of health care that provides broad, comprehensive services to the members for a fixed, prepaid fee. A typical HMO has the following characteristics:
  a. Organized plan to deliver health services to the members.
  b. Broad comprehensive health services.
  c. Fixed prepaid fee.
  d. Dual choice.
  e. Physicians generally not compensated by fee-for-service.
- A preferred provider organization (PPO) can be defined as a group of health-care providers that contracts with employers, insurers, or other third-party payers to provide health-care services to the group members at a reduced fee.

QUESTIONS FOR REVIEW

1. Describe the nature of group insurance plans and show how group insurance differs from individual insurance.
2. Describe the basic underwriting principles that are followed in group insurance.
3. Explain the eligibility requirements that are commonly required in group insurance plans.
4. Describe the major forms of group life insurance.
5. How is the problem of providing life insurance on retired employees met in group insurance?
6. Describe the major features of group major medical insurance.

7. Explain the types of deductibles that are commonly found in group major medical plans.
8. Explain the nature and purpose of the coordination-of-benefits provision that is commonly found in group health insurance plans.
9. Describe the basic characteristics of group short-term and long-term disability income plans.
10. Describe the cost controls that are used in group dental insurance plans.

QUESTIONS FOR DISCUSSION

1. *a.* Although individual underwriting and evidence of insurability are not usually required in group life insurance, there are several factors inherent in the group approach that result in favorable mortality experience. Explain these factors.
   b. Under what circumstances can an insurer require individual evidence of insurability in a group life insurance plan?
2. Compare group term life insurance with group paid-up insurance with respect to each of the following:
   a. continuance of coverage.
   b. use of employer contributions.
   c. right to convert.
3. Compare group short-term disability income plans with long-term disability income plans with respect to each of the following:
   a. benefit period.
   b. definition of disability.
   c. availability of other benefits.
4. Compare a supplemental group major medical plan with a comprehensive major medical plan with respect to each of the following:
   a. use of deductibles.
   b. use of coinsurance.
   c. use of a stop-limit.
5. When group dental insurance plans are initially installed, the insurer is exposed to a high degree of adverse selection. Describe several features that are incorporated into group dental insurance plans to make this coverage feasible despite the existence of adverse selection.
6. *a.* Health maintenance organizations (HMOs) can be viewed as an acceptable alternative to the traditional forms of health care for consumers.
      1. Describe two basic types of HMOs.
      2. What are the advantages of HMOs?
      3. What are the disadvantages of HMOs?
   b. Explain the major characteristics of preferred provider organizations (PPOs).
   c. How does a preferred provider organization (PPO) differ from a health maintenance organization (HMO)?

KEY CONCEPTS AND TERMS TO KNOW

Master contract
Experience rating
Noncontributory
Contributory
Probationary period
Eligibility period
Group term
Group creditor
Group paid-up
Group ordinary
Survivor income benefit insurance (SIBI)
Supplemental major medical insurance
Comprehensive major medical insurance
Individual deductible
Calendar-year deductible
Schedule approach
Relative value schedule
Coordination-of-benefits provision
Stop-loss limit
Corridor deductible
Occupational disability
Nonoccupational disability
Pension accrual benefit
Cost-of-living adjustment
Comprehensive dental insurance
Schedule plan in dental insurance
Predetermination of benefits provision
Health maintenance organization (HMO)
Preferred provider organizatoin (PPO)

SUGGESTIONS FOR ADDITIONAL READING

Beam, Jr., Burton T. *Group Insurance: Basic Concepts and Alternatives*, 2nd ed. Bryn Mawr, Pennsylvania: The American College, 1984, chapters 1–8.

Beam, Jr., Burton T. and John J. McFadden. *Employee Benefits*. Homewood, Illinois: Richard D. Irwin, Inc., 1985, chapters 4–12.

Greene, Mark R. and Henry A. Laskey, "The Health Care Cost Containment Effort—How Successful?" *Benefits Quarterly*, Vol. 1, No. 1 (First Quarter 1985), pp. 9–16.

Hall, Jr., Charles P. "What Is Happening in Health Care Cost Containment?" *Benefits Quarterly*, Vol. 1, No. 1 (First Quarter 1985), pp. 1–8.

Handel, Bernard. *New Directions in Welfare Plan Benefits: Instituting Health Care Cost Containment Programs*. Brookfield, WI: International Foundation of Employee Benefit Plans, 1984.

Hewitt Associates. *Company Practices in Health Care Cost Management*. Lincolnshire, IL: Hewitt Associates, 1984.

International Foundation of Employee Benefit Plans. *Health Care Cost Management: Issues, Strategies and Current Practices: Final Report and Fact Book*. Brookfield, WI: International Foundation of Employee Benefit Plans, 1984.

Rosenbloom, Jerry S., ed. *The Handbook of Employee Benefits: Design, Funding, and Administration*. Homewood, Illinois: Richard D. Irwin, 1984, chapters 4–20.

Rosenbloom, Jerry S. and G. Victor Hallman. *Employee Benefit Planning*. Englewood Cliffs, New Jersey: Prentice-Hall, Inc., 1981.

Spencer, Bruce. *Group Benefits in a Changing Society*, 2nd ed. Chicago, Illinois: Charles D. Spencer and Associates, 1978.

NOTES

1. David W. Gregg, "Fundamental Characteristics of Group Insurance," in Davis W. Gregg and Vane B. Lucas, eds., *Life and Health Insurance Handbook,* 3rd ed. (Homewood, Illinois: Richard D. Irwin, Inc., 1973), pp. 352-53. See also, Burton T. Beam, Jr. and John J. McFadden, *Employee Benefits* (Homewood, IL: Richard D. Irwin, 1985), chapters 4–12.
2. Gregg, pp. 362–63.
3. Gregg, pp. 354–60.
4. American Council of Life Insurance, *1983 Life Insurance Fact Book,* p. 27.
5. William G. Williams, "Group Life Insurance," in *Life and Health Insurance Handbook,* pp. 372–411.
6. In a few states, the terminating employee is allowed to purchase term insurance for a limited period (such as one year) after which he or she must convert to some form of cash-value insurance.
7. Edward R. Hall, "Group Ordinary Life Insurance (Section 79 Plans)," in *Employee Benefit Planning: Readings* (Bryn Mawr, Pennsylvania: The American College, 1979), p. R. 21.1.
8. If the group ordinary plan meets certain requirements specified in the Internal Revenue Code, premiums paid by the employer for the first $50,000 of group term life insurance are not considered taxable income to the employees.
9. A detailed explanation of SIBI plans can be found in Bruce Spencer, *Group Benefits in a Changing Society,* 2nd ed. (Chicago, Illinois: Charles D. Spencer and Associates, 1978), pp. 73–84.
10. Health Insurance Institute, *New Group Health Insurance, Based on Surveys by the Health Insurance Institute, Policies Issued in 1979* (Washington, D.C.: Health Insurance Institute, n.d.), p. 4.
11. See Morton D. Miller, "Group Disability Income Insurance," in *Life and Health Insurance Handbook,* pp. 395–403.
12. Some short-term plans also cover occupational disabilities, especially if the state workers' compensation benefits are considered inadequate.
13. The 1978 amendments apply only to employers with fifteen or more employees. Employees subject to the law must also provide group medical-expense benefits for pregnancy and childbirth on the same basis as other illnesses.
14. See Miller, pp. 403–407.
15. Health Insurance Association of America, *Source Book of Health Insurance Data, 1982–1983,* Table 1.8, p. 20.
16. Charles P. Hall, Jr., "Group Medical Expense Insurance: An Update," *CLU Course HS 303, Group Insurance and Social Insurance* (Bryn Mawr, Pennsylvania: The American College, 1979), p. 4.35.
17. Hall, p. 4.35. See also Spencer, pp. 246–56.
18. *Source Book of Health Insurance Data, 1982–1983,* p. 8.
19. George E. Rejda, *Social Insurance and Economic Security,* 2nd ed. (Englewood Cliffs, New Jersey: Prentice-Hall, 1984), pp. 217–20.
20. Beam, Jr. and McFadden, pp. 144–45.

CHAPTER 23

ADDITIONAL TOPICS IN EMPLOYEE BENEFIT PLANS

"As the population of the country matures, several strains will be placed on our already burdened retirement system."

President's Commission on Pension Policy, Coming of Age: Toward a National Retirement Income Policy

STUDENT LEARNING OBJECTIVES

After studying this chapter, you should be able to:

- Explain the basic features of private pension plans, including:
  a. eligibility requirements
  b. retirement ages
  c. vesting rules
- Distinguish between a defined contribution and defined benefit pension plan.
- Describe the major types of qualified private pension plans that are used by employers today.
- Explain the major features of Retirement Plans for the Self-Employed.
- Describe the basic characteristics of the Individual Retirement Account (IRA).
- Explain the major features of a Simplified Employee Pension plan (SEP).
- Explain the basic characteristic of a Qualified Voluntary Employee Contribution (QVEC) plan and a Section 401(k) plan.

In this chapter, we will continue our discussion of employee benefit plans. We will first discuss the fundamentals of private pension plans. We will then consider retirement plans for self-employed individuals. We will conclude the chapter by examining the basic characteristics of Individual Retirement Accounts (IRAs) and Simplified Employee Pension plans (SEPs).

FUNDAMENTALS OF PRIVATE PENSION PLANS

About half of the private work force is currently covered by private pension plans.[1] These plans have an enormous social and economic impact on the nation. Substantial amounts of retirement income are paid to retired workers and their dependents, which enhances their economic security during retirement. Private pension plans are also an important source of capital funds in the financial markets. Private pension assets currently are in excess of $1 trillion. These funds are invested in housing developments, shopping centers, new plants, machinery and equipment, and other worthwhile economic investments.

Basic Features of Private Pension Plans

In this section, we will study the basic features of private pension plans.[2] The design of these plans is greatly influenced by federal legislation and the Internal Revenue Code. In particular, the **Employee Retirement Income Security Act of 1974 (ERISA)** has greatly influenced the design of private pension plans. The fundamental purpose of ERISA is to provide greater protection of the pension rights of participating employees. Private pension plans subject to the act must meet certain minimum pension standards. Also, more recently, the Tax Reform Act of 1984 and the Retirement Equity Act of 1984 have had an important impact on private pension plans. The following discussion is based on this legislation.

If private pension plans meet certain requirements both employers and employees receive favorable income-tax treatment. If the plan is a qualified pension plan under the Internal Revenue Code, the employer's contributions are deductible as an ordinary business expense and are not considered taxable income to the employees when the contributions are made. Also, the investment earnings on pension plan assets are not subject to income taxes. The pension benefits attributable to the employer's contributions are not taxed until the employees retire, or until the funds are actually distributed or made available to them.

Internal Revenue coverage requirements In order to receive favorable income-tax treatment, the employer must satisfy certain Internal Revenue requirements. The employer is forbidden to establish eligibility requirements that discriminate in favor of the **prohibited group.** The prohibited group consists of officers, stockholders, and highly paid employees. The pension plan must be for the benefit of the employees or beneficiaries in general and not just for the prohibited group. Accordingly, to avoid discrimination in favor of the prohibited group, the plan must meet the following Internal Revenue coverage requirements:

- **If the plan is noncontributory, at least 70 percent of all employees must be covered.**
- **If the plan is contributory, at least 70 percent of the eligible workers must be covered, and at least 80 percent of them must elect to participate.**

As an alternative to the preceding rules, the employer can establish a pension plan for special classes of employees as long as the Internal Revenue Service rules that the plan does not discriminate in favor of the prohibited group.

Eligibility requirements An employer can establish certain eligibility requirements before the employees can participate in the plan. However, the eligibility requirements cannot be more stringent than those allowed under federal law and the Internal Revenue Code.

Employees generally can be required to

meet the following eligibility requirements before they can participate in the plan:

- Be a full-time employee.
- Meet a minimum age and service requirement.
- Not be beyond a maximum age.

Employees must usually be employed *full-time* before they can participate in the plan. In addition, since a pension plan is designed to benefit employees who will be working permanently for the firm, *a minimum age and service requirement* can also be imposed. The Retirement Equity Act of 1984 requires coverage of all employees who are at least age twenty-one and have one year of service with the firm.[3]

Finally, the employees normally must not be beyond a *certain maximum age* in order to participate in the plan. A defined benefit pension plan can exclude employees who are hired within five years of the normal retirement age. However, if the plan is a defined contribution plan, a maximum age limitation is not allowed.

A **defined contribution plan** is a pension plan in which the contribution rate is fixed, but the benefits are variable. In a **defined benefit plan,** the retirement benefit is known in advance, but the contributions are variable. These plans are discussed later in the chapter.

Retirement ages A typical pension plan has three retirement ages. They are:

- Normal retirement age
- Early retirement age
- Late retirement age

A pension plan has a *normal retirement age* where full pension benefits are paid, and the employee is expected to retire. Most private pension plans have a normal retirement age of sixty-five. However, under federal law,[4] most workers in private industry and in state and local government cannot be forced to retire before age seventy. Thus, age seventy can be used as compulsory retirement age; however, the normal retirement age in most private pension plans is still age sixty-five.

A typical pension plan also has an *early retirement age,* so that employees can retire early on a reduced pension. A typical plan may specify age fifty-five as the early retirement age for a worker with ten years of service. The retirement benefit is actuarially reduced, since the worker's full benefit will not have accrued by the early retirement date. The retirement benefit is reduced, since it must be paid over a longer period.

Finally, many plans have a *late retirement age,* so that the employees can defer retirement until age seventy, or even beyond. Some plans provide for increased pension benefits if retirement is delayed. Other plans, however, pay the same pension benefits that would have been paid at the normal retirement age.

Amount of retirement benefits Most private pension plans are designed to pay retirement benefits, which, together with Social Security benefits, will restore about 50 to 55 percent of the worker's earnings before retirement. This percentage is generally set at a higher level for lower-paid employees, such as 80 or 85 percent of preretirement earnings.[5]

The benefit amount can be based on **career average earnings,** which is an average of the worker's earnings while participating in the plan, or it can be based on **final pay,** which generally is an average of the worker's earnings over a three- to five-year period prior to retirement.

In addition, when a new pension plan is installed, some older workers may be close to retirement. In order to pay more adequate retirement benefits, most plans provide for **past service benefits,** which are pension benefits based on service with the firm prior to the establishment of the plan. The actual amount paid, however, will depend on the benefit formula used to determine benefits.

Benefit formulas Some plans use a defined contribution formula to determine the benefit amount. As stated earlier, *in a defined contribution plan, the contribution rate is fixed, but the retirement benefit is variable.* In most plans, the contribution rate is based on the worker's earnings, such as 6 percent by both the employer and employee. However, the actual retirement benefit will vary depending on the worker's age, earnings, contribution rate, investment income, and normal retirement age.

Defined contribution plans are increasingly being used by business firms. Defined contribution plans are also used by nonprofit organizations and by state and local governments, in which pension costs must be budgeted as a percentage of payroll. However, from the employee's viewpoint, a defined contribution plan has several disadvantages. The retirement benefit can only be estimated in advance of retirement; the formula may produce an inadequate benefit if the worker enters the plan at an advanced age; and greater weight from compound interest is given to the worker's lower earnings at the young ages.[6]

Many corporate pension plans are defined benefit plans. *In a defined benefit plan, the retirement benefit is known in advance, but the contributions will vary depending on the amount necessary to fund the desired benefit.* Several defined benefit formulas are currently in use. They are as follows:[7]

1. *Flat dollar amount for all employees.* This formula is sometimes used in collective bargaining plans by which a flat dollar amount is paid to all employees regardless of their earnings or years of service. Thus, the plan may pay $300 monthly to each worker who retires.
2. *Flat percentage of annual earnings.* Under this formula, the retirement benefit is a fixed percentage of the worker's earnings, such as 25 to 50 percent. The benefit may be based on career average earnings or on final pay. For example, if average monthly earnings over a three-year period prior to retirement are $1,500, and the percentage is 40 percent, the monthly pension is $600.
3. *Flat dollar amount for each year of service.* Under this formula, a flat dollar amount is paid for each year of credited service. For example, the plan may pay $20 monthly at the normal retirement age for each year of credited service. If the employee has thirty years of credited service, the monthly pension is $600.
4. *Percentage of earnings for each year of service.* Under this formula, both earnings and years of service are considered. The employee receives a benefit equal to some percentage of earnings for each year of service. For example, the plan may pay a retirement benefit of 1 percent of career average earnings for each year of participation in the plan. Thus, a worker with thirty years of service and monthly career-average earnings of $1,500 would receive a monthly retirement benefit of $450.

Limits on contributions and benefits ERISA placed several limitations on the amount of annual contributions and benefits under a qualified private pension plan. These limits have been modified by recent federal legislation. At present, under a *defined contribution plan,* the maximum annual addition that can be made to an employee's account is limited to 25 percent of compensation, or $30,000, whichever is lower. The $30,000 limit will be annually adjusted after 1987 to reflect changes in the cost of living.

Under a *defined benefit plan,* the maximum annual benefit is limited to 100 percent of the participant's average compensation for his or her three highest consecutive years of compensation, or $90,000, whichever is lower. The $90,000 limit will also be annually adjusted after 1987 to reflect changes in the cost of living.

Participants in defined benefit plans are protected against the loss of their pension benefits up to certain limits if the pension plan should terminate. As a result of ERISA, the *Pension Benefit Guaranty Corporation* (P.B.G.C.) has been established, which guarantees the payment of basic benefits of a terminated pension plan that are nonforfeitable or vested up to certain limits. The monthly limit in 1984 was $1,602.27. Defined contribution and profit-sharing plans are not insured by the P.B.G.C.

Vesting provisions **Vesting** is another basic characteristic of pension plans. *Vesting refers to the employee's right to the benefits attributable to the employer's contributions if employment terminates prior to retirement.* The employee is always entitled to a refund of his or her contributions plus any investment earnings on the account upon termination of employment. However, the right to the employer's contribution, or benefits attributable to the contributions, depends on the extent to which the vesting has been attained.

ERISA provides for three **minimum vesting standards.** They are:

1. *Ten-year rule.* After 10 years of covered services, the employee must be 100 percent vested, with no vesting or graded vesting prior to that time.
2. *The 5 to 15 rule.* The employee must be at least 25 percent vested after five years of service; then 5 percent each year for the next five years; then 10 percent each year for the next five years. Thus, there is 25 percent vesting after five years, 50 percent vesting after ten years, and full vesting after fifteen years.
3. *Rule of 45.* The employee must be at least 50 percent vested after the earlier of ten years of service, or when age plus service equals forty-five; then 10 percent a year for the next five years when full vesting is attained. For example, a worker age forty with five years of covered service must be at least 50 percent vested, since both figures add up to forty-five. However, a worker with ten years of service must also be at least 50 percent vested, regardless of the age plus service figure.

From the employer's viewpoint, the basic purpose of the vesting requirements is to reduce labor turnover. Employees have an incentive to remain with the firm until a vested status has been attained. If the employees terminate their employment before full vesting is attained, the forfeitures must be used to reduce the employer's future pension contributions.

Funding of pension benefits Most private pension plans use the technique of **advance funding** to fund the promised benefits. *Advance funding means the employer systematically and periodically sets aside funds prior to the employees' retirement.* This type of funding has several important advantages. First, there is increased security of benefits for the active employees, since funds are periodically set aside prior to retirement. Second, the employer's financial outlay is substantially reduced because of compound interest on the pension plan assets. Finally, the pension costs are spread more evenly over the employee's working career, which produces a more equitable charge against the firm's earnings each year. This is in accordance with the accounting principle of matching costs with revenues.

As a result of ERISA, the employer must meet certain minimum funding standards. The employer must make an annual contribution to a pension plan that is at least equal to the normal cost of the plan plus an amount sufficient to amortize the initial past service liability over a maximum period of thirty years.[8] **Normal cost** is the amount necessary to fund the pension costs attributable to the current year's operation of the plan. The **initial past service liability** refers to the total cost of the initial past service credits granted to employees for service prior to establishment of the plan. If the employer fails to meet the minimum funding standard, a tax penalty is imposed.[9]

Integration with Social Security benefits Many private pension plans are integrated with Social Security benefits. This means that Social Security retirement benefits are taken into account in determining the total retirement benefit. Since the employer pays part of the cost of Social Security benefits, it is only logical for the employer to consider the availability of Social

Security retirement benefits in the benefit formula.

An integrated plan cannot discriminate in favor of the prohibited group. To prevent discrimination, the Internal Revenue has prescribed several complex integration rules that employers must follow. Only one of them is described here. Under the *offset method,* the private pension benefit can be reduced by a maximum of 83⅓ percent of the employee's primary insurance amount based on the Social Security law in effect at the time the employee retires. However, as a practical matter, the maximum offset is typically only 50 percent and is applied only to long-service employees.[10]

Top-heavy plans A pension plan that benefits primarily the key employees is called a *top-heavy plan.* A plan is considered top-heavy if the plan's accrued benefit values for the key employees exceed 60 percent of the accrued benefit values for all employees covered under the plan. (Accrued benefit values are measured in terms of benefits for defined benefit plans and account balances for defined contribution plans.)

To reduce the possibility of excess discrimination in favor of key employees, a top-heavy plan must contain additional requirements to retain its qualified status. These requirements include the following:

1. The amount of annual compensation that can be used to determine contributions and benefits under the plan is limited to a maximum of $200,000 (adjusted for increases in the cost of living).
2. A special rapid vesting schedule must be used for nonkey employees (discussed later).
3. A minimum level of benefits and contributions must be provided for nonkey employees.
4. There is a reduced limit on aggregate benefits and contributions for key employees covered by both a defined benefit and defined contribution plan.

This concludes our discussion of the basic features of pension plans. Let us next consider the specific types of pension plans used by employers today.

Types of Pension Plans

An employer must select a funding agency to establish a pension plan. A **funding agency** is a financial institution or individual that provides for the accumulation or administration of funds that will be used to pay pension benefits. If the funding agency is a life insurer, the plan is called an *insured plan.* If the funding agency is a commercial bank or individual trustee, the plan is called a *trust-fund plan.* If both funding agencies are used, the plan is called a *combination plan.*

The major types of pension plans are as follows:

- Individual policy plan
- Group permanent plan
- Deferred group annuity
- Deposit administration plan
- Immediate participation guarantee plan
- Guaranteed investment contract
- Trust-fund plan

Let us briefly examine the major characteristics of these plans.[11]

Individual policy plan The **individual policy plan** is designed for smaller firms. An individual policy is purchased for each employee to provide the promised retirement benefits. A retirement income policy or retirement annuity is typically purchased for each covered employee in income units of $10 of monthly retirement income. If the worker's earnings increase, additional policies are purchased, usually in units of $10 of monthly retirement income. The amount paid at retirement is the sum of the amounts paid under all policies.

Group permanent plan Under a **group permanent plan,** cash-value life insurance is issued on a group basis. This can include an ordinary life policy, life paid-up at age sixty-five, or endowment-at-age-sixty-five policy. The amount of life insurance purchased is usually $1,000 for each $10 of monthly retirement benefits. The cash values in the policy are then used to pay retirement benefits when the worker retires. Since the cash value in the policy may not be sufficient for paying the promised monthly benefit, a conversion fund is frequently used to provide the additional cash that is needed.

Deferred group annuity Under a **deferred group annuity plan**, a single premium deferred annuity is purchased each year equal to the retirement benefit earned for that year. For example, under a defined benefit pension plan, the worker may earn for the current year a monthly retirement benefit of $25 starting at age sixty-five. A deferred annuity in this amount would be purchased for that year. The benefit amount paid at retirement is the sum of the benefits payable under all deferred annuity contracts that have been purchased on the worker's behalf.

Deposit administration plan Under a **deposit administration plan,** no annuity is purchased until the worker retires. All pension contributions are deposited in an unallocated fund. When the worker retires, an immediate annuity is then purchased out of the plan's assets.

A *separate account* is a variation of the deposit administration plan. Under a separate account, the pension funds are segregated, so that the account assets are not commingled with the insurance company's general assets. The pension funds can be invested in an equity account or fixed income account. Insurance companies have developed separate accounts in order to compete more effectively with trust-fund plans that allow pension funds to be invested in common stocks. Because of legal restrictions, insurance companies were limited in the percentage of assets that could be invested in equities. However, as a result of special legislation in the early 1960s, separate accounts can now be established that permit employers to invest the pension funds entirely in common stocks if they desire. In addition, separate accounts were developed so that insurance companies could sell variable annuity plans.

Immediate participation guarantee plan Under an **immediate participation guarantee plan (IPG)**, all pension contributions are deposited in an unallocated fund. The fund immediately reflects any favorable or unfavorable experience with respect to mortality, investments, and expenses. Annuities are not purchased when the workers retire; the pension benefits are paid directly out of the plan's assets. The insurer does not guarantee the adequacy of the fund, and there generally are no minimum interest rate guarantees or guarantee of principal. However, the insurer periodically evaluates the fund to determine if it is sufficient to continue paying benefits promised to the retired workers. If the fund should decline to a level inadequate to fund in full the benefits of the retired workers, annuities would then be purchased for them at that point. Finally, a contingency reserve of the insurer is not required, which reduces the employer's pension contributions.

Guaranteed investment contract A **guaranteed investment contract** is an arrangement in which the insurer guarantees a relatively high interest rate for a number of years on a lump sum deposit. Guaranteed investment contracts have been extremely popular with employers in recent years because of the relatively high interest rate guarantee by the insurer. The rate of return generally is higher than the rates available from most fixed income securities. In addition, the principal is also guaranteed against loss. Finally, most guaranteed investment contracts make annuity options or other payment options available, but the employer is not required to use these options.

Trust-fund plans **Trust-fund plans** are widely used in negotiated collective bargaining and multiemployer pension funds. All pension contributions are deposited with a trustee who invests the funds according to the trust agreement between the employer and trustee. The trustee can be a commercial bank or individual trustee. Annuities are not usually purchased when the employees retire, and the pension benefits are paid directly out of the fund. The trustee does not guarantee the adequacy of the fund, nor are there any guarantees of principal and interest rates. A consulting actuary periodically determines the adequacy of the fund.

Trust-fund plans have attractive advantages to employers. The trustee can be granted broad investment powers, and the funds can be invested in common stocks, fixed income securities, or other investments. In addition, the employer has considerable flexibility in funding, subject to the minimum funding standards of ERISA that we discussed earlier. Also, since the fund is unallocated, labor turnover, mortality, and delayed retirement can be discounted in advance, which reduces the employer's initial pension contribution. However, as we noted earlier, there are no guarantees by the trustee. This also applies to the mortality risk, which is assumed by the employer.

RETIREMENT PLANS FOR THE SELF-EMPLOYED

Sole proprietors and partners can also establish a qualified retirement plan and enjoy most of the favorable tax advantages now available to participants in a qualified corporate pension plan. Retirement plans for the owners of unincorporated business firms are commonly called **Keogh plans** or HR-10 plans. The contributions to the plan are income-tax deductible up to certain limits, and the investment income accumulates income-tax free. The amounts deposited and the investment earnings are not taxed until the funds are actually distributed.

As a result of the Tax Equity and Fiscal Responsibility Act of 1982 (TEFRA), for tax years after 1983, the major differences between Keogh retirement plans for the self-employed (sole proprietors and partners) and qualified corporate retirement plans have generally been eliminated and, with some exceptions, the same rules that apply to qualified corporate pension plans now apply to retirement plans for the self-employed. Let us briefly examine the major characteristics of current Keogh plans.

Limits on Maximum Contributions and Benefits

If the retirement plan is a *defined benefit plan*, the self-employed individual can fund for a maximum annual benefit equal to 100 percent of his or her average compensation for the three highest consecutive years of compensation, or $90,000, whichever is lower. (After 1987, this latter figure will be adjusted annually for increases in the cost of living.)

If the plan is a *defined contribution plan*, the maximum annual contribution is limited to 25 percent of net earned income from self-employment, or $30,000, whichever is lower. (This latter figure will also be annually adjusted after 1987 to reflect cost-of-living changes.) *However, the definition of net earned income from self-employment is now defined to exclude the amount contributed to the Keogh plan. As a result, the maximum annual deduction to a defined contribution Keogh plan is limited to 20 percent of the net self-employment earned income that is shown on the federal income tax return (gross business earnings less allowable deductions).* If the 20 percent figure is used, the resulting amount is equal to 25 percent of net earned income after the contribution is made. This can be made clearer by the following example:

> *Fred has gross self-employment income of $30,000 and business deductions of $10,000. Thus, the net income that he must report on his federal tax return is $20,000. The maximum Keogh contribution that he can make is 20 percent of the figure, or $4,000. This amount is exactly equal to 25 percent of his net earned income after the contribution is made ($4,000/$16,000 = 25%).*

INSIGHT 23.1

When Should IRA Funds Be Invested?

Since the earnings on your IRA accumulate tax-deferred until you begin withdrawals, the earlier in the tax year you invest in an IRA, the sooner your money is growing tax-deferred. The chart below shows the difference investing early in the tax year can make over a period of years.

Future Value of An Annual Investment of $2,000 at 10% Annual Appreciation

	Date of Annual Investment			
Length of Investment Period	**Jan 1**	**June 1**	**Dec 1**	**April 15 of Following Year**
10 Years	$ 35,062	$ 33,467	$ 31,874	$ 29,195
20 Years	126,005	120,271	114,550	109,989
30 Years	361,886	345,429	328,988	319,548

After 30 years, the January investor has $42,338 more in his or her account than the individual who waited until the following April each year to invest in his or her IRA.

Other Recent Changes

The passage of TEFRA resulted in numerous additional changes that have affected retirement plans for the self-employed. They include the following:

1. The earlier limitation on contributions to defined contribution plans (lower of 15 percent of earned income or $15,000) has been repealed.
2. The earlier rule limiting benefit accruals in a defined benefit plan has been repealed.
3. The earlier rule requiring an owner-employee to cover all employees with at least three years of service has been repealed.
4. The 6 percent excise tax on excess contributions on behalf of owner-employees has been repealed.
5. The earlier rule that prohibited an owner-employee who received a premature distribution from participating in the plan for five years has been repealed.
6. A lump sum death benefit now qualifies for the $5,000 death benefit exclusion for federal income tax purposes.
7. The plan trustee does not have to be a bank or other approved financial institution.
8. A plan for the self-employed no longer requires that contributions made on behalf of a participant (other than a self-employed person) must be made at a rate of at least 7.5 percent of compensation if the plan takes into account more than $100,000 in compensation.

Top-heavy plans If a retirement plan for the self-employed is considered top-heavy, the special top-heavy rules discussed earlier also apply. Employers in top-heavy plans are limited to an annual compensation of $200,000 for purposes of calculating benefits or contributions. Also, minimum benefits or pension contributions are required for lower-level employees, and more rapid vesting rules are applied (100 percent vesting after three years, or 20 percent after two years and 20 percent for each year thereafter).

This concludes our discussion of retirement plans for the self-employed. Let us next consider the Individual Retirement Account.

Figure 23.1
$2,000 Annual Contribution to IRA Account Until Retirement at Age 65

Your age when you start an IRA	Your total contribution	Monthly retirement benefits for 10 years	Total paid back to you
25	$80,000	$7,436	$892,300
30	70,000	4,880	585,625
40	50,000	2,019	242,259
50	30,000	733	87,972
60	10,000	156	18,651

Note: The contributions are invested at 8 percent compound interest. Income taxes on the distributions are ignored.

INDIVIDUAL RETIREMENT ACCOUNT (IRA)

Individuals with earned income are eligible to establish an **Individual Retirement Account (IRA)** and receive favorable income tax advantages. An IRA can be established by persons who are not covered under any pension plan. Also, active participants in an existing private or governmental retirement plan and the self-employed are also eligible to establish an IRA. The IRA contributions are income-tax deductible up to certain limits, and the investment earnings accumulate income-tax free.

Eligibility Requirements

There are two basic eligibility requirements for establishing an IRA plan. First, the person must have earned compensation during the year from personal services; investment income does not qualify. Second, a person must be under age seventy and a half. No IRA deduction is allowed for the tax year in which the individual attains age seventy and a half or any later year.

Limitation on Contributions

The maximum annual tax-deductible contribution is limited to 100 percent of compensation, or $2,000, whichever is lower. An IRA plan can also be established for a *nonworking spouse* (spousal IRA). If a nonworking spouse is included, the individual can contribute annually a maximum of 100 percent of compensation up to $2,250. The contributions can be divided between the two accounts in any amount, provided no more than $2,000 is contributed to the account of either spouse.

For a divorced spouse, taxable alimony received is treated as compensation, and the divorced spouse can contribute to an IRA up to the $2,000 or 100 percent limit.

The contributions deposited into an IRA plan can accumulate to sizable amounts, especially if the plan is started at an early age. Figure 23.1 illustrates the amount of monthly retirement income that would be paid to an individual at age sixty-five for ten years if the plan is started at different ages.

Withdrawal of Funds

The amounts deposited in an IRA plan generally cannot be withdrawn before age fifty-nine and a half without incurring a substantial tax penalty. With the exception of death and long-term disability, amounts withdrawn before age fifty-nine and a half are considered a **premature distribution.** There is a penalty tax of 10 percent on a premature distribution in addition to the regular tax that must be paid on the amounts withdrawn.

The distribution must start before the end of the year in which the individual attains age seventy and a half. The amounts distributed are taxed as ordinary income when they are received. However, a five-year income tax averaging rule can be used to minimize taxes.

INSIGHT 23.2

Deferred Compensation: The 401(k) option

A growing number of people are being offered another choice for their retirement savings—salary reduction plans set up by their employers. Such plans, known as 401(k) plans, allow employees to set aside a certain percentage of their earnings in a retirement plan administered by the employer. The plans, which are a type of profit-sharing plan, usually supplement an employer's primary pension plan.

The amount set aside is considered "deferred compensation" and is not taxable until it is withdrawn at retirement. An individual electing this plan would thus be taxed only on his or her earnings minus the amount deferred. If a plan allowed a deferral of 6 percent, for example, an employee earning $35,000 would have a taxable income of only $32,900. He or she would pay Social Security taxes on the full $35,000, however.

Most plans allow employees to defer between 6 and 10 percent of their salaries. Most employers also make matching contributions for their employees.

When a plan is set up, it specifies how the money is to be invested. Usually the employer selects an investment adviser and offers employees a choice of investments, such as a common stock fund, a money-market fund, or an annuity. Employees can often split contributions between the choices.

Although contributions are locked up until an employee reaches age 59½, they can be withdrawn under certain circumstances. If you change jobs, you can take your savings with you. If you keep the money, it becomes taxable. You can avoid current taxes by rolling the money over into an IRA or into an employer's pension plan, if that plan allows it.

If you suffer a "hardship," most plans allow you to withdraw your money (though, of course, it also becomes taxable). In the rules proposed by the IRS, hardship refers to heavy financial

Types of IRA Plans

There are two types of IRA plans. They are:

- Individual retirement account
- Individual retirement annuity

Individual retirement account The individual can establish an individual retirement account which must be either a trust account or custodial account. The plan can be established with a bank, insured credit union, savings and loan institution, or a person who is eligible to be a trustee or custodian. No more than $2,000 can be deposited annually on behalf of any individual, and all contributions must be made in cash. No part of the funds can be used to purchase a life insurance policy.

Individual retirement annuity An individual retirement annuity can also be used to fund an IRA plan. The annuity is purchased from a life insurer and must meet certain requirements. The contract must be nontransferable by the owner. In addition, the annuity must have flexible premiums so that if the worker's earnings change, the IRA contributions can also be changed.

OTHER RETIREMENT PLANS

Other retirement plans can also be established for individuals. They include the following:

- Simplified Employee Pension (SEP)
- Qualified Voluntary Employee Contributions (QVEC)

needs that cannot be met from other sources. (Final rules had not been issued when this issue went to press.)

Some plans allow an employee to borrow against the deferred compensation, but there are restrictions on the amount. A loan must be repaid within five years unless the proceeds are specifically used to purchase a house or to make a home improvement.

Employees can contribute both to a 401(k) plan and to an IRA. If finances permit, it's desirable to do both. "The 401(k) plan is a great thing for employees," says Donald Grubbs, an actuary with the George B. Buck Consulting Actuaries. "If it's available, take as much advantage of it as possible."

If you can contribute to only one plan, your contribution should go to the 401(k) because it offers certain advantages over an IRA. If the plan offers matching employer contributions, that's a big plus. No one gives you a matching amount for money put into an IRA.

A 401(k) also has an important advantage when you withdraw money at retirement. If you withdraw 401(k) money in a lump sum at retirement, you are eligible for 10-year forward averaging (that is, the money is taxed over 10 years as if you received only one-tenth of it each year). Such tax treatment is likely to save you considerable money. Money withdrawn from an IRA is not eligible for that tax treatment.

On the other hand, your money may be less available to you in a 401(k), unless there is a loan provision. With an IRA, you have no hardship test for withdrawal of your money. It is always available in an emergency, though of course you have to pay the IRS's 10 percent penalty, plus other possible penalties for early withdrawal. You can make a withdrawal from a 401(k) plan only after age 59½ or for disability, termination of employment, or hardship.

SOURCE: "Deferred compensation: the 401(k) option."

▶ Section 401(k) plan

Let us briefly examine each of these plans.

Simplified Employee Pension Plan

As a result of the Revenue Act of 1978, a special IRA plan can be established that is funded by employer contributions. A **Simplified Employee Pension (SEP)** is essentially an employer-sponsored IRA that meets certain requirements. The purpose is to reduce the paper work required by employers who wish to cover employees in a pension plan. Under a SEP plan, each employee establishes and owns an individual IRA plan and has fully vested rights. The employer can make an annual maximum tax-deductible contribution equal to 15 percent of the employee's compensation or $30,000, whichever is lower. Thus, if Susan earns $20,000 annually, her employer can make a maximum SEP contribution of $3,000.

Qualified Voluntary Employee Contributions (QVEC) As an alternative to an IRA, an active participant in an employer-sponsored retirement plan is allowed to make voluntary tax-deductible contributions to the employer's plan, provided the employer's plan permits them. The **Qualified Voluntary Employee Contributions (QVEC)** are income-tax deductible up to certain limits, and the investment earnings accumulate income-tax free.

QVECs generally are treated the same as IRAs. Instead of establishing an IRA with a financial institution, the employee voluntarily makes a tax-deductible contribution to the employer's retirement plan. The maximum annual deduction is limited to 100 percent of earnings or $2,000, whichever is lower. A premature distribution of funds prior to age fifty-nine and a half (other than for death or disability) results in a 10 percent penalty on the amounts distributed. Distributions from QVEC plans are taxed as ordinary income similar to the taxation of IRAs.

Section 401(k) plan Section 401(k) of the Internal Revenue Code permits an employer to establish a qualified profit-sharing or thrift plan that allows employees to receive cash or make a tax-deferred contribution to the plan. The funds contributed by the participating employees can be generated by a voluntary salary reduction. The employee's taxable earnings are thereby reduced, and the contributions into the plan accumulate income-tax free. The funds contributed are considered to be a form of deferred compensation and generally are not taxable until withdrawn at retirement.

Section 401(k) plans are becoming increasingly popular as investment vehicles for voluntary employee contributions and have several advantages. The contributions are tax-deferred until withdrawn; the employee has a choice of investments; funds can be withdrawn under certain circumstances, such as a financial hardship; the employee may be allowed to borrow from the plan; and the lump sum distribution at retirement receives favorable federal income tax treatment. If you can afford it, both an IRA and a 401(k) plan can be established. However, if you can afford only one plan, pension experts generally recommend the 401(k) plan instead of an IRA. (See Insight 23.2.)

SUMMARY

- Employees must meet certain eligibility requirements before they can participate in a private pension plan. The eligibility requirements cannot be more stringent than those allowed under ERISA and the Internal Revenue Code. Employees generally must meet the following eligibility requirements.
  a. Be a full-time employee.
  b. Meet a minimum age and service requirement.
  c. Not be beyond a maximum age.
  Current law requires coverage of all employees who are at least age twenty-one and have one year of service with the firm. Under ERISA, a defined benefit plan can exclude employees who are hired within five years of the normal retirement age. If the plan is a defined contribution plan, a maximum age limitation is not allowed.
- Vesting refers to the employee's right to the employer's contributions, or to the benefits attributable to the employer's contribution, if employment is terminated prior to retirement. Under ERISA, the plan must meet one of three vesting standards.
  a. Ten-year rule.
  b. Five to fifteen rule.
  c. Rule of forty-five.
- There are several types of private pension plans. They include the following:
  a. Individual policy plan.
  b. Group permanent plan.
  c. Deferred group annuity.
  d. Deposit administration plan.
  e. Immediate participation guarantee plan.
  f. Guaranteed investment contract.
  g. Trust-fund plan.

- A self-employed individual can establish a Keogh plan for the self-employed (HR-10 plan) and receive favorable federal income-tax treatment. The contributions to the plan are income-tax deductible, and the investment income accumulates income-tax free. The maximum annual contribution to a defined contribution Keogh plan is limited to 20 percent of earned income, or $30,000, whichever is lower.
- Persons with earned income can establish an Individual Retirement Account (IRA). The maximum annual income tax-deductible contribution is limited to the lesser of 100 percent of compensation or $2,000 ($2,250 in the case of a spousal IRA).
- A Simplified Employee Pension (SEP) is a special type of IRA plan to which the employer contributes. The employee establishes and owns an IRA plan. The employer can make an annual tax-deductible contribution of up to 15 percent of the employee's compensation, but not to exceed $30,000.
- A qualified voluntary employee contributions (QVEC) plan permits an employee to make a voluntary tax-deductible contribution to the employer's retirement plan. QVEC plans generally are subject to the same rules as IRAs.
- Section 401(k) of the Internal Revenue Code allows an employer to establish a qualified profit-sharing or thrift plan that allows employees to receive cash or make a tax-deferred contribution to the plan. The employee typically agrees to a salary reduction, which reduces the employee's taxable income. The accounts deposited in the plan accumulate income-tax free.

QUESTIONS FOR REVIEW

1. Explain the Internal Revenue coverage requirements that an employer must meet to have a qualified private pension plan.
2. Describe the favorable federal income tax advantages to the employer and employees in having a qualified corporate pension plan.
3. Explain the three retirement ages that are normally found in private pension plans.
4. What is a defined contribution plan? What is a defined benefit plan?
5. Define vesting.
6. Explain the advantages of advance funding.
7. Briefly describe the major types of private pension plans.
8. Describe the major provisions of the Employee Retirement Security Act of 1974 (ERISA).
9. Explain the basic features of a retirement plan for the self-employed (HR-10 plan).
10. Describe the basic characteristics of the Individual Retirement Account (IRA).

QUESTIONS FOR DISCUSSION

1. *a.* A pension expert stated that "eligibility requirements are those conditions an employee must meet to become a participant in a pension plan." Describe briefly the major types of eligibility requirements that may be used in designing a pension plan.
   b. Describe the different types of defined benefit formulas that can be used in a private pension plan. Give an example of each type in your answer.

2. A corporate private pension plan covered under ERISA must meet certain minimum vesting standards.
   a. Explain the nature and the purpose of vesting in a corporate pension plan.
   b. Describe each of the following vesting standards:
   ten-year rule.
   five to fifteen rule.
   rule of forty-five.
3. Several types of corporate pension plans can be used to provide retirement benefits to employees. Describe the basic characteristics of each of the following types of private pension plans:
   a. group deposit administration.
   b. immediate participation guarantee (IPG) plan.
   c. trust-fund plan.
4. Describe the maximum tax-deductible contribution that can be made to a qualified plan for the self-employed.
5. Under present law, most persons with earned income can establish an Individual Retirement Account (IRA).
   a. Describe the maximum annual tax-deductible contribution that can be made to an Individual Retirement Account.
   b. Explain the various types of funding instruments that can be used to fund an Individual Retirement Account plan.
6. Explain briefly the characteristics of the following plans:
   a. Simplified Employee Pension (SEP).
   b. Qualified voluntary employee contributions (QVEC) plan.
   c. Section 401(k) plan.

KEY CONCEPTS AND TERMS TO KNOW

ERISA
Prohibited group
Career average earnings
Final pay average
Past service benefits
Defined contribution plan
Defined benefit plan
Vesting
Minimum vesting standards under ERISA
Advance funding
Normal cost
Initial past service liability
Funding agency
Individual policy plan
Group permanent plan
Deferred group annuity
Deposit administration plan
Immediate participation guarantee plan
Guaranteed investment contract
Trust-fund plan
Separate account
Keogh plan for the self-employed (HR- 10)
Premature distribution
Individual Retirement Account (IRA)
Simplified Employee Pension (SEP)
Qualified voluntary employee contributions
Section 401(k) plan

SUGGESTIONS FOR ADDITIONAL READING

Allen, Jr., Everett, Joseph J. Melone, and Jerry S. Rosenbloom. *Pension Planning,* 5th ed. Homewood, Illinois: Richard D. Irwin, Inc., 1984.

Beam, Jr., Burton T. and John J. McFadden. *Employee Benefits.* Homewood, Illinois: Richard D. Irwin, Inc., 1985, chapters 15–24.

Bodie, Zvi and John B. Shoven, eds. *Financial Aspects of the United States Pension System.* Chicago, Illinois: University of Chicago Press, 1983.

Consumers Union. "IRA: Costs, Benefits, Problems," *Consumer Reports,* Vol. 45, No. 1 (January 1980), pp. 40–46.

Kotlikoff, Laurence J. and Daniel E. Smith. *Pensions in the American Economy.* Chicago, Illinois: University of Chicago Press, 1983.

McGill, Dan M. *Fundamentals of Private Pensions,* 5th ed. Homewood, Illinois: Richard D. Irwin, Inc., 1984.

Mehr, Robert I. and Sandra G. Gustavson. *Life Insurance: Theory and Practice,* 3rd ed. Dallas, Texas: Business Publications, Inc., 1984, chapters 16 and 17.

President's Commission on Pension Policy. *Coming of Age: Toward a National Retirement Income Policy.* Washington, D.C.: President's Commission on Pension Policy, 1981.

Rosenbloom, Jerry S., ed. *The Handbook of Employee Benefits: Design, Funding, and Administration.* Homewood, Illinois: Richard D. Irwin, Inc., 1984, chapters 27–53.

Sutton, Nancy A. "Do Employee Benefit Plans Reduce Labor Turnover?" *Benefits Quarterly,* Vol. 1, No. 2 (Second Quarter 1985), pp. 16–22.

NOTES

1. President's Commission on Pension Policy, *Coming of Age: Toward a National Retirement Income Policy* (Washington, D.C.: President's Commission on Pension Policy, 1981), p. 12.
2. A detailed discussion of the basic features of private pension plans can be found in Everett T. Allen, Jr., Joseph J. Melone, and Jerry S. Rosenbloom, *Pension Planning,* 5th ed. (Homewood, Illinois: Richard D. Irwin, Inc., 1984), chapters 4, 5, and 6.
3. A three-year service requirement can be imposed if there is full and immediate vesting.
4. Age Discrimination in Employment Act Amendments of 1978.
5. Allen, p. 84.
6. Allen, pp. 87–89.
7. Allen, pp. 90–93.
8. Pension plans and multiemployer plans in existence on January 1, 1974, have a maximum period of forty years to amortize the initial past service liability.
9. There is a 5 percent excise tax on the accumulated funding deficiency, which increases to 100 percent if the deficiency is not corrected after notification by the IRS.
10. Dan M. McGill, *Fundamentals of Private Pensions,* 5th ed. (Homewood, Illinois: Richard D. Irwin, Inc., 1984), pp. 180–81.
11. Specific details of these plans can be found in Allen, chapters 9, 10, 11, and 12.

CHAPTER 24

SOCIAL INSURANCE

"A multitude of errors in thinking surround our social insurance programs."

George E. Rejda, Social Insurance and Economic Security

STUDENT LEARNING OBJECTIVES

After studying this chapter, you should be able to:

- Explain the reasons for social insurance programs.
- Describe the basic characteristics of social insurance.
- Explain the major provisions of the Old-Age, Survivors, Disability, and Health Insurance (OASDHI) program.
- Describe the basic objectives and important provisions of state unemployment insurance programs.
- Explain the basic objectives and major provisions of workers' compensation insurance.

In this chapter, we begin our study of social insurance programs in the United States. *Social insurance programs* are compulsory government insurance programs that have certain characteristics that distinguish them from private insurance and other government insurance programs. Social insurance programs provide considerable financial protection against the social risks of premature death, old age, unemployment, occupational and nonoccupational disability, and catastrophic medical expenses of the aged and disabled.

We will first discuss the nature of social insurance programs and their basic characteristics. We will next consider the Old-Age, Survivors, Disability, and Health Insurance (OASDHI) program, commonly known as Social Security. The OASDHI program is a massive social insurance program that affects the lives of millions of Americans. We will end the chapter by describing the major provisions of state unemployment insurance and workers' compensation programs that pay benefits to workers who are unemployed or occupationally disabled.

NATURE OF SOCIAL INSURANCE

In this section, we will briefly discuss the nature of social insurance. This includes a discussion of the reasons for social insurance and the basic characteristics of social insurance.

Reasons for Social Insurance

Although the United States has a highly developed system of private insurance, social insurance programs are also necessary. This is true for three reasons. First, social insurance programs are often enacted into law in order to solve a complex social problem. A social problem affects most or all of society and is so serious that direct government intervention is necessary. For example, the Social Security program came into existence as a result of the Great Depression of the 1930s, when massive unemployment and widespread poverty required a direct government attack on economic insecurity.

Social insurance programs are also necessary because certain perils are difficult to insure privately. For example, the peril of unemployment cannot be privately insured, since it does not completely meet the requirements of an insurable risk. However, unemployment can be publicly insured by state unemployment insurance programs.

Finally, social insurance programs are necessary to provide a base of economic security to the population. The social insurance programs provide a layer of financial security to most persons against the long-term consequences of premature death, old age, occupational and nonoccupational disability, and unemployment. These events can cause great economic insecurity because of the loss of income and additional expenses.

Basic Characteristics of Social Insurance

Social insurance programs have certain characteristics that distinguish them from other government insurance programs. They are:[1]

- Compulsory programs
- Floor of income
- Emphasis on social adequacy rather than individual equity
- Benefits loosely related to earnings
- Benefits prescribed by law
- No needs test
- Full funding unnecessary
- Financially self-supporting

Let us briefly examine each characteristic.

Compulsory programs With few exceptions, social insurance programs are compulsory. A compulsory program has two major advantages. First, the goal of providing a floor of income to the population can be achieved more easily. Second, adverse selection is reduced, since both healthy and unhealthy lives are covered.

Floor of income Social insurance programs generally are designed to provide only a floor of income with respect to the risks that are covered. Most persons are expected to supplement social insurance benefits with their own personal program of savings, investments, and private insurance.

The concept of a floor of income is difficult to define precisely, and there is considerable disagreement concerning the minimum and maximum level of benefits that should be paid. One extreme view is that the floor of income should be so low as to be virtually nonexistent. Another extreme view is that the social insurance benefit by itself should be high enough to provide a comfortable standard of living, so that private and group insurance benefits would be unnecessary. A more realistic view is that the social insurance benefit, when combined with other income and financial assets, should be sufficient to maintain a reasonable standard of living for most persons. Any group whose basic needs are still unmet would be provided for by supplemental public assistance benefits.

Social adequacy rather than individual equity Social insurance programs pay benefits based on social adequacy rather than on individual equity. **Social adequacy** means that the benefits paid should provide a certain standard of living to all contributors. This means that the benefits paid are heavily weighted in favor of certain groups, such as low-income persons, large families, the presently retired aged, and those near retirement when the program first starts. In technical terms, the actuarial value of the benefits received by these groups exceeds the actuarial value of their contributions. In contrast, the **individual equity** principle is followed in private insurance. Individual equity means that contributors receive benefits directly related to their contributions; the actuarial value of the benefits is closely related to the actuarial value of the contributions. Although social insurance programs do not completely ignore individual equity considerations, the benefits are paid largely on the basis of social adequacy.

The basic purpose of the social adequacy principle is to provide a floor of income to all covered persons. If low-income persons received social insurance benefits actuarially equal to the value of their tax contributions (individual equity principle), the benefits paid would be so low that the basic objective of providing a floor of income to everyone would not be achieved.

Benefits loosely related to earnings Social insurance benefits are also related to the worker's earnings. The higher the worker's covered earnings, the greater will be the benefits. The relationship between higher earnings and higher benefits is loose and disproportionate, but it does exist. Thus, some consideration is given to individual equity.

Benefits prescribed by law Social insurance programs are prescribed by law. The benefits or benefit formulas, as well as the eligibility requirements, are established by law. In addition, the administration or supervision of the plan is performed by government.

No needs test Social insurance benefits are paid as a matter of right without any demonstration of need. A formal **needs test** is not required. A needs test is used in public assistance—welfare applicants must show their income and financial assets are below certain levels. By contrast, applicants for social insurance benefits have a statutory right to the benefits if they fulfill certain eligibility requirements.

Full funding not necessary It is not necessary for social insurance programs to be fully funded. A **fully funded program** means that the value of the accumulated assets under the plan will be sufficient to discharge all liabilities for the benefit rights accrued to date under the plan. For example, the trust funds of the Social Security program are not fully funded. The trust funds are designed to be used as emergency buffers, which can be drawn down temporarily when contribution inflows and benefit outflows are not in balance. The OASDI trust fund balance at the end of fiscal year 1984 totalled $32.2 billion.[2] To be fully funded a trust fund in excess of $5 trillion would be required.

A fully funded Social Security program is unnecessary for several reasons. First, the program is expected to operate indefinitely and will not terminate in the predictable future. Since it will not terminate, full funding is unnecessary. Second, since the Social Security program is compulsory, new entrants will always enter the program and pay taxes to support it. Third, the taxing and borrowing powers of the federal government can be used to raise additional revenues if the program has financial problems. Finally, from an economic viewpoint, full funding is undesirable.[3] In contrast, private pension plans must emphasize full funding, since private pension plans can and do terminate. Thus, to protect the pension rights of active and retired workers, private plans should be fully funded.

Financially self-supporting Social insurance programs are designed to be financially self-supporting. This means that the program should be largely financed from the contributions of covered employees, employers, the self-employed, and interest on the trust-fund investments.

OLD-AGE, SURVIVORS, DISABILITY, AND HEALTH INSURANCE (OASDHI)

The OASDHI program is the most important social insurance program in the United States. It was enacted into law as a result of the Social Security Act of 1935. More than nine out of ten workers are working in occupations covered by Social Security. About 36 million persons, or about one out of six persons in the country, receive monthly benefit checks. Also, about 27 million persons age sixty-five or over and about three million disabled persons under age sixty-five are covered for their medical expenses under the Medicare program. Let us briefly examine the major provisions of the current law.[4]

Covered Occupations

The Social Security program is a compulsory program that covers almost all gainfully employed workers. The covered occupations include the following groups:

1. *Employees in private firms.* Almost all private sector employees are covered under the program. An estimated 96 percent of employees in the private sector were covered under the program in 1980.[5]
2. *Federal civilian employees.* Beginning in 1984, newly hired federal employees of the federal government are covered on a compulsory basis. Most federal civilian employees hired before 1984 are covered under the Civil Service Retirement System and are not required to contribute to the OASDI program (although they must contribute to the Hospital Insurance program).
3. *State and local government employees.* State and local government employees can be covered by a voluntary agreement between the state and federal government. About 70 percent of all state and local government employees and their families have protection under the Social Security program. The reason for elective coverage is that a state cannot be taxed without its consent.

   In addition, under current law, the states are now prohibited from terminating coverage of state and local government employees.
4. *Employees of nonprofit organizations.* Beginning in 1984, all employees of nonprofit charitable, educational, and religious organizations are now covered on a compulsory basis.
5. *Self-employment.* Self-employed persons are covered on a compulsory basis if their

net annual earnings are $400 or more. Self-employed farmers are also covered if their net annual earnings are at least $400. There is an alternate reporting system for low-income farmers based on gross income.

6. *Household workers.* Household workers are covered if they receive cash wages of $50 or more in a calendar quarter from any employer.
7. *Other groups.* Ministers are automatically covered unless they elect out because of conscience or religious principles. Persons on active duty in the military uniformed services are also covered on a compulsory basis. In addition, employees receiving cash tips of $20 or more in a month from one employer are covered. Finally, railroad workers subject to the Railroad Retirement Act are not required to pay OASDI taxes directly. However, because of certain coordinating provisions, railroad employees are, in reality, covered compulsorily for OASDI and HI.

Certain groups are excluded from coverage. Except in a few states, police officers with their own retirement system cannot be covered under the program. Other occupations that can be excluded include student nurses; college students working for sororities, fraternities, or college clubs; persons employed by their spouses; children under age twenty-one employed by their parents; and newspaper carriers under age eighteen.

Determination of Insured Status

Before you or your family can receive benefits, you must have credit for a certain amount of work in covered employment. For 1985, covered employees and the self-employed receive one **quarter of coverage** for each $410 in covered annual earnings. No more than four quarters of coverage can be credited for the year. The amount of covered earnings needed for a quarter of coverage will automatically increase in the future as average wages increase.

To become eligible for the various benefits, you must attain an insured status. There are three principal types of insured status: (1) fully insured, (2) currently insured, and (3) disability insured. Retirement benefits require a fully insured status; some survivor benefits require either a fully insured or currently insured status; however, certain survivor benefits require a fully insured status. Disability benefits require a disability insured status.

Fully insured You are **fully insured** if you meet one of the following tests: (1) You have forty quarters of coverage, or (2) you have one quarter of coverage for each year after 1950 (or after age twenty-one, if later) up to the year you die, become disabled, or attain age sixty-two. A minimum of six quarters is required under the second test. For example, if you work during high school, college, or later, you are fully insured after acquiring forty quarters of coverage, or ten years of work. You are then fully insured for life even though you never work again in covered employment.

A fully insured status can also be attained under the second test. For example, a worker who attains age sixty-two in 1986 needs thirty-five quarters of coverage to be fully insured. Eventually, all workers will need forty quarters of coverage to be fully insured for retirement benefits.

Currently insured A **currently insured** status is easy to attain. You are currently insured if you have at least six quarters of coverage out of the last thirteen quarters ending with the quarter of death, disability, or entitlement to retirement benefits.

Disability insured You are **insured for disability benefits** if you are fully insured and have at least twenty quarters of coverage out of the last forty quarters ending with the quarter in which the disability occurs.

Special rules apply to younger workers and to the blind to make it easier for them to qualify for disability benefits. If you are between the ages of twenty-four and thirty-one, you must have credit for half the time between your twenty-first birthday and the time that you become disabled. If you are under age twenty-four, you need only six quarters of coverage out of the last twelve quarters. Blind persons are required only to have a fully insured status. They are not required to meet the recent work test requirement that applies to other disability applicants.

Types of Benefits

The Social Security program has four principal benefits. They are:

- Retirement benefits
- Survivor benefits
- Disability benefits
- Medicare benefits

Retirement benefits Social Security retirement benefits are an important source of income to most retired workers. Without these benefits, financial insecurity among the aged would be substantially increased.

Normal retirement age The normal retirement age for full benefits is age sixty-five. However, starting in the year 2000, the normal retirement age will be gradually increased until it reaches age 67 in 2027. The new retirement age will affect people born in 1938 and later (see Figure 24.1). The higher retirement age is designed to recognize the increase in longevity and thus improves the long-term financial solvency of the program when the World War II "baby boom" generation reaches retirement age.

Figure 24.1
Future Social Security Retirement Age

Year of birth	Attainment of age 62	Retirement age (year/months)	Date of attainment of retirement age[1]/	Age-62 benefit as percent of PIA[2]/
1937 and before	1999 and before	65/0	n.a.	80.0
1938	2000	65/2	March 1, 2003	79.2
1939	2001	65/4	May 1, 2004	78.3
1940	2002	65/6	July 1, 2005	77.5
1941	2003	65/8	September 1, 2006	76.7
1942	2004	65/10	November 1, 2007	75.8
1943	2005	66/0	January 1, 2009	75.0
1943–1954	2005–2016	66/0	January 1, 2009–2020	75.0
1955	2017	66/2	March 1, 2021	74.2
1956	2018	66/4	May 1, 2022	73.3
1957	2019	66/6	July 1, 2023	72.5
1958	2020	66/8	September 1, 2024	71.7
1959	2021	66/10	November 1, 2025	70.8
1960 and after	2022 and after	67/0	January 1, 2027 and after	70.0

[1] Birth date assumed to be January 2 of year (for benefit-entitlement purposes, SSA considers people born on the first day of a month to have attained a given age in the prior month). For later months of birth, add number of months elapsing after January up to birth month.

[2] Applies present-law reduction factor ($\frac{5}{9}$ of 1 percent per month) for the first 36 months' receipt of early retirement benefits and new reduction factor of $\frac{5}{12}$ of 1 percent per month for additional months.

SOURCE: Social Security Administration, *SSA Program Circular, Public Information*, No. 958, April 1983.

Early retirement age Workers and their spouses can retire as early as age sixty-two with actuarially reduced benefits. The benefit payable at age sixty-five is reduced 5/9 of 1 percent for each of the first thirty-six months that the person is below the normal retirement age at the time of retirement and by 5/12 of 1 percent for additional months as the retirement age increases. Thus, at present, when the normal retirement age is sixty-five, a worker retiring at age sixty-two receives only 80 percent of the full benefit.

The actuarial reduction in benefits for early retirement at age sixty-two will gradually be increased in the future from 20 to 30 percent when the new higher normal retirement age provisions become fully effective (see Figure 24.1).

Monthly retirement benefits Monthly retirement benefits can be paid to retired workers and their dependents. Eligible persons include the following:

1. *Retired worker.* Monthly retirement benefits can be paid at the normal retirement age (currently age sixty-five) to a fully insured worker; as stated earlier, reduced benefits can be paid as early as age sixty-two.
2. *Spouse of retired worker.* The spouse of a retired worker can also receive monthly benefits if she or he is at least age sixty-two and has been married to the retired worker for at least one year. A divorced spouse is also eligible for benefits based on the retired worker's earnings if she or he is at least age sixty-two, and the marriage has lasted at least ten years.

   Beginning in 1985, a divorced spouse age sixty-two or over who has been divorced for at least two years can receive benefits based on the earnings of a former spouse who is eligible for retirement benefits even though the former spouse has not retired or applied for benefits.
3. *Unmarried children under age eighteen.* Monthly benefits can also be paid to unmarried children of a retired worker who are under age eighteen (or under nineteen if full-time high-school students).
4. *Unmarried disabled children.* Unmarried disabled children age eighteen or over are also eligible for benefits based on the retired worker's earnings if they were severely disabled before age twenty-two and continue to remain disabled.
5. *Spouse with dependent children under age sixteen.* A spouse at any age can receive a monthly benefit if she or he is caring for an eligible child under age sixteen (or a child of any age who was disabled before age twenty-two) who is receiving a benefit based on the retired worker's earnings. The mother's or father's benefit terminates when the youngest child attains age sixteen (unless she or he is caring for a child disabled before age twenty-two).

Benefit amounts The monthly retirement benefit is based on the worker's **primary insurance amount** (PIA), which is the monthly amount paid to a retired worker at the normal retirement age (currently age sixty-five) or to a disabled worker. The PIA, in turn, is based on the worker's **average indexed monthly earnings.** Prior to the 1977 amendments to the Social Security Act, a technical flaw existed in the provision for computing the initial benefit. During periods of inflation, covered workers benefited twice. First the benefit table was adjusted upward to reflect the inflation. Second, since workers' wages tend to increase during inflationary periods, this would also produce higher future benefits. As a result, some workers retiring in the distant future would have received retirement benefits that exceeded 100 percent of their earnings in the year prior to retirement. Long-run costs would have increased sharply. To correct this flaw, the new AIME method for determining benefits was developed.

The wage-indexing method is designed to assure that monthly cash benefits will reflect changes in wage levels over the worker's lifetime, so that the benefits paid will have a relatively constant relationship to the worker's earnings before retirement, disability, or death. The result is that workers who retire today and workers who will retire in the future will have about the same proportion of their earnings restored by OASDHI retirement benefits.

Let us briefly see how wages are indexed. *Earnings are indexed by multiplying the actual earnings for the year being indexed by the ratio of average wages in the second year before the worker reaches age sixty-two, becomes disabled, or dies to average wages in the year being indexed.* For example, assume that Sam retired at age sixty-two in 1983. The significant year for setting the index factor is the second year before he attained age sixty-two (1981). If Sam's actual wages were $3,000 in 1956, the amount is multiplied by the ratio of average annual wages in the national economy in 1981 to average annual wages in 1956. Thus, Sam's indexed earnings for 1956 are $11,697.36. This can be summarized as follows:

$$\underset{\text{(actual earnings in 1956)}}{\$3{,}000} \times \frac{\$13{,}773.10 \text{ (average annual wages in 1981)}}{\$\ 3532.36 \text{ (average annual wages in 1956)}} = \underset{\text{(indexed earnings for 1956)}}{\$11{,}697.36}$$

This procedure is carried out for each year in the measuring period, except that earnings for and after the indexing year are counted in actual dollar amounts.

Figure 24.2 provides some examples of monthly cash benefits for selected beneficiary categories for 1984.

Figure 24.2
Examples of Monthly Social Security Benefits

Average benefits awarded (February 1985)	
Retired workers	$ 431.50[a]
Disabled workers	456.52
Aged widows and widowers	418.13
Children of deceased workers	322.76
Maximum benefits (1985)	
Retired worker reaching age 65 in 1985	$ 717.00
Retired worker reaching age 62 in 1985	591.00
Maximum family benefits, retired worker, age 65 in 1985	1,255.00
Maximum family benefits, retired worker, age 62 in 1985	1,145.00
Worker disabled in 1985	909.00
Maximum family benefits for a worker who becomes disabled in 1985	1,363.00
Maximum family benefits to survivors of a worker who dies in 1985 (family of three or more)	1,633.00

[a] Represents amount before final rounding of benefits.

SOURCE: Social Security Administration, *Monthly Benefit Statistics, Summary Program Data*, April 19, 1985, Table 1, p. 1; Social Security Administration, *Your Social Security* (January 1985), p. 21; and Social Security Administration, *Thinking About Retiring* (January 1985), p. 9.

Delayed retirement credit To encourage working beyond age sixty-five, a delayed retirement credit is available. The worker's primary insurance amount is increased 3 percent for each year (1/4 of 1 percent for each month) of delayed retirement beyond the normal retirement age (currently age sixty-five) and up to age seventy. (The delayed retirement credit is only 1 percent for those who attained age sixty-five before 1982). The worker's additional benefit also increases the benefits paid to surviving spouses.

The delayed retirement credit will gradually be increased in the future from 3 to 8 percent. Starting for workers who attain age sixty-five in 1990, the delayed retirement credit will be increased gradually until it reaches 8 percent for people who reach the normal retirement age in 2009 (then age sixty-six).

Automatic cost-of-living adjustment The monthly cash benefits are automatically adjusted each year for specified changes in the cost of living, which maintains the real purchasing power of the benefits during inflationary periods. In general, whenever the Consumer Price Index on a quarterly basis increases by at least 3 percent from the third quarter of the previous year to the third quarter of the present year, the benefits are automatically increased for December, payable early in the next January by the same percentage, provided Congress has not enacted a general benefit increase, and the stabilizer provisions are not operative (discussed later). If an automatic cost-of-living adjustment is made, the taxable wage base and earnings test (discussed later) are also automatically adjusted.

A *financial stabilizer* is now built into the system, which helps to protect the Social Security trust funds during periods of adverse economic conditions during which the trust funds may be relatively low and the CPI is increasing more rapidly than average wages. Beginning with the cost-of-living increase payable for December 1984 benefits, if the balance in the Social Security trust funds is below 15 percent of the total amount required to pay benefits for the next year (20 percent beginning with the December 1989 increase), the cost-of-living increase will be based on the *lower* of the increase in the CPI or the increase in average wages. If a benefit increase is based on the increase in average wages, a "catch up" benefit increase will be made in any year when the combined trust fund balance reaches 32 percent of expected expenditures.

Earnings test The Social Security program has an **earnings test (retirement test)** that can result in a loss of monthly cash benefits. If a beneficiary has earnings in excess of some maximum limit, he or she will lose some or all of the benefits. *The purposes of the earnings test are to restrict monthly cash benefits only to those persons who have lost their earned income and to hold down the costs of the program.*

In 1985, beneficiaries ages sixty-five through sixty-nine can earn a maximum of $7,320 with no loss of benefits. A different exempt amount applies to beneficiaries under age sixty-five. In 1985, beneficiaries under age sixty-five can earn $5,400 with no loss of benefits. The annual exempt amounts will automatically increase each year to keep pace with increases in average wages if there is a benefit increase for the preceding December.

If the beneficiary's earnings exceed the annual exempt amount, $1 in benefits is withheld for each $2 of earnings above the exempt amount. Beginning in 1990, $1 of benefits will be withheld for each $3 of earnings in excess of the annual exempt amount for beneficiaries age sixty-five and over. However, this change does not apply to beneficiaries under age sixty-five. Finally, beginning in 2003, the age at which the lower withholding rate applies will also increase as the retirement age increases.

The earnings test has three major exceptions. First, persons age seventy and older can earn any amount and receive full benefits. Second, the earnings test does not apply to investment income, dividends, interest, rents, or annuity payments. The purpose of this exception is to encourage private savings and investments as supplements to the Social Security benefits. Finally, a special monthly earnings test is used for the *initial year of retirement* if it produces a more favorable result than the annual test. Under this special test, the monthly exempt amount is one-twelfth of the annual exempt amount. For the initial year of retirement, regardless of total earnings for the year, full benefits are paid to a beneficiary who neither earns more than the monthly exempt amount ($610 in 1985 for persons age sixty-five through sixty-nine and $450 for those under age sixty-five) nor performs substantial services in self-employment. The purpose of the special monthly test is to pay full retirement benefits, starting with the first month of retirement, to the worker who retires in the middle or near the end of the year. Otherwise, the worker would lose some or all of the benefits if he or she retires after earning the maximum allowed under the annual test.

Survivor benefits Survivor benefits can be paid to the dependents of a deceased worker. The deceased worker must be either fully or currently insured, but for certain survivor benefits, a fully insured status is required. The benefits provide considerable protection in terms of private insurance equivalents. A male age thirty with average earnings and a wife and two children has insurance protection worth at least $150,000. Also, the benefits are inflation proof because of the cost-of-living provision.

Survivor benefits can be paid to certain family members. They include the following:

1. *Unmarried children under age eighteen.* Survivor benefits can be paid to unmarried children under age eighteen (under nineteen if full-time high-school students). The deceased parent must be either fully or currently insured.
2. *Unmarried disabled children.* Unmarried children age eighteen or over who become severely disabled before age twenty-two are also eligible for survivor benefits based on the deceased parent's earnings.
3. *Surviving spouse with children under age sixteen.* A widow, widower, or surviving divorced spouse is also entitled to a monthly benefit if she or he is caring for an eligible child under age sixteen (or disabled) who is receiving a benefit based on the deceased worker's earnings. The benefits terminate for the surviving spouse when the youngest child reaches age sixteen or the disabled child dies, marries, or is no longer disabled.
4. *Surviving spouse age sixty or over.* The surviving spouse age sixty or over is also eligible for survivor benefits. The deceased worker must be fully insured. A surviving divorced wife age sixty or older is also eligible for survivor benefits if the marriage lasted at least ten years.
5. *Disabled widow or widower, ages fifty to fifty-nine.* A disabled widow, widower, or surviving divorced spouse who is age fifty or older can also receive survivor benefits under certain conditions. The person must be disabled at the time of the worker's death or become disabled no later than seven years after the worker's death, or within seven years after the mother's or father's benefits end (as per item 3). The deceased must be fully insured. Finally, a surviving divorced spouse must have been married to a deceased spouse for at least ten years.
6. *Dependent parents.* Dependent parents age sixty-two and over can also receive survivor benefits based on the deceased's earnings. The deceased worker must be fully insured.
7. *Lump-sum death benefit.* A lump-sum death benefit of $255 can also be paid when a worker dies. The benefit, however, can only be made if there is an eligible surviving widow, widower, or entitled child.

Disability benefits The third principal benefit is the payment of disability income benefits to disabled workers who meet certain eligibility requirements. A disabled worker must satisfy the following eligibility requirements:

- Be disability-insured
- Meet a five-month waiting period
- Satisfy the definition of disability

A disabled worker must be disability-insured. We have already explained the meaning of a disability-insured status. The disabled worker must also meet a five-month waiting period. Benefits begin after a waiting period of five full calendar months. Therefore, the first payment is for the sixth full month of disability.

The definition of disability stated in the law must also be met. A strict definition of disability is used in the OASDHI program. The following definition is used: *The worker must have a physical or mental condition that prevents him or her from doing any substantial gainful work and is expected to last (or has lasted) at least twelve months or is expected to result in death.* The impairment must be so severe that the worker is prevented from doing any substantial gainful work in the national economy. In determining whether a person can do substantial gainful work, his or her age, education, training, and work experience can be taken into consideration. If the disabled person cannot work at his or her own occupation but can engage in other substantial gainful work, the disability claim will not be allowed.[6]

The monthly disability-income benefit is equal to the worker's full primary insurance amount. Benefits can also be paid to eligible dependents. They include unmarried children under age eighteen; unmarried disabled children age eighteen or older who became disabled before age twenty-two; a wife at any age if she is caring for a child who is under age sixteen (or who is disabled); and a wife or husband age sixty-two or older even if there are no children present.

Medicare benefits The fourth major benefit is the payment of Medicare benefits to eligible persons. Almost all persons age sixty-five and older are eligible for Medicare benefits. Medicare benefits are also available to disabled persons under age sixty-five who have been entitled to disability benefits for at least twenty-four calendar months (they need not be continuous). Persons under age sixty-five who need long-term kidney dialysis treatment or a kidney transplant are also covered by the Medicare program.

The Medicare program consists of two parts—Hospital Insurance (Part A) and Supplementary Medical Insurance (Part B).

1. *Hospital Insurance (Part A).* **Hospital insurance** provides four principal benefits: (1) inpatient hospital care, (2) skilled nursing facility care, (3) home health care, and (4) hospice care.

Inpatient hospital care is provided to a patient in a hospital for up to ninety days for each benefit period. A benefit period, or spell of illness, begins when the patient first enters the hospital and ends when he or she has been out of the hospital or skilled nursing facility for sixty consecutive days. For benefit periods beginning in 1985, the patient must pay an initial deductible of $400 for the first sixty days. For the sixty-first through ninetieth day of hospitalization, in 1985 a daily coinsurance charge of $100 must be paid. If the patient is still hospitalized after ninety days, a *lifetime reserve* of sixty additional days can be used. A daily coinsurance charge of $200 must be paid for each day of lifetime reserve used in 1985. The deductible and coinsurance charges are automatically adjusted each year to reflect changes in hospital costs.

Inpatient care in a skilled nursing facility is also available. The patient must be hospitalized for at least three days to be eligible for coverage, and confinement must be for medical reasons. A maximum of 100 days of coverage is provided. The first twenty days of covered services are paid in full. For the next eighty days, in 1985, the patient must pay a daily coinsurance charge of $50.

Home health care services can be provided in the patient's home by visiting nurses, physical therapists, speech therapists, and other health professionals. Part A now covers an unlimited number of home health visits made under a plan of treatment established by the patient's physician.

Under certain conditions, Hospital Insurance also pays for hospice care for terminally ill beneficiaries if the care is provided by a hospice certified by Medicare.

Special benefit periods apply to hospice care. Hospital Insurance pays for a maximum of two ninety-day periods and one thirty-day period. (If a patient still requires hospice care after the hospice periods are exhausted, the hospice must continue care unless the patient no longer wants hospice services.)

During the hospice benefit period, Medicare pays the full cost of all covered services for the terminal illness. *There are no deductibles or copayments except for limited cost sharing for outpatient drugs and inpatient respite care.*[7] *The patient pays 5 percent of the cost of outpatient drugs or $5 for each prescription, whichever is lower. For inpatient respite care, the patient pays 5 percent of the cost, up to a total of $400 (1985 amount) during a period that begins when the hospice plan is first chosen and ends fourteen days after such care is cancelled.*

2. *Supplementary Medical Insurance (Part B).* **Supplementary Medical Insurance** (SMI), or Part B of Medicare, is a voluntary program that covers physicians' fees and other related medical services. In general, most persons covered under HI are automatically enrolled for SMI unless they voluntarily refuse the coverage. In 1985, the insured person must pay a monthly premium of $15.50 for the coverage, which is supplemented by the federal government out of its general revenues (which currently meet about 75 percent of total costs). The SMI monthly premium is changed each year, generally based on increases in the level of cash benefits and changes in medical costs.

SMI pays for several types of services when they are considered to be medically necessary. First, *physicians' services* are covered in the doctor's office, hospital, or elsewhere. Medical supplies also furnished by a doctor in his or her office, services of the office nurse, and drugs administered by a doctor are also covered.

Outpatient hospital services for diagnosis and treatment are also covered, such as care in an emergency room or outpatient clinic in a hospital. Laboratory tests, X-rays, and diagnostic hospital services as an outpatient are also covered.

Also, an unlimited number of *home health visits* can be provided if certain conditions are met. The patient must be confined to the home and must require part-time skilled nursing care, or physical or speech therapy. A physician must determine that the home health care services are medically necessary, and the services must be provided by a home health agency participating in Medicare. It is not necessary for the patient to be hospitalized first to be covered for home health care visits under either Part A or Part B.

Finally, *other medical and health care services* are covered. These services include diagnostic tests, X-rays and radiation treatment, limited ambulance services, prosthetic devices, physical therapy and speech pathology services, hospital equipment and other durable medical equipment used at home, and supplies for fractures.

Supplementary Medical Insurance pays 80 percent of the *recognized charges* for covered medical services after the patient pays a $75 calendar-year deductible. Recognized charges or approved charges are the amounts actually approved by the Medicare carrier. In determining the amount allowed, reasonable charges are based on the *customary charges* of the physician or supplier but cannot be higher than the *prevailing charges,* which are the charges made by other physicians or suppliers in the geographical area where the service is provided. Recognized or approved charges are updated annually according to an economic index formula that considers the cost of maintaining a medical practice and increases in general earnings levels. However, because of a time lag in the determination of recognized charges and high rates of inflation, the amounts approved are often less than the actual

INSIGHT 24.1

How Are Social Security Benefits Taxed?

Beginning in 1984, up to half of the Social Security benefits is subject to the federal income tax if the beneficiary's combined income exceeds certain base amounts. The base amounts are $25,000 for a single taxpayer, $32,000 for married taxpayers filing jointly, and zero for married taxpayers filing separately.

In determining the amount of income that must be counted, the taxpayer must count his or her adjusted gross income under present law, plus all nontaxable interest income (such as interest from a municipal bond), plus half of the Social Security benefits. The total combined income is then compared with the base amount. *The amount of Social Security benefits that must be included in gross income is the lower of (1) half of the Social Security benefits or (2) half of the excess of the taxpayer's combined income over the base amount.* This can be made clear by the following examples:

Example 1. Jim and Mary, both 66, have an adjusted gross income of $35,000 and Social Security benefits of $10,000. The amount of Social Security benefits that is included in income is the lower of (1) $5,000 (half the benefits) or (2) $4,000 (half of the excess of $35,000 plus $5,000 over $32,000). In this case, $4,000 of benefits must be included in the couple's gross income.

Example 2. Betty and Ed, both age 66, have an adjusted gross income of $25,000 and Social Security benefits of $9,000. None of the benefits is taxable, since their countable income is under $32,000.

The taxes are collected by the Treasury as part of the income tax and are credited to the OASDI trust funds. The new law will actually affect only upper-income beneficiaries, or about 10 percent of the Social Security beneficiaries in 1984. This provision will increase trust fund revenues by an estimated $27 billion in additional revenue through the decade of the 1980s.

charges of doctors and suppliers. Because of the various deductibles, coinsurance, exclusions, and limitations on charges, Medicare pays slightly less than 40 percent of the medical expenses of the aged as a group. The major reason for this relatively low percentage is that "medical expenses of the aged" are defined to include custodial nursing home care, which is excluded by Medicare.

Taxation of benefits Part of the monthly cash benefits is now subject to federal income taxation for certain beneficiaries. Up to half of the monthly benefits is subject to the federal income tax if the beneficiary's adjusted gross income for federal tax purposes, plus nontaxable interest income, plus half of the Social Security benefits, exceeds certain base amounts (see Insight 24.1). The base amounts are $25,000 for a single taxpayer, $32,000 for married taxpayers, and zero for a couple filing separately if they lived together any part of the year. The purpose of this provision is to improve the long-range financial solvency of the OASDI trust funds by taxing part of the benefits paid to upper-income beneficiaries.

Financing

The OASDI and HI programs are based on *current-cost financing*, which is essentially pay-as-you-go financing with limited trust funds. A covered worker pays a payroll tax on earnings up to some specified maximum limit, and the amount is matched by an identical contribution from the employer. The self-employed pay a contribution rate that is twice the combined OASDHI employee-employer contribution rate (reduced by tax credits).

In 1985, the worker paid a tax contribution rate of 7.05 percent on a maximum taxable earnings base of $39,600. This amount is matched by an identical contribution from the employer. The self-employed pay a gross rate of 14.10 percent (11.8 percent net) on the same earnings base. The earnings base will automatically increase in the future if benefits are increased according to the cost-of-living provisions. The earnings base will increase based on changes in average wages in the national economy.

All payroll taxes and SMI premiums are deposited into four federal trust funds. Contributions for retirement, survivors, and disability benefits are deposited into the Old-Age and Survivors Insurance (OASI) and Disability Insurance (DI) trust funds. Contributions for financing hospital insurance are deposited into the Hospital Insurance trust fund (HI). Monthly premiums to finance supplemental medical insurance, along with the federal government's contribution, are deposited in the Supplementary Medical Insurance trust fund (SMI). All benefits and administrative expenses are paid out of the trust funds. The excess contributions not needed for current benefits and administrative expenses are invested in interest-bearing securities of the federal government.

The fundamental purpose of the trust funds is to serve as emergency buffer funds that can be drawn on when outflows for benefits and expenses exceed contribution inflows.

Figures 24.3 and 24.4 show the OASDHI contribution rates for covered employees, employers, and the self-employed. The contribution rates will increase sharply in the future, especially for the self-employed.

Figure 24.3
OASDHI Employee and Employer Contribution Rates (each)

Year	OASDHI	HI	Total
1984	5.70%	1.30%	7.00%[a]
1985	5.70	1.35	7.05
1986–87	5.70	1.45	7.15
1988–89	6.06	1.45	7.51
1990 and after	6.20	1.45	7.65

[a] Because of a tax credit of 0.3 percent for employees in 1984, the effective withholding rate for employees is 6.7 percent. The employer's contribution rate is 7 percent.

SOURCE: Social Security Administration.

Figure 24.4
OASDHI Self-employed Contribution Rates[a]

Year	OASDHI	HI	Total
1984	11.40%	2.60%	14.00%
1985	11.40	2.70	14.10
1986–1987	11.40	2.90	14.30
1988–1989	12.12	2.90	15.02
1990 and after	12.40	2.90	15.30

[a] Because of tax credits, the net tax rate is 11.3 percent in 1984, 11.8 percent in 1985, 12.3 percent in 1986 and 1987, and 13.02 percent in 1988 and 1989. After 1989, the tax credit will be replaced by special provisions designed to treat the self-employed in much the same manner that employees and employers are treated for Social Security and income tax purposes under present law.

SOURCE: Social Security Administration.

Problems and Issues

Numerous problems and issues are associated with the current Social Security program. They include the following:

1. *Financial condition and Social Security.* Prior to the 1983 amendments, the Social Security program had been experiencing a serious financial problem. Since the early 1970s, the Social Security program had been paying out more in benefits than had been collected in taxes. The cash flow problem was due largely to relatively high inflation rates and poor economic performance of the 1970s. However, as a result of the 1983 amendments, which provided for mandatory coverage of newly hired federal employees, higher tax rates, a higher normal retirement age, taxation of part of the cash benefits, and other changes, the financial position of the program has been materially improved. Based on the 1984 Board of Trustees report, actuarial estimates indicate that monthly OASDI benefits can be paid on time well into the next century on the basis of four sets of economic and demographic assumptions. Over the next seventy-five years, the OASDI program is considered to be in close actuarial balance based on the intermediate-B set of cost assumptions.[8]

   The financial condition of the Medicare program, however, is a matter of deep concern. Based on the 1984 Board of Trustees report, the present financing schedule for HI is barely adequate to ensure the payment of benefits through the end of the decade if the assumptions underlying the estimates are realized. The HI trust fund will be exhausted in 1991 based on the intermediate assumptions. Based on the pessimistic assumptions, the HI trust fund will be exhausted in 1989. Even if the optimistic assumptions are used, the HI trust fund will be exhausted in 1995. To bring the HI program into close actuarial balance for the twenty-five year projection period under the intermediate-B assumptions, disbursements must be reduced by 32 percent, or income must be increased by 48 percent.[9]

   In addition, although the SMI program is considered actuarially sound at the present time, the Board of Trustees is deeply concerned about the rapid growth in the cost of the program and the extent to which general revenues have become the major source of financing. In 1983, general revenues accounted for 75 percent of the total income under the program.

   Some social insurance experts believe that the future long-run financial condition of the Social Security program is bleak (see Insight 24.2) and that drastic changes in financing and benefits are necessary to maintain the future solvency of the system.

2. *Diagnosis related groups under Medicare.* Another important issue is the extent to which payment for inpatient hospital services under Medicare can be held down under a new *prospective payment system.*[10] Under this system, hospital care is classified into 467 diagnosis related groups (DRG), and a single payment amount is paid for each type of care depending on the diagnosis group in which the case is placed. Thus, a flat uniform amount will be paid to each hospital for the same type of care or treatment. (However, the amount paid would vary among nine different geographical locations and by urban and rural facilities.) The new system was gradually phased in over a three-year period beginning on October 1, 1983.

   The purpose of the new DRG system is to create financial incentive to encourage hospitals to operate more efficiently. Hospitals would be allowed to keep payment amounts that exceed their costs, but they would be required to absorb any costs in excess of the DRG flat amounts. As a result of the new system, hospitals are discharging Medicare patients sooner, tests and services ordered by physicians are being carefully scrutinized, and hospitals are now being more cost conscious.

3. *Continuing disability investigation re-*

view. The 1980 amendments required the Social Security Administration to reevaluate periodically each disability claim, since it was discovered earlier that as many as one in five disability beneficiaries might be collecting benefits improperly. As a result, over one million disabled workers had their continuing eligibility reviewed, and 45 percent of them were told that they were ineligible for benefits. However, in many cases, the determination was made erroneously, and about two-thirds of those who appealed their termination had their benefits restored.[11]

As a result of the review procedures used, the OASDI disability program has been plunged into administrative chaos. In twenty states, the federal courts have intervened and have substituted a court-ordered review standard for the procedures used by the Social Security Administration. In nine other states, governors have declared a self-imposed moratorium on processing disability reviews.[12] As a result of loud and vocal criticism, new legislation has been enacted that would make it more difficult for disability examiners to terminate benefits for disabled beneficiaries. Under the new rules, with some exceptions, disability benefits cannot be cut off unless the government has substantial evidence that the person's condition has improved and he or she is capable of doing some work again.

UNEMPLOYMENT INSURANCE

Unemployment insurance programs are federal-state programs that pay weekly cash benefits to workers who are involuntarily unemployed. Each state has its own unemployment insurance program. The various state programs are due to the unemployment insurance provisions of the Social Security Act of 1935.

Objectives of Unemployment Insurance

Unemployment insurance has several basic objectives. They are:

- Provide cash income during involuntary unemployment.
- Help unemployed workers find jobs.
- Encourage employers to stabilize employment.
- Help stabilize the economy.

Weekly cash benefits are paid to unemployed workers during periods of **short-term involuntary unemployment,** thus helping unemployed workers maintain their economic security. A second objective is to help unemployed workers find jobs; applicants for benefits must register for work at local employment offices, and officials of the U.S. Employment Service provide assistance in finding suitable jobs. A third objective is to encourage employers to stabilize their employment through experience rating (discussed later). Finally, unemployment benefits help stabilize the economy during recessionary periods.

Coverage

Most private firms, state and local governments, and nonprofit organizations are covered for unemployment benefits. A *private firm* is subject to the federal unemployment tax if it employs one or more employees in each of at least twenty weeks during the calendar year (or preceding calendar year), or it pays wages of $1,500 or more during a calendar quarter of either year. *State and local governments* are not subject to the federal unemployment tax, but the state program must make unemployment insurance benefits available to state and local government employees.

Agricultural firms are covered if they have a quarterly payroll of at least $20,000 or employ ten or more workers in at least twenty weeks of the year. *Domestic employment* in a private household is covered if the employer pays domestic wages of $1,000 or more in a calendar quarter.

Eligibility Requirements

An unemployed worker must meet the following eligibility requirements:[13]

- Have qualifying wages and employment

INSIGHT 24.2

Social Security's Bleak Future

The Social Security Trustees issued their annual reports on the system's financial status on April 5, 1984. Most of us are too busy to read these three separate reports containing thousands of statistics in their hundreds of pages. But everyone in the employee benefit business should read Table F3 in Appendix F on page 131 of the "Report on the Old-Age and Survivors Insurance and Disability Insurance Trust Funds."

It shows the projected income and outgo for the Old-Age, Survivors and Disability Insurance and Hospital Insurance programs as a percentage of payroll that is subject to the Social Security tax. An extract of figures from Table F3 is as follows:

Year	Outgo	Income	Excess of Income Over Outgo
1984	14%	14%	—
1995	15	16	+1%
2010	16	16	—
2020	20	16	−4
2040	25	16	−9

These figures represent only the portion of Social Security that is financed (primarily) by the FICA tax paid by employers and employees: that is, the Old-Age, Survivors, Disability, and Hospital Insurance benefits (usually referred to as OASDI and HI benefits). The figures do not include Supplementary Medical Insurance (SMI) benefits, which are financed largely by general revenue.

The cost of SMI benefits, currently equivalent to about 1 percent of taxable payroll, will probably rise to between 3 percent and 6 percent of payroll during the projection period, depending upon how much the "deductible" is increased as medical costs rise.

Payroll taxes

The income shown in the table is made up primarily of payroll taxes but is supplemented by small amounts of general revenue. For example, in 1984 the employer payroll tax is 7 percent and the employee tax is 6.7 percent, for a total of 13.7 percent; supplemented by general revenue equivalent to 0.5 percent of payroll. In 1990 and later the employer tax is 7.65 percent and the employee tax is 7.65 percent, for a total of 15.3 percent; supplemented by general revenue of less than one percent of payroll.

The projections in Table F3 are based upon the Alternative II-B assumptions about future de-

- Be able and available for work
- Actively seek work
- Be free from disqualification
- Serve a one-week waiting period

The applicant must have earned qualifying wages of a specified amount during his or her base period, or must have worked a certain number of weeks or calendar quarters during the base period, or have some combination of both. The base period is generally a four-quarter or fifty-two week period prior to the period of unemployment. The purpose of this requirement is to limit unemployment benefits to workers with a current attachment to the labor force.

The applicant must also be physically and mentally capable of working and must be avail-

mographic and economic conditions—the so-called "intermediate" assumptions. Under the less optimistic Alternative III assumptions, projections (not all of which are published) indicate that costs would eventually become about 40 percent to 45 percent of taxable payroll, while the scheduled income would still be only about 16 percent of payroll.

An analysis of these figures indicates that during the first half of the 21st century, taxes would have to be 40 percent higher, on the average, than those currently scheduled in law according to the Alternative II-B projections. According to the Alternative III projections, taxes would have to average about 80 percent higher than those currently scheduled in law.

Stated another way, tax rates are scheduled to rise in 1985, 1986, 1988, and 1990 to an ultimate level of 7.65 percent from employers and 7.65 percent from employees, but that will not be enough. (Self-employed taxes are scheduled to rise from 11.30 percent to 15.30 percent, or the sum of the employee and employer taxes.) Under the Alternative II-B projections, employee taxes would have to rise to an ultimate level of about 12 percent of pay if benefit promises are honored. Under the Alternative III projections, employee taxes would have to rise to about 20 percent of pay. Employer taxes would, of course, have to rise to an equal amount.

Based upon these projections, the long-range financial picture for Social Security is indeed bleak. Social Security has promised far more (40 percent to 80 percent) than can be provided by the taxes scheduled in present law; therefore, for today's youth, taxes must be increased substantially or benefits must be reduced substantially.

This bad news is in sharp contrast to equivocal statements by many commentators that seem designed to lull the public into a false sense of security. Good news can be reported only by limiting the time horizon and by ignoring Hospital Insurance, which is a life annuity—paid in kind rather than cash—for persons aged 65 and over and certain disabled persons. Future Hospital Insurance benefits will have a value equal to more than half the value of the cash benefits. Accordingly, taxpayers are vitally interested in whether their **entire** retirement benefit, not just the cash portion of it, will be paid as promised.

Significant information

It is to the credit of the authors of the OASDI Report that they have included Table F3 showing a projection of future income and outgo for the **entire** retirement benefit, both the OASDI and HI segments. It will be to the credit of everyone in the employee benefit business who is interested in the long-range financial health of Social Security to study Table F3 and communicate its significance to as many people as will listen.

SOURCE: "Social Security's Bleak Future" by A. Haeworth Robertson from *National Underwriter, The Life and Health Insurance Edition,* 1984. Reprinted by permission.

able for work. The claimant must register for work at a public employment office and actively seek work.

In addition, the applicant must not be disqualified from receiving benefits by actions such as voluntarily quitting his or her job without good cause, being discharged for misconduct, or refusing suitable work.

Finally, a one-week waiting period must be satisfied in most states. All but eleven states require a waiting period of one week of total unemployment before unemployment insurance benefits are payable.

Benefits

A weekly cash benefit is paid for each week of total unemployment. The benefit paid varies with the worker's past wages, within certain minimum and maximum dollar amounts. *Most states use a formula that pays benefits based on a fraction of the worker's wages paid during the highest base-period calendar quarter.* A typical fraction is one-twenty-sixth of the highest-quarter wages. This results in the payment of benefits equal to 50 percent of the worker's full-time wage in the highest quarter (subject to minimum and maximum amounts). Several states also pay a dependent's allowance for certain dependents.

As of January 1985, the maximum weekly benefit ranged from $84 ($141 with dependents) in Indiana to $294 (including dependents) in Massachusetts. Most states pay regular unemployment benefits for a maximum duration of twenty-six weeks, although a few states pay benefits for a slightly longer duration.

During periods of high unemployment, some workers exhaust their regular unemployment benefits. A permanent federal-state program of *extended benefits* has been established that pays additional benefits to unemployed workers who have exhausted their regular benefits during periods of high unemployment in individual states. Under the **extended benefits program,** claimants can receive up to thirteen additional weeks of benefits, or one-half the total amount of regular benefits, whichever is less. There is an overall limit of thirty-nine weeks for both regular and extended benefits. The costs of the extended benefits are shared equally by the federal government and the states.

Financing

State unemployment insurance programs are financed largely by payroll taxes paid by employers on the covered wages of employees. Four states (Alabama, Alaska, New Jersey, and Pennsylvania) also require the employees to contribute. All tax contributions are deposited in the federal Unemployment Trust Fund. Each state has a separate account, which is credited with the unemployment-tax contributions and the state's share of investment income. Unemployment benefits are paid out of each state's account.

For 1985, each covered employer must pay a federal payroll tax of 6.2 percent on the first $7,000 of annual wages paid to each covered employee. The employers can credit toward the federal tax any state contributions paid under an approved unemployment insurance program and any tax savings under an approved experience-rating plan. The total employer credit is limited to a maximum of 5.4 percent. The remaining 0.8 percent is paid to the federal government and used for state and federal administrative expenses, for financing the federal government's share of the extended benefits program, and for maintaining a loan fund from which states can temporarily borrow when their accounts are depleted.

Because of a desire to strengthen their unemployment reserves and maintain fund solvency, many jurisdictions have a higher taxable wage base that exceeds federal standards. In 1985, thirty-four jurisdictions had a taxable wage base in excess of $7,000 of annual wages paid to each covered worker.

Experience rating is also used, whereby firms with favorable employment records pay reduced tax rates. Experience rating is highly controversial. The major argument in support of experience rating is that it provides some firms with a financial incentive to stabilize their employment. However, some cyclical and seasonal firms have little control over their employment, and experience rating provides little financial incentive for them to stabilize employment. Also, labor unions are strongly opposed to experience rating, since some business firms resist benefit increases and also contest some valid claims.

Problems and Issues

Numerous problems and issues are associated with unemployment insurance programs. Some important problems are summarized as follows:

1. *Small proportion receiving benefits.* Only a small proportion of the total unemployed at any time receive unemployment benefits. For example, in September 1982, a period of high unemployment, about 11.3

million persons were unemployed in an average week. However, for the week ending October 2, 1982, only about 4.6 million persons, or about 41 percent of the unemployed, received regular state unemployment benefits.[14]

Several reasons explain why a relatively small proportion of the total unemployed receive unemployment insurance benefits. Many unemployed persons are new entrants or reentrants into the labor force and have not earned qualifying wages; some work in noncovered occupations; many are initially denied benefits because of a one-week waiting period in most states; others are disqualified for various reasons; and many remain unemployed after they exhaust their benefits. Thus, the effectiveness of state unemployment insurance programs as a primary defense against short-term unemployment can be seriously questioned.

2. *Inadequate financing.* Many state unemployment insurance programs are inadequately financed, and their reserve accounts have been seriously depleted. During recent recessions, many states found their reserve funds inadequate for meeting the increased cost of benefits due to high unemployment and a longer duration of payments. States are permitted to borrow from the federal unemployment account if their accounts decline to a level where benefit obligations cannot be met. During the recession period of 1974–1976, twenty-three states depleted their unemployment reserves, which forced them to borrow $4.6 billion from the federal loan fund. In 1980, fifteen states still owed more than $4.3 billion.[15]

   Some suggestions for improving the financing of unemployment insurance programs include increasing the taxable wage base, higher contribution rates, more stringent eligibility requirements, and reducing fraud and overpayments. Also, the states must now pay interest on loans from the federal unemployment account.

3. *Disincentives to work.* Unemployment insurance programs provide some disincentives to work. Researchers have found that unemployment insurance programs may result in a higher unemployment rate and a longer duration of unemployment.[16] For many unemployed workers, the cost of remaining unemployed is not high. Unemployed workers are not required to take any job, and the unemployment benefits provide time to find another job in their field of training. Work-related expenses are reduced and for some workers, the weekly benefits restore a relatively large proportion of the take-home pay, especially if dependents' allowances are paid.

WORKERS' COMPENSATION

Thousands of workers are disabled or die each year because of job-related injuries or occupational disease. In 1983 alone, there were 1.9 million occupational injuries, or about nineteen injuries for each 1,000 workers. During the same period, 11,300 workers died from job-related injuries.[17] In addition to pain and suffering, disabled workers are confronted with the serious problems of loss of income, payment of medical expenses, partial or permanent loss of bodily functions or limbs, and job separation.

Workers' compensation is a social insurance program that provides medical care, cash benefits, and rehabilitation services to workers who are disabled from job-related accidents or disease. The benefits are extremely important in reducing economic insecurity that may result from an occupational disability.

Development of Workers' Compensation

Under the *common law of industrial accidents,* dating back to 1837, workers injured on the job had to sue their employers and prove negligence before they could collect damages. However, an employer could use three common law defenses to block the injured worker's lawsuit. Under the **contributory negligence doctrine,** the injured worker could not collect damages if he or she contributed in any way to the injury. Under the **fellow-servant doctrine**, the injured worker could not collect if the injury resulted from the negligence of a fellow worker. And under the **assumption-of-risk doctrine,** the injured worker could not collect if he or she had advance knowledge of the dangers inherent in a particular occupation. As a result of the harsh common law, relatively few disabled workers collected adequate amounts for their injuries.

The enactment of *employer-liability laws* between 1885 and 1910 was the next step in the development of workers' compensation. These laws reduced the effectiveness of the common-law defenses, improved the legal position of injured workers, and required employers to provide safe working conditions for their employees. However, injured workers were still required to sue their employers and prove negligence before they could collect for their injuries.

Finally, the states passed *workers' compensation laws* as a solution to the growing problem of work-related accidents. In 1908, the federal government passed a workers' compensation law covering certain federal employees, and by 1911, ten states had passed similar laws. All states today have workers' compensation laws.

Workers' compensation is based on the fundamental principle of liability without fault. *The employer is held absolutely liable for the occupational injuries or disease suffered by the workers, regardless of who is at fault.* Disabled workers are paid for their injuries according to a schedule of benefits established by law. They are not required to sue their employers to collect benefits. The laws provide for the prompt payment of benefits to disabled workers regardless of fault and with a minimum of legal formality. The costs of workers' compensation benefits are therefore considered to be a normal cost of production, which is included in the price of the product.

Objectives of Workers' Compensation

State workers' compensation laws have several basic objectives. They are:[18]

- Broad coverage of employees for occupational injury and disease
- Substantial protection against the loss of income
- Sufficient medical care and rehabilitation services
- Encouragement of safety
- Reduction in litigation

A fundamental objective is to provide broad coverage of employees for occupational injury and disease. This objective has largely been met. In 1982, workers' compensation laws covered about 87 percent of all wage and salaried workers.[19]

A second objective is to provide substantial protection against the loss of income. The workers' compensation cash benefits are designed to restore a substantial proportion of the disabled worker's lost earnings, so that the disabled worker's previous standard of living can be maintained.

A third objective is to provide sufficient medical care and rehabilitation services to injured workers. Workers' compensation laws require employers to pay hospital, surgical, and other medical costs incurred by injured workers. Also, the laws provide for rehabilitation services to disabled employees so that they can be restored to productive employment. It is estimated that a dollar spent on rehabilitation services can save as much as $10 in claim payments if the disabled worker is reemployed.[20]

Another objective is to encourage firms to reduce work-related accidents and to develop sound safety programs. Experience rating is used to encourage firms to reduce occupational accidents and disease, since firms with superior accident records pay relatively lower workers' compensation premiums.

Finally, workers' compensation laws are designed to reduce litigation. The benefits are paid promptly to disabled workers without requiring them to sue their employers. The objective is to reduce or eliminate the payment of legal fees to attorneys and time-consuming and expensive trials and appeals.

Types of Law

Workers' compensation laws are either compulsory or elective. Most states have compulsory laws that require covered employers to provide specified benefits to workers who are disabled from a job-related accident or disease.

Three states (New Jersey, South Carolina, and Texas) have elective laws, whereby the employer can either elect or reject the workers' compensation law. If the employer rejects the act and the injured employee sues for damages based on the employer's negligence, the employer is deprived of the three common-law defenses. In such a case, the injured worker has only to establish the employer's negligence to collect damages.

Complying with the Law

Employers can comply with the law by purchasing a workers' compensation insurance policy, by self-insuring, or by obtaining insurance from a monopoly or competitive state fund.

Most firms purchase a workers' compensation policy from a private insurer. The policy guarantees the benefits that the employer must legally provide to workers who are occupationally disabled.

Self-insurance is allowed in most states. Many large firms prefer to self-insure their workers' compensation losses and avoid the administrative costs associated with workers' compensation contracts. In addition, group self-insurance may be available to smaller firms that pool their risks and liabilities.

Finally, workers' compensation insurance can be purchased from a state fund in certain states. In six states, covered employers must purchase the workers' compensation insurance from a monopoly state fund. In thirteen states, employers can purchase the insurance either from a competitive state fund or from private insurers.[21]

Covered Occupations

Most industrial occupations are covered by a workers' compensation law. However, certain occupations are excluded, or coverage is incomplete. Some states have numerical exemptions, whereby small firms with fewer than a specified number of employees (typically three to five) are not required to provide workers' compensation benefits. Also, because of the nature of the work, most states exclude or provide incomplete coverage for farm workers, domestic servants, and casual employees. However, employers can voluntarily cover employees who are in an exempted class.

Eligibility Requirements

Two principal eligibility requirements must be met to receive workers' compensation benefits. First, the disabled person must work in a covered occupation. Second, the worker must have a job-related accident or disease. *This means that the injury or disease must arise out of and in the course of employment.* The courts have gradually broadened the meaning of this term over time. The following situations are usually covered under a typical workers' compensation law:

1. The employee is injured while performing specified duties at a specified location.
2. An employee who travels is injured while engaging in activities that benefit the employer.
3. The employee is on the premises and is injured going to the work area.
4. The employee has a heart attack while lifting some heavy boxes.

Certain injuries, however, generally are not compensable under a workers' compensation law.

An employee who is injured in an automobile accident while going to or from work generally is not covered. Injury due to employee intoxication is usually not compensable, and self-inflicted injuries are also excluded.

The states also provide broad coverage of occupational disease. Until recently, most states covered only certain occupational diseases. However, because of the growing number of chemicals and other substances that can cause occupational disease, it is impractical for the states to list each covered disease. Instead, most states provide full coverage for all occupational diseases.

Types of Benefits

Workers' compensation laws provide four principal benefits. They are:[22]

- Medical care
- Disability income
- Death benefits
- Rehabilitation services

Medical care Medical care is covered in full in all states. Medical benefits accounted for about 29 percent of all workers' compensation benefits paid in 1981.

Disability income Disability-income benefits are payable after the disabled worker satisfies a waiting period ranging from two to seven days. If the worker is still disabled after a certain number of days or weeks, most states pay benefits retroactively to the date of injury.

The weekly benefit amount is based on a percentage of the workers' average weekly wage, typically 66.7 percent, and the degree of disability. There are four classifications of disability: (1) temporary total, (2) permanent total, (3) temporary partial, and (4) permanent partial. Most states have minimum and maximum dollar limits on weekly benefits. For example, a worker in Nebraska may break a leg and be off work for three months. He or she would receive a maximum of $200 weekly during the period of disability.

In most states and the District of Columbia, the maximum weekly benefits are adjusted each year according to changes in the state's average weekly wage. In addition, the majority of states have a maximum weekly benefit of 100 percent or more of the statewide weekly wage.

Death benefits Death benefits are also paid if the worker is killed on the job. Two types of benefits are paid. First, a burial allowance is paid, ranging from $300 to $4,680. Second, cash-income payments can be paid to eligible surviving dependents. A weekly benefit based on a proportion of the deceased worker's wages (typically 66.7 percent) is usually paid to a surviving spouse for life or until she or he marries. Upon remarriage, the widow or widower typically gets two years of payments in a lump sum. A weekly benefit can also be paid to each dependent child under age eighteen or until a later age, such as age twenty-two, if the child is a full-time student.

Rehabilitation services Rehabilitation services are available in all states to restore disabled workers to productive employment. In addition to weekly disability benefits, workers who are being rehabilitated are compensated for board, lodging, travel, books, and equipment. Training allowances are also paid in some states.

Second-injury Funds

All states have **second-injury funds.** The purpose is to encourage employers to hire handicapped workers. If a second-injury fund did not exist, employers would be reluctant to hire handicapped workers because of the higher benefits that might have to be paid if a second injury occurs.

For example, assume that a worker with a preexisting injury is injured in a work-related accident. The second injury, when combined with the first injury, produces a disability greater than that caused by the second injury alone. Thus, the amount of workers' compensation ben-

INSIGHT 24.3

How Florida Pays Wage Loss Benefits

To hold down the rapid increase in workers' compensation costs, Florida enacted into law in 1979 an innovative *wage-loss concept.* With few exceptions, *the wage-loss concept bases benefits on the wages actually lost because of the injury.* To determine the amount of lost wages, the worker's actual current earnings are subtracted from 85 percent of the impaired employee's average monthly wage before the injury. The difference is then multiplied by 95 percent, and the result is the amount actually paid. This can be illustrated by the following example:

Pre-injury wage: $1,000 × 85%—	$850
Post-injury wage:	−500
	350
	× .95
	1750
	3150
Actual benefit paid:	$332.50

Florida's new law undoubtedly will be carefully monitored by the other states. The results to date are highly encouraging. Premiums paid by employers have been reduced, many minor claims have been eliminated, maximum benefits have been increased, and employers have a greater incentive to hire disabled workers.

SOURCE: Adaptation of "How Florida Pays Wage Loss Benefits" from *Journal of American Insurance,* Summer, 1982.

efits that must be paid is higher than if only the second injury had occurred. The employer pays only for the second injury, and the second-injury fund pays for the remainder of the benefit award.

Problems and Issues

In 1972, the National Commission on State Workmen's Compensation Laws published a report that was highly critical of state workers' compensation laws.[23] Since that time, workers' compensation programs have been substantially improved. Weekly cash benefits have been substantially increased; there are fewer limits on medical care; few states today have numerical exemptions and elective laws; and restrictions on occupational disease are rapidly disappearing. Despite this progress, two critical problems have emerged that require immediate attention. They are summarized as follows:

1. *Rapid increase in costs.* Workers' compensation costs are rising rapidly in many states. For example, in California, workers' compensation costs increased 400 percent from 1970 to 1980, and the average manual workers' compensation rate paid by employers increased from $1.77 to $3.22 per $100 of payroll.[24] In 1982 alone, employers in all states paid $22.5 billion to protect workers against job-related disabilities.[25] The sharp increase in costs is due largely to three factors: (1) rapid increase in inflation, which results in wage increases and higher medical costs; (2) substantial improvements in coverage and benefits under state workers' compensation laws; and (3) the impact of the federal black lung program introduced in 1970. As a result of substantially increased costs, some smaller firms are finding it in-

creasingly difficult to pay for workers' compensation insurance.

2. *Cumulative injury.* Workers' compensation laws earlier excluded all ordinary diseases to which the general public was exposed. However, an increasing number of states now consider cumulative injury to be part of an occupational disease. *Cumulative injury* means that the employer is liable if any continuing circumstance of employment plays a part in an illness of any kind. For example, a worker may file a claim for job-related emphysema. All costs of a cumulative injury claim for emphysema due to the job would be charged to the employer even though the worker smokes three packs of cigarettes daily. Cumulative injury claims have increased over time, especially by workers who are near retirement or who do not expect to continue working. If current trends in cumulative injury continue, the entire workers' compensation system may be in jeopardy. Litigation will increase; there will be widespread compensation for disabilities that are not work-related; and there will be a substantially higher average cost per claim.[26]

SUMMARY

- Social insurance programs are compulsory insurance programs that have certain characteristics that distinguish them from other government insurance programs. Social insurance programs have the following characteristics:
  a. Compulsory programs.
  b. Floor of income.
  c. Emphasis on social adequacy rather than individual equity.
  d. Benefits related to earnings.
  e. Benefits prescribed by law.
  f. No needs test.
  g. Full funding unnecessary.
  h. Financially self-supporting.
- The OASDHI program is the most important social insurance program in the United States. Four principal types of benefits are provided:
  a. Retirement benefits.
  b. Survivor benefits.
  c. Disability benefits.
  d. Medicare benefits.
- Unemployment insurance programs are federal-state programs that pay weekly cash benefits to workers who are involuntarily unemployed. Unemployment programs have several objectives. They are:
  a. Provide cash income to unemployed workers during periods of involuntary unemployment.
  b. Help unemployed workers find jobs.
  c. Encourage employers to stabilize employment.
  d. Help stabilize the economy.
- Unemployed workers must meet certain eligibility requirements to receive weekly cash benefits. They are:
  a. Have qualifying wages or be employed for a specified period during the base period.
  b. Be able and available for work.

c. Actively seek work.
d. Be free from disqualification.
e. Serve a one-week waiting period in most states.

- State workers' compensation laws typically pay the following benefits:
  a. Unlimited medical care.
  b. Weekly disability income benefits.
  c. Death benefits to survivors.
  d. Rehabilitation services.
- Workers' compensation is a social insurance program that provides medical care, cash benefits, and rehabilitation services to workers who are disabled from job-related accidents or disease. Workers' compensation laws have the following objectives:
  a. Broad coverage of employees for occupational injury and disease.
  b. Substantial protection against the loss of income.
  c. Sufficient medical care and rehabilitation services.
  d. Encouragement of safety.
  e. Reduction in litigation.

QUESTIONS FOR REVIEW

1. Why are social insurance programs necessary?
2. Describe the basic characteristics of social insurance programs.
3. Explain the meaning of fully insured, currently insured, and disability insured under the OASDHI program.
4. Describe briefly the major benefits under the OASDHI program.
5. Why are wages indexed for purposes of determining monthly income benefits under the OASDHI program?
6. Is the OASDHI program financially sound at the present time? Explain your answer.
7. Describe the basic objectives of unemployment insurance programs.
8. Explain the eligibility requirements that must be satisfied to collect unemployment insurance benefits.
9. Describe the basic objectives of workers' compensation laws.
10. List the major benefits that are provided under a typical workers' compensation law.

QUESTIONS FOR DISCUSSION

1. A social insurance author stated that "the OASDHI program need not be fully funded, but private pension plans must emphasize full funding." Do you agree or disagree with the author's statement? Explain your answer.
2. Many elderly persons are fearful that the OASDHI program is going broke.
   a. Explain how the OASDHI program is financed.
   b. Do you believe the program is going broke? Explain your answer.

3. The earnings (retirement) test is one of the most controversial issues in the OASDHI program.
   a. Describe the nature of the earnings test.
   b. What are the purposes of the earnings test?
4. A critic of unemployment insurance stated that "unemployment insurance programs are designed to maintain the economic security of unemployed workers, but there are some critical problems that must be resolved."
   a. Are all forms of unemployment covered under state unemployment insurance programs? Explain.
   b. Describe some situations that may disqualify a person for unemployment benefits.
   c. Are all unemployed persons receiving unemployment insurance benefits at the present time? Explain your answer.
5. Workers' compensation laws provide considerable financial protection to workers who are injured on the job or have an occupational disease.
   a. Explain the fundamental principle on which workers' compensation laws are based.
   b. Explain the nature and purpose of second-injury funds.
   c. Explain the problem of *cumulative injury* that is now present in workers' compensation programs.

KEY CONCEPTS AND TERMS TO KNOW

Social adequacy
Individual equity
Full funding
Needs test
Quarter of coverage
Fully insured
Currently insured
Disability insured
Primary insurance amount
Average indexed monthly earnings
Earnings test (retirement test)
Hospital Insurance
Supplementary Medical Insurance
Short-term involuntary unemployment
Extended benefits program
Experience rating
Contributory negligence doctrine
Fellow-servant doctrine
Assumption-of-risk doctrine
Liability without fault principle
Monopoly and competitive state funds
Second-injury fund

SUGGESTIONS FOR ADDITIONAL READING

Becker, Joseph M. *Unemployment Benefits: Should There Be a Compulsory Federal Standard?* Washington, D.C.: American Enterprise Institute for Public Policy Research, 1980.

Magowan, Peter A. "The Workers' Compensation Mess," *Nation's Business* (June 1983), pp. 30–33.

Murray, Michael L. "Workers' Compensation—A Benefit Out of Time," *Benefits Quarterly*, Vol. 2, No. 2 (Second Quarter 1985), pp. 8–15.

Myers, Robert J. "Will Social Security Have Another Financing Crisis Soon?" *Benefits Quarterly*, Vol. 1, No. 1 (First Quarter 1985), pp. 22–25.

Myers, Robert J. *Social Security*, 3rd ed. Homewood, IL: Richard D. Irwin, Inc., 1985.

Rejda, George E. "Should the Social Security Earnings Test Be Abolished?" *Journal of Pension Planning & Compliance*, Vol. 9, No. 2 (April 1983).

Rejda, George E. *Social Insurance and Economic Security,* 2nd ed. Englewood Cliffs, New Jersey: Prentice-Hall, Inc., 1984.

Rejda, George E. "Taxation of Social Security Benefits: A Critical Evaluation," *Benefits Quarterly,* Vol. 1, No. 2 (Second Quarter 1985), pp. 30–35.

Rejda, George E. and James R. Schmidt. "The Impact of the Social Security Program on Private Pension Contributions," *The Journal of Risk and Insurance,* Vol. 47, No. 4 (December 1979).

Rejda, George E. and James R. Schmidt. "The Impact of Social Security and ERISA on Insured Private Pension Contributions," *The Journal of Risk and Insurance,* Vol. 51, No. 4 (December 1984), pp. 640–51.

Robertson, A. Haeworth. "The Outlook for Social Security," *Journal of the American Society of CLU,* Vol. 39, No. 3 (May 1985), pp. 72–75.

Williams, Jr., C. Arthur, John G. Turnbull, and Earl F. Cheit. *Economic and Social Security: Social Insurance and Other Approaches,* 5th ed. New York: John Wiley & Sons, 1982.

NOTES

1. George E. Rejda, *Social Insurance and Economic Security,* 2nd ed. Englewood Cliffs, New Jersey: Prentice-Hall, Inc., 1984), pp. 19–28.
2. Robert J. Myers, "Will Social Security Have Another Financing Crisis Soon?" *Benefits Quarterly,* Vol. 1, No. 1 (First Quarter 1985), Table 1, p. 24.
3. Full funding would require substantially higher Social Security taxes, which would be deflationary and would result in substantial unemployment.
4. See Rejda, chapters 5 and 6, for a complete discussion of the Social Security program. This section is based largely on this source.
5. Rejda, p. 97.
6. A more liberal rule applies to blind workers. A blind worker age fifty-five or older must be unable to perform work that requires skills or abilities comparable to those required by the work he or she did regularly before age fifty-five (or became blind, if later). However, a more stringent test applies to a disabled widow, widower, or surviving divorced wife. They are considered disabled if they cannot engage in "any gainful activity" (rather than "substantial gainful activity," which applies to disabled workers).
7. Respite care is a short-term inpatient stay that may be necessary for the patient in order to give temporary relief to the person who regularly assists with home care. Inpatient respite care is limited each time to stays of no more than five days in a row.
8. Office of the Actuary, Social Security Administration, *Old-Age Survivors, and Disability Insurance Program: Summary of the 1984 Trustees Report,* April 5, 1984, p. 1.
9. Health Care Financing Administration, Bureau of Data Management and Strategy, *Summary of the 1984 Annual Reports of the Medicare Board of Trustees,* April, 1984, p. 12.
10. Rejda, p. 247.
11. *Press Release,* No. 84-12, United States Senate Committee on Finance, May 16, 1984.
12. *Press Release,* No. 84-12.
13. Rejda, pp. 354–56.
14. Rejda, p. 377.
15. Rejda, p. 379.
16. John Basson and Wesley Mellow found that persons receiving unemployment compensation benefits were unemployed an average of 7.7 weeks longer than those who were not receiving benefits. They concluded that the unemployment rate of 7.4 percent in May 1976 was 1.3 percentage points higher than it would have been in the absence of unemployment compensation benefits. See Edwin G. Dolan, *Basic Economics,* 2nd ed. (Hinsdale, Illinois: The Dryden Press, 1980), pp. 278–79.
17. Insurance Information Institute, *Insurance Facts, 1984/85 Property/Casualty Fact Book,* p. 84.
18. National Commission on State Workmen's Compensation Laws, *The Report of the National Commission on State Workmen's Compensation Laws* (Washington, D.C.: U.S. Government Printing Office, 1972), pp. 35–40.
19. Daniel N. Price, "Workers' Compensation Program Experience, 1982," *Social Security Bulletin,* Vol. 47, No. 12 (December 1984), p. 7.

20. Insurance Company of North America, "What Ails Workers' Compensation?" *Wall Street Journal*, August 4, 1981, p. 9.
21. Monopoly state funds are in Nevada, North Dakota, Ohio, Washington, West Virginia, and Wyoming. The thirteen states that permit workers' compensation insurance to be purchased from a competitive state fund are Arizona, California, Colorado, Idaho, Maryland, Michigan, Minnesota, Montana, New York, Oklahoma, Oregon, Pennsylvania, and Utah.
22. For a description of current workers' compensation programs, see Chamber of Commerce of the United States, *Analysis of Workers' Compensation Laws*, 1984 edition (Washington, D.C.: Chamber of Commerce of the United States, 1984). This volume is published annually.
23. National Commission on State Workmens' Compensation Laws, pp. 35–40.
24. Alfred G. Haggerty, "California Workers' Comp: A System in Crisis," *National Underwriter*, Property and Casualty edition, May 25, 1984, p. 12.
25. Price, p. 12.
26. Insurance Company of North America, "Impact of Health Hazards at Work," *Wall Street Journal*, December 9, 1980, p. 23.

PART

5

THE INSURANCE INDUSTRY

CHAPTER 25

TYPES OF INSURERS AND MARKETING SYSTEMS

"A good agent or broker is worth his weight in gold; a bad one can be a disaster."

Herbert S. Denenberg, The Shopper's Guide

STUDENT LEARNING OBJECTIVES

After studying this chapter, you should be able to:

- Describe the major types of private insurers in the United States, including
  - Stock companies
  - Mutual companies
  - Reciprocal exchange
  - Lloyd's Associations
- Describe the basic characteristics of the New York Insurance Exchange and Free-Trade Zone.
- Explain the legal distinction between agents and brokers.
- Describe the basic marketing systems for selling life insurance, including
  - General agency system
  - Branch office system
- Explain the different marketing systems for selling property and liability insurance, including
  - Independent agency system
  - Exclusive agency system
  - Direct writing
  - Mail order
- Describe the basic characteristics of mass merchandising, and explain the advantages and disadvantages of this marketing method.

In this chapter, we begin our study of the private insurance industry. The industry is divided into three broad categories: life insurance, health insurance, and property and liability insurance. Private insurers have a tremendous impact on the American economy. The industry provides jobs to about 2.0 million individuals, and it controls assets of about $904 billion. However, its major impact on the American economy is the economic and financial security provided to millions of individuals and business firms.

In this chapter, we will first discuss the basic types of private insurers operating in the United States today. We will then examine the various marketing systems for selling insurance, and consider the role of agents and brokers in the sales process. We will conclude the chapter by discussing some newer marketing methods, such as mass merchandising.

TYPES OF PRIVATE INSURERS

A large number of private insurers are currently operating in the United States. At the end of 1983, an estimated 2,125 legal reserve life insurers were doing business in the United States. In early 1984, some 3,474 companies were operating as property and liability insurers. Most property and liability business is written by about 900 companies that operate in all or most states.[1]

In this section, we will examine the major types of private insurers operating in the United States. In terms of legal ownership, the major types of private insurers are as follows:

- Stock companies
- Mutual companies
- Reciprocal exchange
- Lloyd's Associations
- New York Insurance Exchange

Stock Companies

A stock company is a corporation owned by stockholders who participate in the profits and losses of the company. The stockholders elect a board of directors who appoint the executive officers to run the company. The board of directors has the ultimate responsibility for the company's financial success.

The types of insurance that a stock company can write are determined by its charter. In property and liability insurance, the majority of stock companies are multiple-line insurers which write most types of insurance, with the exception of life and health insurance. Some states, however, also permit the writing of life and health insurance. Depending on the types of insurance written, a stock company must meet the state's minimum capital and surplus requirements, which are designed to protect the policyowners against unfavorable underwriting and investment experience.

A stock insurer cannot issue an assessable policy. An assessable policy permits the insurer to assess the policyowners additional premiums if losses are excessive. Instead, the stockholders must bear all losses. But they also share in the profits: if the business is profitable, dividends can be declared and paid to the stockholders based on the amount of common stock ownership.

Stock companies predominate in the property and liability insurance industry, especially with respect to commercial lines of insurance. Stock insurers account for about three-fourths of the property and liability premiums written by private insurers. The stock companies typically market their insurance by using the independent agency system of distribution (discussed later).

Mutual Companies

*A **mutual insurer** is a corporation owned by the policyowners; there are no stockholders.* The policyowners elect the board of directors, which appoints the executives who manage the company. Since relatively few policyowners bother to vote, the board of directors has effective management control of the company.

A mutual company may pay a dividend or give a rate reduction in advance. In life insurance, a dividend is largely a refund of a redundant premium which can be paid if the mortality, investment, and operating experience of the company is favorable. However, since the mortality and investment experience cannot be guaranteed, the dividends legally cannot be guaranteed by the companies. About 6 percent of the life insurance companies are mutuals, but they account for about 56 percent of the assets of U.S. life insurers and about 43 percent of life insurance in force.[2] Thus, mutual life insurers predominate in the life insurance industry.

Let us next consider the different types of mutual insurers in existence today. The major types of mutual insurers are:

- Assessment mutual
- Advance premium mutual
- Factory mutual
- Farm mutual
- Perpetual mutual
- Fraternal insurer

Assessment mutual *An* ***assessment mutual*** *is a company that has the right to assess policyowners for losses and expenses.* Assessment mutuals generally can be classified into three categories.[3] First, a *pure assessment mutual* does not charge a premium in advance, but assesses each policyowner after a loss occurs. Pure assessment mutuals are rare today because of the practical problem of collecting the assessments after a loss occurs. Those companies that are still in existence are smaller insurers that typically write only a limited number of perils, such as fire and windstorm, and confine their operation to a limited geographical area.

A second type of assessment mutual charges a low initial premium that should be sufficient to pay claims and expenses in most years. In those years during which the premiums are insufficient, the company can assess each policyowner an additional amount. The additional assessment may be limited to one additional premium, or it may be a multiple of the initial premium. Most companies of this second type are smaller insurers that write only basic types of insurance, such as fire insurance on dwellings in part of the state.

An assessment mutual may charge an initial premium that is sufficient to pay claims and expenses each year, except in very unusual circumstances. The company, however, can assess the policyowners if the experience is unfavorable. Many companies have never assessed their policyowners, but the right to do so increases their financial strength. Since the initial premiums generally are more than sufficient to pay claims and expenses, most companies have paid dividends to their policyowners. Companies in this third category tend to write more complex lines of insurance than the smaller assessment mutuals referred to earlier.

Advance premium mutual An ***advance premium mutual*** *is owned by the policyowners, but it does not issue an assessable policy.* Once the company's surplus exceeds a certain amount (difference between assets and liabilities), the states will not permit a mutual company to issue an assessable policy. The advance premium mutual generally is larger and financially stronger than the assessment mutual described earlier. The premiums charged are expected to be sufficient to pay all claims and expenses. Any additional costs because of poor experience are paid out of the company's surplus.

In life insurance, most mutual insurers pay dividends annually to the policyowners. In property and liability insurance, dividends to policyowners are not paid on a regular basis. The companies instead charge lower initial premiums that are closer to the actual amount needed for claims and expenses.

Factory mutual A ***factory mutual*** *is a specialized company that insures only superior properties.* There is great emphasis on loss prevention, and before a factory can be insured, it must meet high underwriting standards. The factory typically must be of superior construction, have an approved sprinkler system, and meet other requirements.

A factory mutual provides periodic inspection and engineering services to its insureds. Since the costs of these loss control services are high, only the larger risks are eligible for the insurance. The insurance contracts provide broad coverage, and coinsurance normally is not used.

A distinct characteristic of factory mutual insurance is a relatively high initial premium. The premium paid will substantially exceed the amounts needed for claims and expenses. At the end of the period, a large percentage of the initial premium—typically 65 percent or more—is refunded as a dividend to the policyowner. As a result, the insureds receive their protection at relatively low cost because of the great emphasis on loss prevention.

Farm mutual *A* ***farm mutual*** *is a local company that insures farm property in a limited geographic area, such as a county or state.* Most farm mutuals are smaller companies that issue assessable policies similar to those discussed earlier. Some farm mutuals provide for unlimited assessments, while others limit the assessments to a certain dollar amount or to a certain multiple of the premium.

Perpetual mutual A small number of companies provide property insurance with no expiration date. The insurance is **perpetual.** A large premium deposit is required, and the investment earnings on the deposit are expected to be sufficient for paying all claims and expenses. The premium is paid only once, and dividends may be paid after the policy has been in force for several years. The policy remains in force forever unless it is cancelled by the insured or insurer.

Perpetual insurance has a major tax advantage for a high-income taxpayer, since the investment earnings on the premium deposit are not taxed to the insured. In effect, the insurance is purchased with tax-free dollars. On the other hand, perpetual insurance has certain disadvantages. A large premium deposit is required; only a small number of companies offer the insurance in a limited geographical area; and the types of insurance available are limited.[4] Fire insurance is a major form of insurance typically available from a perpetual mutual.

Fraternal insurer *A* ***fraternal insurer*** *is a mutual company that provides life and health insurance to members of a social organization.* To qualify as a fraternal insurer under a state's insurance code, the insurer must have some type of social organization in existence, such as a lodge, or religious, charitable, or benevolent society. Examples of fraternals are the Knights of Columbus, Catholic Workmen, Independent Order of Foresters, and Aid Association for Lutherans.

Fraternal insurers sell only life and health insurance to their members. The assessment principle was originally used to pay death claims, but assessments were later abandoned when some fraternals experienced financial problems. Today, most fraternals operate on the basis of the level premium and legal reserve system that is used by commercial life insurers.

Since fraternals are nonprofit or charitable organizations, they are usually exempt from federal income taxes and many state and local taxes as well.

Reciprocal Exchange

A ***reciprocal*** *can be defined as an unincorporated mutual.* A reciprocal insurer has several distinct characteristics.[5] *First, in its pure form, insurance is exchanged among the members; each member of the reciprocal insures the other members and, in turn, is insured by them.* Thus, there is an exchange of insurance promises—hence the name, reciprocal exchange.

Second, a reciprocal is managed by an attorney-in-fact. The attorney-in-fact is usually a corporation that is authorized by the subscribers to seek new members, pay losses, collect premiums, handle reinsurance arrangements, invest the funds, and perform other administrative duties. The attorney-in-fact normally is compensated based on a percentage of the gross premiums paid by the subscribers and investment earnings for the year, such as 25 percent. However, the attorney-in-fact is not personally liable for the payment of claims and is not the insurer. The reciprocal exchange is the insurer.

Third, the reciprocal can be a pure or modified reciprocal. In the purest form, a separate account is kept for each subscriber. The account is credited with the subscriber's premiums and share of investment earnings, and debited for the subscriber's share of losses and expenses. The subscriber can be assessed an additional amount if the balance in the account is insufficient to cover his or her obligations. A dividend may be paid, however, if the balance in the account is large. The balance in the account is paid to the subscriber if membership in the reciprocal is terminated. Thus, in its purest form, insurance is provided "at cost" to the subscriber.

In the modified form, a reciprocal is similar to an advance premium mutual. An individual account may be supplemented or replaced by an undivided surplus account. If individual accounts are not kept, a withdrawing subscriber does not receive any refund. If the undivided surplus funds are large, the reciprocal may then issue nonassessable policies.

There are about fifty reciprocal exchanges. Most of them are relatively small and account for only a small percentage of the total property and liability insurance premiums written. In addition, most reciprocals specialize in a limited number of lines of insurance. However, a few reciprocals are multiple-line insurers and can be large. Farmers Insurance Exchange in Los Angeles and United Services Automobile Association are large reciprocals specializing in automobile insurance.

Lloyd's Association

Insurance can also be obtained through a **Lloyd's Association,** which is an organization of individuals who underwrite insurance on a cooperative basis. There are two basic types of Lloyd's Associations: (1) Lloyd's of London, and (2) American Lloyds.

Lloyd's of London Lloyd's of London is famous for writing insurance on heterogeneous exposure units such as a pianist's fingers, a Kentucky Derby winner's legs, an extravagant outdoor reception, an actor's life, and a hole-in-one in a professional golf tournament. Lloyd's of London, however, is also very important worldwide in ocean marine insurance and reinsurance.

Lloyd's of London has several important characteristics. *The first characteristic is that, technically, Lloyd's of London is not an insurance company, but is an association that provides certain services to the members who write insurance as individuals.* Lloyd's by itself does not write insurance, but the individual members do. In this respect, Lloyd's is similar to the New York Stock Exchange, which does not buy or sell securities but provides a marketplace and other services to its members.

A second characteristic is that Lloyd's of London is operated by syndicates and individual underwriters who are members of the syndicates. The syndicates tend to specialize in marine, aviation, automobile, or other property liability lines. Only a small part of the total business of Lloyd's covers the unusual exposure units that have made Lloyd's famous. Life insurance accounts for only a small part of the total business and is usually limited to short-term contracts.

A third characteristic is that the individual underwriters have unlimited liability with respect to the insurance they write as individuals. Each underwriter is responsible only for his or her agreed-upon share of the loss and is not responsible for the other members' share. Thus, membership is usually limited to wealthy individuals with a high net worth who pledge their personal assets to pay losses.

In addition, the underwriters must meet stringent financial requirements. Each underwriter must make a substantial underwriting deposit. All premiums are deposited into a premium trust fund, and withdrawals are allowed only for claims and expenses. Premiums received during a calendar year must remain on deposit for two years after the close of the calendar year. A central guarantee fund pays the loss if an individual underwriter is financially insolvent.

A final characteristic is that Lloyd's is licensed only in a small number of states. In the other states, Lloyd's must operate as a non-admitted insurer.[6] This means that a surplus line broker or agent can place business with Lloyd's, but only if the insurance cannot be obtained from an admitted company in the state. Despite this lack of licensing, business in the United States accounts for 60 percent of Lloyd's premiums.[7] In particular, Lloyd's of London reinsures a large number of American insurers, and is an important professional reinsurer.

To illustrate in a simplified fashion how Lloyd's operates, consider the following example.[8] Jack Willhoft is going into business and wants $1 million of products liability insurance on a new roller skate that he is manufacturing. An agent locates a company in the United States that will sell him $100,000 of products liability insurance. Since another American company cannot be found to write the remaining insurance, the agent contacts a surplus line broker who arranges to place the remaining $900,000 of products liability insurance with Lloyd's of London. Information about Jack's roller skating business is submitted to a Lloyd's broker, who then presents the proposal to a syndicate specializing in high-risk products liability insurance. A lead underwriter then determines the initial premium rate. Let us assume that the lead syndicate takes $100,000 of the desired $900,000 of insurance. Each member of the syndicate will take his or her agreed-upon share. The Lloyd's broker will then contact the other syndicates as well. The second syndicate may take $50,000, the third, $10,000, and so on, until the entire $900,000 is placed. Each member of the various syndicates takes his or her respective share of the insurance, and each pays his or her share of any loss. Finally, the policy is prepared, issued, and the insurance is in force. What we have witnessed here is a sophisticated version of the pooling technique that we discussed in Chapter 2.

American Lloyds Private underwriters in the United States have formed associations similar to Lloyd's of London. The American Lloyds associations, however, have no connection with Lloyd's of London and differ from Lloyd's in many respects. First, the number of individual underwriters is smaller than Lloyd's of London. Second, the liability of the underwriter is often limited. Each underwriter is responsible only for his or her share of the loss and not that of any insolvent member. Third, the personal net worth and financial strength of an underwriter are considerably lower than that of a Lloyd's underwriter. Fourth, an American Lloyds association does not operate through a syndicate, but is managed by an attorney-in-fact. Finally, the financial reputation of an American Lloyds association is not as good as Lloyd's of London. Several associations have failed, and some states, such as New York, forbid the formation of new associations.

New York Insurance Exchange

To provide a domestic alternative to Lloyd's of London and to expand underwriting capacity in the United States insurance markets, New York enacted legislation creating the New York Insurance Exchange and the Free-Trade Zone. As a result of this legislation, American insurers are expected to compete more effectively in the world-wide insurance markets, especially with Lloyd's of London. Let us first consider the Free-Trade Zone.[9]

Free-Trade Zone *The **Free-Trade Zone** refers to a market where large or unusual insurance contracts are exempt from the filing regulations in New York state.* Like most states, New York requires insurers to file their premium rates and policy forms with the state insurance department, which has the authority to approve or disapprove the filings. Under the law, specifically licensed insurers can now write certain types of insurance contracts that are free from the rate and policy-form filing requirements. The delay that filing requirements have imposed upon New York insurers in the past is now eliminated, and American insurers can now compete more effectively in the overseas insurance markets.[10] In particular, American insurers should be able to compete more effectively with Lloyd's of London.

Lloyd's of London is subject to relatively little rate and form regulation by the British gov-

INSIGHT 25.1

Money, Prestige Draw Wealthy Investors to Lloyd's of London Despite Big Risks

To most people, insurance is something they buy to protect what they've got. But at Lloyd's of London, some wealthy individuals, including a growing number of Americans, are taking a riskier approach. They're betting they can increase their wealth by participating in syndicates that sell insurance, for everything from supertankers to a quarterback's arm.

Since the Lloyd's insurance exchange was founded in the late 17th century, it has relied on individual investors to put up the capital needed to underwrite coverage. Today it is the world's biggest insurance market, with 26,000 individual members and more than $8 billion in premium capacity. Membership, once strictly British, was opened to foreigners in 1969.

But becoming a member still isn't easy, and the pitfalls can be enormous. Individual members have only limited control over their investments, and losses can more than wipe out the capital they commit. Moreover, it takes 3½ years to withdraw fully from Lloyd's, no matter how urgent the request.

For the right investors, "Lloyd's can be a good way to diversify your assets," says John Rayer, a partner in the British accounting firm of Robson Rhodes. In a spectrum of investments ranging from ultrasafe bank accounts to riskier possibilities like race horses, he places Lloyd's in the middle, on a par with real estate.

Minimum of $120,000

Lloyd's members are required to have a net worth of at least 100,000 pounds, about $120,000 at current exchange rates. But market professionals say life at the minimum can be a little nerve-wracking. They advise having a net worth of at least $250,000.

Members aren't expected to know all the intricacies of insurance. A managing agent decides which syndicates one should participate in. Then professional underwriters run the syndicates on a day-to-day basis. The members' role is mainly that of passive investors who put up the capital needed to safeguard against big claims. Once a year, the agents tell the members how much they have made—or lost.

Average annual returns in recent years have ranged from 6% to 15%. But the return can be even larger because capital committed to Lloyd's needn't actually be tied up in London. It can consist of a guarantee against the investor's stock portfolio or other assets. "Lloyd's can provide a second income on your assets," says Bill Goodier, a director of Willis, Faber & Dumas Ltd., a British insurance broker.

Not all syndicates earn money, however. Yesterday, for instance, the head of a Lloyd's syndicate that helped underwrite insurance for the malfunctioning satellite launched this week by the space shuttle said claims could total $92 million. Moreover, Lloyd's members face unlimited liability for any losses their syndicates run up. In a couple of cases, losses have totaled as much as four times the amount of capital committed.

Market professionals say investors can reduce the risk by spreading their capital among a half-dozen or more Lloyd's syndicates. That way a loss in one can be offset by gains in others. Some insurance against syndicate losses is also available, but it is expensive. "Unlimited liability is a very real feature of Lloyd's," cautions John Watkins, a partner at the London accounting firm of Neville Russell.

Despite the risks, the number of American members of Lloyd's has grown 19% in the past year, to 2,011. The exchange is most popular with insurance professionals, but accountants say Lloyd's is also attracting other affluent Americans, from farmers to lawyers.

To join Lloyd's, investors must be sponsored by an existing member who has known them for a year. But this British clubbiness is giving way. Several Lloyd's membership groups make regular recruiting visits to the U.S., and prospective new members are automatically introduced to potential "sponsors."

Once approved, investors pay a membership fee of 3,000 pounds (about $3,600) and commit at least 100,000 pounds in capital. Most new members just use a bank letter of credit, which can cost as little as $1,000.

Picking an Agent

The next step is picking an agent. Big accounting firms usually can make recommendations. It is also helpful to find out which syndicates an agent has selected in past years and check their performance ratings, as compiled by the London-based Association of Lloyd's Members.

Once in Lloyd's, the watchword is patience. The first return won't come for three years, because syndicates don't close each year's accounts until three years later. That allows syndicates time to sort out complex claims.

This protracted bookkeeping can be especially vexing if one ever wants to leave Lloyd's. "If you submitted a resignation letter now," says Neville Russell's Mr. Watkins, "it wouldn't take full effect until the books were closed for 1985, in mid-1988. And the tax considerations could linger on for another year."

U.S. and British Taxes

There are also some tax and foreign exchange considerations. Both the U.S. and Britain regard Lloyd's income as taxable. But accountants note that if the British taxes are paid first, they can be used, dollar-for-dollar, to offset U.S. taxes.

Meanwhile, advisers say, a rising or falling dollar won't affect an American's earnings from Lloyd's as much as one might think. That's because as much as 70% of Lloyd's business is done in the U.S. The syndicates' dollar earnings are just briefly translated into pounds, before U.S. members reconvert them back to dollars when they cash their income checks.

For all the headaches, Lloyd's offers a few perquisites. "Some people join Lloyd's even though they don't need the money and never will," says Neville Russell's Mr. Watkins. Lloyd's is "an exclusive club," full of celebrities and the English aristocracy, he says. "People like to be able to tell their friends they're in it."

Besides, Mr. Watkins says, members are encouraged to keep in regular contact with their managing agents. For American clients he says, that can translate into a tax-deductible trip to Europe "at least every two or three years."

SOURCE: "Money, Prestige Draw Wealthy Investors to Lloyd's of London Despite Big Risks" by George Anders from *Wall Street Journal*.

ernment. By contrast, American insurers have been handicapped in the past when they have tried to write insurance on unusual risks or on large, complex risks because of the restrictions placed on them by the states where they are licensed to do business. *By eliminating the rate and policy-form filing requirements for certain insurance contracts, the Free-Trade Zone will eliminate this competitive disadvantage.* In particular, brokers and their clients will benefit from the increased speed and flexibility made possible by the law.

The types of insurance that can be written in the Free-Trade Zone are primary contracts on large commercial exposures with annual premiums of $100,000 or more, and unusual or hard-to-place business with annual premiums considerably less than $100,000. Examples of insurance contracts that can be written in the Free-Trade Zone are aircraft insurance; liability insurance for failure of an alarm system; insurance on amusement parks, fairgrounds, and carnivals; professional liability insurance; insurance on catfish farms; insurrection insurance; liability insurance for violation of a fair employment practice law; oil spill insurance; and vacation rain insurance.

The Free-Trade Zone is not intended to replace the normal insurance markets. Life insurance, annuities and health insurance can be written only if the New York Superintendent of Insurance gives authorization. Personal lines of insurance generally cannot be written in the Free-Trade Zone and be exempt from rate and form filings. Also, workers' compensation insurance, employer's liability insurance, title insurance, and mortgage guarantee insurance are not exempt from the rate and policy-form filings.

In addition to deregulation of the filing requirements, the law also provides that all insurance contracts on property or exposures located outside the United States are exempt from New York's state premium tax and franchise tax on insurance companies. The exemption from premium and franchise taxes does not apply to title insurance or accident and health insurance. However, the law removes a major tax impediment to the placement of overseas business with New York insurers.

New York Insurance Exchange The law also created the **New York Insurance Exchange** which opened for business on March 31, 1980. The Insurance Exchange is a large trading floor where underwriting syndicates offer all types of insurance, and brokers shop among the various syndicates to place business for the clients they represent.

The major purposes of the Insurance Exchange are to provide a central facility for the relatively rapid placement of risks, and to provide an efficient new market to help increase worldwide insurance capacity.

The types of business conducted on the Insurance Exchange include (1) primary insurance on large or unusual risks that have been rejected by the Free-Trade Zone, (2) all types of reinsurance, and (3) primary coverage on risks located outside of the United States.

Individuals, corporations, insurance companies, and other groups are permitted to form syndicates to write insurance on the Insurance Exchange. But the financial requirements for forming a syndicate are strict. Minimum capital for a syndicate writing either life and health insurance or property and liability insurance is $3,550,000. If a syndicate wants to write all types of insurance, the minimum capital requirement is $6,550,000. The Insurance Exchange also has a security fund to protect insureds against the insolvency of a member syndicate.

The New York Insurance Exchange provides several benefits to corporations, brokers, insurers, and investors. The major benefits are summarized as follows:

1. There is now available a centralized and efficient facility for placing large amounts of insurance with a minimum of insurance regulation.
2. American insurers can become fully competitive in the worldwide insurance markets for the first time.

3. There is increased underwriting capacity in the United States insurance markets.
4. Additional opportunities are available for investors to invest in the insurance business.

Finally, other states are considering or have passed legislation creating an insurance exchange. The Illinois Insurance Exchange is now operating in Chicago, and the Insurance Exchange of the Americas is operating in Miami, Florida.

This concludes our discussion of the different types of insurers. Let us next consider agents and brokers.

AGENTS AND BROKERS

Insurers are in business to make money. This means that insurance must be sold to profitable insureds. A successful sales force is the key to the company's financial success. Most policies today are sold by agents and brokers. Let us briefly examine the legal status of agents and brokers.

Agents

An **agent** is someone who legally represents the insurer and has the authority to act on the insurer's behalf. As we noted in Chapter 4, an agent can bind the principal by expressed powers, by implied powers, and by apparent authority. If you buy insurance, you will probably purchase the insurance from an agent. However, there is an important difference between a life insurance agent and a property and liability insurance agent. A life insurance agent does not usually have the authority to bind the company. He or she is merely a soliciting agent who induces persons to apply for life insurance. The applicant for life insurance must normally be approved by the company before the insurance is in force.

In contrast, a property and liability insurance agent typically has the power to bind the company immediately with respect to certain types of coverage. *This is normally done by a binder, which is temporary evidence of insurance until the policy is actually issued.* Binders can be oral or written. For example, if you telephone an agent and request insurance on your motorcycle, the insurance can be in force immediately.

Brokers

In contrast to an agent who represents the company, a **broker** is someone who legally represents the insured. A broker legally does not have the authority to bind the insurer. Instead, the broker can solicit or accept applications for insurance and then attempt to place the coverage with an appropriate insurer. But the insurance is not in force until the company accepts the business.

A broker is paid a commission from the insurers where the business is placed. Many brokers are also licensed as agents, so that they have the authority to bind their companies as agents.

Brokers are extremely important in property and liability insurance at the present time. Large brokerage firms, such as Marsh and McLennan, and Alexander and Alexander, have knowledge of highly specialized insurance markets, provide risk management and loss control services, and control the accounts of large corporate insurance buyers.

Brokers are also important in the surplus lines markets. *Surplus line refers to any type of insurance for which there is no available market within the state, and the coverage must be placed with a non-admitted insurer. A* ***non-admitted insurer*** *is a company not licensed to do business in the state. A* ***surplus line broker*** *is a special type of broker who is licensed to place business with a non-admitted insurer.* An individual may be unable to obtain the coverage from an admitted insurer because the loss exposure is too great, or the required amount of insurance is too large. A surplus line broker has the authority to place the business with a surplus line insurer if the coverage cannot be obtained in the state from an admitted company.

TYPES OF MARKETING SYSTEMS

Marketing systems are the various methods of selling insurance to consumers and business firms. In this section, we will examine the various marketing systems that are used to sell insurance. Let us first consider marketing systems in life insurance.

Life Insurance Marketing Systems

Two basic methods for selling life insurance are used today. They are:

- General agency system
- Branch office system

General agency system Under the **general agency system,** the general agent is an independent businessperson who represents only one insurer. The general agent is in charge of a territory and is responsible for hiring, training, and motivating new agents. The general agent receives a commission based on the amount of business produced.

There are two types of general agency systems.[11] Under the *pure general agency* system, which is largely theoretical since it is used by only a few insurers, the general agent is responsible for hiring and training new agents in a given territory. The general agent receives a commission based on the amount of business produced, plus a collection fee for premium billing and record-keeping expenses. The general agent is also responsible for all expenses, including office expenses and the financing of new agents. The difference between the general agent's commissions and commissions paid to the subagents is used to pay the agency expenses and also to provide a profit. The general agent is generally free of all home office controls, including those which apply to the selection and training of new agents.

Under the *modified general agency system,* which is more common, financial assistance is provided to the general agent. The company pays all or part of the expenses of hiring and training new agents, and thus has considerable control over the selection of agents and their training. The company may also provide an allowance for agency office expenses and other expenses.

Branch office system The **branch office system** is increasing in importance as a method for selling insurance, especially among the larger life insurers. It is becoming more important because it gives the insurer greater direct control over product marketing and servicing, and over the hiring and training of agents.

Under the branch office system, branch offices are established in various areas. The branch manager has the responsibility for hiring and training new agents. However, the branch manager is considered an *employee* of the company, who typically is paid a salary and a bonus based on the volume and quality of the insurance sold and the number of new productive agents added. Under this system, the company pays the expenses of the branch office, including the financing of new agents. The Metropolitan Life, New York Life, and Prudential are examples of insurers using the branch office system.

Property and Liability Insurance Marketing Systems

There are four basic systems for marketing property and liability insurance. They are:

- Independent agency system
- Exclusive agency system
- Direct writer
- Mail order

Let us briefly examine the major characteristics of these systems.[12]

Independent agency system The **independent agency system,** which is sometimes called the American Agency system, has several basic characteristics. *First, the agent is an independent businessperson who represents several companies.* For example, Vern may be an independent agent who represents the Insurance Company of North America, Ohio Casualty, The St. Paul Companies, United Fire and Casualty, Empire Fire and Marine, and Great Plains Insurance. Vern is authorized to write business on behalf of these companies and in turn is paid a

INSIGHT 25.2

Life Insurance Selling as a Career

Selling life insurance is a tough job, and only a relatively small number of new life insurance agents succeed. Out of 100 new life agents hired, more than 40 percent will quit or be terminated during their first year. At the end of five years, fewer than 15 percent are still in the business.

Most companies use various psychological and aptitude tests to select potentially successful agents. The tests are imperfect tools at best, but two traits of a successful life insurance agent have been identified. One is empathy, which enables an agent to "read" a client's feelings and attitudes. The other is the agent's ego. Most successful agents will never take no for an answer, are not easily discouraged, and will work harder at making a sale if the prospect initially says no. Thus, the fear of rejection does not bother the successful agent.

The companies today finance new agents for the first few years in the form of a guaranteed draw. Average income for a new agent is about $14,000 for the first year and more than $25,000 after five years. However, the highly successful agents who belong to the elite Million Dollar Round Table earn considerably higher incomes. This is an organization of members who consistently sell at least $2.25 million of life insurance annually. Members of this elite group typically earn more than $50,000 annually, and annual earnings of $100,000 or more are not uncommon.

Agents in the life insurance industry will earn incomes well below these figures. However, for the unusual, highly talented agent, the financial rewards are great.

commission based on the amount of business produced.

Second, the agency owns the ***expirations or renewal rights to the business.*** If a policy comes up for renewal, the agent can place the business with another insurer if he or she chooses to do so. Likewise, if the contract with an insurer is terminated, the agency can place the business with other companies.

Third, the independent agent is compensated by commissions that vary by line of insurance. For example, the agent may receive a 20 percent commission on homeowners insurance but only 8 percent on a workers' compensation policy. The commission rate on renewal business typically is the same as new business. If a lower renewal rate is paid, the insurer would lose business, since the agent would place the insurance with another company. A second commission called a **contingent or profit- sharing commission** is also paid which is based on a favorable loss ratio.

The commission method of compensating agents has been criticized on two grounds:[13]

1. It creates a conflict of interest. By placing the business with the lowest-cost company, the client benefits, but the agent's commission is lower.
2. The commission is not necessarily related to the effort. A high premium policy results in a high commission even though it may require little effort by the agent.

To correct for these defects, a negotiated fee system has been proposed. The insurer would quote a premium net of commissions, and the agent would then negotiate a fee with the insured based on the amount of effort required.

Independent agents perform several functions. They are frequently authorized to adjust small claims, typically up to $500. The larger agencies may also provide loss control services to the insureds, such as accident prevention and fire control engineers. Also, for some lines, the agency may bill the policyowners and collect the premiums. However, most companies have resorted to **direct billing,** by which the policyowner is billed directly by the insurer and then remits the premium to the company. Many agents have resisted direct billing because they feel that it is a threat to the ownership of their expirations, and that it results in the payment of reduced commissions that may not be completely offset by lower agency expenses.

Examples of companies using the independent agency system are the Hartford, Fireman's Fund, Insurance Company of North America, Travelers, and Royal Globe.

Exclusive agency system *Under this system, the agent represents only one company or group of companies under common ownership.* The agent is prohibited by contract from representing other insurers if insurance can be placed with the exclusive agency company.

Agents under the **exclusive agency system** do not usually own the expirations or renewal rights to the policies. There is some variation, however, in this regard. Some insurers do not give their agents any ownership rights in the expirations. Other companies may grant limited ownership of expirations while the agency contract is in force, but this interest terminates when the agency contract is terminated.[14] As a general rule, exclusive agents have little or no ownership rights in the expirations. In contrast, under the independent agency system, the agency has complete ownership of the expirations.

Another difference is the payment of commissions. Exclusive agency companies generally pay a lower commission rate on renewal business than on new business. For example, a 15 percent commission may be paid on new business, but only 7 percent on renewal business. This results in a strong financial incentive for the agent to write new business and is one factor that helps explain the rapid growth of the exclusive agency companies. In contrast, as we noted earlier, companies using the independent agency system typically pay the same commission rate on new and renewal business.

Also, exclusive agency companies provide strong supportive services to the new agent. The new agent usually starts as an employee during a training period to learn the business. After the training period, the agent becomes an independent contractor who is then paid on a commission basis. Prior to that time, the future agent is an employee who is dependent on the financial support of the company.[15]

The functions performed by exclusive agents vary among the companies. Some companies limit exclusive agents to selling insurance, while others permit them to adjust small first-party claims as well. Virtually all exclusive agency insurers use the direct billing method and are responsible for issuance of the policy.

Examples of exclusive agency companies include State Farm, Allstate,[16] American Family, Nationwide, Prudential of America, and Farmers Insurance.

Direct writer A direct writer is often erroneously confused with an exclusive agency company. *A* ***direct writer*** *is a company in which the salesperson is an employee of the insurer, not an independent contractor.* The company pays all of the selling expenses, including payment of the employee's salary and Social Security taxes. Similar to exclusive agents, an employee of a direct writer represents only one insurer.

Employees of direct writers are usually compensated on a "salary plus" arrangement. Some companies pay a basic salary plus a commission directly related to the amount of insurance sold. Others pay a salary and a bonus that represent both selling and service activities of the employee. And some pay only a straight salary.[17]

Examples of direct writers include Liberty Mutual, Employers of Wausau, and American Mutual Liability Insurance. Many automobile clubs also use the direct-writing system, by which employees are used to sell insurance. Examples are the Detroit Auto Exchange and Inter-Insurance Exchange of the Auto Club of Southern California.

Mail order companies *A* ***mail order*** *company is a company that sells through the mails or* *other mass media,* such as newspapers and magazines, radio, or television. No agents are used to sell the insurance.

Mail order insurance has several advantages to the insurer. Lower selling expenses are incurred because market segmentation can be more precise, and underwriting can be more selective. Mailing lists can be prepared to identify groups that are likely to have fewer claims than average. However, the major disadvantage is that the insurance sold must be limited to the simple lines of insurance, such as automobile and homeowners insurance. Another disadvantage is the possibility of a slower rate of growth because the insured has no personal contact with an agent.[18]

From the consumer's viewpoint, the absence of an agent and selective underwriting can result in much lower insurance costs. However, the principal disadvantage is the lack of personal service from an agent. Examples of insurers using the mail order system are Government Employees Insurance Company, United Services Automobile Association, Colonial Penn, and AMICA Mutual Insurance.

Market shares In recent years, the independent agency companies have experienced a substantial decline in their share of the total property and liability insurance market. Starting from a virtual monopoly at the turn of the century, the independent agency companies' share of total property and liability premiums declined to about 67 percent by 1975.[19] The decline was especially sharp in the personal lines market, especially the market for automobile insurance and homeowners insurance.

The exclusive agency companies, direct writers, and mail order insurers as a group have experienced a substantial increase in their share of premiums written in the personal lines market. For example, more than 50 percent of total private passenger automobile liability insurance premiums are written by exclusive agency companies, direct writers, and mail order insurers.

There are three major reasons for this spectacular growth in the personal lines market.[20] *First, these companies as a group tend to have lower total expense ratios than the independent agency companies.* Part of this is due to differences in commission rates. As we noted earlier, exclusive agency companies have lower commission rates on renewal business than the independent agency companies.

Second, these companies were among the first to use direct billing, mechanization of policy writing, and other internal service functions. This has enabled them to reduce their expenses and prices.

Third, the combined effects of a large automobile insurance market and relative simplicity of the market have enabled the companies to build up large agency forces with a minimum of delay and financial expense. Exclusive agency companies, direct writers, and mail order insurers initially concentrated on automobile insurance. This is a large market, for private passenger automobile insurance alone accounts for about 35 percent of total property and liability premiums. This line of insurance is relatively simple to sell and service when compared with the commercial lines market. As a result of their initial success with automobile insurance, these companies also sold homeowners insurance to the same customers, since homeowners insurance possessed many of the marketing characteristics of automobile insurance. This has resulted in additional growth in the personal lines market.

In contrast, independent agency companies dominate the commercial lines market and account for more than 90 percent of the premiums written in this market. The commercial lines markets are highly specialized markets that require a great deal of skill and knowledge in providing proper insurance coverages and risk management services to business firms. Independent agency companies have highly specialized agents and loss control specialists to service this market effectively. Although the exclusive agency companies and direct writers have made some inroads into the commercial lines market, the independent agency companies as a group still continue to dominate this market.

MASS MERCHANDISING

In recent years, several property and liability insurers have used mass merchandising to market their insurance. ***Mass merchandising*** *is a plan for insuring individual members of a group under a single program of insurance at reduced premiums.*[21] The insurance is sold on a group basis to employees of firms and to members of labor unions, trade associations, social clubs, and professional organizations. Thus, property and liability insurance is sold to individual members of a group using group insurance marketing methods. Both personal lines and commercial lines of insurance have been marketed by the mass merchandising technique. However, there has been greater interest in the mass merchandising of personal lines of insurance, especially automobile and homeowners insurance.

Basic Characteristics

Mass merchandising plans have several basic characteristics.[22] They are:

- Property and liability insurance is sold to individual members of a group.
- There is individual underwriting.
- Lower premiums generally are charged.
- Premiums are paid by payroll deduction.
- Employers do not usually contribute to the plan.

The first characteristic is that property and liability insurance is sold to individual members of a group. Automobile and homeowners insurance are popular lines of insurance that have been emphasized in most mass merchandising plans. For example, an employer may sponsor an automobile insurance plan for the employees. The insurance is then sold to eligible employees within the firm.

A second characteristic is individual underwriting of each applicant. A member of the group who applies for the coverage must meet the insurer's underwriting standards. In most plans, the insurer normally can reject applicants who do not meet the company's underwriting standards. However, in a mass merchandising plan, the insurer may have more liberal underwriting standards than those applied to persons who apply for comparable insurance on an individual basis.

A third characteristic is that lower premiums generally are paid for the insurance than under a comparable plan of insurance that is individually marketed. The premium reductions typically range from 5 percent to 15 percent. The reduction is possible because of a lower commission scale, savings in administrative expenses because of payroll deduction, and more efficient use of a computerized accounting system.

A fourth characteristic is that premiums are paid by payroll deduction. The employee therefore has a convenient method for paying premiums, because the premiums are paid out of the employee's earnings.

Finally, in most plans, the employers do not contribute to the plan. The employees pay the entire cost. One obstacle is an unfavorable tax consequence to the employees. With few exceptions, employer contributions to the group property and liability plans are considered taxable income to the employees.[23]

Advantages and Disadvantages of Mass Merchandising

Mass merchandising has both advantages and disadvantages. From the viewpoint of the individual employee or member of a group, a mass merchandising plan has the following advantages:

- Lower cost
- Convenience of payroll deduction
- Relaxation of underwriting standards
- Availability of insurance counseling by the group representatives

However, a mass merchandising plan could result in the following disadvantages to the individual employee:

- Possible disclosure of adverse personal information to the employer (such as a drunk driving conviction)

- Less choice in the selection of insurance coverage and amounts
- Termination of the plan by the insurer or employer and possible difficulty in obtaining comparable insurance on an individual basis

The future of mass merchandising is cloudy at present. Some insurers have decided against marketing a mass merchandising plan, while other insurers have terminated many individual plans. This pessimism is due to poor underwriting results, high start-up costs, volatility in insurance sales as large blocks of business are added or lost, decline in surplus because of stock market declines during certain periods (which has reduced the willingness of companies to experiment with mass merchandising), and the alienation of insurance agents. Most independent agents strongly oppose mass merchandising plans because they believe that their incomes are adversely affected, that the market for individual personal lines of insurance is being reduced, and that their ownership of expirations is threatened.

SUMMARY

- There are several basic types of insurers. They are:
  a. Stock companies.
  b. Mutual companies.
  c. Reciprocal exchange.
  d. Lloyd's Associations.
  e. New York Insurance Exchange
- The New York Insurance Exchange is a centralized facility where underwriting syndicates offer all types of insurance, and brokers shop among the various syndicates to place business for the clients they represent. The Insurance Exchange is designed to provide an efficient new market to help increase worldwide insurance capacity and enable United States insurers to compete more effectively in the world insurance markets.
- An agent is someone who legally represents the insurer and has the authority to act on the insurer's behalf. In contrast, a broker is someone who legally represents the insured.
- *Surplus lines* refer to any type of insurance for which there is no available market within the state, and the coverage must be placed with a non-admitted insurer. A *non-admitted insurer* is a company not licensed to do business in the state. A *surplus line broker* is a special type of broker who is licensed to place business with a non-admitted insurer.
- In life insurance, there are two basic marketing systems. They are:
  a. General agency system.
  b. Branch office system.
- In property and liability insurance, there are four basic marketing systems. They are:
  a. Independent agency system.
  b. Exclusive agency system.
  c. Direct writer.
  d. Mail order.
- Mass merchandising is a plan by which property and liability insurance is sold on a group basis. Individual members of a group are insured under a single program of insurance at reduced premiums. There is, however, individual underwriting.

QUESTIONS FOR REVIEW

1. What is a stock insurance company?
2. Explain the major features of a mutual insurer. List the basic types of mutual insurers.
3. Describe the major features of Lloyd's of London.
4. Explain the basic characteristics of a *reciprocal exchange* and *fraternal insurer*.
5. Explain the *nature* and *purposes* of the New York Insurance Exchange.
6. What is the legal distinction between an agent and a broker?
7. Describe the major features of the general agency system and branch office system in life insurance marketing.
8. Explain briefly the basic characteristics of the following marketing systems in property and liability insurance:
   a. independent agency system.
   b. exclusive agency system.
   c. direct writer.
   d. mail order.
9. Who owns the policy expirations or renewal rights to the business under the independent agency system?
10. Why have the independent agency companies experienced a substantial decline in their share of the personal lines market for property and liability insurance?

QUESTIONS FOR DISCUSSION

1. Compare a stock insurer with a mutual insurer with respect to each of the following:
   a. legal ownership of the company.
   b. right to assess policyowners.
   c. payment of dividends.
2. An insurance author stated that "Lloyd's of London is an association that provides certain services to the members who write insurance as individuals." Describe Lloyd's of London with respect to each of the following:
   a. nature of the operation.
   b. types of insurance written.
   c. financial safeguards to protect insureds.
3. New York enacted legislation creating the New York Insurance Exchange and Free-Trade Zone. Explain the reasons for the establishment of the New York Insurance Exchange.
4. Property and liability insurance can be marketed under different marketing systems. Compare the *independent agency system* with the *exclusive agency system* with respect to each of the following:
   a. legal status of the agents.
   b. number of companies represented.
   c. ownership of policy expirations.

5. Mass merchandising is a plan for insuring individual members of a group under a single program of insurance at reduced premiums.
   a. Describe the major features of a mass merchandising plan.
   b. From the viewpoint of the insured, explain the possible advantages and disadvantages of a mass merchandising plan.

KEY CONCEPTS AND TERMS TO KNOW

Stock company
Mutual insurer
Reciprocal exchange
Lloyd's Associations
Fraternal insurer
Assessment mutual
Advance premium mutual
Factory mutual
Farm mutual
Perpetual mutual
Free-Trade zone
New York Insurance Exchange
Agent
Broker
Surplus line broker
Nonadmitted insurer
General agency system
Branch office system
Independent agency system
Expirations or renewal rights to business
Contingent or profit-sharing commission
Exclusive agency system
Direct writer
Mail order insurer
Direct billing
Mass Merchandising

SUGGESTIONS FOR ADDITIONAL READING

Bickelhaupt, David L. *General Insurance*, 11th ed. Homewood, Illinois: Richard D. Irwin, Inc., 1983, chapter 25.

Crane, Frederick G. *Insurance Principles and Practices*, 2nd ed. New York: John Wiley & Sons, 1984, chapters 19 and 22.

Cummins, J. David and Jack VanDerhei. "A Note on the Relative Efficiency of Property-Liability Insurance Distribution Systems," *The Bell Journal of Economics*, Vol. 10, No. 9 (Autumn 1979).

Greene, Mark R. and James S. Trieschmann. *Risk and Insurance*, 6th ed. Cincinnati, Ohio: Southwestern Publishing Company, 1984, chapter 5.

Stevens, Thomas L. "Legal Structure of Insurance Exchanges," *The Forum*, Vol. 17, No. 4 (Spring 1982).

Webb, Bernard L., J. J. Launie, Willis Park Rokes, and Norman A. Baglini. *Insurance Company Operations*, 2nd ed. Volume I. Malvern, Pennsylvania: American Institute for Property and Liability Underwriters, 1983.

Williams, Jr., C. Arthur and Richard M. Heins. *Risk Management and Insurance*, 5th ed. New York: McGraw-Hill Book Company, 1985, chapter 26.

NOTES

1. Insurance Information Institute, *1984–85 Property Casualty Fact Book*, p. 5; American Council of Life Insurance, *1984 Life Insurance Fact Book*, p. 88.
2. *1984 Life Insurance Fact Book*, pp. 88–89.
3. C. Arthur Williams, Jr., George L. Head, and G. William Glendenning, *Principles of Risk Management and Insurance*, Volume I (Malvern, Pennsylvania: American Institute for Property and Liability Underwriters, 1978), p. 308.

4. Williams, Jr., p. 310.
5. Williams, Jr., pp. 308–309.
6. A nonadmitted insurer is one which is not licensed to do business in a state.
7. Williams, Jr., p. 307.
8. For a more detailed explanation of this process, the interested student should consult Frederick G. Crane, *Insurance Principles and Practices* (New York: John Wiley & Sons, 1980), pp. 429–30.
9. *Insurance Decisions, The New York Insurance Free Trade Zone* (Philadelphia, Pennsylvania: Insurance Company of North America, n.d.) pp. 1–12.
10. Although filing requirements are eliminated, the law does not eliminate all New York regulation of rates and policy forms. Policies written on risks located or resident in New York State, which are exempted from filing because of the Free-Trade Zone law, must meet the *minimum policy provisions* as set forth in the state's insurance laws and regulations. For example, a fire policy written in the Free-Trade Zone must still include the 165-line standard provisions in the standard fire policy.
11. Dan M. McGill, *Life Insurance*, rev. ed. (Homewood, Illinois: Richard D. Irwin, 1967), pp. 836–39.
12. Bernard L. Webb, J. J. Launie, Willis Park Rokes, and Norman A. Baglini, *Insurance Company Operations*, Volume I (Malvern, Pennsylvania: American Institute for Property and Liability Underwriters, 1978), pp. 64–76.
13. Webb, p. 70.
14. Webb, p. 73.
15. George B. Flanigan, Joseph E. Johnson, Ellen P. Thrower, and Steven N. Weisbart, *Marketing Systems Employed in Property and Liability Insurance: An Empirical Analysis*. Working Papers in Business Administration, Center for Applied Research, University of North Carolina at Greensboro (January, 1979), p. 5.
16. Allstate also employs the independent agency system. Independent agents in small towns where no Sears and Roebuck stores are located have been appointed agents to represent Allstate.
17. Flanigan, p. 6.
18. Webb, p. 75.
19. Webb, p. 90.
20. Webb, pp. 92–99.
21. Webb, p. 119.
22. For a detailed explanation of mass merchandising, the interested student should consult Webb, pp. 119–34. See also Ronald C. Horn, "Collective Merchandising of Insurance," *Topical Outline, Insurance 21, General Principles of Insurance* (Malvern, Pennsylvania: Insurance Institute of America, 1978), pp. 34–37.
23. Group legal expense insurance is an exception. Employer contributions are not considered taxable income to the employees.

INSURANCE COMPANY OPERATIONS

"There's more to insurance than sales."
Carol Kesner, Kemper Insurance Group, Insurance Careers

STUDENT LEARNING OBJECTIVES

After studying this chapter, you should be able to:

- Explain the rate making function.
- Define underwriting and explain the steps in the underwriting process.
- Explain the meaning of "production."
- Describe the objectives of claim settlement and the various steps in the settlement of a claim.
- Explain the reasons for reinsurance and the different types of reinsurance treaties.
- Describe the electronic data processing function.
- Explain the importance of insurance company investments and describe the different types of investments.

We will continue our discussion of insurance company operations in this chapter. In addition to the marketing function discussed in Chapter 25, insurers engage in a wide variety of additional activities. We will first discuss the rate making function. We will then consider the important function of underwriting. We will also see how claims are settled and paid. The reinsurance operations of insurers will also be discussed in some detail. We will conclude the chapter by describing some miscellaneous functions of insurers.

INSURANCE COMPANY OPERATIONS

The most important insurance company operations consist of the following:[1]

- Rate making
- Underwriting
- Production
- Claim settlement
- Reinsurance
- Electronic data processing
- Investments
- Accounting

In addition to the preceding, insurers engage in other operations as well, such as legal services and loss-control services. Let us briefly discuss each of these operations.

RATE MAKING

Rate making, which is one of the most important functions of an insurance company, refers to the pricing of insurance. Insurance pricing differs considerably from the pricing of other products. When other products are sold, the company knows in advance what its costs of production are, so that a price can be established to cover all costs and yield a profit to the company. However, the insurance company does not know in advance what its actual costs are going to be. The premium charged for the insurance may be inadequate for paying all claims and expenses during the policy period, because it is only after the period of protection has expired that the company can determine its actual losses and expenses. Of course, the company hopes that the premium paid in advance will be sufficient to pay all claims and expenses and yield a profit.

The person who determines the premium rates is known as an *actuary*. An actuary is a highly skilled mathematician who is involved in all phases of insurance company operations, including planning, pricing, and research. In life insurance, the actuary studies important statistical data on births, deaths, marriages, disease, employment, retirement, and accidents. Based on this information, the actuary determines premium rates for life and health insurance policies. The objectives are to calculate premiums that will make the business profitable, enable it to compete effectively with other insurers, and allow it to pay claims and expenses as they occur. A life insurance actuary must also determine the legal reserves a company needs for future obligations.[2]

Professional certification as an actuary is attained by passing a series of examinations administered by the Society of Actuaries, which qualifies the actuary as a Fellow of the Society of Actuaries. In addition to ratemaking, life insurance actuaries are also closely involved in the marketing, sales, investment, and financial operations of the company.

In property and liability insurance, actuaries also determine premium rates for different lines of insurance. The rates are determined by the company's past loss experience and by industry statistics. In addition to the company's own loss data, statistics on hurricanes, tornadoes, fires, diseases, crime rates, traffic accidents, and the cost of living are also carefully analyzed. Some companies use their own data in establishing premium rates. Other companies are members of rating bureaus, and bureau rates are used. A **rating bureau** is an organization supported by insurers that computes premium rates for the member companies. A member company submits data that is pooled with the loss and expense experience of other member companies. Some companies use the bureau rates calculated by the rating bureau; others use **deviated rates**, by which the bureau rate may be discounted. For example, a company may deviate from the bureau rate by 15 percent in determining automobile liability insurance premiums.

Actuaries in property and liability insurance also determine the adequacy of loss reserves,[3] allocate expenses, and compile statistics for company management and for state regulatory officials. Also, actuaries help resolve management problems in underwriting, sales, claims, and product development. We will examine these functional areas later in the chapter.

To become a certified actuary in property and liability insurance, the individual must pass a series of examinations administered by the Casualty Actuarial Society. Successful completion of the examinations enables the actuary to become a Fellow of the Casualty Actuarial Society.

UNDERWRITING

One of the most important functions of an insurance company is the underwriting function. ***Underwriting** can be defined as the selection and classification of profitable insureds.* The underwriter is the person who decides to accept or reject an application for insurance. The fundamental objective of underwriting is to produce a safe and profitable distribution of business for the company. The underwriter constantly strives to select certain types of business and to reject others in order to obtain a profitable portfolio of business.

Statement of Underwriting Policy

Underwriting starts with a clear statement of underwriting policy. A company must establish an underwriting policy that is consistent with company objectives. The objective may be a large volume of business with low unit profits or a smaller volume at a larger unit of profit. The company must define classes of business that are acceptable, borderline, or prohibited. The amounts of insurance that can be written on acceptable and borderline business must also be determined.

The company's underwriting policy is determined by top level management in charge of underwriting. The **desk underwriters**—persons who make daily decisions concerning the acceptance or rejection of business—are expected to follow official company policy. The underwriting policy is stated in detail in an *underwriting guide* that specifies the lines of insurance to be written; territories to be developed; forms and rating plans to be used; acceptable, borderline, and prohibited business; amounts of insurance to be written; business that requires approval by a senior underwriter; and other underwriting details.

Basic Underwriting Principles

As we noted earlier, the goal of underwriting is to produce a profitable volume of business. To achieve this goal, certain underwriting principles are followed. Three important principles are as follows:

- Selection of insureds according to the company's underwriting standards
- Proper balance within each rate classification
- Equity among policyowners

The first principle is that the underwriter must select prospective insureds according to the company's underwriting standards. This means that the company does not wish to have claims in excess of those provided for in the rating structure. The underwriters should select only those insureds whose actual loss experience will not exceed the loss experience assumed in the rating structure. For example, a factory mutual may wish to insure only high-grade factories, and expects that its actual loss experience will be well below average. Underwriting standards are established with respect to eligible factories, and a rate is established based on a relatively low loss ratio.[4] Assume that the expected loss ratio is established at 30 percent, and the rate is set accordingly. The underwriters ideally should insure only those factories that can meet the stringent underwriting requirements, so that the actual loss ratio for the group will not exceed 30 percent.

The purpose of the underwriting standards is to reduce adverse selection against the company. There is an old saying in underwriting, "select or be selected against." Without underwriting standards, those persons who are likely to have an early loss will apply for insurance. The group would then contain a disproportionate number of substandard insureds, and the underwriting results would be unprofitable.

The second underwriting principle is to have a proper balance within each rate classification. This means that a below-average insured in an underwriting class should be offset by an above-average insured, so that on balance, the class or manual rate for the group as a whole will be adequate for paying all claims and expenses. For example, much of the underwriting today is **class underwriting**, especially for personal lines of insurance. Exposure units with similar loss-producing characteristics are grouped together and placed in the same underwriting class. Each exposure unit within the class is charged the same rate. However, all exposure units are not completely identical. Some will be above average for the class as a whole, while others will be below average. The underwriter must then select a proper balance of insureds so that the class rate (average rate) will be adequate for paying all claims and expenses.

A final underwriting principle is equity among the policyowners. This means that equitable rates should be charged, and each group of policyowners should pay its own way in terms of losses and expenses. Stated differently, one group of policyowners should not unduly subsidize another group. For example, a group of twenty-year-old persons and a group of eighty-year-old persons should not pay the same premium rate for life insurance. If identical rates were charged to both groups, the younger persons would be subsidizing the older persons. This would be inequitable. Once the younger persons became aware that they were being overcharged, they would seek other insurers whose classification systems are more equitable. The first company would then end up with a disproportionate number of older, unhealthy persons, and the underwriting results would be unprofitable. Thus, because of competition, there must be rate equity among the policyholders.

Steps in Underwriting

After the company's underwriting policy is established, it must be communicated to the sales force. Initial underwriting starts with the agent in the field. Let us briefly examine the agent's role in underwriting.

Agent as first underwriter The agent is the first underwriter. This is often called field underwriting. The agent is told what types of business to solicit, borderline business, and prohibited or undesirable business. For example, in automobile insurance, an agent may be told not to solicit applicants who have a driving while intoxicated conviction, who are youthful single drivers under age twenty-one, or who are young drivers who own high-powered sports cars. In fire insurance, certain exposures, such as bowling alleys and restaurants, may have to be submitted to a company underwriter for approval.

In property and liability insurance, the agent often has authority to bind the company immediately, subject to subsequent disapproval of the application by a company underwriter. Thus, it is important that the agent follow company policy when soliciting applicants for insurance. To encourage a submission of only profitable business, a *contingent or profit-sharing commission* is often paid based on the agent's favorable loss experience.

In life insurance, the agent must also solicit applicants in accordance with the company's underwriting policy. The agent may be told not to solicit applicants who are drug addicts, alcoholics, ex-convicts, or persons working in hazardous occupations.

Sources of underwriting information The underwriter requires certain types of information in deciding whether to accept or reject an applicant for insurance. The type of information varies by line of insurance. For example, in fire insurance, both the physical features of the property and personal characteristics of the applicant must be considered. Physical features include the type of construction, occupancy of the building, location, quality of fire protection, water supply, and exposure from surrounding buildings. With respect to personal characteristics of the applicant, information that reveals the presence of *moral* or *morale hazard* is particularly important. The underwriter wants to screen out applicants who may intentionally cause a loss or inflate a claim beyond its actual value. Likewise, the underwriter wants to avoid insuring persons who are careless in protecting their property because of insurance. Thus, the applicant's present financial condition, living habits, past loss record, and moral character are especially important in the underwriting process.

Underwriting information can be obtained from a wide variety of sources. The most important sources include the following:

- Application
- Agent's report
- Inspection report
- Physical inspection
- Physical examination and attending physician's report
- Medical Information Bureau

The *application* is a basic source of information to the underwriter. The application varies depending on the type of insurance, but it is designed to reveal important underwriting information. For example, in life insurance, the application will show the individual's age, sex, weight, occupation, personal and family health history, and any hazardous hobbies, such as sky diving or scuba diving.

An **agent's report** is another source of information. Most companies require the agent to give an evaluation of the prospective insured. For example, in life insurance, the agent may be asked to state how long he or she has known the applicant, to estimate the applicant's annual income and net worth, to judge whether the applicant plans to lapse or surrender existing life insurance, and to determine whether the application is the result of the agent's solicitation.

An **inspection report** may be required, especially if the underwriter suspects moral hazard. An outside firm investigates the applicant for insurance and makes a detailed report to the company. The report may include the applicant's present financial condition, drinking habits, marital status, amount of outstanding debts, delinquent bills, policy record, felony convictions, and additional information, such as whether the applicant has ever declared bankruptcy. The Equifax Service is an example of a national organization that provides investigative services to insurers.

A *physical inspection* may also be required before the application is approved. In property and liability insurance, the agent or company representative may physically inspect the building or plant to be insured, and submit a report to the company underwriter. For example, in workers' compensation insurance, an inspection may reveal unsafe working conditions, such as dangerous machinery or slippery floors; violation of safety rules, such as not wearing goggles when a grinding machine is used; and an excessively dusty or toxic plant or one with an excessive noise level.

In life insurance, a *physical examination* is a major source of information to the underwriter. The physical examination will reveal whether the applicant is overweight, has high blood pressure, or has any abnormalities in the heart, respiratory system, urinary system, or other parts of the body. An *attending physician's report* may also be required, which is a report from a physician who has treated the applicant in the past.

A final source of underwriting information in life insurance is a **Medical Information Bureau (MIB) report**. Companies that belong to the bureau report any health impairments, which are then recorded and made available to member companies. For example, if an applicant for life insurance has high blood pressure, this information would be recorded in the MIB files, which are coded and do not reveal the decision made by the submitting company.

Making an underwriting decision After the underwriter evaluates the information, an underwriting decision must be made. There are three basic underwriting decisions with respect to an initial application for insurance. They are:

- Accept the application
- Accept the application subject to certain restrictions or modifications
- Reject the application

The underwriter can accept the application, and recommend that the policy be issued. A second decision is to accept the application subject to certain restrictions or modifications. Several examples can illustrate this type of decision. Before a burglary and theft policy is issued, the applicant may be required to improve the property by placing iron bars on windows or by installing an approved central alarm system; the applicant may be refused a homeowners policy and offered a more limited dwelling and contents policy; a different rating plan may be offered; the amount of insurance requested may be reduced; a large deductible may be inserted in the policy; or a substandard rate may be charged if the applicant is substandard in health. If the applicant agrees to the modifications or restrictions, the policy is then issued.

Finally, the application can be rejected. However, excessive and unjustified rejection of applications reduces the company's profitability and alienates the agents who solicited the business. If an application is rejected, the rejection must be based on a clear failure to meet the company's underwriting standards.

Other Underwriting Considerations

Other factors are also considered in underwriting. They include the following:

1. *Rate adequacy and underwriting.* If rates are considered adequate for a class, companies are more willing to underwrite new business. However, if rates are inadequate, prudent underwriting requires a more conservative approach to the acceptance of new business. If moral hazard is excessive, the business generally cannot be insured at any rate.
2. *Reinsurance and underwriting.* Availability of reinsurance facilities may result in more liberal underwriting. However, if reinsurance cannot be obtained on favorable terms, the underwriting may be more restrictive.
3. *Renewal underwriting.* In life insurance, policies are not cancellable. In property and liability insurance, most policies can be cancelled or not renewed. If the loss experience is unfavorable, the company may either cancel or not review the policy. Many states have placed restrictions on the company's right to cancel.

PRODUCTION

The term *production* refers to the sales and marketing activities of insurers. Agents who sell insurance are frequently referred to as **producers**. This word is used because an insurance company can be legally chartered, personnel hired, and policy forms printed, but nothing is produced until a policy is sold. The key to the company's financial success is an effective sales force.

Agency Department

Most companies have an agency or sales department. This department is responsible for recruiting, training, and supervising general agents, branch office managers, and local agents.

Special agents may also be appointed. A **special agent** is a highly specialized technician who provides local agents in the field with technical help and assistance with their marketing problems. For example, a special agent may explain a new policy form or a special rating plan to agents in the field.

In addition to development of an effective sales force, an insurance company also engages in a wide variety of marketing activities. These activities include the development of marketing philosophy and the company's perception of its role in the market place; identification of short-run and long-run production goals; marketing research; development of new insurance products to meet the changing needs of consumers and business firms; developing new marketing strategies; and advertising the company's products.

Professionalism in Selling

The marketing of insurance has been characterized by a distinct trend toward professionalism in recent years. This means that the modern agent should be a competent professional who has a high degree of technical knowledge in a particular area of insurance and who also places the needs of his or her clients first. The professional agent identifies potential insureds, analyzes their insurance needs, and recommends the best solution to the problem. After the sale, the agent has the responsibility to provide follow-up service to clients to keep their insurance programs up to date. Finally, a professional agent abides by a code of ethics.

Several organizations have developed professional programs for agents and other personnel in the insurance industry. In life and health insurance, The American College has established the **Chartered Life Underwriter (CLU)** program. This is a professional program that requires an individual to pass ten examinations to receive the CLU designation. A minimum of three years' experience in life or health insurance is also required. The ten professional courses are:

1. Financial Services: Environment and Professions
2. Income Taxation
3. Economics
4. Financial Statement Analysis/Individual Insurance Benefits
5. Insurance Environment and Operations
6. Group Benefits and Social Insurance
7. Pensions and Other Retirement Benefits
8. Investments
9. Estate and Gift Tax Planning
10. Planning for Business Owners and Professionals

A similar professional program exists in property and liability insurance. The American Institute for Property and Liability Underwriters has established the **Chartered Property and Casualty Underwriter (CPCU)** program. The CPCU program also requires an individual to pass ten examinations. The ten-semester curriculum is made up of the following courses:

1. CPCU 1: Principles of Risk Management and Insurance
2. CPCU 2: Personal Risk Management and Insurance
3. CPCU 3: Commercial Property Risk Management and Insurance
4. CPCU 4: Commercial Liability Risk Management and Insurance
5. CPCU 5: Insurance Company Operations
6. CPCU 6: The Legal Environment of Insurance
7. CPCU 7: Management
8. CPCU 8: Accounting and Finance
9. CPCU 9: Economics
10. CPCU 10: Insurance Issues and Professional Ethics

CLAIM SETTLEMENT

Every insurance company has a claims division or department for settling claims. In this section, we will examine the basic objectives in settling claims, the different types of claim adjustors, and the various steps in the claim-settlement process.

Basic Objectives in Claim Settlement

From the company's viewpoint, there are several basic objectives in settling claims. They include the following:[5]

- Verification of a covered loss
- Fair and prompt payment of claims
- Personal assistance to the insured

The first objective in settling claims is to verify that a covered loss has occurred. This involves determining whether a specific person or property is covered under the policy, and the extent of the coverage. We will examine this objective in greater detail later in the chapter.

The second objective is the fair and prompt payment of claims. If a valid claim is denied, the fundamental social and contractual purpose of protecting the insured is defeated. Also, the company's reputation may be harmed, and the sales of new policies may be adversely affected. Fair payment means that the company should avoid excessive claim settlements and should also resist the payment of fraudulent claims. Excessive claim payments or payment of fraudulent claims will ultimately result in higher premiums. If the company follows a liberal claims policy, all policyowners will suffer because a rate increase will become necessary.

Many states have passed laws that prohibit unfair claim practices. These laws are patterned after the National Association of Insurance Commissioners' Model Act. Some unfair claim practices prohibited by these laws include the following:[6]

1. Refusing to pay claims without conducting a reasonable investigation based upon all available information.
2. Not attempting in good faith to effectuate prompt, fair, and equitable settlements of claims in which liability has become reasonably clear.
3. Compelling insureds to institute litigation to recover amounts due under an insurance policy by offering substantially less than the amounts ultimately recovered in actions brought by such insureds.

A third objective is to provide personal assistance to the insured after a covered loss occurs. Aside from any contractual obligations, the company should also provide personal assistance and comfort to the insured after a loss occurs. In many cases, a covered loss may result in death or severe injury to family members. Assistance by claims personnel during such a crisis can be especially helpful. For example, after a fire, the claims adjustor can help the family find temporary housing; a cash advance may be paid to purchase new clothing; if a death occurs from the fire, assistance in filing a death claim can be provided; transportation can also be made available; and overall emotional support can be provided to the family.

Types of Claim Adjustors

The person who adjusts a claim is known as a **claim adjustor.** The major types of adjustors include the following:

- Agent
- Company adjustor
- Independent adjustor
- Adjustment bureau
- Public adjustor

An *agent* often has authority to settle small first-party claims up to some maximum limit.[7] The insured submits the claim directly to the agent, who has the authority to pay it up to some specified amount, such as $500. This approach to claim settlement has three advantages: it is speedy, it reduces adjustment expenses, and it preserves the policyowner's good will.

A **company adjustor** can settle a claim. The

adjustor is usually a salaried employee who represents only one company. After notice of the loss is received, the company adjustor will investigate the claim, determine the amount of loss, and arrange for payment.

An **independent adjustor** can also be used to settle claims. An independent adjustor is a person who offers his or her services to insurance companies and is compensated by a fee. The company may use an independent adjustor in certain geographical areas where the volume of claims is too low to justify a branch office with a staff of full-time adjustors. An independent adjustor may also be used in highly specialized areas where a company adjustor with the necessary technical skills and knowledge is not available.

An **adjustment bureau** can be used to settle claims. An adjustment bureau is an organization for adjusting claims that is supported by insurers that use their services. Claims personnel employed by an adjustment bureau are highly trained individuals who adjust claims on a full-time basis. An adjustment bureau is frequently used when a catastrophic loss occurs in a given geographical area, and a large number of claims are submitted at the same time. Some national adjustment bureaus are the General Adjustment Bureau (GAB Services, Inc.), Crawford and Company, and Underwriters Adjusting Company.

Finally, a **public adjustor** can be used to settle a claim. *A public adjustor, however, represents the insured rather than the insurance company and is paid a fee based on the amount of the claim settlement.* A public adjustor may be employed by the insured if a complex loss situation occurs, and technical assistance is needed, and also, in those cases where the insured and insurer cannot resolve a dispute over a claim.

Steps in Settlement of a Claim

There are several important steps in settling a claim. They are:

- Notice of loss to the company
- Investigation of the claim
- Filing a proof of loss
- Decision concerning payment

Notice of loss The first step is to notify the company of a loss. A provision concerning notice of loss is usually stated in the policy. A typical provision requires the insured to give notice immediately or as soon as possible after the loss has occurred. For example, the standard fire policy requires the insured to give immediate written notice to the company; a medical-expense health insurance policy may require the insured to give notice within thirty days after the occurrence of a loss, or as soon afterward as is reasonably possible; and the personal auto policy requires that the company must be notified promptly of how, when, and where the accident or loss happened. The notice must also include the names and addresses of any injured persons and witnesses.

Investigation of the claim After notice is received, the next step is to investigate the claim. An adjustor must determine that a covered loss has occurred, and must also determine the amount of the loss. A series of questions must be answered before the claim is approved. The most important questions include the following:[8]

1. Did the loss occur while the policy was in force?
2. Does the policy cover the peril that caused the loss?
3. Does the policy cover the property destroyed or damaged in the loss?
4. Is the claimant entitled to recover?
5. Did the loss occur at an insured location?
6. Is the type of loss covered?

Proof of loss A proof of loss must be filed with the company before the claim is paid. A proof of loss is a sworn statement by the insured that substantiates the loss. For example, under the homeowners policy, the insured must file a proof of loss that indicates the time and cause of

INSIGHT 26.1

Insurers Use Police Tactics to Snare Doctors Who File False Claims

This was no ordinary criminal investigation.

For one thing, the suspects were doctors—nine podiatrists who worked at Family Foot Care Centers in and around this city. The method was also unconventional: Investigators wearing microphones posed as patients to collect evidence of unnecessary surgery and fraudulent billing.

But most unusually, the main investigators in this 1983 case weren't law-enforcement officers, but employees of Blue Cross/Blue Shield of Northern Ohio. Their work in this case, with help from federal postal inspectors and prosecutors, has led to one mail-fraud conviction. More indictments are expected soon, even though former officials of the now-defunct podiatry centers deny all charges.

Health-insurance companies are getting tough. "We're dealing with some pretty sophisticated people and some sophisticated ways to steal money," says William H. Huston, director of this Blue Cross plan's fraud squad, and a former Michigan state policeman.

Fraud units are growing among medical insurers not just to weed out suspicious claims but to build criminal cases against doctors, and other health-care providers and sometimes even subscribers whom they suspect of cheating.

In the past, insurance companies could simply pass the costs of undetected fraud to their subscribers through higher rates. But in today's competitive health-care market, insurers must contain costs, and some of them say a hard line on fraud will save millions of dollars, mainly by deterrence.

Ripe for Plucking

Insurers agree that they've been an easy mark, taking for granted the integrity of doctors' claims. "It was easy for providers to exploit that trust," says Ralph Jeffrey, claims director for Metropolitan Life Insurance Co. Practices like overbilling or billing for work not done are hard to detect.

And the insurers' traditional response when they did find unjustified payouts—merely to ask for the money back and then often settle for less-than-full recovery—did nothing to deter fraud, say the tougher new insurance-fraud cops.

"We treat it as a felony," says Jim Garcia, director of Aetna Life Insurance Co.'s fraud squad, which is one of the largest, with 10 full-time and 100 part-time investigators. Since June 1982, when the squad was established, Aetna has identified $20 million in fraudulent billings. (It pays out about $7 billion a year in medical claims.) Aetna recovered $1.7 million last year, and its fraud investigations led to 132 convictions, about half of them of providers.

Although performing unnecessary surgery isn't a crime, using the U.S. mail to bill for it is.

Other companies' squads have grown less quickly, but they take the same approach. Metropolitan Life's four-member unit recovered $200,000 last year and led to seven indictments, three against health-care providers. The company may add one or two more investigators soon, realizing "there's more out there than we've discovered," says Mr. Jeffrey.

Not all insurance companies have joined in this push. For example, George Miller, a claims official for Prudential Insurance Co. of America, shies from even using the word "fraud" in describing his auditors' function.

"The only person who can use that word, as we've been reminded by counsel, is a judge," says Mr. Miller. "We use euphemisms like 'possible discrepancies.'" He adds, "We still hold that a good, solid claim exam is the best way to turn up abuse."

And Prudential doesn't even routinely prosecute the abusers it does catch. "In most cases, we get our money back, so there's no loss," Mr. Miller says.

But a few fraud squads have grown downright police-like in their philosophy and tactics, such as Mr. Huston's Blue Cross/Blue Shield unit here. Mr. Huston and his seven-member squad have an annual budget of about $400,000, and they operate a toll-free telephone hotline that gets about 100 calls a month alleging fraud. Most don't pan out, but Mr. Huston says the hotline is the source of most investigations, including the Family Foot Care case.

After receiving complaints of expensive, unnecessary surgery at the centers in early 1983, the unit ran a computer check and found that the clinic's nine doctors received about 25% of Blue Cross/Blue Shield's payouts to podiatrists, though they constituted only 3.2% of those specialists in the Cleveland area.

"We knew we had our teeth into a piece of meat," says Doug Fowler, an investigator and former policeman. The squad met with more than 100 patients, and later, with postal inspectors, decided to pose as patients at Family Foot Care clinics. They conducted more than 70 such visits. "We'd go in with symptoms like stinky feet," says Mr. Fowler.

The agents had previously been pronounced healthy by independent podiatrists, but "some of our agents were told (by Family Foot Care) they needed surgery that day," Mr. Fowler says.

Going After Subscribers

Family Foot Care now has new owners and a new name. But Edgar Huler, former chief operating officer of the clinics, insists that the charges against the nine podiatrists are "totally without foundation." Mr. Huler says "everything I observed was ethical and morally justified" at Family Foot Care, despite the conviction of one doctor, David S. Tarr, last December for mail fraud.

Mr. Huston's squad also goes after subscriber fraud, as when people lend their Blue Cross/Blue Shield cards to uninsured friends. But that's a secondary priority: "How much can the individual subscriber get from you?" asks Nancy Russo, an investigator.

Getting a busy prosecutor interested in an insurance case usually requires a big-money fraud, and those almost always involve providers. But Mr. Huston is sensitive to the appearance of "using the prosecutor's office as a collection agency." He avoids that, he says, by consistently pushing prosecution and not seeking repayments from a fraud suspect.

So far, the medical establishment has reacted cautiously. Hart F. Page, executive director of the Ohio Medical Association, says, "Certainly insurance companies have a right to investigate," but he's concerned that allegations could leak out during an investigation and ruin a doctor's reputation before the matter gets to court.

And when the New York Blue Cross fraud squad sought an endorsement from the state medical society, its officials balked. "The data didn't really specify to what degree physicians are involved" in fraud, says Mario Mangini, acting director of the society's medical services division. "Before going before our membership, we'd like to have some hard facts," he says.

Fraud investigators are quick to state that most doctors and other providers are honest in their billing. But Mr. Jeffrey of Metropolitan Life says, "We are foolish if we overlook fraud or pretend that it doesn't exist."

SOURCE: From "Insurers Use Police Tactics to Snare Doctors Who File False Claims," by David Mills. Reprinted by permission of the *Wall Street Journal*,

the loss, interest of the insured and others in the damaged property, other insurance that may cover the loss, and any change in title or occupancy of the property during the term of the policy.

Decision concerning payment After the claim is investigated, the adjustor must make a decision concerning payment. There are three possible decisions. First, the claim can be paid. In most cases, the claim is paid promptly according to the terms of the policy. Second, the claim can be denied. The adjustor may feel that the policy does not cover the loss, or that the claim is fraudulent. Finally, the claim may be valid, but there may be a dispute between the insured and insurer over the amount to be paid. In the case of a dispute, a policy provision may specify how the dispute is to be resolved. For example, if a dispute arises under a homeowners policy, both the insured and insurer select an independent appraiser. The two appraisers or a court of law then appoint an umpire. An agreement by any two of the three is then binding on all parties.

REINSURANCE

Reinsurance is another important insurance company operation. In this section, we will study the meaning of reinsurance, the reasons why reinsurance is used, and the different types of reinsurance contracts. Before we proceed, however, certain definitions should be clearly understood.

Definitions

***Reinsurance** is the shifting of part or all of the insurance originally written by one insurer to another insurer.* The company that initially writes the business is called the **ceding company** or primary insurer. The company that accepts part or all of the insurance from the ceding company is called the *reinsurer*. The amount of insurance retained by the ceding company for its own account is called the **net retention** or retention limit. The amount of the insurance ceded to the reinsurer is known as the **cession**. Finally, the reinsurer may obtain reinsurance from another company. This is known as a **retrocession**.

Reasons for Reinsurance

Reinsurance is used for several reasons. The most important reasons include the following:

- Increase underwriting capacity
- Stabilize profits
- Reduce the unearned premium reserve
- Provide protection against a catastrophic loss

In addition, reinsurance is used to retire from a territory or class of business and to obtain underwriting advice from the reinsurer.

Increase in underwriting capacity Reinsurance is used to increase the company's underwriting capacity to write new business. A company may be asked to assume liability for losses in excess of its retention limit. Without reinsurance, the agent would have to place large amounts of insurance with several companies. This is awkward and may create ill will on behalf of the policyowner. Reinsurance permits the primary company to issue a single policy in excess of its retention limit, thereby increasing its capacity.

Stabilization of profits Reinsurance is also used to stabilize profits. A company may wish to avoid large fluctuations in annual loss experience. Loss experience can fluctuate widely because of social and economic conditions, natural disasters, and chance. Reinsurance can be used to level out the effects of poor loss experience. For example, reinsurance may be used to cover a single, large loss. If a large, unexpected loss occurs, the reinsurer would pay the loss in excess of some specified limit. Another arrangement would be to have the reinsurer reimburse the ceding company for losses that exceed a specified loss ratio during a given year. For example, a company may wish to stabilize its loss ratio at 70 percent.

The reinsurer then agrees to reimburse the ceding company for part or all of the losses in excess of 70 percent up to some maximum limit.

Reduction in the unearned premium reserve Reinsurance is also used to reduce the level of the unearned premium reserve. For some companies, especially newer and smaller companies, the ability to write large amounts of new insurance may be restricted by the unearned premium reserve requirement. *The* ***unearned premium reserve*** *is a liability reserve on the company's balance sheet that represents the unearned portion of gross premiums on all outstanding policies at the time of valuation.*[9] In effect, the unearned premium reserve reflects the fact that premiums are paid in advance, but the period of protection has not yet expired. As time goes on, part of the premium is earned, while the remainder is unearned. It is only after the period of protection expires that the premium is fully earned.

As we stated earlier, a company's ability to grow may be restricted by the unearned premium reserve requirement. This is because the entire *gross premium* must be placed in the unearned premium reserve when the policy is first written. However, the company will incur relatively heavy first-year acquisition expenses in the form of commissions, state premium taxes, underwriting expenses, expenses in issuing the policy, and other expenses. In calculating the amount of the unearned premium reserve, there is no allowance for these first-year acquisition expenses, and the company must pay them out of its surplus. (Policyholder's surplus is the difference between assets and liabilities.) For example, a one-year fire insurance policy with an annual premium of $1,200 may be written on January 1. The entire $1,200 must be placed in the unearned premium reserve. At the end of each month, one-twelfth of the premium, or $100, is earned and the remainder is unearned. On December 31, the entire premium is fully earned. However, assume that first-year acquisition expenses are 30 percent of the gross premium, or $360. This amount will come out of the company's surplus. Thus, the more business it writes, the greater is the drain on its surplus. The company's ability to write new business could eventually be impaired.

Reinsurance can be used to reduce the level of the unearned premium reserve required by law. In the preceding example, if half the business were reinsured, the unearned premium reserve for that policy would be only $600 rather than $1,200. This temporarily increases the surplus position of a company and improves the ratio of surplus to net premiums written, thereby permitting the company to continue to grow.[10]

Protection against a catastrophic loss Reinsurance is also used to provide protection against a catastrophic loss. Insurers are exposed to catastrophic losses because of tornadoes, hurricanes, earthquakes, industrial explosions, commercial airline disasters, and similar losses. Catastrophe reinsurance can provide protection to the ceding company that experiences a catastrophic loss. The reinsurer pays for losses that exceed a certain amount up to some specified maximum limit.

Other reasons for reinsurance Reinsurance is also used to retire from the business or from a given line of insurance. Reinsurance permits the liabilities for existing insurance to be transferred to another company; thus, the policyowner's coverage remains undisturbed.

Finally, reinsurance can be used to obtain the underwriting advice and assistance of the reinsurer. A company may wish to write a new line of insurance, but it may have little experience with respect to underwriting the line. The reinsurer often can provide valuable assistance with respect to rating, retention limits, policy coverages, and other underwriting details.

Types of Reinsurance

There are two principal forms of reinsurance contracts. They are: (1) facultative reinsurance, and

(2) automatic treaty. Let us briefly examine each of these categories.

Facultative reinsurance ***Facultative reinsurance** is an optional, case-by-case method used when the primary company receives an application for insurance that exceeds its retention limit.* Before the policy is issued, the primary company shops around for reinsurance and contacts several reinsurers. However, the primary company is under no obligation to cede insurance, and the reinsurer is under no obligation to accept the insurance. But if a willing reinsurer can be found, the primary company and reinsurer can then enter into a valid contract.

Facultative reinsurance is frequently used when a large amount of insurance is desired. Before the application is accepted, the primary company determines if reinsurance can be obtained. If available, the policy may then be written. For example, before a property insurer accepts an application for $20 million of hull insurance on a commercial jet, it may first determine if facultative reinsurance is available.

Facultative reinsurance has the advantage of flexibility, since a reinsurance contract can be arranged to fit any kind of case. In addition, facultative reinsurance can increase the company's capacity to write large amounts of insurance. The reinsurance tends to stabilize the company's operations by shifting large losses to the reinsurer.

However, the major disadvantage of facultative reinsurance is that it is uncertain. The ceding company does not know in advance if a reinsurer will accept any part of the insurance. There is also a further disadvantage of delay, since the policy will not be issued until reinsurance is obtained. In times of bad loss experience, the reinsurance market tends to dry up. Therefore, facultative reinsurance has the further disadvantage of being unreliable.

Automatic treaty *Under an **automatic treaty**, the primary company must cede insurance to the reinsurer, and the reinsurer must accept.* If the business falls within the scope of the agreement, it is automatically reinsured according to the terms of the treaty.

An automatic treaty has several advantages to the primary company. It is automatic, and no uncertainty or delay is involved. It is also economical, since it is not necessary to shop around for reinsurance before the policy is written.

However, an automatic treaty could be unprofitable to the reinsurer. The reinsurer generally has no knowledge about the individual applicant and must rely on the underwriting judgment of the primary company. The primary insurer may write bad business and then reinsure it. Also, the premium received by the reinsurer may be inadequate. Thus, if the primary company has a poor selection of risks or charges inadequate rates, the reinsurer could incur a loss.

There are several types of automatic reinsurance treaties. Some common arrangements include the following:

- Quota share
- Surplus share
- Excess of loss
- Reinsurance pool

Quota-share treaty Under a quota-share treaty, the ceding company and reinsurer agree to share losses and premiums based on some proportion. *The ceding company's retention limit is stated as a percentage rather than as a dollar amount.* Losses and premiums are then shared based on this percentage. For example, Apex Fire and Geneva Re may enter into a quota-share treaty whereby losses are shared 50 percent and 50 percent, respectively. Thus, if a $12,000 loss occurs, Apex Fire pays $6,000, and Geneva Re pays the remaining $6,000.

Premiums are also shared based on the same percentage used to pay losses. However, the reinsurer pays a **ceding commission** to the primary company to help compensate for the first-year acquisition expenses in writing the business. Thus, in the previous example, Geneva Re would receive 50 percent of the premium less a ceding commission that is paid to Apex Fire.

The major advantage of quota-share reinsurance is that the unearned premium reserve is reduced. For smaller companies and other insurers that wish to reduce a surplus drain, a quota-share treaty can be especially effective. The principal disadvantage is that a large share of potentially profitable business is ceded to the reinsurer.

Surplus-share treaty Under a **surplus-share treaty**, the reinsurer agrees to accept insurance in excess of the ceding company's retention limit, up to some maximum amount. *The retention limit is referred to as a line and is stated as a dollar amount.* If the amount of insurance on a given policy exceeds the retention limit, the excess insurance is ceded to the reinsurer up to some maximum limit. The primary company and reinsurer then share losses and premiums based on the fraction of total insurance retained by each party. Each party pays its respective share of any loss regardless of its size.

For example, assume that Apex Fire has a retention limit of $200,000 (called a line) for a single policy, and that four lines, or $800,000, are ceded to Geneva Re. Apex Fire now has a total underwriting capacity of $1 million on any single exposure. Assume that an agent writes a $500,000 fire insurance policy. Apex Fire takes the first $200,000 of insurance, or two-fifths, and Geneva Re takes the remaining $300,000, or three-fifths. These fractions then determine the amount of loss paid by each party. If a $5,000 loss occurs, Apex Fire pays $2,000 (two-fifths), and Geneva Re pays the remaining $3,000 (three-fifths). This can be summarized as follows:

Apex Fire	$ 200,000 (one line)
Geneve Re	800,000 (four lines)
Total underwriting capacity	$1,000,000

$500,000 policy	Apex Fire	$200,000 (2/5)
	Geneva Re	$300,000 (3/5)

$5,000 loss	Apex Fire	$2,000 (2/5)
	Geneva Re	$3,000 (3/5)

Under a surplus-share treaty, premiums are shared based on the same fraction of loss paid by each party. The reinsurer also pays a ceding commission to the primary company to help compensate for the first-year acquisition expenses.

The principal advantage of a surplus-share treaty is to increase the primary company's underwriting capacity. The major disadvantage is the increase in administrative expenses. The surplus-share treaty is complex and requires extensive paper work, since a list of policies being reinsured must be maintained and furnished periodically to the reinsurer.[11]

Excess-of-loss treaty An **excess-of-loss treaty** is designed largely for a catastrophic loss. Losses in excess of the retention limit are paid by the reinsurer up to some maximum limit. The excess-of-loss treaty can be written to cover (1) a single exposure, (2) a single occurrence, such as a catastrophic loss from a tornado or hurricane, or (3) excess losses when the primary insurer's cumulative losses exceed a certain amount during some stated time period, such as a year. For example, assume that Apex Fire wants protection from a hurricane or tornado loss in excess of $1 million. Assume that an excess-of-loss treaty is written with Franklin Re to cover single occurrences during a specified time period. Franklin Re agrees to pay all losses exceeding $1 million but only to a maximum of $10 million. If a $5 million hurricane loss occurs, Franklin Re would pay $4 million.

Reinsurance pool Reinsurance can also be provided by a **reinsurance pool**. *A reinsurance pool is an organization of insurers that underwrites reinsurance on a joint basis.* Reinsurance pools have been formed because a single insurer alone may not have the financial capacity to write large amounts of insurance, but the companies as a group can combine their financial resources to obtain the necessary capacity. For example, the combined hull and liability loss exposures on a fully loaded DC-10 commercial jet can exceed $300 million if the jet should crash. Such high limits are usually beyond the financial capability of a single company. However, a reinsurance pool for aviation insurance can provide the necessary capacity. In addition to aviation insurance, reinsurance pools also exist for nuclear energy exposures, oil refineries, marine insurance, insurance in foreign countries, and numerous other types of exposures.

The method for sharing losses and premiums varies depending on the type of reinsurance pool. Pools work in two ways.[12] First, each pool member may agree to pay a certain percentage of every loss. For example, if one company has a policyholder that incurs a $100,000 loss, and there are 50 members in the pool, each company would pay 2 percent or $2,000 of the loss, depending on the agreement.

A second arrangement is similar to the excess loss reinsurance treaty. Each pool member is responsible for its own losses below a certain amount. Losses exceeding that amount are shared by all members in the pool.

ELECTRONIC DATA PROCESSING

Another important functional area is electronic data processing (EDP). Use of the computer has revolutionalized the insurance industry by speeding up the processing of information and by eliminating many routine tasks. The computer is now used in accounting, policy processing, premium notices, information retrieval, telecommunications, simulation studies, market analysis, forecasting sales, and training and education. Information can quickly be obtained with respect to premium volume, claims, loss ratios, investments, and underwriting results.

There are several different jobs in electronic data processing. A *systems analyst* reviews the various tasks performed by hand and develops methods of placing them on the computer. The systems analyst confers with others to determine their information needs and types of data to be processed. The analyst also analyzes problems in terms of system capacities and requirements, and decides how the computer can best be used to solve the problem.

A *programmer* works with information pertaining to claims, premiums, investments, personnel needs, and other financial data. The programmer translates this information into "impulse language," which is fed and stored in the computer. The computer is then programmed or instructed concerning the various tasks it is to perform.

Finally, a *data processor* uses a machine similar to a typewriter and records the data on cards or tapes that are fed into the computer. Some data processing systems permit the processor to feed information directly into the computer. The computer can then "read" the information stored in its system.

Because of the vast amount of statistical information and financial data that must be processed and analyzed, the need for electronic data processing personnel is expected to increase sharply during the 1980s.

INVESTMENTS

The investment function is an extremely important function in the overall operations of insurance companies. Since premiums are paid in advance, they can be invested until needed to pay claims and expenses. Let us briefly examine the investment operations of life and property and liability insurers.

Life Insurance Investments

At the end of 1983, U.S. life insurers held assets of about $655 billion.[13] The funds available for investment are derived primarily from premium income, investment earnings, and maturing investments that must be reinvested.

Life insurance investments have an important economic and social impact on the nation. First, life insurance contracts are long-term in nature, and the liabilities of life insurers extend over long periods of time, such as fifty or sixty years. Most life insurance investments are therefore long-term in nature. The primary investment objective is safety of principal. Thus, in 1983, about 59 percent of the assets were invested in mortgages and corporate bonds, which are long-term investments. Only about 10 percent of the assets were invested in stocks, which are subject to wide fluctuations in value. Government securities, real estate, policy loans, and miscellaneous assets accounted for the remaining 31 percent.[14]

Second, investment income is extremely important in reducing the cost of insurance to policyowners. The premiums policyowners pay for life insurance are lower than the actual cost of insurance because the premiums can be invested and earn interest. The interest earned on investments is reflected in the payment of dividends to policyowners, which reduces the cost of life insurance.

Third, life insurance premiums are an important source of capital funds to the economy. These funds are invested in shopping centers, housing developments, office buildings, hospitals, new plants, and other economic investments.

Finally, in recent years, many life insurers have become more aggressive investors. Investments are now being made in warrants or leveraged buyouts, venture capital situations, gas and oil, financial futures market, and other aggressive investments. (See Insight 26.2.)

Property and Liability Insurance Investments

In 1983, property and liability insurers held assets of about $267 billion, and net premiums written were about $109 billion.[15] As we noted earlier, these premiums are usually paid in advance, and they can be invested until needed for claims and expenses.

Two important points must be stressed when the investments of property and liability insurers are analyzed. *First, in contrast to life insurance, property and liability insurance contracts are short-term in nature.* The policy period in most contracts is one year or less. In addition, claims are settled quickly. With the exception of some liability claims that extend over long periods, most property and liability claims are paid within a relatively short period. Also, in contrast to life insurance contracts, which are generally fixed in amount, property and liability claim payments are more variable. The amounts paid can vary widely depending on inflation, medical costs, construction costs, automobile repair costs, economic conditions, and changing value judgments by society. For these reasons, the investment objective of *liquidity* is extremely important to property and liability insurers.

The second point to remember is that investment income is extremely important in offsetting any unfavorable underwriting experience. The investment of capital and surplus funds, along with the funds set aside for loss reserves and the unearned premium reserve, generate investment earnings that usually permit a company to continue its insurance operations despite an underwriting deficit. For example, in 1983, property and liability insurers incurred an overall net underwriting loss of $9.87 billion. However, net investment income was $15.97 billion. The combined net income after taxes was $3.87 billion.[16] Thus, despite a large underwriting loss, the business overall was still profitable.

OTHER INSURANCE COMPANY FUNCTIONS

In addition to the functions described earlier, insurers also perform other functions. They include accounting, legal, and loss control services.

Accounting Department

The accounting department is responsible for the financial accounting operations of an insurer. Accountants prepare financial statements, develop budgets, analyze the company's financial operations, and keep track of the millions of dollars that flow into and out of a typical company each year. Periodic reports are prepared dealing with premium income, operating expenses, claims, in-

INSIGHT 26.2

Insurers Plan to Use Futures Trades As Tool Against Interest Rate Rises

Like most companies, Kemper Investors Life Insurance Co. has never traded a contract in the risky financial-futures market.

But the Kemper Corp. subsidiary has sunk $1 million into a computer futures-accounting system for Kenneth Urbaszewski, its bond manager. These days, Mr. Urbaszewski's desk-top computer screen is as likely to flash a price from the volatile Treasury bond futures market as one for the staid insurance industry's bread-and-butter investments, corporate bonds.

Kemper is one of dozens of life-insurance companies planning to use the futures market to hedge against interest rate rises. In the past, futures trading by insurance companies was against the law in nearly all states, but regulatory barriers are falling in at least 10 states, including Illinois where Kemper is based. Regulators will still limit the amount of hedging insurers can do, however. The movement to futures trading is part of an overall broadening of investment powers sought by the $580-billion life-insurance industry in an effort to remain competitive with banks and brokerage houses in deregulated financial markets.

"These guys are out in full force" in favor of futures trading, says N. Barry Greenhouse, special assistant to the superintendent of insurance in New York, where final futures-trading rules are due soon, as they are in Illinois. "It's the insurance for insurance companies," Mr. Greenhouse says.

Dozens of insurance executives like Mr. Urbaszewski are devising trading strategies designed to protect their investment portfolios against another flare-up of interest rates. Mr. Urbaszewski, for example, says he'll sell Treasury bond futures to protect his fixed-rate corporate bonds. If rates rise, lowering the value of his corporate bonds, the profit on his futures-market position should at least partially offset that loss. Such a trading strategy is called hedging.

In futures trading, participants buy or sell contracts for future delivery of a range of financial instruments and raw materials. Most contracts are offset by opposite transactions in the market before delivery occurs. The leverage is high; a trader typically needs to post only about 5% to 15% of the face value of a contract to begin trading.

Life-insurance executives in several states have pressed in recent years for legislation to allow them to use futures. Kemper in Illinois, Pacific Mutual Life Insurance Co. in California, and Equitable Life Assurance Society of the U.S. in New York led the battle in their states.

The attraction of futures markets as a hedging tool has grown with interest-rate volatility. After October 1979, when a shift in Federal Reserve Board policy permitted interest rates to rise to records, the life-insurance industry suffered a severe liquidity crunch. The value of many companies' fixed-rate bonds and mortgages dropped, and policyholders withdrew money to invest in higher yielding government notes. Before the crunch was over, some companies were nearly out of cash and feared a run. Even giant Aetna Life & Casualty Co. sold commercial paper for the first time to raise more cash.

Since then, most life insurers have increased their liquidity by holding bonds that can be sold more easily and making fewer long-term loans. But many life-insurance executives, still mindful of the beating their fixed-rate portfolios took during the interest-rate spiral of 1979 and 1980, think their best defense against another such crisis is financial futures.

"It's prudent for a company holding the life savings of people to put the risk off on someone else," says Walter Gerken, chairman and chief executive officer of Pacific Mutual. Adds Patricia Owens, a newly installed vice president in charge of futures trading at Equitable: "An insurance company is in the business of taking insurance risks, not investment risks."

Both Equitable and Pacific Mutual say they're planning to trade futures regularly.

Some companies, such as Life Insurance Co. of Virginia, based in Richmond, Va., are already hedging major portions of their portfolios in futures. Virginia was among the first states to permit futures trading by insurers.

At Kemper Investors, Mr. Urbaszewski says lowering the company's interest-rate risk by using futures will allow it to increase its credit risk. Therefore, he plans to as much as triple the amount of lower-grade corporate bonds the company holds. Bonds with lower credit ratings have a higher yield.

The use of futures will permit Kemper Investors to assess both interest-rate and credit risk more accurately, Mr. Urbaszewski says. "It's a scientific method of investing in bonds." Before insurers won futures-trading powers, he adds, they were investing "by the seat of the pants."

Not everyone is as enthusiastic. Some question whether credit risk and interest-rate risk can be traded off. And insurance executives concede that futures trading holds pitfalls.

The simplest hedge can be undercut when, departing from the customary pattern, the cash market for corporate bonds doesn't move in lockstep with the futures market for government bonds, for example.

Some state regulators caution that the insurance companies' relatively inexperienced futures traders could get burned in the tricky futures markets. As big institutional hedgers, insurers need post only about $2,500 to secure a contract controlling $100,000 face value in Treasury bonds. A price move of the two-point daily permissible limit could wipe out four-fifths of that margin money.

Also, smaller or less-sophisticated insurers run the risk of being bamboozled into excessive futures-trading positions by slick brokers hungry for trading commissions, cautions James Hanson, assistant deputy director of the Illinois Department of Insurance.

Or a financially troubled insurer "may decide to take a fling and make it all up in the futures market," warns Franklin R. Edwards, director of the Futures Center at Columbia University in New York. Hedgers have turned into speculators before. Several major agricultural companies, including Cook Industries Inc. in the late 1970s and Farmers Export Co. in 1980, lost millions of dollars when their grain-futures positions grew from hedges to speculation. Speculative trading of futures by insurers is forbidden by all states.

Despite the flurry of preparation, insurers' moves into futures are expected to be gradual.

For now, New York law allows hedging of only 2% of assets and California only 5%; Illinois law is generally more liberal, with futures positions tied to a company's capital. Under these rules, Pacific Mutual could hold roughly 1,500 contracts controlling $150 million in Treasury bonds, and Equitable about 6,000 contracts controlling $600 million face value in bonds. That's not very much. Contracts controlling more than $7 billion in bonds change hands on a slow day.

SOURCE: From "Insurers Plan to Use Futures Trades As Tool Against Interest Rate Rises," by Jeff Bailey. Reprinted by permission of the *Wall Street Journal*,

vestment income, and dividends to policyowners. Accountants also prepare state and federal income-tax returns and file an annual convention statement for review by state regulatory officials.

Legal Department

Another important function of insurance companies is the legal function. In many property and liability insurance companies, the legal department is often part of the claims department. The attorneys may serve as defense counsel for the company if claims are litigated. Also, attorneys are involved in subrogation cases, when the insurer attempts to collect from a negligent third party who caused a loss. In life insurance, attorneys are widely used in advanced underwriting and estate planning.

Attorneys are also involved in other legal activities. An insurance policy is a legal contract that must comply with state and federal laws. The legal department must therefore review a new policy before it is marketed to the public. Also, the legal department must draft the legal language and policy provisions that appear in insurance policies. Other activities include legal assistance to actuarial personnel who testify at rate hearings; reviewing advertising and other published materials; providing general legal advice concerning taxation, marketing, investments, and insurance laws; and lobbying for legislation favorable to the insurance industry.

Finally, attorneys must keep abreast of the frequent changes in state and federal laws that affect the company and its policyowners. These include laws on consumerism, cost disclosure, affirmative action programs, truth in advertising, and similar legislation.

Loss Control Department

The loss control department is responsible for helping individuals and firms reduce the frequency and severity of losses. Loss control is an important part of risk management, and a typical property and liability insurer provides numerous loss control services. These services include advice on alarm systems, automatic sprinklers, fire prevention, occupational safety and health, reduction of occupational exposures, prevention of boiler explosions, and other loss prevention activities. In addition, the loss control department can provide valuable advice on the construction of a new building or plant to make it safer and more resistive to damage, which can result in a substantial rate reduction.

SUMMARY

- Rate making refers to the pricing of insurance. Insurance rates are determined by persons called actuaries.
- Underwriting refers to the selection and classification of profitable insureds. There are several important underwriting principles. They are:
  a. Selection of insureds according to the company's underwriting standards.
  b. Proper balance within each rate classification.
  c. Equity among policyowners.
- In determining whether to accept or reject an applicant for insurance, underwriters have several sources of information. They include the application, agent's report, inspection report, physical inspection, physical examination, attending physician's report, and the Medical Information Bureau.
- Production refers to the sales and marketing activities of insurers. Agents who sell insurance are called producers.

- From the insurer's viewpoint, there are several basic objectives in settling claims. They are:
  a. Verification of a covered loss.
  b. Fair and prompt payment of claims.
  c. Personal assistance to the insured.
- The person who adjusts a claim is known as a claims adjustor. The major types of adjustors are:
  a. Agent.
  b. Company adjustor.
  c. Independent adjustor.
  d. Adjustment bureau.
  e. Public adjustor.
- Several steps are involved in settling a claim. They are:
  a. Notice of loss must be given to the company.
  b. The claim is investigated by the company.
  c. A proof of loss must be filed.
  d. A decision is made concerning payment.
- Reinsurance is the shifting of part or all of the insurance originally written by one insurer to another insurer. Reinsurance is used for several reasons. They are:
  a. To increase the company's underwriting capacity.
  b. To stabilize profits.
  c. To reduce the unearned premium reserve.
  d. To provide protection against a catastrophic loss.
- *Facultative reinsurance* means the primary company shops around for reinsurance. The primary company is under no obligation to reinsure, and the reinsurer is under no obligation to accept the insurance. But if the primary company and reinsurer enter into a valid contract, it is known as a facultative treaty. In contrast, under an *automatic* treaty, if the business falls within the scope of the agreement, the primary company must cede insurance to the reinsurer, and the reinsurer must accept.
- The most important types of automatic reinsurance treaties are:
  a. Quota share.
  b. Surplus share.
  c. Excess of loss.
  d. Reinsurance pool.
- Other important insurance company operations include electronic data processing, investments, accounting, legal services, and loss control services. Because of the growth of risk management, loss control services provided by property and liability insurers have become increasingly more important in recent years.

QUESTIONS FOR REVIEW

1. Briefly describe the rate making function.
2. Define underwriting. Explain several important underwriting principles.
3. Describe the sources of information available to underwriters.

4. Explain the meaning of production.
5. What are the objectives in the settlement of claims?
6. Describe the steps in the claim-settlement process.
7. Define reinsurance. Why is reinsurance used?
8. Distinguish between a facultative treaty and an automatic treaty.
9. Describe the following types of automatic treaties:
   a. Quota-share treaty.
   b. Surplus-share treaty.
   c. Excess-of-loss treaty.
   d. Reinsurance pool.
10. Briefly describe the following insurance company operations:
   a. Electronic data processing.
   b. Accounting.
   c. Legal services.
   d. Loss control.

QUESTIONS FOR DISCUSSION

1. *a.* The underwriting function is often misunderstood by the public. Explain the basic objectives of the underwriting function.
   b. How does the underwriting department handle the problem of adverse selection?
2. *a.* If a loss occurs, the claims adjustor must determine if the loss is covered by the policy. Explain the items of coverage that the claims adjustor must check to determine if the loss is covered under the policy.
   b. Explain the difference between a claims adjustor employed by an insurance company and a public adjustor.
3. *a.* Explain the nature and purpose of a special agent.
   b. Describe the various marketing activities of insurance companies.
4. Reinsurance can be used to solve several problems. In each of the following situations, indicate the type of reinsurance plan the primary company should use, and explain the reasons for your answer.
   a. Company A is an established insurer and is primarily interested in protecting the company from a catastrophic loss arising out of a single occurrence.
   b. Company B is a rapidly growing company and desires a plan of reinsurance that will reduce the financial drain on the company's surplus from writing a large amount of new business.
5. Apex Fire enters into a first surplus-line reinsurance treaty with Geneva Re. Apex Fire has a retention limit of $100,000 and four lines of insurance are ceded to Geneva Re. A building is insured with Apex Fire in the amount of $300,000. If a $30,000 loss occurs, how much will the primary company and reinsurer pay? Explain your answer.
6. Explain the major differences between life insurance company investments and property and liability insurance company investments.

KEY CONCEPTS AND TERMS TO KNOW

Rate making
Rating bureau
Deviated rates
Underwriting
Desk underwriter
Class underwriting
Agent's report
Inspection report
Medical Information Bureau report
Producer
Special agent
Chartered Life Underwriter (CLU)
Chartered Property and Casualty Underwriter (CPCU)
Claim adjustor
Company adjustor
Independent adjustor
Adjustment bureau
Public adjustor
Reinsurance
Ceding company
Net retention
Cession
Retrocession
Unearned premium reserve
Facultative reinsurance
Automatic treaty
Quota-share treaty
Surplus-share treaty
Excess-of-loss treaty
Reinsurance pool
Ceding commission

SUGGESTIONS FOR ADDITIONAL READING

Donaldson, James H. *Casualty Claim Practice,* 4th ed. Homewood, IL: Richard D. Irwin, Inc., 1984.

Holton, Robert B. *Underwriting Principles and Practices,* 2nd ed. Cincinnati, OH: The National Underwriter Co., 1982.

Rokes, Willis Parks. *Human Relations in Handling Insurance Claims,* 2nd ed. Homewood, IL: Richard D. Irwin, Inc., 1981.

Webb, Bernard L., J. J. Launie, Willis Park Rokes, and Norman A. Baglini. *Insurance Company Operations,* 3rd ed., Volumes I and II. Malvern, Pennsylvania: American Institute for Property and Liability Underwriters, 1984.

NOTES

1. A detailed discussion of these functions can be found in *Insurance Careers, The Career-Directed Magazine for College Students,* 1980 ed. (Spring/Summer/Fall/Winter 1980).
2. A legal reserve is a liability item on a company's balance sheet that measures the insurer's obligations to its policyowners. State laws require a company to maintain policy reserves at a level that is sufficient to pay all policy obligations as they fall due.
3. In property and liability insurance, a loss reserve is an estimated liability item that represents an amount for claims reported but not yet paid, claims in the process of settlement, and claims that have already occurred but have not been reported. See Chapter 27 for a further discussion of loss reserves.
4. A loss ratio is the ratio of incurred losses to earned premiums. For example, if incurred losses are $70 and earned premiums are $100, the loss ratio is .70, or 70 percent.
5. For additional information on claim settlement, the interested student should consult Bernard L. Webb, J. J. Launie, Willis Park Rokes, and Norman A. Baglini, *Insurance Company Operations,* Volume II (Malvern, Pennsylvania: American Institute for Property and Liability Underwriters, 1978), chapter 12, pp. 277–337.
6. Webb, pp. 288–89.
7. A first-party claim is a claim submitted by the insured to the insurer, such as fire damage to property owned by the insured.

8. Robert I. Mehr and Emerson Cammack, *Principles of Insurance*, 6th ed. (Homewood, Illinois: Richard D. Irwin, Inc., 1976), pp. 558–59.
9. Mehr, p. 684. The unearned premium reserve is discussed in greater detail in Chapter 27.
10. In property and liability insurance, a basic rule is that a company can safely write $2 of new net premiums (written premiums less reinsurance premiums) for each $1 of policyowner's surplus.
11. The list of reinsured policies is known as a *bordereaux*.
12. Insurance Information Institute, *Sharing the Risk* (New York: Insurance Information Institute, 1981), pp. 103–104.
13. American Council of Life Insurance, *1984 Life Insurance Fact Book*, p. 67.
14. *1984 Life Insurance Fact Book*, p. 68.
15. Insurance Information Institute, *Insurance Facts, 1984–85 Property/Casualty Fact Book*, pp. 16–17.
16. *Insurance Facts*, p. 6.

CHAPTER 27

INSURANCE PRICING

"Actuaries hold an insurance company's profits in their hands."

Insurance Careers

STUDENT LEARNING OBJECTIVES

After studying this chapter, you should be able to:

- Explain the major objectives of rate making.
- Describe the basic rate making methods that are used in property and liability insurance, which include:
  - judgment rating
  - class rating
  - merit rating
- Explain how an underwriting profit or loss for a property and liability insurer is determined.
- Explain the basic concepts of rate making that are used in life insurance, which include:
  - net single premium
  - net level premium
  - gross premium
- Describe the various reserves that insurers are required to maintain by law.

Insurance pricing or rate making is one of the most important functions of an insurance company. Actuaries hold the profits of an insurance company in their hand. They must determine the proper price a company should charge for its insurance, the expenses that will be incurred, and whether the company should offer a particular line of insurance. Actuaries must examine vast amounts of statistics and loss data to determine the proper price that should be charged. Actuaries are also involved in the calculation of certain reserves that insurers must maintain by law.

In this chapter, we will study the fundamentals of rate making. We will first discuss the objectives of rate making. We will next examine the major rate making methods that are used in property and liability insurance and in life insurance. We will conclude the chapter by describing the various types of reserves that insurers must maintain by law.

OBJECTIVES OF RATE MAKING

Rate making or insurance pricing has several basic objectives. Since insurance rates—primarily property and liability rates—are regulated by the states, certain statutory or regulatory requirements must be satisfied. Also, due to the overall goal of profitability, certain business objectives must be stressed in rate making. Thus, rate making goals can be classified into two basic categories—regulatory objectives and business objectives.

Regulatory Objectives

The goal of insurance regulation is to protect the public. All states except Illinois have rating laws that require insurance rates to meet certain standards. In general, the rates charged by insurers must be:

- Adequate
- Not excessive
- Not unfairly discriminatory

Adequate rates The first regulatory requirement is that rates must be adequate. *This means the rates charged by insurers should be high enough to pay all losses and expenses.* If rates are inadequate, a company may become insolvent and fail. As a result, policyowners, beneficiaries, and third-party claimants may be financially harmed if their claims are not paid. However, rate adequacy is complicated by the fact that the company does not know its actual costs when the policy is first sold. The premium is paid in advance, but it may not be sufficient to pay all claims and expenses during the policy period. It is only after the period of protection has expired that a company can determine its actual costs.

Not excessive The second regulatory requirement is that the rates must not be excessive. *This means that the rates should not be so high that policyowners are paying more than the actual value of their protection.* Exorbitant prices are not in the public interest.

Not unfairly discriminatory The third regulatory requirement is that the rates must not be unfairly discriminatory. *This means that exposures that are similar with respect to losses and expenses should be charged the same rates, and dissimilar exposures should be charged different rates.* If two significantly different exposures are charged the same rates, this would be considered unfair rate discrimination. For example, in individual life insurance, if a male age twenty and another male age eighty are placed in the same underwriting class and charged the same rate, the younger person would be subsidizing the older person and would be unfairly discriminated against.

We will examine rate regulation and rating laws in greater detail in Chapter 28.

Business Objectives

Insurers are also guided by certain business objectives in designing a rating system. The rating system should also meet the following objectives:[1]

- Simple
- Stable
- Responsive
- Encourage loss prevention

Simple The rating system should be easy to understand. This is necessary so that producers can quote premiums with a minimum of time and expense. This is especially important in the personal lines market, where the relatively small premiums do not justify a large amount of time and expense in the preparation of premium quotations. In addition, commercial insurance purchasers should understand how their premiums are determined so that they can take active steps to reduce their insurance costs.

Stable Rates should be stable over short periods so that consumer satisfaction can be maintained. If rates change rapidly, insurance consumers may become irritated and dissatisfied. They may then look to government to control the rates or to enact a government insurance program.

Responsive The rates should also be responsive over time to changing loss exposures and changing economic conditions. In order to meet the objective of rate adequacy, the rates must increase when loss exposures increase. For example, as a city grows, automobile insurance rates should increase to reflect the greater traffic and increased frequency of automobile accidents. Likewise, the rates should reflect changing economic conditions. Thus, if inflation causes liability awards to increase, liability insurance rates should be increased to reflect this trend.

Encourage loss prevention The rating system should also encourage loss prevention activities that reduce both loss frequency and severity. This is important since loss prevention tends to keep insurance affordable. Profits are also stabilized. As you will see later, certain rating systems provide a strong financial incentive to the insured to engage in loss prevention.

BASIC DEFINITIONS

Before we proceed, you should be familiar with some basic terms that are widely used in rate making. A **rate** is the price per unit of insurance. An **exposure unit** is the unit of measurement used in insurance pricing. It varies by line of insurance. For example, in fire insurance, the exposure unit is $100 of coverage; in workers' compensation insurance, it is $100 of payroll; in products liability insurance, it is $1,000 of sales; and in automobile collision insurance, it is one car-year, which is one car insured for a year.

The **pure premium** refers to that portion of the rate needed to pay losses and loss-adjustment expenses. **Loading** refers to the amount that must be added to the pure premium for expenses, profit, and a margin for contingencies. Thus, the **gross rate** consists of the pure premium and a loading element. Finally, the **gross premium** paid by the insured consists of the gross rate multiplied by the number of exposure units. Thus, if the gross rate for fire insurance is 10 cents per $100 of fire insurance, the gross premium for a $500,000 building would be $500.

RATE MAKING IN PROPERTY AND LIABILITY INSURANCE

There are three basic rate making methods in property and liability insurance—judgment, class, and merit rating. Merit rating in turn can be broken down into schedule rating, experience rating, and retrospective rating. Thus, the basic rating methods can be conveniently classified as follows:[2]

- Judgment rating
- Class rating

- ▶ Merit rating
  - Schedule rating
  - Experience rating
  - Retrospective rating

Judgment Rating

***Judgment rating** means that each exposure is individually evaluated, and the rate is determined largely by the underwriter's judgment.* This method is used when the loss exposures are so diverse that a class rate cannot be calculated, or when credible loss statistics are not available. For example, when the astronauts made their first flight to the moon, they were covered by life insurance. However, since loss data on deaths in outer space were not available, the premiums charged were judgment rated.

Judgment rating is widely used in ocean marine insurance and in some lines of inland marine insurance. Since the various ocean-going vessels, ports of destination, cargoes carried, and dangerous waters are so diverse, ocean marine rates are determined largely by judgment.

Class Rating

The second type of rating method is class rating. Most rates used today are class rates. ***Class rating** means exposures with similar characteristics are placed in the same underwriting class, and each is charged the same rate.* The rate charged reflects the *average loss experience* for the class as a whole. Class rating is based on the assumption that future losses to insureds will be determined largely by the same set of factors. For example, the major classification factors in life insurance are age, sex, and health. Accordingly, healthy persons who are the same age and sex are placed in the same underwriting class and charged the same rate for life insurance.

The major advantage of class rating is that it is simple to apply. Also, premium quotations can be quickly obtained. As such, it is ideal for the personal lines market.

Class rating is often called **manual rating,** since the various rates are published in a rating manual. Class rating is widely used in fire and homeowners insurance, private passenger automobile insurance, workers' compensation, and life and health insurance.

There are two basic methods for determining class rates. They are the pure premium and loss ratio methods. Let us briefly examine each of these methods.

1. *Pure premium method.* We noted earlier that the pure premium is that portion of the gross rate needed to pay losses and loss-adjustment expenses. *The pure premium can be determined by dividing the dollar amount of incurred losses and loss-adjustment expenses by the number of exposure units.* Incurred losses include all losses paid during the accounting period, plus amounts held as reserves for the future payment of losses that have already occurred during the same period. Thus, incurred losses include all losses that occur during the accounting period whether or not they have been paid by the end of the period. Loss-adjustment expenses are the expenses incurred by the company in adjusting losses during the same accounting period.

To illustrate how a pure premium can be derived, assume that in automobile collision insurance, 500,000 automobiles in a given underwriting class generate incurred losses and loss-adjustment expenses of $30 million over a one-year period. The pure premium is $60. This can be illustrated by the following:

$$\text{Pure premium} = \frac{\text{Incurred losses and loss-adjustment expenses}}{\text{Number of exposure units}}$$
$$= \frac{\$30{,}000{,}000}{500{,}000}$$
$$= \$60$$

The final step is to add a loading for expenses, underwriting profit, and a margin for contingencies. Typical expenses include commissions, initial underwriting expenses, overhead expenses, and premium taxes. The expense loading is usually expressed as a percentage of the gross rate and is called the expense ratio. *The **expense ratio** is that proportion of the gross rate available for expenses and profit.* The final gross rate can be determined by dividing the pure premium by one minus the expense ratio.[3] For example, if we assume that expenses are 40 percent of the gross rate, the final gross rate is $100.00. This can be illustrated by the following:

$$\text{Gross rate} = \frac{\text{Pure premium}}{1 - \text{Expense ratio}}$$
$$= \frac{\$60}{1 - .40}$$
$$= \$100.00$$

2. *Loss ratio method.* Under the **loss ratio** method, the actual loss ratio is compared with the expected loss ratio, and the rate is adjusted accordingly. *The actual loss ratio is the ratio of incurred losses and loss-adjustment expenses to **earned premiums**.*[4] *The expected loss ratio is the percentage of the premiums that is expected to be used to pay losses.* For example, assume that a line of insurance has incurred losses and loss-adjustment expenses in the amount of $800,000, and earned premiums are $1 million. The actual loss ratio is .80, or 80 percent. If the expected loss ratio is .70 or 70 percent, the rate must be increased 14.3 percent. This can be illustrated by the following:

$$\text{Rate change} = \frac{A - E}{E}$$

$$\text{Where } A = \text{Actual loss ratio}$$
$$E = \text{Expected loss ratio}$$

$$= \frac{.80 - .70}{.70}$$
$$= .143 \text{ or } 14.3\%$$

Merit Rating

The third principal type of rating method is merit rating. ***Merit rating** is a rating plan by which class rates (manual rates) are adjusted upward or downward based on individual loss experience.* Merit rating is based on the assumption that the loss experience of a particular insured will differ substantially from the loss experience of other insureds. Thus, class rates are modified upward or downward depending on individual loss experience.

As we noted earlier, there are several different types of merit rating plans. They are:

- Schedule rating
- Experience rating
- Retrospective rating

Schedule rating

*Under a **schedule rating** plan, each exposure is individually rated. A basis rate is determined for each exposure, which is then modified by debits or credits for undesirable or desirable physical features.* Schedule rating is based on the assumption that certain physical characteristics of the insured's operations will influence the insured's future loss experience. Thus, the physical characteristics of the exposure to be insured are extremely important in schedule rating.

Schedule rating is widely used in commercial fire insurance for large industrial plants, large commercial office buildings and apartment houses, and similar structures. Each building is individually rated based on the following factors:

- Construction
- Occupancy
- Protection
- Exposure
- Maintenance

Construction refers to the physical characteristics of the building. A building may be constructed with frame, brick, fire-resistive, or fire-proof materials. A frame building is charged a higher rate than a brick or fire-resistive building. Also, tall buildings and buildings with large open areas may receive debits because of the greater difficulty of putting out or containing a fire.

Occupancy refers to use of the building. The

probability of a fire is greatly influenced by its use. For example, open flame and sparks from torches and welding can quickly cause a fire. Also, if highly combustible materials or chemicals are stored in the building, the fire will be more difficult to contain.

Protection refers to the quality of the city's water supply and fire department. It also includes protective devices installed in the insured building. The Insurance Services Office (ISO) has prepared a *Grading Schedule for Municipal Fire Protection* that grades cities and towns from one to ten based on their water supply and quality of fire-fighting facilities. The higher the grade, the poorer is the protection. Schedule rating also considers private protection devices. Rate credits are given for a fire alarm system, security guard, automatic sprinkler system, fire extinguishers, and similar protective devices.

Exposure refers to the possibility that the insured building will be damaged or destroyed from a fire that starts in an adjacent building and spreads to the insured building. The greater the exposure from surrounding buildings, the greater are the charges applied.

Finally, *maintenance* refers to the housekeeping and overall maintenance of the building. Debits are applied for poor housekeeping and maintenance. Thus, debits may be given if flammable materials such as oily rags are scattered about.

Schedule rating has the principal advantage of identifying and charging for those physical characteristics of a building that can contribute to a loss. As such, the premium charged should reflect more accurately the insured's loss exposure. Schedule rating also encourages loss prevention, since credits are given for protective devices, such as an automatic sprinkler system.

Schedule rating, however, has several disadvantages. First, higher administrative expenses are incurred, since each building must be individually rated. Second, schedule rating may be improperly used if unjustified rate credits are granted because of competition from other insurers. Finally, schedule rating is not effective when human factors are more important in causing losses than physical factors, such as in workers' compensation insurance.

Experience rating Experience rating is another form of merit rating. *Under an **experience rating** plan, the class or manual rate is adjusted upward or downward based on past loss experience.* The most distinctive characteristic of experience rating is that *the insured's past loss experience is used to determine the premium for the next policy period.* The loss experience over the past three years is typically used to determine the premium for the next policy year. If the insured's loss experience is better than the average for the class as a whole, the class rate is reduced. If the loss experience is worse than the class average, the rate is increased. In determining the magnitude of the rate change, the actual loss experience is modified by a *credibility factor*[5] based on the volume of experience.

For example, let us assume that a retail firm has a general liability insurance policy that is experience rated. Annual premiums are $30,000, and the expected loss ratio is 30 percent. If the actual loss ratio over the past three years is 20 percent, and the credibility factor (C) is .29, the firm will receive a premium reduction of 14.5 percent. This can be illustrated by the following:

$$\text{Premium change} = \frac{A - E}{E} \times C$$

$$= \frac{.20 - .30 \times .29}{.20}$$

$$= -14.5\%$$

Thus, the new premium for the next policy period is $25,650. As you can see, experience rating provides a financial incentive to reduce losses, since premiums can be reduced by favorable loss experience.

Experience rating generally is limited only to larger firms that generate a sufficiently high volume of premiums and more credible experience. Smaller firms are normally ineligible for experience rating. This rating system is frequently used in general liability insurance, workers' compensation, commercial automobile liability insurance, and group health insurance.

Retrospective rating The final form of merit rating is retrospective rating. *Under a **retrospective rating** plan, the insured's loss experience during the current policy period determines the actual premium paid for that period.* Under this rating plan, the insured is charged a minimum and a maximum premium. If actual losses during the current policy period are small, the minimum premium is paid. If losses are large, the maximum premium is paid. The actual premium paid generally will fall somewhere between the minimum and maximum premium, depending on the insured's loss experience during the current policy period. Retrospective rating is widely used in workers' compensation insurance, general liability insurance, automobile liability and physical damage insurance, and burglary and glass insurance.

RATE MAKING IN LIFE INSURANCE

Our discussion of rate making so far has applied largely to property and liability insurance. In this section, we will briefly examine the fundamentals of life insurance rate making. The following concepts will be discussed:[6]

- Net single premium
- Net level premium
- Gross premium

Net Single Premium

Life insurance policies can be purchased with a single premium, or by the payment of annual, semiannual, quarterly, or monthly premiums. Although relatively few policies are purchased with a single premium, the NSP forms the foundation for the calculation of all life insurance premiums.

*The **net single premium** can be defined as the present value of the future death benefit.* It is that sum which, together with compound interest, will be sufficient to pay all death claims. In calculating the NSP, only mortality and investment income are considered. Insurance company expenses or the loading element are considered later, when the gross premium is calculated.

The NSP is based on three basic assumptions: (1) premiums are paid at the beginning of the policy year, (2) death claims are paid at the end of the policy year, and (3) the death rate is uniform throughout the year.

Certain assumptions must also be made concerning the probability of death at each attained age. Although life insurers generally develop their own mortality data, we will use the 1958 Commissioners Standard Ordinary Mortality Table in our illustrations. (See Figure 27.1.)

Also, since we are assuming that premiums are paid in advance, and that death claims are paid at the end of the policy year, the amount needed to pay death benefits can be discounted for compound interest. Life insurers generally assume interest rates ranging from 2.5 percent to 4 percent or more in their premium calculations. We will assume that the amounts needed for death claims can be discounted annually at 2.5 percent compound interest.

Term insurance The NSP for term insurance can be easily calculated. The period of protection is only for a specified period or to a stated age. The face amount is paid if the insured dies within the specified period, but nothing is paid if he or she does not die within the period.

Let us first consider the NSP for *yearly renewable term insurance*. Assume that a $1,000 yearly renewable term insurance policy is issued to a person, age thirty-five. *The cost of each year's insurance is determined by multiplying the probability of death by the amount of insurance multiplied by the present value of $1 for the time period the funds are held.* By referring to the 1958 C.S.O. Mortality Table in Figure 27.1, we see that out of 10 million persons alive at age zero, 9,373,807 million are still alive at the beginning of age thirty-five. Of this number, 23,528 persons will die during the year. Therefore, the probability that a person age thirty-five will die

Figure 27.1
Commissioners 1958 Standard Ordinary Mortality Table

Age	No. living at beginning of designated year	No. dying during designated year	Age	No. living at beginning of designated year	No. dying during designated year
0	10,000,000	70,800	50	8,762,306	72,902
1	9,929,200	17,475	51	8,689,404	79,160
2	9,911,725	15,066	52	8,610,244	85,758
3	9,896,659	14,449	53	8,524,486	92,832
4	9,882,210	13,835	54	8,431,654	100,337
5	9,868,375	13,322	55	8,331,317	108,307
6	9,855,053	12,812	56	8,223,010	116,849
7	9,842,241	12,401	57	8,106,161	125,970
8	9,829,840	12,091	58	7,980,191	135,663
9	9,817,749	11,879	59	7,844,528	145,830
10	9,805,870	11,865	60	7,698,698	156,592
11	9,794,005	12,047	61	7,542,106	167,736
12	9,781,958	12,325	62	7,374,370	179,271
13	9,769,633	12,896	63	7,195,099	191,174
14	9,756,737	13,562	64	7,003,925	203,394
15	9,743,175	14,225	65	6,800,531	215,917
16	9,728,950	14,983	66	6,584,614	228,749
17	9,713,967	15,737	67	6,355,865	241,777
18	9,698,230	16,390	68	6,114,088	254,835
19	9,681,840	16,846	69	5,859,253	267,241
20	9,664,994	17,300	70	5,592,012	278,426
21	9,647,694	17,655	71	5,313,586	287,731
22	9,630,039	17,912	72	5,025,855	294,766
23	9,612,127	18,167	73	4,731,089	299,289
24	9,593,960	18,324	74	4,431,800	301,894
25	9,575,636	18,481	75	4,129,906	303,011
26	9,557,155	18,732	76	3,826,895	303,014
27	9,538,423	18,981	77	3,523,881	301,997
28	9,519,442	19,324	78	3,221,884	299,829
29	9,500,118	19,760	79	2,922,055	295,683
30	9,480,358	20,193	80	2,626,372	288,848
31	9,460,165	20,718	81	2,337,524	278,983
32	9,439,447	21,239	82	2,058,541	265,902
33	9,418,208	21,850	83	1,792,639	249,858
34	9,396,358	22,551	84	1,542,781	231,433
35	9,373,807	23,528	85	1,311,348	211,311
36	9,350,279	24,685	86	1,100,037	190,108
37	9,325,594	26,112	87	909,929	168,455
38	9,299,482	27,991	88	741,474	146,997
39	9,271,491	30,132	89	594,477	126,303
40	9,241,359	32,622	90	468,174	106,809
41	9,208,737	35,362	91	361,365	88,813
42	9,173,375	38,253	92	272,552	72,480
43	9,135,122	41,382	93	200,072	57,881
44	9,093,740	44,741	94	142,191	45,026
45	9,048,999	48,412	95	97,165	34,128
46	9,000,587	52,473	96	63,037	25,250
47	8,948,114	56,910	97	37,787	18,456
48	8,891,204	61,794	98	19,331	12,916
49	8,829,410	67,104	99	6415	6415

Source: The American College.

during the year is 23,528/9,373,807. This fraction is then multiplied by $1,000 to determine the amount of money the insurer must have on hand from each policyowner at the end of the year to pay death claims. However, since premiums are paid in advance, and death claims are paid at the end of the year, the amount needed can be discounted for one year of interest. From Figure 27.2, we see that the present value of $1 at 2.5 percent interest is .975610. Thus, if the probability of death at age thirty-five is multiplied by $1,000, and this sum is discounted for one year's interest, the resulting net single premium is $2.45. This calculation is summarized as follows:

Age 35

$$\frac{23{,}528}{9{,}373{,}807} \times \$1{,}000 \times .97561 = \$2.45 \text{ (NSP)}$$

If $2.45 is collected in advance from each of the 9,373,807 persons who are alive at age thirty-five, this amount together with compound interest will be sufficient to pay all death claims.

If the policy is renewed for another year, the NSP at age thirty-six would be calculated as follows:

Age 36

$$\frac{24{,}685}{9{,}350{,}279} \times \$1{,}000 \times .97561 = \$2.58 \text{ (NSP)}$$

The NSP for a yearly renewable term insurance policy issued at age thirty-six is $2.58. Premiums for subsequent years are calculated in the same manner.

Let us next consider the NSP for a *five-year term insurance policy* in the amount of $1,000 issued to a person age thirty-five. In this case, the company must pay the death claim if the insured dies any time within the five-year period. However, any death claims are paid at the end of the year in which they occur, not at the end of the five-year period. Consequently, the cost of each year's mortality must be computed separately and then added together to determine the net single premium.

The cost of insurance for the first year is determined exactly as before, when we calculated the net single premium for yearly renewable term insurance. Thus, we have the following equation:

Age 35

$$\frac{23{,}528}{9{,}373{,}807} \times \$1{,}000 \times .97651 = \$2.45$$

(cost of insurance
for the first year)

The next step is to determine the cost of insurance for the second year. Referring back to Figure 27.1, we see that at age thirty-six, 24,685 people will die during the year. Thus, for the 9,373,807 persons who are alive at age thirty-five, the probability of dying during age thirty-six is 24,685/9,373,807. Note that the denominator does not change but remains the same for each probability fraction. Since the amount needed to pay second-year death claims will not be needed for two years, it can be discounted for two years at 2.5 percent interest. Thus, for the second year, we have the following calculation:

Age 36

$$\frac{24{,}685}{9{,}373{,}807} \times \$1{,}000 \times .951814 = \$2.51$$

(cost of insurance
for the second year)

For each of the remaining three years, we follow the same procedure. (See Figure 27.3.) If the insurer collects $13.09 in a single premium from each of the 9,373,807 persons who are alive at age thirty-five that sum together with compound interest will be sufficient to pay all death claims during the five-year period.

Ordinary life insurance In calculating the NSP for an ordinary life policy, the same method

Figure 27.2
Present Value of $1 at Various Rates of Compound Interest Due

End of year	2 percent	2½ percent	3 percent	End of year	2 percent	2½ percent	3 percent
1	0.980392	0.975610	0.970874	51	0.364243	0.283846	0.221463
2	0.961169	0.951814	0.942596	52	0.357101	0.276923	0.215013
3	0.942322	0.928599	0.915142	53	0.350099	0.270169	0.208750
4	0.923845	0.905951	0.888487	54	0.343234	0.263579	0.202670
5	0.905731	0.883854	0.862609	55	0.336504	0.257151	0.196767
6	0.887971	0.862297	0.837484	56	0.329906	0.250879	0.191036
7	0.870560	0.841265	0.813092	57	0.323437	0.244760	0.185472
8	0.853490	0.820747	0.789409	58	0.317095	0.238790	0.180070
9	0.836755	0.800728	0.766417	59	0.310878	0.232966	0.174825
10	0.820348	0.781198	0.744094	60	0.304782	0.227284	0.169733
11	0.804263	0.762145	0.722421	61	0.298806	0.221740	0.164789
12	0.788493	0.743556	0.701380	62	0.292947	0.216332	0.159990
13	0.773033	0.725420	0.680951	63	0.287203	0.211055	0.155330
14	0.757875	0.707727	0.661118	64	0.281572	0.205908	0.150806
15	0.743015	0.690466	0.641862	65	0.276051	0.200886	0.146413
16	0.728446	0.673625	0.623167	66	0.270638	0.195986	0.142149
17	0.714163	0.657195	0.605016	67	0.265331	0.191206	0.138009
18	0.700159	0.641166	0.587395	68	0.260129	0.186542	0.133989
19	0.686431	0.625528	0.570286	69	0.255028	0.181992	0.130086
20	0.672971	0.610271	0.553676	70	0.250028	0.177554	0.126297
21	0.659776	0.595386	0.537549	71	0.245125	0.173223	0.122619
22	0.646839	0.580865	0.521893	72	0.240319	0.168998	0.119047
23	0.634156	0.566697	0.506692	73	0.235607	0.164876	0.115580
24	0.621721	0.552875	0.491934	74	0.230987	0.160855	0.112214
25	0.609531	0.539391	0.477606	75	0.226458	0.156931	0.108945
26	0.597579	0.526235	0.463693	76	0.222017	0.153104	0.105772
27	0.585862	0.513400	0.450189	77	0.217664	0.149370	0.102691
28	0.574375	0.500878	0.437077	78	0.213396	0.145726	0.099700
29	0.563112	0.488661	0.424346	79	0.209212	0.142172	0.096796
30	0.552071	0.476743	0.411987	80	0.205110	0.138705	0.093977
31	0.541246	0.465115	0.399987	81	0.201088	0.135322	0.091240
32	0.530633	0.453771	0.388337	82	0.197145	0.132021	0.088528
33	0.520229	0.442703	0.377026	83	0.193279	0.128801	0.086002
34	0.510028	0.431905	0.366045	84	0.189490	0.125659	0.083497
35	0.500028	0.421371	0.355383	85	0.185774	0.122595	0.081065
36	0.490223	0.411094	0.345032	86	0.182132	0.119605	0.078704
37	0.480611	0.401067	0.334983	87	0.178560	0.116687	0.076412
38	0.471187	0.391285	0.325226	88	0.175059	0.113841	0.074186
39	0.461948	0.381741	0.315754	89	0.171627	0.111065	0.072026
40	0.452890	0.372431	0.306557	90	0.168261	0.108356	0.069928
41	0.444010	0.363347	0.297628	91	0.164962	0.105713	0.067891
42	0.435304	0.354485	0.288959	92	0.161728	0.103135	0.065914
43	0.426769	0.345839	0.280543	93	0.158556	0.100619	0.063994
44	0.418401	0.337404	0.272372	94	0.155448	0.098165	0.062130
45	0.410197	0.329174	0.264439	95	0.152400	0.095771	0.060320
46	0.402154	0.321146	0.256737	96	0.149411	0.093435	0.058563
47	0.394268	0.313313	0.249259	97	0.146482	0.091156	0.056858
48	0.386538	0.305671	0.241999	98	0.143610	0.088933	0.055202
49	0.378958	0.298216	0.234950	99	0.140794	0.086764	0.053594
50	0.371528	0.290942	0.228107	100	0.138033	0.084647	0.052033

Source: The American College.

Figure 27.3
Figuring the NSP for a Five-year Term Insurance Policy

Age	Probability of death		Amount of insurance		Present value of $1 at 2.5 percent		Cost of insurance
35	$\frac{23{,}528}{9{,}373{,}807}$	×	$1,000	×	.975610	=	$2.45 (year 1)
36	$\frac{24{,}685}{9{,}373{,}807}$	×	$1,000	×	.951814	=	$2.51 (year 2)
37	$\frac{26{,}112}{9{,}373{,}807}$	×	$1,000	×	.928599	=	$2.59 (year 3)
38	$\frac{27{,}991}{9{,}373{,}807}$	×	$1,000	×	.905951	=	$2.70 (year 4)
39	$\frac{30{,}132}{9{,}373{,}807}$	×	$1,000	×	.883854	=	$2.84 (year 5)
					NSP	=	$13.09

described earlier for the five-year term policy is used except that the calculations are carried out to the end of the mortality table (age 99). Thus, in our illustration, the NSP for a $1,000 ordinary life insurance policy issued at age thirty-five would be $420.13.

Net Level Premium

Most life insurance policies are not purchased with a single premium because of the large amount of cash that is required. Consumers generally prefer to pay for their insurance in installment payments, since this is a more convenient method of payment. If premiums are paid annually, the net single premium must be converted into a **net annual level premium (NALP)**, which must be the mathematical equivalent of the net single premium. The net annual level premium cannot be determined by simply dividing the net single premium by the number of years over which the premiums are to be paid. Such a division would produce an insufficient premium. This is true for two reasons. First, the net single premium is based on the assumption that the entire premium is paid in advance at the beginning of the period. If premiums are paid in installments, and some persons die prematurely, the company would suffer the loss of future premiums.

Second, installment payments result in the loss of interest income because of the smaller amounts that are invested. Thus, the mathematical adjustment for the loss of premiums and interest is accomplished by dividing the net single premium by the present value of an appropriate life annuity due of $1. To be more precise, *the net annual level premium is determined by dividing the net single premium by the present value of a life annuity due of $1 for the premium-paying period.* Thus, we obtain the following:

$$\text{NALP} = \frac{\text{NSP}}{\text{PVLAD of \$1 for the premium-paying period}}$$

The concept of a life annuity due requires a brief explanation. The annual premium payments can be viewed as being similar to a life annuity, except that the payments flow from the insured to the insurer. Both life annuity payments and premium payments are similar in that both are paid during the lifetime of a specified individual, or for a stated period of time. Both cease upon death (unless the annuity has a refund feature), and both are discounted for compound interest. The major exception is that the first premium is due immediately (since premiums are paid in advance), while the first annuity payment is due one payment interval from the date of purchase.[7] Thus, the annual premium payments are the equivalent of a regular life annuity plus one payment that is made immediately. However, in order to distinguish the premium payments from the annuity payments, we refer to the series of premium payments as a *life annuity due.* If the annual level premiums are to be paid for life—such as in an ordinary life policy—the premium is called a **whole life annuity due.** If the annual premiums are to be paid for only a temporary period—such as in the case of term insurance or limited payment policies—the premium is called a **temporary life annuity due.**[8]

Term insurance Let us first consider the net annual level premium for a five-year term insurance policy in the amount of $1,000 issued at age thirty-five. We noted earlier that the net single premium for a five-year term insurance policy at age thirty-five is $13.09. This sum must be divided by the present value of a five-year *temporary life annuity due of $1.* For the first year, a $1 payment is due immediately. For the second year, we must determine the probability that a person age thirty-five will still be *alive* at age thirty-six to make the second payment of $1. Referring to Figure 27.1, we see that 9,373,807 persons are alive at age thirty-five. Of this number, 9,350,279 are still alive at age thirty-six. Thus, the probability of survival is 9,350,279 (number alive at age 36)/9,373,807 (number alive at age 35). This fraction is multiplied by $1, and the resulting sum is then discounted for one year's interest. Thus, the present value of the second payment is $0.97. Similar calculations are performed for the remaining three years. The various calculations are summarized as follows:

Age 35 $1 due immediately = $1.00

$$\text{Age 36} \frac{9{,}350{,}279}{9{,}373{,}807} \times \$1 \times .975610 = 0.973161$$

$$\text{Age 37} \frac{9{,}325{,}594}{9{,}373{,}807} \times \$1 \times .951814 = 0.946918$$

$$\text{Age 38} \frac{9{,}299{,}482}{9{,}373{,}807} \times \$1 \times .928599 = 0.921236$$

$$\text{Age 39} \frac{9{,}271{,}491}{9{,}373{,}807} \times \$1 \times .905951 = 0.896062$$

PVLAD of $1 = $4.737

The present value of a five-year temporary life annuity due of $1 at age thirty-five is $4.74. If the net single premium of $13.09 is divided by $4.74, the net annual level premium is $2.76.

$$\text{NALP} = \frac{\text{NSP}}{\text{PVLAD of \$1}} = \frac{\$13.09}{\$\ 4.74} = \$2.76$$

Ordinary life insurance The net annual level premium for a $1,000 ordinary life insurance policy issued at age thirty-five is calculated in a similar manner. The same procedure is used except that the calculations are extended to the end of the mortality table. Thus, we must calculate the present value of a *whole life annuity due of $1* for ages thirty-five through ninety-nine. If the calculations are performed, the present value of a whole life annuity due of $1 at age thirty-five is $23.77. The net single premium ($420.13) is then divided by the present value of a whole life annuity due of $1 at age thirty-five ($23.77), and the net annual level premium is $17.67.

Gross Premium

The gross premium is determined by adding a loading allowance to the net level premium. The loading must cover all operating expenses, provide a margin for contingencies, and in the case of stock life insurers, provide for a contribution to profits. If the policy is a participating policy, the loading must also reflect a margin for dividends.

Three major types of expenses are reflected in the loading allowance. They are:[9] (1) production expenses, (2) distribution expenses, and (3) maintenance expenses. Production expenses are the expenses incurred before the agent delivers the policy, such as policy printing costs, underwriting expenses, and the cost of the medical examination. Distribution expenses are largely selling expenses, such as the first-year commission, advertising, and agency allowances. Maintenance expenses are the expenses incurred after the policy is issued, such as renewal commissions, costs of collecting renewal premiums, and state premium taxes.

RESERVES IN PROPERTY AND LIABILITY INSURANCE

The remainder of this chapter will focus largely on the various financial reserves of insurance companies. The companies are required by law to maintain minimum reserves on their balance sheets. Since premiums are paid in advance, but the period of protection extends into the future, insurers must establish certain reserves to assure that the premiums collected in advance will be available to pay future losses.

Property and liability insurers are required to maintain two principal types of financial reserves. They are:

- Unearned premium reserve
- Loss reserves

Unearned Premium Reserve

The unearned premium reserve is the principal liability item on the company's balance sheet. As we noted in Chapter 26, *the **unearned premium reserve** is a liability reserve that represents the unearned portion of gross premiums on all outstanding policies at the time of valuation.* An insurer is required by law to place the entire gross premium in the unearned premium reserve when the policy is first written, and renewal premiums must be placed in the same reserve. In effect, the unearned premium reserve reflects the fact that premiums are paid in advance, but the period of protection has not expired. As time goes on, part of the gross premium is considered earned, while the remainder is unearned. It is only after a period of protection has expired that the gross premium is fully earned.

Reasons for the unearned premium reserve *The fundamental purpose of the unearned premium reserve is to pay for losses that occur during the policy period.* As we mentioned earlier, premiums are paid in advance, but the period of protection extends into the future. To assure policyowners that future losses will be paid, the unearned premium reserve is required.

The unearned premium reserve is also needed so that premium refunds can be paid to the policyowners in the event of cancellation. If the insurer cancels, a full pro rata premium refund based on the unexpired portion of the policy term must be paid to the policyowner. If the policyowner cancels, a premium refund based on the short-rate table is paid. In any event, the unearned premium reserve must be adequate so that premium refunds can be made in the event of cancellation.

Also, if the business is reinsured, the unearned premium reserve serves as the basis for determining the amount that must be paid to the reinsurer for carrying the reinsured policies to the end of their terms. In practice, however, the amount paid to the reinsurer may be considerably less than the unearned premium reserve, since the reinsurer does not incur heavy first-year acquisition expenses in acquiring the reinsured policies.

Methods of calculation Several methods can be used to calculate the earned premium reserve. Only one of them is described here.[10] Under the **annual pro rata method,** it is assumed that the policies are written uniformly throughout the year. For purposes of determining the unearned premium reserve, it is assumed that all policies are issued on 1 July, which is the average issue date. Therefore, on 31 December, the unearned premium reserve for all one-year policies is one-half of the premium income attributable to these policies. For two-year policies, the unearned premium reserve is three-fourths of the premium income, and for three-year policies, it is five-sixths of the premium income.

Equity in unearned premium reserve We noted earlier that the law requires an insurer to place the entire gross premium in the unearned premium reserve. This results in a redundant or excessive reserve, since most of the expenses incurred in writing the business are incurred when the policy is first written. Relatively little expense is incurred after the policy is issued. When the policy is first written, the company incurs relatively heavy expenses due to agents' commissions, state premium taxes, underwriting expenses, costs of issuing the policy, and other expenses. However, because of emphasis on insurer solvency, the law prohibits an insurer from taking credit in advance for these prepaid expenses. Although the premium is being earned gradually over the policy period, the initial acquisition and underwriting expenses cannot be amortized over the same period. Instead, they are treated as a cash expense, to be charged off immediately. Therefore, since the unearned premium reserve must be established on the basis of a gross premium rather than net premium, it is substantially overstated. *This overstatement or redundancy in the unearned premium reserve is called the* ***equity in the unearned premium reserve.*** Authorities estimate that the unearned premium reserve may be overstated by 20 to 40 percent, with 35 percent being a typical or average estimate of the equity in this reserve.

Effect on underwriting profit or loss The equity in the unearned premium reserve is extremely important in determining the true underwriting profit or loss of a property-liability insurer. For example, let us assume that a new fire insurance company begins operating on January 1. It plans to sell only one-year fire insurance policies. In establishing the rates, the company has an expected loss ratio of 60 percent, an expected expense ratio of 35 percent, and expects to earn an underwriting profit of 5 percent.[11] We will also assume that the business is written uniformly throughout the year, and the annual pro rata method is used to determine the unearned premium reserve. During the year, $10 million of fire insurance premiums are written. Losses incurred and loss adjustment expenses incurred total $3 million, and expenses incurred are $3.5 million.[12] On December 31, what is the company's underwriting profit or loss? The law requires the company to usc a *statutory underwriting formula* to determine its underwriting results. Investment gains or losses are not considered in the formula. The statutory formula is as follows:

$$\text{Statutory underwriting profit or loss} = \begin{matrix}\text{Earned}\\\text{premiums}\end{matrix} - \begin{matrix}\text{Losses incurred and}\\\text{loss adjustment}\\\text{expenses incurred}\end{matrix} - \begin{matrix}\text{Expenses}\\\text{incurred}\end{matrix}$$

In our illustration, the company has a statutory underwriting loss of $1.5 million. This can be illustrated as follows:

($000 omitted)

Premiums written		$10,000
Deduct unearned premiums		5,000
Earned premiums		$5,000
Losses incurred	$3,000	
Expenses incurred	$3,500	
Total losses and expenses		$6,500
Statutory underwriting loss		($1,500)

Although the company's actual loss and expense experience conforms exactly to the experience anticipated in the rating structure, it has a statutory underwriting loss rather than a 5 percent underwriting profit. This is due to the statutory method for determining a profit or loss. As we noted earlier, the first-year acquisition expenses cannot be amortized over the policy term but must be immediately written off as a cash expense. In our example, this produces a statutory underwriting loss.

The statutory underwriting loss of $1.5 million is a charge against the company's surplus. Thus, a rapidly growing company will experience a surplus drain because of a continuous increase in the unearned premium reserve. The opposite is true for a company whose premium volume is declining. The company will have a gain in its surplus account as the business runs off the books. The equity in the unearned premium reserve will flow into the company's surplus with the passage of time as the policy terms run off. Thus, to correct for the distortion that may result from the statutory formula, an **adjusted underwriting profit or loss** (called a trade profit or loss) is often used by financial analysts to determine the true underwriting results.

One method for determining the company's adjusted underwriting profit or loss is to *consider the equity in the unearned premium reserve.* The increased equity in the unearned premium reserve can be added to the statutory profit or loss to determine the adjusted underwriting profit or loss. In our earlier illustration, the company experienced an increase of $5 million in the unearned premium reserve. If we assume an estimated equity of 35 percent of the *increase* in the unearned premium reserve, the company has an adjusted underwriting profit rather than a loss. This can be illustrated as follows:

($000 omitted)

Statutory underwriting loss	$1,500
Equity in the unearned premium reserve	1,750
Adjusted underwriting profit	250

After adjusting the statutory formula for the equity in the unearned premium reserve, the company has an adjusted underwriting profit of $250,000, which is exactly 5 percent of earned premiums.

Loss Reserves

The loss reserve is another important liability reserve for property-liability insurers. A loss reserve is the estimated cost of settling claims that have already occurred but have not been paid as of the valuation date. *More specifically, the **loss reserve** is an estimated amount for (1) claims reported and adjusted but not yet paid, (2) claims reported and filed but not yet adjusted, and (3) claims incurred but not yet reported to the company.* The loss reserve is especially important to casualty insurers because bodily injury and property damage liability lawsuits may take a long time to settle—often several years. In contrast, fire insurance claims, automobile collision and comprehensive losses, and other property insurance claims are settled more quickly; hence loss reserves are relatively smaller for property insurers.

There are four principal methods for estimating the size of the loss reserve.[13] They are:

- Individual estimate method
- Average value method
- Loss ratio method
- Tabular value method

Under the individual estimate method, a loss reserve is established for each claim. This method is used when a number of claims in a particular line of insurance is too small, or when the variation in claims is too large, to assign an average value to each claim.

Under the average value method, an average value is assigned to each claim. This method is used when the number of claims is large, the average amount of each claim is relatively small, and the claims are quickly settled. For example, loss reserves for automobile physical damage claims are often based on this method.

Under the loss ratio method, a statutory formula based on the expected loss ratio is used to

INSIGHT 27.1

How Profitable is the Property and Liability Insurance Industry?

Because of keen competition, the profits in the property and liability insurance industry have been below the average of all U.S. industries in recent years. However, in some years, the property and liability industry has outperformed other industries, including those that are financially oriented.

One measure of profitability is the annual rate of return (net income from all sources after taxes) on net worth. The following table is based on data compiled by Citibank of New York and compares the average annual rates of return on stockholder owned property and liability insurers with other major industries in the United States.

Average Annual Rates of Return on Net Income After Taxes as Percent of Net Worth*, Selected Industries

	Property/Casualty Insurance						
Year	GAAP Accounting	Statutory Accounting	Diversified Financial	Banks	Utilities	Transportation	All* Industries
1974	6.1%	6.5%	7.5%	12.8%	9.8%	6.5%	13.6%
1975	2.4	2.7	8.9	12.1	9.9	3.7	11.6
1976	10.0	8.9	12.1	11.5	10.6	8.8	13.3
1977	19.0	21.3	16.7	11.6	11.1	10.1	13.5
1978	18.1	20.5	17.3	12.9	11.3	13.3	14.3
1979	15.5	17.4	17.5	14.1	12.0	13.2	15.9
1980	13.1	14.7	14.0	13.4	11.7	11.3	14.4
1981	11.8	13.3	11.4	13.0	12.7	13.3	13.8
1982	8.8	9.3	10.0	12.0	12.5	7.9	10.9
1983	8.3	9.1	12.3	11.4	8.8	10.7	10.6
Average: 1974–83	11.3%	12.4%	12.8%	12.5%	11.0%	9.9%	13.2%

*Median for Fortune 500 U.S. Industrial Corporations.

SOURCES: Property/casualty insurance data: GAAP accounting basis. Insurance Services Office. Statutory accounting rate of return calculated by Insurance Information Institute, based on A.M. Best data. All other industry figures based on Fortune Magazine data: rates of return are figure averages, except for All industries, which is the median.

SOURCE: Adaptation of "Average Annual Rates of Return on Net Income After Taxes as Percent of Net Worth, Selected Industries" from *Insurance Facts*, 1984–1985 Edition. Reprinted with permission.

estimate the loss reserve. The expected loss ratio is multiplied by premiums earned during some time period. Losses and loss adjustment expenses that have been paid to date are then subtracted from the ultimate loss figure to determine the current loss reserve. This method is required by law for certain lines of insurance, such as workers' compensation and liability insurance claims.

Finally, the tabular value method is used to estimate loss reserves for certain claims for which the amounts paid will depend on the length of life, duration of disability, remarriage of the beneficiary, and similar factors. This method is often used to establish loss reserves involving total permanent disability, partial permanent disability, survivorship benefits, and similar claims. The loss reserve is called a *tabular reserve* because the duration of the benefit period is based on data derived from mortality, morbidity, and remarriage tables.

LIFE INSURANCE POLICY RESERVES

Policy reserves are the major liability item of life insurers. In this section, we will briefly examine the nature, purposes, and types of life insurance policy reserves.[14]

Nature of the Reserve

Under a level premium plan of life insurance, the premiums paid during the early years of the contract are higher than is necessary to pay death claims, while those paid during the later years are insufficient to pay death claims. The excess or redundant premiums collected during the early years of the contract must be accounted for and held for future payment to the policyowners' beneficiary. The redundant premiums paid during the early years result in the creation of a policy reserve. ***Policy reserves** are a liability item on the company's balance sheet that must be offset by assets equal to that amount.* Policy reserves are considered a liability item because they represent an obligation by the company to pay future policy benefits to policyowners. The policy reserves held by the company plus future premiums and future interest earnings will enable the company to pay all future policy benefits if the actual experience conforms to the actuarial assumptions used in calculating the reserve. Policy reserves are often called *legal reserves,* since state insurance laws specify the minimum basis for calculating them.

Purposes of the Reserve

The policy reserve has two fundamental purposes. *First, it is a formal recognition of the company's obligation to pay future benefits.* As we noted earlier, the policy reserve plus future premiums and interest earnings must be sufficient to pay all future policy benefits.

Second, the reserve is a legal test of the company's solvency. The company must hold assets equal to its legal reserves and other liabilities. This is the legal test of the company's ability to meet its present and future obligations to its policyowners. Policy reserves should not, therefore, be viewed as a fund. Rather, they are a liability item that must be offset by "funds" or assets. About 80 percent of the company's assets are needed to offset its reserve liabilities.

Definition of the Reserve

The reserve can be defined as the difference between the present value of future benefits and the present value of future net premiums. We noted earlier that the net single premium is equal to the present value of future benefits. At the inception of the policy, the net single premium is also equal to the present value of future net premiums. The net single premium can be converted into a series of annual installment payments without changing this relationship. However, once the first installment premium payment is made, this is no longer true. The present value of future benefits and the present value of future net premiums are no longer equal to each other. The present value of future benefits will increase over time, since the date of death is drawing closer, while the present value of future net premiums will decline, since fewer premiums will be paid. Thus, the difference between the two is the policy reserve.

This can be illustrated by Figure 27.4, which shows the reserve for an ordinary life policy issued at age thirty-five. At the inception of the policy, the net single premium is equal to the present value of future benefits and the present value of future net premiums.

The present value of future benefits increases over time, while the present value of future net premiums declines and the reserve is the difference between them. At age 100, the reserve is equal to the policy face amount. If the insured is

Figure 27.4 Prospective Reserve—Ordinary Life Insurance

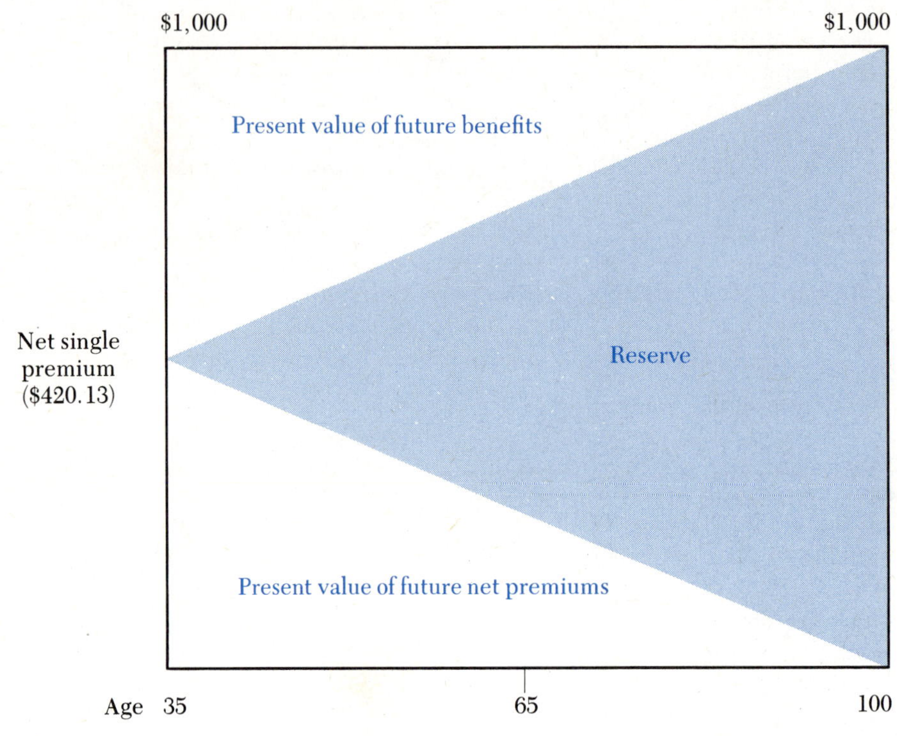

still alive at that time, the face amount of insurance is paid to the policyowner.

Types of Reserves

The reserve can be viewed either retrospectively or prospectively. If we refer to the past experience, the reserve is known as a retrospective reserve. *The **retrospective reserve** represents the net premiums collected by the insurer for a particular block of policies, plus interest earnings at an assumed rate, less the amounts paid out as death claims.*[15] Thus, the retrospective reserve is the excess of the net premiums accumulated at interest over the death claims paid out.

The reserve can also be viewed prospectively when we look to the future. *The **prospective reserve** is the difference between the present value of future benefits and the present value of future net premiums.* We explained this concept earlier when we examined the nature of the reserve. The retrospective and prospective methods are the mathematical equivalent of each other. Both methods will produce the same level of reserves at the end of any given year if the same set of actuarial assumptions is used.

Reserves can also be classified based on the time of valuation. At the time the reserves are valued, they can be classified as terminal, initial, and mean. *A **terminal reserve** is the reserve at the end of any given policy year.* It is used by companies to determine cash surrender values and also to determine the net amount at risk for purposes of determining dividends. *The **initial re-**

***serve** is the reserve at the beginning of any policy year*. It is equal to the preceding terminal reserve plus the net level annual premium for the current year. The initial reserve is also used by companies to determine dividends. *Finally, the **mean reserve** is the average of the terminal and initial reserves*. It is used to indicate the company's reserve liabilities on its annual statement.

SUMMARY

- State rating laws require insurance rates to meet certain standards. The rates charged by insurers must be adequate, not excessive, and not unfairly discriminatory.
- The rating system should also meet certain business objectives. The rates should be simple, stable, responsive, and should encourage loss prevention.
- Judgment rating means that each exposure is individually evaluated, and the rate is determined largely by the underwriter's judgment.
- Class rating means that exposures with similar characteristics are placed in the same underwriting class, and each is charged the same rate. The rate charged reflects the average loss experience for the class as a whole. Most personal lines of insurance are class rated.
- Merit rating is a rating plan by which class rates are adjusted upward or downward based on individual loss experience. It is based on the assumption that the loss experience of a particular insured will differ substantially from the loss experience of other insureds.
- There are three types of merit rating plans. They are:
  a. Schedule rating.
  b. Experience rating.
  c. Retrospective rating.
  Under *schedule rating*, each exposure is individually rated, and debits and credits are applied based on the physical characteristics of the exposure to be insured.
  Experience rating means that the insured's past loss experience is used to determine the premium for the next policy period. *Retrospective rating* means the insured's loss experience during the current policy period determines the actual premium paid for that period.
- In life insurance rate making, the *net single premium* is the present value of the future death benefit. The *net annual level premium* must be the mathematical equivalent of the net single premium. The net annual level premium is determined by dividing the net single premium by the present value of a life annuity due of $1 for the premium-paying period. A loading for expenses must be added to the net annual level premium to determine the gross premium paid by the insured.
- The unearned premium reserve in property and liability insurance is a liability reserve that represents the unearned portion of gross premiums on all outstanding policies at the time of valuation. The fundamental purpose of the unearned premium reserve is to pay for losses that occur during the policy period.
- A loss reserve is the estimated cost of settling claims that have already occurred but have not been paid as of the valuation date. There are several methods for estimating the size of the loss reserve. They are:
  a. Individual estimate method.
  b. Average value method.

c. Loss ratio method.
d. Tabular value method.

▶ In life insurance, a policy reserve is defined as the difference between the present value of future benefits and the present value of future net premiums. Policy reserves or legal reserves are a formal recognition of the company's obligation to pay future benefits. Also, the reserve is a legal test of the company's solvency, since the company must hold assets equal to its legal reserves and other liabilities.

QUESTIONS FOR REVIEW

1. Describe the major objectives of rate making.
2. Explain the meaning of judgment rating.
3. What is class rating?
4. What is merit rating? Describe the three types of merit rating plans.
5. Explain the concept of the net single premium in life insurance.
6. How is the net annual level premium computed?
7. What is the gross premium and how is it determined?
8. Explain the nature and purposes of the unearned premium reserve in property and liability insurance.
9. What is a loss reserve? Describe the various types of loss reserves in property and liability insurance.
10. Describe the nature of a policy reserve (legal reserve) in life insurance.

QUESTIONS FOR DISCUSSION

1. Class rates (manual rates) are widely used in personal lines of insurance.
   a. Briefly describe the principal methods of determining class rates.
   b. Explain the advantages of class rating to insurers.
2. Merit rating is used in property and liability insurance where the final premium paid depends at least partly on the loss experience of the individual insured. Describe the major features of each of the following types of merit rating plans:
   a. Schedule rating.
   b. Experience rating.
   c. Retrospective rating.
3. A property and liability insurer has a redundancy or equity in its unearned premium reserve.
   a. Explain the reasons for the unearned premium reserve in property and liability insurance.
   b. Explain how the redundancy or equity in the unearned premium reserve arises.
4. Property and liability insurers are required to maintain certain types of loss reserves.
   a. Explain the nature of a loss reserve in property and liability insurance.
   b. Briefly describe the following types of loss reserves:
      1. individual estimate method.
      2. average value method.

5. Using the information given below:

Commissioners 1958 Standard Ordinary Mortality Table

Age	Number living at beginning of designated year	Number dying during designated year	Present value of $1 at 2.5%	
			Year	Factor
40	9,241,359	32,622	1	.9756
41	9,208,737	35,362	2	.9518
42	9,173,375	38,253	3	.9286
43	9,135,122	41,382	4	.9060
44	9,093,740	44,741	5	.8839

a. Compute the net single premium for a five-year term insurance policy in the amount of $1,000 issued at age forty.

b. Compute the net annual level premium for the same policy.

NOTE: In answering questions *(a)* and *(b)*, do not make multiplications, divisions, or additions. Merely indicate the results by the letters "A", "B", "C", and so on.

KEY CONCEPTS AND TERMS TO KNOW

Rate
Exposure unit
Pure premium
Loading
Gross rate
Gross premium
Judgment rating
Class rating (manual rating)
Merit rating
Schedule rating
Loss ratio
Expense ratio
Earned premiums
Net single premium
Net level premium
Whole life annuity due
Temporary life annuity due
Unearned premium reserve
Annual pro rata method
Equity in unearned premium reserve
Experience rating
Retrospective rating
Adjusted underwriting profit or loss
Loss reserve
Policy reserves
Retrospective reserve
Prospective reserve
Terminal reserve
Initial reserve
Mean reserve

SUGGESTIONS FOR ADDITIONAL READING

Insurance Information Institute. *Basic Concepts of Accounting and Taxation of Property/Casualty Insurance Companies.* New York: Insurance Information Institute, 1984.

McGill, Dan M. *Life Insurance*, rev. ed. Homewood, Illinois: Richard D. Irwin, Inc., 1967, chapters 10 and 11.

Mehr, Robert I. and Emerson Cammack, *Principles of Insurance*, 7th ed. Homewood, Illinois: Richard D. Irwin, Inc., 1980, chapter 24.

Mehr, Robert I. and Sandra G. Gustavson. *Life Insurance Theory and Practice*, 3rd ed. Homewood, Illinois: Richard D. Irwin, Inc., 1984, chapters 24 and 25.

Troxel, Terrie E. and Cormick L. Breslin. *Property-Liability Insurance Accounting and Finance*, 2nd ed. Malvern, Pennsylvania: American Institute for Property and Liability Underwriters, 1983.

Webb, Bernard L., J. J. Launie, Willis Park Rokes, and Norman A. Baglini. *Insurance Company Operations*, 3rd ed., Volume II. Malvern, Pennsylvania: American Institute for Property and Liability Underwriters, 1984.

Williams, Jr., C. Arthur and Richard M. Heins. *Risk Management and Insurance*, 5th ed. New York: McGraw-Hill Book Company, 1985, chapter 28.

NOTES

1. Bernard L. Webb, J. J. Launie, Willis Park Rokes, and Norman A. Baglini, *Insurance Company Operations*, Volume II (Malvern, Pennsylvania: American Institute for Property and Liability Underwriters, 1978), pp. 2–8.
2. The basic rate making methods are discussed in some detail in Webb, pp. 8–61. The author drew heavily on this source in preparing this section.
3. An equivalent method for determining the final rate is to divide the pure premium by the permissible loss ratio. The *permissible loss ratio* is the same as the expected loss ratio. If the expense ratio is .40, the permissible loss ratio is 1 − .40, or .60. Thus, if the pure premium of $60 is divided by the permissible loss ratio of .60, the resulting gross rate is also $100.

$$\text{Gross rate} = \frac{\text{Pure premium}}{\text{Permissible loss ratio}} = \frac{\$60}{.60} = \$100$$

4. Earned premiums are the premiums actually earned by a company during the accounting period, rather than the premiums written during the same period.
5. The credibility factor (C) refers to the statistical reliability of the data. It ranges from a value of 0 to 1 and increases as the number of claims increases. If the actuary believes that the data are highly reliable and can accurately predict future losses, a credibility factor of 1 can be used. However, if the data are not completely reliable as a predictor of future losses, a credibility factor of less than 1 is used.
6. These concepts are discussed in Dan M. McGill, *Life Insurance*, rev. ed. (Homewood, Illinois: Richard D. Irwin, 1967), pp. 182–274. The author drew heavily on this source in preparing this section.
7. For example, if an immediate life annuity is purchased with annual payments, the first payment would be due one year from the purchase date.
8. McGill, p. 208.
9. McGill, pp. 247–48.
10. For the various methods of calculating the unearned premium reserve, see Cormick L. Breslin and Terrie E. Troxel, *Property-Liability Insurance Accounting and Finance* (Malvern, Pennsylvania: American Institute for Property and Liability Underwriters, 1978), pp. 172–75.
11. The loss ratio is the ratio of losses and loss-adjustment expenses to *earned premiums*. However, the expense ratio is the ratio of expenses incurred to *written premiums*.
12. Expenses incurred of $3.5 million are based on written premiums. Remember that the expense ratio is the ratio of expenses incurred to written premiums ($ 3,500,000/$10,000,000 = 35%).
13. Breslin, pp. 148–50.
14. Life insurance reserves are discussed in greater detail in McGill, pp. 218–45.
15. McGill, p. 219.

CHAPTER 28 GOVERNMENT REGULATION OF INSURANCE

"There are serious shortcomings in state laws and regulatory activities with respect to protecting the interests of insurance consumers . . . ."

General Accounting Office

STUDENT LEARNING OBJECTIVES

After studying this chapter, you should be able to:

- Explain the reasons why insurance companies are regulated.
- Describe the historical development of insurance regulation and indicate those legal cases that have had a profound impact on insurers.
- Explain the various methods for regulating insurers.
- Describe the areas that are specifically regulated.
- Explain the objectives of rate regulation and the different types of rating laws.
- Discuss some current issues in insurance regulation.

REASONS FOR INSURANCE REGULATION

Insurers are regulated by the states for several reasons. They include the following:

- Maintain insurer solvency
- Inadequate consumer knowledge
- Ensure reasonable rates
- Make insurance available

Maintain Insurer Solvency

Insurance regulation is necessary to maintain the solvency of insurers. This goal is called **solidity** by which regulation aims at preserving or enhancing the financial strength of insurers.[1] Solvency is important for two reasons. First, premiums are paid in advance, but the period of protection extends into the future. If a company goes bankrupt and a future claim is not paid, the insurance protection paid for in advance is worthless. Therefore, to ensure that future losses will be paid, the financial strength of insurers must be carefully monitored, and policyowners, beneficiaries, and third-party claimants must be protected against insolvencies.

A second reason for stressing solvency is that individuals can be exposed to great economic insecurity if insurers fail and claims are not paid. For example, if the insured's home is totally destroyed in a tornado, and the loss is not paid, he or she may be financially ruined. Thus, because of the possibility of great financial hardship to insureds, beneficiaries, and third-party claimants, regulation must stress insurer solvency.

Inadequate Consumer Knowledge

Regulation is also necessary because of inadequate consumer knowledge. Insurance contracts are technical, legal documents that contain complex clauses and provisions. Without regulation, an unscrupulous insurer could draft a contract so restrictive and legalistic that it would be worthless.

Furthermore, most consumers do not have adequate information for comparing and determining the monetary value of different insurance contracts. It is difficult to compare dissimilar policies with different premiums because the necessary price and policy information is not readily available. For example, health insurance policies vary widely by cost, coverages, and benefits, and the average consumer would find it difficult to evaluate a particular policy based on the premium alone.

Finally, without good information, consumers cannot select the best insurance product. This can reduce the impact that consumers have on insurance markets, and can also reduce the competitive incentive of insurers to improve product quality and lower price. Thus, regulation is needed to produce the same market effect that results from knowledgeable consumers who are purchasing products in highly competitive markets.[2]

Ensure Reasonable Rates

Regulation is also necessary to ensure reasonable rates. This means that the rates charged for insurance should be neither excessively high nor low. The rates should not be so high that consumers are being exploited by paying more than the value of the coverage. Nor should the rates be so low that the solvency of insurers is threatened. However, whether a rate is too high or too low is often difficult for the regulators to resolve. Rate regulation is an extremely complex issue. We will examine the various rating philosophies and different types of rating laws later in the chapter.

Make Insurance Available

A more recent regulatory goal is to make insurance available to all persons who need it.[3] Insurers are often unwilling to insure all applicants for a given type of insurance because of underwriting losses, inadequate rates, adverse selection, and a host of additional factors. However, the public interest may require regulators to take actions that expand private insurance markets to make insurance more readily available. If private insurers are unable or unwilling to supply the needed coverages, then government insurance programs may be necessary.

HISTORICAL DEVELOPMENT OF INSURANCE REGULATION

In this section, we will briefly review the development of insurance regulation by the states. You should pay careful attention to certain landmark legal decisions that have had a profound impact on insurance regulation.

Early Regulatory Efforts

Insurance regulation first began when state legislatures granted *charters* to new insurers, which authorized their formation and operation. The new companies initially were subject to few regulatory controls. The charters required only that the companies issued periodic reports and provided public information concerning their financial condition. In 1837, state regulation became more formal when Massachusetts passed legislation requiring insurers to maintain reserves for financial stability.

The creation of state insurance commissions was the next step in insurance regulation. In 1841, New Hampshire became the first state to create a separate insurance commission to regulate insurers. Other states followed. In 1859, New York created a separate administrative agency headed by a single superintendent who was given broad licensing and investigative powers. Thus, initial insurance regulation developed under the jurisdiction and supervision of the states.

Paul v. Virginia

The case of ***Paul v. Virginia*** in 1869 was a landmark legal decision that established the right of the states to regulate insurance.[4] Samuel Paul was an agent in Virginia who represented several New York insurers. Paul was fined $50 for selling fire insurance in Virginia without a license. He appealed the case on the grounds that Virginia's law was unconstitutional. He argued that since insurance was interstate commerce, only the federal government had the right to regulate insurance under the commerce clause of the U.S. Constitution. The Supreme Court disagreed. The Court ruled that issuance of an insurance policy was not interstate commerce. Therefore, the insurance industry was not subject to the commerce clause of the Constitution. *Thus, the legal significance of* Paul v. Virginia *was that insurance was not interstate commerce, and that the states rather than the federal government had the right to regulate the insurance industry.* This landmark legal decision stood for about seventy-five years until it was reversed by the Supreme Court in 1944.

South-Eastern Underwriters Association Case

The precedent set in *Paul v. Virginia*, which held that insurance is not interstate commerce, was overturned by the Supreme Court in 1944. The **South-Eastern Underwriters Association (SEUA)** was a cooperative rating bureau that was found guilty of price fixing and other violations of the Sherman Antitrust Act. *In the SEUA case, the Supreme Court ruled that insurance was interstate commerce when conducted across state lines and was subject to federal regulation.*[5] The Court's decision that insurance was interstate commerce and subject to federal antitrust laws caused considerable turmoil for the industry and state regulators, for it raised serious doubts concerning the legality of private rating bureaus and the power of the states to regulate and tax the insurance industry.

McCarran-Ferguson Act

To resolve the confusion and doubt that existed after the *SEUA* decision, Congress passed the **McCarran-Ferguson Act** (Public Law 15) in 1945. The McCarran Act states that continued regulation and taxation of the insurance industry by the states are in the public interest. It also states that federal antitrust laws apply to insurance only to the extent that the insurance industry is not regulated by state law. Therefore, as long as state regulation is in effect, federal antitrust laws will not apply to insurance. However, the exemption from antitrust laws is not absolute. The Sherman Act forbids any acts or agreements to boycott, coerce, or intimidate. In these areas, insurers are still subject to federal law.

At present, the states still have the primary responsibility for regulating insurance. However, Congress can repeal the McCarran Act, which would then give the federal government authority over the insurance industry. There have been strong pressures from a few insurers to repeal the McCarran Act, but Congress to date has not done so. We will examine this important issue later in the chapter.

METHODS FOR REGULATING INSURERS

Three principal methods are used to regulate insurers. They are:

- Legislation
- Courts
- State insurance departments

Let us briefly examine each of these methods.

Legislation

All states have insurance laws that regulate the operations of insurers. These laws regulate (1) formation of insurance companies, (2) licensing of agents and brokers, (3) financial requirements for maintaining solvency, (4) insurance rates, (5) sales and claim practices, (6) taxation, and (7) rehabilitation or liquidation of insurers. Also, laws have been passed to protect the rights of consumers, such as laws restricting the right of insurers to cancel and laws making insurance more widely available.

In addition to state laws, insurance companies are subject to regulation by certain federal agencies and laws. Only a few are mentioned here. The Federal Trade Commission has authority to regulate mail-order insurers in those states where they are not licensed to do business. The Securities and Exchange Commission has regulations concerning the sale of variable annuities and has jurisdiction over the sale of insurance company securities to the public. And the Employee Retirement Income Security Act of 1974 (ERISA) applies to the private pension plans of insurers.

Courts

Insurance companies are also regulated by the courts. State and federal courts periodically hand down decisions concerning the constitutionality of state insurance laws, the interpretation of policy clauses and provisions, and the legality of administrative actions by state departments. As such, the various court decisions can affect the market conduct and operations of insurers in an important way.

State Insurance Departments

Companies are also regulated by state insurance departments. Each state and the District of Columbia have a separate insurance department or bureau. In most states, an *insurance commissioner*, who is typically appointed by the governor, has the responsibility for administering the state insurance laws. Through administrative rulings, the state insurance commissioner wields considerable power over the companies doing business in the state. The insurance commissioner has the power to hold hearings, issue cease-and-desist orders, and revoke or suspend an insurer's license to do business.

The state insurance commissioners belong to an important national association known as the **National Association of Insurance Commissioners (NAIC).** The NAIC, founded in 1871, meets periodically to discuss industry problems that might require legislation or regulation. The NAIC has drafted model laws in various areas and has recommended adoption of these proposals by state legislatures. Although the NAIC has no legal authority to force the states to adopt the recommendations, most states have accepted all or part of them.

WHAT AREAS ARE REGULATED?

Insurers are subject to numerous laws and regulations. The principal areas regulated include the following:

- Formation and licensing of insurers
- Financial regulation
- Rate regulation

- Policy forms
- Sales practices and consumer protection

Formation and Licensing of Insurers

All states have requirements for the formation and licensing of insurers. A new insurer is normally formed by incorporation. The company receives a charter or certificate of incorporation from the state, which authorizes its formation and legal existence.

After being formed, the company must be licensed before it can do business. The licensing requirements for insurers are more stringent than those imposed on other new firms. A higher degree of honesty, managerial competence, and financial strength is required than for other firms. If the company is a capital stock insurer, it must meet certain minimum capital and surplus requirements, which vary by state and by line of insurance. A new mutual insurer must meet a minimum surplus requirement (rather than capital and surplus since there are no stockholders), and other requirements as well.

A license can be issued to a domestic, foreign, or alien insurer. A **domestic insurer** is a company domiciled in the state; it must be licensed in the state as well as in other states where it does business. A **foreign insurer** or out-of-state insurer is a company chartered by another state; it must also be licensed to do business in the state. An **alien insurer** is a company chartered by a foreign country. It must also meet certain licensing requirements. In general, the licensing requirements for out-of-state (foreign) and alien insurers are at least as high as those for domestic insurers.[6]

Financial Regulation

In addition to minimum capital and surplus requirements, insurance companies are subject to other financial regulations as well. These financial regulations are designed to maintain the solvency of insurers.

Admitted assets An insurer must have sufficient assets to offset its liabilities. Only admitted assets can be shown on the company's balance sheet. **Admitted assets** are those that state law allows an insurer to show on its statutory balance sheet in determining its financial condition. All other assets are nonadmitted.

Most assets are classified as admitted assets. These include cash, bonds, common and preferred stocks, mortgages, real estate, and other legal investments. In the valuation of these assets, *cash* is valued at its face amount. *Bonds* not in default are carried at amortized values. (Bonds in default are valued at market.) *Common stocks* are valued according to the NAIC's *Valuation of Securities,* which generally are the market values on December 31. *Mortgages* are valued based on the amount of outstanding debt. Finally, *real estate* can be valued at market value or at book value (original cost less depreciation).

Reserves Reserves are liability items on a company's balance sheet and reflect obligations that must be met in the future. The states have regulations that prescribe the methods by which these reserves are to be calculated. The various methods for calculating reserves were discussed in Chapter 27.

Surplus The surplus position of a company is also carefully monitored. **Policyholders' surplus** is the difference between a company's assets and its liabilities. The surplus of a capital stock insurer consists of two items: (1) a capital stock account that represents the values of the shares issued to the stockholders, and (2) paid-in surplus that represents amounts paid in by stockholders in excess of the par value of the stock. Both items together represent policyholders' surplus. Since a mutual insurer has no stockholders, policyholders' surplus is simply the difference between assets and liabilities.

In property and liability insurance, policyholders' surplus is important for several reasons.[7] First, the amount of new business a company can write is limited by the amount of its policyholders' surplus. One rule of thumb is the **Kenney rule,** by which a property-liability insurer can safely write $2 of new net premiums for each $1 of policyholders' surplus.[8] Second, policyholders' surplus is necessary to offset any substantial underwriting or investment losses. Finally, policyholders' surplus is required to offset any deficiency in loss reserves that may occur over time.

In life insurance, policyholders' surplus is less important because of substantial safety margins in the calculation of premiums and dividends, conservative interest assumptions used in calculating legal reserves, conservative valuation of investments, greater stability in operations over time, and less likelihood of a catastrophic loss.

Investments Insurance company investments are regulated with respect to types, quality, and percentage of assets or surplus that can be invested in different assets. The basic purpose of these regulations is to prevent insurers from making unsound investments that could threaten the company's solvency and harm the policyowners.

1. *Life insurers.* Laws regulating life insurance investments generally are of two types.[9] First, the laws specify the types of investments in which life insurers can invest, and they generally specify maximum limits on each type of investment based on a percentage of assets or surplus. Life insurers typically invest in common and preferred stocks, bonds, mortgages, real estate, and policy loans. All states have limits on common stock investments. For example, in New York, common stock investments are limited to a maximum of 10 percent of total assets, or 100 percent of surplus, whichever is lower.

The second type of law specifies eligibility standards for specific investments. For example, with respect to public utility bonds, Nebraska requires the issuing company to earn at least one and one-half times its fixed charges on all debt during the past year. The objective of these laws is to hold life insurers to conservative investment standards in their investment policies.

2. *Property-liability insurers.* Property and liability insurers are subject to fewer restrictions in their investments than life insurers. The actual restrictions vary among the states, and only general limitations are discussed here.[10] First, with respect to minimum capital requirements, the funds can be invested in federal, state, or municipal bonds, or bonds and notes secured by mortgages and trust deeds.

Second, with respect to the unearned premium and loss reserves, the funds required to offset these liabilities can be invested in the same assets that qualify for the minimum capital requirements. Any excess funds over the minimum capital requirements and reserve liabilities can be invested in the common stock of solvent insurers.

Finally, investments in real estate generally are limited to home office buildings or other property where business is conducted.

Limitations on expenses In life insurance, some states place limitations on the amounts that can be spent in acquiring new business and maintaining old business. These laws are extremely complex, and in general, they limit the amounts that can be spent on acquisition expenses, commissions, bonuses, service fees, and other expenses. New York's law is far-reaching in this regard, since companies doing business in New York must abide by the expense limitations on contracts written in other states.

The purpose of expense limitation laws is to prevent wasteful price competition that would result in life insurers competing with each other by offering higher commissions to agents. Thus, the laws have the effect of holding down the cost of life insurance to consumers.

Dividend policy In life insurance, the annual gain from operations can be distributed in the form of dividends to policyowners, or it can be added to the company's surplus for present and future needs. Many states limit the amount of surplus a participating life insurer can accumulate to a maximum of 10 percent of policy reserves.

The purpose of this limitation is to prevent life insurers from accumulating a substantial surplus at the expense of policyowner dividends.

Reports and examinations Annual reports and examinations are also used to maintain insurer solvency. Each company must file an annual report (known as a **convention blank**) with the state insurance department in those states where it does business. The annual report provides detailed financial information to regulatory officials with respect to assets, liabilities, reserves, investments, claim payments, and other information.

Insurance companies are also periodically examined by the states. A domestic insurer is normally examined at least once every three to five years by the state insurance department. Licensed out-of-state and alien insurers are also periodically examined. In order to avoid duplication of effort and unnecessary expenses, the United States is divided into six zones, and each zone includes several states. The company is examined by a team of examiners from the different state insurance departments under the general supervision of the state insurance department of the home state. The report is then distributed to each of the states where the company does business.

Liquidation of insurers If a company is technically insolvent, the state insurance department assumes control of the company. With proper management, the company may be successfully rehabilitated. If the company cannot be rehabilitated, it is liquidated according to the state's insurance code.

A number of states have adopted the Uniform Insurers Liquidation Act. The Act is designed to achieve uniformity among the states in the liquidation of assets and payment of claims of a defunct insurer. The result is that all creditors are treated equally in each state where the insolvent insurer has conducted business.

If a company becomes insolvent, some claims may still be unpaid. All states have established **insurance guaranty funds** that provide for the payments of unpaid claims of insolvent insurers. In most states, the insolvency fund covers only property and liability insurers; life insurers generally are not included. Between 1969 and 1983, eighty-four property and casualty companies became insolvent, including four that failed in 1983.

The *assessment method* is used to raise the necessary funds to pay unpaid claims. In most states, a company can be assessed a maximum of 2 percent of net premiums written in the state. Thus, the companies are assessed after the insolvency occurs. New York is an exception, because it permanently maintains a preassessment solvency fund, by which the companies are assessed prior to any insolvency. Excluding New York, the state guaranty funds have paid out more than $453 million because of insolvent insurers.

Rate Regulation

With the exception of Illinois, all states have rating laws that require insurance rates to meet certain statutory standards. As we noted in Chapter 27, the rates are required to be adequate, reasonable (not excessive), and not unfairly discriminatory. However, there are wide variations among the states with respect to implementation of these objectives.

Rate regulation is far from uniform. The various types of rating laws include the following:[11]

- State-made rates
- Mandatory bureau rates
- Prior approval laws
- File-and-use laws
- No-filing laws

State-made rates State-made rates are the most rigid form of rate regulation. A state agency sets the rates, and all licensed insurers in the state must use these rates. Texas uses this system at present. However, under Texas law, certain rate deviations are permitted; this results in some price competition. Massachusetts also uses state-made rates for automobile insurance.

Mandatory bureau rates This system is almost as rigid as state-made rates. A rating bureau determines the rates, and all insurers are required by law to use the rates; however, rate deviations are permitted. Mandatory bureau rates are used in North Carolina for fire and automobile insurance.

Prior approval laws The majority of states have some type of prior approval law for regulating rates. Under a **prior approval law,** the rates must be filed and approved by the state insurance department before they can be used. Insurance companies have criticized prior approval laws on several grounds. There is often considerable delay in obtaining a needed rate increase, since state insurance departments are often understaffed. Also, the rate increase that is granted may be inadequate, and needed rate increases can be denied for political purposes. Finally, the statistical data required by the state insurance department to support a rate increase may not be readily available.

File-and-use laws This type of law is more liberal than the laws discussed earlier. Under a **file-and-use law,** the companies are required only to file the rates with the state insurance department, and they can be used immediately. Regulatory authorities have the authority to disapprove the rates later if they violate state law. This type of rating law overcomes the problem of delay which exists under a prior approval law.

No-filing laws No-filing laws or open competition laws are the most liberal of all rating laws. California was the first state to enact such a law. Under a **no-filing law,** insurers are not required to file their rates at all with the state insurance department. However, the companies may be required to furnish rate schedules and supporting data to state officials. The fundamental assumption underlying a no-filing law is that open competition in the market place will ensure that rates are reasonable and insurance is available. Thus, market forces will determine the price and availability of insurance rather than the discretionary acts of regulatory officials.

Life insurance rate regulation Our discussion of rate regulation so far applies primarily to property and liability insurance. Life insurance rates are not directly regulated by the states.[12] Rate adequacy in life insurance is indirectly achieved by regulations that require legal reserves to be at least a minimum size. Minimum legal reserve requirements then affect the rates that must be charged to pay death claims and expenses.

Policy Forms

The regulation of new policy forms is another important area of insurance regulation. Because insurance contracts are technical and complex, the state insurance commissioner has the authority to approve or disapprove new policy forms before the contracts are sold to the public. The purpose is to protect the public from misleading, deceptive, and unfair provisions.

Sales Practices and Consumer Protection

In order to protect consumers, the sales practices of insurers are also regulated. This area is regulated by laws concerning the licensing of agents and brokers, and by laws prohibiting twisting, rebating, and unfair trade practices.

Licensing of agents and brokers All states require agents and brokers to be licensed. In most states, the applicant must pass a written examination or complete a specific course of study. The examinations are usually given under the direction of the state insurance department. The purpose of the examination is to ensure that the applicant possesses some knowledge of insurance law and of the contracts that he or she intends to sell. If the agent is incompetent or dishonest, the state insurance commissioner has the authority to suspend or revoke the agent's license; this provides a powerful control over the agent's behavior.

Twisting All states forbid twisting. **Twisting** is the inducement of a policyowner to drop an existing policy in another company due to misrepresentation or incomplete information. Twisting laws apply largely to life insurance policies; the objective here is to prevent policyowners from being financially harmed by replacing one life insurance policy with another.

Most states have replacement regulations that are designed to provide policyowners with enough information to make an informed decision concerning the replacement of an existing policy. These laws are based on the premise that replacement of an existing life insurance policy generally is not in the policyowner's best interest. For example, a new front-end load of commissions and expenses must be paid; a new incontestable clause and suicide clause must be satisfied; and higher premiums based on the policyowner's higher attained age may have to be paid. However, the basic premise that replacement of an existing life insurance policy is undesirable is being challenged by many researchers. *In some cases, switching policies can be financially justified.* In a comprehensive study of the replacement of life insurance contracts, William Scheel and Jack VanDerhei found that the majority of the replacements studied were acceptable; that is, there were cost savings to policyowners. The authors conclude that their data provide no support for the commonly held viewpoint of state insurance commissioners that replacements generally are undesirable.[13]

Rebating Most state insurance codes also forbid rebating. **Rebating** is giving a premium reduction or some other financial advantage to an individual as an inducement to purchase the policy. One obvious example is a partial refund of the agent's commission to the insured. The basic purpose of antirebate laws is to ensure fair and equitable treatment of all policyowners by preventing one insured from obtaining an unfair price advantage over another.

Unfair trade practices Insurance laws prohibit a wide variety of unfair trade practices, including misrepresentation, twisting, rebating, deceptive or false advertising, inequitable claim settlement, and unfair discrimination. The state insurance commissioner has the legal authority to stop companies from engaging in unfair trade practices. The company can be fined, an injunction can be obtained, or, in serious cases, the insurer's license can be suspended or revoked.

Complaint division State insurance departments typically have a complaint division or department for handling consumer complaints. The department or individual will investigate the complaint and try to obtain a response from the offending insurer or agency. Most consumer complaints involve claims. A company may refuse to pay a claim, or may dispute the amount payable. Although state insurance departments are highly responsive to individual complaints, they generally lack direct authority to order insurers to pay disputed claims where factual questions are an issue. In a study of complaint handling, the General Accounting Office found that most consumer complaints are viewed as valid, and that the majority of them are resolved in favor of consumers.[14] In your own personal insurance program, you should phone or write your state insurance department if you feel you are being treated unfairly by a company or agent.

Readable policies Greater protection of the consumer is also evidenced by the trend toward readable policies. In order to make insurance contracts more understandable, the states have approved policies in which the language is less technical, and therefore is simpler and easier to understand. The development of more readable policies will undoubtedly benefit most consumers.

Shoppers' guides Several states, including New York, Pennsylvania, and Wisconsin, have published shoppers' guides for insurance consumers. These guides provide useful information concerning the types of insurance contracts to buy, saving money on insurance, selection of a company and agent, filing a claim, resolving disputes, and other practical tips. The guides often furnish valuable information with respect to premiums charged by different companies for similar policies, so that consumers can make meaningful cost comparisons among the companies. Cost information on automobile insurance, homeowners insurance, and life insurance can help consumers purchase policies from low-cost companies.

This concludes our discussion of protection of the consumer. Let us next consider how insurance companies are taxed.

TAXATION OF INSURERS

Insurance companies pay numerous local, state, and federal taxes. Two important taxes are the federal income tax and state premium tax. Insurance companies pay federal income taxes based on complex formulas and rules established by federal legislation and the Internal Revenue Service.

Premium Tax

In addition, all states levy a premium tax on gross premiums received from policyowners. The tax rates range from a low of 1.4 percent to a high of 4 percent, with 2 percent being the most common.

The primary purpose of the premium tax is to raise revenues for the states, not to provide funds for insurance regulation. Most state insurance department budgets are less than 5 percent of the premium taxes collected. However, critics of state regulation argue that if state regulation is to become more effective, more money must be spent on insurance regulation.

Most states have *retaliatory tax laws* that affect premium taxes and other taxes. For example, assume that the premium tax is 2 percent in Nebraska and 3 percent in Iowa. If insurers domiciled in Nebraska are required to pay a 3 percent premium tax on business written in Iowa, then domestic insurers in Iowa doing business in Nebraska must also pay 3 percent even though Nebraska's rate is 2 percent. Thus, the purpose of a retaliatory tax law is to protect domestic insurers in the state from excessive taxation by other states where they do business. At the present time, retaliatory tax laws are under attack in the courts.

STATE VERSUS FEDERAL REGULATION

Critics of state regulation argue that the McCarran Act should be repealed and replaced by federal regulation. However, the insurance industry and state regulators are adamantly opposed to additional federal regulation. Let us first examine the alleged advantages of federal regulation.

Advantages of Federal Regulation

Advocates of federal regulation present the following arguments in support of their position:

1. *Uniformity of laws.* Federal regulation can provide greater uniformity of laws. Under state regulation, companies doing business in more than one state must observe different state laws. Under federal regulation, the laws would be uniform.
2. *Greater efficiency.* It is argued that federal regulation would be more efficient. A company doing business nationally would deal with only one federal agency rather than with numerous insurance departments. Also, the federal agency would be less likely to yield to industry pressures, especially those reflecting the views of local companies. Federal regulation would also be less expensive to administer.
3. *More competent regulators.* Federal regulation would attract higher quality personnel who would do a superior job of regulating the companies. The higher salaries and prestige would attract more highly talented and skilled individuals.

Advantages of State Regulation

Supporters of state regulation also offer convincing arguments for continued regulation of insurance by the states. The major advantages claimed for state regulation are as follows:

1. *Greater responsiveness to local needs.* Local needs vary widely and state regulators can respond more quickly to local needs. In contrast, under federal regulation, "red tape" and government bureaucracy would result in considerable delay in solving problems at the local level.
2. *Uniformity of laws by NAIC.* Uniformity of laws can be achieved by the model laws and proposals of the NAIC. Thus, there is reasonable uniformity of state laws in important areas at the present time.
3. *Greater opportunity for innovation.* State regulation provides greater opportunities for innovation in regulation. An individual state can experiment with a new innovation, and if it fails, only that state is affected. In contrast, poor federal legislation would affect all the states.
4. *Unknown consequences of federal regulation.* State regulation is already in existence, and its strengths and weaknesses are well known. In contrast, the consequences of federal regulation on consumers and the insurance industry are unknown.
5. *Decentralization of political power.* State regulation results in a decentralization of political power. Federal regulation would result in further encroachment of the federal government on the economy and a corresponding dilution of states' rights.

Shortcomings of State Regulation

In a study assessing the effectiveness of insurance regulation by state insurance departments, the General Accounting Office found evidence that both contradicts and supports the arguments for state regulation of insurance. On the negative side, the General Accounting Office found a number of serious shortcomings. They include the following:[15]

1. *Inadequate protection of consumers.* Most state insurance departments do not have systematic procedures for determining whether consumers are being treated properly with respect to claim payments, rate setting, and protection from unfair discrimination.
2. *Defects in financial regulation.* Other than the early warning system, most states have not enacted the changes recommended by the NAIC with respect to financial regulation. Some states may not have specialized examiners, and few states have the capacity to conduct computerized audits.
3. *Improvements needed in handling complaints.* Although many states prepare complaint ratios (ratio of complaints to premiums) for each company, few states publicize the ratios or make them widely available to consumers. Most states do not maintain a system by which complaints are coded, analyzed, and fed into the examination process.
4. *Lack of standards in market conduct examination.* Market conduct examinations refer to insurance department examinations of consumer matters such as claims handling, underwriting, advertising, and other trade practices. Serious deficiencies are found in many market conduct examination reports. The most serious defect is the lack of explicit standards in evaluating the market conduct of insurers.
5. *Insurance availability.* Only a minority of urban states have conducted studies to determine if property and liability insurance availability is a serious problem in their states.
6. *Regulators overly responsive to insurance industry.* State insurance departments are overly responsive to the insurance company at the expense of consumers. Insurance regulation is not characterized by an "arm's-length" relationship between regulators and the regulated. Half of the state insurance commissioners were previously employed in the insurance industry, and

> about the same proportion return to the industry after leaving office. Moreover, the NAIC meetings and advisory committees are numerically dominated by insurance representatives.

Despite those shortcomings, the GAO also points out some positive aspects of state regulation, which support the case for continued regulation of the insurance industry by the states. First, considerable uniformity in regulation is provided by the NAIC. Second, none of the insurance executives interviewed in the study believed that compliance with different state laws imposes significant costs on the companies. Third, there is evidence that the threat of federal regulation has forced state regulators to do a better job. Finally, there is considerable evidence that state insurance departments effectively respond to unique insurance needs at the local level, especially in the areas of medical malpractice and commercial liability insurance.

Repeal of the McCarran Act

Because of defects in state regulation, there are growing pressures on Congress to repeal the McCarran Act. The National Commission for the Review of Antitrust Rules and Procedures has recommended that the broad antitrust immunity granted insurers under the McCarran Act should be repealed. The Senate Judiciary Antitrust Subcommittee has also proposed legislation that would substantially affect the insurance industry. The proposed legislation has three purposes. First, the immunity from federal antitrust laws not granted insurers under the McCarran Act would be repealed. Second, open price competition would be encouraged by restricting the use of bureau rates or rates made jointly by an association of insurers. Finally, federal minimum standards would be established to ensure nondiscrimination in insurance pricing, full availability of essential property and casualty coverages, and the elimination of unfair and excessive rate differentials between insureds.

However, it is questionable whether federal standards will substantially upgrade the quality of insurance regulation. The past record of federal regulation of industries is poor. Federal regulation of industries—such as the railroads, airlines, and trucking—has been uniformly destructive to competition, for it has obstructed entry into an industry, entrenched the market power of large companies, and resulted in a cozy relationship between the regulators and the regulated.[16]

CURRENT ISSUES IN INSURANCE REGULATION

Several important issues in insurance regulation are being debated at the present time. They include:

- Life insurance cost disclosure
- Automobile insurance rate classification systems
- Banks entering insurance

Life Insurance Cost Disclosure

An important regulatory issue is life insurance cost disclosure. Consumer advocates maintain that meaningful cost information on life insurance policies should be provided to consumers. However, the types of cost data to be provided and the manner in which the data are to be presented are highly controversial issues.

NAIC cost disclosure recommendations Based on the NAIC model regulation, cost data based on the interest-adjusted method must be provided to the purchasers of life insurance. The buyer of a cash-value policy must be given both a net-payment cost index and a surrender-cost index.

Although the life insurance industry strongly supports the NAIC proposal, consumer advocates argue that additional information is necessary. In particular, Professor Joseph Belth, a highly visible and nationally known life insurance critic, points out several defects in the NAIC model regulation. They include the following:[17]

1. The NAIC proposal provides no periodic

disclosure to policyowners after the sale is made, which provides opportunities for exploitation of long-time policyowners.

2. No price information is provided after twenty years, which may lead to certain forms of actuarial manipulation that show favorable policy results when the policy is not favorable in price.
3. No rate-of-return information on cash values is required. Thus, consumers are kept ignorant about the rates of return on the savings element in cash value policies.
4. There is no requirement for disclosing the cost to policyowners if premiums are paid monthly, quarterly, or semiannually.

Federal Trade Commission Report In a highly controversial report, the Federal Trade Commission has recommended that the life insurance industry should be required to disclose the average annual rates of return on all cash-value and annuity contracts and also to provide other types of cost information in a simple and effective manner.[18]

The FTC maintains that several serious consumer problems exist with respect to the purchase and ownership of life insurance. They include the following:

1. *Low rates of return.* The rate of return consumers receive on the savings component of cash-value policies is often low. Based on the Linton yield method, the five-year rates of return on new cash value policies issued in 1977 range from a minus 9 percent to a minus 19 percent; the ten-year rates are around 1 percent; and the twenty-year rates range from 2 percent to 4.5 percent. Based on a different method, the industry-wide average rate of return on ordinary life policies in 1977 was approximately 1.3 percent.
2. *Substantial loss to policyowners because of early terminations.* Consumers lose substantial amounts because of termination of whole life policies during the first few years. About 20 percent of the new policies purchased lapse within the first two years. Because of the heavy front-end load for acquisition and sales expenses, and no cash values in most policies for the first year, early terminations result in substantial losses to consumers.
3. *Wide variation in cost of similar policies.* The cost of similar whole life policies varies widely among the companies. The FTC estimates that for a $25,000 whole life policy, the consumer can save as much as $4,700 over a twenty-year period by purchasing a low- rather than high-cost policy.

Industry response to FTC report The life insurance industry angrily denounced the FTC report as erroneous, misleading, and highly biased in favor of term insurance. Trade associations assailed the FTC for its attack on cash-value life insurance,[19] and urged Congress to curtail funding of the FTC.

In particular, insurance industry spokesmen maintained that the 1.3 percent return on all ordinary life insurance policies in 1977 was completely meaningless. They argued that the figure of 1.3 percent was based on questionable methods and assumptions—for example, newly issued and older policies were lumped together, and the inclusion of term insurance in the calculation reduced the resulting interest rate.[20]

The industry also voiced strong opposition to the FTC recommendation that cash-value policies should show average annual rates of return. It was argued that the calculation and disclosure of a rate of return would only confuse the policyowners. Also, the information would be expensive to prepare, and the costs would have to be passed on to the policyowners.

Finally, the industry argued that disclosure of the rates of return would require an improper separation of a whole life policy into a savings account and decreasing term insurance. This separation is viewed as improper because a whole life policy is an inseparable contract and can be viewed only as a whole.

Response from consumer advocates The arguments presented by the life insurance industry against disclosing annual rates-of-return data are not convincing to many consumer advocates. Professor Joseph Belth argues that life insurers oppose rigorous price disclosure for several reasons. First, many companies charge substantially higher prices than other companies for similar policies. Second, deceptive sales practices are widely used in the marketing of life insurance. Third, some companies are selling life insurance policies that may be manipulated to appear lower in price than they really are. Finally, many companies are using pricing practices that favor the purchasers of new life insurance policies at the expense of long-time policyowners.[21]

Thus, the heated debate on the nature of price disclosure in life insurance continues into the 1980s. The consumer advocates, led by Joseph Belth, will continue to press for annual rates-of-return information. Likewise, the life insurance industry—as represented by the politically powerful American Council of Life Insurance—will vigorously oppose such disclosures. In the future, state regulatory officials may feel that annual rate-of-return data will be valuable to insurance consumers. However, until that time comes, Joseph Belth and his followers will continue to be heard.

Automobile Insurance Rate Classification Systems

The process of classifying drivers based on certain rating factors is another controversial issue in insurance regulation. In particular, the use of age, sex, and marital status as rating factors in automobile insurance is highly controversial.[22] Based on these factors, younger drivers pay more for their insurance than older drivers; young male drivers pay more than female drivers in the same age category; and unmarried drivers pay more than married drivers.

Several states prohibit the use of age and sex as classification factors in automobile insurance. However, automobile insurers strongly defend these factors. Two principal arguments are presented in defense of age and sex as classification factors. First, it is argued that age and sex factors clearly identify those groups who are likely to have higher-than-average loss costs, and therefore, that such groups should pay higher premiums for protection. Based on age, in 1983, drivers under age twenty-five comprised about 21 percent of all motorists in the United States, but they accounted for about 36 percent of all accidents.[23] And younger male drivers as a group have a poorer accident record than females in the same age category. Therefore, since younger drivers as a group have a disproportionate number of automobile accidents, especially younger male drivers, it is only fair and equitable to charge them higher rates.

Second, insurers argue that it is fair and economically sound for groups to pay premiums based on the expected losses for their own group. To spread these loss costs more widely by eliminating certain rating factors (for example, age and sex) would result in unfair cross subsidies—low-risk groups would be subsidizing high-risk groups by being forced to pay higher premiums than under the present system. Thus, the high-risk groups would be unfairly subsidized at the expense of low-risk groups. In most cases, younger unmarried male drivers who account for a disproportionate number of automobile accidents would receive substantial rate reductions, while rates for the other groups would be increased.

However, social critics argue that age and sex should be prohibited as classification factors in automobile insurance. They present arguments based on concepts of social equity and fairness to defend their position. First, using age and sex as classification factors results in unfair discrimination because these are factors over which persons have no control. Since age and sex are not within a person's control, they cannot provide anyone with an incentive to drive more carefully. Thus, other factors should be used to determine automobile insurance rates, such as years of driving experience and the individual's driving record.

Second, critics argue that the present system

is defective, since younger drivers with good records can be inadvertently misclassified. As a result, they are substantially overcharged for their protection. Because classification systems are imprecise, and the various classes are not completely homogeneous, each class will inevitably contain drivers whose records are substantially better than the average of the class and drivers whose records are worse. It is argued that a great injustice is done to a younger driver with a good record who is incorrectly placed in a high-risk group. The greatest overcharges are likely to occur in the highest-rated driver classes, since these classes are the least homogeneous. Thus, in some territories where four-figure premiums are common, a youthful driver with a good record who is misclassified may be overcharged by several hundreds or even thousands of dollars. Stated differently, since a certain number of younger drivers will be misclassified and overcharged anyway, should the pricing errors be of the type where a relatively small number of drivers are overcharged several hundred dollars annually, or should they be of the type where a large number of drivers are overcharged only $10 to $20 annually.[24]

At present, most states have not been persuaded by these arguments. Consequently, most states continue to permit age and sex to be used as rating factors in automobile insurance.

Finally, the issue of sex as a rating variable is not confined only to automobile insurance. At the present time, many groups are opposed to differentiated rates based on sex in all areas of insurance, and the use of "unisex" rating factors is being widely promoted. (See Insight 28.1.)

Banks Entering Insurance Industry

A hotly debated regulatory issue is the extent to which commercial banks should be allowed to enter the insurance business. Because of deregulation of the banking industry, new computer technology, and rapid growth of financial services, the distinction between commercial banks and other financial institutions is rapidly being blurred. Commercial banks in recent years have expressed an increased willingness to sell and underwrite insurance.

Commercial banks argue that they should be allowed to sell and underwrite insurance based on three principal arguments. They are:[25]

1. *Consumer convenience.* Consumers should be given a choice of where and how they buy insurance and the convenience of purchasing insurance at their local banks.
2. *Other industries have entered insurance.* The banks also argue that other industries have entered the insurance industry, including oil companies, department stores, baby food companies, railroads, and even piano companies. Thus, commercial banks should be given the same right to enter the insurance business.
3. *Insurers can purchase banks.* It is also argued that insurers can now acquire banks, and, therefore, banks should have the right to acquire insurance companies.

However, consumer groups, labor unions, and the insurance industry are strongly opposed to the further entry of banks into the insurance business. They present several arguments to support their position, which include the following:

1. *Increased risk to depositors.* Critics argue that allowing banks to write insurance will result in a dangerous pyramiding of risks in a single operation of banking and insurance, which can affect the security of bank depositors. Critics point out that at least forty-nine banks in the United States failed during the first eight months of 1984, which is the highest since 1939. Bank failures included the Continental Illinois National Bank, which required a massive infusion of $7.5 billion by the Federal Deposit Insurance Corporation to protect depositors. Thus, critics argue that combining insurance, especially property and liability insurance, which is highly volatile, with banking can adversely affect the depositors and policyholders.

INSIGHT 28.1

Unisex Insurance

From state capitals to Washington, D.C., battles are being waged over the issue of sex discrimination in insurance.

The fights focus on unisex legislation that would alter long-standing methods used by the insurance industry to set rates—a system that considers sex as one of many valid factors in computing the price of insurance.

Opponents of unisex insurance claim that the current system is fair, arguing that different rates for men and women are justified because of proven actuarial differences between the sexes.

Because women outlive men by about eight years, for example, women pay lower premiums for life insurance. This also means, however, that they receive less annuity income per premium dollar than men.

Other statistics show that women, particularly those under 25, have fewer automobile accidents than men of the same age and marital status. Therefore, they pay lower premiums for car insurance.

And finally, women pay higher premiums for health insurance because data demonstrates that those under 55 run up more medical bills than men.

Proponents of unisex insurance contend that the system is inherently unfair since it penalizes women for a condition over which they have no control: their sex.

Critics of sex-based rates say that there is no such thing as fair discrimination. They say that the insurance industry should base actuarial tables on objective data such as mileage driven, smoking and drinking habits, weight, and individual driving records; considerations of gender should be prohibited as a matter of social policy.

Unisex bills that would prohibit insurance companies from using sex-based cost factors in setting premium and benefit levels have been introduced in both the U.S. Senate and the House. The insurance industry won the first legislative fight in late March when the House Energy and Commerce Committee approved a bill that would exempt any insurance that isn't connected with employment.

Only a handful of states have embodied the unisex principle in law. Hawaii, North Carolina, Massachusetts and Michigan forbid automobile insurance costs based on sex. And Montana recently became the first state to enact legislation banning discrimination on the basis of sex or marital status in all insurance policies and retirement plans; it will go into effect in 1985.

Landmark decisions also have been handed down by the U.S. Supreme Court. In 1978 the court ruled it illegal for a company to require larger contributions to a pension plan by females than by male employees for equal benefits at retirement. And in 1983 the court ruled that a

2. *Higher concentration of economic power.* The banking industry is now highly concentrated, since a relatively small proportion of large banks account for the bulk of the business. Critics argue that allowing banks to write or sell insurance will increase their economic power, and concentration in banking will be further increased. Big banks would also be big in insurance.
3. *Threat to survival of independent agents.* Independent agents argue that their finan-

company could not provide lower retirement benefits to women employees than to men after both sexes had made equal contributions to a pension plan.

The insurance industry argues that unisex insurance would impose tremendous financial liabilities upon women. Advocates claim, however, that women already pay an average of $16,000 more than men over a lifetime for the same product.

The three principal types of insurance that currently use sex as a rating factor are:

Automobile Insurance

Unisex rating in automobile insurance would increase costs for women from 18% to 66%, according to the Transamerica Occidental Life Insurance Co.

The American Academy of Actuaries says that unisex rates would increase auto premiums for young women drivers by more than $700 million annually.

The National Organization for Women contends that the insurance industry's $700 million estimate applies only to prices charged for insuring drivers under 21 and that it includes heavy surcharges on insurance coverage for young men. NOW claims that these surcharges disappear entirely at ages 25 to 30, depending on marital status, and that women, therefore, subsidize men for most of their driving lifetime.

Life Insurance

The actuaries' group estimates that under unisex rates women will pay $360 million more annually in increased life insurance premiums, with rates for individual women increasing up to 50%. This, they say, will be necessary to subsidize lowered premiums for men.

Women now get favored rates because their life expectancy is longer.

The Women's Equity Action League argues, however, that the contention that women live nearly eight years longer than men is misleading. WEAL says that for men and women aged 65, the difference is about four years.

Health Insurance

Women are charged more than men for individual health and disability insurance because, on the average, their claims are larger. Insurers point out, however, that most women obtain health insurance on a group basis from their employers or are included in the group coverage of their spouses.

For women who need individual coverage, the American Academy of Actuaries estimates that under unisex rates they will pay $69 million a year less for medical insurance.

However the debate ends, the issue of sex discrimination in insurance is not likely to disappear soon.

SOURCE: "Unisex Insurance," *Dollar$ense* (Summer 1984, page 15). © 1984 E. F. Baumer & Company.

cial survival is threatened if banks are allowed to enter the insurance business. Independent agents would lose their present customers to banks. The fear of being financially hurt is especially strong among independent agents who reside in small, rural areas; these agents fear the loss of their customers to local commercial banks.

4. *Coercion of debtors.* It is also argued that debtors could be coerced into buying insurance from a commercial bank as a tie-in sale. It is argued that bank customers

could be induced to buy credit life and health insurance, mortgage insurance, homeowners insurance, and automobile insurance when they borrow from the bank. Since local banks control the market for bank loans, they would also control the local markets for insurance.

The issue of banks entering insurance is not likely to disappear soon. The opposition by commercial insurers and independent agents is strong and vocal and is likely to intensify. However, the banking industry will not concede without vigorous fights. Banks have numerous locations at which they can make substantial profits by selling insurance; the banking industry is well-represented politically with powerful lobbyists, and the distinct trend to providing increased financial services to banking customers is likely to continue. For these reasons, the issue of banks entering insurance is likely to become even more intense in the future.

SUMMARY

- The insurance industry is regulated for several reasons. They are:
  a. Maintain insurer solvency.
  b. Inadequate consumer knowledge.
  c. Insure reasonable rates.
  d. Make insurance available.
- The insurance industry is regulated by the states. The McCarran Act states that continued regulation and taxation of the insurance industry by the states are in the public interest.
- Three principal methods are used to regulate the insurance industry. They are:
  a. Legislation.
  b. Courts.
  c. State insurance departments.
- The principal areas that are regulated include the following:
  a. Formation and licensing of insurers.
  b. Financial regulation.
  c. Rate regulation.
  d. Policy forms.
  e. Sales practices and consumer protection.
- With the exception of Illinois, all states have rating laws that require rates to be adequate, reasonable (not excessive), and not unfairly discriminatory. The principal types of rating laws are as follows:
  a. State-made rates.
  b. Mandatory bureau rates.
  c. Prior approval laws.
  d. File-and-use laws.
  e. No filing laws.
- Insurers must pay a state premium tax on gross premiums. The primary purpose is to raise revenues for the state and not to provide funds for insurance regulation.
- State versus federal regulation is an issue that has evoked considerable debate. The alleged advantages of federal regulation include the following:
  a. Uniformity of laws.
  b. Greater efficiency.
  c. More competent regulations.

- The advantages of state regulation include the following:
  a. Greater responsiveness to local needs.
  b. Uniformity of laws by NAIC.
  c. Greater opportunity for innovation.
  d. Unknown consequences of federal regulation.
  e. Decentralization of political power.
- Critics argue that state regulation of insurance has serious shortcomings. They include the following:
  a. Inadequate protection of consumers.
  b. Defects in financial regulation.
  c. Improvements needed in handling complaints.
  d. Lack of standards in market conduct examination.
  e. Insurance availability studies conducted only in a minority of states.
  f. Regulators overly responsive to insurance industry.
- Several current issues in insurance regulation are being debated at the present time. They include:
  a. Life insurance cost disclosure.
  b. Automobile insurance rate classification systems.
  c. Banks entering insurance industry.

QUESTIONS FOR REVIEW

1. Explain the reasons why insurance companies are regulated.
2. Describe briefly the historical development of insurance regulation by the states. Point out some important legal decisions in your answer.
3. What methods are used to regulate insurance companies?
4. Describe the areas of operation that are regulated by the states.
5. Explain the different types of rating laws.
6. Briefly describe how insurers are taxed.
7. Explain the principal arguments for federal regulation of the insurance industry. What are the major arguments in support of state regulation?
8. Briefly describe some deficiencies in state regulation of the insurance industry.
9. Explain the arguments for and against the use of age and sex as rating factors in automobile insurance.
10. Explain the major arguments for and against expansion of commercial banks into the insurance business.

QUESTIONS FOR DISCUSSION

1. Certain legal cases are significant in insurance regulation. Explain the legal significance of each of the following United States Supreme Court decisions with respect to regulation of the insurance industry by the states:
   a. Paul v. Virginia.

b. South-Eastern Underwriters Association Case.
c. McCarran-Ferguson Act.

2. State rating laws vary. Some states have file-and-use laws, while others have prior approval laws. A few states require state-made rates to be used. Explain how a file-and-use law differs from:
   a. a prior approval law.
   b. state-made rates.
3. *a.* One important goal of insurance regulation is to maintain the solvency of insurers. Describe the specific financial areas of operations that are regulated by the states.
   b. Describe some specific areas of regulation or activities of state insurance departments that aim directly at protection of the consumer.
4. Life insurance cost disclosure is a highly controversial issue in insurance regulation.
   a. What types of cost information do you believe should be provided to the purchasers of life insurance?
   b. Explain the arguments presented by life insurers that oppose providing annual-rates-of-return data to the policyowners.
5. Joseph, age twenty, is single. He feels that he is being discriminated against because he must pay more for his automobile insurance than a married person the same age. Do you believe that Joseph is being discriminated against in automobile insurance because of his age and sex? Explain your answer.

KEY CONCEPTS AND TERMS TO KNOW

Solidity
Paul v. Virginia
South-Eastern Underwriters Association
McCarran-Ferguson Act
Admitted assets
Policyholders' surplus
Kenney rule
Convention blank
Insurance guaranty fund

SUGGESTIONS FOR ADDITIONAL READINGS

Beck, Lowell R. "Insurance Business Could Be a Risky Policy for Banks," *Wall Street Journal*, February 21, 1984, p. 28.

Bickelhaupt, David L. *General Insurance*, 11th ed. Homewood, Illinois: Richard D. Irwin, Inc., 1983, chapter 28.

Bureau of Consumer Protection, Bureau of Economics. *Life Insurance Cost Disclosure: Staff Report to the Federal Trade Commission.* Washington, D.C.: U.S. Government Printing Office, 1979.

Division of Insurance, Commonwealth of Massachusetts. *Automobile Insurance Risk Classification: Equity and Accuracy.* Boston, Massachusetts: Massachusetts Division of Insurance, 1978.

Fenske, Doris. "Can the Insurance Industry Be Deregulated?" *Best's Review*, Property/Casualty Insurance ed., Vol. 82, No. 9 (January 1982).

General Accounting Office. *Issues and Needed Improvements in State Regulation of the Insurance Business (Executive Summary).* Washington, D.C.: U.S. General Accounting Office, 1979.

Greene, Mark R. and James S. Trieschmann. *Risk and Insurance*, 6th ed. Cincinnati, OH: Southwestern Publishing Co., 1984, chapter 26.

Harrington, Scott. "The Impact of Rate Regulation on Automobile Insurance Loss Ratios: Some New Empirical Evidence," *Journal of Insurance Regulation*, Vol. 3, No. 2 (December 1984).

Harrington, Scott. "The Impact of Rate Regulation on Prices and Underwriting Results in the Property-Liability Insurance Industry: A Survey," *The Journal of Risk and Insurance*, Vol. 51, No. 4 (December 1984).

Insurance Information Institute. *Insurance Issues*. New York: Insurance Information Institute, June, 1982.

Mehr, Robert I. and Emerson Cammack. *Principles of Insurance*, 7th ed. Homewood, Illinois: Richard D. Irwin, Inc., 1980, chapters 27 and 28.

Sherwood, David J. "Bank's Arguments Unsupported," *National Underwriter*, Property and Casualty Insurance ed., July 20, 1984, pp. 35–41.

Wallace, Francis K. "Unisex Automobile Rating: The Michigan Experience," *Journal of Insurance Regulation*, Vol. 3, No. 2 (December 1984).

Williams, Jr., C. Arthur and Richard M. Heins. *Risk Management and Insurance*, 5th ed. New York: McGraw-Hill Book Company, 1985, chapter 34.

Witt, Robert C. and Harry Miller. "Is Auto Insurance Rate Regulation Necessary," *Best's Review*, Property/Casualty Insurance ed., Vol. 81, No. 8 (December 1980).

NOTES

1. Spencer L. Kimball, "The Regulation of Insurance," in Spencer L. Kimball and Herbert S. Denenberg, eds., *Insurance, Government and Social Policy* (Homewood, Illinois: Richard D. Irwin, 1969), p. 4.
2. General Accounting Office, *Issues and Needed Improvements in State Regulation of the Insurance Business (Executive Summary)* (Washington, D.C.: U.S. General Accounting Office, 1979), p. 7. The author drew heavily on this report in preparing this chapter.
3. Frederick G. Crane, *Insurance Principles and Practices*, 2nd ed. (New York: John Wiley & Sons, 1984), p. 461.
4. *Paul v. Virginia*, 8 Wall. 183 (1869).
5. *U.S. v. South-Eastern Underwriters Association*, 322 U.S. 533 (1944).
6. David L. Bickelhaupt, *General Insurance*, 10th ed. (Homewood, Illinois: Richard D. Irwin, 1979), p. 207.
7. Robert I. Mehr and Emerson Cammack, *Principles of Insurance*, 7th ed. (Homewood, Illinois: Richard D. Irwin, 1980), pp. 702–704.
8. See Roger Kenney, *Fundamentals of Fire and Casualty Insurance Strength*, 4th ed. (Dedham, Massachusetts: The Kenney Insurance Studies, 1967).
9. George T. Conklin, Jr., "Company Investments," in Davis W. Gregg and Vane B. Lucas, eds., *Life and Health Insurance Handbook*, 3rd ed. (Homewood, Illinois: Richard D. Irwin, 1973), p. 1025.
10. S. S. Huebner, Kenneth Black, Jr., and Robert S. Cline, *Property and Liability Insurance*, 2nd ed. (Englewood Cliffs, New Jersey: Prentice-Hall, Inc., 1976), pp. 684–85.
11. Bernard L. Webb, J. J. Launie, Willis Park Rokes, and Norman A. Baglini, *Insurance Company Operations*, Volume II (Malvern, Pennsylvania: American Institute for Property and Liability Underwriters, 1978), pp. 47–55.
12. There are exceptions. Maximum credit life insurance rates are regulated in all states. Also, a few states, including New York, have regulations concerning minimum first-year premiums under group term insurance. New York also limits the contributions an employee may pay for group life insurance.
13. William C. Scheel and Jack VanDerhei, "Replacement of Life Insurance: Its Regulation and Current Activity," *The Journal of Risk and Insurance*, Vol. 45, No. 2 (June 1978).
14. General Accounting Office, pp. 16–17.
15. General Accounting Office, pp. i–viii.
16. Willis P. Rokes, "Should the McCarran-Ferguson Act be Repealed?" Paper delivered at the annual meeting of the Midwest Business Administration Association, Chicago, Illinois, March 27, 1980.
17. "Belth Backs President's FTC Stance," *The National Underwriter, Life and Health Insurance Edition* (February 23, 1980), pp. 17, 20.
18. *Life Insurance Cost Disclosure: Staff Report to the Federal Trade Commission* (Washington, D.C.: U.S. Government Printing Office, 1979), pp. 21–68.
19. For example, see Blake T. Newton, Jr., "The Misleading Report on Life Insurance Cost Disclosure of the Federal Trade Commission Staff," *CLU Journal* (October 1979), Vol. 33, No. 4, pp. 12–22.

20. The choice of assumptions is questionable. For example, Louis Garfin, chief actuary and vice president of the Pacific Mutual Life, says the FTC staff used assumptions in computing the 1.3 percent return that were completely different from those used for similar calculations elsewhere in the report. The available assumptions could have produced a wide range of implied rates ranging from a negative fraction of 1 percent to a higher return in excess of 9 percent. The assumptions selected by the FTC produced the 1.3 percent return near the bottom of the range. See Louis Garfin, "FTC, Regulation and a Time for Statesmanship, Part 1," *The National Underwriter, Life and Health Edition,* March 1, 1980, pp. 9–10.
21. "Belth Backs President's Stance," p. 17.
22. For a complete discussion of this issue, see General Accounting Office, pp. 26–33, and Natalie Shayer, "Driver Classification in Automobile Insurance," in *Automobile Insurance Rate Classification: Equity and Accuracy* (Boston, Massachusetts: Division of Insurance, 1978), pp. 1–24.
23. Insurance Information Institute, *Insurance Facts, 1984–85 Property/Casualty Fact Book,* p. 75.
24. General Accounting Office, p. 29. For a further discussion, the interested student should consult Joseph Ferreira, Jr., "Identifying Equitable Insurance Premiums for Risk Classes: An Alternative to the Classical Approach," *Automobile Insurance Risk Classification: Equity and Accuracy* (Boston, Massachusetts: Division of Insurance, 1978), pp. 74–120.
25. David J. Sherwood, "Banks Arguments Unsupported," *National Underwriter,* Property & Casualty ed., July 20, 1984, p. 40.

GLOSSARY

A

Absolute liability Liability for damages even though fault or negligence cannot be proven, for example, in such situations as occupational injury of employees under a workers' compensation law; also called strict liability.

Accident A loss-causing event that is sudden, unforeseen, and unintentional; compare with *Occurrence*.

Accidental bodily injury Bodily injury resulting from an act whose result was accidental or unexpected.

Actual cash value Value of property at the time of its damage or loss, determined by subtracting depreciation of the item from its replacement cost.

Actual loss ratio See *Loss ratio*.

Adjustable life insurance Insurance contract that permits certain changes to be made in amount of life insurance, premiums, period of protection, and duration of the premium-paying period.

Adjustment bureau Organization for adjusting insurance claims that is supported by insurers using the bureau's services.

Advance funding Pension provision through which the employer systematically and periodically sets aside funds prior to the employees' retirement.

Advance premium mutual Mutual insurance company owned by the policyowners that does not issue assessable policies but charges premiums expected to be sufficient to pay all claims and expenses.

Adverse selection Process in which the exercise of choice by insureds leads to higher-than-average loss levels since those with a greater probability of experiencing a loss are most likely to seek that kind of insurance.

Agent Someone who legally represents the insurer, has the authority to act on the insurer's behalf, and can bind the principal by expressed powers, by implied powers, and by apparent authority.

Aggregate deductible Deductible in some property and health insurance contracts providing that all covered losses during a year be added together and that the insurer pay only the amount in excess of the aggregate deductible amount.

Alien insurer Insurance company chartered by a foreign country and meeting certain licensing requirements.

All-risk coverage Coverage by an insurance contract that promises to cover all losses except those specifically excluded in the policy.

Annuitant Person who receives the periodic payment of an annuity.

Annuity Periodic payment to an individual that continues for a fixed period or for the duration of a designated life or lives.

Assessment mutual Mutual insurance company that has the right to assess policyowners for losses and expenses.

Assignment Means of protecting a mortgagee's interest in property being insured by having the insured assign the policy to the mortgagee; also refers to transfer of ownership of the policy to another person or party.

Assumption of risk doctrine Defense against a negligence claim that bars recovery for damages if a person understands and recognizes the danger inherent in a particular activity or occupation.

Attractive nuisance Condition that can attract and injure children; occupants of land on which such a condition exists are liable for injuries to children.

Automatic premium loan Cash borrowed from a life insurance policy's cash value to pay an overdue premium after the grace period for paying the premium has expired.

Automatic treaty Method of reinsurance in which the primary company must cede insurance to the reinsurer and the reinsurer must accept and is automatically reinsured according to the terms of the treaty.

Automobile insurance plan Formerly called assigned risk plan; method of providing automobile insurance to persons considered to be high-risk drivers who cannot obtain protection in the voluntary market; insurers are assigned their share of such drivers based on the proportion of automobile insurance written in the state.

Average indexed monthly earnings Under the OASDHI program, the person's actual earnings are indexed to determine his or her Primary Insurance Amount (PIA).

Avoidance See *Loss avoidance*.

B

Bailees' customer policy Policy that covers the loss or

damage to the property of customers regardless of a bailee's legal liability.

Basic form See *Dwelling Property 1; Homeowners 1 policy.*

Binder Authorization of coverage by an agent given before the company has formally approved a policy; provides evidence that the insurance is in force.

Blackout period The period during which Social Security benefits are not paid to a widow—between the time the youngest child reaches age sixteen and the widow's sixtieth birthday.

Blanket coverage Coverage provided for commercial property insurance that may refer to a specific amount applied to property at different locations or to coverage of different types of property at the same location.

Blanket position bond Type of fidelity bond that covers all employees automatically; the limit of liability applies to each employee. Compare with *Commercial blanket bond.*

Blue Cross plans Nonprofit, community-oriented, prepayment plans that provide health insurance coverage primarily for hospital services.

Blue Shield plans Nonprofit, prepayment plans that provide health insurance coverage mainly for physician services.

Bodily injury liability Liability for injury to another person caused by the insured's negligence.

Branch office system Type of life insurance marketing system under which branch offices are established in various areas, with a salaried branch manager as an employee of each, responsible for hiring and training new agents.

Broad form See *Dwelling Property 2 policy; Homeowners 2 policy.*

Broker Someone who legally represents the insured, soliciting or accepting applications for insurance that are not in force until the company accepts the business.

Burglary Unlawful taking of property from within the premises by someone who uses actual force or violence to gain entry, leaving visible marks of entry on the exterior.

Businessowners policy Package policy specifically designed to meet the basic property and liability insurance needs of smaller business firms in one contract.

C

Calendar-year deductible Amount payable by an insured during a calendar year before a group or individual health insurance policy begins to pay for medical expenses.

Captive insurer Insurance company established and owned by a parent firm in order to insure its loss exposures while reducing premium costs, providing easier access to a reinsurer, and perhaps easing tax burdens.

Cash surrender value Amount payable to the owner of a life insurance policy should he or she decide it is no longer wanted; calculated separately from the legal reserve.

Casualty insurance Field of insurance that covers whatever is not covered by fire, marine, and life insurers; includes automobile, liability, burglary and theft, workers' compensation, glass, and health insurance.

Ceding company Insurer who writes the policy initially and later shifts part or all of the coverage to a reinsurer.

Cession Amount of the insurance ceded to a reinsurer by the original insuring company in a reinsurance operation.

Change of occupation clause Provision in a health insurance policy stipulating that if the insured changes to a more hazardous occupation, the benefits are reduced on the basis of the amount of benefits the premium would have purchased for the more hazardous occupation.

Chartered Life Underwriter (CLU) An individual who has attained a high degree of technical competency in the field of life and health insurance and who is expected to abide by a code of ethics; must have a minimum of three years of experience in life or health insurance sales and have passed ten professional examinations administered by the American College.

Chartered Property and Casualty Underwriter (CPCU) Professional who has attained a high degree of technical competency in property and liability insurance and has passed ten professional examinations administered by the American Institute for Property and Liability Underwriters.

Class rating Ratemaking method in which similar insureds are placed in the same underwriting class and each is charged the same rate; also called manual rating.

CLU See *Chartered Life Underwriter.*

Coinsurance Provision common in commercial property insurance contracts that requires the insured to maintain insurance on the property at a stated percentage of its actual cash value; payment for a loss is determined by multiplying the amount of the loss by the fraction derived from the amount of insurance required. If the coinsurance requirement is not met at the time of loss, the insured will be penalized.

Coinsurance is also used to refer to the percentage participation clause in health insurance.

Collision loss Damages to an automobile caused by contact with another object; such losses are paid by the insurer regardless of fault.

Commercial blanket bond Type of fidelity bond that covers all employees automatically; its limit of liability is a maximum applying to any single loss regardless of number of employees involved. Compare with *Blanket position bond.*

Comparative negligence law Law enacted by many jurisdictions permitting an injured person to recover damages even though he or she may have contributed to the accident; the financial burden is shared by both parties according to their respective degrees of fault.

Completed operations Liability arising out of faulty work performed away from the premises after the work or operations are completed; applicable to contractors, plumbers, electricians, and repair shops.

Comprehensive Dishonesty, Disappearance, and Destruction (3D) Policy Crime insurance policy providing protection, at the insured's option, of up to eighteen coverages. Coverages for employee dishonesty, loss inside or outside premises, money orders and counterfeit paper currency, and depositor's forgery are printed in the policy; others may be added.

Comprehensive major medical insurance Type of group plan combining basic plan benefis and major medical insurance in one policy.

Compulsory insurance law Law protecing accident victims against irresponsible motorists by requiring owners and operators of automobiles to carry certain types of liability insurance in order to drive legally within the state.

Concealment Deliberate failure of an applicant for insurance to reveal a material fact to the insurer.

Conditionally renewable Continuance provision of a health insurance policy that stipulates the company cannot cancel the policy during its term but can refuse to renew under certain contractually stated conditions.

Conditions Provisions inserted in an insurance contract that qualify or place limitations on the insurer's promise to perform.

Condominium unit owners form See *Homeowners 6 policy.*

Consequential loss Loss occurring as the consequence of some other loss; often called an indirect loss.

Contents broad form See *Homeowners 4 policy.*

Contingent beneficiary Beneficiary of a life insurance policy who is entitled to receive the policy proceeds upon the insured's death if the primary beneficiary dies before the insured or one who receives the remaining payments if the primary beneficiary dies before receiving the guaranteed number of payments.

Contingent liability Liability arising out of work done by independent contractors for a firm; the firm may be liable if the activity is illegal, the situation does not permit delegation of authority, or the work is inherently dangerous.

Contract bond Type of surety bond guaranteeing that the principal will fulfill all contractual obligations.

Contractual liability Legal liability of another party that the business firm agrees to assume by a written or oral contract.

Contribution by equal shares Type of other-insurance provision often found in liability insurance contracts that requires each company to share equally in the loss until the share of each insurer equals the lowest limit of liability under any policy or until the full amount of loss is paid.

Contributory negligence law Common law defense blocking an injured person from recovering damages if he or she has contributed in any way to the accident.

Contributory plan Group life, health, or pension plan in which the employees pay part of the premiums.

Convertible Term life insurance that can be exchanged for a permanent life insurance policy without evidence of insurability.

Coordination-of-benefits provision Provision of a group medical expense plan that prevents overinsurance and duplication of benefits when one person is covered under more than one group plan.

Corridor deductible Major medical plan deductible that excludes benefits provided by a basic plan if both a basic and a group major medical expense policy are in force; applies only to eligible medical expenses not covered by the basic medical expense plan and is applied only after basic plan benefits are exhausted.

Coverage for damage to your auto That part of the personal auto policy insuring payment for damage or theft of the insured automobile; it includes comprehensive and, at the buyer's option, collision insurance in the same insuring agreement.

CPCU See *Chartered Property and Casualty Underwriter (CPCU).*

Currently insured Status of a covered person under the Old-Age, Survivors, Disability, and Health Insurance (OASDHI) program who has at least six quarters of coverage out of the last thirteen quarters, ending with the quarter of death, disability, or entitlement.

D

Damage to property of others Damage covered up to $500 per occurrence for an insured who damages another's property; payment is made despite the lack of legal liability; coverage is included in Section II of the homeowners policy.

Declarations Statements in an insurance contract that provide information about the property or life to be insured and used for underwriting and rating purposes and identification of the property or life to be insured.

Deferred group annuity Type of allocated pension plan in which a single premium deferred annuity is purchased each year and is equal to the retirement benefit for that year.

Defined benefit plan Type of pension plan in which the retirement benefit is known in advance but the contributions vary depending on the amount necessary to fund the desired benefit.

Defined contribution plan Type of pension plan in which the contribution rate is fixed but the retirement benefit is variable.

Dental insurance Individual or group plan that helps pay costs of normal dental care as well as damage to teeth from an accident.

Dependency period Period of time following the readjustment period during which the surviving spouse's children are under eighteen and therefore dependent upon the parent.

Deposit administration plan Type of pension plan in which all pension contributions are deposited in an unallocated fund; an annuity is purchased only when the employee retires.

Difference in conditions (DIC) insurance All-risk policy that covers other perils not insured by basic property insurance contracts, supplemental to and excluding the coverage provided by underlying contracts.

Direct loss Loss that results directly from an insured peril.

Direct writer Insurance company in which the salesperson is an employee of the insurer, not an independent contractor, and which pays all selling expenses, including salary.

Disability income rider Benefit that can be added to a life insurance policy providing payment of monthly disability income benefits of $10 for each $1,000 of insurance, if the insured becomes totally disabled.

Disability insured Status of an individual who is insured for disability benefits under the Old-Age, Survivors, Disability and Health Insurance (OASDHI) program; the covered person must be fully insured and have at least twenty quarters of coverage out of the last forty, ending with the quarter in which the disability occurs. Fewer quarters are required for persons under age thirty.

Disappearing deductible Deductible in an insurance contract that provides for a decreasing deductible amount as the size of the loss increases, so that small claims are not paid but large losses are paid in full.

Dividend options Ways in which life insurance dividends can be taken, including cash, reduction of premiums, accumulation of cash at interest, paid-up additions, or term insurance.

Domestic insurer Insurance company domiciled and licensed in the state in which it does business.

Double indemnity rider Benefit that can be added to a life insurance policy doubling the face amount of life insurance if death occurs as the result of an accident.

Dram-shop law Law that imputes negligence to the owner of a business that sells liquor in the case that an intoxicated customer causes injury or property damage to another person; usually excluded from general liability policies.

Driver education credit Student discount or reduction in premium amount for which young drivers become eligible upon completion of a driver education course.

Dwelling Property 1 Property insurance policy that insures the dwelling at actual cash value, other structures, personal property, fair rental value, and certain other coverages; covers a limited number of perils.

Dwelling Property 2 Property insurance policy that insures the dwelling and other structures at replacement cost; it adds additional coverages and has a greater list of covered perils than the Dwelling Property 1 policy.

Dwelling Property 3 Property insurance policy providing all-risk coverage on the dwelling and other structures and named-perils coverage on personal property; it provides the greatest protection of the three property insurance forms.

E

Earnings test Test under the Old-Age, Survivors, Disability, and Health Insurance (OASDHI) program that reduces monthly benefits to those persons who have earned income in excess of the maximum allowed; also called retirement test.

Economatic policy Special type of participating whole life insurance in which the dividends are used to buy term insurance or paid-up additions equal to the difference between the face amount of the policy and some guaranteed amount.

Educational endowment Life insurance policy purchased by parents for children under a specified age; the policy matures as an endowment at age eighteen to provide funds for college.

Elements of a negligent act Four elements an injured person must show to prove negligence: existence of a legal duty to use reasonable care, failure to perform that duty, damages or injury to the claimant, and proximate cause relationship between the negligent act and the damage.

Eligibility period Brief period of time following a probationary period during which an employee can sign up for group insurance without furnishing evidence of insurability.

Elimination (waiting period) Waiting period in health insurance during which time benefits are not paid; also a period of time that must be met before benefits are actually payable.

Employee Retirement Income Security Act (ERISA) Legislation passed in 1974 applying to most private pension and welfare plans that requires certain minimum standards of such plans to protect participating employees.

Endorsement Written provision that adds to, deletes, or modifies the provisions in the original contract; also see *Rider*.

Endowment insurance Type of life insurance that pays the face amount of insurance to beneficiary if the insured dies within a specified period or to the insured if he or she survives to the end of the period; combines features of level term insurance and a pure endowment.

Equity in unearned premium reserve Amount by which an unearned premium reserve is overstated because it is established on the basis of gross premium rather than net premium.

ERISA See *Employee Retirement Income Security Act (ERISA)*.

Estate planning Process designed to conserve estate assets before and after death, distribute property according to an individual's wishes, minimize federal estate and state inheritance taxes, provide estate liquidity to meet costs of estate settlement, and provide for the family's financial needs.

Estoppel Legal doctrine that prevents a person from denying the truth of a previous representation of fact, especially when such representation has been relied upon by the one to whom the statement was made.

Exclusions Listing in an insurance contract of the perils, losses, and property excluded from coverage.

Exclusive agency system Type of insurance marketing system under which the agent represents only one company or group of companies under common ownership.

Expense ratio That proportion of the gross rate available for expenses and profit; ratio of expenses incurred to premiums written.

Experience rating (1) Means of rating group life and health insurance plans that uses the loss experience of the group to determine the premiums to be charged. (2) As applied to property and liability insurance by which the firm's past loss experience determines the premium for the next policy period. (3) As applied to state unemployment insurance programs, controversial procedure providing firms with favorable employment records with reduced unemployment tax rates.

Exposure unit Unit of measurement used in insurance pricing.

Extended coverage perils Specific group of perils covered by a property insurance policy, including fire or lightning, internal explosion, windstorm or hail, explosion, riot or civil commotion, aircraft, vehicles, and smoke damage.

Extended nonowned coverage Endorsement that can be added to an automobile liability insurance policy that covers the insured while driving any nonowned automobile on a regular basis.

Extended unemployment insurance benefits Additional cash benefits paid through federal-state unemployment insurance programs to workers who are involuntarily unemployed and who have exhausted their regular weekly cash benefits during periods of high unemployment.

Extra expense insurance Type of business interruption insurance that covers the extra expenses incurred to continue operations after a loss has occurred.

F

Factory mutual Mutual insurance company insuring only properties that meet high underwriting standards with great emphasis on loss prevention.

Facultative reinsurance Optional, case-by-case method of reinsurance used when the primary company receives an application for insurance that exceeds its retention limit.

Fair Access to Insurance Requirements (FAIR) plan Federal property insurance plan that provides basic property insurance to property owners in riot-prone areas who are unable to obtain insurance in the normal markets; each state with such a plan has a central placement facility and a reinsurance association or pool; participating insurers are eligible for federal riot reinsurance from the National Insurance Development Fund.

Fair rental value Amount payable to an insured homeowner for loss of rental income due to damage that makes the premises uninhabitable.

Family automobile policy Auto insurance policy type being phased out in most states in favor of the easier-to-read personal auto policy.

Family income policy Special life insurance policy combining decreasing term and whole life insurance; it pays monthly income of $10 for each $1000 of life insurance if the insured dies within the specified period, then pays face amount at the end of the period.

Family maintenance policy Special life insurance policy combining level term and whole life insurance; it pays a monthly income of $10 for each $1,000 of life insurance for a definite period of time, if the insured dies within the family maintenance period, then pays the face amount at the end of the period.

Family policy Special life insurance policy that insures all family members in one policy; husband or wife is insured under a whole life policy, and the spouse and children are insured by term insurance.

Family purpose doctrine Concept that imputes negligence committed by immediate family members while operating a family car to the owner of the car.

Farm mutual Local mutual insurance company that insures farm property in a limited geographical area primarily through assessable policies.

Federal crime insurance Federal crime insurance program subsidized by the federal government in those high-crime areas where it has been determined that insurance is not available at affordable rates; it is sold by licensed agents and brokers in eligible states, but the Federal Insurance Administration is the insurer.

Federal flood insurance Insurance provided by the Federal Insurance Administration at subsidized rates to persons who reside in flood zones and whose community joins the program and agrees to establish and enforce flood control and land-use measures.

Federal surety bond Type of surety bond required by federal agencies that regulate the actions of business firms; it guarantees that the bonded party will comply with federal standards, pay all taxes or duties accrued, or pay the penalty if the bondholder fails to do so.

Fellow-servant doctrine Common law defense blocking an injured employee from collecting workers' compensation benefits if he or she sustained an injury caused in any way by the negligence of a fellow worker.

Fidelity bond Bond that protects an employer against dishonest or fraudulent acts of employees, such as embezzlement, fraud, or theft of money.

File-and-use law Law for regulating insurance rates under which companies are required to file the rates with the state insurance department before putting them into effect.

Financial responsibility law Law that requires persons involved in automobile accidents involving certain circumstances to furnish proof of financial responsibility up to a minimum dollar limit or face having driving privileges revoked or suspended.

Fire As covered by the standard fire policy, a combustion accompanied by a flame or glow, which escapes its normal confines to cause damage.

Fire legal liability Liability of a firm or person for fire damage caused by negligence of and damage to property of others.

Floaters Commercial fire insurance policies that cover personal property that can be moved from one location to another for both transportation perils and perils affecting property at a fixed location.

Foreign insurer Insurance company chartered by one state but licensed to do business in another.

Fortuitous loss Unforeseen and unexpected loss that occurs as a result of chance.

Franchise deductible Deductible commonly found in marine insurance contracts providing that the insurer has no liability if the loss is under a certain amount, but once this amount is reached, the entire loss is paid in full.

Fraternal insurer Mutual insurance company that provides life and health insurance to members of a social organization.

Free-Trade Zone New York market created by law in 1978 in which large or unusual insurance contracts—primarily on large commercial exposures—are exempt from the rate and policy-form filing regulations of that state.

Fully insured Insured status of a covered person under the Old-Age, Survivors, Disability, and Health Insurance (OASDHI) program if he or she meets certain criteria: has forty quarters of coverage or has one quarter of coverage for each year after 1950 or after age twenty-one, if later, up to the time of qualification.

G

General agency system Type of life insurance marketing system in which the general agent is an independent businessperson who represents only one insurer, is in charge of a territory, and is responsible for hiring, training, and motivating new agents.
General average loss In ocean marine insurance, a loss incurred for the common good that is shared by all parties to the venture.
General damages Money amount awarded by a jury as a result of a negligent act to compensate for losses that cannot be specifically itemized, such as pain and suffering.
Good student discount Reduction of automobile premium for a young driver who ranks in the upper 20 percent of his or her class, has a B or 3.0 average, or is on the Dean's list or honor roll; it is based on the premise that good students are better drivers.
Grace period Period of time during which a policyowner may pay an overdue premium without allowing the policy to lapse.
Gross earnings form Type of business interruption insurance that covers the loss of gross earnings less any expenses that can be discontinued during the shutdown period.
Gross premium Amount paid by the insured for his or her policy, determined by the sum of the pure premium and a loading element.
Group creditor life insurance Life insurance provided debtors by a lending institution to provide for the cancellation of any outstanding debt should the borrower die; normally term insurance limited to the amount of the loan.
Group major medical plan See *Supplementary major medical insurance.*
Group ordinary life insurance Group insurance plan providing life insurance for employees; traditional whole life policy is split into decreasing insurance protection and increasing cash values.
Group paid-up life insurance Accumulating units of single premium whole life insurance and decreasing term insurance, which together equal the face amount of the policy; provided through a group life insurance plan.
Group permanent plan Type of pension plan in which cash-value life insurance is issued on a group basis and cash values in each policy are used to pay retirement benefits when a worker retires.
Group survivor income benefit insurance (SIBI) See *Survivor income benefit insurance.*
Group term life insurance Most common form of group life insurance; yearly renewable term insurance on employees during their working careers.
Guaranteed purchase option Benefit that can be added to a life insurance policy permitting the insured to purchase additional amounts of life insurance at specified times in the future without requiring evidence of insurability.
Guaranteed renewable Continuance provision of a health insurance policy in which the company guarantees to renew the policy to a stated age, typically sixty-five, and whose renewal is at the insured's option; premiums can be increased for broad classes of insureds.

H

Hazard Condition that creates or increases the chance of loss.
Health maintenance organization (HMO) Organized system of health care that provides comprehensive health services to its members for a fixed, prepaid fee by leasing or ownership of medical facilities and agreements with hospitals and physicians.
High-risk automobile insurer Company that specializes in insuring motorists who have poor driving records or have been cancelled or refused insurance.
HMO See *Health maintenance organization (HMO).*
Hold-harmless agreement Clause written into a contract by which one party agrees to release another party from all legal liability, such as a retailer who agrees to release the manufacturer from legal liability if the product injures someone.
Homeowners 1 policy Homeowners insurance policy that requires a minimum of $15,000 of insurance on the dwelling and insures the dwelling and other structures as well as personal property on the basis of replacement cost; personal liability insurance is also provided.
Homeowners 2 policy Homeowners insurance policy that duplicates the Homeowners 1 form and adds additional perils in its coverage.
Homeowners 3 policy Homeowners insurance policy

that covers the dwelling and other structures on an all-risk basis and personal property on a named-perils basis.

Homeowners 4 policy Homeowners insurance policy that applies to tenants renting a home or apartment; covers the tenant's personal property and provides personal-liability insurance.

Homeowners 6 policy Homeowners insurance policy that covers only personal property of the insured condominium owner on a broad form, named-perils basis.

Homeowners 8 policy Homeowner policy that is designed for older homes. Dwelling and other structures are indemnified on the basis of repair cost using common construction materials and methods.

Hospital expense insurance Private health insurance that pays for medical expenses incurred while in a hospital—both a daily hospital benefit for room and board and benefits for miscellaneous expenses.

Hospital insurance (HI) That part of the Medicare program that provides inpatient hospital care, inpatient care in a skilled nursing facility, and home health services.

HR-10 plan See *Keogh plan for the self-employed (HR- 10) plan.*

Hull insurance (1) Class of ocean marine insurance that covers physical damage to the ship or vessel insured; typically written on an all-risk basis. (2) Physical damage insurance on aircraft—similar to collision insurance in an automobile policy.

Human life value For purposes of life insurance, the present value of the family's share of the deceased breadwinner's earnings.

I

Immediate participation guarantee (IPG) plan Type of pension plan in which all pension contributions are deposited in an unallocated fund and used directly to pay benefits to retirees.

Imputed negligence Case in which responsibility for damage can be transferred from the negligent party to another person, such as an employer.

Incontestable clause Contractual provision in a life insurance policy stating that the company cannot contest the policy after it has been in force two years during the insured's lifetime.

Indemnification Compensation to the victim of a loss, in whole or in part, by payment, repair, or replacement.

Indemnity Legal principle that specifies an insured should not collect more than the actual cash value of a loss but should be restored to approximately the same financial position as existed before the loss.

Independent agency system Type of property and liability insurance marketing system, sometimes called the American Agency system, in which the agent is an independent businessperson representing several companies; the agency owns the expirations or renewal rights to the business, and the agent is compensated by commissions that vary by lines of insurance.

Indirect loss See *Consequential loss.*

Individual bond Type of fidelity bond that specifically names an employee, so that coverage applies only to that person.

Individual deductible Amount that an insured and each person of his or her family covered by the policy must pay before the group or individual medical insurance policy begins to pay for medical expenses.

Individual policy plan Type of pension plan in which an individual policy is purchased for each employee to provide the promised retirement benefit.

Individual Retirement Account (IRA) Individual retirement plan that can be established by a person with earned income. An IRA plan enjoys favorable income tax advantages. The maximum annual tax-deductible contribution is the lower of 100 percent of compensation or $2,000 ($2,250 with a nonworking spouse).

Industrial life insurance See *Home service life insurance.*

Inflation-guard endorsement Endorsement added at the insured's request to a homeowners policy to increase periodically the face amount of insurance on the dwelling and other policy coverages by a specified percentage.

Inland marine insurance Transportation insurance that provides protection for goods shipped on land, including imports, exports, domestic shipments, and instrumentalities of transportation as well as an option to insure fine arts, jewelry, and furs.

Insurance Pooling of fortuitous losses by transfer of risks to insurers who agree to indemnify insureds for such losses, to provide other pecuniary benefits on their occurrence, or to render services connected with the risk.

Insurance guaranty funds State funds that provide for the payment of unpaid claims of insolvent insurers.

Insuring agreement That part of an insurance contract that summarizes the major promises of the insurer.

Interest-adjusted method Means of determining cost to an insured of a life insurance policy that considers the time cost of money by applying an interest factor to each element of cost; see *Net payment cost index; Surrender cost index.*
IPG plan See *Immediate participation guarantee (IPG) plan.*
IRA See *Individual Retirement Account (IRA).*
Irrevocable beneficiary Beneficiary designation allowing no change to be made in the beneficiary of an insurance policy without the irrevocable beneficiary's consent.

J

Joint underwriting association (JUA) Organization of all automobile insurers operating in a state that makes automobile insurance available to high-risk drivers through a specially designed policy and predetermined rates.
Judgment rating Ratemaking method for which each exposure is individually evaluated and which is determined largely by the underwriters' judgment.
Judicial bond Type of surety bond used for court proceedings and guaranteeing that the party bonded will fulfill certain obligations specified by law, for example, fiduciary responsibilities.
Jumping juvenile insurance policy Life insurance purchased by parents for children under a specified age; provides permanent life insurance which increases in face value five times at age twenty-one with no increase in premium.

K

Kenney rule Concept permitting a property-liability insurer to write $2 of new net premiums for each $1 of policyholders' surplus.
Keogh plan for the self-employed (HR-10) plan Plan individually adopted by self-employed persons that allows a maximum annual contribution to a defined contribution plan equal to 20 percent of net earned income. If a defined benefit plan is used, the self-employed person can fund for a maximum annual benefit equal to 100 percent of average compensation for the three highest consecutive years of earnings or $90,000, whichever is lower; also applies to employees of the self-employed person.

L

Last clear chance rule Statutory modification of the contributory negligence law allowing the claimant endangered by his or her own negligence to recover damages from a defendant if the defendant had a last clear chance to avoid the accident but failed to do so.
Law of large numbers Concept that the greater the number of exposures, the more closely will actual results approach the probable results expected from an infinite number of exposures.
Legal reserve Liability item on a life insurer's balance sheet; it represents the redundant or excessive premiums paid under the level-premium method during the early years. Assets must be accumulated to offset the legal reserve liability. Purpose of the legal reserve is to provide lifetime protection.
Liability coverage That part of the personal auto policy that protects a covered person against a suit or claim for bodily injury or property damage arising out of negligent operation of an automobile; a single or split limit for bodily injury and property damage liability is applied on a per accident basis.
Liability without fault principle Principle on which workers' compensation is based, holding the employer absolutely liable for occupational injuries or disease suffered by workers, regardless of who is at fault.
License and permit bond Type of surety bond guaranteeing that the person bonded will comply with all laws and regulations that govern his or her activities.
Life insurance programming Systematic method of determining the insured's financial goals, which are translated into specific amounts of life insurance, then periodically reviewed for possible changes.
Limited-payment insurance Type of whole life insurance providing protection throughout the insured's lifetime and for which relatively high premiums are paid only for a limited period.
Liquor liability law See *Dram-shop law.*
Loading The amount that must be added to the pure premium for expenses, profit, and a margin for contingencies.
Loss avoidance A risk management technique whereby a situation or activity that may result in a loss for a firm is avoided or abandoned, thus reducing the chance of loss to zero.
Loss control Risk management activities that reduce both the frequency and severity of losses for a firm or organization.
Loss exposure Situation which threatens potential

loss to a firm or organization, through physical damage to property, loss of income due to such damage, liability lawsuits arising from harm to others, loss through criminal acts or employee dishonesty, or loss due to death of key employees.

Loss payable clause Means of protecting a mortgagee's interest in property by directing the insurer to make a loss payment to the mortgagee in the event of a loss.

Loss ratio The ratio of incurred losses and loss-adjustment expenses to earned premiums.

Loss reserve Amount set aside by property-liability insurers for claims reported and adjusted but not yet paid, claims reported and filed but not yet adjusted, and claims incurred but not yet reported to the company.

M

Mail order insurer Type of insurance company that sells policies through the mail or other mass media, eliminating need for agents.

Major medical insurance Health insurance designed to pay a large proportion of the covered expenses of a catastrophic illness or injury.

Manual rating See *Class rating*.

Manuscript policy Policy designed for a firm's specific needs and requirements.

Mass merchandising Plan for insuring individual members of a group, such as employees of firms or members of labor unions, under a single program of insurance at reduced premiums; property and liability insurance is sold to individual members using group insurance marketing methods.

Maximum possible loss Worst loss that could possibly happen to a firm in its lifetime.

Maximum probable loss Worst loss that is likely to happen to a firm during its lifetime.

McCarran-Ferguson Act Federal law passed in 1945 stating that continued regulation and taxation of the insurance industry by the states are in the public interest and that federal antitrust laws apply to insurance only to the extent that the industry is not regulated by state law.

Medical Information Bureau (MIB) Bureau whose purpose is to supply underwriting information in life insurance to member companies, which report any health impairments of an applicant for insurance.

Medical payments coverage That part of the personal auto policy that pays all reasonable medical and general expenses incurred by a covered person within three years from the date of an accident.

Medical payments to others Pays for medical expenses of others under the homeowners policy in the event that a person (not a resident) is accidentally injured on the premises, or by the activities of an insured, resident employee, or animal owned by or in the care of an insured.

Mercantile Open Stock Burglary Policy Crime insurance policy that covers loss of merchandise, furniture, fixtures, and equipment from a burglary, attempted burglary, or robbery of a watchman only when the premises are closed; designed for businesses that have high-value merchandise easily stolen and converted into cash.

Mercantile Robbery Policy Crime insurance policy that covers the loss of money, securities, and other property from a robbery or attempted robbery; coverage can be written for robbery inside or outside the premises, or both.

Mercantile Safe Burglary Policy Crime insurance policy that covers the loss of money, securities, and other property from within a locked vault or safe as a result of a burglary; also covers damage to the safe or vault.

Merit rating Ratemaking method in which class rates are adjusted upward or downward on the basis of individual loss experience.

MIB See *Medical Information Bureau (MIB)*.

Misstatement of age clause Contractual provision in an insurance policy stating that, if the insured's age is misstated, the amount payable is the amount that the premium would have purchased at the correct age.

Mobilehome insurance A package policy that provides property insurance and personal-liability insurance to the owners of mobile homes. A special endorsement is added to HO 2 or HO 3.

Modified life policy Whole life policy for which premiums are reduced for the first three to five years and are higher thereafter.

Money and Securities Broad Form Crime insurance policy that provides broad coverage for destruction, disappearance, or wrongful abstraction of money and securities, plus limited coverage on other property; coverage for loss inside and outside the premises can be written together or separately.

Moral hazard Dishonesty or character defects in an individual that increase the chance of loss.

Morale hazard Carelessness or indifference to a loss because of the existence of insurance.

Multi-car discount Reduction in automobile insurance premium for insured who owns two or more automobiles, on the basis that two such autos owned by the same person will not be driven as frequently as only one.
Multiple-line insurance Type of insurance that combines several lines of insurance in one contract, for example, fire insurance and liability insurance.
Mutual insurer Insurance corporation owned by the policyowners, who elect the board of directors, which appoints managing executives and which may pay a dividend or give a rate reduction in advance to insureds.

N

NAIC See *National Association of Insurance Commissioners (NAIC).*
NALP See *Net annual level premium (NALP).*
Name schedule bond Type of fidelity bond that specifically names each person to be bonded, at a specified amount.
Named-perils coverage Coverage by an insurance contract that promises to pay only for those losses caused by perils specifically listed in the policy.
National Association of Insurance Commissioners (NAIC) Group founded in 1871 that meets periodically to discuss industry problems and draft model laws in areas it has recommended to state legislatures for adoption.
Nationwide Marine Definition Statement drafted in 1933 by inland marine insurers to define the property that marine insurers can write; has been revised two times.
Needs approach Method for estimating amount of life insurance appropriate for a family by analyzing various family needs that must be met if the family head should die and converting them into specific amounts of life insurance; financial assets are considered in determining the amount of life insurance needed.
Negligence Failure to exercise the standard of care required of a reasonably prudent person to protect others from harm.
Net amount at risk Concept associated with a level-premium life insurance policy; calculated as the difference between the face amount of the policy and the legal reserve.
Net annual level premium (NALP) Annual level premium for a life insurance policy with no expense loading; mathematically equivalent to the net single premium.
Net payment cost index Means of measuring the cost of an insurance policy to an insured if death occurs at the end of some specified time period after taking into consideration the time value of money.
Net retention See *Retention limit.*
Net single premium Present value of the future death benefit of a life insurance policy.
New York Insurance Exchange Large trading floor where underwriting syndicates offer various types of insurance and brokers shop to place business for clients they represent; created in 1978 by New York law.
No-fault automobile insurance Insurance plan providing that, after an automobile accident, each party collects from his or her own insurer regardless of fault.
No filing law Law for regulating insurance rates under which insurers are not required to file rates at all with the state insurance department but may be required to furnish rate schedules and supporting data to state officials.
Noncancellable Continuance provision of a health insurance policy stipulating that the policy cannot be cancelled, that the renewal is guaranteed, and that the premium rates cannot be increased.
Noncontributory Employer pays the entire cost of a group insurance or private pension plan; all eligible employees are covered.
Nonforfeiture law State law requiring insurance companies to provide at least a minimum nonforfeiture value to policyowners who surrender their cash-value policies.
Nonforfeiture options Ways in which a cash-value life policy can get payment when it is surrendered, including cash value, reduced paid-up insurance, or extended term insurance.
Noninsurance transfer One of the various methods other than insurance by which a pure risk and its potential financial consequences can be transferred to another party; for example, contracts, leases, and hold-harmless agreements.

O

Objective risk Relative variation of actual loss from expected loss, which varies inversely with the square root of the number of cases under observation.
Occurrence Loss-causing event that may occur over some period of time; compare with *Accident.*

Ocean marine insurance Type of insurance that provides protection for all types of ocean-going vessels and their cargoes as well as legal liability of owners and shippers.

Ordinary life insurance Type of whole life insurance providing protection throughout the insured's lifetime and for which premiums are paid throughout the insured's lifetime.

Other than a collision loss Optional benefit that can be added to the personal auto policy; all physical damage losses to the automobile other than a collision are covered, including losses from missiles, fire, explosion, windstorm, riot, contact with a bird or animal, and glass breakage. Theft is also covered.

P

P & I Insurance See *Protection and indemnity (P & I) insurance.*

Package policy Policy that combines two or more separate contracts of insurance in one policy; for example, homeowners insurance.

Partial disability Inability of the insured to perform one or more important duties of his or her occupation.

Participating policy Life insurance policy that pays dividends to the policyowners.

Paul v. Virginia Landmark legal decision of 1869 establishing the right of the states, and not the federal government, to regulate insurance; ruled that insurance was not interstate commerce.

Percentage participation clause Provision in a health insurance policy that requires the insured to pay a certain percentage of eligible medical expenses in excess of the deductible; also called coinsurance.

Peril Cause or source of loss.

Perpetual mutual Mutual insurance company providing property insurance with no expiration date, requiring a large one-time premium deposit.

Personal injury Injury for which legal liability arises (such as for false arrest, detention or imprisonment, malicious prosecution, libel, slander, defamation of character, violation of the right of privacy, and unlawful entry or eviction) and which may be covered by an endorsement to the homeowners policy.

Personal liability insurance Liability insurance that protects the insured for an amount up to policy limits against a claim or suit for damages because of bodily injury or property damage caused by the insured's negligence. This coverage is provided by section II of the homeowners policy.

Personal umbrella policy Policy designed to provide protection against a catastrophic lawsuit or judgment, whose coverage ranges from $1 million to $10 million and extends to the entire family anywhere in the world. Insurance is excess over underlying coverages.

Physical hazard Condition that increases the chance of loss.

Physicians' expense insurance See *Regular medical expense insurance.*

PIA See *Primary insurance amount (PIA).*

Policy loan Cash value of a life insurance policy that can be borrowed by the policyowner in lieu of surrendering the policy.

Policyholders' surplus Difference between an insurance company's assets and its liabilities.

Pooling Spreading of losses incurred by the few over the entire group, so that in the process, average loss is substituted for actual loss.

Position schedule bond Type of fidelity bond that lists the various positions and numbers of employees occupying them to be bonded.

Preexisting condition Physical or mental condition of an insured that existed prior to issuance of a policy.

Preexisting condition clause Contractual provision of a health insurance policy stating that preexisting conditions are not covered or are covered only after the policy has been in force for a specified period.

Preferred provider organization (PPO) New health care delivery system whereby the employer or insurer enters into contracts with certain physicians, hospitals, and other health-care providers to provide health-care services at a reduced fee.

Premises and operations coverage In a general liability insurance policy, the coverage that protects a firm for legal liability arising out of the ownership and maintenance of the premises and its business operations.

Primary beneficiary Beneficiary of a life insurance policy who is first entitled to receive the policy proceeds upon the insured's death.

Primary and excess insurance Type of others-insurance provision that requires the primary insurer to pay first in the case of a loss; when the policy limits under the primary policy are exhausted, the excess insurer pays.

Primary insurance amount (PIA) Monthly amount paid to a retired worker at age sixty-five or to a disabled worker eligible for benefits under the Old-Age, Survivors, Disability, and Health Insurance (OASDHI) program.

Prior approval law Law for regulating insurance rates under which the rates must be filed and approved by the state insurance department before they can be used.

Pro rata liability clause Clause in the standard fire policy that makes each company insuring the same interest in a property liable according to the proportion that its insurance bears to the total amount of insurance on the property.

Probationary period (1) Waiting period of one to six months required of an employee before he or she is allowed to participate in a group insurance plan. (2) Specified number of days after a health insurance policy is issued during which time sickness is not covered.

Products liability The legal liability of manufacturers, wholesalers, and retailers to persons who are injured or who incur property damage from defective products.

Professional liability Liability incurred by a professional such as a physician, nurse, attorney, or architect for negligent acts occurring as professional services are performed; homeowners policies do not cover these exposures, but a professional liability policy may be purchased.

Property damage liability Liability for damages to others' property caused by the insured's negligence.

Property and liability insurance Coverage which falls into the category of fire, marine, or casualty insurance or fidelity and surety bonds.

Prospective reserve In life insurance, the difference between the present value of future benefits and the present value of future net premiums.

Protection and indemnity (P & I) insurance Coverage that can be added as a separate contract to an ocean marine insurance policy to provide broad, comprehensive liability insurance for property damage and bodily injury to third parties.

Proximate cause Factor causing damage to property for which there is an unbroken chain of events between the occurrence of an insured peril and damage or destruction of the property.

Public official bond Type of surety bond guaranteeing that public officials will faithfully perform their duties for the protection of the public.

Punitive damages Money amount awarded by a jury as a result of a negligent act to punish the tortfeasor and deter others from committing the same wrongful act.

Pure premium That portion of the insurance rate needed to pay losses and loss-adjustment expenses.

Pure risk Situation in which there is only the possibility of loss.

R

Rate Price per unit of insurance.

Ratemaking Process by which insurance pricing or premium rates are determined for an insurance company.

Rating factors Factors considered by an insurer in order to determine premiums; major factors in automobile insurance include territory, age, sex, marital status, and use of the automobile.

RDC See *Running down clause (RDC).*

Readjustment period One to two year period immediately following the breadwinner's death during which time the family receives approximately the same amount of income it received while the breadwinner was alive.

Rebating An illegal practice of giving a premium reduction or some other financial advantage to an individual as an inducement to purchase the policy.

Reciprocal exchange Unincorporated mutual insuring organization in which insurance is exchanged among members and which is managed by an attorney-in-fact.

Recurrent disability clause Provision in a health insurance policy that considers a second disability as a continuation of the first disability if the insured has not returned to work on a full-time basis for six months.

Redlining Refusal by insurers to insure certain risks because of their location; term stemming from the belief that some insurers draw red lines around inner-city neighborhoods that they will not insure.

Regular medical expense insurance Health insurance that pays a benefit for nonsurgical care provided by a physician in the hospital, the patient's home, or the doctor's office; also called *physicians' expense insurance.*

Reinstatement clause Contractual provision in a life insurance policy that permits the owner to reinstate a lapsed policy if requirements are fulfilled; for example, evidence of insurability is required and overdue premiums plus interest must be paid.

Reinstatement provision Provision of a health insurance policy that allows the insured to reinstate a lapsed policy by payment of premium either without an application or with an application.

Reinsurance The shifting of part or all of the insurance originally written by one insurer to another insurer.

Reinsurance facility Pool for placing high-risk automobile drivers that arranges for a company to accept all applicants for insurance; underwriting losses are shared by all automobile insurers in the state.

Relation of earnings to insurance clause Provision in most guaranteed renewable or noncancellable health insurance policies stating that if disability income benefits payable from all policies exceed the insured's monthly earnings at the time of disability, or average monthly earnings for two years preceding the disability, the company's liability is limited to the proportion of policy benefits that such earnings bear to the total disability benefits of all contracts; also called average earnings clause.

Relative value schedule Variation of the schedule approach in which units or points are assigned to each operation on the basis of degree of difficulty and a conversion factor is used to convert the relative value into an amount paid the surgeon; see also *Schedule approach.*

Renewable Capable of being renewed for additional periods of time without evidence of insurability being required.

Renewable at insurer's option Continuance provision of a health insurance policy that stipulates the company cannot cancel during the policy term and the insurer has the option to renew the policy for another period; the company can refuse to renew the policy.

Rent insurance Type of business interruption insurance that covers the insured against the reduction in rents when a building is untenantable because of loss from an insured peril.

Rental value insurance Type of business interruption insurance that indemnifies the occupant for the loss of the use of damaged premises in the amount it would cost to rent similar quarters.

Replacement cost insurance Property insurance by which the insured is indemnified on the basis of replacement cost with no deduction for depreciation.

Replacement cost provisions Provisions in a homeowners policy for payment of full replacement cost of the damaged building at the time of loss with no deduction for depreciation; coverage of at least 80 percent of the replacement cost of the building must have been purchased.

Reporting form Coverage for commercial property insurance that requires the insured to report monthly or quarterly the value of the insured inventory, with automatic adjustment of insurance amount to cover the accurately reported inventory.

Representations Statements made by an applicant for insurance regarding, for example, occupation, state of health, and family history.

Res ipsa loquitor Literally, the thing speaks for itself; doctrine permitting an injured person to collect damages without proving negligence if the injury is one that normally does not occur in the absence of negligence, if the defendant has superior knowledge of the cause of the accident, if the injured party cannot prove negligence, if the defendant has exclusive control over the instrumentality causing the accident, and if the injured party has not contributed to the accident.

Residual market plan Plan through which motorists who cannot obtain automobile insurance in the normal markets may be insured.

Retention Risk management technique wherein the firm retains part or all of the losses resulting from a given loss exposure; used when no other method is available, the worst possible loss is not serious, and losses are highly predictable.

Retention limit Amount of insurance retained by a ceding company for its own account in a reinsurance operation.

Retirement test See *Earnings test.*

Retrocession Process by which a reinsurer obtains reinsurance from another company; see also *Reinsurance.*

Retrospective rating Type of merit rating method in which the insured's loss experience during the current policy period determines the actual premium paid for that period.

Revocable beneficiary Beneficiary designation allowing the policyowner the right to change the beneficiary without consent of the previous beneficiary.

Rider Term used in insurance contracts to describe a document that amends or changes the original policy; see also *Endorsement.*

Risk Uncertainty concerning the occurrence of a loss.

Risk analysis questionnaire Checklist of key questions to aid in discovery of hidden loss exposures common to many firms.

Risk management Executive decisions concerning the management of pure risks, made through systematic identification and analysis of loss exposures and search for the best methods of handling them.

Robbery Unlawful taking of another person's property by violence or the threat of violence.

Running down clause (RDC) Clause in an ocean marine insurance policy that covers the owner's legal liability if the ship causes damage to another ship or its cargo.

S

Safe driver plan Plan through which automobile premiums paid are based on the insured's driving record and on the records of those living with the insured; most states have such plans.

Savings bank life insurance Life insurance sold over the counter in mutual savings banks; as of publication, available to residents of Massachusetts, New York, and Connecticut.

Schedule Refers to property specifically listed in a schedule and a certain amount of insurance applies.

Schedule approach Means of compensating a physician who performs surgery on an insured in a medical group plan by listing various surgical operations and specifying a maximum dollar amount for each procedure.

Schedule rating Type of merit rating method in which each exposure is individually rated and given a basis rate which is then modified by debits or credits for undesirable or desirable physical features.

Scheduled personal property endorsement Special coverage added at the insured's request to a homeowners policy to include all-risk coverage for items specifically listed; used to insure valuable property such as jewelry, furs, and paintings.

Second-injury fund State fund paying the excess amount of benefit awarded an employee for a second injury if the disability is greater than that caused by the second injury alone; its purpose is to encourage employers to hire handicapped workers.

Self-insurance Retention program that possesses a large number of homogeneous exposure units and provides for payment of losses through earmarked liquid assets or a captive insurer.

SEP Plan See *Simplified Employee Pension (SEP) Plan.*

Separate account Pension plan arrangement in which pension funds are segregated so that account assets are not commingled with insurance company's general assets and can be invested separately.

Service benefits Health insurance benefits that pay hospital charges or payment for care received by the insured directly to the hospital or providers of care. The plan provides service rather than cash benefits to the insured.

Settlement options Ways in which life insurance policy proceeds can be paid other than in a lump sum, including interest, fixed period, fixed amount, and life income options.

SEUA Case See *South-Eastern Underwriters Association (SEUA) Case.*

Short-rate table Schedule used by insurers to refund premium upon policy cancellation; it refunds less than a pro rata amount to cover insurer's expenses in issuing and printing the policy and to offset adverse selection.

SIBI See *Survivor income benefit insurance (SIBI).*

Simplified Employee Pension (SEP) Plan Special type of IRA established by employees that reduces paperwork required of employers in other pension plans.

SMI See *Supplementary Medical Insurance (SMI).*

SMP policy See *Special multi-peril (SMP) policy.*

Social insurance Government insurance programs with certain characteristics that distinguish them from other government insurance programs. Programs are generally compulsory; specific earmarked taxes fund the programs; benefits are heavily weighted in favor of low income groups; and programs are designed to achieve certain social goals.

South-Eastern Underwriters Association (SEUA) Case Legal landmark decision of 1944 overruling the *Paul v. Virginia* ruling and finding that insurance was interstate commerce when conducted across state lines and was subject to federal regulation.

Special agent Highly trained marketing employee of an insurance company's sales or agency department who provides local agents in the field with technical help and assistance with their marketing problems.

Special damages Money amount awarded by a jury as a result of a negligent act to compensate claimant for determinable, itemized losses.

Special form See *Dwelling Property 3 policy; Homeowners 3 policy.*

Special multi-peril (SMP) policy Package policy that covers most commercial property and liability loss exposures in a single contract.

Special policies Special life insurance policies that may require purchase of a minimum amount, feature reduced rates as policy size increases, or apply to preferred risk groups.

Specific coverage Coverage provided for property insurance in which a definite amount of insurance applies to a specific item of property; form commonly used to insure property at a fixed location.

Speculative risk Situation in which both profit and loss are clear possibilities.

Standard mortgage clause Clause appended to the standard fire policy that entitles the mortgagee to receive a loss payment from the insurer regardless of policy violation by the insured, to receive ten days written notice of cancellation, and to sue under the policy in its own name; it also imposes certain duties on the mortgagee, such as responsibility for paying premiums if the mortgager fails to do so.

Stock insurer Company owned by stockholders who share in the profits of the company; stock insurers do not issue assessable policies.

Stop-loss limit Modification of the coinsurance provision in major medical plans that places a dollar limit on the maximum amount that an individual must pay rather than requiring that the insured pay a deductible and 20 percent of all expenses in excess of deductible.

Storekeepers Burglary and Robbery Policy Package policy for small retail firms insuring against robbery inside or outside the premises, kidnapping, burglary of a safe or robbery of a watchman, theft from a night depository or residence, and damage.

Straight deductible Deductible in an insurance contract that specifies the insured must pay a certain number of dollars of loss before the insurer is required to make a payment.

Strict liability See *Absolute liability*.

Subjective risk Uncertainty based on one's mental condition or state of mind.

Subrogation Substitution of the insurer in place of the insured for the purpose of claiming indemnity from a negligent third person for a loss covered by insurance.

Suicide clause Contractual provision in a life insurance policy stating that if the insured commits suicide within two years after the policy is issued, the face amount of insurance will not be paid; only premiums paid will be refunded.

Supplemental major medical insurance Group health insurance plan that supplements the benefits provided by a basic medical expense plan but that provides more comprehensive benefits with higher limits.

Supplementary Medical Insurance (SMI) That part of Medicare program that covers physicians' fees and other related medical services; most eligible Medicare recipients are automatically included unless they voluntarily refuse this coverage.

Surety Party who agrees to answer for the debt, default, or obligation of another in the purchase of a bond.

Surety bond Bond that provides monetary compensation if the bonded party fails to perform certain acts.

Surgical expense insurance Health insurance that provides for payment of physicians' fees for surgical operations performed in a hospital or elsewhere.

Surplus line broker Specialized insurance broker licensed to place business with a nonadmitted insurer or a company not licensed to do business in the state.

Surplus lines market Type of insurance for which there is no available market within the state, so that coverage must be placed with a company not licensed to do business there.

Surrender cost index Means of measuring the cost of an insurance policy to an insured if the policy is surrendered at the end of some specified time period after taking into consideration the time value of money.

Survivor income benefit insurance (SIBI) Group insurance plan that pays monthly income benefits to eligible dependents if a covered employee dies; no lump sum is paid.

T

Term insurance Type of life insurance that provides protection for a temporary, specified number of years; it is renewable and usually convertible.

Theft Any act of stealing; see also *Burglary; Robbery*.

3D Policy See *Comprehensive Dishonesty, Disappearance, and Destruction (3D) Policy*.

Time limit on certain defenses clause Provision in a health insurance policy that prohibits the company from cancelling the policy or denying a claim on the basis of a preexisting condition or misstatement in the application after the policy has been in force for two or three years; proof of fraudulent misstatement allows denial of claim.

Total disability Condition of an insured that makes him or her completely unable to perform all duties of the insured's own occupation or unable to perform the duties of any occupation for which the insured is reasonably fitted by training, education, and experience.

Traditional net cost method Traditional method of determining cost to an insured of a life insurance policy, determined by subtracting the total dividends received and cash value at end of a period from the total premiums paid during that period.

Trust Arrangement whereby property is legally transferred to a trustee who manages it for the benefit of named beneficiaries for their security and in order to insure competent management of estate property.

Trust-fund plan Type of pension plan in which all pension contributions are deposited with a trustee who invests the funds according to a trust agreement between employer and trustee. Benefits are paid directly out of the trust fund.

Twisting Illegal practice of inducing a policyowner to drop an existing policy in one company and take out a new policy in another through misrepresentation or incomplete information.

U

UCR See *Usual, customary, and reasonable (UCR) charges.*

Underinsured motorists coverage Coverage that can be added to the personal auto policy; coverage applies to bodily injury to an insured who is injured by an uninsured motorist or by someone with inadequate liability limits. Under this provision, the injured insured can recover the difference between the actual damages for a bodily injury and the amount of liability insurance paid by the negligent driver's insurer. See also *Uninsured motorists coverage.*

Underwriting The selection and classification of profitable insured's through a clearly stated company policy consistent with company objectives.

Unearned premium reserve Liability reserve of an insurance company that represents the unearned part of gross premiums on all outstanding policies at time of valuation.

Unified tax credit Estate tax credit that can be used to reduce the amount of the federal estate tax.

Uninsured motorists coverage That part of the personal auto policy designed to insure against bodily injury caused by an uninsured motorist, a hit-and-run driver, or a driver whose company is insolvent.

Universal life insurance A special whole life contract that combines flexible premium deposits with monthly renewable term insurance. The contract is an interest-sensitive product that unbundles the insurance, savings, and expense components.

Unsatisfied judgment fund Fund established by a state to compensate accident victims who have exhausted all other means of recovery; as of date of publication, only five states had such laws.

Usual, customary, and reasonable (UCR) charges Amounts payable for health care referring, respectively, to the physician's normal charge for a specific procedure, the amount charged for the same procedure by physicians with similar training in the same area, and the amount considered reasonable if the physician's usual charge does not exceed the customary charge.

V

Valued policy Policy that pays the face amount of insurance, regardless of actual cash value, if a total loss occurs.

Valued policy law Law requiring payment to an insured of the face amount of insurance if a total loss to real property occurs from a peril specified in the law, even though the policy may state that only actual cash value will be paid.

Variable annuity Annuity whose periodic lifetime payments vary depending on the level of common stock prices and based on the assumption that cost of living and common stock prices are correlated in the long run; its purpose is to provide an inflation hedge.

Variable life insurance Life insurance policy in which the death benefit varies according to the investment experience of a separate account maintained by the insurer and which maintains the real purchasing power of the death benefit.

Vesting Characteristic of pension plans guaranteeing the employee's right to part or all of the benefits attributable to the employer's contributions if employment terminates prior to retirement.

Vicarious liability Responsibility for damage done by the driver of an automobile that is imputed to the vehicle's owner.

W

Waiver Voluntary relinquishment of a known legal right.

Waiver of premium rider Benefit that can be added to a life insurance policy providing for waiver of all premiums coming due during a period of total disability of the insured.

War clause Restriction in a life insurance policy that excludes payment if the insured dies as a direct result of war.

Warranty Clause in an insurance contract that prescribes, as a condition of the insurer's liability, the existence of a fact affecting the risk.

Workers' compensation insurance Insurance that covers payment of all workers' compensation and other benefits that the employer must legally provide to covered employees who are occupationally disabled.

Appendix A Standard Fire Policy

STANDARD FIRE INSURANCE POLICY for Alabama, Alaska, Arizona, Arkansas, Colorado, Connecticut, Delaware, District of Columbia, Florida, Georgia, Hawaii, Idaho, Illinois, Indiana, Iowa, Kansas, Kentucky, Louisiana, Maine, Maryland, Michigan, Mississippi, Missouri, Montana, Nebraska, Nevada, New Hampshire, New Jersey, New Mexico, New York, North Carolina, North Dakota, Ohio, Oklahoma, Oregon, Pennsylvania, Rhode Island, South Carolina, South Dakota, Tennessee, Utah, Vermont, Virginia, Washington, West Virginia, Wisconsin and Wyoming. 1

No. NONASSESSABLE

STANDARD FIRE POLICY

Insured's Name and Mailing Address

Policy Term: INCEPTION (Mo. Day Year) EXPIRATION (Mo. Day Year) YEARS

$ Div. on Exp. Pol. Renewal of

It is important that the written portions of all policies covering the same property read exactly alike. If they do not, they should be made uniform at once.

INSURANCE IS PROVIDED AGAINST ONLY THOSE PERILS AND FOR ONLY THOSE COVERAGES INDICATED BELOW BY A PREMIUM CHARGE AND AGAINST OTHER PERILS AND FOR OTHER COVERAGES ONLY WHEN ENDORSED HEREON OR ADDED HERETO.

Item No.	DESCRIPTION AND LOCATION OF PROPERTY COVERED Show address (No., Street, City, County, State, Zip Code), construction, type of roof and occupancy of building(s) covered or containing property covered. If occupied as a dwelling state if building is a seasonal or farm dwelling. If commercial state exact nature of product (and whether manufacturer, wholesaler or retailer) or the service or activity involved.	Protection Class	Dwelling Business Only: No. of Families	Feet From Hydrant	Miles From Fire Dept.	Zone
1.						

Item No.	PERIL(S) INSURED AGAINST AND COVERAGE(S) PROVIDED (INSERT NAME OF EACH)	Per Cent of Co-Insurance Applicable	Deductible Amount	Amount of Insurance	Rate	Prepaid or Installment Premium Due At Inception	Installment Premium Due At Each Anniversary
1.	FIRE AND LIGHTNING			$		$	$
	EXTENDED COVERAGE			XXXXXXX			

Special provision applicable only in State of Mississippi—**Total Insurance**—See form attached—
Item 1, $; Item 2, $; Item 3, $

TOTAL(S) $ $

Special provision applicable only in State of So. Carolina—**Valuation Clause**—See form attached—
Item , $; Item , $; Item , $

TOTAL PREMIUM FOR POLICY TERM PAID IN INSTALLMENTS $

Subject to Form No(s). **attached hereto.**

INSERT FORM NUMBER(S) AND EDITION DATE(S)

Mortgage Clause: Subject to the provisions of the mortgage clause attached hereto, loss, if any, on building items, shall be payable to:

INSERT NAME(S) OR MORTGAGEE(S) AND MAILING ADDRESS(ES)

COUNTERSIGNATURE DATE	AGENCY AT	AGENT

IN CONSIDERATION OF THE PROVISIONS AND STIPULATIONS HEREIN OR ADDED HERETO AND OF the premium above specified, this Company, for the term of *years specified above* from *inception date shown above* At Noon (Standard Time) to *expiration date shown above* At Noon (Standard Time) at location of property involved, to an amount not exceeding the amount(s) above specified, does insure *the insured named above* and legal representatives, to the extent of the actual cash value of the property at the time of loss, but not exceeding the amount which it would cost to repair or replace the property with material of like kind and quality within a reasonable time after such loss, without allowance for any increased cost of repair or reconstruction by reason of any ordinance or law regulating construction or repair, and without compensation for loss resulting from interruption of business or manufacture, nor in any event for more than the interest of the insured, against all **DIRECT LOSS BY FIRE, LIGHTNING AND BY REMOVAL FROM PREMISES ENDANGERED BY THE PERILS INSURED AGAINST IN THIS POLICY, EXCEPT AS HEREINAFTER PROVIDED,** to the property described herein while located or contained as described in this policy, or pro rata for five days at each proper place to which any of the property shall necessarily be removed for preservation from the perils insured against in this policy, but not elsewhere.

Assignment of this policy shall not be valid except with the written consent of this Company.

This policy is made and accepted subject to the foregoing provisions and stipulations and those hereinafter stated, which are hereby made a part of this policy, together with such other provisions, stipulations and agreements as may be added hereto, as provided in this policy.

TAB-3

"Standard Fire Policy" from *Study Kit for Students of Insurance*. Reprinted with permission from Alliance of American Insurers.

2

Concealment, fraud. This entire policy shall be void if, whether before or after a loss, the insured has wilfully concealed or misrepresented any material fact or circumstance concerning this insurance or the subject thereof, or the interest of the insured therein, or in case of any fraud or false swearing by the insured relating thereto.

Uninsurable and excepted property. This policy shall not cover accounts, bills, currency, deeds, evidences of debt, money or securities; nor, unless specifically named hereon in writing, bullion or manuscripts.

Perils not included. This Company shall not be liable for loss by fire or other perils insured against in this policy caused, directly or indirectly, by: (a) enemy attack by armed forces, including action taken by military, naval or air forces in resisting an actual or an immediately impending enemy attack; (b) invasion; (c) insurrection; (d) rebellion; (e) revolution; (f) civil war; (g) usurped power; (h) order of any civil authority except acts of destruction at the time of and for the purpose of preventing the spread of fire, provided that such fire did not originate from any of the perils excluded by this policy; (i) neglect of the insured to use all reasonable means to save and preserve the property at and after a loss, or when the property is endangered by fire in neighboring premises; (j) nor shall this Company be liable for loss by theft.

Other Insurance. Other insurance may be prohibited or the amount of insurance may be limited by endorsement attached hereto.

Conditions suspending or restricting insurance. Unless otherwise provided in writing added hereto this Company shall not be liable for loss occurring

(a) while the hazard is increased by any means within the control or knowledge of the insured; or

(b) while a described building, whether intended for occupancy by owner or tenant, is vacant or unoccupied beyond a period of sixty consecutive days; or

(c) as a result of explosion or riot, unless fire ensue, and in that event for loss by fire only.

Other perils or subjects. Any other peril to be insured against or subject of insurance to be covered in this policy shall be by endorsement in writing hereon or added hereto.

Added provisions. The extent of the application of insurance under this policy and of the contribution to be made by this Company in case of loss, and any other provision or agreement not inconsistent with the provisions of this policy, may be provided for in writing added hereto, but no provision may be waived except such as by the terms of this policy is subject to change.

Waiver provisions. No permission affecting this insurance shall exist, or waiver of any provision be valid, unless granted herein or expressed in writing added hereto. No provision, stipulation or forfeiture shall be held to be waived by any requirement or proceeding on the part of this Company relating to appraisal or to any examination provided for herein.

Cancellation of policy. This policy shall be cancelled at any time at the request of the insured, in which case this Company shall, upon demand and surrender of this policy, refund the excess of paid premium above the customary short rates for the expired time. This policy may be cancelled at any time by this Company by giving to the insured a five days' written notice of cancellation with or without tender of the excess of paid premium above the pro rata premium for the expired time, which excess, if not tendered, shall be refunded on demand. Notice of cancellation shall state that said excess premium (if not tendered) will be refunded on demand.

Mortgagee interests and obligations. If loss hereunder is made payable, in whole or in part, to a designated mortgagee not named herein as the insured, such interest in this policy may be cancelled by giving to such mortgagee a ten days' written notice of cancellation.

If the insured fails to render proof of loss such mortgagee, upon notice, shall render proof of loss in the form herein specified within sixty (60) days thereafter and shall be subject to the provisions hereof relating to appraisal and time of payment and of bringing suit. If this Company shall claim that no liability existed as to the mortgagor or owner, it shall, to the extent of payment of loss to the mortgagee, be subrogated to all the mortgagee's rights of recovery, but without impairing mortgagee's right to sue; or it may pay off the mortgage debt and require an assignment thereof and of the mortgage. Other provisions relating to the interests and obligations of such mortgagee may be added hereto by agreement in writing.

Pro rata liability. This Company shall not be liable for a greater proportion of any loss than the amount hereby insured shall bear to the whole insurance covering the property against the peril involved, whether collectible or not.

Requirements in case loss occurs. The insured shall give immediate written notice to this Company of any loss, protect the property from further damage, forthwith separate the damaged and undamaged personal property, put it in the best possible order, furnish a complete inventory of the destroyed, damaged and undamaged property, showing in detail quantities, costs, actual cash value and amount of loss claimed; **and within sixty days after the loss, unless such time is extended in writing by this Company, the insured shall render to this Company a proof of loss,** signed and sworn to by the insured, stating the knowledge and belief of the insured as to the following: the time and origin of the loss, the interest of the insured and of all others in the property, the actual cash value of each item thereof and the amount of loss thereto, all encumbrances thereon, all other contracts of insurance, whether valid or not, covering any of said property, any changes in the title, use, occupation, location, possession or exposures of said property since the issuing of this policy, by whom and for what purpose any building herein described and the several parts thereof were occupied at the time of loss and whether or not it then stood on leased ground, and shall furnish a copy of all the descriptions and schedules in all policies and, if required, verified plans and specifications of any building, fixtures or machinery destroyed or damaged. The insured, as often as may be reasonably required, shall exhibit to any person designated by this Company all that remains of any property herein described, and submit to examinations under oath by any person named by this Company, and subscribe the same; and, as often as may be reasonably required, shall produce for examination all books of account, bills, invoices and other vouchers, or certified copies thereof if originals be lost, at such reasonable time and place as may be designated by this Company or its representative, and shall permit extracts and copies thereof to be made.

Appraisal. In case the insured and this Company shall fail to agree as to the actual cash value or the amount of loss, then, on the written demand of either, each shall select a competent and disinterested appraiser and notify the other of the appraiser selected within twenty days of such demand. The appraisers shall first select a competent and disinterested umpire; and failing for fifteen days to agree upon such umpire, then, on request of the insured or this Company, such umpire shall be selected by a judge of a court of record in the state in which the property covered is located. The appraisers shall then appraise the loss, stating separately actual cash value and loss to each item; and, failing to agree, shall submit their differences, only, to the umpire. An award in writing, so itemized, of any two when filed with this Company shall determine the amount of actual cash value and loss. Each appraiser shall be paid by the party selecting him and the expenses of appraisal and umpire shall be paid by the parties equally.

Company's options. It shall be optional with this Company to take all, or any part, of the property at the agreed or appraised value, and also to repair, rebuild or replace the property destroyed or damaged with other of like kind and quality within a reasonable time, on giving notice of its intention so to do within thirty days after the receipt of the proof of loss herein required.

Abandonment. There can be no abandonment to this Company of any property.

When loss payable. The amount of loss for which this Company may be liable shall be payable sixty days after proof of loss, as herein provided, is received by this Company and ascertainment of the loss is made either by agreement between the insured and this Company expressed in writing or by the filing with this Company of an award as herein provided.

Suit. No suit or action on this policy for the recovery of any claim shall be sustainable in any court of law or equity unless all the requirements of this policy shall have been complied with, and unless commenced within twelve months next after inception of the loss.

Subrogation. This Company may require from the insured an assignment of all right of recovery against any party for loss to the extent that payment therefor is made by this Company.

IN WITNESS WHEREOF, this Company has executed and attested these presents; but this policy shall not be valid unless countersigned by the duly authorized Agent of this Company at the agency hereinbefore mentioned.

Appendix B Homeowners 3 Special Form

Homeowners 3
Special Form
Ed. 4-84

AGREEMENT

We will provide the insurance described in this policy in return for the premium and compliance with all applicable provisions of this policy.

DEFINITIONS

In this policy, "you" and "your" refer to the "named insured" shown in the Declarations and the spouse if a resident of the same household. "We," "us" and "our" refer to the Company providing this insurance. In addition, certain words and phrases are defined as follows:

1. **"bodily injury"** means bodily harm, sickness or disease, including required care, loss of services and death that results.

2. **"business"** includes trade, profession or occupation.

3. **"insured"** means you and residents of your household who are:

   a. your relatives; or

   b. other persons under the age of 21 and in the care of any person named above.

   Under Section II, **"insured"** also means:

   c. with respect to animals or watercraft to which this policy applies, any person or organization legally responsible for these animals or watercraft which are owned by you or any person included in 3a or 3b above. A person or organization using or having custody of these animals or watercraft in the course of any **business** or without consent of the owner is not an **insured;**

   d. with respect to any vehicle to which this policy applies:

      (1) persons while engaged in your employ or that of any person included in 3a or 3b above; or

      (2) other persons using the vehicle on an **insured location** with your consent.

4. **"insured location"** means:

   a. the **residence premises;**

   b. the part of other premises, other structures and grounds used by you as a residence and:

      (1) which is shown in the Declarations; or

      (2) which is acquired by you during the policy period for your use as a residence;

   c. any premises used by you in connection with a premises in 4a or 4b above;

   d. any part of a premises:

      (1) not owned by an **insured;** and

      (2) where an **insured** is temporarily residing;

   e. vacant land, other than farm land, owned by or rented to an **insured;**

   f. land owned by or rented to an **insured** on which a one or two family dwelling is being built as a residence for an **insured;**

   g. individual or family cemetery plots or burial vaults of an **insured**; or

   h. any part of a premises occasionally rented to an **insured** for other than **business** use.

5. **"occurrence"** means an accident, including exposure to conditions, which results, during the policy period, in:

   a. **bodily injury;** or

   b. **property damage.**

6. **"property damage"** means physical injury to, destruction of, or loss of use of tangible property.

7. **"residence employee"** means:

   a. an employee of an **insured** whose duties are related to the maintenance or use of the **residence premises,** including household or domestic services; or

   b. one who performs similar duties elsewhere not related to the **business** of an **insured.**

8. "residence premises" means:

a. the one family dwelling, other structures, and grounds; or

b. that part of any other building;

where you reside and which is shown as the **"residence premises"** in the Declarations.

"Residence premises" also means a two family dwelling where you reside in at least one of the family units and which is shown as the **"residence premises"** in the Declarations.

SECTION I—PROPERTY COVERAGES

COVERAGE A—Dwelling

We cover:

1. the dwelling on the **residence premises** shown in the Declarations, including structures attached to the dwelling; and
2. materials and supplies located on or next to the **residence premises** used to construct, alter or repair the dwelling or other structures on the **residence premises.**

This coverage does not apply to land, including land on which the dwelling is located.

COVERAGE B—Other Structures

We cover other structures on the **residence premises** set apart from the dwelling by clear space. This includes structures connected to the dwelling by only a fence, utility line, or similar connection.

This coverage does not apply to land, including land on which the other structures are located.

We do not cover other structures:

1. used in whole or in part for **business;** or
2. rented or held for rental to any person not a tenant of the dwelling, unless used solely as a private garage.

The limit of liability for this coverage will not be more than 10% of the limit of liability that applies to Coverage A. Use of this coverage does not reduce the Coverage A limit of liability.

COVERAGE C—Personal Property

We cover personal property owned or used by an **insured** while it is anywhere in the world. At your request, we will cover personal property owned by:

1. others while the property is on the part of the **residence premises** occupied by an **insured;**
2. a guest or a **residence employee,** while the property is in any residence occupied by an **insured.**

Our limit of liability for personal property usually located at an **insured's** residence, other than the **residence premises,** is 10% of the limit of liability for Coverage C, or $1000, whichever is greater. Personal property in a newly acquired principal residence is not subject to this limitation for the 30 days from the time you begin to move the property there.

Special Limits of Liability. These limits do not increase the Coverage C limit of liability. The special limit for each numbered category below is the total limit for each loss for all property in that category.

1. $200 on money, bank notes, bullion, gold other than goldware, silver other than silverware, platinum, coins and medals.
2. $1000 on securities, accounts, deeds, evidences of debt, letters of credit, notes other than bank notes, manuscripts, passports, tickets and stamps.
3. $1000 on watercraft, including their trailers, furnishings, equipment and outboard motors.
4. $1000 on trailers not used with watercraft.
5. $1000 on grave markers.
6. $1000 for loss by theft of jewelry, watches, furs, precious and semi-precious stones.
7. $2000 for loss by theft of firearms.
8. $2500 for loss by theft of silverware, silver-plated ware, goldware, gold-plated ware and pewterware. This includes flatware, hollowware, tea sets, trays and trophies made of or including silver, gold or pewter.
9. $2500 on property, on the **residence premises,** used at any time or in any manner for any **business** purpose.
10. $250 on property, away from the **residence premises,** used at any time or in any manner for any **business** purpose.

Property Not Covered. We do not cover:

1. articles separately described and specifically insured in this or other insurance;
2. animals, birds or fish;
3. motor vehicles or all other motorized land conveyances. This includes:
   a. equipment and accessories; or
   b. any device or instrument for the transmitting, recording, receiving or reproduction of sound or pictures which is operated by power from the electrical system of motor vehicles or all other motorized land conveyances, including:
      (1) accessories or antennas; or
      (2) tapes, wires, records, discs or other media for use with any such device or instrument;

   while in or upon the vehicle or conveyance.

   We do cover vehicles or conveyances not subject to motor vehicle registration which are:

   a. used to service an **insured's** residence; or
   b. designed for assisting the handicapped;
4. aircraft and parts. Aircraft means any contrivance used or designed for flight, except model or hobby aircraft not used or designed to carry people or cargo;
5. property of roomers, boarders and other tenants, except property of roomers and boarders related to an **insured;**
6. property in an apartment regularly rented or held for rental to others by an **insured;**
7. property rented or held for rental to others off the **residence premises;**
8. a. books of account, drawings or other paper records; or
   b. electronic data processing tapes, wires, records, discs or other software media;

   containing **business** data. But, we do cover the cost of blank or unexposed records and media;
9. credit cards or fund transfer cards except as provided in Additional Coverages 6.

COVERAGE D—Loss Of Use

The limit of liability for Coverage D is the total limit for all the coverages that follow.

1. If a loss covered under this Section makes that part of the **residence premises** where you reside not fit to live in, we cover, at your choice, either of the following. However, if the **residence premises** is not your principal place of residence, we will not provide the option under paragraph b. below.
   a. **Additional Living Expense,** meaning any necessary increase in living expenses incurred by you so that your household can maintain its normal standard of living; or
   b. **Fair Rental Value,** meaning the fair rental value of that part of the **residence premises** where you reside less any expenses that do not continue while the premises is not fit to live in.

   Payment under a. or b. will be for the shortest time required to repair or replace the damage or, if you permanently relocate, the shortest time required for your household to settle elsewhere.
2. If a loss covered under this Section makes that part of the **residence premises** rented to others or held for rental by you not fit to live in, we cover the:

   Fair Rental Value, meaning the fair rental value of that part of the **residence premises** rented to others or held for rental by you less any expenses that do not continue while the premises is not fit to live in.

   Payment will be for the shortest time required to repair or replace that part of the premises rented or held for rental.
3. If a civil authority prohibits you from use of the **residence premises** as a result of direct damage to neighboring premises by a Peril Insured Against in this policy, we cover the Additional Living Expense or Fair Rental Value loss as provided under 1 and 2 above for no more than two weeks.

The periods of time under 1, 2 and 3 above are not limited by expiration of this policy.

We do not cover loss or expense due to cancellation of a lease or agreement.

ADDITIONAL COVERAGES

1. **Debris Removal.** We will pay your reasonable expense for the removal of:
   a. debris of covered property if a Peril Insured Against causes the loss; or
   b. ash, dust or particles from a volcanic eruption that has caused direct loss to a building or property contained in a building.

   This expense is included in the limit of liability that applies to the damaged property. If the amount to be paid for the actual damage to the property plus the debris removal expense is more than the limit of liability for the damaged property, an additional 5% of that limit of liability is available for debris removal expense.

We will also pay your reasonable expense for the removal of fallen trees from the **residence premises** if:

a. coverage is not afforded under Additional Coverages 3. Trees, Shrubs and Other Plants for the peril causing the loss; or

b. the tree is not covered by this policy;

provided the tree damages covered property and a Peril Insured Against under Coverage C causes the tree to fall. Our limit of liability for this coverage will not be more than $500 in the aggregate for any one loss.

2. **Reasonable Repairs.** We will pay the reasonable cost incurred by you for necessary repairs made solely to protect covered property from further damage if a Peril Insured Against causes the loss. This coverage does not increase the limit of liability that applies to the property being repaired.

3. **Trees, Shrubs and Other Plants.** We cover trees, shrubs, plants or lawns, on the **residence premises,** for loss caused by the following Perils Insured Against: Fire or lightning, Explosion, Riot or civil commotion, Aircraft, Vehicles not owned or operated by a resident of the **residence premises,** Vandalism or malicious mischief or Theft.

   The limit of liability for this coverage will not be more than 5% of the limit of liability that applies to the dwelling, or more than $500 for any one tree, shrub or plant. We do not cover property grown for **business** purposes.

   This coverage is additional insurance.

4. **Fire Department Service Charge.** We will pay up to $500 for your liability assumed by contract or agreement for fire department charges incurred when the fire department is called to save or protect covered property from a Peril Insured Against. We do not cover fire department service charges if the property is located within the limits of the city, municipality or protection district furnishing the fire department response.

   This coverage is additional insurance. No deductible applies to this coverage.

5. **Property Removed.** We insure covered property against direct loss from any cause while being removed from a premises endangered by a Peril Insured Against and for no more than 30 days while removed. This coverage does not change the limit of liability that applies to the property being removed.

6. **Credit Card, Fund Transfer Card, Forgery and Counterfeit Money.**

   We will pay up to $500 for:

   a. the legal obligation of an **insured** to pay because of the theft or unauthorized use of credit cards issued to or registered in an **insured's** name;

   b. loss resulting from theft or unauthorized use of a fund transfer card used for deposit, withdrawal or transfer of funds, issued to or registered in an **insured's** name;

   c. loss to an **insured** caused by forgery or alteration of any check or negotiable instrument; and

   d. loss to an **insured** through acceptance in good faith of counterfeit United States or Canadian paper currency.

   We do not cover use of a credit card or fund transfer card:

   a. by a resident of your household;

   b. by a person who has been entrusted with either type of card; or

   c. if an **insured** has not complied with all terms and conditions under which the cards are issued.

   All loss resulting from a series of acts committed by any one person or in which any one person is concerned or implicated is considered to be one loss.

   We do not cover loss arising out of **business** use or dishonesty of an **insured.**

   This coverage is additional insurance. No deductible applies to this coverage.

   Defense:

   a. We may investigate and settle any claim or suit that we decide is appropriate. Our duty to defend a claim or suit ends when the amount we pay for the loss equals our limit of liability.

   b. If a suit is brought against an **insured** for liability under the Credit Card or Fund Transfer Card coverage, we will provide a defense at our expense by counsel of our choice.

   c. We have the option to defend at our expense an **insured** or an **insured's** bank against any suit for the enforcement of payment under the Forgery coverage.

7. **Loss Assessment.** We will pay up to $1000 for your share of any loss assessment charged during the policy period against you by a corporation or association of property owners. This only applies when the assessment is made as a result of each direct loss to the property, owned by all members collectively, caused by a Peril Insured Against under Coverage A—Dwelling, other than earthquake or land shock waves or tremors before, during or after a volcanic eruption.

   This coverage applies only to loss assessments charged against you as owner or tenant of the **residence premises.**

   We do not cover loss assessments charged against you or a corporation or association of property owners by any governmental body.

8. Collapse. We insure for direct physical loss to covered property involving collapse of a building or any part of a building caused only by one or more of the following:

a. Perils Insured Against in Coverage C—Personal Property. These perils apply to covered building and personal property for loss insured by this additional coverage;

b. hidden decay;

c. hidden insect or vermin damage;

d. weight of contents, equipment, animals or people;

e. weight of rain which collects on a roof; or

f. use of defective material or methods in construction, remodeling or renovation if the collapse occurs during the course of the construction, remodeling or renovation.

Loss to an awning, fence, patio, pavement, swimming pool, underground pipe, flue, drain, cesspool, septic tank, foundation, retaining wall, bulkhead, pier, wharf or dock is not included under items b, c, d, e, and f unless the loss is a direct result of the collapse of a building.

Collapse does not include settling, cracking, shrinking, bulging or expansion.

This coverage does not increase the limit of liability applying to the damaged covered property.

SECTION I—PERILS INSURED AGAINST

COVERAGE A—DWELLING and
COVERAGE B—OTHER STRUCTURES

We insure against risks of direct loss to property described in Coverages A and B only if that loss is a physical loss to property; however, we do not insure loss:

1. involving collapse, other than as provided in Additional Coverage 8;

2. caused by:

a. freezing of a plumbing, heating, air conditioning or automatic fire protective sprinkler system or of a household appliance, or by discharge, leakage or overflow from within the system or appliance caused by freezing. This exclusion applies only while the dwelling is vacant, unoccupied or being constructed unless you have used reasonable care to:

(1) maintain heat in the building; or

(2) shut off the water supply and drain the system and appliances of water;

b. freezing, thawing, pressure or weight of water or ice, whether driven by wind or not, to a:

(1) fence, pavement, patio or swimming pool;

(2) foundation, retaining wall or bulkhead; or

(3) pier, wharf or dock;

c. theft in or to a dwelling under construction, or of materials and supplies for use in the construction until the dwelling is finished and occupied;

d. vandalism and malicious mischief or breakage of glass and safety glazing materials if the dwelling has been vacant for more than 30 consecutive days immediately before the loss. A dwelling being constructed is not considered vacant;

e. constant or repeated seepage or leakage of water or steam over a period of weeks, months or years from within a plumbing, heating, air conditioning or automatic fire protective sprinkler system or from within a household appliance;

f. (1) wear and tear, marring, deterioration;

(2) inherent vice, latent defect, mechanical breakdown;

(3) smog, rust, mold, wet or dry rot;

(4) smoke from agricultural smudging or industrial operations;

(5) release, discharge or dispersal of contaminants or pollutants;

(6) settling, cracking, shrinking, bulging or expansion of pavements, patios, foundations, walls, floors, roofs or ceilings; or

(7) birds, vermin, rodents, insects or domestic animals.

If any of these cause water damage not otherwise excluded, from a plumbing, heating, air conditioning or automatic fire protective sprinkler system or household appliance, we cover loss caused by the water including the cost of tearing out and replacing any part of a building necessary to repair the system or appliance. We do not cover loss to the system or appliance from which this water escaped.

3. excluded under Section I—Exclusions.

Under items 1 and 2, any ensuing loss to property described in Coverages A and B not excluded or excepted in this policy is covered.

COVERAGE C—PERSONAL PROPERTY

We insure for direct physical loss to the property described in Coverage C caused by a peril listed below unless the loss is excluded in Section I—Exclusions.

1. **Fire or lightning.**
2. **Windstorm or hail.**

   This peril does not include loss to the property contained in a building caused by rain, snow, sleet, sand or dust unless the direct force of wind or hail damages the building causing an opening in a roof or wall and the rain, snow, sleet, sand or dust enters through this opening.

   This peril includes loss to watercraft and their trailers, furnishings, equipment, and outboard motors, only while inside a fully enclosed building.
3. **Explosion.**
4. **Riot or civil commotion.**
5. **Aircraft,** including self-propelled missiles and spacecraft.
6. **Vehicles.**
7. **Smoke,** meaning sudden and accidental damage from smoke.

   This peril does not include loss caused by smoke from agricultural smudging or industrial operations.
8. **Vandalism or malicious mischief.**
9. **Theft,** including attempted theft and loss of property from a known place when it is likely that the property has been stolen.

   This peril does not include loss caused by theft:

   a. committed by an **insured;**

   b. in or to a dwelling under construction, or of materials and supplies for use in the construction until the dwelling is finished and occupied; or

   c. from that part of a **residence premises** rented by an **insured** to other than an **insured.**

   This peril does not include loss caused by theft that occurs off the **residence premises** of:

   a. property while at any other residence owned by, rented to, or occupied by an **insured,** except while an **insured** is temporarily living there. Property of a student who is an **insured** is covered while at a residence away from home if the student has been there at any time during the 45 days immediately before the loss;

   b. watercraft, including their furnishings, equipment and outboard motors; or

   c. trailers and campers.
10. **Falling objects.**

    This peril does not include loss to property contained in a building unless the roof or an outside wall of the building is first damaged by a falling object. Damage to the falling object itself is not included.
11. **Weight of ice, snow or sleet** which causes damage to property contained in a building.
12. **Accidental discharge or overflow of water or steam** from within a plumbing, heating, air conditioning or automatic fire protective sprinkler system or from within a household appliance.

    This peril does not include loss:

    a. to the system or appliance from which the water or steam escaped;

    b. caused by or resulting from freezing except as provided in the peril of freezing below; or

    c. on the **residence premises** caused by accidental discharge or overflow which occurs off the **residence premises.**
13. **Sudden and accidental tearing apart, cracking, burning or bulging** of a steam or hot water heating system, an air conditioning or automatic fire protective sprinkler system, or an appliance for heating water.

    We do not cover loss caused by or resulting from freezing under this peril.
14. **Freezing** of a plumbing, heating, air conditioning or automatic fire protective sprinkler system or of a household appliance.

    This peril does not include loss on the **residence premises** while the dwelling is unoccupied, unless you have used reasonable care to:

    a. maintain heat in the building; or

    b. shut off the water supply and drain the system and appliances of water.
15. **Sudden and accidental damage from artificially generated electrical current.**

    This peril does not include loss to a tube, transistor or similar electronic component.
16. **Damage by glass or safety glazing material** which is part of a building, storm door or storm window.

    This peril does not include loss on the **residence premises** if the dwelling has been vacant for more than 30 consecutive days immediately before the loss. A dwelling being constructed is not considered vacant.
17. **Volcanic Eruption** other than loss caused by earthquake, land shock waves or tremors.

SECTION I—EXCLUSIONS

1. We do not insure for loss caused directly or indirectly by any of the following. Such loss is excluded regardless of any other cause or event contributing concurrently or in any sequence to the loss.

   a. **Ordinance or Law,** meaning enforcement of any ordinance or law regulating the construc tion, repair, or demolition of a building or other structure, unless specifically provided under this policy.

   b. **Earth Movement,** meaning earthquake including land shock waves or tremors before, during or after a volcanic eruption; landslide; mudflow; earth sinking, rising or shifting; unless direct loss by:

      (1) fire;

      (2) explosion; or

      (3) breakage of glass or safety glazing material which is part of a building, storm door or storm window;

      ensues and then we will pay only for the ensuing loss.

      This exclusion does not apply to loss by theft.

   c. **Water Damage,** meaning:

      (1) flood, surface water, waves, tidal water, overflow of a body of water, or spray from any of these, whether or not driven by wind;

      (2) water which backs up through sewers or drains; or

      (3) water below the surface of the ground, including water which exerts pressure on or seeps or leaks through a building, sidewalk, driveway, foundation, swimming pool or other structure.

      Direct loss by fire, explosion or theft resulting from water damage is covered.

   d. **Power Failure,** meaning the failure of power or other utility service if the failure takes place off the **residence premises.** But, if a Peril Insured Against ensues on the **residence premises,** we will pay only for that ensuing loss.

   e. **Neglect,** meaning neglect of the **insured** to use all reasonable means to save and preserve property at and after the time of a loss.

   f. **War,** including undeclared war, civil war, insurrection, rebellion, revolution, warlike act by a military force or military personnel, destruction or seizure or use for a military purpose, and including any consequence of any of these. Discharge of a nuclear weapon will be deemed a warlike act even if accidental.

   g. **Nuclear Hazard,** to the extent set forth in the Nuclear Hazard Clause of Section I—Conditions.

   h. **Intentional Loss,** meaning any loss arising out of any act committed:

      (1) by or at the direction of an **insured;** and

      (2) with the intent to cause a loss.

2. We do not insure for loss to property described in Coverages A and B caused by any of the following. However, any ensuing loss to property described in Coverages A and B not excluded or excepted in this policy is covered.

   a. **Weather conditions.** However, this exclusion only applies if weather conditions contribute in any way with a cause or event excluded in paragraph 1. above to produce the loss;

   b. **Acts or decisions,** including the failure to act or decide, of any person, group, organization or governmental body;

   c. **Faulty, inadequate or defective:**

      (1) planning, zoning, development, surveying, siting;

      (2) design, specifications, workmanship, repair, construction, renovation, remodeling, grading, compaction;

      (3) materials used in repair, construction, renovation or remodeling; or

      (4) maintenance;

      of part or all of any property whether on or off the **residence premises.**

SECTION I—CONDITIONS

1. **Insurable Interest and Limit of Liability.** Even if more than one person has an insurable interest in the property covered, we will not be liable in any one loss:

   a. to the **insured** for more than the amount of the **insured's** interest at the time of loss; or

   b. for more than the applicable limit of liability.

2. **Your Duties After Loss.** In case of a loss to covered property, you must see that the following are done:

   a. give prompt notice to us or our agent;

   b. notify the police in case of loss by theft;

   c. notify the credit card or fund transfer card company in case of loss under Credit Card or Fund Transfer Card coverage;

   d. (1) protect the property from further damage;

      (2) make reasonable and necessary repairs to protect the property; and

      (3) keep an accurate record of repair expenses;

   e. prepare an inventory of damaged personal property showing the quantity, description, actual cash value and amount of loss. Attach all bills, receipts and related documents that justify the figures in the inventory;

   f. as often as we reasonably require:

      (1) show the damaged property;

      (2) provide us with records and documents we request and permit us to make copies; and

      (3) submit to questions under oath and sign and swear to them;

   g. send to us, within 60 days after our request, your signed, sworn proof of loss which sets forth, to the best of your knowledge and belief:

      (1) the time and cause of loss;

      (2) the interest of the **insured** and all others in the property involved and all liens on the property;

      (3) other insurance which may cover the loss;

      (4) changes in title or occupancy of the property during the term of the policy;

      (5) specifications of damaged buildings and detailed repair estimates;

      (6) the inventory of damaged personal property described in 2e above;

      (7) receipts for additional living expenses incurred and records that support the fair rental value loss; and

      (8) evidence or affidavit that supports a claim under the Credit Card, Fund Transfer Card, Forgery and Counterfeit Money coverage, stating the amount and cause of loss.

3. **Loss Settlement.** Covered property losses are settled as follows:

   a. (1) Personal property;

      (2) Awnings, carpeting, household appliances, outdoor antennas and outdoor equipment, whether or not attached to buildings; and

      (3) Structures that are not buildings;

   at actual cash value at the time of loss but not more than the amount required to repair or replace.

   b. Buildings under Coverage A or B at replacement cost without deduction for depreciation, subject to the following:

      (1) If, at the time of loss, the amount of insurance in this policy on the damaged building is 80% or more of the full replacement cost of the building immediately before the loss, we will pay the cost to repair or replace, after application of deductible and without deduction for depreciation, but not more than the least of the following amounts:

         (a) the limit of liability under this policy that applies to the building;

         (b) the replacement cost of that part of the building damaged for like construction and use on the same premises; or

         (c) the necessary amount actually spent to repair or replace the damaged building.

(2) If, at the time of loss, the amount of insurance in this policy on the damaged building is less than 80% of the full replacement cost of the building immediately before the loss, we will pay the greater of the following amounts, but not more than the limit of liability under this policy that applies to the building:

(a) the actual cash value of that part of the building damaged; or

(b) that proportion of the cost to repair or replace, after application of deductible and without deduction for depreciation, that part of the building damaged, which the total amount of insurance in this policy on the damaged building bears to 80% of the replacement cost of the building.

(3) To determine the amount of insurance required to equal 80% of the full replacement cost of the building immediately before the loss, do not include the value of:

(a) excavations, foundations, piers or any supports which are below the undersurface of the lowest basement floor;

(b) those supports in (a) above which are below the surface of the ground inside the foundation walls, if there is no basement; and

(c) underground flues, pipes, wiring and drains.

(4) We will pay no more than the actual cash value of the damage unless:

(a) actual repair or replacement is complete; or

(b) the cost to repair or replace the damage is both:

(i) less than 5% of the amount of insurance in this policy on the building; and

(ii) less than $1000.

(5) You may disregard the replacement cost loss settlement provisions and make claim under this policy for loss or damage to buildings on an actual cash value basis. You may then make claim within 180 days after loss for any additional liability on a replacement cost basis.

4. **Loss to a Pair or Set.** In case of loss to a pair or set we may elect to:

a. repair or replace any part to restore the pair or set to its value before the loss; or

b. pay the difference between actual cash value of the property before and after the loss.

5. **Glass Replacement.** Loss for damage to glass caused by a Peril Insured Against will be settled on the basis of replacement with safety glazing materials when required by ordinance or law.

6. **Appraisal.** If you and we fail to agree on the amount of loss, either may demand an appraisal of the loss. In this event, each party will choose a competent appraiser within 20 days after receiving a written request from the other. The two appraisers will choose an umpire. If they cannot agree upon an umpire within 15 days, you or we may request that the choice be made by a judge of a court of record in the state where the **residence premises** is located. The appraisers will separately set the amount of loss. If the appraisers submit a written report of an agreement to us, the amount agreed upon will be the amount of loss. If they fail to agree, they will submit their differences to the umpire. A decision agreed to by any two will set the amount of loss.

Each party will:

a. pay its own appraiser; and

b. bear the other expenses of the appraisal and umpire equally.

7. **Other Insurance.** If a loss covered by this policy is also covered by other insurance, we will pay only the proportion of the loss that the limit of liability that applies under this policy bears to the total amount of insurance covering the loss.

8. **Suit Against Us.** No action can be brought unless the policy provisions have been complied with and the action is started within one year after the date of loss.

9. **Our Option.** If we give you written notice within 30 days after we receive your signed, sworn proof of loss, we may repair or replace any part of the damaged property with like property.

10. **Loss Payment.** We will adjust all losses with you. We will pay you unless some other person is named in the policy or is legally entitled to receive payment. Loss will be payable 60 days after we receive your proof of loss and:

a. reach an agreement with you;

b. there is an entry of a final judgment; or

c. there is a filing of an appraisal award with us.

11. **Abandonment of Property.** We need not accept any property abandoned by an **insured.**

12. Mortgage Clause.

The word "mortgagee" includes trustee.

If a mortgagee is named in this policy, any loss payable under Coverage A or B will be paid to the mortgagee and you, as interests appear. If more than one mortgagee is named, the order of payment will be the same as the order of precedence of the mortgages.

If we deny your claim, that denial will not apply to a valid claim of the mortgagee, if the mortgagee:

a. notifies us of any change in ownership, occupancy or substantial change in risk of which the mortgagee is aware;

b. pays any premium due under this policy on demand if you have neglected to pay the premium; and

c. submits a signed, sworn statement of loss within 60 days after receiving notice from us of your failure to do so. Policy conditions relating to Appraisal, Suit Against Us and Loss Payment apply to the mortgagee.

If the policy is cancelled or not renewed by us, the mortgagee will be notified at least 10 days before the date cancellation or nonrenewal takes effect.

If we pay the mortgagee for any loss and deny payment to you:

a. we are subrogated to all the rights of the mortgagee granted under the mortgage on the property; or

b. at our option, we may pay to the mortgagee the whole principal on the mortgage plus any accrued interest. In this event, we will receive a full assignment and transfer of the mortgage and all securities held as collateral to the mortgage debt.

Subrogation will not impair the right of the mortgagee to recover the full amount of the mortgagee's claim.

13. No Benefit to Bailee. We will not recognize any assignment or grant any coverage that benefits a person or organization holding, storing or moving property for a fee regardless of any other provision of this policy.

14. Nuclear Hazard Clause.

a. "Nuclear Hazard" means any nuclear reaction, radiation, or radioactive contamination, all whether controlled or uncontrolled or however caused, or any consequence of any of these.

b. Loss caused by the nuclear hazard will not be considered loss caused by fire, explosion, or smoke, whether these perils are specifically named in or otherwise included within the Perils Insured Against in Section I.

c. This policy does not apply under Section I to loss caused directly or indirectly by nuclear hazard, except that direct loss by fire resulting from the nuclear hazard is covered.

15. Recovered Property. If you or we recover any property for which we have made payment under this policy, you or we will notify the other of the recovery. At your option, the property will be returned to or retained by you or it will become our property. If the recovered property is returned to or retained by you, the loss payment will be adjusted based on the amount you received for the recovered property.

16. Volcanic Eruption Period. One or more volcanic eruptions that occur within a 72-hour period will be considered as one volcanic eruption.

SECTION II—LIABILITY COVERAGES

COVERAGE E — Personal Liability

If a claim is made or a suit is brought against an **insured** for damages because of **bodily injury** or **property damage** caused by an **occurrence** to which this coverage applies, we will:

1. pay up to our limit of liability for the damages for which the **insured** is legally liable; and

2. provide a defense at our expense by counsel of our choice, even if the suit is groundless, false or fraudulent. We may investigate and settle any claim or suit that we decide is appropriate. Our duty to settle or defend ends when the amount we pay for damages resulting from the **occurrence** equals our limit of liability.

COVERAGE F — Medical Payments To Others

We will pay the necessary medical expenses that are incurred or medically ascertained within three years from the date of an accident causing **bodily injury.** Medical expenses means reasonable charges for medical, surgical, x-ray, dental, ambulance, hospital, professional nursing, prosthetic devices and funeral services. This coverage does not apply to you or regular residents of your household except **residence employees.** As to others, this coverage applies only:

1. to a person on the **insured location** with the permission of an **insured;** or

2. to a person off the **insured location,** if the **bodily injury:**

a. arises out of a condition on the **insured location** or the ways immediately adjoining;

b. is caused by the activities of an **insured;**

c. is caused by a **residence employee** in the course of the **residence employee's** employment by an **insured;** or

d. is caused by an animal owned by or in the care of an **insured.**

SECTION II—EXCLUSIONS

1. Coverage E — Personal Liability and Coverage F — Medical Payments to Others do not apply to **bodily injury** or **property damage:**

a. which is expected or intended by the **insured;**

b. arising out of **business** pursuits of an **insured** or the rental or holding for rental of any part of any premises by an **insured.**

This exclusion does not apply to:

(1) activities which are usual to non-**business** pursuits; or

(2) the rental or holding for rental of an **insured location:**

(a) on an occasional basis if used only as a residence;

(b) in part for use only as a residence, unless a single family unit is intended for use by the occupying family to lodge more than two roomers or boarders; or

(c) in part, as an office, school, studio or private garage;

c. arising out of the rendering of or failure to render professional services;

d. arising out of a premises:

(1) owned by an **insured;**

(2) rented to an **insured;** or

(3) rented to others by an **insured;**

that is not an **insured location;**

e. arising out of:

(1) the ownership, maintenance, use, loading or unloading of motor vehicles or all other motorized land conveyances, including trailers, owned or operated by or rented or loaned to an **insured;**

(2) the entrustment by an **insured** of a motor vehicle or any other motorized land conveyance to any person; or

(3) statutorily imposed vicarious parental liability for the actions of a child or minor using a conveyance excluded in paragraph (1) or (2) above.

This exclusion does not apply to:

(1) a trailer not towed by or carried on a motorized land conveyance.

(2) a motorized land conveyance designed for recreational use off public roads, not subject to motor vehicle registration and:

(a) not owned by an **insured;** or

(b) owned by an **insured** and on an **insured location.**

(3) a motorized golf cart when used to play golf on a golf course.

(4) a vehicle or conveyance not subject to motor vehicle registration which is:

(a) used to service an **insured's** residence;

(b) designed for assisting the handicapped; or

(c) in dead storage on an **insured location.**

f. arising out of:

(1) the ownership, maintenance, use, loading or unloading of a watercraft described below;

(2) the entrustment by an **insured** of a watercraft described below to any person; or

(3) statutorily imposed vicarious parental liability for the actions of a child or minor using a watercraft described below.

Watercraft:

(1) with inboard or inboard-outdrive motor power owned by an **insured;**

(2) with inboard or inboard-outdrive motor power of more than 50 horsepower rented to an **insured;**

(3) that is a sailing vessel, with or without auxiliary power, 26 feet or more in length owned by or rented to an **insured;** or

(4) powered by one or more outboard motors with more than 25 total horsepower if the outboard motor is owned by an **insured.** But, outboard motors of more than 25 total horsepower are covered for the policy period if:

(a) you acquire them prior to the policy period and:

(i) you declare them at policy inception; or

(ii) your intention to insure is reported to us in writing within 45 days after you acquire the outboard motors.

(b) you acquire them during the policy period.

This exclusion does not apply while the watercraft is stored.

g. arising out of:

(1) the ownership, maintenance, use, loading or unloading of an aircraft;

(2) the entrustment by an **insured** of an aircraft to any person; or

(3) statutorily imposed vicarious parental liability for the actions of a child or minor using an aircraft.

An aircraft means any contrivance used or designed for flight, except model or hobby aircraft not used or designed to carry people or cargo.

h. caused directly or indirectly by war, including undeclared war, civil war, insurrection, rebellion, revolution, warlike act by a military force or military personnel, destruction or seizure or use for a military purpose, and including any consequence of any of these. Discharge of a nuclear weapon will be deemed a warlike act even if accidental.

Exclusions d., e., f., and g. do not apply to **bodily injury** to a **residence employee** arising out of and in the course of the **residence employee's** employment by an **insured.**

2. **Coverage E — Personal Liability,** does not apply to:

a. liability:

(1) for your share of any loss assessment charged against all members of an association, corporation or community of property owners;

(2) under any contract or agreement. However, this exclusion does not apply to written contracts:

(a) that directly relate to the ownership, maintenance or use of an **insured location;** or

(b) where the liability of others is assumed by the **insured** prior to an **occurrence;**

unless excluded in (1) above or elsewhere in this policy;

b. **property damage** to property owned by the **insured;**

c. **property damage** to property rented to, occupied or used by or in the care of the **insured.** This exclusion does not apply to **property damage** caused by fire, smoke or explosion;

d. **bodily injury** to any person eligible to receive any benefits:

(1) voluntarily provided; or

(2) required to be provided;

by the **insured** under any:

(1) workers' compensation law;

(2) non-occupational disability law; or

(3) occupational disease law;

e. **bodily injury** or **property damage** for which an **insured** under this policy:

(1) is also an insured under a nuclear energy liability policy; or

(2) would be an insured under that policy but for the exhaustion of its limit of liability.

A nuclear energy liability policy is one issued by:

(1) American Nuclear Insurers;

(2) Mutual Atomic Energy Liability Underwriters;

(3) Nuclear Insurance Association of Canada;

or any of their successors; or

f. **bodily injury** to you or an **insured** within the meaning of part a. or b. of **"insured"** as defined.

3. **Coverage F—Medical Payments to Others,** does not apply to **bodily injury:**

   a. to a **residence employee** if the **bodily injury:**

      (1) occurs off the **insured location;** and

      (2) does not arise out of or in the course of the **residence employee's** employment by an **insured;**

   b. to any person eligible to receive benefits:

      (1) voluntarily provided; or

      (2) required to be provided;

      under any:

      (1) workers' compensation law;

      (2) non-occupational disability law; or

      (3) occupational disease law;

   c. from any:

      (1) nuclear reaction;

      (2) nuclear radiation; or

      (3) radioactive contamination;

      all whether controlled or uncontrolled or however caused; or

      (4) any consequence of any of these.

   d. to any person, other than a **residence employee** of an **insured,** regularly residing on any part of the **insured location.**

SECTION II—ADDITIONAL COVERAGES

We cover the following in addition to the limits of liability:

1. **Claim Expenses.** We pay:

   a. expenses we incur and costs taxed against an **insured** in any suit we defend;

   b. premiums on bonds required in a suit we defend, but not for bond amounts more than the limit of liability for Coverage E. We need not apply for or furnish any bond;

   c. reasonable expenses incurred by an **insured** at our request, including actual loss of earnings (but not loss of other income) up to $50 per day, for assisting us in the investigation or defense of a claim or suit;

   d. interest on the entire judgment which accrues after entry of the judgment and before we pay or tender, or deposit in court that part of the judgment which does not exceed the limit of liability that applies;

   e. prejudgment interest awarded against the **insured** on that part of the judgment we pay. If we make an offer to pay the applicable limit of liability, we will not pay any prejudgment interest based on that period of time after the offer.

2. **First Aid Expenses.** We will pay expenses for first aid to others incurred by an **insured** for **bodily injury** covered under this policy. We will not pay for first aid to you or any other **insured.**

3. **Damage to Property of Others.** We will pay, at replacement cost, up to $500 per **occurrence** for **property damage** to property of others caused by an **insured.**

   We will not pay for **property damage:**

   a. to the extent of any amount recoverable under Section I of this policy;

   b. caused intentionally by an **insured** who is 13 years of age or older;

   c. to property owned by an **insured;**

   d. to property owned by or rented to a tenant of an **insured** or a resident in your household; or

   e. arising out of:

      (1) **business** pursuits;

      (2) any act or omission in connection with a premises owned, rented or controlled by an **insured,** other than the **insured location;** or

      (3) the ownership, maintenance, or use of aircraft, watercraft or motor vehicles or all other motorized land conveyances.

      This exclusion does not apply to a motorized land conveyance designed for recreational use off public roads, not subject to motor vehicle registration and not owned by an **insured.**

4. **Loss Assessment.** We will pay up to $1000 for your share of any loss assessment charged during the policy period against you by a corporation or association of property owners, when the assessment is made as a result of:

   a. each **occurrence** to which Section II of this policy would apply;

b. liability for each act of a director, officer or trustee in the capacity as a director, officer or trustee, provided:

(1) the director, officer or trustee is elected by the members of a corporation or association of property owners; and

(2) the director, officer or trustee serves without deriving any income from the exercise of duties which are solely on behalf of a corporation or association of property owners.

This coverage applies only to loss assessments charged against you as owner or tenant of the **residence premises.**

We do not cover loss assessments charged against you or a corporation or association of property owners by any governmental body.

Section II — Coverage E — Personal Liability Exclusion 2.a.(1) does not apply to this coverage.

SECTION II—CONDITIONS

1. **Limit of Liability.** Our total liability under Coverage E for all damages resulting from any one **occurrence** will not be more than the limit of liability for Coverage E as shown in the Declarations. This limit is the same regardless of the number of **insureds,** claims made or persons injured.

   Our total liability under Coverage F for all medical expense payable for **bodily injury** to one person as the result of one accident will not be more than the limit of liability for Coverage F as shown in the Declarations.

2. **Severability of Insurance.** This insurance applies separately to each **insured.** This condition will not increase our limit of liability for any one **occurrence.**

3. **Duties After Loss.** In case of an accident or **occurrence,** the **insured** will perform the following duties that apply. You will help us by seeing that these duties are performed:

   a. give written notice to us or our agent as soon as is practical, which sets forth:

      (1) the identity of the policy and **insured;**

      (2) reasonably available information on the time, place and circumstances of the accident or **occurrence;** and

      (3) names and addresses of any claimants and witnesses;

   b. promptly forward to us every notice, demand, summons or other process relating to the accident or **occurrence;**

   c. at our request, help us:

      (1) to make settlement;

      (2) to enforce any right of contribution or indemnity against any person or organization who may be liable to an **insured;**

      (3) with the conduct of suits and attend hearings and trials;

      (4) to secure and give evidence and obtain the attendance of witnesses;

   d. under the coverage — Damage to Property of Others — submit to us within 60 days after the loss, a sworn statement of loss and show the damaged property, if in the **insured's** control;

   e. the **insured** will not, except at the **insured's** own cost, voluntarily make payment, assume obligation or incur expense other than for first aid to others at the time of the **bodily injury.**

4. **Duties of an Injured Person—Coverage F—Medical Payments to Others.**

   The injured person or someone acting for the injured person will:

   a. give us written proof of claim, under oath if required, as soon as is practical; and

   b. authorize us to obtain copies of medical reports and records.

   The injured person will submit to a physical exam by a doctor of our choice when and as often as we reasonably require.

5. **Payment of Claim—Coverage F—Medical Payments to Others.** Payment under this coverage is not an admission of liability by an **insured** or us.

6. **Suit Against Us.** No action can be brought against us unless there has been compliance with the policy provisions.

   No one will have the right to join us as a party to any action against an **insured.** Also, no action with respect to Coverage E can be brought against us until the obligation of the **insured** has been determined by final judgment or agreement signed by us.

7. **Bankruptcy of an Insured.** Bankruptcy or insolvency of an **insured** will not relieve us of our obligations under this policy.

8. **Other Insurance — Coverage E — Personal Liability.** This insurance is excess over other valid and collectible insurance except insurance written specifically to cover as excess over the limits of liability that apply in this policy.

SECTIONS I AND II—CONDITIONS

1. **Policy Period.** This policy applies only to loss in Section I or **bodily injury** or **property damage** in Section II, which occurs during the policy period.

2. **Concealment or Fraud.** We do not provide coverage for an **insured** who has:

   a. intentionally concealed or misrepresented any material fact or circumstance; or

   b. made false statements or engaged in fraudulent conduct;

   relating to this insurance.

3. **Liberalization Clause.** If we adopt a revision which would broaden the coverage under this policy without additional premium within 60 days prior to or during the policy period, the broadened coverage will immediately apply to this policy.

4. **Waiver or Change of Policy Provisions.**

   A waiver or change of a provision of this policy must be in writing by us to be valid. Our request for an appraisal or examination will not waive any of our rights.

5. **Cancellation.**

   a. You may cancel this policy at any time by returning it to us or by letting us know in writing of the date cancellation is to take effect.

   b. We may cancel this policy only for the reasons stated below by letting you know in writing of the date cancellation takes effect. This cancellation notice may be delivered to you, or mailed to you at your mailing address shown in the Declarations.

      Proof of mailing will be sufficient proof of notice.

      (1) When you have not paid the premium, we may cancel at any time by letting you know at least 10 days before the date cancellation takes effect.

      (2) When this policy has been in effect for less than 60 days and is not a renewal with us, we may cancel for any reason by letting you know at least 10 days before the date cancellation takes effect.

      (3) When this policy has been in effect for 60 days or more, or at any time if it is a renewal with us, we may cancel:

         (a) if there has been a material misrepresentation of fact which if known to us would have caused us not to issue the policy; or

         (b) if the risk has changed substantially since the policy was issued.

         This can be done by letting you know at least 30 days before the date cancellation takes effect.

      (4) When this policy is written for a period of more than one year, we may cancel for any reason at anniversary by letting you know at least 30 days before the date cancellation takes effect.

   c. When this policy is cancelled, the premium for the period from the date of cancellation to the expiration date will be refunded pro rata.

   d. If the return premium is not refunded with the notice of cancellation or when this policy is returned to us, we will refund it within a reasonable time after the date cancellation takes effect.

6. **Non-Renewal.** We may elect not to renew this policy. We may do so by delivering to you, or mailing to you at your mailing address shown in the Declarations, written notice at least 30 days before the expiration date of this policy. Proof of mailing will be sufficient proof of notice.

7. **Assignment.** Assignment of this policy will not be valid unless we give our written consent.

8. **Subrogation.** An **insured** may waive in writing before a loss all rights of recovery against any person. If not waived, we may require an assignment of rights of recovery for a loss to the extent that payment is made by us.

   If an assignment is sought, an **insured** must sign and deliver all related papers and cooperate with us.

   Subrogation does not apply under Section II to Medical Payments to Others or Damage to Property of Others.

9. **Death.** If any person named in the Declarations or the spouse, if a resident of the same household, dies:

   a. we insure the legal representative of the deceased but only with respect to the premises and property of the deceased covered under the policy at the time of death;

   b. **insured** includes:

      (1) any member of your household who is an **insured** at the time of your death, but only while a resident of the **residence premises;** and

      (2) with respect to your property, the person having proper temporary custody of the property until appointment and qualification of a legal representative.

Appendix C Personal Auto Policy

PERSONAL AUTO POLICY

AGREEMENT

In return for payment of the premium and subject to all the terms of this policy, we agree with you as follows:

DEFINITIONS

Throughout this policy, "you" and "your" refer to:

1. The "named insured" shown in the Declarations; and
2. The spouse if a resident of the same household.

"We", "us" and "our" refer to the Company providing this insurance.

For purposes of this policy, a private passenger type auto shall be deemed to be owned by a person if leased:

1. Under a written agreement to that person; and
2. For a continuous period of at least 6 months.

Other words and phrases are defined. They are boldfaced when used.

"Family member" means a person related to you by blood, marriage or adoption who is a resident of your household. This includes a ward or foster child.

"Occupying" means in, upon, getting in, on, out or off.

"Trailer" means a vehicle designed to be pulled by a:

1. Private passenger auto; or
2. Pickup, panel truck, or van.

It also means a farm wagon or farm implement while towed by a vehicle listed in 1. or 2. above.

"Your covered auto" means:

1. Any vehicle shown in the Declarations.
2. Any of the following types of vehicles on the date you become the owner:
   a. a private passenger auto; or
   b. a pickup, panel truck or van, not used in any business or occupation other than farming or ranching.

   This provision applies only if you:
   a. acquire the vehicle during the policy period; and
   b. ask us to insure it within 30 days after you become the owner.

   If the vehicle you acquire replaces one shown in the Declarations, it will have the same coverage as the vehicle it replaced. You must ask us to insure a replacement vehicle within 30 days only if you wish to add or continue Coverage for Damage to Your Auto.

   If the vehicle you acquire is in addition to any shown in the Declarations, it will have the broadest coverage we now provide for any vehicle shown in the Declarations.
3. Any **trailer** you own.
4. Any auto or **trailer** you do not own while used as a temporary substitute for any other vehicle described in this definition which is out of normal use because of its:
   a. breakdown;
   b. repair;
   c. servicing;
   d. loss; or
   e. destruction.

PART A—LIABILITY COVERAGE

INSURING AGREEMENT

We will pay damages for bodily injury or property damage for which any **covered person** becomes legally responsible because of an auto accident. We will settle or defend, as we consider appropriate, any claim or suit asking for these damages. In addition to our limit of liability, we will pay all defense costs we incur. Our duty to settle or defend ends when our limit of liability for this coverage has been exhausted.

INSURING AGREEMENT (Continued)

"Covered person" as used in this Part means:

1. You or any **family member** for the ownership, maintenance or use of any auto or **trailer.**

2. Any person using **your covered auto.**

3. For **your covered auto,** any person or organization but only with respect to legal responsibility for acts or omissions of a person for whom coverage is afforded under this Part.

4. For any auto or **trailer,** other than **your covered auto,** any person or organization but only with respect to legal responsibility for acts or omissions of you or any **family member** for whom coverage is afforded under this Part. This provision applies only if the person or organization does not own or hire the auto or **trailer.**

SUPPLEMENTARY PAYMENTS

In addition to our limit of liability, we will pay on behalf of a **covered person:**

1. Up to $250 for the cost of bail bonds required because of an accident, including related traffic law violations. The accident must result in bodily injury or property damage covered under this policy.

2. Premiums on appeal bonds and bonds to release attachments in any suit we defend.

3. Interest accruing after a judgment is entered in any suit we defend. Our duty to pay interest ends when we offer to pay that part of the judgment which does not exceed our limit of liability for this coverage.

4. Up to $50 a day for loss of earnings, but not other income, because of attendance at hearings or trials at our request.

5. Other reasonable expenses incurred at our request.

EXCLUSIONS

A. We do not provide Liability Coverage for any person:

1. Who intentionally causes bodily injury or property damage.

2. For damage to property owned or being transported by that person.

3. For damage to property:

   a. rented to;

   b. used by; or

   c. in the care of;

that person.

This exclusion does not apply to damage to:

   a. a residence or private garage; or

   b. any of the following type vehicles not owned by or furnished or available for the regular use of you or any **family member:**

      (1) private passenger autos;

      (2) **trailers;** or

      (3) pickups, panel trucks, or vans.

4. For bodily injury to an employee of that person during the course of employment. This exclusion does not apply to bodily injury to a domestic employee unless workers' compensation benefits are required or available for that domestic employee.

5. For that person's liability arising out of the ownership or operation of a vehicle while it is being used to carry persons or property for a fee. This exclusion does not apply to a share-the-expense car pool.

6. While employed or otherwise engaged in the business or occupation of:

   a. selling;

   b. repairing;

   c. servicing;

   d. storing; or

   e. parking;

vehicles designed for use mainly on public highways. This includes road testing and delivery. This exclusion does not apply to the ownership, maintenance or use of **your covered auto** by:

   a. you;

   b. any **family member;** or

   c. any partner, agent or employee of you or any **family member.**

EXCLUSIONS
(Continued)

7. Maintaining or using any vehicle while that person is employed or otherwise engaged in any business or occupation not described in Exclusion 6. This exclusion does not apply to the maintenance or use of a:
   a. private passenger auto;
   b. pickup, panel truck or van that you own; or
   c. **trailer** used with a vehicle described in a. or b. above.
8. Using a vehicle without a reasonable belief that that person is entitled to do so.
9. For bodily injury or property damage for which that person:
   a. is an insured under a nuclear energy liability policy; or
   b. would be an insured under a nuclear energy liability policy but for its termination upon exhaustion of its limit of liability.

A nuclear energy liability policy is a policy issued by any of the following or their successors:
   a. Nuclear Energy Liability Insurance Association;
   b. Mutual Atomic Energy Liability Underwriters; or
   c. Nuclear Insurance Association of Canada.

B. We do not provide Liability Coverage for the ownership, maintenance or use of:
1. Any motorized vehicle having less than four wheels.
2. Any vehicle, other than **your covered auto,** which is:
   a. owned by you; or
   b. furnished or available for your regular use.
3. Any vehicle, other than **your covered auto,** which is:
   a. owned by any **family member;** or
   b. furnished or available for the regular use of any **family member.**

However, this exclusion does not apply to your maintenance or use of any vehicle which is:
   a. owned by a **family member;** or
   b. furnished or available for the regular use of a **family member.**

LIMIT OF LIABILITY

The limit of liability shown in the Declarations for this coverage is our maximum limit of liability for all damages resulting from any one auto accident. This is the most we will pay regardless of the number of:
1. **Covered persons;**
2. Claims made;
3. Vehicles or premiums shown in the Declarations; or
4. Vehicles involved in the auto accident.

We will apply the limit of liability to provide any separate limits required by law for bodily injury and property damage liability. However, this provision will not change our total limit of liability.

OUT OF STATE COVERAGE

If an auto accident to which this policy applies occurs in any state or province other than the one in which **your covered auto** is principally garaged, we will interpret your policy for that accident as follows:

If the state or province has:
1. A financial responsibility or similar law specifying limits of liability for bodily injury or property damage higher than the limit shown in the Declarations, your policy will provide the higher specified limit.
2. A compulsory insurance or similar law requiring a nonresident to maintain insurance whenever the nonresident uses a vehicle in that state or province, your policy will provide at least the required minimum amounts and types of coverage.

No one will be entitled to duplicate payments for the same elements of loss.

FINANCIAL RESPONSIBILITY REQUIRED

When this policy is certified as future proof of financial responsibility, this policy shall comply with the law to the extent required.

OTHER INSURANCE

If there is other applicable liability insurance we will pay only our share of the loss. Our share is the proportion that our limit of liability bears to the total of all applicable limits. However, any insurance we provide for a vehicle you do not own shall be excess over any other collectible insurance.

PART B—MEDICAL PAYMENTS COVERAGE

INSURING AGREEMENT

We will pay reasonable expenses incurred for necessary medical and funeral services because of bodily injury:

1. Caused by accident; and
2. Sustained by a **covered person.**

We will pay only those expenses incurred within 3 years from the date of the accident.

"Covered person" as used in this Part means:

1. You or any **family member:**
   a. while **occupying;** or
   b. as a pedestrian when struck by;

   a motor vehicle designed for use mainly on public roads or a trailer of any type.
2. Any other person while **occupying your covered auto.**

EXCLUSIONS

We do not provide Medical Payments Coverage for any person for bodily injury:

1. Sustained while **occupying** any motorized vehicle having less than four wheels.
2. Sustained while **occupying your covered auto** when it is being used to carry persons or property for a fee. This exclusion does not apply to a share-the-expense car pool.
3. Sustained while **occupying** any vehicle located for use as a residence or premises.
4. Occurring during the course of employment if workers' compensation benefits are required or available for the bodily injury.
5. Sustained while **occupying** or, when struck by, any vehicle (other than **your covered auto**) which is:
   a. owned by you; or
   b. furnished or available for your regular use.
6. Sustained while **occupying** or, when struck by, any vehicle (other than **your covered auto**) which is:
   a. owned by any **family member;** or
   b. furnished or available for the regular use of any **family member.**

   However, this exclusion does not apply to you.
7. Sustained while **occupying** a vehicle without a reasonable belief that that person is entitled to do so.
8. Sustained while **occupying** a vehicle when it is being used in the business or occupation of a **covered person.** This exclusion does not apply to bodily injury sustained while **occupying** a:
   a. private passenger auto;
   b. pickup, panel truck, or van that you own; or
   c. **trailer** used with a vehicle described in a. or b. above.
9. Caused by or as a consequence of:
   a. discharge of a nuclear weapon (even if accidental);
   b. war (declared or undeclared);
   c. civil war;
   d. insurrection; or
   e. rebellion or revolution.
10. From or as a consequence of the following, whether controlled or uncontrolled or however caused:
    a. nuclear reaction;
    b. radiation; or
    c. radioactive contamination.

LIMIT OF LIABILITY

The limit of liability shown in the Declarations for this coverage is our maximum limit of liability for each person injured in any one accident. This is the most we will pay regardless of the number of:

1. **Covered persons;**
2. Claims made;
3. Vehicles or premiums shown in the Declarations; or
4. Vehicles involved in the accident.

Any amounts otherwise payable for expenses under this coverage shall be reduced by any amounts paid or payable for the same expenses under Part A or Part C.

No payment will be made unless the injured person or that person's legal representative agrees in writing that any payment shall be applied toward any settlement or judgment that person receives under Part A or Part C.

OTHER INSURANCE

If there is other applicable auto medical payments insurance we will pay only our share of the loss. Our share is the proportion that our limit of liability bears to the total of all applicable limits. However, any insurance we provide with respect to a vehicle you do not own shall be excess over any other collectible auto insurance providing payments for medical or funeral expenses.

PART C—UNINSURED MOTORISTS COVERAGE

INSURING AGREEMENT

We will pay damages which a **covered person** is legally entitled to recover from the owner or operator of an **uninsured motor vehicle** because of bodily injury:

1. Sustained by a **covered person;** and
2. Caused by an accident.

The owner's or operator's liability for these damages must arise out of the ownership, maintenance or use of the **uninsured motor vehicle.**

Any judgment for damages arising out of a suit brought without our written consent is not binding on us.

"Covered person" as used in this Part means:

1. You or any **family member.**
2. Any other person **occupying your covered auto.**
3. Any person for damages that person is entitled to recover because of bodily injury to which this coverage applies sustained by a person described in 1. or 2. above.

"Uninsured motor vehicle" means a land motor vehicle or trailer of any type:

1. To which no bodily injury liability bond or policy applies at the time of the accident.
2. To which a bodily injury liability bond or policy applies at the time of the accident. In this case its limit for bodily injury liability must be less than the minimum limit for bodily injury liability specified by the financial responsibility law of the state in which **your covered auto** is principally garaged.
3. Which is a hit and run vehicle whose operator or owner cannot be identified and which hits:
   a. you or any **family member;**
   b. a vehicle which you or any **family member** are **occupying;** or
   c. **your covered auto.**
4. To which a bodily injury liability bond or policy applies at the time of the accident but the bonding or insuring company:
   a. denies coverage; or
   b. is or becomes insolvent.

However, **"uninsured motor vehicle"** does not include any vehicle or equipment:

1. Owned by or furnished or available for the regular use of you or any **family member.**
2. Owned or operated by a self-insurer under any applicable motor vehicle law.
3. Owned by any governmental unit or agency.
4. Operated on rails or crawler treads.
5. Designed mainly for use off public roads while not on public roads.
6. While located for use as a residence or premises.

EXCLUSIONS

A. We do not provide Uninsured Motorists Coverage for bodily injury sustained by any person:

1. While **occupying,** or when struck by, any motor vehicle owned by you or any **family member** which is not insured for this coverage under this policy. This includes a trailer of any type used with that vehicle.

2. If that person or the legal representative settles the bodily injury claim without our consent.

3. While **occupying your covered auto** when it is being used to carry persons or property for a fee. This exclusion does not apply to a share-the-expense car pool.

4. Using a vehicle without a reasonable belief that that person is entitled to do so.

B. This coverage shall not apply directly or indirectly to benefit any insurer or self-insurer under any of the following or similar law:

1. workers' compensation law; or

2. disability benefits law.

LIMIT OF LIABILITY

The limit of liability shown in the Declarations for this coverage is our maximum limit of liability for all damages resulting from any one accident. This is the most we will pay regardless of the number of:

1. **Covered persons;**

2. Claims made;

3. Vehicles or premiums shown in the Declarations; or

4. Vehicles involved in the accident.

Any amounts otherwise payable for damages under this coverage shall be reduced by all sums:

1. Paid because of the bodily injury by or on behalf of persons or organizations who may be legally responsible. This includes all sums paid under Part A; and

2. Paid or payable because of the bodily injury under any of the following or similar law:

   a. workers' compensation law; or

   b. disability benefits law.

Any payment under this coverage will reduce any amount that person is entitled to recover for the same damages under Part A.

OTHER INSURANCE

If there is other applicable similar insurance we will pay only our share of the loss. Our share is the proportion that our limit of liability bears to the total of all applicable limits. However, any insurance we provide with respect to a vehicle you do not own shall be excess over any other collectible insurance.

ARBITRATION

If we and a **covered person** do not agree:

1. Whether that person is legally entitled to recover damages under this Part; or

2. As to the amount of damages;

either party may make a written demand for arbitration. In this event, each party will select an arbitrator. The two arbitrators will select a third. If they cannot agree within 30 days, either may request that selection be made by a judge of a court having jurisdiction. Each party will:

1. Pay the expenses it incurs; and

2. Bear the expenses of the third arbitrator equally.

Unless both parties agree otherwise, arbitration will take place in the county in which the **covered person** lives. Local rules of law as to procedure and evidence will apply. A decision agreed to by two of the arbitrators will be binding as to:

1. Whether the **covered person** is legally entitled to recover damages; and

2. The amount of damages. This applies only if the amount does not exceed the minimum limit for bodily injury liability specified by the financial responsibility law of the state in which **your covered auto** is principally garaged. If the amount exceeds that limit, either party may demand the right to a trial. This demand must be made within 60 days of the arbitrators' decision. If this demand is not made, the amount of damages agreed to by the arbitrators will be binding.

PART D—COVERAGE FOR DAMAGE TO YOUR AUTO

INSURING AGREEMENT

We will pay for direct and accidental loss to **your covered auto,** including its equipment, minus any applicable deductible shown in the Declarations. However, we will pay for loss caused by **collision** only if the Declarations indicate that Collision Coverage is provided.

"Collision" means the upset, or collision with another object of **your covered auto.** However, loss caused by the following are not considered **"collision"**:

1. Missiles or falling objects;
2. Fire;
3. Theft or larceny;
4. Explosion or earthquake;
5. Windstorm;
6. Hail, water or flood;
7. Malicious mischief or vandalism;
8. Riot or civil commotion;
9. Contact with bird or animal; or
10. Breakage of glass.

If breakage of glass is caused by a **collision,** you may elect to have it considered a loss caused by **collision.**

TRANSPORTATION EXPENSES

In addition, we will pay up to $10 per day, to a maximum of $300, for transportation expenses incurred by you. This applies only in the event of the total theft of **your covered auto.** We will pay only transportation expenses incurred during the period:

1. Beginning 48 hours after the theft; and
2. Ending when **your covered auto** is returned to use or we pay for its loss.

EXCLUSIONS

We will not pay for:

1. Loss to **your covered auto** which occurs while it is used to carry persons or property for a fee. This exclusion does not apply to a share-the-expense car pool.
2. Damage due and confined to:
   a. wear and tear;
   b. freezing;
   c. mechanical or electrical breakdown or failure; or
   d. road damage to tires.

   This exclusion does not apply if the damage results from the total theft of **your covered auto.**
3. Loss due to or as a consequence of:
   a. radioactive contamination;
   b. discharge of any nuclear weapon (even if accidental);
   c. war (declared or undeclared);
   d. civil war;
   e. insurrection; or
   f. rebellion or revolution.
4. Loss to equipment designed for the reproduction of sound. This exclusion does not apply if the equipment is permanently installed in **your covered auto.**
5. Loss to tapes, records or other devices for use with equipment designed for the reproduction of sound.
6. Loss to a camper body or **trailer** not shown in the Declarations. This exclusion does not apply to a camper body or **trailer** you:
   a. acquire during the policy period; and
   b. ask us to insure within 30 days after you become the owner.
7. Loss to any vehicle while used as a temporary substitute for a vehicle you own which is out of normal use because of its:
   a. breakdown;
   b. repair;
   c. servicing;
   d. loss; or
   e. destruction.
8. Loss to:
   a. TV antennas;
   b. awnings or cabanas; or
   c. equipment designed to create additional living facilities.

EXCLUSIONS (Continued)

9. Loss to any of the following or their accessories:
   a. citizens band radio;
   b. two-way mobile radio;
   c. telephone; or
   d. scanning monitor receiver.

This exclusion does not apply if the equipment is permanently installed in the opening of the dash or console of the auto. This opening must be normally used by the auto manufacturer for the installation of a radio.

10. Loss to any custom furnishings or equipment in or upon any pickup, panel truck or van. Custom furnishings or equipment include but are not limited to:
    a. special carpeting and insulation, furniture, bars or television receivers;
    b. facilities for cooking and sleeping;
    c. height-extending roofs; or
    d. custom murals, paintings or other decals or graphics.

LIMIT OF LIABILITY

Our limit of liability for loss will be the lesser of the:
1. Actual cash value of the stolen or damaged property; or
2. Amount necessary to repair or replace the property.

PAYMENT OF LOSS

We may pay for loss in money or repair or replace the damaged or stolen property. We may, at our expense, return any stolen property to:
1. You; or
2. The address shown in this policy.

If we return stolen property we will pay for any damage resulting from the theft. We may keep all or part of the property at an agreed or appraised value.

NO BENEFIT TO BAILEE

This insurance shall not directly or indirectly benefit any carrier or other bailee for hire.

OTHER INSURANCE

If other insurance also covers the loss we will pay only our share of the loss. Our share is the proportion that our limit of liability bears to the total of all applicable limits.

APPRAISAL

If we and you do not agree on the amount of loss, either may demand an appraisal of the loss. In this event, each party will select a competent appraiser. The two appraisers will select an umpire. The appraisers will state separately the actual cash value and the amount of loss. If they fail to agree, they will submit their differences to the umpire. A decision agreed to by any two will be binding. Each party will:
1. Pay its chosen appraiser; and
2. Bear the expenses of the appraisal and umpire equally.

We do not waive any of our rights under this policy by agreeing to an appraisal.

PART E—DUTIES AFTER AN ACCIDENT OR LOSS

GENERAL DUTIES

We must be notified promptly of how, when and where the accident or loss happened. Notice should also include the names and addresses of any injured persons and of any witnesses.

A person seeking any coverage must:
1. Cooperate with us in the investigation, settlement or defense of any claim or suit.
2. Promptly send us copies of any notices or legal papers received in connection with the accident or loss.
3. Submit, as often as we reasonably require, to physical exams by physicians we select. We will pay for these exams.
4. Authorize us to obtain:
   a. medical reports; and
   b. other pertinent records.
5. Submit a proof of loss when required by us.

ADDITIONAL DUTIES FOR UNINSURED MOTORISTS COVERAGE

A person seeking Uninsured Motorists Coverage must also:

1. Promptly notify the police if a hit and run driver is involved.
2. Promptly send us copies of the legal papers if a suit is brought.

ADDITIONAL DUTIES FOR COVERAGE FOR DAMAGE TO YOUR AUTO

A person seeking Coverage for Damage to Your Auto must also:

1. Take reasonable steps after loss to protect **your covered auto** and its equipment from further loss. We will pay reasonable expenses incurred to do this.
2. Promptly notify the police if **your covered auto** is stolen.
3. Permit us to inspect and appraise the damaged property before its repair or disposal.

PART F—GENERAL PROVISIONS

BANKRUPTCY

Bankruptcy or insolvency of the **covered person** shall not relieve us of any obligations under this policy.

CHANGES

This policy contains all the agreements between you and us. Its terms may not be changed or waived except by endorsement issued by us. If a change requires a premium adjustment, we will adjust the premium as of the effective date of change.

We may revise this policy form to provide more coverage without additional premium charge. If we do this your policy will automatically provide the additional coverage as of the date the revision is effective in your state.

LEGAL ACTION AGAINST US

No legal action may be brought against us until there has been full compliance with all the terms of this policy. In addition, under Part A, no legal action may be brought against us until:

1. We agree in writing that the **covered person** has an obligation to pay; or
2. The amount of that obligation has been finally determined by judgment after trial.

No person or organization has any right under this policy to bring us into any action to determine the liability of a **covered person.**

OUR RIGHT TO RECOVER PAYMENT

A. If we make a payment under this policy and the person to or for whom payment was made has a right to recover damages from another we shall be subrogated to that right. That person shall do:

1. Whatever is necessary to enable us to exercise our rights; and
2. Nothing after loss to prejudice them.

However, our rights in this paragraph do not apply under Part D, against any person using **your covered auto** with a reasonable belief that that person is entitled to do so.

B. If we make a payment under this policy and the person to or for whom payment is made recovers damages from another, that person shall:

1. Hold in trust for us the proceeds of the recovery; and
2. Reimburse us to the extent of our payment.

POLICY PERIOD AND TERRITORY

This policy applies only to accidents and losses which occur:

1. During the policy period as shown in the Declarations; and
2. Within the policy territory.

The policy territory is:

1. The United States of America, its territories or possessions;
2. Puerto Rico; or
3. Canada.

This policy also applies to loss to, or accidents involving, **your covered auto** while being transported between their ports.

TERMINATION

Cancellation. This policy may be cancelled during the policy period as follows:

1. The named insured shown in the Declarations may cancel by:
   a. returning this policy to us; or
   b. giving us advance written notice of the date cancellation is to take effect.

TERMINATION
(Continued)

2. We may cancel by mailing to the named insured shown in the Declarations at the address shown in this policy:

a. at least 10 days notice:

(1) if cancellation is for nonpayment of premium; or

(2) if notice is mailed during the first 60 days this policy is in effect and this is not a renewal or continuation policy; or

b. at least 20 days notice in all other cases.

3. After this policy is in effect for 60 days, or if this is a renewal or continuation policy, we will cancel only:

a. for nonpayment of premium; or

b. if your driver's license or that of:

(1) any driver who lives with you; or

(2) any driver who customarily uses **your covered auto;**

has been suspended or revoked. This must have occurred:

(1) during the policy period; or

(2) since the last anniversary of the original effective date if the policy period is other than 1 year.

Nonrenewal. If we decide not to renew or continue this policy, we will mail notice to the named insured shown in the Declarations at the address shown in this policy. Notice will be mailed at least 20 days before the end of the policy period. If the policy period is other than 1 year, we will have the right not to renew or continue it only at each anniversary of its original effective date.

Automatic Termination. If we offer to renew or continue and you or your representative do not accept, this policy will automatically terminate at the end of the current policy period. Failure to pay the required renewal or continuation premium when due shall mean that you have not accepted our offer.

If you obtain other insurance on **your covered auto,** any similar insurance provided by this policy will terminate as to that auto on the effective date of the other insurance.

Other Termination Provisions.

1. If the law in effect in your state at the time this policy is issued, renewed or continued:

a. requires a longer notice period;

b. requires a special form of or procedure for giving notice; or

c. modifies any of the stated termination reasons;

we will comply with those requirements.

2. We may deliver any notice instead of mailing it. Proof of mailing of any notice shall be sufficient proof of notice.

3. If this policy is cancelled, you may be entitled to a premium refund. If so, we will send you the refund. The premium refund, if any, will be computed according to our manuals. However, making or offering to make the refund is not a condition of cancellation.

4. The effective date of cancellation stated in the notice shall become the end of the policy period.

TRANSFER OF YOUR INTEREST IN THIS POLICY

Your rights and duties under this policy may not be assigned without our written consent. However, if a named insured shown in the Declarations dies, coverage will be provided for:

1. The surviving spouse if resident in the same household at the time of death. Coverage applies to the spouse as if a named insured shown in the Declarations; or

2. The legal representative of the deceased person as if a named insured shown in the Declarations. This applies only with respect to the representative's legal responsibility to maintain or use **your covered auto.**

Coverage will only be provided until the end of the policy period.

TWO OR MORE AUTO POLICIES

If this policy and any other auto insurance policy issued to you by us apply to the same accident, the maximum limit of our liability under all the policies shall not exceed the highest applicable limit of liability under any one policy.

Appendix D Whole Life Policy

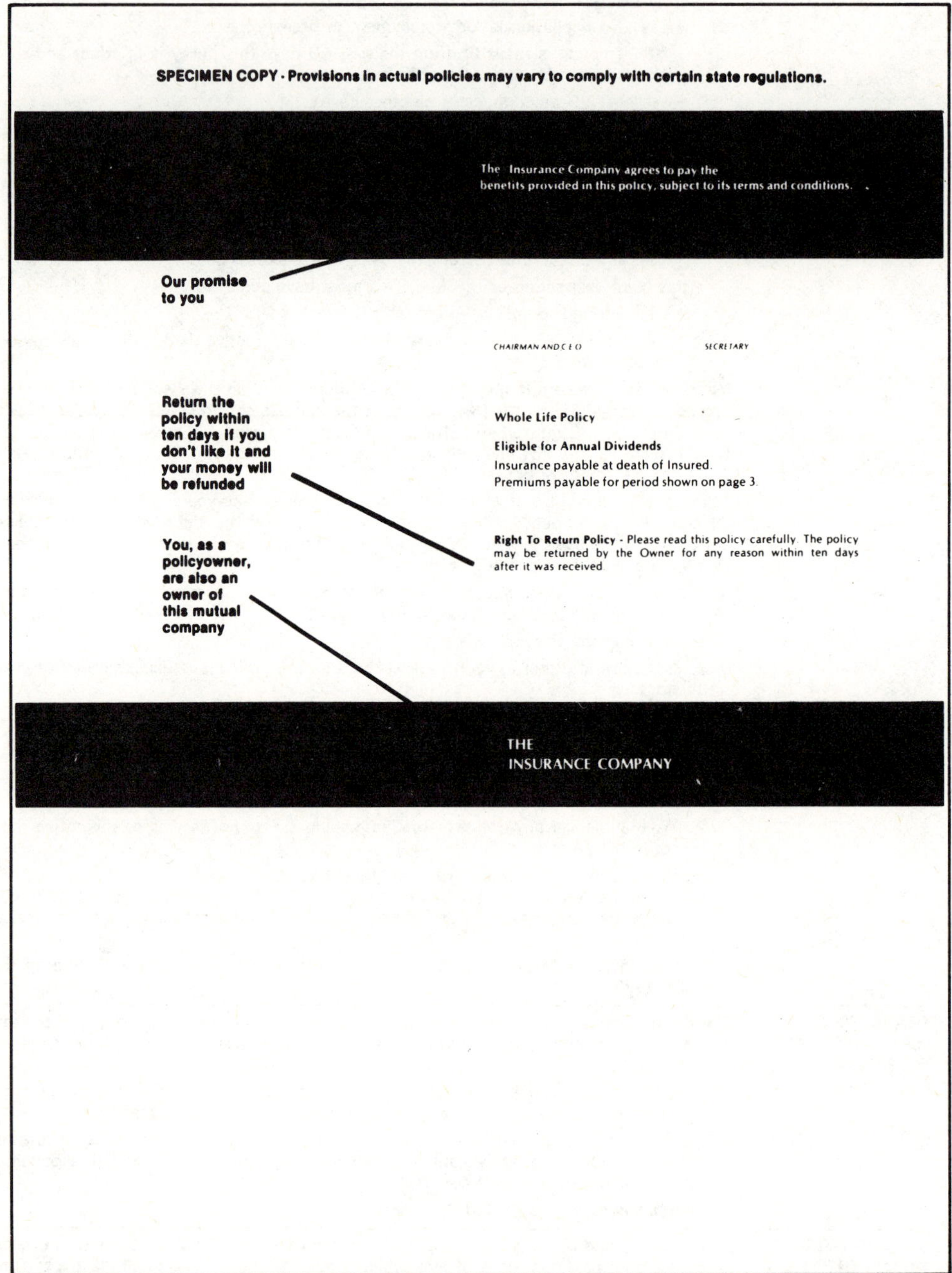
SPECIMEN COPY - Provisions in actual policies may vary to comply with certain state regulations.

The Insurance Company agrees to pay the
benefits provided in this policy, subject to its terms and conditions.

Our promise to you

CHAIRMAN AND C E O
SECRETARY

Return the policy within ten days if you don't like it and your money will be refunded

Whole Life Policy

Eligible for Annual Dividends

Insurance payable at death of Insured.
Premiums payable for period shown on page 3.

You, as a policyowner, are also an owner of this mutual company

Right To Return Policy - Please read this policy carefully. The policy may be returned by the Owner for any reason within ten days after it was received.

THE
INSURANCE COMPANY

"Whole Life Policy" reprinted with permission by Northwestern Mutual Life.

This policy is a legal contract between the Owner and Life Insurance Company.
Read your policy carefully.

Table of Contents — **Guide to Policy Provisions**

ENDORSEMENTS

To be made only by the Company at the Home Office

Pages 3 and 4 show our minimum guarantees to you

BENEFITS AND PREMIUMS

DATE OF ISSUE JANUARY 1, 1982

	AMOUNT	ANNUAL PREMIUM	PAYABLE FOR
PLAN AND ADDITIONAL BENEFITS			
WHOLE LIFE PAID UP AT 90	$100,000	$1,837.00	55 YEARS

A PREMIUM IS PAYABLE ON THE POLICY DATE AND EVERY 12 POLICY MONTHS THEREAFTER.

THE FIRST PREMIUM IS $1,837.00.

THIS POLICY IS ISSUED IN A STANDARD PREMIUM CLASS.

DIRECT BENEFICIARY JANE M. DOE, WIFE OF THE INSURED

OWNER JOHN J. DOE, THE INSURED

INSURED	JOHN J. DOE	AGE AND SEX	35 MALE
POLICY DATE	JANUARY 1, 1982	POLICY NUMBER	1 000 001
PLAN	WHOLE LIFE PAID UP AT 90	AMOUNT	$ 100,000

Type of policy you bought

PAGE 3

Your policy's "I.D."

TABLE OF GUARANTEED VALUES

END OF POLICY YEAR	JANUARY 1,	CASH VALUE	PAID-UP INSURANCE	$100,000 EXTENDED TERM INSURANCE TO
1	1983	$ 0	$ 0	--
2	1984	913	3,100	JUN 30, 1986
3	1985	2,283	7,600	JUN 18, 1990
4	1986	3,689	11,900	OCT 9, 1993
5	1987	5,134	16,100	AUG 3, 1996
6	1988	6,613	20,100	APR 26, 1999
7	1989	8,129	23,900	OCT 9, 2001
8	1990	9,680	27,600	DEC 3, 2003
9	1991	11,266	31,200	OCT 31, 2005
10	1992	12,888	34,600	JUL 19, 2007
11	1993	14,484	37,700	JAN 20, 2009
12	1994	16,111	40,700	JUN 6, 2010
13	1995	17,768	43,600	SEP 16, 2011
14	1996	19,452	46,300	NOV 23, 2012
15	1997	21,163	49,000	JAN 3, 2014
16	1998	22,898	51,500	JAN 18, 2015
17	1999	24,655	53,900	JAN 10, 2016
18	2000	26,434	56,200	DEC 15, 2016
19	2001	28,233	58,500	NOV 2, 2017
20	2002	30,050	60,600	SEP 6, 2018
AGE 60	2007	39,327	69,900	JUL 5, 2022
AGE 65	2012	48,663	77,300	NOV 21, 2025
AGE 70	2017	57,613	83,000	JAN 4, 2029

VALUES SHOWN AT END OF POLICY YEAR DO NOT REFLECT ANY PREMIUM DUE ON THAT POLICY ANNIVERSARY. VALUES ARE INCREASED BY PAID-UP ADDITIONS AND DIVIDEND ACCUMULATIONS AND DECREASED BY POLICY DEBT.

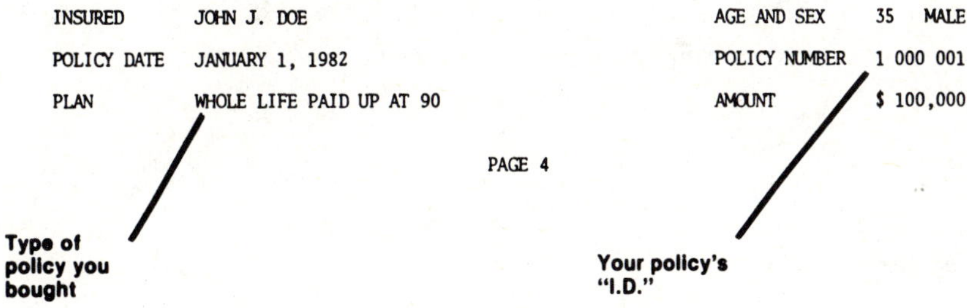

INSURED	JOHN J. DOE	AGE AND SEX	35 MALE
POLICY DATE	JANUARY 1, 1982	POLICY NUMBER	1 000 001
PLAN	WHOLE LIFE PAID UP AT 90	AMOUNT	$ 100,000

PAGE 4

SECTION 1. THE CONTRACT

The contract is made up of the policy and the application

1.1 LIFE INSURANCE BENEFIT

The Insurance Company will pay a benefit on the death of the Insured. Subject to the terms and conditions of the policy:

- payment of the plan Amount shown on page 3 will be made after proof of the death of the Insured is received at the Home Office; and
- payment will be made to the beneficiary or other payee under Sections 8 and 9.

1.2 ENTIRE CONTRACT; CHANGES

This policy with the attached application is the entire contract. Statements in the application are representations and not warranties. A change in the policy is valid only if it is approved by an officer of the Company. The Company may require that the policy be sent to it for endorsement to show a change. No agent has the authority to change the policy or to waive any of its terms.

The company's defense against misrepresentation ends two years after the policy is issued

1.3 INCONTESTABILITY

The Company will not contest this policy after it has been in force during the lifetime of the Insured for two years from the Date of Issue. In issuing the policy, the Company has relied on the application. While the policy is contestable, the Company, on the basis of a misstatement in the application, may rescind the policy or deny a claim.

The company's defense against suicide ends one year after the policy is issued

1.4 SUICIDE

If the Insured dies by suicide within one year from the Date of Issue, the amount payable by the Company will be limited to the premiums paid.

1.5 DATES

The contestable and suicide periods begin with the Date of Issue. Policy months, years and anniversaries are computed from the Policy Date. Both dates are shown on page 3.

1.6 MISSTATEMENT OF AGE OR SEX

If the age or sex of the Insured has been misstated, the amount payable will be the amount which the premiums paid would have purchased at the correct age and sex.

1.7 PAYMENTS BY THE COMPANY

All payments by the Company under this policy are payable at its Home Office.

SECTION 2. OWNERSHIP

2.1 THE OWNER

The Owner is named on page 3. All policy rights may be exercised by the Owner, his successor or his transferee:

- without the consent of any beneficiary.
- while the Insured is living and, after his death, only as provided in Sections 8 and 9.

Policy can have a new owner

2.2 TRANSFER OF OWNERSHIP

The Owner may transfer the ownership of this policy. Written proof of transfer satisfactory to the Company must be received at its Home Office. The transfer will then take effect as of the date it was signed. The Company may require that the policy be sent to it for endorsement to show the transfer.

Policy may be assigned as security for a loan

2.3 COLLATERAL ASSIGNMENT

The Owner may assign this policy as collateral security. The Company is not responsible for the validity or effect of a collateral assignment. The Company will not be responsible to an assignee for any payment or other action taken by the Company before receipt of the assignment in writing at its Home Office.

The interest of any beneficiary will be subject to any collateral assignment made either before or after the beneficiary is named.

A collateral assignee is not an Owner. A collateral assignment is not a transfer of ownership. Ownership can be transferred only by complying with Section 2.2.

SECTION 3. PREMIUMS AND REINSTATEMENT

3.1 PREMIUMS

Payment. All premiums after the first are payable at the Home Office or to an authorized agent. A premium must be paid on or before its due date. A receipt signed by an officer of the Company will be furnished on request.

Frequency. Premiums may be paid every 3, 6 or 12 months at the published rates of the Company. A change in premium frequency will take effect when the Company accepts a premium on a new frequency. Premiums may be paid on any other frequency approved by the Company.

You have 31 days beyond the due date to pay your premium

Grace Period. A grace period of 31 days will be allowed to pay a premium that is not paid on its due date. The policy will be in full force during this period. If the Insured dies during the grace period, any overdue premium will be paid from the proceeds of the policy.

If the premium is not paid within the grace period, the policy will terminate as of the due date unless it continues as extended term or paid-up insurance under Section 5.2 or 5.3.

Premium Refund at Death. The Company will refund that portion of any premium paid for a period beyond the date of the Insured's death. The refund will be part of the policy proceeds.

How to reinstate your policy

3.2 REINSTATEMENT

The policy may be reinstated within five years after the due date of the overdue premium. This may not be done if the policy was surrendered for its cash surrender value.

Within 31 days after the grace period, the policy will be reinstated when the overdue premium is paid. This payment must be made while the Insured is living.

Beyond 31 days after the grace period, the policy will be reinstated if:

- evidence of insurability is given that is satisfactory to the Company; and
- all unpaid premiums are paid with interest from the due date of each premium. Interest is at an annual effective rate of 6%.

Any policy debt on the due date of the overdue premium, with interest from that date, must be repaid or reinstated.

SECTION 4. DIVIDENDS

You receive any dividends annually

4.1 ANNUAL DIVIDENDS

This policy will share in the divisible surplus of the Company. This surplus is determined each year. The policy's share will be credited as a dividend on the policy anniversary.

4.2 USE OF DIVIDENDS

Dividends may be paid in cash or used for one of the following:

This popular way to use dividends provides additional insurance

- **Paid-up Additions.** Dividends will purchase paid-up additional insurance. Paid-up additions share in the divisible surplus.
- **Dividend Accumulations.** Dividends will accumulate at interest. Interest is credited at an annual effective rate of 3½%. The Company may set a higher rate.
- **Premium Payment.** Dividends will be used to reduce premiums. If the balance of a premium is not paid, or if this policy is in force as paid-up insurance, the dividend will purchase paid-up additions.

Another popular way to use dividends is to reduce premiums

Other uses of dividends may be made available by the Company.

If no direction is given for the use of dividends, they will purchase paid-up additions.

4.3 ADDITIONS AND ACCUMULATIONS

Paid-up additions and dividend accumulations increase the policy's cash value. They are payable as part of the policy proceeds. Additions may be surrendered and accumulations may be withdrawn unless they are used for a loan, for extended term insurance or for paid-up insurance.

4.4 DIVIDEND AT DEATH

A dividend for the period from the beginning of the policy year to the date of the Insured's death will be payable as part of the policy proceeds.

6

The rights you have if you no longer want to pay premiums

SECTION 5. CASH VALUE, EXTENDED TERM INSURANCE AND PAID-UP INSURANCE

You can take cash

5.1 CASH VALUE

The cash value for this policy, when all premiums due have been paid, will be the sum of:

- the cash value from the Table of Guaranteed Values;
- the cash value of any paid-up additions; and
- the amount of any dividend accumulations.

The cash value within three months after the due date of any unpaid premium will be the cash value on that due date reduced by any later surrender of paid-up additions and by any later withdrawal of dividend accumulations. After that, the cash value will be the cash value of the insurance then in force, plus the cash value of any paid-up additions and any dividend accumulations.

The cash value of any extended term insurance, paid-up insurance or paid-up additions will be the net single premium for that insurance at the attained age of the Insured.

You can take term insurance for a period of time determined by the amount of the cash surrender value

5.2 EXTENDED TERM INSURANCE

If any premium is unpaid at the end of the grace period, this policy will be in force as extended term insurance. The amount of this term insurance will be the plan Amount of the policy, plus any paid-up additions and dividend accumulations, less any policy debt. The term insurance will start as of the due date of the unpaid premium. The period of term insurance will be determined by using the cash surrender value as a net single premium at the attained age of the Insured. If the term insurance would extend to or beyond age 100, paid-up insurance will be provided instead. Extended term insurance does not share in divisible surplus.

If the extended term insurance is surrendered within 31 days after a policy anniversary, the cash value will not be less than the cash value on that anniversary.

You can take a dividend paying policy, good for life, requiring no further premium payment, in an amount determined by the cash value

5.3 PAID-UP INSURANCE

Paid-up insurance may be selected in place of extended term insurance. A written request must be received at the Home Office no later than three months after the due date of an unpaid premium. The amount of insurance will be determined by using the cash value as a net single premium at the attained age of the Insured. Any policy debt will continue. Paid-up insurance will share in divisible surplus.

5.4 CASH SURRENDER

The Owner may surrender this policy for its cash surrender value. The cash surrender value is the cash value less any policy debt. A written surrender of all claims, satisfactory to the Company, will be required. The date of surrender will be the date of receipt at the Home Office of the written surrender. The policy will terminate and the cash surrender value will be determined as of the date of surrender. The Company may require that the policy be sent to it.

The Company may defer paying the cash surrender value for up to six months from the date of surrender. If payment is deferred for 30 days or more, interest will be paid on the cash surrender value at an annual effective rate of 4% from the date of surrender to the date of payment.

See page 4

5.5 TABLE OF GUARANTEED VALUES

Cash values, paid-up insurance and extended term insurance are shown on page 4 for the end of the policy years indicated. These values assume that all premiums due have been paid for the number of years stated. They do not reflect paid-up additions, dividend accumulations or policy debt. Values during a policy year will reflect any portion of the year's premium paid and the time elapsed in that year.

Values for policy years not shown are calculated on the same basis as those on page 4. A list of these values will be furnished on request. A detailed statement of the method of calculation of all values has been filed with the insurance supervisory official of the state in which this policy is delivered. It will be furnished on request. All values are at least as great as those required by that state.

5.6 BASIS OF VALUES

The cash value for policy years not shown on page 4 equals the reserve calculated on the Commissioners Reserve Valuation Method. Net single premiums are based on the Commissioners 1958 Standard Ordinary Mortality Table, except that for the first ten years of any period of extended term insurance the Commissioners 1958 Extended Term Insurance Table is used. Interest is based on an annual effective rate of 4%. Calculations assume the continuous payment of premiums and the immediate payment of claims.

SECTION 6. LOANS

You can borrow money from the company, the maximum amount to be determined by the loan value

6.1 POLICY AND PREMIUM LOANS

The Owner may obtain a loan from the Company in an amount that is not more than the loan value.

Policy Loan. The loan may be obtained on written request. No loan will be made if the policy is in force as extended term insurance. The Company may defer making the loan for up to six months unless the loan is to be used to pay premiums due the Company.

Premium Loan. If the premium loan provision is in effect on this policy, a loan will be made to pay an overdue premium. If the loan value is not large enough to pay the overdue premium, a premium will be paid for any other frequency permitted by this policy for which the loan value is large enough. The Owner may elect or revoke the premium loan provision by written request received at the Home Office.

Two important facts about loans:

1. **Indebtedness is subtracted at death from the insurance proceeds**
2. **Despite the loan, cash values continue to grow on a dividend paying basis**

6.2 LOAN VALUE

The loan value is the smaller of a. or b., less any policy debt and any premium then due or billed; a. and b. are defined as:

a. the cash value one year after the date of the loan, assuming all premiums due within that year are paid, less interest to one year from the date of the loan.

b. the cash value on the due date of the first premium not yet billed that is due after the date of the loan, less interest from the date of the loan to that premium due date.

6.3 POLICY DEBT

Policy debt consists of all outstanding loans and accrued interest. It may be paid to the Company at any time.

If the policy debt equals or exceeds the cash value, this policy will terminate. Termination occurs 31 days after a notice has been mailed to the Owner and to any assignee on record at the Home Office.

6.4 LOAN INTEREST

Interest is payable at an annual effective rate of 8%. The Company may establish a lower rate for any period during which a loan is outstanding.

Interest accrues and is payable on a daily basis from the date of the loan on policy loans and from the premium due date on premium loans. Unpaid interest is added to the loan.

SECTION 7. CHANGE OF POLICY

You can change the plan, keeping the original issue age

7.1 CHANGE OF PLAN

The Owner may change this policy to any permanent life insurance plan agreed to by the Owner and the Company by:

- paying the required costs; and
- meeting any other conditions set by the Company.

You can change the policy to insure the life of another person, e.g., wife to husband, one business partner to another

7.2 CHANGE OF INSURED

Exchange. The Owner may exchange this policy for a new policy on the life of a new insured by:

- paying the required costs; and
- meeting any other conditions set by the Company, including the following:

  a. on the date of exchange, the new insured's age may not be more than 75;

  b. the proposed new insured must be insurable; and

  c. the Owner must have an insurable interest in the life of the new insured.

Date of Exchange. The date of exchange will be the later of:

- the date of the request to exchange; or
- the date of the medical examination (or the non-medical application).

The New Policy. The new policy will take effect on the date of exchange. When the new policy takes effect, this policy terminates. The policy date of the new policy will be the later of:

- the Policy Date of this policy; or
- the first anniversary of this policy after the date of birth of the new insured.

The contestable and suicide periods in the new policy start on the date of exchange.

The new amount of insurance will be set so that the cash value of this policy and the cash value of the new policy are the same on the date of exchange. If either policy has no cash value, the amount will be set so that the premiums are the same.

Any policy debt or assignment of this policy will continue on the new policy.

As an aid to estate and tax planning, a third party policyowner can change beneficiaries after the death of the insured

Marital deduction provision valuable in cases where spouse is direct beneficiary

Living successor beneficiaries provided for by contract

This clause may safeguard policy proceeds

SECTION 8. BENEFICIARIES

8.1 DEFINITION OF BENEFICIARIES

The term "beneficiaries" as used in this policy includes direct beneficiaries, contingent beneficiaries and further payees.

8.2 NAMING AND CHANGE OF BENEFICIARIES

By Owner. The Owner may name and change the beneficiaries of death proceeds:

- while the Insured is living.
- during the first 60 days after the date of death of the Insured, if the Insured just before his death was not the Owner. No one may change this naming of a direct beneficiary during this 60 days.

By Direct Beneficiary. A direct beneficiary may name and change the contingent beneficiaries and further payees of his share of the proceeds:

- if the direct beneficiary is the Owner;
- if, at any time after the death of the Insured, no contingent beneficiary or further payee of that share is living; or
- if, after the death of the Insured, the direct beneficiary elects a payment plan. The interest of any other beneficiary in the share of that direct beneficiary will end.

These direct beneficiary rights are subject to the Owner's rights during the above 60 days.

By Spouse (Marital Deduction Provision).

- **Power to Appoint.** The spouse of the Insured will have the power alone and in all events to appoint all amounts payable to the spouse under the policy if:
  a. the Insured just before his death was the Owner; and
  b. the spouse is a direct beneficiary; and
  c. the spouse survives the Insured.
- **To Whom Spouse Can Appoint.** Under this power, the spouse can appoint:
  a. to the estate of the spouse; or
  b. to any other persons as contingent beneficiaries and further payees.
- **Effect of Exercise.** As to the amounts appointed, the exercise of this power will:
  a. revoke any other designation of beneficiaries;
  b. revoke any election of payment plan as it applies to them; and
  c. cause any provision to the contrary in Section 8 or 9 of this policy to be of no effect.

Effective Date. A naming or change of a beneficiary will be made on receipt at the Home Office of a written request that is acceptable to the Company. The request will then take effect as of the date that it was signed. The Company is not responsible for any payment or other action that is taken by it before the receipt of the request. The Company may require that the policy be sent to it to be endorsed to show the naming or change.

8.3 SUCCESSION IN INTEREST OF BENEFICIARIES

Direct Beneficiaries. The proceeds of this policy will be payable in equal shares to the direct beneficiaries who survive and receive payment. If a direct beneficiary dies before he receives all or part of his full share, the unpaid part of his share will be payable in equal shares to the other direct beneficiaries who survive and receive payment.

Contingent Beneficiaries. At the death of all of the direct beneficiaries, the proceeds, or the present value of any unpaid payments under a payment plan, will be payable in equal shares to the contingent beneficiaries who survive and receive payment. If a contingent beneficiary dies before he receives all or part of his full share, the unpaid part of his share will be payable in equal shares to the other contingent beneficiaries who survive and receive payment.

Further Payees. At the death of all of the direct and contingent beneficiaries, the proceeds, or the present value of any unpaid payments under a payment plan, will be paid in one sum:

- in equal shares to the further payees who survive and receive payment; or
- if no further payees survive and receive payment, to the estate of the last to die of all of the direct and contingent beneficiaries.

Owner or His Estate. If no beneficiaries are alive when the Insured dies, the proceeds will be paid to the Owner or to his estate.

8.4 GENERAL

Transfer of Ownership. A transfer of ownership of itself will not change the interest of a beneficiary.

Claims of Creditors. So far as allowed by law, no amount payable under this policy will be subject to the claims of creditors of a beneficiary.

Succession under Payment Plans. A direct or contingent beneficiary who succeeds to an interest in a payment plan will continue under the terms of the plan.

Wide range of payment plans: Interest only, installment income or life income

SECTION 9. PAYMENT OF POLICY BENEFITS

9.1 PAYMENT OF PROCEEDS

Interest is paid on policy proceeds from the date of death

Proceeds that are payable due to the death of the Insured will be paid under the payment plan that takes effect on the date of death. The Interest Income Plan (Option A) will be in effect if no payment plan has been elected. Interest will accumulate from the date of death until a payment plan is elected or the proceeds are withdrawn in cash.

Proceeds from the surrender of this policy will be paid in cash or under a payment plan that is elected.

9.2 PAYMENT PLANS

Interest Income Plan (Option A). The proceeds will earn interest which may be received each month or accumulated. The first payment is due one month after the date on which the plan takes effect. Interest that has accumulated may be withdrawn at any time. Part or all of the proceeds may be withdrawn at any time.

Installment Income Plans. Payments will be made each month on the terms of the plan that is elected. The first payment is due on the date that the plan takes effect.

- **Specified Period (Option B).** The proceeds with interest will be paid over a period of from one to 30 years. The present value of any unpaid installments may be withdrawn at any time.
- **Specified Amount (Option D).** Payments of not less than $10.00 per $1,000 of proceeds will be made until all of the proceeds with interest have been paid. The balance may be withdrawn at any time.

Proceeds under these payment plans continue to earn interest

Life Income Plans. Payments will be made each month on the terms of the plan that is elected. The first payment is due on the date that the plan takes effect. Proof of the date of birth, acceptable to the Company, must be furnished for each person on whose life the payments are based.

- **Single Life Income (Option C).** Payments will be made for a chosen period and, after that, for the life of the person on whose life the payments are based. The choices for the period are:
  a. zero years;
  b. 10 years;
  c. 20 years; or
  d. a refund period which continues until the sum of the payments that have been made is equal to the proceeds that were placed under the plan.
- **Joint and Survivor Life Income (Option E).** Payments are based on the lives of two persons. Level payments will be made for a period of 10 years and, after that, for as long as one or both of the persons are living.
- **Other Selections.** The Company may offer other selections under the Life Income Plans.
- **Withdrawal.** The present value of any unpaid payments that are to be made for the chosen period (Option C) or the 10 year period (Option E) may be withdrawn only after the death of all of the persons on whose lives the payments are based.
- **Limitations.** A direct or contingent beneficiary who is a natural person may be paid under a Life Income Plan only if the payments depend on his life. A corporation may be paid under a Life Income Plan only if the payments depend on the life of the Insured or, after the death of the Insured, on the life of his spouse or his dependent.

Payment Frequency. On request, payments will be made once every 3, 6 or 12 months instead of each month.

Transfer between Payment Plans. A beneficiary who is receiving payment under a plan which includes the right to withdraw may transfer the amount withdrawable to any other plan that is available.

Minimum Payment. The Company may limit the election of a payment plan to one that results in payments of at least $50.

If payments under a payment plan are or become less than $50, the Company may change the frequency of payments. If the payments are being made once every 12 months and are less than $50, the Company may pay the present value or the balance of the payment plan.

9.3 PAYMENT PLAN RATES

Interest Income and Installment Income Plans. Proceeds will earn interest at rates declared each year by the Company. None of these rates will be less than an annual effective rate of 3½%. Interest of more than 3½% will increase the amount of the payments or, for the Specified Amount Plan (Option D), increase the number of payments. The present value of any unpaid installments will be based on the 3½% rate of interest.

The Company may offer guaranteed rates of interest higher than 3½% with conditions on withdrawal.

Life income rates vary with investment conditions but a minimum rate is guaranteed. Once a payment plan has been elected, that rate is assured thereafter

Life Income Plans. Payments will be based on rates declared by the Company. These rates will provide at least as much income as would the Company's rates, on the date that the payment plan takes effect, for a single premium immediate annuity contract, with no charge for issue expenses. Payments under these rates will not be less than the amounts that are described in Minimum Payment Rates.

Minimum Payment Rates. The minimum payment rates for the Installment Income Plans (Options B and D) and the Life Income Plans (Options C and E) are shown in the Minimum Payment Rate Table.

Your beneficiary, who has the right to withdraw, can change payment plans

Your beneficiary can put additional funds into any payment plan chosen

Our guarantees to you for installment income plans

The Life Income Plan payment rates in that table depend on the sex and on the adjusted age of each person on whose life the payments are based. The adjusted age is:

- the age on the birthday that is nearest to the date on which the payment plan takes effect; plus
- the age adjustment shown below for the number of policy years that have elapsed from the Policy Date to the date that the payment plan takes effect. A part of a policy year is counted as a full year.

POLICY YEARS ELAPSED	AGE ADJUSTMENT	POLICY YEARS ELAPSED	AGE ADJUSTMENT
1 to 10	+8	31 to 35	−1
11 to 15	+6	36 to 40	−2
16 to 20	+4	41 to 45	−3
21 to 25	+2	46 to 50	−4
26 to 30	0	51 or more	−5

9.4 EFFECTIVE DATE FOR PAYMENT PLAN

A payment plan that is elected will take effect on the date of death of the Insured if:

- the plan is elected by the Owner for death proceeds; and
- the election is received at the Home Office while the Insured is living.

In all other cases, a payment plan that is elected will take effect:

- on the date the election is received at the Home Office; or
- on a later date, if requested.

9.5 PAYMENT PLAN ELECTIONS

For Death Proceeds By Owner. The Owner may elect payment plans for death proceeds:

- while the Insured is living.
- during the first 60 days after the date of death of the Insured, if the Insured just before his death was not the Owner. No one may change this election made during those 60 days.

For Death Proceeds By Direct or Contingent Beneficiary. A direct or contingent beneficiary may elect payment plans for death proceeds payable to him if no payment plan that has been elected is in effect. This right is subject to the Owner's rights during the above 60 days.

For Surrender Proceeds. The Owner may elect payment plans for surrender proceeds. The Owner will be the direct beneficiary.

9.6 INCREASE OF MONTHLY INCOME

A direct beneficiary who is to receive proceeds under a payment plan may increase the amount of the monthly payments. This is done by the payment of an annuity premium to the Company at the time the payment plan elected under Section 9.5 takes effect. The amount that will be applied under the payment plan will be the net premium. The net premium is the annuity premium less a charge of not more than 2% and less any premium tax. The net premium will be applied under the same payment plan and at the same rates as the proceeds. The Company may limit this net premium to an amount that is equal to the direct beneficiary's share of the proceeds payable under this policy.

MINIMUM PAYMENT RATE TABLE

Minimum Monthly Income Payments Per $1,000 Proceeds

INSTALLMENT INCOME PLANS (Options B and D)

PERIOD (YEARS)	MONTHLY PAYMENT	PERIOD (YEARS)	MONTHLY PAYMENT	PERIOD (YEARS)	MONTHLY PAYMENT
1	$84.65	11	$ 9.09	21	$ 5.56
2	43.05	12	8.46	22	5.39
3	29.19	13	7.94	23	5.24
4	22.27	14	7.49	24	5.09
5	18.12	15	7.10	25	4.96
6	15.35	16	6.76	26	4.84
7	13.38	17	6.47	27	4.73
8	11.90	18	6.20	28	4.63
9	10.75	19	5.97	29	4.53
10	9.83	20	5.75	30	4.45

Our guarantees to you for life income plans

MINIMUM PAYMENT RATE TABLE

Minimum Monthly Income Payments Per $1,000 Proceeds

LIFE INCOME PLANS (Options C and E)

SINGLE LIFE MONTHLY PAYMENTS (Option C)									
MALE ADJUSTED AGE*	CHOSEN PERIOD (YEARS)				FEMALE ADJUSTED AGE*	CHOSEN PERIOD (YEARS)			
	ZERO	10	20	REFUND		ZERO	10	20	REFUND
55	$ 5.39	$ 5.24	$ 4.85	$ 5.00	55	$ 4.75	$ 4.70	$ 4.53	$ 4.57
56	5.51	5.34	4.91	5.09	56	4.85	4.78	4.59	4.64
57	5.63	5.45	4.97	5.19	57	4.94	4.87	4.66	4.72
58	5.77	5.56	5.03	5.29	58	5.05	4.97	4.73	4.81
59	5.91	5.68	5.10	5.39	59	5.16	5.07	4.80	4.90
60	6.06	5.80	5.16	5.50	60	5.27	5.17	4.87	4.99
61	6.22	5.93	5.21	5.62	61	5.40	5.28	4.94	5.09
62	6.39	6.07	5.27	5.74	62	5.53	5.40	5.01	5.20
63	6.58	6.21	5.33	5.87	63	5.67	5.52	5.08	5.31
64	6.77	6.35	5.38	6.01	64	5.82	5.66	5.15	5.43
65	6.99	6.50	5.43	6.16	65	5.97	5.80	5.22	5.55
66	7.21	6.66	5.48	6.31	66	6.14	5.95	5.28	5.69
67	7.46	6.83	5.52	6.47	67	6.31	6.10	5.35	5.83
68	7.72	7.00	5.56	6.65	68	6.50	6.27	5.40	5.99
69	7.97	7.17	5.60	6.83	69	6.70	6.45	5.46	6.15
70	8.23	7.35	5.63	7.03	70	6.90	6.63	5.51	6.32
71	8.49	7.53	5.66	7.23	71	7.11	6.82	5.55	6.51
72	8.76	7.71	5.68	7.45	72	7.33	7.02	5.59	6.71
73	9.03	7.89	5.70	7.69	73	7.55	7.22	5.62	6.92
74	9.30	8.07	5.72	7.94	74	7.79	7.43	5.65	7.15
75	9.57	8.25	5.73	8.21	75	8.02	7.64	5.68	7.39
76	9.85	8.43	5.74	8.49	76	8.26	7.85	5.69	7.65
77	10.11	8.60	5.74	8.80	77	8.48	8.05	5.71	7.92
78	10.38	8.77	5.75	9.13	78	8.72	8.26	5.72	8.21
79	10.64	8.93	5.75	9.48	79	8.94	8.45	5.73	8.52
80	10.90	9.08	5.75	9.85	80	9.16	8.64	5.74	8.85
81	11.13	9.21	5.75	10.26	81	9.36	8.81	5.74	9.21
82	11.36	9.34	5.75	10.70	82	9.53	8.96	5.75	9.57
83	11.55	9.44	5.75	11.17	83	9.70	9.10	5.75	9.97
84	11.75	9.54	5.75	11.70	84	9.85	9.22	5.75	10.39
85 and over	11.92	9.61	5.75	12.26	85 and over	9.98	9.33	5.75	10.81

	JOINT AND SURVIVOR MONTHLY PAYMENTS (Option E)						
MALE ADJUSTED AGE*	FEMALE ADJUSTED AGE*						
	55	60	65	70	75	80	85 and over
55	$4.33	$4.55	$4.76	$4.94	$5.08	$5.17	$5.22
60	4.45	4.73	5.03	5.30	5.53	5.68	5.76
65	4.54	4.89	5.28	5.68	6.04	6.29	6.43
70	4.61	5.01	5.49	6.04	6.57	6.97	7.20
75	4.66	5.09	5.65	6.32	7.04	7.65	8.02
80	4.68	5.14	5.74	6.51	7.39	8.20	8.72
85 and over	4.69	5.16	5.78	6.60	7.57	8.52	9.15

*See Section 9.3.

Appendix E Disability Income Policy

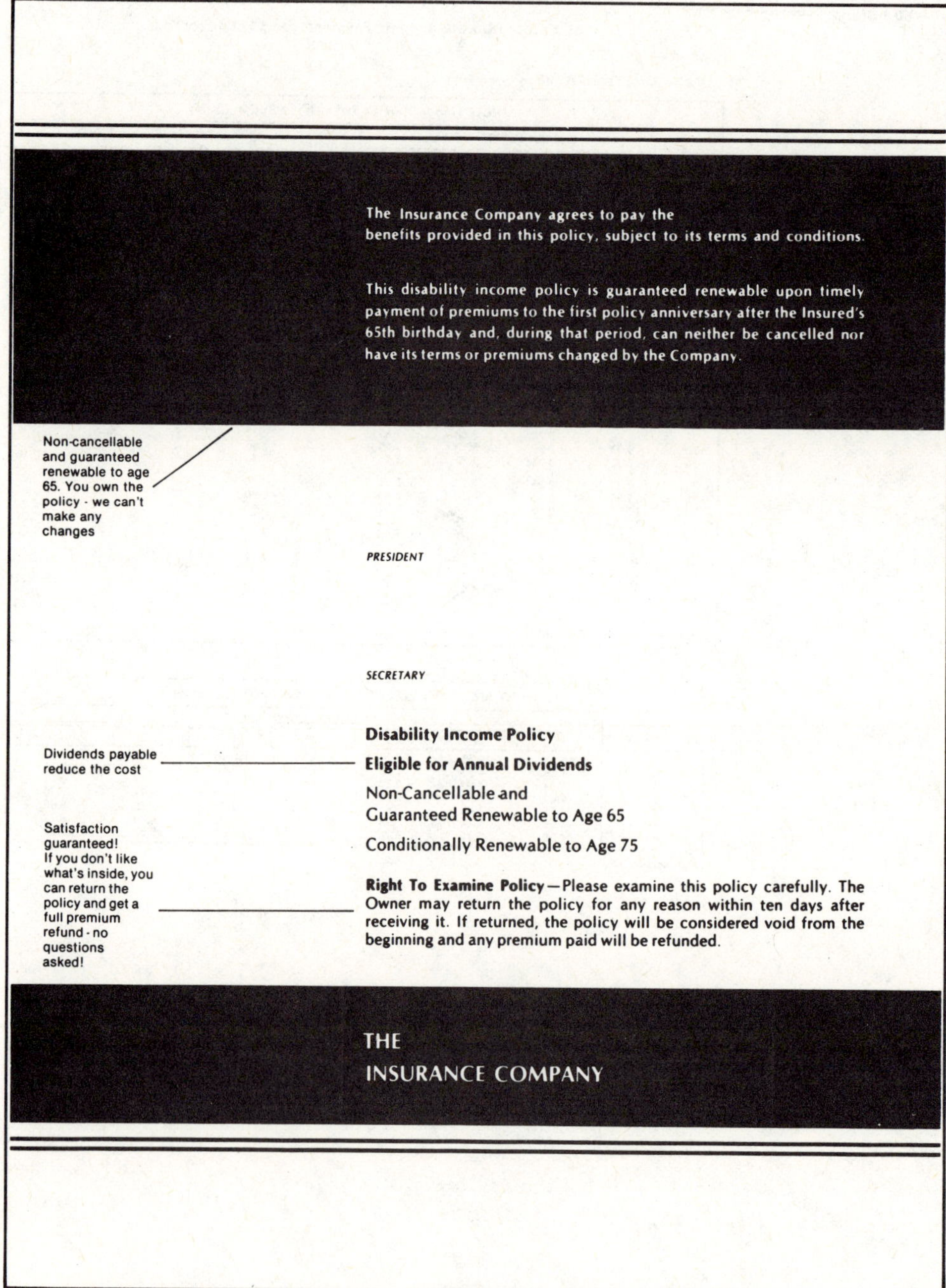
The Insurance Company agrees to pay the benefits provided in this policy, subject to its terms and conditions.

This disability income policy is guaranteed renewable upon timely payment of premiums to the first policy anniversary after the Insured's 65th birthday and, during that period, can neither be cancelled nor have its terms or premiums changed by the Company.

Non-cancellable and guaranteed renewable to age 65. You own the policy - we can't make any changes

PRESIDENT

SECRETARY

Disability Income Policy

Eligible for Annual Dividends

Dividends payable reduce the cost

Non-Cancellable and
Guaranteed Renewable to Age 65

Conditionally Renewable to Age 75

Right To Examine Policy—Please examine this policy carefully. The Owner may return the policy for any reason within ten days after receiving it. If returned, the policy will be considered void from the beginning and any premium paid will be refunded.

Satisfaction guaranteed! If you don't like what's inside, you can return the policy and get a full premium refund - no questions asked!

THE
INSURANCE COMPANY

This policy is a legal contract between the Owner and **Life Insurance Company.**
Read your policy carefully.

Guide To Policy Provisions

Complete directory

ENDORSEMENTS
To be made only by the Company at the Home Office

The details of your policy

SCHEDULE OF BENEFITS AND PREMIUMS

DATE OF ISSUE - FEBRUARY 8, 1983

PLAN AND ADDITIONAL BENEFITS	FULL BENEFIT PER MONTH	ANNUAL PREMIUM	YEARS PAYABLE
DISABILITY INCOME	$ 1,000	$ 275.30	36
ADDITIONAL PURCHASE AMOUNT EACH PURCHASE DATE	1,000	42.50	20
LIFETIME BENEFIT		63.90	30
INDEXED INCOME BENEFIT		75.40	35
SOCIAL SECURITY SUBSTITUTE BENEFIT	800	159.92	35
INDEXED INCOME BENEFIT		36.24	35

RENEWAL OF COVERAGE BEYOND AGE 65 MAY REQUIRE AN INCREASE IN THE PREMIUM. SEE SECTION 3.

A PREMIUM IS PAYABLE ON THE POLICY DATE AND EVERY 12 MONTHS THEREAFTER.

THE FIRST PREMIUM IS $653.26.

BEGINNING DATE	91ST DAY OF DISABILITY IN THE FIRST 180 DAYS AFTER THE START OF DISABILITY.
MAXIMUM BENEFIT PERIOD	TO FEBRUARY 8, 2019, BUT NOT LESS THAN 24 MONTHS OF BENEFITS.
INITIAL PERIOD	60 MONTHS OF BENEFITS, BUT NOT MORE THAN 24 MONTHS OF BENEFITS AFTER FEBRUARY 8, 2017.

OWNER JOHN J DOE, THE INSURED

INSURED	JOHN J DOE	AGE AND SEX	30 MALE
POLICY DATE	FEBRUARY 8, 1983	POLICY NUMBER	D 100 001

EXCLUSIONS—SEE SECTION 2.

PAGE 3

AMENDMENT TO SECTION 1. BENEFITS

As of the Date of Issue or January 1, 1982, whichever is later, the paragraph in Section 1.4, relating to The Meaning of "Earned Income Before Disability" is amended to read as follows:

The Meaning of "Earned Income Before Disability." During the first 12 months of a disability, Earned Income Before Disability is the Base Income of the Insured, defined below. After the first 12 months of a disability, Earned Income Before Disability is the Base Income of the Insured:

Earned Income Before Disability is indexed by yearly changes in the CPI

- multiplied by the Index, defined below, for the fourth month before the most recent anniversary of the start of disability; and
- divided by the Index for the fourth month before the start of disability.

At no time will Earned Income Before Disability be less than the Base Income of the Insured.

The Base Income of the Insured is the average monthly Earned Income of the Insured. This average is determined by using the 12 consecutive month period with the greatest amount of Earned Income in the 24 month period before the start of disability.

The Index will be the monthly *Consumer Price Index for All Urban Consumers, United States City Average, All Items.* This Index is published by the Bureau of Labor Statistics. If the method for determining this Consumer Price Index is changed, or if it is no longer published, the Index will be some other index found by the Company to serve the same purpose.

Paid during partial disability - no total disability required

Covers both total and partial disability

Protected in your occupation

You get the higher benefit

An unknown sickness is covered

You don't have to be continuously disabled - see "beginning date" Page 3

Benefits tied to loss of earned income

NEW! No earnings loss required - you choose the benefit!

Covered in your occupation*

After 6 months, based on earnings loss

Initial period

Only current earnings counted. Money received during disability for work before disability does not reduce the benefit

SECTION 1. BENEFITS

1.1 GENERAL TERMS

This policy provides benefits when the Insured is totally or partially disabled. Section 1 describes the benefits of the policy and tells when they are payable. It also gives the meaning of several important terms that are used in the policy.

Disabilities Covered By The Policy. Benefits are provided for the Insured's total or partial disability only if:

- the Insured becomes disabled while this policy is in force;
- the Insured is under the care of a licensed physician other than himself; and
- the disability results from an accident that occurs, or from a sickness that first appears, while this policy is in force. A sickness is considered to have appeared if it would have caused a prudent person to seek medical attention.

Benefit Terms. The Schedule of Benefits and Premiums (page 3) has a number of important terms that are used in this policy. These terms are:

Full Benefit. This is the maximum amount of monthly income payable under the policy.

Beginning Date. This is the date on which benefits begin to accrue after the Insured becomes disabled. Benefits are not payable for the time the Insured is disabled before the Beginning Date.

Maximum Benefit Period. This is the longest period of time that benefits are payable for disability. After the Beginning Date, benefits continue to be payable for as long as the Insured remains disabled or until the end of the Maximum Benefit Period, if sooner. In determining the maximum length of time for which benefits are payable, periods of total and partial disability are added together.

Initial Period. This is a period of time that starts on the Beginning Date and continues, while the Insured is disabled, for the length of time shown on page 3. The definition of total disability changes after the Initial Period.

Occupation. The words "his occupation" mean the occupation of the Insured at the time he becomes disabled. If the Insured is regularly engaged in more than one occupation, the words "his occupation" include all of the occupations of the Insured at the time he becomes disabled.

1.2 FULL BENEFIT FOR TOTAL DISABILITY

The Full Benefit is payable for each month of total disability between the Beginning Date and the end of the Maximum Benefit Period. During the Initial Period, the Insured is totally disabled when he is unable to perform the principal duties of his occupation. After the Initial Period, the Insured is totally disabled when he is unable to perform the principal duties of his occupation and is not gainfully employed in any occupation.

Benefit Amount For Partial Month. When a total disability lasts for a part of a month, 1/30th of the Full Benefit will be payable for each day of total disability.

1.3 PROPORTIONATE BENEFIT FOR PARTIAL DISABILITY

The Proportionate Benefit is payable for each month of partial disability between the Beginning Date and the end of the Maximum Benefit Period. The Insured is partially disabled when:

- he is unable to perform one or more of the principal duties of his occupation; or
- he is unable to spend as much time at his occupation as he did before the disability started.

After the Proportionate Benefit has been payable for six months, there is a 25% Loss of Earned Income requirement, as explained in Section 1.4.

If the Insured qualifies for both the Full and Proportionate Benefit, the Full Benefit only will be paid.

Benefit Amount For Partial Month. When a partial disability lasts for a part of a month, 1/30th of the Proportionate Benefit will be payable for each day of partial disability.

1.4 HOW THE PROPORTIONATE BENEFIT IS DETERMINED

The Proportionate Benefit is intended to compensate for a Loss of Earned Income to the extent it is caused by the Insured's disability. The Benefit is determined by comparing (a) the Insured's Earned Income while he is disabled with (b) his Earned Income before the disability started. The amount of the Benefit each month is the Full Benefit multiplied by the Loss of Earned Income and divided by the Earned Income Before Disability. The maximum amount payable is 100% of the Full Benefit.

Choice of Benefit Amount for First Six Months. For each of the first six months in which a Proportionate Benefit is payable, the Owner may choose either:

- to receive 50% of the Full Benefit; or
- to have the amount of the Benefit based on the Insured's Loss of Earned Income.

The Owner may alternate between these two choices as to each of the six months. However, the Owner may not change his choice after the Benefit is paid for that month.

25% Loss of Earned Income Required After Six Months. After the first six months in which a Proportionate Benefit is payable, the amount of Benefit is based only on the Loss of Earned Income. A Benefit is not payable unless the Loss of Earned Income is at least 25% of the Insured's Earned Income Before Disability.

The Meaning of "Loss of Earned Income". This is:

- the Insured's Earned Income Before Disability; less
- his Earned Income for the month for which the Benefit is claimed. Earned Income is credited to the period in which it is earned, not the period in which income is actually received.

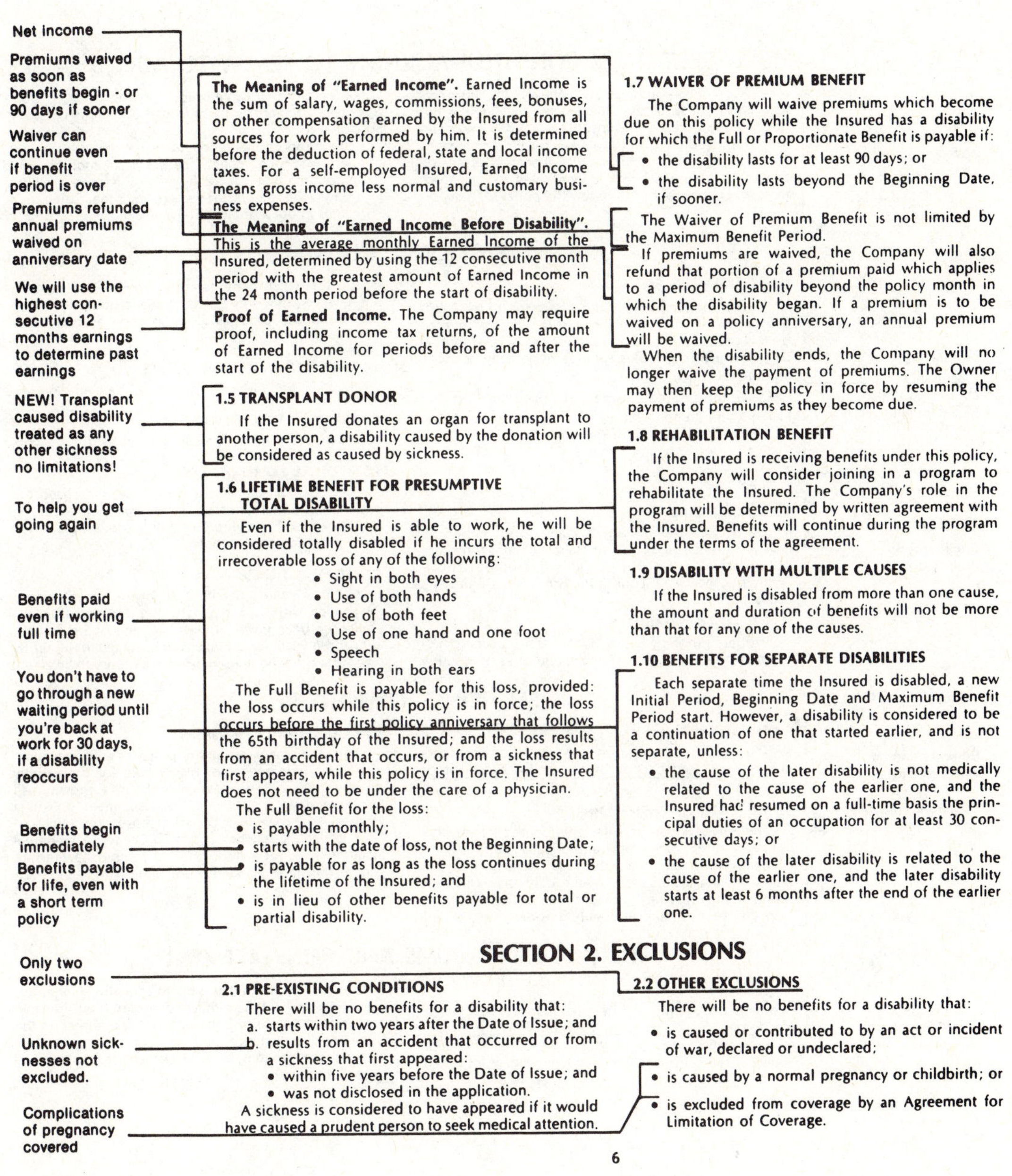

The Meaning of "Earned Income". Earned Income is the sum of salary, wages, commissions, fees, bonuses, or other compensation earned by the Insured from all sources for work performed by him. It is determined before the deduction of federal, state and local income taxes. For a self-employed Insured, Earned Income means gross income less normal and customary business expenses.

The Meaning of "Earned Income Before Disability". This is the average monthly Earned Income of the Insured, determined by using the 12 consecutive month period with the greatest amount of Earned Income in the 24 month period before the start of disability.

Proof of Earned Income. The Company may require proof, including income tax returns, of the amount of Earned Income for periods before and after the start of the disability.

1.5 TRANSPLANT DONOR

If the Insured donates an organ for transplant to another person, a disability caused by the donation will be considered as caused by sickness.

1.6 LIFETIME BENEFIT FOR PRESUMPTIVE TOTAL DISABILITY

Even if the Insured is able to work, he will be considered totally disabled if he incurs the total and irrecoverable loss of any of the following:

- Sight in both eyes
- Use of both hands
- Use of both feet
- Use of one hand and one foot
- Speech
- Hearing in both ears

The Full Benefit is payable for this loss, provided: the loss occurs while this policy is in force; the loss occurs before the first policy anniversary that follows the 65th birthday of the Insured; and the loss results from an accident that occurs, or from a sickness that first appears, while this policy is in force. The Insured does not need to be under the care of a physician.

The Full Benefit for the loss:

- is payable monthly;
- starts with the date of loss, not the Beginning Date;
- is payable for as long as the loss continues during the lifetime of the Insured; and
- is in lieu of other benefits payable for total or partial disability.

1.7 WAIVER OF PREMIUM BENEFIT

The Company will waive premiums which become due on this policy while the Insured has a disability for which the Full or Proportionate Benefit is payable if:

- the disability lasts for at least 90 days; or
- the disability lasts beyond the Beginning Date, if sooner.

The Waiver of Premium Benefit is not limited by the Maximum Benefit Period.

If premiums are waived, the Company will also refund that portion of a premium paid which applies to a period of disability beyond the policy month in which the disability began. If a premium is to be waived on a policy anniversary, an annual premium will be waived.

When the disability ends, the Company will no longer waive the payment of premiums. The Owner may then keep the policy in force by resuming the payment of premiums as they become due.

1.8 REHABILITATION BENEFIT

If the Insured is receiving benefits under this policy, the Company will consider joining in a program to rehabilitate the Insured. The Company's role in the program will be determined by written agreement with the Insured. Benefits will continue during the program under the terms of the agreement.

1.9 DISABILITY WITH MULTIPLE CAUSES

If the Insured is disabled from more than one cause, the amount and duration of benefits will not be more than that for any one of the causes.

1.10 BENEFITS FOR SEPARATE DISABILITIES

Each separate time the Insured is disabled, a new Initial Period, Beginning Date and Maximum Benefit Period start. However, a disability is considered to be a continuation of one that started earlier, and is not separate, unless:

- the cause of the later disability is not medically related to the cause of the earlier one, and the Insured had resumed on a full-time basis the principal duties of an occupation for at least 30 consecutive days; or
- the cause of the later disability is related to the cause of the earlier one, and the later disability starts at least 6 months after the end of the earlier one.

SECTION 2. EXCLUSIONS

2.1 PRE-EXISTING CONDITIONS

There will be no benefits for a disability that:

a. starts within two years after the Date of Issue; and
b. results from an accident that occurred or from a sickness that first appeared:
   - within five years before the Date of Issue; and
   - was not disclosed in the application.

A sickness is considered to have appeared if it would have caused a prudent person to seek medical attention.

2.2 OTHER EXCLUSIONS

There will be no benefits for a disability that:

- is caused or contributed to by an act or incident of war, declared or undeclared;
- is caused by a normal pregnancy or childbirth; or
- is excluded from coverage by an Agreement for Limitation of Coverage.

6

SECTION 3. CONDITIONAL RIGHT TO RENEW TO AGE 75

It is possible to keep your coverage to age 75

On each policy anniversary between the Insured's 65th and 75th birthdays, the Owner may renew this policy for one year if the Insured is actively and gainfully employed on a full-time basis on the anniversary. This right to renew ends on the first anniversary on which the Insured is not so employed or on which the Owner chooses not to renew the policy.

For a policy that is renewed:

- a Full Benefit is payable if the Insured is totally disabled;
- the Proportionate Benefit is not payable;
- the Maximum Benefit Period is 24 months; and
- the premium for each year of renewal will be based on the Insured's age and the Company's rates in use at the time of renewal.

SECTION 4. CLAIMS

You have a reasonable amount of time to file a claim

4.1 NOTICE OF CLAIM

Written notice of claim must be given to the Company within 60 days after the start of any loss covered by this policy. If the notice cannot be given within 60 days, it must be given as soon as reasonably possible. The notice should:

- give the Insured's name and policy number; and
- be sent to the Home Office or be given to an authorized agent of the Company.

Spells out our obligation

4.2 CLAIM FORMS

The Company will furnish claim forms within 15 days after receiving notice of claim. If claim forms are not furnished within that period, written proof of disability may be made without the use of the Company's forms.

4.3 PROOF OF DISABILITY

Written proof of disability must be given to the Company within 90 days after the end of each monthly period for which benefits are claimed. If the proof is not given within this 90 days, the claim will not be affected if the proof is given as soon as reasonably possible.

4.4 TIME OF PAYMENT OF CLAIMS

Benefits due under this policy will be paid monthly.

4.5 PAYMENT OF CLAIMS

Benefits will be paid to the Owner or to his estate.

4.6 MEDICAL EXAMINATION

The Company, at its own expense, may have the Insured examined as often as reasonably necessary in connection with a claim. This will be done by a physician of the Company's choice.

4.7 LEGAL ACTIONS

No legal action may be brought for benefits under this policy within 60 days after written proof of disability has been given. No legal action may be brought after three years (or a longer period that is required by law) from the time written proof is required to be given.

SECTION 5. OWNERSHIP

Benefits can be assigned

Ownership provision gives owner flexibility

5.1 THE OWNER

The Owner is named on page 3. All policy rights may be exercised by the Owner, or his successor or transferee.

5.2 TRANSFER OF OWNERSHIP

The Owner may transfer the ownership of this policy. Written proof of transfer satisfactory to the Company must be received at its Home Office. The transfer will take effect as of the date it was signed. The Company may require that the policy be sent to its Home Office for endorsement to show the transfer.

5.3 COLLATERAL ASSIGNMENT

The Owner may assign this policy as collateral security. The Company is not responsible for the validity or effect of a collateral assignment. The Company will be charged with notice of the assignment only if a written assignment is received at the Home Office.

A collateral assignee is not an Owner. A collateral assignment is not a transfer of ownership. Ownership can be transferred only by complying with Section 5.2.

SECTION 6. PREMIUMS AND REINSTATEMENT

You can change the premium frequency

6.1 PREMIUMS

Payment. All premiums after the first are payable at the Home Office or to an authorized agent. A premium must be paid on or before its due date. A receipt signed by an officer of the Company will be furnished on request.

Frequency. Premiums may be paid annually, semi-annually or quarterly at the published rates of the Company. A change in premium frequency will take effect on the Company's acceptance of the premium for the new frequency. Premiums may be paid on any other frequency approved by the Company.

Full coverage during the grace period, if you forget to pay the premium

Grace Period. A grace period of 31 days will be allowed for payment of a premium that is not paid on its due date. This policy will be in full force during this period.

If the premium is not paid within the grace period, the policy will terminate as of the due date.

One of the few disability policies with this provision

Premium Refund at Death. The Company will refund that portion of any premium paid for a period beyond the date of the Insured's death.

6.2 REINSTATEMENT

Coverage starts immediately after reinstatement

An extra 31 days to reinstate without evidence of insurability

Within Late Payment Period. The late payment period is the first 31 days after the grace period. Within the late payment period, the policy will be reinstated as of the date the overdue premium is paid. No evidence of insurability will be required.

After the Late Payment Period. After the late payment period, the cost to reinstate must be paid to the Company. The Company may also require an application for reinstatement and evidence of insurability. The policy will be reinstated as of the date the cost to reinstate was paid to the Company if:

- the application is approved by the Company; or
- notice that the application has been disapproved is not given within 45 days.

The policy will be reinstated as of the date the Company accepts payment of the cost to reinstate if the Company does not require an application.

Coverage. If no evidence of insurability is required, the reinstated policy will cover only a disability that starts after the date of reinstatement. If evidence of insurability is required:

- the reinstated policy will cover only a disability that results from an accident that occurs, or from a sickness that first appears, after the date of reinstatement; and
- the Company may attach new provisions and limitations to the policy at the time of reinstatement. All other rights of the Owner and the Company will remain the same.

You can reinstate upon discharge - guaranteed

Duty With Armed Forces. If the policy terminates while the Insured is on active duty with the armed forces of any nation or group of nations, the policy may be reinstated without evidence of insurability. The policy will be reinstated as of the date a written request and the cost to reinstate are received by the Company. The request must be received:

- no later than 90 days after the Insured's release from active duty; and
- no later than 5 years after the due date of the unpaid premium.

SECTION 7. THE CONTRACT

7.1 ENTIRE CONTRACT; CHANGES

This policy with the application and attached endorsements is the entire contract between the Owner and the Company. No change in this policy is valid unless approved by an officer of the Company. The Company may require that the policy be sent to it to be endorsed to show a change. No agent has authority to change the policy or to waive any of its provisions.

Protection for you

7.2 INCONTESTABILITY

If disability starts after 2 years, company can't use any misstatement as a defense

In issuing this policy, the Company has relied on the application. The Company may rescind the policy or deny a claim due to a misstatement in the application. However, after this policy has been in force for two years from the Date of Issue, no misstatement in the application may be used to rescind the policy or to deny a claim for a disability that starts after the two year period.

7.3 CHANGE OF PLAN

You have the right to change to a different policy

The Owner may change this policy to any plan of disability insurance agreed to by the Owner and the Company. The change will be subject to:

- payment of required costs; and
- compliance with other conditions required by the Company.

All premiums and dividends after the date of change will be the same as though the new plan had been in effect since the Policy Date.

7.4 MISSTATED AGE OR SEX

If the age or sex of the Insured has been misstated, the benefits will be those which the premiums paid would have purchased at the correct age and sex.

7.5 CONFORMITY WITH STATE STATUTES

Any provisions of this policy which, on the Date of Issue, are in conflict with the statutes of the state in which the Owner resides on that Date are amended to conform to such statutes.

Participates annually in divisible surplus

7.6 DIVIDENDS

This policy will share in the divisible surplus, if any, of the Company. Divisible surplus is determined annually. This policy's share will be credited as an annual dividend.

Dividends will be:

- used to reduce premiums; or
- paid to the Owner when premiums are being waived.

7.7 DATES

The effective date of this policy is the Date of Issue. Policy months, years and anniversaries are computed from the Policy Date. Both dates are shown on page 3 of this policy.

ADDITIONAL PURCHASE BENEFIT

No physical insurability required

Automatic purchase dates up to age 50!

Subject to financial underwriting at time of exercise

You can purchase additional coverage at these times, too.

Choose any benefit period then available

You can exercise two options at the same time

1. THE BENEFIT

The Company will issue additional disability income insurance policies on the Insured, subject to the terms and conditions below. The Company will not refuse to issue these new policies due to changes in the Insured's health, activities, or occupation that occur after the Date of Issue of this policy. However, as explained in section 4 of this Benefit, issue of these new policies is subject to the Company's financial underwriting standards.

In this Benefit, the words "this policy" mean the policy to which this Benefit is attached.

The premium for this Benefit is shown on page 3.

2. PURCHASE DATES

The Owner may purchase a new policy as of each Purchase Date that occurs after the Policy Date. There is a Purchase Date on each policy anniversary that is nearest the Insured's 25th, 30th, 35th, 40th, 45th, and 50th birthdays. The right to purchase a new policy as of a Purchase Date:

- expires on the 30th day after that Date; and
- may be used at an earlier time as an advance purchase.

The Company must receive an application and the first premium for each new policy not more than 60 days before, nor more than 30 days after, a Purchase Date.

3. ADVANCE PURCHASE

A new policy may be purchased before a Purchase Date, on the occurrence of certain events, if:

- this policy has been in force for at least two years; and
- the purchase is made more than two years after the last purchase of a new policy under this Benefit.

An advance purchase of a new policy may be made within 90 days after these events:

- the Insured's marriage;
- the birth of the Insured's child;
- the completion by the Insured of the legal adoption of a child; or
- an increase in the Insured's annual earned income of at least 25% since the Company last issued a disability income policy on the Insured.

An advance purchase of a second new policy may also be made at the same time a new policy is purchased as of a Purchase Date or on the occurrence of one of the events listed above.

To make an advance purchase of a new policy, there must be a future Purchase Date that has not been used. A new policy purchased in advance is in lieu of the new policy that otherwise could be purchased as of the next unused Purchase Date.

The Company must receive an application and the first premium for the new policy not more than 90 days after the marriage, birth, adoption, or increase in income. The application must include proof of the marriage, birth, adoption or increase in income.

4. TERMS OF NEW POLICY

The terms below will apply to each new policy purchased under this Benefit.

In General. Each new policy will be in the form and have the same terms as policies being issued at the time of purchase by the Company as to new insureds. The terms available for each new policy will be based on the classification of risk of this policy. As provided in the following paragraphs, the Owner may choose for each new policy:

- the amount of Full Benefit;
- the Maximum Benefit Period;
- the Beginning Date; and
- additional benefits.

Limitations on Amount and Type of Coverage. A new policy or additional benefit will be issued under this Benefit only if, based on the Company's issue rules in effect at the time the new policy or benefit is to be issued, the Company would issue the new policy or benefit to new insureds having the same income and having the same amount and types of disability insurance as the Insured. A policy designed for employer-funded disability income plans will be issued only if this policy is of a similar type.

Full Benefit. For each new policy:

- the minimum Full Benefit per month that may be purchased will be $200; and
- the maximum Full Benefit per month that may be purchased will be the Additional Purchase Benefit amount shown on page 3. The Owner may request a single new policy with a Full Benefit of up to twice the Additional Purchase Benefit amount shown on page 3 when the Owner has the right to purchase two new policies at the same time, as provided in Advance Purchase (see section 3 of this Benefit).

Maximum Benefit Period. The Owner may choose any Maximum Benefit Period for which the Insured qualifies under the Company's financial underwriting standards in effect at the time the new policy is purchased.

Beginning Date. The Owner may choose any Beginning Date offered at the time the new policy is purchased, provided the Beginning Date is not earlier than that of this policy.

If you can't use it, you can get your premiums back.

The new policy will pay benefits for a covered disability that starts after the new policy is issued.

For an existing disability, if premiums are being waived under the original policy, they'll be waived under the new policy as well.

Additional Benefits. Other than the Additional Purchase Benefit, each new policy may be issued with additional benefits:

- which are then a part of this policy; and
- which are then available to new insureds having the same income and having the same amount and types of disability insurance as the Insured.

Limitations of Coverage. Each new policy will include any Agreement for Limitation of Coverage that is a part of this policy.

No Benefit for Existing Disability. The new policy will cover a disability that starts after the new policy is issued if it is caused by an accident that occurs, or a sickness that first appears, after this policy was issued. The new policy will not cover a disability that exists at the time the new policy is issued.

Premium. The premium for each new policy is determined as of its date of issue by:

- the Company's premium rates then in effect;
- the plan and amount of insurance issued;
- the Insured's age at the time of issue; and
- the classification of risk of this policy.

Waiver of Premium. If premiums are being waived for this policy at the time a new policy is purchased under this Benefit, premiums will also be waived for the new policy for as long as they continue to be waived for this policy.

Effective Date. Each new policy issued will be in force at the time the Company receives the application or the first premium, whichever is later.

5. PREMIUM REFUND

The Company will refund to the Owner all of the premiums paid for this Benefit if:

- the Owner applies for the refund within 90 days after the policy anniversary nearest the Insured's 50th birthday; and
- the Owner supplies proof that:
  (1) the Insured has never qualified for a new policy under the limitations stated in section 4 of this Benefit; and
  (2) the Insured has not purchased a disability income insurance policy from any company while this Benefit was in force.

6. TERMINATION

This Benefit will terminate:

- on the termination of this policy;
- on the policy anniversary nearest the Insured's 50th birthday;
- on the use of the final Purchase Date by advance purchase; or
- on receipt at the Home Office of the Owner's written request within 31 days of a premium due date.

Secretary

THE LIFE

INSURANCE COMPANY

LIFETIME BENEFIT

Full benefit can be paid for either accident and/or sickness — for life!

1. THE BENEFIT

The Full Benefit is payable for total disability as long as total disability continues during the lifetime of the Insured:

- if the Insured is totally disabled on the policy anniversary that is nearest his 60th birthday; and
- if that total disability of the Insured continues beyond the first policy anniversary that follows his 65th birthday.

The premium for this Benefit is shown on page 3.

2. TERMINATION

This Benefit will terminate:

- on the termination of this policy;
- on the policy anniversary nearest the Insured's 60th birthday unless the Insured is then totally disabled; or
- on receipt at the Home Office of the Owner's written request within 31 days of a premium due date.

Increases the Full Benefit when disability benefits are not available from Social Security

SOCIAL SECURITY SUBSTITUTE BENEFIT

You must apply for Social Security benefits

1. THE BENEFIT

The purpose of this Benefit is to increase the amount of monthly income payable under the policy when disability benefits are not available from Social Security. This increase can occur only while this Benefit is in force. When the Full Benefit is payable under the policy or is used to determine the amount of the Proportionate Benefit, it is increased by either:

- the amount of this Benefit when the Insured is not entitled to Social Security benefits based on his disability; or
- 40% of the amount of this Benefit when the Insured, but no member of his family, is entitled to Social Security benefits based on the Insured's disability.

The premium for and the amount of this Benefit are shown on page 3.

2. EXCEPTIONS

The Full Benefit is not increased by the terms of this Benefit:

- when both the Insured and at least one member of his family are entitled to Social Security benefits based on the disability of the Insured;
- when the Insured has elected to receive retirement benefits from Social Security; or
- after the first policy anniversary that follows the 65th birthday of the Insured. At that time, this Benefit will terminate.

3. PROOF OF SOCIAL SECURITY BENEFITS

For the Full Benefit to be increased by the terms of this Benefit, evidence as required by this section 3 must be given to the Company. These requirements are in addition to those set out in the Claims Section of the policy.

Covers both total and partial disability

Entitlement to Benefits. At the request of the Company, written proof must be given to the Company that the Insured is not entitled at that time to Social Security benefits based on his disability. The proof must show:

- that the Insured has applied for Social Security benefits based on his disability; and
- the decision made by Social Security on the application.

If the Insured's application is denied and he appears to the Company to be entitled to Social Security benefits, the proof must show:

- that he has asked for a reconsideration of the decision; and
- if the decision is not changed, that he has appealed the decision further.

The Company must also be given the Insured's written authorization to obtain information from Social Security about his claim.

Benefits Pending Decision by Social Security. Once the Insured has applied for benefits from Social Security, the Full Benefit will be increased under the terms of this Benefit:

- for six months; or
- until he receives the decision from Social Security, if sooner.

If the increases have been stopped because the six months have passed and Social Security later denies the Insured's claim, the Company then will pay those increases that would have been paid under this Benefit had they not been stopped.

Change in Status. The Company must be notified at the time there is a change in the Insured's entitlement to Social Security benefits based on the status of his disability.

Member of Family. When a member of the Insured's family may be entitled to Social Security benefits based on the Insured's disability, the terms of this section 3 as to the Insured also apply to that member.

4. ADDITIONAL DEFINITIONS

Social Security. The words "Social Security" mean the program established under the federal Social Security Act in its present form or as it may be amended or replaced in whole or in part.

Member of Family. A member of the Insured's family is one who is entitled to Social Security benefits due to a relationship to the Insured.

5. TERMINATION

This Benefit will terminate:

- on the termination of this policy;
- on the first policy anniversary that follows the 65th birthday of the Insured;
- on receipt at the Home Office of the Owner's written request within 31 days of a premium due date.

Secretary

THE LIFE INSURANCE COMPANY

INDEXED INCOME BENEFIT

Your benefit can increase along with the Cost of Living

The indexed benefit will stay level beyond age 65

Both total and partial benefits can increase

The CPI will be used to determine the indexed benefit.

Benefit can increase up to 8% a year. A catchup feature is included.

Social Security Substitute benefit will also be indexed.

1. THE BENEFIT

The Company will provide an indexed benefit in place of the benefit that would be payable under Section 1 of the policy. During the first 12 months of a disability, the indexed benefit will be the benefit that would be payable under Section 1 of the policy. After that, the indexed benefit will be based on changes in consumer price levels, subject to certain limits explained in section 2 of this Benefit. The indexed benefit will be determined by using the Index in section 3.

The premium for this Benefit is shown on page 3.

2. HOW THE INDEXED BENEFIT IS DETERMINED

Starting on the first anniversary of the start of disability and subject to the limits described in this section, the indexed benefit for each month will be:

- the benefit that would be payable for that month under Section 1 of the policy;
- multiplied by the Index for the fourth month before the most recent anniversary of the start of disability; and
- divided by the Index for the fourth month before the start of disability.

Limit on Monthly Benefit. Subject to the maximum and minimum limits below, the largest indexed benefit for each month will be determined by:

- taking 8% of the benefit that would be payable for that month under Section 1 of the policy;
- multiplying that amount by the number of full years of continuing disability; and
- adding that result to the benefit that would be payable for that month under Section 1 of the policy.

Maximum and Minimum Limits. The amount of the indexed benefit for each month will not be:

- more than 200% of the benefit that would be payable for that month under Section 1 of the policy; or
- less than 100% of that benefit.

Separate Disabilities. Each separate time the Insured is disabled under the terms of the policy, the indexed benefit will be determined as though there had been no prior disability.

Limit if Lifetime Benefit. If the Lifetime Benefit or the Lifetime Benefit for Presumptive Total Disability is a part of the policy, any indexed benefit that is payable after the Maximum Benefit Period shown in page 3:

- will be the indexed benefit paid for the last month of that Maximum Benefit Period; and
- will remain level and will not change up or down.

Conditional Renewal Excluded. If the policy is in force under a Conditional Right to Renew to Age 75, there will not be an indexed benefit.

3. INDEX

The Index used to find the indexed benefit will be the monthly *Consumer Price Index for All Urban Consumers, United States City Average, All Items.* This Index is published by the Bureau of Labor Statistics.

If the method for determining this Consumer Price Index is changed, or if it is no longer published, the Index will be some other index found by the Company to serve the same purpose.

4. SOCIAL SECURITY SUBSTITUTE BENEFIT

If the Social Security Substitute Benefit is a part of this policy, "the benefit that would be payable for that month under Section 1 of the policy" means that benefit as increased by the terms of the Social Security Substitute Benefit. However, this applies only up to the first policy anniversary that follows the 65th birthday of the Insured; after that anniversary, no benefit is increased by the Social Security Substitute Benefit.

5. TERMINATION

This Benefit will terminate:

- on the termination of this policy;
- on the later of:
  (1) the first policy anniversary that follows the Insured's 65th birthday; or
  (2) the end of the Maximum Benefit Period shown on page 3; or
- on the receipt at the Home Office of the Owner's written request within 31 days of a premium due date.

Appendix F Universal Life Policy

FLEXIBLE-PREMIUM (UNIVERSAL) LIFE INSURANCE POLICY

Flexible-Premium Life Insurance Policy

Life insurance payable if the insured dies before the Final Date of Policy. Accumulation Fund payable on the Final Date.

Adjustable death benefit.

Premiums payable while the insured is alive and before the Final Date of Policy. Premiums must be sufficient to keep the policy in force.

Not eligible for dividends.

10-Day Right to Examine Policy—Please read this policy. You may return this policy to us or to the sales representative through whom you bought it within 10 days from the date you receive it. If you return it within the 10-day period, the policy will be void from the beginning. We will refund any premium paid.

See Table of Contents and Company address on back cover.

POLICY SPECIFICATIONS

DATE OF POLICY.............................

INSURED'S AGE AND SEX....................

FINAL DATE OF POLICY.....................POLICY ANNIVERSARY AT AGE 95

DEATH BENEFIT...............................OPTION (SEE PAGE 5)

OWNER...SEE APPLICATION

BENEFICIARY AND
CONTINGENT BENEFICIARY...................SEE APPLICATION

POLICY CLASSIFICATION......................

INSURED

SPECIFIED
FACE AMOUNT
OF INSURANCE..... —AS OF DATE OF POLICY ..POLICY NUMBER

PLAN................FLEXIBLE-PREMIUM LIFE

THIS POLICY PROVIDES LIFE INSURANCE COVERAGE UNTIL THE FINAL DATE IF SUFFICIENT PREMIUMS ARE PAID. THE PLANNED PREMIUM SHOWN BELOW MAY NEED TO BE INCREASED TO KEEP THIS POLICY AND COVERAGE IN FORCE.

PLANNED PREMIUM OF —PAYABLE

(TOTAL PREMIUM FOR LIFE INSURANCE BENEFIT, ANY SUPPLEMENTAL RATING AND ANY ADDITIONAL BENEFITS LISTED BELOW)

ADDITIONAL BENEFITS

FORM 7-82 MIAC 401. 402. 403. 404.

"Flexible-Premium (Universal) Life Insurance Policy" from *Policy Kit for Students of Insurance*. Reprinted with permission from Alliance of American Insurers.

Table of Guaranteed Maximum Rates For Each $1,000 of Term Insurance
(See "Cost of Term Insurance" Provision on page 6.)

Age Male	Age Female	Monthly Rate*	Age Male	Age Female	Monthly Rate*	Age Male	Age Female	Monthly Rate*
0	—	.370	33	36	.196	79	82	9.320
1	—	.136	34	37	.204	80	83	10.174
2	—	.124	35	38	.214	81	84	11.088
3	—	.119	36	39	.227	82	85	12.053
4	—	.114	37	40	.242	83	86	13.070
5	—	.110	38	41	.261	84	87	14.146
6	—	.106	39	42	.283	85	88	15.289
7	—	.103	40	43	.307	86	89	16.509
8	—	.101	41	44	.334	87	90	17.822
9	—	.100	42	45	.363	88	91	19.256
10	—	.101	43	46	.394	89	92	20.852
11	—	.103	44	47	.429	90	93	22.665
—	0	.329	45	48	.467	91	94	24.769
—	1	.128	46	49	.509	92	—	27.258
—	2	.115	47	50	.556	93	—	30.251
—	3	.110	48	51	.608	94	—	34.025
—	4	.105	49	52	.666			
—	5	.101	50	53	.729			
—	6	.097	51	54	.798			
—	7	.094	52	55	.873			
—	8	.092	53	56	.955			
—	9	.092	54	57	1.044			
—	10	.092	55	58	1.141			
—	11	.094	56	59	1.249			
—	12	.096	57	60	1.367			
—	13	.099	58	61	1.496			
—	14	.102	59	62	1.638			
12	15	.107	60	63	1.794			
13	16	.113	61	64	1.963			
14	17	.118	62	65	2.148			
15	18	.125	63	66	2.351			
16	19	.131	64	67	2.573			
17	20	.138	65	68	2.819			
18	21	.143	66	69	3.091			
19	22	.147	67	70	3.392			
20	23	.151	68	71	3.722			
21	24	.153	69	72	4.076			
22	25	.156	70	73	4.452			
23	26	.158	71	74	4.843			
24	27	.160	72	75	5.248			
25	28	.162	73	76	5.671			
26	29	.164	74	77	6.124			
27	30	.167	75	78	6.623			
28	31	.171	76	79	7.183			
29	32	.175	77	80	7.817			
30	33	.180	78	81	8.532			
31	34	.185						
32	35	.190						

*If there is a supplemental rating for the life insurance benefit, as shown on page 3, the monthly deduction for such supplemental rating must be added to the monthly rate determined from this table.

401-82

Understanding This Policy

"You" and "your" refer to the owner of this policy.

"We", "us" and "our" refer to Metropolitan Insurance and Annuity Company.

The "insured" named on page 3 is the person at whose death the insurance proceeds will be payable.

The "Specified Face Amount of Insurance" as of the date of policy is shown on page 3. A new page 3 will be issued to show any change in the Specified Face Amount of Insurance that has occurred at your request.

The "Date of Policy" is shown on page 3.

The "Final Date of Policy" is the policy anniversary on which the insured is age 95.

Policy years and months are measured from the date of policy. For example, if the date of policy is May 5, 1990, the first policy month ends June 4, 1990, and the first policy year ends May 4, 1991. Similarly, the first monthly anniversary is June 5, 1990, and the first policy anniversary is May 5, 1991.

The "accumulation fund" forms the basis for the benefits provided under your policy. Computation of the accumulation fund is described on page 6.

The "Designated Office" is our Executive Office at One Madison Avenue, New York, N. Y. 10010. We may, by written notice, name other offices within the United States to serve as Designated Offices.

To make this policy clear and easy to read, we have left out many cross-references and conditional statements. Therefore, the provisions of the policy must be read as a whole. For example, our payment of the insurance proceeds (see page 5) depends upon the payment of sufficient premiums (see page 7).

To exercise your rights, you should follow the procedures stated in this policy. If you want to request a payment, adjust the death benefit, change a beneficiary, change an address or request any other action by us, you should do so on the forms prepared for each purpose. You can get these forms from your sales representative or our Designated Office.

Payment When Insured Dies

Insurance Proceeds—If the insured dies before the Final Date of Policy, an amount of money, called the insurance proceeds, will be payable to the beneficiary. The insurance proceeds are the sum of:

- The death benefit described below.

  PLUS

- Any insurance on the insured's life that may be provided by riders to this policy.

  MINUS

- Any policy loan and loan interest.

We will pay the insurance proceeds to the beneficiary after we receive proof of death and a proper written claim.

Death Benefit—The death benefit under the policy will be either (1) or (2) below, whichever is chosen and is in effect on the date of death:

1. Under Option A, the greater of:

   (a) the Specified Face Amount of Insurance;

   or

   (b) 110% of the accumulation fund on the date of death.

2. Under Option B:

   The Specified Face Amount of Insurance;

   PLUS

   The accumulation fund on the date of death.

Death Benefit Adjustment—At any time after the first policy year while this policy is in force, you may change the death benefit option or change (either increase or decrease) the Specified Face Amount of Insurance, subject to the following.

1. In the event of a change in the death benefit option, we will change the Specified Face Amount of Insurance as needed.
2. The Specified Face Amount of Insurance may not be reduced to less than \$50,000 during the first 5 policy years or to less than \$25,000 after the 5th policy year.
3. For any change which would increase the death benefit, you must provide evidence satisfactory to us of the insurability of the insured. Also, the increased death benefit will be subject to a charge of \$3 for each \$1,000 of insurance increase. We will deduct this charge from the accumulation fund as of the date the increase takes effect.
4. No change in the death benefit will take effect unless the accumulation fund, after the change, is sufficient to keep this policy in force for at least 2 months. Subject to this condition, a request for a change in the death benefit will take effect on the monthly anniversary which coincides with or next follows: (a) if evidence of insurability is required, the date we approve the request; or (b) if not, the date of the request.
5. We will issue a new page 3 for this policy showing the change. We may require that you send us this policy to make the change.

402-82

Computation of Accumulation Fund

Accumulation Fund—The value of the accumulation fund is as follows:

- On the date of policy—91% of the first premium;

  MINUS

  The monthly deduction for the first month.
- On any monthly anniversary—The value on the last monthly anniversary;

  PLUS

  One month's interest on such value at the currently applicable rates;

  PLUS

  91% of the premiums received since the last monthly anniversary;

  MINUS

  The monthly deduction for the month beginning on the current monthly anniversary.
- On other than a monthly anniversary—The value on the last monthly anniversary;

  PLUS

  91% of the premiums received since the last monthly anniversary.

Note: The 9% deduction from premiums is an expense charge.

If you make a partial cash withdrawal (see page 7), the accumulation fund defined above will be reduced by the amount of such withdrawal.

Monthly Deduction—The deduction for any policy month is the sum of the following amounts, determined as of the beginning of that month:

- The monthly cost of the term insurance (See Cost of Term Insurance on page 6).
- The monthly cost of any benefits provided by riders.
- For each of the first 12 policy months only, a charge of $35 plus $.25 for each $1,000 of Specified Face Amount of Insurance.

Interest Rate—The guaranteed interest rate used to determine the accumulation fund is .32737% a month, compounded monthly. This is equivalent to a rate of 4% a year, compounded annually.

Interest will be credited to the accumulation fund each month as follows:

- At the guaranteed interest rate on the first $1,000 in the accumulation fund.
- In the manner and at the rate we set from time to time, on amounts in excess of $1,000 in the accumulation fund. The rate we set will never be less than the guaranteed interest rate.
- If there is a loan against this policy, interest on that portion of the accumulation fund in excess of $1,000 that equals the loan will be at a rate we set. The rate with respect to the amount of the loan will never be less than the guaranteed interest rate.

Example—Suppose the accumulation fund is $10,000 and there is a policy loan of $2,000. If we set the annual interest rates at 10% for amounts over $1,000 in the accumulation fund and at 6% for the amount of any loan, then interest would be credited: at the rate of 4% on the first $1,000; at the rate of 6% on the next $2,000 representing the amount of the loan; and at the rate of 10% on the remaining $7,000.

Cost of Term Insurance—Under either death benefit option, the amount of term insurance for any policy month is equal to:

- The death benefit divided by 1.0032737;

  MINUS
- The accumulation fund.

The accumulation fund used in this calculation is the accumulation fund at the beginning of the policy month before the deduction for the monthly cost of term insurance, but after the deductions for riders and any other charges.

The cost of the term insurance for any policy month is equal to the amount of term insurance multiplied by the monthly term insurance rate. Monthly term insurance rates will be set by us from time to time, based on the insured's age, sex, and underwriting class. But these rates will never be more than the maximum rates shown in the table on page 4.

Payments During Insured's Lifetime

Payment on Final Date of Policy—If the insured is alive on the Final Date of Policy, we will pay you the accumulation fund minus any policy loan and loan interest. Coverage under this policy will then end.

Cash Value—Your policy has a cash value while the insured is alive.

The cash value at any time during the first policy year will equal:

- The accumulation fund;

  MINUS

- $35 times the number of full policy months left in that year;

  MINUS

- Any policy loan and loan interest.

After the first policy year, the cash value at any time will

- The accumulation fund;

  MINUS

- The interest in excess of the guaranteed rate credited to the fund during the last 12 policy months;

  MINUS

- Any policy loan and loan interest.

Full and Partial Cash Withdrawal—We will pay you all or part of the cash value after we receive your request at our Designated Office. The cash value will be determined as of the date we receive your request. If you request and are paid the full cash value, this policy and all our obligations under it will end. We may require surrender of this policy before we pay you the full cash value.

Each partial withdrawal of cash value must be at least $250. When a partial withdrawal is made, we will reduce the accumulation fund by the amount of the partial withdrawal. If Option A is in effect, we will also reduce the Specified Face Amount of Insurance by the amount of the partial withdrawal; and a new page 3 will then be issued. We may require that you send us this policy to make the change.

If you request a partial withdrawal which would reduce the cash value to less than $500, we will treat it as a request for a full cash withdrawal. Also, if Option A is in effect and the Specified Face Amount of Insurance would be reduced to less than $50,000 during the first 5 policy years, or to less than $25,000 thereafter, we will treat your request as a request for a full cash withdrawal.

Policy Loan—You may also get cash from us by taking a policy loan. If there is an existing loan you can increase it. The most you can borrow at any time is the cash value on the next monthly anniversary, less the monthly deduction for the following month.

Loan interest is charged daily at the rate of 8% a year, and is due at the end of each policy year. Interest not paid within 31 days after it is due will be added to the amount of the loan. It will be added as of the due date and will bear interest at the same rate as the rest of the loan.

A loan will affect the interest rate we credit to amounts over $1,000 in the accumulation fund (see "Interest Rate" on page 6).

Loan Repayment—You may repay all or part (but not less than $25) of a policy loan at any time while the insured is alive and this policy is in force. If any payment you make to us is intended as a loan repayment, rather than a premium payment, you must tell us this when you make the payment.

Failure to repay a policy loan or to pay loan interest will not terminate this policy unless the accumulation fund, minus the policy loan and loan interest, is insufficient to pay the monthly deduction due on a monthly anniversary. In that case, the Grace Period provision will apply (see page 8).

Deferment—We may delay paying a full or partial cash withdrawal for up to 6 months from the date we receive a request for payment. If we delay for 30 days or more, interest will be paid from the date we receive the request at a rate not less than 3% a year.

We also may delay making a policy loan, except for a loan to pay a premium, for up to 6 months from the date you request the loan.

Premiums

Premium Payments—Premiums may be paid at our Designated Office or to our sales representative. A receipt signed by our President or Secretary and countersigned by the sales representative will be given for a premium paid to the sales representative.

The first premium is due on the date of policy and will be credited as of that date. No insurance will take effect before the first premium is paid. Other premiums may be paid at any time while the policy is in force and before the Final Date of Policy and in any amount and subject to the limits described below.

We will send premium notices, if you request in writing, according to the planned premium shown on page 3. You may skip planned premium payments or change their frequency and amount if the accumulation fund is large enough to keep your policy in force.

402-82

Premiums (Continued)

Limits—The first premium may not be less than the planned premium shown on page 3. Each premium payment after the first must be at least $250 ($50 for a Check-O-Matic payment).

We may increase these minimum premium limits. No increase will take effect until 90 days after notice is sent

The total premiums paid in a policy year may not exceed the maximum we set for that year.

Grace Period—If the accumulation fund on any monthly anniversary, minus any policy loan and loan interest, is less than the monthly deduction for that month, there will be a grace period of 61 days after that anniversary to pay an amount that will cover the monthly deduction. We will send you a notice at the start of the grace period. We will also send a notice to any assignee on our records.

If we do not receive a sufficient amount by the end of the grace period, your policy will then end without value.

If the insured dies during the grace period, we will pay the insurance proceeds minus any overdue monthly deduction.

Reinstatement—If the grace period has ended and you have not paid the required premium and have not surrendered your policy for its cash value, you may reinstate this policy while the insured is alive if you:

1. Ask for reinstatement within 3 years after the end of the grace period;
2. Provide evidence of insurability satisfactory to us;
3. Pay a sufficient amount to keep the policy in force for at least 2 months after the date of reinstatement;
4. If the grace period began during the first policy year, pay: (a) an amount sufficient to cover the unpaid portion of the charges applicable during the first 12 policy months; plus (b) interest on such amount to the date of reinstatement at the rate of 6% a year.

The effective date of the reinstated policy will be the monthly anniversary following the date we approve the reinstatement application. If we approve it on a monthly anniversary, the effective date will be that anniversary.

Ownership and Beneficiary

Owner—As owner, you may exercise all rights under your policy while the insured is alive. You may name a contingent owner who would become the owner if you should die before the insured.

Change of Ownership—You may name a new owner at any time. If a new owner is named, any earlier choice of a contingent owner, beneficiary, contingent beneficiary or optional income plan will be canceled, unless you specify otherwise.

Beneficiary—The beneficiary is the person or persons to whom the insurance proceeds are payable when the insured dies. You may name a contingent beneficiary to become the beneficiary if all the beneficiaries die while the insured is alive. If no beneficiary or contingent beneficiary is named, or if none is alive when the insured dies, the owner (or the owner's estate) will be the beneficiary. While the insured is alive, the owner may change any beneficiary or contingent beneficiary.

If more than one beneficiary is alive when the insured dies, we will pay them in equal shares, unless you have chosen otherwise.

How to Change the Owner or the Beneficiary—You may change the owner, contingent owner, beneficiary or contingent beneficiary of this policy by written notice or assignment of the policy. No change is binding on us until it is recorded at our Designated Office. Once recorded, the change binds us as of the date you signed it. The change will not apply to any payment made by us before we recorded your request. We may require that you send us this policy to make the change.

Collateral Assignment—Your policy may be assigned as collateral. All rights under the policy will be transferred to the extent of the assignee's interest. We are not bound by any assignment unless it is in writing and is recorded at our Designated Office. We are not responsible for the validity of any assignment.

402-82

General Provisions

The Contract—This policy includes any riders and, with the application attached when the policy is issued, makes up the entire contract. All statements in the application will be representations and not warranties. No statement will be used to contest the policy unless it appears in the application.

Limitation on Sales Representative's Authority—No sales representative or other person except our President, a Vice-President, or the Secretary may (a) make or change any contract of insurance; or (b) make any binding promises about policy benefits; or (c) change or waive any of the terms of this policy. Any change is valid only if made in writing and signed by our President, a Vice-President, or the Secretary.

Incontestability—We will not contest the validity of your policy after it has been in force during the insured's lifetime for 2 years from the date of policy. We will not contest the validity of any increase in the death benefit after such increase has been in force during the insured's lifetime for 2 years from its effective date.

Suicide—The insurance proceeds will not be paid if the insured commits suicide, while sane or insane, within 2 years from the date of policy. Instead we will pay the beneficiary an amount equal to all premiums paid, without interest, less any policy loan and loan interest and less any partial cash withdrawals. If the insured commits suicide, while sane or insane, more than 2 years after the date of this policy but within 2 years from the effective date of any increase in the death benefit, our liability with respect to such increase will be limited to its cost.

Age and Sex—If the insured's age or sex on the date of the policy is not correct as shown on page 3, we will adjust the benefits under this policy. The adjusted benefits will be those that the premiums paid would have provided at the correct age and sex.

Nonparticipation—This policy is not eligible for dividends; it does not participate in any distribution of our surplus.

Computation of Values—The minimum accumulation fund and policy reserves are computed using interest at the rate of 4% a year. These values and the maximum term insurance rates shown on page 4 are based on the 1958 Commissioners Standard Ordinary Mortality Table, age last birthday for male lives. For female lives, they are based on that table set back 3 years at ages 15 and older and on the female extension of that table at ages under 15.

We have filed a detailed statement of the method of computation with the insurance supervisory official of the state in which this policy is delivered. The values under this policy are equal to or greater than those required by the law of that state.

Annual Reports—Each year we will send you a report showing the current death benefit, accumulation fund and cash value for this policy.

It will also show the amount and type of credits to and deductions from the accumulation fund during the past policy year.

The report will also include any other information required by state laws and regulations.

Illustration of Future Benefits—At any time, we will provide an illustration of the future benefits and values under your policy. You must ask in writing for this illustration and pay the service fee set by us.

Optional Income Plans

The insurance proceeds when the insured dies, or the amount payable on the Final Date of Policy, instead of being paid in one sum may be applied under one or more of the following income plans. Also, at any time before the Final Date and while the insured is alive, you may ask us to:

(a) Apply the full cash value of this policy under a non-life income plan;

or

(b) Apply the accumulation fund of this policy, minus any policy loan and loan interest, under a life income plan.

Non-Life Income Plans

Option 1. *Interest Income*
The amount applied will earn interest which will be paid monthly. Withdrawals of at least $500 each may be made at any time by written request.

Option 2. *Instalment Income for a Stated Period*
Monthly instalment payments will be made so that the amount applied, with interest, will be paid over the period chosen (from 1 to 30 years).

Option 2A. *Instalment Income of a Stated Amount*
Monthly instalment payments of a chosen amount will be made until the entire amount applied, with interest, is paid.

Life Income Plans

Option 3. *Single Life Income—Guaranteed Payment Period*

Monthly payments will be made during the lifetime of the payee with a chosen guaranteed payment period of 10, 15 or 20 years.

Option 3A. *Single Life Income—Guaranteed Return*
Monthly payments will be made during the lifetime of the payee. If the payee dies before the total amount applied under this plan has been paid, the remainder will be paid in one sum as a death benefit.

Option 4. *Joint and Survivor Life Income*
Monthly payments will be made jointly to two persons while they are both alive and will continue during the remaining lifetime of the survivor. A total payment period of 10 years is guaranteed.

Other Frequencies and Plans—Instead of monthly payments, you may choose to have payments made quarterly, semiannually or annually. Other income plans may be arranged with us.

Choice of Income Plans—A choice of an income plan for insurance proceeds made by you in writing and recorded by us while the insured is alive will take effect when the insured dies. A choice of an income plan for the amount payable on the Final Date of Policy will take effect on such date. All other choices of income plans will take effect when recorded by us or later, if requested. When an income plan starts, we will issue a contract that will describe the terms of the plan. We may require that you send us this policy. We may also require proof of the payee's age

Income plans for insurance proceeds may be chosen

1. By you during the lifetime of the insured.
2. By the beneficiary, within one year after the date the insured died and before any payment has been made. if no election was in effect on the date of death.

Income plans for the amount payable on the Final Date of Policy may be chosen by you:

1. On or before the Final Date of Policy.
2. Within one year after the Final Date of Policy and before any payment has been made.

A choice of an income plan will not become effective unless each payment under the plan would be at least $50.

Limitations—If the payee is not a natural person. the choice of an income plan will be subject to our approval An assignment for a loan will modify a prior choice of income plan. The amount due the assignee will be payable in one sum and the balance will be applied under the income plan.

Income plan payments may not be assigned and, to the extent permitted by law, will not be subject to the claims of creditors.

Income Plan Rates—Amounts applied under non-life income plans will earn interest at a rate we set from time to time. That rate will never be less than 3% a year.

Life income plan payments will be based on a rate set by us and in effect on the date the amount to be applied becomes payable.

Optional Income Plans (Continued)

Minimum Payments under Optional Income Plans—Monthly payments under Options 2, 3, 3A and 4 for each $1,000 applied will not be less than the amounts shown in the following Tables.

Option 2. *Instalment Income for a Stated Period*
Monthly Payments for each $1,000 Applied

Years Chosen	Minimum Amount of Each Monthly Payment	Years Chosen	Minimum Amount of Each Monthly Payment	Years Chosen	Minimum Amount of Each Monthly Payment
1	$84.47	11	$8.86	21	$5.32
2	42.86	12	8.24	22	5.15
3	28.99	13	7.71	23	4.99
4	22.06	14	7.26	24	4.84
5	17.91	15	6.87	25	4.71
6	15.14	16	6.53	26	4.59
7	13.16	17	6.23	27	4.47
8	11.68	18	5.96	28	4.37
9	10.53	19	5.73	29	4.27
10	9.61	20	5.51	30	4.18

To determine the minimum amount for quarterly payment, multiply the above monthly payment by 2.99; for semiannual by 5.96; and for annual by 11.84.

Payee's Age	**Option 3.** *Single Life Income*—Guaranteed Payment Period. Minimum Amount of each Monthly Payment for each $1,000 Applied — Guaranteed Payment Period: 10 years		15 years		20 years		**Option 3A.** *Single Life Income*—Guaranteed Return. Minimum Amount of each Monthly Payment for each $1,000 Applied	
	Male	Female	Male	Female	Male	Female	Male	Female
50	$4.50	$4.09	$4.40	$4.05	$4.28	$3.99	$4.24	$3.96
55	4.96	4.49	4.80	4.41	4.58	4.31	4.61	4.29
60	5.53	4.99	5.25	4.86	4.90	4.67	5.07	4.72
65	6.25	5.67	5.75	5.40	5.18	5.03	5.67	5.28
70	7.11	6.55	6.23	5.99	5.39	5.31	6.46	6.04
75	8.03	7.60	6.61	6.48	5.49	5.45	7.54	7.06
80	8.87	8.60	6.81	6.74	5.51	5.50	9.01	8.44
85 and over	9.40	9.22	6.86	6.84	5.51	5.51	11.14	10.26

Option 4. *Joint and Survivor Life Income*—Guaranteed Period of 10 years
Minimum Amount of each Monthly Payment for each $1,000 Applied

Age of Both Payees	One Male and One Female	Two Males	Two Females
50	$3.77	$3.92	$3.67
55	4.09	4.27	3.97
60	4.52	4.73	4.37
65	5.10	5.35	4.91
70	5.90	6.18	5.68
75	6.95	7.21	6.72

On request, we will provide additional information about amounts of minimum payments.

404-82

Index

I

J

K

L

T

U